Infants, Children, and Adolescents

Infants, Children, and Adolescents

SIXTH EDITION

Laura E. Berk
Illinois State University

PEARSON

Boston | New York | San Francisco
Mexico City | Montreal | Toronto | London | Madrid | Munich | Paris
Hong Kong | Singapore | Tokyo | Cape Town | Sydney

To Melissa and Peter, in honor of their marriage and with love

Managing Editor: Mirella Misiaszek
Development Editor: Judy Ashkenaz
Editorial Assistants: Courtney Mullen,
  Liz Tassell, Jennifer DeMambro
Executive Marketing Manager: Pamela Laskey
Production Supervisor: Patrick Cash-Peterson
Composition Buyer: Linda Cox

Manufacturing Manager: Megan Cochran
Cover Director: Linda Knowles
Designer: Joyce Weston Designs
Photo Researcher: Sarah Evertson—ImageQuest
Copyeditor: Margaret Pinette
Proofreader: Bill Heckman

Milestones of Development Table
photo credits:

Page 290: column 1: © Ariel Skelley/ Getty Images/Blend Images; column 2: © Marcus Mok/Getty Images/Asia Images; column 3: © Ellen Senisi

Page 291: column 1 top: © LWA-Dann Tardif/CORBIS; column 1 bottom: © Myrleen Ferguson Cate/PhotoEdit; column 2: ©© Geri Engberg/The Image Works; column 3: © Laura Dwight/ CORBIS

Page 408: column 1: © Don Smetzer/ PhotoEdit; column 2: © John-Francis Bourke/zefa/CORBIS; column 3: © Retna/Index Stock

Page 409: column 1 top: © Peter Hvizdak/The Image Works; column 1 bottom: © Gideon Mendel/CORBIS; column 2: © David Madison/Getty Images/Photographer's Choice; column 3 top: © Don Hammond/Design Pics/ CORBIS; column 3 bottom: © Brand X Pictures/Jupiter Images

Page 526: column 1: © Dennis MacDonald/PhotoEdit; column 2; © Nancy R Cohen/Getty Images/Digital Vision; column 3: © David Young-Wolff/Getty Images/Photographer's Choice

Page 527: column 1 top: CP PHOTO/Paul Chiasson; column 1

bottom: Toronto Star/Firstlight; column 2: © David Young-Wolff/PhotoEdit; column 3 top: © Gideon Mendel/ CORBIS; column 3 bottom: © Thomas Downs/Lonely Planet Images

Page 638: column 1: © Cathrine Wessel/ CORBIS; column 2; © Leland Bobbé/ CORBIS; column 3: © Kayte M. Deioma/PhotoEdit

Page 639: column 1 top: © Steve Skjold/ Alamy; column 1 bottom: © David Young-Wolff/PhotoEdit; column 2: © ournal-Courier/Clayton Stalter/The Image Works; column 3 top: © Don Smetzer/Getty Images/Stone; column 3 bottom: © Ariel Skelley/CORBIS

For related titles and support materials, visit our online catalog at www.ablongman.com

Portions of this book are also published under the title Infants and Children: Prenatal Through Middle Childhood, Sixth Edition, by Laura E. Berk, copyright © 2008, 2005, 2002, 1999, 1996, 1994 by Pearson Education, Inc.

Library of Congress Cataloging-in-Publication Data
Berk, Laura E.
  Infants, children, and adolescents / Laura E. Berk.—6th ed.
    p. cm.
  Includes bibliographical references and index.
  ISBN-13: 978-0-205-51138-9 (alk. paper)
  ISBN-10: 0-205-51138-4 (alk. paper)
  1. Child development. 2. Infants—Development. 3. Adolescence. I. Title.
  RJ131.B387 2008
  618.92—dc22

                                                      2007023431

Printed in the United States of America

10 9 8 7 6 5 4 3 2 1   VH   11 10 09 08 07

About The Author

Laura E. Berk is a distinguished professor of psychology at Illinois State University, where she has taught child and human development to both undergraduate and graduate students for more than three decades. She received her bachelor's degree in psychology from the University of California, Berkeley, and her master's and doctoral degrees in child development and educational psychology from the University of Chicago. She has been a visiting scholar at Cornell University, UCLA, Stanford University, and the University of South Australia.

Berk has published widely on the effects of school environments on children's development, the development of private speech, and most recently, the role of make-believe play in development. Her research has been funded by the U.S. Office of Education and the National Institute of Child Health and Human Development. It has appeared in many prominent journals, including *Child Development, Developmental Psychology, Merrill-Palmer Quarterly, Journal of Abnormal Child Psychology, Development and Psychopathology,* and *Early Childhood Research Quarterly.* Her empirical studies have attracted the attention of the general public, leading to contributions to *Psychology Today* and *Scientific American.*

Berk has served as research editor for *Young Children* and consulting editor for *Early Childhood Research Quarterly* and the *Journal of Cognitive Education and Psychology.* She is a frequent contributor to edited volumes on early childhood development, having recently authored chapters on the importance of parenting, on make-believe play and self-regulation, and on the kindergarten child. She has also written the chapter on development for *The Many Faces of Psychological Research in the Twenty-First Century* (Society for the Teaching of Psychology), the chapter on social development for *The Chicago Companion to the Child,* the article on Vygotsky for the *Encyclopedia of Cognitive Science,* and the chapter on storytelling as a teaching strategy for *Voices of Experience: Memorable Talks from the National Institute on the Teaching of Psychology* (Association for Psychological Science).

Berk's books include *Private Speech: From Social Interaction to Self-Regulation, Scaffolding Children's Learning: Vygotsky and Early Childhood Education,* and *Landscapes of Development: An Anthology of Readings.* In addition to *Infants, Children, and Adolescents,* she is author of the best-selling texts *Child Development* and *Development Through the Lifespan,* published by Allyn and Bacon. Her book for parents and teachers is *Awakening Children's Minds: How Parents and Teachers Can Make a Difference.*

Berk is active in work for children's causes. In addition to service in her home community, she is a member of the national board of directors of Jumpstart, a nonprofit organization that provides early literacy intervention to thousands of low-income preschoolers across the United States, using college and university students as interveners. Berk is a fellow of the American Psychological Association, Division, 7: Developmental Psychology.

Brief Contents

List of Features

Contents

PART V
Middle Childhood: Six to Eleven Years

CHAPTER 11
PHYSICAL DEVELOPMENT IN MIDDLE CHILDHOOD   410

CHAPTER 12
COGNITIVE DEVELOPMENT IN MIDDLE CHILDHOOD   436

CHAPTER 13
EMOTIONAL AND SOCIAL DEVELOPMENT IN MIDDLE CHILDHOOD   480

PART VI
Adolescence: The Transition to Adulthood

CHAPTER 14
PHYSICAL DEVELOPMENT IN ADOLESCENCE   528

CHAPTER 15
COGNITIVE DEVELOPMENT IN ADOLESCENCE   564

CHAPTER 16
EMOTIONAL AND SOCIAL DEVELOPMENT IN ADOLESCENCE   596

CHAPTER 17
EMERGING ADULTHOOD   640

A Personal Note to Students

My more than 30 years of teaching child development have brought me in contact with thousands of students like you—students with diverse college majors, future goals, interests, and needs. Some are affiliated with my own department, psychology, but many come from other related fields—education, sociology, anthropology, family studies, social service, nursing, and biology, to name just a few. Each semester, my students' aspirations have proved to be as varied as their fields of study. Many look toward careers in applied work—teaching, caregiving, nursing, counseling, social work, school psychology, and program administration. Some want to teach, and a few want to do research. Most hope someday to become parents, whereas others are already parents who come with a desire to better understand and rear their children. And almost all arrive with a deep curiosity about how they themselves developed from tiny infants into the complex human beings they are today.

My goal in preparing this sixth edition of *Infants, Children, and Adolescents* is to provide a textbook that meets the instructional goals of your course as well as your personal interests and needs. To achieve these objectives, I have grounded this book in a carefully selected body of classic and current theory and research brought to life with stories and vignettes about children and families, most of whom I have known personally. In addition, the text highlights the joint contributions of biology and environment to the developing child, explains how the research process helps solve real-world problems, illustrates commonalities and differences among ethnic groups and cultures, and pays special attention to policy issues that are crucial for safeguarding children's well-being in today's world. Woven throughout the text is a unique pedagogical program that will assist you in mastering information, integrating the various aspects of development, critically examining controversial issues, applying what you have learned, and relating the information to your own life.

I hope that learning about child development will be as rewarding for you as I have found it over the years. I would like to know what you think about both the field of child development and this book. I welcome your comments; please feel free to send them to me at Department of Psychology, Box 4620, Illinois State University, Normal, IL 61790, or care of the publisher, who will forward them to me.

Laura E. Berk

Preface for Instructors

My decision to write *Infants, Children, and Adolescents* was inspired by a wealth of professional and personal experiences. First and foremost were the interests and concerns of hundreds of students of child development with whom I have worked in more than three decades of college teaching. I aimed for a text that is intellectually stimulating, that provides depth as well as breadth of coverage, that portrays the complexities of child development with clarity and excitement, and that is relevant and useful in building a bridge from theory and research to children's everyday lives. Instructor and student enthusiasm for the book not only has been among my greatest sources of pride and satisfaction, but also has inspired me to rethink and improve each edition.

The 15 years since *Infants, Children, and Adolescents* first appeared have been a period of unprecedented expansion and change in theory and research. This sixth edition represents these rapidly transforming aspects of the field, with a wealth of new content and teaching tools:

■ *Diverse pathways of change are highlighted.* Investigators have reached broad consensus that variations in biological makeup, everyday tasks, and the people who support children in mastery of those tasks lead to wide individual differences in children's paths of change and resulting competencies. This edition pays more attention to variability in development and to recent theories—including ecological, sociocultural, and dynamic systems—that attempt to explain it. Multicultural and cross-cultural findings, including international comparisons, are enhanced throughout the text and in revised and expanded Cultural Influences boxes.

■ *The complex, bidirectional relationship between biology and environment is given greater attention.* Accumulating evidence on development of the brain, motor skills, cognitive competencies, temperament, and developmental problems underscores the way biological factors emerge in, are modified by, and share power with experience. The interconnection between biology and environment is revisited throughout the text narrative and in Biology and Environment boxes with new and updated topics.

■ *Inclusion of interdisciplinary research is expanded.* The move toward viewing thoughts, feelings, and behavior as an integrated whole, affected by a wide array of influences in biology, social context, and culture, has motivated developmental researchers to strengthen their ties with other fields of psychology and with other disciplines. Topics and findings included in this edition increasingly reflect the contributions of educational psychology, social psychology, health psychology, clinical psychology, neuropsychology, biology, pediatrics, sociology, anthropology, social service, and other fields.

■ *The links among theory, research, and applications—a theme of this book since its inception—are strengthened.* As researchers intensify their efforts to generate findings that can be applied to real-life situations, I have placed even greater weight on social policy issues and sound theory- and research-based practices. Further applications are provided in the Applying What We Know tables, which give students concrete ways of building bridges between their learning and the real world.

■ *The educational context of development becomes a stronger focus.* The home, school, and community are featured as vital educational contexts in which the child develops. Research on effective teaching practices appears in many chapters and in new and revised Social Issues: Education boxes.

■ *The role of active student learning is made more explicit.* A new Take a Moment... feature, built into the chapter narrative, asks students to think deeply and critically as they read. Ask Yourself questions at the end of each major section have been revised and expanded to promote four approaches to engaging actively with the subject matter: *Review, Apply, Connect,* and *Reflect.* This feature assists students in reflecting on what they have read from multiple vantage points.

Text Philosophy

The basic approach of this book has been shaped by my own professional and personal history as a teacher, researcher, and parent. It consists of seven philosophical ingredients that I regard as essential for students to emerge from a course with a thorough understanding of child development:

1. An understanding of major theories and the strengths and shortcomings of each. The first chapter begins by emphasizing that only knowledge of multiple theories can do justice to the richness of child development. As I take up each age period and domain of development, I present a variety of theoretical perspectives, indicate how each highlights previously overlooked facets of development, and discuss research that evaluates it. Consideration of contrasting theories also serves as the context for an even-handed analysis of many controversial issues.

2. An appreciation of research strategies for investigating child development. To evaluate theories, students must have a firm grounding in research methods and designs. In addition to a special section in Chapter 1 covering research strategies, throughout the book numerous studies are discussed in sufficient detail for students to use what they have learned to critically assess the findings, conclusions, and implications of research.

3. Knowledge of both the sequence of child development and the processes that underlie it. Students are provided with a description of the organized sequence of development along with processes of change. An understanding of process—how complex interactions of biological and environmental events produce development—has been the focus of most recent research. Accordingly, the text reflects this emphasis. But new information about the timetable of change has also emerged. In many ways, children have proved to be far more competent than they were believed to be in the past. Current evidence on the sequence and timing of development, along with its implications for process, is presented throughout the book.

4. An appreciation of the impact of context and culture on child development. A wealth of research indicates that children live in rich physical and social contexts that affect all domains of development. In each chapter, students travel to distant parts of the world as I review a growing body of cross-cultural evidence. The text narrative also discusses many findings on socioeconomically and ethnically diverse children within the United States and Canada, and on children with varying abilities and disabilities. Besides highlighting the role of immediate settings, such as family, neighborhood, and school, I make a concerted effort to underscore the impact of larger social structures—societal values, laws, and government programs—on children's well-being.

5. An understanding of the joint contributions of biology and environment to development. The field recognizes more powerfully than ever before the joint roles of hereditary/constitutional and environmental factors—that these contributions to development combine in complex ways and cannot be separated in a simple manner. Numerous examples of how biological dispositions can be maintained as well as transformed by social contexts are presented throughout the book.

6. A sense of the interdependency of all domains of development—physical, cognitive, emotional, and social. Every chapter takes an integrated approach to understanding children. I show how physical, cognitive, emotional, and social development are interwoven. Within the text narrative and in a special series of Ask Yourself *Connect* questions at the end of major sections, students are referred to other sections of the book to deepen their grasp of relationships among various aspects of change.

7. An appreciation of the interrelatedness of theory, research, and applications. Throughout this book, I emphasize that theories of child development and the research stimulated by them provide the foundation for sound, effective practices with children. The links among theory, research, and applications are reinforced by an organizational format in which theory and research are presented first, followed by practical implications. In addition, a current focus in the field—harnessing child development knowledge to shape social policies that support children's needs—is reflected in every chapter. The text

addresses the current condition of children in the United States, Canada, and around the world and shows how theory and research have combined with public interest to spark successful interventions.

Text Organization

I have chosen a chronological organization for this text. The chronological approach assists students in thoroughly understanding each age period. It also eases the task of integrating the various domains of development because each is discussed in close proximity. At the same time, a chronologically organized book requires that theories covering several age periods be presented piecemeal. This creates a challenge for students, who must link the various parts together. To assist with this task, I frequently remind students of important earlier achievements before discussing new developments, referring back to related sections with page references. Also, chapters devoted to the same topic (for example, cognitive development) are similarly organized, making it easier for students to draw connections across age periods and construct an overall view of developmental change.

New Coverage in the Sixth Edition

Child development is a fascinating and ever-changing field of study, with constantly emerging new discoveries and refinements in existing knowledge. The sixth edition represents this burgeoning contemporary literature, with more than 2,000 new citations. Cutting-edge topics throughout the text underscore the book's major themes. Here is a sampling:

CHAPTER 1 • New, applied examples of the contributions of behaviorism and social learning theory • Introduction to developmental cognitive neuroscience as a new area of investigation • New examples of research using systematic observation, structured interviews, and correlational research • Revised Cultural Influences box on immigrant youths • Revised section on sequential designs, including a new example and visual illustration • New section on combining experimental and developmental designs, including an illustration in a new Social Issues box answering the question, Can musical experiences enhance intelligence?

CHAPTER 2 • Updated discussion of basic genetics, including incomplete dominance • New evidence on the changing proportion of male to female births • Inclusion of both germline and somatic mutation, with implications for modifiability of the genotype and gene-environment interaction • New evidence on genetic treatment of disease • Updated section on development of adopted children • New section on affluence, family functioning, and development • Enhanced attention to the impact of poverty on development • Updated research on neighborhood influences on physical and mental health of children and adults • Updated section on public policies and child development • New Social Issues: Education box on worldwide education of girls and its transforming impact on current and future generations • Updated and enhanced discussion of environmental influences on gene expression

CHAPTER 3 • New evidence on family size and children's intellectual development • Updated research on fetal sensory and behavioral capacities • Expanded and updated consideration of a wide range of teratogens • Inclusion of the new designation for harmful effects of prenatal alcohol exposure—fetal alcohol spectrum disorder—and its associated three diagnoses: fetal alcohol syndrome (FAS), partial fetal alcohol syndrome (PFAS), and alcohol-related neurodevelopmental disorder (ARND) • New Cultural Influences box on how culturally sensitive prenatal care promotes healthy pregnancies • New evidence on the long-term consequences of emotional stress during pregnancy • New findings on older maternal age and prenatal and birth complications • Expanded section on preparing for parenthood

CHAPTER 4 • New research on natural childbirth practices, including positions for delivery and water birth • New findings on oxygen deprivation during childbirth, head-cooling treatment to reduce brain injury, and developmental consequences • Updated discussion of preterm and low-birth-weight infants, including long-term developmental outcomes for very low-birth-weight babies • Updated Social Issues: Health box on health care and other policies for parents and newborn babies, including cross-national infant mortality rates and consideration of the importance of generous parental leave • Updated Biology and Environment box on sudden infant death syndrome, including protective sleeping practices • New research on infant crying, including a nurse home-visiting program to reduce colic • New research on fetal and newborn pain perception • New findings on the impact of the prenatal environment on newborn odor preferences • Expanded consideration of the father's influence on family adjustment and newborn care • New section addressing the transition to parenthood for the growing number of single mothers • Revised and expanded Biology and Environment box on parental depression and child development, including both maternal and paternal postpartum depression

CHAPTER 5 • Introduction to major methods of assessing brain functioning, including EEG, ERPs, FMRI, PET, and NIROT • New research on infants born with cataracts and children adopted from Romanian orphanages, bearing on the question of whether infancy is a sensitive period of development • New evidence on infants' and toddlers' eating habits and early risk for obesity • New findings on newborn imita-

tion in humans and chimpanzees • New dynamic systems research on development of reaching • New findings on development of infant speech perception, including infants' capacity to analyze the speech stream • New Biology and Environment box on "tuning in" to familiar speech, faces, and music during the second half of the first year, suggesting a sensitive period for culture-specific learning • New evidence on development of object perception, including infants' capacity to keep track of objects' paths of movement

CHAPTER 6 • New research on deferred imitation in toddlerhood • New evidence on infants' understanding of object permanence, including neurophysiological findings • Inclusion of the most recent edition of the Bayley Scales of Infant Development (Bayley-III) • Updated findings on quality of child care in the United States and Canada, with consequences for cognitive and language development • New research on early intervention for poverty-stricken families with infants and toddlers, including Early Head Start • New findings on language areas in the brain • New research on vocabulary development • New evidence on how intermodal stimulation supports infants' efforts to make sense of language • Updated findings on SES variations in language progress • New Social Issues: Education box on the impact of parent–child interaction on language and cognitive development of deaf children

CHAPTER 7 • New research on the self-regulatory dimension of temperament—effortful control • New research on parents' tendency to emphasize differences in temperament between siblings • Enhanced consideration of cultural variations in sensitive caregiving, with implications for attachment security • New research on the joint contribution of infant characteristics and parental sensitivity to attachment security • Expanded section on fathers' involvement with infants • New section on grandparent primary caregivers and children's development • Updated Social Issues: Health box on the influences of quality of child care and long child-care hours on attachment and later development • Expanded and updated section on development of self-awareness and self-recognition in the first two years, with implications for emotional and social development • Updated consideration of development of compliance and self-control, with increased attention to the influence of parenting

CHAPTER 8 • New research on factors linked to child tooth decay, and its incidence among North American children varying in SES • Updated consideration of advances in brain development in early childhood, with emphasis on the cerebellum and the hippocampus • New Biology and Environment box on low-level lead exposure and children's development • New findings on the relationship of nutritional deficiencies to mental development and behavior problems • Updated statistics and research on childhood immunization • New findings on the contribution of child temperament and parenting practices to unintentional injury in early childhood • Updated Cultural Influences box on child health care in the United States and other Western nations

CHAPTER 9 • New research on development of categorization • Enhanced discussion of development of autobiographical memory, including the influence of the parent–child relationship • Updated research on factors that affect development of accurate, efficient problem-solving strategies • New evidence on cognitive attainments and social experiences (including parents' mental-state talk) that contribute to mastery of false belief • Updated research on early development of counting and math concepts • Updated Biology and Environment box on "mindblindness" and autism, including explanations for deficient theory of mind among children with autism • Expanded section on educational media, including effects of television and computers on cognitive development and academic learning • Expanded and updated research on the diverse strategies preschoolers use to figure out word meanings • New findings on the gradual development of grammatical skills, with implications for theoretical controversies

CHAPTER 10 • Enhanced explanation of the I-self and me-self, with an illustrative figure • New research on the contributions of parent–child conversations about the past to early self-concept • New findings on preschoolers' understanding of the self as existing continuously over time • New evidence on the contribution of attachment to parent–child narratives about emotions and, thus, to emotional understanding • Updated consideration of emotional self-regulation in early childhood, including effortful control • New evidence on the importance of social skills and friendships in fostering children's successful transition to school • New Cultural Influences box on ethnic differences in the consequences of physical punishment • Revised and updated consideration of types of aggression, including physical, verbal, and relational forms • Updated discussion of violent media and development of aggression • New evidence on gender-stereotyped learning in early childhood, including the influence of parents and same-sex peer associations • New Social Issues: Education box on children's learning of gender stereotypes through mother–child conversations • Updated discussion of gender schema theory, noting individual differences among children in gender-schematic processing • New findings on the harmful impact of parental psychological control on children's adjustment

CHAPTER 11 • Revised and updated section on overweight and obesity, including rapid increase in developing nations • New findings on mild nutritional deficiencies and children's cognitive functioning • Updated evidence on outcomes of participation in youth sports programs • Updated Social Issues: Education box on children's understanding of health and illness • New Social Issues: Education box on benefits of school recess

CHAPTER 12 • New research on cultural influences on operational thought and cognitive maps • Revised and updated Biology and Environment box on children with attention-deficit hyperactivity disorder • Updated findings on relationships between aspects of information processing and

children's IQs • Expanded section on mathematical development, with implications for math education • Description of the new Stanford-Binet Intelligence Scales, Fifth Edition • New Social Issues: Education box on emotional intelligence • Expanded treatment of language development in middle childhood, with special attention to narrative • Updated research on bilingual development, including code switching • Expanded and updated section on computers and academic learning • New research on inclusive classrooms and children with learning difficulties

CHAPTER 13 • New findings on parental beliefs about ability and children's achievement-related attributions • New section on school-age children's grasp of individual rights, with implications for moral understanding • New section on children's understanding of diversity and inequality, including research on development of racial and ethnic prejudice and strategies for reducing children's prejudices • New findings on peer acceptance, including implications of peer-acceptance categories for bullying and victimization • New evidence on development of gender identity in middle childhood, with implications for emotional adjustment • New findings on cultural variations in gender typing in sex-segregated peer groups • Enhanced attention to parenting of school-age children, including the consequences of paternal involvement for children's development • New evidence on children's eyewitness testimony, including factors that contribute to children's suggestibility

CHAPTER 14 • New statistics and evidence on teenage use of performance-enhancing drugs • Updated research on adolescent brain development • New evidence on implications of pubertal timing for psychological adjustment in adolescence and adulthood • Updated evidence on factors that contribute to anorexia nervosa and treatment outcomes • New findings on personal and environmental factors that contribute to adolescent sports-related injuries • Discussion of the Internet as a hazardous "sex educator," including adolescents' exposure to pornography on the Internet • New research on cultural variations in parent–adolescent conversations about sex • New evidence on the long-term consequences of adolescent parenthood and on prevention strategies • New Social Issues: Health box on intergenerational continuity in adolescent parenthood • Updated statistics on adolescent alcohol and drug use, and new findings on contributing factors

CHAPTER 15 • New findings on the influence of schooling on development of propositional thought • Expanded and updated research on adolescent decision making • Updated consideration of factors contributing to sex differences in verbal, mathematical, and spatial abilities • New research on the impact of school transitions on adjustment • Updated Social Issues: Education box on implications of high-stakes testing for students' learning • New research on ethnic variations in peer support for school achievement • Updated findings on factors contributing to high school dropout by low-SES ethnic minority students • Enhanced consideration of gender differences in vocational choice • New findings on consequences of part-time work for adolescent adjustment

CHAPTER 16 • Updated and enhanced section on development of self-esteem in adolescence • New research on identity statuses, cognitive styles, and adjustment • Updated Cultural Influences box on identity development among ethnic minority youths • Revised evaluation of Kohlberg's stages • New section on adolescents' coordination of moral, social-conventional, and personal concerns • Updated section on religious involvement and moral development • Expanded and updated section on parenting and adolescent autonomy • Inclusion of the impact of acculturative stress on adjustment of ethnic minority teenagers • New findings on sibling relationships in adolescence • New research on gender differences in communication between friends, with implications for friendship stability • New section on Internet friendships

• Updated section on dating • New evidence on wide-ranging problems of adolescents who bend easily to peer influence

CHAPTER 17 • Expanded attention to SES and ethnic variation in the experience of emerging adulthood • Updated research on cognitive changes, including development of epistemic cognition • Enhanced consideration of identity development, with special attention to in-depth evaluation of commitments and the role of personal agency in exploration and commitment certainty • New findings on changing conceptions of close relationships and the process of forging a romantic partnership • Enhanced attention to gender differences in career development • New section on college experience and career development among ethnic minority emerging adults, including the influence of college support services and racial biases in career opportunities • Enhanced discussion of the contribution of a secure, affectionate bond with parents to adaptive functioning in emerging adulthood

Pedagogical Features

Maintaining a highly accessible writing style–one that is lucid and engaging without being simplistic–continues to be one of my major goals. I frequently converse with students, encouraging them to relate what they read to their own lives. In doing so, I hope to make the study of child development involving and pleasurable.

CHAPTER INTRODUCTIONS AND VIGNETTES ABOUT CHILDREN To provide a helpful preview of chapter content, I include an outline and overview of chapter content in each chapter introduction. To help students construct a clear image of development and to enliven the text narrative, each chronological age division is unified by case examples woven throughout that set of chapters. For example, within the infancy and toddlerhood section, we'll look in on three children, observe dramatic changes and striking individual differences, and address the impact of family background, child-rearing practices, and parents' and children's life experiences on development. Besides a set of main characters, many additional vignettes offer vivid examples of development among children and adolescents.

END-OF-CHAPTER SUMMARIES Comprehensive end-of-chapter summaries, organized according to the major divisions of each chapter and highlighting important terms, remind students of key points in the text discussion. Review questions are included in the summary to encourage active study.

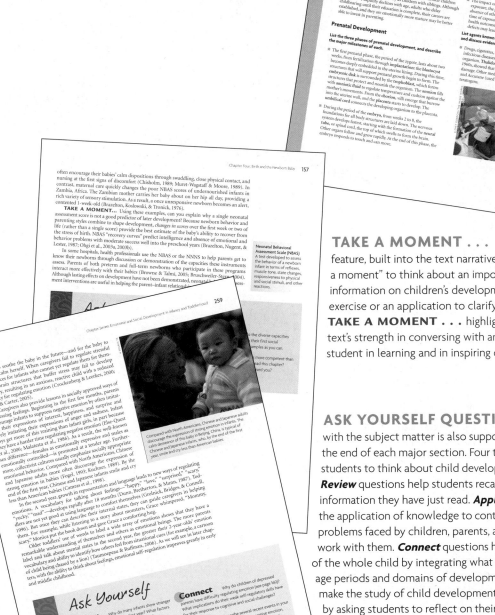

TAKE A MOMENT . . . This new active-learning feature, built into the text narrative, asks students to "take a moment" to think about an important point, integrate information on children's development, or engage in an exercise or an application to clarify a challenging concept. **TAKE A MOMENT . . .** highlights and reinforces the text's strength in conversing with and actively engaging the student in learning and in inspiring critical thinking.

ASK YOURSELF QUESTIONS Active engagement with the subject matter is also supported by study questions at the end of each major section. Four types of questions prompt students to think about child development in diverse ways: *Review* questions help students recall and comprehend information they have just read. *Apply* questions encourage the application of knowledge to controversial issues and problems faced by children, parents, and professionals who work with them. *Connect* questions help students build an image of the whole child by integrating what they have learned across age periods and domains of development. *Reflect* questions make the study of child development personally meaningful by asking students to reflect on their own development and life experiences. Each question is answered on the text's MyDevelopmentLab website.

THREE TYPES OF THEMATIC BOXES accentuate
the philosophical themes of this book:

- **SOCIAL ISSUES** boxes discuss the impact of social conditions on children and emphasize the need for sensitive social policies to ensure their well-being. They are divided into two types: (1) *Social Issues: Education* boxes, greatly expanded in this edition, focus on home, school, and community influences on children's learning—for example, *Worldwide Education of Girls: Transforming Current and Future Generations; Parent-Child Interaction: Impact on Language and Cognitive Development of Deaf Children; School Recess—A Time to Play, a Time to Learn;* and *High-Stakes Testing.* (2) *Social Issues: Health* boxes address values and practices relevant to children's physical and mental health. Examples include *A Cross-National Perspective on Health Care and Other Policies for Parents and Newborn Babies; Children's Eyewitness Testimony;* and *Like Parent, Like Child: Intergenerational Continuity in Adolescent Parenthood*

- **BIOLOGY AND ENVIRONMENT** boxes highlight the growing attention to the complex, bidirectional relationship between biology and environment. Examples include *Brain Plasticity: Insights from Research on Brain-Damaged Children and Adults; "Tuning In" to Familiar Speech, Faces, and Music: A Sensitive Period for Culture-Specific Learning; Low-Level Lead Exposure and Children's Development; "Mindblindness" and Autism;* and *Bullies and Their Victims.*

- **CULTURAL INFLUENCES** boxes have been expanded and updated to deepen attention to culture threaded throughout the text. They highlight both cross-cultural and multicultural variations in child development—for example, *The African-American Extended Family; Culturally Sensitive Care Promotes Healthy Pregnancies; Cultural Variation in Infant Sleeping Arrangements; Ethnic Differences in the Consequences of Physical Punishment;* and *The Impact of Ethnic and Political Violence on Children.*

APPLYING WHAT WE KNOW TABLES

In this new feature, I summarize research-based applications on many issues, speaking directly to students as parents or future parents and to those pursuing different careers or areas of study, such as teaching, health care, counseling, or social work. They include: *Do's and Don'ts for a Healthy Pregnancy; Keeping Infants and Toddlers Safe; Supporting Emergent Literacy in Early Childhood; Regulating TV and Computer Use;* and *Parenting Practices That Foster Adolescent Competence.*

MILESTONES TABLES A Milestones table appears at the end of each age division of the text. These tables summarize major physical, cognitive, language, emotional, and social attainments, providing a convenient aid for reviewing the chronology of child development.

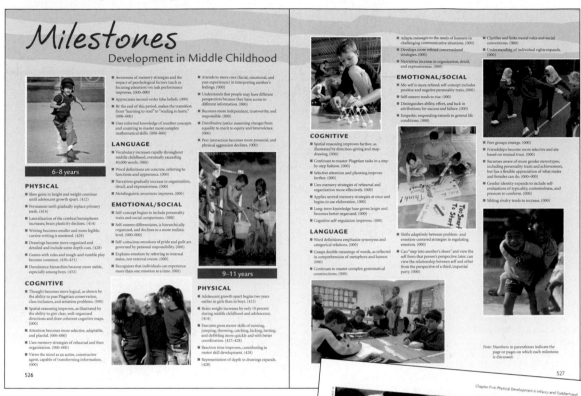

ART AND PHOTO PROGRAM

A thoroughly revised art style presents concepts and research findings with clarity and attractiveness, thereby aiding student understanding and retention. The illustration program greatly increases the number of photos compared to the previous edition. Each has been carefully selected to portray the text discussion and to represent the diversity of children around the world.

KEY TERMS WITH DEFINITIONS, END-OF-CHAPTER TERM LIST, AND END-OF-BOOK GLOSSARY Mastery of terms that make up the central vocabulary of the field is promoted through key-term and concept definitions, which appear in the text margins, in a page-referenced end-of-chapter term list, and in a page-referenced end-of-book glossary.

Acknowledgments

The dedicated contributions of a great many individuals helped make this book a reality and contributed to refinements and improvements in this sixth edition. An impressive cast of reviewers provided many helpful suggestions, constructive criticisms, and encouragement and enthusiasm for the organization and content of the text. I am grateful to each one of them.

Reviewers for the First Through Fifth Editions

Mark B. Alcorn, University of Northern Colorado
Armin W. Arndt, Eastern Washington University
Lamia Barakat, Drexel University
Cecelia Benelli, Western Illinois University
Kathleen Bey, Palm Beach Community College
Donald Bowers, Community College of Philadelphia
Michele Y. Breault, Truman State University
Jerry Bruce, Sam Houston State College
Lanthan D. Camblin, University of Cincinnati
Joseph J. Campos, University of California, Berkeley
Linda A. Camras, DePaul University

Lynn Caruso, Seneca College
Nancy Taylor Coghill, University of Southwest Louisiana
Diane Brothers Cook, Gainesville College
Jennifer Cook, Kent State University
Roswell Cox, Berea College
Ronald Craig, Edinboro University of Pennsylvania
Zoe Ann Davidson, Alabama A & M University
Sheridan DeWolf, Grossmont College
Matthew DiCintio, Delaware County Community College
Constance DiMaria-Kross, Union County College
Bronwyn Fees, Kansas State University
F. Richard Ferraro, University of North Dakota
Kathleen Fite, Southwest Texas State University
Trisha Folds-Bennett, College of Charleston
Nancy Freeman, University of South Carolina
Eugene Geist, Ohio University
Kristine Hansen, University of Winnipeg
Vivian Harper, San Joaquin Delta College
Algea Harrison, Oakland University
Janice Hartgrove-Freile, North Harris Community College
Vernon Haynes, Youngstown State University
Bert Hayslip, Jr., University of North Texas
Sandra Hellyer, Butler University

Joan Herwig, Iowa State University
Paula Hillmann, University of Wisconsin, Waukesha
Christie Honeycutt, Stanly Community College
Malia Huchendorf, Normandale Community College
Lisa Huffman, Ball State University
Clementine Hansley Hurt, Radford University
Joline Jones, Worcester State University
Kate Kenney, Howard Community College
Shirin Khosropour, Austin Community College
John S. Klein, Castleton State College
Claire Kopp, Claremont Graduate School
Eugene Krebs, California State University, Fresno
Carole Kremer, Hudson Valley Community College
Gary W. Ladd, University of Illinois, Urbana-Champaign
Deborah Laible, Southern Methodist University
Linda Lavine, State University of New York at Cortland
Sara Lawrence, California State University, Northridge
Gail Lee, Jersey City State College
Judith R. Levine, State University of New York at Farmingdale
David Lockwood, Humber College
Frank Manis, University of Southern California
Martin Marino, Atlantic Cape Community College
Mary Ann McLaughlin, Clarion University of Pennsylvania
Annie McManus, Parkland College
Cloe Merrill, Weber State University
Rich Metzger, University of Tennessee at Chattanooga
Karla Miley, Black Hawk College

Jennifer Trapp Myers, University of Michigan
Virginia Navarro, University of Missouri, St. Louis
Peter V. Oliver, University of Hartford
Behnaz Pakizegi, William Patterson University
Virginia Parsons, Carroll College
Joe M. Price, San Diego State University
Cathy Proctor-Castillo, Long Beach Community College
Mary Kay Reed, York College of Pennsylvania
Alan Russell, Flinders University
Tizrah Schutzengel, Bergen Community College
Johnna Shapiro, Illinois Wesleyan University
Gregory Smith, Dickinson College
Thomas Spencer, San Francisco State University
Carolyn Spies, Bloomfield College
Kathy Stansbury, University of New Mexico
Connie Steele, University of Tennessee, Knoxville
Janet Strayer, Simon Fraser University
Marcia Summers, Ball State University
Christy Teranishi, Texas A&M International University
Connie K. Varnhagen, University of Alberta
Judith Ward, Central Connecticut State University
Shawn Ward, Le Moyne College
Alida Westman, Eastern Michigan University
Colin William, Columbus State Community College
Belinda Wholeben, Rockford College
Sue Williams, Southwest Texas State University
Deborah Winters, New Mexico State University

Reviewers for the Sixth Edition

Scott Adler, York University
Joseph Allen, University of Virginia
William Aquilino, University of Wisconsin
Lamia Barakat, Drexel University
Heather Bouchey, University of Vermont
Gustavo Carlo, University of Nebraska-Lincoln
Raymond Collings, SUNY Cortland
Jacque Eccles, University of Michigan
Ronald Craig, Edinboro University of Pennsylvania
Peter Flynn, Northern Essex Community College
Jayne Gackenbach, MacEwan University
Eugene Geist, Ohio University
Sabine Gerhardt, University of Akron
Kristine Hansen, University of Winnipeg
Sandra Hellyer, Butler University

Lisa Huffman, Ball State University
Scott Johnson, New York University
Joline Jones, Worcester State University
David Lockwood, Humber College
Larry Nelson, Brigham Young University
Peggy Norwood, Red Rocks Community College
Behnaz Pakizegi, William Paterson University
Julie Poehlmann, University of Wisconsin - Madison
Kavita Prakash, Heritage College
Verna Raab, Mount Royal College
Raghu Rao, University of Minnesota
Michael Rodman, Middlesex Community College
Delores Smith, University of Tennessee
Daniel Swingley, University of Pennsylvania
Dennis Thompson, Georgia State University
Tracy Thorndike-Christ, Western Washington University
Athena Vouloumanos, McGill University

Colleagues and students at Illinois State University aided my research and contributed significantly to the text's supplements. Richard Payne, Department of Politics and Government, is a kind and devoted friend with whom I have shared many profitable discussions about the writing process, the condition of children and families, and other topics that have significantly influenced my perspective on child development and social policy. Sara Harris joined me in prkeparing the Instructor's Resource Manual, The Child Development in Action Observation Video Guide, and A Window on Lifespan Development Video Guide, bringing to these tasks enthusiasm, imagination, depth of knowledge, and impressive writing skill. Sara's outstanding, dedicated work in ensuring the quality and accuracy of assessments and other ancillary materials has been invaluable. Trisha Mann's outstanding, dedicated work in conducting literature searches and revising the Grade Aid study guide has contributed immeasurably to the currency of the text and the usefulness of its study tools. Sarah Bartosik and CindyBet Pérez-Martinez spent countless hours gathering and organizing library materials.

The supplements package also benefited from the talents and diligence of several other individuals. Gabrielle Principe of Ursinus College and Tom Finn of Bentley College authored a superb test bank, and Mark Seidl, Ph.D. prepared the Grade Aid practice tests with great concern for clarity and accuracy. Elizabeth Hurley designed and wrote a highly attractive and useful PowerPoint presentation.

Among Allyn and Bacon's editorial team, Tom Pauken, editor of the fifth edition, continues to influence my work on this text in important ways. Although he has moved on to a career in university teaching, I value our continued friendship, his deep concern for children's welfare, and his inspiring periodic letters chronicling his thoughts and experiences as a devoted father of a young child. Mirella Misiaszek, Managing Editor, oversaw the multifaceted tasks of coordinating the sixth edition—arranging for manuscript reviews, text supplements, photo illustrations, and other essential tasks.

Judy Ashkenaz, Development Editor, worked closely with me as I wrote each chapter, making sure that every thought and concept would be precisely expressed and well-developed. Judy's keen writing and editing skills and impressive knowledge of developmental issues made the editing an exceptional learning experience and pleasure. I am grateful also for her contributions to the photo captions and the Instructor's Resource Manual. Margaret Pinette and Bill Heckman provided outstanding copyediting and proofreading. Sara Evertson obtained the exceptional photos that so aptly illustrate the text narrative.

I would like to express a heartfelt thank you to Pamela Laskey, Executive Marketing Manager, for her exceptional work in marketing my texts. Pam has made sure that accurate and clear information about my books and their ancillaries reached Allyn and Bacon's sales force and that the needs of prospective and current adopters were met. Words cannot do justice to her marketing savvy and skill and to everything that she has contributed to the quality and broad distribution of *Infants, Children, and Adolescents*.

A final word of gratitude goes to my family, whose love, patience, and understanding have enabled me to be wife, mother, teacher, researcher, and text author at the same time. My sons, David and Peter, grew up with my child development texts, passing from childhood to adolescence and then to emerging and young adulthood as successive editions were written. David has a special connection with the books' subject matter as an elementary school teacher. Peter, an attorney, is about to be married to an exceptionally talented, caring, and beautiful bride. Both continue to enhance my understanding through reflections on events and progress in their own lives. I thank them for helping me grasp the awe-inspiring continuities and discontinuities in development in a most profound and personally enriching way. My husband, Ken, willingly made room for yet another time-consuming endeavor in our life together and communicated his belief in its importance in a great many unspoken, caring ways.

Laura E. Berk

Supplementary Materials

Instructor Supplements

A variety of teaching tools are available for qualified instructors in organizing lectures, planning demonstrations and examinations, and ensuring student comprehension.

MYDEVELOPMENTLAB This interactive and instructive multimedia resource can be used as a supplement to a classroom course or to completely administer an online course. Prepared in collaboration with Laura E. Berk, MyDevelopmentLab includes a variety of assessments that enable continuous evaluation of students' learning. Extensive video footage, multimedia simulations, biographies of major figures in the field, and interactive activities that are unique to *Infants, Children, and Adolescents* are also included. The power of MyDevelopmentLab lies in its design as an all-inclusive teaching and learning tool. For a sampling of its rich content, contact your Allyn and Bacon publisher's representative.

INSTRUCTOR'S CLASSROOM KIT, VOLUME I AND II AND CD-ROM A comprehensive instructional resource, this classroom kit includes all print supplements. Supplements for Chapters 1 to 7 are in Volume I, those for Chapters 8 to 17 in Volume II. Organized by chapter, each volume contains the Instructor's Manual, Test Bank, Grade Aid Study Guide with Practice Tests, and slides from the PowerPoint presentation.

- **Instructor's Resource Manual (IRM)** This thoroughly revised IRM can be used by first-time or experienced instructors to enrich classroom experiences. Each chapter includes a Chapter-at-a-Glance grid, Brief Chapter Summary, Learning Objectives, detailed Lecture Outlines, Lecture Enhancements, Learning Activities, Ask Yourself questions with answers, Suggested Student Readings, Transparencies list, and Media Materials list.
- **Test Bank.** The Test Bank contains over 2,000 multiple-choice questions, each of which is page-referenced to chapter content and classified by type (factual, applied, or conceptual). Each chapter also includes a selection of essay questions and sample answers.
- **Grade Aid with Practice Tests** This helpful study guide offers Chapter Summaries, Learning Objectives, Study Questions organized according to major headings in the text, Crossword Puzzles for mastering important terms, and two multiple-choice Practice Tests per chapter.

- **PowerPoint Presentation** The PowerPoint presentation contains illustrations and outlines of key topics for each text chapter from the text, presented in a clear and visually attractive format.
- **Instructor's Resource CD-ROM** Electronic versions of all the resources in the Instructor's Classroom Kit are made available on this easy-to-use CD.

COMPUTERIZED TEST BANK This computerized version of the Test Bank, in easy-to-use TestGen software, lets you prepare tests for printing as well as for network and online testing. It has full editing capability. Test items are also available in CourseCompass, Blackboard, and WebCT formats.

"INFANTS, CHILDREN, AND ADOLESCENTS IN ACTION" OBSERVATION PROGRAM This real-life videotape is over two hours in length and contains hundreds of observation segments that illustrate the many theories, concepts, and milestones of child development. An Observation Guide helps students use the video in conjunction with the textbook, deepening their understanding and applying what they have learned to everyday life.

"A WINDOW ON LIFESPAN DEVELOPMENT" RUNNING OBSERVATIONAL FOOTAGE VIDEO This video complements the Observation Program described above through more than two hours of unscripted footage on many aspects of child development. Examples of new content include *Supporting Early Language Learning, False Belief,* and *Emerging Adulthood.* An accompanying Video Guide is also available.

TRANSPARENCIES Two hundred full-color transparencies taken from the text and other sources are referenced in the IRM for the most appropriate use in your classroom presentations.

Student Supplements

Beyond the study aids found in the textbook, Allyn and Bacon offers a number of supplements for students:

MYDEVELOPMENTLAB This interactive and instructive multimedia resource is an all-inclusive learning tool. Prepared in collaboration with Laura E. Berk, MyDevelopmentLab engages users and reinforces learning through controlled assessments, extensive video footage, multimedia simulations, biographies of major figures in the field, and interactive activities that are unique to *Infants, Children, and Adolescents*. Easy to use, MyDevelopmentLab meets the individual learning needs of every student. For a sampling of its rich content, visit *www.mdevelopmentlab.com.*

GRADE AID WITH PRACTICE TESTS This helpful study guide offers Chapter Summaries, Learning Objectives, Study Questions organized according to major headings in the text, Crossword Puzzles for mastering important terms, and two multiple-choice Practice Tests per chapter.

MILESTONES STUDY CARDS Adapted from the popular Milestones tables featured in the text, these colorfully illustrated study cards outline key developmental attainments. Easy-to-use, they assist students in integrating the various domains of development and constructing a vision of the whole developing child.

RESEARCHNAVIGATOR—NOW INCLUDED IN MYDEVELOPMENTLAB Through three exclusive databases, this intuitive search interface provides extensive help with the research process, enabling students to make the most of their research time. EBSCO's *ContentSelect* Academic Journal Database permits a discipline-specific search through professional and popular journals. Also included are the *New York Times* Search-by-Subject Archive and *Best of the Web* Link Library. To examine the features of Research Navigator, visit *www.researchnavigator.com.*

About the Chapter Opening Art

I would like to extend grateful acknowledgments to the International Museum of Children's Art, Oslo, Norway, and to the International Child Art Foundation, Washington, DC, for the exceptional cover image and chapter opening art, which depict the talents, concerns, and viewpoints of young artists from around the world. The awe-inspiring collection of children's art gracing this text expresses family, school, and community themes; good times and personal triumphs; profound appreciation for beauty; and great depth of emotion. I am pleased to share this window into children's creativity, insightfulness, sensitivity, and compassion with readers.

My appreciation, also, to Joel Bergner for permission to include his breathtaking mural in the opening of Chapter 17, Emerging Adulthood. Joel is recipient of the 2004 Public Community Mural Award, San Francisco, California.

Infants, Children, and Adolescents

Chapter 1

By depicting himself in traditional Pakistani clothing, this artist conveys identification with and pride in his culture. The "magical rainbow," he comments, represents his desire to create "a greener and more peaceful world." Chapter 1 will introduce you to a rainbow of theories—a multiplicity of ways of thinking about and studying children's development.

"Magical Paintbrush"
Salaar Khan
10 years, Pakistan

Reprinted with permission from the International Child Art Foundation, Washington, D.C.

History, Theory, and Research Strategies

N ot long ago, I left my Midwestern home to live for a year near the small city in northern California where I spent my childhood. One morning, I visited the neighborhood where I grew up—a place I had not seen since I was 12 years old.

I stood at the entrance to my old schoolyard. Buildings and grounds that had looked large to me as a child now seemed strangely small. I peered through the window of my first-grade classroom. The desks were no longer arranged in rows but grouped in intimate clusters. Computers rested against the far wall, near where I once sat. I walked my old route home from school, the distance shrunken by my longer stride. I stopped in front of my best friend Kathryn's house, where we once drew sidewalk pictures, crossed the street to play kickball, and produced plays in the garage. In place of the small shop where I had purchased penny candy stood a child-care center, filled with the voices and vigorous activity of toddlers and preschoolers.

As I walked, I reflected on early experiences that contributed to who and what I am today—weekends helping my father in his downtown clothing shop, the year my mother studied to become a high school teacher, moments of companionship and rivalry with my sister and brother, Sunday outings to museums and the seashore, and visits to my grandmother's house, where I became someone extra special.

As I passed the homes of my childhood friends, I thought of what I knew about their present lives. Kathryn, star student and president of our sixth-grade class—today a successful corporate lawyer and mother of two. Shy, withdrawn Phil, cruelly teased because of his cleft lip—now owner of a thriving chain of hardware stores and member of the city council. Julio, immigrant from Mexico who joined our class in third grade—today director of an elementary school bilingual education program and single parent of an adopted Mexican boy. And finally, my next-door neighbor Rick, who picked fights at recess, struggled with reading, repeated fourth grade, dropped out of high school, and (so I heard) moved from one job to another over the following ten years.

As you begin this course in child development, perhaps you, too, wonder about some of the same questions that crossed my mind during that nostalgic neighborhood walk:

■ In what ways are children's home, school, and neighborhood experiences the same today as they were in generations past, and in what ways are they different?

- How is the infant and young child's perception of the world the same as the adult's, and how is it different?
- What determines the features that humans have in common and those that make each of us unique—physically, mentally, and behaviorally?
- How did Julio, transplanted at age 8 to a new culture, master its language and customs and succeed in its society, yet remain strongly identified with his ethnic community?
- Why do some of us, like Kathryn and Rick, retain the same styles of responding that characterized us as children, whereas others, like Phil, change in essential ways?
- How do cultural changes—employed mothers, child care, divorce, smaller families, and new technologies—affect children's characteristics?

These are central questions addressed by **child development,** an area of study devoted to understanding constancy and change from conception through adolescence. Child development is part of a larger, interdisciplinary field known as **developmental science,** which includes all changes we experience throughout the lifespan (Lerner, 2006). Great diversity characterizes the interests and concerns of the thousands of investigators who study child development. But all have a common goal: to describe and identify those factors that influence the consistencies and changes in young people during the first two decades of life.

The Field of Child Development

Theories have practical value in helping us improve the welfare and treatment of children. For example, theories have contributed to new approaches to education that emphasize exploration, discovery, and collaboration.

child development A field of study devoted to understanding all aspects of human constancy and change from conception through adolescence.

developmental science An interdisciplinary field devoted to the study of all changes we experience throughout the lifespan.

Look again at the questions just listed, and you will see that they are not just of scientific interest. Each has *applied,* or practical, importance as well. In fact, scientific curiosity is just one factor that led child development to become the exciting field of study it is today. Research about development has also been stimulated by social pressures to better the lives of children. For example, the beginning of public education in the early twentieth century led to a demand for knowledge about what and how to teach children of different ages. Pediatricians' interest in improving children's health required an understanding of physical growth and nutrition. The social service profession's desire to treat children's anxieties and behavior problems required information about personality and social development. And parents have continually asked for advice about child-rearing practices and experiences that would promote the well-being of their child.

Our large storehouse of information about child development is *interdisciplinary*. It has grown through the combined efforts of people from many fields. Because of the need to solve everyday problems concerning children, researchers from psychology, sociology, anthropology, biology, and neuroscience have joined forces with professionals from education, family studies, medicine, public health, and social service—to name just a few. The field of child development, as it exists today, is a monument to the contributions of these many disciplines. Its body of knowledge is not just scientifically important but relevant and useful.

Domains of Development

To make the vast, interdisciplinary study of human constancy and change more orderly and convenient, development is often divided into three broad domains: *physical, cognitive,* and *emotional and social*. Refer to Figure 1.1 for a description and illustration of each. Within each period from infancy through adolescence, we will consider the three domains in the order just listed. Yet the domains are not really distinct. Rather, they combine in an integrated, holistic fashion to yield the living, growing child. Furthermore, each domain influences and is influenced by the others. For example, in Chapter 5 you will see that new motor capacities, such as reaching,

Emotional and Social Development
Changes in emotional communication, self-understanding, knowledge about other people, interpersonal skills, friendships, intimate relationships, and moral reasoning and behavior

Physical Development
Changes in body size, proportions, appearance, functioning of body systems, perceptual and motor capacities, and physical health

Cognitive Development
Changes in intellectual abilities, including attention, memory, academic and everyday knowledge, problem solving, imagination, creativity, and language

FIGURE 1.1

Major domains of development. The three domains are not really distinct. Rather, they overlap and interact.

sitting, crawling, and walking (physical), contribute greatly to infants' understanding of their surroundings (cognitive). When babies think and act more competently, adults stimulate them more with games, language, and expressions of delight at their new achievements (emotional and social). These enriched experiences, in turn, promote all aspects of development.

Although each chapter focuses on a particular domain, you will encounter instances of the interwoven nature of all domains on nearly every page of this book. Also, look for the *Ask Yourself* feature at the end of major sections, designed to deepen your understanding. Within it, I have included *Review* questions, which help you recall and think about information you have just read; *Apply* questions, which encourage you to apply your knowledge to controversial issues and problems faced by parents, teachers, and children; *Connect* questions, which help you form a coherent, unified picture of child development; and *Reflect* questions, which invite you to reflect on your own development and that of people you know well.

Periods of Development

Besides distinguishing and integrating the three domains, another dilemma arises in discussing development: how to divide the flow of time into sensible, manageable parts. Researchers usually use the following age periods, according to which I have organized this book. Each brings with it new capacities and social expectations that serve as important transitions in major theories:

- *The prenatal period: from conception to birth.* In this 9-month period, the most rapid time of change, a one-celled organism is transformed into a human baby with remarkable capacities for adjusting to life in the surrounding world.

© UWE OMMER/FAMILIES/TASCHEN ED.

Child development is so dramatic that researchers divide it into periods. These brothers and sisters in Sikkim, India, photographed with their parents, illustrate, from left, early childhood, adolescence, infancy, and middle childhood.

- *Infancy and toddlerhood: from birth to 2 years.* This period brings dramatic changes in the body and brain that support the emergence of a wide array of motor, perceptual, and intellectual capacities; the beginnings of language; and first intimate ties to others.
- *Early childhood: from 2 to 6 years.* The body becomes longer and leaner, motor skills are refined, and children become more self-controlled and self-sufficient. Make-believe play blossoms, supporting every aspect of psychological development. Thought and language expand at an astounding pace, a sense of morality becomes evident, and children establish ties with peers.
- *Middle childhood: from 6 to 11 years.* Children learn about the wider world and master new responsibilities that increasingly resemble those they will perform as adults. Hallmarks of this period are improved athletic abilities, participation in organized games with rules, more logical thought processes, mastery of basic literacy skills, and advances in understanding the self, morality, and friendship.
- *Adolescence: from 11 to 18 years.* This period initiates the transition to adulthood. Puberty leads to an adult-sized body and sexual maturity. Thought becomes abstract and idealistic, and schooling is increasingly directed toward preparation for higher education and the world of work. Young people begin to establish autonomy from the family and to define personal values and goals.

For many contemporary youth in industrialized nations, the transition to adult roles has become increasingly prolonged—so much so that some researchers have posited a new period of development called *emerging adulthood,* which spans ages 18 to 25. Although emerging adults have moved beyond adolescence, they have not yet fully assumed adult roles. Rather, during higher education and sometimes beyond, these young people intensify their exploration of options in love, career, and personal values before making enduring commitments. Because the period of emerging adulthood surfaced only during the past few decades, researchers have just begun to study it (Arnett, 2003, 2004; Arnett & Tanner, 2006). Perhaps it is *your* period of development. In Chapter 17, we will consider milestones of emerging adulthood, which build on adolescent attainments.

With this introduction in mind, let's turn to some basic issues that have captivated, puzzled, and sparked debate among child development theorists. Then our discussion will trace the emergence of the field and survey major theories. We will return to each contemporary theory in greater detail in later chapters.

Basic Issues

Research on child development did not begin until the late nineteenth and early twentieth centuries. But ideas about how children grow and change have a much longer history. As these speculations combined with research, they inspired the construction of *theories* of development. A **theory** is an orderly, integrated set of statements that describes, explains, and predicts behavior. For example, a good theory of infant–caregiver attachment would (1) *describe* the behaviors of babies around 6 to 8 months of age as they seek the affection and comfort of a familiar adult, (2) *explain* how and why infants develop this strong desire to bond with a caregiver, and (3) *predict* the consequences of this emotional bond for future relationships.

Theories are vital tools for two reasons. First, they provide organizing frameworks for our observations of children. In other words, they *guide and give meaning* to what we see. Second, theories that are verified by research often serve as a sound basis for practical action. Once a

theory An orderly, integrated set of statements that describes, explains, and predicts behavior.

theory helps us *understand* development, we are in a much better position *to know how to improve* the welfare and treatment of children.

As we will see later, theories are influenced by the cultural values and belief systems of their times. But theories differ in one important way from mere opinion or belief: A theory's continued existence depends on *scientific verification*. This means that the theory must be tested using a fair set of research procedures agreed on by the scientific community, and its findings must endure, or be replicated, over time.

Within the field of child development, many theories offer very different ideas about what children are like and how they change. The study of child development provides no ultimate truth because investigators do not always agree on the meaning of what they see. Also, children are complex beings; they change physically, cognitively, emotionally, and socially. No single theory has explained all these aspects. But the existence of many theories helps advance knowledge because researchers are continually trying to support, contradict, and integrate these different points of view.

Although there are many theories, we can easily organize them by looking at the stand they take on three basic issues: (1) Is the course of development continuous or discontinuous? (2) Does one course of development characterize all children, or are there many possible courses? (3) Are genetic or environmental factors more important in influencing development? Let's look closely at each of these issues.

Continuous or Discontinuous Development?

Recently, the mother of 20-month-old Angelo reported to me with amazement that her young son had pushed a toy car across the living room floor while making a motorlike sound, "Brmmmm, brmmmm," for the first time. When he hit a nearby wall with a bang, Angelo let go of the car, exclaimed, "C'ash," and laughed heartily.

"How come Angelo can pretend, but he couldn't a few months ago?" queried his mother. "And I wonder what 'Brmmmm, brmmmm' and 'Crash!' mean to Angelo? Does he understand motorlike sounds and collision the same way I do?"

Angelo's mother has raised a puzzling issue about development: How can we best describe the differences in capacities and behavior between small infants, young children, adolescents, and adults? As Figure 1.2 illustrates, most major theories recognize two possibilities.

One view holds that infants and preschoolers respond to the world in much the same way as adults do. The difference between the immature and the mature being is simply one of *amount or complexity*. For example, little Angelo's thinking may be just as logical and well-organized as our own. Perhaps (as his mother reports) he can sort objects into simple categories, recognize whether he has more of one kind than of another, and remember where he left his favorite toy at child care

(a) Continuous Development   **(b) Discontinuous Development**

FIGURE 1.2

Is development continuous or discontinuous? (a) Some theorists believe that development is a smooth, continuous process. Children gradually add more of the same types of skills. (b) Other theorists think that development takes place in discontinuous stages. Children change rapidly as they step up to a new level of development and then change very little for a while. With each step, the child interprets and responds to the world in a qualitatively different way.

the week before. Angelo's only limitation may be that he cannot perform these skills with as much information and precision as we can. If this is so, then Angelo's development is **continuous**—a process of gradually augmenting the same types of skills that were there to begin with.

According to a second view, Angelo's thoughts, emotions, and behavior differ considerably from those of adults. His development is **discontinuous**—a process in which new ways of understanding and responding to the world emerge at specific times. From this perspective, Angelo is not yet able to organize objects or remember and interpret experiences as we do. Instead, he will move through a series of developmental steps, each with unique features, until he reaches the highest level of functioning.

Theories that accept the discontinuous perspective regard development as taking place in **stages**—*qualitative* changes in thinking, feeling, and behaving that characterize specific periods of development. In stage theories, development is much like climbing a staircase, with each step corresponding to a more mature, reorganized way of functioning. The stage concept also assumes that children undergo periods of rapid transformation as they step up from one stage to the next, alternating with plateaus during which they stand solidly within a stage. In other words, change is fairly sudden rather than gradual and ongoing.

Does development actually occur in a neat, orderly sequence of stages? This ambitious assumption has faced significant challenges. We will review some influential stage theories later in this chapter.

One Course of Development or Many?

Stage theorists assume that people everywhere follow the same sequence of development. For example, in the domain of cognition, a stage theorist might try to identify the common influences that lead children to represent their world through language and make-believe play in early childhood, to think more logically and systematically in middle childhood, and to reason abstractly in adolescence.

At the same time, the field of child development is becoming increasingly aware that children grow up in distinct **contexts**—unique combinations of personal and environmental circumstances that can result in different paths of change. For example, a shy child who fears social encounters develops in very different contexts from those of an outgoing agemate who readily seeks out other people (Kagan, 2003). Children in non-Western village societies have experiences in their families and communities that differ sharply from those of children in large Western cities. These different circumstances foster different cognitive capacities, social skills, and feelings about the self and others (Shweder et al., 2006).

As you will see, contemporary theorists regard the contexts that mold development as many-layered and complex. On the personal side, these include heredity and biological makeup. On the environmental side, they include both immediate settings—home, child-care center, school, and neighborhood—and circumstances that are more remote from children's everyday lives: community resources, societal values and priorities, and historical time period. Finally, researchers today are more conscious than ever before of cultural diversity in development.

Relative Influence of Nature and Nurture?

In addition to describing the course of child development, each theory takes a stand on a major question about its underlying causes: Are genetic or environmental factors more important in influencing development? This is the age-old **nature–nurture controversy**. By *nature*, we mean inborn biological givens—the hereditary information we receive from our parents at the moment of conception. By *nurture*, we mean the complex forces of the physical and social world that influence our biological makeup and psychological experiences before and after birth.

Although all theories grant at least some role to both nature and nurture, they vary in emphasis. Consider the following questions: Is the older child's ability to think in more complex ways largely the result of an inborn timetable of growth, or is it primarily influenced by stimulation from parents and teachers? Do children acquire language because they are genetically predisposed to do so or because parents intensively teach them from an early age? And

continuous development A view that regards development as a cumulative process of gradually augmenting the same types of skills that were there to begin with.

discontinuous development A view of development as a process in which new ways of understanding and responding to the world emerge at specific times.

stage A qualitative change in thinking, feeling, and behaving that characterizes a specific period of development.

contexts Unique combinations of personal and environmental circumstances that can result in markedly different paths of change.

nature–nurture controversy Debate among theorists about whether genetic or environmental factors are more important in development.

what accounts for the vast individual differences among children—in height, weight, physical coordination, intelligence, personality, and social skills? Is nature or nurture more responsible?

A theory's position on the roles of nature and nurture affects how it explains individual differences. Some theorists emphasize *stability*—that children who are high or low in a characteristic (such as verbal ability, anxiety, or sociability) will remain so at later ages. These theorists typically stress the importance of *heredity*. If they do regard environment as important, they usually point to *early experiences* as establishing a lifelong pattern of behavior. Powerful negative events in the first few years, they argue, cannot be fully overcome by later, more positive ones (Bowlby, 1980; Johnson, 2000; Sroufe, Egeland, & Kreutzer, 1990). Other theorists, taking a more optimistic view, emphasize that *change* is possible and even likely if new experiences support it (Greenspan & Shanker, 2004; Masten & Reed, 2002; Nelson, 2002).

Throughout this book, you will see that investigators disagree, often sharply, on the question of *stability versus change*. Their answers have great applied significance. If you believe that development is largely due to nature, then providing experiences aimed at promoting change would seem to be of little value. If, on the other hand, you are convinced of the supreme importance of early experience, then you would intervene as soon as possible, offering high-quality stimulation and support to ensure that children develop at their best. Finally, if you think that environment is profoundly influential throughout development, you would provide assistance any time children or adolescents face difficulties, believing that, with the help of favorable life circumstances, they can recover from early negative events.

A Balanced Point of View

So far, we have discussed basic issues of child development in terms of extremes—solutions favoring one side or the other. But as we trace the unfolding of the field in the rest of this chapter, you will see that the positions of many theorists have softened. Today, some theorists believe that both continuous and discontinuous changes occur. Many acknowledge that development has both universal features and features unique to the individual and his or her contexts. And a growing number regard heredity and environment as inseparably interwoven, each affecting the potential of the other to modify the child's traits and capacities (Cole, 2006; Gottlieb, Wahlsten, & Lickliter, 2006; Huttenlocher, 2002; Lerner, 2006; Rutter, 2002). We will discuss these new ideas about nature and nurture in Chapter 2.

Finally, as you will see later in this book, the relative impact of early and later experiences varies greatly from one domain of development to another and even—as the Biology and Environment box on page 10 indicates—across individuals! Because of the complex network of factors contributing to human change and the challenge of isolating the effects of each, many theoretical points of view have gathered research support. Although debate continues, this circumstance has also sparked more balanced visions of child development.

Ask Yourself

Review   Why are there many theories of child development? Cite three basic issues on which almost all theories take a stand.

Apply   Anna, a high school counselor, has devised a program that integrates classroom learning with vocational training to help adolescents at risk for school dropout stay in school and transition smoothly to work life. What is Anna's position on *stability versus change* in development? Explain.

Connect   Provide an example of how one domain of development (physical, cognitive, or emotional/social) can affect development in another domain.

Reflect   Cite an aspect of your development that differs from a parent's or a grandparent's when he or she was your age. How might contexts explain this difference?

Biology and Environment

Resilient Children

John and his best friend Gary grew up in a run-down, crime-ridden inner-city neighborhood. By age 10, each had experienced years of family conflict followed by parental divorce. Reared for the rest of childhood and adolescence in mother-headed households, John and Gary rarely saw their fathers. Both achieved poorly, dropped out of high school, and were in and out of trouble with the police.

Then their paths diverged. By age 30, John had fathered two children with women he never married, had spent time in prison, was unemployed, and drank alcohol heavily. In contrast, Gary had returned to finish high school, had studied auto mechanics at a community college, and became manager of a gas station and repair shop. Married with two children, he had saved his earnings and bought a home. He was happy, healthy, and well-adapted to life.

A wealth of evidence shows that environmental risks—poverty, negative family interactions and parental divorce, job loss, mental illness, and drug abuse—predispose children to future problems (Masten & Gewirtz, 2006; Sameroff, 2006). Why did Gary "beat the odds" and come through unscathed?

New evidence on **resilience**—the ability to adapt effectively in the face of threats to development—is receiving increasing attention as investigators look for ways to protect young people from the damaging effects of stressful life conditions (Masten & Powell, 2003). This interest has been inspired by several long-term studies on the relationship of life stressors in childhood to competence and adjustment in adolescence and adulthood (Fergusson & Horwood, 2003; Masten et al., 1995; Werner & Smith, 2001). In each study, some individuals were shielded from negative outcomes, whereas others had lasting problems. Four broad factors seemed to offer protection from the damaging effects of stressful life events.

Personal Characteristics

A child's biologically endowed characteristics can reduce exposure to risk or lead to experiences that compensate for early stressful events. High intelligence and socially valued talents (in music or athletics, for example) increase the chances that a child will have rewarding experiences at school and in the community that offset the impact of a stressful home life. Temperament is particularly powerful. Children

with easygoing, sociable dispositions have an optimistic outlook on life and a special capacity to adapt to change—qualities that elicit positive responses from others. In contrast, emotionally reactive and irritable children often tax the patience of people around them (Masten & Reed, 2002; Werner, 2005). For example, both John and Gary moved several times during their childhoods. Each time, John became anxious and angry. Gary looked forward to making new friends and exploring new parts of the neighborhood.

A Warm Parental Relationship

A close relationship with at least one parent who provides warmth, appropriately high expectations, monitoring of the child's activities, and an organized home environment fosters resilience (Masten & Shaffer, 2006). But this factor (as well as the next one) is not independent of children's personal characteristics. Children who are relaxed, socially responsive, and able to deal with change are easier to rear and more likely to enjoy positive relationships with parents and other people. At the same time, some children may develop more attractive dispositions as a result of parental warmth and attention (Conger & Conger, 2002).

Social Support Outside the Immediate Family

The most consistent asset of resilient children is a strong bond to a competent, caring adult. For children who do not have a close bond with either parent, a grandparent, aunt, uncle, or teacher who forms a special relationship with the child can promote resilience (Masten & Reed, 2002). Gary received support in adolescence from his grandfather, who listened to Gary's concerns and helped him solve problems. In addition, Gary's grandfather had a stable marriage and work life and handled stressors skillfully. Consequently, he served as a model of effective coping.

Associations with rule-abiding peers who value school achievement are also linked to resilience. But children who have positive relationships with adults are far more likely to establish these supportive peer ties.

This boy's special relationship with his grandmother promotes resilience. By providing social support, she helps him cope with stress and solve problems constructively.

Community Resources and Opportunities

Community supports—good schools, convenient and affordable health care and social services, libraries, and recreation centers—foster both parent's and children's well-being. In addition, opportunities to participate in community life help older children and adolescents overcome adversity. Extracurricular activities at school, religious youth groups, scouting, and other organizations teach important social skills, such as cooperation, leadership, and contributing to others' welfare. As participants acquire these competencies, they gain in self-reliance, self-esteem, and community commitment (Benson et al., 2006). As a college student, Gary volunteered for Habitat for Humanity, joining a team building affordable housing in low-income neighborhoods. Community involvement offered Gary additional opportunities to form meaningful relationships, which further strengthened his resilience.

Research on resilience highlights the complex connections between heredity and environment. Armed with positive characteristics stemming from innate endowment, favorable rearing experiences, or both, children and adolescents can act to reduce stressful situations.

But when many risks pile up, they are increasingly difficult to overcome (Quyen et al., 1998). Therefore, interventions must reduce risks and enhance children's protective relationships at home, in school, and in the community. This means attending to both the person and the environment—strengthening children's capacities while also reducing hazardous experiences.

Historical Foundations

Contemporary theories of child development are the result of centuries of change in Western cultural values, philosophical thinking about children, and scientific progress. To understand the field as it exists today, we must return to its early beginnings—to ideas about children that long preceded scientific child study and that linger as important forces in current theory and research.

Medieval Times

Childhood was regarded as a separate period of life as early as medieval Europe—the sixth through the fifteenth centuries. Medieval painters often depicted children wearing loose, comfortable gowns, playing games, and looking up to adults. Written texts contained terms that distinguished children under age 7 or 8 from other people and that recognized even young teenagers as not fully mature. By the fourteenth century, manuals offering advice on many aspects of child care, including health, feeding, clothing, and games, were common (Alexandre-Bidon & Lett, 1997; Lett, 1997). Laws recognized that children needed protection from people who might mistreat them, and courts exercised leniency with lawbreaking youths because of their tender years (Hanawalt, 1993).

In sum, in medieval times, if not before, clear awareness existed of children as vulnerable beings and of childhood as a distinct developmental period. Religious writings, however, contained contradictory depictions of children's basic nature, sometimes portraying them as possessed by the devil and in need of purification, at other times as innocent and close to angels (Hanawalt, 2003). Both ideas foreshadowed later views of childhood.

THE ART ARCHIVE/BIBLIOTHÈQUE UNIVERSITAIRE DE MÉDECINE, MONTPELLIER/DAGLI ORTI

As early as medieval times, adults viewed childhood as a distinct developmental period. The children in this fourteenth-century image, painted in a book of songs, are dressed in loose, comfortable gowns as they play a lively game of Blind Man's Bluff.

The Reformation

In the sixteenth century, the Puritan belief in original sin gave rise to the view that children were born evil and stubborn and had to be civilized (Shahar, 1990). Harsh, restrictive child-rearing practices were recommended to tame the depraved child. Children were dressed in stiff, uncomfortable clothing that held them in adultlike postures, and disobedient students were routinely beaten by their schoolmasters. Nevertheless, love and affection for their children prevented most Puritan parents from using extremely repressive measures (Moran & Vinovskis, 1986).

As the Puritans emigrated from England to the United States, they brought the belief that child rearing was one of their most important obligations. Although they continued to regard the child's soul as tainted by original sin, they tried to teach their sons and daughters to use reason to tell right from wrong (Clarke-Stewart, 1998). As they trained their children in self-reliance and self-control, Puritan parents gradually adopted a moderate balance between severity and permissiveness.

Philosophies of the Enlightenment

The seventeenth-century Enlightenment brought new philosophies that emphasized ideals of human dignity and respect. Conceptions of childhood were more humane than those of the past.

JOHN LOCKE ■ The writings of British philosopher John Locke (1632–1704) served as the forerunner of a twentieth-century perspective that we will discuss shortly: behaviorism. Locke viewed the child as a **tabula rasa**—Latin for "blank slate." According to this idea, children begin

resilience The ability to adapt effectively in the face of threats to development.

tabula rasa Locke's view of the child as a "blank slate" whose character is shaped entirely by experience.

as nothing at all; their characters are shaped entirely by experience. Locke (1690/1892) saw parents as rational tutors who can mold the child however they wish through careful instruction, effective example, and rewards for good behavior. He was ahead of his time in recommending child-rearing practices that present-day research supports. For example, he recommended the use of praise and approval, rather than money or sweets, as rewards. He also opposed physical punishment: "The child repeatedly beaten in school cannot look upon books and teachers without experiencing fear and anger." Locke's philosophy led to a change from harshness toward children to kindness and compassion.

Look carefully at Locke's ideas, and you will see that he regarded development as *continuous*: Adultlike behaviors are gradually built up through the warm, consistent teachings of parents. His view of the child as a tabula rasa led him to champion *nurture*—the power of the environment to shape the child. And his faith in nurture suggests the possibility of *many courses of development* and of *change at later ages* due to new experiences. Finally, Locke's philosophy characterizes children as doing little to influence their own destiny, which is written on "blank slates" by others. This vision of a passive child has been discarded. All contemporary theories view children as active, purposeful beings who contribute substantially to their own development.

JEAN-JACQUES ROUSSEAU ■ In the eighteenth century, French philosopher Jean-Jacques Rousseau (1712–1778) introduced a new view of childhood. Children, Rousseau claimed, are not blank slates to be filled by adult instruction. Instead, they are **noble savages,** naturally endowed with a sense of right and wrong and an innate plan for orderly, healthy growth. Unlike Locke, Rousseau believed that children's built-in moral sense and unique ways of thinking and feeling would only be harmed by adult training. His was a child-centered philosophy in which the adult should be receptive to the child's needs at each of four stages of development: infancy, childhood, late childhood, and adolescence.

Rousseau's philosophy includes two influential concepts. The first is the concept of *stage*, which we discussed earlier. The second is the concept of **maturation,** which refers to a genetically determined, naturally unfolding course of growth. In contrast to Locke, Rousseau saw children as determining their own destinies. And he viewed development as a *discontinuous, stagewise* process that follows a *single, unified course* mapped out by *nature*.

Scientific Beginnings

The study of child development evolved quickly in the late nineteenth and early twentieth centuries. Early observations of children were soon followed by improved methods and theories. Each advance contributed to the firm foundation on which the field rests today.

DARWIN: FOREFATHER OF SCIENTIFIC CHILD STUDY ■ British naturalist Charles Darwin (1809–1882) joined an expedition to distant parts of the world, where he observed infinite variation among plant and animal species. He also saw that within a species, no two individuals are exactly alike. From these observations, he constructed his famous *theory of evolution*.

The theory emphasized two related principles: *natural selection* and *survival of the fittest*. Darwin explained that certain species survive in particular parts of the world because they have characteristics that fit with, or are adapted to, their surroundings. Other species die off because they are not as well-suited to their environments. Individuals within a species who best meet the environment's survival requirements live long enough to reproduce and pass their more beneficial characteristics to future generations. Darwin's emphasis on the adaptive value of physical characteristics and behavior eventually found its way into important developmental theories.

During his explorations, Darwin discovered that early prenatal growth is strikingly similar in many species. Other scientists concluded from Darwin's observation that the development of the human child followed the same general plan as the evolution of the human species. Although this belief eventually proved inaccurate, efforts to chart parallels between child growth and human evolution prompted researchers to make careful observations of all aspects of children's behavior. Out of these first attempts to document an idea about development, scientific child study was born.

noble savage Rousseau's view of the child as naturally endowed with a sense of right and wrong and an innate plan for orderly, healthy growth.

maturation A genetically determined, naturally unfolding course of growth.

normative approach An approach in which age-related averages are computed to represent typical development.

THE NORMATIVE PERIOD ■ G. Stanley Hall (1844–1924), one of the most influential American psychologists of the early twentieth century, is generally regarded as the founder of the child-study movement (Cairns & Cairns, 2006). Inspired by Darwin's work, Hall and his well-known student Arnold Gesell (1880–1961) devised theories based on evolutionary ideas. These early leaders regarded development as a genetically determined process that unfolds automatically, much like a flower (Gesell, 1933; Hall, 1904).

Hall and Gesell are remembered less for their one-sided theories than for their intensive efforts to describe all aspects of child development. They launched the **normative approach,** in which measures of behavior are taken on large numbers of individuals and age-related averages are computed to represent typical development. Using this procedure, Hall constructed elaborate questionnaires asking children of different ages almost everything they could tell about themselves—interests, fears, imaginary playmates, dreams, friendships, everyday knowledge, and more. Similarly, through observations and parental interviews, Gesell collected detailed normative information on the motor achievements, social behaviors, and personality characteristics of infants and children.

Gesell was also among the first to make knowledge about child development meaningful to parents. If, as he believed, the timetable of development is the product of millions of years of evolution, then children are naturally knowledgeable about their needs. His child-rearing advice, in the tradition of Rousseau, recommended sensitivity to children's cues (Thelen & Adolph, 1992). Along with Benjamin Spock's *Baby and Child Care,* Gesell's books became a central part of a rapidly expanding popular literature for parents.

THE MENTAL TESTING MOVEMENT ■ While Hall and Gesell were developing their theories and methods in the United States, French psychologist Alfred Binet (1857–1911) was also taking a normative approach to child development, but for a different reason. In the early 1900s, Binet and his colleague Theodore Simon were asked by Paris school officials to find a way to identify children with learning problems who needed to be placed in special classes. To address these practical educational concerns, Binet and Simon constructed the first successful intelligence test.

Binet began with a well-developed theory of intelligence. Capturing the complexity of children's thinking, he defined intelligence as good judgment, planning, and critical reflection (Sternberg & Jarvin, 2003). Then he created age-graded test items that directly measured these abilities.

In 1916, at Stanford University, Binet's test was adapted for use with English-speaking children. Since then, the English version has been known as the *Stanford-Binet Intelligence Scale.* Besides providing a score that could successfully predict school achievement, the Binet test sparked tremendous interest in individual differences in development. Comparisons of the scores of children who vary in gender, ethnicity, birth order, family background, and other characteristics became a major focus of research. And intelligence tests rose quickly to the forefront of the nature–nurture controversy.

Theories of child development have sparked an extensive parenting-advice literature. This new mother is learning what to expect in her baby's first year.

Ask Yourself

Review   Suppose we could arrange a debate between John Locke and Jean-Jacques Rousseau on the nature–nurture controversy. Summarize the argument that each historical figure is likely to present.

Connect   What do the ideas of Rousseau, Darwin, and Hall have in common?

Reflect   Find out whether your parents read Gesell, Spock, or other parenting advice books when you were growing up. What questions most concerned them? Do you think today's parents have concerns that differ from those of your parents? Explain.

Mid-Twentieth-Century Theories

In the mid-twentieth century, the field of child development expanded. A variety of theories emerged, each of which continues to have followers today. In these theories, the European concern with the child's inner thoughts and feelings contrasts sharply with the North American academic focus on scientific precision and concrete, observable behavior.

The Psychoanalytic Perspective

By the 1930s and 1940s, parents were increasingly seeking professional help in dealing with children's emotional difficulties. The earlier normative movement had answered the question, What are children like? Now another question had to be addressed: How and why do children become the way they are? To treat psychological problems, psychiatrists and social workers turned to an emerging approach to personality development that emphasized the unique history of each child.

According to the **psychoanalytic perspective,** children move through a series of stages in which they confront conflicts between biological drives and social expectations. How these conflicts are resolved determines the person's ability to learn, to get along with others, and to cope with anxiety. Although many individuals contributed to the psychoanalytic perspective, two have been especially influential: Sigmund Freud, founder of the psychoanalytic movement, and Erik Erikson.

FREUD'S THEORY ■ Freud (1856–1939), a Viennese physician, sought a cure for emotionally troubled adults by having them talk freely about painful events of their childhoods. Working with these remembrances, Freud examined the unconscious motivations of his patients and constructed his **psychosexual theory,** which emphasizes that how parents manage their child's sexual and aggressive drives in the first few years of life is crucial for healthy personality development.

In Freud's theory, three parts of the personality—id, ego, and superego—become integrated during a sequence of five stages, summarized in Table 1.1. The *id,* the largest portion of the mind, is the source of basic biological needs and desires. The *ego,* the conscious, rational part of personality, emerges in early infancy to redirect the id's impulses so that they are discharged in acceptable ways. Between 3 and 6 years of age, the *superego,* or conscience, develops through interactions with parents, who insist that children conform to the values of society. Now the ego faces the increasingly complex task of reconciling the demands of the id, the external world, and conscience (Freud, 1923/1974)—for example, the id impulse to grab an attractive toy from a playmate, versus the superego's awareness that such behavior is wrong. According to Freud, the relations established between id, ego, and superego during the preschool years determine the individual's basic personality.

Freud (1938/1973) believed that during childhood, sexual impulses shift their focus from the oral to the anal to the genital regions of the body. In each stage, parents walk a fine line between permitting too much or too little gratification of their child's basic needs. If parents strike an appropriate balance, then children grow into well-adjusted adults with the capacity for mature sexual behavior and investment in family life.

Freud's theory was the first to stress the influence of the early parent–child relationship on development. But his perspective was eventually criticized. First, it overemphasized the influence of sexual feelings in development. Second, because it was based on the problems of sexually repressed, well-to-do adults in nineteenth-century Victorian society, it did not apply in other cultures. Finally, Freud had not studied children directly.

ERIKSON'S THEORY ■ Several of Freud's followers took what was useful from his theory and improved on his vision. The most important of these neo-Freudians is Erik Erikson (1902–1994), who expanded the picture of development at each stage. In his **psychosocial theory,** Erikson emphasized that in addition to mediating between id impulses and superego demands, the ego

psychoanalytic perspective Freud's view of personality development, in which children move through a series of stages in which they confront conflicts between biological drives and social expectations. The way these conflicts are resolved determines psychological adjustment.

psychosexual theory Freud's theory, which emphasizes that how parents manage children's sexual and aggressive drives in the first few years of life is crucial for healthy personality development.

psychosocial theory Erikson's theory, which emphasizes that at each Freudian stage, individuals not only develop a unique personality but also acquire attitudes and skills that help them become active, contributing members of their society.

TABLE 1.1 Freud's Psychosexual Stages

PSYCHOSEXUAL STAGE	PERIOD OF DEVELOPMENT	DESCRIPTION
Oral	Birth–1 year	The new ego directs the baby's sucking activities toward breast or bottle. If oral needs are not met appropriately, the individual may develop such habits as thumb sucking, fingernail biting, and pencil chewing in childhood and overeating and smoking in later life.
Anal	1–3 years	Toddlers and preschoolers enjoy holding and releasing urine and feces. Toilet training becomes a major issue between parent and child. If parents insist that children be trained before they are ready, or if they make too few demands, conflicts about anal control may appear in the form of extreme orderliness and cleanliness or messiness and disorder.
Phallic	3–6 years	As preschoolers take pleasure in genital stimulation, Freud's Oedipus conflict for boys and Electra conflict for girls arise: Children feel a sexual desire for the other-sex parent. To avoid punishment, they give up this desire and adopt the same-sex parent's characteristics and values. As a result, the superego is formed, and children feel guilty each time they violate its standards.
Latency	6–11 years	Sexual instincts die down, and the superego develops further. The child acquires new social values from adults and same-sex peers outside the family.
Genital	Adolescence	With puberty, the sexual impulses of the phallic stage reappear. If development has been successful during earlier stages, it leads to marriage, mature sexuality, and the birth and rearing of children. This stage extends through adulthood.

acquires attitudes and skills that make the individual an active, contributing member of society. A basic psychological conflict, which is resolved along a continuum from positive to negative, determines healthy or maladaptive outcomes at each stage. As Table 1.2 on page 16 shows, Erikson's first five stages parallel Freud's stages, but Erikson added three adult stages. He was one of the first to recognize the lifespan nature of development.

Unlike Freud, Erikson pointed out that normal development must be understood in relation to each culture's life situation. For example, in the 1940s, he observed that Yurok Indians of the U.S. northwest coast deprived babies of breastfeeding for the first 10 days after birth and instead fed them a thin soup. At age 6 months, infants were abruptly weaned—if necessary, by having the mother leave for a few days. From our cultural vantage point, these practices may seem cruel. But Erikson explained that the Yurok lived in a world in which salmon fill the river just once a year, a circumstance requiring the development of considerable self-restraint for survival. In this way, he showed that child rearing is responsive to the competencies valued and needed by the child's society.

CONTRIBUTIONS AND LIMITATIONS OF PSYCHOANALYTIC THEORY ■ A special strength of the psychoanalytic perspective is its emphasis on the individual's unique life history as worthy of study and understanding. Consistent with this view, psychoanalytic theorists accept the *clinical,* or *case study, method,* which synthesizes information from a variety of sources into a detailed picture of the personality of a single child. (We will discuss the clinical method further at the end of this chapter.) Psychoanalytic theory has also inspired a wealth of research on many aspects of emotional and social development, including infant–caregiver attachment, aggression, sibling relationships, child-rearing practices, morality, gender roles, and adolescent identity.

© FRANS LEMMENS/ZEFA/CORBIS

Erik Erikson believed that child rearing can be understood only in relation to the competencies valued and needed by the individual's society. This boy fishing with his father in the Inle Lake in Myanmar is learning skills that he will need as an adult in his culture.

TABLE 1.2   Erikson's Psychosocial Stages, with Corresponding Psychosexual Stages Indicated

PSYCHOSOCIAL STAGE	PERIOD OF DEVELOPMENT	DESCRIPTION
Basic trust versus mistrust (Oral)	Birth–1 year	From warm, responsive care, infants gain a sense of trust, or confidence, that the world is good. Mistrust occurs when infants have to wait too long for comfort and are handled harshly.
Autonomy versus shame and doubt (Anal)	1–3 years	Using new mental and motor skills, children want to choose and decide for themselves. Autonomy is fostered when parents permit reasonable free choice and do not force or shame the child.
Initiative versus guilt (Phallic)	3–6 years	Through make-believe play, children experiment with the kind of person they can become. Initiative—a sense of ambition and responsibility—develops when parents support their child's new sense of purpose. The danger is that parents will demand too much self-control, which leads to overcontrol, meaning too much guilt.
Industry versus inferiority (Latency)	6–11 years	At school, children develop the capacity to work and cooperate with others. Inferiority develops when negative experiences at home, at school, or with peers lead to feelings of incompetence.
Identity versus role confusion (Genital)	Adolescence	The adolescent tries to answer the questions, Who am I, and what is my place in society? By exploring values and vocational goals, the young person forms a personal identity. The negative outcome is confusion about future adult roles.
Intimacy versus isolation	Emerging adulthood	As the quest for identity continues, young people also work on establishing intimate ties to others. Because of earlier disappointments, some individuals cannot form close relationships and remain isolated.
Generativity versus stagnation	Adulthood	Generativity means giving to the next generation through child rearing, caring for other people, or productive work. The person who fails in these ways feels an absence of meaningful accomplishment.
Integrity versus despair	Old age	In this final stage, individuals reflect on the kind of person they have been. Integrity results from feeling that life was worth living as it happened. Old people who are dissatisfied with their lives fear death.

Erik Erikson
© OLIVE PIERCE/BLACK STAR

behaviorism An approach that regards directly observable events—stimuli and responses—as the appropriate focus of study and that views the development of behavior as taking place through classical and operant conditioning.

social learning theory An approach that emphasizes the role of modeling, or observational learning, in the development of behavior.

Despite its extensive contributions, the psychoanalytic perspective is no longer in the mainstream of child development research. Psychoanalytic theorists may have become isolated from the rest of the field because they were so strongly committed to the clinical approach that they failed to consider other methods. In addition, many psychoanalytic ideas, such as psychosexual stages and ego functioning, are too vague to be tested empirically (Crain, 2005; Thomas, 2005). Nevertheless, Erikson's broad outline of psychosocial change captures the essence of personality development during childhood and adolescence. Consequently, we will return to it in later chapters.

Behaviorism and Social Learning Theory

As the psychoanalytic perspective gained prominence, child study was also influenced by a very different perspective. According to **behaviorism,** directly observable events—stimuli and responses—are the appropriate focus of study. North American behaviorism began in the early twentieth century with the work of psychologist John Watson (1878–1958), who wanted to create an objective science of psychology.

TRADITIONAL BEHAVIORISM ■ Watson was inspired by Russian physiologist Ivan Pavlov's studies of animal learning. Pavlov knew that dogs release saliva as an innate reflex when they are given food. But he noticed that his dogs started salivating before they tasted any food—when they saw the trainer who usually fed them. The dogs, Pavlov reasoned, must have learned to associate a neutral stimulus (the trainer) with another stimulus (food) that produces a reflexive response (salivation). Because of this association, the neutral stimulus alone could bring about a response resembling the reflex. Eager to test this idea, Pavlov successfully taught dogs to salivate at the sound of a bell by pairing it with the presentation of food. He had discovered *classical conditioning*.

Watson wanted to find out if classical conditioning could be applied to children's behavior. In a historic experiment, he taught Albert, an 11-month-old infant, to fear a neutral stimulus—a soft white rat—by presenting it several times with a sharp, loud sound, which naturally scared the baby. Little Albert, who at first had reached out eagerly to touch the furry rat, began to cry and turn his head away at the sight of it (Watson & Raynor, 1920). In fact, Albert's fear was so intense that researchers eventually challenged the ethics of studies like this one. Consistent with Locke's tabula rasa, Watson concluded that environment is the supreme force in development and that adults can mold children's behavior by carefully controlling stimulus–response associations. He viewed development as continuous—a gradual increase with age in the number and strength of these associations.

Another form of behaviorism was B. F. Skinner's (1904–1990) *operant conditioning theory*. According to Skinner, the frequency of a behavior can be increased by following it with a wide variety of *reinforcers*, such as food, praise, a friendly smile, or a new toy. It can also be decreased through *punishment*, such as disapproval or withdrawal of privileges. As a result of Skinner's work, operant conditioning became a broadly applied learning principle, which we will consider further when we explore the infant's learning capacities in Chapter 5.

SOCIAL LEARNING THEORY ■ Psychologists wondered whether behaviorism might offer a more direct and effective explanation of the development of children's social behavior than the less precise concepts of psychoanalytic theory. This sparked approaches that built on the principles of conditioning, offering expanded views of how children and adults acquire new responses.

Several kinds of **social learning theory** emerged. The most influential, devised by Albert Bandura (1977), emphasizes *modeling*, also known as *imitation* or *observational learning*, as a powerful source of development. The baby who claps her hands after her mother does so, the child who angrily hits a playmate in the same way that he has been punished at home, and the teenager who wears the same clothes and hairstyle as her friends at school are all displaying observational learning.

Bandura's work continues to influence much research on children's social development. But today, like the field of child development as a whole, his theory stresses the importance of *cognition*, or thinking. Bandura has shown that children's ability to listen, remember, and abstract general rules from complex sets of observed behavior affects their imitation and learning. In fact, the most recent revision of Bandura's (1992, 2001) theory places such strong emphasis on how children think about themselves and other people that he calls it a *social-cognitive* rather than a social learning approach.

Social learning theory recognizes that children acquire many skills through modeling. By observing and imitating her mother's behavior, this Vietnamese preschooler is becoming a skilled user of chopsticks.

In Bandura's revised view, children gradually become more selective in what they imitate. From watching others engage in self-praise and self-blame and through feedback about the worth of their own actions, children develop *personal standards* for behavior and a *sense of self-efficacy*—the belief that their own abilities and characteristics will help them succeed. These cognitions guide responses in particular situations (Bandura, 1999, 2001). For example, imagine a parent who often remarks, "I'm glad I kept working on that task, even though it was hard," and who encourages persistence by saying, "I know you can do a good job on that homework!" Soon the child starts to view herself as hardworking and high-achieving and selects people with these characteristics as models. In this way, as children acquire attitudes, values, and convictions about themselves, they control their own learning and behavior.

CONTRIBUTIONS AND LIMITATIONS OF BEHAVIORISM AND SOCIAL LEARNING THEORY ■
Behaviorism and social learning theory have had a major impact on practices with children. **Behavior modification** consists of procedures that combine conditioning and modeling to eliminate undesirable behaviors and increase desirable responses. It has been used to relieve a wide range of serious developmental problems, such as persistent aggression, language delays, and extreme fears (Martin & Pear, 2007).

Behavior modification is also effective in dealing with common, everyday difficulties, including poor time management; unwanted habits such as nail biting and smoking; and anxiety over such recurrent events as test-taking, public speaking, and medical and dental treatments. In one study, researchers reduced 4- and 5-year-olds' unruliness in a preschool classroom by reinforcing them with tokens (which they could exchange for candy) when they behaved appropriately and punishing them by taking away tokens when they screamed, threw objects, attacked other children, or refused to comply with a teacher's request (Conyers et al., 2004). In another investigation, children with acute burn injuries played a virtual reality game while nurses engaged in the painful process of changing their bandages. Visual images and sound effects delivered though a headset made the children feel as if they were in a fantasy world. As the game reinforced children's concentration and pleasure, it distracted them from the medical procedure, causing their pain and anxiety to drop sharply compared with dressing changes in which the game was unavailable (Das et al., 2005).

Nevertheless, many theorists believe that behaviorism and social learning theory offer too narrow a view of important environmental influences. These extend beyond immediate reinforcements and modeled behaviors to children's rich physical and social worlds. Behaviorism and social learning theory have also been criticized for underestimating children's contributions to their own development. Bandura, with his emphasis on cognition, is unique among theorists whose work grew out of the behaviorist tradition in granting children an active role in their own learning.

Piaget's Cognitive-Developmental Theory

If one individual has influenced the contemporary field of child development more than any other, it is Swiss cognitive theorist Jean Piaget (1896–1980). North American investigators had been aware of Piaget's work since 1930. But they did not grant it much attention until the 1960s, mainly because Piaget's ideas were at odds with behaviorism, which dominated North American psychology in the mid-twentieth century (Cairns & Cairns, 2006). Piaget did not believe that children's learning depends on reinforcers, such as rewards from adults. According to his **cognitive-developmental theory,** children actively construct knowledge as they manipulate and explore their world.

PIAGET'S STAGES ■ Piaget's view of development was greatly influenced by his early training in biology. Central to his theory is the biological concept of *adaptation* (Piaget, 1971). Just as structures of the body are adapted to fit with the environment, so structures of the mind develop to better fit with, or represent, the external world. In infancy and early childhood, Piaget claimed, children's understanding is different from adults'. For example, he believed that young babies do not realize that an object hidden from view—a favorite toy or even the

behavior modification
Procedures that combine conditioning and modeling to eliminate undesirable behaviors and increase desirable responses.

cognitive-developmental theory An approach introduced by Piaget that views children as actively constructing knowledge as they manipulate and explore their world and that regards cognitive development as taking place in stages.

mother—continues to exist. He also concluded that preschoolers' thinking is full of faulty logic. For example, children younger than age 7 commonly say that the amount of a liquid changes when it is poured into a different-shaped container. According to Piaget, children eventually revise these incorrect ideas in their ongoing efforts to achieve an *equilibrium,* or balance, between internal structures and information they encounter in their every-day worlds.

In Piaget's theory, as the brain develops and children's experiences expand, they move through four broad stages, each characterized by quali-tatively distinct ways of thinking. Table 1.3 on page 20 provides a brief description of Piaget's stages. Cognitive development begins in the *sensorimotor stage* with the baby's use of the senses and movements to explore the world. These action patterns evolve into the symbolic but illog-ical thinking of the preschooler in the *preoperational stage*. Then cognition is transformed into the more organized reasoning of the school-age child in the *concrete operational stage*. Finally, in the *formal operational stage,* thought becomes the abstract, systematic reasoning system of the adoles-cent and adult.

Piaget devised special methods for investigating how children think. Early in his career, he carefully observed his three infant children and also presented them with everyday problems, such as an attractive object that could be grasped, mouthed, kicked, or searched for. From their responses, Piaget derived his ideas about cognitive changes during the first two years. To study childhood and adolescent thought, Piaget adapted the clinical method of psychoanalysis, conducting open-ended *clinical interviews* in which a child's initial response to a task served as the basis for Piaget's next question. We will look more closely at this technique when we discuss research methods later in this chapter.

In Piaget's sensorimotor stage, babies learn by acting on the world. As this 1-year-old bangs a mallet on a xylophone, he discovers that his movements have predictable effects on objects and that objects influence one another in regular ways.

CONTRIBUTIONS AND LIMITATIONS OF PIAGET'S THEORY ■ Piaget convinced the field that children are active learners whose minds consist of rich structures of knowledge. Besides investi-gating children's understanding of the physical world, Piaget explored their reasoning about the social world. His stages have sparked a wealth of research on children's conceptions of themselves,

In Piaget's preoperational stage, preschoolers represent their earlier sensorimotor discoveries with symbols, and language and make-believe play develop rapidly. These 3-year-olds create an imaginative play scene with dolls and stuffed animals.

In Piaget's concrete operational stage, school-age children think in an organized, logical fashion about concrete objects. These 7-year-olds understand that the amount of milk remains the same after being poured into a differently shaped container, even though its appear-ance changes.

TABLE 1.3	Piaget's Stages of Cognitive Development	
STAGE	**PERIOD OF DEVELOPMENT**	**DESCRIPTION**
Sensorimotor	Birth–2 years	Infants "think" by acting on the world with their eyes, ears, hands, and mouth. As a result, they invent ways of solving sensorimotor problems, such as pulling a lever to hear the sound of a music box, finding hidden toys, and putting objects in and taking them out of containers.
Preoperational	2–7 years	Preschool children use symbols to represent their earlier sensorimotor discoveries. Development of language and make-believe play takes place. However, thinking lacks the logic of the two remaining stages.
Concrete operational	7–11 years	Children's reasoning becomes logical. School-age children understand that a certain amount of lemonade or play dough remains the same even after its appearance changes. They also organize objects into hierarchies of classes and subclasses. However, thinking falls short of adult intelligence. It is not yet abstract.
Formal operational	11 years on	The capacity for abstract, systematic thinking enables adolescents, when faced with a problem, to start with a hypothesis, deduce testable inferences, and isolate and combine variables to see which inferences are confirmed. Adolescents can also evaluate the logic of verbal statements without referring to real-world circumstances.

Jean Piaget

© BETTMANN/CORBIS

other people, and human relationships. In practical terms, Piaget's theory encouraged the development of educational philosophies and programs that emphasize children's discovery learning and direct contact with the environment.

Despite Piaget's overwhelming contributions, his theory has been challenged. Research indicates that Piaget underestimated the competencies of infants and preschoolers. When young children are given tasks scaled down in difficulty and relevant to their everyday experiences, their understanding appears closer to that of the older child and adult than Piaget assumed. This discovery has led many researchers to conclude that the maturity of children's thinking may depend on their familiarity with the task presented and the complexity of knowledge sampled. Furthermore, many studies show that children's performance on Piagetian problems can be improved with training—findings that call into question Piaget's assumption that discovery learning rather than adult teaching is the best way to foster development (Klahr & Nigam, 2004; Siegler & Sventina, 2006). Critics also point out that Piaget's stagewise account pays insufficient attention to social and cultural influences—and the resulting wide variation in thinking that exists among children of the same age.

Today, the field of child development is divided over its loyalty to Piaget's ideas. Those who continue to find merit in Piaget's stages often accept a modified view—one in which changes in children's thinking take place more gradually than Piaget believed (Case, 1998; Demetriou et al., 2002; Fischer & Bidell, 2006; Halford & Andrews, 2006). Among those who disagree with Piaget's stage sequence, some have embraced an approach that emphasizes continuous gains in children's cognition: information processing. And still others have been drawn to

© SYRACUSE NEWSPAPERS/LI-HUA LAN/THE IMAGE WORKS

In Piaget's formal operational stage, adolescents think systematically and abstractly. These high school students, who have entered a science competition, must construct a lightweight model tower that can support up to 60 pounds. They solve the problem by generating hypotheses about procedures that might work, isolating and combining relevant variables, and conducting systematic tests to observe their real-world consequences.

theories that highlight the role of children's social and cultural contexts. We take up these approaches in the next section.

Ask Yourself

Review   What aspect of behaviorism made it attractive to critics of psychoanalytic theory? How did Piaget's theory respond to a major limitation of behaviorism?

Apply   A 4-year-old becomes frightened of the dark and refuses to go to sleep at night. How would a psychoanalyst and a behaviorist differ in their views of how this problem developed?

Connect   Although social learning theory focuses on social development and Piaget's theory on cognitive development, each has enhanced our understanding of other domains. Mention an additional domain addressed by each theory.

Recent Theoretical Perspectives

New ways of understanding the child are constantly emerging—questioning, building on, and enhancing the discoveries of earlier theories. Today, a burst of fresh approaches and research emphases is broadening our understanding of children's development.

Information Processing

In the 1970s and 1980s, researchers turned to the field of cognitive psychology for ways to understand the development of children's thinking. The design of digital computers that use mathematically specified steps to solve problems suggested to psychologists that the human mind might also be viewed as a symbol-manipulating system through which information flows—a perspective called **information processing** (Klahr & MacWhinney, 1998; Munakata, 2006). From the time information is presented to the senses at input until it emerges as a behavioral response at output, information is actively coded, transformed, and organized.

CONCERN WITH RIGOR AND PRECISION ■ Information-processing researchers often use flowcharts to map the precise steps individuals use to solve problems and complete tasks, much like the plans devised by programmers to get computers to perform a series of "mental operations" (Siegler & Alibali, 2005). To see the usefulness of this approach, let's look at an example.

In a study of problem solving, a researcher provided a pile of blocks varying in size, shape, and weight and asked school-age children to build a bridge across a "river" (painted on a floor mat) that was too wide for any single block to span (Thornton, 1999). Figure 1.3 on page 22 shows one solution to the problem: Two planklike blocks span the water, each held in place by the counterweight of heavy blocks on the bridge's towers. Whereas older children easily built successful bridges, only one 5-year-old did. Careful tracking of her efforts revealed that she repeatedly tried unsuccessful strategies, such as pushing two planks together and pressing down on their ends to hold them in place. But eventually, her experimentation triggered the idea of using the blocks as counterweights. Her mistaken procedures helped her understand why the counterweight approach worked.

Many information-processing models exist. Some, like the one just considered, track children's mastery of one or a few tasks. Others describe the human cognitive system as a whole

information processing
An approach that views the human mind as a symbol-manipulating system through which information flows and that regards cognitive development as a continuous process.

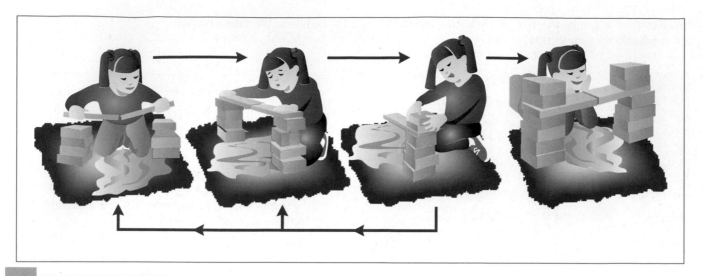

FIGURE 1.3

Information-processing flowchart showing the steps that a 5-year-old used to solve a bridge-building problem. Her task was to use blocks varying in size, shape, and weight, some of which were planklike, to construct a bridge across a "river" (painted on a floor mat) too wide for any single block to span. The child discovered how to counterweight and balance the bridge. The arrows reveal that even after building a successful counterweight, she returned to earlier, unsuccessful strategies, which seemed to help her understand why the counterweight approach worked. (Adapted from Thornton, 1999.)

developmental cognitive neuroscience An area of investigation that brings together researchers from psychology, biology, neuroscience, and medicine to study the relationship between changes in the brain and the developing child's cognitive processing and behavior patterns.

ethology An approach concerned with the adaptive, or survival, value of behavior and its evolutionary history.

sensitive period A time that is optimal for certain capacities to emerge and in which the individual is especially responsive to environmental influences.

(Atkinson & Shiffrin, 1968; Lockhart & Craik, 1990). These general models are used as guides for asking questions about broad age changes in children's thinking: Does a child's ability to solve problems become more organized and "planful" with age? What strategies do younger and older children use to remember new information, and how do those strategies affect children's recall?

The information-processing approach is also being used to clarify the processing of social information. For example, flowcharts exist that track the steps children use to solve social problems (such as how to enter an ongoing play group) and acquire gender-linked preferences and behaviors (Crick & Dodge, 1994; Liben & Bigler, 2002). If we can identify how social problem solving and gender stereotyping arise in childhood, then we can design interventions that promote more favorable social development.

Like Piaget's theory, the information-processing approach regards children as active, sense-making beings who modify their own thinking in response to environmental demands (Halford, 2005; Munakata, 2006). But unlike Piaget's theory, it does not divide development into stages. Rather, the thought processes studied—perception, attention, memory, categorization of information, planning, problem solving, and comprehension of written and spoken prose—are regarded as similar at all ages but present to a lesser or greater extent. Therefore, the view of development is one of continuous change.

A great strength of the information-processing approach is its commitment to rigorous research methods. Because it has provided precise accounts of how children of different ages engage in many aspects of thinking, its findings have led to teaching methods that help children approach academic tasks in more advanced ways (Blumenfeld, Marx, & Harris, 2006). But information processing has fallen short in some respects. It has been better at analyzing thinking into its components than at putting them back together into a comprehensive theory. And it virtually ignores aspects of children's cognition that are not linear and logical, such as imagination and creativity (Birney et al., 2005).

DEVELOPMENTAL COGNITIVE NEUROSCIENCE ■ Over the past two decades, as information-processing research has expanded, a new area of investigation has arisen, called **developmental**

cognitive neuroscience. It brings together researchers from psychology, biology, neuroscience, and medicine to study the relationship between changes in the brain and the developing child's cognitive processing and behavior patterns.

Improved methods for analyzing brain activity while children perform various tasks have greatly enhanced knowledge of relationships between brain functioning and behavior (Johnson, 2005). Armed with these brain-imaging techniques (which we will consider in Chapter 5), neuroscientists are tackling questions like these: How do specific experiences at various ages influence the growth and organization of the young child's brain? What transformations in the brain make it harder for adolescents and adults than for children to acquire a second language?

Neuroscientists are making rapid progress in identifying the types of experiences that support or undermine brain development at various ages. They are also clarifying the brain bases of many learning and behavior disorders, and they are contributing to effective treatments for children with disabilities by examining the impact of various intervention techniques on both brain functioning and behavior (Munakata, Casey, & Diamond, 2004). Although much remains to be discovered, developmental cognitive neuroscience is already transforming our understanding of development and yielding major practical applications.

An advantage of having many theories is that they encourage researchers to attend to previously neglected dimensions of children's lives. The final four perspectives we will discuss focus on *contexts* for development. The first of these views emphasizes that the development of many capacities is influenced by our long evolutionary history.

Ethology and Evolutionary Developmental Psychology

Ethology is concerned with the adaptive, or survival, value of behavior and its evolutionary history (Hinde, 1992). Its roots can be traced to the work of Darwin. Two European zoologists, Konrad Lorenz and Niko Tinbergen, laid its modern foundations. Watching diverse animal species in their natural habitats, Lorenz and Tinbergen observed behavior patterns that promote survival. The best known of these is *imprinting,* the early following behavior of certain baby birds, such as geese, which ensures that the young will stay close to the mother and be fed and protected from danger. Imprinting takes place during an early, restricted period of development. If the mother goose is absent during this time but an object resembling her in important features is present, young goslings may imprint on it instead (Lorenz, 1952).

Observations of imprinting led to a major concept in child development: the *critical period.* It is a limited time span during which the child is biologically prepared to acquire certain adaptive behaviors but needs the support of an appropriately stimulating environment. Many researchers have investigated whether complex cognitive and social behaviors must be learned during certain periods. For example, if children are deprived of adequate food or physical and social stimulation during their early years, will their intelligence be impaired? If language is not mastered in early childhood, is the child's capacity to acquire it reduced?

© AP IMAGES

In later chapters, you will discover that the term *sensitive period* applies better to human development than the strict notion of a critical period (Bornstein, 1989). A **sensitive period** is a time that is optimal for certain capacities to emerge and in which the individual is especially responsive to environmental influences. However, its boundaries are less well-defined than are those of a critical period. Development can occur later, but it is harder to induce.

Inspired by observations of imprinting, British psychoanalyst John Bowlby (1969) applied ethological theory to understanding the human infant–caregiver relationship. He argued that

Ethology focuses on the adaptive, or survival, value of behavior and on similarities between human behavior and that of other species, especially our primate relatives. Observing this mother cuddling her 8-day-old infant helps us understand the human-infant caregiver relationship.

infant smiling, babbling, grasping, and crying are built-in social signals that encourage the caregiver to approach, care for, and interact with the baby. By keeping the parent near, these behaviors help ensure that the baby will be fed, protected from danger, and provided with the stimulation and affection necessary for healthy growth. The development of attachment in human infants is a lengthy process involving changes in psychological structures that lead the baby to form a deep affectionate tie with the caregiver (Thompson, 2006). In Chapter 7, we will consider how infant, caregiver, and family context contribute to attachment and how attachment influences later development.

Observations by ethologists have shown that many aspects of children's social behavior, including emotional expressions, aggression, cooperation, and social play, resemble those of our primate relatives. Recently, researchers have extended this effort in a new area of research called **evolutionary developmental psychology.** It seeks to understand the adaptive value of species-wide cognitive, emotional, and social competencies as those competencies change with age. Evolutionary developmental psychologists ask questions like these: What role does the newborn's visual preference for facelike stimuli play in survival? Does it support older infants' capacity to distinguish familiar caregivers from unfamiliar people? Why do children play in gender-segregated groups? What do they learn from such play that might lead to adult gender-typed behaviors, such as male dominance and female investment in caregiving?

As these examples suggest, evolutionary psychologists are not just concerned with the genetic and biological basis of development. They realize that humans' large brain and extended childhood resulted from the need to master an increasingly complex environment, so they are also interested in learning (Bjorklund & Blasi, 2005). And they realize that today's lifestyles differ so radically from those of our evolutionary ancestors that certain evolved behaviors, such as life-threatening risk-taking by adolescents and male-to-male violence, are no longer adaptive (Bjorklund & Pellegrini, 2002; Blasi & Bjorklund, 2003). By clarifying the origins and development of such behaviors, evolutionary developmental psychology may help spark more effective interventions.

In sum, evolutionary psychologists want to understand the entire *organism–environment system.* The next contextual perspective we will discuss, Vygotsky's sociocultural theory, serves as an excellent complement to the evolutionary viewpoint because it highlights the social and cultural dimensions of children's experiences.

Vygotsky's Sociocultural Theory

The field of child development has recently seen a dramatic increase in studies addressing the cultural context of children's lives. Investigations that make comparisons across cultures, and between ethnic groups within cultures, provide insight into whether developmental pathways apply to all children or are limited to particular environmental conditions (Cole, 2005).

Today, much research is examining the relationship of *culturally specific beliefs and practices* to development. The contributions of Russian psychologist Lev Vygotsky (1896–1934) have played a major role in this trend. Vygotsky's (1934/1987) perspective, known as **sociocultural theory,** focuses on how *culture*—the values, beliefs, customs, and skills of a social group—is transmitted to the next generation. According to Vygotsky, *social interaction*—in particular, cooperative dialogues with more knowledgeable members of society—is necessary for children to acquire the ways of thinking and behaving that make up a community's culture (Rowe & Wertsch, 2002). Vygotsky believed that as adults and more expert peers help children master culturally meaningful activities, the communication between them becomes part of children's thinking. As children internalize features of these dialogues, they can use the language within them to guide their own thought and actions and to acquire new skills (Berk & Harris, 2003). The young child instructing herself while working a puzzle or preparing a table for dinner has begun to produce the same kinds of guiding comments that an adult previously used to help her master important tasks.

Vygotsky's theory has been especially influential in the study of children's cognition. Vygotsky agreed with Piaget that children are active, constructive beings. But whereas Piaget

COURTESY OF JAMES V. WERTSCH/ CLARK UNIVERSITY

According to Lev Vygotsky, shown here with his daughter, many cognitive processes and skills are socially transferred from more knowledgeable members of society to children. Vygotsky's sociocultural theory helps explain the wide cultural variation in cognitive competencies.

emphasized children's independent efforts to make sense of their world, Vygotsky viewed cognitive development as a *socially mediated process,* in which children depend on assistance from adults and more expert peers as they tackle new challenges.

In Vygotsky's theory, children undergo certain stage-wise changes. For example, when they acquire language, they gain in ability to participate in dialogues with others, and mastery of culturally valued competencies surges forward. When children enter school, they spend much time discussing language, literacy, and other academic concepts—experiences that encourage them to reflect on their own thinking (Bodrova & Leong, 2007; Kozulin, 2003). As a result, they gain dramatically in reasoning and problem solving.

At the same time, Vygotsky stressed that dialogues with experts lead to continuous changes in thinking that vary greatly from culture to culture. Consistent with this view, a major finding of cross-cultural research is that cultures select different tasks for children's learning (Rogoff, 2003). Social interaction surrounding those tasks leads to competencies essential for success in a par-

With her grandmother's guidance, a Navajo girl learns to use a vertical weaving loom. She is acquiring a culturally valued skill through interacting with an older, more expert weaver.

ticular culture. For example, in industrialized nations, teachers help people learn to read, drive a car, or use a computer. Among the Zinacanteco Indians of southern Mexico, adult experts guide young girls as they master complicated weaving techniques (Greenfield, 2004; Greenfield, Maynard, & Childs, 2000). In Brazil and other developing nations, child candy sellers with little or no schooling develop sophisticated mathematical abilities as the result of buying candy from wholesalers, pricing it in collaboration with adults and experienced peers, and bargaining with customers on city streets (Saxe, 1988).

Research stimulated by Vygotsky's theory reveals that children in every culture develop unique strengths. But Vygotsky's emphasis on culture and social experience led him to neglect the biological side of development. Although he recognized the importance of heredity and brain growth, he said little about their role in cognitive change. Furthermore, Vygotsky's focus on social transmission of knowledge meant that, compared with other theorists, he placed less emphasis on children's capacity to shape their own development. Followers of Vygotsky stress that children actively participate in the conversations and social activities from which their development springs. From these joint experiences, they not only acquire culturally valued practices but also modify and transform those practices (Rogoff, 1998, 2003). Contemporary sociocultural theorists grant the individual and society balanced, mutually influential roles.

Ecological Systems Theory

Urie Bronfenbrenner (1917–2005) is responsible for an approach to child development that has moved to the forefront of the field over the past two decades because it offers the most differentiated and complete account of contextual influences on children's development. **Ecological systems theory** views the child as developing within a complex system of relationships affected by multiple levels of the surrounding environment. Since the child's biologically influenced dispositions join with environmental forces to mold development, Bronfenbrenner recently characterized his perspective as a *bioecological model* (Bronfenbrenner, 2005; Bronfenbrenner & Morris, 2006).

Bronfenbrenner envisioned the environment as a series of nested structures, including but also extending beyond the home, school, and neighborhood settings in which children spend their everyday lives (see Figure 1.4 on page 26). Each layer of the environment is viewed as having a powerful impact on development.

evolutionary developmental psychology An approach that seeks to understand the adaptive value of species-wide cognitive, emotional, and social competencies as those competencies change with age.

sociocultural theory Vygotsky's theory, in which children acquire the ways of thinking and behaving that make up a community's culture through cooperative dialogues with more knowledgeable members of their society.

ecological systems theory Bronfenbrenner's approach, which views the child as developing within a complex system of relationships affected by multiple levels of the surrounding environment, from immediate settings of family and school to broad cultural values and programs.

FIGURE 1.4

Structure of the environment in ecological systems theory. The *microsystem* concerns relations between the child and the immediate environment; the *mesosystem,* connections among immediate settings; the *exosystem,* social settings that affect but do not contain the child; and the *macrosystem,* the values, laws, customs, and resources of the culture that affect activities and interactions at all inner layers. The *chronosystem* (not pictured) is not a specific context. Instead, it refers to the dynamic, ever-changing nature of the person's environment.

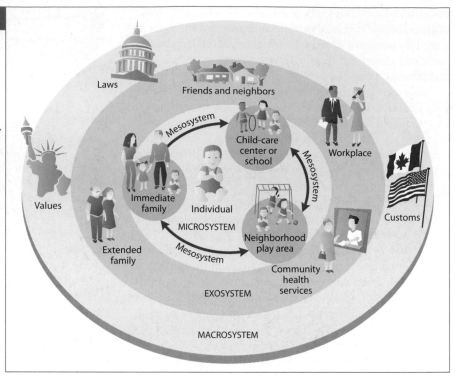

THE MICROSYSTEM ■ The innermost level of the environment, the **microsystem,** consists of activities and interaction patterns in the child's immediate surroundings. Bronfenbrenner emphasizes that to understand child development at this level, we must keep in mind that all relationships are *bidirectional:* Adults affect children's behavior, but children's biologically and socially influenced characteristics—their physical attributes, personalities, and capacities—also affect adults' behavior. A friendly, attentive child is likely to evoke positive, patient reactions from parents, whereas a distractible child is more likely to receive restriction and punishment. When these reciprocal interactions occur often over time, they have an enduring impact on development (Collins et al., 2000; Crockenberg & Leerkes, 2003).

At the same time, *third parties*—other individuals in the microsystem—affect the quality of any two-person relationship. If they are supportive, then interaction is enhanced. For example, when parents encourage each other in their child-rearing roles, each engages in more effective parenting. In contrast, marital conflict is associated with inconsistent discipline and hostile reactions toward children. In response, children typically become hostile, and their adjustment suffers (Hetherington & Stanley-Hagen, 2002).

microsystem In ecological systems theory, the innermost level of the environment, consisting of activities and interaction patterns in the child's immediate surroundings.

mesosystem In ecological systems theory, connections between children's immediate settings.

exosystem In ecological systems theory, social settings that do not contain children but that affect children's experiences in immediate settings. Examples are parents' workplace, health and welfare services available in the community, and parents' social networks.

THE MESOSYSTEM ■ The second level of Bronfenbrenner's model, the **mesosystem,** encompasses connections between microsystems, such as home, school, neighborhood, and child-care center. For example, a child's academic progress depends not just on activities that take place in classrooms but also on parent involvement in school life and on the extent to which academic learning is carried over into the home (Epstein & Sanders, 2002). Similarly, parent–child interaction at home is likely to affect caregiver–child interaction in the child-care setting, and vice versa. Each relationship is more likely to support development when there are links between home and child care, in the form of visits and cooperative exchanges of information.

THE EXOSYSTEM ■ The **exosystem** consists of social settings that do not contain children but that nevertheless affect children's experiences in immediate settings. These can be formal organizations, such as parents' workplaces, their religious institutions, and health and welfare services in the community. For example, parents' work settings can support child rearing and, indirectly, enhance development through flexible work schedules, paid maternity and paternity leave, and sick leave for parents whose children are ill. Exosystem supports also can be informal, such as parents' social networks—friends and extended-family members who provide advice, companionship, and even financial assistance. Research confirms the negative impact of a breakdown in exosystem activities. Families who are affected by unemployment or socially isolated, with few personal or community-based ties, show increased rates of conflict and child abuse (Wekerle & Wolfe, 2003).

THE MACROSYSTEM ■ The outermost level of Bronfenbrenner's model, the **macrosystem,** consists of cultural values, laws, customs, and resources. The priority that the macrosystem gives to children's needs affects the support they receive at inner levels of the environment. For example, in countries that require generous workplace benefits for employed parents and high-quality standards for child care, children are more likely to have favorable experiences in their immediate settings. As you will see in later chapters, such programs are far less available in the United States than in Canada and other industrialized nations (Children's Defense Fund, 2006; Kamerman, 2000).

AN EVER-CHANGING SYSTEM ■ According to Bronfenbrenner, the environment is not a static force that affects children in a uniform way. Instead, it is ever-changing. Important life events, such as the birth of a sibling, the beginning of school, a move to a new neighborhood, or parents' divorce, modify existing relationships between children and their environments, producing new conditions that affect development. In addition, the timing of environmental change affects its impact. The arrival of a new sibling has very different consequences for a homebound toddler than for a school-age child with many relationships and activities beyond the family.

Bronfenbrenner called the temporal dimension of his model the **chronosystem** (the prefix *chrono-* means "time"). Changes in life events can be imposed on the child, as in the examples just given. Alternatively, they can arise from within the child, since as children get older they select, modify, and create many of their own settings and experiences. How they do so depends on their physical, intellectual, and personality characteristics and their environmental opportunities. Therefore, in ecological systems theory, development is neither entirely controlled by environmental circumstances nor driven solely by inner dispositions. Rather, children and their environments form a network of interdependent effects. Notice how our discussion of resilient children on page 10 illustrates this idea. You will see many more examples in this book.

In ecological systems theory, development occurs within a complex system of relationships affected by multiple levels of the environment. This father greets his daughter at the end of the school day. The girl's experiences at school (microsystem) and the father's experiences at work (exosystem) affect father-daughter interaction.

New Directions: Development as a Dynamic System

Today, researchers recognize both consistency and variability in children's development and want to do a better job of explaining variation. Consequently, a new wave of theorists has adopted a **dynamic systems perspective.** According to this view, the child's mind, body, and physical and social worlds form an *integrated system* that guides mastery of new skills. The system is *dynamic,* or constantly in motion. A change in any part of it—from brain maturation to physical and social surroundings—disrupts the current organism–environment relationship. When this happens, the child actively reorganizes his or her behavior so the various components of the system work together again but in a more complex, effective way (Fischer & Bidell, 2006; Spencer & Schöner, 2003; Thelen & Smith, 2006).

Researchers adopting a dynamic systems perspective try to find out just how children attain new levels of organization by studying their behavior while they are in transition (Thelen & Corbetta, 2002). For example, when presented with an attractive toy, how does a 3-month-old baby who engages in many, varied movements discover how to reach for it? On hearing a new word, how does a 2-year-old figure out the category of objects or events to which it refers?

macrosystem In ecological systems theory, cultural values, laws, customs, and resources that influence experiences and interactions at inner levels of the environment.

chronosystem In ecological systems theory, temporal changes in children's environments, which produce new conditions that affect development. These changes can be imposed externally or arise from within the child.

dynamic systems perspective A view that regards the child's mind, body, and physical and social worlds as a dynamic, integrated system. A change in any part of the system leads the child to reorganize his behavior so the various components of the system work together again but in a more complex and effective way.

FIGURE 1.5

The dynamic systems view of development. Rather than envisioning a single line of stagewise or continuous change (refer to Figure 1.2 on page 7), dynamic systems theorists conceive of development as a web of fibers branching out in many directions. Each strand in the web represents a skill within the major domains of development—physical, cognitive, and emotional/social. The differing directions of the strands signify possible variations in paths and outcomes as the child masters skills necessary to participate in diverse contexts. The interconnections of the strands within the vertical windows portray stagelike changes—periods of major transformation in which various skills work together as a functioning whole. As the web expands, skills become more numerous, complex, and effective. (Adapted from Fischer & Bidell, 2006.)

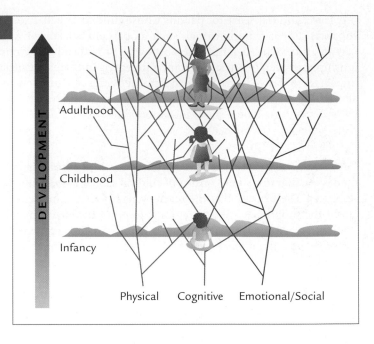

The dynamic systems perspective views the child's mind, body, and physical and social worlds as a continuously reorganizing, integrated system. A change in any part of the system disrupts the current organism-environment relationship. As this girl experiences the physical, cognitive, and emotional changes of early adolescence, she and her mother must devise new, more mature ways of relating to each other.

Dynamic systems theorists acknowledge that a common human genetic heritage and basic regularities in children's physical and social worlds yield certain universal, broad outlines of development. But biological makeup, everyday tasks, and the people who support children in mastery of those tasks vary greatly, leading to wide individual differences in specific skills. Even when children master the same skills, such as walking, talking, or adding and subtracting, they often do so in unique ways. And because children build competencies by engaging in real activities in real contexts, different skills vary in maturity within the same child. From this perspective, development cannot be characterized as a single line of change. As Figure 1.5 shows, it is more like a web of fibers branching out in many directions, each representing a different skill area that may undergo both continuous and stagewise transformations (Fischer & Bidell, 2006).

The dynamic systems view has been inspired by other scientific disciplines, especially biology and physics. It also draws on information-processing and contextual theories—evolutionary developmental psychology, sociocultural theory, and ecological systems theory. Dynamic systems research is still in its early stages. The perspective has been applied largely to children's motor and cognitive skills, but some investigators have drawn on it to explain emotional and social development as well (Campos, Frankel, & Camras, 2004; Fogel, 2000; Lewis, 2000). Consider the young teenager, whose body and reasoning powers are changing massively and who also is confronting the challenges of secondary school. Researchers following parent–child interaction over time found that the transition to adolescence disrupted family communication. It became unstable and variable for several years—a mix of positive, neutral, and negative exchanges. Gradually, as parent and adolescent devised new, more mature ways of relating to one another, the system reorganized and stabilized. Once again, interaction became predictable and mostly positive (Granic et al., 2003).

As dynamic systems research illustrates, today investigators are tracking and analyzing development in all its complexity. In doing so, they hope to move closer to an all-encompassing approach to understanding change.

Ask Yourself

Review   What features of Vygotsky's sociocultural theory distinguish it from Piaget's theory and from information processing?

Review   Explain how each recent theoretical perspective regards children as active contributors to their own development.

Connect   Return to the Biology and Environment box on page 10. How does the story of John and Gary illustrate bidirectional influences within the microsystem, as described in ecological systems theory?

Reflect   To illustrate the chronosystem in ecological systems theory, select an important event from your childhood, such as a move to a new neighborhood, a class with an inspiring teacher, or parental divorce. How did the event affect you? How might its impact have differed had you been five years younger? How about five years older?

Comparing Child Development Theories

In the preceding sections, we reviewed theoretical perspectives in child development research. They differ in many respects. First, they focus on different domains of development. Some, such as the psychoanalytic perspective and ethology, emphasize emotional and social development. Others, such as Piaget's cognitive-developmental theory, information processing, and Vygotsky's sociocultural theory, stress changes in thinking. The remaining approaches— behaviorism, social learning theory, evolutionary developmental psychology, ecological systems theory, and the dynamic systems perspective—discuss many aspects of children's functioning. Second, every theory contains a point of view about child development. **TAKE A MOMENT...** As we conclude our review of theoretical perspectives, identify the stand that each theory takes on the controversial issues presented at the beginning of this chapter. Then check your analysis of the theories against Table 1.4 on page 30.

Finally, we have seen that every theory has strengths and limitations. Perhaps you found that you are attracted to some theories, but you have doubts about others. As you read more about child development in later chapters, you may find it useful to keep a notebook in which you test your own theoretical likes and dislikes against the evidence. Don't be surprised if you revise your ideas many times, just as theorists have done throughout the past century. By the end of the course, you will have built your own personal perspective on child development. Very likely, it will be an *eclectic position*, or blend of several theories, since every viewpoint we have considered has contributed to what we know about children.

Studying the Child

In every science, theories, like those we have just reviewed, guide the collection of information, its interpretation, and its application to real-life situations. In fact, research usually begins with a *hypothesis*, or prediction, drawn directly from a theory. But theories and hypotheses are only the beginning of the many activities that result in sound evidence on child development. Conducting research according to scientifically accepted procedures involves many steps and choices. Investigators must decide which participants, and how many, to include. Then they

TABLE 1.4   Stances of Major Theories on Basic Issues in Child Development

THEORY	CONTINUOUS OR DISCONTINUOUS DEVELOPMENT?	ONE COURSE OF DEVELOPMENT OR MANY?	NATURE OR NURTURE AS MORE IMPORTANT?
Psychoanalytic perspective	*Discontinuous:* Psychosexual and psychosocial development takes place in stages.	*One course:* Stages are assumed to be universal.	*Both nature and nurture:* Innate impulses are channeled and controlled through child-rearing experiences. *Early experiences* set the course of later development.
Behaviorism and social learning theory	*Continuous:* Development involves an increase in learned behaviors.	*Many possible courses:* Behaviors reinforced and modeled may vary from child to child.	*Emphasis on nurture:* Development results from conditioning and modeling. *Both early and later experiences* are important.
Piaget's cognitive-developmental theory	*Discontinuous:* Cognitive development takes place in stages.	*One course:* Stages are assumed to be universal.	*Both nature and nurture:* Development occurs as the brain matures and children exercise their innate drive to discover reality in a generally stimulating environment. *Both early and later experiences* are important.
Information processing	*Continuous:* Children gradually improve in perception, attention, memory, and problem-solving skills.	*One course:* Changes studied characterize most or all children.	*Both nature and nurture:* Children are active, sense-making beings who modify their thinking as the brain matures and they confront new environmental demands. *Both early and later experiences* are important.
Ethology and evolutionary developmental psychology	*Both continuous and discontinuous:* Children gradually develop a wider range of adaptive behaviors. Sensitive periods occur, in which qualitatively distinct capacities emerge fairly suddenly.	*One course:* Adaptive behaviors and sensitive periods apply to all members of a species.	*Both nature and nurture:* Evolution and heredity influence behavior, and learning lends greater flexibility and adaptiveness to it. In sensitive periods, *early experiences* set the course of later development.
Vygotsky's sociocultural theory	*Both continuous and discontinuous:* Language acquisition and schooling lead to stagewise changes. Dialogues with more expert members of society also lead to continuous changes that vary from culture to culture.	*Many possible courses:* Socially mediated changes in thought and behavior vary from culture to culture.	*Both nature and nurture:* Heredity, brain growth, and dialogues with more expert members of society jointly contribute to development. *Both early and later experiences* are important.
Ecological systems theory	*Not specified.*	*Many possible courses:* Children's characteristics join with environmental forces at multiple levels to mold development in unique ways.	*Both nature and nurture:* Children's characteristics and the reactions of others affect each other in a bidirectional fashion. Layers of the environment influence child-rearing experiences. *Both early and later experiences* are important.
Dynamic systems perspective	*Both continuous and discontinuous:* Change in the system is always ongoing. Stagelike transformations occur as children reorganize their behavior so components of the system work as a functioning whole.	*Many possible courses:* Biological makeup, everyday tasks, and social experiences vary, yielding wide individual differences in specific skills.	*Both nature and nurture:* The child's mind, body, and physical and social surroundings form an integrated system that guides mastery of new skills. *Both early and later experiences* are important.

must figure out what the participants will be asked to do and when, where, and how many times each will be seen. Finally, they must examine and draw conclusions from their data.

In the following sections, we look at research strategies commonly used to study children. We begin with *methods of gathering information*—the specific activities of participants, such as taking tests, answering questionnaires, responding to interviews, or being observed. Then we turn to *research designs*—overall plans for research studies that permit the best possible test of the investigator's hypothesis. Finally, we discuss special ethical issues involved in doing research on children.

At this point, you may be wondering, Why learn about research strategies? Why not leave these matters to research specialists and concentrate on what is already known about the child and how this knowledge can be applied? There are two reasons. First, each of us must be a wise and critical consumer of knowledge. Knowing the strengths and limitations of various research strategies is important in separating dependable information from misleading results. Second, individuals who work directly with children may be in a unique position to build bridges between research and practice by conducting studies, either on their own or in partnership with experienced investigators. Community agencies such as schools, mental health facilities, and parks and recreation programs sometimes collaborate with researchers in designing, implementing, and evaluating interventions aimed at enhancing children's development (Lerner, Fisher, & Weinberg, 2000). To broaden these efforts, a basic understanding of the research process is essential.

Common Methods of Gathering Information

How does a researcher choose a basic approach to gathering information about children? Common methods include systematic observation, self-reports (such as questionnaires and interviews), clinical or case studies of a single child, and ethnographies of the life circumstances of a specific group of children. As you read about these methods, you may find it helpful to refer to Table 1.5 on page 32, which summarizes the strengths and limitations of each.

SYSTEMATIC OBSERVATION ■ Observations of the behavior of children, and of adults who are important in their lives, can be made in different ways. One approach is to go into the field, or natural environment, and observe the behavior of interest—a method called **naturalistic observation.**

A study of preschoolers' responses to their peers' distress provides a good example of this technique (Farver & Branstetter, 1994). Observing 3- and 4-year-olds in child-care centers, the researchers recorded each instance of a child crying and the reactions of nearby children—whether they ignored, watched curiously, commented on the child's unhappiness, scolded or teased, or shared, helped, or expressed sympathy. Caregiver behaviors—explaining why a child was crying, mediating conflict, or offering comfort—were noted to see if adult sensitivity was related to children's caring responses. A strong relationship emerged. The great strength of naturalistic observation is that investigators can see directly the everyday behaviors they hope to explain.

Naturalistic observation also has a major limitation: Not all individuals have the same opportunity to display a particular behavior in everyday life. In the study just mentioned, some children might have witnessed a child crying more often than others or been exposed to more cues for positive social responses from caregivers. For this reason, they might have displayed more compassion.

Researchers commonly deal with this difficulty by making **structured observations,** in which the investigator sets up a laboratory situation that evokes the behavior of interest so that every participant has an equal opportunity to display the response. In one study, 2-year-olds'

This researcher is using naturalistic observation—recording children's behavior in the field, or natural environment. One limitation of this method is that some children may have more opportunities than others to display the behavior of interest.

naturalistic observation
A method in which the researcher goes into the natural environment to observe the behavior of interest.

structured observations
A method in which the investigator sets up a laboratory situation that evokes the behavior of interest so that every participant has an equal opportunity to display the response.

TABLE 1.5   Strengths and Limitations of Common Information-Gathering Methods

METHOD	DESCRIPTION	STRENGTHS	LIMITATIONS
Systematic Observation			
Naturalistic observation	Observation of behavior in natural contexts.	Reflects participants' everyday behaviors.	Cannot control conditions under which participants are observed.
Structured observation	Observation of behavior in a laboratory, where conditions are the same for all participants.	Grants each participant an equal opportunity to display the behavior of interest. Permits study of behaviors rarely seen in everyday life.	May not yield observations typical of participants' behavior in everyday life.
Self-Reports			
Clinical interview	Flexible interviewing procedure in which the investigator obtains a complete account of the participant's thoughts.	Comes as close as possible to the way participants think in everyday life. Great breadth and depth of information can be obtained in a short time.	May not result in accurate reporting of information. Flexible procedure makes comparing individuals' responses difficult.
Structured interview, questionnaires, and tests	Self-report instruments in which each participant is asked the same questions in the same way.	Permits comparisons of participants' responses and efficient data collection. Researchers can specify answer alternatives that participants might not think of in an open-ended interview.	Does not yield the same depth of information as a clinical interview. Responses are still subject to inaccurate reporting.
Clinical, or Case Study, Method	A full picture of a single individual's psychological functioning, obtained by combining interviews, observations, and sometimes test scores.	Provides rich, descriptive insights into processes of development.	May be biased by researchers' theoretical preferences. Findings cannot be applied to individuals other than the participant.
Ethnography	Participant observation of a culture or distinct social group. By making extensive field notes, the researcher tries to capture the culture's unique values and social processes.	Provides a more complete and accurate description than can be derived from a single observational visit, interview, or questionnaire.	May be biased by researcher's values and theoretical preferences. Findings cannot be applied to individuals and settings other than the ones studied.

emotional reactions to harm that they thought they had caused were observed by asking them to take care of a rag doll that had been modified so its leg would fall off when the child picked it up. To make the child feel at fault, once the leg detached, an adult "talked for" the doll by saying, "Ow!" Researchers recorded children's facial expressions of sadness and concern for the injured doll, efforts to help the doll, and body tension—responses that indicated remorse and a desire to make amends. In addition, mothers were asked to engage in brief conversations about emotions with their children (Garner, 2003). Toddlers whose mothers more often explained the causes and consequences of emotion were more likely to express concern for the injured doll.

Structured observation permits greater control over the research situation than does naturalistic observation. In addition, the method is especially useful for studying behaviors—such as parent–child or friendship interactions—that investigators rarely have an opportunity to see in everyday life. When aggressive and nonaggressive 10-year-old boys were observed playing games with their best friend in a laboratory, the aggressive boys and their friends more often violated game rules, cheated, and encouraged each other to engage in these dishonest acts. In addition, observers rated these boys' interactions as angrier and less cooperative than

clinical interview An interview method in which the researcher uses a flexible, conversational style to probe for the participant's point of view.

structured interview An interview method in which each participant is asked the same questions in the same way.

the interactions of nonaggressive boys (Bagwell & Coie, 2004). The researchers concluded that aggressive boys' close peer ties provide a context in which they practice hostility and other negative behaviors, which may contribute to increased antisocial behavior.

The procedures used to collect systematic observations vary, depending on the purpose of the research. Some investigators choose to describe the entire behavior stream—everything said and done over a certain time period. In one of my own studies, I wanted to find out how sensitive, responsive, and verbally stimulating caregivers were with children in child-care centers (Berk, 1985). In this case, everything each caregiver said and did—even the amount of time spent away from children, taking a coffee break or talking on the phone—was important. In other studies, only one or a few kinds of behavior are needed, so researchers can use more efficient procedures in which they record only specified events or mark off behaviors on checklists.

Systematic observation provides invaluable information on how children and adults behave, but it tells us little about the reasoning behind their responses. For this kind of information, researchers must turn to self-report techniques.

SELF-REPORTS: INTERVIEWS AND QUESTIONNAIRES ■ Self-reports ask research participants to provide information on their perceptions, thoughts, abilities, feelings, attitudes, beliefs, and past experiences. They range from relatively unstructured interviews to highly structured interviews, questionnaires, and tests.

In a **clinical interview,** a flexible, conversational style is used to probe for the participant's point of view. Consider the following example, in which Piaget questioned a 5-year-old child about his understanding of dreams:

> *Where does the dream come from?*—I think you sleep so well that you dream.—*Does it come from us or from outside?*—From outside. —*When you are in bed and you dream, where is the dream?*—In my bed, under the blanket. I don't really know. If it was in my stomach, the bones would be in the way and I shouldn't see it.—*Is the dream there when you sleep?*—Yes, it is in the bed beside me. (Piaget, 1926/1930, pp. 97–98)

The clinical interview has two major strengths. First, it permits people to display their thoughts in terms that are as close as possible to the way they think in everyday life. Second, the clinical interview can provide a large amount of information in a fairly brief period. For example, in an hour-long session, we can obtain a wide range of child-rearing information from a parent—much more than we could capture by observing for the same amount of time.

A major limitation of the clinical interview has to do with the accuracy with which people report their thoughts, feelings, and experiences. Some participants, desiring to please the interviewer, may make up answers. When asked about past events, some may have trouble recalling exactly what happened. And because the clinical interview depends on verbal ability and expressiveness, it may underestimate the capacities of individuals who have difficulty putting their thoughts into words.

The clinical interview has also been criticized because of its flexibility. When questions are phrased differently for each participant, different responses may reflect the manner of interviewing rather than real differences in the way people think about a topic. **Structured interviews,** in which each participant is asked the same questions in the same way, eliminate this problem. In addition, these instruments are much more efficient. Answers are briefer, and researchers can obtain written responses from an entire group of children or parents at the same time. Furthermore, by listing answer alternatives, researchers can indicate the specific activities and behaviors they are interested in—ones that participants might not think of in an open-ended clinical interview. For example, when parents were asked what they considered "the most important thing for children to prepare them for life,"

Using the clinical, or case study, method, this researcher combines interviews with the mother and observations and testing of the child to construct an in-depth picture of one child's psychological functioning. A major drawback is that investigators' theoretical preferences may bias what they see and conclude.

62 percent checked "to think for themselves" when this alternative appeared on a list. Yet only 5 percent thought of it during a clinical interview (Schwarz, 1999).

Nevertheless, structured interviews do not yield the same depth of information as a clinical interview. And they can still be affected by inaccurate reporting.

THE CLINICAL, OR CASE STUDY, METHOD ■ An outgrowth of psychoanalytic theory, the **clinical,** or **case study, method** brings together a wide range of information on one child, including interviews, observations, and sometimes test scores. The aim is to obtain as complete a picture as possible of that child's psychological functioning and the experiences that led up to it.

The clinical method is well-suited to studying the development of certain types of individuals who are few in number but vary widely in characteristics. For example, the method has been used to find out what contributes to the accomplishments of *prodigies*—extremely gifted children who attain adult competence in a field before age 10 (Moran & Gardner, 2006). Consider Adam, a boy who read, wrote, and composed musical pieces before he was out of diapers. By age 4, Adam was deeply involved in mastering human symbol systems—French, German, Russian, Sanskrit, Greek, the computer programming language BASIC, ancient hieroglyphs, music, and mathematics. Adam's parents provided a home rich in stimulation and reared him with affection, firmness, and humor. They searched for schools in which he could both develop his abilities and form rewarding social relationships. He graduated from college at age 18 and continued to pursue musical composition. Would Adam have realized his potential without the chance combination of his special gift and nurturing, committed parents? Probably not, researchers concluded (Goldsmith, 2000).

The clinical method yields richly detailed case narratives that offer valuable insights into the multiplicity of factors affecting development. Nevertheless, like all other methods, it has drawbacks. Because information often is collected unsystematically and subjectively, researchers' theoretical preferences may bias their interpretations. In addition, investigators cannot assume that their conclusions apply, or generalize, to anyone other than the child studied (Stanovich, 2004). Even when patterns emerge across several cases, it is wise to confirm them with other research strategies.

METHODS FOR STUDYING CULTURE ■ To study the impact of culture on child development, researchers adjust the methods just considered or tap procedures specially devised for cross-cultural and multicultural research. Which approach investigators choose depends on their research goals (Triandis, 1998).

Sometimes researchers are interested in characteristics that are believed to be universal but that vary in degree from one culture to the next. These investigators might ask, Do parents make greater maturity demands of children in some cultures than in others? How strong are gender stereotypes in different nations? In each instance, several cultural groups will be compared, and all participants must be questioned or observed in the same way. Therefore, researchers draw on the self-report and observational procedures we have already considered, adapting them through translation so they can be understood in each cultural context. For example, to study cultural variation in parenting attitudes, the same questionnaire, asking for ratings on such items as "I often hug and kiss my child" or "I scold my child when his/her behavior does not meet my expectations," is given to all participants (Wu et al., 2002).

At other times, researchers want to uncover the *cultural meanings* of children's and adults' behaviors by becoming as familiar as possible with their way of life. To achieve this goal, researchers rely on a method borrowed from the field of anthropology—**ethnography.** Like the clinical method, ethnographic research is a descriptive, qualitative technique. But instead of aiming to understand a single individual, it is directed toward understanding a culture or a distinct social group through *participant observation.* Typically, the researcher spends months and sometimes years in the cultural community, participating in its daily life. Extensive field notes are gathered, consisting of a mix of observations, self-reports from members of the culture, and careful interpretations by the investigator (Miller, Hengst, & Wang, 2003; Shweder et al., 2006). Later, these notes are put together into a description of the community that tries to capture its unique values and social processes.

clinical, or **case study, method** A method in which the researcher attempts to understand an individual child by combining interview data, observations, and sometimes test scores.

ethnography A method in which the researcher attempts to understand the unique values and social processes of a culture or a distinct social group through participant observation—living with its members and taking field notes over an extended period of time.

The ethnographic method assumes that by entering into close contact with a social group, researchers can understand the beliefs and behaviors of its members in a way that is not possible with an observational visit, interview, or questionnaire. Some ethnographies take in many aspects of children's experience, as one researcher did in describing what it is like to grow up in a small American town. Others focus on one or a few settings, such as home, school, or neighborhood life (LeVine et al., 1994; Peshkin, 1978, 1997; Valdés, 1998). And still others are limited to a particular practice, such as uncovering cultural and religious influences on children's make-believe play. For example, ethnographic findings reveal that East Indian Hindu parents encourage preschoolers to communicate with "invisible" characters. They regard this activity as linked to *karma* (the cycle of birth and death) and believe that the child may be remembering a past life. In contrast, Christian fundamentalist parents often discourage children from pretending to be unreal characters, believing that such play promotes dangerous spiritual ideas and deceitful behavior (Taylor & Carlson, 2000). Researchers may supplement traditional self-report and observational methods with ethnography if they suspect that unique meanings underlie cultural differences, as the Cultural Influences box on page 36 reveals.

Ethnographers strive to minimize their influence on the culture they are studying by becoming part of it. Nevertheless, as with clinical research, investigators' cultural values and theoretical commitments sometimes lead them to observe selectively or misinterpret what they see. Finally, the findings of ethnographic studies cannot be assumed to generalize beyond the people and settings in which the research was conducted.

This Western ethnographer is spending months living among the Efe people of the Republic of Congo. Here he observes a group of young children sharing food. Among the Efe, cooperation and generosity are highly valued and encouraged at an early age.

Ask Yourself

Review   Why might a researcher choose structured observation over naturalistic observation? How about the reverse? What might lead the researcher to opt for clinical interviewing over systematic observation?

Apply   A researcher wants to study the thoughts and feelings of children who have a parent on active duty in the military. Which method is best-suited for investigating this question? Why?

Connect   What strengths and limitations do the clinical, or case study, method and ethnography have in common?

General Research Designs

In deciding on a research design, investigators choose a way of setting up a study that permits them to test their hypotheses with the greatest degree of certainty possible. Two main designs are used in all research on human behavior: *correlational* and *experimental.*

CORRELATIONAL DESIGN ■ In a **correlational design,** researchers gather information on individuals, generally in natural life circumstances, and make no effort to alter their experiences. Then they look at relationships between participants' characteristics and their behavior or development. Suppose we want to answer such questions as, Do parents' styles of interacting with their children have any bearing on children's intelligence? Does attending a child-care center promote children's friendliness with peers? How do child abuse and neglect affect

correlational design
A research design in which the researcher gathers information on individuals without altering participants' experiences and then examines relationships between variables. Does not permit inferences about cause and effect.

Cultural Influences

Immigrant Youths: Amazing Adaptation

This Hmong girl from southeast Asia is performing a cultural dance at an ethnic festival in St. Paul, Minnesota, where many Hmong immigrants have settled. Cultural values that engender allegiance to family and community promote high achievement and protect many immigrant youths from involvement in risky behaviors.

During the past quarter century, a rising tide of immigrants has come to North America, fleeing war and persecution in their homelands or seeking better life chances. Today, one-fifth of the U.S. youth population has foreign-born parents; nearly one-third of these youths are foreign born themselves, mostly from Asia and Latin America. In Canada, too, immigrant youths—mostly from Asia, Africa, the Middle East, and Europe—are the fastest-growing segment of the Canadian population (Service Canada, 2005; Suarez-Orozco, Todorova, & Qin, 2006).

How well are immigrant youths adapting to their new country? To find out, researchers use multiple research methods—academic testing, questionnaires assessing psychological adjustment, and in-depth ethnographies.

Academic Achievement and Adjustment

Although educators and laypeople often assume that the transition to a new country has a negative impact on psychological well-being, evidence reveals that many children of immigrant parents from diverse countries adapt amazingly well. Students who are first generation (foreign-born) or second generation (American- or Canadian-born, with immigrant parents) often achieve in school as well as or better than students of native-born parents (Fuligni, 2004; Saucier et al., 2002). Findings on psychological adjustment are similar. Compared with their agemates, adolescents from immigrant families are less likely to commit delinquent and violent acts, to use drugs and alcohol, or to have early sex. They are also less likely to be obese or to have missed school because of illness. And they feel as positively about themselves as do young people with native-born parents. These successes do not depend on having extensive time to adjust to a new way of life. Recently arrived high school students do as well in school and report just as favorable self-esteem as those who came at younger ages (Fuligni, 1998; Saucier et al., 2002).

These outcomes are strongest for Chinese, Filipino, Japanese, Korean, and East Indian youths, less dramatic for other ethnicities (Fuligni, 2004; Louie, 2001; Portes & Rumbaut, 2005). And a minority of young people—especially of certain ethnicities, including Cambodians and Laotians—deviate from these favorable patterns, showing high rates of school failure and dropout, delinquency, teenage parenthood, and drug use (Zhou & Xiong, 2005). Variations in parental economic resources and education contribute to these trends. Still, many first- and second-generation youths from ethnic groups that face considerable financial hardship (such as Mexican and Vietnamese) are successful (Fuligni & Yoshikawa, 2003). Factors other than income are responsible—notably, family values and strong ethnic-community ties.

Family and Ethnic-Community Influences

Ethnographies reveal that immigrant parents view education as the surest way to improve life chances (Goldenberg et al., 2001; Louie, 2001). Aware of the challenges their children face, they typically emphasize trying hard. They remind their children that, because educational opportunities were not available in their native countries, they themselves are often limited to menial jobs.

Adolescents from these families internalize their parents' valuing of academic achievement, endorsing it more strongly than agemates with native-born parents (Asakawa, 2001; Fuligni, 2004). Because minority ethnicities usually stress allegiance to family and community over individual goals, first- and second-generation young people often feel a strong sense of obligation to their parents. They view school success as an important way of repaying their parents for the hardships they have endured (Fuligni, Yip, & Tseng, 2002; Suárez-Orozco & Suárez-Orozco, 2001). Both family relationships and school achievement protect these youths from delinquency, early sexual activity, drug use, and other risky behaviors (see the Biology and Environment box on page 10).

Immigrant parents of successful youths typically develop close ties to an ethnic community, which exerts additional control through a high consensus on values and constant monitoring of young people's activities. The comments of Vietnamese teenagers capture the power of these family and community forces:

■ *Thuy Trang, age 14, middle-school Student of the Year:* When my parents first emigrated from Vietnam, they spent every waking hour working hard to support a family. They have sacrificed for me, and I am willing to do anything for them.

■ *Elizabeth, age 16, straight-A student, like her two older sisters:* My parents know pretty much all the kids in the neighborhood. Everybody here knows everybody else. It's hard to get away with much. (Zhou & Bankston, 1998, pp. 93, 130)

The experiences of high-achieving, well-adjusted immigrant youths are not problem-free. Adolescents who had arrived in Canada within the previous five years described their first year as "very difficult" because they did not yet speak either English or French—Canada's two official languages—and felt socially isolated (Hanvey & Kunz, 2000). Young immigrants also encounter racial and ethnic prejudices and experience tensions between family values and the new culture—challenges we will take up in Chapter 16. In the long term, however, family and community cohesion, supervision, and high expectations promote favorable outcomes.

children's feelings about themselves and their relationships with peers? In these and many other instances, the conditions of interest are difficult or impossible to arrange and control and must be studied as they currently exist.

Correlational studies have one major limitation: We cannot infer cause and effect. For example, if we find that parental interaction is related to children's intelligence, we would not know whether parents' behavior actually *causes* intellectual differences among children. In fact, the opposite is possible. The behaviors of highly intelligent children may be so attractive that they cause parents to interact more favorably. Or a third variable that we did not even consider, such as amount of noise and distraction in the home, may cause changes in both parental interaction and children's intelligence.

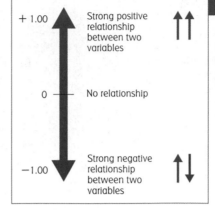

FIGURE 1.6

The meaning of correlation coefficients. The magnitude of the number indicates the *strength* of the relationship. The sign of the number (+ or −) indicates the *direction* of the relationship.

+1.00 — Strong positive relationship between two variables

0 — No relationship

−1.00 — Strong negative relationship between two variables

In correlational studies, and in other types of research designs, investigators often examine relationships by using a **correlation coefficient**—a number that describes how two measures, or variables, are associated with one another. We will encounter the correlation coefficient in discussing research findings throughout this book. So let's look at what it is and how it is interpreted. A correlation coefficient can range in value from +1.00 to −1.00. The *magnitude, or size, of the number* shows the *strength of the relationship.* A zero correlation indicates no relationship, but the closer the value is to either +1.00 or −1.00, the stronger the relationship (see Figure 1.6). For instance, a correlation of −.78 is high, −.52 is moderate, and −.18 is low. Note, however that correlations of +.52 and −.52 are equally strong. The *sign of the number* refers to the *direction of the relationship.* A positive sign (+) means that as one variable *increases,* the other also *increases.* A negative sign (−) indicates that as one variable *increases,* the other *decreases.*

Let's look at some examples of how a correlation coefficient works. One researcher reported a +.55 correlation between a measure of maternal language stimulation and the size of children's vocabularies at age 2 years (Hoff, 2003). This is a moderate correlation, which indicates that mothers who spoke more to their infants had children who were more advanced in language development. In two other studies, child-rearing practices were related to toddlers' compliance in consistent ways. First, maternal warmth and sensitivity during play correlated positively (+.34) with 2-year-olds' willingness to comply with their mother's directive to clean up toys (Feldman & Klein, 2003). And second, the extent to which mothers interrupted and controlled their 3-year-old's play correlated negatively (−.23) with children's compliance (Whiteside-Mansell et al., 2003).

All these investigations found a relationship between parenting and young children's behavior. Are you tempted to conclude that parenting influenced children's responses? Although the researchers suspected this was so, they could not be sure about cause and effect in any of the studies. But finding a relationship in a correlational study suggests that tracking down its cause—with a more powerful experimental strategy, if possible—would be worthwhile.

EXPERIMENTAL DESIGN ■ An **experimental design** permits inferences about cause and effect because researchers use an evenhanded procedure to assign people to two or more treatment conditions. In an experiment, the events and behaviors of interest are divided into two types: independent and dependent variables. The **independent variable** is the one the investigator expects to cause changes in another variable. The **dependent variable** is the one the investigator expects to be influenced by the independent variable. Cause-and-effect relationships can be detected because the researcher directly *controls* or *manipulates* changes in the independent variable by exposing participants to the treatment conditions. Then the researcher compares their performance on measures of the dependent variable.

In one *laboratory experiment,* researchers explored the impact of adults' angry interactions on children's adjustment (El-Sheikh, Cummings, & Reiter, 1996). They hypothesized that the way angry encounters end (independent variable) affects children's emotional reactions

correlation coefficient A number, ranging from +1.00 to −1.00, that describes the strength and direction of the relationship between two variables.

experimental design A research design in which the investigator randomly assigns participants to treatment conditions. Permits inferences about cause and effect.

independent variable The variable the researcher expects to cause changes in another variable in an experiment.

dependent variable The variable the investigator expects to be influenced by the independent variable in an experiment.

FIGURE 1.7

Does the way adults end their angry encounters affect children's emotional reactions?

A laboratory experiment showed that children who previously witnessed adults resolving their disputes by apologizing and compromising are more likely to decline in distress when witnessing subsequent adult conflicts than are children who witnessed adults leaving their arguments unresolved. Notice in this graph that only 10 percent of children in the unresolved-anger treatment declined in distress (see bar on left), whereas 42 percent of children in the resolved-anger treatment did so (see bar on right). (Adapted from El-Sheikh, Cummings, & Reiter, 1996.)

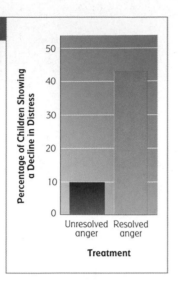

Graph: Percentage of Children Showing a Decline in Distress (y-axis, 0 to 50) by Treatment (x-axis: Unresolved anger, Resolved anger)

© BRIAN SUMMERS/GETTY IMAGES/FIRST LIGHT

In field experiments, researchers assign participants to different treatment conditions in natural settings. For example, a researcher might use this design to investigate the effects of two different styles of caregiver behavior—nurturant versus emotionally reserved—on children's helpfulness and cooperativeness in child-care centers.

(dependent variable). Four- and 5-year-olds were brought one at a time to a laboratory, accompanied by their mothers. One group was exposed to an *unresolved-anger treatment,* in which two adult actors entered the room and argued but did not work out their disagreements. The other group witnessed a *resolved-anger treatment,* in which the adults ended their disputes by apologizing and compromising. As Figure 1.7 shows, when they witnessed a follow-up adult conflict, more children in the resolved-anger treatment showed a decline in distress, as measured by fewer anxious facial expressions, less freezing in place, and less seeking of closeness to their mothers. The experiment revealed that anger resolution can reduce the stressful impact of adult conflict on children.

In experimental studies, investigators must take special precautions to control for participants' characteristics that could reduce the accuracy of their findings. For example, in the study just described, if more children from homes high in parental conflict ended up in the unresolved-anger treatment, we could not tell what produced the results—the independent variable or the children's backgrounds. To protect against this problem, researchers engage in **random assignment** of participants to treatment conditions. By using an unbiased procedure, such as drawing numbers out of a hat or flipping a coin, investigators increase the chances that participants' characteristics will be equally distributed across treatment groups.

Sometimes researchers combine random assignment with another technique called *matching.* In this procedure, participants are measured before the experiment on the factor in question—in our example, exposure to parental conflict. Then children from homes high and low in parental conflict are assigned in equal numbers to each treatment condition. In this way, the experimental groups are deliberately matched, or made equivalent, on characteristics that are likely to distort the results.

MODIFIED EXPERIMENTAL DESIGNS: FIELD AND NATURAL EXPERIMENTS ■

Most experiments are conducted in laboratories, where researchers can achieve the maximum possible control over treatment conditions. But as we have already indicated, findings obtained in laboratories may not apply to everyday situations. In *field experiments,* investigators capitalize on rare opportunities to assign participants randomly to treatment conditions in natural settings. In the experiment just described, we can conclude that the emotional climate established by adults affects children's behavior in the laboratory. But does it also do so in daily life?

Another study helps answer this question (Yarrow, Scott, & Waxler, 1973). This time, the research was carried out in a child-care center. A caregiver deliberately interacted differently with two groups of preschoolers. In one condition (the *nurturant treatment*), she modeled many instances of warmth and helpfulness. In the second condition (the *control,* since it involved no treatment), she behaved as usual, with no special emphasis on concern for others. Two weeks later, the researchers created several situations that called for helpfulness. For example, a visiting mother asked each child to watch her baby for a few moments, but the baby's toys had fallen out of the playpen. The investigators found that children exposed to the nurturant treatment were much more likely than those in the control condition to return toys to the baby.

TABLE 1.6	**Strengths and Limitations of Research Designs**		
DESIGN	**DESCRIPTION**	**STRENGTHS**	**LIMITATIONS**
General			
Correlational	The investigator obtains information on participants without altering their experiences.	Permits study of relationships between variables.	Does not permit inferences about cause-and-effect relationships.
Experimental	The investigator manipulates an independent variable and looks at its effect on a dependent variable; can be conducted in the laboratory or in the natural environment.	Permits inferences about cause-and-effect relationships.	When conducted in the laboratory, findings may not apply to the real world. When conducted in the field, control is usually weaker, and results may be due to variables other than the treatment.
Developmental			
Longitudinal	The investigator studies the same group of participants repeatedly at different ages.	Permits study of common patterns and individual differences in development and relationships between early and later events and behaviors.	Age-related changes may be distorted because of dropout and test-wiseness of participants and because of cohort effects.
Cross-sectional	The investigator studies groups of participants differing in age at the same point in time.	More efficient than the longitudinal design.	Does not permit study of individual developmental trends. Age differences may be distorted because of cohort effects.
Sequential design	The investigator follows a sequence of samples (two or more age groups), collecting data on them at the same points in time.	Permits both longitudinal and cross-sectional comparisons. Reveals cohort effects. Permits tracking of age-related changes more efficiently than the longitudinal design.	May have the same problems as longitudinal and cross-sectional strategies, but the design itself helps identify difficulties.
Microgenetic design	The investigator presents children with a novel task and follows their mastery over a series of closely spaced sessions.	Offers insights into the process of development.	Requires intensive study of participants' moment-by-moment behaviors. The time required for participants to change is difficult to anticipate. Practice effects may distort developmental trends.

Often researchers cannot randomly assign participants and manipulate conditions in the real world, as these investigators were able to do. Sometimes they can compromise by conducting *natural,* or *quasi-, experiments.* Treatments that already exist, such as different family environments, child-care centers, or schools, are compared. These studies differ from correlational research only in that groups of participants are carefully chosen to ensure that their characteristics are as much alike as possible. In this way, investigators rule out as best they can alternative explanations for their treatment effects. But despite these efforts, natural experiments are unable to achieve the precision and rigor of true experimental research.

To help you compare correlational and experimental designs, Table 1.6 summarizes their strengths and limitations. It also includes an overview of designs for studying development, to which we now turn.

random assignment An unbiased procedure for assigning participants to treatment groups, which increases the chances that participants' characteristics will be equally distributed across treatment conditions in an experiment.

Designs for Studying Development

Scientists interested in child development require information about the way research participants change over time. To answer questions about development, they must extend correlational and experimental approaches to include measurements at different ages. Longitudinal and cross-sectional designs are special *developmental research strategies.* In each, age comparisons form the basis of the research plan.

THE LONGITUDINAL DESIGN ■ In a **longitudinal design,** participants are studied repeatedly at different ages, and changes are noted as the participants get older. The time spanned may be relatively short (a few months to several years) or very long (a decade or even a lifetime). The longitudinal approach has two major strengths. First, because it tracks the performance of each person over time, researchers can identify common patterns as well as individual differences in development. Second, longitudinal studies permit investigators to examine relationships between early and later events and behaviors. Let's illustrate these ideas.

A group of researchers wondered whether children who display extreme personality styles—either angry and explosive or shy and withdrawn—retain the same dispositions when they become adults. In addition, the researchers wanted to know what kinds of experiences promote stability or change in personality and what consequences explosiveness and shyness have for long-term adjustment. To answer these questions, the researchers delved into the archives of the Guidance Study, a well-known longitudinal investigation that was initiated in 1928 at the University of California, Berkeley, and continued for several decades (Caspi, Elder, & Bem, 1987, 1988).

Results revealed that the two personality styles were moderately stable. Between ages 8 and 30, a good number of individuals remained the same, whereas others changed substantially. When stability did occur, it appeared to be due to a "snowballing effect," in which children evoked responses from adults and peers that acted to maintain their dispositions. Explosive youngsters were likely to be treated with anger, whereas shy children were apt to be ignored. As a result, the two types of children came to view their social worlds differently. Explosive children regarded others as hostile; shy children regarded them as unfriendly (Caspi & Roberts, 2001). Together, these factors led explosive children to sustain or increase their unruliness and shy children to continue to withdraw.

Persistence of extreme personality styles affected many areas of adult adjustment. For men, the results of early explosiveness were most apparent in their work lives, in the form of conflicts with supervisors, frequent job changes, and unemployment. Since few women in this sample of an earlier generation worked after marriage, their family lives were most affected. Explosive girls grew up to be hotheaded wives and parents who were especially prone to divorce. Sex differences in the long-term consequences of shyness were even greater. Men who had been withdrawn in childhood were delayed in marrying, becoming fathers, and developing stable careers. However, because a withdrawn, unassertive style was socially acceptable for females in the mid-twentieth century, women who had shy personalities showed no special adjustment problems.

PROBLEMS IN CONDUCTING LONGITUDINAL RESEARCH ■ Despite their strengths, longitudinal investigations pose a number of problems. For example, participants may move away or drop out of the research for other reasons. This often leads to biased samples that no longer represent the populations to whom researchers would like to generalize their findings. Also, from repeated study, people may become "test-wise." Their performance may improve as a result of *practice effects*—better test-taking skills and increased familiarity with the test—not because of factors commonly associated with development.

The most widely discussed threat to the accuracy of longitudinal findings is cultural–historical change, commonly called **cohort effects.** Longitudinal studies examine the development of *cohorts*—children born at the same time, who are influenced by particular cultural and historical conditions. Results based on one cohort may not apply to children developing at

longitudinal design A research design in which participants are studied repeatedly at different ages.

cohort effects The effects of cultural-historical change on the accuracy of longitudinal and cross-sectional findings. Children born in a particular time period are influenced by a particular set of cultural and historical conditions.

other times. For example, look back at the findings on female shyness described in the previous section, which were gathered in the 1950s. Today's shy young women tend to be poorly adjusted—a difference that may be due to changes in gender roles in Western societies. Shy adults, whether male or female, feel more depressed, have fewer social supports, and may do less well in educational and career attainment than their agemates (Caspi, 2000; Caspi et al., 2003). Similarly, a longitudinal study of social development would probably result in quite different findings if it were carried out in the first decade of the twenty-first century, around the time of World War II, or during the Great Depression of the 1930s.

Cohort effects don't just operate broadly on an entire generation. They also occur when specific experiences influence some children but not others in the same generation. For example, children who witnessed the terrorist attacks of September 11, 2001, either because they were near Ground Zero or because they saw injury and death on TV, were far more likely than other children to display persistent emotional problems, including intense fear, anxiety, and depression (Saylor et al., 2003). A study of one New York City sample suggested that as many as one-fourth of the city's children were affected (Hoven, Mandell, & Duarte, 2003).

These children, who were victims of the December 2004 tsunami in Indonesia, participate in art therapy to help them cope with the loss of family members. This powerfully destructive historical event is a cohort effect, with profound consequences for development.

THE CROSS-SECTIONAL DESIGN ■ The length of time it takes for many behaviors to change, even in limited longitudinal studies, has led researchers to turn to a more efficient strategy for studying development. In the **cross-sectional design,** groups of people differing in age are studied at the same point in time. Because participants are measured only once, researchers need not be concerned about such difficulties as participant dropout or practice effects.

An investigation in which students in grades 3, 6, 9, and 12 filled out a questionnaire asking about their sibling relationships provides a good illustration (Buhrmester & Furman, 1990). Findings revealed that sibling interaction was characterized by greater equality and less power assertion with age. Also, feelings of sibling companionship declined during adolescence. The researchers thought that several factors contributed to these age differences. As later-born children become more competent and independent, they no longer need, and are probably less willing to accept, direction from older siblings. And as adolescents move from psychological dependence on the family to greater involvement with peers, they may have less time and emotional need to invest in siblings. As you will see in Chapter 16, subsequent research has confirmed these intriguing ideas about the development of sibling relationships.

PROBLEMS IN CONDUCTING CROSS-SECTIONAL RESEARCH ■ Despite its convenience, the cross-sectional design does not provide evidence about change at the level at which it actually occurs: the individual (Kraemer et al., 2000). For example, in the cross-sectional study of sibling relationships just discussed, comparisons are limited to age-group averages. We cannot tell if important individual differences exist. Indeed, longitudinal findings reveal that adolescents vary considerably in the changing quality of their sibling relationships. Although many become more distant, others become more supportive and intimate, still others more rivalrous and antagonistic (Branje et al., 2004; Dunn, Slomkowski, & Beardsall, 1994).

Cross-sectional studies—especially those that cover a wide age span—have another problem. Like longitudinal research, they can be threatened by cohort effects. For example, comparisons of 5-year-old cohorts and 15-year-old cohorts—groups born and reared in different years—may not

cross-sectional design A research design in which groups of people differing in age are studied at the same point in time.

really represent age-related changes. Instead, they may reflect unique experiences associated with the time period in which the age groups were growing up.

IMPROVING DEVELOPMENTAL DESIGNS ■ Researchers have devised ways of building on the strengths and minimizing the weaknesses of longitudinal and cross-sectional approaches. Several modified developmental designs have resulted.

Sequential Designs. To overcome some of the limitations of traditional developmental designs, investigators sometimes use **sequential designs,** in which they conduct several similar cross-sectional or longitudinal studies (called *sequences*) at varying times. As the illustration in Figure 1.8 reveals, some sequential designs combine longitudinal and cross-sectional strategies, an approach that has three advantages:

■ We can find out whether cohort effects are operating by comparing participants of the same age who were born in different years. In Figure 1.8, for example, we can compare the longitudinal samples at seventh, eighth, and ninth grades. If they do not differ, we can rule out cohort effects.
■ We can make both longitudinal and cross-sectional comparisons. If outcomes are similar, we can be especially confident about the findings.
■ The design is efficient. In our example, we can find out about change over a five-year period by following each cohort for three years.

In a study that used the design in Figure 1.8, researchers wanted to find out if family harmony changed as young people experienced the dramatic physical and psychological changes of adolescence (Baer, 2002). A questionnaire assessing emotional bonding among family members was given to three adolescent cohorts, each born a year apart. In longitudinal follow-ups, each cohort again responded to the questionnaire during the following two years.

Findings for the three cohorts converged: All reported (1) a slight decline in family harmony with grade and (2) similar levels of family harmony as they reached the same grade, confirming that there were no cohort effects. Therefore, the researchers concluded that family closeness diminishes steadily from sixth to tenth grade, noting, however, that the change is

FIGURE 1.8

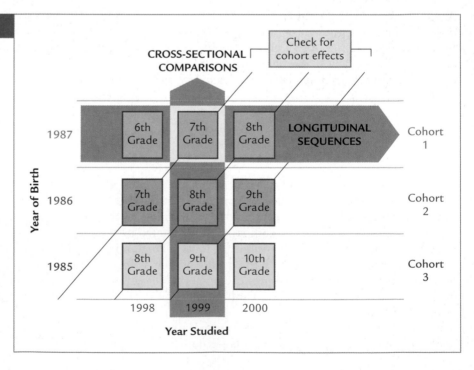

Example of a sequential design. Three cohorts, born in 1985 (blue), 1986 (pink), and 1987 (green), respectively, are followed longitudinally for three years. Testing the cohorts in overlapping grades enables researchers to check for cohort effects by comparing participants born in different years when they reach the same grade (see diagonals). In a study using this design, same-grade adolescents who were members of different cohorts scored similarly on a questionnaire assessing family harmony, indicating no cohort effects. By following each cohort for just three years, the investigator could infer a developmental trend across five years, from sixth to tenth grade.

mild—not enough to threaten supportive family ties. **TAKE A MOMENT...** Turn back to our discussion of parent–adolescent communication as a dynamic system on page 28 and our consideration of adolescent sibling relationships on page 41. How are those results helpful in interpreting the outcomes of the sequential study just described?

Examining Microcosms of Development. In the examples of developmental research we have discussed, observations of children are fairly widely spaced. When we observe once a year or every few years, we can describe development, but we cannot easily capture the processes that produce it. The **microgenetic design,** an adaptation of the longitudinal approach, presents children with a novel task and follows their mastery over a series of closely spaced sessions. Within this "microcosm" of development, researchers observe how change occurs (Kuhn, 1995; Siegler & Crowley, 1991). The microgenetic design is especially useful for studying cognitive development—for example, the strategies children use to acquire new knowledge in reading, mathematics, and science (Siegler, 2002, 2006). As you will see in Chapter 5, the microgenetic design has also been used to trace infants' mastery of motor skills.

Nevertheless, microgenetic studies are difficult to carry out. Researchers must pore over hours of recorded information, analyzing each participant's behavior many times. In addition, the time required for children to change is hard to anticipate. It depends on a careful match between the child's capabilities and the demands of the task. Finally, as in other longitudinal research, practice effects can distort microgenetic findings. But when researchers overcome these challenges, they reap the benefits of seeing development as it takes place.

In a block-gluing project, these 5-year-olds experiment with balance, observe the results with rapt attention, and—if the structure tumbles—take corrective steps. What strategies do they use, and how do they become proficient at the task? A microgenetic design, which permits researchers to follow children's mastery of a challenging task, is uniquely suited to answering these questions.

Combining Experimental and Developmental Designs. Perhaps you noticed that all the examples of longitudinal and cross-sectional research we have considered permit only correlational, not causal, inferences. Yet causal information is also desirable, both for testing theories and for finding ways to enhance development. Sometimes researchers can explore the causal link between experiences and development by experimentally manipulating the experiences. If, as a result, development improves, then we have strong evidence for a causal association. Today, research that combines an experimental strategy with either a longitudinal or a cross-sectional approach is increasingly common. For an example, refer to the Social Issues: Education box on page 44.

Ethics in Research on Children

Research into human behavior creates ethical issues because, unfortunately, the quest for scientific knowledge can sometimes exploit people. When children take part in research, the ethical concerns are especially complex. Children are more vulnerable than adults to physical and psychological harm. In addition, immaturity makes it difficult or impossible for children to evaluate for themselves what participation in research will mean. For these reasons, special ethical guidelines for research on children have been developed by the federal government, by funding agencies, and by research-oriented associations such as the American Psychological Association (2002), the Canadian Psychological Association (2000), and the Society for Research in Child Development (1993).

sequential design A research design in which several similar cross-sectional or longitudinal studies (called *sequences*) are conducted at varying times.

microgenetic design A research design in which investigators present children with a novel task and follow their mastery over a series of closely spaced sessions.

Social Issues: Education

Can Musical Experiences Enhance Intelligence?

In a 1993 experiment, researchers reported that college students who listened to a Mozart sonata for a few minutes just before taking a test of spatial reasoning abilities did better on the test than students who took the test after listening to relaxation instructions or sitting in silence (Rauscher, Shaw, & Ky, 1993). Strains of Mozart, the investigators concluded, seem to induce changes in the brain that "warm up" neural connections, thereby improving thinking. But the gain in performance, widely publicized as the "Mozart effect," lasted only 15 minutes and proved difficult to replicate. Rather than involving a real change in ability, Mozart seemed

Children who take music lessons over many weeks gain in mental test performance compared to children who take drama lessons or who receive no lessons at all. To make music, children must engage in diverse intellectually challenging activities—reading musical notation, memorizing lengthy passages, analyzing musical structures, and mastering technical skills.

to improve arousal and mood, yielding better concentration on the test (Schellenberg, 2005).

Despite mounting evidence that the Mozart effect was uncertain at best, the media and politicians were enthralled with the idea that a brief exposure of the brain to classical music in infancy, when neural connections are forming rapidly, might yield lifelong intellectual

benefits. Soon Georgia, Tennessee, and South Dakota began providing free CDs for every newborn baby leaving the hospital. Yet no studies of the Mozart effect have ever been conducted on infants! And an experiment with school-age children failed to yield any intellectual gains as a result of simply listening to music (McKelvie & Low, 2002).

Research suggests that to produce lasting gains in mental test scores, interventions must be long-lasting and involve children's active participation. Consequently, Glenn Schellenberg (2004) wondered, can music lessons enhance intelligence? Children who take music lessons must practice regularly, engage in extended focused attention, read music, memorize lengthy musical passages, understand diverse musical structures, and master technical skills. These experiences might foster cognitive processing, particularly during childhood, when regions of the brain are taking on specialized functions and are highly sensitive to environmental influences.

Schellenberg recruited 132 6-year-olds—children just old enough for formal lessons. First, the children took an intelligence test and were rated on social maturity, permitting the researchers to see whether music lessons would affect some aspects of development but not others. Next, the children were randomly assigned to one of four experimental conditions. Two were music groups; one received piano lessons and the other voice lessons. The third group took drama lessons—a condition that shed light on whether intellectual gains were unique to musical experiences. The fourth group—a no-lessons control—was offered music lessons the following year. All music and drama instruction took place at the prestigious Royal Conservatory of Music in Toronto, where experienced teachers taught the children in small groups. After 36 weeks of lessons, a longitudinal follow-up was conducted: The children's intelligence and social maturity were assessed again.

All four groups gained in mental test performance, probably because the participants had just entered grade school, which usually leads to an increase in intelligence test scores. But the two music groups consistently gained more than the drama and no-lesson control groups (see Figure 1.9). Their advantage, though

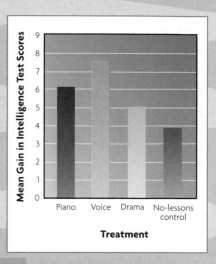

FIGURE 1.9

Music lessons promote gains in intelligence. In a study that combined experimental and longitudinal research strategies, children's mental test performance was tracked longitudinally, before and after they experienced one of four conditions: (1) piano lessons, (2) voice lessons, (3) drama lessons, and (4) no lessons. Children in the two groups receiving music lessons showed greater gains in test scores.

just a few points, extended across many mental abilities, including verbal and spatial skills and speed of thinking. At the same time, only the drama group improved in social maturity.

In sum, active, sustained musical experiences can lead to small increases in intelligence among 6-year-olds that do not arise from comparable drama lessons. But other enrichment activities with similar properties, such as reading, science, math, and chess programs, may confer similar benefits. All demand that children invest far more time and effort than they would in listening to a Mozart sonata. Nevertheless—despite absence of evidence to support their claims—music companies persist in selling CDs entitled "Tune Your Brain with Mozart," "Music for Accelerating Learning," and "Mozart for Newborns: A Bright Beginning."

TABLE 1.7	Children's Research Rights
RESEARCH RIGHT	**DESCRIPTION**
Protection from harm	Children have the right to be protected from physical or psychological harm in research. If in doubt about the harmful effects of research, investigators should seek the opinion of others. When harm seems possible, investigators should find other means for obtaining the desired information or abandon the research.
Informed consent	All research participants, including children, have the right to have explained to them, in language appropriate to their level of understanding, all aspects of the research that may affect their willingness to participate. When children are participants, informed consent of parents as well as others who act on the child's behalf (such as school officials) should be obtained, preferably in writing. Children, and the adults responsible for them, have the right to discontinue participation in the research at any time.
Privacy	Children have the right to concealment of their identity on all information collected in the course of research. They also have this right with respect to written reports and any informal discussions about the research.
Knowledge of results	Children have the right to be informed of the results of research in language that is appropriate to their level of understanding.
Beneficial treatments	If experimental treatments believed to be beneficial are under investigation, children in control groups have the right to alternative beneficial treatments if they are available.

Sources: American Psychological Association, 2002; Canadian Psychological Association, 2000; Society for Research in Child Development, 1993.

Table 1.7 presents a summary of children's basic research rights. **TAKE A MOMENT...** Once you have examined them, read about the following research situations, each of which poses a serious ethical dilemma. What precautions do you think should be taken in each instance? Is either so threatening to children's well-being that it should not be carried out?

- To study children's willingness to separate from their caregivers, an investigator decides to ask mothers of 1- and 2-year-olds to leave their child alone briefly in an unfamiliar playroom. The researcher knows that these circumstances will upset some children.
- In a study of moral development, a researcher wants to assess children's ability to resist temptation by videotaping their behavior without their knowledge. She promises 7-year-olds an attractive prize for solving difficult puzzles but tells them not to look at a classmate's correct solutions, which are deliberately placed at the back of the room. Telling children ahead of time that cheating is being studied or that their behavior is being monitored will defeat the purpose of the study.

Did you find it difficult to evaluate these examples? Virtually every organization that has devised ethical principles for research has concluded that conflicts arising in research situations do not have simple right or wrong answers. The ultimate responsibility for the ethical integrity of research lies with the investigator. But researchers are advised—and often required—to seek advice from others. Committees for this purpose exist in colleges, universities, and other institutions. These review boards balance the costs of the research to participants in terms of time, stress, and inconvenience against the study's value for advancing knowledge and improving conditions of life. If any risks to the safety and welfare of participants outweigh the worth of the research, then preference is always given to the interests of the participants.

The ethical principle of *informed consent* requires special interpretation when participants cannot fully appreciate the research goals and activities. Parental consent is meant to protect the safety of children whose ability to decide is not yet mature. In addition, researchers should obtain the agreement of other individuals who act on children's behalf, such as institutional officials when research is conducted in schools, child-care centers, or hospitals. This is especially important when research includes special groups, such as abused children, whose parents may not always represent their best interests (Fisher, 1993; Thompson, 1990b).

As soon as children are old enough to appreciate the purpose of the research, and certainly by 7 years of age, their own informed consent should be obtained in addition to parental

© ED BOCK/CORBIS

This researcher takes special precautions as she prepares a young child to participate in research. Because children rely on a basic faith in adults, she must explain carefully that information will be kept confidential and make sure the child understands that he can end his participation anytime, for any reason.

consent. Around age 7, changes in children's thinking permit them to better understand basic scientific principles and the needs of others. Researchers should respect and enhance these capacities by giving school-age children a full explanation of research activities in language they can understand (Fisher, 1993). Extra care must be taken when telling children that the information they provide will be kept confidential and that they can end their participation at any time. Children may not understand or believe these promises (Abramovitch et al., 1995; Bruzzese & Fisher, 2003). And in certain ethnic minority communities, where deference to authority, maintaining pleasant relationships, and meeting the needs of a guest (the researcher) are highly valued, children and parents may be particularly likely to consent when they would rather not do so (Fisher et al., 2002).

Finally, young children rely on a basic faith in adults to feel secure in unfamiliar situations. For this reason, they may find some types of research particularly disturbing. All ethical guidelines advise that special precautions be taken in the use of deception and concealment, as occurs when researchers observe children from behind one-way mirrors, give them false feedback about their performance, or do not tell them the truth regarding what the research is about. When these procedures are used with adults, *debriefing*, in which the researcher provides a full account and justification of the activities, occurs after the research session is over. Debriefing should also be done with children, but it rarely works as well. Despite explanations, children may leave the research situation questioning the honesty of adults. Ethical standards permit deception in research with children if investigators satisfy institutional committees that such practices are necessary. Nevertheless, because deception may have serious emotional consequences for some youngsters, many child development specialists believe that researchers should come up with other research strategies when children are involved.

Ask Yourself

Review   Explain how cohort effects can distort the findings of both longitudinal and cross-sectional studies. How does the sequential design reveal cohort effects?

Apply   A researcher compares children who went to summer leadership camps with children who attended athletic camps. She finds that those who attended leadership camps are friendlier. Should the investigator tell parents that sending children to leadership camps will cause them to be more sociable? Why or why not?

Connect   Review the experiment on music lessons and intelligence reported in the Social Issues: Education box on page 44. Why was it ethically important for the researchers to offer music lessons to the no-lessons control group during the year after completion of the study? (*Hint:* Refer to Table 1.7.)

Reflect   Suppose a researcher asks you to enroll your baby in a ten-year longitudinal study. What factors would lead you to agree and to stay involved? Do your answers shed light on why longitudinal studies often have biased samples? Explain.

Summary

The Field of Child Development

What is the field of child development, and what factors stimulated its expansion?

■ **Child development** is an area of study devoted to understanding constancy and change from conception through adolescence. It is part of a larger interdisciplinary field known as **developmental science**, which includes all changes we experience throughout the lifespan. Research on child development has been stimulated both by scientific curiosity and by social pressures to better children's lives.

How can we divide child development into sensible, manageable periods and domains?

■ Development is often divided into three broad domains: (1) physical development, (2) cognitive development, and (3) emotional and social development. These domains are not really distinct; rather, they combine in an integrated, holistic fashion.

© DAVID YOUNG-WOLFF/ PHOTOEDIT

■ Researchers generally divide the flow of time into the following age periods, which serve as important transitions in major theories: (1) the prenatal period (conception to birth), (2) infancy and toddlerhood (birth to 2 years), (3) early childhood (2 to 6 years), (4) middle childhood (6 to 11 years), and (5) adolescence (11 to 18 years). To describe the prolonged transition to adulthood typical of contemporary young people in industrialized nations, researchers have posited a new period of development, emerging adulthood, spanning ages 18 to 25.

Basic Issues

Identify three basic issues on which theories of child development take a stand.

■ Each **theory** of child development takes a stand on three fundamental issues: (1) Is development a **continuous** process, or is it **discontinuous**, following a series of distinct **stages**? (2) Does one general course of development characterize all children, or are there many possible courses, influenced by the distinct **contexts** in which children grow up? (3) Is development primarily influenced by genetic or environmental factors (the **nature–nurture controversy**)?

■ Recent theories take a balanced stand on these issues. And contemporary researchers realize that answers may vary across domains of development and even, as research on **resilience** illustrates, across individuals.

Historical Foundations

Describe major historical influences on modern theories of child development.

■ Contemporary theories of child development have roots extending far into the past. As early as medieval times, the sixth through the fifteenth centuries, childhood was regarded as a separate phase of life.

■ In the sixteenth and seventeenth centuries, the Puritan conception of original sin led to a harsh philosophy of child rearing, based on the view that children were born evil and had to be civilized through repressive measures.

■ The seventeenth-century Enlightenment brought a new emphasis on human dignity and respect that led to more humane conceptions of childhood. Locke's notion of the child as a **tabula rasa** ("blank slate") provided the basis for twentieth-century behaviorism, while Rousseau's idea that children were **noble savages** foreshadowed the concepts of stage and **maturation**.

■ Inspired by Darwin's theory of evolution, efforts to observe the child directly began in the late nineteenth and early twentieth centuries. Soon after, Hall and Gesell introduced the **normative approach**, which produced a large body of descriptive facts about children. In the early 1900s, Binet and Simon constructed the first successful intelligence test, which sparked interest in individual differences in development and led to a heated controversy over nature versus nurture.

Mid-Twentieth-Century Theories

What theories influenced child development research in the mid-twentieth century?

■ In the 1930s and 1940s, psychiatrists and social workers turned to the **psychoanalytic perspective** for help in treating children's emotional problems. In Freud's **psychosexual theory**, children move through five stages, during which three portions of the personality—id, ego, and superego—become integrated.

■ Erikson's **psychosocial theory** builds on Freud's theory, emphasizing the development of culturally relevant attitudes and skills and—with the addition of three adult stages—the lifespan nature of development. Despite its extensive contributions, the psychoanalytic perspective is no longer in the mainstream of child development research.

■ As the psychoanalytic perspective gained in prominence, **behaviorism** emerged, focusing on directly observable events (stimuli and responses) in an effort to create an objective science of psychology. B. F. Skinner's *operant conditioning theory* emphasizes the role of reinforcement and punishment in increasing or decreasing the frequency of a behavior.

■ A related approach, Albert Bandura's **social learning theory,** focuses on modeling as the major means through which children and adults acquire new responses. Its most recent revision stresses the role of cognition, or thinking, in children's imitation and learning and, therefore, is known as a social-cognitive rather than a social learning approach.

© MARGOT GRANITSAS/THE IMAGE WORKS

■ Behaviorism and social learning theory gave rise to techniques of **behavior modification** to eliminate undesirable behaviors and increase desirable responses.

■ Piaget's **cognitive-developmental theory** emphasizes that children actively construct knowledge as they manipulate and explore their world. According to Piaget, children move through four stages, beginning with the baby's sensorimotor action patterns and ending with the abstract, systematic reasoning system of the adolescent and adult. Piaget's work has stimulated a wealth of research on children's thinking and has encouraged educational programs that emphasize children's discovery learning.

Recent Theoretical Perspectives

Describe recent theoretical perspectives on child development.

■ **Information processing** views the mind as a complex symbol-manipulating system, much like a computer. This approach helps investigators achieve a detailed understanding of what children of different ages do when faced with tasks and problems.

■ Over the past two decades, researchers in **developmental cognitive neuroscience** have begun to study the relationship between changes in the brain and the developing child's cognitive processing and behavior patterns. They have made progress in identifying the types of experiences to which the brain is sensitive at various ages and in clarifying the brain bases of many learning and behavior disorders.

■ Three perspectives place special emphasis on contexts for development. **Ethology** stresses the evolutionary origins and adaptive value of behavior and inspired the **sensitive period** concept. In a new area of research called **evolutionary developmental psychology,** researchers have extended this emphasis, seeking to understand the adaptiveness of species-wide competencies as they change over time.

■ Vygotsky's **sociocultural theory**, which views cognitive development as a socially influenced process, has enhanced our understanding of cultural variation. Through cooperative dialogues with more expert members of society, children come to use language to guide their own thought and actions and acquire culturally relevant knowledge and skills.

■ **Ecological systems theory** views the child as developing within a complex system of relationships affected by multiple, nested layers of the surrounding environment—**microsystem, mesosystem, exosystem,** and **macrosystem.** Each of these levels is seen as a major influence on children's well-being. The **chronosystem** represents the dynamic, ever-changing nature of children and their experiences.

■ Inspired by ideas in other sciences and recent perspectives in child development, a new wave of theorists has adopted a **dynamic systems perspective** to account for wide variation in development. According to this view, the mind, body, and physical and social worlds form an integrated system that guides mastery of new skills. A change in any part of the system prompts the child to reorganize her behavior so the various components work together again but in a more complex, effective way.

Comparing Child Development Theories

Identify the stand taken by each major theory on the basic issues of child development.

■ Theories that are major forces in child development research vary in their focus on different domains of development, in their view of

how development occurs, and in their strengths and weaknesses. (For a full summary, see Table 1.4 on page 30.)

Studying the Child

Describe methods commonly used to gather information on children.

■ **Naturalistic observations,** which are gathered in everyday environments, permit researchers to see directly the everyday behaviors they hope to explain. In contrast, **structured observations** take place in laboratories, where every participant has an equal opportunity to display the behaviors of interest.

■ Self-report methods can be flexible and open-ended like the **clinical interview,** which permits participants to express their thoughts in ways similar to their thinking in everyday life. Alternatively, **structured interviews,** tests, and questionnaires are more efficient and permit researchers to specify activities and behaviors that participants might not think of in an open-ended interview.

■ Investigators use the **clinical,** or **case study, method** to obtain an in-depth understanding of a single child. It involves synthesizing a wide range of information, including interviews, observations, and sometimes test scores.

■ A growing interest in the impact of culture has prompted researchers to adapt observational and self-report methods to permit direct comparisons of cultures. To uncover the cultural meanings of children's and adults' behaviors, researchers rely on **ethnography,** a technique borrowed from anthropology, which uses participant observation to capture the unique values and social processes of a culture or distinct social group.

Distinguish between correlational and experimental research designs, noting the strengths and limitations of each.

■ The **correlational design** examines relationships between variables, generally as they occur in natural life circumstances, without altering participants' experiences. The **correlation coefficient** describes how two measures, or variables, are associated with one another. Correlational studies do not permit inferences about cause and effect, but they can be helpful in identifying relationships that are worth exploring with a more powerful experimental strategy.

■ An **experimental design** permits inferences about cause and effect. Researchers manipulate an **independent variable** by exposing participants to two or more treatment conditions. Then they determine what effect this variable has on a **dependent variable. Random assignment** reduces the chances that characteristics of participants will affect the accuracy of experimental findings.

■ To achieve high degrees of control, most experiments are conducted in laboratories, but their findings may not apply to everyday life. Field and natural, or quasi-, experiments compare treatments in natural environments. But these approaches are less rigorous than laboratory experiments.

Describe designs for studying development, noting the strengths and limitations of each.

■ In a **longitudinal design,** participants are studied repeatedly at different ages, revealing common patterns as well as individual differences in development and the relationship between early and later events and behaviors. Researchers conducting longitudinal research may face problems with biased samples and practice effects. Their findings are also subject to **cohort effects**—the influence of particular cultural and historical conditions, which can make it difficult to generalize findings to children developing at other times, or to children who did not experience a specific event.

■ The **cross-sectional design** offers an efficient approach to investigating development. However, it is limited to comparisons of age-group averages and does not provide evidence about individual change. Findings of cross-sectional research also can be distorted by cohort effects, especially when they cover a wide age span.

■ **Sequential designs** can overcome some of the limitations of traditional developmental designs. By comparing participants of the same age who were born in different years, investigators can find out if cohort effects are operating. When sequential designs combine longitudinal and cross-sectional strategies, researchers can see if outcomes are similar, for added confidence in their findings.

■ In the **microgenetic design,** an adaptation of the longitudinal approach, researchers track change as it occurs for unique insights into processes of development. However, the time required for children to change is hard to anticipate, and practice effects can bias findings.

■ When researchers combine experimental and developmental designs, they can examine causal influences on development. This combined strategy is increasingly common today.

What special ethical concerns arise in doing research on children?

■ Because of their immaturity, children are especially vulnerable to harm and often cannot evaluate the risks and benefits of research. Ethical guidelines and special committees that weigh the risks and benefits of research help ensure that children's research rights are protected. Besides obtaining consent from parents and others who act on children's behalf, researchers should seek the informed consent of children 7 years and older.

■ The use of deception in research with children is especially risky because it may undermine their basic faith in the trustworthiness of adults.

Important Terms and Concepts

behavior modification (p. 18)
behaviorism (p. 16)
child development (p. 4)
chronosystem (p. 27)
clinical interview (p. 33)
clinical, or case study, method (p. 34)
cognitive-developmental theory (p. 18)
cohort effects (p. 40)
contexts (p. 8)
continuous development (p. 8)
correlation coefficient (p. 37)
correlational design (p. 35)
cross-sectional design (p. 41)
dependent variable (p. 37)
developmental cognitive neuroscience (p. 22)
developmental science (p. 4)
discontinuous development (p. 8)

dynamic systems perspective (p. 27)
ecological systems theory (p. 25)
ethnography (p. 34)
ethology (p. 23)
evolutionary developmental
   psychology (p. 24)
exosystem (p. 26)
experimental design (p. 37)
independent variable (p. 37)
information processing (p. 21)
longitudinal design (p. 40)
macrosystem (p. 27)
maturation (p. 12)
mesosystem (p. 26)
microgenetic design (p. 43)
microsystem (p. 26)
naturalistic observation (p. 31)

nature–nurture controversy (p. 8)
noble savage (p. 12)
normative approach (p. 13)
psychoanalytic perspective (p. 14)
psychosexual theory (p. 14)
psychosocial theory (p. 14)
random assignment (p. 38)
resilience (p. 10)
sensitive period (p. 23)
sequential design (p. 42)
social learning theory (p. 17)
sociocultural theory (p. 24)
stage (p. 8)
structured interview (p. 33)
structured observation (p. 31)
tabula rasa (p. 11)
theory (p. 6)

Chapter 2

This urban scene, with trains, planes, boats, buses, and pedestrians going about their business, captures the bustling complexity of contemporary city life. Chapter 2 will introduce you to a similarly complex blend of forces—genetic, family, school, neighborhood, and societal—that influence child development.

Reprinted with permission from the International Museum of Children's Art, Oslo, Norway

"The Spirited City"
Wong Hiu Kit
8 years, Hong Kong, China

Biological and Environmental Foundations

phenotype The individual's
physical and behavioral
characteristics, which are
determined by both genetic
and environmental factors.

genotype An individual's
genetic makeup.

"It's a girl," announces the doctor, holding up the squalling little creature as her new parents gaze with amazement at their miraculous creation. "A girl! We've named her Sarah!" exclaims the proud father to eager relatives waiting for news of their new family member.

As we join these parents in thinking about how this wondrous being came into existence and imagining her future, we are struck by many questions. How could this baby, equipped with everything necessary for life outside the womb, have developed from the union of two tiny cells? What ensures that Sarah will, in due time, roll over, reach for objects, walk, talk, make friends, imagine, and create—just like other typical children born before her? Why is she a girl and not a boy, dark-haired rather than blond, calm and cuddly instead of wiry and energetic? What difference will it make that Sarah is given a name and place in one family, community, nation, and culture rather than another?

To answer these questions, this chapter takes a close look at the foundations of development: heredity and environment. Because nature has prepared us for survival, all humans have features in common. Yet each of us is also unique. **TAKE A MOMENT …** Think about several children you know well, and jot down the most obvious physical and behavioral similarities between them and their parents. Did you find that one child shows combined features of both parents, another resembles just one parent, whereas a third is not like either parent? These directly observable characteristics are called **phenotypes.** They depend in part on the individual's **genotype**—the complex blend of genetic information that determines our species and influences all our unique characteristics. Yet phenotypes are also affected by each person's lifelong history of experiences.

We begin our discussion at the moment of conception, an event that establishes the hereditary makeup of the new individual. First we review basic genetic principles that help explain similarities and differences among children in appearance and behavior. Then we turn to aspects of the environment that play powerful roles in children's lives. You will quickly see that both nature and nurture affect all aspects of development. In fact, some findings and conclusions may surprise you. For example, many people believe that when children inherit unfavorable characteristics, not much can be done to help them. Others are convinced that the damage done to a child by a harmful environment can easily be corrected. As we will see, neither of these assumptions is true. In the final section of this chapter, we take up the question of how nature and nurture work *together* to shape the course of development.

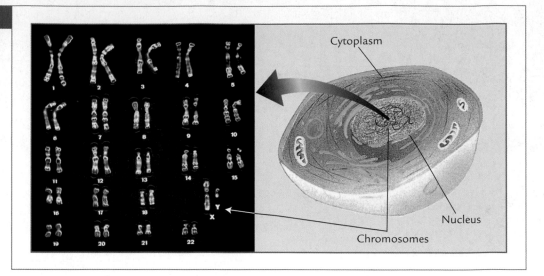

FIGURE 2.1

A karyotype, or photograph, of human chromosomes. The 46 chromosomes shown on the left were isolated from a human cell, stained, greatly magnified, and arranged in pairs according to decreasing size of the upper "arm" of each chromosome. Note the twenty-third pair, XY. The cell donor is a male. In a female, the twenty-third pair would be XX. (© CNRI/Science Photo Library/Photo Researchers, Inc.)

Genetic Foundations

Each of us is made up of trillions of units called *cells*. Within the cell is a control center, or *nucleus,* that contains rodlike structures called **chromosomes**, which store and transmit genetic information. Human chromosomes come in 23 matching pairs (an exception is the XY pair in males, which we will discuss shortly). Each member of a pair corresponds to the other in size, shape, and genetic functions. One is inherited from the mother and one from the father (see Figure 2.1).

The Genetic Code

Chromosomes are made up of a chemical substance called **deoxyribonucleic acid** or **DNA**. As Figure 2.2 shows, DNA is a long, double-stranded molecule that looks like a twisted ladder. Each rung of the ladder consists of a pair of chemical substances called *bases*. Although the bases always pair up in the same way across the ladder rungs—A with T and C with G—they can occur in any order along its sides. It is this sequence of base pairs that provides genetic instructions. A **gene** is a segment of DNA along the length of the chromosome. Genes can be of different lengths—perhaps 100 to several thousand ladder rungs long. An estimated 20,000 to 25,000 genes lie along the human chromosomes (International Human Genome Sequencing Consortium, 2004).

We share some of our genetic makeup with even the simplest organisms, such as bacteria and molds, and most of it with other mammals, especially primates. Between 98 and 99 percent of chimpanzee and human DNA is identical. This means that only a small portion of our heredity is responsible for the traits that make us human, from our upright gait to our extraordinary language and cognitive capacities. And the genetic variation from one human to the next is even less! Individuals around the world are about 99.1 percent genetically identical (Gibbons, 1998; Gibbons et al., 2004). Only a tiny quantity of DNA contributes to human variation in traits and capacities.

A unique feature of DNA is that it can duplicate itself through a process called **mitosis.** This special ability permits a single cell, formed at conception, to develop into a complex human being composed of a great many cells. Refer again to Figure 2.2, and you will see that during mitosis, the chromosomes copy themselves. As a result, each new body cell contains the same number of chromosomes and identical genetic information.

chromosomes Rodlike structures in the cell nucleus that store and transmit genetic information.

deoxyribonucleic acid (DNA) Long, double-stranded molecules that make up chromosomes.

gene A segment of a DNA molecule that contains hereditary instructions.

mitosis The process of cell duplication, in which each new cell receives an exact copy of the original chromosomes.

FIGURE 2.2

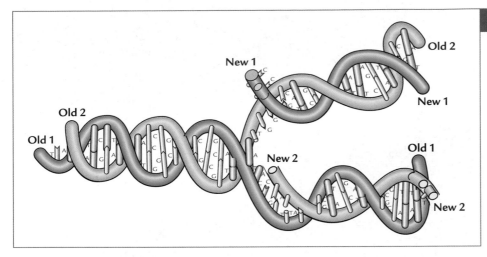

DNA's ladderlike structure. This figure shows that the pairings of bases across the rungs of the ladder are very specific: Adenine (A) always appears with thymine (T), and cytosine (C) always appears with guanine (G). Here, the DNA ladder duplicates by splitting down the middle of its ladder rungs. Each free base picks up a new complementary partner from the area surrounding the cell nucleus.

Genes accomplish their task by sending instructions for making a rich assortment of proteins to the *cytoplasm,* the area surrounding the cell nucleus. Proteins, which trigger chemical reactions throughout the body, are the biological foundation on which our characteristics are built. How do humans, with far fewer genes than scientists once thought (only twice as many as the worm or fly), manage to develop into such complex beings? The answer lies in the proteins our genes make, which break up and reassemble in staggering variety—about 10 to 20 million altogether. Simpler species have far fewer proteins. Furthermore, the communication system between the cell nucleus and cytoplasm, which fine-tunes gene activity, is more intricate in humans than in simpler organisms. Within the cell, a wide range of environmental factors modify gene expression (Strachan & Read, 2004). So even at this microscopic level, biological events are the result of *both* genetic and nongenetic forces.

The Sex Cells

New individuals are created when two special cells called **gametes,** or sex cells—the sperm and ovum—combine. A gamete contains only 23 chromosomes, half as many as a regular body cell. Gametes are formed through a cell division process called **meiosis,** which halves the number of chromosomes normally present in body cells, thereby ensuring that a constant quantity of genetic material is transmitted from one generation to the next. When sperm and ovum unite at conception, the cell that results, called a **zygote,** will again have 46 chromosomes.

The steps involved in meiosis are shown in Figure 2.3 on page 54. First, the chromosomes pair up, and each one copies itself. Then a special event called **crossing over** occurs, in which chromosomes next to each other break at one or more points along their length and exchange segments, so that genes from one are replaced by genes from another. This shuffling of genes creates new hereditary combinations. Next, the chromosome pairs separate into different cells, but chance determines which member of each pair will gather with others and end up in the same gamete. Finally, each chromosome leaves its partner and becomes part of a gamete containing only 23 chromosomes instead of the usual 46.

These events make the likelihood extremely low—about 1 in 700 trillion—that nontwin offspring of the same two parents will be genetically identical (Gould & Keeton, 1996). Therefore, meiosis helps us understand why siblings differ, even though they also have features in common because their genotypes come from the same pool of parental genes. The genetic variability produced by meiosis is important in an evolutionary sense: Because it generates offspring that vary in phenotype, it increases the chances that at least some members of a species will cope successfully with ever-changing environments and will survive.

In the male, four sperm are produced when meiosis is complete. Also, the cells from which sperm arise are produced continuously throughout life. For this reason, a healthy man can father a child at any age after sexual maturity. In the female, meiosis results in just one ovum;

gametes Human sperm and ova, which contain half as many chromosomes as regular body cells.

meiosis The process of cell division through which gametes are formed and in which the number of chromosomes in each cell is halved.

zygote The newly fertilized cell formed by the union of sperm and ovum at conception.

crossing over During meiosis, the exchange of genes between chromosomes next to each other.

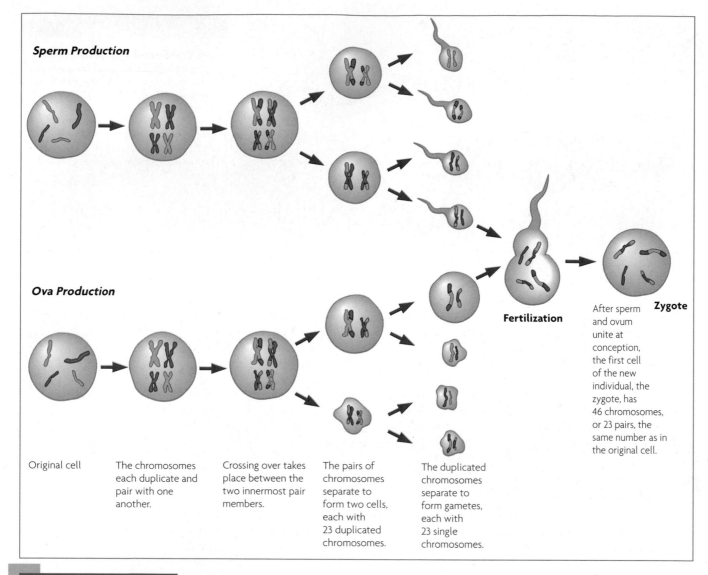

Sperm Production

Ova Production

Fertilization

Zygote

After sperm and ovum unite at conception, the first cell of the new individual, the zygote, has 46 chromosomes, or 23 pairs, the same number as in the original cell.

Original cell	The chromosomes each duplicate and pair with one another.	Crossing over takes place between the two innermost pair members.	The pairs of chromosomes separate to form two cells, each with 23 duplicated chromosomes.	The duplicated chromosomes separate to form gametes, each with 23 single chromosomes.

FIGURE 2.3

The cell division process of meiosis, leading to gamete formation. (Here, original cells are depicted with two rather than the full complement of 23 pairs.) Meiosis creates gametes with only half the usual number of chromosomes. When sperm and ovum unite at conception, the first cell of the new individual (the zygote) has the correct, full number of chromosomes.

the remaining genetic material degenerates. In addition, the female is born with all her ova already present in her ovaries, and she can bear children for only three to four decades. Still, there are plenty of female sex cells. About 1 to 2 million are present at birth, 40,000 remain at adolescence, and approximately 350 to 450 will mature during a woman's childbearing years (Moore & Persaud, 2003).

autosomes The 22 matching chromosome pairs in each human cell.

sex chromosomes The twenty-third pair of chromosomes, which determines the sex of the child—in females, called XX; in males, called XY.

Boy or Girl?

Return to Figure 2.1, and note that 22 of the 23 pairs of chromosomes are matching pairs, called **autosomes.** Geneticists number these from longest (1) to shortest (22). The twenty-third pair consists of **sex chromosomes.** In females, this pair is called XX; in males, it is called XY. The X is a relatively large chromosome, whereas the Y is short and carries little genetic material. When gametes form in males, the X and Y chromosomes separate into different

TABLE 2.1	Maternal Factors Linked to Fraternal Twinning
FACTOR	**DESCRIPTION**
Ethnicity	Occurs in 4 per 1,000 births among Asians, 8 per 1,000 births among whites, 12 to 16 per 1,000 births among blacks[a]
Family history of twinning	Occurs more often among women whose mothers and sisters gave birth to fraternal twins
Age	Rises with maternal age, peaking between 35 and 39 years, and then rapidly falls
Nutrition	Occurs less often among women with poor diets; occurs more often among women who are tall and overweight or of normal weight as opposed to slight body build
Number of births	Is more likely with each additional birth
Season and geographic region	Increases with exposure to sunlight: Occurs more often in conceptions during summer months and in regions near the equator
Fertility drugs and in vitro fertilization	Is more likely with fertility hormones and in vitro fertilization (see page 66), which also increase the chances of triplets to quintuplets

[a]Worldwide rates, not including multiple births resulting from use of fertility drugs.

Sources: Bortolus et al., 1999; Hall, 2003.

sperm cells. The gametes that form in females all carry an X chromosome. Therefore, the sex of the new organism is determined by whether an X-bearing or a Y-bearing sperm fertilizes the ovum. In fact, scientists have isolated three genes on the Y chromosome that are crucial for male sexual development—one that switches on the production of male hormones and two involved in the formation of male sex organs. But they also know that other genes, yet to be discovered, are involved in the development of sexual characteristics (Cotinot et al., 2002).

Multiple Births

Ruth and Peter, a couple I know well, tried for several years to have a child, without success. When Ruth reached age 33, her doctor prescribed a fertility drug, and Ruth gave birth to twins—Jeannie and Jason. Jeannie and Jason are **fraternal**, or **dizygotic, twins,** the most common type of multiple birth, resulting from the release and fertilization of two ova. Fraternal twins, who are genetically no more alike than ordinary siblings, account for 1 in every 62 births in the United States and 1 in every 80 births in Canada (Statistics Canada, 2006d; U.S. Department of Health and Human Services, 2006). Older maternal age, fertility drugs, and in vitro fertilization (to be discussed shortly) are major causes of the dramatic rise in fraternal twinning and other multiple births in industrialized nations over the past several decades (Machin, 2005; Russell et al., 2003). As Table 2.1 indicates, other genetic and environmental factors also increase the chances of bearing fraternal twins.

Twins can be created in another way. Sometimes a zygote that has started to duplicate separates into two clusters of cells that develop into two individuals. These are called **identical,** or **monozygotic, twins** because they have the same genetic makeup. The frequency of identical twins is unrelated to the factors listed in Table 2.1. It is the same around the world—about 1 in every 330 births (Hall, 2003). Animal research has uncovered a variety of environmental influences that induce this type of twinning, including temperature changes, variation in oxygen levels, and late fertilization of the ovum. The causes of identical twinning in humans, however, are unclear.

During their early years, children of single births often are healthier and develop more rapidly than twins. Jeannie and Jason were born early (as are most twins)—three weeks before Ruth's due date (Blickstein, 2002). As you will see in Chapter 4, like other premature infants, they required special care after birth. When the twins came home from the hospital, Ruth and Peter had to divide time between them. Perhaps because neither baby got quite as much attention as

fraternal, or **dizygotic, twins** Twins resulting from the release and fertilization of two ova. They are genetically no more alike than ordinary siblings.

identical, or **monozygotic, twins** Twins that result when a zygote, during the early stages of cell duplication, divides in two. They have the same genetic makeup.

These identical, or monozygotic, twins were created when a duplicating zygote separated into two clusters of cells, and two individuals with the same genetic makeup developed. Identical twins look alike, and as we will see later in this chapter, tend to resemble each other in a variety of psychological characteristics.

the average single infant, Jeannie and Jason walked and talked several months later than other children their age, although both caught up in development by middle childhood (Lytton & Gallagher, 2002).

Patterns of Genetic Inheritance

Jeannie has her parents' dark, straight hair, whereas Jason is curly-haired and blond. Patterns of genetic inheritance—the way genes from each parent interact—explain these outcomes. Recall that except for the XY pair in males, all chromosomes come in corresponding pairs. Two forms of each gene occur at the same place on the chromosomes, one inherited from the mother and one from the father. Each form of a gene is called an **allele.** If the alleles from both parents are alike, the child is **homozygous** and will display the inherited trait. If the alleles are different, the child is **heterozygous,** and relationships between the alleles determine the phenotype.

DOMINANT–RECESSIVE INHERITANCE ■ In many heterozygous pairings, **dominant–recessive inheritance** occurs: Only one allele affects the child's characteristics. It is called *dominant;* the second allele, which has no effect, is called *recessive.* Hair color is an example. The allele for dark hair is dominant (we can represent it with a capital *D*), whereas the one for blond hair is recessive (symbolized by a lowercase *b*). A child who inherits a homozygous pair of dominant alleles *(DD)* and a child who inherits a heterozygous pair *(Db)* will both be dark-haired, even though their genotypes differ. Blond hair (like Jason's) can result only from having two recessive alleles *(bb).* Still, heterozygous individuals with just one recessive allele *(Db)* can pass that trait to their children. Therefore, they are called **carriers** of the trait.

Some human characteristics that follow the rules of dominant–recessive inheritance are listed in Table 2.2 and Table 2.3 on page 58. As you can see, many disabilities and diseases are the product of recessive alleles. One of the most frequently occurring recessive disorders is *phenylketonuria,* or *PKU.* It affects the way the body breaks down proteins contained in many foods. Infants born with two recessive alleles lack an enzyme that converts one of the basic amino acids that make up proteins (phenylalanine) into a byproduct essential for body functioning (tyrosine). Without this enzyme, phenylalanine quickly builds to toxic levels that damage the central nervous system. By 1 year, infants with PKU are permanently retarded.

Despite its potentially damaging effects, PKU provides an excellent illustration of the fact that inheriting unfavorable genes does not always lead to an untreatable condition. All U.S. states and Canadian provinces require that each newborn be given a blood test for PKU. If the disease is found, doctors place the baby on a diet low in phenylalanine. Children who receive this treatment nevertheless show mild deficits in certain cognitive skills, such as memory, planning, and problem solving, because even small amounts of phenylalanine interfere with brain functioning (Antshel, 2003; Luciana, Sullivan, & Nelson, 2001). But as long as dietary treatment begins early and continues, children with PKU usually attain an average level of intelligence and have a normal lifespan.

In dominant–recessive inheritance, if we know the genetic makeup of the parents, we can predict the percentage of children in a family who are likely to display or be carriers of a trait. Figure 2.4 on page 59 illustrates this for PKU. For a child to inherit the condition, each parent must have a recessive allele *(p).* As the figure also illustrates, single genes often affect more than one trait. Because of their inability to convert phenylalanine into tyrosine (which is responsible for pigmentation), children with PKU usually have light hair and blue eyes. Furthermore, children vary in the degree to which phenylalanine accumulates in their tissues and in the extent to which they respond to treatment. This is due to the action of **modifier genes,** which enhance or dilute the effects of other genes.

allele Each of two forms of a gene located at the same place on the autosomes.

homozygous Having two identical alleles at the same place on a pair of chromosomes.

heterozygous Having two different alleles at the same place on a pair of chromosomes.

dominant–recessive inheritance A pattern of inheritance in which, under heterozygous conditions, the influence of only one allele is apparent.

carrier A heterozygous individual who can pass a recessive trait to his or her children.

modifier genes Genes that can enhance or dilute the effects of other genes.

Only rarely are serious diseases due to dominant alleles. Think about why this is so. Children who inherited the dominant allele would always develop the disorder. They seldom live long enough to reproduce, and the harmful dominant allele is eliminated from the family's heredity in a single generation. Some dominant disorders, however, do persist. One of them is *Huntington disease,* a condition in which the central nervous system degenerates. Why has this disorder endured? Its symptoms usually do not appear until age 35 or later, after the person has passed the dominant allele to his or her children.

INCOMPLETE DOMINANCE ■ In some heterozygous circumstances, the dominant–recessive relationship does not hold completely. Instead, we see **incomplete dominance,** a pattern of inheritance in which both alleles are expressed in the phenotype, resulting in a combined trait, or one that is intermediate between the two.

The *sickle cell trait,* a heterozygous condition present in many black Africans, provides an example. *Sickle cell anemia* (see Table 2.3) occurs in full form when a child inherits two recessive alleles. They cause the usually round red blood cells to become sickle (crescent-moon) shaped, especially under low-oxygen conditions. The sickled cells clog the blood vessels and block the flow of blood, causing intense pain, swelling, and tissue damage. Despite medical advances that today allow 85 percent of affected children to survive to adulthood, North Americans with sickle cell anemia have a life expectancy of only 55 years (Quinn, Rogers, & Buchanan, 2004). Heterozygous individuals are protected from the disease under most circumstances. However, when they experience oxygen deprivation—for example, at high altitudes or after intense physical exercise—the single recessive allele asserts itself, and a temporary, mild form of the illness occurs.

The sickle cell allele is common among black Africans for a special reason. Carriers of it are more resistant to malaria than individuals with two alleles for normal red blood cells. In Africa, where malaria is common, these carriers have survived and reproduced more frequently than others, leading the gene to be maintained in the black population. In regions of the world where the risk of malaria is low, the frequency of the gene is declining. For example, compared with 20 percent of black Africans, only 8 percent of African Americans are carriers. The carrier rate is believed to be slightly higher in Canada than in the United States because a greater proportion of African Canadians are recent immigrants (Goldbloom, 2004).

X-LINKED INHERITANCE ■ Males and females have an equal chance of inheriting recessive disorders carried on the autosomes, such as PKU and sickle cell anemia. But when a harmful allele is carried on the X chromosome, **X-linked inheritance** applies. Males are more likely to be affected because their sex chromosomes do not match. In females, any recessive allele on one X chromosome has a good chance of being suppressed by a dominant allele on the other X. But the Y chromosome is only about one-third as long and therefore lacks many corresponding alleles to override those on the X. A well-known example is *hemophilia,* a disorder in which the blood fails to clot normally. Figure 2.5 on page 59 shows its greater likelihood of inheritance by male children whose mothers carry the abnormal allele.

Besides X-linked disorders, many sex differences reveal the male to be at a disadvantage. Rates of miscarriage, infant and childhood deaths, birth defects, learning disabilities, behavior

TABLE 2.2	Examples of Dominant and Recessive Characteristics
DOMINANT	**RECESSIVE**
Dark hair	Blond hair
Normal hair	Pattern baldness
Curly hair	Straight hair
Nonred hair	Red hair
Facial dimples	No dimples
Normal hearing	Some forms of deafness
Normal vision	Nearsightedness
Farsightedness	Normal vision
Normal vision	Congenital eye cataracts
Normally pigmented skin	Albinism
Double-jointedness	Normal joints
Type A blood	Type O blood
Type B blood	Type O blood
Rh-positive blood	Rh-negative blood

Note: Many normal characteristics that were previously thought to be due to dominant–recessive inheritance, such as eye color, are now regarded as due to multiple genes. For the characteristics listed here, there still seems to be general agreement that the simple dominant–recessive relationship holds.

Source: McKusick, 2002.

incomplete dominance
A pattern of inheritance in which both alleles are expressed in the phenotype, resulting in a combined trait, or one that is intermediate between the two.

X-linked inheritance
A pattern of inheritance in which a recessive gene is carried on the X chromosome, so that males are more likely to be affected.

TABLE 2.3 Examples of Dominant and Recessive Diseases

DISEASE	DESCRIPTION	MODE OF INHERITANCE	INCIDENCE	TREATMENT
Autosomal Diseases				
Cooley's anemia	Pale appearance, retarded physical growth, and lethargic behavior begin in infancy.	Recessive	1 in 500 births to parents of Mediterranean descent	Frequent blood transfusion; death from complications usually occurs by adolescence.
Cystic fibrosis	Lungs, liver, and pancreas secrete large amounts of thick mucus, leading to breathing and digestive difficulties.	Recessive	1 in 2,000 to 2,500 Caucasian births; 1 in 16,000 births to North Americans of African descent	Bronchial drainage, prompt treatment of respiratory infection, dietary management. Advances in medical care allow survival with good life quality into adulthood.
Phenylketonuria (PKU)	Inability to metabolize the amino acid phenylalanine, contained in many proteins, causes severe central nervous system damage in the first year of life.	Recessive	1 in 8,000 births	Placing the child on a special diet results in average intelligence and normal lifespan. Subtle difficulties with planning and problem solving are often present.
Sickle cell anemia	Abnormal sickling of red blood cells causes oxygen deprivation, pain, swelling, and tissue damage. Anemia and susceptibility to infections, especially pneumonia, occur.	Recessive	1 in 600 births to North Americans of African descent	Blood transfusions, painkillers, prompt treatment of infection. No known cure; 50 percent die by age 20.
Tay-Sachs disease	Central nervous system degeneration, with onset at about 6 months, leads to poor muscle tone, blindness, deafness, and convulsions.	Recessive	1 in 3,600 births to Jews of European descent and to French Canadians	None; death by 3 to 4 years of age.
Huntington disease	Central nervous system degeneration leads to muscular coordination difficulties, mental deterioration, and personality changes. Symptoms usually do not appear until age 35 or later.	Dominant	1 in 18,000 to 25,000 births	None; death 10 to 20 years after symptom onset.
Marfan syndrome	Tall, slender build; thin, elongated arms and legs; and heart defects and eye abnormalities, especially of the lens. Excessive lengthening of the body results in a variety of skeletal defects.	Dominant	1 in 20,000 births	Correction of heart and eye defects sometimes possible. Death from heart failure in early adulthood is common.
X-Linked Diseases				
Duchenne muscular dystrophy	This degenerative muscle disease causes abnormal gait, with loss of ability to walk between 7 and 13 years of age.	Recessive	1 in 3,000 to 5,000 male births	None; death from respiratory infection or weakening of the heart muscle usually occurs in adolescence.
Hemophilia	Blood fails to clot normally; can lead to severe internal bleeding and tissue damage.	Recessive	1 in 4,000 to 7,000 male births	Blood transfusions; safety precautions to prevent injury.
Diabetes insipidus	Insufficient production of the hormone vasopressin results in excessive thirst and urination. Dehydration can cause central nervous system damage.	Recessive	1 in 2,500 male births	Hormone replacement.

Note: For recessive disorders, carrier status can be detected in prospective parents through a blood test or genetic analyses. For all disorders listed, prenatal diagnosis is available (see page 63).

Sources: Behrman, Kliegman, & Arvin, 1996; Chodirker et al., 2001; Gott, 1998; Grody, 1999; Knoers et al., 1993; McKusick, 2002; Schulman & Black, 1997.

FIGURE 2.4

Dominant–recessive mode of inheritance, as illustrated by PKU. When both parents are heterozygous carriers of the recessive gene *(p)*, we can predict that 25 percent of their offspring are likely to be normal *(NN)*, 50 percent are likely to be carriers *(Np)*, and 25 percent are likely to inherit the disorder *(pp)*. Notice that the PKU-affected child, in contrast to his siblings, has light hair. The recessive gene for PKU affects more than one trait. It also leads to fair coloring.

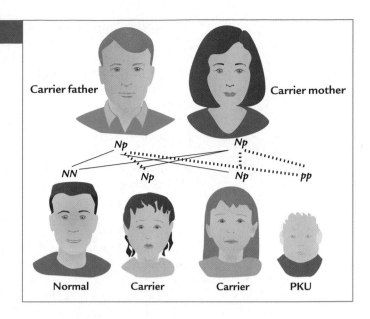

disorders, and mental retardation are greater for boys (Butler & Meaney, 2005). It is possible that these sex differences can be traced to the genetic code. The female, with two X chromosomes, benefits from a greater variety of genes. Nature, however, seems to have adjusted for the male's disadvantage. Worldwide, about 105 boys are born for every 100 girls, and judging from miscarriage and abortion statistics, an even greater number of boys are conceived (Pyeritz, 1998).

Nevertheless, in recent decades the proportion of male births has declined in many industrialized countries, including the United States, Canada, and European nations (Jongbloet et al., 2001). Some researchers attribute the trend to a rise in stressful living conditions, which heighten spontaneous abortions, especially of male fetuses. In a test of this hypothesis, male-to-female birth ratios in East Germany were examined between 1946 and 1999. The ratio was lowest in 1991, the year that the country's economy collapsed (Catalano, 2003). Similarly, in a California study spanning the decade of the 1990s, the percentage of male fetal deaths increased in months in which unemployment (a major stressor) also rose above its typical level (Catalano et al., 2005).

GENETIC IMPRINTING ■ More than 1,000 human characteristics follow the rules of dominant–recessive and incomplete-dominance inheritance (McKusick, 2002). In these cases, whichever parent contributes a gene to the new individual, the gene responds in the same way. Geneticists, however, have identified some exceptions. In **genetic imprinting**, alleles are *imprinted*, or chemically *marked*, in such a way that one pair member (either the mother's or the father's) is activated, regardless of its makeup. The imprint is often temporary; it may be erased in the next generation, and it may not occur in all individuals (Everman & Cassidy, 2000).

Imprinting helps us understand certain puzzling genetic patterns. For example, children are more likely to develop diabetes if their father, rather than their mother, suffers from it. And people with asthma or hay fever tend to have mothers, not fathers, with the illness. Scientists do not yet know what causes this parent-specific genetic transmission. At times, it reveals itself in heartbreaking ways. Imprinting is involved in several childhood cancers and in *Prader-Willi syndrome,* a disorder with symptoms of mental retardation and severe obesity (Hanel & Wevrick, 2001). It may also explain why Huntington disease, when inherited from the father, tends to emerge at an earlier age and to progress more rapidly (Navarrete, Martinez, & Salamanca, 1994).

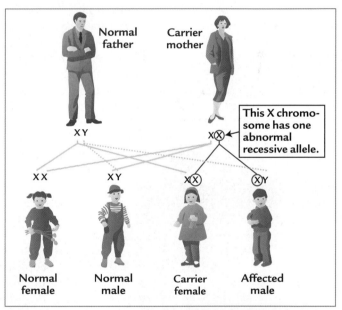

FIGURE 2.5

X-linked inheritance. In the example shown here, the allele on the father's X chromosome is normal. The mother has one normal and one abnormal recessive allele on her X chromosomes. By looking at the possible combinations of the parents' alleles, we can predict that 50 percent of male children are likely to have the disorder, and 50 percent of female children are likely to be carriers of it.

genetic imprinting A pattern of inheritance in which alleles are imprinted, or chemically marked, in such a way that one pair member is activated, regardless of its makeup.

Genetic imprinting can also operate on the sex chromosomes, as *fragile X syndrome*—the most common inherited cause of mental retardation—reveals. In this disorder, an abnormal repetition of a sequence of DNA bases occurs in a special spot on the X chromosome, damaging a particular gene. Fragile X syndrome has been linked to 2 to 3 percent of cases of autism, a serious disorder usually diagnosed in early childhood that involves impaired social interaction, delayed or absent language and communication, and repetitive motor behavior (Goodlin-Jones et al., 2004). Research reveals that the defective gene at the fragile site is expressed only when it is passed from mother to child (Reiss & Dant, 2003).

MUTATION ■ How are harmful genes created in the first place? The answer is **mutation,** a sudden but permanent change in a segment of DNA. A mutation may affect only one or two genes, or it may involve many genes, as in the chromosomal disorders we will discuss shortly. Some mutations occur spontaneously, simply by chance. Others are caused by hazardous environmental agents.

Although nonionizing forms of radiation—electromagnetic waves and microwaves—have no demonstrated impact on DNA, ionizing (high-energy) radiation is an established cause of mutation. Women who receive repeated doses before conception are more likely to miscarry or give birth to children with hereditary defects. The incidence of genetic abnormalities, such as physical malformations and childhood cancer, is also higher in children whose fathers are exposed to radiation in their occupation. However, infrequent and mild exposure to radiation does not cause genetic damage (Jacquet, 2004). Rather, high doses over a long period impair DNA.

The examples just given illustrate *germline mutation,* which takes place in the cells that give rise to gametes. When the affected individual mates, the defective DNA is passed on to the next generation. In a second type, called *somatic mutation,* normal body cells mutate, an event that can occur at any time of life. The DNA defect appears in every cell derived from the affected body cell, eventually becoming widespread enough to cause disease (such as cancer) or disability.

It is easy to see how disorders that run in families can result from germline mutation. But somatic mutation may be involved in these disorders as well. Some people harbor a genetic susceptibility that causes certain body cells to mutate easily in the presence of triggering events (Weiss, 2005). This helps explain why some individuals develop serious illnesses (such as cancer) as a result of smoking, exposure to pollutants, or psychological stress, while others do not.

POLYGENIC INHERITANCE ■ So far, we have discussed patterns of inheritance in which people either display a particular trait or do not. These cut-and-dried individual differences are much easier to trace to their genetic origins than are characteristics that vary continuously among people, such as height, weight, intelligence, and personality. These traits are due to **polygenic inheritance,** in which many genes affect the characteristic in question. Polygenic inheritance is complex, and much about it is still unknown. In the final section of this chapter, we discuss how researchers infer the influence of heredity on human attributes when they do not know the precise patterns of inheritance.

The boy on the right has facial features typical of children with Down syndrome. Despite his impaired intellectual development, he is doing well because he is growing up in a stimulating home where he is loved and accepted and receives attention from family members, including his older, typically developing brother.

Chromosomal Abnormalities

Besides harmful recessive alleles, abnormalities of the chromosomes are a major cause of serious developmental problems. Most chromosomal defects result from mistakes during meiosis, when the ovum and sperm are formed. A chromosome pair does not separate properly, or part of a chromosome breaks off. Since these errors involve far more DNA than problems due to single genes, they usually produce many physical and mental symptoms.

DOWN SYNDROME ■ The most common chromosomal disorder, occurring in 1 out of every 1,000 live births, is *Down syndrome.* In 95 percent of cases, it results from a failure of the twenty-first pair of chromosomes to separate during meiosis, so the new individual inherits three of these chromosomes rather than the normal two. For this reason, Down syndrome is sometimes called *trisomy 21*. In other, less frequent forms, an extra twenty-first chromosome is attached to part of another chromosome (called *translocation* pattern). Or an error occurs during the early stages of mitosis, causing some but not all body cells to have the defective chromosomal makeup (called *mosaic* pattern) (Saitta & Zackai, 2005). Because less genetic material is involved in the mosaic type, symptoms of the disorder are less extreme.

The consequences of Down syndrome include mental retardation, memory and speech problems, limited vocabulary, and slow motor development. Affected individuals also have distinct physical features—a short, stocky build; a flattened face; a protruding tongue; almond-shaped eyes; and an unusual crease running across the palm of the hand. In addition, infants with Down syndrome often are born with eye cataracts, hearing loss, and heart and intestinal defects. Because of medical advances, fewer individuals with Down syndrome die early than was the case in the past. Many survive into their fifties and a few into their sixties to eighties (Roizen & Patterson, 2003). However, more than half of affected individuals who live past age 40 show symptoms of *Alzheimer's disease,* the most common form of dementia (Menendez, 2005). Genes on chromosome 21 are linked to this disorder.

TABLE 2.4	Risk of Giving Birth to a Down Syndrome Child by Maternal Age
MATERNAL AGE	**RISK**
20	1 in 1,900 births
25	1 in 1,200
30	1 in 900
33	1 in 600
36	1 in 280
39	1 in 130
42	1 in 65
45	1 in 30
48	1 in 15

Note: The risk of giving birth to a Down syndrome baby after age 35 has increased slightly over the past 20 years as a result of improved medical interventions during pregnancy and consequent greater likelihood that a Down syndrome fetus will survive to be liveborn.

Sources: Adapted from Halliday et al., 1995; Meyers et al., 1997.

Caring for a baby with Down syndrome poses extra challenges for parents. Facial deformities often lead to breathing and feeding difficulties. Also, these infants smile less readily, show poorer eye-to-eye contact, and explore objects less persistently. But when parents encourage them to engage with their surroundings, Down syndrome children develop more favorably (Sigman, 1999). They also benefit from infant and preschool intervention programs, although emotional, social, and motor skills improve more than intellectual performance (Carr, 2002). Clearly, environmental factors affect how well children with Down syndrome fare.

As Table 2.4 shows, the risk of bearing a Down syndrome baby rises dramatically with maternal age. Why is this so? Geneticists believe that the ova, present in the woman's body since her own prenatal period, weaken over time. As a result, chromosomes do not separate properly as they complete the process of meiosis at conception. But in about 5 to 10 percent of cases, the extra genetic material originates with the father. The reasons for this mutation are unknown. Some studies suggest a role for advanced paternal age, while others show no age effects (Dzurova & Pikhart, 2005; Fisch et al., 2003; Muller et al., 2000).

ABNORMALITIES OF THE SEX CHROMOSOMES ■ Disorders of the autosomes other than Down syndrome usually disrupt development so severely that miscarriage occurs. When such babies are born, they rarely survive beyond early childhood. In contrast, abnormalities of the sex chromosomes usually lead to fewer problems. In fact, sex chromosome disorders often are not recognized until adolescence when, in some deviations, puberty is delayed. The most common problems involve the presence of an extra chromosome (either X or Y) or the absence of one X in females.

Research has discredited a variety of myths about individuals with sex chromosome disorders. For example, as Table 2.5 on page 62 reveals, males with *XYY syndrome* are not necessarily more aggressive and antisocial than XY males. And most children with sex chromosome disorders do not suffer from mental retardation. Rather, their intellectual problems are usually

mutation A sudden but permanent change in a segment of DNA.

polygenic inheritance A pattern of inheritance in which many genes affect the characteristic in question.

TABLE 2.5	Sex Chromosomal Disorders		
DISORDER	**DESCRIPTION**	**INCIDENCE**	**TREATMENT**
XYY syndrome	Extra Y chromosome. Above-average height, large teeth, and sometimes severe acne. Intelligence, male sexual development, and fertility are normal.	1 in 1,000 male births	No special treatment necessary.
Triple X syndrome (XXX)	Extra X chromosome. Tallness and impaired verbal intelligence. Female sexual development and fertility are normal.	1 in 500 to 1,250 female births	Special education to treat verbal ability problems.
Klinefelter syndrome (XXY)	Extra X chromosome. Tallness, body fat distribution resembling females, incomplete development of sex characteristics at puberty, sterility, and impaired verbal intelligence.	1 in 900 male births	Hormone therapy at puberty to stimulate development of sex characteristics; special education to treat verbal ability problems.
Turner syndrome (XO)	Missing X chromosome. Short stature, webbed neck, incomplete development of sex characteristics at puberty, sterility, and impaired spatial intelligence.	1 in 2,500 to 8,000 female births	Hormone therapy in childhood to stimulate physical growth and at puberty to promote development of sex characteristics; special education to treat spatial ability problems.

Sources: Geerts, Steyaert, & Fryns, 2003; Rovet et al., 1996; Saitta & Zackai, 2005; Simpson et al., 2003.

very specific. Verbal difficulties—for example, with reading and vocabulary—are common among girls with *triple X syndrome* and boys with *Klinefelter syndrome,* both of whom inherit an extra X chromosome. In contrast, girls with *Turner syndrome,* who are missing an X, have trouble with spatial relationships—for example, drawing pictures, telling right from left, following travel directions, and noticing changes in facial expressions (Geschwind et al., 2000; Lawrence et al., 2003; Simpson et al., 2003). These findings tell us that adding to or subtracting from the usual number of X chromosomes results in particular intellectual deficits. At present, geneticists do not know why.

Ask Yourself

Review   Explain the genetic origins of PKU and Down syndrome. Cite evidence indicating that both heredity and environment contribute to the development of children with these disorders.

Review   Using your knowledge of X-linked inheritance, explain why males are more vulnerable to miscarriage, infant death, genetic disorders, and other problems.

Apply   Gilbert's genetic makeup is homozygous for dark hair. Jan's is homozygous for blond hair. What color is Gilbert's hair? How about Jan's? What proportion of their children are likely to be dark-haired? Explain.

Connect   Referring to ecological systems theory (Chapter 1, pages 25–27), explain why parents of children with genetic disorders often experience increased stress. What factors, within and beyond the family, can help these parents support their children's development?

Reproductive Choices

Two years after they married, Ted and Marianne gave birth to their first child. Kendra appeared to be a healthy infant, but by 4 months her growth had slowed, and she was diagnosed as having Tay-Sachs disease (see Table 2.3). When Kendra died at 2 years of age, Ted and Marianne were devastated. Although they did not want to bring another infant into the world who would endure such suffering, they badly wanted to have a child. They began to avoid family get-togethers, where little nieces and nephews were constant reminders of the void in their lives.

In the past, many couples with genetic disorders in their families chose not to bear a child at all rather than risk the birth of an abnormal baby. Today, genetic counseling and prenatal diagnosis help people make informed decisions about conceiving, carrying a pregnancy to term, or adopting a child.

Genetic Counseling

Genetic counseling is a communication process designed to help couples assess their chances of giving birth to a baby with a hereditary disorder and choose the best course of action in view of risks and family goals (Hodgson & Spriggs, 2005). Individuals likely to seek counseling are those who have had difficulties bearing children—for example, repeated miscarriages—or who know that genetic problems exist in their families. In addition, women who delay childbearing past age 35 are often candidates for genetic counseling. After this time, the overall rate of chromosomal abnormalities rises sharply, from 1 in every 190 to as many as 1 in every 20 pregnancies at age 43 (Wille et al., 2004). But some experts argue that maternal needs, not age, should determine referral for genetic counseling. Because younger mothers give birth in far higher numbers than older mothers, they bear the majority of babies with genetic defects (Berkowitz, Roberts, & Minkoff, 2006).

If a family history of mental retardation, psychological disorders, physical defects, or inherited diseases exists, the genetic counselor interviews the couple and prepares a *pedigree,* a picture of the family tree in which affected relatives are identified. The pedigree is used to estimate the likelihood that parents will have an abnormal child, using the genetic principles discussed earlier in this chapter. For many disorders, blood tests or genetic analyses can reveal whether the parent is a carrier of the harmful gene. Carrier detection is possible for all the recessive diseases listed in Table 2.3, as well as others, and for fragile X syndrome.

When all the relevant information is in, the genetic counselor helps people consider appropriate options. These include taking a chance and conceiving, choosing from among a variety of reproductive technologies (see the Biology and Environment box on pages 66–67), or adopting a child.

Prenatal Diagnosis and Fetal Medicine

If couples who might bear an abnormal child decide to conceive, several **prenatal diagnostic methods**—medical procedures that permit detection of developmental problems before birth—are available (see Table 2.6 on page 64). Women of advanced maternal age are prime candidates for *amniocentesis* or *chorionic villus sampling* (see Figure 2.6 on page 65). Except for *maternal blood analysis,* prenatal diagnosis should not be used routinely, since other methods have some chance of injuring the developing organism.

Prenatal diagnosis has led to advances in fetal medicine. For example, by inserting a needle into the uterus, doctors can administer drugs to the fetus. Surgery has been performed to repair such problems as heart, lung, and diaphragm malformations; urinary tract obstructions; and neural defects (Hanson, Corbet, & Ballard, 2005). Fetuses with blood disorders have been given blood transfusions. And those with immune deficiencies have received bone marrow transplants that succeeded in creating a normally functioning immune system (Williams, 2006).

genetic counseling A communication process designed to help couples assess their chances of giving birth to a baby with a hereditary disorder and choose the best course of action in view of risks and family goals.

prenatal diagnostic methods Medical procedures that permit detection of developmental problems before birth.

TABLE 2.6   **Prenatal Diagnostic Methods**

METHOD	DESCRIPTION
Amniocentesis	The most widely used technique. A hollow needle is inserted through the abdominal wall to obtain a sample of fluid in the uterus. Cells are examined for genetic defects. Can be performed by the 14th week after conception; 1 to 2 more weeks are required for test results. Small risk of miscarriage.
Chorionic villus sampling	A procedure that can be used if results are desired or needed very early in pregnancy. A thin tube is inserted into the uterus through the vagina, or a hollow needle is inserted through the abdominal wall. A small plug of tissue is removed from the end of one or more chorionic villi, the hairlike projections on the membrane surrounding the developing organism. Cells are examined for genetic defects. Can be performed at 9 weeks after conception, and results are available within 24 hours. Entails a slightly greater risk of miscarriage than does amniocentesis. Also associated with a small risk of limb deformities, which increases the earlier the procedure is performed.
Fetoscopy	A small tube with a light source at one end is inserted into the uterus to inspect the fetus for defects of the limbs and face. Also allows a sample of fetal blood to be obtained, permitting diagnosis of such disorders as hemophilia and sickle cell anemia as well as neural defects (see below). Usually performed between 15 and 18 weeks after conception, but can be done as early as 5 weeks. Entails some risk of miscarriage.
Ultrasound	High-frequency sound waves are beamed at the uterus; their reflection is translated into a picture on a video screen that reveals the size, shape, and placement of the fetus. By itself, permits assessment of fetal age, detection of multiple pregnancies, and identification of gross physical defects. Also used to guide amniocentesis, chorionic villus sampling, and fetoscopy. When used five or more times, may increase the chances of low birth weight.
Maternal blood analysis	By the second month of pregnancy, some of the developing organism's cells enter the maternal bloodstream. An elevated level of alpha-fetoprotein may indicate kidney disease, abnormal closure of the esophagus, or neural tube defects, such as anencephaly (absence of most of the brain) and spina bifida (bulging of the spinal cord from the spinal column). Isolated cells can be examined for genetic defects.
Preimplantation genetic diagnosis	After in vitro fertilization and duplication of the zygote into a cluster of about eight to ten cells, one or two cells are removed and examined for hereditary defects. Only if that sample is free of detectable genetic disorders is the fertilized ovum implanted in the woman's uterus.

Sources: Bianchi, 2005; Kumar & O'Brien, 2003; Moore & Persaud, 2003; Newnham et al., 1993; Sermon, Van Steirteghem, & Liebaers, 2004.

© ABRAHAM MENASHE INC.

The mother of this girl with cystic fibrosis has learned to provide the time-consuming physical care her daughter needs. Here, she pounds on the child's chest with open palms to clear the child's lungs of thick mucus. In the future, such children may benefit from the discovery of new gene-based treatments for hereditary disorders.

These techniques frequently result in complications, the most common being premature labor and miscarriage (Flake, 2003). Yet parents may be willing to try almost any option, even one with only a slim chance of success. Currently, the medical profession is struggling with how to help parents make informed decisions about fetal surgery. One suggestion is that the advice of an independent counselor be provided—a doctor or nurse who understands the risks but is not involved in doing research on or performing the procedure.

Advances in *genetic engineering* also offer new hope for correcting hereditary defects. As part of the Human Genome Project—an ambitious international research program aimed at deciphering the chemical makeup of human genetic material (genome)—researchers have mapped the sequence of all human DNA base pairs. Using this information, they are "annotating" the genome—identifying all its genes and their functions, including their protein products and what these products do. A major goal is to understand the estimated 4,000 human disorders, those due to single genes and those resulting from a complex interplay of multiple genes and environmental factors.

Already, thousands of genes have been identified, including those involved in hundreds of diseases, such as cystic fibrosis; Duchenne muscular dystrophy; Huntington disease; Marfan syndrome; heart, digestive, blood, eye, and nervous system abnormalities; and many forms of cancer (National Institutes of Health, 2006). As a result, new treatments are being explored, such as *gene therapy*—correcting genetic abnormalities by delivering DNA carrying a functional gene to the cells. In recent experiments, gene therapy relieved symptoms in hemophilia patients and in patients with severe immune system dysfunction. A few, however, experienced serious side effects (Ralph, Harrington, & Pandha, 2004). In another approach,

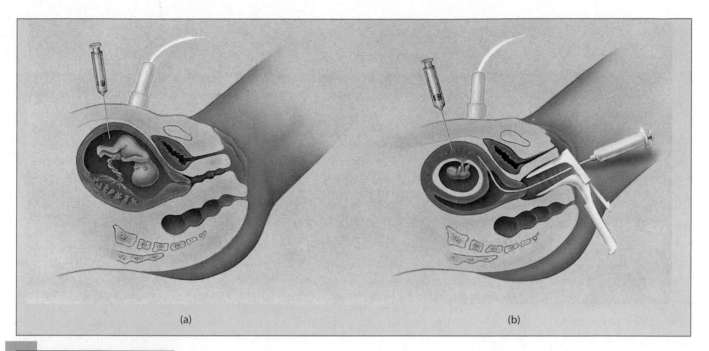

(a)   (b)

FIGURE 2.6

Amniocentesis and chorionic villus sampling.   Today, hundreds of defects and diseases can be detected before birth using these two procedures. (a) In amniocentesis, a hollow needle is inserted through the abdominal wall into the uterus during the fourteenth week after conception, or later. Fluid is withdrawn, and fetal cells are cultured, a process that takes about one to two weeks. (b) Chorionic villus sampling can be performed much earlier in pregnancy, at nine weeks after conception, and results are available within 24 hours. Two approaches to obtaining a sample of chorionic villus are shown: inserting a thin tube through the vagina into the uterus and inserting a needle through the abdominal wall. In both amniocentesis and chorionic villus sampling, an ultrasound scanner is used for guidance.   (From K. L. Moore & T. V. N. Persaud, 2003, *Before We Are Born*, 6th ed., Philadelphia: Saunders, p. 87. Adapted by permission of the publisher and author.)

called *proteomics*, scientists modify gene-specified proteins involved in disease (Bradshaw & Burlingame, 2005).

Genetic treatments seem some distance away for most single-gene defects, however, and farther off for diseases involving multiple genes that combine in complex ways with each other and the environment. Applying What We Know on page 68 summarizes steps that prospective parents can take before conception to protect the genetic health of their child.

The Alternative of Adoption

Adults who are infertile, who are likely to pass along a genetic disorder, or who are older and single but want a family are turning to adoption in increasing numbers. Those who have children by birth, too, sometimes choose to expand their families through adoption. Adoption agencies try to ensure a good fit by seeking parents of the same ethnic and religious background as the child and, where possible, trying to choose parents who are the same age as typical biological parents. Because the availability of healthy babies has declined (fewer young unwed mothers give up their babies than in the past), more people in North America and Western Europe are adopting from other countries or accepting children who are past infancy or who have known developmental problems (Schweiger & O'Brien, 2005).

Adopted children and adolescents—whether or not they are born in their adoptive parents' country—tend to have more learning and emotional difficulties than other children, a difference that increases with the child's age at time of adoption (Brodzinsky & Pinderhughes, 2002; Nickman, Rosenfeld, & Fine, 2005). There are many possible reasons for adoptees' more problematic childhoods. The biological mother may have been unable to care for the child because of problems believed to be partly genetic, such as alcoholism or severe depression. She may have passed this tendency to her offspring. Or perhaps she experienced stress, poor diet,

Biology and Environment

The Pros and Cons of Reproductive Technologies

Some couples decide not to risk pregnancy because of a history of genetic disease. Many others—in fact, one-sixth of all couples who try to conceive—discover that they are sterile. And some never-married adults and gay and lesbian partners want to bear children. Today, increasing numbers of individuals are turning to alternative methods of conception—technologies that, although they fulfill the wish for parenthood, have become the subject of heated debate.

Donor Insemination and In Vitro Fertilization

For several decades, *donor insemination*—injection of sperm from an anonymous man into a woman—has been used to overcome male reproductive difficulties. In recent years, it has also permitted women without a male partner to become pregnant. Donor insemination is 70 to 80 percent successful, resulting in 30,000 to 50,000 births in North America each year (Reynolds et al., 2003; Wright et al., 2004).

In vitro fertilization is another reproductive technology that has become increasingly common. Since the first "test tube" baby was born in England in 1978, 1 percent of all children in developed countries—about 40,000 babies in the United States and 3,500 babies in Canada—have been conceived through this technique annually (Jackson, Gibson, & Wu, 2004; Sutcliffe, 2002). With in vitro fertilization, a woman is given hormones, which stimulate the ripening of several ova. These are removed surgically and placed in a dish of nutrients, to which sperm are added. Once an ovum is fertilized and begins to duplicate into several cells, it is injected into the mother's uterus.

By mixing and matching gametes, pregnancies can be brought about when either or both partners have a reproductive problem. Usually, in vitro fertilization is used to treat women whose fallopian tubes are permanently damaged. But a recently developed technique permits a single sperm to be injected directly into an ovum, thereby overcoming most male fertility problems. And a "sex sorter" method helps ensure that couples who carry X-linked diseases (which usually affect males) have a daughter. Fertilized ova and sperm can even be frozen and stored in embryo banks for use at some future time, thereby guaranteeing healthy

zygotes should age or illness lead to fertility problems.

The overall success rate of in vitro fertilization is about 30 percent. However, success declines steadily with age, from 40 percent in women younger than age 35 to 7 percent in women age 43 and older (Wright et al., 2004).

Children conceived through these methods may be genetically unrelated to one or both of their parents. In addition, most parents who have used in vitro fertilization do not tell their children about their origins, even though health professionals now encourage them to do so. Does lack of genetic ties or secrecy surrounding these techniques interfere with parent–child relationships? Perhaps because of a strong desire for parenthood, caregiving is actually somewhat warmer for young children conceived through donor insemination or in vitro fertilization. And in vitro infants are as securely attached to their parents, and in vitro children and adolescents as well-adjusted, as their counterparts who were naturally conceived (Golombok & MacCallum, 2003; Golombok et al., 2004).

Although donor insemination and in vitro fertilization have many benefits, serious questions have arisen about their use. Most U.S. states and Canadian provinces have few legal guidelines for these procedures. As a result, donors are not always screened for genetic or sexually transmitted diseases. In many countries, including the United States and Canada, doctors are not required to keep records of donor characteristics (Richards, 2004). Canada, however, does retain a file on donor identities, permitting contact only in cases of serious disease, where knowledge of the child's genetic background might be helpful for medical reasons (Bioethics Consultative Committee, 2003). Another concern is that the in vitro "sex sorter" method will lead to parental sex selection, thereby eroding the moral value that boys and girls are equally precious.

Finally, more than 50 percent of in vitro procedures result in multiple births. Most are twins, but 9 percent are triplets and higher-order multiples. Consequently, among in vitro babies, the rate of low birth weight is 2.6 times higher than in the general population (Jackson, Gibson, & Wu, 2004). Risk of major birth defects also doubles, probably because of multiple factors, including drugs used to induce ripening of ova

and maintain the pregnancy and delays in fertilizing the ova outside the womb (Machin, 2005). In sum, in vitro fertilization poses greater risks than natural conception to infant survival and healthy development.

Surrogate Motherhood

An even more controversial form of medically assisted conception is *surrogate motherhood*. Typically in this procedure, sperm from a man whose wife is infertile are used to inseminate a woman, called a surrogate, who is paid a fee for her childbearing services. In return, the surrogate agrees to turn the baby over to the man (who is the natural father). The child is then adopted by his wife.

Although most of these arrangements proceed smoothly, those that end up in court highlight serious risks for all concerned. In one case, both parties rejected the infant with severe disabilities that resulted from the pregnancy. In several others, the surrogate mother wanted to keep the baby, or the couple changed their mind during the pregnancy. These children came into the world in the midst of conflict that threatened to last for years.

Because surrogacy usually involves the wealthy as contractors for infants and the less economically advantaged as surrogates, it may promote exploitation of financially needy women. In addition, most surrogates already have children of their own, who may be deeply affected by the pregnancy. Knowledge that their mother would give away a baby for profit may cause these children to worry about the security of their own family circumstances.

New Reproductive Frontiers

Reproductive technologies are evolving faster than societies can weigh the ethics of these procedures. Doctors have used donor ova from younger women in combination with in vitro fertilization to help postmenopausal women become pregnant. Most recipients are in their forties, but several women in their fifties and sixties have given birth. These cases raise questions about bringing children into the world whose parents may not live to see them reach adulthood. Based on U.S. life expectancy data, one in three mothers and one in two fathers having a baby at age 55 will die before their child enters college (U.S. Census Bureau, 2007b).

Currently, experts are debating other reproductive options. At donor banks, customers can select ova or sperm on the basis of physical characteristics and even IQ. And scientists are devising ways to alter the DNA of human ova, sperm, and embryos to protect against hereditary disorders—techniques that could be used to engineer other desired characteristics. Many worry that these practices are dangerous steps toward selective breeding through "designer babies"—controlling offspring traits by manipulating genetic makeup.

Furthermore, scientists have successfully cloned (made multiple copies of) fertilized ova in sheep, cattle, and monkeys, and they are working on effective ways to do so in humans. By providing extra ova for injection, cloning might improve the success rate of in vitro fertilization. But it also raises the possibility of mass-producing genetically identical people. Therefore, it is widely condemned.

Although new reproductive technologies permit many barren couples to rear healthy newborn babies, laws are needed to regulate such practices. In Australia, New Zealand, Sweden, and Switzerland, individuals conceived with donated gametes have a right to information about their genetic origins (Frith, 2001). Pressure from those working in the field of assisted reproduction may soon lead to a similar policy in the United States and Canada. Australia, Canada, and the Netherlands prohibit any genetic alteration of human gametes, with other nations following suit (Bernier & Grégoire, 2004). But some scientists argue that this total ban is too restrictive because it interferes with serving therapeutic needs.

In the case of surrogate motherhood, the ethical problems are so complex that 18 U.S. states have sharply restricted the practice, and Australia, Canada, and many European nations have banned it, arguing that the status of a baby should not be a matter of commercial arrangement and that the body's reproductive system should not be rented or sold (Chen, 2003; McGee, 1997). Denmark, France, and Great Britain have prohibited in vitro fertilization for women past menopause (Bioethics Consultative Committee, 2003). At present, nothing is known about the psychological consequences of being a product of these procedures. Research on how such children grow up, including what they know and how they feel about their origins, is important for weighing the pros and cons of these techniques.

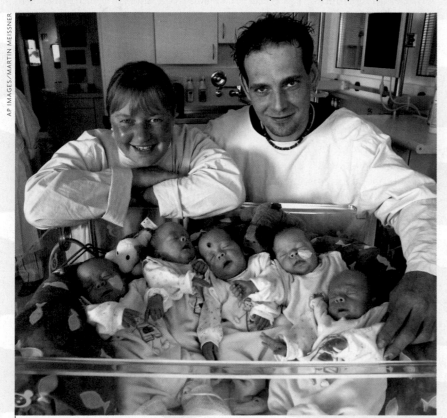

Reproductive technologies can pose grave ethical dilemmas. In vitro fertilization and fertility drugs often lead to multiple fetuses, with higher risks of low birth weight and major birth defects than in natural conception. This German couple are parents of quintuplets. Although the babies are now in good condition, at birth they averaged only 2 pounds (940 grams) each. When severe pregnancy complications are likely, doctors may even recommend aborting one or more fetuses to save the others.

or inadequate medical care during pregnancy—factors that can affect the child (as you will see in Chapter 3). Furthermore, children adopted after infancy often have a history of conflict-ridden family relationships, lack of parental affection, neglect and abuse, or deprived institutional rearing. Finally, adoptive parents and children, who are genetically unrelated, are less alike in intelligence and personality than biological relatives—differences that may threaten family harmony.

Despite these risks, most adopted children fare well, and those with problems usually make rapid progress (Bimmel et al., 2003; Johnson, 2002). In a study of internationally adopted children in the Netherlands, sensitive maternal care and secure attachment in infancy predicted cognitive and social competence at age 7 (Stams, Juffer, & van IJzendoorn, 2002).

© GERI ENGBERG/THE IMAGE WORKS

Adoption is one option for adults who are infertile or have a family history of genetic disorders. This couple, who adopted a child from China, can promote her successful adjustment by helping her learn about her birth heritage.

Overall, international adoptees fare much better in development than birth siblings or institutionalized agemates who stay behind. And if they were adopted in infancy, by middle childhood their mental test scores resemble those of their nonbiological siblings and school classmates, although they tend to achieve less well in school, to have more learning problems that require special treatment, and to be slightly delayed in language skills (van IJzendoorn, Juffer, & Poelhuis, 2005). Children adopted at older ages develop feelings of trust and affection for their adoptive parents as they come to feel loved and supported in their new families (Sherrill & Pinderhughes, 1999). But later-adopted children, as we will see in Chapter 5, are more likely to have persistent cognitive, emotional, and social problems.

By adolescence adoptees' lives often are complicated by unresolved curiosity about their roots. Some have difficulty accepting the possibility that they may never know their birth parents. Others worry about what they would do if their birth parents suddenly reappeared. Nevertheless, the decision to search for birth parents is usually postponed until early adulthood, when marriage and childbirth may trigger it. Despite concerns about their origins, most adoptees appear well-adjusted as adults. And as long as their parents took steps to help them learn about their heritage in childhood, young people adopted into a different ethnic group or culture generally develop identities that are healthy blends of their birth and rearing backgrounds (Nickman et al., 2005; Yoon, 2004).

As we conclude our discussion of reproductive choices, perhaps you are wondering how things turned out for Ted and Marianne. Through genetic counseling, Marianne discovered a history of Tay-Sachs disease on her mother's side of the family. Ted had a distant cousin who died of the disorder. The genetic counselor explained that the chances of giving birth to another affected baby were 1 in 4. Ted and Marianne took the risk. Their son Douglas is now 12 years old. Although Douglas is a carrier of the recessive allele, he is a normal, healthy boy. In a few years, Ted and Marianne will tell Douglas about his genetic history and explain the importance of genetic counseling and testing before he has children of his own.

Applying What We Know

Steps Prospective Parents Can Take Before Conception to Increase the Chances of a Healthy Baby

RECOMMENDATION	EXPLANATION
Arrange for a physical exam.	A physical exam before conception permits detection of diseases and other medical problems that might reduce fertility, be difficult to treat after the onset of pregnancy, or affect the developing organism.
Consider your genetic makeup.	Find out if anyone in your family has had a child with a genetic disease or disability. If so, seek genetic counseling before conception.
Reduce or eliminate toxins under your control.	Since the developing organism is highly sensitive to damaging environmental agents during the early weeks of pregnancy (see Chapter 3), couples trying to conceive should avoid drugs, alcohol, cigarette smoke, radiation, pollution, chemical substances in the home and workplace, and infectious diseases. Furthermore, stay away from ionizing radiation and some industrial chemicals that are known to cause mutations.
Ensure proper nutrition.	A doctor-recommended vitamin–mineral supplement, begun before conception, helps prevent many prenatal problems. It should include folic acid, which reduces the chances of neural tube defects, prematurity, and low birth weight (see Chapter 3, page 116).
Consult a physician after 12 months of unsuccessful efforts at conception.	Long periods of infertility may be due to undiagnosed spontaneous abortions, which can be caused by genetic defects in either partner. If a physical exam reveals a healthy reproductive system, seek genetic counseling.

Ask Yourself

Review   Why is genetic counseling called a *communication process*? Who should seek it?

Apply   Imagine that you must counsel a couple considering in vitro fertilization using the wife's ova and sperm from an anonymous man to overcome the husband's infertility. What medical and ethical risks would you raise?

Connect   How does research on adoption reveal resilience? Which of the factors related to resilience (see Chapter 1, page 10) is central in positive outcomes for adoptees?

Reflect   Imagine that you are a woman who is a carrier of fragile X syndrome but who wants to have children. Would you become pregnant, adopt, use a surrogate mother, or give up your desire for parenthood? If you became pregnant, would you opt for prenatal diagnosis? Explain your decisions.

Environmental Contexts for Development

Just as complex as the genetic inheritance that sets the stage for development is the surrounding environment—a many-layered set of influences that combine to help or hinder physical and psychological well-being. **TAKE A MOMENT...** Think back to your own childhood, and jot down a brief description of people and events that had a significant impact on your development. Do the items on your list resemble those of my students, who mostly mention experiences that involve their families? This emphasis is not surprising, since the family is the first and longest-lasting context for development. Other influences that make most students' top ten are friends, neighbors, school, and community and religious organizations.

Return to Bronfenbrenner's ecological systems theory, discussed on pages 25–27 in Chapter 1. It emphasizes that environments extending beyond the *microsystem*—the immediate settings just mentioned—powerfully affect development. Indeed, my students rarely mention one very important context. Its impact is so pervasive that we seldom stop to think about it in our daily lives. This is the *macrosystem*, or broad social climate of society—its values and programs that support and protect children's development. All families need help in rearing their children—through affordable housing and health care, safe neighborhoods, good schools, well-equipped recreational facilities, and high-quality child care and other services that permit parents to meet both work and family responsibilities. And some families, because of poverty or special tragedies, need considerably more help than others.

In the following sections, we take up these contexts for development. Because they affect every age and aspect of change, we will return to them in later chapters. For now, our discussion emphasizes that besides heredity, environments can enhance or create risks for development.

The Family

In power and breadth of influence, no context equals the family. The family introduces children to the physical world by providing opportunities for play and exploration of objects. It also creates unique bonds between people. Attachments to parents and siblings are usually lifelong and serve as models for relationships in the wider world. Within the family, children learn the language, skills, and social and moral values of their culture. And people of all ages turn to family members for information, assistance, and pleasurable interaction. Warm, gratifying family ties predict psychological health throughout development. In contrast, isolation or alienation from the family is often associated with developmental problems (Deković & Buist, 2005; Parke & Buriel, 2006).

Contemporary researchers view the family as a network of interdependent relationships (Bronfenbrenner & Morris, 2006; Lerner et al., 2002). Recall from ecological systems theory that *bidirectional influences* exist in which the behaviors of each family member affect those of

© JOUANNEAU THOMAS/CORBIS SYGMA

The family is a network of interdependent relationships, in which each person's behavior influences that of others. The positive mealtime atmosphere of this extended family in Baghdad, Iraq, is the result of many forces, including parents who respond to children with warmth and patience, grandparents who support parents in their child-rearing roles, and children who have developed cooperative dispositions.

others. Indeed, the very term *system* implies that the responses of all family members are related. These system influences operate both directly and indirectly.

DIRECT INFLUENCES ■ Recently, as I passed through the checkout counter at the supermarket, I witnessed two episodes, each an example of how parents and children directly affect each other:

■ Four-year-old Danny stood next to tempting rows of candy as his mother lifted groceries from her cart onto the counter. "Pleeeeease, can I have it, Mom?" Danny begged, holding up a large package of bubble gum. "Do you have a dollar? Just one?"

"No, not today," his mother answered. "Remember, we picked out your special cereal. That's what I need the dollar for." Gently taking the bubble gum from his hand, Danny's mother handed him the box of cereal. "Here, let's pay," she said, lifting Danny so he could see the cash register.

■ Three-year-old Meg was sitting in the shopping cart while her mother transferred groceries to the counter. Suddenly Meg turned around, grabbed a bunch of bananas, and started pulling them apart.

"Stop it, Meg!" shouted her mother, snatching the bananas from Meg's hand. But as she turned her attention to swiping her debit card, Meg reached for a chocolate bar from a nearby shelf. "Meg, how many times have I told you, *don't touch!*" Loosening the candy from her tight little fist, Meg's mother slapped her hand. Meg's face turned red with anger as she began to wail.

These observations fit with a wealth of research on the family system. Many studies show that when parents' requests are firm but made with warmth and affection, children tend to cooperate. And when children willingly comply, their parents are likely to be warm and gentle in the future. In contrast, children whose parents discipline harshly and impatiently are more likely to refuse and rebel. And because children's misbehavior is stressful, parents may increase their use of punishment, leading to more unruliness by the child (Stormshak et al., 2000; Whiteside-Mansell et al., 2003). In each case, the behavior of one family member helps sustain a form of interaction in the other that either promotes or undermines children's well-being.

INDIRECT INFLUENCES ■ The impact of family relationships on child development becomes even more complicated when we consider that interaction between any two members is affected by others present in the setting. Bronfenbrenner calls these indirect influences the effect of *third parties* (see Chapter 1, page 26).

Third parties can serve as supports for or barriers to development. For example, parents who have a warm, considerate marital relationship tend to cooperate in child rearing, praise and stimulate children more, and nag and scold them less. In contrast, parents whose marriage is tense and hostile often interfere with one another's child-rearing efforts, are less responsive to children's needs, and are more likely to criticize, express anger, and punish (Cox, Paley, & Harter, 2001; McHale et al., 2002). Children who are chronically exposed to angry, unresolved parental conflict have serious emotional problems (Harold et al., 2004). These include both internalizing difficulties (especially among girls), such as feeling worried and afraid and trying to repair their parents' relationship, and externalizing difficulties (especially among boys), including verbal and physical aggression (Davies & Lindsay, 2004). These child problems can further disrupt parents' marital relationship.

Yet even when marital conflict strains children's adjustment, other family members may help restore effective interaction. As a case in point, grandparents can promote children's development both directly, by responding warmly to the child, and indirectly, by providing parents with child-rearing advice, models of child-rearing skills, and even financial assistance. Of course, as with any indirect influence, grandparents can sometimes be harmful. When quarrelsome relations exist between parents and grandparents, parent–child communication may suffer.

ADAPTING TO CHANGE ■ Think back to the *chronosystem* in Bronfenbrenner's theory (see page 27 in Chapter 1). The interplay of forces within the family is dynamic and ever-changing, as each member adapts to the development of other members.

For example, as children acquire new skills, parents adjust the way they treat their more competent youngsters. **TAKE A MOMENT...** The next time you have a chance, notice the way a parent relates to a tiny baby as compared with a walking, talking toddler. During the first few months, parents spend much time feeding, changing, bathing, and cuddling the infant. Within a year, things change dramatically. The 1-year-old points, shows, names objects, and makes his way through the household cupboards. In response, parents devote less time to physical care and more to talking, playing games, and disciplining. These new ways of interacting, in turn, encourage the child's expanding motor, cognitive, and social skills.

Parents' development affects children as well. In Chapter 14, we will see that the rise in parent–child conflict that often occurs in early adolescence is not solely due to teenagers' striving for independence. This is a time when most parents of adolescents have reached middle age and—conscious that their children will soon leave home and establish their own lives—are reconsidering their own commitments (Steinberg & Silk, 2002). Consequently, while the adolescent presses for greater autonomy, the parent presses for more togetherness. This imbalance promotes friction, which parent and teenager gradually resolve by accommodating to changes in each other. Indeed, no social unit other than the family is required to adjust to such vast changes in its members.

Historical time period also contributes to a dynamic family system. In recent decades, a declining birth rate, a high divorce rate, expansion of women's roles, greater acceptance of homosexuality, and postponement of parenthood have led to a smaller family size and a greater number of single parents, remarried parents, gay and lesbian parents, employed mothers, and dual-earner families. Clearly, families in industrialized nations have become more diverse than ever before. In later chapters we will take up these family forms, emphasizing how each affects family relationships and, ultimately, children's development.

Nevertheless, some general patterns in family functioning do exist. In the United States, Canada, and other industrialized nations, one important source of these consistencies is socioeconomic status.

Socioeconomic Status and Family Functioning

People in industrialized nations are stratified on the basis of what they do at work and how much they earn for doing it—factors that determine their social position and economic well-being. Researchers assess a family's standing on this continuum through an index called **socioeconomic status (SES)**, which combines three related, but not completely overlapping, variables: (1) years of education and (2) the prestige of one's job and the skill it requires, both of which measure social status, and (3) income, which measures economic status. As SES rises and falls, parents and children face changing circumstances that profoundly affect family functioning.

SES is linked to timing of parenthood and to family size. People who work in skilled and semiskilled manual occupations (for example, construction workers, truck drivers, and custodians) tend to marry and have children earlier, as well as give birth to more children, than people in professional and technical occupations. The two groups also differ in child-rearing values and expectations. For example, when asked about personal qualities they desire for their children, lower-SES parents tend to emphasize external characteristics, such as obedience, politeness, neatness, and cleanliness. In contrast, higher-SES parents emphasize psychological traits, such as curiosity, happiness, self-direction, and cognitive and social maturity (Duncan & Magnuson, 2003; Hoff, Laursen, & Tardif, 2002; Tudge et al., 2000).

These differences are reflected in family interaction. Parents higher in SES talk to and stimulate their infants and preschoolers more and grant them greater freedom to explore. With older children, higher-SES parents use more warmth, explanations, and verbal praise and set higher developmental goals. Commands ("You do that because I told you to"), criticism, and physical punishment all occur more often in low-SES households (Bradley & Corwyn, 2003).

socioeconomic status (SES) A measure of a family's social position and economic well-being that combines three related variables: years of education, the prestige of and skill required by one's job, and income.

Social Issues: Education

Worldwide Education of Girls: Transforming Current and Future Generations

When a new school opened in the Egyptian village of Beni Shara'an, Ahmen, an illiterate shopkeeper, immediately enrolled his 8-year-old daughter Rawia (Bellamy, 2004, p. 19). Until that day, Rawia had divided her days between back-breaking farming and confinement to her home.

Before long, Rawia's advancing language, literacy, and reasoning skills transformed her family's quality of life. "My store accounts were in a mess, but soon Rawia started straightening out the books," Ahmen recalled. She also began helping her older sister learn to read and write and explaining to her family the instructions on prescription medicines. In addition, Rawia began to envision a better life for herself. "When I grow up," she told her father, "I want to be a doctor. Or maybe a teacher."

Over the past century, the percentage of children in the developing world who go to school has increased from a small minority of boys to a majority of all children in most regions. Still, some 135 million 7- to 18-year-olds, most of them poverty-stricken girls, receive no education at all. Millions of others, again mostly girls, drop out before completing the first three grades (Gordon, 2003).

Although schooling is vital for all children, educating girls has an especially powerful impact on the welfare of families, societies, and future generations. The diverse benefits of girls' schooling largely accrue in two ways: (1) through enhanced verbal skills—reading, writing, and oral communication; and (2) through empowerment—a growing desire to improve their life (LeVine, LeVine, & Schnell, 2001).

Family Health

Education equips people with the communicative skills and confidence to seek health services and to benefit from public health information. As a result, years of schooling strongly predicts women's preventive health behavior: prenatal visits, child immunizations, healthy diet, and sanitary practices (Dexter, LeVine, & Velasco, 1998; LeVine et al., 2004; Peña, Wall, & Person, 2000). In addition, because educated women have more life opportunities, they are more likely to take advantage of family planning services, delay childbearing, and have more widely spaced and fewer children (Caldwell, 1999). All these practices are linked to increased maternal and child survival and family health.

Family Relationships and Parenting

In developed and developing nations alike, the empowerment that springs from education is associated with more equitable husband–wife relationships and a reduction in harsh disciplining of children (LeVine et al., 1991; LeVine, LeVine, & Schnell, 2001). Also, educated mothers engage in more verbal stimulation and teaching of literacy skills to their children, which fosters success in school, higher educational attainment, and economic gains in the next generation. Regions of the world that have invested more in girls' education, such as Southeast Asia and Latin America, tend to have higher levels of economic development (King & Mason, 2001).

According to a recent United Nations report, educating girls is the most effective means of combating the most profound, global threats to human development: poverty, maternal and child mortality, and disease (Bellamy, 2004). Rawia got the chance to go to school because of an Egyptian national initiative, which led to the establishment of several thousand one-classroom schools in rural areas with the poorest record in educating girls. Because of cultural beliefs about gender roles or reluctance to give up a daughter's work at home, parents sometimes resist. But when governments create employment possibilities for women and provide information about the benefits of education for girls, the overwhelming majority of parents—including the very poor—choose to send their daughters to school, and some make great sacrifices to do so (Narayan et al., 2000).

© TOPHAM/LAUREN GOODSMITH/THE IMAGE WORKS

For these girls in the Taza region of Mauritania, attending school will dramatically improve their life opportunities and the welfare of their nation. In both developed and developing nations, education of girls leads to changes in family income and relationships that carry over to health, education, and economic gains in the next generation.

Education also contributes to SES differences in family interaction. Higher-SES parents' interest in verbal stimulation and nurturing inner traits is supported by years of schooling, during which they learned to think about abstract, subjective ideas (Uribe, LeVine, & LeVine, 1994). In diverse cultures around the world, as the Social Issues: Education box on page 72 makes clear, education of women in particular fosters patterns of thinking that greatly improve quality of life, for both parents and children.

Because of limited education and low social status, many lower-SES parents feel a sense of powerlessness and lack of influence in their relationships beyond the home. At work, for example, they must obey rules made by others in positions of power and authority. When they get home, their parent–child interaction seems to duplicate these experiences—but now they are in the authority role. Higher levels of stress, along with a stronger belief in the value of physical punishment, contribute to low-SES parents' greater use of coercive discipline (Pinderhughes et al., 2000). Higher-SES parents, in contrast, have more control over their own lives. At work, they are used to making independent decisions and convincing others of their point of view. At home, they teach these skills to their children (Greenberger, O'Neil, & Nagel, 1994).

As early as the second year of life, higher SES is associated with enhanced cognitive and language development and with reduced incidence of emotional and behavior problems. And throughout childhood and adolescence, higher-SES children do better in school (Bradley & Corwyn, 2003). As a result, they attain higher levels of education, which greatly enhances their opportunities for a prosperous adult life. Researchers believe that differences in family functioning have much to do with these outcomes.

Children growing up in affluent families are at risk for academic and other difficulties if their parents are physically and emotionally unavailable. The simple routine of eating dinner together is associated with a reduction in adjustment problems.

Affluence

Despite their advanced education and great material wealth, affluent parents—those in highly prestigious occupations with six-figure annual incomes—too often fail to engage in family interaction and parenting that promote development. In several studies, researchers tracked the adjustment of youths growing up in wealthy suburbs (Luthar & Latendresse, 2005a). By seventh grade, many showed serious problems that worsened in high school. Their school grades were poor, and they were more likely than low-SES youths to engage in alcohol and drug use and to report high levels of anxiety and depression (Luthar & Becker, 2002). Furthermore, among affluent (but not low-SES) teenagers, substance use was correlated with anxiety and depression, suggesting that wealthy youths took drugs to self-medicate—a practice that predicts persistent abuse (Luthar & Sexton, 2004).

Why are so many affluent youths troubled? Compared to their better-adjusted counterparts, poorly adjusted affluent young people report less emotional closeness and supervision from their parents, who lead professionally and socially demanding lives. As a group, wealthy parents are nearly as physically and emotionally unavailable to their youngsters as parents coping with serious financial strain. At the same time, these parents often make excessive demands for achievement (Luthar & Becker, 2002). Adolescents whose parents value their accomplishments more than their character are more likely to have academic and emotional problems.

For both affluent and low-SES youths, a simple routine—eating dinner with parents—is associated with a reduction in adjustment difficulties, even after many other aspects of parenting are controlled (see Figure 2.7) (Luthar & Latendresse, 2005b).

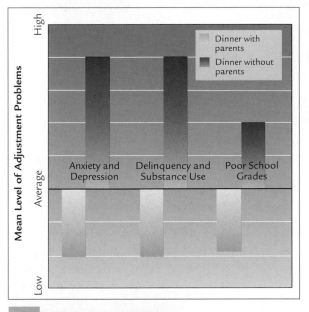

FIGURE 2.7

Relationship of regularly eating dinner with parents to affluent youths' adjustment problems. Compared with sixth graders who often ate dinner with their parents, those who rarely did so were far more likely to display anxiety and depression, delinquency and substance use, and poor school grades, even after many other aspects of parenting were controlled. In this study, frequent family mealtimes also protected low-SES youths from delinquency and substance use and from classroom learning problems. (Adapted from Luthar & Latendresse, 2005b.)

Interventions that make wealthy parents aware of the high costs of a competitive lifestyle and minimal family time are badly needed.

Poverty

When families slip into poverty, development is seriously threatened. Consider the case of Zinnia Mae, who grew up in a close-knit black community located in a small southeastern American city (Heath, 1990). As unemployment struck in the 1980s and citizens moved away, 16-year-old Zinnia Mae caught a ride to Atlanta. Two years later, she was the mother of a daughter and twin boys. She had moved into high-rise public housing.

All of Zinnia Mae's days were much the same. She worried constantly about scraping together enough money to put food on the table, finding baby-sitters so she could go to the laundry or grocery, freeing herself from growing debt, and finding the twins' father, who had stopped sending money. To relieve loneliness and anxiety, she watched TV and talked with a few friends on the phone. Her most frequent words were, "I'm so tired." The children had only one set meal (breakfast); otherwise, they ate whenever they were hungry or bored. Their play space was limited to the living room sofa and a mattress on the floor. Toys consisted of scraps of a blanket, spoons and food cartons, a small rubber ball, a few plastic cars, and a roller skate abandoned in the building.

At the researcher's request, Zinnia Mae agreed to tape record her interactions with her children. Cut off from family and community ties and overwhelmed by financial strains and feelings of helplessness, she found herself unable to join in activities with her children. In 500 hours of tape, she started a conversation with her children only 18 times.

Although poverty rates in the United States and Canada declined slightly in the 1990s, in recent years they have risen (UNICEF, 2005a). Today, about 12 percent of people in Canada and 13 percent in the United States are affected. Those hit hardest are parents under age 25 with young children and elderly people who live alone. Poverty is also magnified among ethnic minorities and women. For example, 18 percent of American and Canadian children are poor, rates that climb to 32 percent for Native-American children, 34 percent for African-American and Hispanic children, and 60 percent for Canadian Aboriginal children.[1] For single mothers with preschool children, the poverty rate in both countries is nearly 50 percent (Canada Campaign 2000, 2005; U.S. Census Bureau, 2007b).

Joblessness, a high divorce rate, a high rate of adolescent parenthood, and (as we will see later) inadequate government programs to meet family needs are responsible for these disheartening statistics. The poverty rate is higher among children than any other age group. And of all Western nations, the United States has the highest percentage of extremely poor children. More than 6 percent of American children live in deep poverty (well below the poverty threshold, the income level judged necessary for a minimum living standard), compared with 2.5 percent in Canada. However, these circumstances are worrisome in both countries because the earlier poverty begins, the deeper it is, and the longer it lasts, the more devastating are its effects. Children of poverty are more likely than other children to suffer from lifelong poor physical health, persistent deficits in cognitive development and academic achievement, high school dropout, mental illness, and antisocial behavior (Children's Defense Fund, 2006; Dearing, McCartney, & Taylor, 2006; Ryan, Fauth, & Brooks-Gunn, 2006).

The constant stresses that accompany poverty gradually weaken the family system. Poor families have many daily hassles—bills to pay, the car breaking down, loss of welfare and unemployment payments, something stolen from the house, to name just a few. When daily crises arise, parents become depressed, irritable, and distracted, warmth and sensitivity

This mother and child were evacuated in the aftermath of Hurricane Katrina, which devastated the southern Gulf Coast of the United States in 2005. For low-income families, the destruction and dislocation caused by a natural disaster is especially likely to result in long-term homelessness, impoverishment, and emotional stress.

© MICHAEL AINSWORTH/DALLAS MORNING NEWS/CORBIS

---

[1] Aboriginal peoples in Canada include three groups: (1) First Nations, or Native Canadian peoples; (2) Inuit, most of whom live in northern Canada; and (3) Métis, or people of mixed Native Canadian and European descent.

decline, hostile interactions increase, and children's development suffers (Evans, 2006; Mistry et al., 2004). Negative outcomes are especially severe in single-parent families and those that must live in poor housing and dangerous neighborhoods—conditions that make everyday existence even more difficult, while reducing social supports that assist in coping with economic hardship (Leventhal & Brooks-Gunn, 2003).

Besides poverty, another problem—one that has become more common in the past 25 years—has reduced the life chances of many children. On any given night, approximately 35,000 people in Canada and 350,000 people in the United States have no place to live (Pohl, 2001; Wright, 1999). An estimated 25 to 40 percent of the homeless are families with children (Kidd & Scrimenti, 2004). The rise in homelessness is mostly due to two factors: a decline in the availability of government-supported low-cost housing and the release of large numbers of mentally ill people from hospitals, without an increase in community treatment programs to help them adjust to ordinary life and get better.

Most homeless families consist of women with children under age 5. Besides health problems (which affect most homeless people), homeless children suffer from developmental delays and serious emotional stress due to their harsh, insecure daily lives (Bratt, 2002; Pardeck, 2005). An estimated 25 to 30 percent of those who are old enough do not go to school. Those who do enroll achieve less well than other poverty-stricken children because of poor attendance and severe health and emotional difficulties (Vostanis, Grattan, & Cumella, 1997).

Beyond the Family: Neighborhoods and Schools

As the concepts of the mesosystem and the exosystem in ecological systems theory make clear, ties between family and community are vital for children's well-being. From our discussion of poverty, perhaps you can see why. In poverty-stricken urban areas, community life is usually disrupted. Families move often, parks and playgrounds are in disarray, and community centers providing organized leisure activities do not exist. In such neighborhoods, family violence, child abuse and neglect, children's problem behavior, youth antisocial activity, and adult criminality are especially high (Brody et al., 2003; Kohen et al., 2002). In contrast, strong family ties to the community—as indicated by frequent contact with friends and relatives and regular church, synagogue, or mosque attendance—reduce family stress and adjustment problems (Boardman, 2004; Magnuson & Duncan, 2002).

NEIGHBORHOODS ■ To look at the functions of communities in the lives of children, let's begin with the neighborhood. **TAKE A MOMENT...** What were your childhood experiences like in the yards, streets, and parks surrounding your home? How did you spend your time, whom did you get to know, and how important were these moments to you?

Neighborhoods offer resources and social ties that play an important part in children's development. In several studies, low-SES families were randomly assigned vouchers to move out of public housing into neighborhoods varying widely in affluence. Compared with their peers who remained in poverty-stricken areas, children and youths who moved into low-poverty neighborhoods showed substantially better physical and mental health and school achievement (Goering, 2003; Leventhal & Brooks-Gunn, 2003).

Neighborhood resources have a greater impact on economically disadvantaged than on well-to-do young people. Higher-SES families are less dependent on their immediate surroundings for social support, education, and leisure pursuits. They can afford to transport their children to lessons and entertainment and even, if necessary, to

Neighborhood resources are important influences on children's development and well-being. A young girl proudly carries the Canadian flag in the Chinese New Year parade in the Chinatown district of Vancouver, British Columbia. The event fosters self-confidence, cooperation, and identification with her community and culture.

better-quality schools in distant parts of the community (Elliott et al., 1996). In low-income neighborhoods, in-school and after-school programs that substitute for lack of other resources by providing art, music, sports, scouting, and other enrichment activities are associated with improved school performance and a reduction in emotional and behavior problems in middle childhood (Peters, Petrunka, & Arnold, 2003; Vandell & Posner, 1999). Neighborhood organizations, such as religious youth groups and special-interest clubs, contribute to favorable development in adolescence, including self-confidence, school achievement, and educational aspirations (Gonzales et al., 1996).

In areas riddled with unemployment, crime, and population turnover, social ties linking families to one another and to other institutions are often weak or absent. Informal social controls—adults who keep an eye on children's play activities and who intervene when they see young people skipping school or behaving antisocially—are likely to disintegrate. Unstable, poverty-stricken neighborhoods also introduce stressors that undermine parental warmth, involvement, and supervision and increase parental harshness and inconsistency. And when a run-down, impoverished neighborhood combines with poor parenting, child behavior problems and youth antisocial activity are especially high (Brody et al., 2003; Kohen et al., 2002).

The Better Beginnings, Better Futures Project of Ontario, Canada, is a government-sponsored set of pilot programs aimed at preventing the dire consequences of neighborhood poverty. The most successful of these efforts, using a local elementary school as its base, provided children with in-class and summer enrichment activities. Workers also visited each child's parents regularly, informed them about community resources, and encouraged their involvement in the child's school and neighborhood life (Peters, 2005; Peters, Petrunka, & Arnold, 2003). An evaluation after four years revealed wide-ranging benefits—gains in neighborhood satisfaction, family functioning, effective parenting, and children's reading skills, along with a reduction in emotional and behavior problems.

SCHOOLS ■ Unlike the informal worlds of family and neighborhood, school is a formal institution designed to transmit knowledge and skills that children need to become productive members of their society. Children in the developed world spend many hours in school—6 hours a day, 5 days a week, 36 weeks a year—a total of about 14,000 hours, on average, by high school graduation. And today, because many children younger than age 5 attend "school-like" child-care centers or preschools, the impact of schooling begins even earlier and is more powerful than these figures suggest.

Schools are complex social systems that affect many aspects of development. Schools differ in their physical environments—student body size, number of children per class, and space available for work and play. They also vary in their educational philosophies—whether teachers regard children as passive learners to be molded by adult instruction; as active, curious beings who determine their own learning; or as collaborative partners assisted by adult experts, who guide their mastery of new skills. Finally, the social life of schools varies—for example, in the degree to which students cooperate or compete; in the extent to which students of different abilities, SES, and ethnic backgrounds learn together; and in whether classrooms, hallways, and play yards are safe, humane settings or are riddled with violence (Evans, 2006). We will discuss each of these aspects of schooling in later chapters.

Regular parent–school contact supports development at all ages. Students whose parents are involved in school activities and attend

© JACK KURTZ/THE IMAGE WORKS

Students gather for an assembly at the Thomas J. Pappas School in Phoenix, Arizona. The school provides vital supports for extremely needy children and their families. Although all its students are homeless, parent–teacher contact occurs often. And classrooms are exciting contexts for learning that stress effective communication, problem solving, responsibility, and cultural awareness.

parent–teacher conferences show better academic achievement. Higher-SES parents, whose backgrounds and values are similar to those of teachers, are more likely to make phone calls and visits to school. In contrast, low-SES and ethnic minority parents often feel uncomfortable about coming to school, and daily stressors reduce the energy they have for school involvement (Epstein & Sanders, 2002; Hill & Taylor, 2004). Parent–teacher contact is also more frequent in small towns, where most citizens know each other and schools serve as centers of community life (Peshkin, 1994). Teachers and administrators must take extra steps with low-SES and ethnic minority families and in urban areas to build supportive family–school ties.

When these efforts lead to cultures of good parenting and teaching, they deliver an extra boost to children's well-being. For example, students attending schools with many highly involved parents achieve especially well (Darling & Steinberg, 1997). And when excellent education becomes a team effort of teachers, administrators, and community members, its effects on learning are stronger and reach many more students (Brown, 1997; Hauser-Cram et al., 2006).

The Cultural Context

Our discussion in Chapter 1 emphasized that child development can be fully understood only when viewed in its larger cultural context. In the following sections, we expand on this important theme by taking up the role of the macrosystem in development. First, we discuss ways that cultural values and practices affect environmental contexts for development. Then we consider how healthy development depends on laws and government programs that shield children from harm and foster their well-being.

CULTURAL VALUES AND PRACTICES ■ Cultures shape family interaction, school experiences, and community settings beyond the home—in short, all aspects of daily life. Many of us remain blind to aspects of our own cultural heritage until we see them in relation to the practices of others.

TAKE A MOMENT... Consider the question, Who should be responsible for rearing young children? How would you answer it? Here are some typical responses from my students: "If parents decide to have a baby, then they should be ready to care for it." "Most people are not happy about others intruding into family life." These statements reflect a widely held opinion in North America—that the care and rearing of young children, and paying for that care, are the duty of parents, and only parents. This view has a long history—one in which independence, self-reliance, and the privacy of family life emerged as central North American values (Halfon & McLearn, 2002). It is one reason, among others, that the public has been slow to endorse publicly supported benefits for all families, such as high-quality child care. And it has also contributed to the large number of American and Canadian children who remain poor, even though their parents are gainfully employed (Pohl, 2002; Zigler & Hall, 2000).

Although the culture as a whole may value independence and privacy, not all citizens share the same values. Many belong to **subcultures**—groups of people with beliefs and customs that differ from those of the larger culture. Many ethnic minority groups in the United States and Canada have cooperative family structures, which help protect their members from the harmful effects of poverty. As the Cultural Influences box on page 78 indicates, the African-American tradition of **extended-family households,** in which parent and child live with one or more adult relatives, is a vital feature of black family life that has enabled its members to survive, despite a long history of prejudice and economic deprivation. Within the extended family, grandparents play meaningful roles in guiding younger generations; adults with employment, marital, or child-rearing difficulties receive assistance and emotional support; and caregiving is enhanced for children and the elderly. Active and involved extended families also characterize other minorities, such as Asian, Native-American, Hispanic, and Canadian Aboriginal subcultures (Becker et al., 2003; Harrison et al., 1994).

Our discussion so far reflects a broad dimension on which cultures and subcultures differ: the extent to which collectivism versus individualism is emphasized. In **collectivist societies,** people define themselves as part of a group and stress group over individual goals. In **individualistic societies,** people think of themselves as separate entities and are largely concerned

subculture A group of people with beliefs and customs that differ from those of the larger culture.

extended-family household A household in which parent and child live with one or more adult relatives.

collectivist societies Societies in which people define themselves as part of a group and stress group over individual goals.

individualistic societies Societies in which people think of themselves as separate entities and are largely concerned with their own personal needs.

Cultural Influences

The African-American Extended Family

The African-American extended family can be traced to the African heritage of most black Americans. In many African societies, newly married couples do not start their own households. Instead, they live with a large extended family, which assists its members with all aspects of daily life. This tradition of maintaining a broad network of kinship ties traveled to North America during the period of slavery. Since then, it has served as a protective shield against the destructive impact of poverty and racial prejudice on African-American family life. Today, more black than white adults have relatives other than their own children living in the same household. African-American parents also live closer to kin, often establish familylike relationships with friends and neighbors, see more relatives during the week, and perceive them as more important in their lives (Boyd-Franklin, 2006; Kane, 2000).

By providing emotional support and sharing income and essential resources, the African-American extended family helps reduce the stress of poverty and single parenthood. Extended-family members often help with child rearing, and adolescent mothers living in extended families are more likely to complete high school and get a job and less likely to be on welfare than mothers living on their own—factors that in turn benefit children's well-being (Gordon, Chase-Lansdale, & Brooks-Gunn, 2004; Trent & Harlan, 1994).

Strong bonds with extended family members protect the development of many African-American children growing up under conditions of poverty and single parenthood. Extended-family ties also strengthen the transmission of African-American culture.

For single mothers who were very young at the time of their child's birth, extended-family living continues to be associated with more positive mother–child interaction during the preschool years. Otherwise, establishing an independent household with the help of nearby relatives is related to improved child rearing. Perhaps this arrangement permits the more mature teenage mother who has developed effective parenting skills to implement them (Chase-Lansdale, Brooks-Gunn, & Zamsky, 1994). In families rearing adolescents, kinship support increases the likelihood of effective parenting, which is related to adolescents' self-reliance, emotional well-being, and reduced delinquency (Hamilton, 2005; Taylor & Roberts, 1995).

Finally, the extended family plays an important role in transmitting African-American culture. Compared with nuclear-family households (which include only parents and their children), extended-family arrangements place more emphasis on cooperation and on moral and religious values. And older black adults, such as grandparents and great-grandparents, regard educating children about their African heritage as especially important (Mosely-Howard & Evans, 2000; Taylor, 2000). Family reunions—sometimes held in grandparents' and great-grandparents' hometowns in the South—are especially common among African Americans, giving young people a strong sense of their roots (Boyd-Franklin, 2006). These influences strengthen family bonds, enhance children's development, and increase the chances that the extended-family lifestyle will carry over to the next generation.

© JEFF GREENBERG/ALAMY

with their own personal needs (Triandis, 1995). As these definitions suggest, the two cultural patterns are associated with two distinct views of the self. Collectivist societies value an *interdependent self*, which stresses social harmony, obligations and responsibility to others, and collaborative endeavors. In contrast, individualistic societies value an *independent self*, which emphasizes personal exploration, discovery, and achievement and individual choice in relationships. Both interdependence and independence are part of the makeup of every person and occur in varying mixtures (Greenfield et al., 2003; Keller, 2003). But societies vary greatly in the extent to which they emphasize each alternative and—as later chapters will reveal—instill it in their young.

Although individualism tends to increase as cultures become more complex, cross-national differences remain. The United States is strongly individualistic, while Canada falls in

TABLE 2.7	**How Do the United States and Canada Compare to Other Nations on Indicators of Children's Health and Well-Being?**		
INDICATOR	**U.S. RANK**[a]	**CANADIAN RANK**[a]	**SOME COUNTRIES THE UNITED STATES AND CANADA TRAIL**
Childhood poverty[b] (among 23 industrialized nations considered)	23rd	16th	Australia, Czech Republic, Germany, Norway, Sweden, Taiwan
Infant deaths in the first year of life (worldwide)	26th	16th	Hong Kong, Ireland, Singapore, Spain
Teenage pregnancy rate (among 45 industrialized nations considered)	28th	21st	Albania, Australia, Czech Republic, Denmark, Poland, Netherlands
Expenditures on education as a percentage of gross domestic product[c] (among 22 industrialized nations considered)	10th	6th	*For Canada:* Israel, Sweden *For the United States:* Australia, France, New Zealand, Sweden
Expenditures on health as a percentage of gross domestic product[c] (among 22 industrialized nations considered)	16th	4th	*For Canada:* Iceland, Switzerland *For the United States:* Austria, Australia, Hungary, New Zealand

[a]1 = highest, or best, rank.

[b]North American childhood poverty rates—18 percent in both the United States and Canada—greatly exceed those of any of these nations. For example, the rate is 12 percent in Australia, 6 percent in the Czech Republic, 4 percent in Norway, and 2.5 percent in Sweden.

[c]Gross domestic product is the value of all goods and services produced by a nation during a specified time period. It provides an overall measure of a nation's wealth.

Sources: Luxembourg Income Study, 2005; Perie et al., 2000; UNICEF, 2001; U.S. Census Bureau, 2007b; U.S. Department of Education, 2006.

between the United States and most Western European countries, which lean toward collectivism. As we will see next, collectivist versus individualistic values have a powerful impact on a nation's approach to protecting the well-being of its children and families.

PUBLIC POLICIES AND CHILD DEVELOPMENT ■ When widespread social problems arise, such as poverty, homelessness, hunger, and disease, nations attempt to solve them by developing **public policies**—laws and government programs designed to improve current conditions. For example, when poverty increases and families become homeless, a country might decide to build more low-cost housing, raise the minimum wage, and increase welfare benefits. When reports indicate that many children are not achieving well in school, federal and state governments might grant more tax money to school districts, strengthen teacher preparation, and make sure that help reaches children who need it most.

Nevertheless, American and Canadian public policies safeguarding children and youths have lagged behind policies in other developed nations. As Table 2.7 reveals, the United States does not rank well on any key measure of children's health and well-being. Canada, which devotes considerably more of its resources to education and health, fares somewhat better. For example, all Canadian citizens have access to government-funded health care.

The problems of children and youths extend beyond the indicators in Table 2.7. The United States is the only industrialized nation in the world that does not have a universal, publicly funded health care system. Hence, approximately 11 percent of U.S. children—most of them in low-income families—have no health insurance, making children the largest sector of the U.S. uninsured population (Children's Defense Fund, 2006). Furthermore, both the United States and Canada have been slow to move toward national standards and funding for child care. In both countries, much child care is substandard in quality (Goelman et al., 2000; NICHD Early Child Care Research Network, 2000a). In families affected by divorce, weak enforcement of child support payments heightens poverty in mother-headed households. When they finish high school, many North American non-college-bound young people do not have the vocational preparation they need to contribute fully to society. And about 11 percent

public policies Laws and government programs designed to improve current conditions.

of U.S. and Canadian adolescents leave high school without a diploma (Bushnik, Barr-Telford, & Bussiére, 2004; U.S. Department of Education, 2006). Those who do not finish their education are at risk for lifelong poverty.

Why have attempts to help children and youths been difficult to realize in the United States and (to a lesser extent) Canada? A complex set of political and economic forces is involved. Cultural values of self-reliance and privacy have made government hesitant to become involved in family matters. Furthermore, good social programs are expensive, and they must compete for their fair share of a country's economic resources. Children can easily remain unrecognized in this process because they cannot vote or speak out to protect their own interests, as adult citizens do (Ripple & Zigler, 2003). Instead, they must rely on the goodwill of others to make them an important government priority.

Without vigilance from child advocates, policies directed at solving one social problem can work at cross-purposes with children's well-being, leaving them in dire straits or even worsening their condition. Consider, for example, welfare reforms aimed at returning welfare recipients to the workforce. As the Social Issues: Health box on the following page makes clear, these policies can either help or harm children, depending on whether they lift a family out of poverty.

LOOKING TOWARD THE FUTURE ■ Public policies aimed at fostering children's development can be justified on two grounds. The first is that children are the future—the parents, workers, and citizens of tomorrow. Investing in children yields valuable returns to a nation's quality of life (Heckman & Masterov, 2004).

Second, child-oriented policies can be defended on humanitarian grounds—children's basic rights as human beings. In 1989, the United Nations General Assembly, with the assistance of experts from many child-related fields, drew up the *Convention on the Rights of the Child,* a legal agreement among nations that commits each cooperating country to work toward guaranteeing environments that foster children's development, protect them from harm, and enhance their community participation and self-determination. Examples of rights include the highest attainable standard of health; an adequate standard of living; free and compulsory education; a happy, understanding, and loving family life; protection from all forms of abuse and neglect; and freedom of thought, conscience, and religion, subject to appropriate parental guidance and national law.

Canada's Parliament ratified the Convention in 1991. Although the United States played a key role in drawing up the Convention, it is one of only two countries in the world whose legislature has not yet ratified it. (The other is war-torn Somalia, which currently does not have a recognized national government.) American individualism has stood in the way. Opponents maintain that the Convention's provisions would shift the burden of child rearing from the family to the state (Melton, 2005).

Although the worrisome state of many children and families persists, efforts are being made to improve their condition. Throughout this book, we will discuss many successful programs that could be expanded. Also, growing awareness of the gap between what we know and what we do to better children's lives has led experts in child development to join with concerned citizens as advocates for more effective policies. As a result, several influential interest groups devoted to the well-being of children have emerged.

In the United States, the Children's Defense Fund—a private, nonprofit organization founded by Marion Wright Edelman in 1973—engages in research, public education, legal action, drafting of legislation, congressional testimony, and community organizing. Each year, it publishes *The State of America's Children,* which provides a comprehensive analysis of children's condition, including government-sponsored programs that serve children and families and proposals for improving those

PERMISSION GRANTED BY THE CHILDREN'S DEFENSE FUND

The Children's Defense Fund is the most vigorous interest group working for the well-being of children in the United States. It released this poster expressing outrage that millions of American children, most living in poverty or near-poverty, have no health insurance, making children the largest segment of the U.S. uninsured population.

Social Issues: Health

Welfare Reform, Poverty, and Child Development

In the mid-1990s, the United States and Canada both changed their welfare policies, instituting welfare-to-work programs that ended decades of guaranteed government financial aid to needy families. In these new systems, recipients must go to work or face reduced or terminated benefits. The goal is to encourage families on welfare to become self-sufficient. The U.S. program is strictly time-limited: A family can be on welfare for only 24 continuous months, with a lifetime limit of 60 months, and the states can further restrict these benefits. For example, a state can prevent payments from increasing if recipients have more children, and it can deny teenage single mothers any benefits.

Canadian welfare policies, while strongly employment focused, are more flexible. In Ontario, for example, welfare recipients must actively look for a job, participate in community volunteer work while acquiring work skills, and accept any paid work offered if they are physically capable of performing it. Unlike the U.S. policy, however, a Canadian family's benefits increase if family size increases, although several provinces have reduced these payments (National Forum on Welfare to Work, 2004).

Until recently, most evaluations of welfare-to-work programs focused on declines in the number of families on the welfare rolls. By these standards, welfare-to-work seemed to be a resounding success. But as researchers looked more closely, they found that some people made successful transitions to financial independence—typically, those who had more schooling and fewer mental health problems. Others, however, had difficulty meeting work requirements, lost their benefits, and fell deeper into poverty. Consequently, as welfare caseloads declined, the incomes of the poorest single-mother families dropped sharply (Lindsay & Martin, 2003).

Designers of welfare-to-work assumed it would be beneficial to children. But moving off welfare without increasing family income poses serious risks to child development. In one study, mothers who left welfare and also left poverty engaged in more positive parenting, and had preschoolers who showed more favorable cognitive development, compared with working mothers whose incomes remained below the poverty threshold. Among these mothers, harsh, coercive parenting remained high (Smith et al., 2001).

In other research, families who moved from welfare to a combination of welfare and work experienced a greater reduction in young children's behavior problems than families who moved to total reliance on work (Dunifon, Kalil, & Danziger, 2003; Gennetian & Morris, 2003). Why was the welfare–work combination so beneficial? Most welfare recipients must take unstable jobs with erratic work hours and minimal or no benefits. Working while retaining some welfare support probably gave mothers an added sense of economic stability (Kalil, Schweingruber, & Seefeldt, 2001). The resulting lessening of financial anxiety seemed to enhance children's adjustment.

In sum, welfare reform promotes children's development only when it results in a more adequate standard of living. Punitive aspects of welfare-to-work that reduce or cut off benefits push families deeper into poverty, with destructive consequences for children's well-being. Because of a shortage of affordable child care in the United States and Canada (care for one child can consume 50 percent or more of a minimum-wage earner's income), mothers of young children are least able to earn enough by working. Yet poverty is most harmful to development when it occurs early in life (see page 74).

Welfare policies in other Western nations do not just encourage parents to be better providers. They also protect children from the damaging effects of poverty. France, for example, guarantees most of its citizens a modest minimum income. Single parents receive an extra amount during their child's first three years—a benefit that acknowledges a special need for income support during this period. Government-funded, high-quality child care begins at age 3, enabling mothers to go to work knowing that their children are safe and secure (Duncan & Brooks-Gunn, 2000).

Canada offers working parents more generous tax refunds than are available in the United States. Still, widespread poverty in both nations underscores the need for more effective poverty prevention policies—ones that help poor families rear children while they move toward financial independence.

This mother and her sons are able to afford their New Haven, Connecticut, apartment with the help of a U.S. government program that helps make livable housing affordable for needy families. Welfare-to-work programs benefit all family members when they protect children from the effects of growing up in poverty, while helping parents move from reliance on subsidies toward independence.

© PETER HVIZDAK/THE IMAGE WORKS

Campaign 2000 is Canada's public education movement aimed at building national awareness of the extent of child poverty and the need to improve policies benefiting children. This Campaign 2000 poster calls for strengthening a diverse array of community resources that assist families in rearing children.

programs. To learn more about the Children's Defense Fund, visit its website at *www.childrensdefense.org*.

In 1991, Canada initiated a public education movement, called Campaign 2000, to build nation-wide awareness of the extent and consequences of child poverty and to lobby government representatives for improved policies benefiting children. Diverse organizations—including professional, religious, health, and labor groups at national, provincial, and community levels—have joined forces to work toward campaign goals: raising basic living standards so no child lives in poverty, ensuring each child affordable, appropriate housing, and strengthening child care and other community resources that assist families in rearing children. Consult *www.campaign2000.ca* to explore the work of Campaign 2000, including its annual *Report Card on Child Poverty in Canada*.

Besides strong advocacy, public policies that enhance child development depend on policy-relevant research that documents needs and evaluates programs to spark improvements (refer back to the Social Issues: Health box on page 81 for an example). Today, more researchers are collaborating with community and government agencies to enhance the social relevance of their investigations. They are also doing a better job of disseminating their findings to the public, through television documentaries, newspaper stories, magazine articles, websites, and direct reports to government officials. In these ways, they are helping to create the sense of immediacy about the condition of children and families that is necessary to spur a society into action.

Ask Yourself

Review   Links between family and community are essential for children's well-being. Provide examples and research findings from our discussion that support this idea.

Apply   Check your local newspaper or one or two national news magazines or news websites to see how often articles on the condition of children and families appear. Why is it important for researchers to communicate with the general public about children's needs?

Connect   How does poverty affect the functioning of the family system, placing all aspects of development at risk?

Reflect   Do you agree with the widespread North American sentiment that government should not become involved in family life? Explain.

Understanding the Relationship Between Heredity and Environment

Throughout this chapter, we have discussed a wide variety of genetic and environmental influences, each of which has the power to alter the course of development. Yet children who are born into the same family (and who therefore share both genes and environments) often are quite different in characteristics. We also know that some children are affected more than others by their homes, neighborhoods, and communities. In some cases, a child who is given many advantages nevertheless does poorly, while another, growing up in unfavorable rearing conditions, does well. How do scientists explain the impact of heredity and environment when they seem to work in so many different ways?

Behavioral genetics is a field devoted to uncovering the contributions of nature and nurture to this diversity in human traits and abilities. All contemporary researchers agree that both heredity and environment are involved in every aspect of development. But for polygenic traits (those due to many genes) such as intelligence and personality, scientists are a long way from knowing the precise hereditary influences involved. Although they are making progress in identifying the multiple variations in DNA sequences associated with complex traits, so far these genetic markers explain only a small amount of variation in human behavior, and a minority of cases of most psychological disorders (Plomin, 2005; Plomin et al., 2003). For the most part, scientists are still limited to investigating the impact of genes on complex characteristics indirectly.

Some believe that it is useful and possible to answer the question of *how much each factor contributes* to differences among children. A growing consensus, however, regards that question as unanswerable. These investigators believe that heredity and environment are inseparable (Gottlieb, Wahlsten, & Lickliter, 2006). The important question, they maintain, is *how nature and nurture work together*. Let's consider each position in turn.

The Question, "How Much?"

Researchers use two methods—heritability estimates and concordance rates—to infer the role of heredity in complex human characteristics. Let's look closely at the information these procedures yield, along with their limitations.

HERITABILITY ■ **Heritability estimates** measure the extent to which individual differences in complex traits in a specific population are due to genetic factors. We will take a brief look at heritability findings on intelligence and personality here and will return to them in later chapters, when we consider these topics in greater detail. Heritability estimates are obtained from **kinship studies,** which compare the characteristics of family members. The most common type of kinship study compares identical twins, who share all their genes, with fraternal twins, who share only some. If people who are genetically more alike are also more similar in intelligence and personality, then the researcher assumes that heredity plays an important role.

Kinship studies of intelligence provide some of the most controversial findings in the field of child development. Some experts claim a strong genetic influence, whereas others believe that heredity is barely involved. Currently, most kinship findings support a moderate role for heredity. When many twin studies are examined, correlations between the scores of identical twins are consistently higher than those of fraternal twins. In a summary of more than 13,000 twin pairs, the average correlation was .86 for identical twins and .60 for fraternal twins (Plomin & Spinath, 2004).

Researchers use a complex statistical procedure to compare these correlations, arriving at a heritability estimate ranging from 0 to 1.00. The value for intelligence is about .50 for child and adolescent twin samples in Western industrialized nations. This suggests that differences in genetic makeup explain half the variation in intelligence (Plomin, 1994). Adopted children's mental test scores are more strongly related to their biological parents' scores than to those of their adoptive parents, offering further support for the role of heredity (Petrill & Deater-Deckard, 2004; Plomin et al., 1997).

Heritability research also reveals that genetic factors are important in personality. For frequently studied traits, such as sociability, anxiety, agreeableness, and activity level, heritability estimates obtained on child and adolescent and young adult twins are moderate, at .40 to .50 (Bouchard, 2004; Caspi & Shiner, 2006; Rothbart & Bates, 2006).

behavioral genetics A field devoted to uncovering the contributions of nature and nurture to the diversity in human traits and abilities.

heritability estimate A statistic that measures the extent to which individual differences in complex traits in a specific population are due to genetic factors.

kinship studies Studies comparing the characteristics of family members to determine the importance of heredity in complex human characteristics.

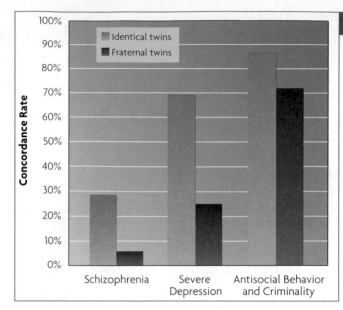

FIGURE 2.8

Concordance rates for schizophrenia, severe depression, and antisocial behavior and criminality. We know that heredity plays some role in schizophrenia and is even more influential in severe depression because the concordance rate is much higher for identical than for fraternal twins. We also see that heredity contributes less to antisocial behavior and criminality because the difference between identical and fraternal twins' concordance rates is smaller. (From Gottesman, 1991; McGuffin & Sargeant, 1991; Torrey et al., 1994.)

CONCORDANCE ■ A second measure used to infer the contribution of heredity to complex characteristics is the **concordance rate**—the percentage of instances in which both twins show a trait when it is present in one twin. Researchers typically use concordance to study the contribution of heredity to emotional and behavior disorders, which can be judged as either present or absent.

A concordance rate ranges from 0 to 100 percent. A score of 0 indicates that if one twin has the trait, the other twin never has it. A score of 100 means that if one twin has the trait, the other one always has it. When a concordance rate is much higher for identical twins than for fraternal twins, heredity is believed to play a major role. As Figure 2.8 reveals, twin studies of schizophrenia (a disorder involving delusions and hallucinations, difficulty distinguishing fantasy from reality, and irrational and inappropriate behaviors) and severe depression show this pattern of findings. Look carefully at the figure, and you will see that the influence of heredity on antisocial behavior and criminality, though apparent, is less strong: The difference between concordance rates for identical and fraternal twins is smaller. Again, adoption studies support these results. Biological relatives of schizophrenic and depressed adoptees are more likely than adoptive relatives to share the same disorder (Plomin et al., 2001; Tienari et al., 2003).

Taken together, concordance and adoption research suggests that the tendency for schizophrenia, depression, and criminality to run in families is partly due to genetic factors. But we also know that environment is involved: If heredity were the only influence, the concordance rate for identical twins would be 100 percent. We have seen that environmental stressors, such as poverty, family conflict, and a disorganized home and neighborhood life, are often associated with emotional and behavior problems. You will encounter many more examples of this relationship throughout this book.

LIMITATIONS OF HERITABILITY AND CONCORDANCE ■ Serious questions have been raised about the accuracy of heritability estimates and concordance rates. The accuracy of both measures depends on the extent to which the twin pairs studied reflect genetic and environmental variation in the population. Within a population in which all people have very similar home, school, and community experiences, individual differences in intelligence and personality would be largely genetic, and heritability estimates would be close to 1.00. Conversely, the more environments vary, the more likely they are to account for individual differences, yielding lower heritability estimates (Plomin, 1994). In twin studies, most of the twin pairs studied are reared together under highly similar conditions. Even when separated twins are available for study, social service agencies often place them in advantaged homes that are alike in many ways (Rutter et al., 2001). Because the environments of most twin pairs are less diverse than those of the general population, heritability estimates are likely to exaggerate the role of heredity.

Heritability estimates are controversial measures because they can easily be misapplied. For example, high heritabilities have been used to suggest that ethnic differences in intelligence, such as the poorer performance of black children compared to white children, have a genetic basis (Jensen, 1969, 1985, 1998). Yet this line of reasoning is widely regarded as incorrect.

concordance rate The percentage of instances in which both members of a twin pair show a trait when it is present in one pair member, used to study the contribution of heredity to emotional and behavior disorders.

Adriana and Tamara, identical twins born in Mexico, were separated at birth and adopted into different homes in the New York City area. They were unaware of each other's existence until age 20, when they met through a mutual acquaintance. The twins discovered that they were similar in many ways, ranging from academic achievement to a love of dancing and similar taste in clothing. The study of identical twins reared apart reveals that heredity contributes to many psychological characteristics. But generalizing from twin evidence to the population is controversial.

© JACQUIE HEMMERDINGER/THE NEW YORK TIMES

Heritabilities computed on mostly white twin samples do not tell us what causes test score differences between ethnic groups. We have already seen that large economic and cultural differences are involved. In Chapter 12, we will discuss research indicating that when black children are adopted into economically advantaged homes at an early age, their scores are well above average and substantially higher than those of children growing up in impoverished families.

Perhaps the most serious criticism of heritability estimates and concordance rates has to do with their limited usefulness. They are interesting statistics but give us no precise information on how intelligence and personality develop or how children might respond to environments designed to help them develop as far as possible (Rutter, 2002; Wachs, 1999). Indeed, the heritability of intelligence increases as parental education and income increase— that is, as children grow up in conditions that allow them to make the most of their genetic endowment. In disadvantaged environments, children are prevented from realizing their potential. Consequently, enhancing their experiences through interventions—such as parent education and high-quality preschool or child care—has a greater impact on development (Bronfenbrenner & Morris, 2006; Turkheimer et al., 2003).

According to one group of experts, heritability estimates have too many problems to yield any firm conclusions about the relative strength of nature and nurture (Collins et al., 2000). Although these statistics confirm that heredity contributes to complex traits, they do not tell us how environment can modify genetic influences.

The Question, "How?"

Today, most researchers view development as the result of a dynamic interplay between heredity and environment. How do nature and nurture work together? Several concepts shed light on this question.

REACTION RANGE  The first of these ideas is **range of reaction,** or each person's unique, genetically determined response to the environment (Gottesman, 1963). Let's explore this idea in Figure 2.9 on page 86. Reaction range can apply to any characteristic; here it is illustrated for intelligence. Notice that when environments vary from extremely unstimulating to highly enriched, Ben's intelligence increases steadily, Linda's rises sharply and then falls off, and Ron's begins to increase only after the environment becomes modestly stimulating.

Reaction range highlights two important points. First, it shows that because each of us has a unique genetic makeup, we respond differently to the same environment. Note in Figure 2.9 how a poor environment results in similarly low scores for all three individuals. But when the environment provides an intermediate level of stimulation, Linda is by far the best-performing child. And in a highly enriched environment, Ben does best, followed by Ron, both of whom now outperform Linda.

Second, often different genetic–environmental combinations can make two people look the same! For example, if Linda is reared in a minimally stimulating environment, her score will be about 100—average for children in general. Ben and Ron can also obtain this score, but

range of reaction Each person's unique, genetically determined response to a range of environmental conditions.

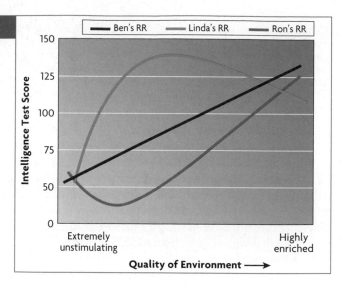

Ben's RR   Linda's RR   Ron's RR

FIGURE 2.9

Intellectual ranges of reaction (RR) for three children in environments that vary from extremely unstimulating to highly enriched. Each child, because of his or her genetic makeup, responds differently as quality of the environment changes. Ben's intelligence test score increases steadily, Linda's rises sharply and then falls off, and Ron's begins to increase only after the environment becomes modestly stimulating. (Adapted from Wahlsten, 1994.)

to do so they must grow up in a fairly enriched home. In sum, range of reaction reveals that unique blends of heredity and environment lead to both similarities and differences in behavior (Gottlieb, Wahlsten, & Lickliter, 2006).

CANALIZATION ■ The concept of canalization provides another way of understanding how heredity and environment combine. **Canalization** is the tendency of heredity to restrict the development of some characteristics to just one or a few outcomes. A behavior that is strongly canalized develops similarly in a wide range of environments; only strong environmental forces can change it (Waddington, 1957). For example, infant perceptual and motor development seems to be strongly canalized because all normal human babies eventually roll over, reach for objects, sit up, crawl, and walk. It takes extreme conditions to modify these behaviors or cause them not to appear. In contrast, intelligence and personality are less strongly canalized; they vary much more with changes in the environment.

When we look at behaviors that are constrained by heredity, we can see that canalization is highly adaptive. Through it, nature ensures that children will develop certain species-typical skills under a wide range of rearing conditions, thereby promoting survival.

GENETIC–ENVIRONMENTAL CORRELATION ■ A major problem in trying to separate heredity and environment is that they are often correlated (Plomin et al., 2001; Scarr & McCartney, 1983). According to the concept of **genetic–environmental correlation,** our genes influence the environments to which we are exposed. The way this happens changes with age.

Passive and Evocative Correlation. At younger ages, two types of genetic–environmental correlation are common. The first is called *passive* correlation because the child has no control over it. Early on, parents provide environments influenced by their own heredity. For example, parents who are good athletes emphasize outdoor activities and enroll their children in swimming and gymnastics. Besides being exposed to an "athletic environment," the children may have inherited their parents' athletic ability. As a result, they are likely to become good athletes for both genetic and environmental reasons.

This mother shares her love of running with her daughter—who also may have inherited her mother's athletic ability. When heredity and environment are correlated, they jointly foster the same capacities, and the influence of one cannot be separated from the influence of the other.

© MYRLEEN FERGUSON CATE/PHOTOEDIT

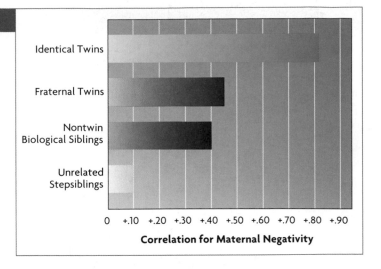

FIGURE 2.10

Similarity in mothers' interactions for pairs of siblings differing in genetic relatedness. The correlations shown are for maternal negativity. The pattern illustrates evocative genetic–environmental correlation. Identical twins evoke highly similar maternal treatment because of their identical heredity. As genetic resemblance between siblings declines, the strength of the correlation drops. Mothers vary their interactions as they respond to each child's unique genetic makeup. (Adapted from Reiss, 2003.)

The second type of genetic–environmental correlation is *evocative*. The responses children evoke from others are influenced by the child's heredity, and these responses strengthen the child's original style. For example, an active, friendly baby is likely to receive more social stimulation than a passive, quiet infant. And a cooperative, attentive child probably receives more patient and sensitive interactions from parents than an inattentive, distractible child. In support of this idea, the less genetically alike siblings are, the more their parents treat them differently, in both warmth and negativity. Thus, parents' treatment of identical twins is highly similar, whereas their treatment of fraternal twins and nontwin biological siblings is only moderately so. And little resemblance exists in parents' warm and negative interactions with unrelated stepsiblings (see Figure 2.10) (Reiss, 2003).

Active Correlation. In older children, *active* genetic–environmental correlation becomes common. As children extend their experiences beyond the immediate family and are given the freedom to make more choices, they actively seek environments that fit with their genetic tendencies. The well-coordinated, muscular child spends more time at after-school sports, the musically talented youngster joins the school orchestra and practices his violin, and the intellectually curious child is a familiar patron at her local library.

This tendency to actively choose environments that complement our heredity is called **niche-picking** (Scarr & McCartney, 1983). Infants and young children cannot do much niche-picking because adults select environments for them. In contrast, older children and adolescents are much more in charge of their environments.

Niche-picking explains why pairs of identical twins reared apart during childhood and later reunited may find, to their surprise, that they have similar hobbies, food preferences, and vocations—a trend that is especially evident when twins' environmental opportunities are similar (Plomin, 1994). Niche-picking also helps us understand why identical twins become somewhat more alike, and fraternal twins and adopted siblings less alike, in intelligence with age (Loehlin, Horn, & Willerman, 1997).

The influence of heredity and environment is not constant but changes over time. With age, genetic factors may become more important in influencing the environments we experience and choose for ourselves.

ENVIRONMENTAL INFLUENCES ON GENE EXPRESSION ■ Notice how, in the concepts just considered, heredity is granted priority. In range of reaction, it *limits* responsiveness to varying environments. In canalization, it *restricts* the development of certain behaviors. Similarly, some theorists regard genetic–environmental correlation as entirely driven by genetics (Harris, 1998;

canalization The tendency of heredity to restrict the development of some characteristics to just one or a few outcomes.

genetic–environmental correlation The idea that heredity influences the environments to which individuals are exposed.

niche-picking A type of genetic–environmental correlation in which individuals actively choose environments that complement their heredity.

FIGURE 2.11

The epigenetic framework. Development takes place through ongoing, bidirectional exchanges between heredity and all levels of the environment. Genes affect behavior and experiences. Experiences and behavior also affect gene expression. (Adapted from Gottlieb, 2000.)

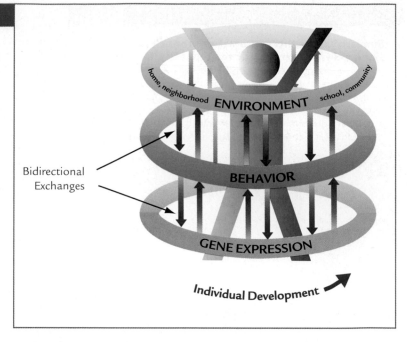

Bidirectional Exchanges

Rowe, 1994). They believe that children's genetic makeup causes them to receive, evoke, or seek experiences that actualize their inborn tendencies.

Others argue that heredity does not dictate children's experiences or development in a rigid way. In one study, boys with a genetic tendency toward antisocial behavior (based on the presence of a gene on the X chromosome known to predispose both animals and humans to aggression) were no more aggressive than boys without this gene, *unless* they also had a history of severe child abuse (Caspi et al., 2002). Boys with and without the gene did not differ in their experience of abuse, indicating that the "aggressive genotype" did not increase exposure to abuse.

Furthermore, parents and other caring adults can *uncouple* unfavorable genetic–environmental correlations. They often provide children with positive experiences that modify the expression of heredity, yielding favorable outcomes. For example, in a study that tracked the development of 5-year-old identical twins, pair members tended to resemble each other in level of aggression. And the more aggression they displayed, the more maternal anger and criticism they received (a genetic–environmental correlation). Nevertheless, some mothers treated their twins differently. When followed up at age 7, twins who had been targets of more maternal negativity engaged in even more antisocial behavior. In contrast, their better-treated, genetically identical counterparts showed a reduction in disruptive acts (Caspi et al., 2004). Good parenting protected them from a spiraling, antisocial course of development.

Accumulating evidence reveals that the relationship between heredity and environment is not a one-way street, from genes to environment to behavior. Rather, like other system influences considered in this and the previous chapter, it is *bidirectional*: Genes affect children's behavior and experiences, but their experiences and behavior also affect gene expression (Gottlieb, 2000, 2003; Rutter, 2006a). Stimulation—both *internal* to the child (activity within the cytoplasm of the cell, hormones released into the bloodstream) and *external* to the child (home, neighborhood, school, and society)—triggers gene activity.

Researchers call this view of the relationship between heredity and environment the *epigenetic framework* (Gottlieb, 1998, 2002). It is depicted in Figure 2.11. **Epigenesis** means development resulting from ongoing, bidirectional exchanges between heredity and all levels of the environment. To illustrate, providing a baby with a healthy diet promotes brain growth, leading to new connections between nerve cells, which transform gene expression. This opens the door to new gene–environment exchanges—for example, advanced exploration of objects and interaction with caregivers, which further enhance brain growth and gene expres-

epigenesis Development of the individual resulting from ongoing, bidirectional exchanges between heredity and all levels of the environment.

sion. These ongoing bidirectional influences foster cognitive and social development. In contrast, harmful environments can dampen gene expression, at times so profoundly that later experiences can do little to change characteristics (such as intelligence and personality) that originally were flexible.

A major reason that researchers are interested in the nature–nurture issue is that they want to improve environments so that children can develop as far as possible. The concept of epigenesis reminds us that development is best understood as a series of complex exchanges between nature and nurture. Although children cannot be changed in any way we might desire, environments can modify genetic influences. The success of any attempt to improve development depends on the characteristics we want to change, the genetic makeup of the child, and the type and timing of our intervention.

Ask Yourself

Review   What is epigenesis, and how does it differ from range of reaction and genetic–environmental correlation? Provide an example of epigenesis.

Apply   Bianca's parents are accomplished musicians. At age 4, Bianca began taking piano lessons. By age 10, she was accompanying the school choir. At age 14, she asked if she could attend a special music high school. Explain how genetic–environmental correlation promoted Bianca's talent.

Connect   Explain how each of the following concepts supports the conclusion that genetic influences on human characteristics are not constant but change over time: somatic mutation (page 60), niche-picking (page 86), and epigenesis (page 88).

Reflect   What aspects of your own development—for example, interests, hobbies, college major, or vocational choice—are probably due to niche-picking? Explain.

Summary

Genetic Foundations

What are genes, and how are they transmitted from one generation to the next?

■ Each individual's **phenotype,** or directly observable characteristics, is a product of both **genotype** and environment. **Chromosomes,** rodlike structures within the cell nucleus, contain our hereditary endowment. Along their length are **genes,** segments of **deoxyribo-nucleic acid (DNA),** that send instructions for making a rich assortment of proteins to the cytoplasm of the cell—a process that makes us distinctly human and influences our development and characteristics.

■ **Gametes,** or sex cells, are produced through a cell division process called **meiosis. Crossing over** and chance assortment of chromosomes into gametes ensure that each receives a unique set of genes from each parent. Once sperm and ovum unite, the resulting **zygote** starts to develop into a complex human being through cell duplication, or **mitosis.**

■ All but one of the 23 pairs of chromosomes are matching pairs called **autosomes.** The remaining pair are the **sex chromosomes—** XX in females and XY in males. A child's sex is determined by whether an X-bearing or Y-bearing sperm fertilizes the ovum.

■ **Fraternal,** or **dizygotic, twins** result when two ova are released from the mother's ovaries and each is fertilized. When a zygote divides in two during the early stages of cell duplication, **identical,** or **monozygotic, twins** develop.

© RACHEL EPSTEIN/PHOTOEDIT

Describe various patterns of genetic inheritance.

■ A child who inherits the same form of a gene, or **allele,** from both parents, is **homozygous** and will display the inherited trait. When the alleles are different, the child is **heterozygous,** and relationships between the alleles determine the phenotype.

■ In **dominant–recessive inheritance,** only the dominant allele affects the child's phenotype. Individuals who inherit a dominant and a recessive allele become **carriers,** who can pass the recessive trait to their children. A child who inherits two recessive alleles will display the recessive trait. In **incomplete dominance,** both alleles are expressed in the phenotype, resulting in a trait that combines aspects of both. **Modifier genes** enhance or dilute the effects of other genes.

■ When recessive disorders are **X-linked** (carried on the X chromosome), males are more likely to be affected. **Genetic imprinting** is a pattern of inheritance in which one parent's allele is activated, regardless of its makeup.

■ Harmful genes arise from **mutation,** a sudden but permanent change in a DNA segment that can occur spontaneously or be induced by hazardous environmental agents. Germline mutation occurs in the cells that give rise to gametes, so the affected DNA is passed on to the next generation. In somatic mutation, normal body cells mutate—something that can occur at any time of life.

■ Human traits that vary continuously among people, such as intelligence and personality, result from **polygenic inheritance,** meaning that they are influenced by many genes. Scientists must study the influence of heredity on these characteristics indirectly.

Describe major chromosomal abnormalities, and explain how they occur.

■ Most chromosomal abnormalities are due to errors in meiosis. The most common is Down syndrome, which results in physical defects and mental retardation. Disorders of the sex chromosomes—XYY, triple X, Klinefelter, and Turner syndromes—are milder than defects of the autosomes.

Reproductive Choices

What procedures can assist prospective parents in having healthy children?

■ **Genetic counseling** helps couples at risk for giving birth to children with genetic abnormalities consider appropriate reproductive options. **Prenatal diagnostic methods** allow early detection of genetic problems.

■ Reproductive technologies, such as donor insemination, in vitro fertilization, surrogate motherhood, and post-menopausal-assisted childbirth, permit many individuals to become parents who otherwise would not, but they raise serious legal and ethical concerns.

■ Many parents who cannot conceive or who have a high likelihood of transmitting a genetic disorder decide to adopt. Although adopted children tend to have more learning and emotional problems than children in general, in the long run, with warm, sensitive parenting, most adopted children fare well.

Environmental Contexts for Development

Describe family functioning from the perspective of ecological systems theory, along with aspects of the environment that support family well-being and children's development.

■ The family is the child's first and foremost context for development. Ecological systems theory emphasizes that the behaviors of each family member affect those of others, both directly and indirectly. The family system is also dynamic, continually adjusting to the development of its members and to societal change.

■ One source of consistency in family functioning is **socioeconomic status (SES).** Lower SES is linked to earlier timing of parenthood and larger family size. And lower-SES parents often stress external characteristics and practice more restrictive parenting, whereas

higher-SES parents place greater emphasis on psychological traits and engage in warmer, more verbally stimulating interaction.

■ Adjustment problems are seen in children from affluent families whose parents do not provide emotional closeness and supervision. And poverty and homelessness undermine effective parenting and pose serious threats to children's development.

■ Children benefit from supportive ties between the family and the surrounding environment, including neighborhoods that offer constructive leisure activities, high-quality schools that communicate often with parents, and other strong connections between family and community life.

■ The values and practices of cultures and **subcultures** affect all aspects of children's daily lives. **Extended-family households,** in which parent and child live with one or more adult relatives, are common among many ethnic minority groups and can protect children's development under highly stressful conditions.

■ Cultures differ in the extent to which they are **collectivist societies,** which emphasize group needs and goals, versus **individualistic societies,** which emphasize individual well-being over collective goals. Collectivist and individualistic societies take different approaches to developing **public policies** to address social problems, including those affecting children. U.S. and (to a lesser extent) Canadian policies safeguarding children and youths have lagged behind policies in other developed nations.

Understanding the Relationship Between Heredity and Environment

Explain the various ways heredity and environment may combine to influence complex traits.

■ **Behavioral genetics** is a field that examines the contributions of nature and nurture to complex traits. Some researchers seek to determine "how much" each factor contributes to individual differences by computing **heritability estimates** and **concordance rates** from **kinship studies.** Although these measures show that genetic factors contribute to such traits as intelligence and personality, their accuracy and usefulness have been challenged.

■ Most researchers view development as the result of a dynamic interplay between nature and nurture. According to the ideas of **range of reaction** and **canalization,** heredity influences children's responsiveness to varying environments. **Genetic–environmental correlation** and **niche-picking** describe how children's genes affect the environments to which they are exposed. **Epigenesis** reminds us that development is best understood as a series of complex exchanges between nature and nurture.

Important Terms and Concepts

allele (p. 56)
autosomes (p. 54)
behavioral genetics (p. 83)
canalization (p. 86)
carrier (p. 56)
chromosomes (p. 52)
collectivist societies (p. 77)
concordance rate (p. 84)
crossing over (p. 53)
deoxyribonucleic acid (DNA) (p. 52)
dominant–recessive inheritance (p. 56)
epigenesis (p. 88)
extended-family household (p. 77)
fraternal, or dizygotic, twins (p. 55)

gametes (p. 53)
gene (p. 52)
genetic counseling (p. 63)
genetic–environmental correlation (p. 86)
genetic imprinting (p. 59)
genotype (p. 51)
heritability estimate (p. 83)
heterozygous (p. 56)
homozygous (p. 56)
identical, or monozygotic, twins (p. 55)
incomplete dominance (p. 57)
individualistic societies (p. 77)
kinship studies (p. 83)
meiosis (p. 53)

mitosis (p. 52)
modifier genes (p. 56)
mutation (p. 61)
niche-picking (p. 87)
phenotype (p. 51)
polygenic inheritance (p. 61)
prenatal diagnostic methods (p. 63)
public policies (p. 79)
range of reaction (p. 85)
sex chromosomes (p. 54)
socioeconomic status (SES) (p. 71)
subculture (p. 77)
X-linked inheritance (p. 57)
zygote (p. 53)

Chapter 3

A young painter captures the wide-ranging medical and social supports that help ensure that her twin siblings, floating within her mother's protective womb, will be born healthy. How is the one-celled organism gradually transformed into a baby with the capacity to participate in family life? What factors protect or undermine prenatal development? Chapter 3 answers these questions.

"Mother at the Specialist's"
Sonja Zajcikovska
7 years, former Czechoslovakia

Prenatal Development

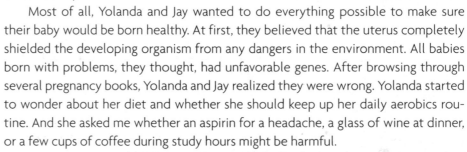

When I met Yolanda and Jay one fall in my child development class, Yolanda was just two months pregnant. After months of wondering if the time in their lives was right, they had decided to have a baby. Both were full of questions: "How does the baby grow before birth?" "When is each organ formed?" "Has its heart begun to beat?" "Can it hear, feel, or sense our presence?"

Most of all, Yolanda and Jay wanted to do everything possible to make sure their baby would be born healthy. At first, they believed that the uterus completely shielded the developing organism from any dangers in the environment. All babies born with problems, they thought, had unfavorable genes. After browsing through several pregnancy books, Yolanda and Jay realized they were wrong. Yolanda started to wonder about her diet and whether she should keep up her daily aerobics routine. And she asked me whether an aspirin for a headache, a glass of wine at dinner, or a few cups of coffee during study hours might be harmful.

In this chapter, we answer Yolanda and Jay's questions, along with a great many more that scientists have asked about the events before birth. We begin our discussion during the time period before pregnancy with these puzzling questions: Why is it that generation after generation, most couples who fall in love and marry want to become parents? And how do they decide whether to have just one child or more than one?

Then we trace prenatal development, paying special attention to environmental supports for healthy growth, as well as damaging influences that threaten the child's health and survival. Finally, we look at how couples prepare psychologically for the arrival of the baby and start to forge a new sense of self as mother or father.

Motivations for Parenthood

TAKE A MOMENT... What, in your view, are the benefits and drawbacks of having children? How large would your ideal family be, and why? As part of her semester project for my class, Yolanda interviewed her grandmother, asking why she had wanted children and how she had settled on a particular family size. Yolanda's grandmother, whose children were born in the 1950s, replied:

> We didn't think much about whether or not to have children in those days.
> We just had them—everybody did. It would have seemed odd not to! I was 22

Individuals from diverse cultures mention many of the same reasons for becoming parents. This couple takes pleasure in an affectionate parent–child relationship and in helping their daughter grow, physically, intellectually, and emotionally.

years old when I had the first of my four children, and I had four because—well, I wouldn't have had just one because we all thought children needed brothers and sisters, and only children could end up spoiled and selfish. Life is more interesting with children, you know. And now that we're older, we've got family we can depend on and grandchildren to enjoy.

Why Have Children?

In some ways, the reasons Yolanda's grandmother wanted children are much like those of contemporary parents. In other ways, they are very different. In the past, the issue of whether to have children was, for many adults, "a biological given or unavoidable cultural demand" (Michaels, 1988, p. 23). Today, in Western industrialized nations, it is a matter of true individual choice. Effective birth control techniques enable adults to avoid having children in most instances. And changing cultural values allow people to remain childless with much less fear of social criticism and rejection than a generation or two ago. In 1950, 78 percent of North American married couples were parents. Today, 70 percent bear children—a choice affected by a complex array of factors including financial circumstances, career goals, personal and religious values, and health conditions (Theil, 2006).

When North Americans are asked about their desire to have children, they mention a variety of advantages and disadvantages, which are listed in Table 3.1. Although some ethnic and regional differences exist, reasons for having children that are most important to all groups include the warm, affectionate relationship and the stimulation and fun that children provide. Also frequently mentioned are growth and learning experiences that children bring into the lives of adults, the desire to have someone carry on after one's own death, and feelings of accomplishment and creativity that come from helping children grow (Cowan & Cowan, 2000; Dion, 1995; O'Laughlin & Anderson, 2001).

TABLE 3.1	Advantages and Disadvantages of Parenthood Mentioned by American Couples

ADVANTAGES	DISADVANTAGES
Giving and receiving warmth and affection	Loss of freedom, being tied down
Experiencing the stimulation and fun that children add to life	Financial strain
Being accepted as a responsible and mature member of the community	Family–work conflict—not enough time to meet both child-rearing and job responsibilities
Experiencing new growth and learning opportunities that add meaning to life	Interference with mother's employment opportunities and career progress
Having someone to provide care in old age	Worries over children's health, safety, and well-being
Gaining a sense of accomplishment and creativity from helping children grow	Risks of bringing up children in a world plagued by crime, war, and pollution
Learning to become less selfish and to sacrifice	Reduced time to spend with husband or wife
Having someone carry on after one's own death	Loss of privacy
Having offspring who help with parents' work or add their own income to the family's resources	Fear that children will turn out badly, through no fault of one's own

Sources: Cowan & Cowan, 2000; O'Laughlin & Anderson, 2001.

Most adults are also aware that having children means years of extra burdens and responsibilities. When asked about the disadvantages of parenthood, they mention "loss of freedom" most often, followed by "financial strain." Indeed, the cost of child rearing is a major factor in modern family planning. According to a conservative estimate, today's new parents will spend about $190,000 in the United States and $170,000 in Canada to rear a child from birth to age 18, and many will incur substantial additional expense for higher education and financial dependency during emerging adulthood—a reality that has contributed to the declining birthrate in industrialized nations (Child Care Advocacy Association of Canada, 2004; U.S. Department of Agriculture, 2005a). Finally, many adults worry greatly about conflict between family and work— not having enough time to meet both child-rearing and job responsibilities (Hewlett, 2003).

Greater freedom to choose whether, when, and how to have children (see the discussion of reproductive choices in Chapter 2) makes contemporary family planning more challenging than it was in Yolanda's grandmother's day. As each partner expects to have equal say, childbearing often becomes a matter of delicate negotiation (Cowan & Cowan, 2000). Yet careful weighing of the pros and cons of having children means that many more couples are making informed and personally meaningful decisions—a trend that should increase the chances that they will have children when ready and will find parenting an enriching experience.

How Large a Family?

In contrast to her grandmother, Yolanda plans to have no more than two children. And she and Jay are talking about whether to limit their family to a single child. In 1960, the average number of children per North American couple was 3.1. Currently, it is 1.8 in the United States; 1.7 in Australia, Great Britain, and Sweden; 1.6 in Canada; 1.4 in Japan and Germany; and 1.3 in Italy (U.S. Census Bureau, 2007a; 2007b). In addition to more effective birth control, a major reason for this decline is that a family size of one or two children is more compatible with a woman's decision to divide her energies between family and work. Marital instability has also contributed to smaller families: More couples today get divorced before their childbearing plans are complete.

Popular advice to prospective parents often recommends limiting family size in the interests of "child quality"—more parental affection, attention, and material resources per child, which enhance children's intellectual development. Do large families make less intelligent children, as prevailing attitudes suggest? Or do less intelligent parents—as a result of heredity, environment, or both— tend to have larger families? To find out researchers turned to a large, two-generation longitudinal study.

Starting in 1972, the U.S. National Longitudinal Survey of Youth (NLSY) followed a representative sample of more than 3,000 14- to 22-year-olds; in 1986 the children of the original participants were added to the investigation. Because both cohorts took intelligence tests, researchers could (1) examine the relationship of sibling birth order within families to mental test scores, to find out whether having more children depresses children's intellectual functioning, and (2) correlate maternal scores with family size, for insight into whether mothers who score poorly are prone to have larger families.

As the horizontal lines in Figure 3.1 reveal, children's mental test performance did not decline with later birth

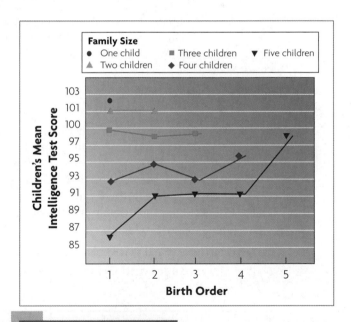

FIGURE 3.1

Relationship of birth order to intelligence. In the U.S. National Longitudinal Survey of Youth, children's intelligence test scores did not decline with later birth order, as would be predicted if large families diluted the quality of children's experiences. To the contrary, in the largest families, the youngest children tended to score higher than their siblings. But note the differences among the lines, which indicate that the larger the family, the lower the scores of all siblings. (From J. L. Rodgers, H. H. Cleveland, E. van den Oord, & D. C. Rowe, 2000, "Resolving the Debate Over Birth Order, Family Size, and Intelligence," *American Psychologist, 55,* p. 607. Copyright © by the American Psychological Association. Reprinted by permission.)

Average family size has declined in recent decades in North America, Western Europe, and other developed nations. But having more children does not—as is commonly believed—reduce children's intelligence and life chances.

order—a finding that contradicts the belief that having more children depresses children's intellectual ability. At the same time, the differences among the lines show that the larger the family, the lower the scores of all siblings. The researchers found that the link between family size and children's scores can be explained by the strong trend for mothers who are low in intelligence to give birth to more children (Rodgers et al., 2000). In other NLSY research, among children of bright, economically advantaged mothers, the family size–intelligence correlation disappeared (Guo & Van-Wey, 1999).

Although many good reasons exist for limiting family size, the concern that additional births will reduce children's intelligence and life chances is not warranted. Rather, young people with lower mental test scores—many of whom dropped out of school, live in poverty, lack hope for their future, and fail to engage in family planning—are most likely to have large families. Return to the Social Issues: Education box on page 72 in Chapter 2 to review the close link between education and family planning. Both are vital for improving children's quality of life.

Is Yolanda's grandmother right when she says that parents who have just one child are likely to end up with a spoiled, selfish youngster? As we will see in Chapter 13, research also challenges this widely held belief. Only children are just as well-adjusted as children with siblings. Still, the one-child family, like all family lifestyles, has both pros and cons. Table 3.2 summarizes results of a survey in which only children and their parents were asked what they liked and disliked about living in a single-child family. The list is a useful one for parents to consider when deciding how many children would best fit their life plans.

Is There a Best Time During Adulthood to Have a Child?

Yolanda's grandmother had her first child in her early twenties. Yolanda, at age 28, is pregnant for the first time. Many people believe that women should, ideally, give birth in their twenties, not only because the risk of having a baby with a chromosomal disorder increases with age (see Chapter 2) but also because younger parents have more energy to keep up with active children.

However, as Figure 3.2 reveals, first births to women in their thirties have increased greatly over the past quarter century. Many people are delaying childbearing until their education is

TABLE 3.2	Advantages and Disadvantages of a One-Child Family		
ADVANTAGES		**DISADVANTAGES**	
Mentioned by Parents	**Mentioned by Children**	**Mentioned by Parents**	**Mentioned by Children**
Having time to pursue one's own interests and career	Having no sibling rivalry	Walking a "tightrope" between healthy attention and overindulgence	Not getting to experience the closeness of a sibling relationship
Less financial pressure	Having more privacy		
	Enjoying greater affluence	Having only one chance to "make good" as a parent	Feeling too much pressure from parents to succeed
Not having to worry about "playing favorites" among children	Having a closer parent–child relationship	Being left childless in case of the child's death	Having no one to help care for parents when they get old

Source: Hawke & Knox, 1978.

complete, their careers are established, and they know they can support a child. Older parents may be somewhat less energetic than they once were, but they are financially better off and emotionally more mature. For these reasons, they may be better able to invest in parenting.

Nevertheless, reproductive capacity does decline with age. Fertility problems among women increase from age 15 to 50, with a sharp rise in the mid-thirties. Between ages 25 and 34, nearly 14 percent of women are affected, a figure that climbs to 26 percent for 35- to 44-year-olds. Age also affects male reproductive capacity. Amount of semen and concentration of sperm in each ejaculation gradually decline after age 30. Consequently, compared to a 25-year-old man, a 45-year-old is 12 times as likely to take more than two years to achieve a conception (Hassan & Killick, 2003; U.S. Department of Health and Human Services, 2006f). Women with demanding careers are especially likely to delay parenthood (Barber, 2001a). Many believe, incorrectly, that if they have difficulty conceiving, they can rely on reproductive technologies. But recall from Chapter 2 that the success of these procedures drops steadily with age. Although no one time during adulthood is best to begin parenthood, individuals who decide to put off childbirth until well into their thirties or early forties risk having fewer children than they desire or none at all.

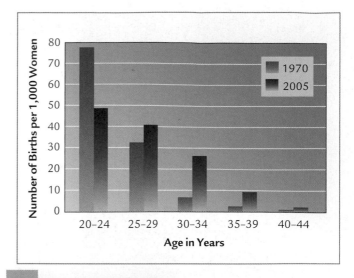

FIGURE 3.2

First births to American women of different ages in 1970 and 2005. The birthrate decreased during this period for women 20 to 24 years of age, whereas it increased for women 25 years of age and older. For women in their thirties, the birthrate more than doubled. Similar trends have occurred in Canada and other industrialized nations. (Adapted from U. S. Department of Health and Human Services, 2006f.)

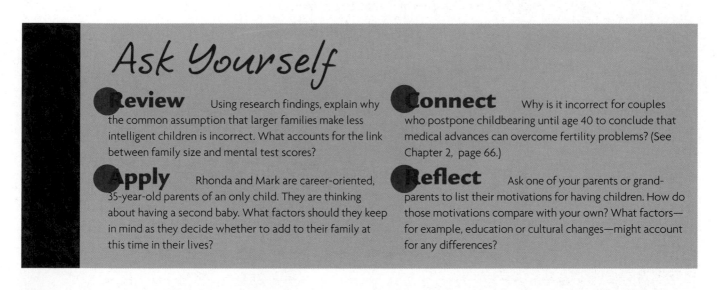

Ask Yourself

Review   Using research findings, explain why the common assumption that larger families make less intelligent children is incorrect. What accounts for the link between family size and mental test scores?

Apply   Rhonda and Mark are career-oriented, 35-year-old parents of an only child. They are thinking about having a second baby. What factors should they keep in mind as they decide whether to add to their family at this time in their lives?

Connect   Why is it incorrect for couples who postpone childbearing until age 40 to conclude that medical advances can overcome fertility problems? (See Chapter 2, page 66.)

Reflect   Ask one of your parents or grandparents to list their motivations for having children. How do those motivations compare with your own? What factors—for example, education or cultural changes—might account for any differences?

Prenatal Development

The sperm and ovum that unite to form the new individual are uniquely suited for the task of reproduction. The ovum is a tiny sphere, measuring $\frac{1}{175}$ inch in diameter, that is barely visible to the naked eye as a dot the size of the period at the end of this sentence. But in its microscopic world, it is a giant—the largest cell in the human body. The ovum's size makes it a perfect target for the much smaller sperm, which measure only $\frac{1}{500}$ inch.

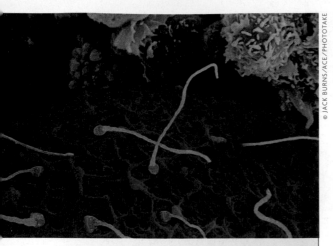

In this photo taken with the aid of a powerful microscope, sperm penetrate the surface of the enormous-looking ovum, the largest cell in the human body. When one sperm is successful at fertilizing the ovum, the resulting zygote will begin duplicating into the new organism.

© JACK BURNS/ACE/PHOTOTAKE

Conception

About once every 28 days, in the middle of a woman's menstrual cycle, an ovum bursts from one of her *ovaries,* two walnut-sized organs located deep inside her abdomen, and is drawn into one of two *fallopian tubes*—long, thin structures that lead to the hollow, soft-lined uterus (see Figure 3.3). While the ovum is traveling, the spot on the ovary from which it was released, now called the *corpus luteum,* secretes hormones that prepare the lining of the uterus to receive a fertilized ovum. If pregnancy does not occur, the corpus luteum shrinks, and the lining of the uterus is discarded two weeks later with menstruation.

The male produces sperm in vast numbers—an average of 300 million a day—in the *testes,* two glands located in the *scrotum,* sacs that lie just behind the penis. In the final process of maturation, each sperm develops a tail that permits it to swim long distances, upstream in the female reproductive tract, through the *cervix* (opening of the uterus), and into the fallopian tube, where fertilization usually takes place. The journey is difficult, and many sperm die. Only 300 to 500 reach the ovum, if one happens to be present. Sperm live for up to 6 days and can lie in wait for the ovum, which survives for only 1 day after being released into the fallopian tube. However, most conceptions result from intercourse during a 3-day period—on the day of or during the 2 days preceding ovulation (Wilcox, Weinberg, & Baird, 1995).

With conception, the story of prenatal development begins to unfold. The vast changes that take place during the 38 weeks of pregnancy are usually divided into three phases: (1) the period of the zygote, (2) the period of the embryo, and (3) the period of the fetus. As we look at what happens in each, you may find it useful to refer to Table 3.3 on page 100, which summarizes major milestones of prenatal development.

FIGURE 3.3

Female reproductive organs, showing fertilization, early cell duplication, and implantation. (Adapted from K. L. Moore and T. V. N. Persaud, 2003, *Before We Are Born,* 6th ed., Philadelphia: Saunders, p. 36. Reprinted by permission of the publisher and authors.)

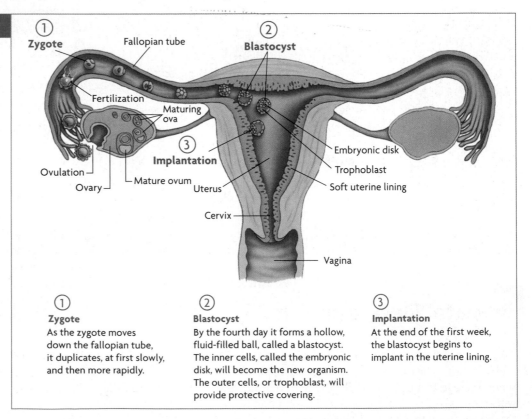

Zygote
As the zygote moves down the fallopian tube, it duplicates, at first slowly, and then more rapidly.

Blastocyst
By the fourth day it forms a hollow, fluid-filled ball, called a blastocyst. The inner cells, called the embryonic disk, will become the new organism. The outer cells, or trophoblast, will provide protective covering.

Implantation
At the end of the first week, the blastocyst begins to implant in the uterine lining.

© LENNART NILSSON, A CHILD IS BORN/BONNIERS

Period of the zygote: seventh to ninth day. The fertilized ovum duplicates at an increasingly rapid rate, forming a hollow ball of cells, or blastocyst, by the fourth day after fertilization. Here the blastocyst, magnified thousands of times, burrows into the uterine lining between the seventh and ninth day.

The Period of the Zygote

The period of the zygote lasts about two weeks, from fertilization until the tiny mass of cells drifts down and out of the fallopian tube and attaches itself to the wall of the uterus. The zygote's first cell duplication is long and drawn out; it is not complete until about 30 hours after conception. Gradually, new cells are added at a faster rate. By the fourth day, 60 to 70 cells exist that form a hollow, fluid-filled ball called a **blastocyst** (refer again to Figure 3.3). The cells on the inside of the blastocyst, called the **embryonic disk,** will become the new organism; the thin outer ring of cells, termed the **trophoblast,** will become the structures that provide protective covering and nourishment.

IMPLANTATION ■ Between the seventh and ninth days, **implantation** occurs: The blastocyst burrows deep into the uterine lining where, surrounded by the woman's nourishing blood, it starts to grow in earnest. At first, the trophoblast (protective outer layer) multiplies fastest. It forms a membrane, called the **amnion,** that encloses the developing organism in **amniotic fluid,** which helps keep the temperature of the prenatal world constant and provides a cushion against any jolts caused by the woman's movement. A *yolk sac* emerges that produces blood cells until the developing liver, spleen, and bone marrow are mature enough to take over this function (Moore & Persaud, 2003).

The events of these first two weeks are delicate and uncertain. As many as 30 percent of zygotes do not survive this period. In some, the sperm and ovum did not join properly. In others, for some unknown reason, cell duplication never begins. By preventing implantation in these cases, nature eliminates most prenatal abnormalities (Sadler, 2006).

THE PLACENTA AND UMBILICAL CORD ■ By the end of the second week, cells of the trophoblast form another protective membrane—the **chorion,** which surrounds the amnion. From the chorion, tiny fingerlike *villi,* or blood vessels, emerge.[1] As these villi burrow into the uterine wall, the placenta starts to develop. By bringing the mother's and the embryo's blood close together, the **placenta** permits food and oxygen to reach the developing organism and waste products to be carried away. A membrane forms that allows these substances to be exchanged but prevents the mother's and the embryo's blood from mixing directly (see Figure 3.4 on page 101).

---

[1] Recall from Chapter 2 that *chorionic villus sampling* is the prenatal diagnostic method that can be performed earliest, at nine weeks after conception. In this procedure, tissues from the ends of the villi are removed and examined for genetic abnormalities.

blastocyst The zygote 4 days after fertilization, when the tiny mass of cells forms a hollow, fluid-filled ball.

embryonic disk A small cluster of cells on the inside of the blastocyst, from which the new organism will develop.

trophoblast The thin outer ring of cells of the blastocyst, which will become the structures that provide protective covering and nourishment to the new organism.

implantation Attachment of the blastocyst to the uterine lining, which occurs 7 to 9 days after fertilization.

amnion The inner membrane that encloses the prenatal organism.

amniotic fluid The fluid that fills the amnion, helping to keep temperature constant and to provide a cushion against jolts caused by the mother's movement.

chorion The outer membrane that surrounds the amnion and sends out tiny, fingerlike villi, from which the placenta begins to develop.

placenta The organ that permits exchange of nutrients and waste products between the bloodstreams of the mother and the embryo, while also preventing the mother's and embryo's blood from mixing directly.

TABLE 3.3	**Major Milestones of Prenatal Development**

TRIMESTER	PERIOD	WEEKS	LENGTH AND WEIGHT	MAJOR EVENTS
First	Zygote	1		The one-celled zygote multiplies and forms a blastocyst.
		2		The blastocyst burrows into the uterine lining. Structures that feed and protect the developing organism begin to form—*amnion, chorion, yolk sac, placenta,* and *umbilical cord.*
	Embryo	3–4	¼ inch (6 mm)	A primitive brain and spinal cord appear. Heart, muscles, ribs, backbone, and digestive tract begin to develop.
		5–8	1 inch (2.5 cm); ½ ounce (4 g)	Many external body structures (face, arms, legs, toes, fingers) and internal organs form. The sense of touch begins to develop, and the embryo can move.
	Fetus	9–12	3 inches (7.6 cm); less than 1 ounce (28 g)	Rapid increase in size begins. Nervous system, organs, and muscles become organized and connected, and new behavioral capacities (kicking, thumb sucking, mouth opening, and rehearsal of breathing) appear. External genitals are well-formed, and the fetus's sex is evident.
Second		13–24	12 inches (30 cm); 1.8 pounds (820 g)	The fetus continues to enlarge rapidly. In the middle of this period, fetal movements can be felt by the mother. Vernix and lanugo keep the fetus's skin from chapping in the amniotic fluid. Most of the brain's neurons are present by 24 weeks. Eyes are sensitive to light, and the fetus reacts to sound.
Third		25–38	20 inches (50 cm); 7.5 pounds (3,400 g)	The fetus has a good chance of survival if born during this time. Size increases. Lungs mature. Rapid brain development causes sensory and behavioral capacities to expand. In the middle of this period, a layer of fat is added under the skin. Antibodies are transmitted from mother to fetus to protect against disease. Most fetuses rotate into an upside-down position in preparation for birth.

Source: Moore & Persaud, 2003.

Photos (from top to bottom): © Claude Cortier/Photo Researchers, Inc.; © G. Moscoso/Photo Researchers, Inc.; © John Watney/Photo Researchers, Inc.; © James Stevenson/Photo Researchers, Inc.; © Lennart Nilsson/*A Child Is Born*/Bonniers.

umbilical cord The long cord that connects the prenatal organism to the placenta, delivering nutrients and removing waste products.

The placenta is connected to the developing organism by the **umbilical cord.** In the period of the zygote, it first appears as a primitive body stalk, but during the course of pregnancy, it grows to a length of 1 to 3 feet. The umbilical cord contains one large vein that delivers blood loaded with nutrients and two arteries that remove waste products. The force of blood flowing through the cord keeps it firm, much like a garden hose, so it seldom tangles while the embryo, like a space-walking astronaut, floats freely in its fluid-filled chamber (Moore & Persaud, 2003).

By the end of the period of the zygote, the developing organism has found food and shelter. Already, it is a very complex being. These dramatic beginnings take place before most mothers know they are pregnant.

FIGURE 3.4

Cross-section of the uterus, showing detail of the placenta. The embryo's blood flows from the umbilical cord arteries into the chorionic villi and returns via the umbilical cord vein. The mother's blood circulates in spaces surrounding the chronic villi. A membrane between the two blood supplies permits food and oxygen to be delivered and waste products to be carried away. The two blood supplies do not mix directly. The umbilical arteries carry oxygen-poor blood (shown in blue) to the placenta, and the umbilical vein carries oxygen-rich blood (shown in red) to the fetus. (Adapted from K. l. Moore and T. V. N. Persaud, 2003, *Before We Are Born*, 6th ed., Philadelphia: Saunders, p. 95. Reprinted by permission of the publisher and authors.)

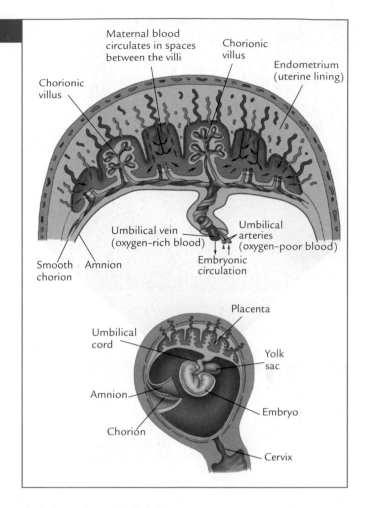

The Period of the Embryo

The period of the **embryo** lasts from implantation through the eighth week of pregnancy. During these brief 6 weeks, the most rapid prenatal changes take place, as the groundwork is laid for all body structures and internal organs. Because all parts of the body are forming, the embryo is especially vulnerable to interference with healthy development. But a short time span of embryonic growth helps limit opportunities for serious harm.

LAST HALF OF THE FIRST MONTH ■ In the first week of this period, the embryonic disk forms three layers of cells: (1) the *ectoderm,* which will become the nervous system and skin; (2) the *mesoderm,* from which will develop the muscles, skeleton, circulatory system, and other internal organs; and (3) the *endoderm,* which will become the digestive system, lungs, urinary tract, and glands. These three layers give rise to all parts of the body.

At first, the nervous system develops fastest. The ectoderm folds over to form the **neural tube,** or spinal cord. At 3½ weeks, the top swells to form the brain. Production of *neurons* (nerve cells that store and transmit information) begins deep inside the neural tube at an astounding pace—more than 250,000 per minute. Once formed, neurons travel along tiny threads to their permanent locations, where they will form the major parts of the brain (Nelson, Thomas, & de Haan, 2006).

While the nervous system is developing, the heart begins to pump blood, and muscles, backbone, ribs, and digestive tract start to appear. At the end of the first month, the curled embryo— only ¼ inch long—consists of millions of organized groups of cells with specific functions.

THE SECOND MONTH ■ In the second month, growth continues rapidly. The eyes, ears, nose, jaw, and neck form. Tiny buds become arms, legs, fingers, and toes. Internal organs are more distinct: The intestines grow, the heart develops separate chambers, and the liver and spleen take over production of blood cells so that the yolk sac is no longer needed. Changing body proportions cause the embryo's posture to become more upright. Now 1 inch long and ⅐ of an ounce in weight, the embryo can sense its world. It responds to touch, particularly in the mouth area and on the soles of the feet. And it can move, although its tiny flutters are still too light to be felt by the mother (Moore & Persaud, 2003).

embryo The prenatal organism from 2 to 8 weeks after conception—the period when the groundwork is laid for all body structures and internal organs.

neural tube The primitive spinal cord that develops from the ectoderm, the top of which swells to form the brain during the period of the embryo.

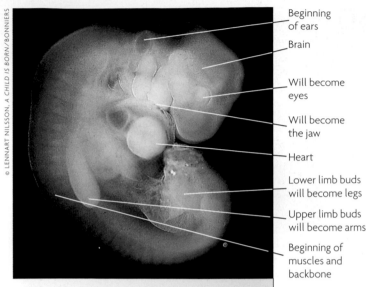

Beginning of ears

Brain

Will become eyes

Will become the jaw

Heart

Lower limb buds will become legs

Upper limb buds will become arms

Beginning of muscles and backbone

Period of the embryo: fourth week. In actual size, this 4-week-old embryo is only ¼ inch long, but many body structures have begun to form.

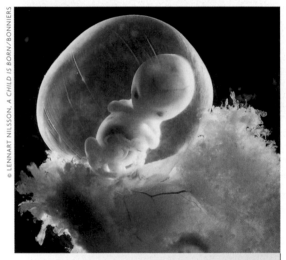

Period of the embryo: seventh week. The embryo's posture is more upright. Body structures—eyes, nose, arms, legs, and internal organs—are more distinct. An embryo of this age responds to touch. It also can move, although at less than one inch long and an ounce in weight, it is still too tiny to be felt by the mother.

fetus The prenatal organism from the ninth week to the end of pregnancy—the period when body structures are completed and dramatic growth in size occurs.

trimesters Three equal time periods in prenatal development, each lasting three months.

The Period of the Fetus

The period of the **fetus,** from the ninth week to the end of pregnancy, is the longest prenatal period. During this "growth and finishing" phase, the developing organism increases rapidly in size, especially from the ninth to the twentieth week.

THE THIRD MONTH ■ In the third month, the organs, muscles, and nervous system start to become organized and connected. When the brain signals, the fetus kicks, bends its arms, forms a fist, curls its toes, opens its mouth, and even sucks its thumb. The tiny lungs begin to expand and contract in an early rehearsal of breathing movements. By the twelfth week, the external genitals are well-formed, and the sex of the fetus is evident (Sadler, 2006). Using ultrasound, Yolanda's doctor could see that she would have a boy (although Yolanda and Jay asked not to be told the fetus's sex). Other finishing touches appear, such as fingernails, toenails, tooth buds, and eyelids that open and close. The heartbeat is now stronger and can be heard through a stethoscope.

Prenatal development is sometimes divided into **trimesters,** or three equal time periods. At the end of the third month, the first trimester is complete.

THE SECOND TRIMESTER ■ By the middle of the second trimester, between 17 and 20 weeks, the new being has grown large enough that the mother can feel its movements. A white, cheeselike substance called **vernix** covers the skin, protecting it from chapping during the long months spent in the amniotic fluid. White, downy hair called **lanugo** also appears, helping the vernix stick to the skin.

At the end of the second trimester, many organs are well-developed. And most of the brain's billions of neurons are in place; few will be produced after this time. However, *glial cells,* which support and feed the neurons, continue to increase at a rapid rate throughout the remaining months of pregnancy, as well as after birth. Consequently, brain weight increases tenfold from the twentieth week until birth (Roelfsema et al., 2004).

Brain growth means new behavioral capacities. The 20-week-old fetus can be stimulated as well as irritated by sounds. And if a doctor looks inside the uterus using fetoscopy (see Chapter 2, page 64), fetuses try to shield their eyes from the light with their hands, indicating that the sense of sight has begun to emerge (Moore & Persaud, 2003). Still, a fetus born at this time cannot survive. Its lungs are immature, and the brain cannot yet control breathing movements or body temperature.

THE THIRD TRIMESTER ■ During the final trimester, a fetus born early has a chance for survival. The point at which the baby can first survive, called the **age of viability,** occurs sometime between 22 and 26 weeks (Moore & Persaud, 2003). A baby born between the seventh and eighth month, however, usually needs oxygen assistance to breathe. Although the brain's respiratory center is now mature, tiny air sacs in the lungs are not yet ready to inflate and exchange carbon dioxide for oxygen.

During the last three months, the brain continues to make great strides. The *cerebral cortex,* the seat of human intelligence, enlarges. Convolutions and grooves in its surface appear, permitting a dramatic increase in surface area without extensive increase in head size. As a result, maximum prenatal brain growth occurs without the full-term baby's head becoming too large to pass through the birth canal. As neurological organization improves, the fetus spends more time awake. At 20 weeks, the fetal heart rate reveals no periods of alertness. But by 28 weeks, fetuses are awake about 11 percent of the time, a figure that rises to 16 percent just before birth (DiPietro et al., 1996). And between 30 and 34 weeks, fetuses show rhythmic alternations between sleep and wakefulness that gradually increase in organization (Rivkees, 2003).

By the end of pregnancy, the fetus also takes on the beginnings of a personality. Higher fetal activity in the last weeks of pregnancy predicts a more active infant in the first month of life—a relationship that, for boys, persists into early childhood (Groome et al., 1999). Fetal activity is linked in other ways to infant temperament. In one study, more active fetuses during the third trimester became 1-year-olds who could better handle frustration and 2-year-olds who were less fearful, in that they more readily interacted with toys and with an unfamiliar adult in a laboratory (DiPietro et al., 2002). Perhaps fetal activity level is an indicator of healthy neurological development, which fosters adaptability in childhood. The relationships just described, however, are only modest. As we will see in Chapter 7, sensitive caregiving can modify the temperaments of children who have difficulty adapting to new experiences.

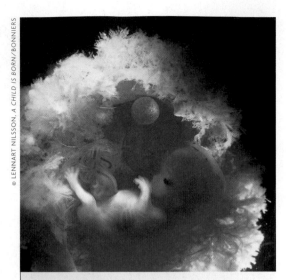

Period of the fetus: eleventh week. The organism increases rapidly in size, and body structures are completed. At 11 weeks, the brain and muscles are better connected. The fetus can kick, bend its arms, open and close its hands and mouth, and suck its thumb. Notice the yolk sac, which shrinks as pregnancy advances. The internal organs have taken over its function of producing blood cells.

The third trimester also brings greater responsiveness to external stimulation. As we will see later when we discuss newborn capacities, from bathing in and swallowing amniotic fluid (its makeup is influenced by the mother's diet), fetuses acquire taste and odor preferences. Between 23 and 30 weeks, connections form between the cerebral cortex and brain regions involved in pain sensitivity. By this time, painkillers should be used in any surgical procedures (Lee et al., 2005). When Yolanda turned on an electric mixer, the fetus reacted with a forceful startle. And by 28 weeks, fetuses blink their eyes in reaction to nearby sounds (Kisilevsky & Low, 1998; Saffran, Werker, & Werner, 2006).

Within the next 6 weeks, fetuses distinguish the tone and rhythm of different voices and sounds: They show systematic heart rate changes in response to a male versus a female speaker, to the mother's voice versus a stranger's, and to a simple familiar melody (descending tones) versus an unfamiliar melody (ascending tones) (Granier-Deferre et al., 2003; Huotilainen et al., 2005; Kisilevsky et al., 2003; Lecanuet et al., 1993). And in one clever study, mothers read aloud Dr. Seuss's lively book *The Cat in the Hat* each day during the last 6 weeks of pregnancy. After birth, their infants learned to turn on recordings of the mother's voice by sucking on nipples. They sucked hardest to hear *The Cat in the Hat*—the sound they had come to know while still in the womb (DeCasper & Spence, 1986).

TAKE A MOMENT... On the basis of these findings, would you recommend that expectant mothers provide fetuses with certain kinds of stimulation to enhance later mental development? Notice how risky it is to draw such conclusions. First, specific forms of fetal stimulation, such as reading aloud or playing classical music, are unlikely to have a long-lasting impact on cognitive development because of the developing child's constantly changing capacities and experiences, which can override the impact of fetal stimulation (Lecanuet, Granier-Deferre, & DeCasper, 2005). Second, although ordinary stimulation contributes to the functioning of sensory systems, excessive input can be dangerous. For example, animal studies indicate that a sensitive period (see page 23 in Chapter 1) exists in which the fetal ear is highly susceptible to injury. During that time, prolonged exposure to sounds that are harmless to the mature ear can permanently damage fetal inner-ear structures (Rubel & Ryals, 1982, 1983).

In the final three months, the fetus gains more than 5 pounds and grows 7 inches. As it fills the uterus, it gradually moves less often. In addition, brain development, which enables the organism to inhibit behavior, contributes to a decline in physical activity (DiPietro et al.,

vernix A white, cheeselike substance that covers the fetus, preventing the skin from chapping due to constant exposure to amniotic fluid.

lanugo White, downy hair that covers the entire body of the fetus, helping the vernix stick to the skin.

age of viability The earliest age at which the fetus can survive if born prematurely, occurring sometime between 22 and 26 weeks.

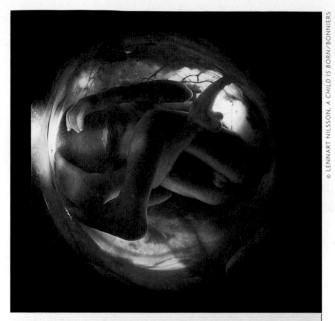

Period of the fetus: twenty-second week This fetus is almost a foot long and weighs slightly more than a pound. Its movements can be felt easily by the mother and other family members who place a hand on her abdomen. The fetus has reached the age of viability; if born, it has a slim chance of surviving.

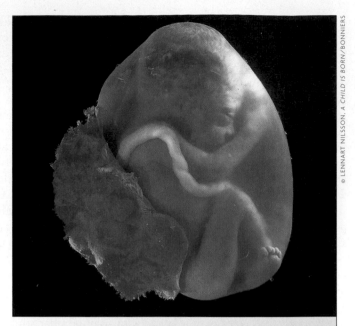

Period of the fetus: thirty-sixth week. This fetus fills the uterus. To support its need for nourishment, the umbilical cord and placenta have grown large. Notice the vernix (cheeselike substance) on the skin, which protects it from chapping. The fetus has accumulated a layer of fat to assist with temperature regulation after birth. In two more weeks, it will be full-term.

1996). In the eighth month, a layer of fat is added to assist with temperature regulation. The fetus also receives antibodies from the mother's blood to protect against illnesses, since the newborn's own immune system will not work well until several months after birth. In the last weeks, most fetuses assume an upside-down position, partly because of the shape of the uterus and partly because the head is heavier than the feet. Growth slows, and birth is about to take place.

Ask Yourself

Review   Why is the period of the embryo regarded as the most dramatic prenatal phase? Why is the period of the fetus called the "growth and finishing" phase?

Apply   Amy, who is two months pregnant, wonders how the developing organism is being fed and what parts of the body have formed. "I don't look

pregnant yet, so does that mean not much development has taken place?" she asks. How would you respond to Amy?

Connect   How is brain development related to fetal capacities and behavior? What implications do individual differences in fetal behavior have for the baby's temperament after birth?

Prenatal Environmental Influences

Although the prenatal environment is far more constant than the world outside the womb, a great many factors can affect the embryo and fetus. Yolanda and Jay learned that they could do a great deal to create a safe environment for development before birth. Let's look at some factors that can influence the prenatal environment.

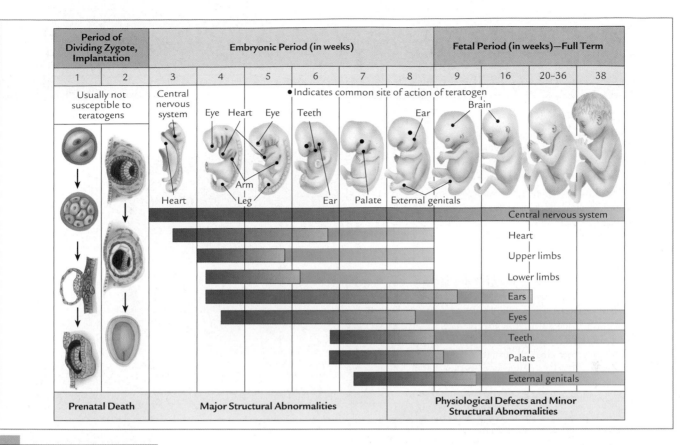

FIGURE 3.5

Sensitive periods in prenatal development. Each organ or structure has a sensitive period, during which its development may be disturbed. Blue horizontal bars indicate highly sensitive periods. Green horizontal bars indicate periods that are somewhat less sensitive to teratogens, although damage can occur. (Adapted from K. L. Moore & T. V. N. Persaud, 2003, *Before We Are Born*, 6th ed., Philadelphia: Saunders, p. 130. Reprinted by permission of the publisher and authors.)

Teratogens

The term **teratogen** refers to any environmental agent that causes damage during the prenatal period. It comes from the Greek word *teras,* meaning "malformation" or "monstrosity." Scientists selected this label because they first learned about harmful prenatal influences from cases in which babies had been profoundly damaged. But the harm done by teratogens is not always simple and straightforward. It depends on the following factors:

- *Dose.* As we discuss particular teratogens, we will see that larger doses over longer time periods usually have more negative effects.
- *Heredity.* The genetic makeup of the mother and the developing organism plays an important role. Some individuals are better able than others to withstand harmful environments.
- *Other negative influences.* The presence of several negative factors at once, such as poor nutrition, lack of medical care, and additional teratogens, can worsen the impact of a single harmful agent.
- *Age.* The effects of teratogens vary with the age of the organism at time of exposure. We can best understand this last idea if we again think of the *sensitive period* concept. Recall that a sensitive period is a limited time span in which a part of the body or a behavior is biologically prepared to develop rapidly. During that time, it is especially sensitive to its surroundings. If the environment is harmful, then damage occurs, and recovery is difficult and sometimes impossible.

Figure 3.5 summarizes prenatal sensitive periods. Look at it carefully, and you will see that some parts of the body, such as the brain and eye, have long sensitive periods that extend

teratogen Any environmental agent that causes damage during the prenatal period.

Biology and Environment

The Prenatal Environment and Health in Later Life

When Michael entered the world 55 years ago, 6 weeks premature and weighing only 4 pounds, the doctor delivering him wasn't sure he would make it. Michael not only survived but enjoyed good health until his mid-forties, when, during a routine medical checkup, he was diagnosed with high blood pressure and type 2 diabetes. Michael had no apparent risk factors for these conditions: He wasn't overweight, didn't smoke, and didn't eat high-fat foods. Nor did the illnesses run in his family. Could the roots of Michael's health problems date back to his prenatal development?

Increasing evidence suggests that prenatal environmental factors—ones that are not toxic (as are tobacco or alcohol) but rather fairly subtle, such as the flow of nutrients and hormones across the placenta—can affect an individual's health decades later.

Low Birth Weight and Heart Disease, Stroke, and Diabetes

Carefully controlled animal experiments reveal that a poorly nourished, underweight fetus experiences changes in body structure and function that greatly increase the risk of cardiovascular disease in adulthood (Franco et al., 2002). To explore this relationship in humans, researchers tapped public records, gathering information on the birth weights of 15,000

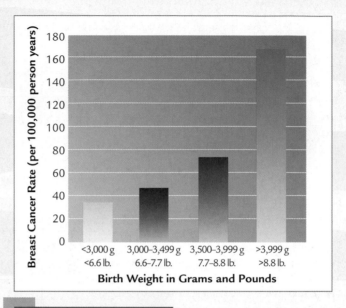

FIGURE 3.6

Relationship of birth weight to breast cancer risk in adulthood. In a study of more than 2,000 British births with follow-ups in adulthood, birth weight predicted breast cancer incidence after many other prenatal and postnatal health risks were controlled. The breast cancer risk was especially high for women whose birth weights were greater than 3,999 grams, or 8.8 pounds. (Adapted from Silva et al., 2004.)

British men and women and the occurrence of disease in middle adulthood. Those weighing less than 5 pounds at birth had a 50 percent greater chance of dying of heart disease and

throughout prenatal development. Other sensitive periods, such as those for the limbs and palate, are much shorter. Figure 3.5 also indicates that we can make some general statements about the timing of harmful influences. In the period of the zygote, before implantation, teratogens rarely have any impact. If they do, the tiny mass of cells is usually so completely damaged that it dies. The embryonic period is the time when serious defects are most likely to occur because the foundations for all body parts are being laid down. During the fetal period, teratogenic damage is usually minor. However, organs such as the brain, ears, eyes, teeth, and genitals can still be strongly affected.

The effects of teratogens go beyond immediate physical damage. Some health effects are subtle and delayed. As the Biology and Environment box above illustrates, they may not show up for decades. Furthermore, psychological consequences may occur indirectly, as a result of physical damage. For example, a defect resulting from drugs the mother took during pregnancy can affect others' reactions to the child as well as the child's ability to explore the environment. Over time, parent–child interaction, peer relations, and opportunities to explore may suffer. These experiences, in turn, can have far-reaching consequences for cognitive, emotional, and social development.

stroke, even after SES and a variety of other health risks were controlled. The connection between birth weight and cardiovascular disease was strongest for people whose weight-to-length ratio at birth was very low—a sign of prenatal growth stunting (Godfrey & Barker, 2000; Martyn, Barker, & Osmond, 1996).

In other large-scale studies, a consistent link between low birth weight and heart disease, stroke, and diabetes in middle adulthood has emerged—for both sexes and in diverse countries, including Finland, India, Jamaica, and the United States (Barker, 2002; Fowden, Giussani, & Forhead, 2005; Godfrey & Barker, 2001). Smallness itself does not cause later health problems; rather, researchers believe, complex factors associated with it are involved.

Some speculate that a poorly nourished fetus diverts large amounts of blood to the brain, causing organs in the abdomen, such as the liver and kidneys (involved in controlling cholesterol and blood pressure), to be undersized (Hales & Ozanne, 2003). The result is heightened later risk for heart disease and stroke. In the case of diabetes, inadequate prenatal nutrition may permanently impair functioning of the pancreas, leading glucose intolerance to rise as the person ages (Wu et al., 2004). Yet another hypothesis, supported by both animal and human research, is that the malfunctioning placentas of some expectant mothers permit high levels of stress hormones to reach the fetus, which retards fetal growth, increases fetal blood pressure, and promotes hyperglycemia (excess blood sugar), predisposing the developing person to later disease (Stocker, Arch, & Cawthorne, 2005).

Finally, prenatally growth-stunted babies often gain excessive weight in childhood, once

Prenatal environmental factors—even subtle ones, such as the flow of nutrients across the placenta—can affect an individual's health in later life. Extremes of both low and high birth weight are associated with diseases of middle adulthood. Individuals who were low- or high-weight at birth should be attentive to health and lifestyle factors that may protect them against these diseases.

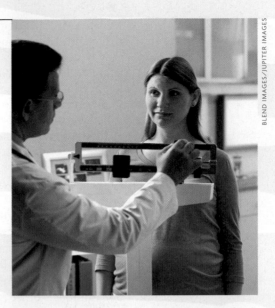

they have access to plentiful food. This excess weight usually persists, greatly increasing the risk of diabetes (Hyppönen, Power, & Smith, 2003).

High Birth Weight and Breast Cancer

The other prenatal growth extreme—high birth weight—is related to breast cancer, the most common malignancy in adult women (Ahlgren et al., 2004; Vatten et al., 2002). In one study of more than 2,000 British women, high birth weight—especially weight above 8.8 pounds—was associated with a greatly increased incidence of breast cancer, even after other cancer risks were controlled (see Figure 3.6) (Silva et al., 2004). Researchers suspect that the culprit is excessive maternal estrogen during pregnancy, which promotes large fetal size and alters beginning breast tissue so that it may respond to estrogen in adulthood by becoming malignant.

High birth weight is also associated with increases in digestive and lymphatic cancers in both men and women (McCormack et al., 2005). As yet, the reasons are unclear.

Prevention

The relationships between prenatal development and later-life illnesses emerging in research do not mean that the illnesses are inevitable. Rather, prenatal environmental conditions *influence* adult health, and the steps we take to protect our health can prevent prenatal risks from becoming reality. Researchers advise individuals who were low-weight at birth to get regular medical checkups and to be attentive to diet, weight, fitness, and stress—controllable factors that contribute to heart disease and adult-onset diabetes. And high-birth-weight women should be conscientious about breast self-exams and mammograms, which permit early detection—and, in many cases, cure—of breast cancer.

Notice how an important idea about development that we discussed in earlier chapters is at work here: *bidirectional influences* between child and environment. Now let's take a look at what scientists have discovered about a variety of teratogens.

PRESCRIPTION AND NONPRESCRIPTION DRUGS ■ In the early 1960s, the world learned a tragic lesson about drugs and prenatal development. At that time, a sedative called **thalidomide** was widely available in Canada, Europe, and South America. When taken by mothers 4 to 6 weeks after conception, thalidomide produced gross deformities of the embryo's developing arms and legs and, less frequently, damage to the ears, heart, kidneys, and genitals. About 7,000 infants worldwide were affected (Moore & Persaud, 2003). As children exposed to thalidomide grew older, many scored below average in intelligence. Perhaps the drug damaged the central nervous system directly. Or the child-rearing conditions of these severely deformed youngsters may have impaired their intellectual development.

thalidomide A sedative widely available in the early 1960s that produced gross deformities of the embryo's arms and legs when taken by expectant mothers 4 to 6 weeks after conception.

Currently, thalidomide is being prescribed to treat *erythema nodosum,* a rare but painful skin inflammation associated with flulike symptoms. It also may prove useful for a variety of other diseases. Consequently, some researchers worry about a resurgence of thalidomide-caused birth defects (Ances, 2002). Turn to the Social Issues: Health box on the following page to find out about a drug, prescribed to treat severe acne, that has sparked similar concerns.

Another medication, a synthetic hormone called *diethylstilbestrol (DES),* was widely prescribed between 1945 and 1970 to prevent miscarriages. As daughters of these mothers reached adolescence and young adulthood, they showed unusually high rates of cancer of the vagina, malformations of the uterus, and infertility. When they tried to have children, their pregnancies more often resulted in prematurity, low birth weight, and miscarriage than those of non-DES-exposed women. Young men showed an increased risk of genital abnormalities and cancer of the testes (Hammes & Laitman, 2003; Palmer et al., 2001).

Any drug with a molecule small enough to penetrate the placental barrier can enter the embryonic or fetal bloodstream. Nevertheless, many pregnant women continue to take over-the-counter medications without consulting their doctors. Aspirin is one of the most common. Several studies suggest that regular aspirin use is linked to low birth weight, infant death around the time of birth, poorer motor development, and lower intelligence test scores in early childhood, although other research fails to confirm these findings (Barr et al., 1990; Kozer et al., 2003; Streissguth et al., 1987). Coffee, tea, cola, and cocoa contain another frequently consumed drug, caffeine. Heavy caffeine intake (more than three cups of coffee per day) is associated with low birth weight, miscarriage, and newborn withdrawal symptoms, such as irritability and vomiting (Klebanoff et al., 2002; Vik et al., 2003). And antidepressant medication taken during the third trimester is linked to increased risk of birth complications, including respiratory distress (Lattimore et al., 2005).

Because children's lives are involved, we must take findings like these seriously. At the same time, we cannot be sure that these frequently used drugs actually cause the problems just mentioned. Often mothers take more than one drug. If the embryo or fetus is injured, it is hard to tell which drug might be responsible or whether other factors correlated with drug taking are really at fault. Until we have more information, the safest course is the one Yolanda took: Avoid these drugs entirely. Unfortunately, many women do not know that they are pregnant during the early weeks of the embryonic period, when exposure to medications (and other teratogens) can be of greatest threat.

ILLEGAL DRUGS ■ The use of highly addictive mood-altering drugs, such as cocaine and heroin, has become more widespread, especially in poverty-stricken inner-city areas, where these drugs provide a temporary escape from a daily life of hopelessness. As many as 3 to 7 percent of American and Canadian babies born in large cities, and 1 to 2 percent of all North American newborns, have been exposed to cocaine prenatally (British Columbia Reproductive Care Program, 2003; Lester et al., 2001).

Babies born to users of cocaine, heroin, or methadone (a less addictive drug used to wean people away from heroin) are at risk for a wide variety of problems, including prematurity, low birth weight, physical defects, breathing difficulties, and death around the time of birth (Behnke et al., 2001; Schuetze & Eiden, 2006; Walker, Rosenberg, & Balaban-Gil, 1999). In addition, these infants arrive drug-addicted. They often are feverish and irritable at birth and have trouble sleeping, and their cries are abnormally shrill and piercing—a common symptom among stressed newborns (Bauer et al., 2005). When mothers with many problems of their own must care for these babies, who are difficult to calm, cuddle, and feed, behavior problems are likely to persist.

Throughout the first year, heroin- and methadone-exposed infants are less attentive to the environment than nonexposed babies, and their motor development is slow. After infancy, some children get better, while others remain jittery and inattentive. The kind of parenting they receive seems to explain why problems last for some of these youngsters but not for others (Cosden, Peerson, & Elliott, 1997).

Evidence on cocaine suggests that some prenatally exposed babies develop lasting difficulties. Cocaine constricts the blood vessels, causing oxygen delivered to the developing organism to fall for 15 minutes following a high dose. It also can alter the production and functioning of

Social Issues: Health

Can a Thalidomide-Like Tragedy Occur Again?
The Teratogenic Effects of Accutane

Twenty-five-year-old Corrine, several weeks pregnant, suffered from severe, disfiguring acne. After several milder medications failed to clear up the inflamed, hard bumps covering her face, Corrine's dermatologist prescribed the drug Accutane, also known by the generic name *isotretinoin*—a vitamin A derivative. Within days, Corinne's acne receded.

We depend on vitamin A for the health of our skin, hair, mucous membranes, and immune system. But in excess, vitamin A and its derivatives are toxic to the developing organism. Taken during the first trimester of pregnancy, Accutane causes extensive damage, including eye, ear, skull, brain, heart, central nervous system, and immune system abnormalities (Honein, Paulozzi, & Erickson, 2001). Corrine's baby was born with multiple defects, including heart disease, facial deformities, and hydrocephalus (accumulation of excess fluid, which compresses and damages the brain). After extensive treatment, including heart surgery, he died at 9 weeks of age.

Accutane is the most widely used teratogenic drug since the thalidomide disaster of nearly a half-century ago (Accutane Action Group Forum, 2003). Since its release in the early 1980s, 12 million people in some 100 countries have been treated with it. Hundreds of thousands of U.S. and Canadian women of childbearing age currently take Accutane, and the number of prescriptions is increasing. Despite its established harmful effects, more than 2,300 reports of drug-exposed pregnancies have occurred in the United States alone. Miscarriage rates among affected women are high, and many others choose to end their pregnancies once they learn about possible prenatal damage. Although the number of babies born with Accutane-caused malformations is not known, at least 162 documented American cases exist (Andresen, 2006).

Accutane's packaging warns users to avoid pregnancy and also states that the drug must not be used by women who are pregnant. Furthermore, early case reports of infants damaged by the drug caused the manufacturer to step up efforts to get doctors to inform patients about the importance of abstaining from intercourse or using two methods of birth control if taking Accutane. The drug

company will even pay for birth control counseling and contraceptives. Why, then, do Accutane-exposed pregnancies continue to occur?

To find out, researchers interviewed women who became pregnant while taking Accutane. Findings revealed that most did not use two forms of contraception, and more than half reported at least one instance in which they used none at all! Either their doctors had failed to communicate the risks, or the patients had not been receptive to the warnings. Furthermore, only half the women had acne severe enough to warrant Accutane treatment (Honein, Paulozzi, & Erickson, 2001). Doctors were overprescribing the drug, using it even to treat mild skin inflammations. Other evidence indicates that some women purchase the medication in foreign countries, use a "leftover" prescription, or "borrow" medication from a friend, without following manufacturer recommendations for monthly pregnancy testing and effective birth control (Robertson et al., 2002).

Unlike thalidomide, which was released before its catastrophic consequences were known, Accutane's teratogenic effects were established when the drug was first marketed. Yet barriers to preventing prenatal exposure persist. Women who become pregnant without planning (about half of all U.S. and Canadian expectant mothers) are less likely to avoid drug taking and less responsive to teratogen counseling (Atanackovic & Koren, 1999). And some patients misinterpret the teratogen symbol that appears on bottles of Accutane and thalidomide: They take it to mean that a woman cannot get pregnant while taking the drug—a conclusion that increases the risk of exposures during pregnancy (Honein et al., 2002).

Notice how a combination of factors—biological, psychological, and environmental—jointly contributes to Accutane prenatal risks. Consequently, multifaceted efforts are needed to prevent Accutane from spiraling into a thalidomide-like tragedy. These include:

■ Restriction of teratogenic drugs to treatment of severe medical conditions, for which there are no alternatives

■ Improved public and patient education about teratogenic effects and protective strategies
■ Interventions that promote widespread, effective contraceptive use

In 2005, the U.S. federal government required that doctors enter every patient who takes Accutane into an Internet database. Before a prescription can be filled, patients must verify that their doctors counseled them about risks and performed pregnancy tests. Patients must also pledge that they will not share Accutane with anyone and will stop taking it if they get pregnant, miss a menstrual period, or stop using two birth control methods (Healy, 2005).

Accutane is the most widely used, potent teratogenic drug in the industrialized world. If a woman becomes pregnant and takes the drug during the first trimester, her baby is likely to suffer from multiple, severe physical defects. Accutane-exposed pregnancies continue to occur because doctors sometimes fail to communicate the risks and patients are not always receptive to warnings. And many women misinterpret the teratogen symbol that appears on Accutane bottles as indicating that a woman cannot get pregnant while using the drug!

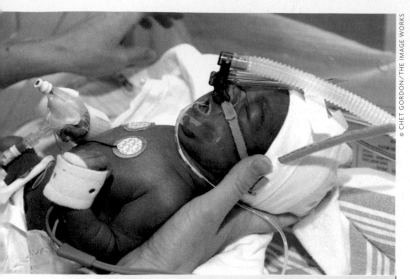

This 3-day-old infant, who was born many weeks before his due date and is underweight, breathes with the aid of a respirator. Prematurity and low birth weight can result from a variety of environmental influences during pregnancy, including maternal drug use and cigarette smoking. Babies born prematurely are at increased risk for later physical, emotional, and behavioral problems and school learning deficits.

fetal alcohol spectrum disorder (FASD) A range of physical, mental, and behavioral outcomes caused by prenatal alcohol exposure.

fetal alcohol syndrome (FAS) The most severe form of fetal alcohol spectrum disorder, distinguished by slow physical growth, facial abnormalities, and brain injury; usually seen in children whose mothers consumed large amounts of alcohol during most or all of pregnancy.

partial fetal alcohol syndrome (p-FAS) A form of fetal alcohol spectrum disorder characterized by facial abnormalities and brain injury, but less severe than fetal alcohol syndrome; usually seen in children whose mothers drank alcohol in smaller quantities during pregnancy.

alcohol-related neuro-developmental disorder (ARND) The least severe form of fetal alcohol spectrum disorder, involving brain injury, but with typical physical growth and absence of facial abnormalities.

neurons and the chemical balance in the fetus's brain. These effects may contribute to an array of cocaine-associated physical defects, including eye, bone, genital, urinary tract, kidney, and heart deformities; hemorrhages and seizures; and severe growth retardation (Covington et al., 2002; Feng, 2005; Mayes, 1999). Several studies report perceptual, motor, attention, memory, and language problems in infancy that persist into the preschool years (Lester et al., 2003; Noland et al., 2005; Singer et al., 2002a, 2002b, 2004).

But other investigations reveal no major negative effects of prenatal cocaine exposure (Behnke et al., 2006; Frank et al., 2005; Hurt et al., 2005). These contradictory findings indicate how difficult it is to isolate the precise damage caused by illegal drugs. Cocaine users vary greatly in the amount, potency, and purity of the cocaine they ingest. Also, they often take several drugs, display other high-risk behaviors, suffer from poverty and other stresses, and engage in insensitive caregiving. The joint impact of these factors worsens outcomes for children (Alessandri, Bendersky, & Lewis, 1998; Carta et al., 2001). But researchers have yet to determine exactly what accounts for findings of cocaine-related damage in some studies but not in others.

Another illegal drug, marijuana, is used more widely than heroin and cocaine. Studies examining its relationship to low birth weight and prematurity reveal mixed findings (Fried, 1993). Several researchers have linked prenatal marijuana exposure to smaller head size (a measure of brain growth); to sleep, attention, memory, and academic achievement difficulties and to depression in childhood; and to poorer problem-solving performance in adolescence (Dahl et al., 1995; Goldschmidt et al., 2004; Gray et al., 2005; Huizink & Mulder, 2006). As with cocaine, however, lasting consequences are not well-established. Overall, the effects of illegal drugs are far less consistent than the impact of two legal substances to which we now turn: tobacco and alcohol.

TOBACCO ■ Although smoking has declined in Western nations, an estimated 12 percent of American women and 17 percent of Canadian women smoke during their pregnancies (Martin et al., 2006; Millar & Hill, 2004). The best-known effect of smoking during the prenatal period is low birth weight. But the likelihood of other serious consequences, such as miscarriage, prematurity, impaired heart rate and breathing during sleep, infant death, and asthma and cancer later in childhood, is also increased (Franco et al., 2000; Jaakkola & Gissler, 2004). The more cigarettes a mother smokes, the greater the chances that her baby will be affected. If a pregnant woman decides to stop smoking at any time, even during the last trimester, she immediately reduces the likelihood that her infant will be born underweight and suffer from future problems (Klesges et al., 2001).

Even when a baby of a smoking mother appears to be born in good physical condition, slight behavioral abnormalities may threaten the child's development. Newborns of smoking mothers are less attentive to sounds, display more muscle tension, are more excitable when touched and visually stimulated, and more often have colic (persistent crying)—findings that suggest subtle negative effects on brain development (Law et al., 2003; Sondergaard et al., 2002). Furthermore, an unresponsive, restless baby may not evoke the kind of interaction from adults that promotes healthy psychological development. Some studies report that prenatally exposed children and adolescents have shorter attention spans, poorer memories, lower mental test scores, and more behavior problems (Fried, Watkinson, & Gray, 2003; Huizink & Mulder, 2006; Thapar et al., 2003). However, other factors closely associated with smoking, such as lower maternal education and income levels, may contribute to these outcomes (Ernst, Moolchan, & Robinson, 2001).

Exactly how can smoking harm the fetus? Nicotine, the addictive substance in tobacco, constricts blood vessels, lessens blood flow to the uterus, and causes the placenta to grow abnormally. This reduces the transfer of nutrients, so the fetus gains weight poorly. Also, nicotine raises the concentration of carbon monoxide in the bloodstreams of both mother and fetus. Carbon monoxide displaces oxygen from red blood cells, damaging the central nervous system and slowing body growth in the fetuses of laboratory animals (Friedman, 1996). Similar effects may occur in humans.

From one-third to one-half of nonsmoking pregnant women are "passive smokers" because their husbands, relatives, or co-workers use cigarettes. Passive smoking is also related to low birth weight, infant death, childhood respiratory illnesses, and possible long-term impairments in attention and learning (Hanke, Sobala, & Kalinka, 2004; Makin, Fried, & Watkinson, 1991; Pattenden et al., 2006). Clearly, expectant mothers should avoid smoke-filled environments.

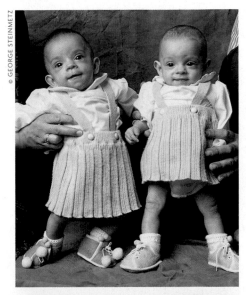

ALCOHOL ■ In his moving book *The Broken Cord*, Michael Dorris (1989), a Dartmouth University anthropology professor, described what it was like to raise his adopted son Abel (called Adam in the book), whose biological mother died of alcohol poisoning shortly after his birth. A Sioux Indian, Abel was born with **fetal alcohol spectrum disorder (FASD)**, a term that encompasses a range of physical, mental, and behavioral outcomes caused by prenatal alcohol exposure. As Table 3.4 on page 112 shows, children with FASD are given one of three diagnoses, which vary in severity:

1. **Fetal alcohol syndrome (FAS)**, distinguished by (a) slow physical growth, (b) a pattern of three facial abnormalities (short eyelid openings; a thin upper lip; a smooth or flattened philtrum, or indentation running from the bottom of the nose to the center of the upper lip), and (c) brain injury, evident in a small head and impairment in at least three areas of functioning—for example, memory, language and communication, attention span and activity level (overactivity), planning and reasoning, motor coordination, or social skills. Other defects—of the eyes, ears, nose, throat, heart, genitals, urinary tract, or immune system—may also be present. Abel was diagnosed as having FAS. As is typical for this disorder, his mother drank heavily throughout pregnancy.

2. **Partial fetal alcohol syndrome (p-FAS)**, characterized by (a) two of the three facial abnormalities just mentioned and (b) brain injury, again evident in at least three areas of impaired functioning. Mothers of children with p-FAS generally drank alcohol in smaller quantities, and children's defects vary with the timing and length of alcohol exposure. Furthermore, recent evidence suggests that paternal alcohol use around the time of conception may alter gene expression (see page 88 in Chapter 2), thereby contributing to symptoms (Abel, 2004).

3. **Alcohol-related neurodevelopmental disorder (ARND)**, in which at least three areas of mental functioning are impaired, despite typical physical growth and absence of facial abnormalities. Again, prenatal alcohol exposure, though confirmed, is less pervasive than in FAS (Chudley et al., 2005; Loock et al., 2005).

(Top) The mother of these twin baby girls drank heavily during pregnancy. Their short eyelid openings, thin upper lip, and smooth philtrum (indentation running from the bottom of the nose to the center of the upper lip) are typical of fetal alcohol syndrome (FAS). (Bottom) The adolescent girl shown here also has symptoms of FAS. Because the prenatal brain damage caused by alcohol is permanent, she has great difficulty learning in school and adapting to everyday challenges.

Even when provided with enriched diets, FAS babies fail to catch up in physical size during infancy or childhood. Mental impairment associated with all three FASD diagnoses is also permanent: In his teens and twenties, Abel Dorris had trouble concentrating and keeping a routine job, and he suffered from poor judgment. For example, he would buy something and not wait for change or wander off in the middle of a task. He died in 1991, at age 23, after being hit by a car.

The more alcohol a woman consumes during pregnancy, the poorer the child's motor coordination, speed of information processing, reasoning, and intelligence and achievement test scores during the preschool and school years (Burden, Jacobson, & Jacobson, 2005; Korkman, Kettunen, & Autti-Raemoe, 2003). In adolescence and early adulthood, FASD is associated with

TABLE 3.4	**Fetal Alcohol Spectrum Disorder: Criteria for Diagnosis**		
	DIAGNOSTIC CATEGORY		
Criteria	**FAS**	**p-FAS**	**ARND**
Slow physical growth	Yes	No	No
Facial abnormalities: • Short eyelid openings • Thin upper lip • Smooth or flattened philtrum	All three are present	Two of the three are present	None are present
Brain injury	Impairment in a minimum of three areas of functioning	Impairment in a minimum of three areas of functioning	Impairment in a minimum of three areas of functioning

Source: Loock et al., 2005.

persisting motor coordination deficits, poor school performance, trouble with the law, inappropriate sexual behavior, alcohol and drug abuse, and lasting mental health problems (Baer et al., 2003; Connor et al., 2006; Howell et al., 2006; Streissguth et al., 2004).

How does alcohol produce its devastating effects? First, it interferes with cell duplication and migration in the primitive neural tube. Brain-imaging research reveals arrested brain growth, structural damage, and abnormalities in the electrical and chemical activity involved in transferring messages from one part of the brain to another (Bookstein et al., 2002; Riley, McGee, & Sowell, 2004). Second, the body uses large quantities of oxygen to metabolize alcohol. A pregnant woman's heavy drinking draws away oxygen that the developing organism needs for cell growth.

About one-fourth of American and Canadian mothers reported drinking some alcohol during their pregnancies. As with heroin and cocaine, alcohol abuse is higher in poverty-stricken women (Bearer et al., 2005; Health Canada, 2006b). On some Native-American and Canadian First Nations reservations, the incidence of FAS is as high as 10 percent (Silverman et al., 2001). Unfortunately, when affected girls later become pregnant, the poor judgment caused by the syndrome often prevents them from understanding why they themselves should avoid alcohol. As a result, the tragic cycle is likely to be repeated in the next generation.

How much alcohol is safe during pregnancy? Even mild drinking, less than one drink per day, is associated with reduced head size and body growth among children followed into adolescence (Day et al., 2002; Jacobson et al., 2004). Recall that other factors—both genetic and environmental—can make some fetuses more vulnerable to teratogens. Therefore, no amount of alcohol is safe. Couples planning a pregnancy and expectant mothers should avoid alcohol entirely.

RADIATION ■ In Chapter 2, we saw that ionizing radiation can cause mutation, damaging DNA in ova and sperm. When mothers are exposed to radiation during pregnancy, the embryo or fetus can suffer additional harm. Defects due to radiation were tragically apparent in the children born to pregnant Japanese women who survived the bombing of Hiroshima and Nagasaki during World War II. Similar abnormalities surfaced in the nine months following the 1986 Chernobyl, Ukraine, nuclear power plant accident. After each disaster, the incidence of miscarriage and babies born with underdeveloped brains, physical deformities, and slow physical growth rose dramatically (Hoffmann, 2001; Schull, 2003).

Even when a radiation-exposed baby seems normal, problems may appear later. For example, even low-level radiation, as the result of industrial leakage or medical X-rays, can increase the risk of childhood cancer (Fattibene et al., 1999). In middle childhood, prenatally exposed Chernobyl children had abnormal brain-wave activity, lower intelligence test scores, and rates of language and emotional disorders two to three times greater than those of nonexposed Russian children. Furthermore, the more tension parents reported, due to forced evacuation from their homes and worries about living in irradiated areas, the poorer their children's emotional functioning (Kolominsky, Igumnov, & Drozdovitch, 1999; Loganovskaja & Loganovsky, 1999). Stressful rearing conditions seemed to combine with the damaging effects of prenatal radiation to impair children's development.

Women should do their best to avoid medical X-rays during pregnancy. If dental, thyroid, chest, or other X-rays are necessary, insisting on the use of an abdominal X-ray shield is a key protective measure.

ENVIRONMENTAL POLLUTION ■ Yolanda and Jay like to refinish antique furniture in their garage, and Jay enjoys growing fruit trees in the backyard. When Yolanda became pregnant, they postponed work on several pieces of furniture, and Jay did not spray the fruit trees in the fall or spring of that year. Continuing to do so, they learned, might expose Yolanda and the embryo or fetus to chemical levels thousands of times greater than judged safe by the federal government.

In industrialized nations, an astounding number of potentially dangerous chemicals are released into the environment. More than 75,000 are in common use in the United States, and many new pollutants are introduced each year. When 10 newborns were randomly selected from U.S. hospitals for analysis of umbilical cord blood, researchers uncovered a startling array of industrial contaminants— 287 in all! They concluded that many babies are "born polluted" by chemicals that not only impair prenatal development but also increase the chances of life-threatening diseases and health problems later on (Houlihan et al., 2005).

One established teratogen is *mercury*. In the 1950s, an industrial plant released waste containing high levels of mercury into a bay providing food and water for the town of Minimata, Japan. Many children born at the time displayed physical deformities, mental retardation, abnormal speech, difficulty in chewing and swallowing, and uncoordinated movements. Autopsies of those who died revealed widespread brain damage. High levels of prenatal mercury exposure disrupt production and migration of neurons (Clarkson, Magos, & Myers, 2003; Hubbs-Tait et al., 2005). Pregnant women are wise to avoid eating long-lived predatory fish, such as swordfish, albacore tuna, and shark, which are heavily contaminated with mercury.

This child's mother was just a few weeks pregnant during the Chernobyl nuclear power plant disaster. Radiation exposure probably is responsible for his limb deformities. He also is at risk for low intelligence and language and emotional disorders.

For many years, *polychlorinated biphenyls (PCBs)* were used to insulate electrical equipment, until research showed that, like mercury, they found their way into waterways and entered the food supply. In Taiwan, prenatal exposure to very high levels of PCBs in rice oil resulted in low birth weight, discolored skin, deformities of the gums and nails, brain-wave abnormalities, and delayed cognitive development (Chen & Hsu, 1994; Chen et al., 1994). Steady, low-level PCB exposure is also harmful. Women who frequently ate PCB-contaminated fish, compared with those who ate little or no fish, had infants with lower birth weights, smaller heads, persisting attention and memory difficulties, and lower intelligence test scores in childhood (Jacobson & Jacobson, 2003; Stewart et al., 2000; Walkowiak et al., 2001).

Another teratogen, *lead,* is present in paint flaking off the walls of old buildings and in certain materials used in industrial occupations. High levels of prenatal lead exposure are consistently related to prematurity, low birth weight, brain damage, and a wide variety of physical defects. Even low levels may be dangerous. In some studies, affected babies showed slightly poorer mental and motor development. In one investigation, unfavorable effects—in the form of increased delinquent and antisocial behaviors—were evident in adolescence (Bellinger, 2005; Dietrich et al., 2001).

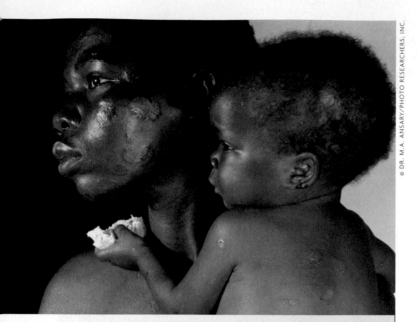

This South African mother and infant have AIDS. Both have extensive ringworm skin rashes. Antiviral drugs that have dramatically reduced prenatal AIDS transmission in Western nations are not widely available in Africa, where most new infections occur, more than half affecting women.

INFECTIOUS DISEASE ■ During her first prenatal visit, Yolanda's doctor asked her if she and Jay had already had measles, mumps, chicken pox, and several other illnesses. In addition, Yolanda was checked for the presence of several infections—and for good reason. As you can see in Table 3.5, certain diseases are major causes of miscarriage and birth defects.

Viruses. Five percent of women catch a virus of some sort while pregnant. Most of these illnesses, such as the common cold and various strains of the flu, have no impact on the embryo or fetus. A few, however, can result in extensive damage. The best known of these is **rubella,** otherwise known as three-day, or German, measles. In the mid-1960s, a worldwide rubella epidemic led to the birth of more than 20,000 North American babies with serious defects. Consistent with the sensitive-period concept, the greatest damage occurs when rubella strikes during the embryonic period. Over 50 percent of infants whose mothers become ill during that time show eye cataracts; deafness; heart, genital, urinary, and intestinal defects; and mental retardation (Eberhart-Phillips, Frederick, & Baron, 1993). Infection during the fetal period is less likely to be harmful, but low birth weight, hearing loss, and bone defects may still occur. And the brain abnormalities resulting from prenatal rubella increase the risk of severe mental illness, especially schizophrenia, in adulthood (Brown & Susser, 2002).

Although vaccination against rubella in infancy and childhood is now routine, about 10 to 20 percent of women in North America and Western Europe lack the rubella antibody. Thus, new disease outbreaks are possible (Health Canada, 2002; Pebody et al., 2000).

The *human immunodeficiency virus (HIV),* which can lead to **acquired immune deficiency syndrome (AIDS),** a disease that destroys the immune system, has infected increasing numbers of women over the past two decades. Currently, women account for one-fourth of cases in North America, Western Europe, and East Asia. Although the incidence of AIDS has declined in industrialized nations, the disease is rampant in developing countries, where 95 percent of new infections occur, more than half of which affect women. In South Africa, for example, one-fourth of all pregnant women are HIV-positive (Kasmauski & Jaret, 2003; Quinn & Overbaugh, 2005). HIV-infected expectant mothers pass the deadly virus to the fetus 20 to 30 percent of the time.

AIDS progresses rapidly in infants. By 6 months, weight loss, diarrhea, and repeated respiratory illnesses are common. The virus also causes brain damage, as indicated by seizures, gradual loss in brain weight, and delayed mental and motor development. Most prenatal AIDS babies survive for only 5 to 8 months after the appearance of these symptoms (O'Rahilly & Müller, 2001). The antiviral drug zidovudine (ZDV) reduces prenatal AIDS transmission by as much as 95 percent, with no harmful consequences of drug treatment for children (Culnane et al., 1999). It has led to a dramatic decline in prenatally acquired AIDS in Western nations, but ZDV is not widely available in impoverished regions of the world (United Nations, 2006).

As Table 3.5 reveals, the developing organism is especially sensitive to the family of herpes viruses, for which no vaccine or treatment exists. Among these, *cytomegalovirus* (the most frequent prenatal infection, transmitted through respiratory or sexual contact, often without symptoms) and *herpes simplex 2* (which is sexually transmitted) are especially dangerous. In both, the virus invades the mother's genital tract, infecting babies either during pregnancy or at birth. Both diseases often have no symptoms, very mild symptoms, or symptoms with which people are unfamiliar, thereby increasing the likelihood of contagion. Pregnant women who are not in a mutually monogamous relationship are at greatest risk.

rubella Three-day, or German, measles; responsible for a wide variety of prenatal abnormalities, especially when it strikes during the embryonic period.

acquired immune deficiency syndrome (AIDS) A viral infection that destroys the immune system and is spread through transfer of body fluids from one person to another; it can be transmitted prenatally.

TABLE 3.5	Effects of Some Infectious Diseases During Pregnancy			
DISEASE	MISCARRIAGE	PHYSICAL MALFORMATIONS	MENTAL RETARDATION	LOW BIRTH WEIGHT AND PREMATURITY
Viral				
Acquired immune deficiency syndrome (AIDS)	0	?	+	?
Chicken pox	0	+	+	+
Cytomegalovirus	+	+	+	+
Herpes simplex 2 (genital herpes)	+	+	+	+
Mumps	+	?	0	0
Rubella (German measles)	+	+	+	+
Bacterial				
Chlamydia	+	?	0	+
Syphilis	+	+	+	?
Tuberculosis	+	?	+	+
Parasitic				
Malaria	+	0	0	+
Toxoplasmosis	+	+	+	+

+ = established finding, 0 = no present evidence, ? = possible effect that is not clearly established.
Sources: Behrman, Kliegman, & Jenson, 2000; Jones, Lopez, & Wilson, 2003; Mardh, 2002; O'Rahilly & Müller, 2001.

Bacterial and Parasitic Diseases. Table 3.5 also includes several bacterial and parasitic diseases. Among the most common is **toxoplasmosis,** an infection caused by a parasite found in many animals. Pregnant women may become infected from eating raw or undercooked meat or from contact with the feces of infected cats. About 40 percent of women who have the disease transmit it to the developing organism. If it strikes during the first trimester, it is likely to cause eye and brain damage. Infection during the second and third trimesters is linked to mild visual and cognitive impairments. And about 80 percent of affected newborns with no obvious signs of damage develop learning or visual disabilities in later life (Jones, Lopez, & Wilson, 2003). Expectant mothers can avoid toxoplasmosis by making sure that the meat they eat is well-cooked, having pet cats checked for the disease, and turning over the care of litter boxes to other family members.

Other Maternal Factors

Besides avoiding teratogens, expectant parents can support the embryo and fetus in other ways. Regular exercise, good nutrition, and emotional well-being of the mother are essential. Problems that may result from maternal and fetal blood type differences can be prevented. Finally, many prospective parents wonder how a mother's age affects the course of pregnancy. We examine each of these factors in the following sections.

EXERCISE ■ Yolanda continued her half-hour of aerobics three times a week into the third trimester, although her doctor cautioned against bouncing, jolting, and jogging movements that might subject the fetus to too many shocks and startles. In healthy, physically fit women, regular moderate exercise, such as walking, swimming, biking, or an aerobic workout, is related to increased birth weight (Leiferman & Evenson, 2003). However, very frequent, vigorous, extended exercise—working up a sweat for more than 30 minutes, four or five days a

toxoplasmosis A parasitic disease caused by eating raw or undercooked meat or through contact with the feces of infected cats; during the first trimester, it leads to eye and brain damage.

An instructor leads a nutrition class for poor urban women and their children in Madras, India. By promoting a proper diet during pregnancy, the class helps prevent prenatal malnutrition. Mothers also learn how breastfeeding can protect their newborn baby's healthy growth (see Chapter 5, pages 178–180).

week, especially late in pregnancy—results in lower birth weight than in healthy controls (Clapp et al., 2002; Pivarnik, 1998). Hospital-sponsored childbirth education programs frequently offer exercise classes and suggest appropriate routines that help prepare for labor and delivery.

During the last trimester, when the abdomen grows very large, mothers have difficulty moving freely and often must cut back on exercise. Most women, however, do not engage in sufficient moderate exercise during pregnancy to promote their own and their baby's health (Hausenblas & Downs, 2005). An expectant mother who remains fit experiences fewer physical discomforts, such as back pain, upward pressure on the chest, or difficulty breathing in the final weeks.

Pregnant women with health problems, such as circulatory difficulties or a history of miscarriages, should consult their doctors about fitness routines. For these mothers, exercise (especially the wrong kind) can endanger the pregnancy.

NUTRITION ■ During the prenatal period, when children are growing more rapidly than at any other time, they depend totally on the mother for nutrients. A healthy diet, consisting of a gradual increase in calories—an extra 100 calories a day in the first trimester, 265 in the second, and 430 in the third—resulting in a weight gain of 25 to 30 pounds (10 to 13.5 kilograms), helps ensure the health of mother and baby (Reifsnider & Gill, 2000).

Consequences of Prenatal Malnutrition. During World War II, a severe famine occurred in the Netherlands, giving scientists a rare opportunity to study the impact of nutrition on prenatal development. Findings revealed that the sensitive-period concept operates with nutrition, just as it does with teratogens. Women affected by the famine during the first trimester were more likely to have miscarriages or give birth to babies with physical defects. When women were past the first trimester, fetuses usually survived, but many were born underweight and had small heads (Stein et al., 1975).

We now know that prenatal malnutrition can cause serious damage to the central nervous system. The poorer the mother's diet, the greater the loss in brain weight, especially if malnutrition occurred during the third trimester. During that time, the brain is increasing rapidly in size, and for it to reach its full potential, the mother must have a diet high in all the basic nutrients (Morgane et al., 1993). An inadequate diet during pregnancy can also distort the structure of other organs, including the liver, kidney, and pancreas, resulting in lifelong health problems (refer again to the Biology and Environment box on pages 106–107).

Because poor nutrition suppresses development of the immune system, prenatally malnourished babies frequently catch respiratory illnesses (Chandra, 1991). In addition, they often are irritable and unresponsive to stimulation. Like drug-addicted newborns, they have a high-pitched cry that is particularly distressing to their caregivers. In poverty-stricken families, these effects quickly combine with a stressful home life. With age, low intelligence test scores and serious learning problems become more apparent (Pollitt, 1996).

Prevention and Treatment. Many studies show that providing pregnant women with adequate food has a substantial impact on the health of their newborn babies. Yet the growth demands of the prenatal period require more than just increased quantity of food. Vitamin–mineral enrichment is also crucial.

For example, folic acid can prevent abnormalities of the neural tube, such as anencephaly and spina bifida (see Table 2.6 on page 64). In a study of nearly 2,000 women in seven countries who had previously given birth to a baby with a neural tube defect, half were randomly selected to receive a daily folic acid supplement around the time of conception, and half received a mixture of other vitamins or no supplement. The folic acid group showed 72 percent fewer neural tube defects (MCR Vitamin Study Research Group, 1991). In addition, adequate folate intake during the last 10 weeks of pregnancy cuts in half the risk of premature delivery and low birth weight (Scholl, Hediger, & Belsky, 1996).

Because of these findings, U.S. and Canadian government guidelines recommend that all women of childbearing age consume 0.4 milligrams of folic acid per day. For women who have previously had a pregnancy affected by neural tube defect, the recommended amount is 4 milligrams of folate per day beginning one month before conception and continuing through the first trimester, with some experts recommending 5 milligrams (dosage must be carefully monitored, as excessive intake can be harmful) (American Academy of Pediatrics, 2006). About half of North American pregnancies are unplanned, so government regulations mandate that bread, flour, rice, pasta, and other grain products be fortified with folic acid.

Other vitamins and minerals also have established benefits. Enriching women's diets with calcium helps prevent maternal high blood pressure and premature births (Repke, 1992). Adequate magnesium and zinc reduce the risk of many prenatal and birth complications (Durlach, 2004; Kontic-Vucinic, Sulovic, & Radunovic, 2006; Spätling & Spätling, 1988). Fortifying table salt with iodine virtually eradicates cretinism—a condition of stunted growth and cognitive impairment, caused by prenatal iodine deficiency, that is a common cause of mental retardation in many parts of the world (Maberly, Haxton, & van der Haar, 2003). And sufficient vitamin C and iron beginning early in pregnancy promote growth of the placenta and healthy birth weight (Mathews, Yudkin, & Neil, 1999). Nevertheless, a supplement program should complement, not replace, efforts to improve maternal diets during pregnancy. For women who do not get enough food or an adequate variety of foods, multivitamin tablets are a necessary, but not a sufficient, intervention.

When poor nutrition continues throughout pregnancy, infants usually require more than dietary improvement. In response to their tired, restless behavior, parents tend to be less sensitive and stimulating. The babies, in turn, become even more passive and withdrawn. Successful interventions must break this cycle of apathetic caregiver–baby interaction. Some do so by teaching parents how to interact effectively with their infants; others focus on stimulating infants to promote active engagement with their physical and social surroundings (Grantham-McGregor et al., 1994; Grantham-McGregor, Schofield, & Powell, 1987).

Although prenatal malnutrition is highest in poverty-stricken regions of the world, it is not limited to developing countries. The U.S. Special Supplemental Food Program for Women, Infants, and Children (WIC), which provides food packages and nutrition education to low-income pregnant women, reaches about 90 percent of those who qualify because of their extremely low incomes. But many U.S. women who need nutrition intervention are not eligible (U.S. Department of Agriculture, 2005c). The Canadian Prenatal Nutrition Program (CPNP), which provides counseling, social support, access to health care, and shelter, as well as food, to all pregnant women in need, regardless of income, reaches nearly 10 percent of expectant mothers in Canada (Health Canada, 2006a).

EMOTIONAL STRESS ■ When women experience severe emotional stress during pregnancy, their babies are at risk for a wide variety of difficulties. Intense prenatal anxiety is associated with a higher rate of miscarriage, prematurity, low birth weight, infant respiratory illness and digestive disturbances, and irritability during the first three years (Mulder et al., 2002; Wadhwa, Sandman, & Garite, 2001). It is also related to several commonly occurring physical defects, such as cleft lip and palate, heart deformities, and pyloric stenosis (tightening of the infant's stomach outlet, which must be treated surgically) (Carmichael & Shaw, 2000).

How can maternal stress affect the developing organism? **TAKE A MOMENT...** To understand this process, list the changes you sensed in your own body the last time you were under stress. When we experience fear and anxiety, stimulant hormones released into our bloodstream cause us to be "poised for action." Large amounts of blood are sent to parts of the

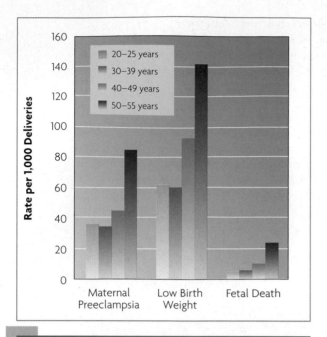

FIGURE 3.7

Relationship of maternal age to prenatal and birth complications. Complications increase after age 40, with a sharp rise between 50 and 55 years. See page 119 for a description of toxemia. (Adapted from Salihu et al., 2003.)

body involved in the defensive response—the brain, the heart, and muscles in the arms, legs, and trunk. Blood flow to other organs, including the uterus, is reduced. As a result, the fetus is deprived of a full supply of oxygen and nutrients.

Stress hormones also cross the placenta, causing a dramatic rise in fetal heart rate and activity (Monk et al., 2000, 2004). They may permanently alter fetal neurological functioning as well, thereby heightening stress reactivity in later life. In one study, researchers identified mothers who had been directly exposed to the September 11, 2001, World Trade Center collapse during their pregnancies. At age 9 months, their babies were tested for saliva concentrations of *cortisol,* a hormone involved in regulating the stress response. Infants whose mothers had reacted to the disaster with severe anxiety had cortisol levels that were abnormally low—a symptom of reduced physiological capacity to manage stress (Yehuda et al., 2005). Consistent with this finding, maternal emotional stress during pregnancy predicts anxiety, short attention span, anger, aggression, and overactivity among preschool and school-age children, above and beyond the impact of other risks, such as maternal smoking during pregnancy, low birth weight, postnatal maternal anxiety, and low SES (de Weerth & Buitelaar, 2005; Glover & O'Connor, 2005; Van den Bergh, 2004).

But stress-related prenatal complications are greatly reduced when mothers receive support from husbands, other family members, and friends (Federenko & Wadhwa, 2004). The link between social support and positive pregnancy outcomes is particularly strong for low-income women, who often lead highly stressful lives (Hoffman & Hatch, 1996). Enhancing supportive social networks for pregnant mothers can help prevent prenatal complications.

BLOOD INCOMPATIBILITY ■ When the inherited blood types of mother and fetus differ, serious problems sometimes result. The most common cause of these difficulties is **Rh factor incompatibility.** When the mother is Rh-negative (lacks the protein) and the father is Rh-positive (has the protein), the baby may inherit the father's Rh-positive blood type. (Recall from Table 2.2 on page 57 that Rh-positive blood is dominant and Rh-negative blood is recessive, so the chances are good that a baby will be Rh-positive.) If even a little of a fetus's Rh-positive blood crosses the placenta into the Rh-negative mother's bloodstream, she begins to form antibodies to the foreign Rh protein. If these enter the fetus's system, they destroy red blood cells, reducing the oxygen supply to organs and tissues. Mental retardation, miscarriage, heart damage, and infant death can occur.

Because it takes time for the mother to produce Rh antibodies, firstborn children are rarely affected. The danger increases with each additional pregnancy. Fortunately, Rh incompatibility can be prevented in most cases. After the birth of each Rh-positive baby, Rh-negative mothers are routinely given a vaccine to prevent the buildup of antibodies. In emergency cases, blood transfusions can be performed immediately after delivery or, if necessary, even before birth.

Rh factor incompatibility A condition that arises when the fetus's blood contains the Rh protein but the mother's blood does not, causing the mother to build up antibodies, which, if they return to the fetus's system, destroy red blood cells, reducing the oxygen supply to organs and tissues.

MATERNAL AGE AND PREVIOUS BIRTHS ■ Recall that women who delay having children until their thirties or forties face increased risk of infertility, miscarriage, and babies born with chromosomal defects (see Chapter 2). Are other pregnancy complications also more common for older mothers? Research consistently indicates that healthy women in their thirties have about the same rates of prenatal and birth problems as those in their twenties (Bianco et al., 1996; Dildy et al., 1996; Prysak, Lorenz, & Kisly, 1995). Thereafter, as Figure 3.7 reveals, complication rates increase, with a sharp rise among women age 50 to 55—an age at which, because of menopause (end of menstruation) and aging reproductive organs, few women can conceive naturally (Salihu et al., 2003).

In the case of teenage mothers, does physical immaturity cause prenatal problems? Again, research shows that it does not. As we will see in Chapter 14, nature tries to ensure that once a girl can conceive, she is physically ready to carry and give birth to a baby. Infants born to teenagers have a higher rate of problems, but not directly because of maternal age. Most pregnant teenagers come from low-income backgrounds, where stress, poor nutrition, and health problems are common. Also, many are afraid to seek medical care or, in the United States, do not have access to care because they lack health insurance (U.S. Department of Health and Human Services, 2006i).

The Importance of Prenatal Health Care

Yolanda had her first prenatal appointment three weeks after missing her menstrual period. After that, she visited the doctor's office once a month until she was seven months pregnant, then twice during the eighth month. As birth grew near, Yolanda's appointments increased to once a week. The doctor kept track of her general health, her weight gain, and the capacity of her uterus and cervix to support the fetus. The fetus's growth was also carefully monitored.

Yolanda's pregnancy, like most others, was free of complications. But unexpected difficulties can arise, especially if mothers have health problems. For example,

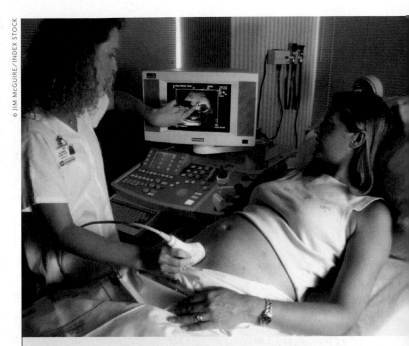

During a routine prenatal visit, this doctor uses ultrasound to show an expectant mother an image of her fetus and to evaluate its development. All pregnant women should receive early and regular prenatal care to protect their own health and the health of their babies.

women with diabetes need careful monitoring. Extra sugar in the diabetic mother's bloodstream causes the fetus to grow larger than average, making pregnancy and birth problems more common. Another complication, experienced by 5 to 10 percent of pregnant women, is **toxemia** (sometimes called *preeclampsia*), in which blood pressure increases sharply and the face, hands, and feet swell in the second half of pregnancy. If untreated, toxemia can cause convulsions in the mother and fetal death. Usually, hospitalization, bed rest, and drugs can lower blood pressure to a safe level (Vidaeff, Carroll, & Ramin, 2005). If not, the baby must be delivered at once.

Despite steady improvement over the past decade, unfortunately, 16 percent of pregnant women in the United States wait until after the first trimester to seek prenatal care, and nearly 4 percent receive none at all. As Figure 3.8 on page 120 shows, inadequate care is far more common among adolescent and low-income, ethnic minority mothers. Their infants are three times as likely to be born underweight and five times as likely to die as are babies of mothers who receive early medical attention (Child Trends, 2007). Why do these mothers delay going to the doctor? One reason is that they lack health insurance. Although the very poorest of these mothers are eligible for government-sponsored health services, many low-income women do not qualify. As we will see when we take up birth complications in Chapter 4, in countries where affordable medical care is universally available, such as Australia, Canada, Japan, and the Western European countries, late-care pregnancies and maternal and infant health problems are greatly reduced.

Besides financial hardship, some mothers have other reasons for not seeking early prenatal care. When researchers asked women who first went to the doctor late in pregnancy why they waited so long, they mentioned a wide variety of obstacles. These included both *situational barriers*—difficulty finding a doctor, getting an appointment, and arranging transportation, and insensitive or unsatisfying experiences with clinic staff—and *personal barriers*—psychological stress, the demands of taking care of other young children, family crises, lack of knowledge about signs of pregnancy and benefits of prenatal care, and ambivalence about the pregnancy. Many were also engaging in high-risk behaviors, such as smoking and drug abuse, and did not want to reveal those behaviors to health professionals (Daniels, Noe, & Mayberry,

toxemia An illness of the last half of pregnancy, also known as preeclampsia, in which the mother's blood pressure increases sharply; if untreated, it can cause convulsions in the mother and death of the fetus.

FIGURE 3.8

Expectant mothers in the United States with late (after the first trimester) or no prenatal care. Nearly one-fourth of low-income, ethnic minority mothers, and more than 40 percent of adolescent mothers, receive inadequate prenatal care. Weak health insurance policies and lack of culturally sensitive prenatal care contribute to this dire situation. (From U. S. Department of Health and Human Services, 2006i.)

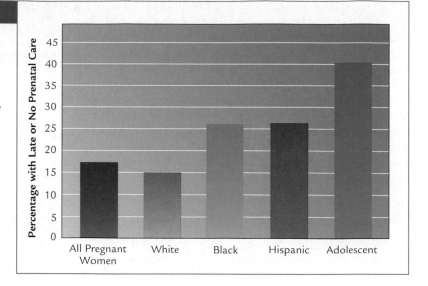

2006; Maupin et al., 2004). These women, who had little or no prenatal care, were among those who needed it most!

Clearly, public education about the importance of early and sustained prenatal care for all pregnant women is badly needed. For women who are young, less educated, low-income, or under stress and therefore at risk for inadequate prenatal care, assistance in making appointments, drop-in child-care centers, and convenient, free or low-cost transportation—are vital. See also the Cultural Influences box on the following page, about the importance of culturally sensitive health-care practices. Finally, Applying What We Know below lists "do's and don'ts" for a healthy pregnancy, based on our discussion of the prenatal environment.

Applying What We Know

Do's and Don'ts for a Healthy Pregnancy

DO

Do make sure that you have been vaccinated against infectious diseases dangerous to the embryo and fetus, such as rubella, before you get pregnant. Most vaccinations are not safe during pregnancy.

Do see a doctor as soon as you suspect that you are pregnant—within a few weeks after a missed menstrual period.

Do continue to get regular medical checkups throughout pregnancy.

Do obtain literature from your doctor, local library, and bookstore about prenatal development and care. Ask questions about anything you do not understand.

Do eat a well-balanced diet and take vitamin–mineral supplements, as prescribed by your doctor, both prior to and during pregnancy. On average, a woman should increase her intake by 100 calories a day in the first trimester, 265 in the second, and 430 in the third. Gain 25 to 30 pounds gradually.

Do keep physically fit through mild exercise. If possible, join a special exercise class for expectant mothers.

Do avoid emotional stress. If you are a single parent, find a relative or friend on whom you can count for emotional support.

Do get plenty of rest. An overtired mother is at risk for pregnancy complications.

Do enroll in a prenatal and childbirth education class along with your partner. When parents know what to expect, the nine months before birth can be one of the most joyful times of life.

DON'T

Don't take any drugs without consulting your doctor.

Don't smoke. If you have already smoked during part of your pregnancy, cut down or (better yet) quit. If other members of your family are smokers, ask them to quit or to smoke outside.

Don't drink alcohol from the time you decide to get pregnant. If you find it difficult to give up alcohol, ask for help from your doctor, local family service agency, or nearest chapter of Alcoholics Anonymous.

Don't engage in activities that might expose your embryo or fetus to environmental hazards, such as radiation or chemical pollutants. If you work in an occupation that involves these agents, ask for a safer assignment or a leave of absence.

Don't engage in activities that might expose your embryo or fetus to harmful infectious diseases, such as toxoplasmosis.

Don't choose pregnancy as a time to go on a diet.

Don't gain too much weight during pregnancy. A very large weight gain is associated with complications.

Cultural Influences

Culturally Sensitive Prenatal Care Promotes Healthy Pregnancies

Jasmine, three months pregnant, arrived at a public health clinic for her first prenatal visit despite a host of barriers: She was a 19-year-old single mother of an 8-month-old and felt overwhelmed at discovering that she was pregnant again. Unfortunately, Jasmine's experience discouraged her from returning for additional checkups. The nurse at the reception desk remarked insensitively, "You pregnant again?" And the doctor rushed through the exam and spoke rapidly in English to Jasmine, a native Spanish speaker, who comprehended little of what he said. Jasmine did not make another appointment until she was within two weeks of giving birth.

In several studies, low-SES ethnic minority expectant and new mothers were asked to describe their prenatal-care visits. Many mentioned long hours sitting in waiting rooms; harsh, belittling interactions with medical staff; and impersonal, hurried checkups that discouraged them from asking questions—events that discouraged them from sustaining regular prenatal health care (Daniels & Mayberry, 2006). One mother commented:

> Sometimes they check you really fast and really rough, and they don't ask you anything. They just check rudely and quickly and they do it so fast . . . after a few visits I stopped trying to ask anything and just wanted to get it over as quickly as possible. (Tandon, Parillo, & Keefer, 2005, pp. 315–316)

Hispanic women who had recently immigrated to the United States reported communication difficulties that prevented them from fully grasping health information. As one woman stated, "It took a lot of effort asking where I needed to go to get something or to understand what they were saying . . . but nobody would try to help me. I never want to go back" (p. 316).

Lack of patient-sensitive care is particularly disturbing to ethnic minority women from cultures that emphasize warm, personalized styles of interaction and a relaxed sense of time. Consequently, even when these

In a culturally sensitive approach to prenatal care, women whose babies are due at about the same time receive a medical checkup followed by a group session, scheduled at regular intervals from the third or fourth prenatal month until birth. A trained leader establishes a relaxed communication atmosphere, delivers important health information and answers questions, and encourages participants to form a social network of support—a prenatal-care style that is far more effective with minority expectant mothers than traditional medical appointments.

mothers have ready access to health care, they are likely to avoid it. A great need exists for prenatal care that is responsive to cultural values and practices.

A recently devised strategy known as *group prenatal care* is highly effective in serving minority expectant mothers (Massey, Rising, & Ickovics, 2006). It provides 8 to 12 women, whose babies are due at about the same time, with 10 two-hour prenatal care sessions, scheduled regularly from the third to fourth prenatal month until birth. After a half-hour medical checkup, the women bring their questions to a group discussion that focuses on important health issues, such as nutrition, exercise, stress management, and childbirth preparation. A trained group leader conducts group activities in the participants'

native language and encourages them to develop a social network for information and emotional support.

Group prenatal care is responsive to minority women who have culturally based expectations for a relaxed, informal communication atmosphere that allows ample time to build trusting relationships. Evaluations reveal that compared with mothers receiving a series of traditional 15-minute appointments, those in group care engage in more health-promoting and fewer health-damaging behaviors. They also give birth to babies with a reduced incidence of prematurity and low birth weight—major predictors of newborn survival and healthy development (Grady & Bloom, 2004; Ickovics et al., 2003).

Ask Yourself

Review   Why is it difficult to determine the effects of some environmental agents, such as drugs and pollution, on the embryo and fetus?

Apply   Nora, pregnant for the first time, has heard about the teratogenic impact of alcohol and tobacco. But she still believes that a few cigarettes and a glass of wine a day won't be harmful. Provide Nora with research-based reasons for not smoking or drinking.

Connect   How do teratogens illustrate the notion of epigenesis, presented in Chapter 2, that environments can affect gene expression (see page 88 to review).

Reflect   If you had to choose five environmental influences in a campaign aimed at promoting healthy prenatal development, which ones would you choose, and why?

Preparing for Parenthood

Although we have discussed many ways that development can be thrown off course during the prenatal period, over 90 percent of pregnancies in industrialized nations result in healthy newborn babies. For most expectant parents, the prenatal period is not a time of medical hazard. Rather, it is a period of major life change accompanied by excitement, anticipation, and looking inward. The nine months before birth not only permit the fetus to grow but also give men and women time to develop a new sense of themselves as mothers and fathers.

This period of psychological preparation is vital. In one study, more than 100 first-time expectant married couples, varying widely in age and SES, were interviewed about their pregnancy experiences. Participants reported a wide range of reactions to learning they were expecting. Nearly two-thirds were positive, about one-third mixed or neutral, and only a handful negative (Feeney et al., 2001). An unplanned pregnancy was especially likely to spark negative or ambivalent feelings. But as the pregnancy moved along, these reactions subsided. By the third trimester, no participants felt negatively, and only about 10 percent remained mixed or neutral. Couples' increasingly upbeat attitudes reflected acceptance of parenthood—a coming to terms with this imminent, radical change in their lives.

How effectively individuals construct a parental identity during pregnancy has important consequences for the parent–child relationship. A great many factors contribute to the personal adjustments that take place.

Seeking Information

We know most about how mothers adapt to the psychological challenges of pregnancy, although some evidence suggests that fathers use many of the same techniques. One common strategy is to seek information, as Yolanda and Jay did when they read books on pregnancy and childbirth and enrolled in my class. In fact, expectant mothers regard books as an extremely valuable source of information, rating them as second in importance only to their doctors. And the more a pregnant woman seeks information—by reading, accessing relevant websites, asking friends, consulting her own mother, or attending a prenatal class—the more confident she tends to feel about her own ability to be a good mother (Cowan & Cowan, 2000; Deutsch et al., 1988).

The Baby Becomes a Reality

At the beginning of pregnancy, the baby seems far in the future. Except for a missed period and some morning sickness (nausea that most women experience during the first trimester), the woman's body has not changed much. But gradually, her abdomen enlarges, and the baby starts to become a reality. A major turning point occurs when expectant parents have concrete proof that a fetus is, indeed, developing inside the uterus. For Yolanda and Jay, this happened 13 weeks into the pregnancy, when their doctor showed them an ultrasound image. As Jay described the experience, "We saw it, these little hands and feet waving and kicking. It had the cord and everything. It's really a baby in there!" Sensing the fetus's movements for the first time can be just as thrilling. Of course, the mother feels these "kicks" first, but soon after, the father (and siblings) can participate by touching her abdomen.

Parents get to know the fetus as an individual through these signs of life. And both may form an emotional attachment to the new being, dream about the future parent–infant relationship, and discuss names. In a Swedish study, the stronger mothers' and fathers' attachment to their fetus, the more positively they related to each other and to their baby after birth, and the more upbeat the baby's mood at age 8 months (White et al., 1999).

As these prospective parents shop for baby clothes together, they begin to develop a sense of themselves as mother and father. In this way, they construct a parental identity, becoming emotionally attached to their child and dreaming about the future parent–infant relationship.

Models of Effective Parenthood

As pregnancy proceeds, expectant parents think about important models of parenthood in their own lives. When men and women have had good relationships with their own parents, they are more likely to develop positive images of themselves as parents during pregnancy (Deutsch et al., 1988). These images, in turn, predict harmonious marital communication and effective parenting during infancy and early childhood (Curran et al., 2005; Klitzing et al., 1999; McHale et al., 2004).

If their own parental relationships are mixed or negative, expectant mothers and fathers may have trouble building a healthy picture of themselves as parents. Some adults handle this challenge by seeking other examples of effective parenthood. One expectant father named Roger shared these thoughts with his wife and several couples, who met regularly with a counselor to talk about their concerns during pregnancy:

> I rethink past experiences with my father and my family and am aware of how I was raised. I just think I don't want to do that again, I want to change that; I don't want to be like my father in that way. I wish there had been more connection and closeness and a lot more respect for who I was. For me, my father-in-law combines spontaneity, sincerity, and warmth. He is a mix of empathy and warmth plus stepping back and being objective that I want to be as a father. (Colman & Colman, 1991, p. 148)

Like Roger, many people come to terms with negative experiences in their own childhood, recognize that other options are available to them, and build healthier and happier relationships with their children (Main, 2000; Thompson, 2006). Roger achieved this understanding after participating in a special intervention program for expectant mothers and fathers.

This expectant mother's positive relationship with her own mother makes it easier for her to develop a positive image of herself as a parent. But even when expectant parents do not have positive memories of their childhoods, they often can come to terms with these disappointments and decide to create healthier, happier relationships with their children.

Couples who take part in such programs feel better about themselves and their marital relationships, regard the demands of caring for the new baby as less stressful, and adapt more easily when family problems arise (Glade, Bean, & Vira, 2005).

The Parental Relationship

The most important preparation for parenthood takes place in the context of the parents' relationship. Expectant couples who are unhappy in their marriages and who have difficulty working out their differences continue to be distant, dissatisfied, and poor problem solvers after the baby is born (Cowan & Cowan, 2000; Curran et al., 2005). Deciding to have a baby in hopes of improving a troubled relationship is a serious mistake. In a troubled marriage, pregnancy adds to rather than lessens family conflict (Perren et al., 2005).

When a couple's relationship is faring well and both partners want and planned for the baby, the excitement of a first pregnancy may bring husband and wife closer (Feeney et al., 2001). At the same time, pregnancy does change a marriage. Expectant parents must adjust their established roles to make room for children. In addition, each partner is likely to develop new expectations of the other. Women look for greater demonstrations of affection, interest in the pregnancy, and help with household chores. They see these behaviors as important signs of continued acceptance of themselves, the pregnancy, and the baby to come. Similarly, men are particularly sensitive to expressions of warmth from their partner. These reassure them of a central place in the new mother's emotional life after the baby is born (Cowan & Cowan, 2000).

When a relationship rests on a solid foundation of love and respect, parents are well-equipped for the challenges of pregnancy. They are also prepared to handle the much more demanding changes that will take place as soon as the baby is born.

Ask Yourself

Apply   Muriel, who is expecting her first child, recalls her own mother as cold and distant. Muriel is worried about whether she will be effective at caring for her new baby. What factors during pregnancy are related to maternal behavior?

Reflect   Ask your parents and/or your grandparents to describe attitudes and experiences that fostered or interfered with their capacity to build a positive parental identity when they were expecting their first child. Do you think building a healthy picture of oneself as a parent is more challenging today than it was in your parents' or grandparents' generation?

Summary

Motivations for Parenthood

How has decision making about childbearing changed over the past half-century, and what are the consequences for child rearing and child development?

■ Today, adults in Western industrialized nations have greater freedom to choose whether, when, and how to have children, and they are more likely to weigh the advantages and disadvantages of becoming parents. In industrialized nations, family size has declined over the past half-century. But no link has been found between later birth order and lower mental test performance. Rather, less intelligent parents—as a result of heredity, environment, or both—tend to have larger families.

■ When couples limit their families to just one child, their children are just as well-adjusted socially as children with siblings. Although reproductive capacity declines with age, adults who delay childbearing until their education is complete, their careers are established, and they are emotionally more mature may be better able to invest in parenting.

Prenatal Development

List the three phases of prenatal development, and describe the major milestones of each.

■ The first prenatal phase, the period of the zygote, lasts about two weeks, from fertilization through **implantation:** the **blastocyst** becomes deeply embedded in the uterine lining. During this time, structures that will support prenatal growth begin to form. The **embryonic disk** is surrounded by the **trophoblast,** which forms structures that protect and nourish the organism. The **amnion** fills with **amniotic fluid** to regulate temperature and cushion against the mother's movements. From the **chorion,** villi emerge that burrow into the uterine wall, and the **placenta** starts to develop. The **umbilical cord** connects the developing organism to the placenta.

■ During the period of the **embryo,** from weeks 2 to 8, the foundations for all body structures are laid down. The nervous system develops fastest, starting with the formation of the **neural tube,** or spinal cord, the top of which swells to form the brain. Other organs follow and grow rapidly. At the end of this phase, the embryo responds to touch and can move.

■ The period of the **fetus,** from the ninth week until the end of pregnancy, involves a dramatic increase in body size and completion of physical structures. By the middle of the second **trimester,** the mother can feel movement. The fetus becomes covered with **vernix,** which protects the skin from chapping. White, downy hair called **lanugo** helps the vernix stick to the skin. At the end of the second trimester, production of neurons in the brain is complete.

■ Between 22 and 26 weeks, at the beginning of the third trimester, the baby reaches the **age of viability** and is able to survive if born early. The brain continues to develop rapidly, and new sensory and behavioral capacities emerge. Gradually the lungs mature, the fetus fills the uterus, and birth is near.

Prenatal Environmental Influences

What are teratogens, and what factors influence their impact?

■ **Teratogens** are environmental agents that cause damage during the prenatal period. Their effects conform to the sensitive period concept. The developing organism is especially vulnerable during the embryonic period, when all essential body structures are emerging rapidly.

■ The impact of teratogens varies with the amount and length of exposure, the genetic makeup of mother and fetus, the presence or absence of other harmful agents, and the age of the organism at time of exposure. In addition to immediate physical damage, some health outcomes may appear later in development, and physical defects may lead to psychological consequences as well.

List agents known to be or suspected of being teratogens, and discuss evidence supporting their harmful impact.

■ Drugs, cigarettes, alcohol, radiation, environmental pollution, and infectious diseases are teratogens that can endanger the developing organism. **Thalidomide,** a sedative widely available in the early 1960s, showed that drugs could cross the placenta, causing serious damage. Other medications, including diethylstilbestrol (DES) and Accutane (used to treat severe acne), are also known teratogens.

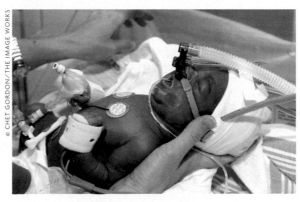

- Babies born to users of heroin, methadone, or cocaine are at risk for prematurity, low birth weight, and physical defects, and are born drug-addicted, displaying withdrawal symptoms. In some studies, cocaine is associated with lasting difficulties, while others show no major negative effects. Findings are also mixed on the effects of marijuana use during pregnancy.

- Infants whose parents use tobacco are often born underweight and may have attention, learning, and behavior problems in early childhood. When mothers consume alcohol in large quantities, children may be born with **fetal alcohol spectrum disorder (FASD)**, a term that includes a range of physical, mental, and behavioral outcomes caused by prenatal alcohol exposure. In the most severe form, **fetal alcohol syndrome (FAS)**, effects include slow physical growth, facial abnormalities, and impairment in mental functioning. Pregnant women who consume smaller quantities of alcohol may bear children with less severe forms of FASD—**partial fetal alcohol syndrome (p-FAS)** or **alcohol-related neurodevelopmental disorder (ARND)**.

- Prenatal exposure to high levels of radiation, mercury, lead, and PCBs leads to physical malformations and severe brain damage. Low-level exposure to these teratogens has also been linked to diverse impairments, including cognitive and language deficits and emotional and behavior disorders.

- Among infectious diseases, **rubella** causes a wide variety of abnormalities, which vary with its time of occurrence during pregnancy. The human immuno-deficiency virus (HIV), responsible for **acquired immune deficiency syndrome (AIDS),** can be transmitted prenatally, resulting in brain damage and early death. Cytomegalovirus (the most frequent prenatal infection) and herpes simplex 2 are also devastating to the fetus. **Toxoplasmosis,** a parasitic infection, may lead to eye and brain damage when a mother contracts it in the first trimester; in the second and third trimesters it can cause mild visual and cognitive impairments.

Describe the impact of other maternal factors on prenatal development.

- In healthy, physically fit pregnant women, regular moderate exercise contributes to general health and readiness for childbirth and is related to higher birth weight. However, very vigorous exercise results in lower birth weight.

- When an expectant mother's diet is inadequate, low birth weight and damage to the brain and other organs are major concerns.

Vitamin–mineral supplementation, including folate, beginning before conception and continuing during pregnancy can prevent prenatal and birth complications.

- Severe emotional stress is linked to many pregnancy complications and may permanently alter fetal neurological functioning. Its impact can be reduced by providing the mother with emotional support.

- **Rh factor incompatibility**—an Rh-positive fetus developing within an Rh-negative mother—can lead to oxygen deprivation, brain and heart damage, and infant death.

- Aside from the risk of chromosomal abnormalities in older women, maternal age through the early forties is not a major cause of prenatal problems. Rather, poor health and environmental risks associated with poverty are the strongest predictors of pregnancy complications in both teenagers and older women.

Why is early and regular health care vital during the prenatal period?

- Unexpected difficulties, such as **toxemia,** can arise, especially when pregnant women have health problems to begin with. Prenatal care is especially crucial for those women least likely to seek it—in particular, those who are young or poverty-stricken. Among low-SES ethnic minority mothers, culturally sensitive health-care practices—such as group prenatal care—can lead to more health-promoting behaviors.

Preparing for Parenthood

What factors contribute to preparation for parenthood during the prenatal period?

- Over the course of pregnancy, reactions to expectant parenthood become increasingly positive. Mothers and fathers prepare for their new role by seeking information from books and other sources. Ultrasound images, fetal movements, and the mother's enlarging abdomen make the baby a reality, and parents may form an emotional attachment to the new being. They also rely on effective models of parenthood to build images of themselves as mothers and fathers.

- The most important preparation for parenthood takes place in the context of the couple's relationship. During the nine months preceding birth, parents adjust their roles and their expectations of each other as they prepare to welcome the baby into the family.

Important Terms and Concepts

acquired immune deficiency syndrome (AIDS) (p. 114)

age of viability (p. 102)

alcohol-related neurodevelopmental disorder (ARND) (p. 111)

amnion (p. 99)

amniotic fluid (p. 99)

blastocyst (p. 99)

chorion (p. 99)

embryo (p. 101)

embryonic disk (p. 99)

fetal alcohol spectrum disorder (FASD) (p. 111)

fetal alcohol syndrome (FAS) (p. 111)

fetus (p. 102)

implantation (p. 99)

lanugo (p. 102)

neural tube (p. 101)

partial fetal alcohol syndrome (p-FAS) (p. 111)

placenta (p. 99)

Rh factor incompatibility (p. 118)

rubella (p. 114)

teratogen (p. 105)

thalidomide (p. 107)

toxemia (p. 119)

toxoplasmosis (p. 115)

trimesters (p. 102)

trophoblast (p. 99)

umbilical cord (p. 100)

vernix (p. 102)

Chapter 4

Birth and the Newborn Baby

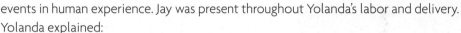

A
lthough Yolanda and Jay completed my course three months before their baby was born, both agreed to return the following spring to share with my next class their reactions to birth and new parenthood. Two-week-old Joshua came along as well. Yolanda and Jay's story revealed that the birth of a baby is one of the most dramatic and emotional events in human experience. Jay was present throughout Yolanda's labor and delivery. Yolanda explained:

> By morning, we knew I was in labor. It was Thursday, so we went in for my usual weekly appointment. The doctor said, yes, the baby was on the way, but it would be a while. He told us to go home and relax, and come to the hospital in three or four hours. We checked in at 3 in the afternoon; Joshua arrived at 2 o'clock the next morning. When, finally, I was ready to deliver, it went quickly; a half hour or so and some good hard pushes, and there he was! His face was red and puffy, and his head was misshapen, but I thought, "Our son! I can't believe he's really here."

Jay was also elated by Joshua's birth. "I wanted to support Yolanda and to experience as much as I could. It was awesome, indescribable," he said, holding little Joshua over his shoulder and patting and kissing him gently.

In this chapter we explore the experience of childbirth, from both the parents' and the baby's points of view. As recently as forty years ago, the birth process was treated more like an illness than a natural part of life. Today, women in industrialized nations have many choices about where and how they give birth, and hospitals go to great lengths to make the arrival of a new baby a rewarding, family-centered event.

Joshua reaped the benefits of Yolanda and Jay's careful attention to his needs during pregnancy. He was strong, alert, and healthy at birth. Nevertheless, the birth process does not always go smoothly. We will consider the pros and cons of medical interventions, such as pain-relieving drugs and surgical deliveries, designed to ease a difficult birth and protect the health of mother and baby. Our discussion also addresses the problems of infants born underweight or too early.

Finally, Yolanda and Jay spoke candidly about how their lives had changed since Joshua's arrival. "It's exciting and wonderful," reflected Yolanda, "but the adjustments are enormous. I wasn't quite prepared for the intensity of Joshua's 24-hour-a-day demands." In the concluding sections of this chapter, we look closely at the remarkable capacities of newborns to adapt to the external world and to communicate their needs. We also consider how parents adjust to the realities of everyday life with a new baby.

The Stages of Childbirth

It is not surprising that childbirth is often referred to as labor. It is the hardest physical work that a woman may ever do. A complex series of hormonal changes between mother and fetus initiates the process. Yolanda's whole system, which for nine months supported and protected Joshua's growth, now turned toward a new goal: getting him safely out of the uterus.

The events that lead to childbirth begin slowly in the ninth month of pregnancy and gradually pick up speed. Several signs indicate that labor is near:

- Yolanda occasionally felt the upper part of her uterus contract. These contractions are often called *false labor* or *prelabor* because they remain brief and unpredictable for several weeks.
- About two weeks before birth, an event called *lightening* occurred; Joshua's head dropped low into the uterus. Yolanda's cervix had begun to soften in preparation for delivery and no longer supported Joshua's weight so easily.
- A sure sign that labor is only hours or days away is the *bloody show*. As the cervix begins to open, the plug of mucus that sealed it during pregnancy is released, producing a reddish discharge. Soon after, contractions of the uterus become more frequent, and mother and baby have entered the first of three stages of labor (see Figure 4.1).

FIGURE 4.1

The three stages of labor.

Stage 1

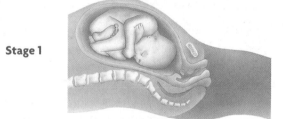

(a) Dilation and Effacement of the Cervix
Contractions of the uterus cause dilation and effacement of the cervix.

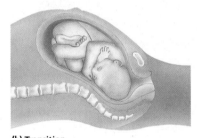

(b) Transition
Transition is reached when the frequency and strength of the contractions are at their peak and the cervix opens completely.

Stage 2

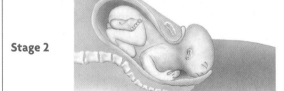

(c) Pushing
With each contraction, the mother pushes, forcing the baby down the birth canal, and the head appears.

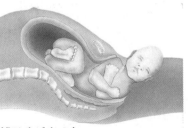

(d) Birth of the Baby
Near the end of Stage 2, the shoulders emerge, followed quickly by the rest of the baby's body.

Stage 3

(e) Delivery of the Placenta
With a few final pushes, the placenta is delivered.

Stage 1: Dilation and Effacement of the Cervix

Stage 1 is the longest, lasting an average of 12 to 14 hours with a first birth and 4 to 6 hours with later births. **Dilation and effacement of the cervix** take place—that is, as uterine contractions gradually become more frequent and powerful, they cause the cervix to open (dilate) and thin (efface), forming a clear channel from the uterus into the birth canal, or vagina. The uterine contractions that open the cervix are forceful and regular, starting out 10 to 20 minutes apart and lasting about 15 to 20 seconds. Gradually, they get closer together, occurring every 2 to 3 minutes, and become more powerful, persisting for as long as 60 seconds.

During this stage, Yolanda could do nothing to speed up the process. Jay held her hand, provided sips of juice and water, and helped her get comfortable. Throughout the first few hours, Yolanda walked, stood, or sat upright. As the contractions became more intense, she leaned against pillows or lay on her side.

The climax of Stage 1 is a brief phase called **transition,** in which the frequency and strength of contractions are at their peak and the cervix opens completely. Although transition is the most uncomfortable part of childbirth, it is especially important that the mother relax. If she tenses or bears down with her muscles before the cervix is completely dilated and effaced, she may bruise the cervix and slow the progress of labor.

Stage 2: Delivery of the Baby

In Stage 2, which lasts about 50 minutes for a first baby and 20 minutes in later births, the infant is born. Strong contractions of the uterus continue, but the mother also feels a natural urge to squeeze and push with her abdominal muscles. As she does so with each contraction, she forces the baby down and out.

Between contractions, Yolanda dozed lightly. As each wave came, "I pushed with all my might," she said. When the doctor announced that the baby's head was *crowning*—the vaginal opening had stretched around the entire head—Yolanda felt renewed energy; she knew that soon the baby would arrive. Quickly, with several more pushes, Joshua's forehead, nose, and chin emerged, then his upper body and trunk. The doctor held him up, wet with amniotic fluid and still attached to the umbilical cord. As air rushed into his lungs, Joshua cried. When the umbilical cord stopped pulsing, it was clamped and cut. A nurse placed Joshua on Yolanda's chest, where she and Jay could see, touch, and gently talk to him. Then the nurse wrapped Joshua snugly, to help with temperature regulation.

Stage 3: Birth of the Placenta

Stage 3 brings labor to an end. A few final contractions and pushes cause the placenta to separate from the wall of the uterus and be delivered in about 5 to 10 minutes. Yolanda and Jay were surprised at the large size of the thick 1½-pound red-gray organ, which had taken care of Joshua's basic needs for the previous nine months.

The Baby's Adaptation to Labor and Delivery

At first glance, labor and delivery seem like a dangerous ordeal for the baby. The strong contractions of Yolanda's uterus exposed Joshua's head to a great deal of pressure, and they squeezed the placenta and the umbilical cord repeatedly. Each time, Joshua's supply of oxygen was temporarily reduced.

Fortunately, healthy babies are equipped to withstand these traumas. The force of the contractions causes the infant to produce high levels of stress hormones. Recall from Chapter 3 that during pregnancy, the effects of maternal stress can endanger the baby. In contrast, during childbirth, the infant's production of cortisol and other stress hormones is adaptive. It helps the baby withstand oxygen deprivation by sending a rich supply of blood to the brain and heart (Gluckman, Sizonenko, & Bassett, 1999). In addition, it prepares the baby to breathe

dilation and effacement of the cervix Widening and thinning of the cervix during the first stage of labor.

transition Climax of the first stage of labor, in which the frequency and strength of contractions are at their peak and the cervix opens completely.

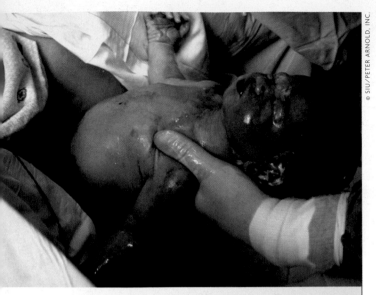

To accommodate the well-developed brain, a newborn's head is large in relation to the trunk and legs. In addition, the round face, with its chubby cheeks and big eyes, induces adults to approach, pick up, and cuddle the newborn.

effectively by causing the lungs to absorb any remaining fluid and by expanding the bronchial tubes (passages leading to the lungs). Finally, stress hormones arouse the infant into alertness. Joshua was born wide-awake, ready to interact with the surrounding world (Lagercrantz & Slotkin, 1986).

The Newborn Baby's Appearance

Parents are often surprised at the odd-looking newborn—a far cry from the storybook image they may have had in their minds. The average newborn is 20 inches long and 7½ pounds in weight; boys tend to be slightly longer and heavier than girls. The head is large in comparison to the trunk and legs, which are short and bowed. Proportionally, if your head were as large as that of a newborn infant, you would be balancing something about the size of a watermelon between your shoulders! This combination of a large head (with its well-developed brain) and a small body means that human infants learn quickly in the first few months of life. But unlike most other mammals, they cannot get around on their own until much later.

Even though newborn babies may not match parents' idealized image, some features do make them attractive. Their round faces, chubby cheeks, large foreheads, and big eyes make adults feel like picking them up and cuddling them (Berman, 1980).

Assessing the Newborn's Physical Condition: The Apgar Scale

Infants who have difficulty making the transition to life outside the uterus must be given special help at once. To assess the newborn's physical condition quickly, doctors and nurses use the **Apgar Scale.** As Table 4.1 shows, a rating of 0, 1, or 2 on each of five characteristics is made at 1 minute and again at 5 minutes after birth. A combined Apgar score of 7 or better indicates that the infant is in good physical condition. If the score is between 4 and 6, the baby requires assistance in establishing breathing and other vital signs. If the score is 3 or below, the infant is in serious danger and requires emergency medical attention. Two Apgar ratings are given because some babies have trouble adjusting at first but do quite well after a few minutes (Apgar, 1953).

Ask Yourself

Review   Name and briefly describe the three stages of labor.

Apply   On seeing her newborn baby for the first time, Caroline exclaimed, "Why is she so out of proportion?" What observations prompted Caroline to ask this question? Explain why her baby's appearance is adaptive.

Connect   Contrast the positive impact of the baby's production of stress hormones during childbirth with the negative impact of maternal stress on the fetus, discussed on page 117 in Chapter 3.

TABLE 4.1   **The Apgar Scale**

	SCORE		
SIGN[a]	**0**	**1**	**2**
Heart rate	No heartbeat	Under 100 beats per minute	100 to 140 beats per minute
Respiratory effort	No breathing for 60 seconds	Irregular, shallow breathing	Strong breathing and crying
Reflex irritability (sneezing, coughing, and grimacing)	No response	Weak reflexive response	Strong reflexive response
Muscle tone	Completely limp	Weak movements of arms and legs	Strong movements of arms and legs
Color[b]	Blue body, arms, and legs	Body pink with blue arms and legs	Body, arms, and legs completely pink

[a]To remember these signs, you may find it helpful to use a technique in which the original labels are reordered and renamed as follows: color = Appearance, heart rate = Pulse, reflex irritability = Grimace, muscle tone = Activity, and respiratory effort = Respiration. Together, the first letters of the new labels spell **Apgar**.

[b]The skin tone of nonwhite babies makes it difficult to apply the "pink" color criterion. However, newborns of all races can be rated for pinkish glow resulting from the flow of oxygen through body tissues.

Source: Apgar, 1953.

Approaches to Childbirth

Childbirth practices, like other aspects of family life, are molded by the society of which mother and baby are a part. In many village and tribal cultures, expectant mothers are well-acquainted with the childbirth process. For example, the Jarara of South America and the Pukapukans of the Pacific Islands treat birth as a vital part of daily life. The Jarara mother gives birth in full view of the entire community, including small children. The Pukapukan girl is so familiar with the events of labor and delivery that she can frequently be seen playing at it. Using a coconut to represent the baby, she stuffs it inside her dress, imitates the mother's pushing, and lets the nut fall at the proper moment. In most nonindustrialized cultures, women are assisted—though often not by medical personnel—during labor and delivery. Among the Mayans of the Yucatán, the mother leans against the body of a woman called the "head helper," who supports her weight and breathes with her during each contraction (Jordan, 1993; Mead & Newton, 1967).

In Western nations, childbirth has changed dramatically over the centuries. Before the late 1800s, birth usually took place at home and was a family-centered event. The industrial revolution brought greater crowding to cities, along with new health problems. As a result, childbirth moved from home to hospital, where the health of mothers and babies could be protected. Once doctors assumed responsibility for childbirth, women's knowledge of it declined, and relatives and friends were no longer welcome to participate (Borst, 1995).

By the 1950s and 1960s, women had begun to question the medical procedures that had come to be used routinely during labor and delivery. Many felt that routine use of strong drugs and delivery instruments had robbed them of a precious experience and was often neither necessary nor safe for the baby. Gradually, a natural childbirth movement arose in Europe and spread to North America. Its purpose was to make hospital birth as comfortable and rewarding for mothers as possible. Carrying this theme further, most hospitals today offer birth centers that are centered and homelike. *Freestanding birth centers,* which permit greater maternal control over labor and delivery, including choice of delivery positions, presence of family members and friends, and early contact between parents and baby, also exist. However, they offer less backup medical care than hospitals. And a small number of North American women are rejecting institutional birth entirely and choosing to have their babies at home.

Apgar Scale A rating used to assess the newborn baby's physical condition immediately after birth.

Let's take a closer look at two childbirth approaches that have gained popularity in recent years: natural childbirth and home delivery.

Natural, or Prepared, Childbirth

Yolanda and Jay chose **natural, or prepared, childbirth**—a group of techniques aimed at reducing pain and medical intervention and making childbirth as rewarding an experience as possible. Most natural childbirth programs draw on methods developed by Grantly Dick-Read (1959) in England and Fernand Lamaze (1958) in France. These physicians recognized that cultural attitudes had taught women to fear the birth experience. An anxious, frightened woman in labor tenses her muscles, turning the mild pain that sometimes accompanies strong contractions into a great deal of pain.

In a typical natural childbirth program, the expectant mother and a companion (a partner, a relative, or a friend) participate in three activities:

- *Classes.* Yolanda and Jay attended a series of classes in which they learned about the anatomy and physiology of labor and delivery. Knowledge about the birth process reduces a mother's fear.
- *Relaxation and breathing techniques.* During each class, Yolanda was taught relaxation and breathing exercises aimed at counteracting the pain of uterine contractions.
- *Labor coach.* Jay learned how to help Yolanda during childbirth by reminding her to relax and breathe, massaging her back, supporting her body, and offering encouragement and affection.

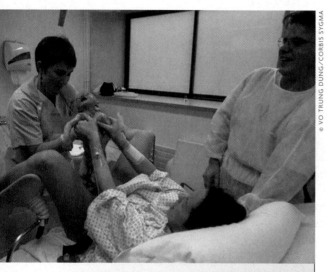

© VO TRUNG DUNG/CORBIS SYGMA

In a hospital birth center, this mother and father welcome their newborn baby, delivered by the midwife just moments before. The father's support is a vital part of natural childbirth techniques in Western nations. Natural childbirth is associated with shorter labors and fewer birth complications and offers parents a more rewarding birth experience.

natural, or prepared, childbirth An approach designed to reduce pain and medical intervention and to make childbirth a rewarding experience for parents.

Studies reveal many benefits for mothers who experience natural childbirth compared with those who do not. Because mothers feel more in control of labor and delivery, their attitudes toward the childbirth experience are more positive. They also feel less pain. As a result, they require less pain-relieving medication—very little or none at all (Taylor, 2002; Waldenström, 1999).

SOCIAL SUPPORT AND NATURAL CHILDBIRTH ■ Social support is important to the success of natural childbirth techniques. In Guatemalan and American hospitals that routinely isolated patients during childbirth, some mothers were randomly assigned a trained companion who stayed with them throughout labor and delivery, talking to them, holding their hands, and rubbing their backs to promote relaxation. These mothers had fewer birth complications, and their labors were several hours shorter than those of women who did not have supportive companionship. Guatemalan mothers who received support also interacted more positively with their babies after delivery, talking, smiling, and gently stroking (Kennell et al., 1991; Sosa et al., 1980). Other studies indicate that mothers who are supported during labor less often have cesarean (surgical) deliveries, and their babies' Apgar scores are higher (Sauls, 2002).

The continuous rather than intermittent support of a trained companion during labor and delivery strengthens these outcomes. It is particularly helpful during a first childbirth, when mothers are more anxious (DiMatteo & Kahn, 1997; Scott, Berkowitz, & Klaus, 1999). And this aspect of natural childbirth makes Western hospital-birth customs more acceptable to women from parts of the world where assistance from family and community members is the norm (Granot et al., 1996).

POSITIONS FOR DELIVERY ■ When natural childbirth is combined with delivery in a birth center or at home, mothers often give birth in an upright, sitting position rather than lying flat on their backs with their feet in stirrups (the traditional hospital delivery room practice). Use of special stools to enable an upright birth has become more common. One type of birthing stool permits the partner to sit behind the mother, providing physical support (see Figure 4.2).

Research findings favor the sitting position. When mothers are upright, labor is shortened because pushing is easier and more effective. The baby benefits from a richer supply of oxygen because blood flow to the placenta is increased. Because the mother can see the delivery, she can track the effectiveness of each contraction in pushing the baby out of the birth canal (Kelly, Terry, & Naglieri, 1999). This helps her work with the doctor or midwife to ensure that the baby's head and shoulders emerge slowly, which reduces the chances of tearing the mother's tissues and, thus, the need for an *episiotomy* (incision that increases the size of the vaginal opening). Compared with those who give birth lying on their backs, women who choose a partner-supported stool birth are less likely to use pain-relieving medication (Eberhard, Stein, & Geissbuehler, 2005).

In another increasingly popular method, water birth, the mother sits in a warm tub of water, which supports her weight, relaxes her, and provides her with the freedom to move into any position she finds most comfortable. Recent evidence indicates that water birth is associated with a shorter labor, a lower episiotomy rate, and a greater likelihood of medication-free delivery than both back-lying and birthing-stool approaches (Eberhard, Stein, & Geissbuehler, 2005; Thoeni et al., 2005). As long as they are carefully managed by health professionals, water births pose no additional risk of infection or safety to mothers or babies.

FIGURE 4.2

A birthing stool. The mother gives birth in an upright posture. Her partner can sit behind, supporting her body.

Home Delivery

Home birth has always been popular in certain industrialized nations, such as England, the Netherlands, and Sweden. The number of North American women choosing to have their babies at home rose during the 1970s and 1980s but nevertheless remains small, at about 1 percent (Studelska, 2006). Although some home births are attended by doctors, many more are handled by *certified nurse–midwives,* who have degrees in nursing and additional training in childbirth management.

The joys and perils of home delivery are well illustrated by the story I heard from Don, who was painting my house as I worked on this book. "Our first child was delivered in the hospital," Don told me. "Even though I was present, Kathy and I found the atmosphere to be rigid and insensitive. We wanted a warmer, more personal birth environment." With the coaching of a nurse–midwife, Don delivered their second child, Cindy, at their farmhouse, three miles out of town. Three years later, when Kathy went into labor with Marnie, their third child, a heavy snowstorm prevented the midwife from reaching the house on time, so Don delivered the baby alone. The birth was difficult, and Marnie failed to breathe for several minutes. With great effort, Don managed to revive her. But the frightening memory of Marnie's limp, blue body convinced Don and Kathy to return to the hospital to have their last child. By then, the hospital's birth practices had changed, and the event was a rewarding one for both parents.

Don and Kathy's experience raises the question of whether it is just as safe to give birth at home as in a hospital. For healthy women who are assisted by a well-trained doctor or midwife, the answer is yes, since complications rarely occur (Johnson & Daviss, 2005; Vedam, 2003). However, if attendants are not carefully trained and prepared to handle emergencies, the rate of infant death is high (Mehlmadrona & Madrona, 1997). When mothers are at risk for any kind of complication, the appropriate place for labor and delivery is the hospital, where life-saving treatment is available.

© FRANCE KEYSER/IN VISU/CORBIS

This woman has chosen to have a water birth, an increasingly popular childbirth option. Sitting in a warm tub of water relaxes the mother, supports her weight, and gives her the freedom to move into a comfortable position.

Medical Interventions

Medical interventions during childbirth occur in both industrialized and nonindustrialized cultures. For example, some tribal and village societies have discovered labor-inducing drugs and devised surgical techniques to deliver babies (Jordan, 1993). Yet childbirth in North America, more so than elsewhere in the world, is a medically monitored and controlled event. Use of some medical procedures has reached epic proportions—in part because of rising rates of multiple births and other high-risk deliveries, which are associated with increased maternal age and use of fertility treatments. But births unaffected by these factors are also highly medicalized.

What medical techniques are doctors likely to use during labor and delivery? When are they justified, and what dangers do they pose to mothers and babies?

Fetal Monitoring

Fetal monitors are electronic instruments that track the baby's heart rate during labor. An abnormal heartbeat pattern may indicate that the baby is in distress due to lack of oxygen and needs to be delivered immediately. Most U.S. hospitals require continuous fetal monitoring; it is used in over 80 percent of American births. In Canada, continuous monitoring is usually reserved for babies at risk for birth complications (Natale & Dodman, 2003; Liston et al., 2002). The most popular type of monitor is strapped across the mother's abdomen throughout labor. A second, more accurate method involves threading a recording device through the cervix and placing it directly under the baby's scalp.

Fetal monitoring is a safe medical procedure that has saved the lives of many babies in high-risk situations. But in healthy pregnancies, it does not reduce the already low rates of infant brain damage and death (Priddy, 2004). Furthermore, most infants have some heartbeat irregularities during labor, and critics worry that fetal monitors identify many babies as in danger who, in fact, are not. Monitoring is linked to an increase in the number of instrument and cesarean (surgical) deliveries, practices we will discuss shortly (Thacker & Stroup, 2003). In addition, some women complain that the devices are uncomfortable and interfere with the normal course of labor.

Still, fetal monitors will probably continue to be used routinely in the United States, even though they are not necessary in most cases. Doctors fear that they will be sued for malpractice if an infant dies or is born with problems and they cannot show that they did everything possible to protect the baby.

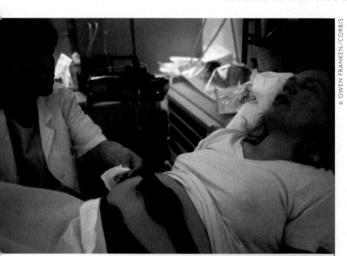

This mother wears a fetal monitor strapped across her abdomen throughout labor. The monitor uses ultrasound to record fetal heart rate. In high-risk situations, fetal monitoring saves many lives. But it also may lead to an increase in unnecessary instrument and cesarean (surgical) deliveries.

© OWEN FRANKEN/CORBIS

Labor and Delivery Medication

Some form of medication is used in more than 80 percent of North American births (Sharma & Leveno, 2003). **Analgesics,** drugs used to relieve pain, may be given in mild doses during labor to help a mother relax. **Anesthetics** are a stronger type of painkiller that blocks sensation. Currently, the most common approach to controlling pain during labor is *epidural analgesia,* in which a regional pain-relieving drug is delivered continuously through a catheter into a small space in the lower spine. Unlike older spinal block procedures, which numb the entire lower half of the body, epidural analgesia limits pain reduction to the pelvic region. Because the mother retains the capacity to feel the pressure of the contractions and to move her trunk and legs, she is able to push during the second stage of labor.

Although pain-relieving drugs help women cope with childbirth and enable doctors to perform essential medical interventions, they also can cause problems. Epidural analgesia, for example, weakens uterine contractions. As a result, labor is prolonged. And because drugs rapidly

fetal monitors Electronic instruments that track the baby's heart rate during labor.

analgesics Mild pain-relieving drugs.

anesthetics Strong painkillers that block sensation.

cross the placenta, exposed newborns tend to have lower Apgar scores, to be sleepy and withdrawn, to suck poorly during feedings, and to be irritable when awake (Caton et al., 2002; Eltzschig, Lieberman, & Camann, 2003; Emory, Schlackman, & Fiano, 1996).

Do heavy doses of childbirth medication have a lasting impact on physical and mental development? Some researchers have claimed so (Brackbill, McManus, & Woodward, 1985), but their findings have been challenged (Golub, 1996; Riordan et al., 2000). Use of medication may be related to other risk factors that could account for the long-term consequences in some studies, but more research is needed to sort out these effects. Meanwhile, the negative impact of these drugs on the newborn's adjustment supports the current trend to limit their use.

Instrument Delivery

Forceps, metal clamps placed around the baby's head to pull the infant from the birth canal, have been used since the sixteenth century to speed up delivery (see Figure 4.3). A more recent instrument, the **vacuum extractor,** consists of a plastic cup (placed on the baby's head) attached to a suction tube. Instrument delivery is appropriate if the mother's pushing during the second stage of labor does not move the baby through the birth canal in a reasonable period of time.

Instrument use has declined considerably over the past decade, partly because doctors more often deliver babies surgically when labor problems arise. Nevertheless, forceps and vacuum extractors continue to be used in about 7 percent of American and 17 percent of Canadian births, compared with less than 5 percent in Western Europe (Martin et al., 2002; Wen et al., 2001). These figures suggest that instruments are applied too freely in North American hospitals.

Using forceps to pull the baby through most or all of the birth canal greatly increases the risk of brain damage. As a result, forceps are seldom used this way today. Low-forceps delivery (carried out when the baby is most of the way through the vagina) is associated with risk of injury to the baby's head and the mother's tissues. Vacuum extractors are less likely to tear the mother's tissues. Cup suction does cause bleeding beneath the baby's skin and external to the skull in about 6 percent of cases. However, few of these newborns experience serious complications (Johnson et al., 2004; Putta & Spencer, 2000). Still, neither method should be used when mothers can be encouraged to deliver normally and there is no special reason to hurry the birth.

Induced Labor

An **induced labor** is one that is started artificially, usually by breaking the amnion, or bag of waters (an event that typically occurs naturally in the first stage of labor), and giving the mother synthetic oxytocin, a hormone that stimulates contractions. About 20 percent of North American labors are induced—a figure that has more than doubled over the past decade (Sanchez-Ramos, 2005).

Induced labors are justified when continuing the pregnancy threatens the well-being of mother or baby. Often, though, they are performed for the doctor's or the patient's convenience—a major reason they have increased. An induced labor often proceeds differently from a naturally occurring one. Contractions are longer, harder, and closer together, increasing the possibility of inadequate oxygen supply to the baby. In addition, mothers often find it more difficult to stay in control of an induced labor, even when they have been coached in natural childbirth techniques. As a result, labor and delivery medication is likely to be used in larger amounts, and the chances of instrument delivery are slightly greater (Cammu et al., 2002; Hoffman et al., 2006).

Occasionally, induction is performed before the mother is physically ready to give birth, and the procedure fails. When this happens, a cesarean delivery is necessary. The rate of cesareans is nearly twice as great in induced labors as in spontaneous labors (Dublin et al., 2000). A placental hormone called *corticotropin-releasing hormone (CRH)* helps predict the success of induction procedures. Mothers with high levels of CRH are more likely to respond well than are those whose CRH levels are low (Smith, 1999).

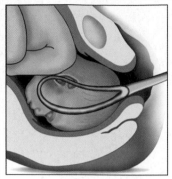

Forceps

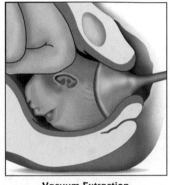

Vacuum Extraction

FIGURE 4.3

Instrument delivery. The pressure that must be applied to pull the infant from the birth canal with forceps involves risk of injury to the baby's head. An alternative method, the vacuum extractor, is less likely than forceps to injure the mother's tissues. Scalp injuries, however, are common.

forceps Metal clamps placed around a baby's head to pull the infant from the birth canal.

vacuum extractor A plastic cup attached to a suction tube, used to help deliver a baby.

induced labor A labor started artificially by breaking the amnion and giving the mother a hormone that stimulates contractions.

Cesarean Delivery

A **cesarean delivery** is a surgical birth; the doctor makes an incision in the mother's abdomen and lifts the baby out of the uterus. It received its name from the belief that Roman emperor Julius Caesar was born this way. Forty years ago, cesarean delivery was rare. Since then, cesarean rates have climbed internationally, reaching 15 percent in Finland, 19 percent in Canada and New Zealand, 21 percent in Australia, and 30 percent in the United States (Canadian Institute for Health Information, 2005; U.S. Department of Health and Human Services, 2006b). And in some Latin American countries, cesareans have skyrocketed, accounting for 27 percent of births in Brazil and 40 percent in Chile (ICAN, 2003).

Cesareans have always been warranted by medical emergencies, such as Rh incompatibility, premature separation of the placenta from the uterus, or serious maternal illness or infection (for example, the herpes simplex 2 virus, which can infect the baby during a vaginal delivery). Cesareans are also justified when babies are in **breech position,** turned so that the buttocks or feet would be delivered first (about 1 in every 25 births). The breech position increases the chances of squeezing of the umbilical cord as the large head moves through the birth canal, thereby depriving the infant of oxygen. Head injuries are also more likely (Golfier et al., 2001). But the infant's exact position (which can be felt by the doctor) makes a difference. Certain breech babies fare just as well with a normal delivery as with a cesarean (Giuliani et al., 2002). Sometimes, too, the doctor can gently turn the baby into a head-down position during the early part of labor.

Until recently, many women who have had a cesarean have been offered the option of a vaginal birth in subsequent pregnancies. But new evidence indicates that compared with repeated cesareans, a natural labor after a cesarean is associated with slightly increased rates of rupture of the uterus and infant death (Gerten et al., 2005). If labor is induced, these risks multiply (Smith et al., 2002b). As a result, the rule, "Once a cesarean, always a cesarean," is making a comeback.

Repeated cesareans, however, do not explain the worldwide rise in cesarean deliveries. Instead, medical control over childbirth is largely responsible. Because many needless cesareans are performed, pregnant women should ask questions about the procedure when choosing a doctor. Although the operation itself is safe, mother and baby require more time for recovery. Anesthetic may have crossed the placenta, making cesarean newborns sleepy and unresponsive and putting them at increased risk for breathing difficulties (McDonagh, Osterweil, & Guise, 2005).

cesarean delivery A surgical delivery in which the doctor makes an incision in the mother's abdomen and lifts the baby out of the uterus.

breech position A position of the baby in the uterus that would cause the buttocks or feet to be delivered first.

Ask Yourself

Review   Describe the features and benefits of natural childbirth. What aspect contributes greatly to favorable outcomes, and why?

Apply   Sharon, a heavy smoker, has just arrived at the hospital in labor. Which one of the medical interventions discussed in the preceding sections is her doctor justified in using? (For help in answering this question, review the prenatal effects of tobacco on page 110 in Chapter 3.)

Connect   Use of any one medical intervention during labor increases the chances that others will also be used. Provide as many examples as you can to illustrate this idea.

Reflect   If you were an expectant parent, would you choose home birth? Why or why not?

Birth Complications

We have seen that some babies—in particular, those whose mothers are in poor health, do not receive good medical care, or have a history of pregnancy problems—are especially likely to experience birth complications. Inadequate oxygen, a pregnancy that ends too early, and a baby who is born underweight are serious risks to development that we have touched on many times. A baby remaining in the uterus too long is yet another risk. Let's look at the impact of each complication on later development.

Oxygen Deprivation

Some years ago, I got to know 4-year-old Melinda and her mother, Judy, both of whom participated in a special program for children with disabilities at our laboratory school. Melinda has **cerebral palsy,** a general term for a variety of problems that result from brain damage before, during, or just after birth. Difficulties in muscle coordination are always involved, such as a clumsy walk, uncontrolled movements, and unclear speech. The disorder can range from very mild tremors to severe crippling and mental retardation. One out of every 500 North American children has cerebral palsy. About 10 percent of these youngsters experienced **anoxia,** or inadequate oxygen supply, along with a buildup of harmful acids and deficiency of vital blood substrates, as a result of decreased maternal blood supply during labor and delivery (Anslow, 1998; Bracci, Perrone, & Buonocore, 2006).

Melinda walks with a halting, lumbering gait and has difficulty keeping her balance. "Some mothers don't know how the palsy happened," confided Judy, "but I do. I got pregnant accidentally, and my boyfriend didn't want to have anything to do with it. I was frightened and alone most of the time. I arrived at the hospital at the last minute. Melinda was breech, and the cord was wrapped around her neck."

Squeezing of the umbilical cord, as in Melinda's case, is one cause of anoxia. Another cause is *placenta abruptio,* or premature separation of the placenta, a life-threatening event with a high rate of infant death (Matsuda, Maeda, & Kouno, 2003). Teratogens that cause constriction of blood vessels and abnormal development of the placenta, such as tobacco and cocaine, are related to it (Ovelese & Ananth, 2006). Just as serious is *placenta previa,* a condition caused by implantation of the blastocyst so low in the uterus that the placenta covers the cervical opening. As the cervix dilates and effaces in the third trimester, part of the placenta may detach. Women who have had previous cesareans or who are carrying multiple fetuses are at increased risk (Ovelese & Smulian, 2006). Although placenta abruptio and placenta previa occur in only 1 to 2 percent of births, they can cause severe hemorrhaging, which requires that an emergency cesarean be performed.

In still other instances, the birth seems to go along all right, but the baby fails to start breathing within a few minutes. Healthy newborns can survive periods of little or no oxygen longer than adults can; they reduce their metabolic rate, thereby conserving the limited oxygen available. Nevertheless, brain damage is likely if a baby is suffering from infection and therefore cannot initiate these protective reactions or if regular breathing is delayed more than 10 minutes (Kendall & Peebles, 2005). **TAKE A MOMENT...** Can you think of other possible causes of oxygen deprivation that you learned about as you studied prenatal development and birth?

After initial brain injury from anoxia, another phase of cell death can occur several hours later. Currently, researchers are experimenting with ways to prevent this secondary damage. Cooling the brain by several degrees and administering growth factors (substances naturally produced by the brain to promote recovery from injury) are effective in newborn rats, pigs, and sheep (Gunn, 2000; Jatana et al., 2006). Similarly, compared with routine treatment, placing anoxic human newborns in a head-cooling device shortly after birth for 72 hours substantially reduced brain injury (detected through brain scans) and increased scores on a newborn behavioral assessment (Lin et al., 2006). And in another study, having anoxic newborns lie on a precooled water blanket resulted in an 18 percent reduction in rate of death or of moderate to severe disability at 18- to 22-month follow-up (Shankaran et al., 2005).

How do children who experience anoxia during labor and delivery fare as they get older? Research suggests that the greater the oxygen deprivation, the poorer children's cognitive and language skills in early and middle childhood (Hopkins-Golightly, Raz, & Sander, 2003). Although effects of even mild to moderate anoxia often persist, many children do improve over time (Bass et al., 2004; Raz, Shah, & Sander, 1996). In Melinda's case, her physical disability was permanent, but with warm, stimulating intervention services, she was just slightly behind in mental development as a preschooler.

When development is severely impaired, the anoxia was probably extreme. Perhaps it was caused by prenatal insult to the baby's respiratory system, or it may have happened because the

cerebral palsy A general term for a variety of problems, all involving muscle coordination, that result from brain damage before, during, or just after birth.

anoxia Inadequate oxygen supply.

Use of this head-cooling device, known as CoolCap, helps prevent brain damage in oxygen-deprived newborns.

OLYMPIC COOL-CAP® SYSTEM IMAGE COURTESY OF NATUS MEDICAL INCORPORATED

infant's lungs were not yet mature enough to breathe. For example, infants born more than 6 weeks early commonly have **respiratory distress syndrome** (otherwise known as *hyaline membrane disease*). Their tiny lungs are so poorly developed that the air sacs collapse, causing serious breathing difficulties. Today, mechanical respirators keep many such infants alive. In spite of these measures, some babies suffer permanent brain damage from lack of oxygen, and in other cases their delicate lungs are harmed by the treatment itself. Respiratory distress syndrome is only one of many risks for babies born too soon, as we will see in the following section.

Preterm and Low-Birth-Weight Infants

Janet, almost six months pregnant, and her husband, Rick, boarded a flight in Hartford, Connecticut, on their way to a vacation in Hawaii. During a stopover in San Francisco, Janet told Rick she was bleeding. Rushed to a hospital, she gave birth to Keith, who weighed less than 1½ pounds. Delivered 23 weeks after conception, he had barely reached the age of viability (see Chapter 3, page 102).

During Keith's first month, he experienced one crisis after another. Three days after birth, an ultrasound scan suggested that fragile blood vessels feeding Keith's brain had hemorrhaged, a complication that can cause brain damage. Within three weeks, Keith had surgery to close a heart valve that seals automatically in full-term babies. Keith's immature immune system made infections difficult to contain. Repeated illnesses and the drugs used to treat them caused permanent hearing loss. Keith also had respiratory distress syndrome and breathed with the help of a respirator. Soon there was evidence of lung damage. More than three months of hospitalization passed before Keith's rough course of complications and treatment eased.

Babies born three weeks or more before the end of a full 38-week pregnancy or who weigh less than 5½ pounds (2,500 grams) have for many years been referred to as "premature." A wealth of research indicates that premature babies are at risk for many problems. Birth weight is the best available predictor of infant survival and healthy development. Many newborns who weigh less than 3⅓ pounds (1,500 grams) experience difficulties that are not overcome, an effect that becomes stronger as birth weight decreases (Laptook et al., 2005; Minde, 2000). Frequent illness, inattention, overactivity, sensory impairments, poor motor coordination, language delays, low intelligence test scores, deficits in school learning, and emotional and behavior problems are some of the difficulties that persist through childhood and adolescence and into adulthood (Grunau, Whitfield, & Fay, 2004; Hack et al., 2002; Lefebvre, Mazurier, & Tessier, 2005).

About 1 in 13 American infants and 1 in 18 Canadian infants are born underweight. The problem can occur unexpectedly, as it did for Janet and Rick. But it is highest among poverty-stricken women (Children's Defense Fund, 2006; Statistics Canada, 2006a). These mothers, as indicated in Chapter 3, are more likely to be undernourished and exposed to other harmful environmental influences—factors strongly linked to low birth weight. In addition, they often do not receive the prenatal care necessary to protect their vulnerable babies.

Recall from Chapter 2 that prematurity is also common among twins, who are usually born about three weeks early. Because space inside the uterus is restricted, they gain less weight than singletons after the twentieth week of pregnancy.

PRETERM VERSUS SMALL-FOR-DATE INFANTS ■ Although low-birth-weight infants face many obstacles to healthy development, most go on to lead normal lives; about half of those who weighed only a couple of pounds at birth have no disability (see Figure 4.4). To better understand why some babies do better than others, researchers divide them into two groups. **Preterm infants** are born several weeks or more before their due date. Although they are small, their weight may still be appropriate, based on time spent in the uterus. **Small-for-date infants** are below their expected weight when length of the pregnancy is taken into account. Some small-for-date infants are actually full-term. Others are preterm babies who are especially underweight.

Of the two types of babies, small-for-date infants usually have more serious problems. During the first year, they are more likely to die, catch infections, and show evidence of brain

respiratory distress syndrome A disorder of preterm infants in which the lungs are so immature that the air sacs collapse, causing serious breathing difficulties.

preterm infants Infants born several weeks or more before their due date.

small-for-date infants Infants whose birth weight is below normal when length of the pregnancy is taken into account.

damage. By middle childhood, they have lower intelligence test scores, are less attentive, achieve more poorly in school, and are socially immature (Hediger et al., 2002; O'Keefe et al., 2003). Small-for-date infants probably experienced inadequate nutrition before birth. Perhaps their mothers did not eat properly, the placenta did not function normally, or the babies themselves had defects that prevented them from growing as they should. In some of these babies, an abnormally functioning placenta permitted ready transfer of stress hormones from mother to fetus. Consequently, small-for-date infants are especially likely to suffer from prenatal neurological impairments that permanently weaken their capacity to manage stress (Wust et al., 2005).

Even among preterm newborns whose weight is appropriate for length of pregnancy, just 7 more days—from 34 to 35 weeks—can contribute greatly to infant health. Compared to babies born at 34 weeks, those born at 35 weeks show substantially reduced rates of illness, costly medical procedures, and lengthy hospital stays (although they need greater medical intervention than full-term babies) (Gladstone & Katz, 2004). And despite being relatively low-risk for disabilities, a substantial number of 34-week preterms are well below average in physical growth and mildly to moderately delayed in cognitive development in early and middle childhood (de Haan et al., 2000; Pietz et al., 2004). Yet doctors often induce births several weeks preterm, under the misconception that these babies are developmentally "mature."

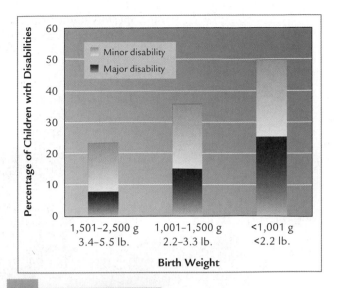

FIGURE 4.4

Incidence of major and minor disabilities by birth weight, obtained from studies of low-birth-weight children at school age. *Major disabilities* include cerebral palsy, mental retardation, and vision and hearing impairments. *Minor disabilities* include slightly below-average intelligence, learning disabilities (usually in reading, spelling, and math), mild difficulties in motor control, and behavior problems (including poor attention and impulse control, aggressiveness, noncompliance, depression, passivity, anxiety, and difficulty separating from parents). (Adapted from D'Agostino & Clifford, 1998.)

CONSEQUENCES FOR CAREGIVING ■ Imagine a scrawny, thin-skinned infant whose body is only a little larger than the size of your hand. You try to play with the baby by stroking and talking softly, but he is sleepy and unresponsive. When you feed him, he sucks poorly. During the short, unpredictable periods in which he is awake, he is usually irritable.

The appearance and behavior of preterm babies can lead parents to be less sensitive and responsive in caring for them. Compared to full-term infants, preterm babies—especially those who are very ill at birth—are less often held close, touched, and talked to gently. At times, mothers of these infants resort to interfering pokes and verbal commands, in an effort to obtain a higher level of response from the baby (Barratt, Roach, & Leavitt, 1996). This may explain why preterm babies as a group are at risk for child abuse. When they are born to isolated, poverty-stricken mothers who cannot provide good nutrition, health care, and parenting, the likelihood of unfavorable outcomes increases. In contrast, parents with stable life circumstances and social supports usually can overcome the stresses of caring for a preterm infant. In these cases, even sick preterm babies have a good chance of catching up in development by middle childhood (Ment et al., 2003).

These findings suggest that how well preterm babies develop has a great deal to do with the parent–child relationship. Consequently, interventions directed at supporting both sides of this tie are more likely to help these infants recover.

INTERVENTIONS FOR PRETERM INFANTS ■ A preterm baby is cared for in a special Plexiglas-enclosed bed called an *isolette*. Temperature is carefully controlled because these infants cannot yet regulate their own body temperature effectively. To help protect the baby from infection, air is filtered before it enters the isolette. When a preterm infant is fed through a stomach tube, breathes with the aid of a respirator, and receives medication through an intravenous needle, the isolette can be very isolating indeed! Physical needs that otherwise would lead to close contact and other human stimulation are met mechanically.

Special Infant Stimulation. At one time doctors believed that stimulating such fragile babies could be harmful. Now we know that in proper doses, certain kinds of stimulation can help preterm infants develop. In some intensive care nurseries, preterm babies can be seen rocking in suspended hammocks or lying on waterbeds designed to replace the gentle motion they would have received while still in the mother's uterus. Other forms of stimulation have also been used—an attractive mobile or a tape recording of a heartbeat, soft music, or the mother's voice. These experiences promote faster weight gain, more predictable sleep patterns, and greater alertness (Arnon et al., 2006; Marshall-Baker, Lickliter, & Cooper, 1998; Standley, 1998).

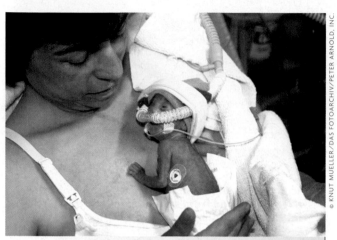

This mother is practicing "kangaroo care" with her preterm baby in the intensive care nursery. By holding the infant close to her chest, she promotes oxygenation of the baby's body, temperature regulation, feeding, alertness, and more favorable development. At the same time, she gains confidence in her ability to meet her fragile newborn's needs.

Touch is an especially important form of stimulation. In baby animals, touching the skin releases certain brain chemicals that support physical growth—effects believed to occur in humans as well. When preterm infants were gently massaged several times each day in the hospital, they gained weight faster and, at the end of the first year, were more advanced in mental and motor development than preterm babies not given this stimulation (Field, 2001; Field, Hernandez-Reif, & Freedman, 2004).

In developing countries where hospitalization is not always possible, skin-to-skin "kangaroo care" is the most readily available intervention for promoting the survival and recovery of preterm babies. It involves placing the infant in a vertical position between the mother's breasts or next to the father's chest (under the parent's clothing) so the parent's body functions as a human incubator. Kangaroo care offers fathers a unique opportunity to increase their involvement in caring for the preterm newborn. Because of its many physical and psychological benefits, the technique is used often in Western nations as a supplement to hospital intensive care.

Kangaroo skin-to-skin contact fosters improved oxygenation of the baby's body, temperature regulation, sleep, feeding, alertness, and infant survival (Feldman & Eidelman, 2003). In addition, the kangaroo position provides the baby with gentle stimulation of all sensory modalities: hearing (through the parent's voice), smell (through proximity of the parent's body), touch (through skin-to-skin contact), and visual (through the upright position). Mothers and fathers practicing kangaroo care feel more confident about caring for their fragile babies, interact more sensitively and affectionately, and feel more attached to them (Dodd, 2005; Feldman et al., 2002, 2003). Together, these factors may explain why preterm babies given many hours of kangaroo care in their early weeks, compared to those given little or no such care, score higher on measures of mental and motor development during the first year (Charpak, Ruiz-Peláez, & Figueroa, 2005; Tessier et al., 2003). Because of its diverse benefits, more than 80 percent of North American hospital nurseries now offer kangaroo care to preterm newborns (Engler et al., 2002).

Training Parents in Infant Caregiving Skills. Interventions that support parents of preterm infants generally teach them about the infant's characteristics and promote caregiving skills. For parents with the economic and personal resources to care for a preterm infant, just a few sessions of coaching in recognizing and responding to the baby's needs are linked to steady gains in mental test performance that, after several years, equal those of full-term children (Achenbach et al., 1990). Warm parenting that helps preterm infants sustain attention (for example, gently commenting on and showing the baby features of a toy) is especially helpful in promoting early cognitive and language development (Smith et al., 1996).

When preterm infants live in stressed, low-income households, long-term intensive intervention is necessary. In the Infant Health and Development Project, preterm babies born into poverty received a comprehensive intervention that combined medical follow-up, weekly parent training sessions, and cognitively stimulating child care from 1 to 3 years of age. More than four times as many intervention children as no-intervention controls (39 versus 9 percent) were within normal range at age 3 in intelligence, psychological adjustment, and physical growth (Bradley et al., 1994). In addition, mothers in the intervention group were more affectionate and more often encouraged play and cognitive mastery in their children—one reason their 3-year-olds may have been developing so favorably (McCarton, 1998).

At ages 5 and 8, children who had attended the child-care program regularly—for more than 350 days over the three-year period—continued to show better intellectual functioning. The more they attended, the higher they scored, with greater gains among those whose birth weights were higher—between 4½ and 5½ pounds (2,001 to 2,500 grams) (see Figure 4.5). In contrast, children who attended only sporadically gained little or even lost ground (Hill, Brooks-Gunn, & Waldfogel, 2003). These findings confirm that babies who are both preterm and economically disadvantaged require *intensive* intervention. And special strategies, such as extra adult–child interaction, may be necessary to achieve lasting changes in children with the lowest birth weights.

VERY LOW BIRTH WEIGHT, ENVIRONMENTAL ADVANTAGES, AND LONG-TERM OUTCOMES ■ Although very low-birth-weight individuals often have lasting problems, in a Canadian study, participants who weighed between 1 and 2.2 pounds (500 to 1,000 grams) at birth were doing well as young adults (Saigal et al., 2006). At 22 to 25 years of age, they resembled normal-birth-weight individuals in educational attainment, rates of marriage and parenthood, and (for those who had no neurological or sensory impairments) employment status. What explains these excellent outcomes? Researchers believe that home, school, and societal advantages are largely responsible (Hack & Klein, 2006). Most participants in this study were reared in two-parent middle-SES homes, attended good schools where they received special services, and benefited from Canada's universal health care system.

Nevertheless, even the best environments cannot "fix" the enormous biological risks associated with very low birth weight. Think back to Keith, the very sick baby you met at the beginning of this section. Despite advanced medical technology and new ways of helping parents, all but a few infants born as early and with as low a birth weight as Keith either die or end up with serious disabilities (Mathews & Mac-Dorman, 2006). Six months after he was born, Keith died without ever having left the hospital.

Keith's premature birth was unavoidable, but the high rate of underweight babies in the United States—one of the worst in the industrialized world—could be greatly reduced by improving the health and social conditions described in the Social Issues: Health box on pages 144–145. Fortunately, today we can save many preterm babies, but an even better course of action would be to prevent this serious threat to infant survival and development before it happens.

Birth Complications, Parenting, and Resilience

In the preceding sections, we considered a variety of birth complications. Now let's try to put the evidence together. Can any general principles help us understand how infants who survive a traumatic birth are likely to develop? A landmark study carried out in Hawaii provides answers to this question.

In 1955, Emmy Werner began to follow the development of nearly 700 infants on the island of Kauai who experienced either mild, moderate, or severe birth complications. Each was matched, on the basis of SES and ethnicity, with a healthy newborn (Werner &

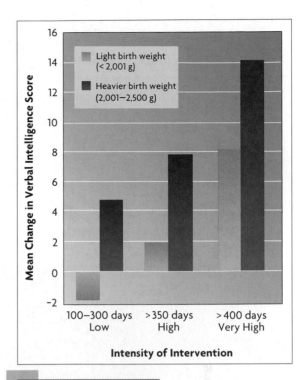

FIGURE 4.5

Influence of intensity of early intervention for low-income, preterm babies on intellectual functioning at age 8. Infants born preterm received cognitively stimulating child care from 1 through 3 years of age. Those who attended the program sporadically either gained little in intellectual functioning (heavier-weight babies) or lost ground (lighter-weight babies). The more children attended, the greater their intellectual gains. Heavier babies consistently gained more than light babies. But boosting the intensity of intervention above 400 days led to a dramatic increase in the performance of the light-weight group. (Adapted from Hill, Brooks-Gunn, & Waldfogel, 2003.)

Social Issues: Health

A Cross-National Perspective on Health Care and Other Policies for Parents and Newborn Babies

Infant mortality—the number of deaths in the first year of life per 1,000 live births—is an index used around the world to assess the overall health of a nation's children. The United States has the most up-to-date health care technology in the world, including a newborn intensive care capacity per number of births far exceeding that of other industrialized nations (Thompson, Goodman, & Little, 2002). Nevertheless, it has made less progress in reducing infant deaths than many other countries. Over the past three decades, it has slipped in the international rankings, from seventh in the 1950s to twenty-sixth in 2006. Members of America's poor ethnic minorities are at greatest risk. African-American and Native-American babies are twice as likely as white infants to die in the first year of life (U.S. Census Bureau, 2007b).

Canada, in contrast, has achieved one of the lowest infant mortality rates in the world. It ranks sixteenth and falls only slightly behind top-ranked countries. Still, infant mortality among Canada's lowest-income groups is much higher than the national figure. First Nations babies die at twice the rate, and Inuit babies at three times the rate, of Canadian babies in general (Smylie, 2001; Statistics Canada, 2005f).

Neonatal mortality, the rate of death within the first month of life, accounts for 67 percent of the infant death rate in the United States and for 80 percent in Canada. Two factors are largely responsible for neonatal mortality. The first is serious physical defects, most of which cannot be prevented. The percentage of babies born with physical defects is about the same in all ethnic and income groups. The second leading cause of neonatal mortality is low birth weight, which is largely preventable. African-American, Native-American, and Canadian Aboriginal babies are more than twice as likely as white infants to be born early and underweight (Health Canada, 2004b; U.S. Census Bureau, 2007b).

Widespread poverty and, in the United States, weak health care programs for mothers and young children are largely responsible for these trends. Each country listed in Figure 4.6 that outranks the United States in infant survival provides all its citizens with government-sponsored health care benefits. And each takes extra steps to make sure that pregnant mothers and babies have access to good nutrition, high-quality medical care, and social and economic supports that promote effective parenting.

For example, all Western European nations guarantee women a certain number of prenatal visits at very low or no cost. After a baby is born, a health professional routinely visits the home to provide counseling about infant care and to arrange continuing medical services. Home assistance is especially extensive in the Netherlands. For a token fee, each mother is granted a specially trained maternity helper, who assists with infant care, shopping, housekeeping, meal preparation, and the care of other children during the days after delivery (Bradley & Bray, 1996; Kamerman, 1993).

Paid, job-protected employment leave is another vital societal intervention for new parents. Canadian mothers are eligible for 15 weeks' maternity leave at 55 percent of prior earnings, and Canadian mothers or fathers are eligible for an additional 35 weeks of parental leave at the same rate. Paid leave is widely available in other industrialized nations as well. Sweden has the most generous parental leave program in the world. Parents have the right to paid birth leave of two weeks for fathers plus 18 months of paid leave to share between them—the first 12 months at 80 percent of prior earnings, the next three months at a modest flat rate, and the final three months unpaid (Seward, Yeats, & Zottarelli, 2002). Even less-developed

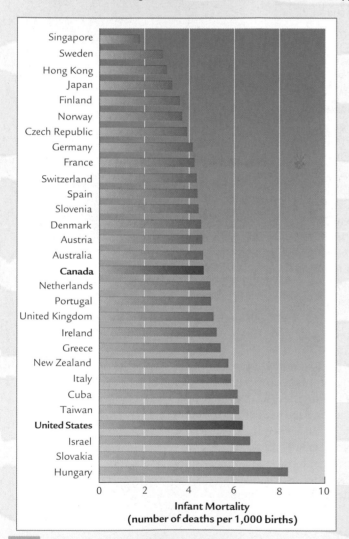

FIGURE 4.6

Infant mortality in 29 nations. Despite its advanced health care technology, the United States ranks poorly. It is twenty-sixth in the world, with a death rate of 6.6 infants per 1,000 births. Canada, which provides all its citizens government-funded health care, ranks fifteenth. Its infant death rate is 4.8 per 1,000 births. (Adapted from U.S. Census Bureau, 2007a.)

nations provide parental leave benefits. For example, in the People's Republic of China, a new mother is granted three months' leave at regular pay. Furthermore, many countries supplement basic paid leave. In Germany, for example, after a fully paid three-month leave, a parent may take two more years at a modest flat rate and a third year at no pay (Waldfogel, 2001).

Yet in the United States, the federal government mandates *only 12 weeks of unpaid leave* for employees in companies with at least 50 workers. Most women, however, work in smaller businesses (Hewlett, 2003). And because of financial pressures, many new mothers who are eligible for unpaid work leave take far less than 12 weeks, while new fathers tend to take little or none at all (Han & Waldfogel, 2003). In 2002, California became the first state to guarantee a mother or father paid leave—up to six weeks at half salary, regardless of the size of the company.

Nevertheless, research indicates that six weeks of childbirth leave (the norm in the United States) is not enough. When a family is stressed by a baby's arrival, a leave of six weeks or less is linked to maternal anxiety, depression, sense of role overload (conflict between work and family responsibilities), and negative interactions with the baby. A longer leave (12 weeks or more) predicts favorable maternal mental health, supportive marital interaction, and sensitive, responsive caregiving (Feldman, Sussman, & Zigler, 2004; Hyde et al., 2001). Single women and their babies are most hurt by the absence of a generous national paid-leave policy. These mothers, who are usually the sole source of support for their families, can least afford to take time from their jobs.

In countries with low infant mortality rates, expectant mothers need not wonder how they will get health care and other resources to support their baby's development. The

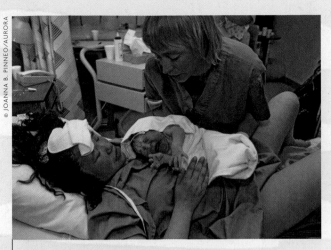

This Inuit mother, from Baffin Island in northernmost Canada, experienced pregnancy complications and had to be flown 190 miles to deliver her son. Limited access to health care and social services in remote areas compromises the futures of many Inuit newborns.

powerful impact of universal, high-quality health care, generous parental leave, and other social services on maternal and infant well-being provides strong justification for these policies.

Smith, 1982). Findings showed that the likelihood of long-term difficulties increased if birth trauma was severe. But among mildly to moderately stressed children, those growing up in stable families did almost as well on measures of intelligence and psychological adjustment as those with no birth problems. Those exposed to poverty, family disorganization, and mentally ill parents often developed serious learning difficulties, behavior problems, and emotional disturbance.

The Kauai study tells us that as long as birth injuries are not overwhelming, a supportive home can restore children's growth. But the most intriguing cases in this study were the handful of exceptions. A few children with serious birth complications and troubled family environments grew into competent adults who fared as well as controls in career attainment and psychological adjustment. Werner found that these children relied on factors outside the family and within themselves to overcome stress. Some had attractive personalities that drew positive responses from relatives, neighbors, and peers. In other instances, a grandparent, aunt, uncle, or baby-sitter provided the needed emotional support (Werner, 1989, 2001; Werner & Smith, 1992).

Do these outcomes remind you of the characteristics of resilient children, discussed in Chapter 1? The Kauai study and other similar investigations reveal that the impact of early biological risks often wanes as children's personal characteristics and social experiences contribute increasingly to their functioning (Laucht, Esser, & Schmidt, 1997; Resnick et al., 1999). In sum, when the overall balance of life events tips toward the favorable side, children with serious birth problems can develop successfully. And when negative factors outweigh positive ones, even a sturdy newborn can become a lifelong casualty.

infant mortality Number of deaths in the first year of life per 1,000 live births.

neonatal mortality Number of deaths in the first month of life per 1,000 live births.

Ask Yourself

Review   Sensitive care can help preterm infants recover, but unfortunately they are less likely than full-term newborns to receive such care. Explain why.

Apply   Cecilia and Adena each gave birth to a three-pound baby seven weeks preterm. Cecilia is single and on welfare. Adena and her husband are happily married and earn a good income. Plan an intervention appropriate for helping each baby develop.

Connect   List factors discussed in this chapter and in Chapter 3 that increase the chances that an infant will be born underweight. How many of these factors could be prevented by better health care for mothers and babies?

Reflect   Many people object to the use of extraordinary medical measures to save extremely low-birth-weight babies because of their high risk for serious and persistent developmental problems. Do you agree or disagree? Explain.

Precious Moments After Birth

© SEAN CAYTON/THE IMAGE WORKS

This father displays great affection for and involvement with his newborn baby. Like mothers, fathers typically express their elation by touching, looking at, talking to, and kissing the infant.

Yolanda and Jay's account of Joshua's birth revealed that the time spent holding and touching him right after delivery was filled with intense emotion. A mother given her infant at this time will usually stroke the baby gently, look into the infant's eyes, and talk softly (Klaus & Kennell, 1982). Fathers respond similarly. Most are overjoyed at the birth of the baby; characterize the experience as "awesome," "indescribable," or "unforgettable"; and display intense interest in their newborn child (Bader, 1995; Rose, 2000). Regardless of SES or participation in childbirth classes, fathers touch, look at, talk to, and kiss their newborn infants just as much as mothers do. When they hold the baby, they sometimes exceed mothers in stimulation and affection (Parke & Tinsley, 1981).

Certain parental hormonal changes in the presence of the newborn help foster parents' involvement and sensitivity. Toward the end of pregnancy, mothers begin producing *oxytocin,* a hormone that causes the breasts to "let down" milk and heightens responsiveness to the baby (Russell, Douglas, & Ingram, 2001). And in several studies, first-time fathers showed hormonal changes around the time of birth that were compatible with those of mothers—specifically, slight increases in *prolactin* (a hormone that stimulates milk production in females) and *estrogens* (sex hormones produced in larger quantities in females) and a drop in *androgens* (sex hormones produced in larger quantities in males). In animal and human research, these changes are associated with positive emotional reactions to infants and with paternal caregiving (Storey et al., 2000; Wynne-Edwards, 2001).

But do human parents require close physical contact in the hours after birth for **bonding,** or feelings of affection and concern for the infant, to develop—as many animal species do? Current evidence shows that the human parent–infant relationship does not depend on a precise, early period of togetherness. Some parents report sudden, deep feelings of affection on first holding their babies. For others, these emotions emerge gradually (Lamb, 1994). In adoptive parents, a warm, affectionate relationship can develop even if the child enters the family months or years after birth (see page 00 in Chapter 2). Human bonding is a complex process that depends on many factors, not just on what happens during a short sensitive period.

Still, contact with the baby after birth may be one of several factors that helps build a good parent–infant relationship. Research shows that mothers learn to discriminate their newborn baby from other infants on the basis of touch, smell, and sight (a photograph) after as little as one hour of contact (Kaitz et al., 1987, 1988, 1993a). Fathers, as well, can recognize their baby by touch and sight after brief exposure (Bader & Phillips, 2002; Kaitz et al., 1993b). This early recognition probably facilitates responsiveness to the infant.

Clearly, early contact supports parental engagement with the newborn, although it is neither necessary nor a guarantee of it. Realizing this, today hospitals offer **rooming in,** in which the infant stays in the mother's hospital room all or most of the time. If parents do not choose this option or cannot do so for medical reasons, there is no evidence that their competence as caregivers will be compromised or that the baby will suffer emotionally.

The Newborn Baby's Capacities

As recently as the mid-twentieth century, scientists considered the newborn baby to be a passive, disorganized being who could see, hear, feel, and do very little. Today we know that this image is wrong. Newborn infants have a remarkable set of capacities that are crucial for survival and for evoking adult attention and care. In relating to the physical and social world, babies are active from the very start.

Reflexes

A **reflex** is an inborn, automatic response to a particular form of stimulation. Reflexes are the newborn baby's most obvious organized patterns of behavior. As Jay placed Joshua on a table in my classroom, we saw several. When Jay bumped the side of the table, Joshua reacted by flinging his arms wide and bringing them back toward his body. As Yolanda stroked Joshua's cheek, he turned his head in her direction. When she put her finger in Joshua's palm, he grabbed on tightly. **TAKE A MOMENT...** Look at Table 4.2 on page 148 and see if you can name the newborn reflexes that Joshua displayed. Then let's consider the meaning and purpose of these curious behaviors.

ADAPTIVE VALUE OF REFLEXES ■ Some reflexes have survival value. The rooting reflex helps a breastfed baby find the mother's nipple. Babies display it only when hungry and touched by another person, not when they touch themselves (Rochat & Hespos, 1997). And if sucking were not automatic, our species would be unlikely to survive for a single generation! At birth, babies adjust their sucking pressure to how easily milk flows from the nipple (Craig & Lee, 1999). The swimming reflex helps a baby who is accidentally dropped into a body of water stay afloat, increasing the chances of retrieval by the caregiver.

Other reflexes probably helped babies survive during our evolutionary past. For example, the Moro, or "embracing," reflex is believed to have helped infants cling to their mothers when they were carried about all day. If the baby happened to lose support, the reflex caused the infant to embrace and, along with the palmar grasp reflex (so strong during the first week that it can support the baby's entire weight), regain its hold on the mother's body (Kessen, 1967; Prechtl, 1958).

Several reflexes help parents and infants establish gratifying interaction. A baby who searches for and successfully finds the nipple, sucks easily during feedings, and grasps when her hand is touched encourages parents to respond lovingly and feel competent as caregivers. Reflexes can also help parents comfort the baby because they permit infants to control distress and amount of stimulation. For example, on short trips with Joshua to the grocery store, Yolanda brought along a pacifier. If he became fussy, sucking helped quiet him until she could feed, change, or hold and rock him.

REFLEXES AND THE DEVELOPMENT OF MOTOR SKILLS ■ A few reflexes form the basis for complex motor skills that will develop later. For example, the tonic neck reflex may prepare the baby for voluntary reaching. When infants lie on their backs in this "fencing position," they naturally gaze at the hand in front of their eyes. The reflex may encourage them to combine vision with arm movements and, eventually, reach for objects (Knobloch & Pasamanick, 1974).

The palmar grasp reflex is so strong during the first week after birth that many infants can use it to support their entire weight.

bonding Parents' feelings of affection and concern for the newborn baby.

rooming in An arrangement in which the newborn baby stays in the mother's hospital room all or most of the time.

reflex An inborn, automatic response to a particular form of stimulation.

TABLE 4.2   Some Newborn Reflexes

REFLEX	STIMULATION	RESPONSE	AGE OF DISAPPEARANCE	FUNCTION
Eye blink	Shine bright light at eyes or clap hand near head	Infant quickly closes eyelids	Permanent	Protects infant from strong stimulation
Rooting	Stroke cheek near corner of mouth	Head turns toward source of stimulation	3 weeks (becomes voluntary head turning at this time)	Helps infant find the nipple
Sucking	Place finger in infant's mouth	Infant sucks finger rhythmically	Replaced by voluntary sucking after 4 months	Permits feeding
Swimming	Place infant face down in pool of water	Baby paddles and kicks in swimming motion	4–6 months	Helps infant survive if dropped into water
Moro	Hold infant horizontally on back and let head drop slightly, or produce a sudden loud sound against surface supporting infant	Infant makes an "embracing" motion by arching back, extending legs, throwing arms outward, and then bringing arms in toward the body	6 months	In human evolutionary past, may have helped infant cling to mother
Palmar grasp	Place finger in infant's hand and press against palm	Spontaneous grasp of finger	3–4 months	Prepares infant for voluntary grasping
Tonic neck	Turn baby's head to one side while infant is lying awake on back	Infant lies in a "fencing position." One arm is extended in front of eyes on side to which head is turned, other arm is flexed	4 months	May prepare infant for voluntary reaching
Stepping	Hold infant under arms and permit bare feet to touch a flat surface	Infant lifts one foot after another in stepping response	2 months in infants who gain weight quickly; sustained in lighter infants	Prepares infant for voluntary walking
Babinski	Stroke sole of foot from toe toward heel	Toes fan out and curl as foot twists in	8–12 months	Unknown

Sources: Knobloch & Pasamanick, 1974; Prechtl & Beintema, 1965; Thelen, Fisher, & Ridley-Johnson, 1984.

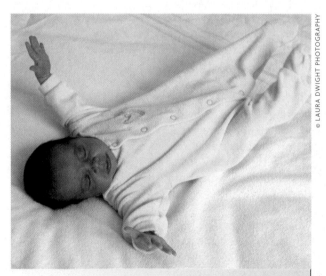

© LAURA DWIGHT PHOTOGRAPHY

In the Moro reflex, loss of support or a sudden loud sound causes this baby to arch her back, extend her arms outward, and then bring them in toward her body.

Certain reflexes—such as the palmar grasp, swimming, and stepping—drop out early, but the motor functions involved are renewed later. The stepping reflex, for example, looks like a primitive walking response. Unlike other reflexes, it appears in a wide range of situations—with the newborn's body in a sideway or upside-down position, with feet touching walls or ceilings and even with legs dangling in the air (Adolph & Berger, 2006). One reason that babies frequently engage in the alternating leg movements of stepping is their ease compared with other movement patterns; repetitive movement of one leg or of both legs at once requires more effort.

In infants who gain weight quickly in the weeks after birth, stepping drops out because thigh and calf muscles are not strong enough to lift the baby's chubby legs. But if the lower part of the infant's body is dipped in water, the reflex reappears because the buoyancy of the water lightens the load on the baby's muscles (Thelen, Fisher, & Ridley-Johnson, 1984). When stepping is exercised regularly, babies display more spontaneous stepping movements and gain muscle strength. Consequently, they tend to walk several weeks earlier than if stepping is not

This baby shows the Babinski reflex. When an adult strokes the sole of the foot, the toes fan out. Then they curl as the foot twists in.

When held upright under the arms, newborn babies show reflexive stepping movements.

practiced (Zelazo et al., 1993). However, there is no special need for infants to practice the stepping reflex—all normal babies walk in due time.

In the case of the swimming reflex, trying to build on it is risky. Although young babies placed in a swimming pool will paddle and kick, they swallow large amounts of water. This lowers the concentration of salt in the baby's blood, which can cause brain swelling and seizures. Despite this remarkable reflex, swimming lessons are best postponed until at least 3 years of age.

THE IMPORTANCE OF ASSESSING NEWBORN REFLEXES ■ Look at Table 4.2 again, and you will see that most newborn reflexes disappear during the first six months. Researchers believe that this is due to a gradual increase in voluntary control over behavior as the cerebral cortex develops. Pediatricians test reflexes carefully, especially if a newborn has experienced birth trauma, because reflexes can reveal the health of the baby's nervous system. Weak or absent reflexes, overly rigid or exaggerated reflexes, and reflexes that persist beyond the point in development when they should normally disappear can signal brain damage (Schott & Rossor, 2003; Zafeiriou, 2000). However, individual differences in reflexive responses exist that are not cause for concern. An observer must assess newborn reflexes along with other characteristics to accurately distinguish normal from abnormal central nervous system functioning (Touwen, 1984).

States

Throughout the day and night, newborn infants move in and out of the five **states of arousal,** or degrees of sleep and wakefulness, described in Table 4.3 on page 150. During the first month, these states alternate frequently. The most fleeting is quiet alertness, which usually moves quickly toward fussing and crying. Much to the relief of their fatigued parents, newborns spend the greatest amount of time asleep—about 16 to 18 hours a day. Newborns—even those who are four to six weeks preterm—sleep more at night than during the day (Rivkees, 2003). Nevertheless, their sleep–wake cycles are affected more by fullness–hunger than by darkness–light (Davis, Parker, & Montgomery, 2004; Goodlin-Jones, Burnham, & Anders, 2000).

However, striking individual differences in daily rhythms exist that affect parents' attitudes toward and interactions with the baby. A few newborns sleep for long periods, increasing the energy their well-rested parents have for sensitive, responsive care. Other babies cry a great deal, and their parents must exert great effort to soothe them. If these parents do not succeed, they may feel less competent and less positive toward their infant. Babies who spend more time alert probably receive more social stimulation and opportunities to explore and therefore may have a slight advantage in mental development (Gertner et al., 2002).

Of the states listed in Table 4.3 the two extremes—sleep and crying—have been of greatest interest to researchers. Each tells us something about normal and abnormal early development.

states of arousal Different degrees of sleep and wakefulness.

SLEEP ■ One day, Yolanda and Jay watched Joshua while he slept and wondered why his eyelids and body twitched and his rate of breathing varied. Sleep is made up of at least two states.

TABLE 4.3   Infant States of Arousal

STATE	DESCRIPTION	DAILY DURATION IN NEWBORN
Regular, or NREM, sleep	The infant is at full rest and shows little or no body activity. The eyelids are closed, no eye movements occur, the face is relaxed, and breathing is slow and regular.	8–9 hours
Irregular, or REM, sleep	Gentle limb movements, occasional stirring, and facial grimacing occur. Although the eyelids are closed, occasional rapid eye movements can be seen beneath them. Breathing is irregular.	8–9 hours
Drowsiness	The infant is either falling asleep or waking up. Body is less active than in irregular sleep but more active than in regular sleep. The eyes open and close; when open, they have a glazed look. Breathing is even but somewhat faster than in regular sleep.	Varies
Quiet alertness	The infant's body is relatively inactive, with eyes open and attentive. Breathing is even.	2–3 hours
Waking activity and crying	The infant shows frequent bursts of uncoordinated body activity. Breathing is very irregular. Face may be relaxed or tense and wrinkled. Crying may occur.	1–4 hours

Source: Wolff, 1966.

rapid-eye-movement (REM) sleep An "irregular" sleep state in which brain-wave activity is similar to that of the waking state.

non-rapid-eye-movement (NREM) sleep A "regular" sleep state in which the body is quiet and heart rate, breathing, and brain-wave activity are slow and regular.

sudden infant death syndrome (SIDS) The unexpected death, usually during the night, of an infant younger than 1 year of age that remains unexplained after thorough investigation.

Yolanda and Jay happened to observe irregular, or **rapid-eye-movement (REM), sleep,** in which brain-wave activity is remarkably similar to that of the waking state. The eyes dart beneath the lids; heart rate, blood pressure, and breathing are uneven; and slight body movements occur. The expression "sleeping like a baby" was probably not meant to describe this state! In contrast, during regular, or **non-rapid-eye-movement (NREM), sleep,** the body is almost motionless, and heart rate, breathing, and brain-wave activity are slow and even.

Like children and adults, newborns alternate between REM and NREM sleep. However, they spend far more time in the REM state than they ever will again. REM sleep accounts for 50 percent of the newborn baby's sleep time. By 3 to 5 years, it has declined to an adultlike level of 20 percent (Louis et al., 1997).

Why do young infants spend so much time in REM sleep? In older children and adults, the REM state is associated with dreaming. Babies probably do not dream, at least not in the same way we do. But researchers believe that the stimulation of REM sleep is vital for growth of the central nervous system. Young infants seem to have a special need for this stimulation because they spend so little time in an alert state, when they can get input from the environment. In support of this idea, the percentage of REM sleep is especially great in the fetus and in preterm babies, who are even less able than full-term newborns to take advantage of external stimulation (de Weerd & van den Bossche, 2003; Peirano, Algarin, & Uauy, 2003).

Whereas the brain-wave activity of REM sleep safeguards the central nervous system, the rapid eye movements protect the health of the eye. Eye movements cause the vitreous (gelatin-like substance within the eye) to circulate, thereby delivering oxygen to parts of the eye that do not have their own blood supply. During sleep, when the eyes and the vitreous are still, visual structures are at risk for anoxia. As the brain cycles through REM-sleep periods, rapid eye movements stir up the vitreous, ensuring that the eye is fully oxygenated (Blumberg & Lucas, 1996).

Because the normal sleep behavior of the newborn baby is organized and patterned, observations of sleep states can help identify central nervous system abnormalities. In infants who are brain-damaged or who have experienced serious birth trauma, disturbed REM–NREM sleep cycles are often present. Babies with poor sleep organization are likely to be behaviorally disorganized and, therefore, to have difficulty learning and eliciting caregiver interactions that enhance their development. In follow-ups during the preschool years, they show delayed motor, cognitive, and language development (de Weerd & van den Bossche, 2003; Feldman, 2006; Holditch-Davis, Belyea, & Edwards, 2005). And the brain-functioning problems that underlie newborn sleep irregularities may culminate in sudden infant death syndrome, a major cause of infant mortality (see the Social Issues: Health box on the following page).

Social Issues: Health

The Mysterious Tragedy of Sudden Infant Death Syndrome

Millie awoke with a start one morning and looked at the clock. It was 7:30, and Sasha had missed both her night waking and her early morning feeding. Wondering if she was all right, Millie and her husband, Stuart, tiptoed into the room. Sasha lay still, curled up under her blanket. She had died silently during her sleep.

Sasha was a victim of **sudden infant death syndrome (SIDS),** the unexpected death, usually during the night, of an infant younger than 1 year of age that remains unexplained after thorough investigation. In industrialized nations, SIDS is the leading cause of infant mortality between 1 week and 12 months. Its incidence peaks between ages 2 and 4 months (Health Canada, 2004d; Hamilton et al., 2005).

Although the precise cause of SIDS is not known, its victims usually show physical problems from the very beginning. Early medical records of SIDS babies reveal higher rates of prematurity and low birth weight, poor Apgar scores, and limp muscle tone. Abnormal heart rate and respiration and disturbances in sleep–wake cycles are also involved (Daley, 2004; Kato et al., 2003). At the time of death, many SIDS babies have a mild respiratory infection (Samuels, 2003). This seems to increase the chances of respiratory failure in an already vulnerable baby.

One hypothesis about the cause of SIDS is that problems in brain functioning prevent these infants from learning how to respond when their survival is threatened—for example, when respiration is suddenly interrupted. Between 2 and 4 months, when SIDS is most likely, reflexes decline and are replaced by voluntary, learned responses. Respiratory and muscular weaknesses may stop SIDS babies from acquiring behaviors that replace defensive reflexes (Lipsitt, 2003). As a result, when breathing difficulties occur during sleep, these infants do not wake up, shift their position, or cry out for help. Instead, they simply give in to oxygen deprivation and death. In support of this interpretation, autopsies reveal that SIDS babies, more often than other infants, show abnor-

malities in brain centers that control breathing and arousal (Paterson et al., 2006).

In an effort to reduce the occurrence of SIDS, researchers are studying environmental factors related to it. Maternal cigarette smoking, both during and after pregnancy, as well as smoking by other caregivers, strongly predicts the disorder. Babies exposed to cigarette smoke have more respiratory infections, arouse less easily from sleep, and are twice as likely as non-exposed infants to die of SIDS (Anderson, Johnson, & Batal, 2005; Horne et al., 2004). Prenatal abuse of drugs that depress central nervous system functioning (opiates and barbiturates) increases the risk of SIDS tenfold (Kandall et al., 1993). SIDS babies are also more likely to sleep on their stomachs than on their backs and often are wrapped very warmly in clothing and blankets (Hauck et al., 2003).

Researchers suspect that nicotine, depressant drugs, excessive body warmth, and respiratory infection all lead to physiological stress, which disrupts the normal sleep pattern. When sleep-deprived infants experience a sleep "rebound," they sleep more deeply, which results in loss of muscle tone in the airway passages. In at-risk babies, the airway may collapse, and the infant may fail to arouse sufficiently to reestablish breathing (Simpson, 2001). In other cases, healthy babies sleeping down in soft bedding may die from continually breathing their own exhaled breath.

Quitting smoking, changing an infant's sleeping position, and removing a few bedclothes can reduce the incidence of SIDS. For example, if women refrained from smoking while pregnant, an estimated 30 percent of SIDS cases would be prevented. Public education campaigns that encourage parents to put their infants down on their backs have cut the incidence of SIDS in half in many Western nations (Byard & Krous, 2003). Another protective measure is pacifier use: Sleeping babies who suck arouse more easily in response to breathing and heart-rate irregularities (Hauck, Omojokun, & Siadaty, 2005). Nevertheless, compared with

white infants, SIDS rates are two to six times as high in poverty-stricken minority groups, where parental stress, substance abuse, and lack of knowledge about preventive sleep practices are widespread (Pickett, Luo, & Lauderdale, 2005).

When SIDS does occur, surviving family members require a great deal of help to overcome a sudden and unexpected death. As Millie commented six months after Sasha's death, "It's the worst crisis we've ever been through. What's helped us most are the comforting words of others who've experienced the same tragedy."

© ROYALTY-FREE/CORBIS

Public education campaigns encouraging parents to put their infants down on their backs to sleep have helped to reduce the incidence of SIDS, which has dropped by half in many Western nations. Research also confirms the value of using a pacifier. If breathing or heart-rate irregularities occur, infants who suck wake from sleep more easily.

CRYING ■ Crying is the first way that babies communicate, letting parents know that they need food, comfort, and stimulation. During the weeks after birth, all babies seem to have some fussy periods when they are difficult to console. But most of the time, the nature of the cry, combined with the experiences that led up to it, helps guide parents toward its cause. The baby's cry is actually a complex stimulus that varies in intensity, from a whimper to a message of all-out distress (Gustafson, Wood, &

Green, 2000). As early as the first few weeks, infants can be identified by the unique vocal "signature" of their cry, which helps parents locate their baby from a distance (Gustafson, Green, & Cleland, 1994).

Young infants usually cry because of physical needs. Hunger is the most common cause, but babies may also cry in response to temperature change when undressed, a sudden noise, or a painful stimulus. Newborns (as well as older babies) often cry at the sound of another crying baby (Dondi, Simion, & Caltran, 1999). Some researchers believe that this response reflects an inborn capacity to react to the suffering of others. Furthermore, crying typically increases during the early weeks, peaks at about 6 weeks, and then declines. Because this trend appears in many cultures with vastly different infant care practices, researchers believe that normal readjustments of the central nervous system underlie it (Barr, 2001).

TAKE A MOMENT... The next time you hear a baby cry, notice your own reaction. The sound stimulates strong feelings of arousal and discomfort in men and women, parents and nonparents alike (Murray, 1985). This powerful response is probably innately programmed to help ensure that babies receive the care and protection they need to survive.

Soothing Crying Infants. Although parents do not always interpret their baby's cry correctly, their accuracy improves with experience. Fortunately, there are many ways to soothe a crying baby when feeding and diaper changing do not work (see Applying What We Know on the following page). The technique that Western parents usually try first, lifting the baby to the shoulder and rocking or walking, is most effective.

Another common soothing method is swaddling—wrapping the baby snugly in a blanket. The Quechua, who live in the cold, high-altitude desert regions of Peru, dress young babies in several layers of clothing and blankets that cover the head and body. The result—a warm pouch placed on the mother's back that moves rhythmically as she walks—reduces crying and promotes sleep. It also allows the baby to conserve energy for early growth in the harsh Peruvian highlands (Tronick, Thomas, & Daltabuit, 1994).

To soothe her crying infant, this mother holds her baby upright against her gently moving body. Besides encouraging infants to stop crying, this technique causes them to become quietly alert and attentive to the environment.

In many tribal and village societies and in non-Western developed nations, infants spend most of the day and night in close physical contact with their caregivers. Among the !Kung of the desert regions of Botswana, Africa, mothers carry their young babies in grass-lined, animal-skin slings hung on their hips, so the infants can see their surroundings and can nurse at will. Japanese mothers also spend much time holding their babies (Small, 1998). Infants in these cultures show shorter bouts of crying than their North American counterparts (Barr, 2001).

But not all research indicates that rapid parental responsiveness reduces infant crying (van IJzendoorn & Hubbard, 2000). The conditions that prompt crying are complex, and parents must make reasoned choices about what to do on the basis of culturally accepted practices, the suspected reason for the cry, and the context in which it occurs—for example, in the privacy of their own home or while having dinner at a restaurant. Fortunately, with age, crying declines. Virtually all researchers agree that parents can lessen older babies' need to cry by encouraging more mature ways of expressing their desires, such as gestures and vocalizations.

Abnormal Crying. Like reflexes and sleep patterns, the infant's cry offers a clue to central nervous system distress. The cries of brain-damaged babies and those who have experienced prenatal and birth complications are often shrill, piercing, and shorter in duration than the cries of healthy infants (Boukydis & Lester, 1998; Green, Irwin, & Gustafson, 2000). Even newborns with a fairly common problem—*colic,* or persistent crying—tend to have high-pitched, harsh-sounding cries (Zeskind & Barr, 1997). Although the cause of colic is unknown, certain newborns, who react especially strongly to unpleasant stimuli, are susceptible. Because their crying is intense, they find it harder to calm down than other babies. Colic generally subsides between 3 and 6 months (Barr et al., 2005; St James-Roberts et al., 2003).

In an intervention aimed at reducing colic, nurses made periodic home visits, providing parents with help in identifying their baby's early warning signs of becoming overly aroused, in using effective soothing techniques, and in modifying light, noise, and activity in the home to promote predictable sleep–wake cycles (Keefe et al., 2005). Colicky infants who received the intervention spent far less time crying than no-intervention controls—1.3 versus 3 hours per day.

Applying What We Know

Soothing a Crying Baby

TECHNIQUE	EXPLANATION
Lift the baby to the shoulder and rock or walk.	This provides a combination of physical contact, upright posture, and motion. It is the most effective soothing technique, causing young infants to become quietly alert.
Swaddle the baby.	Restricting movement and increasing warmth often soothe a young infant.
Offer a pacifier, preferably sweetened with a sugar solution.	Sucking helps babies control their own level of arousal. Sucking a sweetened pacifier relieves pain and quiets a crying infant.
Talk softly or play rhythmic sounds.	Continuous, monotonous, rhythmic sounds (such as a clock ticking, a fan whirring, or peaceful music) are more effective than intermittent sounds.
Take the baby for a short car ride or a walk in a baby carriage; swing the baby in a cradle.	Gentle, rhythmic motion of any kind helps lull the baby to sleep.
Massage the baby's body.	Stroke the baby's torso and limbs with continuous, gentle motions. This technique is used in some non-Western cultures to relax the baby's muscles.
Combine several of the methods just listed.	Stimulating several of the baby's senses at once is often more effective than stimulating only one.
If these methods do not work, let the baby cry for a short period.	Occasionally, a baby responds well to just being put down and will, after a few minutes, fall asleep.

Sources: Blass, 1999; Campos, 1989; Lester, 1985; Reisman, 1987.

Most parents try to respond to a crying baby's call for help with extra care and attention, but sometimes the cry is so unpleasant and the infant so difficult to soothe that parents become frustrated, resentful, and angry. Preterm and ill babies are more likely to be abused by highly stressed parents, who sometimes mention a high-pitched, grating cry as one factor that caused them to lose control and harm the baby (Zeskind & Lester, 2001). We will discuss a host of additional influences on child abuse in Chapter 10.

Sensory Capacities

On his visit to my class, Joshua looked wide-eyed at my bright pink blouse and turned to the sound of his mother's voice. During feedings, he lets Yolanda know by the way he sucks that he prefers the taste of breast milk to a bottle of plain water. Clearly, Joshua has some well-developed sensory capacities. In the following sections, we explore the newborn baby's responsiveness to touch, taste, smell, sound, and visual stimulation.

TOUCH ■ In our discussion of preterm infants, we saw that touch helps stimulate early physical growth. And as we will see in Chapter 7, it is vital for emotional development as well. Therefore, it is not surprising that sensitivity to touch is well developed at birth.

The reflexes listed in Table 4.2 on page 148 reveal that the newborn baby responds to touch, especially around the mouth, on the palms, and on the soles of the feet. During the prenatal period, these areas, along with the genitals, are the first to become sensitive to touch (Humphrey, 1978; Streri, 2005). Using their palms, newborns can even distinguish the shapes of small objects (a prism versus a cylinder), as indicated by their tendency to hold on longer to an object with an unfamiliar shape than to a familiar-shaped object (Streri, Lhote, & Dutilleul, 2000).

At birth, infants are quite sensitive to pain. If male newborns are circumcised, anesthetic is sometimes not used because of the risk of giving drugs to a very young infant. Babies often respond with a high-pitched, stressful cry and a dramatic rise in heart rate, blood pressure, palm sweating, pupil dilation, and muscle tension (Jorgensen, 1999; Warnock & Sandrin, 2004). Recent research establishing the safety of certain local anesthetics for newborns promises to ease the stress of these procedures. Offering a nipple that delivers a

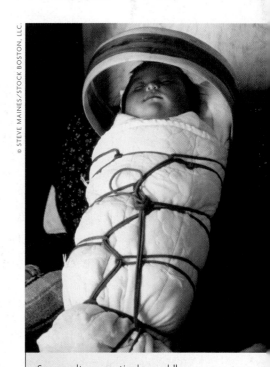

© STEVE MAINES/STOCK BOSTON, LLC.

Some cultures routinely swaddle young infants, restricting movement and increasing warmth by wrapping blankets tightly around the body. This Navajo baby rests on a traditional cradle board that can be strapped to the mother's back. Swaddling reduces crying and promotes sleep.

sugar solution is also helpful; it quickly reduces crying and discomfort in young babies. And combining the sweet liquid with gentle holding by the parent lessens pain even more. Research on infant mammals indicates that physical touch releases *endorphins*—painkilling chemicals in the brain (Gormally et al., 2001).

Allowing a newborn to endure severe pain overwhelms the nervous system with stress hormones, which can disrupt the child's developing capacity to handle common, everyday stressors. The result is heightened pain sensitivity, sleep disturbances, feeding problems, and difficulty calming down when upset (Mitchell & Boss, 2002).

TASTE AND SMELL ■ Facial expressions reveal that newborns can distinguish several basic tastes. Like adults, they relax their facial muscles in response to sweetness, purse their lips when the taste is sour, and show a distinct archlike mouth opening when it is bitter (Steiner, 1979; Steiner et al., 2001). These reactions are important for survival: The food that best supports the infant's early growth is the sweet-tasting milk of the mother's breast. Not until 4 months do babies prefer a salty taste to plain water, a change that may prepare them to accept solid foods (Mennella & Beauchamp, 1998).

Nevertheless, newborns can readily learn to like a taste that at first evoked either a neutral or a negative response. For example, babies allergic to cow's milk formula who are given a soy or other vegetable-based substitute (typically very strong and bitter-tasting) soon prefer it to regular formula. A taste previously disliked can come to be preferred when it is paired with relief of hunger (Harris, 1997).

As with taste, certain odor preferences are present at birth. For example, the smell of bananas or chocolate causes a relaxed, pleasant facial expression, whereas the odor of rotten eggs makes the infant frown (Steiner, 1979). During pregnancy, the amniotic fluid is rich in tastes and smells that vary with the mother's diet—early experiences that influence newborns' preferences. In a study carried out in the Alsatian region of France, where anise is frequently used to flavor foods, researchers tested newborns for their reaction to the anise odor (Schaal, Marlier, & Soussignan, 2000). The mothers of some babies had regularly consumed anise during the last two weeks of pregnancy; the other mothers had never consumed it. When presented with the anise odor on the day of birth, the babies of non-anise-consuming mothers were far more likely to turn away than the babies of anise-consuming mothers (see Figure 4.7). These different reactions were still apparent four days later, even though all mothers had refrained from consuming anise during this time.

In many mammals, the sense of smell plays an important role in feeding and in protecting the young from predators by helping mothers and babies identify each other. Although smell is less well-developed in humans, traces of its survival value remain. Newborns given a choice between the smell of their own mother's amniotic fluid and that of another mother spend more time oriented toward the familiar fluid (Marlier, Schaal, & Soussignan, 1998). The smell of the mother's amniotic fluid is comforting; babies exposed to it cry less than babies who are not (Varendi et al., 1998).

Immediately after birth, infants placed face-down between their mother's breasts latch on to a nipple and begin sucking within an hour. If one breast is washed to remove its natural scent, most newborns move

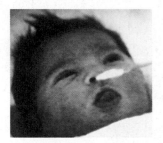
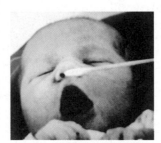

(a) Responses by newborns of anise-consuming mothers

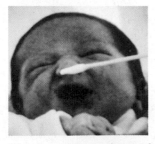
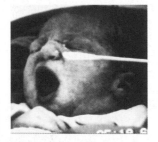

(b) Responses by newborns of non-anise-consuming mothers

FIGURE 4.7

Examples of facial expressions of newborns exposed to the odor of anise whose mothers' diets differed in anise-flavored foods during late pregnancy. (a) Babies of anise-consuming mothers spent more time turning toward the odor and sucking, licking, and chewing. (b) Babies of non-anise-consuming mothers more often turned away with a negative facial expression. (From B. Schaal, L. Marlier, & R. Soussignan, 2000, "Human Foetuses Learn Odours from Their Pregnant Mother's Diet," *Chemical Senses, 25*, p. 731. Reprinted by permission of the authors.)

toward the unwashed breast, indicating that they are guided by smell (Varendi & Porter, 2001). At 4 days of age, breastfed babies prefer the smell of their own mother's breast to that of an unfamiliar lactating woman (Cernoch & Porter, 1985). And both breast- and bottle-fed 3- to 4-day-olds orient more and display more mouthing to the smell of unfamiliar human milk than to formula milk, indicating that (even without postnatal exposure) the odor of human milk is more attractive to newborns (Marlier & Schaal, 2005). Newborns' dual attraction to the odors of their mother and of breast milk helps them locate an appropriate food source and, in the process, distinguish their caregiver from other people.

HEARING ■ Although conduction of sound through the structures of the ear and transmission of auditory information to the brain are inefficient at birth, newborn infants can hear a wide variety of sounds, and this sensitivity improves greatly over the first few months (Saffran, Werker, & Werner, 2006; Tharpe & Ashmead, 2001). At birth, infants prefer complex sounds, such as noises and voices, to pure tones. And babies only a few days old can tell the difference between a variety of sound patterns: a series of tones arranged in ascending versus descending order; utterances with two versus three syllables; the stress patterns of words, such as "*ma-ma*" versus "ma-*ma*"; happy-sounding speech as opposed to speech with negative or neutral emotional qualities; and even two languages spoken by the same bilingual speaker, as long as those languages differ in their rhythmic features—for example, French from Russian (Mastropieri & Turkewitz, 1999; Ramus, 2002; Sansavini, Bertoncini, & Giovanelli, 1997; Trehub, 2001).

Young infants listen longer to human speech than to structurally similar nonspeech sounds (Vouloumanos & Werker, 2004). And they can detect the sounds of any human language. Newborns make fine-grained distinctions among many speech sounds. For example, when given a nipple that turns on a recording of the "*ba*" sound, babies suck vigorously for a while, then slow down as the novelty wears off. When the sound switches to "*ga*," sucking picks up, indicating that infants detect this subtle difference. Using this method, researchers have found only a few speech sounds that newborns cannot discriminate. Their ability to perceive sounds not found in their own language is more precise than an adult's (Aldridge, Stillman, & Bower, 2001; Jusczyk & Luce, 2002). These capacities reveal that the baby is marvelously prepared for the awesome task of acquiring language.

Responsiveness to sound also supports the newborn baby's exploration of the environment. Infants as young as 3 days turn their eyes and head in the general direction of a sound. The ability to identify the precise location of a sound improves greatly over the first 6 months and shows further gains through the preschool years (Litovsky & Ashmead, 1997).

TAKE A MOMENT... Listen carefully to yourself the next time you talk to a young baby. You will probably speak in a high-pitched, expressive voice and use a rising tone at the ends of phrases and sentences. Adults probably communicate this way with infants because they notice that babies are more attentive when they do so. Indeed, newborns prefer speech with these characteristics (Saffran, Werker, & Werner, 2006). In addition, newborn babies will suck more on a nipple to hear a recording of their own mother's voice than that of an unfamiliar woman and to hear their native language as opposed to a rhythmically distinct foreign language (Moon, Cooper, & Fifer, 1993; Spence & DeCasper, 1987). These preferences may have developed from hearing the muffled sounds of the mother's voice before birth.

VISION ■ Vision is the least developed of the senses at birth. Visual structures in both the eye and the brain are not yet fully formed. For example, cells in the *retina*, the membrane lining the inside of the eye that captures light and transforms it into messages that are sent to the brain, are not as mature or densely packed as they will be in several months. And the optic nerve that relays these messages, and visual centers in the brain that receive them, will not be adultlike for several years. Furthermore, the muscles of the lens, which permit us to adjust our visual focus to varying distances, are weak (Kellman & Arterberry, 2006).

As a result, newborn babies cannot focus their eyes well, and their **visual acuity,** or fineness of discrimination, is limited. At birth, infants perceive objects at a distance of 20 feet about as clearly as adults do at 600 feet (Slater, 2001). In addition, unlike adults (who see nearby objects most clearly), newborn babies see unclearly across a wide range of distances

visual acuity Fineness of visual discrimination.

FIGURE 4.8

View of the human face by the newborn and the adult. The newborn baby's limited focusing ability and poor visual acuity lead the mother's face, even when viewed from close up, to look much like the fuzzy image in (a) than the clear image in (b). Also, newborn infants have some color vision, although they have difficulty discriminating colors. Researchers speculate that colors probably appear similar, but less intense, to newborns than to older infants and adults. (From Hainline, 1998; Slater, 2001.)

(a) Newborn View   (b) Adult View

(Banks, 1980; Hainline, 1998). As a result, images such as the parent's face, even from close up, look like the blurry image in Figure 4.8. Nevertheless, as we will see in Chapter 5, newborns can detect human faces. And as with their preference for their mother's smell and voice, from repeated exposures they quickly learn to prefer her face to that of an unfamiliar woman, although they are sensitive to its broad outlines rather than its fine-grained features (Bartrip, Morton, & de Schonen, 2001; Walton, Armstrong, & Bower, 1998).

Although newborn infants cannot see well, they actively explore their environment by scanning it for interesting sights and tracking moving objects. However, their eye movements are slow and inaccurate (von Hofsten & Rosander, 1998). Joshua's captivation with my pink blouse reveals that he is attracted to bright objects. Nevertheless, once newborns focus on an object, they tend to look only at a single feature—for example, the corner of a triangle instead of the entire shape. And although newborn babies prefer to look at colored rather than gray stimuli, they are not yet good at discriminating colors. It will take about 4 months for color vision to become adultlike (Adams & Courage, 1998; Kellman & Arterberry, 2006).

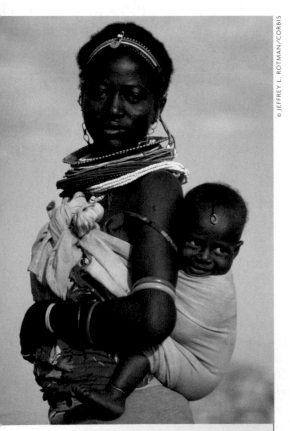

Similar to women in the Zambian culture, this mother of the El Molo people of northern Kenya carries her baby about all day, providing close physical contact, a rich variety of stimulation ,and ready feeding.

Neonatal Behavioral Assessment

A variety of instruments permit doctors, nurses, and researchers to assess the behavior of newborn babies. The most widely used of these tests, T. Berry Brazelton's **Neonatal Behavioral Assessment Scale (NBAS),** evaluates the baby's reflexes, muscle tone, state changes, responsiveness to physical and social stimuli, and other reactions (Brazelton & Nugent, 1995). A recently developed instrument consisting of similar items, called the *Neonatal Intensive Care Unit Network Neurobehavioral Scale (NNNS),* is specially designed for use with newborns at risk for developmental problems—because of low birth weight, preterm delivery, prenatal substance exposure, or other conditions (Lester & Tronick, 2004). Scores are used to recommend appropriate interventions and to guide parents in meeting their baby's unique needs.

The NBAS has been given to many infants around the world. As a result, researchers have learned about individual and cultural differences in newborn behavior and how child-rearing practices can maintain or change a baby's reactions. For example, NBAS scores of Asian and Native-American babies reveal that they are less irritable than Caucasian infants. Mothers in these cultures often encourage their babies' calm dispositions through swaddling, close physical contact, and nursing at the first signs of discomfort (Chisholm, 1989; Muret-Wagstaff & Moore, 1989). In contrast, maternal care quickly changes the poor NBAS scores of undernourished infants in Zambia, Africa. The Zambian mother carries her baby about on her hip all day, providing a rich variety of sensory stimulation. As a result, a once unresponsive newborn becomes an alert, contented 1-week-old (Brazelton, Koslowski, & Tronick, 1976).

TAKE A MOMENT... Using these examples, can you explain why a single neonatal assessment score is not a good predictor of later development? Because newborn behavior and parenting styles combine to shape development, *changes in scores* over the first week or two of life (rather than a single score) provide the best estimate of the baby's ability to recover from the stress of birth. NBAS "recovery curves" predict intelligence and absence of emotional and behavior problems with moderate success well into the preschool years (Brazelton, Nugent, & Lester, 1987; Ohgi et al., 2003a, 2003b).

In some hospitals, health professionals use the NBAS or the NNNS to help parents get to know their newborns through discussion or demonstration of the capacities these instruments assess. Parents of both preterm and full-term newborns who participate in these programs interact more effectively with their babies (Browne & Talmi, 2005; Bruschweiler-Stern, 2004). Although lasting effects on development have not been demonstrated, neonatal behavioral assessment interventions are useful in helping the parent–infant relationship get off to a good start.

Neonatal Behavioral Assessment Scale (NBAS) A test developed to assess the behavior of a newborn infant in terms of reflexes, muscle tone, state changes, responsiveness to physical and social stimuli, and other reactions.

Ask Yourself

Review What functions does REM sleep serve in young infants? Can sleep tell us anything about the health of the newborn's central nervous system? Explain.

Apply After a difficult delivery, Jackie observes her 2-day-old daughter, Kelly, being given the NBAS. Kelly scores poorly on many items. Seeing this, Jackie wonders if Kelly will develop normally. How would you respond to Jackie's concern?

Connect How do the diverse capacities of newborn babies contribute to their first social relationships? Provide as many examples as you can.

Reflect Are newborns more competent than you thought they were before you read this chapter? Which of their capacities most surprised you?

The Transition to Parenthood

The early weeks after a new baby enters the family are full of profound changes. The mother needs to recover from childbirth and adjust to massive hormone shifts in her body. If she is breastfeeding, energies must be devoted to working out this intimate relationship. The father must become a part of this new threesome while supporting the mother in her recovery. At times, he may feel ambivalent about the baby, who constantly demands and gets the mother's attention.

While all this is going on, the tiny infant is assertive about his urgent physical needs, demanding to be fed, changed, and comforted at odd times of the day and night. The family schedule becomes irregular and uncertain. Yolanda spoke candidly about the changes she and Jay experienced:

> When we brought Joshua home, he seemed so small and helpless, and we worried about whether we would be able to take proper care of him. It took us 20 minutes to change the first diaper. I rarely feel rested because I'm up two to four times every night, and I spend a good part of my waking hours trying to anticipate Joshua's rhythms and needs. If Jay weren't so willing to help by holding and walking Joshua, I think I'd find it much harder.

Changes in the Family System

The demands of new parenthood—constant caregiving, added financial responsibilities, and less time for couples to devote to one another—usually cause the gender roles of husband and wife to become more traditional (Cowan & Cowan, 2000; Salmela-Aro et al., 2000). This is true even for couples like Yolanda and Jay, who are strongly committed to gender equality and are used to sharing household tasks. Yolanda took a leave of absence from work, whereas Jay's career continued as it had before. As a result, Yolanda spent more time at home with the baby, while Jay focused more on his provider role.

For most new parents, however, the arrival of a baby does not cause significant marital strain. Marriages that are gratifying and supportive tend to remain so, resembling childless marriages in overall happiness (Feeney et al., 2001; Miller, 2000). But troubled marriages usually become more distressed after a baby is born. In a study of newlyweds who were interviewed annually for six years, the husband's affection, expression of "we-ness" (values and goals similar to his wife's), and awareness of his wife's daily life predicted mothers' stable or increasing marital satisfaction after childbirth. In contrast, the husband's negativity and the couple's out-of-control conflict predicted a drop in mothers' satisfaction (Shapiro, Gottman, & Carrere, 2000). For some new parents, adjustment problems are severe (see the Biology and Environment box on page 160).

Also, violated expectations about division of labor in the home affect family well-being. In dual-earner marriages, the larger the difference between men's and women's caregiving responsibilities, the greater the decline in marital satisfaction after childbirth, especially for women—with negative consequences for parent–infant interaction. In contrast, sharing caregiving predicts greater parental happiness and sensitivity to the baby (Feldman, 2002; McHale et al., 2004). An exception exists, however, for employed lower-SES women who endorse traditional gender roles. When their husbands help extensively with child care, these mothers tend to report more distress, perhaps because they feel disappointed at being unable to fulfill their desire to do most of the caregiving (Goldberg & Perry-Jenkins, 2003).

Postponing parenthood until the late twenties or thirties, as more couples do today, eases the transition to parenthood. Waiting permits couples to pursue occupational goals and gain life experience. Under these circumstances, men are more enthusiastic about becoming fathers and therefore more willing to participate. And women whose careers are well under way are more likely to encourage their husbands to share housework and child care (Coltrane, 1990; Saginak & Saginak, 2005).

A second birth typically requires that fathers take an even more active role in parenting—by caring for the firstborn while the mother is recuperating and by sharing in the high demands of tending to both a baby and a young child. Consequently, well-functioning families with a newborn second child typically show a pulling back from the traditional division of responsibilities that occurred after the first birth. In a study that tracked parents from the end of pregnancy through the first year after their second child's birth, fathers' willingness to place greater emphasis on the parenting role was strongly linked to mothers' adjustment after the arrival of a second baby (Stewart, 1990). And the support and encouragement of family, friends, and spouse are crucial for fathers' well-being.

Finally, both parents must help their firstborn child adjust. Preschool-age siblings understandably may feel displaced and react with jealousy and anger—a topic we will take up in Chapter 7. For strategies that couples can use to ease the transition to parenthood, refer to Applying What We Know on the following page.

Single-Mother Families

About 37 percent of babies in the United States and Canada are born to single mothers (U.S. Department of Health and Human Services, 2006c; United Nations, 2000). One-third of U.S. and one-fifth of Canadian single-parent births are to teenage mothers. When we take up adolescent parenthood in Chapter 14, we will see that these mothers and their newborns are at high risk for developmental problems.

At the other extreme, planned births and adoptions by single 30- to 45-year-old women are increasing. These mothers are generally financially secure, have readily available social support

Applying What We Know

How Couples Can Ease the Transition to Parenthood

STRATEGY	DESCRIPTION
Devise a plan for sharing household tasks.	As soon as possible, discuss division of household responsibilities. Decide who does a particular chore based on who has the needed skill and time, not gender. Schedule regular times to reevaluate your plan to fit changing family circumstances.
Begin sharing child care right after the baby's arrival.	For fathers, strive to spend equal time with the baby early. For mothers, refrain from imposing your standards on your partner. Instead, share the role of "child-rearing expert" by discussing parenting values and concerns often. Attend a new-parenthood course together.
Talk over conflicts about decision making and responsibilities.	Face conflict through communication. Clarify your feelings and needs, and express them to your partner. Listen and try to understand your partner's point of view. Then be willing to negotiate and compromise.
Establish a balance between work and parenting.	Critically evaluate the time you devote to work in view of new parenthood. If it is too much, try to cut back.
Press for workplace and public policies that assist parents in rearing children.	Difficulties faced by new parents may be partly due to lack of workplace and societal supports. Encourage your employer to provide benefits that help combine work and family roles, such as paid employment leave, flexible work hours, and on-site high-quality, affordable child care. Communicate with lawmakers and other citizens about improving policies for children and families, including paid, job-protected leave to support the transition to parenthood.

from family members and friends, and adapt to parenthood with relative ease. In fact, older single mothers in well-paid occupations who plan carefully for a new baby may encounter fewer parenting difficulties than married couples, largely because their family structure is simpler: They do not have to coordinate parenting roles with a partner, and they have no unfulfilled expectations for shared caregiving (Ambert, 2006). And because of their psychological maturity, these mothers are likely to cope effectively with parenting challenges.

The majority of nonmarital births are unplanned and to women in their twenties. Most of these single mothers have incomes below the poverty level and experience a stressful transition to parenthood. Although many live with the baby's father or another partner, cohabiting relationships in North America are less socially acceptable than those in Western Europe, involve less commitment and cooperation, and are far more likely to break up—especially after an unplanned baby arrives (Fussell & Gauthier, 2005). Furthermore, these single mothers often lack emotional and parenting support—strong predictors of psychological distress and infant caregiving difficulties (Keating-Lefler et al., 2004).

Parent Interventions

Special interventions are available to help parents adjust to life with a new baby. For those who are not at high risk for problems, counselor-led parenting groups are highly effective (Glade, Bean, & Vira, 2005). In one program, first-time expectant couples gathered once a week for six months to discuss their dreams for the family and the changes in relationships sparked by the baby's arrival. Eighteen months after the program ended, participating fathers described themselves as more involved with their child than did fathers in a no-intervention condition. Perhaps because of fathers' caregiving assistance, participating mothers maintained their prebirth satisfaction with family and work roles. Three years after the birth, the marriages of all participating couples were still intact and just as happy as they had

© ARIEL SKELLEY/CORBIS

A growing number of single women in their thirties and early forties are choosing to give birth or adopt a child. If they are financially secure and have social support from friends and family members, they are likely to have a relatively smooth transition to parenthood.

Biology and Environment

Parental Depression and Child Development

For 50 to 80 percent of first-time mothers, the excitement of the baby's arrival gives way to an emotional letdown during the first week after delivery known as the *postpartum* (or after-birth) *blues*. The blues are temporary. They die down as mothers adjust to hormonal changes following childbirth and gain confidence in caring for the baby. But about 10 percent of women do not bounce back so easily. They experience **postpartum depression**, mild to severe feelings of sadness and withdrawal that continue for weeks or months.

Although less recognized and studied, about 4 percent of fathers also report depression after the birth of a child (Deater-Deckard et al., 1998). Either maternal or paternal depression can interfere with effective parenting and seriously impair children's development. Genetic makeup affects an individual's risk of depressive illness, but social and cultural factors are also involved.

Maternal Depression

During Julia's pregnancy, her husband, Kyle, showed so little interest in the baby that Julia worried that having a child might be a mistake.

This depressed mother appears overwhelmed and unresponsive to her infant. If her disengagement continues, the baby is likely to become negative and irritable and, eventually, withdrawn. Over time, this disruption in the parent–child relationship leads to serious emotional and behavior problems.

Then, shortly after Lucy was born, Julia's mood plunged. She felt anxious and weepy, overwhelmed by Lucy's needs, and angry that she no longer had control over her own schedule. When Julia approached Kyle about her own fatigue and his unwillingness to help with the baby, he snapped that she was overreacting to every move he made. Julia's childless friends stopped by just once to see Lucy but did not call again.

Julia's depressed mood quickly affected her baby. In the weeks after birth, infants of depressed mothers sleep poorly, are less attentive to their surroundings, and have elevated levels of the stress hormone cortisol (Field, 1998). The more extreme the depression and the greater the number of stressors in a mother's life (such as marital discord, little or no social support, and poverty), the more the parent–child relationship suffers (Simpson et al., 2003). Julia, for example, rarely smiled at, comforted, or talked to Lucy, who responded to her mother's sad, vacant gaze by turning away, crying, and often looking sad or angry herself (Herrera, Reissland, & Shepherd, 2004; Stanley, Murray, & Stein, 2004). Each time this happened, Julia felt guilty and inadequate, and her depression deepened. By age 6 months, Lucy showed symptoms common in babies of depressed mothers—delays in mental development, an irritable mood, and attachment difficulties (Martins & Gaffan, 2000).

When maternal depression persists, the parent–child relationship worsens. Depressed parents view their infants more negatively than do independent observers (Hart, Field, & Roitfarb, 1999). And they use inconsistent discipline—sometimes lax, at other times too forceful. As we will see in later chapters, children who experience these maladaptive parenting practices often have serious adjustment problems. Some withdraw into a depressive mood themselves; others become impulsive and aggressive (Hay et al., 2003).

Paternal Depression

Like maternal depression, paternal depression is linked to dissatisfaction with marriage and family life after childbirth. In fact, it often follows maternal depression (Bielawska-Batorowicz & Kossakowska-Petrycka, 2006).

In a study of a large representative sample of British parents and babies, researchers assessed depressive symptoms of fathers shortly after birth and again the following year. Then they tracked the development of their children into the preschool years. Persistent paternal depression was a strong predictor of child behavior problems—especially overactivity, defiance, and aggression in boys—even after many other factors, including family SES and maternal depression, had been controlled (Ramchandani et al., 2005).

Although little is known about the precise effects of paternal depression on parenting, well-adjusted fathers are more positive, attentive, and involved with their babies. At older ages, paternal depression is linked to frequent father–child conflict (Kane & Garber, 2004). Over time, children subjected to parental negativity develop a pessimistic world view—one in which they lack self-confidence and perceive their parents and other people as threatening. Children who constantly feel in danger are likely to become overly aroused in stressful situations, easily losing control in the face of cognitive and social challenges (Cummings & Davies, 1994). Although children of depressed parents may inherit a tendency to develop emotional and behavior problems, quality of parenting is a major factor in their adjustment.

Interventions

Early treatment of parental depression is vital to prevent the disorder from interfering with the parent–child relationship. Julia's doctor referred her to a counselor, who helped Julia and Kyle with their marital problems and encouraged them to interact more sensitively with Lucy. Therapy that teaches depressed mothers to engage in emotionally positive, responsive caregiving reduces young children's attachment and developmental problems (Van Doesum, Hosman, & Riksen-Walraven, 2005). At times, antidepressant medication is prescribed. In most cases, mothers bounce back after short-term treatment (Steinberg & Bellavance, 1999). When a depressed parent does not respond to intervention, a warm relationship with the other parent or another caregiver can safeguard children's development (Mezulis, Hyde, & Clark, 2004).

© JANINE WIEDEL PHOTOLIBRARY/ALAMY

been before parenthood. In contrast, 15 percent of couples receiving no intervention had divorced (Cowan & Cowan, 1997, 2000).

High-risk parents struggling with poverty or the birth of a child with disabilities need more intensive interventions. Programs in which a trained intervener visits the home and focuses on enhancing social support and parenting skills have resulted in improved parent–infant interaction and benefits for children's cognitive and social development up to five years after the intervention (Meisels, Dichtelmiller, & Liaw, 1993). Many low-income single parents also require tangible support—money, food, transportation, and affordable child care—to ease stress and allow them to engage in effective caregiving.

When marital relationships are positive, social support is available, and families have sufficient income, the stress caused by the birth of a baby remains manageable. Nevertheless, as one pair of counselors who have worked with many new parents point out, "As long as children are dependent on their parents, those parents find themselves preoccupied with thoughts of their children. This does not keep them from enjoying other aspects of their lives, but it does mean that they never return to being quite the same people they were before they became parents" (Colman & Colman, 1991, p. 198).

postpartum depression
Feelings of sadness and withdrawal that develop shortly after childbirth and continue for weeks or months.

Ask Yourself

Review Explain how persisting postpartum depression seriously impairs children's development.

Apply Derek, father of a 3-year-old and a newborn, reported that he had a harder time adjusting to the birth of his second child than to that of his first child. Explain why this might be so.

Connect Louise has just given birth to her first child. Because her husband works long hours and is seldom available to help, she feels overwhelmed by the pressures of caring for a new baby. Why does Louise's four-week maternity leave pose a risk to her mental health? (*Hint:* Consult the Social Issues: Health box on page 151.)

Reflect If you are a parent, what was the transition to parenthood like for you? What factors helped you adjust to this major life change? What factors made it more difficult? If you are not a parent, pose these questions to someone you know who recently became a parent.

Summary

The Stages of Childbirth

Describe the three stages of childbirth, the baby's adaptation to labor and delivery, and the newborn baby's appearance.

■ In the first stage of childbirth, **dilation and effacement of the cervix** occur as uterine contractions increase in strength and frequency. This stage culminates in **transition,** a brief period in which contractions are at their peak and the cervix opens completely. In the second stage, the mother feels an urge to bear down with her abdominal muscles, and the baby is born. In the final stage, the placenta is delivered.

■ During labor, the force of the contractions causes infants to produce high levels of stress hormones, which help them withstand oxygen deprivation, clear the lungs for breathing, and arouse them into alertness at birth. The **Apgar Scale** is used to assess the baby's physical condition at birth.

■ Newborn infants have large heads, small bodies, and facial features that make adults feel like picking them up and cuddling them.

Approaches to Childbirth

Describe natural childbirth and home delivery, noting benefits and concerns associated with each.

■ In **natural,** or **prepared, childbirth,** the expectant mother and a companion typically attend classes where they learn about labor and delivery, master relaxation and breathing techniques to counteract pain, and prepare for coaching during childbirth.

■ Natural childbirth reduces pain and use of medication and fosters more positive maternal attitudes toward the birth experience. Social support, a vital part of natural childbirth, reduces the length of labor and the incidence of birth complications.

- When mothers can give birth in an upright, sitting position, labor is also shortened, with benefits for both mother and baby.

- Home birth is relatively rare in North America but is more common in some other industrialized nations. It reduces unnecessary medical procedures and permits mothers to exercise greater control over their own care and that of their babies. For a mother who is healthy and is assisted by a well-trained doctor or midwife, giving birth at home is just as safe as giving birth in a hospital.

Medical Interventions

List common medical interventions during childbirth, circumstances that justify their use, and any dangers associated with each.

- Medical interventions during childbirth are more common in North America than anywhere else in the world. When mothers have a history of pregnancy and birth complications, **fetal monitors** help save the lives of many babies. When used routinely, however, they may identify infants as in danger who, in fact, are not. Fetal monitoring is linked to an increase in cesarean deliveries.

- Use of **analgesics** and **anesthetics** to control pain during childbirth can prolong labor and cause newborns to be withdrawn and irritable. Instrument delivery using **forceps** or a **vacuum extractor** may be appropriate if the mother's pushing does not move the infant through the birth canal in a reasonable period of time. Vacuum extractors are less likely than forceps to cause serious complications, but both types of instrument delivery should be avoided if possible.

- **Induced labor** is more difficult than naturally occurring labor and is more likely to be associated with the use of labor and delivery medication and instrument delivery. Inductions should be scheduled only when continuing the pregnancy threatens the well-being of mother or baby.

- **Cesarean deliveries** are justified in cases of medical emergency or serious maternal illness, and when the baby is in **breech position.** A dramatic worldwide rise has occurred in cesarean deliveries, many of which are unnecessary.

Birth Complications

What are the risks of oxygen deprivation, preterm birth, and low birth weight, and what factors can help infants who survive a traumatic birth?

- About 10 percent of children with **cerebral palsy** experienced **anoxia** (oxygen deprivation) and resulting brain damage because of decreased maternal blood supply during labor and delivery. Other causes of anoxia are placenta abruptio and placenta previa. Effects of even mild to moderate anoxia on cognitive and language development are still evident in middle childhood, though many children improve over time.

- Infants born more than 6 weeks early commonly have **respiratory distress syndrome,** which can cause permanent brain damage due to immaturity of the lungs and associated anoxia.

- The incidence of premature births is high among poverty-stricken women and mothers of twins. Compared with **preterm** babies, whose weight is appropriate for time spent in the uterus, **small-for-date** infants have more serious problems. The fragile appearance and unresponsive, irritable behavior of preterm infants can lead parents to be less sensitive and responsive in caring for them.

- Some interventions provide special infant stimulation through gentle motion, attractive mobiles, soothing sounds, massage, and skin-to-skin contact with the caregiver ("kangaroo care") in the intensive care nursery. Others teach parents how to care for and interact with their babies.

- Parents with stable life circumstances and social supports generally need only a few sessions of coaching in caring for a preterm baby to help their child develop favorably. For preterm infants who live in stressed, low-income households, long-term, intensive intervention is necessary. A major cause of **neonatal** and **infant mortality** is low birth weight.

- When babies experience birth trauma, a supportive family environment or relationships with other caring adults can help restore their growth. Even infants with fairly serious birth complications can recover with the help of positive life events.

Precious Moments After Birth

Is close parent–infant contact shortly after birth necessary for bonding?

- Human parents do not require close physical contact with the baby immediately after birth for **bonding** and effective parenting to occur. Nevertheless, early contact supports parents' feelings of caring and affection. Hospital practices that promote parent–infant closeness, such as **rooming in,** may help parents build a good relationship with their newborn.

The Newborn Baby's Capacities

Describe the newborn baby's reflexes and states of arousal, including sleep characteristics and ways to soothe a crying baby.

- **Reflexes** are the newborn baby's most obvious organized patterns of behavior. Some have survival value, others help parents and infants establish gratifying interaction, and still others provide the foundation for voluntary motor skills.

- Although newborns move in and out of five **states of arousal,** they spend most of their time asleep. Sleep includes at least two states: **rapid-eye-movement (REM) sleep** and **non-rapid-eye-movement (NREM) sleep.** Newborns spend about 50 percent of their sleep time in REM sleep, far more than they ever will again. REM sleep provides young infants with stimulation essential for central nervous system development. Rapid eye movements also ensure that structures of the eye remain oxygenated during sleep. Disturbed REM–NREM cycles are a sign of central nervous system abnormalities, which may contribute to **sudden infant death syndrome (SIDS),** a major cause of infant mortality.

■ A crying baby stimulates strong feelings of discomfort in nearby adults. The intensity of the cry and the experiences that led up to it help parents identify what is wrong. Once feeding and diaper changing have been tried, lifting the baby to the shoulder and rocking or walking is the most effective soothing technique. Other helpful soothing methods include swaddling, offering a pacifier, and talking softly.

Describe the newborn baby's sensory capacities.

■ The senses of touch, taste, smell, and sound are well-developed at birth. Newborns can use their palms to distinguish the shapes of small objects. They are also sensitive to pain, prefer sweet tastes and smells, and orient toward the odor of their own mother's amniotic fluid (including odors that reflect the mother's diet), the lactating breast, and human milk rather than formula milk.

■ Newborns can distinguish a few sound patterns, as well as nearly all speech sounds. They are especially responsive to high-pitched expressive voices, their own mother's voice, and speech in their native language and will listen longer to human speech than to structurally similar nonspeech sounds.

■ Vision is the least developed of the newborn's senses. At birth, focusing ability and **visual acuity** are limited. Nevertheless, newborns can detect human faces and prefer their mother's familiar face to the face of a stranger. In exploring the visual field, newborn babies are attracted to bright objects, but they limit their looking to single features. Newborn babies have difficulty discriminating colors.

Why is neonatal behavioral assessment useful?

■ The most widely used instrument for assessing the behavior of the newborn infant, Brazelton's **Neonatal Behavioral Assessment Scale (NBAS),** has helped researchers understand individual and cultural differences in newborn behavior. Sometimes it is used to teach parents about their baby's capacities.

The Transition to Parenthood

Describe typical changes in the family after the birth of a new baby, along with interventions that foster the transition to parenthood.

■ In response to the demands of new parenthood, the gender roles of husband and wife usually become more traditional. Parents in gratifying marriages who continue to support each other's needs generally adapt well. But a large difference between a husband's and wife's caregiving responsibilities can strain the marriage and negatively affect parent–child interaction. Favorable adjustment to a second birth typically requires that fathers take an even more active role in parenting.

■ About 10 percent of women experience **postpartum depression.** If not treated early, it can have serious, lasting consequences for children's development.

■ Most nonmarital births are unplanned and to young mothers who have incomes below the poverty level and experience a stressful transition to parenthood. Planned births and adoptions by financially secure single women in their thirties and forties are increasing. These mothers adapt to new parenthood as well as, and sometimes more favorably than, married couples.

■ When parents are at low risk for problems, counselor-led parenting groups involving discussion of changing family relationships can ease the transition to parenthood. High-risk parents struggling with poverty or the birth of a baby with disabilities are more likely to benefit from intensive home interventions focusing on enhancing social support and parent–infant interaction.

Important Terms and Concepts

Chapter 5

Getting ready for a bath, the baby lifts his arms happily as he senses the physical potential of his growing body. During the first year, infants grow quickly, move on their own, increasingly investigate their surroundings, and make sense of complex sights and sounds.

Reprinted with permission from the International Museum of Children's Art, Oslo, Norway

"Bath"
Erandi Kemini
9 years, Sri Lanka

Physical Development in Infancy and Toddlerhood

On a brilliant June morning, 16-month-old Caitlin emerged from her front door, ready for the short drive to the child-care home where she spent her weekdays while her mother, Carolyn, and her father, David, worked. Clutching a teddy bear in one hand and her mother's arm with the other, Caitlin descended the steps. "One! Two! Threeeee!" Carolyn counted as she helped Caitlin down. "How much she's changed!" Carolyn thought to herself, looking at the child who, not long ago, had been a newborn. With her first steps, Caitlin had passed from *infancy* to *toddlerhood*—a period spanning the second year of life. At first, Caitlin did, indeed, "toddle" with an awkward gait, tipping over frequently. But her face reflected the thrill of conquering a new skill.

As they walked toward the car, Carolyn and Caitlin spotted 3-year-old Eli and his father, Kevin, in the neighboring yard. Eli dashed toward them, waving a bright yellow envelope. Carolyn bent down to open the envelope and took out a card. It read, "Announcing the arrival of Grace Ann. Born: Cambodia. Age: 16 months." Carolyn turned toward Kevin and Eli. "That's wonderful news! When can we see her?"

"Let's wait a few days," Kevin suggested. "Monica's taken Grace to the doctor this morning. She's underweight and malnourished." Kevin described Monica's first night with Grace in a hotel room in Phnom Penh. Grace lay on the bed, withdrawn and fearful. Eventually she fell asleep, gripping crackers in both hands.

Carolyn felt Caitlin's impatient tug at her sleeve. Off they drove to child care, where Vanessa had just dropped off her 18-month-old son, Timmy. Within moments, Caitlin and Timmy were in the sandbox, shoveling sand into plastic cups and buckets with the help of their caregiver, Ginette.

A few weeks later, Grace joined Caitlin and Timmy at Ginette's child-care home. Although still tiny and unable to crawl or walk, she had grown taller and heavier, and her sad, vacant gaze had given way to an alert expression, a ready smile, and an enthusiastic desire to imitate and explore. When Caitlin headed for the sandbox, Grace stretched out her arms, asking Ginette to carry her there, too. Soon Grace was pulling herself up at every opportunity. Finally, at age 18 months, she walked!

This chapter traces physical growth during the first two years—one of the most remarkable and busiest times of development. We will see how rapid changes in the infant's body and brain support learning, motor skills, and perceptual capacities. Caitlin, Grace, and Timmy will join us along the way to illustrate individual differences and environmental influences on physical development.

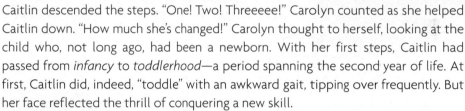

165

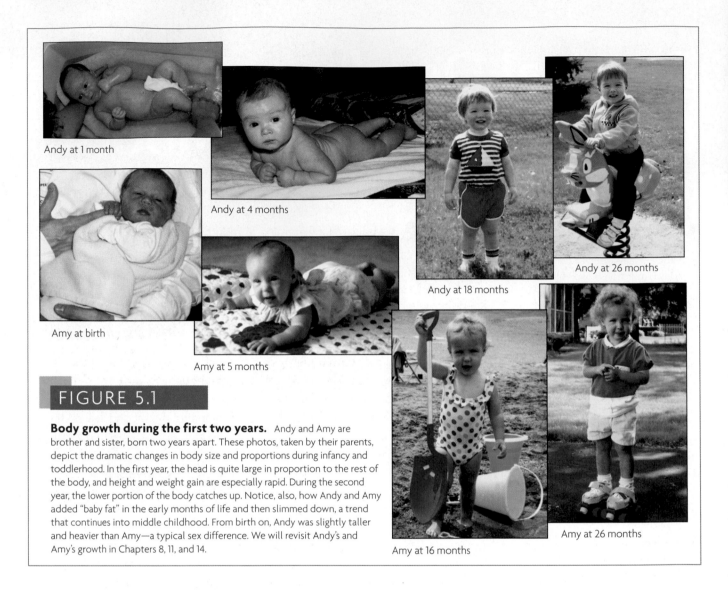

Andy at 1 month

Andy at 4 months

Amy at birth

Amy at 5 months

Andy at 18 months

Andy at 26 months

Amy at 16 months

Amy at 26 months

FIGURE 5.1

Body growth during the first two years. Andy and Amy are brother and sister, born two years apart. These photos, taken by their parents, depict the dramatic changes in body size and proportions during infancy and toddlerhood. In the first year, the head is quite large in proportion to the rest of the body, and height and weight gain are especially rapid. During the second year, the lower portion of the body catches up. Notice, also, how Andy and Amy added "baby fat" in the early months of life and then slimmed down, a trend that continues into middle childhood. From birth on, Andy was slightly taller and heavier than Amy—a typical sex difference. We will revisit Andy's and Amy's growth in Chapters 8, 11, and 14.

cephalocaudal trend An organized pattern of physical growth and motor control that proceeds from head to tail.

proximodistal trend An organized pattern of physical growth and motor control that proceeds from the center of the body outward.

skeletal age An estimate of physical maturity based on development of the bones of the body.

epiphyses Growth centers in the bones where new cartilage cells are produced and gradually harden.

Body Growth

TAKE A MOMENT... The next time you're walking in your neighborhood park or at the mall, observe the contrast between the capabilities of infants and toddlers. One reason for the vast changes in what children can do over the first two years is that their bodies change enormously—faster than at any other time after birth.

Changes in Body Size and Muscle–Fat Makeup

By the end of the first year a typical infant's height is about 32 inches—more than 50 percent greater than at birth. By 2 years, it is 75 percent greater (36 inches). Similarly, by 5 months of age, birth weight has doubled, to about 15 pounds. At 1 year it has tripled, to 22 pounds, and at 2 years it has quadrupled, to about 30 pounds.

Figure 5.1 illustrates this dramatic increase in body size. But rather than making steady gains, infants and toddlers grow in little spurts. In one study, children who were followed over the first 21 months of life went for periods of 7 to 63 days with no growth, then added as much as half an inch in a 24-hour period! Almost always, parents described their babies as irritable and very hungry on the day before the spurt (Lampl, 1993; Lampl, Veldhuis, & Johnson, 1992).

One of the most obvious changes in infants' appearance is their transformation into round, plump babies by the middle of the first year. This early rise in "baby fat," which peaks at about 9 months, helps the infant maintain a constant body temperature. In the second year, most toddlers slim down, a trend that continues into middle childhood (Fomon & Nelson, 2002). In contrast, muscle tissue increases very slowly during infancy and will not reach a peak until adolescence. Babies are not very muscular; their strength and physical coordination are limited.

In infancy, girls are slightly shorter and lighter than boys, with a higher ratio of fat to muscle. These small sex differences persist throughout early and middle childhood and are greatly magnified at adolescence. Ethnic differences in body size are apparent as well. Grace was below the *growth norms* (height and weight averages for children her age). Early malnutrition played a part, but even after substantial catch-up, Grace—as is typical for Asian children—remained below North American norms. In contrast, Timmy is slightly above average in size, as African-American children tend to be (Bogin, 2001).

This comparison between a 4-month-old and a 2-year-old shows that body growth is dramatic during infancy and toddlerhood—faster than at any other time after birth. Height increases by 75 percent, and weight quadruples.

Changes in Body Proportions

As the child's overall size increases, parts of the body grow at different rates. Two growth patterns describe these changes. The first is the **cephalocaudal trend**—from the Latin for "head to tail." During the prenatal period, the head develops more rapidly than the lower part of the body. At birth, the head takes up one-fourth of total body length, the legs only one-third. Notice how, in Figure 5.1, the lower portion of the body catches up. By age 2, the head accounts for only one-fifth and the legs for nearly one-half of total body length.

In the second pattern, the **proximodistal trend,** growth proceeds, literally, from "near to far"—from the center of the body outward. In the prenatal period, the head, chest, and trunk grow first, then the arms and legs, and finally the hands and feet. During infancy and childhood, the arms and legs continue to grow somewhat ahead of the hands and feet.

Skeletal Growth

Children of the same age differ in *rate* of physical growth; some make faster progress toward a mature body size than others. But current body size is not enough to tell us how quickly a child's physical growth is moving along. Although Timmy is larger and heavier than Caitlin and Grace, he is not physically more mature. In a moment, you will see why.

GENERAL SKELETAL GROWTH ■ The best way of estimating a child's physical maturity is to use **skeletal age,** a measure of development of the bones of the body. The embryonic skeleton is first formed out of soft, pliable tissue called *cartilage*. Then, beginning in the sixth week of pregnancy, cartilage cells harden into bone, a gradual process that continues throughout childhood and adolescence (Moore & Persaud, 2003).

Just before birth, special growth centers, called **epiphyses,** appear at the two extreme ends of each of the long bones of the body (see Figure 5.2). Cartilage cells continue to be

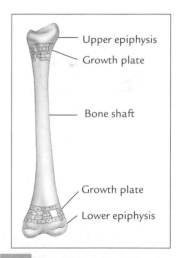

FIGURE 5.2

Diagram of a long bone showing upper and lower epiphyses. Cartilage cells are produced at the growth plates of the epiphyses and gradually harden into bone. (From J. M. Tanner, *Foetus into Man* [2nd ed.], Cambridge, MA: Harvard University Press, p. 32. Copyright © 1990 by J. M. Tanner. All rights reserved. Reprinted by permission of the publisher and author.)

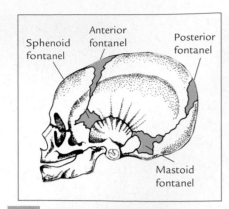

FIGURE 5.3

The skull at birth, showing the fontanels and sutures. The fontanels gradually close during the first two years, forming sutures that permit the skull to expand easily as the brain grows.

fontanels Six gaps, or "soft spots," separating the bones of the skull at birth.

neurons Nerve cells that store and transmit information.

synapses The gaps between neurons, across which chemical messages are sent.

neurotransmitters Chemicals released by neurons that cross the synapse to send messages to other neurons.

synaptic pruning Loss of connective fibers by seldom-stimulated neurons, thereby returning them to an uncommitted state so they can support future development.

glial cells Cells that are responsible for myelination and, in certain instances, also participate directly in neural communication.

myelination A process in which neural fibers are coated with an insulating fatty sheath, myelin, that improves the efficiency of message transfer.

produced at the growth plates of these epiphyses, which increase in number throughout childhood and then, as growth continues, get thinner and disappear. After that, no further growth in bone length is possible. Skeletal age can be estimated by X-raying the bones and seeing the number of epiphyses and the extent to which they are fused.

African-American children tend to be slightly ahead of Caucasian-American children in skeletal age. And girls are considerably ahead of boys—the reason Timmy's skeletal age lags behind that of Caitlin and Grace. At birth, the sexes differ by about 4 to 6 weeks, a gap that widens over infancy and childhood. This is why girls reach their full body size several years before boys (Tanner, Healy, & Cameron, 2001). Girls are advanced in development of other organs as well. This greater physical maturity may contribute to girls' greater resistance to harmful environmental influences. As noted in Chapter 2, girls experience fewer developmental problems than boys and have lower infant and childhood mortality rates.

GROWTH OF THE SKULL ■ Pediatricians routinely measure children's head size between birth and age 2 years, when skull growth is especially rapid because of large increases in brain size. At birth, the bones of the skull are separated by six gaps, or "soft spots," called **fontanels** (see Figure 5.3). The gaps permit the bones to overlap as the large head of the baby passes through the mother's narrow birth canal. You can easily feel the largest gap, the anterior fontanel, which measures slightly more than an inch across at the top of a baby's skull. It gradually shrinks and is filled in during the second year. The other fontanels are smaller and close more quickly. As the skull bones come in contact with one another, they form *sutures,* or seams. These permit the skull to expand easily as the brain grows. The sutures disappear completely in adolescence, when skull growth is complete.

APPEARANCE OF TEETH ■ On average, an African-American baby's first tooth appears at about 4 months, a Caucasian baby's around 6 months, although wide individual differences exist. Timmy's first tooth erupted when he was 2 months old; a few infants do not get their first tooth until 1 year of age. By age 2, the average child has 20 teeth (Carruth et al., 2004). Dental development provides a rough clue to rate of skeletal development: A child who gets teeth early is likely to be advanced in physical maturity.

Brain Development

At birth, the brain is nearer to its adult size than any other physical structure, and it continues to develop at an astounding pace throughout infancy and toddlerhood. We can best understand brain growth by looking at it from two vantage points: (1) the microscopic level of individual brain cells and (2) the larger level of the cerebral cortex, the most complex brain structure and the one responsible for the highly developed intelligence of our species.

Development of Neurons

The human brain has 100 to 200 billion **neurons,** or nerve cells, that store and transmit information, many of which have thousands of direct connections with other neurons. Unlike other body cells, neurons are not tightly packed together. Between them are tiny gaps, or **synapses,** where fibers from different neurons come close together but do not touch (see Figure 5.4 on page 169). Neurons send messages to one another by releasing chemicals called **neurotransmitters,** which cross the synapse.

The basic story of brain growth concerns how neurons develop and form this elaborate communication system. Figure 5.5 summarizes major milestones of brain development. In the prenatal period, neurons are produced in the embryo's primitive neural tube. From there, they migrate to form the major parts of the brain (see Chapter 3, page 101). Once neurons are in place, they differentiate, establishing their unique functions by extending their fibers to form synaptic connections with neighboring cells. During infancy and toddlerhood, neural fibers and synapses increase at an astounding pace (Huttenlocher, 2002; Moore & Persaud, 2003). Because developing neurons require space for these connective structures, a surprising aspect of brain growth is that as synapses form, many surrounding neurons die—20 to 80 percent, depending on the brain region (de Haan & Johnson, 2003; Stiles, 2001a). Fortunately, during the prenatal period, the neural tube produces far more neurons than the brain will ever need.

As neurons form connections, *stimulation* becomes vital to their survival. Neurons that are stimulated by input from the surrounding environment continue to establish new synapses, forming increasingly elaborate systems of communication that support more complex abilities. At first, stimulation results in a massive overabundance of synapses, many of which serve identical functions, thereby ensuring that the child will acquire the motor, cognitive, and social skills that our species needs to survive. Neurons that are seldom stimulated soon lose their synapses, in a process called **synaptic pruning** that returns neurons not needed at the moment to an uncommitted state so they can support future development. In all, about 40 percent of synapses are pruned during childhood and adolescence (Webb, Monk, & Nelson, 2001). For this process to go forward, appropriate stimulation of the child's brain is vital during periods in which the formation of synapses is at its peak (Nelson, Thomas, & de Haan, 2006).

If few neurons are produced after the prenatal period, what causes the dramatic increase in brain size during the first two years? About half the brain's volume is made up of **glial cells,** which are responsible for **myelination,** the coating of neural fibers

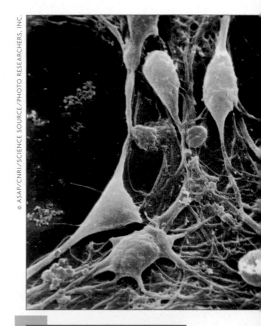

FIGURE 5.4

Neurons and their connective fibers. This photograph of several neurons, taken with the aid of a powerful microscope, shows the elaborate synaptic connections that form with neighboring cells.

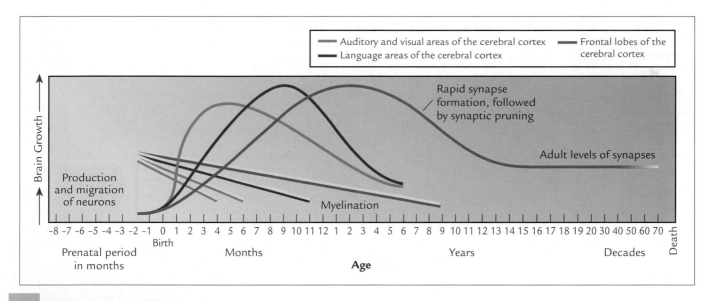

FIGURE 5.5

Major milestones of brain development. Formation of synapses is rapid during the first two years, especially in the auditory, visual, and language areas of the cerebral cortex. The frontal lobes undergo more extended synaptic growth. In each area, overproduction of synapses is followed by synaptic pruning. The frontal lobes are among the last regions to attain adult levels of synaptic connections—in mid- to late adolescence. Myelination occurs at a dramatic pace during the first two years and then at a slower pace through childhood and adolescence. The multiple yellow lines indicate that the timing of myelination varies among different brain areas. For example, neural fibers continue to myelinate over a longer period in the language areas, and especially in the frontal lobes, than in the visual and auditory areas. (Adapted from Thompson & Nelson, 2001).

with an insulating fatty sheath (called *myelin*) that improves the efficiency of message transfer. Certain types of glial cells also participate directly in neural communication, by picking up and passing on neuronal signals and releasing neurotransmitters (LoTurco, 2000). From the end of pregnancy through the second year of life, glial cells multiply rapidly—a process that continues at a slower pace through middle childhood and accelerates again in adolescence. Increases in neural fibers and myelination are responsible for the extraordinary gain in overall size of the brain—from nearly 30 percent of its adult weight at birth to 70 percent by age 2 (Thatcher et al., 1996).

Brain development can be compared to molding a "living sculpture." After neurons and synapses are overproduced, cell death and synaptic pruning sculpt away excess building material to form the mature brain—a process jointly influenced by genetically programmed events and the child's experiences. The resulting sculpture is a set of interconnected regions, each with specific functions—much like countries on a globe that communicate with one another (Johnston et al., 2001). This "geography" of the brain permits researchers to study its organization and the activity of its regions using *neurophysiological* techniques.

Neurophysiological Methods

Table 5.1 describes major methods for measuring brain functioning, Two of these detect changes in *electrical activity* in the cerebral cortex. Researchers can examine *EEG brain-wave patterns* for stability and organization—signs of mature cortical functioning. And as a child processes a particular stimulus, *ERPs* detect the precise location of brain-wave activity—a method often used to study preverbal infants' responsiveness to various stimuli, the impact of experience on specialization of specific brain regions, and atypical brain functioning in children at risk for learning and emotional problems (deRegnier, 2005).

TABLE 5.1	Methods for Measuring Brain Functioning
METHOD	**DESCRIPTION**
Electroencephalogram (EEG)	Electrodes are taped to the scalp to record the stability and organization of electrical brain-wave activity in the brain's outer layers—the cerebral cortex.
Event-related potentials (ERPs)	Using the EEG, the frequency and amplitude of brain waves in response to particular stimuli (such as a picture, music, or speech) are recorded in specific areas of the cerebral cortex.
Functional magnetic resonance imaging (fMRI)	While the person lies quietly inside a tunnel-shaped apparatus that creates a magnetic field, a scanner magnetically detects increased blood flow and oxygen metabolism in areas of the brain as the individual processes particular stimuli. The result is a computerized moving picture of activity anywhere in the brain (not just its outer layers).
Positron Emission Tomography (PET)	After injection or inhalation of a radioactive substance, the individual lies inside a tunnel-shaped apparatus with a scanner that emits fine streams of X-rays, which detect increased blood flow and oxygen metabolism in areas of the brain while the person processes particular stimuli. As with fMRI, the result is a computerized moving picture of activity anywhere in the brain.
Near-Infrared Optical Topography (NIROT)	Using thin, flexible optical fibers attached to the scalp, infrared (invisible) light is beamed at the brain; its absorption by areas of the cerebral cortex varies with changes in blood flow and oxygen metabolism. The optical fibers detect these light-absorption variations while the individual processes particular stimuli, yielding a computerized moving picture of active cortical areas. Unlike fMRI and PET, the NIROT apparatus is compact; an infant or child can sit on the parent's lap or move within limited range during testing.

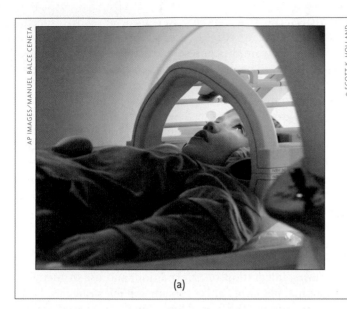

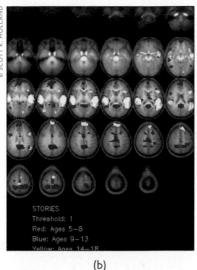

FIGURE 5.6

Measuring brain activity using functional magnetic resonance imaging (fMRI). (a) This 6-year-old is part of a study that uses fMRI to find out how his brain processes light and motion. (b) The fMRI image shows which areas of the boy's brain are active while he views changing visual stimuli.

STORIES
Threshold: 1
Red: Ages 5–8
Blue: Ages 9–13
Yellow: Ages 14–18

(a)   (b)

Neuroimaging techniques, which yield detailed, three-dimensional computerized pictures of the entire brain and its active areas, provide the most precise information about which brain regions are specialized for certain capacities. In both *PET* and *fMRI,* the child must lie quietly inside a tunnel-like apparatus. But unlike PET, fMRI does not depend on X-ray photography, which requires injection of a radioactive substance. Rather, when a child is exposed to a stimulus, fMRI detects increases in blood flow and oxygen metabolism throughout the brain magnetically, yielding a colorful, moving picture of parts of the brain used to perform a given activity (see Figure 5.6 for an example).

PET and fMRI are not suitable for infants and young children, since they require that the child remain as motionless as possible while lying on a narrow plank in an enclosed space for an extended time. A new brain-imaging method that works well in infancy and early childhood is *near infrared optical topography (NIROT),* in which infrared (invisible) light is beamed at regions of the cerebral cortex to measure blood flow and oxygen metabolism while the child attends to a stimulus (refer again to Table 5.1). Because the apparatus consists only of thin, flexible optical fibers attached to the scalp, a baby can sit on the parent's lap and move during testing (Taga et al., 2003).

Neurophysiological methods are powerful tools for uncovering relationships between the brain and psychological development. But like all research methods, they have limitations. Even though a stimulus produces a consistent pattern of brain activity, investigators cannot be certain that an individual has processed it in a certain way. Other methods must be combined with brain-wave and -imaging findings to clarify their meaning (Nicholson, 2006). Now let's turn to the developing organization of the cerebral cortex.

In preparing for an EEG, a researcher applies gel to electrodes before attaching them to a baby's scalp. This method records the stability and organization of electrical brain-wave activity in the cerebral cortex. It can also be used to measure ERPs, the frequency and amplitude of brain waves in particular areas of the cerebral cortex in response to specific stimuli, such as music or speech.

Development of the Cerebral Cortex

The **cerebral cortex** surrounds the rest of the brain, resembling half of a shelled walnut. It is the largest brain structure—accounting for 85 percent of the brain's weight and containing the greatest number of neurons and synapses. Because the cerebral cortex is the last part of the brain to stop growing, it is sensitive to environmental influences for a much longer period than any other part of the brain.

cerebral cortex The largest, most complex structure of the human brain, responsible for the highly developed intelligence of the human species.

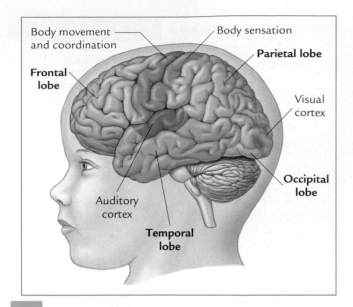

FIGURE 5.7

The left side of the human brain, showing the cerebral cortex. The cortex is divided into different lobes, each of which contains a variety of regions with specific functions. Some major regions are labeled here.

REGIONS OF THE CORTEX ■ Figure 5.7 shows specific functions of regions of the cerebral cortex, such as receiving information from the senses, instructing the body to move, and thinking. The order in which cortical regions develop corresponds to the order in which various capacities emerge in the infant and growing child. For example, a burst of synaptic growth occurs in the auditory and visual cortexes and in areas responsible for body movement over the first year—a period of dramatic gains in auditory and visual perception and mastery of motor skills (Johnson, 2005). Language areas are especially active from late infancy through the preschool years, when language development flourishes (Thompson et al., 2000b).

The cortical regions with the most extended period of development are the *frontal lobes,* which are responsible for thought—in particular, for consciousness, inhibition of impulses, integration of information, and use of memory, reasoning, planning, and problem-solving strategies. From age 2 months on, the frontal lobes function more effectively. But they undergo especially rapid myelination and formation and pruning of synapses during the preschool and school years, yielding an adult level of synaptic connections around mid- to late adolescence (Nelson, 2002; Nelson, Thomas, & de Haan, 2006; Sowell et al., 2002).

LATERALIZATION AND PLASTICITY OF THE CEREBRAL CORTEX ■ The cortex has two *hemispheres,* or sides—left and right—that differ in their functions. Some tasks are done mostly by one hemisphere and some by the other. For example, each hemisphere receives sensory information from the side of the body opposite to it and controls only that side.[1] For most of us, the left hemisphere is largely responsible for verbal abilities (such as spoken and written language) and positive emotion (for example, joy). The right hemisphere handles spatial abilities (judging distances, reading maps, and recognizing geometric shapes) and negative emotion (such as distress) (Banish & Heller, 1998; Nelson & Bosquet, 2000). This pattern may be reversed in left-handed people, but more often, the cerebral cortex of left-handers is less clearly specialized than that of right-handers.

Specialization of the two hemispheres is called **lateralization.** Why are behaviors and abilities lateralized? fMRI studies reveal that the left hemisphere is better at processing information in a sequential, analytic (piece-by-piece) way, a good approach for dealing with communicative information—both verbal (language) and emotional (a joyful smile). In contrast, the right hemisphere is specialized for processing information in a holistic, integrative manner, ideal for making sense of spatial information and regulating negative emotion (Banish, 1998). A lateralized brain is certainly adaptive and may have evolved because it enabled humans to cope more successfully with changing environmental demands (Rogers, 2000). It permits a wider array of functions to be carried out effectively than if both sides processed information in exactly the same way. But it is important to note that the two hemispheres communicate and work together, doing so more rapidly and effectively with age. Thus, the popular notion of a "right-brained" or "left-brained" person is an oversimplification.

Researchers study when brain lateralization occurs to learn more about **brain plasticity.** In a highly *plastic* cerebral cortex, many areas are not yet committed to specific functions. Consequently, the cortex has a high capacity for learning. In addition, if a part of the cortex is damaged, other parts can take over the tasks it would have handled. But once the hemispheres

lateralization Specialization of functions in the two hemispheres of the cerebral cortex.

brain plasticity The capacity of various parts of the cerebral cortex to take over functions of damaged regions.

---

[1] The eyes are an exception. Messages from the right half of each retina go to the right hemisphere; messages from the left half of each retina go to the left hemisphere. Thus, visual information from *both* eyes is received by *both* hemispheres.

lateralize, damage to a specific region means that the abilities it controls cannot be recovered to the same extent or as easily as earlier.

At birth, the hemispheres have already begun to specialize. Most newborns favor the right side of the body in their head position and reflexive reactions (Grattan et al., 1992; Rönnqvist & Hopkins, 1998). Most also show greater ERP brain-wave activity in the left hemisphere while listening to speech sounds or displaying a positive state of arousal. In contrast, the right hemisphere reacts more strongly to nonspeech sounds and to stimuli (such as a sour-tasting fluid) that evoke a negative reaction (Davidson, 1994; Fox & Davidson, 1986).

Nevertheless, research on brain-damaged children and adults offers dramatic evidence for substantial plasticity in the young brain, summarized in the Biology and Environment box on page 174. Furthermore, early experience greatly influences the organization of the cerebral cortex. For example, deaf adults who, as infants and children, learned sign language (a spatial skill) depend more than hearing individuals on the right hemisphere for language processing (Neville & Bavelier, 2002). And toddlers who are advanced in language development show greater left-hemispheric specialization for language than their more slowly developing age-mates. Apparently, the very process of acquiring language promotes lateralization (Casey et al., 2002; Luna et al., 2001; Mills et al., 2005).

In sum, the brain is more plastic during the first few years than at any later time of life. An overabundance of synaptic connections supports brain plasticity and, therefore, young children's ability to learn, which is fundamental to their survival (Nelson, 2000). And although the cortex is genetically programmed for hemispheric specialization, experience greatly influences the rate and success of its advancing organization.

Sensitive Periods in Brain Development

Animal studies confirm that early, extreme sensory deprivation results in permanent brain damage and loss of functions—findings that verify the existence of sensitive periods in brain development. For example, early, varied visual experiences must occur for the brain's visual centers to develop normally. If a 1-month-old kitten is deprived of light for just 3 or 4 days, these areas of the brain degenerate. If the kitten is kept in the dark during the fourth week of life and beyond, the damage is severe and permanent (Crair, Gillespie, & Stryker, 1998). And the general quality of the early environment affects overall brain growth. When animals reared from birth in physically and socially stimulating surroundings are compared with those reared in isolation, the brains of the stimulated animals show much denser synaptic connections (Greenough & Black, 1992).

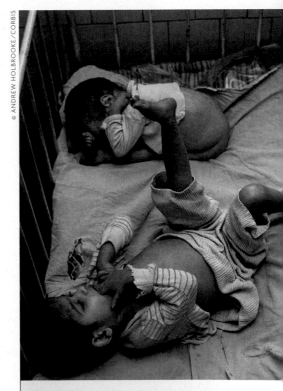

CHILDREN BORN WITH CATARACTS AND ORPHANAGE CHILDREN ■ For ethical reasons, we cannot deliberately deprive some infants of normal rearing experiences and observe the impact on their brains and competencies. Instead, we must turn to natural experiments, in which children were victims of deprived early environments that were later rectified. Such studies have revealed some parallels with the animal evidence just described.

For example, when babies are born with cataracts in both eyes (clouded lenses, preventing clear visual images), those who have corrective surgery within 4 to 6 months show rapid improvement in vision, except for subtle aspects of face perception, which require early visual input to the right hemisphere to develop (Le Grand et al., 2001, 2003). But the longer cataract surgery is postponed beyond infancy, the less complete the recovery in visual skills. And if surgery is delayed until adulthood, vision is severely and permanently impaired (Maurer et al., 1999).

Studies of infants placed in orphanages who were later exposed to ordinary family rearing confirm the importance of a generally stimulating physical and social environment for all domains of development. In one study, researchers followed the progress of a large sample of children transferred between birth and age 3½ from extremely deprived Romanian orphanages to adoptive families in Great

These children in an orphanage in Romania receive very little adult contact and stimulation. The longer they remain in this barren environment, the more they will withdraw and wither, displaying profound impairment in all domains of development.

Biology and Environment

Brain Plasticity: Insights from Research on Brain-Damaged Children and Adults

In the first few years of life, the brain is highly plastic. It can reorganize areas committed to specific functions in a way that the mature brain cannot. Consistently, adults who suffered brain injuries in infancy and early childhood show fewer cognitive impairments than adults with later-occurring injuries (Holland, 2004; Huttenlocher, 2002). Nevertheless, the young brain is not totally plastic. When it is injured, its functioning is compromised. The extent of plasticity depends on several factors, including age at time of injury, site of damage, and skill area.

Brain Plasticity in Infancy and Early Childhood

In a large study of children with injuries to the cerebral cortex that occurred before birth or in the first six months of life, language and spatial skills were assessed repeatedly into adolescence (Akshoomoff et al., 2002; Stiles, 2001a; Stiles et al., 2005). All the children had experienced early brain seizures or hemorrhages. Brain-imaging techniques (fMRI and PET) revealed the precise site of damage.

Regardless of whether injury occurred in the left or right cerebral hemisphere, the children showed delays in language development that persisted until about 3½ years of age. That damage to either hemisphere affected early language competence indicates that at first, language functioning is broadly distributed in the brain. But by age 5, the children caught up in vocabulary and grammatical skills. Undamaged areas—in either the left or the right hemisphere—had taken over these language functions.

Compared with language, spatial skills were more impaired after early brain injury. When preschool through adolescent-age youngsters were asked to copy designs, those with early right-hemispheric damage had trouble with holistic processing—accurately representing the overall shape. In contrast, children with left-hemispheric damage captured the basic shape but omitted fine-grained details. Nevertheless, the children showed improvements in their drawings with age—gains that did not occur in brain-injured adults (Akshoomoff et al., 2002; Stiles et al., 2003).

Clearly, recovery after early brain injury is greater for language than for spatial skills. Why is this so? Researchers speculate that spatial processing is the older of the two capacities in our evolutionary history and, therefore, more lateralized at birth (Stiles, 2001b; Stiles et al., 2002). But early brain injury has far less impact than later injury on *both* language and spatial skills. In sum, the young brain is remarkably plastic.

The Price of High Plasticity in the Young Brain

Despite impressive recovery of language and (to a lesser extent) spatial skills, children with early brain injuries show deficits in a wide variety of complex mental abilities during the school years. For example, their reading and math progress is slow. And in telling stories, they produce simpler narratives than agemates without early brain injuries (although many catch up in narrative skills by early adolescence) (Reilly, Bates, & Marchman, 1998; Reilly et al., 2004). Furthermore, the more brain tissue destroyed in infancy or early childhood, the poorer children score on intelligence tests (Anderson et al., 2006).

High brain plasticity, researchers explain, comes at a price. When healthy brain regions take over the functions of damaged areas, a "crowding effect" occurs: Multiple tasks must be done by a smaller-than-usual volume of brain tissue. Consequently, the brain processes information less quickly and accurately than it would if it were intact. Complex mental abilities of all kinds suffer into middle childhood, and often longer, because performing them well requires considerable space in the cerebral cortex (Huttenlocher, 2002).

Later Plasticity

Brain plasticity is not restricted to early childhood. Although far more limited, reorganization in the brain can occur later, even in adulthood. For example, adult stroke victims often display considerable recovery, especially in response to stimulation of language and motor skills. Brain-imaging techniques reveal that structures adjacent to the permanently damaged area or in the opposite cerebral hemisphere reorganize to support the impaired ability (Bach-y-Rita, 2001; Hallett, 2000).

In infancy and childhood, the goal of brain growth is to form neural connections that ensure mastery of essential skills. Animal research reveals that plasticity is greatest while the brain is forming many new synapses; it declines during synaptic pruning (Kolb & Gibb, 2001). At older ages, specialized brain structures are in place, but after injury they can still reorganize to some degree. The adult brain can produce a small number of new neurons. And when an individual practices relevant tasks, the brain strengthens existing synapses and generates new ones (Nelson, Thomas, & de Haan, 2006). Plasticity seems to be a basic property of the nervous system. Researchers hope to discover how experience and brain plasticity work together throughout life, so they can help people of all ages—with and without brain injuries—develop at their best.

This 8-year-old, who experienced brain damage in infancy, has well-developed language skills but has difficulty with spatial tasks. Still, he has been spared massive impairments in either area because of early, high brain plasticity. The boy's teachers are strengthening his spatial skills by providing him with many activities involving copying and creating designs.

Britain (Beckett et al., 2006; O'Connor et al., 2000; Rutter et al., 1998, 2004). On arrival, most were impaired in all domains of development. By the preschool years, catch-up in physical size was dramatic. Cognitive catch-up, assessed at ages 6 and 11, was impressive for children adopted before 6 months, who attained average mental test scores, performing as well as a comparison group of early-adopted British-born children. But Romanian children who had been institutionalized for more than the first 6 months showed serious intellectual deficits (see Figure 5.8). Although they improved in test scores during middle childhood (perhaps as a result of added time in their adoptive homes and special services at school), they remained substantially below average. Even for adopted children who had experienced adequate early nutrition, both time spent in the institution and poor cognitive functioning were correlated with below-average head size, suggesting that early lack of stimulation damaged the brain (Rutter, 2006b).

Additional evidence shows that the chronic stress of early, deprived orphanage rearing disrupts the brain's capacity to manage stress, with long-term physical and psychological consequences. In another investigation, researchers followed the development of children who had spent their first 8 months or more in Romanian institutions and were then adopted into Canadian homes (Gunnar et al., 2001; Gunnar & Cheatham, 2003). Compared with agemates adopted shortly after birth, these children showed extreme stress reactivity, as indicated by high concentrations of the stress hormone *cortisol* in their saliva—a physiological response linked to illness, retarded physical growth, and learning and behavior problems, including deficits in attention and control of anger and other impulses. The longer the children spent in orphanage care, the higher their cortisol levels—even 6½ years after adoption.

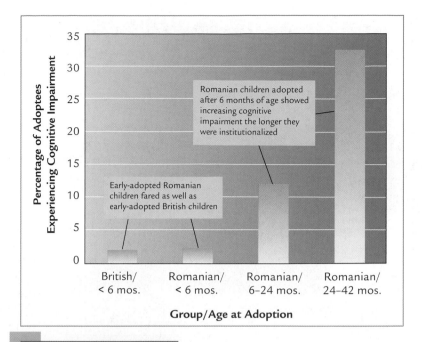

FIGURE 5.8

Relationship of age at adoption to mental test scores at ages 6 and 11 among British and Romanian adoptees. Children transferred from Romanian orphanages to British adoptive homes in the first 6 months of life attained average scores and fared as well as British early-adopted children, suggesting that they had fully recovered from extreme early deprivation. However, children adopted after 6 months performed well below average, and those adopted after age 2 showed persisting serious intellectual deficits. (Adapted from Beckett et al., 2006.)

APPROPRIATE STIMULATION ■ Unlike the orphanage children just described, Grace, whom Monica and Kevin had adopted in Cambodia at 16 months of age, showed favorable progress. Two years earlier, they had adopted Grace's older brother, Eli. When Eli was 2 years old, Monica and Kevin sent a letter and a photo of Eli to his biological mother, describing a bright, happy child. The next day, the Cambodian mother tearfully asked an adoption agency to send her baby daughter to join Eli and his American family. Although Grace's early environment was very depleted, her biological mother's loving care—holding gently, speaking softly, and breastfeeding—may have prevented irreversible damage to her brain.

In addition to impoverished environments, ones that overwhelm children with expectations beyond their current capacities interfere with the brain's potential. In recent years, expensive early learning centers have sprung up, in which infants are trained with letter and number flash cards and slightly older toddlers are given a full curriculum of reading, math, science, art, gym, and more. There is no evidence that these programs yield smarter, better "superbabies" (Hirsh-Pasek & Golinkoff, 2003). To the contrary, trying to prime infants with stimulation for which they are not ready can cause them to withdraw, thereby threatening their interest in learning and creating conditions much like stimulus deprivation!

How, then, can we characterize appropriate stimulation during the early years? To answer this question, researchers distinguish between two types of brain development. The first,

Experience-expectant brain growth takes place naturally, through ordinary, stimulating experiences. These young children exuberantly playing in the autumn leaves enjoy the type of activity that is best for promoting brain development in the early years.

experience-expectant brain growth, refers to the young brain's rapidly developing organization, which depends on ordinary experiences—opportunities to see and touch objects, to hear language and other sounds, and to move about and explore the environment. As a result of millions of years of evolution, the brains of all infants, toddlers, and young children expect to encounter these experiences and, if they do, grow normally. The second type of brain development—**experience-dependent brain growth**—occurs throughout our lives. It consists of additional growth and the refinement of established brain structures as a result of specific learning experiences that vary widely across individuals and cultures (Greenough & Black, 1992). Reading and writing, playing computer games, weaving an intricate rug, and practicing the violin are examples. The brain of a violinist differs in certain ways from the brain of a poet because each has exercised different brain regions for a long time (Thompson & Nelson, 2001).

Experience-expectant brain development takes place early and naturally, as caregivers offer babies and preschoolers age-appropriate play materials and engage them in enjoyable daily routines—a shared meal, a game of peekaboo, a bath before bed, a picture book to talk about, or a song to sing. The resulting growth provides the foundation for later-occurring, experience-dependent development (Huttenlocher, 2002; Shonkoff & Phillips, 2001). No evidence exists for a sensitive period in the first few years of life for mastering skills that depend on extensive training, such as reading, musical performance, or gymnastics (Bruer, 1999). To the contrary, rushing early learning also harms the brain by overwhelming its neural circuits, thereby reducing the brain's sensitivity to the everyday experiences it needs for a healthy start in life.

Changing States of Arousal

Rapid brain growth means that the organization of sleep and wakefulness changes substantially between birth and 2 years, and fussiness and crying also decline. The newborn baby takes round-the-clock naps that total about 16 to 18 hours (Davis, Parker, & Montgomery, 2004). Total sleep time declines slowly; the average 2-year-old still needs 12 to 13 hours. But periods of sleep and wakefulness become fewer but longer, and the sleep–wake pattern increasingly conforms to a night–day schedule. Most 6- to 9-month-olds take two daytime naps; by about 18 months, children generally need only one nap. Finally, between ages 3 and 5, napping subsides (Iglowstein et al., 2003).

These changing arousal patterns are due to brain development, but they are also affected by the social environment. In Western nations, many parents try to get their babies to sleep through the night around 4 months of age by feeding them solid foods before bedtime, then putting them down in a separate, quiet room—practices that may be at odds with young infants' neurological development. Not until the middle of the first year is the secretion of *melatonin,* a hormone within the brain that promotes drowsiness, much greater at night than during the day (Sadeh, 1997).

As the Cultural Influences box on the following page reveals, isolating infants to promote sleep is rare elsewhere in the world. When babies sleep with their parents, their average sleep period remains constant at 3 hours from 1 to 8 months of age. Only at the end of the first year, as REM sleep (the state that usually prompts waking) declines, do infants move in the direction of an adultlike sleep–wake schedule (Ficca et al., 1999).

Even after infants sleep through the night, they continue to wake occasionally. When babies begin to crawl and walk, they often show temporary periods of disrupted sleep (Scher,

experience-expectant brain growth The young brain's rapidly developing organization, which depends on ordinary experiences— opportunities to see and touch objects, to hear language and other sounds, and to move about and explore the environment.

experience-dependent brain growth New growth and refinement of brain structures as a result of specific learning experiences that vary widely across individuals and cultures.

Cultural Influences

Cultural Variation in Infant Sleeping Arrangements

While awaiting the birth of a new baby, North American parents typically furnish a room as the infant's sleeping quarters. For decades, child-rearing advice from experts strongly encouraged the nighttime separation of baby from parent. For example, the most recent edition of Benjamin Spock's *Baby and Child Care* recommends that babies sleep in their own room by 3 months of age, explaining, "By 6 months, a child who regularly sleeps in her parents' room may become dependent on this arrangement" (Spock & Needlman, 2004, p. 60).

Yet parent–infant "cosleeping" is the norm for approximately 90 percent of the world's population, in cultures as diverse as the Japanese, the rural Guatemalan Maya, the Inuit of northwestern Canada, and the !Kung of Botswana. Japanese and Korean children usually lie next to their mothers throughout infancy and early childhood, and many continue to sleep with a parent or other family member until adolescence (Takahashi, 1990; Yang & Hahn, 2002). Among the Maya, mother–infant cosleeping is interrupted only by the birth of a new baby, at which time the older child is moved next to the father or to another bed in the same room (Morelli et al., 1992). Cosleeping is also common in some North American subcultures. African-American children frequently fall asleep with their parents and remain with them for part or all of the night (Brenner et al., 2003). Appalachian children of eastern Kentucky typically sleep with their parents for the first two years of life (Abbott, 1992).

Cultural values—specifically, collectivism versus individualism (see Chapter 2, page 77)—strongly influence infant sleeping arrangements. In one study, researchers interviewed American middle-SES mothers and Guatemalan Mayan mothers about their sleeping practices. Mayan mothers stressed a collectivist perspective, explaining that cosleeping builds a close parent–child bond, which is necessary for children to learn the ways of people around them. In contrast, American mothers conveyed an individualistic perspective, mentioning the importance of instilling early independence, preventing bad habits, and protecting their own privacy (Morelli et al., 1992).

Over the past 15 years, cosleeping has increased dramatically in North America and other Western nations, perhaps because more mothers are breastfeeding. Today the rate of bedsharing among U.S. mothers of young babies may be as high as 50 percent (Willinger et al., 2003). Research suggests that cosleeping evolved to protect infants' survival and health. During the night, cosleeping babies breastfeed three times longer than infants who sleep alone. Because infants arouse to nurse more often when sleeping next to their mothers, some researchers believe that cosleeping may actually help safeguard babies at risk for sudden infant death syndrome (SIDS) (see page 151 in Chapter 4). In Asian cultures where cosleeping is widespread, including Cambodia, China, Japan, Korea, Thailand, and Vietnam, SIDS is rare (McKenna, 2002; McKenna & McDade, 2005). And contrary to popular belief, cosleeping does not reduce mothers' total sleep time, although they experience a greater number of brief awakenings, which permit them to check on their baby (Mao et al., 2004).

Infant sleeping practices affect other aspects of family life. For example, sleep problems are not an issue for Mayan parents. Babies doze off in the midst of ongoing family activities and are carried to bed by their mothers. In contrast, for many North American parents, getting young children ready for bed often requires an elaborate ritual that takes a good part of the evening. Perhaps bedtime struggles, so common in Western homes but rare elsewhere in the world, are related to the stress young children feel when they are required to fall asleep without assistance (Latz, Wolf, & Lozoff, 1999).

Critics of bedsharing warn that cosleeping children will develop emotional problems, especially excessive dependency. Yet a longitudinal study following children from the end of pregnancy through age 18 showed that young people who had bedshared in the early years were no different from others in any aspect of adjustment (Okami, Weisner, & Olmstead, 2002). Another concern is that infants might become trapped under the parent's body or in soft covers, mattresses, or sofas and suffocate. Parents who are obese or who use alcohol, tobacco, or illegal drugs do pose a serious risk to their sleeping babies. Use of quilts and comforters or an overly soft mattress is also hazardous (Willinger et al., 2003).

But with appropriate precautions, parents and infants can cosleep safely (Gessner & Porter, 2006). In cultures where cosleeping is widespread, parents and infants usually sleep with light covering on hard surfaces, such as firm mattresses, floor mats, and wooden planks, or infants sleep in a cradle or hammock next to the parents' bed (McKenna, 2001, 2002; Nelson, Schiefenhoevel, & Haimerl, 2000). Also, infants typically lie on their backs, which promotes arousal if breathing is threatened and helps ensure frequent, easy communication between parent and baby.

This Cambodian father and child sleep together—a practice common in their culture and around the globe. When children fall asleep with their parents, sleep problems are rare during the early years. And many parents who practice cosleeping believe that it helps build a close parent-child bond.

Epstein, & Tirosh, 2004). And studies carried out in Australia, Great Britain, and Israel revealed that night wakings increased between 1½ and 2 years, then declined (Johnson, 1991; Scher et al., 1995). As we will see in Chapter 7, the challenges of the second year—ability to range farther from the familiar caregiver and awareness of the self as separate from others—often prompt anxiety in toddlers, evident in disturbed sleep and clinginess. When parents offer comfort, these behaviors subside.

Ask Yourself

Review   How does stimulation affect early brain development? Cite evidence at the level of neurons and at the level of the cerebral cortex.

Review   How do overproduction of synapses and synaptic pruning support infants' and children's ability to learn?

Apply   Which infant enrichment program would you choose: one that emphasizes gentle talking and touching and social games, or one that includes reading and number drills and classical music lessons? Explain.

Reflect   What is your attitude toward parent–infant cosleeping? Is it influenced by your cultural background? Explain.

Influences on Early Physical Growth

Physical growth, like other aspects of development, results from the continuous and complex interplay between genetic and environmental factors. Heredity, nutrition, relative freedom from disease, and emotional well-being all affect early physical growth.

Heredity

Because identical twins are much more alike in body size than fraternal twins, we know that heredity is important in physical growth (Estourgie-van Burk et al., 2006). When diet and health are adequate, height and rate of physical growth are largely determined by heredity. In fact, as long as negative environmental influences such as poor nutrition or illness are not severe, children and adolescents typically show *catch-up growth*—a return to a genetically determined growth path—once conditions improve. After her adoption, Grace grew rapidly until, at age 2, she was nearly average in size by Cambodian standards. Physical growth is a strongly canalized process (see Chapter 2, page 86). Still, the health of many organs may be permanently compromised by inadequate early nutrition.

Genetic makeup also affects body weight: The weights of adopted children correlate more strongly with those of their biological than of their adoptive parents (Sørensen, Holst, & Stunkard, 1998). At the same time, environment—in particular, nutrition and eating habits—plays an especially important role.

Nutrition

Nutrition is especially crucial for development in the first two years because the baby's brain and body are growing so rapidly. Pound for pound, an infant's energy needs are twice those of an adult. Twenty-five percent of infants' total caloric intake is devoted to growth, and babies need extra calories to keep rapidly developing organs functioning properly (Trahms & Pipes, 1997).

BREASTFEEDING VERSUS BOTTLE-FEEDING ■ Babies not only need enough food; they need the right kind of food. In early infancy, breast milk is ideally suited to their needs, and bottled

Applying What We Know

Reasons to Breastfeed

NUTRITIONAL AND HEALTH ADVANTAGES	EXPLANATION
Provides the correct balance of fat and protein	Compared with the milk of other mammals, human milk is higher in fat and lower in protein. This balance, as well as the unique proteins and fats contained in human milk, is ideal for a rapidly myelinating nervous system.
Ensures nutritional completeness	A mother who breastfeeds need not add other foods to her infant's diet until the baby is 6 months old. The milks of all mammals are low in iron, but the iron contained in breast milk is much more easily absorbed by the baby's system. Consequently, bottle-fed infants need iron-fortified formula.
Helps ensure healthy physical growth	In the first few months, breastfed infants add weight and length slightly faster than bottle-fed infants, who catch up by the end of the first year. One-year-old breastfed babies are leaner (have a higher percentage of muscle to fat), a growth pattern that may help prevent later overweight and obesity.
Protects against many diseases	Breastfeeding transfers antibodies and other infection-fighting agents from mother to child and enhances functioning of the immune system. As a result, compared with bottle-fed infants, breastfed babies have far fewer allergic reactions and respiratory and intestinal illnesses. Breast milk also has anti-inflammatory effects, which reduce the severity of illness symptoms. Infant mortality rates in North American are reduced by 21 percent in breastfed infants.
Protects against faulty jaw development and tooth decay	Sucking the mother's nipple instead of an artificial nipple helps avoid malocclusion, a condition in which the upper and lower jaws do not meet properly. It also protects against tooth decay due to sweet liquid remaining in the mouths of infants who fall asleep while sucking on a bottle.
Ensures digestibility	Because breastfed babies have a different kind of bacteria growing in their intestines than bottle-fed infants, they rarely suffer from constipation or other gastrointestinal problems.
Smooths the transition to solid foods	Breastfed infants accept new solid foods more easily than do bottle-fed infants, perhaps because of their greater experience with a variety of flavors, which pass from the maternal diet into the mother's milk.

Sources: American Academy of Pediatrics, 2005a; Buescher, 2001; Fulhan, Collier, & Duggan, 2003; Kramer et al., 2002, 2003.

formulas try to imitate it. Applying What We Know above summarizes major nutritional and health advantages of breastfeeding.

Because of these benefits, breastfed babies in poverty-stricken regions of the world are much less likely to be malnourished and 6 to 14 times more likely to survive the first year of life. The World Health Organization recommends breastfeeding until age 2 years, with solid foods added at 6 months. These practices, if widely followed, would save the lives of more than a million infants annually. Even breastfeeding for just a few weeks offers some protection against respiratory and intestinal infections, which are devastating to young children in developing countries. Also, because a nursing mother is less likely to get pregnant, breastfeeding helps increase spacing among siblings, a major factor in reducing infant and childhood deaths in nations with widespread poverty (Bellamy, 2005). (Note, however, that breastfeeding is not a reliable method of birth control.)

Yet many mothers in the developing world do not know about these benefits. In Africa, the Middle East, and Latin America, most babies get some breastfeeding, but fewer than 40 percent are exclusively breastfed for the first 6 months. And one-third are fully weaned from the breast before 1 year (Lauer et al., 2004). In place of breast milk, mothers give their babies commercial formula or low-grade nutrients, such as rice water or highly diluted cow or goat milk. Contamination of these foods as a result of poor sanitation is common and often leads to illness and infant death. The United Nations has encouraged all hospitals and maternity units in developing countries to promote breastfeeding as long as mothers do not have viral or bacterial infections (such as HIV or tuberculosis) that can be transmitted to the baby. Today, most developing countries have banned the practice of giving free or subsidized formula to new mothers.

Partly as a result of the natural childbirth movement, breastfeeding has become more common in industrialized nations, especially among well-educated women.

© SEAN SPRAGUE/THE IMAGE WORKS

Breastfeeding is especially important in developing countries. This breastfed baby from Gambia is likely to grow normally during the first year.

By providing nutritious meals and snacks, this toddler's parents support her desire to feed herself while helping her develop healthy eating habits. Limiting her consumption of foods high in sugar, salt, and saturated fats will help protect her from early weight gain, associated with later obesity.

Today, 71 percent of American and 75 percent of Canadian mothers breastfeed. However, about two-thirds of breastfeeding U.S. mothers and nearly half of Canadian mothers stop after a few months (Li et al., 2005; Palda et al., 2004). Breast milk is so easily digestible that a breastfed infant becomes hungry quite often—every 1½ to 2 hours, compared to every 3 or 4 hours for a bottle-fed baby. This makes breastfeeding inconvenient for many employed women. Not surprisingly, mothers who return to work sooner wean their babies from the breast earlier (Arora et al., 2002).

Mothers who cannot be with their babies all the time can still combine breast- and bottle-feeding. U.S. and Canadian national health agencies advise exclusive breastfeeding for the first 6 months. In the United States, recommendations also suggest that breast milk be included in the baby's diet until at least 1 year; in Canada, until 2 years and beyond (Health Canada, 2004c; U.S. Department of Health and Human Services, 2005b).

Women who do not breastfeed sometimes worry that they are depriving their baby of an experience essential for healthy psychological development. Yet breastfed and bottle-fed children in industrialized nations do not differ in emotional adjustment (Fergusson & Woodward, 1999). Some studies report a small advantage in intelligence test performance for children and adolescents who were breastfed, after controlling for many factors. Others, however, find no cognitive benefits (Gómez-Sanchiz et al., 2003; Jain, Concat, & Leventhal, 2002).

ARE CHUBBY BABIES AT RISK FOR LATER OVERWEIGHT AND OBESITY? ■ From early infancy, Timmy was an enthusiastic eater who nursed vigorously and gained weight quickly. By five months, he began reaching for food on his parents' plates. Vanessa wondered: Was she overfeeding Timmy and increasing his chances of being permanently overweight?

Most chubby infants thin out during toddlerhood and the preschool years, as weight gain slows and they become more active. Infants and toddlers can eat nutritious foods freely without risk of becoming overweight. But recent evidence does indicate a strengthening relationship between rapid weight gain in infancy and later obesity (Stettler et al., 2005; Yanovski, 2003). The trend may be due to the rise in overweight and obesity among adults, who promote unhealthy eating habits in their young children. Interviews with more than 3,000 U.S. parents of 4- to 24-month-olds revealed that many routinely served them french fries, pizza, candy, sugary fruit drinks, and soda. For example, 60 percent of 12-month-olds ate candy at least once a day! On average, infants consumed 20 percent and toddlers 30 percent more calories than they needed. At the same time, one-third ate no fruits or vegetables (Briefel et al., 2004).

How can concerned parents prevent their infants from becoming overweight children and adults? One way is to breastfeed for the first six months, which is associated with slower weight gain (Baker et al., 2004; Kalies et al., 2005). Another is to avoid giving them foods loaded with sugar, salt, and saturated fats. Once toddlers learn to walk, climb, and run, parents can also provide plenty of opportunities for energetic play. Finally, because research shows a correlation between excessive television viewing and overweight in older children, parents should limit the time very young children spend in front of the TV.

Malnutrition

Osita is an Ethiopian 2-year-old whose mother has never had to worry about his gaining too much weight. When she weaned him at 1 year, he had little to eat besides starchy rice flour cakes. Soon his belly enlarged, his feet swelled, his hair fell out, and a rash appeared on his skin. His bright-eyed curiosity vanished, and he became irritable and listless.

In developing countries and war-torn areas where food resources are limited, malnutrition is widespread. Recent evidence indicates that about one-third of the world's children suffer from malnutrition before age 5 (Bellamy, 2005). The 9 percent who are severely affected suffer from two dietary diseases.

The baby on the left, of Niger, Africa, has marasmus, a wasted condition caused by a diet low in all essential nutrients. The swollen abdomen of the toddler on the right, who lives in a Rwandan refugee camp, is a symptom of kwashiorkor, which results from a diet very low in protein. If the children survive, they are likely to be growth stunted, to suffer damage to vital organs, and to have lasting impairments in intellectual and emotional development.

Marasmus is a wasted condition of the body caused by a diet low in all essential nutrients. It usually appears in the first year of life when a baby's mother is too malnourished to produce enough breast milk and bottle-feeding is also inadequate. Her starving baby becomes painfully thin and is in danger of dying.

Osita has **kwashiorkor,** caused by an unbalanced diet very low in protein. The disease usually strikes after weaning, between 1 and 3 years of age. It is common in regions where children get just enough calories from starchy foods but little protein. The child's body responds by breaking down its own protein reserves, which causes the swelling and other symptoms that Osita experienced.

Children who survive these extreme forms of malnutrition often grow to be smaller in all body dimensions and suffer from lasting damage to the brain, heart, liver, or other organs (Müller & Krawinkel, 2005). When their diets do improve, they tend to gain excessive weight (Branca & Ferrari, 2002; Martins et al., 2004). A malnourished body protects itself by establishing a low basal metabolism rate, which may endure after nutrition improves. Also, malnutrition may disrupt appetite control centers in the brain, causing the child to overeat when food becomes plentiful.

Learning and behavior are also seriously affected. In one long-term study of marasmic children, an improved diet led to some catch-up growth in height, but not in head size (Stoch et al., 1982). The malnutrition probably interfered with growth of neural fibers and myelination, causing a permanent loss in brain weight. These children score low on intelligence tests, show poor fine-motor coordination, and have difficulty paying attention (Galler et al., 1990; Liu et al., 2003). They also display a more intense stress response to fear-arousing situations, perhaps caused by the constant, gnawing pain of hunger (Fernald & Grantham-McGregor, 1998).

Recall from our discussion of prenatal malnutrition in Chapter 3 that the passivity and irritability of malnourished children worsen the impact of poor diet. These behaviors may appear even when protein-calorie deprivation is only mild to moderate. They also accompany *iron-deficiency anemia,* a condition common among poverty-stricken infants and children that interferes with many central nervous system processes. Withdrawal and listlessness reduce

marasmus A disease usually appearing in the first year of life, caused by a diet low in all essential nutrients, that leads to a wasted condition of the body.

kwashiorkor A disease caused by a diet low in protein that usually appears after weaning, with symptoms including an enlarged belly, swollen feet, hair loss, skin rash, and irritable, listless behavior.

the nutritionally deprived child's ability to pay attention, explore, and evoke sensitive caregiving from parents, whose lives are already disrupted by poverty and stressful living conditions (Grantham-McGregor & Ani, 2001; Lozoff et al., 1998). For this reason, interventions for malnourished children must improve the family situation as well as the child's nutrition.

Inadequate nutrition is not confined to developing countries. Because government-supported supplementary food programs do not reach all families in need, an estimated 13 percent of Canadian children and 16 percent of American children suffer from *food insecurity*—uncertain access to enough food for a healthy, active life. Food insecurity is especially high among single-parent families (30 percent) and low-income ethnic minority families—for example, Hispanic and African Americans (22 percent) and Canadian Aboriginals (31 percent) (Statistics Canada, 2005e; U.S. Department of Agriculture, 2005b). Although few of these children have marasmus or kwashiorkor, their physical growth and ability to learn are still affected.

Emotional Well-Being

We may not think of affection and stimulation as necessary for healthy physical growth, but they are just as vital as food. **Nonorganic failure to thrive,** a growth disorder resulting from lack of parental love, is usually present by 18 months of age. Infants who have it show all the signs of marasmus (Black, 2005). But no organic (or biological) cause for the baby's failure to grow can be found. The baby is offered enough food and has no serious illness.

Lana, an observant nurse at a public health clinic, became concerned about 8-month-old Melanie, who was 3 pounds lighter than she had been at her last checkup. Lana noted that Melanie kept her eyes on nearby adults, anxiously watching their every move, and rarely smiled at her mother (Steward, 2001).

During feeding, diaper changing, and play, Melanie's mother sometimes acted cold and distant, at other times impatient and hostile (Hagekull, Bohlin, & Rydell, 1997). Melanie tried to protect herself by tracking her mother's whereabouts and, when she approached, avoiding her gaze.

Often an unhappy marriage and parental psychological disturbance contribute to these serious caregiving problems (Drotar, Pallotta, & Eckerle, 1994; Duniz et al., 1996). Sometimes the baby is irritable and displays abnormal feeding behaviors, such as poor sucking or vomiting, that stress the parent–child relationship further (Linscheid et al., 2005).

In Melanie's case, her alcoholic father was out of work, and her parents argued constantly. Melanie's mother had little energy to meet Melanie's psychological needs. When treated early, by helping parents or placing the baby in a caring foster home, failure-to-thrive infants show quick catch-up growth. But if the disorder is not corrected in infancy, most of these children remain small and show lasting cognitive and emotional difficulties (Dykman et al., 2001).

nonorganic failure to thrive
A growth disorder, usually present by 18 months of age, caused by lack of affection and stimulation.

Ask Yourself

Review   Explain why breastfeeding can have lifelong consequences for the development of babies born in poverty-stricken regions of the world.

Apply   Ten-month-old Shaun is below-average in height and painfully thin. He has one of two serious growth disorders. Name them, and indicate what clues you would look for to tell which one Shaun has.

Connect   How are bidirectional influences between parent and child involved in the impact of malnutrition on psychological development? After her adoption, how did those influences change for Grace?

Reflect   Imagine that you are the parent of a newborn baby. Describe feeding practices you would use, and ones you would avoid, to prevent overweight and obesity.

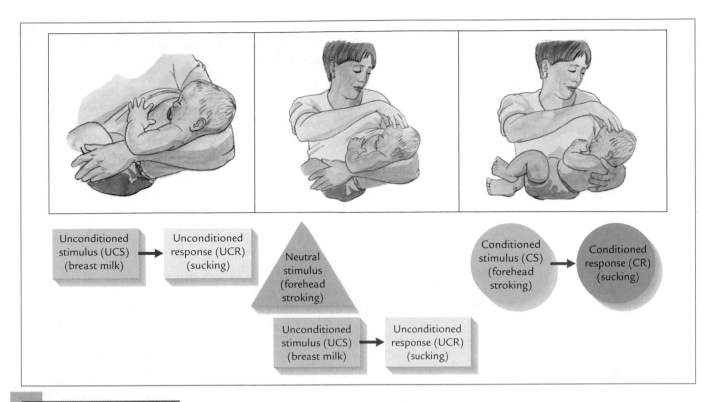

FIGURE 5.9

The steps of classical conditioning. This example shows how Caitlin's mother classically conditioned her to make sucking movements by stroking her forehead at the beginning of feedings.

Learning Capacities

Learning refers to changes in behavior as the result of experience. Babies come into the world with built-in learning capacities that permit them to profit from experience immediately. Infants are capable of two basic forms of learning, which were introduced in Chapter 1: classical and operant conditioning. They also learn through their natural preference for novel stimulation. Finally, shortly after birth, babies learn by observing others; they can imitate the facial expressions and gestures of adults.

Classical Conditioning

Newborn reflexes, discussed in Chapter 4, make **classical conditioning** possible in the young infant. In this form of learning, a neutral stimulus is paired with a stimulus that leads to a reflexive response. Once the baby's nervous system makes the connection between the two stimuli, the neutral stimulus produces the behavior by itself. Classical conditioning helps infants recognize which events usually occur together in the everyday world, so they can anticipate what is about to happen next. As a result, the environment becomes more orderly and predictable. Let's take a closer look at the steps of classical conditioning.

As Carolyn settled down in the rocking chair to nurse Caitlin, she often stroked Caitlin's forehead. Soon Carolyn noticed that each time she did this, Caitlin made active sucking movements. Caitlin had been classically conditioned. Here is how it happened (see Figure 5.9):

1. Before learning takes place, an **unconditioned stimulus (UCS)** must consistently produce a reflexive, or **unconditioned, response (UCR).** In Caitlin's case, sweet breast milk (UCS) resulted in sucking (UCR).

classical conditioning
A form of learning that involves associating a neutral stimulus with a stimulus that leads to a reflexive response.

unconditioned stimulus (UCS) In classical conditioning, a stimulus that leads to a reflexive response.

unconditioned response (UCR) In classical conditioning, a reflexive response that is produced by an unconditioned stimulus.

2. To produce learning, a *neutral stimulus* that does not lead to the reflex is presented just before, or at about the same time as, the UCS. Carolyn stroked Caitlin's forehead as each nursing period began. The stroking (neutral stimulus) was paired with the taste of milk (UCS).

3. If learning has occurred, the neutral stimulus alone produces a response similar to the reflexive response. The neutral stimulus is then called a **conditioned stimulus (CS),** and the response it elicits is called a **conditioned response (CR).** We know that Caitlin has been classically conditioned because stroking her forehead outside the feeding situation (CS) results in sucking (CR).

If the CS is presented alone enough times, without being paired with the UCS, the CR will no longer occur, an outcome called *extinction.* In other words, if Carolyn repeatedly strokes Caitlin's forehead without feeding her, Caitlin will gradually stop sucking in response to stroking.

Young infants can be classically conditioned most easily when the association between two stimuli has survival value. Learning which stimuli regularly accompany feeding improves the infant's ability to get food and survive (Blass, Ganchrow, & Steiner, 1984). In contrast, some responses, such as fear, are very difficult to classically condition in young babies. Until infants have the motor skills to escape unpleasant events, they have no biological need to form these associations. After age 6 months, however, fear is easy to condition. **TAKE A MOMENT...** Return to Chapter 1, page 17, to review John Watson's well-known experiment in which he conditioned Little Albert to withdraw and cry at the sight of a furry white rat. Then test your knowledge of classical conditioning by identifying the UCS, UCR, CS, and CR in Watson's study.

Operant Conditioning

In classical conditioning, babies build expectations about stimulus events in the environment, but they do not influence the stimuli that occur. In **operant conditioning,** infants act, or *operate,* on the environment, and stimuli that follow their behavior change the probability that the behavior will occur again. A stimulus that increases the occurrence of a response is called a **reinforcer.** For example, sweet liquid *reinforces* the sucking response in newborns. Removing a desirable stimulus or presenting an unpleasant one to decrease the occurrence of a response is called **punishment.** A sour-tasting fluid *punishes* newborn babies' sucking response. It causes them to purse their lips and stop sucking entirely.

Many stimuli besides food can serve as reinforcers of infant behavior. For example, newborns will suck faster on a nipple that produces interesting sights and sounds, including visual designs, music, or human voices (Floccia, Christophe, & Bertoncini, 1997). Even preterm babies will seek reinforcing stimulation. In one study, they increased their contact with a soft teddy bear that "breathed" at a rate reflecting the infant's respiration, whereas they decreased their contact with a nonbreathing bear (Thoman & Ingersoll, 1993). As these findings suggest, operant conditioning is a powerful tool for finding out what stimuli babies can perceive and which ones they prefer.

As infants get older, operant conditioning expands to include a wider range of responses and stimuli. For example, researchers have hung special mobiles over the cribs of 2- to 6-month-olds. When the baby's foot is attached to the mobile with a long cord, the infant can, by kicking, make the mobile turn. Under these conditions, it takes only a few minutes for infants to start kicking vigorously (Rovee-Collier, 1999; Rovee-Collier & Barr, 2001). As you will see in Chapter 6, operant conditioning with mobiles is frequently used to study infants' memory and their ability to group similar stimuli into categories. Once babies learn the kicking response, researchers see how long and under what conditions they retain it when exposed again to the original mobile or to mobiles with varying features.

Operant conditioning also plays a vital role in the formation of social relationships. As the baby gazes into the adult's eyes, the adult looks and smiles back, and then the infant looks and smiles again. As the behavior of each partner reinforces the other, both continue their pleasurable interaction. In Chapter 7, we will see that this contingent responsiveness contributes to the development of infant–caregiver attachment.

---

conditioned stimulus (CS) In classical conditioning, a neutral stimulus that, through pairing with an unconditioned stimulus, leads to a new response.

conditioned response (CR) In classical conditioning, an originally reflexive response that is produced by a conditioned stimulus.

operant conditioning A form of learning in which a spontaneous behavior is followed by a stimulus that influences the probability that the behavior will occur again.

reinforcer In operant conditioning, a stimulus that increases the occurrence of a response.

punishment In operant conditioning, removal of a desirable stimulus or presentation of an unpleasant stimulus, which decreases the occurrence of a response.

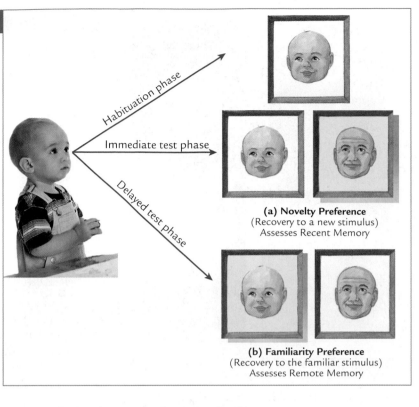

Using habituation to study infant perception and cognition. In the habituation phase, infants view a photo of a baby until their looking declines. In the next phase, infants are again shown the baby photo, but this time it appears alongside a photo of a bald-headed man. (a) When the test phase occurs soon after the habituation phase (within minutes, hours, or days, depending on the age of the infants), participants who remember the baby face and distinguish it from the man's face show a *novelty preference;* they recover to (spent more time looking at) the photo of the man—the new stimulus. (b) When the test phase is delayed for weeks or months, infants who continue to remember the baby face shift to a *familiarity preference;* they recover to the familiar baby face rather than to the novel man's face.

(a) Novelty Preference
(Recovery to a new stimulus)
Assesses Recent Memory

(b) Familiarity Preference
(Recovery to the familiar stimulus)
Assesses Remote Memory

Habituation

At birth, the human brain is set up to be attracted to novelty. Infants tend to respond more strongly to a new element that has entered their environment, an inclination that ensures that they will continually add to their knowledge base. **Habituation** refers to a gradual reduction in the strength of a response due to repetitive stimulation. Looking, heart rate, and respiration rate may all decline, indicating a loss of interest. Once this has occurred, a new stimulus—a change in the environment—causes responsiveness to return to a high level, an increase called **recovery.** For example, when you walk through a familiar space, you notice things that are new and different—a recently hung picture on the wall or a piece of furniture that has been moved. Habituation and recovery promote learning by focusing our attention on those aspects of the environment we know least about.

Researchers studying infants' understanding of the world rely on habituation and recovery more than any other learning capacity. For example, a baby who first *habituates* to a visual pattern (a photo of a baby) and then *recovers* to a new one (a photo of a bald man) appears to remember the first stimulus and perceive the second one as new and different from it. This method of studying infant perception and cognition, illustrated in Figure 5.10, can be used with newborns, including preterm infants. It has even been used to study the fetus's sensitivity to external stimuli—for example, by measuring changes in fetal heart rate when various repeated sounds are presented (Doherty & Hepper, 2000). The capacity to habituate is evident in the third trimester of pregnancy.

Recovery to a new stimulus, or novelty preference, assesses infants' *recent memory.* **TAKE A MOMENT...** Think about what happens when you return to a place you have not seen for a long time. Instead of attending to novelty, you are likely to focus on aspects that are familiar: "I recognize that—I've been here before!" Similarly, with passage of time, infants shift from a novelty preference to a familiarity preference. That is, they recover to the familiar stimulus rather than to a novel stimulus (see Figure 5.10) (Bahrick & Pickens, 1995; Courage & Howe, 1998). By focusing on that shift, researchers can also use habituation to assess *remote memory,* or memory for stimuli to which infants were exposed weeks or months earlier.

With age, babies habituate and recover to stimuli more quickly, indicating that they process information more efficiently. Habituation and recovery have been used to assess a wide range of infant perceptual and cognitive capacities—speech perception, musical and visual pattern perception, object perception, categorization, and knowledge of the social world. But despite the strengths of habituation research, its findings are not clear-cut. When looking, sucking, or

habituation A gradual reduction in the strength of a response as a result of repetitive stimulation.

recovery Following habituation, an increase in responsiveness to a new stimulus.

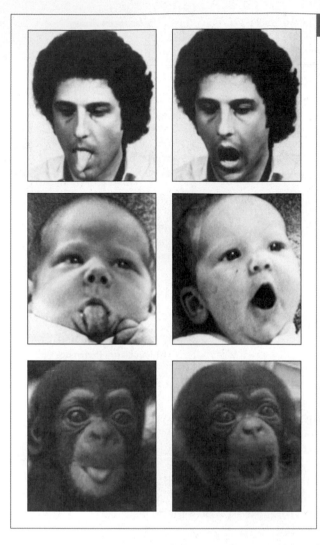

FIGURE 5.11

Imitation by human and chimpanzee newborns. The human infants in the middle row imitating (left) tongue protrusion and (right) mouth opening are 2 to 3 weeks old. The chimpanzee imitating both facial expressions is 2 weeks old. (From A. N. Meltzoff & M. K. Moore, 1977, "Imitation of Facial and Manual Gestures by Human Neonates," *Science, 198*, p. 75; and M. Myowa-Yamakoshi et al., 2004, "Imitation in Neonatal Chimpanzees [*Pan troglodytes*]." *Developmental Science, 7*, p. 440. Copyright 1977 and 1982 by the AAAS, copyright 2004 by Blackwell Publishing Ltd. Reprinted by permission.)

heart rate declines and recovers, what babies actually know about the stimuli to which they responded is sometimes uncertain. We will return to this difficulty in Chapter 6.

Imitation

Babies come into the world with a primitive ability to learn through **imitation**—by copying the behavior of another person. For example, Figure 5.11 shows a human newborn imitating two adult facial expressions (Meltzoff & Moore, 1977). The newborn's capacity to imitate extends to certain gestures, such as head movements, and has been demonstrated in many ethnic groups and cultures (Meltzoff & Kuhl, 1994). As the figure reveals, even newborn chimpanzees, our closest evolutionary ancestors, imitate some behaviors (Myowa-Yamakoshi et al., 2004).

But a few studies have failed to reproduce the human findings (see, for example, Anisfeld et al., 2001). And imitation is harder to induce in babies 2 to 3 months old than just after birth. Therefore, some researchers regard the capacity as little more than an automatic response that declines with age, much like a reflex. Others claim that newborns imitate a variety of facial expressions and head movements with effort and determination, even after short delays—when the adult is no longer demonstrating the behavior (Hayne, 2002; Meltzoff & Moore, 1999). Furthermore, these investigators argue, imitation—unlike reflexes—does not decline. Human babies several months old often do not imitate an adult's behavior right away because they first try to play familiar social games—mutual gazing, cooing, smiling, and waving their arms. But when an adult models a gesture repeatedly, older human infants soon get down to business and imitate (Meltzoff & Moore, 1994). Similarly, imitation declines in baby chimps around 9 weeks of age, when mother–baby mutual gazing and other face-to-face exchanges increase.

According to Andrew Meltzoff, newborns imitate much as older children and adults do—by actively trying to match body movements they *see* with ones they *feel* themselves make (Meltzoff & Decety, 2003). Later we will encounter evidence that young babies are surprisingly good at coordinating information across sensory systems.

Furthermore, scientists have identified specialized cells in many areas of the cerebral cortex of primates—called *mirror neurons*—that underlie these capacities (Rizzolatti & Craighero, 2004). Mirror neurons fire identically when a primate hears or sees an action and when it carries out that action on its own. Humans have especially elaborate systems of mirror neurons, which enable us to observe another person's behavior (such as smiling or throwing a ball) while simulating the behavior in our own brain. Mirror neurons are believed to be the biological basis of a variety of interrelated, complex social abilities, including imitation, empathic sharing of emotions, and understanding others' intentions (Iocaboni et al., 2005).

imitation Learning by copying the behavior of another person.

Still, Meltzoff's view of newborn imitation as a voluntary capacity is controversial. Mirror neurons probably require an extended period of development, and as we will see in Chapter 6, the capacity to imitate improves greatly over the first two years. But however limited it is at birth, imitation is a powerful means of learning (Blasi & Bjorklund, 2003). Using imitation, young infants explore their social world, getting to know people by matching their behavioral states. As babies notice similarities between their own actions and those of others, they start to learn about themselves. By tapping into infants' ability to imitate, adults can get infants to exhibit desirable behaviors. Finally, caregivers take great pleasure in a baby who imitates their facial gestures and actions, which helps get the infant's relationship with parents off to a good start.

Ask Yourself

Review   Provide an example of classical conditioning, of operant conditioning, and of habituation/recovery in young infants. Why is each type of learning useful?

Apply   Nine-month-old Byron has a toy with large, colored push buttons on it. Each time he pushes a button, he hears a nursery tune. Which learning capacity is the manufacturer of this toy taking advantage of? What can Bryon's play with the toy reveal about his perception of sound patterns?

Connect   Infants with nonorganic failure to thrive rarely smile at friendly adults but, instead, anxiously keep track of nearby people. Using the learning capacities discussed in the previous sections, explain these reactions.

Motor Development

Carolyn, Monica, and Vanessa each kept baby books, filling them with proud notations about when their children held up their heads, reached for objects, sat by themselves, and walked alone. Parents are understandably excited about these new motor skills, which allow babies to master their bodies and the environment in new ways. For example, sitting upright gives infants a brand-new perspective on the world. Reaching permits babies to find out about objects by acting on them. And when infants can move on their own, their opportunities for exploration multiply.

Babies' motor achievements have a powerful effect on their social relationships. When Caitlin crawled at 7½ months, Carolyn and David began to restrict her movements. When she walked three days after her first birthday, the first "testing of wills" occurred (Biringen et al., 1995). Despite her mother's warnings, Caitlin sometimes pulled items from shelves that were off limits. "I said, 'Don't do that!'" Carolyn would say firmly, redirecting Caitlin.

At the same time, Carolyn and David increased their expressions of affection and playful activities as Caitlin sought them out for greetings, hugs, and a gleeful game of hide-and-seek (Campos, Kermoian, & Zumbahlen, 1992). Soon after, Caitlin turned the pages of a book and pointed as she and her parents named each picture. Caitlin's delight as she worked on new motor competencies triggered pleasurable reactions in others, which encouraged her efforts further (Mayes & Zigler, 1992). Motor skills, social competencies, cognition, and language developed together and supported one another.

The Sequence of Motor Development

Gross motor development refers to control over actions that help infants get around in the environment, such as crawling, standing, and walking. *Fine motor development* has to do with smaller movements, such as reaching and grasping. Table 5.2 on page 188 shows the average

TABLE 5.2	Gross and Fine Motor Development in the First Two Years	
MOTOR SKILL	**AVERAGE AGE ACHIEVED**	**AGE RANGE IN WHICH 90 PERCENT OF INFANTS ACHIEVE THE SKILL**
When held upright, holds head erect and steady	6 weeks	3 weeks–4 months
When prone, lifts self by arms	2 months	3 weeks–4 months
Rolls from side to back	2 months	3 weeks–5 months
Grasps cube	3 months, 3 weeks	2–7 months
Rolls from back to side	4½ months	2–7 months
Sits alone	7 months	5–9 months
Crawls	7 months	5–11 months
Pulls to stand	8 months	5–12 months
Plays pat-a-cake	9 months, 3 weeks	7–15 months
Stands alone	11 months	9–16 months
Walks alone	11 months, 3 weeks	9–17 months
Builds tower of two cubes	11 months, 3 weeks	10–19 months
Scribbles vigorously	14 months	10–21 months
Walks up stairs with help	16 months	12–23 months
Jumps in place	23 months, 2 weeks	17–30 months
Walks on tiptoe	25 months	16–30 months

Sources: Bayley, 1969, 1993, 2005.

dynamic systems theory of motor development A theory that views new motor skills as reorganizations of previously mastered skills, which lead to more effective ways of exploring and controlling the environment. Each new skill is a joint product of central nervous system development, the body's movement possibilities, the child's goals, and environmental supports for the skill.

age at which infants and toddlers achieve a variety of gross and fine motor skills. It also presents the age range during which most babies accomplish each skill, indicating large individual differences in rate of motor progress. Also, a baby who is a late reacher is not necessarily going to be a late crawler or walker. We would be concerned about a child's development only if many motor skills were seriously delayed.

Look at Table 5.2 once more, and you will see both organization and direction in infants' motor achievements. The *cephalocaudal trend* is evident: Motor control of the head comes before control of the arms and trunk, which comes before control of the legs. You can also see a *proximodistal trend:* Head, trunk, and arm control precedes coordination of the hands and fingers. The similarities between physical and motor development suggest a genetic contribution to motor progress. But as we will see, some motor milestones deviate sharply from these trends.

We must be careful not to think of motor skills as unrelated accomplishments that follow a fixed maturational timetable. Rather, each skill is a product of earlier motor attainments and a contributor to new ones. And children acquire motor skills in highly individual ways. For example, before her adoption, Grace spent most of her days lying in a hammock. Because she was rarely placed on her tummy and on firm surfaces that enabled her to move on her own, she did not try to crawl. As a result, she pulled to a stand and walked before she crawled!

Many influences—both internal and external to the child—join together to support the vast transformations in motor competencies of the first two years. The *dynamic systems perspective,* a relatively recent theoretical approach introduced in Chapter 1 (see pages 27–28), helps us understand how motor development takes place.

Motor Skills as Dynamic Systems

According to **dynamic systems theory of motor development,** mastery of motor skills involves acquiring increasingly complex *systems of action.* When motor skills work as a *system,* separate abilities blend together, each cooperating with others to produce more effective ways of exploring and controlling the environment. For example, control of the head and upper chest combine into sitting with support. Kicking, rocking on all fours, and reaching combine to become crawling. Then crawling, standing, and stepping are united into walking (Thelen, 1989).

Each new skill is a joint product of the following factors: (1) central nervous system development, (2) the body's movement capacities, (3) the goals the child has in mind, and (4) environmental supports for the skill. Change in any element makes the system less stable, and the child starts to explore and select new, more effective motor patterns.

The factors that induce change vary with age. In the early weeks of life, brain and body growth are especially important as infants achieve control over the head, shoulders, and upper torso. Later, the baby's goals (getting a toy or crossing the room) and environmental supports (parental encouragement, objects in the infants' everyday setting) play a greater role. Characteristics of the broader physical world also profoundly influence motor skills. For example, if Caitlin, Grace, and Timmy were reared on the moon, with its reduced gravity, they would prefer jumping to walking or running!

When a skill is first acquired, infants must refine it. For example, in trying to crawl, Caitlin often collapsed on her tummy and moved backward. Soon she figured out how to propel herself forward by alternately pulling with her arms and pushing with her feet, "belly-crawling" in various ways for several weeks (Vereijkin & Adolph, 1999). As they attempt a new skill, most babies move back and forth between its presence and absence: An infant might roll over, sit, crawl, or take a few steps on Monday but not do so again until Friday, and then not again until the following week (Adolph & Berger, 2006). This variability is evidence of loss of stability in the system—in dynamic systems theory, a necessary transition between a less mature and a more mature stable state.

Furthermore, motor mastery involves intense practice. In learning to walk, for example, toddlers practice six or more hours a day, traveling the length of 29 football fields! Gradually their small, unsteady steps change to a longer stride, their feet move closer together, their toes point to the front, and their legs become symmetrically coordinated (Adolph, Vereijken, & Shrout, 2003). As movements are repeated thousands of times, they promote new synaptic connections in the brain that govern motor patterns.

Dynamic systems theory shows us why motor development cannot be genetically determined. Because it is motivated by exploration and the desire to master new tasks, heredity can map it out only at a general level. Rather than being *hardwired* into the nervous system, behaviors are *softly assembled,* allowing for different paths to the same motor skill (Adolph & Berger, 2006; Thelen & Smith, 2006).

Dynamic Motor Systems in Action

To find out how infants acquire motor capacities, researchers conduct microgenetic studies (see Chapter 1, page 43), following babies from their first attempts at a skill until it becomes smooth and effortless. Using this strategy, James Galloway and Esther Thelen (2004) held sounding toys alternately in front of infants' hands and feet, from the time they first showed interest until they engaged in well-coordinated reaching and grasping. As Figure 5.12 shows, the infants, violating the cephalocaudal trend, first explored the toys with their feet—as early as 8 weeks of age, at least a month before reaching with their hands!

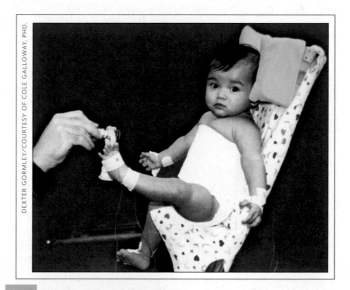

FIGURE 5.12

Reaching "feet first." When sounding toys were held in front of babies' hands and feet, they reached with their feet as early as 8 weeks of age, a month or more before they reached with their hands—a clear violation of the cephalocaudal pattern. Reduced freedom of movement in the hip joint makes leg movements easier to control than arm movements. This 2½-month-old skillfully explores an object with her foot.

This 10-month-old might be considered an early walker, but his rapid motor progress would probably be typical in a culture that deliberately encourages infant crawling, walking, and other gross motor skills.

Why did babies reach "feet first"? Because the hip joint constrains the legs to move less freely than the shoulder joint constrains the arms, infants could more easily control their leg movements. Consequently, foot reaching required far less practice than hand reaching. As these findings confirm, rather than following a strict, predetermined cephalocaudal pattern, the order in which motor skills develop depends on the anatomy of the body part being used, the surrounding environment, and the baby's efforts.

Cultural Variations in Motor Development

Cross-cultural research further illustrates how early movement opportunities and a stimulating environment contribute to motor development. Several decades ago, Wayne Dennis (1960) observed infants in Iranian orphanages who were deprived of the tantalizing surroundings that induce infants to acquire motor skills. These babies spent their days lying on their backs in cribs, without toys to play with—conditions far worse than Grace experienced lying in a hammock in her Cambodian home. As a result, most did not move on their own until after 2 years of age. When they finally did move, the constant experience of lying on their backs led them to scoot in a sitting position rather than crawl on their hands and knees. Because babies who scoot come up against objects such as furniture with their feet, not their hands, they are far less likely to pull themselves to a standing position in preparation for walking. Indeed, by 3 to 4 years of age, only 15 percent of the Iranian orphans were walking alone.

Cultural variations in infant-rearing practices also affect motor development. **TAKE A MOMENT...** Take a quick survey of several parents you know: Should sitting, crawling, and walking be deliberately encouraged? Answers vary widely from culture to culture. Japanese mothers, for example, believe such efforts are unnecessary (Seymour, 1999). And among the Zinacanteco Indians of southern Mexico, rapid motor progress is actively discouraged. Babies who walk before they know enough to keep away from cooking fires and weaving looms are viewed as dangerous to themselves and disruptive to others (Greenfield, 1992).

In contrast, among the Kipsigis of Kenya and the West Indians of Jamaica, babies hold their heads up, sit alone, and walk considerably earlier than North American infants. Kipsigi parents deliberately teach these motor skills. In the first few months, babies are seated in holes dug in the ground, with rolled blankets to keep them upright. Walking is promoted by frequently bouncing babies on their feet (Super, 1981).

Finally, because it decreases exposure to "tummy time," the current Western practice of having babies sleep on their backs to protect them from SIDS (see page 151 in Chapter 4) delays gross motor milestones of rolling, sitting, and crawling (Majnemer & Barr, 2005; Scrutton, 2005). To prevent these delays, caregivers can regularly expose babies to the tummy-lying position during waking hours.

Fine Motor Development: Reaching and Grasping

Of all motor skills, reaching may play the greatest role in infant cognitive development. By grasping things, turning them over, and seeing what happens when they are released, infants learn a great deal about the sights, sounds, and feel of objects.

Reaching and grasping, like many other motor skills, start out as gross, diffuse activity and move toward mastery of fine movements. Figure 5.13 illustrates some milestones of voluntary reaching over the first nine months. Newborns will actively work to bring their hands into their field of vision: In a dimly lit room, they keep their hand within a narrow beam of light, moving the hand when the light beam moves (van der Meer, 1997). Newborns also make poorly coordinated swipes, called **prereaching,** toward an object in front of them, but because of poor arm and hand control, they rarely contact the object. Like newborn reflexes, prereaching drops out around 7 weeks of age. Yet it suggests that babies are biologically prepared to coordinate hand with eye in the act of exploring (Rosander & von Hofsten, 2002; von Hofsten, 2004).

DEVELOPMENT OF REACHING AND GRASPING ■ At about 3 to 4 months, as infants develop the necessary eye, head, and shoulder control, reaching appears as purposeful, forward arm movements in the presence of a nearby toy and gradually improves in accuracy (Bhat, Heathcock,

prereaching The poorly coordinated, primitive reaching movements of newborn babies.

ulnar grasp The clumsy grasp of the young infant, in which the fingers close against the palm.

pincer grasp The well-coordinated grasp that emerges at the end of the first year, involving thumb and index finger opposition.

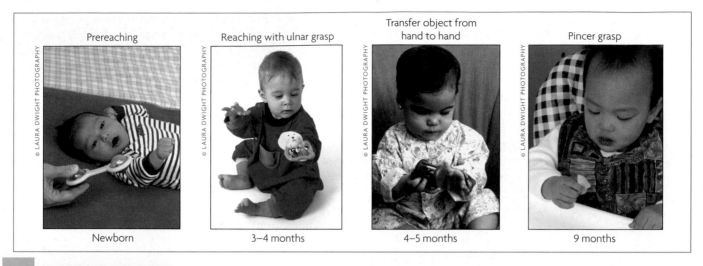

FIGURE 5.13

Some milestones of reaching. The average age at which each skill is attained is given. (Ages from Bayley, 1969; Rochat, 1989.)

& Galloway, 2005; Spencer et al., 2000). By 5 to 6 months, infants reach for an object in a room that has been darkened during the reach by switching off the lights—a skill that improves over the next few months (Clifton et al., 1994; McCarty & Ashmead, 1999). This indicates that the baby does not need to use vision to guide the arms and hands in reaching. Rather, reaching is largely controlled by *proprioception*—our sense of movement and location in space, arising from stimuli within the body. When vision is freed from the basic act of reaching, it can focus on more complex adjustments, such as fine-tuning actions to fit the distance and shape of objects.

Reaching improves as depth perception advances and as infants gain greater control of body posture and arm and hand movements. Four-month-olds aim their reaches ahead of a moving object so they can catch it (von Hofsten, 1993). Around 5 months, babies reduce their efforts when an object is moved beyond their reach (Robin, Berthier, & Clifton, 1996). By 7 months, the arms become more independent: Infants reach for an object by extending one arm rather than both (Fagard & Pezé, 1997). During the next few months, infants become better at reaching for moving objects—ones that spin, change direction, or move closer or farther away (Wentworth, Benson, & Haith, 2000).

Once infants can reach, they modify their grasp. The newborn's grasp reflex is replaced by the **ulnar grasp,** a clumsy motion in which the young infant's fingers close against the palm. Still, even 3-month-olds adjust their grasp to the size and shape of an object—a capacity that improves over the first year as infants orient the hand more precisely and do so in advance of contacting the object (Newman, Atkinson, & Braddick, 2001; Witherington, 2005). Around 4 to 5 months, when infants begin to sit up, both hands become coordinated in exploring objects. Babies of this age can hold an object in one hand while the other scans it with the tips of the fingers, and they frequently transfer objects from hand to hand (Rochat & Goubet, 1995). By the end of the first year, infants use the thumb and index finger in a well-coordinated **pincer grasp.** Then the ability to manipulate objects greatly expands. The 1-year-old can pick up raisins and blades of grass, turn knobs, and open and close small boxes.

Between 8 and 11 months, reaching and grasping are well-practiced. As a result, attention is released from the motor skill to events that occur before and after obtaining the object. For example, 10-month-olds easily modify their reach to anticipate their next action. They reach for a ball faster when they intend to throw it than when they intend to drop it carefully through a narrow tube (Claxton, Keen, & McCarty, 2003). Around this time, too, infants begin to solve simple problems that involve reaching, such as searching for and finding a hidden toy.

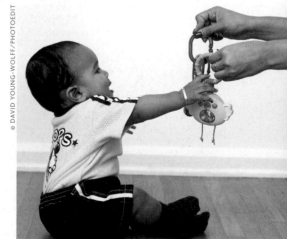

Improved posture—the capacity to sit independently—along with greater independence of the two arms enables this 7-month-old to reach for a tantalizing toy with one hand, rather than both.

EARLY EXPERIENCE AND REACHING ■ Like other motor milestones, reaching is affected by early experience. In a well-known study, institutionalized infants given a moderate amount of visual stimulation—at first, simple designs and, later, a mobile hung over their crib—reached for objects six weeks earlier than infants given nothing to look at. A third group given massive stimulation—patterned crib bumpers and mobiles at an early age—also reached sooner than unstimulated babies. But this heavy enrichment took its toll. These infants looked away and cried a great deal, and they were less advanced in reaching than the moderately stimulated group (White & Held, 1966). Recall from our discussion of brain development that more stimulation is not necessarily better. Trying to push infants beyond their readiness to handle stimulation can undermine the development of important motor skills.

Finally, as motor skills permit infants and toddlers to move about and manipulate objects, caregivers must devote more energy to protecting them from harm. See Applying What We Know below for a variety of suggestions for keeping infants and toddlers safe. In Chapter 8, we will consider the topic of unintentional injuries in greater detail.

Bowel and Bladder Control

More than any other aspect of early muscular development, parents wonder about bowel and bladder control. Two or three generations ago, many mothers tried to toilet train infants, but they only caught the baby's reflexive release of urine or a bowel movement at a convenient moment.

Toilet training is best delayed until the months following the second birthday, when children can consistently identify the signals from a full bladder or rectum and wait for the right

Applying What We Know

Keeping Infants and Toddlers Safe

STRATEGY	DESCRIPTION
Provide safe toys.	Match all toys to the child's age and abilities (see Applying What We Know, Chapter 6, page 219). Inspect all toys for small parts that can be swallowed, sharp edges that can cut, and materials that can shatter.
	Avoid cord-activated toys and toys intended to be attached to a crib or playpen; the infant's neck can become entangled in the cord or clothing can catch on a part of the toy, resulting in strangulation.
	Remove crib mobiles and crib gyms when the baby begins to push up on hands and knees; although researchers often use such toys to investigate infant capacities, the risk of becoming entangled is high.
	Do not let young children play with balloons, which can be inhaled if the child tries to blow them up.
Child-proof all rooms.	Keep toilet lids closed and buckets of water used for cleaning away from infants and toddlers; a curious toddler who tries to play in the water can fall in and drown.
	Keep all medicines, cosmetics, cleaners, paints, glues, and other toxic substances out of reach, preferably in locked cabinets; make sure that medicine bottles have child-resistant safety caps.
	Put safety plugs in all unused electrical outlets.
	Unplug all appliances or remove dials when not in use so the child cannot turn them on. Keep cords for window blinds and curtains out of reach.
	Remove unstable furniture, such as tall floor lamps and freestanding bookshelves.
	When the infant starts to crawl, install safety gates at top and bottom of stairs.
Continuously monitor the infant or toddler.	Never leave a young child alone in the bath or on a changing table, even for a moment. At mealtimes, strap the infant or toddler into a high chair, and do not leave the child unattended in situations that pose any risk of injury.
Use a car seat, following government regulations.	When driving, always strap the infant and young child into a car seat that meets government safety standards. Always have children under age 13 ride in the back seat, and never hold an infant in your arms or permit a child to ride on your lap; in an accident, your body could crush the child as you are thrown forward.
Report any unsafe toys and equipment.	Check with the U.S. Consumer Product Safety Commission, (800) 638-2772, *www.cpsc.gov*, or the Canadian Consumer Product Safety Programme, (613) 957-4467, *www.hc-sc.gc.ca/hecs-sesc/cps*, to stay informed about unsafe toys and equipment. If you discover any products that seem unsafe, report them to these agencies. Each keeps a record of complaints and initiates recalls of dangerous products.

place to open these muscles—physiological developments essential for the child to cooperate with training. A toddler who stays dry for several hours at a time, stops playing during urination or a bowel movement, and is bothered by a wet or full diaper shows signs of readiness. Children whose parents postpone intensive training until the early to middle of the third year are generally fully trained within four months. Starting before 27 months simply makes the process take longer (Blum & Nemeth, 2003; Brazelton & Sparrow, 2004).

Effective training techniques include establishing regular toileting routines (for example, after getting up, after eating, before going to bed), using gentle encouragement, and praising children for their efforts (Christophersen & Mortweet, 2003). As we will see in Chapter 7, pressuring too much in this area, as in others, can negatively affect the toddler's emotional well-being.

Ask Yourself

Review Cite evidence that motor development is not genetically determined but rather is a joint product of biological, psychological, and environmental factors.

Apply Rosanne hung mobiles and pictures above her newborn baby's crib, hoping that this would stimulate her infant's motor development. Is Rosanne doing the right thing? Why or why not?

Connect Provide several examples of how motor development influences infants' and toddlers' social experiences. How do social experiences, in turn, influence motor development?

Reflect Do you favor early, systematic training of infants in motor skills such as crawling, walking, running, hopping, and stair climbing? Why or why not?

Perceptual Development

In Chapter 4, you learned that the senses of touch, taste, smell, and hearing—but not vision— are remarkably well-developed at birth. Now let's turn to a related question: How does perception change over the first year? Our discussion will address hearing and vision, the focus of almost all research. Unfortunately, little evidence exists on how touch, taste, and smell develop after birth. Also, in Chapter 4 we used the word *sensation* to talk about these capacities. It suggests a fairly passive process—what the baby's receptors detect when exposed to stimulation. Now we use the word *perception*, which is active: When we perceive, we organize and interpret what we see.

As we review the perceptual achievements of infancy, you may find it hard to tell where perception leaves off and thinking begins. The research we are about to discuss provides an excellent bridge to the topic of Chapter 6—cognitive development during the first two years.

Hearing

On Timmy's first birthday, Vanessa bought several tapes of nursery songs, and she turned one on each afternoon at naptime. Soon Timmy let her know his favorite tune. If she put on "Twinkle, Twinkle," he stood up in his crib and whimpered until she replaced it with "Jack and Jill." Timmy's behavior illustrates the greatest change in hearing over the first year of life: Babies start to organize sounds into complex patterns.

Between 4 and 7 months, infants have a sense of musical phrasing. They prefer Mozart minuets with pauses between phrases to those with awkward breaks (Krumhansl & Jusczyk, 1990). Around 6 to 7 months, they can distinguish musical tunes on the basis of variations in rhythmic patterns, including beat structure (duple or triple) and accent structure (emphasis on the first

These 6-month-olds already have a sense of musical phrasing and can detect changes in beat and accent structures of melodies.

note of every beat unit or at other positions) (Hannon & Johnson, 2004). And by the end of the first year, infants recognize the same melody when it is played in different keys (Trehub, 2001). As we will see next, 6- to 12-month-olds make comparable discriminations in human speech: They readily detect sound regularities that will facilitate later language learning.

SPEECH PERCEPTION ■ Recall from Chapter 4 that newborns can distinguish nearly all sounds in human languages and that they prefer listening to human speech over nonspeech sounds, and to their native tongue rather than a rhythmically distinct foreign language. As infants listen to people talking, they learn to focus on meaningful sound variations. ERP brain-wave recordings reveal that around 5 months, infants become sensitive to syllable stress patterns in their own language (Weber et al., 2004). Between 6 and 8 months, they start to "screen out" sounds not used in their own language (Anderson, Morgan, & White, 2003; Polka & Werker, 1994). As the Biology and Environment box on the following page explains, this increased responsiveness to native-language sounds is part of a general "tuning" process in the second half of the first year—a possible sensitive period in which babies acquire a range of perceptual skills for picking up socially important information.

Soon after, infants focus on larger speech units that are critical to figuring out meaning. They recognize familiar words in spoken passages and listen longer to speech with clear clause and phrase boundaries (Jusczyk, 2002; Jusczyk & Hohne, 1997; Soderstrom et al., 2003). Around 7 to 9 months, infants extend this sensitivity to speech structure to individual words: They begin to divide the speech stream into wordlike units (Jusczyk, 2002; Saffran, Werker, & Werner, 2006).

ANALYZING THE SPEECH STREAM ■ How do infants make such rapid progress in perceiving the structure of speech? Research reveals that they are impressive *statistical analyzers* of sound patterns. When presented with controlled sequences of nonsense syllables, babies listened for statistical regularities, discriminating syllables that often occur together (indicating that they belong to the same word) from syllables that seldom occur together (indicating a word boundary). Consider the English word sequence *pretty#baby.* After listening to the speech stream for just 1 minute (about 60 words), babies can distinguish a word-internal syllable pair *(pretty)* from a word-external syllable pair *(ty#ba)* (Saffran, Aslin, & Newport, 1996; Saffran & Thiessen, 2003).

Once infants use these statistical learning abilities to locate words, they focus on the words and, between 7 and 9 months, detect regular syllable-stress patterns (Swingley, 2005; Thiessen & Saffran, 2003). For example, English learners often rely on the onset of a strong syllable to indicate a new word, as in "*an*imal" or "*pud*ding." By 10 months, infants can detect words that start with weak syllables, such as "sur*prise,*" by listening for sound regularities before and after the words (Jusczyk, 2001).

Infants also attend to regularities in word sequences. In a study using nonsense words, 7-month-olds distinguished the ABA structure of "ga ti ga" and "li na li" from the ABB structure of "wo fe fe" and "ta la la" (Marcus et al., 1999). They seemed to detect simple word-order rules—a capacity that may eventually help them figure out basic grammar. After extracting these rules, babies generalize them to nonspeech sounds. Seven-month-olds who were exposed to regularities in sequences of nonsense words could identify similar patterns in strings of musical tones and animal sounds. But when presented alone, these stimuli yielded no rule learning (Marcus, Fernandes, & Johnson, 2007). Analyzing speech seems to help babies structure other aspects of their auditory world.

Clearly, babies have a powerful ability to extract regularities from complex, continuous speech. As a result, they acquire a great deal of language-specific knowledge—including a stock of words and other speech structures for which they will later learn meanings—before they start to talk around 12 months of age. As we will see in Chapter 6, adults' style of communicating with infants greatly facilitates analysis of the structure of speech.

Biology and Environment

"Tuning in" to Familiar Speech, Faces, and Music: A Sensitive Period for Culture-Specific Learning

To share experiences with members of their family and community, babies must become skilled at making perceptual discriminations that are meaningful in their culture. As we have seen, at first babies are sensitive to virtually all speech sounds but, around six months, narrow their focus, limiting the distinctions they make to the language they hear and will soon learn.

The ability to perceive faces shows a similar path of development. After habituating to one member of each pair of faces in Figure 5.14, 6-month-olds were shown the familiar and novel face side by side. For both pairs, they recovered to (looked longer at) the novel face, indicating that they could discriminate the individual faces of both humans and monkeys equally well (Pascalis, de Haan, & Nelson, 2002). But at 9 months, infants no longer showed a novelty preference when viewing the monkey pair. Like adults, they could distinguish only the human faces.

This developmental trend appears again in musical rhythm perception. Western adults are accustomed to the even-beat pattern of Western music—repetition of the same rhythmic structure in every measure of a tune—and easily notice rhythmic changes that disrupt this familiar beat. But present them with music that does not follow this typical Western rhythmic form—Baltic folk tunes, for example—and they fail to pick up on rhythmic-pattern deviations (Hannon & Trehub, 2005b). Six-month-olds, however, can detect such disruptions in both Western and non-Western melodies. But by 12 months, after added exposure to Western music, babies are no longer aware of deviations in foreign musical rhythms, although their sensitivity to Western rhythmic structure remains unchanged (Hannon & Trehub, 2005b).

Several weeks of regular interaction with a foreign-language speaker and of daily opportunities to listen to non-Western music fully restore 12-month-olds' sensitivity to wide-ranging speech sounds and music rhythms (Hannon & Trehub, 2005a; Kuhl, Tsao, & Liu, 2003). Adults given similar extensive experiences, by contrast, show little improvement in perceptual sensitivity.

Taken together, these findings suggest a heightened capacity—or sensitive period—in the second half of the first year, when babies are biologically prepared to "zero in" on socially meaningful perceptual distinctions. Notice how, between 6 and 12 months, learning is especially rapid across several domains (speech, faces, and music) and is easily modified by experience. This suggests a broad neurological change—perhaps a special time of experience-expectant brain growth (see page 176) in which babies analyze everyday stimulation of all kinds similarly, in ways that prepare them to participate in their cultural community.

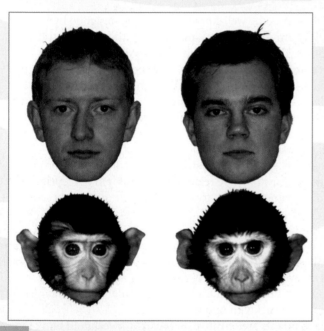

FIGURE 5.14

Discrimination of human and monkey faces. Which of these pairs is easiest for you to tell apart? After habituating to one of the photos in each pair, infants were shown the familiar and the novel face side-by-side. For both pairs, 6-month-olds recovered to (looked longer at) the novel face, indicating that they could discriminate human and monkey faces equally well. By 12 months, babies lost their ability to distinguish the monkey faces. Like adults, they showed a novelty preference only to human stimuli. (Reprinted with permission from O. Pascalis et al., "Is Face Processing Species-Specific During the First Year of Life?" *Science* 296:1321-1323 (Science 17 May 2002) Fig. 1, (c) 2007 AAAS.

Vision

For exploring the environment, humans depend on vision more than any other sense. Although at first a baby's visual world is fragmented, it undergoes extraordinary changes during the first 7 to 8 months of life.

Visual development is supported by rapid maturation of the eye and visual centers in the cerebral cortex. Recall from Chapter 4 that the newborn baby focuses and perceives color poorly. Around 2 months, infants can focus on objects about as well as adults, and their color vision is adultlike by 4 months (Kellman & Arterberry, 2006). Visual acuity (fineness of discrimination) increases steadily throughout the first year, reaching a near-adult level of about 20/20 by

© MARK RICHARDS/PHOTOEDIT

FIGURE 5.15

The visual cliff. Plexiglas covers the deep and shallow sides. By refusing to cross the deep side and showing a preference for the shallow side, this infant demonstrates the ability to perceive depth.

6 months (Slater, 2001). Scanning the environment and tracking moving objects also improve over the first half-year as infants see more clearly and better control their eye movements. In addition, as young infants build an organized perceptual world, they scan more thoroughly and systematically, strategically picking up important information (Johnson, Slemmer, & Amso, 2004; von Hofsten & Rosander, 1998). Consequently, scanning enhances perception, and—in bidirectional fashion—perception also enhances scanning.

As babies explore their visual field, they figure out the characteristics of objects and how they are arranged in space. To understand how they do so, let's examine the development of three aspects of vision: depth, pattern, and object perception.

DEPTH PERCEPTION ■ *Depth perception* is the ability to judge the distance of objects from one another and from ourselves. It is important for understanding the layout of the environment and for guiding motor activity.

Figure 5.15 shows the well-known *visual cliff,* designed by Eleanor Gibson and Richard Walk (1960) and used in the earliest studies of depth perception. It consists of a Plexiglas-covered table with a platform at the center, a "shallow" side with a checkerboard pattern just under the glass, and a "deep" side with a checkerboard several feet below the glass. The researchers found that crawling babies readily crossed the shallow side, but most reacted with fear to the deep side. They concluded that around the time infants crawl, most distinguish deep from shallow surfaces and avoid drop-offs.

The visual cliff shows that crawling and avoidance of drop-offs are linked, but not how they are related or when depth perception first appears. Recent research has looked at babies' ability to detect specific depth cues, using methods that do not require that they crawl.

Emergence of Depth Perception. How do we know when an object is near rather than far away? **TAKE A MOMENT...** Try these exercises to find out. Pick up a small object (such as your cup) and move it toward and away from your face. Did its image grow larger as it approached and smaller as it receded? Next time you take a bike or car ride, notice that nearby objects move past your field of vision more quickly than those far away.

Motion is the first depth cue to which infants are sensitive. Babies 3 to 4 weeks old blink their eyes defensively when an object moves toward their face as though it is going to hit (Nánez & Yonas, 1994). As they are carried about and people and things turn and move before their eyes, infants learn more about depth. By the time they are 3 months old, motion has helped them figure out that objects are not flat but three-dimensional (Arterberry, Craton, & Yonas, 1993).

Binocular depth cues arise because our two eyes have slightly different views of the visual field. The brain blends these two images, resulting in perception of depth. Research in which two overlapping images are projected before the baby, who wears special goggles to ensure that each eye receives only one image, reveals that sensitivity to binocular cues emerges between 2 and 3 months and improves rapidly over the first year (Birch, 1993; Brown & Miracle, 2003). Infants soon make use of binocular cues in their reaching, adjusting arm and hand movements to match the distance of objects from the eyes.

Finally, around 6 to 7 months, infants develop sensitivity to *pictorial depth cues*—the ones artists often use to make a painting look three-dimensional. Examples include lines that create the illusion of perspective, changes in texture (nearby textures are more detailed than faraway ones), overlapping objects (an object partially hidden by another object is perceived to be more distant), and shadows cast on surfaces (indicating a separation in space between the object and the surface) (Sen, Yonas, & Knill, 2001; Yonas, Elieff, & Arterberry, 2002; Yonas & Granrud, 2006).

Why does perception of depth cues emerge in the order just described? Researchers speculate that motor development is involved. For example, control of the head during the early weeks

contrast sensitivity A general principle accounting for early pattern preferences, which states that if babies can detect a difference in contrast between two or more patterns, they will prefer the one with more contrast.

of life may help babies notice motion and binocular cues. Around 5 to 6 months, the ability to turn, poke, and feel the surface of objects may promote perception of pictorial cues (Bushnell & Boudreau, 1993). And as we will see next, one aspect of motor progress—independent movement—plays a vital role in the refinement of depth perception.

Independent Movement and Depth Perception. Just before he reached the 6-month mark, Timmy started crawling. "He's fearless!" exclaimed Vanessa. "If I put him down in the middle of the bed, he crawls right over the edge. The same thing's happened by the stairs." Will Timmy become more wary of the side of the bed and the staircase as he becomes a more experienced crawler? Research suggests that he will. Infants with more crawling experience (regardless of when they started to crawl) are far more likely to refuse to cross the deep side of the visual cliff (Campos et al., 2000).

What do infants learn from crawling that promotes this sensitivity to depth information? Research suggests that from extensive everyday experience, babies gradually figure out how to use depth cues to detect the danger of falling. But because the loss of body control that leads to falling differs greatly for each body position, babies undergo new learning about depth as they master new postures. In one study, 9-month-olds, who were experienced sitters but novice crawlers, were placed on the edge of a shallow drop-off that could be widened (Adolph, 2000, 2002). While in the familiar sitting position, infants avoided leaning out for an attractive toy at distances likely to result in falling. But in the unfamiliar crawling position, they headed over the edge, even when the distance was extremely wide! And newly walking babies, while avoiding sharp drop-offs, careen down slopes and over uneven surfaces without making the necessary postural adjustments, so they fall frequently (Joh & Adolph, 2006; Witherington et al., 2005). As infants discover how to avoid falling in different postures and situations, their understanding of depth expands.

Crawling experience promotes other aspects of three-dimensional understanding. For example, seasoned crawlers are better than their inexperienced agemates at remembering object locations and finding hidden objects (Bai & Bertenthal, 1992; Campos et al., 2000). Why does crawling make such a difference? **TAKE A MOMENT...** Compare your own experience of the environment when you are driven from one place to another with what you experience when you walk or drive yourself. When you move on your own, you are much more aware of landmarks and routes of travel, and you take more careful note of what things look like from different points of view. The same is true for infants.

In fact, crawling promotes a new level of brain organization, as indicated by more organized EEG brain-wave activity in the cerebral cortex. Perhaps crawling strengthens certain neural connections, especially those involved in vision and understanding of space (Bell & Fox, 1996). As the Social Issues: Education box on page 198 reveals, the link between independent movement and spatial knowledge is also evident in a population with very different perceptual experience: infants with severe visual impairments.

PATTERN PERCEPTION ■ Even newborns prefer to look at patterned rather than plain stimuli (Fantz, 1961). As they get older, infants prefer more complex patterns. For example, 3-week-olds look longest at black-and-white checkerboards with a few large squares, whereas 8- and 14-week-olds prefer those with many squares (Brennan, Ames, & Moore, 1966).

A general principle, called **contrast sensitivity,** explains early pattern preferences (Banks & Ginsburg, 1985). *Contrast* refers to the difference in the amount of light between adjacent regions in a pattern. If babies are *sensitive to* (can detect) the contrast in two or more patterns, they prefer the one with more contrast. To understand this idea, look at the checkerboards in the top row of Figure 5.16 on page 199. To us, the one with many small squares has more contrasting elements. Now look at the bottom row, which shows how these checkerboards appear to infants in the first few weeks of life. Because of their poor vision, very young babies cannot resolve the small features in more complex patterns, so they prefer to look at the large, bold checkerboard. Around 2 months, when detection of fine-grained detail has improved, infants become sensitive to the contrast in complex patterns and spend more time looking at them (Gwiazda & Birch, 2001).

As this Sri Lankan baby becomes adept at crawling, she notices how to get from place to place, where objects are in relation to herself and to other objects, and how they appear from different viewpoints.

This 3-month-old looks at stimuli that match his level of visual development. His visual acuity has improved greatly since birth, so he can detect the contrast in complex patterns and spends more time looking at them.

Social Issues: Education

Development of Infants with Severe Visual Impairments

Research on infants who can see little or nothing at all dramatically illustrates the interdependence of vision, motor exploration, social interaction, and understanding of the world. In a longitudinal study, infants with a visual acuity of 20/800 or worse (they had only dim light perception or were blind) were followed through the preschool years. Compared to agemates with less severe visual impairments, they showed serious delays in all aspects of development. Motor and cognitive functioning suffered the most. With age, performance in both domains became increasingly distant from that of other children (Hatton et al., 1997).

What explains these profound developmental delays? Minimal or absent vision can alter the child's experiences in at least two crucial, interrelated ways.

Impact on Motor Exploration and Spatial Understanding

Infants with severe visual impairments attain gross and fine motor milestones many months later than their sighted counterparts (Levtzion-Korach et al., 2000). For example, on average, blind infants do not reach for and manipulate objects until 12 months, crawl until 13 months, or walk until 19 months (compare these averages to the norms in Table 5.2 on page 188). Why is this so?

Infants with severe visual impairments must rely on sound to identify the whereabouts of objects. But sound does not function as a precise clue to object location until much later than vision—around the middle of the first year (Litovsky & Ashmead, 1997). And because infants who cannot see have difficulty engaging their caregivers, adults may not provide them with rich, early exposure to sounding objects. As a result, the baby comes to understand relatively late that there is a world of interesting objects to explore.

Until "reaching on sound" is achieved, infants with severe visual impairments are not motivated to move independently. Because of their own uncertainty and their parents' protection and restraint to prevent injury, blind infants are typically tentative in their movements. These factors delay motor development further.

Motor and cognitive development are closely linked, especially for infants with little or no vision. These babies build an understanding of the location and arrangement of objects in space only after reaching and crawling (Bigelow, 1992). Inability to imitate the motor actions of others presents additional challenges as these children get older, contributing to declines in motor and cognitive progress relative to peers with better vision (Hatton et al., 1997).

Impact on the Caregiver–Infant Relationship

Infants who see poorly have great difficulty evoking stimulating caregiver interaction. They cannot make eye contact, imitate, or pick up nonverbal social cues. Their emotional expressions are muted; for example, their smile is fleeting and unpredictable. And because they cannot gaze in the same direction as a partner, they are greatly delayed in establishing a shared focus of attention on objects as the basis for play (Bigelow, 2003).

Consequently, these infants may receive little adult attention and other stimulation vital for all aspects of development.

When a visually impaired child does not learn how to participate in social interaction during infancy, communication is compromised in early childhood. In an observational study of blind children enrolled in preschools with sighted agemates, the blind children seldom initiated contact with peers and teachers. When they did interact, they had trouble interpreting the meaning of others' reactions and responding appropriately (Preisler, 1991, 1993).

Interventions

Parents, teachers, and caregivers can help infants with minimal vision overcome early developmental delays through stimulating, responsive interaction. Until a close emotional bond with an adult is forged, babies with visual impairments cannot establish vital links with their environments.

Techniques that help infants become aware of their physical and social surroundings include heightened sensory input through combining sound and touch (holding, touching, or bringing the baby's hands to the adult's face while talking or singing), engaging in many repetitions, and consistently reinforcing the infant's efforts to make contact. Manipulative play with objects that make sounds is also vital.

Finally, rich language stimulation can compensate for visual loss (Conti-Ramsden & Pérez-Pereira, 1999). It gives young children a ready means of finding out about objects, events, and behaviors they cannot see. Once language emerges, many children with limited or no vision show impressive rebounds. Some acquire a unique capacity for abstract thinking, and most master social and practical skills that enable them to lead productive, independent lives (Warren, 1994).

COURTESY OF RICH KENNEY, FOUNDATION FOR BLIND CHILDREN

As a result of complications from prematurity, this 2-year-old experienced nearly complete detachment of her retinas and has only minimal light perception. By guiding the child's exploration of a zither through touch and sound, a caregiver helps prevent the developmental delays often associated with severely impaired vision.

FIGURE 5.16

The way two checkerboards differing in complexity look to infants in the first few weeks of life. Because of their poor vision, very young infants cannot resolve the fine detail in the *complex checkerboard*. It appears blurred, like a gray field. The large, *bold checkerboard* appears to have more contrast, so babies prefer to look at it. (Adapted from M. S. Banks & P. Salapatek, 1983, "Infant Visual Perception," in M. M. Haith & J. J. Campos [Eds.], *Handbook of Child Psychology: Vol. 2. Infancy and Developmental Psychobiology* [4th ed.], New York: Wiley, p. 504. Copyright © 1983 by John Wiley & Sons. Reprinted by permission.)

Bold checkerboard   Complex checkerboard

Appearance of checkerboards to very young infants

Combining Pattern Elements. In the early weeks of life, infants respond to the separate parts of a pattern. They stare at single high-contrast features and have difficulty shifting their gaze away toward other interesting stimuli (Hunnius & Geuze, 2004a, 2004b). In exploring drawings of human faces, for example, 1-month-olds often limit themselves to the edges of the stimulus and focus on the hairline or chin. At 2 to 3 months, when scanning ability and contrast sensitivity improve, infants thoroughly explore a pattern's internal features, pausing briefly to look at each part (Bronson, 1994).

Once babies can take in all aspects of a pattern, they integrate the parts into a unified whole. Around 4 months, babies are so good at detecting pattern organization that they perceive subjective boundaries that are not really present. For example, they perceive a square in the center of Figure 5.17a, just as you do (Ghim, 1990). Older infants carry this responsiveness to subjective form even further. For example, 9-month-olds look much longer at an organized series of moving lights that resembles a human being walking than at an upside-down or scrambled version (Bertenthal, 1993). At 12 months, infants can detect familiar objects represented by incomplete drawings, even when as much as two-thirds of the drawing is missing (see Figure 5.17b) (Rose, Jankowski, & Senior, 1997). As these findings reveal, infants' increasing knowledge of objects and actions supports pattern perception.

Face Perception. Infants' tendency to search for structure in a patterned stimulus applies to face perception. Newborns prefer to look at photos and simplified drawings of faces with features arranged naturally (upright) rather than unnaturally (upside down or sideways) (see Figure 5.18a and b on page 200) (Cassia, Turati, & Simion, 2004; Mondloch et al., 1999). They also track a facelike pattern moving across their visual field farther than they track other stimuli (Johnson, 1999). And

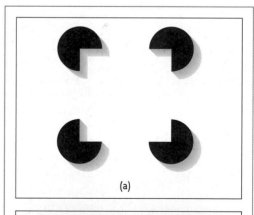

(a)

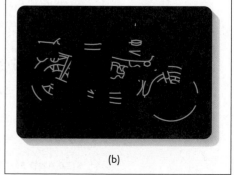

(b)

FIGURE 5.17

Subjective boundaries in visual patterns. (a) Do you perceive a square in the middle of the figure on the left? By 4 months of age, infants do, too. (b) What does the image below, missing two-thirds of its outline, look like to you? By 12 months, infants detect the image of a motorcycle. After habituating to the incomplete motorcycle image, they were shown an intact motorcycle figure paired with a novel form. Twelve-month-olds recovered to (looked longer at) the novel figure, indicating that they recognized the motorcycle pattern on the basis of very little visual information. (Adapted from Ghim, 1990; Rose, Jankowski, & Senior, 1997.)

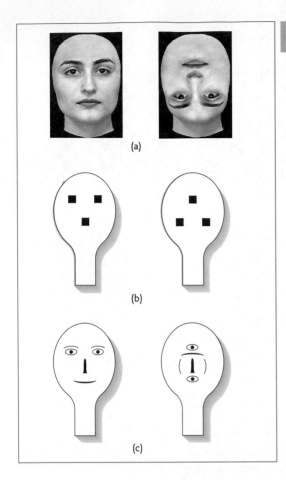

FIGURE 5.18

Early face perception. Newborns prefer to look at the photo of a face (a) and the simple pattern resembling a face (b) over the upside-down versions. (c) When the complex drawing of a face on the left and the equally complex, scrambled version on the right are moved across newborns' visual field, they follow the face longer. But if the two stimuli are stationary, infants show no preference for the face until around 2 months of age. (Cassia, Viola Macchi; Turati, Chiara; Simion, Francesca (2004). Can a nonspecific bias toward top-heavy patterns explain newborns' face preference?. Psychological Science. Blackwell Publishing 15(6), Nov 2004, 379-383.

although their ability to distinguish real faces on the basis of inner features is limited, shortly after birth babies prefer photos of faces with eyes open and a direct gaze (Farroni et al., 2002). Yet another amazing capacity is their tendency to look longer at faces judged by adults as attractive—a preference that may be the origin of the widespread social bias favoring physically attractive people (Slater et al., 2000).

Some researchers believe that these behaviors reflect a built-in capacity to orient toward members of one's own species, just as many newborn animals do (Johnson, 2001a; Slater & Quinn, 2001). Others assert that newborns simply prefer any stimulus in which the most salient elements are arranged horizontally in the upper part of a pattern—like the "eyes" in Figure 5.18b (Turati, 2004). Indeed, newborns do prefer patterns with these characteristics over other arrangements (Cassia, Turati, & Simion, 2004; Simion et al., 2001). But possibly, a bias favoring the facial pattern promotes such preferences. Still other researchers argue that newborns are exposed to faces more often than to other stimuli—early experiences that could quickly "wire" the brain to detect faces and prefer attractive ones (Nelson, 2001).

Although newborns respond to facelike structures, they cannot discriminate a complex facial pattern from other, equally complex patterns (see Figure 5.18c). Nevertheless, from repeated exposures to their mother's face, they quickly learn to prefer her face to that of an unfamiliar woman, although they are sensitive only to its broad outlines. Around 2 months, when they can combine pattern elements into an organized whole, babies prefer a complex drawing of the human face to other equally complex stimulus arrangements (Dannemiller & Stephens, 1988). They also prefer their mother's detailed facial features to those of another woman (Bartrip, Morton, & de Schonen, 2001).

Around 3 months, infants make fine distinctions among the features of different faces—for example, between photographs of two strangers, even when the faces are moderately similar. At 5 months—and strengthening over the second half-year—infants perceive emotional expressions as meaningful wholes. They treat positive faces (happy and surprised) as different from negative ones (sad and fearful) (Bornstein & Arterberry, 2003; Ludemann, 1991). Extensive face-to-face interaction with caregivers undoubtedly contributes to infants' refinement of face perception. And as babies recognize and respond to the expressive behavior of others, face perception supports their earliest social relationships.

Object Perception

Research on pattern perception involves only two-dimensional stimuli, but our environment is made up of stable, three-dimensional objects. Do young infants perceive a world of independently existing objects—knowledge essential for distinguishing among the self, other people, and things?

SIZE AND SHAPE CONSTANCY ■ As we move around the environment, the images that objects cast on our retina constantly change in size and shape. To perceive objects as stable and unchanging, we must translate these varying retinal images into a single representation.

Size constancy—perception of an object's size as the same, despite changes in the size of its retinal image—is evident in the first week of life. To test for it, researchers habituated infants to a small cube at varying distances from the eye, in an effort to desensitize them to changes in the cube's retinal image size and direct their attention to the object's actual size. When the small cube was presented together with a new, large cube—but at different distances so that they cast retinal images of the same size—all babies recovered to (looked longer at) the novel large cube, indicating that they distinguished objects on the basis actual size, not retinal image size (Slater, 2001).

Perception of an object's shape as stable, despite changes in the shape projected on the retina, is called **shape constancy**. Habituation research reveals that it, too, is present within the first week of life, long before babies can actively rotate objects with their hands and view them from different angles (Slater & Johnson, 1999).

In sum, both size and shape constancy seem to be built-in capacities that assist babies in detecting a coherent world of objects. Yet they provide only a partial picture of young infants' object perception.

PERCEPTION OF OBJECT IDENTITY ■ At first, babies rely heavily on motion and spatial arrangement to identify objects (Jusczyk et al., 1999; Spelke & Hermer, 1996). When two objects are touching and either move in unison or stand still, babies younger than 4 months cannot distinguish between them. Infants, of course, are fascinated by moving objects. As they observe objects' motions, they pick up additional information about objects' boundaries, such as shape, color, and texture.

For example, as Figure 5.19 reveals, around 2 months, babies realize that a moving rod whose center is hidden behind a box is a complete rod rather than two rod pieces. Motion, a textured background, alignment of the top and bottom of the rod, and a small box (so most of the rod is visible) are necessary for young infants to infer object unity. They cannot do so without all these cues to heighten the distinction between the objects in the display (Johnson, 2004; Johnson et al., 2002).

As infants become familiar with many types of objects, they rely more on shape, color, and texture and less on motion (Cohen & Cashon, 2001). Babies as young as 4½ months can distinguish between two touching objects on the basis of their features in very simple, easy-to-process situations. And prior exposure to one of the test objects enhances the ability of 4½-month-olds to discern the boundary between two touching objects—a finding that highlights the role of experience (Dueker, Modi, & Needham, 2003; Needham, 2001). In the second half of the first year, the capacity to distinguish objects on the basis of their features extends to more complex displays of objects.

In everyday life, objects frequently move in and out of sight, so infants must keep track of their disappearance and reappearance to perceive their identity. Habituation research, in which a ball moves back and forth behind a screen, reveals that at age 4 months, infants first perceive the ball's path as continuous (Johnson et al., 2003). Once again, experience—watching objects move in and out of view—contributes to this attainment (Johnson, Amso, & Slemmer, 2003). Between 4 and 5 months, infants can monitor increasingly intricate paths of objects. As indicated by their future-oriented eye movements (looking ahead to where they expect an object to reappear from behind a barrier), 5-month-olds even keep track of an object that travels on a curvilinear course at varying speeds (Rosander & von Hofsten, 2004).

Notice that perception of *object unity* in the rod-and-box task (Figure 5.19) is mastered before perception of an *object's continuous path of movement*—a more challenging task. We will revisit these attainments when we take up infants' understanding of object permanence—awareness that an object still exists when hidden—in Chapter 6.

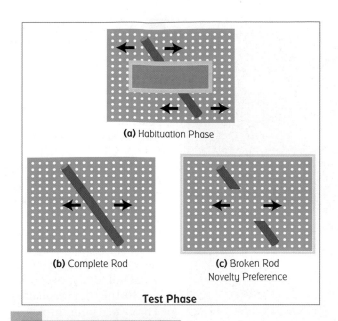

(a) Habituation Phase

(b) Complete Rod

(c) Broken Rod Novelty Preference

Test Phase

FIGURE 5.19

Testing infants' ability to perceive object unity.
(a) Infants were habituated to a rod moving back and forth behind a box against a textured background. Next, they were shown two test displays in alternation: (b) a complete rod and (c) a broken rod with a gap corresponding to the location of the box. Each stimulus was moved back and forth against the textured background, in the same way as the habituation stimulus. Infants 2 months of age and older recovered to (looked longer at) the broken rod than the complete rod. Their novelty preference suggests that they perceive the rod behind the box in the first display as a single unit.   (Adapted from Johnson, 1997.)

size constancy Perception of an object's size as the same, despite changes in the size of its retinal image.

shape constancy Perception of an object's shape as the same, despite changes in the shape projected on the retina.

Babies quickly learn associations between the sights, sounds, and feel of toys, as this 3-month-old is doing, assisted by her mother. Within the first half-year, infants master a remarkable range of intermodal relationships.

intermodal perception
Integration of simultaneous stimulation from more than one sensory system, resulting in perception of such input as an integrated whole.

amodal sensory properties
Information that overlaps two or more sensory systems, such as common rate, rhythm, and duration in visual and auditory input.

differentiation theory The view that perceptual development involves the detection of increasingly fine-grained, invariant features in the environment.

affordances The action possibilities that a situation offers an organism with certain motor capabilities.

Intermodal Perception

Our world provides rich, continuous *intermodal stimulation*—simultaneous input from more than one *modality,* or sensory system. In **intermodal perception,** we make sense of these running streams of light, sound, tactile, odor, and taste information, perceiving them as integrated wholes. We know, for example, that the shape of an object is the same whether we see it or touch it, that lip movements are closely coordinated with the sound of a voice, and that dropping a rigid object on a hard surface will cause a sharp, banging sound.

Recall that newborns turn in the general direction of a sound, and they reach for objects in a primitive way. These behaviors suggest that infants expect sight, sound, and touch to go together. Research reveals that babies perceive input from different sensory systems in a unified way by detecting **amodal sensory properties,** information that is not specific to a single modality but that overlaps two or more sensory systems. Consider the sight and sound of a bouncing ball or the face and voice of a speaking person. In each event, visual and auditory information are conveyed simultaneously and with the same rate, rhythm, duration, and intensity. Newborn babies are highly sensitive to amodal properties. After just one exposure, they learn associations between the sights and sounds of toys, such as a rhythmically jangling rattle (Morrongiello, Fenwick, & Chance, 1998).

Within the first half-year, infants master a remarkable range of intermodal relationships. Three- to 4-month-olds can match faces with voices on the basis of lip–voice synchrony, emotional expression, and even age and gender of the speaker (Bahrick, Netto, & Hernandex-Reif, 1998). Furthermore, recall that 5- to 6-month-olds will reach for an object in a room that has been darkened during their reach—a behavior that illustrates the union of sight and touch. They will also reach for a sounding object in the dark, displaying union of sound and touch (Clifton et al., 1994).

Intermodal sensitivity is crucial for perceptual development. Intermodal stimulation makes amodal properties (such as rhythm) stand out. As a result, inexperienced perceivers notice a meaningful unitary event, such as a hammer's tapping, without being distracted by momentarily irrelevant aspects of the situation, such as the hammer's color or orientation (Bahrick, Lickliter, & Flom, 2004).

In addition to easing perception of the physical world, intermodal perception facilitates processing of the social world. An adult's gentle touch induces an infant to smile and attend to her face (Stack & Muir, 1992). And as 3- to 4-month-olds gaze at an adult's face, they initially require both vocal and visual input to distinguish positive from negative emotional expressions (Walker-Andrews, 1997). Only later do infants discriminate positive from negative emotion in each sensory modality—first in voices (around 4 to 5 months), later (from 5 months on) in faces. Finally, 4- to 6-month-olds build on their extensive face–voice intermodal knowledge, picking up more detailed associations. When interacting with unfamiliar people, they quickly learn and remember their unique face–voice pairings (Bahrick, Hernandez-Reif, & Flom, 2005).

In sum, intermodal perception is a fundamental ability that fosters all aspects of psychological development. Early parent–infant interaction presents the baby with a rich context—consisting of many concurrent sights, sounds, touches, and smells—for expanding intermodal knowledge. And when provided with intermodal stimulation, babies process more information, learn faster, and show better memory (Lickliter & Bahrick, 2000). Intermodal perception is yet another capacity that illustrates infants' active efforts to build an orderly, predictable world.

Understanding Perceptual Development

Now that we have reviewed the development of infant perceptual capacities, how can we put together this diverse array of amazing achievements? Widely accepted answers come from the work of Eleanor and James Gibson. According to the Gibsons' **differentiation theory,** infants actively search for *invariant features* of the environment—those that remain stable—in a constantly changing perceptual world. In pattern perception, for example, young babies search for features that stand out and orient toward faces. Soon they explore internal features, noticing *stable relationships* among those features. As a result, they detect patterns, such as complex designs and individual faces. The development of intermodal perception also reflects this principle. Babies seek out invariant relationships—first, amodal properties, such as common rate and rhythm, in a voice and face, later more detailed associations, such as unique voice–face matches.

The Gibsons described their theory as *differentiation* (where "differentiate" means "analyze" or "break down") because over time, the baby detects finer and finer invariant features among stimuli. In addition to pattern perception and intermodal perception, differentiation applies to depth and object perception: Recall how in each, sensitivity to motion precedes detection of fine-grained features. So one way of understanding perceptual development is to think of it as a built-in tendency to search for order and consistency—a capacity that becomes increasingly fine-tuned with age (Gibson, 1970; Gibson, 1979).

Acting on the environment is vital in perceptual differentiation. According to the Gibsons, perception is guided by the discovery of **affordances**—the action possibilities that a situation offers an organism with certain motor capabilities (Gibson, 2000, 2003). By moving about and exploring the environment, babies figure out which objects can be grasped, squeezed, bounced, or stroked and whether a surface is safe to cross or presents the possibility of falling. Sensitivity to these affordances means that we spend far less time correcting ineffective actions than we would otherwise: It makes our actions future-oriented and largely successful rather than reactive and blundering.

To illustrate, recall how infants' changing capabilities for independent movement affect their perception. When babies crawl, and again when they walk, they gradually realize that a sloping surface *affords the possibility* of falling (see Figure 5.20). With added weeks of practicing each skill, they hesitate to crawl or walk down a risky incline. Experience in trying to keep their balance on various surfaces seems to make crawlers and walkers more aware of the consequences of their movements. Crawlers come to detect when surface slant places so much body weight on their arms that they will fall forward, and walkers come to sense when an incline shifts body weight so their legs and feet can no longer hold them upright (Adolph &Berger, 2006). Each skill leads infants to perceive surfaces in new ways that guide their movements. As a result, they act more competently.

As we conclude this chapter, it is only fair to note that some researchers believe that babies do more than make sense of experience by searching for invariant features and discovering affordances: They also *impose meaning on* what they perceive, constructing categories of objects and events in the surrounding environment. We have seen the glimmerings of this cognitive point of view in this chapter. For example, older babies *interpret* a familiar face as a source of pleasure and affection and a pattern of blinking lights as a moving human being. This cognitive perspective also offers insight into the achievements of infancy. In fact, many researchers combine these two positions, regarding infant development as proceeding from a perceptual to a cognitive emphasis over the first year of life.

FIGURE 5.20

Acting on the environment plays a major role in perceptual differentiation. Crawling and walking change the way babies perceive a sloping surface. The newly crawling infant on the left plunges headlong down the slope. He has not yet learned that it affords the possibility of falling. The toddler on the right, who has been walking for more than a month, approaches the slope cautiously. Experience in trying to remain upright but frequently tumbling over has made him more aware of the consequences of his movements. He perceives the incline differently than he did at a younger age.

Ask Yourself

Review Using examples, explain why intermodal stimulation is vital for infants' developing understanding of their physical and social worlds.

Apply After several weeks of crawling, Ben learned to avoid going headfirst down a steep incline. Now he has started to walk. Can his mother trust him not to try walking down a steep surface? Explain, using the concept of affordances.

Connect According to differentiation theory, perceptual development reflects infants' active search for invariant features. Provide examples from research on hearing, pattern perception, and intermodal perception.

Reflect Are young infants more competent than you thought they were before you read this chapter? List capacities that most surprised you.

Summary

Body Growth

Describe major changes in body size, proportions, muscle–fat makeup, and skeletal growth over the first two years.

- Height and weight gains are greater during the first two years than at any other time after birth. Body fat is laid down quickly during the first nine months, whereas muscle development is slow and gradual. Parts of the body grow at different rates, following the **cephalocaudal** and **proximodistal trends,** resulting in changing body proportions.

- **Skeletal age,** a measure based on the number of **epiphyses** and the extent to which they are fused, is the best way to estimate the child's overall physical maturity. At birth, the bones of an infant's skull are separated by six gaps, or **fontanels,** which permit the skull to expand as the brain grows. The first tooth emerges around age 6 months. By age 2, the average child has 20 teeth.

Brain Development

Describe brain development during infancy and toddlerhood, current methods of measuring brain functioning, and appropriate stimulation to support the brain's potential.

- Early in development, the brain grows faster than any other organ of the body. Once **neurons** are in place, they rapidly form **synapses,** or connections, and release chemicals called **neurotransmitters** that cross synapses to send messages to other neurons. During the peak period of synaptic growth in any brain area, many surrounding neurons die. Stimulation determines which neurons will survive and establish new synapses and which will lose their connective fibers through **synaptic pruning. Glial cells,** which are responsible for **myelination,** multiply dramatically from the end of pregnancy through the second year, contributing to large gains in brain weight.

- Neurophysiological methods for measuring brain functioning include those that detect changes in electrical activity in the cerebral cortex (EEG, ERPs), neuroimaging techniques (PET, fMRI), and NIROT, which uses infrared light and is suitable for infants and young children.

- The **cerebral cortex** is the largest, most complex brain structure and the last to stop growing. Its regions develop in the general order in which various capacities emerge in the growing child, with the frontal lobes having the most extended period of development. The hemispheres of the cerebral cortex specialize, a process called **lateralization.** In the first few years of life, there is high **brain plasticity,** with many areas not yet committed to specific functions.

- Both heredity and early experience contribute to brain organization. Stimulation of the brain is essential during sensitive periods—periods in which the brain is developing most rapidly. Prolonged early deprivation, as in some babies reared in orphanages, can disrupt brain growth and interfere with the brain's capacity to manage stress, with long-term physical and psychological consequences.

- Appropriate early stimulation promotes **experience-expectant brain growth,** which depends on ordinary experiences. No evidence exists for a sensitive period in the first few years for **experience-dependent brain growth**—additional growth and refinement of established brain structures as a result of specific learning experiences. In fact, environments that overwhelm children with inappropriately advanced expectations can undermine the brain's potential.

How does the organization of sleep and wakefulness change over the first two years?

- Infants' changing arousal patterns are primarily affected by brain growth. Periods of sleep and wakefulness become fewer but longer over the first two years, conforming to a night–day schedule.

- The Western practice of isolating young infants to promote sleeping through the night, which is rare elsewhere in the world, may be at odds with their neurological development. When babies sleep with their parents, they shift toward an adultlike sleep–wake schedule only at the end of the first year.

Influences on Early Physical Growth

Cite evidence indicating that heredity, nutrition, and parental affection and stimulation contribute to early physical growth.

- Twin and adoption studies reveal that heredity contributes to body size and rate of physical growth.

- Breast milk is ideally suited to infants' growth needs and offers protection against disease. In poverty-stricken areas of the world, breastfeeding prevents malnutrition and infant death. Breastfed and bottle-fed babies in industrialized nations do not differ in emotional adjustment, but some studies report a small advantage in intelligence test performance for children and adolescents who were breastfed.

- Most infants and toddlers can eat nutritious foods freely without risk of becoming overweight. However, the relationship between rapid weight gain in infancy and obesity at older ages is strengthening, perhaps because of a rise in unhealthy early feeding practices, in which babies are given high-fat foods and sugary drinks.

- **Marasmus** and **kwashiorkor** are dietary diseases caused by malnutrition that affect many children in developing countries. Affected children often suffer from disrupted body and brain growth and intellectual and emotional impairments. **Nonorganic failure to thrive** illustrates the importance of parental affection and stimulation for normal physical growth.

Learning Capacities

Describe infant learning capacities, the conditions under which they occur, and the unique value of each.

- **Classical conditioning** is based on the infant's ability to associate events that usually occur together in the everyday world. In this form of learning, a neutral stimulus is paired with an **unconditioned stimulus (UCS)** that produces a reflexive, **unconditioned response (UCR).** Once learning has occurred, the neutral stimulus, now called the **conditioned stimulus (CS),** alone elicits a similar response, called the **conditioned response (CR).** Young infants can be classically conditioned when the pairing of a CS with a UCS has survival value, as in the feeding situation. However, classical conditioning of fear is difficult before age 6 months.

- In **operant conditioning,** as infants act on their environment, their behavior is followed by **reinforcers,** which increase the occurrence of a preceding behavior. Alternatively, **punishment** involves removing a desirable stimulus or presenting an unpleasant one to decrease the occurrence of a response. In young infants, interesting sights and sounds and pleasurable caregiver interaction serve as effective reinforcers.

- **Habituation** and **recovery** reveal that at birth, babies are attracted to novelty. Novelty preference (recovery to a novel stimulus) assesses recent memory, whereas familiarity preference (recovery to the familiar stimulus) assesses remote memory.

- Newborns also have a primitive ability to imitate adults' facial expressions and gestures. **Imitation** is a powerful means of learning, which contributes to the parent–infant bond. However, whether newborn imitation is a voluntary capacity remains controversial.

Motor Development

Describe the general course of motor development during the first two years, along with factors that influence it.

■ In general, motor development follows the cephalocaudal and proximodistal trends, although some milestones deviate sharply from these patterns. According to **dynamic systems theory of motor development,** children acquire new motor skills by combining existing skills into increasingly complex systems of action. Each new skill is a joint product of central nervous system development, the body's movement possibilities, the child's goals, and environmental supports for the skill.

■ Movement opportunities and a stimulating environment profoundly affect motor development, as shown by research on infants reared in deprived institutions. Cultural values and child-rearing customs contribute to the emergence and refinement of early motor skills.

■ During the first year, infants perfect their reaching and grasping. The poorly coordinated **prereaching** of the newborn period drops out. As depth perception and control of body posture and of arm and hand movements improve, reaching becomes more flexible and accurate, and the clumsy **ulnar grasp** is transformed into a refined **pincer grasp** by the end of the first year.

■ Young children are not physically and psychologically ready for toilet training until the months following their second birthday. Effective training techniques include regular toileting routines, gentle encouragement, and praise.

Perceptual Development

What changes in hearing and in depth, pattern, object, and intermodal perception take place during infancy?

■ Over the first year, infants organize sounds into complex patterns and readily detect sound regularities that facilitate later language learning. They show a preference for listening to human speech over nonspeech, and they gradually become more responsive to the sounds of their own language and use their remarkable ability to analyze the speech stream to detect meaningful units of speech.

■ Rapid maturation of the eye and visual centers in the cerebral cortex supports the development of focusing, color discrimination, and visual acuity during the first few months. The ability to scan the environment and track moving objects also improves.

■ Research on depth perception reveals that responsiveness to motion develops first, followed by sensitivity to binocular and then to pictorial depth cues. Experience in crawling enhances depth perception and other aspects of three-dimensional understanding. However, babies must undergo new learning about depth as they master new postures.

■ **Contrast sensitivity** accounts for infants' early pattern preferences. At first, babies stare at single, high-contrast features. At 2 to 3 months, they thoroughly explore internal features of a pattern and start to detect pattern organization. Over time, they discriminate increasingly complex and meaningful patterns.

■ Newborns prefer to look at photos and simplified drawings of faces, but whether they have a built-in tendency to orient toward human faces is a matter of dispute. Newborns are sensitive to the broad outlines of their mother's face; at 2 months, they recognize and prefer her facial features. Around 3 months, they make fine distinctions between the features of different faces. From 5 months on, they perceive emotional expressions as meaningful wholes.

■ At birth, **size** and **shape constancy** help babies build a coherent world of objects. At first, infants depend on motion and spatial arrangement to identify objects. After 4 months of age, they rely increasingly on other features, such as distinct shape, color, and texture.

■ At 4 months, infants first perceive the path of a ball moving back and forth behind a screen as continuous. Between 4 and 5 months, they can monitor increasingly intricate paths of objects.

■ From the start, infants are capable of **intermodal perception,** quickly combining information across sensory modalities, often after a single exposure to a new situation. Detection of **amodal sensory properties,** such as common rate rhythm, duration, and intensity, may provide the basis for detecting many intermodal matches. Intermodal sensitivity facilitates processing of both the physical and social worlds. And when provided with intermodal stimulation, babies show faster learning.

Explain the Gibsons' differentiation theory of perceptual development.

■ According to **differentiation theory,** perceptual development is a matter of detecting increasingly fine-grained **invariant features** in a constantly changing perceptual world. Perceptual differentiation is guided by discovery of **affordances**—the action possibilities that a situation offers the individual.

Important Terms and Concepts

Chapter 6

This toddler embarks on an expedition of discovery within gloriously animated and colorful surroundings. In Chapter 6, you will see that a stimulating environment combined with the guidance of more mature members of their culture ensures that infants' and toddlers' cognition will develop at its best.

Reprinted with permission from the International Museum of Children's Art, Oslo, Norway

"I Like Flowers"
Ying Yang
7 years, China

Cognitive Development in Infancy and Toddlerhood

When Caitlin, Grace, and Timmy gathered at Ginette's child-care home, the playroom was alive with activity. The three spirited explorers, each nearly 18 months old, were bent on discovery. Grace dropped shapes through holes in a plastic box that Ginette held and adjusted so the harder ones would fall smoothly into place. Once a few shapes were inside, Grace grabbed the box and shook it, squealing with delight as the lid fell open and the shapes scattered around her. The clatter attracted Timmy, who picked up a shape, carried it to the railing at the top of the basement steps, and dropped it overboard, then followed with a teddy bear, a ball, his shoe, and a spoon. Meanwhile, Caitlin pulled open a drawer, unloaded a set of wooden bowls, stacked them in a pile, knocked it over, and then banged two bowls together. With each action, the children seemed to be asking, "How do things work? What makes interesting events happen? Which ones can I control?"

As the toddlers experimented, I could see the beginnings of spoken language—a whole new way of influencing the world. "All gone baw!" Caitlin exclaimed as Timmy tossed the bright red ball down the basement steps. "Bye-bye," Grace chimed in, waving as the ball disappeared from sight. Later in the day, Grace revealed that she could use words and gestures to pretend. "Night-night," she said, putting her head down and closing her eyes, ever so pleased that in make-believe, she could decide for herself when and where to go to bed.

Over the first two years, the small, reflexive newborn baby becomes a self-assertive, purposeful being who solves simple problems and starts to master the most amazing human ability: language. Parents often wonder, How does all this happen so quickly? This question has also captivated researchers, yielding a wealth of findings along with vigorous debate over how to explain the astonishing pace of infant and toddler cognition.

In this chapter we take up three perspectives on early cognitive development: Piaget's *cognitive-developmental theory, information processing*, and Vygotsky's *sociocultural theory*. We also consider the usefulness of tests that measure infants' and toddlers' intellectual progress. Our discussion concludes with the beginnings of language. We will see how toddlers' first words build on early cognitive achievements and how, very soon, new words and expressions greatly increase the speed and flexibility of their thinking. Throughout development, cognition and language mutually support each other.

Piaget's Cognitive-Developmental Theory

Swiss theorist Jean Piaget inspired a vision of children as busy, motivated explorers whose thinking develops as they act directly on the environment. Influenced by his background in biology, Piaget believed that the child's mind forms and modifies psychological structures so they achieve a better fit with external reality. Recall from Chapter 1 that in Piaget's theory, children move through four stages between infancy and adolescence. According to Piaget, all aspects of cognition develop in an integrated fashion, changing in a similar way at about the same time.

Piaget's first stage, the **sensorimotor stage,** spans the first two years of life. As the name of this stage implies, Piaget believed that infants and toddlers "think" with their eyes, ears, hands, and other sensorimotor equipment. They cannot yet carry out many activities inside their heads. But by the end of toddlerhood, children can solve everyday practical problems and represent their experiences in speech, gesture, and play. To appreciate Piaget's view of how these vast changes take place, let's consider some important concepts.

Piaget's Ideas about Cognitive Change

According to Piaget, specific psychological structures—organized ways of making sense of experience called **schemes**—change with age. At first, schemes are sensorimotor action patterns. For example, at 6 months, Timmy dropped objects in a fairly rigid way, simply by letting go of a rattle or teething ring and watching with interest. By 18 months, his "dropping scheme" had become deliberate and creative. In tossing objects down the basement stairs, he threw some in the air, bounced others off walls, released some gently and others forcefully. Soon, instead of just acting on objects, he will show evidence of thinking before he acts. For Piaget, this change marks the transition from sensorimotor to preoperational thought.

In Piaget's theory, two processes, *adaptation* and *organization,* account for changes in schemes.

ADAPTATION ■ TAKE A MOMENT... The next time you have a chance, notice how infants and toddlers tirelessly repeat actions that lead to interesting effects. **Adaptation** involves building schemes through direct interaction with the environment. It consists of two complementary activities: *assimilation* and *accommodation.* During **assimilation,** we use our current schemes to interpret the external world. For example, when Timmy dropped objects, he was assimilating them all into his sensorimotor "dropping scheme." In **accommodation,** we create new schemes or adjust old ones after noticing that our current ways of thinking do not fit the environment completely. When Timmy dropped objects in different ways, he modified his dropping scheme to take account of the varied properties of objects.

According to Piaget, the balance between assimilation and accommodation varies over time. When children are not changing very much, they assimilate more than they accommodate. Piaget called this a state of cognitive *equilibrium,* implying a steady, comfortable condition. During rapid cognitive change, however, children are in a state of *disequilibrium,* or cognitive discomfort. Realizing that new information does not match their current schemes, they shift away from assimilation toward accommodation. Once they have modified their schemes, they move back toward assimilation, exercising their newly changed structures until they are ready to be modified again.

Each time this back-and-forth movement between equilibrium and disequilibrium occurs, more effective schemes are produced. Because the times of greatest accommodation are the earliest ones, the sensorimotor stage is Piaget's most complex period of development.

ORGANIZATION ■ Schemes also change through **organization,** a process that takes place internally, apart from direct contact with the environment. Once children form new schemes, they rearrange them, linking them with other schemes to create a strongly interconnected cognitive system. For example, eventually Timmy will relate "dropping" to "throwing" and to his

sensorimotor stage Piaget's first stage, spanning the first two years of life, during which infants and toddlers "think" with their eyes, ears, hands, and other sensorimotor equipment.

scheme In Piaget's theory, a specific structure, or organized way of making sense of experience, that changes with age.

adaptation In Piaget's theory, the process of building schemes through direct interaction with the environment.

assimilation That part of adaptation in which the external world is interpreted in terms of current schemes.

accommodation That part of adaptation in which new schemes are created and old ones adjusted to produce a better fit with the environment.

organization In Piaget's theory, the internal rearrangement and linking together of schemes so that they form a strongly interconnected cognitive system.

circular reaction In Piaget's theory, a means of building schemes in which infants try to repeat a chance event caused by their own motor activity.

developing understanding of "nearness" and "farness." According to Piaget, schemes reach a true state of equilibrium when they become part of a broad network of structures that can be jointly applied to the surrounding world (Piaget, 1936/1952).

In the following sections, we will first describe infant development as Piaget saw it, noting research that supports his observations. Then we will consider evidence demonstrating that in some ways, babies' cognitive competence is more advanced than Piaget believed.

According to Piaget's theory, the baby's first schemes are motor action patterns. As this 8-month-old takes apart, turns, and bangs these pots and pans, he discovers that his movements have predictable effects on objects and that objects influence one another in predictable ways.

The Sensorimotor Stage

The difference between the newborn baby and the 2-year-old child is so vast that Piaget divided the sensorimotor stage into six substages (see Table 6.1 for a summary). Piaget based this sequence on observations of his own three children—a very small sample. But he watched his son and two daughters carefully and also presented them with everyday problems (such as hidden objects) that helped reveal their understanding of the world.

According to Piaget, at birth infants know so little about their world that they cannot purposefully explore it. The **circular reaction** provides a special means of adapting their first schemes. It involves stumbling onto a new experience caused by the baby's own motor activity. The reaction is "circular" because, as the infant tries to repeat the event again and again, a sensorimotor response that originally occurred by chance becomes strengthened into a new scheme. Consider Caitlin, who at age 2 months accidentally made a smacking sound after a feeding. The sound was new and intriguing, so Caitlin tried to repeat it until, after a few days, she became quite expert at smacking her lips.

At first, the circular reaction centers around the infant's own body. Later it turns outward, toward manipulation of objects. Finally, in the second year, it becomes experimental and creative, aimed at producing novel effects in the environment. Infants' difficulty inhibiting new and interesting behaviors may underlie the circular reaction. This immaturity in inhibition seems to be adaptive, helping to ensure that new skills will not be interrupted before they strengthen (Carey & Markman, 1999). Piaget considered revisions in the circular reaction so important that he named the sensorimotor substages after them (refer again to Table 6.1).

TABLE 6.1	Summary of Piaget's Sensorimotor Stage
SENSORIMOTOR SUBSTAGE	**TYPICAL ADAPTIVE BEHAVIORS**
1. Reflexive schemes (birth–1 month)	Newborn reflexes (see Chapter 4, page 147)
2. Primary circular reactions (1–4 months)	Simple motor habits centered around the infant's own body; limited anticipation of events
3. Secondary circular reactions (4–8 months)	Actions aimed at repeating interesting effects in the surrounding world; imitation of familiar behaviors
4. Coordination of secondary circular reactions (8–12 months)	Intentional, or goal-directed, behavior; ability to find a hidden object in the first location in which it is hidden (object permanence); improved anticipation of events; imitation of behaviors slightly different from those the infant usually performs
5. Tertiary circular reactions (12–18 months)	Exploration of the properties of objects by acting on them in novel ways; imitation of unfamiliar behaviors; ability to search in several locations for a hidden object (accurate A–B search)
6. Mental representation (18 months–2 years)	Internal depictions of objects and events, as indicated by sudden solutions to problems; ability to find an object that has been moved while out of sight (invisible displacement); deferred imitation; and make-believe play

This 2½-month-old sees her hands touch, open, and close. She tries to repeat these movements, in a primary circular reaction that helps her gain voluntary control over her behavior.

When this 4-month-old accidentally hits a toy hung in front of her, her action causes it to swing. Using the secondary circular reaction, she tries to recapture this interesting swinging effect. In the process, she builds a new "hitting scheme."

REPEATING CHANCE BEHAVIORS
■ Piaget saw newborn reflexes as the building blocks of sensorimotor intelligence. In Substage 1, babies suck, grasp, and look in much the same way, no matter what experiences they encounter. In one amusing example, Carolyn described how 2-week-old Caitlin lay on the bed next to her sleeping father. Suddenly, he awoke with a start. Caitlin had latched on and begun to suck on his back!

Around 1 month, as babies enter Substage 2, they start to gain voluntary control over their actions through the *primary circular reaction,* by repeating chance behaviors largely motivated by basic needs. This leads to some simple motor habits, such as sucking their fists or thumbs. Babies of this substage also begin to vary their behavior in response to environmental demands. For example, they open their mouths differently for a nipple than for a spoon. Young infants also start to anticipate events. At age 3 months, when Timmy awoke from his nap, he cried out with hunger. But as soon as Vanessa entered the room, his crying stopped. He knew that feeding time was near.

During Substage 3, from 4 to 8 months, infants sit up and become skilled at reaching for and manipulating objects. These motor achievements play a major role in turning infants' attention outward toward the environment. Using the *secondary circular reaction,* they try to repeat interesting events caused by their own actions. For example, 4-month-old Caitlin accidentally knocked a toy hung in front of her, producing a fascinating swinging motion. Over the next three days, Caitlin tried to repeat this effect and, when she succeeded, gleefully repeated her new "hitting" scheme. Improved control over their own behavior permits infants to imitate others' behavior more effectively. However, 4- to 8-month-olds cannot adapt flexibly and quickly enough to imitate novel behaviors (Kaye & Marcus, 1981). Therefore, although they enjoy watching an adult demonstrate a game of pat-a-cake, they are not yet able to participate.

intentional, or goal-directed, behavior A sequence of actions in which schemes are deliberately combined to solve a problem.

object permanence The understanding that objects continue to exist when they are out of sight.

A-not-B search error The error made by 8- to 12-month-olds who, after an object has been moved from hiding place A to hiding place B, search for it incorrectly in the first hiding place (A).

mental representation Internal depictions of information that the mind can manipulate.

INTENTIONAL BEHAVIOR ■ In Substage 4, 8- to 12-month-olds combine schemes into new, more complex action sequences. As a result, actions that lead to new schemes no longer have a random, hit-or-miss quality—*accidentally* bringing the thumb to the mouth or *happening* to hit the toy. Instead, 8- to 12-month-olds can engage in **intentional,** or **goal-directed, behavior,** coordinating schemes deliberately to solve simple problems. The clearest example is provided by Piaget's famous object-hiding task, in which he shows the baby an attractive toy and then hides it behind his hand or under a cover. Infants of this substage can find the object by coordinating two schemes—"pushing" aside the obstacle and "grasping" the toy. Piaget regarded these *means–end action sequences* as the foundation for all problem solving.

Retrieving hidden objects reveals that infants have begun to master **object permanence,** the understanding that objects continue to exist when they are out of sight. But awareness of object permanence is not yet complete. Babies still make the **A-not-B search error:** If they reach several times for an object at a first hiding place (A), then see it moved to a second (B), they still search for it in the first hiding place (A). Consequently, Piaget concluded that they do not have a clear image of the object as persisting when hidden from view.

Infants of Substage 4, who can better anticipate events, sometimes use their capacity for intentional behavior to try to change those events. At 10 months, Timmy crawled after Vanessa when she put on her coat, whimpering to keep her from leaving. Also, babies can now imitate behaviors slightly different from those they usually perform. After watching someone else, they try to stir with a spoon, push a toy car, or drop raisins into a cup. Again, they draw on intentional behavior, purposefully modifying schemes to fit an observed action (Piaget, 1945/1951).

In Substage 5, from 12 to 18 months, the *tertiary circular reaction,* in which toddlers repeat behaviors with variation, emerges. Recall how Timmy dropped objects over the basement steps, trying this action, then that, then another. Because they approach the world in this deliberately exploratory way, 12- to 18-month-olds become better problem solvers. For example, Grace figured out how to fit a shape through a hole in a container by turning and twisting it until it fell through, and she discovered how to use a stick to get toys that were out of reach. According to Piaget, this capacity to experiment leads to a more advanced understanding of object permanence. Toddlers look for a hidden toy in several locations, displaying an accurate A–B search. Their more flexible action patterns also permit them to imitate many more behaviors, such as stacking blocks, scribbling on paper, and making funny faces.

MENTAL REPRESENTATION ■ Substage 6 brings the ability to create **mental representations**—internal depictions of information that the mind can manipulate. Our most powerful mental representations are of two kinds: (1) *images,* or mental pictures of objects, people, and spaces, and (2) *concepts,* or categories in which similar objects or events are grouped together. We can use a mental image to retrace our steps when we've misplaced something or to imitate someone's behavior long after we've observed it. And by thinking in concepts and labeling them (for example, "ball" for all rounded, movable objects used in play), we become more efficient thinkers, organizing our diverse experiences into meaningful, manageable, and memorable units.

Piaget noted that 18- to 24-month-olds arrive at solutions suddenly rather than through trial-and-error behavior. In doing so, they seem to experiment with actions inside their heads—evidence that they can mentally represent experiences. For example, at 19 months, Grace—after bumping her new push toy against a wall—no longer pushed, pulled, and bumped the toy in a random fashion until it was free to move again. Rather, she paused for a moment as if to "think," then immediately turned the toy in a new direction.

Representation also enables older toddlers to solve advanced object permanence problems involving *invisible displacement*—finding a toy moved while out of sight, such as into a small box while under a cover.

The capacity to find a hidden object emerges between 8 and 12 months, marking a major advance in cognitive development. In coordinating schemes to solve a problem—finding the hidden toy under the pillow—this infant engages in a intentional, goal-directed behavior—the basis of all problem solving.

Using a tertiary circular reaction, this baby twists, turns, and pushes until a block fits through its matching hole in her shape sorter. Between 12 and 18 months, toddlers take a deliberately experimental approach to problem solving, repeating behaviors with variation.

© LAURA DWIGHT/CORBIS

The capacity for mental representation enables this toddler to engage in make-believe play at the toy stove. With the expansion of make-believe toward the end of the second year, the child increasingly relies on mental symbols.

Second, it permits **deferred imitation**—the ability to remember and copy the behavior of models who are not present. And it makes possible **make-believe play,** in which children act out everyday and imaginary activities. Grace's pretending to go to sleep, in the opening to this chapter, illustrates the very simple make-believe of toddlers. Make-believe expands greatly in early childhood, and it is so important for psychological development that we will return to it again. In sum, as the sensorimotor stage draws to a close, mental symbols have become major instruments of thinking.

Follow-Up Research on Infant Cognitive Development

Many studies suggest that infants display a wide array of understandings earlier than Piaget believed. Recall the operant conditioning research reviewed in Chapter 5, in which newborns sucked vigorously on a nipple to gain access to interesting sights and sounds. This behavior, which closely resembles Piaget's secondary circular reaction, shows that babies try to explore and control the external world long before 4 to 8 months. In fact, they do so as soon as they are born.

A major method used to find out what infants know about hidden objects and other aspects of physical reality relies on habituation/recovery, discussed in Chapter 5. In the **violation-of-expectation method,** researchers *habituate* babies to a physical event (expose them to the event until their looking declines). Then they determine whether infants *recover* to (look longer at) an *expected event* (a variation of the first event that follows physical laws) or an *unexpected event* (a variation that violates physical laws). Recovery to the unexpected event suggests that the infant is "surprised" by a deviation from physical reality and, therefore, is aware of that aspect of the physical world.

The violation-of-expectation method is controversial. Some critics believe that it indicates limited awareness of physical events, not the full-blown, conscious understanding that was Piaget's focus in requiring infants to act on their surroundings, as in searching for hidden objects (Munakata, 2001; Thelen & Smith, 1994). Others maintain that the method reveals only babies' perceptual preference for novelty, not their understanding of experience (Bremner & Mareschal, 2004; Hood, 2004; Schilling, 2000). Let's examine this debate in light of recent evidence.

OBJECT PERMANENCE ■ In a series of studies using the violation-of-expectation method, Renée Baillargeon and her collaborators claimed to have found evidence for object permanence in the first few months of life. One of Baillargeon's studies is illustrated in Figure 6.1 (Aguiar & Baillargeon, 1999, 2002; Baillargeon & DeVos, 1991). After habituating to a short and a tall carrot moving behind a screen, infants were given two test events: (1) an *expected event,* in which the short carrot moved behind a screen, could not be seen in its window, and reappeared on the other side, and (2) an *unexpected event,* in which the tall carrot moved behind a screen, could not be seen in its window (although it was taller than the window's lower edge), and reappeared. Infants as young as 2½ to 3½ months looked longer at the unexpected event, suggesting that they had some awareness that an object moved behind a screen would continue to exist.

Additional violation-of-expectation studies yielded similar results (Baillargeon, 2004; Wang, Baillargeon, & Paterson, 2005). But several researchers using similar procedures failed to confirm some of Baillargeon's findings (Bogartz, Shinskey, & Shilling, 2000; Cashon & Cohen, 2000; Cohen & Marks, 2002; Rivera, Wakeley, & Langer, 1999). Baillargeon and others answer that these opposing investigations did not include crucial controls. And they emphasize that infants look longer at a wide variety of unexpected events involving hidden objects (Newcombe, Sluzenski, & Huttenlocher, 2005; Wang, Baillargeon, & Paterson, 2005). Still, critics question what babies' looking preferences tell us about what they actually know.

deferred imitation The ability to remember and copy the behavior of models who are not present.

make-believe play A type of play in which children pretend, acting out everyday and imaginary activities.

violation-of-expectation method A method in which researchers habituate infants to a physical event and then determine whether they recover to (look longer at) an expected event (a variation of the first event that conforms to physical laws) or an unexpected event (a variation that violates physical laws). Recovery to the unexpected event suggests awareness of that aspect of physical reality.

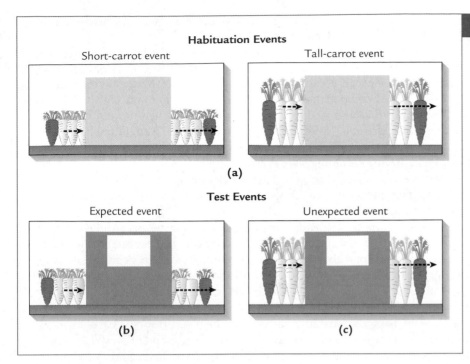

Habituation Events

Short-carrot event

Tall-carrot event

(a)

Test Events

Expected event

Unexpected event

(b)

(c)

FIGURE 6.1

Testing young infants for understanding of object permanence using the violation-of-expectation method. (a) First, infants were habituated to two events: a short carrot and a tall carrot moving behind a yellow screen, on alternate trials. Next, the researchers presented two test events. The color of the screen was changed to help infants notice its window. (b) In the *expected event*, the carrot shorter than the window's lower edge moved behind the blue screen and reappeared on the other side. (c) In the *unexpected event*, the carrot taller than the window's lower edge moved behind the screen and did not appear in the window, but then emerged intact on the other side. Infants as young as 2½ to 3½ months recovered to (looked longer at) the *unexpected event*, suggesting that they had some understanding of object permanence. (Adapted from R. Baillargeon & J. DeVos, 1991, "Object Permanence in Young Infants: Further Evidence," *Child Development, 62*, p. 1230. © The Society for Research in Child Development. Reprinted with permission.)

But recall the findings on object perception presented in Chapter 5: Four-month-olds can track an objects' path of movement as it disappears and reappears from behind a barrier, even gazing ahead to where they expect it to emerge—a behavior suggesting awareness that objects persist when out of view. In other research, investigators measured 6-month-olds' EEG brain-wave activity as they watched two events on a computer screen. In one event, a black square moved until it covered an object, then moved away to reveal the object (object permanence). In the other event, as a black square started to move behind an object, the object appeared to disintegrate (object disappearance) (Kaufman, Csibra, & Johnson, 2005). Only while watching the first event did the infants display an increase in a particular pattern of EEG activity in the right temporal lobe—the very pattern adults exhibit when told to keep in mind a mental image of an object.

If young infants do have some notion of object permanence, how do we explain Piaget's finding that even infants capable of voluntary reaching do not try to search for hidden objects before 8 months of age? Consistent with Piaget's theory, searching for hidden objects is a true cognitive advance because infants solve some object-hiding tasks before others. Ten-month-olds search for an object placed on a table and covered by a cloth before they search for an object that a hand deposits under a cloth (Moore & Meltzoff, 1999). In the second, more difficult task, infants seem to expect the object to reappear in the hand because that is where the object initially disappeared. When the hand emerges without the object, they conclude that there is no other place the object could be. Not until 14 months can most infants infer that the hand deposited the object under the cloth.

Around this time, toddlers demonstrate a thorough understanding of hidden objects. Fourteen-month-olds know that objects continue to exist in their hidden locations even after the infants have left the location. After seeing an object hidden in a cupboard, when the toddlers returned the next day, they correctly searched for the specific object in its original location. When exposed to a similar cupboard in a new room, the infants behaved just as adults do: They saw no reason to search (Moore & Meltzoff, 2004).

SEARCHING FOR OBJECTS HIDDEN IN MORE THAN ONE LOCATION ■ For some years, researchers thought that 8- to 12-month-olds made the A-not-B search error because they had trouble remembering an object's new location after it had been hidden in more than one place. But poor memory cannot fully account for infants' unsuccessful performance. For example, between 6 and 12 months, infants increasingly *look* at the correct location while *reaching* incorrectly (Ahmed & Ruffman, 1998; Hofstadter & Reznick, 1996).

Perhaps babies search at A (where they found the object on previous reaches) instead of at B (its most recent location) because they have trouble inhibiting a previously rewarded motor response (Diamond, Cruttenden, & Neiderman, 1994). In support of this view, the more prior reaches to A, the greater the likelihood that the infant will reach again toward A when the object is hidden at B. Another possibility is that after finding the object several times at A, babies do not attend closely when it is hidden at B (Ruffman & Langman, 2002). A more comprehensive explanation is that a complex, dynamic system of factors—having built a habit of reaching toward A, continuing to look at A, having the hiding place at B look similar to the one at A, and maintaining a constant body posture—increase the chances that the baby will make the A-not-B search error. Research shows that disrupting any one of these factors increases 10-month-olds' accurate searching at B (Thelen et al., 2001).

In sum, mastery of object permanence is a gradual achievement. According to one view, young babies presented with a simple object-hiding task and older babies presented with an A–B search task have a remarkable appreciation of an object's continued existence and location, but at first they have difficulty translating what they know into a successful search strategy (Baillargeon, 2000; Berthier et al., 2001). Another view is that babies' understanding becomes dramatically more complex with age: They must perceive an object's identity by integrating feature and movement information (see Chapter 5, page 201), distinguish the object from the barrier concealing it, keep track of the object's whereabouts, and use this knowledge to obtain the object (Cohen & Cashon, 2006; Meltzoff & Moore, 1998; Munakata & Stedron, 2002). Succeeding at simple object search and A–B search tasks coincides with rapid development of the frontal lobes of the cerebral cortex (Bell, 1998). Also crucial are a wide variety of experiences perceiving, acting on, and remembering objects.

MENTAL REPRESENTATION ■ In Piaget's theory, infants lead purely sensorimotor lives. They cannot represent experience until about 18 months of age. Yet 8-month-olds' ability to recall the location of hidden objects after delays of more than a minute, and 14-month-olds' ability to do so after delays of a day or more, indicate that babies do construct mental representations of objects and their whereabouts (McDonough, 1999; Moore & Meltzoff, 2004). And new studies of deferred imitation and problem solving reveal that representational thought is evident even earlier.

© SPENCER GRANT/PHOTOEDIT

Deferred imitation greatly enriches young children's adaptations to their surrounding world. This toddler has probably seen an adult bathing a younger sibling. Later, she imitates the behavior, having learned through observation what the tub is for.

Deferred Imitation. Piaget studied imitation by noting when his three children demonstrated it in their everyday behavior. Under these conditions, a great deal must be known about the infant's daily life to be sure that deferred imitation—which requires infants to represent another's past behavior—has occurred.

Laboratory research reveals that deferred imitation is present at 6 weeks of age! Infants who watched an unfamiliar adult's facial expression imitated it when exposed to the same adult the next day (Meltzoff & Moore, 1994). As motor capacities improve, infants copy actions with objects. In one study, adults showed 6-month-olds a novel series of actions with a puppet: taking its glove off, shaking the glove to ring a bell inside, and replacing the glove. When tested a day later, infants who had seen the novel actions were far more likely to imitate them. Furthermore, by merely pairing a second, motionless puppet with the first puppet during the demonstration, the researchers induced the infants to generalize the actions to a new, very different-looking puppet (Barr, Marrott, & Rovee-Collier, 2003). Between 6 and 9 months, babies increase the number of novel behaviors they imitate—copying, on average, three out of six presented by an adult (Collie & Hayne, 1999).

Gains in recall, expressed through deferred imitation, are accompanied by changes in brain-wave activity as measured by ERPs. This suggests that improvements in memory storage in the cerebral cortex contribute to these advances (Bauer et al., 2006). Between 12 and 18 months, toddlers use deferred imitation skillfully to enrich their range of schemes. They retain modeled behaviors for at

FIGURE 6.2

Analogical problem solving by 10- to 12-month-olds. After the parent demonstrated the solution to problem (a), infants solved problems (b) and (c) with increasing efficiency, even though these problems differed from problem (a) in all aspects of their superficial features. (From Z. Chen, R. P. Sanchez, & T. Campbell, 1997, "From Beyond to Within Their Grasp: The Rudiments of Analogical Problem Solving in 10- to 13-Month-Olds," *Developmental Psychology, 33,* p. 792. Copyright © 1997 by the American Psychological Association. Reprinted by permission of the publisher and author.)

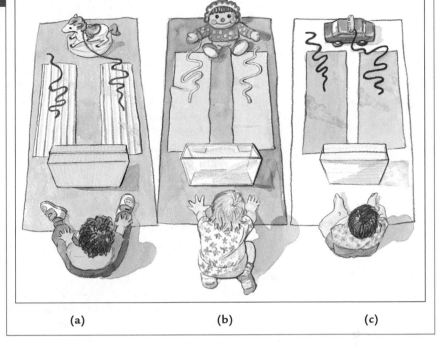

(a)   (b)   (c)

least several months, copy the actions of peers as well as adults, and imitate across a change in context—for example, enact in the home a behavior learned at child care or on TV (Barr & Hayne, 1999; Hayne, Boniface, & Barr, 2000; Klein & Meltzoff, 1999).

Toddlers even imitate rationally, by inferring others' intentions! Fourteen-month-olds are more likely to imitate purposeful than accidental behaviors (Carpenter, Akhtar, & Tomasello, 1998). And they adapt their imitative acts to a model's goals. If 14-month-olds see an adult perform an unusual action for fun (turn on a light with her head, even though her hands are free), they copy the behavior after a week's delay. But if the adult engages in the odd behavior because she *must* (her hands are otherwise occupied), toddlers imitate using a more efficient action (turning on the light with their hand) (Gergely, Bekkering, & Király, 2003). Around 18 months, toddlers can imitate actions an adult *tries* to produce, even if these are not fully realized (Meltzoff, 1995). On one occasion, Ginette attempted to pour some raisins into a small bag but missed, spilling them. A moment later, Grace began dropping the raisins into the bag. She had inferred Ginette's goal to guide her imitative actions (Falck-Ytter, Gredebäck, & von Hofsten, 2006). By age 2, children mimic entire social roles—mommy, daddy, baby—during make-believe play.

Problem Solving. As Piaget indicated, around 7 to 8 months, infants develop intentional means–end action sequences, using them to solve simple problems, such as pulling on a cloth to obtain a toy resting on its far end (Willatts, 1999). Soon after, infants' representational skills permit more effective problem solving than Piaget's theory suggests.

By 10 to 12 months, infants can *solve problems by analogy*—take a strategy from one problem and apply it to other relevant problems. In one study, babies of this age were given three similar problems, each requiring them to overcome a barrier, grasp a string, and pull it to get an attractive toy. The problems differed in all aspects of their specific features (see Figure 6.2). For the first problem, the parent demonstrated the solution and encouraged the infant to imitate. Babies obtained the toy more readily on each additional problem, suggesting that they had formed a flexible mental representation of actions that access an out-of-reach object (Chen, Sanchez, & Campbell, 1997). In another study, 12-month-olds who were repeatedly presented with a spoon in the same orientation (handle to one side) readily adapted their motor actions when the spoon was presented in the opposite orientation (handle to the other side), successfully transporting food to their mouths most of the time (McCarty & Keen, 2005). These findings suggest that at the end of the first year, infants form flexible mental representations of how to use tools to get objects.

With age, children become better at reasoning by analogy, applying relevant strategies across increasingly dissimilar situations (Goswami, 1996). But even in the first year, infants have some ability to move beyond trial-and-error experimentation, represent a solution mentally, and use it in new contexts.

Evaluation of the Sensorimotor Stage

Table 6.2 summarizes the remarkable cognitive attainments we have just considered. **TAKE A MOMENT...** Compare this table with the description of Piaget's sensorimotor substages in Table 6.1 on page 209. You will see that infants anticipate events, actively search for hidden objects, master the A–B object search, flexibly vary their sensorimotor schemes, and engage in make-believe play within Piaget's time frame. Yet other capacities—including secondary circular reactions, first signs of object permanence, deferred imitation, and problem solving by analogy—emerge earlier than Piaget expected.

Notice, also, that the cognitive attainments of infancy and toddlerhood do not develop in the neat, stepwise fashion Piaget predicted. For example, deferred imitation is present long before toddlers can solve Piaget's most advanced object-hiding task. To obtain an object that has been moved while out of sight, infants must go beyond recall of a past event to a more complex form of representation: They must *imagine an event they have not seen* (Rast & Meltzoff, 1995). Yet Piaget assumed that all representational capacities develop at the same time, at the end of the sensorimotor stage.

Disagreements between Piaget's observations and those of recent researchers raise controversial questions about how infant development takes place. Consistent with Piaget's ideas, sensorimotor action helps infants construct some forms of knowledge. For example, in Chapter 5 we saw that experience in crawling enhances depth perception and ability to find hidden objects. Yet we have also seen evidence that infants comprehend a great deal before they are capable of the motor behaviors that Piaget assumed led to those understandings. How can we account for babies' amazing cognitive accomplishments?

ALTERNATIVE EXPLANATIONS ■ Unlike Piaget, who thought young babies constructed all mental representations out of sensorimotor activity, most researchers now believe that young babies have some built-in cognitive equipment for making sense of experience. But intense disagreement exists over how much initial understanding infants have. As we have seen,

TABLE 6.2	Some Cognitive Attainments of Infancy and Toddlerhood
AGE	**COGNITIVE ATTAINMENTS**
Birth–1 month	Secondary circular reactions using limited motor skills, such as sucking a nipple to gain access to interesting sights and sounds
1–4 months	Awareness of many object properties, including object permanence, object solidity, and gravity, as suggested by violation-of-expectation findings; deferred imitation of an adult's facial expression after a short delay (1 day)
4–8 months	Improved physical knowledge and basic numerical knowledge, as suggested by violation-of-expectation findings; deferred imitation of an adult's novel actions on objects over a short delay (1 day)
8–12 months	Ability to search for a hidden object when covered by a cloth, then when a hand deposits it under a cloth; ability to solve sensorimotor problems by analogy to a previous problem
12–18 months	Ability to search in several locations for a hidden object (accurate A–B search); deferred imitation of an adult's novel actions on an object over a long delay (at least several months) and across a change in situation (from child care to home, from TV to everyday life); rational imitation, taking into account the model's intentions
18 months–2 years	Deferred imitation of actions an adult tries to produce, even if these are not fully realized, again indicating a capacity to infer others' intentions; imitation of everyday behaviors in make-believe play

TAKE A MOMENT... Which of the capacities listed in this table indicate that mental representation emerges earlier than Piaget believed?

much evidence on young infants' cognition rests on the violation-of-expectation method. Researchers who lack confidence in this method argue that babies' cognitive starting point is limited. For example, some believe that newborns begin life with a set of biases for attending to certain information and with general-purpose learning procedures—such as powerful techniques for analyzing complex perceptual information. Together, these capacities enable infants to construct a wide variety of schemes (Bahrick, Lickliter, & Flom, 2004; Huttenlocher, 2002; Kirkham, Slemmer, & Johnson, 2002; Mandler, 2004b).

Others, convinced by violation-of-expectation findings, believe that infants start out with impressive understandings. According to this **core knowledge perspective,** babies are born with a set of innate knowledge systems, or *core domains of thought.* Each of these "prewired" understandings permits a ready grasp of new, related information and therefore supports early, rapid development (Carey & Markman, 1999; Leslie, 2004; Spelke & Newport, 1998). Core knowledge theorists argue that infants could not make sense of the varied stimulation around them without having been genetically "set up" in the course of evolution to comprehend its crucial aspects.

Researchers have conducted many studies of infants' *physical knowledge,* including object permanence, object solidity (that one object cannot move through another object), and gravity (that an object will fall without support). Violation-of-expectation findings suggest that in the first few months, infants have some awareness of these basic object properties and quickly build on this knowledge (Baillargeon, 2004; Hespos & Baillargeon, 2001; Luo & Baillargeon, 2005; Spelke, 2000). Researchers have also investigated infants' *numerical knowledge,* or ability to distinguish small quantities (see the Biology and Environment box on page 218). Furthermore, core knowledge theorists assume that *linguistic knowledge* is etched into the structure of the human brain—a possibility we will consider when we take up language development. And infants' early orientation toward people, these theorists point out, initiates swift development of *psychological knowledge*—in particular, understanding of mental states, such as intentions, emotions, desires, and beliefs (see Chapter 7).

But as the Biology and Environment box reveals, studies of young infants' knowledge yield mixed results. And even when violation-of-expectation findings are consistent, critics take issue with the assumption that infants are endowed with *knowledge.* They argue that young infants' looking behaviors may indicate only a perceptual preference, not the existence of concepts and reasoning (Cohen & Cashon, 2006; Haith, 1999). Similarly, investigators of brain development add that little evidence exists for prewiring of complex cognitive functions in the brain (Johnson, 2001b; Nelson, Thomas, & de Haan, 2006). Instead, they say, the cerebral cortex is initially highly plastic and gradually specializes, largely as the result of children's experiences (see Chapter 5, pages 172–173).

Finally, although the core knowledge perspective emphasizes native endowment, it acknowledges that experience is essential for children to extend this initial knowledge. But so far, it has not offered greater clarity than Piaget's theory on how biology and environment jointly produce cognitive change. For example, it says little about which experiences are most important in each domain of thought and how those experiences advance children's thinking. Despite these limitations, the ingenious studies and provocative findings of core knowledge researchers have sharpened the field's focus on clarifying the starting point for human cognition and on carefully tracking the changes that build on it.

Did this toddler acquire the necessary physical knowledge to build a block tower through repeatedly acting on objects, as Piaget assumed? Or did he begin life with considerable innate knowledge, which enables him to understand objects and their relationships quickly, with little hands-on exploration?

PIAGET'S LEGACY ■ Follow-up research on Piaget's sensorimotor stage yields broad agreement on two issues. First, many cognitive changes of infancy are gradual and continuous rather than abrupt and stagelike, as Piaget thought (Bjorklund, 2004; Courage & Howe, 2002). Second, rather than developing together, various aspects of infant cognition change unevenly because of the challenges posed by different types of tasks and infants' varying experiences with them. These ideas serve as the basis for another major approach to cognitive development—*information processing*—which we take up next.

core knowledge perspective A perspective that states that infants are born with a set of innate knowledge systems, or core domains of thought, each of which permits a ready grasp of new, related information.

Biology and Environment

Do Infants Have Built-In Numerical Knowledge?

How does cognition develop so rapidly during the early years of life? According to the *core knowledge perspective*, infants have an inherited foundation of knowledge, which quickly becomes more elaborate as they explore, play, and interact with others. Do infants display numerical understandings so early that some knowledge must be innate? The violation-of-expectation method has been used to answer this question.

In the best known of these studies, illustrated in Figure 6.3, 5-month-olds saw a screen raised to hide a single toy animal, then watched a hand place a second toy behind the screen. Finally the screen was removed to reveal either one toy or two toys. If infants kept track of the two objects, then they should look longer at the one-toy display *(unexpected outcome)*—which is what they did. In additional experiments, 5-month-olds given this task looked longer at three objects than at two. These findings and those of similar investigations suggest that babies can discriminate quantities of single items up to three and use that knowledge to perform simple arithmetic—both addition and subtraction (in which two

objects are covered and one object is removed) (Kobayashi et al., 2004; Kobayashi, Hiraki, & Hasegawa, 2005; Wynn, Bloom, & Chiang, 2002).

Other research shows that 6-month-olds can distinguish among large sets of items, as long as the difference between those sets is very great. For example, they can tell the difference between 8 versus 16 dots, but not between 6 versus 12 (Lipton & Spelke, 2003; Xu & Spelke, 2000). As a result, some researchers believe that infants can represent approximate large-number values, in addition to the small-number discriminations evident in Figure 6.3.

But findings on infants' numerical knowledge, like other violation-of-expectation results, are controversial. Critics question what looking preferences tell us about infants' numerical knowledge. And some researchers report that 5-month-olds cannot add and subtract small quantities. In experiments similar to those just described, looking preferences were inconsistent (Langer, Gillette, & Arriaga, 2003; Wakeley, Rivera, & Langer, 2000). These investigators point out that claims for infants'

knowledge of number concepts is surprising, given other research indicating that before 14 to 16 months, toddlers have difficulty with less-than and greater-than relationships between small sets. And, as we will see in Chapter 9, not until the preschool years do children add and subtract small sets correctly.

Overall, in some studies infants display amazing knowledge, but in others they do not. And if such knowledge is innate, older children should reason in the same way as infants, yet they do not always do so. Core knowledge theorists respond that infant looking behaviors may be more reliable indicators of understanding than older children's verbal and motor behaviors, which may not tap their true competencies (Wynn, 2002). And ERP brain-wave recordings taken while babies view correct and incorrect solutions to simple arithmetic equations reveal a response pattern identical to the pattern adults show when they detect errors (Berger, Tzur, & Posner, 2006). At present, whether babies have innate numerical understandings continues to be hotly debated.

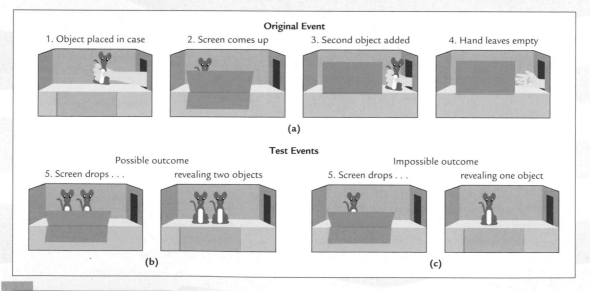

Original Event

1. Object placed in case   2. Screen comes up   3. Second object added   4. Hand leaves empty

(a)

Test Events

Possible outcome

5. Screen drops . . .   revealing two objects

(b)

Impossible outcome

5. Screen drops . . .   revealing one object

(c)

FIGURE 6.3

Testing infants for basic number concepts.   (a) First, infants saw a screen raised in front of a toy animal. Then an identical toy was added behind the screen. Next, the researchers presented two outcomes. (b) In the *expected outcome*, the screen dropped to reveal two toy animals. (c) In the *unexpected outcome*, the screen dropped to reveal one toy animal. Five-month-olds shown the unexpected outcome looked longer than did 5-month-olds shown the expected outcome. The researchers concluded that infants can discriminate the quantities "one" and "two" and use that knowledge to perform simple addition: 1 + 1 = 2. A variation of this procedure suggested that 5-month-olds could also do simple subtraction: 2 − 1 = 1. (From K. Wynn, 1992, "Addition and Subtraction by Human Infants," *Nature, 358,* p. 749. Reprinted by permission.)

Applying What We Know

Play Materials That Support Infant and Toddler Cognitive Development

FROM 2 MONTHS	FROM 6 MONTHS	FROM 1 YEAR
Crib mobile	Squeeze toys	Large dolls
Rattles and other handheld sound-making toys, such as a bell on a handle	Nesting cups	Toy dishes
	Clutch and texture balls	Toy telephone
Adult-operated music boxes, records, tapes, and CDs with gentle, regular rhythms, songs, and lullabies	Stuffed animals and soft-bodied dolls	Hammer-and-peg toy
	Filling and emptying toys	Pull and push toys
	Large and small blocks	Cars and trucks
	Pots, pans, and spoons from the kitchen	Rhythm instruments for shaking and banging, such as bells, cymbals, and drums
	Simple, floating objects for the bath	Simple puzzles
	Picture books	Sandbox, shovel, and pail
		Shallow wading pool and water toys

Note: Return to Applying What We Know in Chapter 5, page 192, to review safety concerns related to toys for infants and toddlers.
Source: Bronson, 1995.

Before we turn to this alternative point of view, let's recognize Piaget's enormous contributions. Although his account of development is no longer fully accepted, contemporary theorists are far from consensus on how to modify or replace it. And they continue to draw inspiration from Piaget's lifelong quest to understand how children acquire new cognitive capacities. Piaget's work inspired a wealth of research on infant cognition, including the studies that challenged his theory. His observations also have been of great practical value. Teachers and caregivers continue to look to the sensorimotor stage for guidelines on how to create developmentally appropriate environments for infants and toddlers. **TAKE A MOMENT...** Now that you are familiar with some milestones of the first two years, what play materials do you think would support the development of sensorimotor and early representational schemes? Prepare a list, justifying it by referring to the cognitive attainments described in the previous sections. Then compare your suggestions to the ones given in Applying What We Know above.

Ask Yourself

Review Using the text discussion on pages 209–212, construct your own table providing an overview of infant and toddler cognitive development. Which entries in your table are consistent with Piaget's sensorimotor stage? Which ones develop earlier than Piaget anticipated?

Apply Mimi's father holds up her favorite teething biscuit, deposits it under a napkin, and shows Mimi his empty hand. Ten-month-old Mimi, looking puzzled, fails to search for the biscuit. Why does Mimi find this object-hiding task difficult?

Connect Recall from Chapter 5 (page 201) that around the middle of the first year, infants become adept at identifying objects by their features (shape, color, and texture) and by their paths of movement, even when they cannot observe the entire path. How might these capacities contribute to infants' understanding of object permanence?

Reflect Which explanation of infants' cognitive competencies do you prefer, and why?

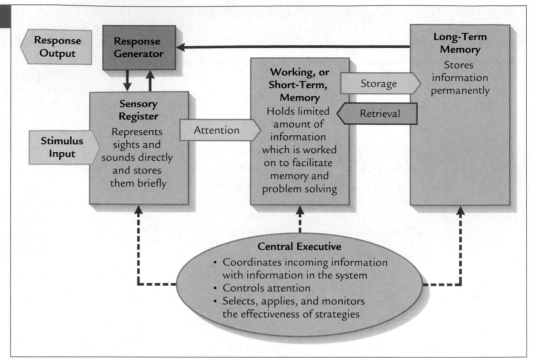

FIGURE 6.4

Model of the human information-processing system. Information flows through three parts of the mental system: the *sensory register; working,* or *short-term, memory*; and *long-term memory*. In each, mental strategies can be used to manipulate information, increasing the efficiency and flexibility of thinking and the chances that information will be retained. The *central executive* is the conscious, reflective part of working memory. It coordinates incoming information already in the system, decides what to attend to, and oversees the use of strategies.

Information Processing

Information-processing researchers agree with Piaget that children are active, inquiring beings. But instead of providing a single, unified theory of cognitive development, they focus on many aspects of thinking, from attention, memory, and categorization skills to complex problem solving.

Recall from Chapter 1 that the information-processing approach frequently relies on computerlike flowcharts to describe the human cognitive system. Information-processing researchers are not satisfied with general concepts, such as assimilation and accommodation, to describe how children think. Instead, they want to know exactly what individuals of different ages do when faced with a task or problem (Birney et al., 2005; Halford, 2002). They find the computer model of human thinking attractive because it is explicit and precise.

Structure of the Information-Processing System

Most information-processing researchers assume that we hold information in three parts of the mental system for processing: the *sensory register; working,* or *short-term, memory*; and *long-term memory* (see Figure 6.4). As information flows through each, we can use **mental strategies** to operate on and transform it, increasing the chances that we will retain information, use it efficiently, and think flexibly, adapting the information to changing circumstances. To understand this more clearly, let's look at each aspect of the mental system.

First, information enters the **sensory register,** where sights and sounds are represented directly and stored briefly. **TAKE A MOMENT...** Look around you, and then close your eyes. An image of what you saw persists for a few seconds, but then it decays, or disappears, unless you use mental strategies to preserve it. For example, by *attending to* some information more carefully than to other information, you increase the chances that it will transfer to the next step of the information-processing system.

In the second part of the mind, **working,** or **short-term, memory,** we actively apply mental strategies as we "work" on a limited amount of information. For example, if you are

mental strategies In information processing, procedures that operate on and transform information, thereby increasing the efficiency and flexibility of thinking and the chances that information will be retained.

sensory register The part of the mental system in which sights and sounds are represented directly and stored briefly before they decay or are transferred to working memory.

working, or **short-term, memory** The part of the mental system where we actively "work" on a limited amount of information, applying mental strategies to ensure that it will be retained.

studying this book effectively, you are taking notes, repeating information to yourself, or grouping pieces of information together. Why do you apply these strategies? The sensory register, though limited, can take in a wide panorama of information. The capacity of working memory is more restricted. Using strategies increases our chances of retaining information. And by meaningfully connecting pieces of information into a single representation, we reduce the number of separate pieces we must attend to, thereby making room in working memory for more. Also, the more thoroughly we learn information, the more *automatically* we use it. Automatic cognitive processing expands working memory by permitting us to focus on other information simultaneously.

To manage its complex activities, a special part of working memory—called the **central executive**—directs the flow of information. It decides what to attend to, coordinates incoming information with information already in the system, and selects, applies, and monitors strategies (Baddeley, 2000; Pressley & Hilden, 2006). The central executive is the conscious, reflective part of our mental system.

The longer we hold information in working memory, the more likely it will transfer to the third and largest storage area—**long-term memory,** our permanent knowledge base, which is unlimited. In fact, we store so much in long-term memory that we sometimes have problems with *retrieval,* or getting information back from the system. To aid retrieval, we apply strategies, just as we do in working memory. Information in long-term memory is *categorized* by its contents, much like a library shelving system that allows us to retrieve items by following the same network of associations used to store them in the first place.

Information-processing researchers believe that the basic structure of the human mental system remains similar throughout life. But the *capacity* of the system—the amount of information that can be retained and processed at once and the speed with which it can be processed—increases, making more complex forms of thinking possible with age (Case, 1998; Kail, 2003). Gains in information-processing capacity are due in part to brain development and in part to improvements in strategies—such as attending to information and categorizing it effectively—that are already developing in the first two years of life.

Attention

How does attention develop in early infancy? Recall from our discussion of perceptual development in Chapter 5 that between 1 and 2 months of age, infants shift from attending to a single high-contrast feature of their visual world to exploring objects and patterns more thoroughly. Besides attending to more aspects of the environment, infants gradually become more efficient at managing their attention, taking in information more quickly with age. Habituation research reveals that preterm and newborn babies require about 3 or 4 minutes to habituate and recover to novel visual stimuli. But by 4 or 5 months, infants require as little as 5 to 10 seconds to take in a complex visual stimulus and recognize that it differs from a previous one (Rose, Feldman, & Janowski, 2001; Slater et al., 1996).

One reason that very young babies' habituation times are so much longer is that they have difficulty disengaging their attention from interesting stimuli (Colombo, 2002). When Carolyn held up a doll dressed in red-and-white checked overalls, 2-month-old Caitlin stared intently until, unable to break her gaze, she burst into tears. The ability to shift attention from one stimulus to another is just as important as attending to a stimulus. By 4 months, infants' attention becomes more flexible—a change believed to be due to development of structures in the cerebral cortex controlling eye movements (Hood, Atkinson, & Braddick, 1998). A few babies do continue to have trouble shifting attention. These "long lookers" get stuck on certain small features of a visual pattern and, consequently, process little information (Colombo, 2002; Colombo et al., 2004). When researchers used a moving red spotlight to

As toddlers become increasingly capable of goal-directed play, sustained attention improves. Adults can promote the development of sustained attention by noting the child's current interest, encouraging it, and prompting the child to stay focused, as this father is doing.

central executive The conscious part of working memory that directs the flow of information through the mental system by deciding what to attend to, coordinating incoming information with information already in the system, and selecting, applying, and monitoring strategies.

long-term memory The part of the mental system that contains our permanent knowledge base.

induce 5-month-old long lookers to attend to all parts of a complex design, the babies started to scan it thoroughly and, as result, improved in performance on habituation tasks (Jankowski, Rose, & Feldman, 2001).

During the first year, infants attend to novel and eye-catching events. With the transition to toddlerhood, children become increasingly capable of intentional behavior (refer back to Piaget's Substage 4, on page 210–211). Consequently, attraction to novelty declines (but does not disappear) and *sustained attention* improves, especially when children play with toys. A toddler who engages in goal-directed behavior even in a limited way, such as stacking blocks or putting them in a container, must sustain attention to reach the goal. As plans and activities gradually become more complex, so does the duration of attention (Ruff & Capozzoli, 2003).

Adults can foster sustained attention by taking note of an infant or toddler's current interest, encouraging it ("Oh, you like that bell!"), and prompting the child to stay focused ("See, it makes a noise!"). Consistently helping babies focus attention at 10 months predicts higher mental test scores at 18 months (Bono & Stifter, 2003). Also, infants and toddlers gradually become more interested in what others are attending to. Later we will see that this joint attention between caregiver and child is important for language development.

Memory

Operant conditioning and habituation provide windows into early memory. Both methods show that retention of visual events increases dramatically over infancy and toddlerhood.

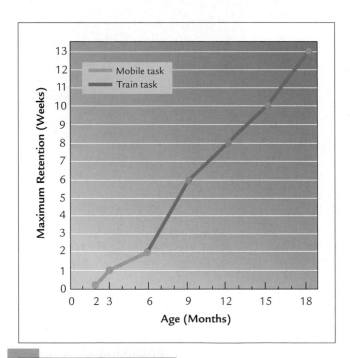

FIGURE 6.5

Increase in retention in two operant conditioning tasks from 2 to 18 months. Two- to 6-month-olds were trained to make a kicking response that turned a mobile. Six- to 18-month-olds were trained to press a lever that made a toy train move around a track. Six-month-olds learned both responses and retained them for an identical length of time, indicating that the tasks are comparable. Consequently, researchers could plot a single line tracking gains in retention of operant responses from 2 to 18 months of age. The line shows that memory improves dramatically. (From C. Rovee-Collier & R. Barr, 2001, "Infant Learning and Memory," in G. Bremner & A. Fogel, eds., *Blackwell Handbook of Infant Development*, Oxford, U.K.: Blackwell, p. 150. Reprinted by permission.)

OPERANT CONDITIONING RESEARCH ■ Using operant conditioning, researchers study infant memory by teaching 2- to 6-month-olds to move a mobile by kicking a foot tied to it with a long cord. Two- to 3-month-olds still remember how to activate the mobile one week after training. By 6 months, memory increases to two weeks (Rovee-Collier, 1999; Rovee-Collier & Bhatt, 1993). Around the middle of the first year, babies can manipulate switches or buttons to control stimulation. When 6- to 18-month-olds pressed a lever to make a toy train move around a track, duration of memory continued to increase with age; 13 weeks after training, 18-month-olds still remembered how to press the lever (Hartshorn et al., 1998b). Figure 6.5 shows this dramatic rise in retention of operant responses over the first year and a half.

Even after 2- to 6-month-olds forget an operant response, they need only a brief prompt—an adult who shakes the mobile—to reinstate the memory (Hildreth & Rovee-Collier, 2002). And when 6-month-olds are given a chance to reactivate the response themselves for just a couple of minutes—jiggling the mobile by kicking or moving the train by lever-pressing—their memory not only returns but also extends dramatically, to about 17 weeks (Hildreth, Sweeney, & Rovee-Collier, 2003). Perhaps permitting the baby to produce the previously learned behavior strengthens memory because it reexposes the child to more aspects of the original learning situation.

At first, infants' memory for operant responses is highly *context-dependent*. If 2- to 6-month-olds are not tested in the same situation in which they were trained—with the same mobile and crib bumper and in the same room—they remember poorly (Boller, Grabelle, & Rovee-Collier, 1995; Hayne & Rovee-Collier, 1995). After 9 months, the importance of context declines. Older infants and toddlers remember how to make the toy train move even when its features are altered and testing takes place in a different room (Hartshorn et al., 1998a; Hayne, Boniface, & Barr, 2000). As babies move on their own and experience frequent changes in context, their memory becomes increasingly *context-free.* They can apply learned responses more flexibly, generalizing them to relevant new situations.

HABITUATION/RECOVERY RESEARCH ■ Habituation/recovery studies show that infants learn and retain a wide variety of information just by watching objects and events, without being physically active. Sometimes, they do so for much longer time spans than in operant conditioning studies. Babies are especially attentive to the movements of objects and people. In one investigation, 5½-month-olds remembered a woman's captivating action (such as blowing bubbles or brushing hair) seven weeks later, as indicated by a *familiarity preference* (see page 185 in Chapter 5) (Bahrick, Gogate, & Ruiz, 2002). In fact, the babies were so attentive to the woman's action that they did not remember her face, even when tested one minute later for a *novelty preference.*

In Chapter 4, we saw that 3- to 5-month-olds are excellent at discriminating faces. But their memory for the faces of unfamiliar people and for other visual patterns is short-lived—at 3 months, only about 24 hours; at the end of the first year, several days to a few weeks (Fagan, 1973; Pascalis, de Haan, & Nelson, 1998). By contrast, 3-month-olds' memory for the unusual movements of objects (such as a metal nut swinging on the end of a string) persists for at least three months (Bahrick, Hernandez-Reif, & Pickens, 1997).

Habituation research confirms that infants need not be physically active to acquire new information. Nevertheless, as illustrated by research presented in Chapter 5 on the facilitating role of crawling in finding hidden objects (see page 197), motor activity does promote certain aspects of learning and memory.

RECALL MEMORY ■ So far, we have discussed only **recognition**—noticing when a stimulus is identical or similar to one previously experienced. It is the simplest form of memory because all that babies have to do is indicate (by looking, kicking, or pressing a lever) whether a new experience is identical or similar to a previous one. **Recall** is more challenging because it involves remembering something without perceptual support. To recall, you must generate a mental image of the past experience. Can infants engage in recall? By the end of the first year, they can, as indicated by their ability to find hidden objects and to imitate the actions of others hours or days after observing the behavior. And like operant responses, babies' imitative behaviors are at first context-dependent, with deferred imitation becoming increasingly flexible and generalizing to new contexts around 9 months (Learmonth, Lamberth, & Rovee-Collier, 2004).

Between 1 and 2 years of age, children's recall of people, places, objects, and actions is excellent. In several studies, 1-year-olds who briefly observed an adult's actions on a novel toy imitated those behaviors one month later. Among 2-year-olds, retention persisted for at least three months (Herbert & Hayne, 2000; Klein & Meltzoff, 1999). Other evidence suggests that toddlers' recall endures even longer—three months for short sequences of adult-modeled actions at 1 year and up to 12 months for sequences observed at 1½ years. Furthermore, the ability to recall an adult's actions on toys in the order in which those actions occurred improves greatly during the second year (Bauer, 2002b; Bauer, 2006). And when toddlers imitate in correct sequence, they remember more (Knopf, Kraus, & Kressley-Mba, 2006). This indicates that they process not just separate actions but relations between actions, using that information to increase their memory.

Long-term recall depends on connections among multiple regions of the cerebral cortex, especially with the frontal lobes. During the second year, these neural circuits develop rapidly (Bauer et al., 2006; Nelson, Thomas, & de Haan, 2006).Yet a puzzling finding is that older children and adults no longer recall their earliest experiences! See the Biology and Environment box on pages 224–225 for a discussion of *infantile amnesia.*

Memory for operant responses improves dramatically over the first 18 months. Here, a 10-month-old baby has learned to press a lever to make a toy train move around a track—a response he is likely to remember when reexposed to the task after an interval as long as six weeks (see Figure 6.5).

recognition The simplest form of memory, which involves noticing whether a new experience is identical or similar to a previous one.

recall The type of memory that involves remembering something without perceptual support.

Biology and Environment

Infantile Amnesia

If toddlers remember many aspects of their everyday lives, how do we explain **infantile amnesia**—that most of us cannot retrieve events that happened to us before age 3? The reason we forget cannot be merely the passage of time, because we can recall many personally meaningful one-time events from both the recent and the distant past: the day a sibling was born, a birthday party, or a move to a new house—recollections known as **autobiographical memory.**

Several complementary explanations of infantile amnesia exist. In one theory, vital changes in the frontal lobes of the cerebral cortex may pave the way for an *explicit* memory system—one in which children remember deliberately rather than *implicitly,* without conscious awareness (Boyer & Diamond, 1992; Rovee-Collier & Barr, 2001). A related conjecture is that older children and adults often use verbal means for storing information, whereas infants' and toddlers' memory processing is largely nonverbal—an incompatibility that may prevent long-term retention of their experiences.

To test this idea, researchers sent two adults to the homes of 2- to 4-year-olds with a highly

unusual toy that the children were likely to remember: The Magic Shrinking Machine, depicted in Figure 6.6. One of the adults showed the child how, after inserting an object in an opening on top of the machine and turning a crank that activated flashing lights and musical sounds, the child could retrieve a smaller, identical object from behind a door on the front of the machine. (The second adult discretely dropped the smaller object down a chute leading to the door.) The child was encouraged to participate as the machine "shrunk" additional objects.

A day later, the researchers tested the children to see how well they recalled the event. Results revealed that their nonverbal memory—based on acting out the "shrinking" event and recognizing the "shrunken" objects in photos—was excellent. But even when they had the vocabulary, children younger than age 3 had trouble describing features of the "shrinking" experience. Verbal recall increased sharply between ages 3 and 4—the period during which children "scramble over the amnesia barrier" (Simcock & Hayne, 2003, p. 813). In a second study, preschoolers could not translate their

nonverbal memory for the game into language six months to one year later, when their language had improved dramatically. Their verbal reports were "frozen in time," reflecting their limited language skill at the time they played the game (Simcock & Hayne, 2002).

These findings help us reconcile infants' and toddlers' remarkable memory skills with infantile amnesia. In the first few years, children rely heavily on nonverbal memory techniques, such as visual images and motor actions. As language develops, children first use words to talk about the here and now. Only after age 3 do they often represent events verbally and discuss them in elaborate conversations with adults. As children encode autobiographical events in verbal form, they increase the later accessibility of those memories because they can use language-based cues to retrieve them (Hayne, 2004).

Other findings suggest that the advent of a clear self-image contributes to the end of infantile amnesia. In longitudinal research, toddlers who were advanced in development of a sense of self demonstrated better verbal memories a year later while conversing about past experiences

---

Categorization

Even young infants can categorize, grouping similar objects and events into a single representation. Categorization helps infants make sense of experience—reduce the enormous amount of new information they encounter every day so they can learn and remember (Cohen, 2003; Oakes & Madole, 2003).

Some creative variations of operant conditioning research with mobiles have been used to find out about infant categorization. One such study is described and illustrated in Figure 6.7. Similar investigations reveal that in the first few months, babies categorize stimuli on the basis of shape, size, and other physical properties (Wasserman & Rovee-Collier, 2001). And by 6 months of age, they can categorize on the basis of two correlated features—for example, the shape and color of the alphabet letter (Bhatt et al., 2004). This ability to categorize using clusters of features prepares babies for acquiring many complex everyday categories.

Habituation/recovery has also been used to study infant categorization. Researchers show babies a series of stimuli belonging to one category and then see whether they recover to (look longer at) a picture that is not a member of the category. Findings reveal that 6- to 12-month-olds structure objects into an impressive array of meaningful categories—food items, furniture, birds, animals, plants, vehicles, kitchen utensils, and spatial location ("above" and "below," "on" and "in") (Casasola, Cohen, & Chiarello, 2003; Mandler & McDonough, 1998; Oakes, Coppage, & Dingel, 1997). Besides organizing the physical world, infants of this age categorize their emotional and social worlds. They sort people and their voices by gender and age (Bahrick, Netto, &

infantile amnesia The inability of most people to recall events that happened to them before age 3.

autobiographical memory Representations of special, one-time events that are long-lasting because they are imbued with personal meaning.

with their mothers (Harley & Reese, 1999). Very likely, both biology and social experience contribute to the decline of infantile amnesia. Brain development and adult–child interaction may jointly foster self-awareness and language, which enable children to talk with adults about significant past experiences (Nelson & Fivush, 2004). As a result, preschoolers begin to construct a long-lasting autobiographical narrative of their lives and enter into the history of their family and community. In Chapters 8 and 12, we will see that deliberate, verbal recall improves greatly during childhood. It undoubtedly supports the success of conversations about the past in structuring children's autobiographical memories.

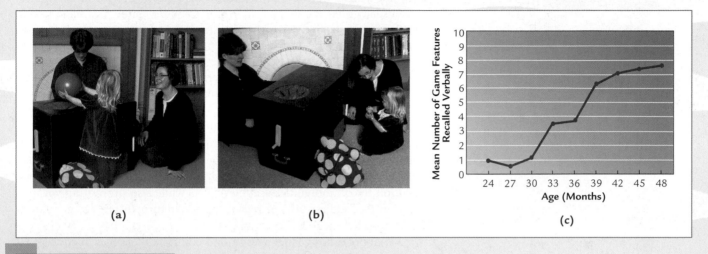

(a)   (b)   (c)

FIGURE 6.6

The Magic Shrinking Machine, used to test young children's verbal and nonverbal memory of an unusual event. After being shown how the machine worked, the child participated in selecting objects from a polka-dot bag, dropping them into the top of the machine (a), and turning a crank, which produced a "shrunken" object (b). When tested the next day, 2- and 4-year-olds' nonverbal memory for the event was excellent. But below 36 months, verbal recall was poor, based on the number of features recalled about the game during an open-ended interview (c). Recall improved between 36 and 48 months, the period during which infantile amnesia subsides. (From G. Simcock & H. Hayne, 2003, "Age-Related Changes in Verbal and Nonverbal Memory During Early Childhood," *Developmental Psychology, 39,* pp. 806, 808. Copyright © by the American Psychological Association. Reprinted by permission.) *Photos:* Ross Coombes/Courtesy of Harlene Hayne.

Hernandez-Reif, 1998; Poulin-DuBois et al., 1994), have begun to distinguish emotional expressions, and can separate people's natural movements from other motions (see Chapter 5, pages 199–200).

Babies' earliest categories are *perceptual*—based on similar overall appearance or prominent object parts—legs for animals, wheels for vehicles. But by the second half of the first year, more categories are *conceptual*—based on common function and behavior (Cohen, 2003; Mandler, 2004). Older infants can even make categorical distinctions when the perceptual contrast between two categories—animals and vehicles—is minimal (for an illustration, see Figure 6.8 on page 226).

In the second year, toddlers become active categorizers. Around 12 months, they touch objects that go together but do not group them. At 16 months, they can group objects into a single category. For example,

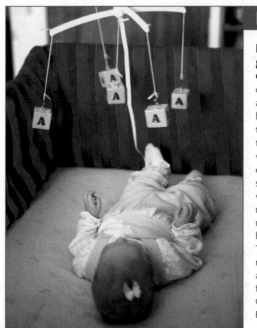

FIGURE 6.7

Investigating infant categorization using operant conditioning. Three-month-olds were taught to kick to move a mobile that was made of small blocks, all with the letter *A* on them. After a delay, kicking returned to a high level only if the babies were shown a mobile whose elements were labeled with the same form (the letter *A*). If the form was changed (from *A*s to *2*s), infants no longer kicked vigorously. While making the mobile move, the babies had grouped together its features. They associated the kicking response with the category *A* and, at later testing, distinguished it from the category *2* (Bhatt, Rovee-Collier, & Weiner, 1994; Hayne, Rovee-Collier, & Perris, 1987).

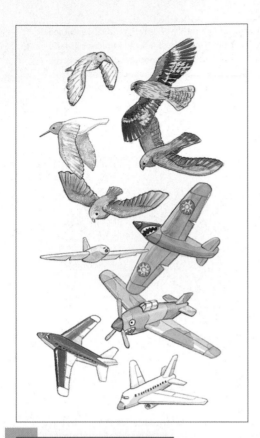

FIGURE 6.8

Categorical distinction made by 9- to 11-month-olds. After infants were given an opportunity to examine (by looking or touching) the objects in one category, they were shown a new object from each of the categories. They recovered to (spent more time looking at or touching) the object from the contrasting category, indicating that they distinguished the birds from the airplanes, despite their perceptual similarity. (Adapted from Mandler & McDonough, 1993.)

when given four balls and four boxes, they put all the balls together but not the boxes. Around 18 months, they sort objects into two classes (Gopnik & Meltzoff, 1987). Compared with habituation/recovery, touching, sorting, and other play behaviors better reveal the meanings that toddlers attach to categories because they are applying those meanings in their everyday activities. For example, after watching an experimenter give a toy dog a drink from a cup, 14-month-olds shown a rabbit and a motorcycle usually offer the drink only to the rabbit (Mandler & McDonough, 1998). Their behavior reveals a clear understanding that certain actions are appropriate for some categories of items (animals) but not others (vehicles).

How does this perceptual-to-conceptual change take place? Although researchers disagree on whether this shift requires a new approach to analyzing experience, most acknowledge that exploration of objects and expanding knowledge of the world contribute to older infants' capacity to move beyond physical features and group objects by their functions and behaviors (Mandler, 2004; Oakes & Madole, 2003). In addition, language both builds on and facilitates categorization. Adult labeling calls infants' attention to commonalities among objects while also promoting vocabulary growth. Toddlers' advancing vocabulary, in turn, fosters categorization (Gelman & Kalish, 2006; Waxman, 2003).

Variations among languages lead to cultural differences in conceptual development. Korean toddlers, who learn a language in which object names are often omitted from sentences, develop object-grouping skills later than their English-speaking counterparts (Gopnik & Choi, 1990). At the same time, Korean contains a commonly used word (*kkita*) that has no English equivalent, referring to a tight fit between objects in contact—a ring on a finger, a cap on a pen, or a puzzle piece—and Korean toddlers are advanced in forming the spatial category "tight-fit" (Choi et al., 1999).

Evaluation of Information-Processing Findings

The information-processing perspective underscores the continuity of human thinking from infancy into adult life. In attending to the environment, remembering everyday events, and categorizing objects, Caitlin, Grace, and Timmy think in ways that are remarkably similar to our own, though their mental processing is far from proficient. Findings on infant memory and categorization join with other research in challenging Piaget's view of early cognitive development. If 3-month-olds can remember events for as long as three months and categorize stimuli, then they must have some ability to mentally represent their experiences.

Information-processing research has contributed greatly to our view of infants and toddlers as sophisticated cognitive beings. But its central strength—analyzing cognition into its components, such as perception, attention, memory, and categorization—is also its greatest drawback: Information processing has had difficulty putting these components back together into a broad, comprehensive theory.

One approach to overcoming this weakness has been to combine Piaget's theory with the information-processing approach, an effort we will take up in Chapter 12. A more recent trend has been the application of a *dynamic systems view* (see Chapter 1, page 27) to early cognition. In this approach, researchers analyze each cognitive attainment to see how it results from a complex system of prior accomplishments and the child's current goals (Courage & Howe, 2002; Spencer & Schöner, 2003; Thelen & Smith, 2006). Once these ideas are fully tested, they may move the field closer to a more powerful view of how the mind of the infant and child develops.

The Social Context of Early Cognitive Development

Look back at the short episode at the beginning of this chapter in which Grace dropped shapes into a container. Notice that she learns about the toy with Ginette's help. With adult support, Grace will gradually become better at matching shapes to openings and dropping them into the container. Then she will be able to perform the activity (and others like it) on her own.

Vygotsky's sociocultural theory emphasizes that children live in rich social and cultural contexts that affect the way their cognitive world is structured (Bodrova & Leong, 2007; Rogoff, 2003). Vygotsky believed that complex mental activities, such as voluntary attention, deliberate memory, categorization, and problem solving, have their origins in social interaction. Through joint activities with more mature members of their society, children master activities and think in ways that have meaning in their culture.

A special Vygotskian concept explains how this happens. The **zone of proximal** (or potential) **development** refers to a range of tasks that the child cannot yet handle alone but can do with the help of more skilled partners. To understand this idea, think of a sensitive adult (such as Ginette) who introduces a child to a new

This father provides gentle physical support and simple words to help his young son put together a puzzle. By bringing the task within the child's zone of proximal development and adjusting his communication to suit the child's needs, the father transfers mental strategies to the child, promoting his cognitive development.

activity. The adult picks a task that the child can master but that is challenging enough that the child cannot do it by herself. Or the adult capitalizes on an activity that the child has chosen. The adult guides and supports, adjusting the level of support offered to fit the child's current level of performance. As the child joins in the interaction and picks up mental strategies, her competence increases, and the adult steps back, permitting the child to take more responsibility for the task. This form of teaching—known as *scaffolding*—promotes learning at all ages, and we will consider it further in Chapter 9.

Vygotsky's ideas have been applied mostly to preschool and school-age children, who are more skilled in language and social communication. Recently, however, his theory has been extended to infancy and toddlerhood. Recall that babies are equipped with capabilities that ensure that caregivers will interact with them. Then adults adjust the environment and their communication in ways that promote learning adapted to their cultural circumstances.

A study by Barbara Rogoff and her collaborators (1984) illustrates this process. Placing a jack-in-the-box nearby, the researchers watched how several adults played with Rogoff's son and daughter over the first two years. In the early months, adults tried to focus the baby's attention by working the toy and, as the bunny popped out, saying something like "My, what happened?" By the end of the first year, when the baby's cognitive and motor skills had improved, interaction centered on how to use the toy: The adults guided the baby's hand in turning the crank and putting the bunny back in the box. During the second year, adults helped from a distance, using gestures and verbal prompts, such as making a turning motion with the hand near the crank. Research indicates that this fine-tuned support is related to advanced play, language, and problem solving during the second year (Bornstein et al., 1992b; Charman et al., 2001; Tamis-LeMonda & Bornstein, 1989).

As early as the first year, cultural variations in social experiences affect mental strategies. In the jack-in-the-box example, adults and children focused their attention on a single activity. This strategy, common in Western middle-SES homes, is well-suited to lessons in which children master skills apart from the everyday situations in which they will later use those skills. In contrast, Guatemalan Mayan adults and babies often attend to several events at once. For example, one 12-month-old skillfully put objects in a jar while watching a passing truck and blowing into a toy whistle his mother had slipped in his mouth (Chavajay & Rogoff, 1999).

zone of proximal development In Vygotsky's theory, a range of tasks that the child cannot yet handle alone but can accomplish with the help of more skilled partners.

Processing several competing events simultaneously may be vital in cultures where children largely learn not through lessons but through keen observation of others' ongoing activities at home, at work, and in public life. Mexican children from low-SES families continue to display this style of attention well into middle childhood (Correa-Chavez, Rogoff, & Arauz, 2005).

Earlier we saw how infants and toddlers create new schemes by acting on the physical world (Piaget) and how certain skills become better-developed as children represent their experiences more efficiently and meaningfully (information processing). Vygotsky adds a third dimension to our understanding by emphasizing that many aspects of cognitive development are socially prompted and encouraged. The Cultural Influences box on the following page presents additional evidence for this idea. And we see even more evidence in the next section, where we look at individual differences in mental development during the first two years.

Ask Yourself

Review Cite evidence that categorization becomes less perceptual and more conceptual with age. What factors support this shift? How can adults promote the development of categorization?

Apply Rosa, who is growing up in a rural Mexican village, played with toys in a more intentional, goal-directed way as a toddler than as an infant. What impact is her more advanced toy play likely to have on her development of attention? How is Rosa's cultural background likely to affect her attention?

Connect Review the research on page 215, indicating that by age 10 to 12 months, infants can solve problems by analogy. How might this capacity be related to a context-free memory, which develops about the same time?

Reflect Describe your earliest autobiographical memory. How old were you when the event occurred? Do your responses fit with research on infantile amnesia?

Individual Differences in Early Mental Development

Because of Grace's deprived early environment, Kevin and Monica had a child psychologist give her one of many tests available for assessing mental development in infants and toddlers. Worried about Timmy's progress, Vanessa also arranged for him to be tested. At age 22 months, he had only a handful of words in his vocabulary, played in a less mature way than Caitlin and Grace, and seemed restless and overactive.

The cognitive theories we have just discussed try to explain the *process* of development—how children's thinking changes. Mental tests, in contrast, focus on cognitive *products*. Their goal is to measure behaviors that reflect development and to arrive at scores that *predict* future performance, such as later intelligence, school achievement, and adult vocational success. This concern with prediction arose nearly a century ago, when French psychologist Alfred Binet designed the first successful intelligence test, which predicted school achievement (see Chapter 1). It inspired the design of many new tests, including ones that measure intelligence at very early ages.

Infant Intelligence Tests

Accurately measuring infants' intelligence is a challenge because young babies cannot answer questions or follow directions. All we can do is present them with stimuli, coax them to respond, and observe their behavior. As a result, most infant tests emphasize perceptual and

Cultural Influences

Social Origins of Make-Believe Play

One of the activities my husband, Ken, used to do with our two sons when they were young was to bake pineapple upside-down cake, a favorite treat. One Sunday afternoon when a cake was in the making, 21-month-old Peter stood on a chair at the kitchen sink, busily pouring water from one cup to another.

"He's in the way, Dad!" complained 4-year-old David, trying to pull Peter away from the sink.

"Maybe if we let him help, he'll give us some room," Ken suggested. As David stirred the batter, Ken poured some into a small bowl for Peter, moved his chair to the side of the sink, and handed him a spoon.

"Here's how you do it, Petey," instructed David, with an air of superiority. Peter watched as David stirred, then tried to copy his motion. When it was time to pour the batter, Ken helped Peter hold and tip the small bowl.

"Time to bake it," said Ken.

"Bake it, bake it," repeated Peter, watching Ken slip the pan into the oven.

Several hours later, we observed one of Peter's earliest instances of make-believe play. He got his pail from the sandbox and, after filling it with a handful of sand, carried it into the kitchen and put it down on the floor in front of the oven. "Bake it, bake it," Peter called to Ken. Together, father and son placed the pretend cake in the oven.

Piaget and his followers concluded that toddlers discover make-believe independently, once they are capable of representational schemes. Vygotsky's theory has challenged this view. He believed that society provides children with opportunities to represent culturally meaningful activities in play. Make-believe, like other complex mental activities, is first learned under the guidance of experts (Berk, 2006b). In the example just described, Peter extended his capacity to represent daily events when Ken drew him into the baking task and helped him act it out in play.

Current evidence supports the idea that early make-believe is the combined result of children's readiness to engage in it and social experiences that promote it. In one observational study of middle-SES American toddlers,

75 to 80 percent of make-believe involved mother–child interaction (Haight & Miller, 1993). At 12 months, make-believe was fairly one-sided: Almost all play episodes were initiated by mothers. By the end of the second year, mothers and children displayed mutual interest in getting make-believe started; half of pretend episodes were initiated by each.

Toddlers' make-believe is more elaborate when adults participate (Keren et al., 2005). They are more likely to combine schemes into complex sequences, as Peter did when he put the sand in the bucket ("making the batter"), carried it into the kitchen, and, with Ken's help, put it in the oven ("baking the cake"). The more parents pretend with their toddlers, the more time their children devote to make-believe. In some collectivist societies, such as Argentina and Japan, mother–toddler other-directed pretending, as in feeding or putting a doll to sleep, is particularly rich in maternal expressions of affection and praise (Bornstein et al., 1999a).

In some cultures, such as those of Indonesia and Mexico, where extended-family households and sibling caregiving are common, make-believe is more frequent and complex with older siblings than with mothers. As early as age 3 to 4, children provide rich, challenging stimulation to their younger brothers and sisters, take these teaching responsibilities seriously, and, with age, become better at them (Zukow-Goldring, 2002). In a study of Zinacanteco Indian children of southern Mexico, by age 8, sibling teachers were highly skilled at showing 2-year-olds how to play at everyday tasks, such as washing and cooking. They often guided toddlers verbally and physically through the task and provided feedback (Maynard, 2002).

Older siblings in Western middle-SES families less often teach deliberately, but they still serve as influential models of playful behavior. In a study of New Zealand families of Western European descent, when both a parent and an older sibling were available, toddlers more often imitated the actions of the sibling, especially when siblings engaged in make-believe or in routines (like answering the phone or raking leaves) that could inspire pretending (Barr & Hayne, 2003).

As we will see in Chapter 9, make-believe is a major means through which children extend their cognitive skills and learn about important activities in their culture. Vygotsky's theory, and the findings that support it, tell us that providing a stimulating environment is not enough to promote early cognitive development. In addition, toddlers must be invited and encouraged by more skilled members of their culture to participate in the social world around them. Parents and teachers can enhance early make-believe by playing often with toddlers, guiding and elaborating their make-believe themes.

© DAVID WOODFALL / WWI / PETER ARNOLD, INC.

In cultures where sibling caregiving is common, make-believe play is more frequent and complex with older siblings than with mothers. As these Venezuelan brothers play with a balsa-wood boat, the older boy provides his younger sibling with rich, challenging stimulation.

© LAURA DWIGHT PHOTOGRAPHY

A trained examiner administers a test based on the Bayley Scales of Infant Development to a baby while her mother looks on. Unlike tests for older children, which assess verbal, conceptual, and problem-solving skills, most infant tests emphasize perceptual and motor responses, which predict later intelligence poorly.

motor responses. But increasingly, new tests are being developed that tap early language, cognition, and social behavior, especially with older infants and toddlers.

One commonly used test, the Bayley Scales of Infant Development, is suitable for children between 1 month and 3½ years. The most recent edition, the Bayley-III, has three main subtests: (1) the Cognitive Scale, which includes such items as attention to familiar and unfamiliar objects, looking for a fallen object, and pretend play; (2) the Language Scale, which taps understanding and expressions of language—for example, recognition of objects and people, following simple directions, and naming objects and pictures; and (3) the Motor Scale, which includes gross and fine motor skills, such as grasping, sitting, stacking blocks, and climbing stairs (Bayley, 2005).

Two additional Bayley-III scales depend on parental report: (4) the Social-Emotional Scale, which asks caregivers about such behaviors as ease of calming, social responsiveness, and imitation in play; and (5) the Adaptive Behavior Scale, which asks about adaptation to the demands of daily life, including communication, self-control, following rules, and getting along with others.

COMPUTING INTELLIGENCE TEST SCORES ■ Intelligence tests for infants, children, and adults are scored in much the same way—by computing an **intelligence quotient (IQ),** which indicates the extent to which the raw score (number of items passed) deviates from the typical performance of same-age individuals. In constructing a test, designers engage in **standardization**—giving the test to a large, representative sample and using the results as the *standard* for interpreting scores. The standardization sample for the Bayley-III included 1,700 infants, toddlers, and young preschoolers, reflecting the U.S. population in SES and ethnic diversity.

Within the standardization sample, performances at each age level form a **normal distribution,** in which most scores cluster around the mean, or average, and progressively fewer fall toward the extremes (see Figure 6.9). This *bell-shaped distribution* results whenever researchers measure individual differences in large samples. When intelligence tests are standardized, the mean IQ is set at 100. An individual's IQ is higher or lower than 100 by an amount that reflects how much his or her test performance deviates from the standardization-sample mean.

The IQ offers a way of finding out whether an individual is ahead, behind, or on time (average) in mental development compared with others of the same age. For example, if Timmy did better than 50 percent of his age-mates, his score will be 100. A child who does better than only 16 percent has an IQ of 85; one who outperforms 98 percent has an IQ of 130. The IQs of 86 percent of individuals fall between 70 and 130; only a few achieve higher or lower scores.

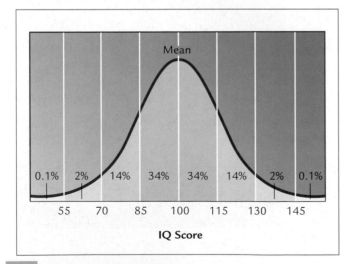

Mean

| 0.1% | 2% | 14% | 34% | 34% | 14% | 2% | 0.1% |

55   70   85   100   115   130   145

IQ Score

FIGURE 6.9

Normal distribution of intelligence test scores. To determine what percentage of same-age individuals in the population a person with a certain IQ outperformed, add the figures to the left of that IQ score. For example, an 8-year-old child with an IQ of 115 scored better than 84 percent of the population of 8-year-olds.

PREDICTING LATER PERFORMANCE FROM INFANT TESTS ■ Many people assume, incorrectly, that IQ is a measure of inborn ability that does not change with age. Despite careful construction, most infant tests predict later intelligence poorly. Longitudinal research reveals that the majority of children show substantial fluctuations in IQ between toddlerhood and adolescence—10 to 20 points in most cases and sometimes much more (McCall, 1993; Weinert & Hany, 2003).

Because infants and toddlers are especially likely to become distracted, fatigued, or bored during testing, their scores often do not reflect their true abilities. In addition, the perceptual and motor items on infant tests differ from the tasks given to older children, which emphasize increasingly complex verbal, conceptual, and problem-solving skills. Because of concerns that infant test scores do not tap the same dimensions of intelligence measured at older ages, they are conservatively labeled **developmental quotients,** or **DQs,** rather than IQs. Not until age 6 do IQ scores become stable, serving as reasonably good predictors of later performance (Hayslip, 1994).

Infant tests are somewhat better at making long-term predictions for extremely low-scoring babies. Today, they are used largely for *screening*—helping to identify for further observation and intervention babies whose very low scores mean that they are likely to have developmental problems in the future.

Because infant tests do not predict later mental test scores for most children, researchers have turned to information-processing measures, such as habituation, to assess early mental progress. Their findings show that speed of habituation and recovery to novel visual stimuli are among the best available infant predictors of IQ from early childhood into adolescence, with correlations ranging from the .30s to the .60s (McCall & Carriger, 1993; Sigman, Cohen, & Beckwith, 1997; Kavsek, 2004). In one study, the speed with which fetal startle reactions in the third trimester of pregnancy declined to a repeatedly presented loud sound was modestly associated with cognitive performance (assessed through recovery to novel photos of human faces) at 6 and 9 months of age (Gaultney & Gingras, 2005).

Habituation and recovery seem to be an especially effective early index of intelligence because they assess memory as well as quickness and flexibility of thinking, which underlie intelligent behavior at all ages (Colombo, 1995; Rose & Feldman, 1997). Piagetian object-permanence tasks are also relatively good predictors of later IQ, perhaps because they, too, reflect a basic intellectual process—problem solving (Rose, Feldman, & Wallace, 1992). The consistency of these findings has prompted designers of the Bayley-III to include items that tap such cognitive skills as habituation/recovery, object permanence, and categorization.

Early Environment and Mental Development

In Chapter 2, we indicated that intelligence is a complex blend of hereditary and environmental influences. Many studies have examined the relationship of environmental factors to infant and toddler mental test scores. As we consider this evidence, you will encounter findings that highlight the role of heredity as well.

HOME ENVIRONMENT ■ The **Home Observation for Measurement of the Environment (HOME)** is a checklist for gathering information about the quality of children's home lives through observation and parental interview (Caldwell & Bradley, 1994). Applying What We Know on page 232 lists the factors measured by HOME during the first three years. Each is positively related to toddlers' mental test performance. Regardless of SES and ethnicity, an organized, stimulating physical setting and parental affection, involvement, and encouragement of new skills repeatedly predict better language and IQ scores in toddlerhood and early childhood (Fuligni, Han, & Brooks-Gunn, 2004; Linver, Martin, & Brooks-Gunn, 2004; Tamis-LeMonda et al., 2004). As the final section of this chapter will reveal, the extent to which parents talk to infants and toddlers is particularly important. It contributes strongly to early language progress, which, in turn, predicts intelligence and academic achievement in elementary school (Hart & Risley, 1995).

Yet we should interpret these correlational findings with caution. In all the studies, children were reared by their biological parents, with whom they share not just a common environment but also a common heredity. Parents who are genetically more intelligent may provide better experiences while also giving birth to genetically brighter children, who evoke more parental stimulation. This hypothesis, which refers to *genetic–environmental correlation* (see Chapter 2, pages 86–87), is supported by research (Saudino & Plomin, 1997). Still, heredity

intelligence quotient, or IQ A score that reflects an individual's performance on an intelligence test compared with the performances of other individuals of the same age.

standardization The practice of giving an intelligence test to a large, representative sample, which serves as the standard for interpreting individual scores.

normal distribution A bell-shaped distribution that results when individual differences are measured in large samples.

developmental quotient, or DQ A score on an infant intelligence test, computed in the same manner as an IQ but based primarily on perceptual and motor responses.

Home Observation for Measurement of the Environment (HOME) A checklist for gathering information about the quality of children's home lives through observation and parental interview.

Applying What We Know

Features of a High-Quality Home Life for Infants and Toddlers: The HOME Infant–Toddler Subscales

HOME SUBSCALE	SAMPLE ITEM
Emotional and verbal responsiveness of the parent	Parent caresses or kisses child at least once during observer's visit.
	Parent spontaneously speaks to child twice or more (excluding scolding) during observer's visit.
Parental acceptance of the child	Parent does not interfere with child's actions or restrict child's movements more than three times during observer's visit.
Organization of the physical environment	Child's play environment appears safe and free of hazards.
Provision of appropriate play materials	Parent provides toys or interesting activities for child during observer's visit.
Parental involvement with the child	Parent tends to keep child within view and to look at child often during observer's visit.
Opportunities for variety in daily stimulation	Child eats at least one meal per day with mother and/or father, according to parental report.
	Child frequently has a chance to get out of house (for example, accompanies parent on trips to grocery store).

Source: Bradley, 1994; Bradley et al., 2001.

does not account for the entire association between home environment and mental test scores. Family living conditions continue to predict children's IQ beyond the contribution of parental IQ and education (Chase-Lansdale et al., 1997; Klebanov et al., 1998). In one study, infants and children growing up in less crowded homes had parents who were far more verbally responsive to them—a major contributor to language, intellectual, and academic progress (Evans, Maxwell, & Hart, 1999).

How can the research summarized so far help us understand Vanessa's concern about Timmy's development? Ben, the psychologist who tested Timmy, found that he scored only slightly below average. Ben talked with Vanessa about her child-rearing practices and watched her play with Timmy. A single parent who worked long hours, Vanessa had little energy for Timmy at the end of the day. Ben also noticed that Vanessa, anxious about Timmy's progress, tended to pressure him, dampening his active behavior and bombarding him with directions: "That's enough ball play. Stack these blocks."

Ben explained that when parents are intrusive in these ways, infants and toddlers are likely to be distractible, play immaturely, and do poorly on mental tests (Bono & Stifter, 2003; Stilson & Harding, 1997). He coached Vanessa in how to interact sensitively with Timmy, while also assuring her that Timmy's current performance need not forecast his future development. Warm, responsive parenting that builds on toddlers' current capacities is a much better indicator than an early mental test score of how children will do later.

© ROBERT BRENNER/PHOTOEDIT

As child care for infants and toddlers has become common, the prevalence of poor-quality child care is cause for concern. But a high-quality child care setting like this one, where well-trained caregivers provide positive, developmentally appropriate stimulation, can be especially beneficial for children from low-SES homes.

INFANT AND TODDLER CHILD CARE ■ Child care for infants and toddlers has become common today, as more than 60 percent of North American mothers with a child under age 2 are employed (Statistics Canada, 2003f; U.S. Census Bureau, 2007b). In addition to the home environment, the quality of child care has an impact on children's mental development. Research in the United States and Canada consistently shows that infants and young children exposed to poor-quality child care—whether they come from middle-class or from low-SES homes—score lower on measures of cognitive and social skills (Hausfather et al., 1997; Kohen et al., 2000; NICHD Early Child Care Research Network, 2000b, 2001, 2003b, 2006).

In contrast, good child care can reduce the negative impact of a stressed, poverty-stricken home life, and it sustains the benefits of growing up in an economically advantaged family (Lamb & Ahnert, 2006; NICHD Early Child Care Research Network, 2003b). In Swedish longitudinal research, entering high-quality child care in infancy and toddlerhood was associated with cognitive, emotional, and social competence in middle childhood and adolescence (Andersson, 1989, 1992; Broberg et al., 1997).

TAKE A MOMENT... Visit several child-care settings, and take notes on what you see. In contrast to most European countries and to Australia and New Zealand, where child care is nationally regulated and funded to ensure its quality, reports on U.S. and Canadian child care raise serious concerns. Standards are set by the individual states and provinces and vary widely. In some places, caregivers need no special training in child development, and one adult is permitted to care for 6 to 12 babies at once (Children's Defense Fund, 2006). In studies of child-care quality in each nation, only 20 to 25 percent of child-care centers and family child-care settings (in which a caregiver cares for children in her home) provided infants and toddlers with sufficiently positive, stimulating experiences to promote healthy psychological development. Most settings offered substandard care (Doherty et al., 2000; Goelman et al., 2000; NICHD Early Child Care Research Network, 2000a, 2004b).

Unfortunately, many children from low-income families experience inadequate child care (Brooks-Gunn, 2004). In the United States, however, settings providing the very worst care tend to serve middle-SES families. These parents are especially likely to place their children in for-profit centers, where quality tends to be lowest. Low-SES children more often attend publicly subsidized, nonprofit centers, which have smaller group sizes and better teacher–child ratios (Lamb & Ahnert, 2006; Phillips, Howes, & Whitebook, 1992), Still, child-care quality for low-SES children varies widely. And probably because of greater access to adult stimulation, infants and toddlers in high-quality family child care score higher than those in center care in cognitive and language development (NICHD Early Child Care Research Network, 2000b).

Refer to Applying What We Know on page 234 for signs of high-quality child care for infants and toddlers, based on standards for **developmentally appropriate practice.** These standards, devised by the U.S. National Association for the Education of Young Children, specify program characteristics that meet the developmental and individual needs of young children, based on both current research and consensus among experts. Caitlin, Grace, and Timmy are fortunate to be in family child care that meets these standards.

Child care in the United States and Canada is affected by a macrosystem of individualistic values and weak government regulation and funding. Furthermore, many parents think that their children's child-care experiences are better than they really are. Because they are unable to identify good care, they do not demand it (Helburn, 1995). In recent years, the U.S. and Canadian federal governments, as well as some states and provinces, have tried to address the child-care crisis by allocating additional funds to subsidize the cost of care, especially for low-income families. Though far from meeting the need, this increase in resources has had a positive impact on child-care quality and accessibility (Canada Campaign 2000, 2003; Children's Defense Fund, 2006). In Canada, the province of Québec leads the nation with universal, government-supported good-quality child care for infants and preschoolers, for which every Québec family pays the same minimal daily fee.

High-quality child care is a cost-effective means of protecting children's well-being. And, much like the programs we are about to consider, excellent child care can also serve as effective early intervention for children whose development is at risk.

Early Intervention for At-Risk Infants and Toddlers

Children living in poverty are likely to show gradual declines in intelligence test scores and to achieve poorly when they reach school age (Bradley et al., 2001; Gutman, Sameroff, & Cole, 2003). These problems are largely due to disorganized, stressful home environments that

developmentally appropriate practice Research-based standards devised by the National Association for the Education of Young Children that specify program characteristics that meet the developmental and individual needs of young children of varying ages.

Applying What We Know

Signs of Developmentally Appropriate Infant and Toddler Child Care

PROGRAM CHARACTERISTIC	SIGNS OF QUALITY
Physical setting	Indoor environment is clean, in good repair, well-lighted, and well-ventilated.
	Fenced outdoor play space is available.
	Setting does not appear overcrowded when children are present.
Toys and equipment	Play materials are appropriate for infants and toddlers and are stored on low shelves within easy reach.
	Cribs, highchairs, infant seats, and child-sized tables and chairs are available.
	Outdoor equipment includes small riding toys, swings, slide, and sandbox.
Caregiver–child ratio	In child-care centers, caregiver–child ratio is no greater than 1 to 3 for infants, and 1 to 6 for toddlers.
	Group size (number of children in one room) is no greater than 6 infants with 2 caregivers and 12 toddlers with 2 caregivers.
	In family child care, caregiver is responsible for no more than 6 children; within this group, no more than 2 are infants and toddlers.
	Staffing is consistent, so infants and toddlers can form relationships with particular caregivers.
Daily activities	Daily schedule includes times for active play, quiet play, naps, snacks, and meals. It is flexible rather than rigid, to meet the needs of individual children.
	Atmosphere is warm and supportive, and children are never left unsupervised.
Interactions among adults and children	Caregivers respond promptly to infants' and toddlers' distress; hold, talk to, sing, and read to them; and interact with them in a manner that respects the individual child's interests and tolerance for stimulation.
Caregiver qualifications	Caregiver has some training in child development, first aid, and safety.
Relationships with parents	Parents are welcome anytime.
	Caregivers talk frequently with parents about children's behavior and development.
Licensing and accreditation	Child-care setting, whether a center or a home, is licensed by the state or province.
	In the United States, voluntary accreditation by the National Academy of Early Childhood Programs (www.naeyc.org/accreditation) or the National Association for Family Child Care (www.nafcc.org) is evidence of an especially high-quality program.
	Canada is working on a voluntary accreditation system, under the leadership of the Canadian Child Care Federation (www.cccf-fcsge.ca).

Sources: Bredekamp & Copple, 1997; National Association for the Education of Young Children, 1998.

undermine children's ability to learn and increase the likelihood that they will remain poor as adults (McLoyd, Aikens, & Burton, 2006). A variety of intervention programs have been developed to break this tragic cycle of poverty. Although most begin during the preschool years (we will discuss these in Chapter 9), a few start during infancy and continue through early childhood.

In center-based interventions, children attend an organized child-care or preschool program where they receive educational, nutritional, and health services and their parents receive child-rearing and other social service supports. In home-based interventions, a skilled adult visits the home and works with parents, providing social support and teaching them how to stimulate a very young child's development. In most programs of either type, participating children score higher than untreated controls on mental tests by age 2. These gains persist as long as the program lasts and occasionally longer. The earlier intervention begins, the longer it lasts, and the greater its scope and intensity (for example, year-round high-quality child care plus generous support services for parents), the better participants' cognitive and academic performance is throughout childhood and adolescence (Brooks-Gunn, 2004; Ramey, Ramey, & Lanzi, 2006; Sweet & Appelbaum, 2004).

FIGURE 6.10

IQ scores of treatment and control children from infancy to 21 years in the Carolina Abecedarian Project. At 1 year, treatment children outperformed controls, an advantage consistently maintained through age 21. The IQ scores of both groups declined gradually during childhood and adolescence—a trend probably due to the damaging impact of poverty on mental development. (Adapted from Campbell et al., 2001.)

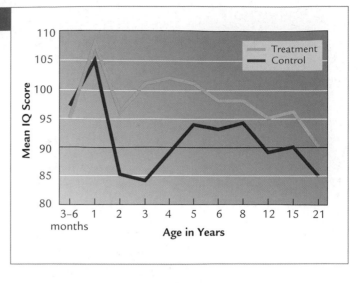

The Carolina Abecedarian Project illustrates these positive outcomes. In the 1970s, more than 100 infants from poverty-stricken families, ranging in age from 3 weeks to 3 months, were randomly assigned to either a treatment group or a control group. Treatment infants were enrolled in full-time, year-round child care through the preschool years. There they received stimulation aimed at promoting motor, cognitive, language, and social skills and, after age 3, literacy and math concepts. Special emphasis was placed on rich, responsive adult–child verbal communication. All children received nutrition and health services; the primary difference between treatment and controls was the intensive child-care experience.

As Figure 6.10 shows, by 12 months of age, the IQs of the two groups diverged. Treatment children maintained their advantage until last tested—at age 21. In addition, throughout their years of schooling, treatment youths achieved considerably higher in reading and math. These gains translated into more years of schooling completed, higher rates of college enrollment and employment in skilled jobs, and lower rates of drug use and adolescent parenthood (Campbell et al., 2001, 2002; Ramey & Ramey, 1999).

Without some form of early intervention, many children born into economically disadvantaged families will not reach their potential. Recognition of this reality led the U.S. Congress to provide limited funding for intervention services directed at infants and toddlers who already have serious developmental problems or who are at risk for problems because of poverty. Early Head Start, begun in 1995, currently has 700 sites serving 62,000 low-income families. It offers an array of coordinated services—child care, educational experiences for infants and toddlers, parenting education, family social support, and health care—delivered through a center-based, home-based, or mixed approach, depending on community needs. A recent evaluation, conducted when children reached age 3, showed that intervention led to warmer, more stimulating parenting, a reduction in harsh discipline, gains in cognitive and language development, and lessening of child aggression. The strongest effects occurred at sites offering a mix of center- and home-based services (Love et al., 2005). Though not yet plentiful enough to meet the need, such programs are a promising beginning.

Intervention programs such as Early Head Start offer coordinated services, including child care, educational experiences for infants and toddlers, parenting education, health care, and social support for families. An evaluation showed that Early Head Start led to warmer, more stimulating parenting, cognitive and language gains, and a decline in harsh discipline and child aggression.

Ask Yourself

Review   What probably accounts for the finding that speed of habituation and recovery to visual stimuli predicts later IQ better than an infant mental test score?

Apply   Fifteen-month-old Joey's developmental quotient (DQ) is 115. His mother wants to know exactly what this means and what she should do at home to support his mental development. How would you respond?

Connect   Using what you learned about brain development in Chapter 5, explain why it is best to initiate intervention for poverty-stricken children in the first two years, rather than later.

Reflect   Suppose you were seeking a child-care setting for your baby. What would you want it to be like, and why?

Language Development

Improvements in perception and cognition during infancy pave the way for an extraordinary human achievement—language. In Chapter 5, we saw that in the second half of the first year, infants make dramatic progress in distinguishing the basic sounds of their language and in segmenting the flow of speech into word and phrase units. They also start to comprehend some word meanings and, around 12 months of age, say their first word. Sometime between 1½ and 2 years, toddlers combine two words (MacWhinney, 2005). By age 6, children have become skilled conversationalists, using a vocabulary of about 10,000 words and speaking in elaborate sentences.

Infants are communicative beings from the very beginning of life, as seen in this interchange between a father and his baby. How will this child accomplish the impressive task of becoming a fluent speaker of his native language within just a few years? Theorists disagree sharply on answers to this question.

© LWA-SHARIE KENNEDY/ZEFA/CORBIS

To appreciate this awesome task, think about the many abilities involved in your own flexible use of language. When you speak, you must select words that match the underlying concepts you want to convey. To be understood, you must pronounce these utterances correctly. Then you must combine them into phrases and sentences using a complex set of grammatical rules. Finally, you must follow the rules of everyday conversation—taking turns, making comments relevant to what your partner just said, and using an appropriate tone of voice. Otherwise, no matter how clear and correct your language, others may refuse to listen to you.

How do infants and toddlers make such remarkable progress in launching these skills? To address this question, let's examine several prominent theories of language development.

Three Theories of Language Development

In the 1950s, researchers did not take seriously the idea that very young children might be able to figure out important properties of the language they hear. As a result, the first two theories of how children acquire language were extreme views. One, *behaviorism*, regards language development as entirely due to environmental influences. The second, *nativism,* assumes that children are "prewired" to master the intricate rules of their language.

THE BEHAVIORIST PERSPECTIVE ■ Behaviorist B. F. Skinner (1957) proposed that language, like any other behavior, is acquired through *operant conditioning.* As the baby makes sounds, parents reinforce those that are most like words with smiles, hugs, and speech in return. For example, at 12 months, my older son, David, often babbled something like "book-a-book-a-dook-a-dook-a-book-a-nook-a-book-aaa." One day as he babbled away, I held up his picture book and said, "Book!" Soon David was saying "book-aaa" in the presence of books.

Some behaviorists believe that children rely on *imitation* to rapidly acquire complex utterances, such as whole phrases and sentences (Moerk, 2000). Imitation can combine with reinforcement to promote language, as when a parent coaxes, "Say 'I want a cookie,'" and delivers praise and a treat after the toddler responds, "Wanna cookie!"

Although reinforcement and imitation contribute to early language development, they are best viewed as supporting rather than fully explaining it. "It's amazing how creative Caitlin is with language," Carolyn remarked one day. "She combines words in ways she's never heard before, like 'needle it' when she wants me to sew up her teddy bear and 'allgone outside' when she has to come in." Carolyn's observations are accurate: Young children create many novel utterances that are not reinforced by or copied from others. And when they do imitate others' language, they do so selectively, focusing mainly on building their vocabularies and on refining aspects of language that they are working on at the moment (Owens, 2005).

THE NATIVIST PERSPECTIVE ■ Linguist Noam Chomsky (1957) proposed a *nativist* account that regards the young child's amazing language skill as a uniquely human accomplishment, etched into the structure of the brain. Focusing on grammar, Chomsky reasoned that the rules for sentence organization are much too complex to be directly taught to or independently discovered by even a cognitively sophisticated young child. Rather, he argued, all children have a **language acquisition device (LAD),** an innate system that contains a *universal grammar,* or set of rules common to all languages. It permits children, as soon as they have acquired sufficient vocabulary, to combine words into grammatically consistent, novel utterances and to understand the meaning of sentences, no matter which language they hear. Because the LAD is specifically suited for language processing, children master the structure of language spontaneously and swiftly. In sharp contrast to the behaviorist view, nativists regard deliberate training by parents as unnecessary (Pinker, 1999).

Are children biologically primed to acquire language? Recall from Chapter 4 that newborn babies are remarkably sensitive to speech sounds. And children everywhere reach major language milestones in a similar sequence—evidence consistent with a biologically based language program (Gleitman & Newport, 1996). Furthermore, the ability to master a grammatically complex language system seems to be unique to humans, as efforts to teach language to nonhuman primates—using either specially devised artificial symbol systems or American Sign Language (ASL), a gestural language used by the deaf—have met with limited success (Miles, 1999). Even after extensive training, chimpanzees (who are closest to humans in terms of evolution) master only a basic vocabulary and short word combinations, and they produce these far less consistently than human preschoolers do (Tomasello, Call, & Hare, 2003).

Evidence for specialized language areas in the brain and a sensitive period for language development have also been interpreted as supporting Chomsky's theory. Let's take a closer look at these findings.

Language Areas in the Brain. Recall from Chapter 5 that for most people, language is housed in the left hemisphere of the cerebral cortex. Within it are two important language-related structures (see Figure 6.11 on page 238). To clarify their functions, researchers have, for several decades, studied adults who experienced damage to these structures and display *aphasias,* or communication disorders. **Broca's area,** located in the left frontal lobe, supports grammatical processing and language production. **Wernicke's area,** located in the left temporal lobe, plays a role in comprehending word meaning.

language acquisition device (LAD) In Chomsky's theory, an innate system that contains a universal grammar, or set of rules common to all languages, that permits children to understand and speak in a rule-oriented fashion as soon as they have learned enough words.

Broca's area A structure located in the left frontal lobe of the cerebral cortex that supports grammatical processing and language production.

Wernicke's area A structure located in the left temporal lobe of the cerebral cortex that plays a role in comprehending word meaning.

FIGURE 6.11

Broca's and Wernicke's areas, in the left hemisphere of the cerebral cortex. (1) Broca's area, located in the frontal lobe, supports grammatical processing and language production. (2) Wernicke's area, located in the temporal lobe, is involved in comprehending word meaning. Contrary to what was once believed, however, neither area is solely or even mainly responsible for these functions. Instead, each cooperates with many other regions of the left hemisphere. Wernicke's area and Broca's area communicate through a bundle of nerve fibers represented by dashed lines in the figure. Among the regions from which Wernicke's area receives impulses is (3) the primary auditory area, where sensations from the ears are sent. Broca's area communicates with motor areas involved in speaking.

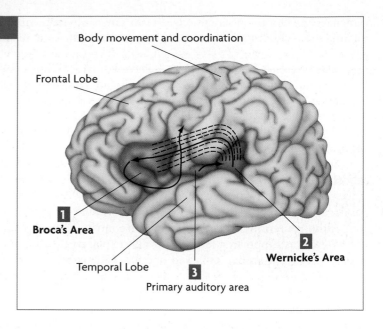

PET and fMRI brain-imaging research, however, suggests more complex relationships between language functions and brain structures. The impaired pronunciation and grammar of patients with Broca's aphasia and the meaningless speech streams of patients with Wernicke's aphasia involve widespread abnormal activity in the left cerebral hemisphere, triggered by the brain damage (Bates et al., 2003). Contrary to long-held belief, then, Broca's and Wernicke's areas are not solely or even mainly responsible for specific language functions. Nevertheless, depending on the site of injury to the adult left hemisphere, language deficits do vary predictably. Damage to frontal-lobe areas usually yields language production problems, damage to areas in the other lobes comprehension problems (Dick et al., 2004).

The broad association of language functions with left-hemispheric regions is consistent with Chomsky's notion of a brain prepared to process language. But critics point out that at birth, the brain is not fully lateralized; it is highly plastic. Language areas in the cerebral cortex *develop* as children acquire language. If the left hemisphere is injured in the early years, other regions take over its language functions. Recall from Chapter 5 that deaf adults who as children learned sign language depend more on the right hemisphere. Thus, left-hemispheric localization (though typical) is not necessary for effective language processing.

Nevertheless, when the young brain allocates language to the right hemisphere—as a result of left-hemispheric damage or learning of sign language—it localizes it in roughly the same regions that typically support language in the left hemisphere (Mueller et al., 1998; Newman et al., 2002). This suggests that those brain structures are uniquely disposed for language processing.

A Sensitive Period for Language Development. Must language be acquired early in life, during an age span in which the brain is particularly responsive to language stimulation? Evidence for a sensitive period that coincides with brain lateralization would support the view that language development has unique biological properties.

To test this idea, researchers have examined the language competence of deaf adults who acquired their first language—American Sign Language (ASL)—at different ages. The later learners, whose parents chose to educate them through the oral method, which relies on speech and lip-reading, did not acquire spoken language because of their profound deafness. And consistent with the sensitive-period notion, those who learned ASL in adolescence or adulthood never became as proficient as those who learned in childhood (Mayberry, 1994; Newport, 1991; Singleton & Newport, 2004). However, no precise age cutoff has been established for a decline in first-language competence.

Is acquiring a second language also harder after a sensitive period has passed? In one study, researchers examined U.S. census data, selecting immigrants from non-English-speaking countries who had resided in the United States for at least ten years. The census form had asked the immigrants to rate how competently they spoke English, from "not at all" to "very well"—self-reports that correlate strongly with objective language measures. As age of immigration increased from infancy and early childhood into adulthood, English proficiency declined (Hakuta, Bialystok, & Wiley, 2003). Furthermore, ERP and fMRI measures of brain activity indicate that second-language processing is less lateralized in older than in younger learners (Neville & Bruer, 2001). However, the capacity to acquire a second language does not drop sharply at a certain age. Rather, a continuous, age-related decrease occurs.

In sum, research on both first- and second-language learning reveals a biologically based time frame for optimum language development. However, the boundaries of this sensitive period remain unclear.

This Cambodian father may never gain as much proficiency in English as his son and daughter, who are growing up in the United States. Although the capacity to learn a second language does not drop sharply at a certain age, childhood seems to be a sensitive period for optimum language development.

LIMITATIONS OF THE NATIVIST PERSPECTIVE ■ Chomsky's theory has had a major impact on current views of language development. It is now widely accepted that humans have a unique, biologically based capacity to acquire language. Still, Chomsky's account of development has been challenged on several grounds.

First, researchers have had great difficulty specifying Chomsky's universal grammar. A major problem is the absence of a complete description of these abstract grammatical structures or even an agreed-on list of how many exist or the best examples of them (Maratsos, 1998; Tomasello, 2003). Critics of Chomsky's theory doubt that one set of rules can account for the extraordinary variation in grammatical forms among the world's languages (Maratsos, 1998; Tomasello, 2003). How children manage to link such rules with the strings of words they hear is also unclear.

Second, Chomsky's assumption that grammatical knowledge is innately determined does not fit with certain observations of language development. Once children begin to use an innate grammatical structure, we would expect them to apply it to all relevant instances in their language. But children refine and generalize many grammatical forms gradually, engaging in much piecemeal learning and making errors along the way. For example, one 3-year-old, in grappling with prepositions, initially added *with* to the verb *open* ("You open with scissors") but not to the word *hit* ("He hit me stick") (Tomasello, 2000, 2003, 2006). As we will see in Chapter 12, complete mastery of some grammatical forms, such as the passive voice, is not achieved until well into middle childhood (Tager-Flusberg, 2005). This suggests that more experimentation and learning are involved than Chomsky assumed.

THE INTERACTIONIST PERSPECTIVE ■ Recent ideas about language development emphasize *interactions* between inner capacities and environmental influences. One type of interactionist theory applies the *information-processing perspective* to language development. A second type emphasizes *social interaction*.

Some information-processing theorists assume that children make sense of their complex language environments by applying powerful cognitive capacities of a general kind (Bates, 2004; Elman, 2001). These theorists note that regions of the brain housing language also govern similar perceptual, motor, and cognitive abilities. For example, damage to parts of the left hemisphere, including Wernicke's area, results in difficulty comprehending both language and other patterned stimuli, such as music and a series of moving lights that depict familiar shapes (Koelsch et al., 2002; Saygin et al., 2004). Other theorists blend this information-processing view with Chomsky's nativist perspective. They agree that infants are amazing analyzers of speech and other information. But, they argue, these capacities probably are not sufficient to

TABLE 6.3 Milestones of Language Development During the First Two Years

APPROXIMATE AGE	MILESTONE
2 months	Infants coo, making pleasant vowel sounds.
4 months on	Infants observe with interest as the caregiver plays turn-taking games, such as pat-a-cake and peekaboo.
6 months on	Infants babble, adding consonants to their cooing sounds and repeating syllables. By 7 months, babbling starts to include many sounds of spoken languages.
8–12 months	Infants comprehend some words.
	Infants become more accurate at establishing joint attention with the caregiver, who often verbally labels what the baby is looking at.
	Infants use preverbal gestures, such as showing and pointing, to influence the behavior of others.
12 months	Babbling includes sound and intonation patterns of the child's language community.
	Infants actively participate in turn-taking games, trading roles with the caregiver.
	Toddlers say their first recognizable word.
18–24 months	Vocabulary expands from about 50 to 200 spoken words.
	Toddlers combine two words.

account for mastery of higher-level aspects of language, such as intricate grammatical structures (Newport & Aslin, 2000).

Still other interactionists emphasize that children's social skills and language experiences are centrally involved in language development. In this social-interactionist view, an active child, well-endowed for making sense of language, strives to communicate. In doing so, she cues her caregivers to provide appropriate language experiences, which help her relate content and structure of language to its social meanings (Bohannon & Bonvillian, 2005; Chapman, 2000).

Among social interactionists, disagreement continues over whether or not children are equipped with specialized language structures (Bloom, 1999; Tomasello, 2003, 2006). But as we chart the course of language development, we will encounter much support for their central premise—that children's social competencies and language experiences greatly affect their language progress. In reality, native endowment, cognitive-processing strategies, and social experience may operate in different balances with respect to each aspect of language: pronunciation, vocabulary, grammar, and communication skills. Table 6.3 provides an overview of early language milestones that we will examine in the next few sections.

Getting Ready to Talk

Before babies say their first word, they make impressive progress toward understanding and speaking their native tongue. They listen attentively to human speech, and they make speech-like sounds. As adults, we can hardly help but respond.

COOING AND BABBLING ■ Around 2 months, babies begin to make vowel-like noises, which are called **cooing** because of their pleasant "oo" quality. Gradually, consonants are added, and around 6 months **babbling** appears, in which infants repeat consonant–vowel combinations in long strings, such as "babababababa" or "nanananana."

Babies everywhere (even those who are deaf) start babbling at about the same age and produce a similar range of early sounds. But for babbling to develop further, infants must be able to hear human speech. A baby with impaired hearing will be greatly delayed in babbling and produce a reduced range of sounds. And a deaf infant not exposed to sign language will not babble at all (Oller, 2000).

cooing Pleasant vowel-like noises made by infants, beginning around 2 months of age.

babbling Repetition of consonant–vowel combinations in long strings, beginning around 6 months of age.

joint attention A state in which child and caregiver attend to the same object or event and the caregiver comments on what the child sees.

In one case, a deaf-born 5-month-old received a *cochlear implant*—an electronic device inserted into the ear that converts external sounds into a signal to stimulate the auditory nerve. She showed typical babbling in infancy and resembled her hearing agemates in language development at 3 to 4 years (Schauwers et al., 2004). But if auditory input is not restored until after age 2 (the usual time for cochlear implant surgery), children remain behind in language development. And if implantation occurs after age 4, language delays are severe and persistent (Govaerts et al., 2002; Svirsky, Teoh, & Neuburger, 2004). These outcomes suggest an early sensitive period for the brain to develop the necessary organization for normal speech processing.

TAKE A MOMENT... When a baby coos or babbles and gazes at you, how do you respond? One day, as I stood in line at the post office behind a mother and her 7-month-old, the baby babbled, and three adults—myself and two people standing beside me—started to talk to the infant. Imitating the baby, we cooed and babbled ourselves, and we also said things like "My, you're a big girl, aren't you? Out to help Mommy mail letters today?" The baby smiled and babbled all the more. As infants listen to spoken language, babbling increases. Around 7 months, it starts to include many sounds of spoken languages. And by 10 months, it reflects the sound and intonation patterns of children's language community, some of which are transferred to their first words (Boysson-Bardies & Vihman, 1991).

Deaf infants exposed to sign language from birth babble with their hands much as hearing infants do through speech (Petitto & Marentette, 1991). Furthermore, hearing babies of deaf, signing parents produce babblelike hand motions with the rhythmic patterns of natural sign languages (Petitto et al., 2001, 2004). This sensitivity to language rhythm, evident not just in perception of speech but also in babbling, whether spoken or signed, supports both discovery and production of meaningful language units.

BECOMING A COMMUNICATOR ■ Besides responding to cooing and babbling, adults interact with infants in many other situations. By 3 to 4 months, infants start to gaze in the same general direction as adults are looking—a skill that becomes more accurate around 10 to 11 months. Around this time, babies become sensitive to adults' precise direction of gaze, suggesting that they realize that others' focus provides information about their communicative intentions (Amano, Kezuka, & Yamamoto, 2004; Brooks & Meltzoff, 2005). Adults also follow the baby's line of vision and comment on what the infant sees. This **joint attention,** in which the child attends to the same object or event as the caregiver, who labels it, contributes greatly to early language development. Infants and toddlers who often experience it sustain attention longer, comprehend more language, produce meaningful gestures and words earlier, and show faster vocabulary development (Carpenter, Nagel, & Tomasello, 1998; Flom & Pick, 2003; Silvén, 2001). Gains in joint attention at the end of the first year suggest that infants are beginning to appreciate that other people have goals, just as they themselves do. This permits the child to establish a "common ground" with the adult, through which the child can figure out the meaning of the adult's verbal labels (Tomasello, 2003).

Around 4 to 6 months, interactions between caregivers and babies begin to include *give-and-take,* as in pat-a-cake and peekaboo games. At first, the parent starts the game and the baby is an amused observer. But even 4-month-olds are sensitive to the structure and timing of these interactions, smiling more to an organized than to a disorganized peekaboo exchange (Rochat, Querido, & Striano, 1999). By 12 months, babies participate actively, trading roles with the caregiver. As they do so, they practice the turn-taking pattern of human conversation, a vital context for acquiring language and communication skills. Infants' play maturity and vocalizations during games predict advanced language progress in the second year (Rome-Flanders & Cronk, 1995).

This 1-year-old baby uses a preverbal gesture to draw his father's attention to the train. His father's verbal response promotes the baby's transition to spoken language.

At the end of the first year, as infants become capable of intentional behavior, they use *preverbal gestures* to attract the attention and interest of adults and to influence their behavior (Liszkowski et al., 2004). For example, Caitlin held up a toy to show it and pointed to the cupboard when she wanted a cookie. Carolyn responded to her gestures and also labeled them ("That's your bear!" "Oh, you want a cookie!"). In this way, toddlers learn that using language leads to desired results. Soon they integrate words with gestures, using the gesture to expand their verbal message, as in pointing to a toy while saying "give" (Capirci et al., 2005). Gradually, gestures recede, and words become dominant. Nevertheless, the earlier toddlers produce these word–gesture combinations, the sooner they combine words later in the second year (Goldin-Meadow & Bucher, 2003).

First Words

In the second half of the first year, infants begin to understand word meanings. When 6-month-olds listened to the words "Mommy" or "Daddy" while looking at side-by-side videos of their parents, they looked longer at the video of the named parent (Tincoff & Jusczyk, 1999). Perhaps you have noticed that when engaged in play with babies, adults frequently offer *intermodal perceptual cues* to the meaning of words—for example, saying "doll" while moving a doll and, sometimes, having the doll touch the infant. In doing so, they provide a supportive learning environment. In two studies, 7-month-olds remembered associations between verbal labels and objects only when they heard the label and saw the object move at the same time (Gogate & Bahrick, 1998, 2001).

First spoken words, around 1 year, build on the sensorimotor foundations Piaget described and on categories children form during infancy and toddlerhood. Earliest words usually refer to important people ("Mama," "Dada"), animals ("doggie," "kitty"), objects that move ("ball," "car"), foods ("milk," "apple"), familiar actions ("bye-bye," "up," "more"), or outcomes of familiar actions ("dirty," "hot," "wet") (Hart, 2004; Nelson, 1973). In their first 50 words, toddlers rarely name things that just *sit there*, like "table" or "vase."

Some early words are linked to specific cognitive achievements. For example, about the time toddlers master advanced object permanence problems, they use disappearance words, such as "all gone." And success and failure expressions ("There!" "Uh-oh!") appear when toddlers can solve sensorimotor problems suddenly rather than through trial and error. According to one pair of researchers, "Children seem to be motivated to acquire words that are relevant to the particular cognitive problems they are working on at the moment" (Gopnik & Meltzoff, 1986, p. 1057).

Besides cognition, emotion influences early word learning. At first, when acquiring a new word for an object, person, or event, 1½-year-olds say it neutrally. To learn, they need to listen carefully, and strong emotion would divert their attention. But as words become better learned, toddlers integrate talking and expressing feelings (Bloom, 1998). "Shoe!" 22-month-old Grace said enthusiastically as Monica tied her shoelaces before an outing. At the end of the second year, toddlers label their emotions with words like "happy," "mad," and "sad"—a development we will consider further in Chapter 7.

When young children first learn words, they sometimes apply them too narrowly, an error called **underextension.** For example, at 16 months, Caitlin used "bear" only to refer to the worn and tattered teddy bear she carried nearly constantly. A more common error is **overextension**—applying a word to a wider collection of objects and events than is appropriate. For example, Grace used "car" for buses, trains, trucks, and fire engines. Toddlers' overextensions reflect their sensitivity to categories. They apply a new word to a group of similar experiences ("dog" for furry, four-legged animals; "open" for opening a door, peeling fruit, and untying shoelaces). This suggests that children sometimes overextend deliberately because they have difficulty recalling or have not acquired a suitable word. And when a word is hard to pronounce, toddlers are likely to substitute a related one they can say (Bloom, 2000). As vocabulary and pronunciation improve, overextensions disappear.

The Two-Word Utterance Phase

At first, toddlers add to their vocabularies slowly, at a rate of one to three words a week. Because rate of word learning between 18 and 24 months of age is so impressive (one or two words per day), many researchers concluded that toddlers undergo *a spurt in vocabulary*—a

underextension An early vocabulary error in which a word is applied too narrowly, to a smaller number of objects and events than is appropriate.

overextension An early vocabulary error in which a word is applied too broadly, to a wider collection of objects and events than is appropriate.

transition from a slower to a faster learning phase. But recent evidence indicates that a spurt characterizes only a minority of young children. Most show a steady, continuous increase in rate of word learning that continues through the preschool years (Ganger & Brent, 2004).

How do toddlers build their vocabularies so quickly? Over the second year, they improve in ability to categorize experience, recall words, and pick up others' social cues to meaning—such as eye gaze, pointing, and handling objects (Dapretto & Bjork, 2000; Golinkoff & Hirsh-Pasek, 2006). Furthermore, as toddlers' experiences broaden, they have a wider range of interesting objects and events to label. For example, children approaching age 2 more often mention places to go ("park," "store"). And as they construct a clearer self-image, they add more words that refer to themselves ("me," "mine," "Katy") and to their own and others' bodies and clothing ("eyes," "mouth," "jacket" (Hart, 2004). In Chapter 9, we will consider young children's multiple, specific strategies for word learning.

When vocabulary approaches 200 words, toddlers transition from word–gesture combinations to joining two words: "Mommy shoe," "go car," "my truck." These two-word utterances are called **telegraphic speech** because, like a telegram, they focus on high-content words and omit smaller, less important ones ("can," "the," "to").

Toddlers typically utter their first words around 1 year. As their experiences broaden, they label more objects and events, first with single words and then using two-word utterances, also known as telegraphic speech.

Children the world over use two-word utterances to express a wide variety of meanings. But they do not yet apply a consistent grammar. Two-word speech consists largely of simple formulas ("want + X," "more + X"), with many different words inserted in the "X" position. Toddlers rarely make gross grammatical errors, such as saying "chair my" instead of "my chair." But we can hear them violating the rules. At 20 months, Caitlin said "more hot" and "more read," expressions not acceptable in English grammar. The word-order regularities in toddlers' two-word utterances are usually copies of adult word pairings, as when Carolyn remarked to Caitlin, "That's *my book*" or "How about *more sandwich?*" (Tomasello, 2003; Tomasello & Brooks, 1999). When 18- to 23-month-olds were taught noun and verb nonsense words (for example, "meek" for a doll and "gop" for a snapping action), they easily combined the new nouns with words they knew well ("more meek"). But they seldom formed word combinations with the new verbs (Tomasello, 2000; Tomasello et al., 1997). This suggests that they did not yet grasp subject–verb and verb–object relations, which are the foundation of grammar.

In sum, toddlers are absorbed in figuring out word meanings and using their limited vocabularies in whatever way possible to get their thoughts across. They first acquire "concrete pieces of language," gradually generalizing to construct the word-order and other grammatical rules of their native tongue (Tomasello, 2006). As we will see in Chapter 7, they make steady progress over the preschool years.

Comprehension versus Production

So far, we have focused on language **production**—the words and word combinations children use. What about **comprehension**—the language they understand? At all ages, comprehension develops ahead of production. A five-month lag exists between the time toddlers comprehend 50 words (around 13 months) and the time they produce that many (around 18 months) (Menyuk, Liebergott, & Schultz, 1995).

Think back to the distinction made earlier in this chapter between two types of memory—recognition and recall. Comprehension requires only that children *recognize* the meaning of a word. But for production, children must *recall*, or actively retrieve from their memories, not only the word but also the concept for which it stands. Still, the two capacities are related. The speed and accuracy of toddlers' comprehension of spoken language increase dramatically over the second year. And toddlers who are faster and more accurate in comprehension tend to show more rapid growth in words understood and produced as they approach age 2 (Fernald, Perfors, & Marchman, 2006). Quick comprehension frees space in working memory for picking up new words and for the more demanding task of using them to communicate.

telegraphic speech
Toddlers' two-word utterances that, like a telegram, omit smaller and less important words.

production In language development, the words and word combinations that children use.

comprehension In language development, the words and word combinations that children understand.

Individual and Cultural Differences

Each child's progress in acquiring language results from a complex blend of biological and environmental influences. For example, earlier we saw that Timmy's spoken language was delayed, in part because of Vanessa's tense, directive communication with him. But Timmy is also a boy, and many studies show that girls are slightly ahead of boys in early vocabulary growth (Fenson et al., 1994). The most common biological explanation is girls' faster rate of physical maturation, which is believed to promote earlier development of the left cerebral hemisphere. Temperament makes a difference, too. Shy toddlers often wait until they understand a great deal before trying to speak. When they finally do speak, their vocabularies increase rapidly, although they remain slightly behind their agemates (Spere et al., 2004).

The surrounding environment also plays a role: The more words caregivers use, the more children learn (Weizman & Snow, 2001). Mothers talk much more to toddler-age girls than to boys, and parents converse less often with shy than with sociable children (Leaper, Anderson, & Sanders, 1998; Patterson & Fisher, 2002). Low-SES children, who receive less verbal stimulation in their homes than higher-SES children, usually have smaller vocabularies (Hoff, 2003)—largely as a result of limited parent–child book reading. On average, a middle-SES child is read to for 1,000 hours between 1 and 5 years, a low-SES child for only 25 hours (Neuman, 2003). As a result, low-SES kindergartners have vocabularies only one-fourth as large as those of their higher-SES agemates (Lee & Burkam, 2002).

Young children have distinct styles of early language learning. Caitlin and Grace, like most toddlers, used a **referential style;** their vocabularies consisted mainly of words that referred to objects. A smaller number of toddlers use an **expressive style;** compared to referential children, they produce many more social formulas and pronouns ("stop it," "thank you," "I want it") uttered as compressed phrases that sound like single words ("Iwannit"). These styles reflect early ideas about the functions of language. Grace, for example, thought words were for naming things. In the week after her adoption, she uttered only a single word in Khmer, her native language. But after two months of listening to English conversation, Grace added words quickly: "Eli," then "doggie," "kitty," "Mama," "Dada," "book," "ball," "car," "cup," "clock," and "chicken"—all within one week. In contrast, expressive-style children believe words are for talking about people's feelings and needs. Referential-style children's vocabularies grow faster because all languages contain many more object labels than social phrases (Bates et al., 1994).

Why does a toddler use a particular language style? Rapidly developing referential-style children often have an especially active interest in exploring objects. They also eagerly imitate their parents' frequent naming of objects, and their parents imitate back—a strategy that supports swift vocabulary growth by helping children remember new labels (Masur & Rodemaker, 1999). Expressive-style children tend to be highly sociable, and their parents more often use verbal routines ("How are you?" "It's no trouble") that support social relationships (Goldfield, 1987). The two language styles are also linked to culture. Object words (nouns) are particularly common in the vocabularies of English-speaking toddlers, but among Chinese and Korean toddlers, words for actions (verbs) and social routines are more numerous. When mothers' speech is examined in each culture, it reflects this difference (Choi & Gopnik, 1995; Tardif, Gelman, & Xu, 1999).

When should parents become concerned if their child talks very little or not at all? If a toddler's development is greatly delayed when compared with the norms in Table 6.3, then parents should consult the child's doctor or a speech and language therapist. Late babbling may be a sign of slow language development calling for early intervention (Oller et al., 1999). Some toddlers who do not follow simple directions or who, after age 2, have difficulty putting their thoughts into words may suffer from a hearing impairment or a language disorder that requires immediate treatment.

Supporting Early Language Development

Consistent with the interactionist view, a rich social environment builds on young children's natural readiness to speak their native tongue. For a summary of how caregivers can consciously support early language learning, see Applying What We Know on the following page. Caregivers also do so unconsciously—through a special style of speech.

Culture influences early styles of language learning. This Chinese mother's conversation with her toddler probably includes many words for actions and social routines, so her child—like other Chinese children—is likely to display an expressive style, focused on strengthening social relationships.

referential style A style of early language learning in which toddlers use language mainly to label objects.

expressive style A style of early language learning in which toddlers use language mainly to talk about their own feelings and needs and those of other people, with an emphasis on social formulas and pronouns.

© DANITA DELIMONT/ALAMY

Applying What We Know

Supporting Early Language Learning

STRATEGY	CONSEQUENCE
Respond to coos and babbles with speech sounds and words.	Encourages experimentation with sounds that can later be blended into first words
	Provides experience with the turn-taking pattern of human conversation
Establish joint attention and comment on what child sees.	Predicts earlier onset of language and faster vocabulary development
Play social games, such as pat-a-cake and peekaboo.	Provides experience with the turn-taking pattern of human conversation
Engage toddlers in joint make-believe play.	Promotes all aspects of conversational dialogue
Engage toddlers in frequent conversations.	Predicts faster early language development and academic success during the school years
Read to toddlers often, engaging them in dialogues about picture books.	Provides exposure to many aspects of language, including vocabulary, grammar, communication skills, and information about written symbols and story structures

Adults in many countries speak to young children in **child-directed speech (CDS),** a form of language made up of short sentences with high-pitched, exaggerated expression, clear pronunciation, distinct pauses between speech segments, clear gestures to support verbal meaning, and repetition of new words in a variety of contexts ("See the ball." "The ball bounced!") (Fernald et al., 1989; O'Neill et al., 2005). Deaf parents use a similar style of communication when signing to their babies (Masataka, 1996). From birth on, infants prefer CDS over other kinds of adult talk, and by 5 months they are more emotionally responsive to it (Aslin, Jusczyk, & Pisoni, 1998).

CDS builds on several communicative strategies we have already considered: joint attention, turn-taking, and caregivers' sensitivity to toddlers' preverbal gestures. Here is an example of Carolyn using CDS with 18-month-old Caitlin as she picked her up from child care:

This mother speaks to her baby in short, clearly pronounced sentences with high-pitched, exaggerated intonation. The use of child-directed speech, common in many cultures, eases early language learning.

Caitlin:	"Go car."
Carolyn:	"Yes, time to go in the car. Where's your jacket?"
Caitlin:	[looks around, walks to the closet] "Dacket!" [*Points to her jacket.*]
Carolyn:	"There's that jacket! [*She helps Caitlin into the jacket.*] On it goes! Let's zip up. [*Zips up the jacket.*] Now, say bye-bye to Grace and Timmy."
Caitlin:	"Bye-bye, G-ace."
Carolyn:	"What about Timmy? Bye to Timmy?"
Caitlin:	"Bye-bye, Te-te."
Carolyn:	"Where's your bear?"
Caitlin:	[*Looks around.*]
Carolyn:	[*Pointing*] "See? Go get the bear. By the sofa." [*Caitlin gets the bear.*]

TAKE A MOMENT... Notice how Carolyn kept her utterance length just ahead of Caitlin's, creating a sensitive match between language stimulation and Caitlin's current capacities. Parents constantly fine-tune the length and content of their utterances in CDS to fit children's needs—adjustments that foster language learning and enable toddlers to join in (Cameron-Faulkner, Lieven, & Tomasello, 2003). As the Social Issues: Education box on page 246 makes clear, when a child's disability makes it difficult for parents to engage in the sensitive communication of CDS, language and cognitive development are drastically delayed.

As we saw earlier, parent–toddler conversation strongly predicts language development and later academic success. It provides many examples of speech just ahead of the child's current level and a sympathetic environment in which children can try out new skills. Dialogues about picture books are particularly effective. They expose children to great breadth of language and literacy knowledge, from vocabulary, grammar, and communication skills to information about written symbols and story structures. From the end of the first year through early childhood, children who experience regular adult–child book reading are substantially

child-directed speech (CDS) A form of language adults use to speak to young children, consisting of short sentences with high-pitched, exaggerated expression, clear pronunciation, distinct pauses between speech segments, clear gestures to support verbal meaning, and repetition of new words in a variety of contexts.

Social Issues: Education

Parent–Child Interaction: Impact on Language and Cognitive Development of Deaf Children

About one in every 1,000 North American infants is born profoundly or fully deaf (Deafness Research Foundation, 2005). When a deaf child cannot participate fully in communication with caregivers, development is severely compromised. Yet the consequences of deafness for children's language and cognition vary with social context, as revealed by comparing two groups of deaf children: those with hearing parents and those with deaf parents.

Over 90 percent of deaf children have hearing parents who are not fluent in sign language. In toddlerhood and early childhood, these children often are delayed in development of language and make-believe play. In middle childhood, many achieve poorly in school and are deficient in social skills. Deaf children of hearing parents frequently display impulse-control problems, as well (Arnold, 1999). Yet deaf children of deaf parents escape these difficulties! Their language (use of sign), play maturity, and impulse control are on a par with hearing children's. After school entry, deaf children of deaf parents learn easily and get along well with adults and peers (Bornstein et al., 1999b; Spencer & Lederberg, 1997).

These differences can be traced to early parent–child communication. Children with limited and less sensitive parental communication lag behind their agemates in achieving verbal control over their behavior—in thinking before they act and in planning. Beginning in infancy, hearing parents of deaf children are less positive, less responsive to the child's efforts to communicate, less effective at achieving joint attention and turn-taking, less involved in play, and more directive and intrusive (Spencer, 2000; Spencer & Meadow-Orlans, 1996). In contrast, the quality of interaction between deaf children and deaf parents resembles that of hearing children and hearing parents.

Hearing parents are not to blame for their deaf child's problems. Rather, they lack experience with visual communication, which enables deaf parents to respond readily to a deaf child's needs. Deaf parents know they must wait for the child to turn toward them before interacting (Loots & Devise, 2003). Hearing parents tend to speak or gesture while the child's attention is directed elsewhere—a strategy that works with a hearing but not with a deaf partner. When the child is confused or unresponsive, hearing parents often feel overwhelmed and become overly controlling (Jamieson, 1995).

The impact of deafness on language and cognitive development can best be understood by considering how it affects parents and other significant people in the child's life. Deaf children need access to language models—deaf adults and peers—to experience natural language learning. And their hearing parents benefit from social support along with training in how to interact sensitively with a nonhearing partner.

Screening techniques can identify deaf babies at birth. Many U.S. states, some Canadian provinces, and an increasing number of Western nations now require that every newborn be tested, enabling immediate enrollment in programs aimed at fostering effective parent–child interaction (Hearing Foundation of Canada, 2006). When children with profound hearing loss start to receive intervention within the first year of life, they show much better language, cognitive, and social development (Yoshinaga-Itano, 2003).

© DAVID YOUNG-WOLFF/PHOTOEDIT

When this mother signs "eat" to her 16-month-old child, who is deaf, he responds with babblelike hand motions, similar to the babbling that hearing infants do through speech. Babbling, whether spoken or signed, supports production of meaningful language.

ahead of their agemates in language skills (Karrass & Braungart-Rieker, 2005; Whitehurst & Lonigan, 1998).

Do social experiences that promote language development remind you of those that strengthen cognitive development in general? CDS and parent–child conversation create a *zone of proximal development* in which children's language expands. In contrast, impatience with and rejection of children's efforts to talk lead them to stop trying and result in immature language skills (Baumwell, Tamis-LeMonda, & Bornstein, 1997). In the next chapter we will see that sensitivity to children's needs and capacities supports their emotional and social development as well.

Ask Yourself

Review Why is the social interactionist perspective attractive to many investigators of language development? Cite evidence that supports it.

Apply Prepare a list of research-based recommendations on how to support language development during the first two years.

Connect Cognition and language are interrelated. List examples of how cognition fosters language development. Next, list examples of how language fosters cognitive development.

Reflect Find an opportunity to speak to an infant or toddler. How did your manner of speaking differ from the way you typically speak to an adult? What features of your speech are likely to promote early language development, and why?

Summary

Piaget's Cognitive-Developmental Theory

According to Piaget, how do schemes change over the course of development?

■ In Piaget's theory, by acting directly on the environment, children move through four stages in which psychological structures, or **schemes,** achieve a better fit with external reality.

■ Schemes change in two ways: through **adaptation,** which is made up of two complementary activities—**assimilation** and **accommodation;** and through **organization,** the internal rearrangement of schemes into a strongly interconnected cognitive system.

Describe the major cognitive achievements of the sensorimotor stage.

■ Piaget's **sensorimotor stage** is divided into six substages. Through the **circular reaction,** the newborn baby's reflexes gradually transform into the more flexible action patterns of the older infant. During Substage 4, infants develop **intentional,** or **goal-directed, behavior** and begin to understand **object permanence.** Substage 5 brings a more flexible, exploratory approach, and babies no longer make the **A-not-B search error.** In Substage 6, sensorimotor development culminates with **mental representation,** as shown by sudden solutions to sensorimotor problems, mastery of object permanence problems involving invisible displacement, **deferred imitation,** and **make-believe play.**

What does follow-up research say about the accuracy of Piaget's sensorimotor stage?

■ Many studies suggest that infants display a variety of understandings earlier than Piaget believed. Some awareness of object permanence, as revealed by the **violation-of-expectation method,** may be evident in the first few months, although searching for hidden objects is a true cognitive advance, as Piaget suggested. Recent studies of deferred imitation and problem solving also suggest that infants are capable of mental representation in the first year.

■ Today, researchers believe that newborns have more built-in equipment for making sense of their world than Piaget assumed. According to the **core knowledge perspective,** infants are born with a set of core domains of thought that support early, rapid cognitive development. Overall, however, findings on the existence of "prewired," ready-made knowledge are mixed, and critics reject the assumption that infants are endowed with knowledge.

■ Nevertheless, broad agreement exists on two issues. First, many cognitive changes of infancy are gradual and continuous rather than stagelike. Second, various aspects of cognition change unevenly, rather than in an integrated fashion.

Information Processing

Describe the information-processing view of cognitive development and the general structure of the information-processing system.

■ Rather than providing a single, unified theory, information-processing researchers study many aspects of thinking. They want to know exactly what individuals of different ages do when faced with a task or problem.

■ Most information-processing researchers assume that we hold information in three parts of the mental system, where **mental strategies** operate on and transform it so that it can be retained and used efficiently. Information enters the **sensory register,** is actively processed in **working,** or **short-term, memory,** and is permanently stored in **long-term memory.** The **central executive**—the conscious, reflective part of our mental system—is a special part of working memory that directs the flow of information.

What changes in attention, memory, and categorization take place over the first two years?

■ With age, infants attend to more aspects of the environment, take information in more quickly, and flexibly shift their attention from one stimulus to another. In the second year, attention to novelty declines and sustained attention improves, especially during play with toys.

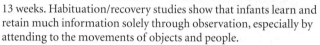

■ Retention of visual events increases dramatically over infancy and toddlerhood. By 6 months, babies have a memory span of two weeks for operant responses; by 18 months, this has increased to 13 weeks. Habituation/recovery studies show that infants learn and retain much information solely through observation, especially by attending to the movements of objects and people.

■ Young infants are capable of **recognition** memory, the simplest form of memory. By the end of the first year, they can also engage in **recall,** remembering without perceptual support. Between 1 and 2 years, recall of people, places, objects, and actions is excellent. Both brain development and social experience probably contribute to the decline of **infantile amnesia** and the emergence of **autobiographical memory.**

■ Infants group stimuli into increasingly complex categories, shifting from a perceptual to a conceptual basis of categorization in the second half of the first year. In the second year, toddlers become active categorizers, spontaneously sorting objects during their play. Babies' exploration of objects, expanding knowledge of the world, and advancing language skills foster categorization.

Describe the contributions and limitations of the information-processing approach to our understanding of early cognitive development.

■ Information-processing findings challenge Piaget's view of infants as purely sensorimotor beings who cannot mentally represent experiences. However, information processing has not yet provided a broad, comprehensive theory of children's thinking.

The Social Context of Early Cognitive Development

How does Vygotsky's concept of the zone of proximal development expand our understanding of early cognitive development?

■ According to Vygotsky's sociocultural theory, complex mental activities originate in social interaction. Through the support and guidance of more skilled partners, infants master tasks within the **zone of proximal development**—that is, tasks just ahead of their current capacities. As early as the first year, cultural variations in social experiences affect mental strategies.

Individual Differences in Early Mental Development

Describe the mental testing approach, the meaning of intelligence test scores, and the extent to which infant tests predict later performance.

■ The mental testing approach measures intellectual development in an effort to predict future performance. The **intelligence quotient,** or **IQ,** is a mental test score that compares an individual's performance with that of a **standardization** sample, whose performances form a **normal,** or bell-shaped, **distribution.** IQ is higher or lower, depending on how much the test-taker's performance deviates from the mean of the standardization sample.

■ Infant tests, which consist largely of perceptual and motor responses, predict later intelligence poorly. As a result, scores on infant tests are called **developmental quotients,** or **DQs,** rather than IQs. Speed of habituation and recovery to visual stimuli and object permanence are better predictors of future performance.

Discuss environmental influences on early mental development, including home, child care, and early intervention for at-risk infants and toddlers.

■ Research with the **Home Observation for Measurement of the Environment (HOME)** hows that an organized, stimulating home environment and parental affection, involvement, and encouragement of new skills repeatedly predict higher mental test scores. Although the HOME–IQ relationship is partly due to heredity, family living conditions also affect mental development.

■ The quality of infant and toddler child care influences cognitive and social skills. Standards for **developmentally appropriate practice** specify program characteristics that meet the developmental needs of young children.

■ Intensive early intervention can prevent the gradual declines in intelligence and the poor academic performance of poverty-stricken children. Findings of the Carolina Abecedarian Project reveal long-lasting advantages in IQ and achievement, which translated into higher educational attainment and skilled employment rates for treatment than control participants.

■ Early Head Start in the United States has led to warmer, more stimulating parenting, a reduction in harsh discipline, cognitive and language gains, and lessening of child aggression. Such programs, however, are not yet plentiful enough to meet the need.

Language Development

Describe three theories of language development, and indicate the emphasis each places on innate abilities and environmental influences.

■ According to the *behaviorist* perspective, parents train children in language skills through operant conditioning and imitation. Behaviorism has difficulty accounting for children's novel utterances.

■ Chomsky's *nativist* theory regards children as endowed with a **language acquisition device (LAD)** containing a universal grammar common to all languages. Consistent with this perspective, a complex language system is unique to humans.

■ Although language-related structures—**Broca's** and **Wernicke's areas**—exist in the left hemisphere of the cerebral cortex, their roles are more complex than previously assumed. But the broad association of left-hemispheric regions is consistent with Chomsky's notion of a brain prepared to process language. Evidence for a sensitive period for language development also supports this view.

■ Difficulty specifying the universal grammar that underlies the vast diversity among languages challenges the nativist perspective. Children's gradual, piecemeal learning of many constructions is also inconsistent with Chomsky's theory.

■ Recent theories suggest that language development results from *interactions* between inner capacities and environmental influences. Some interactionists apply the information-processing perspective to language development. Others emphasize the importance of children's social skills and language experiences.

Describe major milestones of language development in the first two years, individual differences, and ways adults can support infants' and toddlers' emerging capacities.

■ Infants begin **cooing** at 2 months and **babbling** around 6 months. At 10 to 11 months, babies' skill at establishing **joint attention**

improves, and by 12 months they actively engage in turn-taking games and use preverbal gestures. Adults can encourage language progress by responding to infants' coos and babbles, playing turn-taking games, establishing joint attention and labeling what babies see, and responding verbally to their preverbal gestures.

■ In the second half of the first year, infants begin to understand word meanings. Around 12 months, toddlers say their first word. Young children often make errors of **underextension** and **overextension.** Rate of word learning increases steadily, and once vocabulary reaches about 200 words, two-word utterances called **telegraphic speech** appear. At all ages, language **comprehension** develops ahead of **production.**

■ Individual differences in early language development exist. Girls show faster progress than boys, and reserved, cautious toddlers may wait before trying to speak. Low-SES children, who receive less verbal stimulation than higher-SES children, usually have smaller vocabularies.

■ Most toddlers use a **referential style** of language learning, in which early words consist largely of names for objects. A few use an **expressive style,** in which social formulas and pronouns are common and vocabulary grows more slowly.

■ Adults in many cultures speak to young children in **child-directed speech (CDS)**, a simplified form of language that is well suited to their learning needs. Conversation between parent and toddler is one of the best predictors of early language development and academic competence during the school years.

Important Terms and Concepts

accommodation (p. 208)
adaptation (p. 208)
A-not-B search error (p. 211)
assimilation (p. 208)
autobiographical memory (p. 224)
babbling (p. 240)
Broca's area (p. 237)
central executive (p. 221)
child-directed speech (CDS) (p. 245)
circular reaction (p. 209)
comprehension (p. 243)
cooing (p. 240)
core knowledge perspective (p. 217)
deferred imitation (p. 212)
developmental quotient, or DQ (p. 231)
developmentally appropriate practice (p. 233)

expressive style (p. 244)
Home Observation for Measurement of the
    Environment (HOME) (p. 231)
infantile amnesia (p. 224)
intelligence quotient, or IQ (p. 230)
intentional, or goal-directed, behavior
    (p. 210)
joint attention (p. 241)
language acquisition device (LAD) (p. 237)
long-term memory (p. 221)
make-believe play (p. 212)
mental representation (p. 211)
mental strategies (p. 220)
normal distribution (p. 230)
object permanence (p. 210)
organization (p. 208)

overextension (p. 242)
production (p. 243)
recall (p. 223)
recognition (p. 223)
referential style (p. 244)
scheme (p. 208)
sensorimotor stage (p. 208)
sensory register (p. 220)
standardization (p. 230)
telegraphic speech (p. 243)
underextension (p. 242)
violation-of-expectation method
    (p. 212)
Wernicke's area (p. 237)
working, or short-term, memory (p. 220)
zone of proximal development (p. 227)

Chapter 7

"Motherhood"
Nasr Abdulsemih Mahmud
12 years, Egypt

A mother serves as a soft nest of emotional closeness, protecting the baby from danger and supporting her mastery of a complex, colorful environment. The importance of parental love and sensitivity for infants' and toddlers' feelings of security and competence is a major theme of Chapter 7.

Reprinted with permission from the International Museum of Children's Art, Oslo, Norway

Emotional and Social Development in Infancy and Toddlerhood

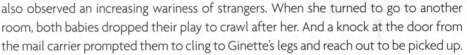

As Caitlin reached 8 months of age, her parents noticed that she had become more fearful. One evening, when Carolyn and David left her with a babysitter, she wailed when they headed for the door—an experience she had accepted easily a few weeks earlier. Caitlin and Timmy's caregiver Ginette also observed an increasing wariness of strangers. When she turned to go to another room, both babies dropped their play to crawl after her. And a knock at the door from the mail carrier prompted them to cling to Ginette's legs and reach out to be picked up.

At the same time, each baby seemed more willful. Removing an object from the hand produced little response at 5 months, but at 8 months Timmy resisted when his mother, Vanessa, took away a table knife he had managed to reach. He burst into angry screams and could not be consoled by the toys she offered in its place.

Monica and Kevin knew little about Grace's development during her first year, except that she had been deeply loved by her destitute, homeless mother. Separation from her, followed by a long journey to an unfamiliar home, had left Grace in shock. At first she was extremely sad, turning away when Monica or Kevin picked her up. She did not smile for over a week. But as Grace's new parents held her close, spoke gently, and satisfied her craving for food, Grace returned their affection. Two weeks after her arrival, her despondency gave way to a sunny, easygoing disposition. She burst into a wide grin, reached out at the sight of Monica and Kevin, and laughed at her brother Eli's funny faces. Among her first words were the names of family members—"Eli," "Mama," and "Dada." As her second birthday approached, she pointed to herself, exclaiming "Gwace!" and laid claim to treasured possessions. "Gwace's chicken!" she would announce at mealtimes, sucking the marrow from the drumstick, a practice she had brought with her from Cambodia.

Taken together, the children's reactions reflect two related aspects of personality that develop during the first two years: close ties to others and a sense of self. We begin with Erikson's psychosocial theory, which provides an overview of personality development during infancy and toddlerhood. Then, as we chart the course of emotional development, we will discover why fear and anger became more apparent in Caitlin's and Timmy's range of emotions by the end of the first year. Our attention then turns to individual differences in temperament. We will examine biological and environmental contributions to these differences and their consequences for future development.

251

Next, we take up attachment to the caregiver, the child's first affectionate tie. We will see how the feelings of security that grow out of this important bond support the child's exploration, sense of independence, and expanding social relationships.

Finally, we focus on early self-development. By the end of toddlerhood, Grace recognized herself in mirrors and photographs, labeled herself as a girl, and showed the beginnings of self-control. "Don't touch!" she instructed herself one day as she resisted the desire to pull a lamp cord out of its socket. Cognitive advances combine with social experiences to produce these changes during the second year.

Erikson's Theory of Infant and Toddler Personality

Our discussion of major theories in Chapter 1 revealed that psychoanalytic theory is no longer in the mainstream of child development research. But one of its lasting contributions is its ability to capture the essence of personality development during each period of development. Recall that Sigmund Freud, founder of the psychoanalytic movement, believed that psychological health and maladjustment could be traced to the early years—in particular, to the child's relationships with parents. Although Freud's preoccupation with the channeling of biological drives and his neglect of important experiences beyond infancy and early childhood came to be heavily criticized, the basic outlines of his theory were accepted and elaborated in several subsequent theories. The most influential is Erik Erikson's *psychosocial theory*, also introduced in Chapter 1.

Basic Trust versus Mistrust

Erikson accepted Freud's emphasis on the importance of feeding, but he expanded and enriched Freud's view. A healthy outcome during infancy, Erikson believed, does not depend on the *amount* of food or oral stimulation offered but rather on the *quality* of caregiving: relieving discomfort promptly and sensitively, holding the infant gently during feedings, waiting patiently until the baby has had enough milk, and weaning when the infant shows less interest in breast or bottle.

Erikson recognized that no parent can be perfectly in tune with the baby's needs. Many factors affect parental responsiveness—feelings of personal happiness, momentary life conditions (for example, additional young children in the family), and culturally valued child-rearing practices. But when the *balance of care* is sympathetic and loving, the psychological conflict of the first year—**basic trust versus mistrust**—is resolved on the positive side. The trusting infant expects the world to be good and gratifying, so he feels confident about venturing out and exploring it. The mistrustful baby cannot count on the kindness and compassion of others, so she protects herself by withdrawing from people and things around her.

Autonomy versus Shame and Doubt

With the transition to toddlerhood, Freud viewed the parent's manner of toilet training, in which children must bring their impulses in line with social requirements, as crucial for personality development. (Return to Chapter 5, pages 192–193, to review how adults can best support toddlers' attainment of bladder and bowel control.)

In Erikson's view, toilet training is only one of many important experiences. The familiar refrains of newly walking, talking toddlers—"No!" "Do it myself!"—reveal that they have entered a period of budding selfhood. They want to decide for themselves, not just in toileting but also in other situations. The conflict of toddlerhood, **autonomy versus shame and doubt,** is

basic trust versus mistrust In Erikson's theory, the psychological conflict of infancy, which is resolved positively when caregiving, especially during feeding, is sympathetic and loving.

autonomy versus shame and doubt In Erikson's theory, the psychological conflict of toddlerhood, which is resolved positively when parents provide young children with suitable guidance and reasonable choices.

resolved favorably when parents provide young children with suitable guidance and reasonable choices. A self-confident, secure 2-year-old has been encouraged not only to use the toilet but also to eat with a spoon and to help pick up his toys. His parents do not criticize or attack him when he fails at these new skills. And they meet his assertions of independence with tolerance and under-standing—for example, by giving him an extra five minutes to finish his play before leaving for the grocery store.

This toddler is intent on using a spoon to feed herself. Toddlers who are allowed to decide and do things for themselves in appropriate situations develop a sense of autonomy—the feeling of being able to control their bodies and act competently on their own.

© MICHAEL NEWMAN/PHOTOEDIT

According to Erikson, the parent who is over- or undercontrolling in toileting is likely to be so in other aspects of the toddler's life as well. The outcome is a child who feels forced and shamed and who doubts his ability to control his impulses and act competently on his own.

In sum, basic trust and autonomy grow out of warm, sensitive parent-ing and reasonable expectations for impulse control starting in the second year. If children emerge from the first few years without sufficient trust in caregivers and without a healthy sense of individuality, the seeds are sown for adjustment problems. Adults who have difficulty establishing intimate ties, who are overly dependent on a loved one, or who continually doubt their own ability to meet new challenges may not have fully mastered the tasks of trust and autonomy during infancy and toddlerhood.

Ask Yourself

Apply   Derek's mother fed him in a warm and loving manner during the first year. But when he became a toddler, she kept him in a playpen for many hours because he got into too much mischief while exploring freely. Use Erikson's theory to evaluate Derek's early experiences.

Connect   Do Erikson's recommendations for fostering autonomy in toddlerhood fit with Vygotsky's concept of the zone of proximal development, described on page 227 in Chapter 6? Explain.

Emotional Development

TAKE A MOMENT... Observe several infants and toddlers, noting the emotions each dis-plays, the cues you rely on to interpret the baby's emotional state, and how caregivers respond. Researchers have conducted many such observations to find out how effectively infants and toddlers convey their emotions and interpret those of others. They have discovered that emo-tions play powerful roles in organizing the attainments that Erikson regarded as so important: social relationships, exploration of the environment, and discovery of the self (Frijda, 2000; Halle, 2003; Saarni et al., 2006).

Think back to the *dynamic systems perspective* introduced in Chapters 1 and 5. As you read about early emotional development in the sections that follow, notice how emotions are an integral part of young children's dynamic systems of action. Emotions energize development. At the same time, they are an aspect of the system that develops, becoming more varied and complex as children reorganize their behavior to attain new goals (Campos, Frankel, & Camras, 2004; Witherington, Campos, & Hertenstein, 2001).

Because infants cannot describe their feelings, determining exactly which emotions they are experiencing is a challenge. Although vocalizations and body movements provide information,

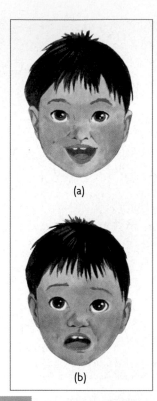

(a)

(b)

FIGURE 7.1

Which emotions are these babies displaying? The MAX (Maximally Discriminative Facial Movement) System is a widely used method for classifying infants' emotional expressions by determining the correspondence between facial muscle movements and basic feeling states. (a) Cheeks raised and corners of the mouth pulled back and up signal happiness. (b) Eyebrows raised, eyes widened, and mouth opened with corners pulled straight back denote fear. (From Izard, 1979.)

basic emotions Emotions such as happiness, interest, surprise, fear, anger, sadness, and disgust that are universal in humans and other primates and have a long evolutionary history of promoting survival.

researchers have relied most on facial expressions. Cross-cultural evidence reveals that people around the world associate photographs of different facial expressions with emotions in the same way (Ekman, 2003; Ekman & Friesen, 1972). These findings inspired researchers to analyze infants' facial patterns to determine the range of emotions they display at different ages. A commonly used method for doing so, the MAX System, is illustrated in Figure 7.1.

Nevertheless, assuming a close correspondence between a pattern of behavior and an underlying emotional state can lead to error. Infants, children, and adults use diverse responses to express a particular emotion. For example, babies on the visual cliff (see page 196 in Chapter 5) generally do not display a fearful facial expression, though they do show other clear signs of fear—drawing back and refusing to crawl over the deep side. Recall, also, from Chapter 5 that the emotional expressions of blind babies, who cannot make eye contact, are muted, prompting parents to withdraw (see page 198). When therapists show parents how blind infants express emotions through finger movements, parents become more interactive (Campos et al., 2006; Fraiberg, 1971). Furthermore, the same general response can express several emotions. For example, depending on the situation, a smile might be conveying joy, embarrassment, contempt, or a social greeting.

In line with the dynamic systems view, emotional expressions are *flexibly organized;* they vary with the person's developing capacities, goals, and context. To infer an emotion accurately, researchers must attend to multiple interacting cues—vocal, facial, gestural, and situational (Lewis, 2000). With these ideas in mind, let's chart the course of early emotional development.

Development of Basic Emotions

Basic emotions—happiness, interest, surprise, fear, anger, sadness, and disgust—are universal in humans and other primates and have a long evolutionary history of promoting survival. Do infants come into the world with the ability to express basic emotions? Although signs of some emotions are present, babies' earliest emotional life consists of little more than two global arousal states: attraction to pleasant stimulation and withdrawal from unpleasant stimulation. Only gradually do emotions become clear, well-organized signals (Camras et al., 2003; Fox, 1991).

The *dynamic systems perspective* helps us understand how this happens: Children coordinate separate skills into more effective, emotionally expressive systems as the central nervous system develops and the child's goals and experiences change. Videotaping the facial expressions of her daughter from 6 to 14 weeks, Linda Camras (1992) found that in the early weeks, the baby displayed a fleeting angry face as she was about to cry and a sad face as her crying waned. These expressions first appeared on the way to or away from full-blown distress and were not clearly linked to the baby's experiences and desires. With age, she was better able to sustain an angry signal when she encountered a blocked goal and a sad signal when she could not overcome an obstacle.

According to one view, sensitive, contingent caregiver communication, in which parents selectively mirror aspects of the baby's diffuse emotional behavior, helps infants construct emotional expressions that more closely resemble those of adults (Gergely & Watson, 1999). Around 6 months, face, gaze, voice, and posture form organized patterns that vary meaningfully with environmental events. For example, Caitlin typically responded to her parents' playful interaction with a joyful face, pleasant babbling, and a relaxed posture, as if to say, "This is fun!" In contrast, an unresponsive parent often evokes a sad face, fussy sounds, and a drooping body (sending the message, "I'm despondent") or an angry face, crying, and "pick-me-up" gestures (as if to say, "Change this unpleasant event!"). In sum, by the middle of the first year, emotional expressions are organized—and therefore able to tell us a great deal about the infant's internal state (Weinberg & Tronick, 1994; Yale et al., 1999).

We will begin by looking at four basic emotions—happiness, anger, sadness, and fear—that have received the most research attention. Later in the chapter, we will examine other emotions that develop in the first two years.

HAPPINESS ■ Happiness—expressed first in blissful smiles, later through exuberant laughter— contributes to many aspects of development. When infants achieve new skills, they smile and laugh, displaying delight in motor and cognitive mastery. The smile also encourages caregivers to be affectionate and stimulating, so the baby smiles even more (Aksan & Kochanska, 2004). Happiness binds parent and baby into a warm, supportive relationship that fosters the infant's developing competence.

During the early weeks, newborn babies smile when full, during sleep, and in response to gentle touches and sounds, such as stroking of the skin, rocking, and the mother's soft, high-pitched voice. By the end of the first month, infants start to smile at dynamic, eye-catching sights, such as a bright object jumping suddenly across their field of vision. And as infants attend to the parent's face, and the parent talks and smiles, babies knit their brows, open their mouths to coo, and move their arms and legs excitedly, gradually becoming more emotionally positive until, between 6 and 10 weeks, the parent's communication evokes a broad grin called the **social smile** (Lavelli & Fogel, 2005; Sroufe & Waters, 1976). Social smiling becomes better organized and stable as babies learn to use it to evoke and sustain pleasurable face-to-face interaction with the parent.

Laughter, which first occurs around 3 to 4 months, reflects faster processing of information than does smiling. But as with smiling, the first laughs occur in response to very active stimuli, such as the parent saying playfully, "I'm gonna get you!" and kissing the baby's tummy. As infants understand more about their world, they laugh at events with subtler elements of surprise. At 10 months, Timmy chuckled as Vanessa played a silent game of peekaboo. At 1 year, he laughed heartily as she crawled on all fours and then walked like a penguin (Sroufe & Wunsch, 1972).

Around the middle of the first year, infants smile and laugh more often when interacting with familiar people, a preference that strengthens the parent–child bond. Like adults, 10- to 12-month-olds have several smiles, which vary with context—a broad, "cheek-raised" smile in response to a parent's greeting; a reserved, muted smile for a friendly stranger; and a "mouth-open" smile during stimulating play (Bolzani et al., 2002; Dickson, Fogel, & Messinger, 1998). And at the end of the first year, the smile becomes a deliberate social signal. Between 8 and 10 months, infants more often interrupt their play with an interesting toy to relay their delight to an attentive adult (Venezia et al., 2004).

ANGER AND SADNESS ■ Newborn babies respond with generalized distress to a variety of unpleasant experiences, including hunger, painful medical procedures, changes in body temperature, and too much or too little stimulation (see Chapter 4). From 4 to 6 months into the second year, angry expressions increase in frequency and intensity. Older infants react with anger in a wider range of situations—when an object is taken away, an expected pleasant event does not occur, their arms are restrained, the caregiver leaves for a brief time, or they are put down for a nap (Camras et al., 1992; Stenberg & Campos, 1990; Sullivan & Lewis, 2003).

Why do angry reactions increase with age? As infants become capable of intentional behavior (see Chapter 6), they want to control their own actions and the effects they produce. Loss of *contingent control*—for example, when pulling on a string at first produces pleasant pictures and music but later is unrelated to these rewarding outcomes—evokes especially strong angry responses (Sullivan & Lewis, 2003). Older infants are also better at identifying who caused them pain or removed a toy. The rise in anger is also adaptive. New motor capacities enable an angry infant to defend herself or overcome an obstacle (Izard & Ackerman, 2000). Finally, anger motivates caregivers to relieve the infant's distress and, in the case of separation, may discourage them from leaving again soon.

Although expressions of sadness also occur in response to pain, removal of an object, and brief separations, they are less common than anger. In contrast, sadness occurs often when infants are deprived of a familiar, loving caregiver (as illustrated by Grace's despondency in the weeks after her adoption) and when parent–infant interaction is seriously disrupted. In several studies, researchers had parents assume either a still-faced, unreactive pose or a depressed emotional state. Their 2- to 7-month-olds tried facial expressions, vocalizations, and body movements to get their mother or father to respond again. When these efforts failed, they turned away, frowned, and cried (Hernandez & Carter, 1996; Moore, Cohn, & Campbell, 2001). The still-face reaction is identical among American, Canadian, and Chinese babies,

This Tibetan baby, snuggled in his father's robe, smiles with delight at onlookers. Infants' smiles and laughter encourage caregivers to respond in kind, binding parent and baby into a warm, supportive relationship that promotes all aspects of development.

social smile The smile evoked by the stimulus of the human face, which first appears between 6 and 10 weeks.

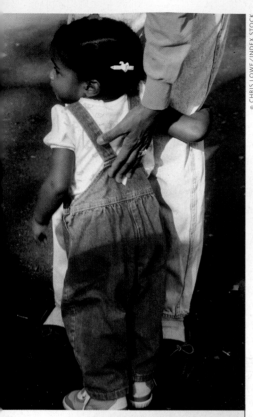

On an outing, this 1-year-old shows stranger anxiety, which increases during the second half of the first year. As infants move on their own, this rise in fear has adaptive value, increasing the chances that they will remain close to the parent and be protected from danger.

suggesting that it is a built-in withdrawal response to caregivers' lack of communication (Kisilevsky et al., 1998). Return to Chapter 4, page 160, and note that infants of depressed parents respond this way. When allowed to persist, a sad, vacant outlook disrupts all aspects of early development.

FEAR ■ Like anger, fear rises during the second half of the first year. Older infants hesitate before playing with a new toy, and newly crawling infants soon show fear of heights (see Chapter 5). But the most frequent expression of fear is to unfamiliar adults, a response called **stranger anxiety.** Many infants and toddlers are quite wary of strangers, although the reaction does not always occur. It depends on several factors: temperament (some babies are generally more fearful), past experiences with strangers, and the current situation (Thompson & Limber, 1991). When an unfamiliar adult picks up the infant in a new situation, stranger anxiety is likely. But if the adult sits still while the baby moves around and a parent is nearby, infants often show positive and curious behavior (Horner, 1980). The stranger's style of interaction—expressing warmth, holding out an attractive toy, playing a familiar game, and approaching slowly rather than abruptly—reduces the baby's fear.

Cross-cultural research reveals that infant-rearing practices can modify stranger anxiety. Among the Efe hunters and gatherers of Congo, West Africa, where the maternal death rate is high, infant survival is safeguarded by a collective caregiving system in which, starting at birth, Efe babies are passed from one adult to another. Consequently, Efe infants show little stranger anxiety (Tronick, Morelli, & Ivey, 1992). In contrast, in Israeli kibbutzim (cooperative agricultural settlements), living in an isolated community subject to terrorist attacks has led to widespread wariness of strangers. By the end of the first year, when infants look to others for cues about how to respond emotionally, kibbutz babies display far greater stranger anxiety than their city-reared counterparts (Saarni et al., 2006).

The rise in fear after 6 months of age keeps newly mobile babies' enthusiasm for exploration in check. Once wariness develops, infants use the familiar caregiver as a **secure base,** or point from which to explore, venturing into the environment and then returning for emotional support. As part of this adaptive system, encounters with strangers lead to conflicting tendencies: approach (indicated by interest and friendliness) and avoidance (indicated by fear). The infant's behavior is a balance between the two.

Eventually, as cognitive development permits toddlers to discriminate more effectively between threatening and nonthreatening people and situations, stranger anxiety and other fears of the first two years decline. This change is adaptive, since adults other than caregivers will be soon be important in children's development. Fear also wanes as children acquire a wider array of strategies for coping with it, as you will see when we discuss emotional self-regulation.

Understanding and Responding to the Emotions of Others

Infants' emotional expressions are closely tied to their ability to interpret the emotional cues of others. We have seen that in the first few months, babies match the feeling tone of the caregiver in face-to-face communication. Some researchers claim that young babies respond in kind to others' emotions through a built-in, automatic process of *emotional contagion* (Stern, 1985). Others, however, believe that infants acquire these emotional contingencies through operant conditioning—for example, by learning that a smile generally triggers caregiver responsiveness and that distress can prompt a diverted caregiver to renew her attentiveness and offer comfort (Saarni et al., 2006).

Around 3 to 4 months, infants have become sensitive to the structure and timing of face-to-face interactions (see Chapter 6, page 241). When they gaze, smile, or vocalize, they expect their social partner to respond in kind (Rochat, Striano, & Blatt, 2002). Within these exchanges, babies become increasingly aware of the range of emotional expressions (Montague & Walker-Andrews, 2001).

stranger anxiety Expression of fear in response to unfamiliar adults, which appears in many babies in the second half of the first year.

secure base Role of the familiar caregiver as a point from which the infant explores the environment, returning for emotional support.

From 5 months on, infants perceive facial expressions as organized patterns (see Chapter 5). Responding to emotional expressions as organized wholes indicates that these signals are becoming meaningful to babies. As skill at establishing joint attention improves (see Chapter 6), infants realize that an emotional expression not only has meaning but is also a meaningful reaction to a specific object or event (Moses et al., 2001; Tomasello, 1999a).

Once these understandings are in place, infants engage in **social referencing**—actively seeking emotional information from a trusted person in an uncertain situation. Beginning at 8 to 10 months, when infants start to evaluate unfamiliar people, objects, and events in terms of their safety and security, social referencing occurs often (Mumme et al., 2006). Many studies show that a caregiver's emotional expression (happy, angry, or fearful) influences whether a 1-year-old will be wary of strangers, play with an unfamiliar toy, or cross the deep side of the visual cliff (Repacholi, 1998; Stenberg, 2003; Striano & Rochat, 2000). The caregiver's voice— either alone or combined with a facial expression—is more effective than a facial expression alone (Mumme, Fernald, & Herrera, 1996; Vaish & Striano, 2004). The voice conveys both emotional and verbal information, and the baby need not turn toward the adult but, instead, can focus on evaluating the novel event. As recall memory and language skills improve, and as parents' warnings to their newly walking youngsters become more frequent and intense, babies retain these emotional messages over longer time intervals. At 11 months, they respond appropriately after a delay of a few minutes, at 14 months after a delay of an hour or more (Hertenstein & Campos, 2004).

Parents can take advantage of social referencing to teach their baby how to react to many everyday events. And around the middle of the second year, as toddlers begin to appreciate that others' emotional reactions may differ from their own, social referencing allows them to compare their own and others' assessments of events. In one study, an adult showed 14- and 18-month-olds broccoli and crackers. In one condition, she acted delighted with the taste of broccoli but disgusted with the taste of crackers. In the other condition, she showed the reverse preference. When asked to share the food, 14-month-olds offered only the type of food they themselves preferred—usually crackers. In contrast, 18-month-olds gave the adult whichever food she appeared to like, regardless of their own preferences (Repacholi & Gopnik, 1997).

In sum, social referencing helps toddlers move beyond simply reacting to others' emotional messages. They use those signals to guide their own actions and to find out about others' intentions, preferences, and desires. These experiences, along with cognitive and language development, help toddlers refine the meanings of emotions of the same valence—for example, happiness versus surprise, anger versus fear—during the second year (Saarni et al., 2006).

Emergence of Self-Conscious Emotions

Besides basic emotions, humans are capable of a second, higher-order set of feelings, including shame, embarrassment, guilt, envy, and pride. These are called **self-conscious emotions** because each involves injury to or enhancement of our sense of self. For example, when we are ashamed or embarrassed, we feel negatively about our behavior, and we want to retreat so that others will no longer notice our failings. We feel guilt when we know that we have harmed someone and want to relieve the other's suffering and repair the relationship. In contrast, pride reflects delight in the self's achievements, and we are inclined to tell others what we have accomplished and to take on further challenges (Saarni et al., 2006).

Self-conscious emotions appear in the middle of the second year, as 18- to 24-month-olds become firmly aware of the self as a separate, unique individual. Toddlers show shame and embarrassment by lowering their eyes, hanging their heads, and hiding their faces with their hands. They show guiltlike reactions, too. After noticing Grace's unhappiness, 22-month-old Caitlin returned a toy she had grabbed and patted her upset playmate. Pride also emerges around this time, and envy by age 3 (Barrett, 2005; Garner, 2003; Lewis et al., 1989). Besides self-awareness, self-conscious emotions require an additional ingredient: adult instruction in *when* to feel proud, ashamed, or guilty. Parents begin this tutoring early when they say, "Look how far you can throw that ball!" or "You should feel ashamed for grabbing that toy!"

social referencing Active seeking of emotional information from a trusted person in deciding how to respond in an uncertain situation.

self-conscious emotions Emotions such as shame, embarrassment, guilt, envy, and pride that involve injury to or enhancement of the sense of self.

This beaming toddler clearly feels a sense of pride at her artistic accomplishment. Pride and other self-conscious emotions appear in the middle of the second year as children become firmly aware of the self as a separate, unique individual.

Self-conscious emotions play important roles in children's achievement-related and moral behaviors. The situations in which adults encourage these feelings vary from culture to culture. In Western individualistic nations, most children are taught to feel pride over personal achievement—throwing a ball the farthest, winning a game, and (later on) getting good grades. In collectivist cultures such as China and Japan, calling attention to purely personal success evokes embarrassment and self-effacement. And violating cultural standards by failing to show concern for others—a parent, a teacher, or an employer—sparks intense shame (Akimoto & Sanbinmatsu, 1999; Lewis, 1992).

Beginnings of Emotional Self-Regulation

Besides expressing a wider range of emotions, infants and toddlers begin to manage their emotional experiences. **Emotional self-regulation** refers to the strategies we use to adjust our emotional state to a comfortable level of intensity so we can accomplish our goals (Eisenberg & Morris, 2002; Eisenberg & Spinrad, 2004). When you remind yourself that an anxiety-provoking event will be over soon or decide not to see a scary horror film, you are engaging in emotional self-regulation.

Emotional self-regulation requires voluntary, effortful management of emotions. This capacity for *effortful control* improves gradually, as the result of development of the cerebral cortex and the assistance of caregivers, who help children manage intense emotion and teach them strategies for doing so (Fox & Calkins, 2003; Rothbart, Posner, & Kieras, 2006). Individual differences in control of emotion are evident in infancy and, by early childhood, play such a vital role in children's adjustment that—as we will see later—effortful control is regarded as a major dimension of temperament. A good start in regulating emotion during the first two years contributes greatly to autonomy and mastery of cognitive and social skills. Poorly regulated toddlers, by contrast, are likely to be delayed in mental development and to have behavior problems in the preschool years and are at risk for long-lasting problems (Eisenberg et al., 2004b; Lawson & Ruff, 2004).

In the early months, infants have only a limited capacity to regulate their emotional states; when their feelings get too intense, they are easily overwhelmed. They depend on the soothing interventions of caregivers for distraction and reorienting of attention—being lifted to the shoulder, rocked, gently stroked, and talked to softly.

Rapid development of the frontal lobes of the cerebral cortex increases the baby's tolerance for stimulation. Between 2 and 4 months, caregivers build on this capacity by initiating face-to-face play and attention to objects. In these interactions, parents arouse pleasure in the baby while adjusting the pace of their own behavior so the infant does not become overwhelmed and distressed. As a result, the baby's tolerance for stimulation increases further (Kopp & Neufeld, 2003).

By 4 to 6 months, the ability to shift attention and to engage in self-soothing help infants control emotion. When faced with a highly stimulating novel event (a toy fire truck with siren blaring and lights flashing), babies who more readily turn away or suck their fingers are less prone to distress (Axia, Bonichini, & Benini, 1999; Crockenberg & Leerkes, 2005). At the end of the first year, crawling and walking enable infants to regulate emotion more effectively by approaching or retreating from various situations. And further gains in attention permit toddlers to sustain interest in their surroundings and in play activities for a longer time (Rothbart & Bates, 2006).

As caregivers help infants regulate their emotional states, they contribute to the child's style of emotional self-regulation. Infants whose parents read and respond contingently and sympathetically to their emotional cues tend to be less fussy, to express more pleasurable emotion, to be more interested in exploration, and to be easier to soothe (Crockenberg & Leerkes, 2004; Eisenberg, Cumberland, & Spinrad, 1998; Volling et al., 2002). In contrast, parents who respond impatiently or angrily or wait to intervene until the infant has become extremely agitated reinforce the baby's rapid rise to intense distress. This makes it harder for

emotional self-regulation Strategies for adjusting our emotional state to a comfortable level of intensity so we can accomplish our goals.

parents to soothe the baby in the future—and for the baby to learn to calm herself. When caregivers fail to regulate stressful experiences for infants who cannot yet regulate them for themselves, brain structures that buffer stress may fail to develop properly, resulting in an anxious, reactive child with a reduced capacity for regulating emotion (Crockenberg & Leerkes, 2000; Little & Carter, 2005).

Caregivers also provide lessons in socially approved ways of expressing feelings. Beginning in the first few months, parents encourage infants to suppress negative emotion by often imitating their expressions of interest, happiness, and surprise and rarely imitating their expressions of anger and sadness. Infant boys get more of this training than infant girls, in part because they have a harder time regulating negative emotion (Else-Quest et al., 2006; Malatesta et al., 1986). As a result, the well-known sex difference—females as emotionally expressive and males as emotionally controlled—is promoted at a tender age. Furthermore, collectivist cultures usually emphasize socially appropriate emotional behavior. Compared with North Americans, Chinese and Japanese adults more often discourage the expression of strong emotion in babies (Fogel, 1993; Kuchner, 1989). By the end of the first year, Chinese and Japanese infants smile and cry less than American babies (Camras et al., 1998).

Compared with North Americans, Chinese and Japanese adults discourage the expression of strong emotion in infants. The calm demeanor of this baby in Beijing, China, is typical of Chinese and Japanese infants, who, by the end of the first year, smile and cry less than American babies.

In the second year, growth in representation and language leads to new ways of regulating emotions. A vocabulary for talking about feelings—"happy," "love," "surprised," "scary," "yucky," "mad"—develops rapidly after 18 months (Dunn, Bretherton, & Munn, 1987). Toddlers are not yet good at using language to comfort themselves (Grolnick, Bridges, & Connell, 1996). But once they can describe their internal states, they can guide caregivers in helping them. For example, while listening to a story about monsters, Grace whimpered, "Mommy, scary." Monica put the book down and gave Grace a comforting hug.

Older toddlers' use of words to label a wide array of emotions shows that they have a remarkable understanding of themselves and others as emotional beings. The more parents label and talk about mental states in the second year, the greater their 2-year-olds' emotion vocabulary and ability to identify how others feel from situational cues (for example, a cartoon of child being chased by a lion) (Taumoepeau & Ruffman, 2006). As we will see in later chapters, with the ability to think about feelings, emotional self-regulation improves greatly in early and middle childhood.

Ask Yourself

Review   Why do many infants show stranger anxiety in the second half of the first year? What factors can increase or decrease wariness of strangers?

Apply   At 14 months, Reggi built a block tower and gleefully knocked it down. But at age 2, he called to his mother and pointed proudly at his tall block tower. What explains this change in Reggie's emotional behavior?

Connect   Why do children of depressed parents have difficulty regulating emotion (see page 160)? What implications do their weak self-regulatory skills have for their response to cognitive and social challenges?

Reflect   Describe several recent events in your own life that required you to manage negative emotion. How did you react in each case? How might your early experiences, gender, and cultural background have influenced your style of emotional self-regulation?

Development of Temperament

From early infancy, Caitlin, Grace, and Timmy showed unique patterns of emotional responding. Caitlin's sociability was unmistakable to everyone who met her. She smiled and laughed while interacting with adults and, in her second year, readily approached other children. Meanwhile, Monica marveled at Grace's calm, relaxed disposition. At 19 months, she sat contentedly in her high chair through a two-hour family celebration at a restaurant. In contrast, Timmy was active and distractible. Vanessa found herself chasing him as he dropped one toy, moved on to the next, and climbed on chairs and tables.

When we describe one person as "upbeat," another as active and energetic, and still others as calm, cautious, or prone to angry outbursts, we are referring to **temperament**—early-appearing, stable individual differences in reactivity and self-regulation. *Reactivity* refers to quickness and intensity of emotional arousal, attention, and motor activity. *Self-regulation,* as we have seen, refers to strategies that modify that reactivity (Rothbart & Bates, 2006). Researchers have become increasingly interested in temperamental differences among children because the psychological traits that make up temperament are believed to form the cornerstone of the adult personality.

In 1956, Alexander Thomas and Stella Chess initiated the New York Longitudinal Study, a groundbreaking investigation of the development of temperament that followed 141 children from early infancy well into adulthood. Results showed that temperament increases a child's chances of experiencing psychological problems or, alternatively, may protect a child from the negative effects of a stressful home life. However, Thomas and Chess (1977) also found that parenting practices can modify children's emotional styles considerably.

These findings stimulated a growing body of research on temperament, including its stability, biological roots, and interaction with child-rearing experiences. Let's begin to explore these issues by looking at the structure, or makeup, of temperament and how it is measured.

The Structure of Temperament

Thomas and Chess's nine dimensions, listed in Table 7.1 on page 261, served as the first influential model of temperament. When detailed descriptions of infants' and children's behavior obtained from parental interviews were rated on these dimensions, certain characteristics clustered together, yielding three types of children:

- The **easy child** (40 percent of the sample) quickly establishes regular routines in infancy, is generally cheerful, and adapts easily to new experiences.
- The **difficult child** (10 percent of the sample) is irregular in daily routines, is slow to accept new experiences, and tends to react negatively and intensely.
- The **slow-to-warm-up child** (15 percent of the sample) is inactive; shows mild, low-key reactions to environmental stimuli; is negative in mood; and adjusts slowly to new experiences.

Note that 35 percent of the children did not fit any of these categories. Instead, they showed unique blends of temperamental characteristics.

The "difficult" pattern has sparked the most interest because it places children at high risk for adjustment problems—both anxious withdrawal and aggressive behavior in early and middle childhood (Bates, Wachs, & Emde, 1994; Ramos et al., 2005; Thomas, Chess, & Birch, 1968). Compared with difficult children, slow-to-warm-up children present fewer problems in the early years. However, they tend to show excessive fearfulness and slow, constricted behavior in the late preschool and school years, when they are expected to respond actively and quickly in classrooms and peer groups (Chess & Thomas, 1984; Schmitz et al., 1999).

Table 7.1 also shows a second model of temperament, developed by Mary Rothbart, which combines overlapping dimensions of Thomas and Chess and other researchers. For example, "distractibility" and "attention span and persistence" are considered opposite ends of the same

temperament Early-appearing, stable individual differences in the quality and intensity of emotional reaction, activity level, attention, and emotional self-regulation.

easy child A child whose temperament is characterized by establishment of regular routines in infancy, general cheerfulness, and easy adaptation to new experiences.

difficult child A child whose temperament is characterized by irregular daily routines, slow acceptance of new experiences, and a tendency to react negatively and intensely.

slow-to-warm-up child A child whose temperament is characterized by inactivity; mild, low-key reactions to environmental stimuli; negative mood; and slow adjustment to new experiences.

effortful control The self-regulatory dimension of temperament, involving voluntary suppression of a dominant, reactive response in order to plan and execute a more adaptive response.

dimension, which is labeled "attention span/persistence." This model also includes a dimension not identified by Thomas and Chess, "irritable distress," which permits reactivity triggered by frustration to be distinguished from reactivity due to fear. And it deletes overly broad dimensions, such as "rhythmicity," "intensity of reaction," and "threshold of responsiveness" (Rothbart, Ahadi, & Evans, 2000; Rothbart & Mauro, 1990). A child who is rhythmic in sleeping is not necessarily rhythmic in eating or bowel habits. And a child who smiles and laughs quickly and intensely is not necessarily quick and intense in fear, irritability, or motor activity.

Notice how Rothbart's dimensions represent the three underlying components included in the definition of temperament: (1) emotion ("fearful distress," "irritable distress," "positive affect," and "soothability"), (2) attention ("attention span/persistence"), and (3) action ("activity level"). According to Rothbart, individuals differ not just in their reactivity on each dimension but also in their effortful capacity to manage that reactivity. **Effortful control,** the self-regulatory dimension of temperament, involves voluntarily suppressing a dominant, reactive response in order to plan and execute a more adaptive response (Rothbart, 2003; Rothbart & Bates, 2006). Variations in effortful control are evident in how effectively a child can focus and shift attention, inhibit impulses, and manage negative emotion.

This child reacts negatively and intensely to a new situation—his mother's request for help carrying the clean laundry. Patient, supportive parenting can help him modify his biologically based temperament and become better at managing his reactivity to new stimuli.

TABLE 7.1   Two Models of Temperament

THOMAS AND CHESS		ROTHBART	
Dimension	**Description**	**Dimension**	**Description**
Activity level	Ratio of active periods to inactive ones	***Reactivity***	
Rhythmicity	Regularity of body functions, such as sleep, wakefulness, hunger, and excretion	Activity level	Level of gross motor activity
		Attention span/persistence	Duration of orienting or interest
Distractibility	Degree to which stimulation from the environment alters behavior—for example, whether crying stops when a toy is offered	Fearful distress	Wariness and distress in response to intense or novel stimuli, including time to adjust to new situations
Approach/withdrawal	Response to a new object, food, or person	Irritable distress	Extent of fussing, crying, and distress when desires are frustrated
Adaptability	Ease with which child adapts to changes in the environment, such as sleeping or eating in a new place	Positive affect	Frequency of expression of happiness and pleasure
Attention span and persistence	Amount of time devoted to an activity, such as watching a mobile or playing with a toy	***Self-regulation***	
Intensity of reaction	Energy level of response, such as laughing, crying, talking, or gross motor activity	Effortful control	Capacity to voluntarily suppress a dominant, reactive response in order to plan and execute a more adaptive response
Threshold of responsiveness	Intensity of stimulation required to evoke a response		
Quality of mood	Amount of friendly, joyful behavior as opposed to unpleasant, unfriendly behavior		

Sources: Left: Thomas & Chess, 1977. Right: Rothbart, Ahadi, & Evans, 2000; Rothbart & Mauro, 1990.

Measuring Temperament

Temperament is often assessed through interviews or questionnaires given to parents, as well as behavior ratings by pediatricians, teachers, and others familiar with the child and direct observations by researchers. Parental reports are convenient and take advantage of parents' depth of knowledge of the child across many situations (Gartstein & Rothbart, 2003). But information from parents has been criticized as being biased. Parents' prebirth expectations for their infant's temperament affect their later reports (Diener, Goldstein, & Mangelsdorf, 1995). And mothers who are anxious and depressed tend to view their babies as more difficult (Forman et al., 2003). Nevertheless, parental reports are moderately related to researchers' observations of children's behavior (Mangelsdorf, Schoppe, & Buur, 2000). And parent perceptions are vital for understanding how parents view and respond to their child.

Although observations by researchers in the home or laboratory avoid the subjectivity of parent reports, they can lead to other inaccuracies. In homes, observers find it hard to capture all relevant information, especially events that are rare but important, such as infants' response to frustration. And in the unfamiliar lab setting, distress-prone children may become too upset to complete the session (Wachs & Bates, 2001). Still, researchers can better control the study of temperament in the lab. And they can conveniently combine observations of behavior with physiological measures to gain insight into the biological basis of temperament.

Most physiological assessments have focused on children who fall at opposite extremes of the positive-affect and fearful-distress dimensions of temperament (refer again to Table 7.1): **inhibited,** or **shy, children,** who react negatively to and withdraw from novel stimuli, and on **uninhibited,** or **sociable, children,** who display positive emotion and approach novel stimuli. As the Biology and Environment box on the following page reveals, biologically based reactivity—evident in heart rate, hormone levels, and EEG brain waves in the frontal region of the cerebral cortex—differentiate children with inhibited and uninhibited temperaments.

Stability of Temperament

Young children who score low or high on attention span, irritability, sociability, shyness, or effortful control tend to respond similarly when assessed again a few years later and, occasionally, even into the adult years (Caspi et al., 2003; Kochanska & Knaack, 2003; Pedlow et al., 1993; Rothbart, Ahadi, & Evans, 2000; Ruff & Rothbart, 1996). However, the overall stability of temperament is low in infancy and toddlerhood and only moderate from the preschool years on (Putnam, Samson, & Rothbart, 2000). Some children remain the same, but many others change.

Why isn't temperament more stable? A major reason is that temperament itself develops with age. To illustrate, let's look at irritability and activity level. Recall from Chapter 4 that most babies fuss and cry in the early months. But as infants better regulate their attention and emotions, many who initially seemed irritable become calm and content. In the case of activity level, the meaning of the behavior changes. At first, an active, wriggling infant tends to be highly aroused and uncomfortable, whereas an inactive baby is often alert and attentive. But as infants move on their own, the reverse is so! An active crawler is usually alert and interested in exploration, whereas a very inactive baby might be fearful and withdrawn.

These inconsistencies help us understand why long-term prediction from early temperament is best achieved after age 3, when the child's system of emotion, attention, and action is better established (Roberts & DelVecchio, 2000). In line with this idea, between 2½ and 3, children perform more consistently across a wide range of tasks requiring effortful control, such as waiting for a reward, lowering their voice to a whisper, succeeding at games like "Simon Says," and selectively attending to one stimulus while ignoring competing stimuli. Researchers believe that around this time, areas in the frontal lobes involved in suppressing impulses develop rapidly (Gerardi-Caulton, 2000; Rothbart & Bates, 2006). Beginning in the preschool years, effortful control predicts children's cognitive and social competence (Rothbart, Posner, & Kieras, 2006).

inhibited, or **shy, child**
A child who tends to react negatively to and withdraw from novel stimuli.

uninhibited, or **sociable, child** A child who tends to display positive emotion and to approach novel stimuli.

Biology and Environment

Development of Shyness and Sociability

Two 4-month-old babies, Larry and Mitch, visited the laboratory of Jerome Kagan, who observed their reactions to a variety of unfamiliar experiences. When exposed to new sights and sounds, such as a moving mobile decorated with colorful toys, Larry tensed his muscles, moved his arms and legs with agitation, and began to cry. In contrast, Mitch remained relaxed and quiet, smiling and cooing at the excitement around him.

As toddlers, Larry and Mitch returned to the laboratory. This time, each experienced a variety of procedures designed to induce uncertainty. Electrodes were placed on their bodies and blood pressure cuffs on their arms to measure heart rate; toy robots, animals, and puppets moved before their eyes; and unfamiliar people entered and behaved in unexpected ways or wore novel costumes. While Larry whimpered and quickly withdrew, Mitch watched with interest, laughed at the strange sights, and approached the toys and strangers.

On a third visit, at age 4½, Larry barely talked or smiled during an interview with an unfamiliar adult. In contrast, Mitch asked questions and communicated his pleasure at each intriguing activity. In a playroom with two unfamiliar peers, Larry pulled back, while Mitch made friends quickly.

In longitudinal research on several hundred Caucasian children, Kagan found that about 20 percent of 4-month-old babies were, like Larry, easily upset by novelty; 40 percent, like Mitch, were comfortable, even delighted, with new experiences. About 20 to 30 percent of these extreme groups retained their temperamental styles as they grew older (Kagan, 2003; Kagan & Saudino, 2001). But most children's dispositions became less extreme over time. Biological makeup and child-rearing experiences jointly influenced stability and change in temperament.

Physiological Correlates of Shyness and Sociability

Kagan believes that individual differences in arousal of the *amygdala*, an inner brain structure that controls avoidance reactions, contribute to these contrasting temperaments. In shy, inhibited children, novel stimuli easily excite the amygdala and its connections to the cerebral cortex and sympathetic nervous system, which prepares the body to act in the face of threat. In sociable, uninhibited children, the same level of stimulation evokes minimal neural excitation (Kagan & Fox, 2006). In support of this theory, while viewing photos of unfamiliar faces, adults who had been classified as inhibited in the second year of life showed greater fMRI activity in the amygdala than adults who had been uninhibited as toddlers (Schwartz et al., 2003). And the two emotional styles are distinguished by additional physiological responses that are known to be mediated by the amygdala:

- *Heart rate.* From the first few weeks of life, the heart rates of shy children are consistently higher than those of sociable children, and they speed up further in response to unfamiliar events (Snidman et al., 1995).
- *Cortisol.* Saliva concentration of cortisol, a hormone that regulates blood pressure and is involved in resistance to stress, tends to be higher in shy than in sociable children (Gunnar & Nelson, 1994).
- *Pupil dilation, blood pressure, and skin surface temperature.* Compared with sociable children, shy children show greater pupil dilation, rise in blood pressure, and cooling of the fingertips when faced with novelty (Kagan et al., 1999).

Another physiological correlate of approach–withdrawal to people and objects is the pattern of EEG brain waves in the frontal lobes of the cerebral cortex. Shy infants and preschoolers show greater EEG activity in the right frontal lobe, which is associated with negative emotional reactivity; sociable children show the opposite pattern (Kagan & Snidman, 2004). Neural activity in the amygdala, which is transmitted to the frontal lobes, contributes to these differences. Inhibited children also show greater generalized activation of the cerebral cortex, an indicator of high emotional arousal and monitoring of new situations for potential threats (Henderson et al., 2004).

Child-Rearing Practices

According to Kagan, extremely shy or sociable children inherit a physiology that biases them toward a particular temperamental style. Yet heritability research indicates that genes contribute only modestly to shyness and sociability (Kagan & Fox, 2006). Experience has a profound impact.

Child-rearing practices affect the chances that an emotionally reactive baby will become a fearful child. Warm, supportive parenting reduces shy infants' and preschoolers' intense physiological reaction to novelty, whereas cold, intrusive parenting heightens anxiety (Rubin, Burgess, & Hastings, 2002). And if parents protect infants who dislike novelty from minor stresses, they make it harder for the child to overcome an urge to retreat. Parents who make appropriate demands for their baby to approach new experiences help the child overcome fear (Rubin et al., 1997).

When inhibition persists, it leads to excessive cautiousness, low self-esteem, and loneliness (Fordham & Stevenson-Hinde, 1999; Rubin, Stewart, & Coplan, 1995). In adolescence, persistent shyness increases the risk of severe anxiety, especially social phobia—intense fear of being humiliated in social situations (Kagan & Fox, 2006). For inhibited children to acquire effective social skills, parenting must be tailored to their temperaments—a theme we will encounter again in this and later chapters.

A strong physiological response to uncertain situations prompts this child to cling to her father. With patient but insistent encouragement, he can modify her reactivity and help her overcome her urge to retreat from unfamiliar events.

Other findings demonstrate that child rearing plays an important role in modifying biologically based temperamental traits. Toddlers and young preschoolers who have fearful or negative, irritable temperaments but experience patient, supportive parenting are better at managing their reactivity and are especially likely to decline in difficultness (Warren & Simmens, 2005).

From the evidence as a whole, we see that many factors affect the extent to which a temperamental style persists, including development of the biological systems on which temperament is based, the child's capacity for effortful control, and rearing experiences. However, children's temperaments rarely change from one extreme to the other: Shy toddlers seldom become highly sociable, and irritable toddlers seldom become easy-going. With these ideas in mind, let's turn to genetic and environmental contributions to temperament and personality.

Genetic Influences

The word *temperament* implies a genetic foundation for individual differences in personality. Research indicates that identical twins are more similar than fraternal twins across a wide range of temperamental traits (activity level, attention span, shyness/sociability, irritability, and effortful control) and personality measures (introversion/extroversion, anxiety, agreeableness, curiosity and imaginativeness, and impulsivity) (Bouchard, 2004; Bouchard & Loehlin, 2001; Caspi & Shiner, 2006; Saudino & Cherny, 2001). In Chapter 2, we noted that heritability estimates derived from twin studies suggest a moderate role for genetic factors in temperament and personality: About half of individual differences have been attributed to differences in genetic makeup.

Consistent ethnic and sex differences in early temperament exist, again implying a role for heredity. Compared with North American Caucasian infants, Asian babies tend to be less active, irritable, and vocal, more easily soothed when upset, and better at quieting themselves (Kagan et al., 1994; Lewis, Ramsay, & Kawakami, 1993). Grace's capacity to remain contentedly seated in her high chair through a long family dinner certainly fits with this evidence.

And Timmy's high rate of activity illustrates a typical sex difference (Gartstein & Rothbart, 2003). From an early age, boys are more active and daring, more irritable when frustrated, more often express high-intensity pleasure in play, and are slightly more impulsive than girls—all factors that contribute to boys' higher injury rates throughout childhood and adolescence. Girls, in contrast, tend to be more anxious and timid. And the large sex difference favoring girls in effortful control undoubtedly contributes to girls' greater compliance and cooperativeness, better school performance, and reduced incidence of behavior problems (Eisenberg et al., 2004a; Else-Quest et al., 2006).

Consistent sex differences in temperament are evident in children's play styles. Boys tend to engage in more active, high-intensity play, which contributes to their higher injury rates. Girls' advantage in effortful control helps explain their greater compliance and cooperativeness.

(a)

(b)

Nevertheless, genetic influences vary with the temperamental trait and with the age of the individual being studied. For example, heritability estimates are much higher for expressions of negative emotion than for positive emotion. And the role of heredity is considerably smaller in infancy than in childhood and later years, when temperament becomes more stable (Wachs & Bates, 2001).

Environmental Influences

Environment also has a powerful influence on temperament. For example, persistent nutritional and emotional deprivation profoundly alters temperament, resulting in maladaptive emotional reactivity. Recall from Chapter 5 that even after dietary improvement, children exposed to severe malnutrition in infancy remain more distractible and fearful than their agemates. And infants reared in deprived orphanages are easily overwhelmed by stressful events. Their poor regulation of emotion results in inattention and weak impulse control, including frequent expressions of anger (see pages 175 and 182).

Other research shows that child rearing is a major factor in whether or not infants and young children maintain their temperamental traits. In fact, heredity and environment often jointly contribute to temperament, since a child's approach to the world affects the experiences to which she is exposed. To see how this works, let's take a second look at ethnic and sex differences in temperament.

Japanese mothers usually say that babies come into the world as independent beings who must learn to rely on their parents through close physical contact. North American mothers typically believe just the opposite—that they must wean the baby away from dependence into autonomy. Consistent with these beliefs, Asian mothers interact gently, soothingly, and gesturally with their babies, whereas Caucasian mothers use a more active, stimulating, verbal approach (Rothbaum et al., 2000a). Also, recall from our discussion of emotional self-regulation that Chinese and Japanese adults discourage babies from expressing strong emotion, which contributes further to their infants' tranquility.

A similar process seems to contribute to sex differences in temperament. Within 24 hours after birth (before they have had much experience with the baby), parents already perceive male and female newborns differently. Sons are rated as larger, coordinated, more alert, and stronger; daughters as softer, more awkward, weaker, and more delicate (Stern & Karraker, 1989; Vogel et al., 1991). In line with these gender-stereotyped beliefs, parents more often encourage their young sons to be physically active and their daughters to seek help and physical closeness—through the toys they provide (trucks and footballs for boys, dolls and tea sets for girls) and through more positive reactions when their child engages in gender-typed play (Ruble, Martin, & Berenbaum, 2006).

In families with several children, an additional influence on temperament is at work. **TAKE A MOMENT...** Ask several parents to tell you about each of their children's personalities; then compare their comments about each child. You will see that parents often look for and emphasize differences between siblings: "She's a lot more active." "He's more sociable." "She's far more persistent." As a result, parents often regard siblings as more distinct than other observers do. In a large study of 1- to 3-year-old twin pairs, parents rated identical twins as resembling each other less in temperament than researchers' ratings indicated. And whereas researchers rated fraternal twins as moderately similar, parents viewed them as somewhat opposite in temperamental style (see Figure 7.2, page 266) (Saudino, 2003).

Parents' tendency to emphasize each child's unique qualities affects their child-rearing practices. In a study of 3-year-old identical twins, mothers' differential treatment of each twin predicted differences between twins in psychological adjustment. The pair member who received more warmth and less punitive parenting was more positive in mood and social behavior and less likely to have behavior problems (Deater-Deckard et al., 2001). Each child, in turn, evokes responses from caregivers that are consistent with parental beliefs and the child's developing temperament.

FIGURE 7.2

Temperament correlations for identical and fraternal twin pairs, as rated by researchers and parents. Parents rated 1- to 3-year-old identical twins as resembling each other less in temperament than did researchers. And whereas researchers rated fraternal twins as moderately similar, parents rated them as somewhat opposing in temperament. The correlations depicted here are for emotional reactivity. Activity level, shyness, and attention span/persistence yielded a similar pattern of findings. (Adapted from Saudino, 2003.)

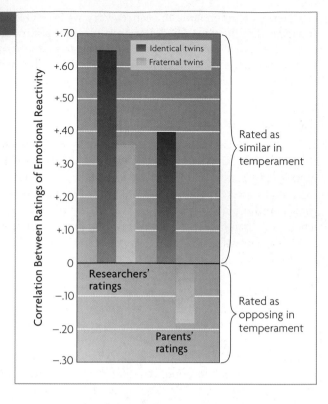

Besides different experiences within the family, siblings have unique experiences with teachers, peers, and others in their community that affect development. And in middle childhood and adolescence, they often seek ways to differ from one another. For all these reasons, both identical and fraternal twins tend to become increasingly dissimilar in personality with age (Loehlin & Martin, 2001; McCartney, Harris, & Bernieri, 1990). In sum, temperament and personality can be understood only in terms of complex interdependencies between genetic and environmental factors.

Temperament and Child Rearing: The Goodness-of-Fit Model

As we have seen, children's temperaments often change with age. This suggests that if a child's disposition interferes with learning or getting along with others, adults can counteract the child's maladaptive behavior. Thomas and Chess (1977) proposed a **goodness-of-fit model** to explain how temperament and environment can together produce favorable outcomes. Goodness of fit involves creating child-rearing environments that recognize each child's temperament while simultaneously encouraging more adaptive functioning.

Goodness of fit helps explain why difficult children (who withdraw from new experiences and react negatively and intensely) are at high risk for later adjustment problems. These children frequently experience parenting that fits poorly with their dispositions. As infants, they are less likely to receive sensitive caregiving (van den Boom & Hoeksma, 1994). By the second year, their parents tend to resort to angry, punitive discipline, which undermines the development of effortful control. As the child reacts with defiance and disobedience, parents become increasingly stressed (Coplan, Bowker, & Cooper, 2003). As a result, they continue their coercive tactics and also discipline inconsistently, sometimes rewarding the child's noncompliance by giving in to it (Calkins, 2002; Lee & Bates, 1985). These practices sustain and even increase the child's irritable, conflict-ridden style. In contrast, when parents are positive and sensitive, which helps babies regulate emotion, difficultness declines by age 2 (Feldman, Greenbaum, & Yirmiya, 1999).

Effective parenting also depends on life conditions. In a comparison of the temperaments of Russian and U.S. babies, Russian infants were more emotionally negative, fearful, and upset when frustrated (Gartstein, Slobodskaya, & Kinsht, 2003). Faced with a depressed national economy, which resulted in longer work hours and increased stress, Russian parents may have lacked time and energy for the patient parenting that protects against difficultness.

goodness-of-fit model
Thomas and Chess's model, which states that an effective match, or "good fit," between a child's temperament and the child-rearing environment leads to more adaptive functioning, whereas a "poor fit" results in adjustment problems.

Cultural values also affect the fit between parenting and child temperament, as research in China illustrates. In the past, collectivist values, which discourage self-assertion, led Chinese adults to evaluate shy children positively, and several studies showed that Chinese children of a decade or two ago appeared adjusted, both academically and socially (Chen, Rubin, & Li, 1995; Chen et al., 1998). But rapid expansion of a competitive economy, which requires assertiveness and sociability for success, may be responsible for a recent reversal in Chinese parents' and teachers' attitudes toward childhood shyness (Xu & Peng, 2001; Yu, 2002). Among Shanghai fourth graders, the association between shyness and adjustment also changed over time. Whereas shyness was positively correlated with teacher-rated competence, peer acceptance, leadership, and academic achievement in 1990, these relationships weakened in 1998 and reversed in 2002, when they mirrored findings of Western research (see Figure 7.3) (Chen et al., 2005). Cultural context makes a difference in whether shy children receive support or disapproval and whether they adjust well or poorly.

An effective match between rearing conditions and child temperament is best accomplished early, before unfavorable temperament–environment relationships produce maladjustment. Both difficult and shy children benefit from warm, accepting parenting that makes firm but reasonable demands for mastering new experiences. With reserved, inactive toddlers, highly stimulating parenting—frequent questioning and pointing out objects—fosters exploration. Yet for highly active toddlers, these same parental behaviors are too directive, dampening their play and exploration (Miceli et al., 1998). Recall from Chapter 6 that Vanessa often behaved in a harsh, directive way with Timmy. A poor fit between her parenting and Timmy's active temperament may have contributed to his tendency to move from one activity to the next with little involvement.

The goodness-of-fit model reminds us that babies have unique dispositions that adults must accept. Parents can neither take full credit for their children's virtues nor be blamed for all their faults. But parents can turn an environment that exaggerates a child's problems into one that builds on the child's strengths. In the following sections, we will see that goodness of fit is also at the heart of infant–caregiver attachment. This first intimate relationship grows out of interaction between parent and baby, to which the emotional styles of both partners contribute.

"Goodness-of-fit" describes the interaction between a child's biologically based temperament and the child-rearing environment. This mother's calm, soothing response will help her child regulate intense emotional reactions and develop more adaptive responses to frustration.

FIGURE 7.3

Changes over time in correlations between shyness and adjustment among Chinese fourth graders. In 1990, shy Chinese children appeared well-adjusted. But as China's market economy expanded and valuing of self-assertion and sociability increased, the direction of the correlations shifted. In 2002, shyness was negatively associated with adjustment. These findings are for teacher-rated competence and peer acceptance. Those for leadership (holding offices in student organizations) and academic achievement changed similarly. (Adapted from Chen et al., 2005.)

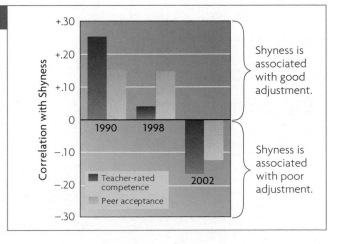

Ask Yourself

Review   How do genetic and environmental factors work together to influence temperament? Cite several examples.

Apply   At 18 months, highly active Jake climbed out of his high chair and had a tantrum when his father insisted that he sit at the table until the meal was finished. Using the concept of goodness of fit, suggest another way of handling Jake.

Connect   Do findings on ethnic and sex differences in temperament illustrate genetic–environmental correlation, discussed on pages 86–87 in Chapter 2? Explain.

Reflect   How would you describe your temperament as a young child? Do you think your temperament has remained stable, or has it changed? What factors might be involved?

Development of Attachment

Attachment is the strong affectionate tie we have for special people in our lives that leads us to experience pleasure and joy when we interact with them and to be comforted by their nearness in times of stress. By the second half of the first year, infants have become attached to familiar people who have responded to their needs. **TAKE A MOMENT...** Watch how babies of this age single out their parents for special attention: When the parent enters the room, the baby breaks into a broad, friendly smile. When she picks him up, he pats her face, explores her hair, and snuggles against her. When he feels anxious or afraid, he crawls into her lap and clings closely.

Freud first suggested that the infant's emotional tie to the mother is the foundation for all later relationships. Contemporary research indicates that—although the infant–parent bond is vitally important—later development is influenced not just by early attachment experiences but also by the continuing quality of the parent–child relationship.

Attachment has also been the subject of intense theoretical debate. Turn back to the description of Erikson's theory at the beginning of this chapter and notice how the *psychoanalytic perspective* regards feeding as the central context in which caregivers and babies build this close emotional bond. *Behaviorism,* too, emphasizes the importance of feeding, but for different reasons. According to a well-known behaviorist account, infants learn to prefer the mother's soft caresses, warm smiles, and tender words because these events are paired with tension relief as she satisfies the baby's hunger.

Although feeding is an important context for building a close relationship, attachment does not depend on hunger satisfaction. In the 1950s, a famous experiment showed that rhesus monkeys reared with terrycloth and wire-mesh "surrogate mothers" clung to the soft terrycloth substitute, even though the wire-mesh "mother" held the bottle and infants had to climb onto it to be fed (Harlow & Zimmerman, 1959). Human infants, too, become attached to family members who seldom feed them, including fathers, siblings, and grandparents. And toddlers in Western cultures who sleep alone and experience frequent daytime separations from their parents sometimes develop strong emotional ties to cuddly objects, such as blankets or teddy bears, that play no role in infant feeding!

Baby monkeys reared with "surrogate mothers" preferred to cling to a soft terrycloth "mother" instead of a wire-mesh "mother" that held a bottle. These findings contradict the drive-reduction explanation of attachment, which assumes that the parent–infant relationship is based on feeding.

Both psychoanalytic and behaviorist accounts of attachment have an additional problem: They emphasize the caregiver's contribution to the attachment relationship, paying little attention to the importance of the infant's characteristics.

Bowlby's Ethological Theory

Today, **ethological theory of attachment,** which recognizes the infant's emotional tie to the caregiver as an evolved response that promotes survival, is the most widely accepted view. John Bowlby (1969), who first applied this idea to the infant–caregiver bond, retained the psychoanalytic idea that quality of attachment to the caregiver has profound implications for the child's feelings of security and capacity to form trusting relationships.

At the same time, Bowlby was inspired by Konrad Lorenz's studies of imprinting in baby geese (see Chapter 1). Bowlby believed that the human infant, like the young of other animal species, is endowed with a set of built-in behaviors that keep the parent nearby to protect the infant from danger and to provide support for exploring and mastering the environment (Waters & Cummings, 2000). Contact with the parent also ensures that the baby will be fed, but Bowlby was careful to point out that feeding is not the basis for attachment. Rather, attachment can best be understood in an evolutionary context in which survival of the species—through ensuring both safety and competence—is of utmost importance.

According to Bowlby, the infant's relationship with the parent begins as a set of innate signals that call the adult to the baby's side. Over time, a true affectionate bond forms, supported by new cognitive and emotional capacities as well as by a history of warm, sensitive care. Attachment develops in four phases:

Separation anxiety increases between 6 and 15 months, when clear-cut infant–caregiver attachment develops. But the occurrence of separation anxiety depends on infant temperament, context, and adult behavior. Here, the child's distress at his mother's departure will probably be short-lived because his caregiver is supportive and sensitive.

1. *Preattachment phase* (birth to 6 weeks). Built-in signals—grasping, smiling, crying, and gazing into the adult's eyes—help bring newborn babies into close contact with other humans, who comfort them. Babies of this age recognize their own mother's smell, voice, and face (see Chapter 4). But they are not yet attached to her, since they do not mind being left with an unfamiliar adult.

2. *"Attachment in the making" phase* (6 weeks to 6 to 8 months). During this phase, infants respond differently to a familiar caregiver than to a stranger. For example, at 4 months, Timmy smiled, laughed, and babbled more freely when interacting with his mother and quieted more quickly when she picked him up. As infants learn that their own actions affect the behavior of those around them, they begin to develop a *sense of trust*—the expectation that the caregiver will respond when signaled—but they still do not protest when separated from her.

3. *"Clear-cut" attachment phase* (6 to 8 months to 18 months to 2 years). Now attachment to the familiar caregiver is evident. Babies display **separation anxiety,** becoming upset when their trusted caregiver leaves. Like stranger anxiety (see page 256), separation anxiety does not always occur; it depends on infant temperament and the current situation. But in many cultures, separation anxiety increases between 6 and 15 months, suggesting that infants have developed a clear understanding that the caregiver continues to exist when not in view. Consistent with this idea, babies who have not yet mastered Piagetian object permanence usually do not become anxious when separated from the parent (Lester et al., 1974).

attachment The strong affectionate tie that humans have for special people in their lives.

ethological theory of attachment Bowlby's theory that the infant's emotional tie to the caregiver is an evolved response that promotes survival.

separation anxiety An infant's distressed reaction to the departure of the familiar caregiver.

Besides protesting the parent's departure, older infants and toddlers try hard to maintain her presence. They approach, follow, and climb on her in preference to others. And they use the familiar caregiver as a secure base from which to explore.

4. *Formation of a reciprocal relationship* (18 months to 2 years and on). By the end of the second year, rapid growth in representation and language enables toddlers to understand the parent's coming and going and to predict her return. As a result, separation protest declines. Instead, children negotiate with the caregiver, using requests and persuasion to alter her goals. For example, at age 2, Caitlin asked Carolyn and David to read her a story before leaving her with a babysitter. The extra time with her parents, along with a better understanding of where they were going ("to have dinner with Uncle Sean") and when they would be back ("right after you go to sleep"), helped Caitlin withstand her parents' absence.

According to Bowlby (1980), out of their experiences during these four phases, children construct an enduring affectionate tie to the caregiver that they can use as a secure base in the parent's absence. This image serves as an **internal working model,** or set of expectations about the availability of attachment figures, their likelihood of providing support during times of stress, and the self's interaction with those figures. The internal working model becomes a vital part of personality, serving as a guide for all future close relationships (Bretherton & Munholland, 1999). Children continually revise and expand their internal working model as their cognitive, emotional, and social capacities increase and as they interact with parents and form other close bonds with adults, siblings, and friends.

Measuring the Security of Attachment

Although all family-reared babies become attached to a familiar caregiver by the second year, the quality of this relationship differs from child to child. Some infants appear relaxed and secure in the presence of the caregiver; they know they can count on her for protection and support. Others seem anxious and uncertain.

A widely used laboratory technique for assessing the quality of attachment between 1 and 2 years of age is the **Strange Situation.** In designing it, Mary Ainsworth and her colleagues reasoned that securely attached infants and toddlers should use the parent as a secure base from which to explore in an unfamiliar playroom. In addition, when the parent leaves, an unfamiliar adult should be less comforting than the parent. Consequently, the Strange Situation takes the baby through eight short episodes, in which brief separations from and reunions with the caregiver occur (see Table 7.2).

Observing infants' responses to these episodes, researchers identified a secure attachment pattern and three patterns of insecurity; a few babies cannot be classified (Ainsworth et al., 1978; Barnett & Vondra, 1999; Main & Solomon, 1990; Thompson, 2006). Although separation anxiety varies among the groups, the baby's reunion responses largely define attachment quality. **TAKE A MOMENT...** From the description at the beginning of this chapter, which pattern do you think Grace displayed after adjusting to her adoptive family?

■ **Secure attachment.** These infants use the parent as a secure base. When separated, they may or may not cry, but if they do, it is because the parent is absent and they prefer her to the stranger. When the parent returns, they actively seek contact, and their crying is reduced immediately. About 60 percent of North American infants in middle-SES families show this pattern. (In low-SES families, a smaller proportion of babies show the secure pattern, with higher proportions falling into the following insecure patterns.)

■ **Avoidant attachment.** These infants seem unresponsive to the parent when she is present. When she leaves, they usually are not distressed, and they react to the stranger in much the same way as to the parent. During reunion, they avoid or are slow to greet the parent, and when picked up, they often fail to cling. About 15 percent of North American infants in middle-SES families show this pattern.

■ **Resistant attachment.** Before separation, these infants seek closeness to the parent and often fail to explore. When the parent leaves, they are usually distressed, and on her return, they combine clinginess with angry, resistive behavior, struggling when held and

internal working model
A set of expectations, derived from early caregiving experiences, about the availability of attachment figures, their likelihood of providing support during times of stress, and the self's interaction with those figures, which becomes a guide for all future close relationships.

Strange Situation A laboratory method used to assess the quality of attachment between age 1 and 2 years by observing the baby's responses to eight short episodes, in which brief separations from and reunions with the caregiver occur in an unfamiliar playroom.

secure attachment The attachment pattern characterizing infants who are distressed by parental separation but are easily comforted by the parent when she returns.

avoidant attachment The attachment pattern characterizing infants who seem unresponsive to the parent when she is present, are usually not distressed when she leaves, and avoid the parent when she returns.

resistant attachment The attachment pattern characterizing infants who seek closeness to the parent before her departure, are usually distressed when she leaves, and combine clinginess with angry, resistive behavior when she returns.

TABLE 7.2   Episodes in the Strange Situation

EPISODE	EVENTS	ATTACHMENT BEHAVIOR OBSERVED
1	Researcher introduces parent and baby to playroom and then leaves.	
2	Parent is seated while baby plays with toys.	Parent as a secure base
3	Stranger enters, is seated, and talks to parent.	Reaction to unfamiliar adult
4	Parent leaves room. Stranger responds to baby and offers comfort if baby is upset.	Separation anxiety
5	Parent returns, greets baby, and offers comfort if necessary. Stranger leaves room.	Reaction to reunion
6	Parent leaves room.	Separation anxiety
7	Stranger enters room and offers comfort.	Ability to be soothed by stranger
8	Parent returns, greets baby, offers comfort if necessary, and tries to reinterest baby in toys.	Reaction to reunion

Note: Episode 1 lasts about 30 seconds; each of the remaining episodes lasts about 3 minutes. Separation episodes are cut short if the baby becomes very upset. Reunion episodes are extended if the baby needs more time to calm down and return to play.

Source: Ainsworth et al., 1978.

sometimes hitting and pushing. Many continue to cry after being picked up and cannot be comforted easily. About 10 percent of North American infants in middle-SES families show this pattern.

■ **Disorganized/disoriented attachment.** This pattern reflects the greatest insecurity. At reunion, these infants show confused, contradictory behaviors—for example, looking away while the parent is holding them or approaching the parent with flat, depressed emotion. Most display a dazed facial expression, and a few cry out unexpectedly after having calmed down or display odd, frozen postures. About 15 percent of North American infants in middle-SES families show this pattern.

Infants' reactions in the Strange Situation closely resemble their use of the parent as a secure base and their response to separation at home (Pederson & Moran, 1996; Pederson et al., 1998). For this reason, the method is a powerful tool for assessing attachment security. Researchers have modified Strange Situation procedures to make them appropriate for preschoolers. The resulting attachment classifications are modestly associated with previously obtained infant assessments (Crittenden, 2000; Main & Cassidy, 1988; Moss, Cyr, & Dubois-Comtois, 2004).

The **Attachment Q-Sort**, an alternative assessment method suitable for children between 1 and 5 years of age, depends on home observations (Waters et al., 1995). Either the parent or a highly trained observer sorts 90 behaviors—such as "Child greets mother with a big smile when she enters the room," "If mother moves very far, child follows along," and "Child uses mother's facial expressions as a good source of information when something looks risky or threatening"—into categories ranging from "highly descriptive" to "not at all descriptive" of the child. Then a score, ranging from high to low in security, is computed.

Because the Q-Sort taps a wider array of attachment-related behaviors than the Strange Situation, it may better reflect the parent–infant relationship in everyday life. However, the Q-sort method is time-consuming, requiring a nonparent informant to spend several hours observing the child before sorting the descriptors, and it does not differentiate between types of insecurity. The Q-Sort responses of expert observers show moderate correspondence with infants' security assessed in the Strange Situation. Without careful training, however, parents' Q-Sort judgments show little relationship with Strange Situation assessments (van IJzendoorn et al., 2004). Parents of insecure children, especially, have difficulty accurately reporting their child's attachment behaviors.

disorganized/disoriented attachment The attachment pattern reflecting the greatest insecurity, characterizing infants who show confused, contradictory behaviors when reunited with the parent after a separation.

Attachment Q-Sort A method for assessing the quality of attachment between ages 1 and 5 years through home observations of a variety of attachment-related behaviors.

Stability of Attachment

Research on the stability of attachment patterns between 1 and 2 years of age yields a wide range of findings. In some studies, as many as 70 to 90 percent of children remain the same in their reactions to parents; in others, only 30 to 40 percent do (Thompson, 2000, 2006). A close look at which babies stay the same and which ones change yields a more consistent picture. Quality of attachment is usually secure and stable for middle-SES babies experiencing favorable life conditions. And infants who move from insecurity to security typically have well-adjusted mothers with positive family and friendship ties. Perhaps many became parents before they were psychologically ready but, with social support, grew into the role. In contrast, in low-SES families with many daily stresses, little social support, and parental psychological problems, attachment status generally moves away from security or changes from one insecure pattern to another (Belsky et al., 1996; Fish, 2004; Vondra, Hommerding, & Shaw, 1999; Vondra et al., 2001).

These findings indicate that securely attached babies more often maintain their attachment status than do insecure babies, whose relationship with the caregiver is, by definition, fragile and uncertain. The exception is disorganized/disoriented attachment—an insecure pattern with high stability in most studies (Barnett, Ganiban, & Cicchetti, 1999; Hesse & Main, 2000; Weinfeld, Whaley, & Egeland, 2004). As you will soon see, many disorganized/disoriented infants experience extremely negative caregiving, which may disrupt emotional self-regulation so severely that confused, ambivalent feelings toward parents persist.

Overall, many children show short-term instability in attachment quality. A few studies reveal high long-term stability from infancy to middle childhood and—on the basis of interviews about relationships with parents—into adolescence and early adulthood (Hamilton, 2000; Waters et al., 2000). But once again, participants came from middle-SES homes, and most probably had stable family lives. Other long-term investigations show little to no stability but, instead, shifts for many participants from security in infancy to insecurity in adolescence and early adulthood. These negative changes in attachment pattern were associated with intervening negative life events, including child maltreatment, parental divorce, parental physical or mental illness, and poor family functioning linked to poverty (Lewis, Feiring, & Rosenthal, 2000; Weinfeld, Sroufe, & Egeland, 2000).

© WOLFGANG KAEHLER/CORBIS

Among the Dogon people of Mali, Africa, mothers stay close to their babies and respond promptly and gently to infant distress. Dogon mothers are almost never overly stimulating or intrusive—practices linked to avoidant attachment. And none of the infants were avoidantly attached to their mothers.

Cultural Variations

Cross-cultural evidence indicates that attachment patterns may have to be interpreted differently in certain cultures. For example, as Figure 7.4 reveals, German infants show considerably more avoidant attachment than American babies do. But German parents encourage their infants to be nonclingy and independent, so the baby's behavior may be an intended outcome of cultural beliefs and practices (Grossmann et al., 1985). In contrast, in a study of infants of the Dogon people of Mali, Africa, none showed avoidant attachment to their mothers (True, Pisani, & Oumar, 2001). Even when grandmothers are primary caregivers (as they are with firstborn sons), Dogan mothers remain available to their babies, holding them close and nursing them promptly in response to hunger and distress.

Similarly, Japanese infants rarely show avoidant attachment (refer again to Figure 7.4). Rather, many are resistantly attached—a reaction that may not represent true insecurity. Japanese mothers rarely leave their babies in others' care, and Japanese parents view the clinginess and attention-seeking that are part of resistant attachment as normal indicators of infant closeness and dependence (Rothbaum et al., 2000b). Likewise, infants in Israeli kibbutzim seldom show avoidant attachment. For these babies, who can sense the fear of unfamiliar people that is pervasive in their communities (see page 256), the Strange Situation probably induces unusual distress (van IJzendoorn & Sagi, 1999). Despite these cultural variations and others, the secure pattern is still the most common attachment classification in all societies studied to date.

Factors That Affect Attachment Security

What factors might influence attachment security? Researchers have looked closely at four important influences: (1) opportunity to form a close relationship, (2) quality of caregiving, (3) the baby's characteristics, and (4) family context, including parents' internal working models.

OPPORTUNITY FOR ATTACHMENT ■ What happens when a baby does not have the opportunity to establish a close tie to a caregiver? In a series of studies, René Spitz (1946) observed institutionalized infants whose mothers had given them up between 3 and 12 months of age. After being placed in a large ward where each shared a nurse with at least seven others, the babies lost weight, wept, withdrew from their surroundings, and had difficulty sleeping. If a consistent caregiver did not replace the mother, the depression deepened rapidly.

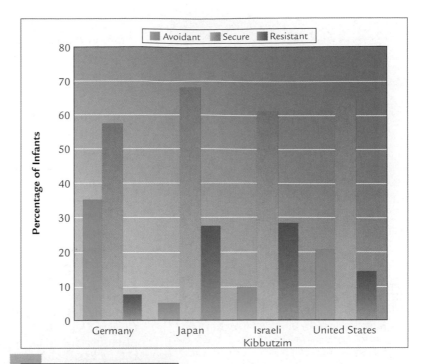

FIGURE 7.4

A cross-cultural comparison of infants' reactions in the Strange Situation. A high percentage of German babies seem avoidantly attached, whereas a substantial number of Japanese and Israeli kibbutz infants appear resistantly attached. Note that these responses may not reflect true insecurity. Instead, they are probably due to cultural differences in child-rearing practices. (Adapted from Sagi et al., 1995; van IJzendoorn & Kroonenberg, 1988)

These institutionalized babies had emotional difficulties because they were prevented from forming a bond with one or a few adults (Rutter, 1996). In another study, researchers followed the development of infants in an institution with a good caregiver–child ratio and a rich selection of books and toys—but where staff turnover was so rapid that the average child had 50 different caregivers by age $4\frac{1}{2}$! Many of these children became "late adoptees" who were placed in homes after age 4. Most developed deep ties with their adoptive parents, indicating that a first attachment bond can develop as late as 4 to 6 years of age (Tizard & Rees, 1975). But these children were more likely to display emotional and social problems, including an excessive desire for adult attention, "overfriendliness" to unfamiliar adults and peers, and few friendships.

Adopted children who spent their first 8 months or more in deprived Romanian orphanages often display these same difficulties (Hodges & Tizard, 1989; O'Connor et al., 2003). Furthermore, as early as 7 months, Romanian orphanage children show reduced ERP brain-wave responsiveness to facial expressions of emotion and have difficulty discriminating such expressions—findings that suggest disrupted formation of neural structures involved in "reading" emotions (Parker et al., 2005). Taken together, the evidence indicates that fully normal emotional development depends on establishing a close, caregiver bond in the early years of life.

QUALITY OF CAREGIVING ■ Dozens of studies report that **sensitive caregiving**—responding promptly, consistently, and appropriately to infants and holding them tenderly and carefully—is moderately related to attachment security in both biological and adoptive mother–infant pairs and in diverse cultures and SES groups (De Wolff & van IJzendoorn, 1997; Posada et al., 2002, 2004; van IJzendoorn et al., 2004). In contrast, insecurely attached infants tend to have mothers who engage in less physical contact, handle them awkwardly or in a "routine" manner, and are sometimes resentful and rejecting (Ainsworth et al., 1978; Isabella, 1993; Pederson & Moran, 1996).

sensitive caregiving
Caregiving that involves prompt, consistent, and appropriate responses to infant signals.

This mother and baby are engaging in a sensitively tuned form of communication called interactional synchrony in which they match emotional states, especially positive ones. Among North American babies, interactional synchrony supports secure attachment. But it does not characterize mother–infant interaction in all cultures.

Also, in several studies of North American babies, a special form of communication called **interactional synchrony** separated the experiences of secure from insecure babies. It is best described as a sensitively tuned "emotional dance," in which the caregiver responds to infant signals in a well-timed, rhythmic, appropriate fashion. In addition, both partners match emotional states, especially the positive ones (Feldman, 2003; Isabella & Belsky, 1991). In one instance, Carolyn responded to Caitlin's excited shaking of a rattle with an enthusiastic "That-a-girl!" Then Caitlin smiled and cooed in return. When Caitlin fussed and cried, Carolyn soothed with gentle touches and soft, sympathetic words.

Earlier we saw that sensitive face-to-face play, in which interactional synchrony occurs, increases babies' sensitivity to others' emotional messages and helps them regulate emotion. But moderate adult–infant coordination is a better predictor of attachment security than "tight" coordination, in which the adult responds to most infant cues (Jaffee et al., 2001). Perhaps warm, sensitive caregivers use a relaxed, flexible style of communication in which they comfortably accept and repair emotional mismatches, returning to a synchronous state.

Cultures vary in their view of sensitivity toward infants. Among the Gusii people of Kenya, for example, mothers rarely cuddle, hug, or interact playfully with their babies, although they are very responsive to their babies' needs. Yet most Gusii infants appear securely attached (LeVine et al., 1994). This suggests that security depends on attentive caregiving, not necessarily on moment-by-moment contingent interaction. Puerto Rican mothers, who highly value obedience and socially appropriate behavior, often physically direct and limit their babies' actions—a caregiving style linked to attachment security in Puerto Rican culture (Carlson & Harwood, 2003). Yet in many Western cultures, such physical control predicts insecurity.

Compared with securely attached infants, avoidant babies tend to receive overstimulating and intrusive care. Their mothers might, for example, talk energetically to them while they are looking away or falling asleep. By avoiding the mother, these infants appear to be escaping from overwhelming interaction. Resistant infants often experience inconsistent care. Their mothers are unresponsive to infant signals. Yet when the baby begins to explore, these mothers interfere, shifting the infant's attention back to themselves. As a result, the baby is overly dependent as well as angry at the mother's lack of involvement (Cassidy & Berlin, 1994; Isabella & Belsky, 1991).

Highly inadequate caregiving is a powerful predictor of disruptions in attachment. Child abuse and neglect (topics we will consider in Chapter 10) are associated with all three forms of attachment insecurity. Among maltreated infants, disorganized/disoriented attachment is especially high (van IJzendoorn, Schuengel, & Bakermans-Kranenburg, 1999). Persistently depressed mothers, mothers with very low marital satisfaction, and parents suffering from a traumatic event, such as serious illness or loss of a loved one, also tend to promote the uncertain behaviors of this pattern (Campbell et al., 2004; Moss et al., 2005; van IJzendoorn, 1995). Observations reveal that these mothers display frightening, contradictory, and other unpleasant behaviors, such as looking scared, mocking or teasing the baby, holding the baby stiffly at a distance, roughly pulling the baby by the arm, or seeking reassurance from the upset child (Goldberg et al., 2003; Lyons-Ruth, Bronfman, & Parsons, 1999). The baby's disorganized behavior reflects his conflicted reaction to the parent, who sometimes comforts but at other times arouses fear.

INFANT CHARACTERISTICS ■ Because attachment is the result of a *relationship* between two partners, infant characteristics should affect how easily it is established. In Chapters 3 and 4 we saw that prematurity, birth complications, and newborn illness make caregiving more taxing. In families under stress, these difficulties are linked to attachment insecurity. In one study, the *combination* of preterm birth and maternal depression—but not preterm birth alone—increased the likelihood of insecure attachment at 12 months (Poehlmann & Fiese, 2001).

interactional synchrony
A form of communication in which the caregiver responds to infant signals in a well-timed, rhythmic, appropriate fashion and both partners match emotional states, especially positive ones.

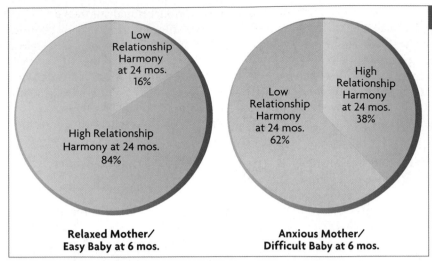

FIGURE 7.5

Influence of mother–infant distress at 6 months on relationship harmony at 24 months. In a study extending over the first two years, the combination of high maternal anxiety and high infant difficultness frequently impaired caregiving, resulting in many mothers and babies with low relationship harmony—characterized by maternal insensitivity and attachment insecurity—in the second year. (Adapted from Symons, 2001.)

Infants with special needs probably require greater parental sensitivity, which stressed parents often cannot provide. But at-risk newborns whose parents have adequate time and patience to care for them fare quite well in attachment security (Cox, Hopkins, & Hans, 2000).

The role of infant temperament in attachment security has been intensely debated. Some researchers believe that infants who are irritable and fearful may simply react to brief separations with intense anxiety, regardless of the parent's sensitivity to the baby (Kagan, 1998; Kagan & Fox, 2006). Consistent with this view, emotionally reactive, difficult babies are more likely to develop later insecure attachments (van IJzendoorn et al., 2004; Vaughn & Bost, 1999). Again, however, other evidence suggests that caregiving is involved. In a study extending from birth to age 2, difficult infants more often had highly anxious mothers—a combination that, by the second year, often resulted in a "disharmonious relationship" characterized by both maternal insensitivity and attachment insecurity (see Figure 7.5) (Symons, 2001). Infant difficultness and maternal anxiety seemed to perpetuate each other, impairing caregiving and the security of the parent–infant bond.

If children's temperaments alone determined attachment quality, we would expect attachment, like temperament, to be at least moderately heritable. Yet the heritability of attachment is virtually nil (O'Connor & Croft, 2001). In fact, about two-thirds of siblings establish similar attachment patterns with their parents, although the siblings often differ in temperament (Dozier et al., 2001). This suggests that most parents try to adjust their caregiving to each child's individual needs. Finally, interventions that teach parents to interact sensitively with difficult-to-care-for infants succeed in enhancing both quality of caregiving and attachment security (Bakermans-Kranenburg, van IJzendoorn, & Juffer, 2003; Velderman et al., 2006).

A major reason that children's characteristics do not show strong relationships with attachment security is that their influence depends on goodness of fit. From this perspective, *many* child attributes can lead to secure attachment as long as caregivers sensitively adjust their behavior to fit the baby's needs (Seifer & Schiller, 1995). But when parents' capacity to do so is strained—by their own personalities or by stressful living conditions—then infants with illnesses, disabilities, and difficult temperaments are at risk for attachment problems.

FAMILY CIRCUMSTANCES ■ Shortly after Timmy's birth, his parents divorced and his father moved to a distant city. As Vanessa began working 50- to 60-hour weeks to make ends meet, she felt harried, distracted, and lonely. On days that she stayed late at the office, a baby-sitter picked Timmy up from Ginette's child-care home and gave him dinner. When Vanessa arrived, just before Timmy's bedtime, instead of reaching out, crawling, or running to her as securely attached babies do, Timmy ignored her.

As Timmy's behavior illustrates, a failing marriage, financial strain, and other stressors can undermine attachment indirectly, by interfering with the sensitivity of parental care. Or they can affect babies' sense of security directly by altering the emotional climate of the family (for example, exposing them to angry adult interactions) or by disrupting familiar daily routines (Raikes & Thompson, 2005; Thompson & Raikes, 2003). Parents who manage to sustain a favorable relationship with their baby despite environmental stressors protect the child's development. Social support fosters attachment security by reducing parental stress and improving the quality of parent–child communication (Belsky & Fearon, 2002b; Moss et al., 2005). Ginette's sensitivity toward Timmy was helpful, as was the parenting advice Vanessa received from Ben, a psychologist. As Timmy turned 2, his relationship with his mother seemed warmer.

PARENTS' INTERNAL WORKING MODELS ■ Parents bring to the family context their own history of attachment experiences, from which they construct internal working models that they apply to the bonds they establish with their babies. Monica, who recalled her mother as tense and preoccupied, expressed regret that they had not had a closer relationship. Is her image of parenthood likely to affect Grace's attachment security?

Researchers assess parents' internal working models by asking them to recall and evaluate childhood memories of attachment experiences. Parents who discuss their childhoods with objectivity and balance, regardless of whether their experiences were positive or negative, tend to have securely attached infants and to behave sensitively toward them. In contrast, parents who dismiss the importance of early relationships or describe them in angry, confused ways usually have insecurely attached babies and engage in less sensitive caregiving (Pederson et al., 1998; Slade et al., 1999; van IJzendoorn, 1995).

But we should not assume any direct transfer of parents' childhood experiences to quality of attachment to their own children. Internal working models are *reconstructed memories* affected by many factors, including other close relationships, personality, and current life satisfaction. Longitudinal research reveals that certain negative life events can weaken the link between an individual's own attachment security in infancy and a secure internal working model in adulthood. And insecurely attached babies who become adults with insecure internal working models often have lives that, based on adulthood self-reports, are filled with family crises (Waters et al., 2000; Weinfield, Sroufe, & Egeland, 2000).

In sum, our early rearing experiences do not destine us to become sensitive or insensitive parents. Rather, the way we *view* our childhoods—our ability to come to terms with negative events, to integrate new information into our working models, and to look back on our own parents in an understanding, forgiving way—appears to be much more influential in how we rear our children than the actual history of care we received (Main, 2000).

ATTACHMENT IN CONTEXT ■ Carolyn and Vanessa returned to work when their babies were 2 to 3 months old. Monica did the same a few weeks after Grace's adoption. When mothers divide their time between work and parenting and place their infants and toddlers in child care, is the quality of attachment affected? See the Social Issues: Health box on the following page for research that addresses this issue.

After reading the box, consider each factor that influences the development of attachment—infant and parent characteristics, the parents' relationship with each other, outside-the-family stressors, the availability of social supports, parents' views of their attachment history, and child-care arrangements. Although attachment builds within the warmth and intimacy of caregiver–infant interaction, it can be fully understood only from an ecological systems perspective (Bornstein, 2002). Return to Chapter 1, pages 25–27, to review Bronfenbrenner's ecological systems theory. Notice how research confirms the importance of each level of the environment for attachment security.

Multiple Attachments

As we have indicated, babies develop attachments to a variety of familiar people—not just mothers, but fathers, grandparents, siblings, and professional caregivers. Although Bowlby (1969) believed that infants are predisposed to direct their attachment behaviors to a single special person, especially when they are distressed, his theory allowed for these multiple attachments.

Social Issues: Health

Does Child Care in Infancy Threaten Attachment Security and Later Adjustment?

Research suggests that infants placed in full-time child care before 12 months of age are more likely than home-reared babies to display insecure attachment—especially avoidance—in the Strange Situation (Belsky, 2001, 2005). Does this mean that infants who experience daily separations from their employed parents and early placement in child care are at risk for developmental problems? Let's look closely at the evidence.

Attachment Quality

In North American studies reporting an association between child care and attachment quality, the rate of insecurity among child-care infants is somewhat higher than among non-child-care infants—about 36 versus 29 percent (Lamb, Sternberg, & Prodromidis, 1992). But not all investigations report that babies in child care differ in attachment quality from those cared for solely by parents (NICHD Early Child Care Research Network, 1997; Roggman et al., 1994). The relationship between child care and emotional well-being depends on both family and child-care experiences.

Family Circumstances

We have seen that family conditions affect attachment security. Many employed women find the pressures of handling two full-time jobs—work and motherhood—stressful. Some mothers, fatigued and anxious because they receive little help from the child's father, may respond less sensitively to their babies, thereby risking the infant's security (Stifter, Coulehan, & Fish, 1993). Other employed parents probably value and encourage their infant's independence. Or their babies may be unfazed by the Strange Situation because they are used to separating from their parents. In these cases, avoidance in the Strange Situation may represent healthy autonomy rather than insecurity (Clarke-Stewart, Allhusen, & Goosens, 2001).

Quality and Extent of Child Care

Long periods spend in poor-quality child care may contribute to a higher rate of insecure attachment. In the U.S. National Institute of Child Health and Development (NICHD) Study of Early Child Care—the largest longitudinal study to date, including more than 1,300 infants and their families—child care alone did not contribute to attachment insecurity. But when babies were exposed to combined home and child-care risk factors—insensitive caregiving at home with insensitive caregiving in child care, long hours in child care, or more than one child-care arrangement—the rate of insecurity increased. Overall, mother–child interaction was more favorable when children attended higher-quality child care and spent fewer hours in child care (NICHD Early Child Care Research Network, 1997, 1999).

Furthermore, when the NICHD sample reached 3 years of age, a history of higher-quality child care predicted better social skills (NICHD Early Child Care Research Network, 2002b). At the same time, at age $4\frac{1}{2}$ to 5, children averaging more than 30 child-care hours per week were somewhat more likely to have behavior problems, especially defiance, disobedience, and aggression (NICHD Early Child Care Research Network, 2003a, 2006). This does not necessarily mean that child care causes behavior problems. Rather, heavy exposure to substandard care, which is widespread in the United States, may promote these difficulties. In Australia, infants enrolled full-time in government-funded, high-quality child care have a higher rate of secure attachment than infants who are informally cared for by relatives, friends, or baby-sitters. And amount of time spent in child care is unrelated to Australian preschoolers' behavior problems (Love et al., 2003).

Still, some children may be particularly stressed by long child-care hours. Many infants, toddlers, and preschoolers attending child-care centers for full days show a mild increase in saliva concentrations of the stress hormone cortisol across the day—a pattern that does not occur on days they spend at home. In one study, children rated as highly fearful by their caregivers experienced an especially sharp increase in cortisol levels (Watamura et al., 2003). Inhibited children may find the social context of child care—the constant company of large numbers of peers—particularly stressful.

Conclusions

Taken together, research suggests that some infants may be at risk for attachment insecurity and adjustment problems due to inadequate child care, long hours in child care, and the joint pressures their mothers experience from full-time employment and parenthood. But it is inappropriate to use these findings to justify a reduction in infant child-care services. When family incomes are limited or mothers who want to work are forced to stay at home, children's emotional security is not promoted.

Instead, it makes sense to increase the availability of high-quality child care, to provide paid employment leave so parents can limit the hours their children spend in child care (see pages 144–145), and to educate parents about the vital role of sensitive caregiving and child-care quality in early emotional development. For child care to foster attachment security, the professional caregiver's relationship with the baby is vital. When caregiver–child ratios are generous, group sizes are small, and caregivers are educated about child development and child rearing, caregivers' interactions are more positive and children develop more favorably (NICHD Early Child Care Research Network, 2000b, 2002a, 2006). Child care with these characteristics can become part of an ecological system that relieves rather than intensifies parental and child stress, thereby promoting healthy attachment and development.

At the end of his day in child care, a toddler eagerly greets his mother. High-quality child care and fewer hours in child care are associated with favorable mother-child interaction, which contributes to attachment security.

© ELLEN B. SENISI

FATHERS ■ An anxious, unhappy 1-year-old who is permitted to choose between the mother and the father as a source of comfort and security will usually choose the mother. But this preference typically declines over the second year. And when babies are not distressed, they approach, vocalize to, and smile equally often at both parents, who in turn are equally responsive to their infant's social bids (Bornstein, 2006; Parke, 2002).

Fathers' sensitive caregiving and interactional synchrony with infants, like mothers', predict attachment security (Lundy, 2003; van IJzendoorn et al., 2004). But in the United States, Canada, and many other cultures, including Australia, India, Israel, Italy, and Japan, mothers and fathers tend to interact differently with their babies: Mothers devote more time to physical care and expressing affection, fathers to playful interaction (Lamb, 1997; Roopnarine et al., 1990).

Mothers and fathers also play differently. Mothers more often provide toys, talk to infants, and gently play conventional games like pat-a-cake and peekaboo. In contrast, fathers—especially with their infant sons—tend to engage in highly arousing physical play with bursts of excitement that increase as play progresses (Feldman, 2003). This stimulating, surprising play style may help prepare babies to venture confidently into the surrounding world and to approach unfamiliar situations, such as play with peers (Paquette, 2004).

In cultures such as Japan, where long work hours prevent most fathers from sharing in infant caregiving, play is a vital context in which fathers build secure attachments (Hewlett, 2004; Schwalb et al., 2004). In many Western nations, however, a strict division of parental roles—mother as caregiver, father as playmate—has changed over the past quarter century in response to women's workforce participation and to cultural valuing of gender equality. Recent surveys indicate that in dual-earner families, U.S. fathers devote 85 percent as much time, and Canadian fathers 75 percent as much time, as mothers do to children—on average, about 3½ hours per day (Pleck & Masciadrelli, 2004; Sandberg & Hofferth, 2001; Zuzanek, 2000). Paternal availability to children is fairly similar across SES and ethnic groups, with one exception: Hispanic fathers spend more time engaged, probably because of the particularly high value that Hispanic cultures place on family involvement (Cabrera & García Coll, 2004; Parke et al., 2004).

Mothers in dual-earner families tend to engage in more playful stimulation of their babies than mothers who are at home full-time (Cox et al., 1992). But fathers who are primary caregivers retain their arousing play style (Lamb & Oppenheim, 1989). These highly involved fathers are less gender-stereotyped in their beliefs; have sympathetic, friendly personalities; often had fathers who were more involved in raising them; and regard parenthood as an especially enriching experience (Cabrera et al., 2000; Levy-Shiff & Israelashvili, 1988).

Fathers' involvement with babies occurs within a complex system of family attitudes and relationships. When both mothers and fathers believe that men are capable of nurturing infants, fathers devote more time to caregiving (Beitel & Parke, 1998). A warm marital bond supports both parents' sensitivity and involvement with babies, but it is particularly important for fathers (Lamb & Lewis, 2004). See the Cultural Influences box on the following page for cross-cultural evidence documenting this conclusion—and also highlighting the powerful role of paternal warmth in children's development.

When parents' troubled lives threaten their children's well-being, grandparents often become primary caregivers. Despite stepping into the parenting role under highly stressful conditions, grandparents who provide physical and emotional care over an extended time form deep attachments with their grandchildren.

GRANDPARENT PRIMARY CAREGIVERS ■ Over the past decade, families in which grandparents are children's primary caregivers have become increasingly common. Nearly 2.4 million U.S. and 75,000 Canadian children—4 to 5 percent of the child population—live apart from parents and with their grandparents (Statistics Canada, 2003a; U.S. Census Bureau, 2007b). The arrangement occurs in all ethnic groups, though more often in African-American, Hispanic, and Canadian Aboriginal families than in Caucasian families. These grandparents (more often women than men) generally step in when parents' troubled lives—as a result of substance abuse, child abuse and neglect, mental illness, or adolescent parenthood—threaten

Cultural Influences

The Powerful Role of Paternal Warmth in Development

Research in diverse cultures demonstrates that fathers' warmth contributes greatly to children's long-term favorable development. In studies of many societies and ethnic groups around the world, researchers coded paternal expressions of love and nurturance—evident in such behaviors as cuddling, hugging, comforting, playing, verbally expressing love, and praising the child's behavior. Fathers' sustained affectionate involvement predicted later cognitive, emotional, and social competence as strongly as did mothers' warmth—and occasionally more strongly (Rohner & Veneziano, 2001; Veneziano, 2003). And in Western cultures, paternal warmth protected children against a wide range of difficulties, including childhood emotional and behavior problems and adolescent substance abuse and delinquency (Grant et al., 2000; Rohner & Brothers, 1999; Tacon & Caldera, 2001).

In families where fathers devote little time to physical caregiving, they express warmth through play. In a German study, fathers' play sensitivity—accepting toddlers' play initiatives, adapting play behaviors to toddlers' capacities, and responding appropriately to toddlers' expressions of emotion—predicted children's secure internal working models of attachment during middle childhood and adolescence (Grossmann et al., 2002). Through play, fathers seemed to transfer to young children a sense of confidence about parental support, which may strengthen their capacity to master many later challenges.

What factors promote paternal warmth? Cross-cultural research reveals a consistent association between the amount of time fathers

spend near infants and toddlers and their expressions of caring and affection (Rohner & Veneziano, 2001). Consider the Aka hunters and gatherers of Central Africa, where fathers spend more time in physical proximity to their babies than in any other known society. Observations reveal that Aka fathers are within arm's reach of infants more than half the day. They pick up, cuddle, and play with their babies at least five times as often as fathers in other hunting-and-gathering societies. Why are Aka fathers so involved? The bond between Aka husband and wife is unusually cooperative and intimate. Throughout the day, couples share hunting, food preparation, and social and leisure activities. The more Aka parents are together, the greater the father's loving interaction with his baby (Hewlett, 1992).

In Western cultures as well, fathers in gratifying marriages spend more time with and interact more effectively with infants. In contrast, marital dissatisfaction is associated with insensitive paternal care (Grych & Clark, 1999; Lundy, 2002). Clearly, mothers' and fathers' warm interactions with each other and with their babies are closely linked. But paternal warmth promotes long-term favorable development,

beyond the influence of maternal warmth (Rohner & Veneziano, 2001). Evidence for the power of fathers' affection, reported in virtually every culture and ethnic group studied, is reason to encourage more men to engage in nurturing care of young children.

This Japanese father engages in the exciting, active play style typical of fathers in many cultures. In both Western and non-Western nations, fathers' warmth predicts long-term favorable development. And in Western societies, it protects against a range of problems in childhood and adolescence.

children's well-being (Fuller-Thomson, 2005; Minkler & Fuller-Thomson, 2005). Often these families take in two or more children.

As a result, grandparents tend to assume the parenting role under highly stressful life circumstances. Absent parents' difficulties generally strain family relationships. Previously unfavorable child-rearing experiences have left their mark on children, and children who are older when they enter grandparent care show high rates of learning difficulties, depression, and antisocial behavior (Mills, Gomez-Smith, & De Leon, 2005). These youngsters also introduce financial burdens into households that are already likely to be low-income. And grandparent caregivers, at a time when they anticipated having more time for spouses, friends, and leisure, instead have less. Not surprisingly, then, many report feeling emotionally drained, depressed, and worried about what will happen to the children if their own health fails (Hayslip et al., 2002; Kolomer & McCallion, 2005).

Although the arrival of a baby brother or sister is a difficult experience for most toddlers and preschoolers, a close emotional bond quickly builds between siblings. This mother's involvement with her young daughter as well as the new baby helps promote a good sibling relationship from the start.

Nevertheless, because they provide physical and emotional care for an extended time and are invested in the child's well-being, grandparent caregivers forge significant attachment relationships with their grandchildren (Poehlmann, 2003). Warm grandparent–grandchild bonds help protect children from worsening adjustment problems, even under conditions of great hardship (Fuller-Thomson & Minkler, 2000). Still, grandparent caregivers have a tremendous need for social and financial support and intervention services for their at-risk grandchildren.

SIBLINGS ■ Despite declines in family size, 80 percent of North American children still grow up with at least one sibling (Dunn, 2004). The arrival of a new baby is a difficult experience for most preschoolers, who—realizing that now they must share their parents' attention and affection—often become demanding, clingy, and deliberately naughty for a time. Attachment security also typically declines, especially for children over age 2 (old enough to feel threatened and displaced) and for those with mothers stressed by marital or psychological problems (Baydar, Greek, & Brooks-Gunn, 1997; Teti et al., 1995).

Yet resentment is only one feature of the rich emotional relationship that soon develops between siblings. Older children also show affection and concern—kissing and patting the baby, and calling out, "Mom, he needs you," when the infant cries. By the end of the baby's first year, babies typically spend much time with older siblings and are comforted by the presence of their preschool-age brother or sister during short parental absences. And in the second year, toddlers often imitate and join in play with older siblings (Barr & Hayne, 2003).

Nevertheless, individual differences in sibling relationships emerge soon after the new baby's arrival. Temperament plays an important role: Conflict is greater when one sibling is emotionally intense or highly active (Brody, Stoneman, & McCoy, 1994; Dunn, 1994). And maternal warmth toward both children is related to positive sibling interaction and to preschoolers' support of a distressed younger sibling (Volling, 2001; Volling & Belsky, 1992). Mothers who frequently play with their children and explain the toddler's wants and needs to the preschool sibling foster sibling cooperation. In contrast, maternal harshness and lack of involvement are linked to antagonistic sibling relationships (Howe, Aquan-Assee, & Bukowski, 2001). Finally, a good marriage is correlated with older preschool siblings' capacity to cope adaptively with jealousy and conflict (Volling, McElwain, & Miller, 2002). Perhaps good communication between parents serves as a model of effective problem solving. It may also foster a generally happy family environment, giving children less reason to feel jealous.

Refer to Applying What We Know on the following page for ways to promote positive relationships between babies and their preschool siblings. Siblings offer a rich social context in which children learn and practice a wide range of skills, including affectionate caring, conflict resolution, and control of hostile and envious feelings.

From Attachment to Peer Sociability

In cultures where agemates have regular contact during the first year of life, peer sociability begins early. By age 6 months, Caitlin and Timmy occasionally looked, reached, smiled, and babbled when they saw one another. These isolated social acts increased until, by the end of the first year, an occasional reciprocal exchange occurred in which the children grinned, gestured, or otherwise imitated a playmate's behavior (Vandell & Mueller, 1995).

Between 1 and 2 years, coordinated interaction occurs more often, largely in the form of mutual imitation involving jumping, chasing, or banging a toy. These imitative, turn-taking games create joint understandings that aid verbal communication. Around age 2, toddlers use words to talk about and influence a peer's behavior, as when Caitlin said to Grace, "Let's play chase," and after the game got going, "Hey, good running!" (Eckerman & Peterman, 2001; Eckerman & Whitehead, 1999). Reciprocal play and positive emotion are especially frequent in

Applying What We Know

Encouraging Affectionate Ties Between Infants and Their Preschool Siblings

SUGGESTION	DESCRIPTION
Spend extra time with the older child.	To minimize the older child's feelings of being deprived of affection and attention, set aside time to spend with her. Fathers can be especially helpful in this regard, planning special outings with the preschooler and taking over care of the baby so the mother can be with the older child.
Handle sibling misbehavior with patience.	Respond patiently to the older sibling's misbehavior and demands for attention, recognizing that these reactions are temporary. Give the preschooler opportunities to feel proud of being more grown-up than the baby. For example, encourage the older child to assist with feeding, bathing, dressing, and offering toys, and show appreciation for these efforts.
Discuss the baby's wants and needs.	By helping the older sibling understand the baby's point of view, parents can promote friendly, considerate behavior. Say, for example, "He's so little that he just can't wait to be fed" or "He's trying to reach his rattle and can't."
Express positive emotion toward your partner and engage in joint problem solving.	By modeling effective problem solving, parents' good communication helps the older sibling cope adaptively with jealousy and conflict. Also, when family life is happy, children have less reason to feel jealous.

toddlers' interactions with familiar agemates, suggesting that they are building true peer relationships (Ross et al., 1992).

Though quite limited, peer sociability is present in the first two years and is promoted by the early caregiver–child bond. Infants who have a warm parental relationship engage in more extended peer exchanges. Through interactions with sensitive adults, these babies learn how to send and interpret emotional signals in their first peer associations (Trevarthen, 2003). Later, as preschoolers, these children display more socially competent behavior (Howes & Matheson, 1992). Similarly, for toddlers in child care, a secure attachment to a stable professional caregiver predicts advanced peer and play behavior (Howes & Hamilton, 1993).

The beginnings of peer sociability emerge in infancy, in the form of touches, smiles, and babbles that gradually develop into coordinated interaction in the second year. Early peer sociability is fostered by a warm, sensitive caregiver child bond.

Attachment and Later Development

According to psychoanalytic and ethological theories, the inner feelings of affection and security that result from a healthy attachment relationship support all aspects of psychological development. In an extensive longitudinal study consistent with this view, Alan Sroufe and his collaborators found that preschoolers who had been securely attached as babies were rated by their teachers as higher in self-esteem, social skills, and empathy than were their insecurely attached counterparts. When studied again at age 11 in summer camp, children who had been secure infants had more favorable relationships with peers, closer friendships, and better social skills, as judged by camp counselors (Elicker, Englund, & Sroufe, 1992; Sroufe, 2002; Sroufe et al., 2005).

For some researchers, these findings seem to indicate that secure attachment in infancy causes improved cognitive, emotional, and social competence in later years. Yet contrary evidence exists. In other longitudinal studies, secure infants sometimes developed more favorably than insecure infants but not always (Lewis, 1997; McCartney et al., 2004; Schneider, Atkinson, & Tardif, 2001; Stams, Juffer, & van IJzendoorn, 2002). Disorganized/disoriented attachment, however, is an exception: It is uniformly related to internalizing problems (fear and anxiety) and externalizing problems (anger and aggression) during the preschool and school years. Disorganized children also show inappropriate role reversals: In an apparent effort to compensate for their parent's confused communication, they use either exaggerated comforting or hostility to try to control the parent's behavior (Lyons-Ruth, 1996; Lyons-Ruth, Easterbrooks, & Cibelli, 1997; Moss et al., 2004, 2006; Moss, Cyr, & Dubois-Comtois, 2004).

What accounts for the inconsistency in research findings on the consequences of early attachment quality? Mounting evidence indicates that *continuity of caregiving* determines whether attachment security is linked to later development (Lamb et al., 1985; Thompson, 2006). Children whose parents respond sensitively not just in infancy but also in later years are likely to develop favorably. In contrast, children whose parents react insensitively or who, over a long period, are exposed to a negative family climate tend to establish lasting patterns of avoidant, resistant, or disorganized behavior and are at greater risk for developmental difficulties.

A close look at the relationship between parenting and children's adjustment in the first few years supports this emphasis on continuity of caregiving. Recall that parents of disorganized/disoriented infants tend to have serious psychological problems and to engage in highly maladaptive caregiving—conditions that usually persist and that are strongly linked to poor adjustment in children (Lyons-Ruth, Bronfman, & Parsons, 1999). And when more than 1,000 children were tracked from age 1 to 3 years, those with histories of secure attachment followed by sensitive parenting scored highest in cognitive, emotional, and social outcomes. Those with histories of insecure attachment followed by insensitive parenting scored lowest, while those with mixed histories of attachment and maternal sensitivity scored in between (Belsky & Fearon, 2002a). Specifically, insecurely attached infants whose mothers became more positive and supportive in early childhood showed signs of developmental recovery.

Does this trend remind you of our discussion of *resilience* in Chapter 1? A child whose parental caregiving improves or who has other compensating affectionate ties can bounce back from adversity. In contrast, a child who experiences tender care in infancy but lacks sympathetic ties later on is at risk for problems.

Although a secure attachment in infancy does not guarantee continued good parenting, it does launch the parent–child relationship on a positive path that is likely to continue. Much research shows that an early warm, positive parent–child tie, sustained over time, promotes many aspects of children's development: a more confident and complex self-concept, more advanced emotional understanding, more favorable relationships with teachers and peers, more effective social skills, a stronger sense of moral responsibility, and higher motivation to achieve in school (Thompson, 2006; Thompson, Easterbrooks, & Padilla-Walker, 2003). But the effects of early attachment security are *conditional*—dependent on the quality of the baby's

Ask Yourself

Review   What factors explain stability in attachment pattern for some children and change for others? Are these factors also involved in the link between attachment in infancy and later development? Explain.

Apply   What attachment pattern did Timmy display when Vanessa arrived home from work, and what factors probably contributed to it?

Connect   Review research on emotional self-regulation on pages 258–259. How do the caregiving experiences of securely attached infants promote the development of emotional self-regulation?

Reflect   How would you characterize your internal working model? What factors, in addition to your early relationship with your parents, might have influenced it?

future relationships. Finally, as you will see again in future chapters, attachment is only one of the complex influences on children's psychological development.

Self-Understanding

Infancy is a rich formative period for the development of physical and social understanding. In Chapter 6, you learned that infants develop an appreciation of the permanence of objects. And in this chapter, we have seen that over the first year, infants recognize and respond appropriately to others' emotions and distinguish familiar from unfamiliar people. That both objects and people achieve an independent, stable existence for the infant implies that knowledge of the self as a separate, permanent entity is also emerging.

Self-Awareness

After Caitlin's bath, Carolyn often held her in front of the bathroom mirror. As early as the first few months, Caitlin smiled and returned friendly behaviors to her image. At what age did she realize that the charming baby gazing and grinning back was really herself?

BEGINNINGS OF SELF-AWARENESS ■ At birth, infants sense that they are physically distinct from their surroundings. For example, newborns display a stronger rooting reflex in response to external stimulation (an adult's finger touching their cheek) than to self-stimulation (their own hand contacting their cheek) (Rochat & Hespos, 1997). Newborns' remarkable capacity for intermodal perception (see page 202 in Chapter 5) supports the beginnings of self-awareness (Rochat, 2003). As they feel their own touch, feel and watch their limbs move, and feel and hear themselves cry, babies experience intermodal matches that differentiate their own body from surrounding bodies and objects.

Over the first few months, infants distinguish their own visual image from other stimuli, but their self-awareness is limited—expressed only in perception and action. When shown two side-by-side video images of their kicking legs, one from their own perspective (camera behind the baby) and one from an observer's perspective (camera in front of the baby), 3-month-olds looked longer at the observer's view (see Figure 7.6a). In another video-image comparison, they looked longer at a reversal of their leg positions than at a normal view (see Figure 7.6b) (Rochat, 1998). This suggests that young babies have a sense of their own body as a distinct entity, since they have habituated to it, as indicated by their interest in novel views of the body. By 4 months, infants look and smile more at video images of others than video images of themselves, indicating that they distinguish between the two and treat another person (as opposed to the self) as a potential social partner (Rochat & Striano, 2002).

SELF-RECOGNITION ■ At the same time, toddlers become consciously aware of the self's physical features. Seeing their image in a mirror, they may act silly or coy, playfully experimenting with the way the self looks (Bullock & Lutkenhaus, 1990).

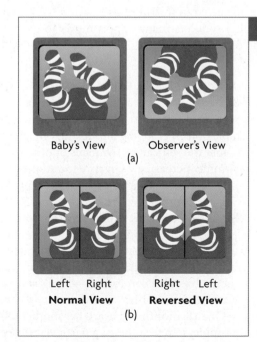

FIGURE 7.6

Three-month-olds' emerging self-awareness, as indicated by reactions to video images. (a) When shown two side-by-side views of their kicking legs, babies looked longer at the novel, observer's view than at their own view. (b) When shown a normal view of their leg positions alongside a reversed view, infants looked longer at the novel, reversed view. (Adapted from Rochat, 1998.)

Baby's View   Observer's View
(a)

Left   Right   Right   Left
Normal View   **Reversed View**
(b)

This 22-month-old, on seeing his changed appearance in a mirror as a result of wearing a new hat, immediately reaches for the hat—a response indicating that he recognizes his unique physical features. He is well aware of himself as a separate being, distinct from other people and objects.

In several studies, toddlers were placed in front of a mirror. Then, each mother rubbed red dye on her infant's nose or forehead. Younger babies touched the mirror as if the red mark had nothing to do with them. But those older than 20 months touched or rubbed their strange-looking noses or foreheads, a response indicating awareness of their unique appearance (Bard et al., 2006; Lewis & Brooks-Gunn, 1979).

Around age 2, self-recognition—identification of the self as a physically unique being—is well under way. Children point to themselves in photos and refer to themselves by name or with a personal pronoun ("I" or "me"). But it will take another year before children grasp the self as extending over time. When shown a live video of themselves, 2- and 3-year-olds quickly reached for a Post-It note stuck on top of their head as they saw it on the screen. But when they saw the note in a video that was replayed a few minutes later, not until age 4 did children remove the note and, when asked who was on TV, say with certainty, "Me" (Povinelli, 2001).

As infants act on the environment, they notice effects that help them sort out self, other people, and objects (Nadel, Prepin, & Okanda, 2005; Rochat, 2001). For example, batting a mobile and seeing it swing in a pattern different from the infant's own actions gives the baby information about the relation between self and physical world. Smiling and vocalizing at a caregiver who smiles and vocalizes back helps specify the relation between self and social world. And watching the movements of one's own hands and feet provides still another kind of feedback—one under much more direct control than other people or objects. The contrast between these experiences helps infants build an image of the self as separate from, but vitally connected to, external reality.

Sensitive caregiving promotes early self-development. Compared to their insecurely attached agemates, securely attached toddlers display more complex self-related actions during play, such as making a doll labeled as the self take a drink or kiss a teddy bear. They also show greater knowledge of their own and their parents' physical features—for example, in labeling of body parts (Pipp, Easterbrooks, & Brown, 1993; Pipp, Easterbrooks, & Harmon, 1992). And 18-month-olds who often establish joint attention with their caregivers are advanced in mirror self-recognition (Nichols, Fox, & Mundy, 2005). Joint attention seems to offer toddlers many opportunities to engage in social referencing—to monitor their own and others' reactions to objects and events—which promotes self-awareness.

SELF-AWARENESS AND EARLY EMOTIONAL AND SOCIAL DEVELOPMENT ■ Self-awareness quickly becomes a central part of children's emotional and social lives. In the final months of first year, as infants start to behave intentionally, they learn that their own goals (touching a breakable object, grabbing a peer's toy) frequently conflict with the goals of others. Soon they realize that the self can be the focus of others' intentions and emotional reactions. As a result, they become increasingly sensitive to variations in caregivers' emotional messages (Thompson, 2006). This sets the stage for social referencing and, in the middle of the second year, the emergence of self-conscious emotions (see page 257).

Self-awareness leads to first efforts to understand another's perspective. We have seen that toddlers increasingly appreciate others' intentions, feelings, and desires. They also show early signs of **empathy**—the ability to understand another's emotional state and *feel with* that person, or respond emotionally in a similar way. For example, toddlers start to give to others what they themselves find comforting—a hug, a reassuring comment, or a favorite doll or blanket (Hoffman, 2000). At the same time, they demonstrate clearer awareness of how to upset others. One 18-month-old heard her mother tell another adult, "Anny (sibling) is really frightened of spiders. In fact, there's a particular toy spider that we've got that she just hates" (Dunn,

empathy The ability to understand another's emotional state and respond emotionally in a similar way—"feeling with" that person.

1989, p. 107). The innocent-looking toddler ran to get the spider from the toy box, returned, and pushed it in front of Anny's face!

Categorizing the Self

By the end of the second year, language becomes a powerful tool in self-development. Because it permits children to represent the self more clearly, it greatly enhances self-awareness. Between 18 and 30 months, children develop a **categorical self** as they categorize themselves and others on the basis of age ("baby," "boy," or "man"), sex ("boy" or "girl"), physical characteristics ("big," "strong"), and even goodness and badness ("I good girl." "Tommy mean!"). They also start to refer to the self's competencies ("Did it!" "I can't") (Stipek, Gralinski, & Kopp, 1990).

Toddlers' use their limited understanding of these social categories to organize their own behavior. For example, children's ability to label their own gender is associated with a sharp rise in gender-stereotyped responses. As early as 18 months, children select and play in a more involved way with toys that are stereotyped for their own gender—dolls and tea sets for girls, trucks and cars for boys. Then parents encourage these preferences by responding more positively when toddlers display them (Ruble, Martin, & Berenbaum, 2006). As we will see in Chapter 10, gender-typed behavior increases dramatically during early childhood.

Self-Control

Self-awareness also contributes to *effortful control*, the extent to which children can inhibit impulses, manage negative emotion, and behave in socially acceptable ways. Indeed, a firmer sense of self may underlie the increasing stability and organization of effortful control in the third year (see page 257). To behave in a self-controlled fashion, children must think of themselves as separate, autonomous beings who can direct their own actions. And they must have the representational and memory capacities to recall a caregiver's directive ("Caitlin, don't touch that light socket!") and apply it to their own behavior.

As these capacities emerge between 12 and 18 months, toddlers first become capable of **compliance:** They show clear awareness of caregivers' wishes and expectations and can obey simple requests and commands. And, as every parent knows, they can also decide to do just the opposite! One way toddlers assert their autonomy is by resisting adult directives. But for most, opposition is far less common than compliance with an eager, willing spirit, which suggests that the child is beginning to adopt the adult's directives as his own (Kochanska, Murray, & Harlan, 2000). Compliance quickly leads to toddlers' first consciencelike verbalizations—for example, correcting the self by saying "No, can't" before reaching for a treat or jumping on the sofa.

Researchers often study the early emergence of self-control by giving children tasks that, like the situations just mentioned, require **delay of gratification**—waiting for an appropriate time and place to engage in a tempting act. Between ages 1½ and 3, children show an increasing capacity to wait before eating a treat, opening a present, or playing with a toy (Vaughn, Kopp, & Krakow, 1984). Children who are advanced in development of attention and language tend to be better at delaying gratification—findings that help explain why girls are typically more self-controlled than boys (Else-Quest et al., 2006). Some toddlers already use verbal and other attention-diverting techniques—talking to themselves, singing, or looking away—to keep from engaging in prohibited acts.

This father is encouraging compliance and the beginnings of self-control. The toddler joins in the task with an eager, willing spirit, which suggests he is beginning to adopt the adult's directive as his own.

categorical self Classification of the self according to prominent ways in which people differ, such as age, sex, physical characteristics, and competencies, that develops between 18 and 30 months.

compliance Voluntary obedience to adult requests and commands.

delay of gratification Ability to wait for an appropriate time and place to engage in a tempting act.

Applying What We Know

Helping Toddlers Develop Compliance and Self-Control

SUGGESTION	RATIONALE
Respond to the toddler with sensitivity and encouragement.	Toddlers whose parents are sensitive and supportive are more compliant and self-controlled.
Provide advance notice when the toddler must stop an enjoyable activity.	Toddlers find it more difficult to stop a pleasant activity that is already under way to wait before engaging in a desired action.
Offer many prompts and reminders.	Toddlers' ability to remember and comply with rules is limited; they need continuous adult oversight.
Respond to self-controlled behavior with verbal and physical approval.	Praise and hugs reinforce appropriate behavior, increasing the likelihood that it will occur again.
Encourage selective and sustained attention (see Chapter 6, pages 221–222).	Development of attention is related to self-control. Children who can shift attention, selectively focusing on one stimulus while ignoring competing stimuli, are better at controlling their emotions and impulses.
Support language development (see Chapter 6, pages 244–246).	Early language development is related to self-control. In the second year, children begin to use language to remind themselves of adult expectations and to delay gratification.
Gradually increase rules in a manner consistent with the toddler's developing capacities.	As cognition and language improve, toddlers can follow more rules related to safety, respect for people and property, family routines, manners, and simple chores.

Toddlers who experience parental warmth and gentle encouragement are more likely to be cooperative and advanced in self-control (Kochanska, Murray, & Harlan, 2000; Lehman et al., 2002). Such parenting—which encourages and models patient, nonimpulsive behavior—is particularly important for temperamentally difficult babies. In one study, anger-prone 7-month-olds with gentle, responsive mothers became eagerly compliant 15-month-olds. Angry infants with insensitive mothers, by contrast, developed into strikingly uncooperative toddlers (Kochanska, Aksan, & Carlson, 2005). **TAKE A MOMENT...** Turn back to page 266, and note how these findings provide yet another example of the importance of goodness-of-fit between temperament and child rearing.

As self-control improves, parents gradually expand the rules they expect toddlers to follow, from safety and respect for property and people to family routines, manners, and simple chores (Gralinski & Kopp, 1993). Still, toddlers' control over their own actions depends on constant parental oversight and reminders. Several prompts ("Remember, we're going to go in just a minute") and gentle insistence were usually necessary to get Caitlin to stop playing so that she and her parents could go on an errand. Applying What We Know above summarizes ways to help toddlers develop compliance and self-control.

As the second year of life drew to a close, Carolyn, Monica, and Vanessa were delighted at their children's readiness to learn the rules of social life. As we will see in Chapter 10, advances in cognition and language, along with parental warmth and reasonable demands for maturity, lead preschoolers to make tremendous strides in this area.

Ask Yourself

Review   Why is insisting that infants comply with parental directives inappropriate? What competencies are necessary for the emergence of compliance and self-control?

Apply   Len, a caregiver of 1- and 2-year-olds, wonders whether toddlers recognize themselves. List signs of self-recognition in the second year that Len can observe.

Connect   What type of early parenting fosters the development of emotional self-regulation, secure attachment, and self-control? Why, in each instance, is it effective?

Summary

Erikson's Theory of Infant and Toddler Personality

What personality changes take place during Erikson's stages of basic trust versus mistrust and autonomy versus shame and doubt?

■ According to Erikson, warm, responsive caregiving leads infants to resolve the psychological conflict of **basic trust versus mistrust** on the positive side. The trusting infant expects the world to be good and gratifying, so he feels confident about exploring it.

■ The conflict of **autonomy versus shame and doubt** is resolved favorably when parents provide appropriate guidance and reasonable choices. The outcome is a self-confident, secure child who can control her impulses and act competently on her own.

■ If children emerge from the first few years without sufficient trust and autonomy, the seeds are sown for adjustment problems.

Emotional Development

Describe the development of basic emotions over the first year, noting the adaptive function of each.

■ During the first half-year, **basic emotions**—happiness, interest, fear, anger, sadness, and disgust—become clear, well-organized signals. The **social smile** appears between 6 and 10 weeks, laughter around 3 to 4 months. Happiness strengthens the parent–child bond and reflects as well as supports physical and cognitive mastery.

■ In the second half of the first year, as infants become capable of intentional behavior and better able to evaluate objects and events, anger increases. It motivates babies to defend themselves and overcome obstacles and prompts caregivers to relieve their distress. Sadness occurs when infants are deprived of the familiar, loving caregiver.

■ Fear, most frequently expressed as **stranger anxiety,** also rises in the second half of the first year, keeping babies' enthusiasm for exploration in check. Once wariness develops, infants use the familiar caregiver as a **secure base** from which to explore.

Summarize changes that occur during the first two years in understanding others' emotions, expression of self-conscious emotions, and emotional self-regulation.

■ The ability to understand others' feelings expands over the first year. From 5 months on, babies perceive facial expressions as organized patterns. Between 8 and 10 months, infants engage in **social referencing,** actively seeking emotional information from caregivers in uncertain situations. By the middle of the second year, infants become aware that others' emotional reactions may differ from their own.

■ During toddlerhood, self-awareness and adult instruction provide the foundation for **self-conscious emotions:** shame, embarrassment, guilt, envy, and pride.

■ Caregivers help infants with **emotional self-regulation** by relieving distress, engaging in stimulating play, and discouraging negative emotion. During the second year, growth in representation and language leads to more effective ways of regulating emotion.

Development of Temperament

What is temperament, and how is it measured?

■ Children differ greatly in **temperament**—early appearing, stable individual differences in reactivity and self-regulation. The New York Longitudinal Study identified three patterns: the **easy child,** the **difficult child,** and the **slow-to-warm-up child.** Difficult children are at high risk for adjustment problems.

■ Rothbart's model of temperament combines characteristics into three underlying components—emotion, attention, and action—that form an integrated system of capacities and limitations. Rothbart's model includes **effortful control,** the ability to regulate one's reactivity.

■ Temperament is assessed through parental reports, behavior ratings by others familiar with the child, and direct observations. A combination of laboratory and physiological measures has been used to identify **inhibited,** or **shy, children,** and, at the other extreme, **uninhibited,** or **sociable, children.**

Discuss the roles of heredity and environment in the stability of temperament, including the goodness-of-fit model.

■ Temperament has low to moderate stability: It develops with age and can be modified by experience. Long-term prediction from early temperament is best achieved after age 3.

■ Twin studies suggest a moderate role of heredity in temperament. Consistent ethnic and sex differences also imply a genetic foundation, but also reflect cultural beliefs and practices as well as parents' perceptions.

■ The **goodness-of-fit model** describes how temperament and environment work together to affect later development. Parenting practices that fit well with the child's temperament help children achieve more adaptive functioning. Cultural values affect goodness of fit, as seen in the recent change in attitudes toward childhood shyness in China.

Development of Attachment

What are the unique features of ethological theory of attachment?

■ The most widely accepted perspective on development of **attachment**—our strong, affectionate tie with special people in our lives—is **ethological theory,** which views babies as biologically prepared to establish emotional bonds with familiar caregivers, who promote survival by ensuring both safety and competence.

■ In early infancy, a set of built-in behaviors encourages the parent to remain close to the baby. Around 6 to 8 months, **separation anxiety** and use of the parent as a secure base indicate the existence of a true attachment bond. Separation anxiety declines as representation and language develop, letting toddlers understand the parent's coming and going. From early caregiving experiences, children construct an **internal working model** that guides all future close relationships.

Cite the four attachment patterns assessed by the Strange Situation and the Attachment Q-Sort, and discuss factors that affect attachment security.

■ Using the **Strange Situation,** a common technique for measuring the quality of attachment between 1 and 2 years of age, researchers have identified four attachment patterns: **secure, avoidant,**

resistant, and **disorganized/disoriented attachment.** The **Attachment Q-Sort,** based on home observations of children between ages 1 and 5, yields a score ranging from low to high security.

■ Securely attached babies in middle-SES families under favorable life conditions more often maintain their attachment pattern than insecure babies. However, the disorganized/disoriented pattern is highly stable. Cultural conditions may affect infants' reactions to the Strange Situation.

■ Attachment security is influenced by the opportunity to form a close relationship, the quality of caregiving, the baby's characteristics, and the family context. Infants who lack the opportunity to form a close bond with one or a few adults show lasting emotional and social problems.

■ **Sensitive caregiving** is moderately related to secure attachment. In some cultures, **interactional synchrony** also characterizes the experiences of securely attached babies. Overstimulating, intrusive care is linked to avoidant attachment, inconsistent care to resistant attachment. Many disorganized/disoriented babies experience extremely negative caregiving.

■ Even ill and temperamentally irritable infants usually become securely attached if parents adapt their caregiving to suit the baby's needs. Family conditions, stress and instability, influence caregiving behavior and attachment security. Parents' internal working models also predict the quality of infants' attachment bonds.

Discuss infants' formation of multiple attachments, and indicate how attachment paves the way for early peer sociability.

■ Infants develop strong affectionate ties to fathers, whose sensitive caregiving predicts attachment security. In families where fathers devote little time to infant care, stimulating, playful interaction is a vital context in which they build secure attachments with babies.

■ Grandparents who serve as primary caregivers for grandchildren, increasingly common, forge significant attachment ties that help protect children with troubled family lives from adjustment problems.

■ Early in the first year, infants start to form rich emotional relationships with siblings that combine rivalry and resentment with affection and sympathetic concern. Individual differences in these relationships are influenced by temperament, parenting practices, and marital quality.

■ Peer sociability begins in infancy with isolated social acts, followed by reciprocal exchanges (largely in the form of mutual imitation) in the second year of life. A warm caregiver–child bond promotes peer sociability.

Describe and interpret the relationship between secure attachment in infancy and cognitive, emotional, and social competence in childhood.

■ Continuity of caregiving is the crucial factor determining whether attachment security is linked to later development. A secure attachment in infancy launches the parent–child relationship on a positive path. But if caregiving improves, children can recover from an insecure attachment history.

Self-Understanding

Describe the development of self-awareness in infancy and toddlerhood, along with the emotional and social capacities it supports.

■ Self-awareness begins at birth, when infants sense that they are physically distinct from their surroundings, and expands over the early months. At first, self-awareness is expressed only in perception and action. Later, self-recognition—identification of the self as a physically unique being—emerges, as toddlers become keenly aware of the self's physical features. By age 2, children point to themselves in photos and refer to themselves by name or a personal pronoun.

■ Self-awareness sets the stage for social referencing and, in the second year, the emergence of self-conscious emotions. It also leads to toddlers' first efforts to appreciate others' perspectives, including early signs of **empathy.** Between 18 and 30 months, as language develops, children develop a **categorical self** based on age, sex, physical characteristics, and competences.

■ Self-awareness also contributes to effortful control and, between 12 and 18 months, to the emergence of **compliance.** Between ages 1½ and 3, **delay of gratification** strengthens. Toddlers who experience parental warmth and gentle encouragement are likely to be advanced in self-control.

Important Terms and Concepts

attachment (p. 268)
Attachment Q-Sort (p. 271)
autonomy versus shame and doubt (p. 252)
avoidant attachment (p. 270)
basic emotions (p. 254)
basic trust versus mistrust (p. 252)
categorical self (p. 285)
compliance (p. 285)
delay of gratification (p. 285)
difficult child (p. 260)
disorganized/disoriented attachment (p. 271)

easy child (p. 260)
effortful control (p. 261)
emotional self-regulation (p. 258)
empathy (p. 284)
ethological theory of attachment (p. 269)
goodness-of-fit model (p. 266)
inhibited, or shy, child (p. 262)
interactional synchrony (p. 274)
internal working model (p. 270)
resistant attachment (p. 270)
secure attachment (p. 270)

secure base (p. 256)
self-conscious emotions (p. 257)
sensitive caregiving (p. 273)
separation anxiety (p. 269)
slow-to-warm-up child (p. 260)
social referencing (p. 257)
social smile (p. 255)
Strange Situation (p. 270)
stranger anxiety (p. 256)
temperament (p. 260)
uninhibited, or sociable, child (p. 262)

Milestones
Development in Infancy and Toddlerhood

Birth–6 months

PHYSICAL

- Height and weight increase rapidly. (166)
- Newborn reflexes decline. (149–151)
- First tooth erupts. (168)
- Synaptic growth and myelination of neural fibers in the brain occur rapidly. (172)
- Sleep is increasingly organized into a night–day schedule. (176)
- Responses can be classically and operantly conditioned. (183–184)
- Habituates to unchanging stimuli; recovers to novel stimuli. (185)
- Holds head up, rolls over, and grasps objects. (188)
- Shows sensitivity to motion and binocular depth cues. (196–197)
- Perceives auditory and visual stimuli as organized patterns. (202)
- Recognizes and prefers human facial pattern; recognizes features of mother's face. (202–203)

COGNITIVE

- Engages in immediate and deferred imitation of adults' facial expressions. (214–215)
- Repeats chance behaviors that lead to interesting results. (210)
- Has some awareness of many physical properties (including object permanence) and basic numerical knowledge. (212)
- Attention becomes more efficient and flexible. (221)
- Recognition memory for visual events improves. (222)

- Memory is context-dependent. (222)
- Forms perceptual categories based on objects' similar features. (225)

LANGUAGE

- Engages in cooing and, by the end of this period, babbling. (240)
- Begins to establish joint attention with caregiver, who labels objects and events. (241)

EMOTIONAL/SOCIAL

- Social smile and laughter emerge. (255)
- Matches feeling tone of caregiver in face-to-face communication and, later, expects matched responses. (256)
- Emotional expressions become well organized and meaningfully related to environmental events. (257)

- Regulates emotion by shifting attention and self-soothing. (258)
- Responds differently to caregiver than to a stranger. (269)
- Shows early signs of self-awareness. (283)

7–12 months

PHYSICAL

- Approaches adultlike sleep–wake schedule. (176)
- Sits alone, crawls, and walks. (188)
- Shows refined pincer grasp. (191)

- "Screens out" sounds not used in own language; perceives meaningful speech. (194)
- Develops sensitivity to pictorial depth cues. (196)
- Relies on shape, color, and texture to distinguish objects from their surroundings. (201)
- Becomes increasingly adept at intermodal perception. (202)

COGNITIVE

- Engages in intentional, or goal-directed, behavior. (210)
- Finds an object hidden in an initial location. (211)
- Engages in deferred imitation of adults' actions with objects. (214)
- Solves simple problems by analogy. (215)
- Memory becomes increasingly context-free. (223)
- Categorizes objects conceptually, by similar function and behavior. (225)

LANGUAGE

- Babbling expands to include sounds of spoken languages and patterns of the child's language community. (241)
- Joint attention with caregiver becomes more accurate. (241)
- Takes turns in games, such as pat-a-cake and peekaboo. (241)
- Comprehends some word meanings. (242)
- Uses preverbal gestures (showing, pointing) to influence others' behavior. (242)

- Around 1 year, says first words. (242)

290

EMOTIONAL/SOCIAL

- Smiling and laughter increase in frequency and expressiveness. (255)

- Anger and fear increase in frequency and intensity. (255–256)
- Stranger anxiety and separation anxiety appear. (256, 269–270)
- Uses caregiver as a secure base for exploration. (270)
- Shows "clear-cut" attachment to a familiar caregiver. (269)
- Detects the meaning of others' emotional expressions and engages in social referencing. (269)
- Regulates emotion by approaching and retreating from stimulation. (258)

13–18 months

PHYSICAL

- Height and weight gain are rapid, but not as great as in first year; toddlers slim down. (166–167)
- Walking is better coordinated. (188)
- Manipulates small objects with improved coordination. (191, 210)

COGNITIVE

- Explores the properties of objects by deliberately acting on them in novel ways. (211)
- Searches in several locations for a hidden object. (211)
- Imitates actions across a change in context— for example, from child care to home. (215)
- Sustained attention improves. (222)
- Recall memory for people, places, objects, and actions improves. (223)
- Sorts objects into categories. (225)

LANGUAGE

- Steadily adds to vocabulary. (242)
- Comprehends 50 words at 13 months; produces 50 words at 18 months. (243)

EMOTIONAL/SOCIAL

- Joins in play with familiar adults, siblings, and peers. (280–281)
- Recognizes image of self in mirror. (283–284)
- Begins to realize that others' emotional reactions may differ from one's own. (284)
- Uses social referencing to better evaluate events and understand emotions of the same valence. (284)
- Shows signs of empathy. (284)
- Complies with simple directives. (285)

19–24 months

PHYSICAL

- Has 20 teeth. (168)
- Brain reaches 70 percent of its adult weight. (170)
- Jumps and walks on tiptoe. (188)
- Manipulates small objects with good coordination. (191, 210)

COGNITIVE

- Solves simple problems suddenly, through representation. (211)

- Finds a hidden object that has been moved while out of sight. (211)
- Engages in make-believe play, using simple actions. (212)
- Engages in deferred imitation of actions an adult tries to produce, even if not fully realized. (215)
- Sorts objects into categories more effectively. (226)

LANGUAGE

- Produces about 200 words. (243)
- Combines two words. (243)

EMOTIONAL/SOCIAL

- Self-conscious emotions (shame, embarrassment, guilt, and pride) emerge. (257)
- Acquires an emotion vocabulary for talking about feelings, aiding emotional self-regulation. (259)
- Begins to tolerate caregiver's absences more easily; separation anxiety declines. (270)
- Starts to use words to influence a playmate's behavior. (280)
- Self-recognition is well under way; identifies self in photos. (284)
- Categorizes self and others on the basis of age, sex, physical characteristics, goodness and badness, and competencies. (285)
- Shows gender-stereotyped toy preferences. (285)
- Self-control emerges. (285)

Note: Numbers in parentheses indicate the page or pages on which each milestone is discussed.

Chapter 8

Expressing pride in mastery of a new motor skill, this artist imagines brushing a lion's teeth, just as she cares for her own teeth. Chapter 8 highlights the close link between early childhood physical growth and other aspects of development.

Reprinted with permission from the International Museum of Children's Art, Oslo, Norway

"The Lion's Toothpaste"
Erika Tomano
3 years, Japan

Physical Development in Early Childhood

For more than a decade, my fourth-floor office window overlooked the preschool and kindergarten play yard of our university laboratory school. On mild fall and spring mornings, the doors of classrooms swung open, and sand table, woodworking bench, easels, and large blocks spilled out into a small, fenced courtyard. Alongside the building was a grassy area with jungle gyms, swings, a playhouse, and a flower garden planted by the children; beyond it, a circular path lined with tricycles and wagons. Each day, the setting was alive with activity.

Even from my distant vantage point, the physical changes of early childhood were evident. Children's bodies were longer and leaner than they had been a year or two earlier. The awkward gait of toddlerhood had disappeared in favor of more refined movements that included running, climbing, jumping, galloping, and skipping. Children scaled the jungle gym, raced across the lawn, turned somersaults, and vigorously pedaled tricycles. Just as impressive as these gross motor achievements were gains in fine motor skills. At the sand table, children built hills, valleys, caves, and roads and prepared trays of pretend cookies and cupcakes. And as they grew older, their paintings at the outdoor easels took on greater structure and detail as family members, houses, trees, birds, sky, monsters, and letterlike forms appeared in the colorful creations.

The years from 2 to 6 are often called "the play years"—aptly so, since play blossoms during this time and supports every aspect of development. Our discussion of early childhood opens with the physical achievements of this period—growth in body size, improvements in motor coordination, and refinements in perception. We pay special attention to biological and environmental factors that support these changes, as well as to their intimate connection with other domains of development. The children I came to know well, first by watching from my office window and later by observing at close range in their classrooms, will provide many examples of developmental trends and individual differences.

Body Growth

In early childhood, the rapid increase in body size of the first two years tapers off into a slower growth pattern. On average, children add 2 to 3 inches in height and about 5 pounds in weight each year. Boys continue to be slightly larger than girls. As

Toddlers and 5-year-olds have very different body shapes. During early childhood, body fat declines, the torso enlarges to better accommodate the internal organs, and the spine straightens. Compared to her younger brother, this girl looks more streamlined. Her body proportions resemble those of an adult.

the "baby fat" that began to decline in toddlerhood drops off further, children gradually become thinner, although girls retain somewhat more body fat than boys, who are slightly more muscular. As the torso lengthens and widens, internal organs tuck neatly inside, and the spine straightens. As Figure 8.1 shows, by age 5 the top-heavy, bowlegged, potbellied toddler has become a more streamlined, flat-tummied, longer-legged child with body proportions similar to those of adults. Consequently, posture and balance improve—changes that support the gains in motor coordination.

Individual differences in body size are even more apparent during early childhood than in infancy and toddlerhood. Speeding around the bike path in the play yard, 5-year-old Darryl—at 48 inches tall and 55 pounds—towered over his kindergarten classmates. At the doctor's office, he was, as his mother put it, "off the growth charts" compared with the average North American 5-year-old boy, who is 43 inches tall and weighs 42 pounds. Priti, an Asian-Indian child, was unusually small because of genetic factors linked to her cultural ancestry. And Lynette and Hal, two Caucasian children with impoverished home lives, were well below average for reasons we will discuss shortly.

The existence of these variations in body size reminds us that growth norms for one population are not good standards for children elsewhere in the world. Consider the Efe of the Republic of Congo, whose typical adult height is less than 5 feet. Between 1 and 6 years, Efe children's growth tapers off to a greater extent than that of most other preschoolers. By age 5, the average Efe child is shorter than more than 97 percent of North American 5-year-olds. For genetic reasons, the impact of hormones controlling body size is reduced in Efe children (Bailey, 1991). The Efe's small size probably evolved because it reduced their caloric requirements in the face of food scarcity in the rain forests of Central Africa and permitted them to move easily through the dense forest underbrush (Shea & Bailey, 1996). So we should not view Efe children's short stature as a sign of problems with growth or health. But for other extremely slow-growing children, such as Lynette and Hal, these concerns are warranted.

Skeletal Growth

The skeletal changes of infancy continue throughout early childhood. Between ages 2 and 6, approximately 45 new *epiphyses*—or growth centers, in which cartilage hardens into bone—emerge in various parts of the skeleton. Other epiphyses will appear in middle childhood. X-rays of these growth centers enable doctors to estimate children's *skeletal age*, or progress toward physical maturity (see page 167 in Chapter 5)—information helpful in diagnosing growth disorders.

By the end of the preschool years, children start to lose their primary, or "baby," teeth. The age at which they do so is heavily influenced by genetic factors. For example, girls, who are ahead of boys in physical development, lose their primary teeth sooner. Cultural ancestry also makes a difference. North American children typically get their first secondary (permanent) tooth at 6½ years, children in Ghana at just over 5 years, and children in Hong Kong around the sixth birthday (Burns, 2000). But nutritional factors also influence dental development. Prolonged malnutrition delays the appearance of permanent teeth, whereas overweight and obesity accelerate it (Hilgers et al., 2006).

Care of primary teeth is essential because diseased baby teeth can affect the health of permanent teeth. Brushing consistently, avoiding sugary foods, drinking fluoridated water, and getting topical fluoride treatments and sealants (plastic coatings that protect tooth surfaces) prevent cavities. Another factor is protection from exposure to tobacco smoke, which

Andy at 3 years

Andy at 4 years

Andy at 5 years

Andy at 5¾ years

Amy at 3 years

Amy at 3½ years

Amy at 4½ years

Amy at 5½ years

FIGURE 8.1

Body growth during early childhood. Andy and Amy grew more slowly during the preschool years than they did in infancy and toddlerhood (see Chapter 5, page 166). By age 5, their bodies became more streamlined, flat-tummied, and longer-legged. Boys continue to be slightly taller and heavier and more muscular than girls. But generally, the two sexes are similar in body proportions and physical capacities.

suppresses children's immune system, including the ability to fight bacteria responsible for tooth decay. The risk associated with this suppression is greatest in infancy and early childhood, when the immune system is not yet fully mature (Aligne et al., 2003). Young children in homes with regular smokers are three times more likely than their agemates to have decayed teeth, even after other factors that influence dental health have been controlled (Shenkin et al., 2004).

Although tooth decay has declined sharply over the past 40 years, an estimated 40 percent of North American 5-year-olds have at least some affected teeth (Neurath, 2005). Among poverty-stricken preschoolers, cavities advance especially rapidly, affecting an average of 2.5 teeth per year. By the time American and Canadian young people graduate from high school,

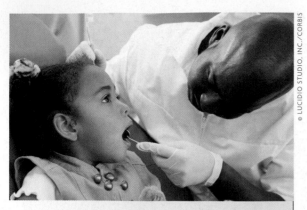

Regular dental checkups are important for preschoolers. Diseased primary teeth can affect the long-term health of permanent teeth, which start to appear at the end of the preschool years.

about 80 percent have decayed or filled teeth (World Health Organization, 2003, 2004). Causes include poor diet and inadequate health care—factors that are more likely to affect low-SES children.

Asynchronies in Physical Growth

As Figure 8.2 shows, physical growth is *asynchronous:* Body systems differ in their patterns of growth. Body size (as measured by height and weight) and a variety of internal organs follow the **general growth curve:** rapid growth during infancy, slower gains in early and middle childhood, and rapid growth again during adolescence. The genitals develop slowly from birth to age 4, change little throughout middle childhood, and then grow rapidly during adolescence. In contrast, the lymph glands grow at an astounding pace in infancy and childhood; in adolescence, lymph tissue declines. The lymph system helps fight infection and assists with absorption of nutrients, thereby supporting children's health and survival.

Figure 8.2 illustrates another growth trend with which you are already familiar: During the first few years, the brain grows faster than any other part of the body. Let's look at some highlights of brain development in early childhood.

Brain Development

Between ages 2 and 6, the brain increases from 70 percent of its adult weight to 90 percent. At the same time, preschoolers improve in a wide variety of skills—physical coordination, perception, attention, memory, language, logical thinking, and imagination.

In addition to increasing in weight, the brain undergoes much reshaping and refining. By age 4, many parts of the cortex have overproduced synapses. In some regions, such as the frontal lobes, the number of synapses is nearly double the adult value. Together, synaptic growth and myelination of neural fibers result in a high energy need. In fact, fMRI evidence reveals that energy metabolism in the cerebral cortex reaches a peak around this age (Huttenlocher, 2002; Johnson, 1998).

Recall from Chapter 5 that overabundance of synaptic connections supports *plasticity* of the young brain, helping to ensure that the child will acquire certain abilities even if some areas are damaged. *Synaptic pruning* follows: Neurons that are seldom stimulated lose their connective fibers, and the number of synapses is reduced (see page 169). As the structures of stimulated neurons become more elaborate and require more space, surrounding neurons die, and brain plasticity declines. By age 8 to 10, energy consumption of most cortical regions declines to near-adult levels (Nelson, 2002).

EEG and fMRI measures of neural activity in various cortical regions reveal especially rapid growth from 3 to 6 years in frontal-lobe

FIGURE 8.2

Growth of three different organ systems and tissues contrasted with the body's general growth. Growth is plotted in terms of percentage of change from birth to 20 years. Note that the growth of lymph tissue rises to nearly twice its adult level by the end of childhood. Then it declines. (Reprinted by permission of the publisher from J. M. Tanner, 1990, *Foetus into Man*, 2nd ed., Cambridge, MA: Harvard University Press, p. 16. Copyright © 1990 by J. M. Tanner. All rights reserved.)

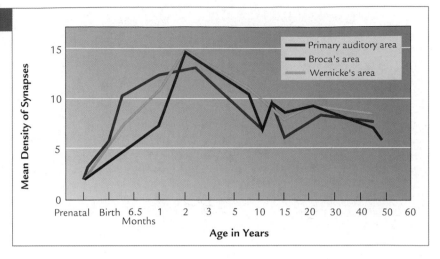

FIGURE 8.3

Age-related changes in synaptic density of three areas of the cerebral cortex involved in language processing. Density of synapses in all three areas rises sharply during the first three years—the same period in which children rapidly develop language skills. As a result of pruning, density of synapses falls during the late preschool and school years. During this time, plasticity of the cerebral cortex is reduced. (Adapted from P. R. Huttenlocher, 2000, "Synaptogenesis in Human Cerebral Cortex and the Concept of Critical Periods," in N. A. Fox, L. A. Leavitt, & J. G. Warhol, eds., *The Role of Early Experience in Development*, p. 21. St. Louis, MO: Johnson & Johnson Pediatric Institute. Reprinted by permission.)

areas devoted to attention and planning and organizing behavior. Furthermore, for most children, the left hemisphere is especially active between 3 and 6 years, then levels off. In contrast, right-hemispheric activity increases steadily throughout early and middle childhood, with a slight spurt between ages 8 and 10 (Thatcher, Walker, & Giudice, 1987; Thompson et al., 2000a). Studies of the brains of children who have died confirm these trends. For example, Figure 8.3 shows age-related changes in density of synapses in three left-hemispheric cortical areas involved in language processing: the primary auditory area, Broca's area, and Wernicke's area. (To review the location of these structures, refer to page 238.) Notice how synaptic density rises during the first three years and then, as a result of pruning, falls to an adult level around age 10.

These findings fit nicely with what we know about several aspects of cognitive development. Early childhood is a time of marked gains on tasks that depend on the frontal cortex—ones that require inhibiting impulses and substituting thoughtful responses (Diamond, 2004; Nelson, Thomas, & de Haan, 2006). Further, language skills (typically housed in the left hemisphere) increase at an astonishing pace in early childhood, and they support children's increasing control over behavior, also mediated by the frontal lobes. In contrast, spatial skills (usually located in the right hemisphere), such as giving directions, drawing pictures, and recognizing geometric shapes, develop gradually over childhood and adolescence.

Differences in rate of development between the two hemispheres suggest that they are continuing to *lateralize* (specialize in functions). Let's take a closer look at brain lateralization during early childhood by focusing on handedness.

Handedness

On a visit to the preschool, I watched 3-year-old Moira as she drew pictures, worked puzzles, joined in snack time, and played outside. Unlike most of her classmates, Moira does most things—drawing, eating, and zipping her jacket—with her left hand. But she uses her right hand for a few activities, such as throwing a ball. Research on handedness, along with other evidence covered in Chapter 5, supports the joint contribution of nature and nurture to brain lateralization.

By the end of the first year, children typically display a hand preference that, over the next few years, gradually extends to a wider range of skills (Hinojosa, Sheu, & Michael, 2003). Handedness reflects the greater capacity of one side of the brain—the individual's **dominant cerebral hemisphere**—to carry out skilled motor action. Other important abilities are generally located on the dominant side as well. For right-handed people—in Western nations, 90 percent of the population—language is housed in the left hemisphere, with hand control. For the left-handed 10 percent, language is occasionally located in the right hemisphere or, more often, shared between the hemispheres (Szaflarski et al., 2002). This indicates that the brains of left-handers tend to be less strongly lateralized than those of right-handers. Consistent with this idea, many

general growth curve
Curve representing overall changes in body size—rapid growth during infancy, slower gains in early and middle childhood, and rapid growth again during adolescence.

dominant cerebral hemisphere The hemisphere of the brain responsible for skilled motor action—in right-handed individuals, the left hemisphere.

Twins typically lie in the uterus in opposite orientations, which may explain why they are more often opposite-handed than are ordinary siblings. Although left-handedness is associated with certain developmental problems, atypical lateralization is probably not responsible. Most left-handers show typical development, and some show outstanding verbal or mathematical talent.

left-handed individuals (like Moira) are also *ambidextrous*. Although they prefer their left hand, they sometimes use their right hand skillfully as well (McManus et al., 1988).

Left-handed parents show only a weak tendency to have left-handed children. One genetic theory proposes that most children inherit a gene that *biases* them for right-handedness and a left-dominant cerebral hemisphere. But that bias is not strong enough to overcome experiences that might sway children toward a left-hand preference (Annett, 2002).

Even prenatal events may profoundly affect handedness. Both identical and fraternal twins are more likely than ordinary siblings to differ in hand preference, probably because twins usually lie in opposite orientations in the uterus (Derom et al., 1996). The orientation of most singleton fetuses—facing toward the left—is believed to promote greater control over movements on the body's right side (Previc, 1991).

Handedness also involves practice. Newborns' bias in head position causes them to spend more time looking at and using one hand, which contributes to greater skillfulness of that hand (Hinojosa, Sheu, & Michael, 2003). Handedness is strongest for complex skills requiring extensive training, such as eating with utensils, writing, and engaging in athletic activities. Also, wide cultural differences exist in rates of left-handedness. In Tanzania, Africa, where children are physically restrained and punished for favoring the left hand, less than 1 percent of adults are left-handed (Provins, 1997).

Although left-handedness occurs more frequently among severely retarded and mentally ill people than in the general population, atypical brain lateralization is probably not responsible for these individuals' problems. Rather, early damage to the left hemisphere may have caused their disabilities while also leading to a shift in handedness. In support of this idea, left-handedness is associated with prenatal and birth difficulties that can result in brain damage, including prolonged labor, prematurity, Rh incompatibility, and breech delivery (O'Callaghan et al., 1993; Powls et al., 1996).

Most left-handers, however, have no developmental problems—in fact, unusual lateralization may have certain advantages. Left- and mixed-handed young people are more likely than their right-handed agemates to develop outstanding verbal and mathematical talents (Flannery & Liederman, 1995). More even distribution of cognitive functions across both hemispheres may be responsible.

Other Advances in Brain Development

Besides the cerebral cortex, several other areas of the brain make strides during early childhood (see Figure 8.4). All of these changes involve establishing links between parts of the brain, increasing the coordinated functioning of the central nervous system.

cerebellum A brain structure that aids in balance and control of body movement.

reticular formation A brain structure that maintains alertness and consciousness.

hippocampus An inner-brain structure that plays a vital role in memory and in spatial images we use to help us find our way.

corpus callosum The large bundle of fibers connecting the two hemispheres of the brain.

At the rear and base of the brain is the **cerebellum**, a structure that aids in balance and control of body movement. Fibers linking the cerebellum to the cerebral cortex grow and myelinate from birth through the preschool years. This change contributes to dramatic gains in motor coordination: By the end of the preschool years, children can play hopscotch, throw a ball with a well-organized set of movements, and print letters of the alphabet. Connections between the cerebellum and the cerebral cortex also support thinking (Diamond, 2000): Children with damage to the cerebellum usually display both motor and cognitive deficits, including problems with memory, planning, and language (Noterdaeme et al., 2002; Riva & Giorgi, 2000).

The **reticular formation**, a structure in the brain stem that maintains alertness and consciousness, generates synapses and myelinates throughout early childhood and into adolescence.

FIGURE 8.4

Cross section of the human brain, showing the location of the cerebellum, the reticular formation, the hippocampus, and the corpus callosum. These structures undergo considerable development during early childhood. Also shown is the pituitary gland, which secretes hormones that control body growth (see page 301).

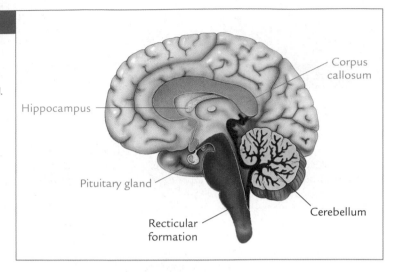

Neurons in the reticular formation send out fibers to other areas of the brain. Many go to the frontal lobes of the cerebral cortex, contributing to improvements in sustained, controlled attention.

An inner-brain structure called the **hippocampus**—which plays a vital role in memory and in images of space that help us find our way—undergoes rapid formation of synapses and myelination in the second half of the first year, when recall memory and independent movement emerge (see page 169 in Chapter 5). Over the preschool and elementary school years, the hippocampus, along with surrounding areas of the cerebral cortex, continues its swift development, establishing connections with one another and with the frontal lobes (Nelson, Thomas, & de Haan, 2006). These changes make possible the dramatic gains in memory and spatial understanding of early and middle childhood—ability to use strategies to store and retrieve information, expansion of autobiographical memory (which brings an end to infantile amnesia), and drawing and reading of maps (which we will take up in Chapter 9).

The **corpus callosum** is a large bundle of fibers that connects the two cerebral hemispheres. Production of synapses and myelination of the corpus callosum increase at 1 year, peak between 3 and 6 years, then continue at a slower pace through middle childhood and adolescence (Thompson et al., 2000a). The corpus callosum supports smooth coordination of movements on both sides of the body and integration of many aspects of thinking, including perception, attention, memory, language, and problem solving. The more complex the task, the more critical is communication between the hemispheres.

In early childhood, changes in the corpus callosum and other brain structures enhance communication between different parts of the brain, enabling children to perform increasingly complex tasks—like this board game—that require integration of attention, memory, language, and problem solving.

Ask Yourself

Review   What aspects of brain development support the tremendous gains in language, thinking, and motor control of early childhood?

Connect   What stance on the nature–nurture issue does evidence on development of handedness support? Document your answer with research findings.

Apply   Both Crystal and Shana are shorter and lighter than 97 percent of North American 4-year-old girls. What are the possible causes of their very short stature?

Reflect   How early, and to what extent, did you experience tooth decay in childhood? What factors might have been responsible?

Biology and Environment

Low-Level Lead Exposure and Children's Development

Lead is a highly toxic element that, at blood levels exceeding 60 μg/dL (micrograms per deciliter), causes brain swelling and hemorrhaging. Risk of death rises as blood-lead level exceeds 100 μg/dL. Before 1980, exposure to lead resulted from the use of lead-based paints for the interiors of residences (where infants and young children often ate paint chips that flaked off walls) and from the use of leaded gasoline (car exhaust resulted in a highly breathable form of lead). The passage of laws limiting the lead content of paint and mandating lead-free gasoline led to a sharp decline in children's

AP IMAGES/MOHAMED El-DAKHAKHNY

lead levels, from an average of 15 μg/dL in 1980 to 1.9 μg/dL today (Centers for Disease Control and Prevention, 2005; Meyer et al., 2003).

But in neighborhoods near industries that use lead production processes, or where lead-based paint remains in older homes, children's blood levels are still markedly elevated. About 16 percent of low-SES children who live in large central cities, and 37 percent of African-American children in these areas, have blood-lead levels exceeding 10 μg/dL (the official "level of concern" in the United States and Canada), warranting immediate efforts to reduce exposure (Centers for Disease Control and Prevention, 2005; Health Canada, 2006c).

How much lead exposure is too much? Is lead contamination a "silent epidemic," impairing children's mental functioning even in small quantities? Until recently, answers were unclear. Studies reporting a negative relationship between children's current lead levels and cognitive performance had serious limita-

tions. Researchers knew nothing about children's history of lead exposure and often failed to control for factors associated with both blood-lead levels and mental test scores (such as SES, home environmental quality, and nutrition) that might account for the findings.

Over the past two decades, seven longitudinal studies of the developmental consequences of lead have been conducted—three in the United States, two in Australia, one in Mexico City, and one in Yugoslavia. Some focused on inner-city, low-SES minority children, others on middle- and upper-middle SES suburban children, and one on children living close to a lead smelter. Each tracked children's lead exposure over an extended time and included relevant controls.

Consistent findings emerged: In five sites, negative relationships between lead exposure and children's IQs emerged (Hubbs-Tait et al., 2006). Higher blood levels were also associated with deficits in verbal and visual-motor skills and with distractibility, overactivity, poor organization, and behavior problems. And an array of findings suggested that persistent childhood lead exposure contributes to antisocial behavior in adolescence (Dietrich et al., 2001; Needleman et al., 2002; Nevin, 2000; Stretesky & Lynch, 2001).

These children play near a cement factory in Cairo, Egypt, which ranks among the worlds most polluted cities in levels of lead and other toxins. Longitudinal studies consistently show lasting negative effects of lead exposure, including learning impairments and behavior problems.

Influences on Physical Growth and Health

As we discuss growth and health during early childhood, you will encounter some familiar themes. Heredity remains important, but environmental factors continue to play a crucial role. Emotional well-being, restful sleep, good nutrition, relative freedom from disease, and physical safety are essential. And as the Biology and Environment box illustrates, environmental pollutants can threaten children's healthy development. The extent to which low-level lead—one of the most common—undermines children's mental and emotional functioning is the focus of intensive research.

Heredity and Hormones

The impact of heredity on physical growth is evident throughout childhood. Children's physical size and rate of growth are related to those of their parents (Bogin, 2001). Genes influence

The investigations did not agree on an age period of greatest vulnerability. In some, relationships were strongest in toddlerhood and early childhood; in others, at the most recently studied age—suggesting cumulative effects over time. Still other studies reported a similar susceptibility to lead-related cognitive deficits from infancy through adolescence. Overall, poorer mental test scores associated with lead exposure persisted over time and seemed to be permanent. Children given drugs to induce excretion of lead (chelation) did not improve in long-term outcomes (Dietrich et al., 2004; Rogan et al., 2001). And negative lead-related cognitive consequences were evident at all levels of exposure—even below 10 µg/dL (Lamphear et al., 2005).

Although the overall impact of low-level lead exposure on all outcomes is modest, in three longitudinal investigations, cognitive consequences were much greater for low-SES than higher-SES children (see, for example, Figure 8.5) (Bellinger, Leviton, & Sloman, 1990; Ris et al., 2004; Tong, McMichael, & Baghurst, 2000). A stressed, disorganized home life seems to heighten lead-induced damage, whereas an organized, stimulating home and school may offset it. Dietary factors can also magnify or reduce lead's toxic effects. Iron deficiency, common in low-SES children, increases lead concentration in the blood, whereas iron supplements decrease it. Similarly, exposed children absorb less lead when their diets contain enough zinc (Noonan et al., 2003; Wolf, Jimenez, & Lozoff, 2003; Wright et al., 2003).

In sum, lead impairs learning and contributes to behavior problems—findings confirmed by rigorous animal experiments (Cory-Slechta, 2003; Delville, 1999; Li et al., 2003). Low-SES

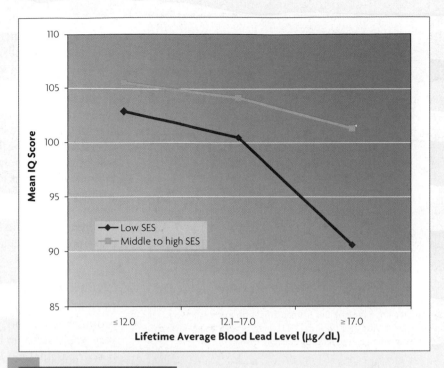

FIGURE 8.5

Relationship of lifetime average lead exposure to 11-to-13-year-old IQ by SES. In this study, conducted in the lead-smelting city of Port Pirie, Australia, blood-lead levels of 375 children were measured repeatedly from birth to age 11 to 13. Among both low-SES and higher-SES participants, increases in lifetime average blood-lead concentrations were associated with poorer mental test scores. But the lead-exposure-related drop in IQ was much greater for low-SES children. (Adapted from Tong, McMichael, & Baghurst, 2000.)

children are more likely both to live in lead-contaminated areas and to experience additional risks that magnify lead-induced damage. Because lead is a stable element, its release into the air and soil is difficult to reverse. Therefore, in addition to laws that control lead pollution and limit children's exposure, interventions that reduce the negative impact of lead—through involved parenting, better schools, and dietary enrichment—are vital.

growth by controlling the body's production of hormones. The **pituitary gland**, located at the base of the brain (refer to Figure 8.4), plays a critical role by releasing two hormones that induce growth.

The first, **growth hormone (GH)**, is necessary from birth on for development of all body tissues except the central nervous system and genitals. Children who lack GH reach an average mature height of only 4 feet, 4 inches. When treated early with injections of GH, such children show catch-up growth and then grow at a normal rate, becoming much taller than they would have without treatment (Saenger, 2003).

The availability of synthetic GH has also made it possible to treat short, normal-GH children with hormone injections, in hopes of increasing their final height. Thousands of parents, concerned that their children will suffer social stigma because of their shortness, have sought this GH therapy. But most normal-GH children given GH treatment grow only slightly taller than their previously predicted mature height (Guyda, 1999). And contrary to popular belief, normal-GH short children are not deficient in self-esteem or other aspects of psychological

pituitary gland A gland located near the base of the brain that releases hormones affecting physical growth.

growth hormone (GH) A pituitary hormone that affects the development of all body tissues except the central nervous system and the genitals.

When a child is extremely short because of growth hormone (GH) deficiency, early treatment with injections of GH leads to substantial gains in height. But little justification exists for using this treatment with short, normal-GH children, who do not differ from their agemates in psychological adjustment.

adjustment (Sandberg & Voss, 2002). So despite the existence of "heightism" in Western cultures, little justification exists for medically intervening in short stature that is merely the result of biologically normal human diversity.

A second pituitary hormone, **thyroid-stimulating hormone (TSH)**, prompts the thyroid gland in the neck to release *thyroxine*, which is necessary for brain development and for GH to have its full impact on body size. Infants born with a deficiency of thyroxine must receive it at once, or they will be mentally retarded. Once the most rapid period of brain development is complete, children with too little thyroxine grow at a below-average rate, but the central nervous system is no longer affected. With prompt treatment, such children catch up in body growth and eventually reach normal size (Salerno et al., 2001).

Emotional Well-Being

In childhood as in infancy, emotional well-being can have a profound effect on growth and health. Preschoolers with very stressful home lives (due to divorce, financial difficulties, or parental job loss) suffer more respiratory and intestinal illnesses and more unintentional injuries than others (Cohen & Herbert, 1996; Kemeny, 2003).

Extreme emotional deprivation can interfere with the production of GH and lead to **psychosocial dwarfism**, a growth disorder that appears between ages 2 and 15. Typical characteristics include very short stature, decreased GH secretion, immature skeletal age, and serious adjustment problems, which help distinguish psychosocial dwarfism from normal shortness (Doeker et al., 1999; Voss, Mulligan, & Betts, 1998). Lynette, the 4-year-old mentioned earlier in this chapter, was diagnosed with this condition. She was placed in foster care after child welfare authorities discovered that she spent most of the day at home alone, unsupervised, and also might have been physically abused. When children like Lynette are removed from their emotionally inadequate environments, their GH levels quickly return to normal, and they grow rapidly. But if treatment is delayed, the dwarfism can be permanent.

Sleep Habits and Problems

Sleep contributes to body growth, since GH is released during the child's sleeping hours. A well-rested child is better able to play, learn, and contribute positively to family functioning. Also, children who sleep poorly disrupt their parents' sleep, which can contribute to significant family stress—a major reason that sleep difficulties are among the most common concerns parents raise with their preschooler's doctor (Mindell, Owens, & Carskadon, 1999; Mindell, 2005).

On average, total sleep declines in early childhood; 2- and 3-year-olds sleep 11 to 12 hours, 4- to 6-year-olds 10 to 11 hours (National Sleep Foundation, 2004). Younger preschoolers typically take a 1- to 2-hour nap in the early afternoon, although their daytime sleep needs vary widely. Some continue to take two naps, as they did in toddlerhood; others give up napping entirely. Most children stop napping between ages 3 and 4, although a quiet play period or rest after lunch helps them rejuvenate for the rest of the day (Howard & Wong, 2001). In some cultures, daytime naps persist through adulthood.

Western preschoolers often become rigid about bedtime rituals, such as using the toilet, listening to a story, getting a drink of water, taking a security object to bed, and hugging and kissing before turning off the light. These practices, which can take as long as 30 minutes, help young children adjust to feelings of uneasiness at being left by themselves in a darkened room. Difficulty falling asleep—calling to the parent or asking for another drink of water—is common in early childhood. When it occurs repeatedly, it is usually due to typical fears of the preschool

thyroid-stimulating hormone (TSH) A pituitary hormone that stimulates the thyroid gland to release thyroxine, which is necessary for normal brain development and body growth.

psychosocial dwarfism A growth disorder, observed between 2 and 15 years of age, characterized by very short stature, decreased GH secretion, immature skeletal age, and serious adjustment problems.

years or to parental problems in setting bedtime limits. The problem usually subsides when parents follow the recommendations given in Applying What We Know below. Intense bedtime struggles sometimes result from family turmoil, as children worry about how their parents may get along when they are asleep and not available to distract them. In these cases, addressing family stress and conflict is the key to improving children's sleep.

In early childhood, parent–child cosleeping remains the usual practice in non-Western cultures and many ethnic minority groups. North American Caucasian parents who cosleep with their preschoolers tend to be reluctant to tell others about the practice, out of fear of disapproval, so how many do so is uncertain. In most cases, cosleeping is not associated with problems during the preschool years, other than more frequent night wakings by parents due to children's movements during sleep (Gaylor et al., 2005; Thiedke, 2001). Western cosleeping children generally ask to sleep in their own bed by age 6 or 7.

Finally, most children waken during the night from time to time, and those who cannot return to sleep on their own may suffer from a sleep disorder. Because young children have vivid imaginations and difficulty separating fantasy from reality, *nightmares* are common; half of 3- to 6-year-olds experience them from time to time. And about 4 percent of children are frequent *sleepwalkers,* who are unaware of their wanderings during the night. Gently awakening and returning the child to bed helps avoid self-injury. *Sleep terrors,* which affect 3 percent of young children, are perhaps

Parents of preschoolers often report that their children have sleep difficulties. Bedtime rituals, such as a story and a hug and kiss before turning out the light, help young children adjust to falling asleep in a room by themselves.

Applying What We Know

Helping Young Children Get a Good Night's Sleep

STRATEGY	EXPLANATION
Establish a regular bedtime, early enough to ensure, on average, 10 to 11 hours of nightly sleep.	Children who go to sleep too late in the evening—after 9:30 or 10 P.M.—get less sleep than those who go to sleep earlier and are sleepier and more irritable during the day.
Provide special bedtime attire.	Changing into bedtime attire, such as pajamas or a nightshirt, provides the child with clear psychological separation between daytime and bedtime.
Avoid watching television or playing computer games before bedtime.	Preschoolers' difficulty distinguishing fantasy from reality can lead to disturbing thoughts and emotions that interfere with sleep.
If the child resists going to bed, respond with kind but firm insistence.	Discuss the next day's activities with the child, emphasizing that tomorrow will be a good day. Initiate the bedtime ritual without introducing other enjoyable activities and, if necessary, stay with the child until he or she falls asleep.
If the child awakens repeatedly during the night, establish a routine to follow.	Respond to an upset child. Letting preschoolers cry themselves to sleep undermines trust in the parent and, instead of enhancing self-control, increases clingy and demanding behavior during the day. Use a predictable, but boring, routine that ends with the last two or three steps of the child's bedtime ritual—rubbing the child's back, hugging and kissing the child, and sitting quietly with the child until he or she returns to sleep.
Do not give a child who resists sleep over-the-counter sleeping medication of any kind.	These brain-altering chemicals can affect children differently than adults. They also cause "rebound" insomnia—sleeplessness after medication is discontinued. And they prevent children from developing their own effective strategies for falling asleep. Children with sleep disorders may require prescription medication, which must be carefully supervised by the child's doctor.

Sources: Mindell, 2005; Owens, Rosen, & Mindell, 2003.

the most upsetting sleep problem to parents. In these panic-stricken arousals from deep sleep, the child may scream, thrash, speak incoherently, show a sharp rise in heart rate and breathing, and initially be unresponsive to parents' attempts to comfort. Sleepwalking and sleep terrors tend to run in families, suggesting a genetic influence (Guilleminault et al., 2003; Thorpy & Yager, 2001). But they can also be triggered by stress or extreme fatigue.

Fortunately, sleep disorders of early childhood usually subside without treatment. In the few cases that persist, children require a medical and psychological evaluation. Their disturbed sleep may be a sign of neurological or emotional difficulties (Gregory et al., 2004). And the resulting daytime sleepiness often contributes to attention, learning, and behavior problems.

Nutrition

With the transition to early childhood, appetite tends to become unpredictable. Preschoolers eat well at one meal and barely touch their food at the next. And many become picky eaters. One father I know wistfully recalled how his son, as a toddler, eagerly sampled Chinese food: "He ate rice, chicken chow mein, egg rolls—and now, at age 3, the only thing he'll try is the ice cream!"

Preschoolers' appetites decline because their growth has slowed. Their wariness of new foods is also adaptive: If they stick to familiar foods, they are less likely to swallow dangerous substances when adults are not around to protect them (Birch & Fisher, 1995). Parents need not worry about variations in amount eaten from meal to meal. Over the course of a day, preschoolers compensate for eating little at one meal by eating more at a later one (Hursti, 1999).

Though they eat less, preschoolers need a high-quality diet, including the same foods adults need, but in smaller amounts. Milk and milk products, meat or meat alternatives (such as eggs, dried peas or beans, and peanut butter), vegetables and fruits, and breads and cereals should be included. Fats, oils, and salt should be kept to a minimum because of their link to high blood pressure and heart disease in adulthood. Foods high in sugar should also be avoided. In addition to causing tooth decay, they lessen young children's appetite for healthy foods and increase their risk of overweight and obesity—a topic we will take up in Chapter 11.

The social environment powerfully influences young children's food preferences. Children tend to imitate the food choices and eating practices of people they admire, both adults and peers. For example, mothers who drink milk or soft drinks tend to have 5-year-old daughters with a similar beverage preference (Fisher et al., 2001). In Mexico, where children see family members delighting in the taste of peppery foods, preschoolers enthusiastically eat chili peppers, whereas most North American children reject them (Birch, Zimmerman, & Hind, 1980).

Repeated, unpressured exposure to a new food also increases acceptance (Fuller et al., 2005). In one study, preschoolers were given one of three versions of a food they had never eaten before (sweet, salty, or plain tofu). After 8 to 15 exposures, they readily ate the food. But they preferred the version they had already tasted. For example, children in the "sweet" condition liked sweet tofu best, and those in the "plain" condition liked plain tofu best (Sullivan & Birch, 1990). These findings reveal that adding sugar or salt in hopes of increasing a young child's willingness to eat healthy foods simply strengthens the child's desire for a sugary or salty taste. Similarly, offering children sweet fruit or soft drinks promotes "milk avoidance." Compared to their milk-drinking agemates, milk-avoiders are shorter in stature and have a lower bone density—a condition that leads to a lifelong reduction in strength and to increased risk of bone fractures (Black et al., 2002).

The emotional climate at mealtimes has a powerful impact on children's eating habits. When parents are worried

This Quechua child of the Peruvian highlands enthusiastically shares a soup made from bitter-tasting potatoes with her father. She has already acquired a taste for the foods that are commonly served in her culture.

© MARC GARANGER/CORBIS

Applying What We Know

Encouraging Good Nutrition in Early Childhood

SUGGESTION	DESCRIPTION
Offer a varied, healthy diet.	Provide a well-balanced variety of nutritious foods that are colorful and attractively served. Avoid serving sweets and "junk" foods as a regular part of meals and snacks.
Offer predictable meals as well as several snacks each day.	Preschoolers' stomachs are small, and they may not be able to eat enough in three meals to satisfy their energy requirements. They benefit from extra opportunities to eat.
Offer small portions, and permit the child to serve him- or herself and to ask for seconds.	When too much food is put on the plate, preschoolers often overeat, increasing the risk of obesity. On average, preschoolers consume 25 percent less at a meal when permitted to serve themselves.
Offer new foods early in a meal and repeatedly at subsequent meals, and respond with patience if the child rejects the food.	Introduce new foods before the child's appetite is satisfied. Let children see you eat and enjoy the new food. If the child rejects it, accept the refusal and serve it again at another meal. As foods become more familiar, they are more readily accepted.
Keep mealtimes pleasant, and include the child in mealtime conversations.	A pleasant, relaxed eating environment helps children develop positive attitudes about food. Refrain from constantly offering food and prompting eating because these practices are associated with excessively fast eating and overeating. Avoid confrontations over disliked foods and table manners, which may lead to refusal to eat.
Avoid using food as a reward and forbidding access to certain foods.	Saying "No dessert until you clean your plate" tells children that they must eat regardless of whether they are hungry and that dessert is the best part of the meal. Restricting access to a food increases children's valuing of that food and efforts to obtain it.

Sources: Birch, 1999; Fisher, Rolls, & Birch, 2003; Spruijt-Metz et al., 2002.

about how well their preschoolers are eating, meals can become unpleasant and stressful. Offering bribes ("Finish your vegetables, and you can have an extra cookie"), as some parents do, causes children to like the healthy food less and the treat more. Although children's healthy eating depends on a healthy food environment, too much parental control over children's eating limits their opportunities to develop self-control, thereby promoting overeating (Birch, Fisher, & Davison, 2003). For ways to encourage healthy, varied eating in young children, refer to Applying What We Know above.

Finally, as indicated in earlier chapters, many children in North America and in developing countries lack access to sufficient high-quality food to support healthy growth. Five-year-old Hal rode a bus from a poor neighborhood to our laboratory preschool. His mother's welfare check barely covered her rent, let alone food. Hal's diet was deficient in protein and in essential vitamins and minerals—iron (to prevent anemia), calcium (to support development of bones and teeth), zinc (to support immune system functioning, neural communication, and cell duplication), vitamin A (to help maintain eyes, skin, and a variety of internal organs), and vitamin C (to facilitate iron absorption and wound healing). These are the most common dietary deficiencies of the preschool years (Ganji, Hampl, & Betts, 2003).

Hal was small for his age, pale, inattentive, and unruly at preschool. By the school years, North American low-SES children are, on average, about ½ to 1 inch shorter than their economically advantaged counterparts (Cecil et al., 2005; Yip, Scanlon, & Trowbridge, 1993). And throughout childhood and adolescence, a nutritionally deficient diet is associated with attention difficulties, poorer mental test scores, and behavior problems—especially hyperactivity and aggression—even after family factors that might account for these relationships (such as stressors, parental psychological health, education, warmth, and stimulation of the child) are controlled (Liu et al., 2004; Pollitt, 2001; Slack & Yoo, 2005).

Infectious Disease

Two weeks into the school year, I looked outside my window and noticed that Hal was absent from the play yard. Several weeks passed, and I still did not see him, so I asked Leslie, his

These street children in Calcutta, India, are at risk for disease resulting from unsanitary food and contaminated water. Disease, in turn, contributes to malnutrition, with negative consequences for both physical and cognitive development.

preschool teacher, what was wrong. "Hal's been hospitalized with the measles," she explained. "He's had difficulty recovering—lost weight when there wasn't much to lose in the first place." In well-nourished children, ordinary childhood illnesses have no effect on physical growth. But when children are undernourished, disease interacts with malnutrition in a vicious spiral, with potentially severe consequences.

INFECTIOUS DISEASE AND MALNUTRITION ■ Hal's reaction to the measles would be commonplace in developing nations, where a large proportion of the population lives in poverty and children do not receive routine immunizations. Illnesses such as measles and chicken pox, which typically do not appear until after age 3 in industrialized nations, occur much earlier. Poor diet depresses the body's immune system, making children far more susceptible to disease. Of the 10 million annual deaths of children under age 5 worldwide, 98 percent are in developing countries, and 70 percent are due to infectious diseases (World Health Organization, 2005).

Disease, in turn, is a major contributor to malnutrition, hindering both physical growth and cognitive development. Illness reduces appetite and limits the body's ability to absorb foods, especially in children with intestinal infections. In developing countries, widespread diarrhea, resulting from unsafe water and contaminated foods, leads to several million childhood deaths each year (Tharpar & Sanderson, 2004). Studies carried out in the slums and shantytowns of Brazil and Peru reveal that the more persistent diarrhea is in early childhood, the shorter children are in height and the lower they score on mental tests during the school years (Checkley et al., 2003; Niehaus et al., 2002).

Most developmental impairments and deaths due to diarrhea can be prevented with nearly cost-free *oral rehydration therapy (ORT)*, in which sick children are given a glucose, salt, and water solution that quickly replaces fluids the body loses. Since 1990, public health workers have taught nearly half the families in the developing world how to administer ORT. Also, supplements of zinc (essential for immune system functioning), which cost only 30 cents for a month's supply, substantially reduce the incidence of severe and prolonged diarrhea (Bhandari et al., 2002). Because of these interventions, the lives of millions of children are saved each year.

IMMUNIZATION ■ In industrialized nations, childhood diseases have declined dramatically over the past half-century, largely because of widespread immunization of infants and young children. Hal got the measles because, unlike his classmates from more advantaged homes, he did not receive a full program of immunizations.

About 20 percent of American infants and toddlers are not fully immunized. Of the 80 percent who receive a complete schedule of vaccinations in the first two years, some do not receive the immunizations they need later, in early childhood. Overall, 24 percent of American preschoolers lack essential immunizations, a rate that rises to 27 percent for poverty-stricken children and is especially high for Native Americans, at 33 percent. Many of these preschoolers do not receive full protection until age 5 or 6, when it is required for school entry (U.S. Department of Health and Human Services, 2006h). In contrast, fewer than 10 percent of preschoolers lack immunizations in Denmark and Norway, and fewer than 7 percent in Great Britain, Canada, the Netherlands, and Sweden (United Nations, 2002; UNICEF, 2006).

Why does the United States lag behind these other countries in immunization? In earlier chapters, we noted that many children in the United States do not have access to the health care they need. The Cultural Influences box on the following page compares child health care in the United States with that in other Western nations.

Inability to pay for vaccines is only one cause of inadequate immunization. Parents with stressful daily lives often fail to schedule vaccination appointments, and those without a

Cultural Influences

Child Health Care in the United States and Other Western Nations

In the United States, strongly individualistic values, which emphasize parental responsibility for the care and rearing of children, join with powerful economic interests in the medical community to prevent government-sponsored health services from being offered to all American children. Health insurance in the United States is generally an optional, employment-related fringe benefit. Businesses that rely on low-wage and part-time help often do not insure their employees; others do not cover employees' family members, including children.

The largest U.S. public health insurance program, Medicaid, serves only very-low-income people. This leaves about 8 million children (9 percent of the child population), many of whom have working parents, uninsured and, therefore, without affordable health care (U.S. Census Bureau, 2007b). In the United States, uninsured children are three times as likely as insured children to go without needed doctor visits (Newachek et al., 2002). Consequently, an estimated one-third of children younger than age 5 who come from economically disadvantaged families are in less than very good health. Partly because of weak health care services, 13 percent of children living in poverty have activity limitations due to chronic illnesses—a rate nearly double the national average (U.S. Department of Health and Human Services, 2006e).

The inadequacies of U.S. child health care stand in sharp contrast to services provided in Australia, Canada, New Zealand, Western Europe, and other industrialized nations, where government-sponsored health insurance is regarded as a fundamental human right and is made available to all citizens. Let's look at two examples.

In the Netherlands, every child receives free medical examinations from birth through adolescence. Children's health care also includes parental counseling in nutrition, disease prevention, and child development (de Winter, Balledux, & de Mare, 1997). The Netherlands achieves its extraordinarily high childhood immunization rate by giving parents of every newborn baby a written schedule that shows exactly when and where the child should be immunized. If a parent does not bring the child at the specified time,

a public health nurse calls the family. When appointments are missed repeatedly, the nurse goes to the home to ensure that the child receives the recommended immunizations (de Pree-Geerlings, de Pree, & Bulk-Bunschoten, 2001).

In Norway, federal law requires that all communities establish well-baby and child clinics and that health checkups occur three times in the first year, then at ages 2 and 4. On other occasions, children are seen by specialized nurses who monitor their development, provide immunizations, and counsel parents on physical and mental health (AWC Oslo, 2005). Although citizens pay a small fee for routine medical visits, hospital services are free.

Currently, many organizations, government officials, and concerned citizens committed to improving child health are working to guarantee every American child basic health care. Under the State Children's Health Insurance Program (SCHIP), launched in 1997, the states receive $4 billion a year in federal matching funds for upgrading children's health insurance. State control over program implementation enables each state to adapt insurance coverage to meet its unique needs. But it also means that child advocates must continually exert pressure for family-friendly policies. For example, a state can require that families share health care costs, despite the fact that for low-income parents, even a small premium or copayment generally makes SCHIP unaffordable. Currently, many states are experiencing funding shortfalls and, without additional government allocations, will have to reduce SCHIP enrollment or medical coverage rates (Trapp, 2007).

Even many insured U.S. children do not see a doctor regularly. Parents with no health benefits of their own are less inclined to make

Poverty-stricken, publicly insured U.S. children and their parents often endure long waits in crowded public clinics to receive health care services. Because many American doctors refuse to take public-aid patients, such children frequently do not have a primary care physician, and they receive lower-quality care than their more economically advantaged, privately insured agemates.

appointments for their children. And because of low insurance-reimbursement rates, many doctors refuse to take public-aid patients. As a result, children with public insurance frequently do not have a primary care physician. Instead, they endure long waits in crowded public health clinics, and their parents often say they cannot gain access to needed services (Dombrowski, Lantz, & Freed, 2004; Hughes & Ng, 2003).

Finally, millions of eligible children are not enrolled in SCHIP because their parents either do not understand the eligibility requirements or find the application process confusing. Clearly, the United States has a long way to go to ensure that all its children receive excellent health care.

primary care physician do not want to endure long waits in crowded U.S. public health clinics. Misconceptions about vaccine safety also contribute—for example, the notion that vaccines do not work or that they weaken the immune system (Gellin, Maibach, & Marcuse, 2000). Furthermore, some parents have been influenced by media reports suggesting a link between the measles–mumps–rubella vaccine and a rise in the number of children diagnosed with autism, although large-scale studies show no such association (Dales, Hammer, & Smith, 2001; Richler et al., 2006; Stehr-Green et al., 2003). In areas where many parents have refused to immunize their children, disease outbreaks of whooping cough and rubella have occurred, with life-threatening consequences (Tuyen & Bisgard, 2003). Public education programs directed at increasing parental knowledge about the importance of timely immunizations are badly needed.

A final point regarding communicable disease in early childhood deserves mention. Childhood illness rises with child-care attendance. On average, a child-care infant becomes sick 9 to 10 times a year, a child-care preschool child 6 to 7 times. The diseases that spread most rapidly are those most frequently suffered by young children—diarrhea and respiratory infections. The risk that a respiratory infection will result in *otitis media,* or middle ear infection, is almost double that for children remaining at home (Nafstad et al., 1999). To learn about the consequences of otitis media and how to prevent it, consult the Social Issues: Health box on the following page.

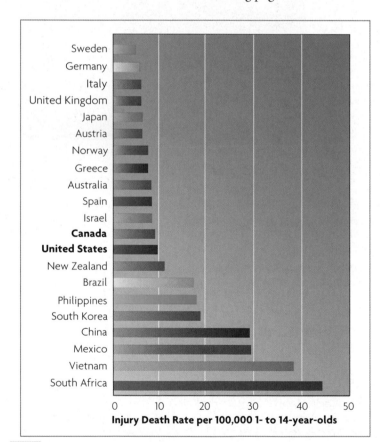

FIGURE 8.6

International death rates due to unintentional injury among 1- to 14-year-olds. Compared with other industrialized nations, the United States and Canada have high injury death rates, largely because of widespread childhood poverty and shortages of high-quality child care. Injury death rates are many times higher in developing nations, where poverty, rapid population growth, overcrowding in cities, and inadequate safety measures endanger children's lives. (Adapted from Health Canada, 2005a; Safe Kids Worldwide, 2002; Towner & Towner, 2002.)

Childhood Injuries

More than any other child in the preschool classroom, 3-year-old Tommy had trouble sitting still and paying attention. Instead, he darted from one place and activity to another. One day, I read in our local newspaper that Tommy had narrowly escaped serious injury when he put his mother's car in gear while she was outside scraping ice from its windows. The vehicle rolled through a guardrail and over the side of a 10-foot concrete underpass, where it hung until rescue workers arrived. Police charged Tommy's mother with failing to use a restraint seat for a child younger than age 8.

Unintentional injuries—auto collisions, pedestrian accidents, drownings, poisonings, firearm wounds, burns, falls, and swallowing of foreign objects—are the leading causes of childhood mortality in industrialized nations. As Figure 8.6 reveals, the United States and, to a lesser extent, Canada rank poorly in these largely preventable events. In North America, nearly 40 percent of childhood deaths and 70 percent of adolescent deaths are due to injury (Children's Defense Fund, 2006; Health Canada, 2005a). And among injured children and youths who survive, thousands suffer pain, brain damage, and permanent physical disabilities.

Auto and traffic accidents, drownings, burns, falls, and poisonings are the most common injuries during early childhood. Motor vehicle collisions are by far the most frequent source of injury at all ages, ranking as the leading cause of death among children more than 1 year old.

FACTORS RELATED TO CHILDHOOD INJURIES ■
The common view of childhood injuries as "accidental"

Social Issues: Health

Otitis Media and Development

During his first year in child care, 2-year-old Alex caught five colds, had the flu on two occasions, and experienced repeated *otitis media* (middle ear infection). Alex is not unusual. By age 3, 75 percent of North American children have had respiratory illnesses that resulted in at least one bout of otitis media; nearly half of these have had three or more bouts (Aronson & Henderson, 2006). Although antibiotics eliminate the bacteria responsible for otitis media, they do not reduce fluid buildup in the middle ear, which causes mild to moderate hearing loss that can last for weeks or months.

The incidence of otitis media is greatest between 6 months and 3 years, when children are first acquiring language. Frequent infections predict delayed language progress in early childhood and poorer academic performance after school entry that, in one study, was still evident in adolescence (Bennett et al., 2001; Casby, 2001; Miccio et al., 2002).

How might otitis media disrupt language and academic progress? Difficulties in perceiving and processing speech sounds, particularly in noisy settings, may be responsible (Polka & Rvachew, 2005). Children with many bouts are less attentive to others' speech and less persistent at tasks (Asbjornsen et al., 2005; Petinou et al., 2001). Their distractibility may result from an inability to make out what people around them are saying—which, in turn, may reduce the quality of others' interactions with them.

Because otitis media is so widespread, current evidence argues strongly in favor of early prevention. Crowded living conditions and exposure to cigarette smoke and other pollutants are linked to the disease, probably accounting for its high incidence among low-SES children. And child care creates opportunities for close contact, greatly increasing otitis media episodes.

Early otitis media can be prevented in the following ways:

- *Preventive doses of xylitol, a sweetener derived from birch bark.* Research in Finland revealed that children given a daily dose of xylitol, in gum or syrup form, showed a 30 to 40 percent drop in otitis media compared with controls given gum or syrup without the sweetener. Xylitol appears to have natural bacteria-fighting ingredients (Blazek-O'Neill, 2005). However, dosage must be carefully monitored—too much xylitol can cause abdominal pain and diarrhea.
- *Frequent screening for the disease, followed by prompt medical intervention.* Plastic tubes that drain the inner ear often are used to treat chronic otitis media, although their effectiveness has been disputed.
- *Child-care settings that control infection.* Because infants and young children often put toys in their mouths, these objects should be rinsed frequently with a disinfectant. Spacious, well-ventilated rooms and small group sizes also limit spread of the disease.
- *Verbally stimulating adult–child interaction.* Developmental problems associated with otitis media are reduced or eliminated in high-quality child-care centers. When caregivers are verbally stimulating and keep noise to a minimum, children have more opportunities to hear, and benefit from, spoken language (Roberts et al., 1998; Vernon-Feagans, Hurley, & Yont, 2002).

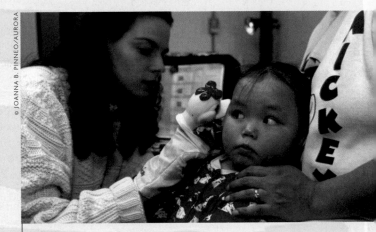

© JOANNA B. PINNEO/AURORA

This 2-year-old Inuit child of Canada's Northwest Territory has her hearing tested. Frequent otitis media infections can lead to persistent hearing problems, which interfere with language development and later academic progress. About one-fourth of Inuit children are affected.

suggests that they are due to chance and cannot be prevented (Sleet & Mercy, 2003). In fact, these injuries occur within a complex *ecological system* of individual, family, community, and societal influences—and we can do something about them.

As Tommy's case suggests, individual differences exist in the safety of children's behaviors. Because of their higher activity level and sensation seeking, and their greater willingness to take risks, boys are 1.5 times more likely to be injured than girls, and their injuries are more severe (National Safe Kids Campaign, 2005). Parents realize that they need to take more steps to protect their young sons than daughters from injury, and most do so. Still, mothers judge the chances of preventing injury in sons to be lower—a belief that may keep them from exercising sufficient oversight and control over the most injury-prone boys (Morrongiello & Kiriakou, 2004; Morrongiello, Ondejko, & Littlejohn, 2004).

Children with other temperamental characteristics—irritability, inattentiveness, and negative mood—are also at greater risk for injury (Matheny, 1991; Schwebel et al., 2004). As we

Boys' higher activity level and sensation seeking and greater willingness to take risks explain why they are more likely than girls to be injured, and to experience severe injuries.

saw in Chapter 7, children with these traits present child-rearing challenges. They are likely to protest when placed in auto seat restraints, to refuse to take a companion's hand when crossing the street, and to disobey after repeated instruction and discipline.

Other factors strongly associated with injury are poverty, low parental education, and more children in the home (Ramsay et al., 2003). Parents who must cope with many daily stresses often have little time and energy to monitor the safety of their youngsters. And their homes and neighborhoods are likely to be noisy, crowded, and run-down, posing further risks (Dal Santo et al., 2004).

Broad societal conditions also affect childhood injury. In developing countries, the rate of death from injury before age 15 is five times higher than in developed nations and soon may exceed disease as the leading cause of childhood mortality. Widespread poverty, rapid population growth, overcrowding in cities, and heavy road traffic combined with weak safety measures are major causes. Safety devices, such as car safety seats and bicycle helmets, are neither readily available nor affordable. To purchase a child safety seat requires more than 100 hours of wages in Vietnam and 53 hours in China, but only 2.5 hours in the United States (Safe Kids Worldwide, 2002).

Why, among developed nations, are injury rates so high in Canada and the United States? Major factors are poverty, shortages of high-quality child care (to supervise children in their parents' absence), and—especially in the United States—a high rate of births to teenagers, who are neither psychologically nor financially ready for parenthood. But North American children from advantaged families are also at somewhat greater risk for injury than children in Western Europe (Safe Kids Worldwide, 2002). This indicates that besides reducing poverty and teenage pregnancy and upgrading the status of child care, additional steps are needed to ensure children's safety.

PREVENTING CHILDHOOD INJURIES ■ Childhood injuries have many causes, so a variety of approaches are needed to control them. Laws prevent many injuries by requiring car safety seats, child-resistant caps on medicine bottles, flameproof clothing, and fencing around backyard swimming pools (the site of 50 percent of early childhood drownings) (Brenner, 2003). Communities can help by modifying their physical environments. Providing inexpensive and widely available public transportation can reduce the amount of time that children spend in cars. Playgrounds, a common site of injury, can be covered with protective surfaces (National Safe Kids Campaign, 2005). Families living in high-rise apartment buildings can be given free,

Motor vehicle collisions are the most frequent source of unintentional injury at all ages, including early childhood. American parents, who place a high value on individual rights and personal freedom, often ignore familiar safety practices, such as proper use of car safety seats.

easily installed window guards to prevent falls. And widespread media and information campaigns can inform parents and children about safety issues.

But even though they know better, many parents and children behave in ways that compromise safety. For example, about 10 percent of Canadian parents and 40 percent of American parents (like Tommy's mother) fail to place their preschoolers in car safety seats (Howard, 2002). And when parents do use safety seats, 82 percent either install or use them incorrectly (Howard, 2002; National Safe Kids Campaign, 2005). Americans, especially, seem willing to ignore familiar safety practices, perhaps because of the high value they place on individual rights and personal freedom (Damashek & Peterson, 2002).

Many North American parents begin relying on children's knowledge of safety rules, rather than monitoring and controlling access to hazards, as early as 2 or 3 years of age—a premature transition associated with a rise in home injuries (Morrongiello, Ondejko, & Littlejohn, 2004). But even older preschoolers spontaneously recall only about half the safety

Applying What We Know

Reducing Unintentional Injuries in Early Childhood

SUGGESTION	DESCRIPTION
Provide age-appropriate supervision and safety instruction.	Despite increasing understanding and self-control, preschoolers need nearly constant supervision. Establish and enforce safety rules, explain the reasons behind them, and praise children for following them, thereby encouraging the child to remember and obey.
Know the child's temperament.	Children who are unusually active, distractible, negative, or curious have more than their share of injuries and need extra monitoring.
Eliminate the most serious dangers from the home.	Examine all spaces for safety. For example, in the kitchen, store dangerous products in high cabinets out of sight, and keep sharp implements in a latched drawer. Remove guns; if that is impossible, store them unloaded in a locked cabinet. Always accompany young preschoolers to the bathroom, and keep all medicines in containers with safety caps.
During automobile travel, always restrain the child properly in the back seat of the car.	Use an age-appropriate, properly installed car safety seat or booster seat up to age 8 or until the child is 4 feet 9 inches tall, and strap the child in correctly every time. Children should always ride in the back seat; passenger-side air bags in the front seat deploy so forcefully that they can cause injury or death to a child.
Select safe playground equipment and sites.	Make sure sand, wood chips, or rubberized matting has been placed under swings, seesaws, and jungle gyms. Check yards for dangerous plants. Always supervise outdoor play.
Be extra cautious around water.	Constantly observe children during water play; even shallow inflatable pools are frequent sites of drownings. While they are swimming, young children's heads should not be immersed in water; they may swallow so much that they develop water intoxication, which can lead to convulsions and death.
Practice safety around animals.	Wait to get a pet until the child is mature enough to handle and care for it—usually around age 5 or 6. Never leave a young child alone with an animal; bites often occur during playful roughhousing. Model and teach humane pet treatment.

Source: Damashek & Peterson, 2002.

rules their parents teach them. And even with well-learned rules, they need supervision to ensure that they comply (Morrongiello, Midgett, & Shields, 2001).

Programs based on *behavior modification* (modeling and reinforcement) have been used to improve parent and child safety practices. But such efforts focus narrowly on specific risks. Attention must also be paid to family conditions that can prevent childhood injury: relieving crowding in the home, providing social supports to ease parental stress, and teaching parents to use effective discipline—a topic we will take up in Chapter 10. Positive parenting—an affectionate, supportive relationship with the child; consistent, reasonable expectations for maturity; and oversight—substantially reduces injury rates, especially in overactive and temperamentally difficult children (Schwebel et al., 2004). But to implement these strategies, parents must have ample time and emotional resources as well as relevant skills. Refer to Applying What We Know above for ways to minimize unintentional injuries in early childhood.

Ask Yourself

Review What sleep problems can Western parents anticipate during the preschool years, and what factors contribute to those problems?

Apply One day, Leslie prepared a new snack to serve at preschool: celery stuffed with ricotta cheese and pineapple. The first time she served it, few children touched it. How can Leslie encourage her students to accept the snack? What tactics should she avoid?

Connect Using research on malnutrition or on unintentional injuries, show how physical growth and health in early childhood result from a continuous, complex interplay between heredity and environment.

Reflect Ask a parent or other family member whether, as a preschooler, you were a picky eater, suffered from many infectious diseases, or sustained any serious injuries. In each instance, what factors might have been responsible?

Motor Development

TAKE A MOMENT... Observe several 2- to 6-year-olds at play in a neighborhood park, preschool, or child-care center. You will see that an explosion of new motor skills occurs in early childhood, each of which builds on the simpler movement patterns of toddlerhood.

During the preschool years, children continue to integrate previously acquired skills into more complex, *dynamic systems*. Then they revise each new skill as their bodies grow larger and stronger, their central nervous systems develop, their environments present new challenges, and they set new goals, aided by gains in perceptual and cognitive capacities.

Gross Motor Development

As children's bodies become more streamlined and less top-heavy, their center of gravity shifts downward, toward the trunk. As a result, balance improves greatly, paving the way for new motor skills involving large muscles of the body. By age 2, preschoolers' gaits become smooth and rhythmic—secure enough that soon they leave the ground, at first by running and later by jumping, hopping, galloping, and skipping.

As children become steadier on their feet, their arms and torsos are freed to experiment with new skills—throwing and catching balls, steering tricycles, and swinging on horizontal bars and rings. Then upper- and lower-body skills combine into more refined actions. Five- and 6-year-olds simultaneously steer and pedal a tricycle and flexibly move their whole body when jumping. By the end of the preschool years, all skills are performed with greater speed and endurance. Table 8.1 provides an overview of gross motor development in early childhood.

Changes in ball skills provide an excellent illustration of preschoolers' gross motor progress. **TAKE A MOMENT...** Play a game of catch with a 2- or 3-year-old, and watch the child's body. Young preschoolers stand still, facing the target, throwing with their arm thrust forward. Catching is equally awkward. Two-year-olds extend their arms and hands rigidly, using

TABLE 8.1	Changes in Gross and Fine Motor Skills During Early Childhood	
AGE	**GROSS MOTOR SKILLS**	**FINE MOTOR SKILLS**
2–3 years	Walks more rhythmically; hurried walk changes to run Jumps, hops, throws, and catches with rigid upper body Pushes riding toy with feet; little steering	Puts on and removes simple items of clothing Zips and unzips large zippers Uses spoon effectively

3–4 years	Walks up stairs, alternating feet, and down stairs, leading
	  with one foot
	Jumps and hops, flexing upper body
	Throws and catches with slight involvement of upper body;
	  still catches by trapping ball against chest
	Pedals and steers tricycle
		Fastens and unfastens large buttons
		Serves self food without assistance
		Uses scissors
		Copies vertical line and circle
		Draws first picture of person, using tadpole image

4–5 years	Walks down stairs, alternating feet Runs more smoothly Gallops and skips with one foot Throws ball with increased body rotation and transfer of weight on feet; catches ball with hands Rides tricycle rapidly, steers smoothly	Uses fork effectively Cuts with scissors following line Copies triangle, cross, and some letters
5–6 years	Increases running speed Gallops more smoothly; engages in true skipping Displays mature throwing and catching pattern Rides bicycle with training wheels	Uses knife to cut soft food Ties shoes Draws person with six parts Copies some numbers and simple words

Sources: Cratty, 1986; Malina & Bouchard, 1991; Haywood & Getchell, 2005.

FIGURE 8.7

Changes in catching during early childhood. At age 2, children extend their arms rigidly, and the ball tends to bounce off the body. At age 3, they flex their elbows in preparation for catching, trapping the ball against the chest. By ages 5 and 6, children involve the entire body. Instead of pressing the ball against the chest, they catch it with only the hands and fingers.

| 2 Years | 3 Years | 5–6 Years |

them as a single unit to trap the ball. By age 3, children flex their elbows enough to trap the ball against the chest. But if the ball arrives too quickly, they cannot adapt, and it may bounce off the body (Haywood & Getchell, 2005).

Gradually, children call on the shoulders, torso, trunk, and legs to support throwing and catching. By age 4, the body rotates as the child throws, and at 5 years, preschoolers shift their weight forward, stepping as they release the ball. As a result, the ball travels faster and farther. When the ball is returned, older preschoolers predict its place of landing by moving forward, backward, or sideways (see Figure 8.7). Soon, they will catch it with their hands and fingers, "giving" with arms and body to absorb the force of the ball.

Fine Motor Development

Like gross motor development, fine motor skills take a giant leap forward in the preschool years. Because control of the hands and fingers improves, young children put puzzles together, build with small blocks, cut and paste, and string beads. To parents, fine motor progress is most apparent in two areas: (1) children's care of their own bodies, and (2) the drawings and paintings that fill the walls at home, child care, and preschool.

SELF-HELP SKILLS ■ As Table 8.1 shows, young children gradually become self-sufficient at dressing and feeding. Two-year-olds put on and take off simple items of clothing. By age 3, children can do so well enough to take care of toileting needs by themselves. Between ages 4 and 5, children can dress and undress without supervision. At mealtimes, young preschoolers use a spoon well, and they can serve themselves. By age 4 they are adept with a fork, and around 5 to 6 years they can use a knife to cut soft foods. Roomy clothing with large buttons and zippers and child-sized eating utensils help children master these skills.

Preschoolers get great satisfaction from managing their own bodies. They are proud of their independence, and their new skills also make life easier for adults. But parents must be patient about these abilities. When tired and in a hurry, young children often revert to eating with their fingers. And the 3-year-old who dresses himself in the morning sometimes ends up with his shirt on inside out, his pants on backward, and his left snow boot on his right foot! Perhaps the most complex self-help skill of early childhood is shoe tying, mastered around age 6. Success requires a longer attention span, memory for an intricate series of hand movements, and the dexterity to perform them. Shoe tying illustrates the close connection between cognitive and motor development. Drawing and writing offer additional examples.

DRAWING ■ When given crayon and paper, even toddlers scribble in imitation of others. As the young child's ability to mentally represent the world expands, marks on the page take on meaning. A variety of factors combine with fine motor control in the development of children's artful representations (Golomb, 2004). These include the realization that pictures can serve as symbols, improved planning and spatial understanding, and the emphasis that the child's culture places on artistic expression.

Typically, drawing progresses through the following sequence:

1. *Scribbles.* Western children begin to draw during the second year. At first, the intended representation is contained in gestures rather than in the resulting marks on the page. For

Putting on and fastening clothing is challenging but rewarding to preschoolers. Young children enjoy a new sense of independence when they can dress themselves.

© LAURA DWIGHT PHOTOGRAPHY

As cognitive and fine motor skills advance, children include more conventional figures in their drawings and paintings. The human figure in this girl's painting has a distinct head and body with arms and legs, and an array of distinctive features—eyes, nose, mouth, hair, and hands.

example, one 18-month-old made her crayon hop and, as it produced a series of dots, explained, "Rabbit goes hop-hop" (Winner, 1986).

2. *First representational forms.* Around age 3, children's scribbles start to become pictures. Often children make a gesture with the crayon, notice that they have drawn a recognizable shape, and then decide to label it. In one case, a 2-year-old made some random marks on a page and then, realizing the resemblance between his scribbles and noodles, named the creation "chicken pie and noodles" (Winner, 1986).

Few 3-year-olds spontaneously draw so others can tell what their picture represents. However, after an adult demonstrated how pictures can be used to stand for objects in a game, more 3-year-olds drew recognizable forms (Callaghan & Rankin, 2002). Western parents and teachers spend much time promoting 2- and 3-year-olds' language and make-believe play but relatively little time showing them how they can use drawings to represent their world. When adults draw with children and point out the resemblances between drawings and objects, preschoolers' pictures become more comprehensible and detailed (Braswell & Callanan, 2003).

A major milestone in drawing occurs when children use lines to represent the boundaries of objects. This enables 3- and 4-year-olds to draw their first picture of a person. Look at the tadpole image—a circular shape with lines attached—on the left in Figure 8.8. Fine motor and cognitive limitations lead the preschooler to create this universal image, which reduces the figure to the simplest form that still looks human. Four-year-olds add features, such as eyes, nose, mouth, hair, fingers, and feet, as the tadpole drawings illustrate.

3. *More realistic drawings.* Young children do not demand that a drawing be realistic. But as cognitive and fine motor skills improve, they learn to desire greater realism. As a result, they create more complex drawings, like the one by a 6-year-old shown on the right in Figure 8.8. Older preschoolers include more conventional figures, in which the head and

FIGURE 8.8

Examples of young children's drawings.   The universal tadpolelike shape that children use to draw their first picture of a person is shown on the left. The tadpole soon becomes an anchor for greater detail as arms, fingers, toes, and facial features sprout from the basic shape. By the end of the preschool years, children produce more complex, differentiated pictures like the one on the right, drawn by a 6-year-old child.   (Tadpole drawings from H. Gardner, 1980, *Artful Scribbles: The Significance of Children's Drawings*, New York: Basic Books, p. 64. Reprinted by permission of Basic Books, a division of HarperCollins Publishers, Inc. Six-year-old's picture from E. Winner, August 1986, "Where Pelicans Kiss Seals," *Psychology Today, 20*[8], p. 35. Reprinted with permission from *Psychology Today* magazine. Copyright © 1986 Sussex Publishers, Inc.)

body are differentiated and arms and legs appear. (Note the human and animal figures in the 6-year-old's drawing.) Still, because they have just begun to represent depth, their drawings contain perceptual distortions (Braine et al., 1993).

Greater realism in drawing occurs gradually, as perception, language (ability to describe visual details), memory, and fine motor capacities improve (Toomela, 2002). Drawing of geometric objects follows the steps illustrated in Figure 8.9. (1) Three- to 7-year olds draw a single unit to stand for an object. To represent a cube, they draw a square; to represent a cylinder, they draw a circle, an oval, or a rectangle. (2) During the late preschool and school years, children represent salient object parts. They draw several squares to stand for a cube's sides and draw two circles and some lines to represent a cylinder. However, the parts are not joined properly. (3) Older school-age children and adolescents integrate object parts into a realistic whole (Toomela, 1999).

Preschoolers' free depiction of reality makes their artwork look fanciful and inventive. When accomplished artists try to represent people and objects freely, they often must work hard to achieve what they did effortlessly as 5- and 6-year-olds.

CULTURAL VARIATIONS IN DEVELOPMENT OF DRAWING ■ In cultures with rich artistic traditions, children create elaborate drawings that reflect the conventions of their culture. For example, the women of Walbiri, an Aboriginal group in Australia, draw symbols in sand to illustrate stories for preschoolers. Walbiri children often mix these symbols with more realistic images (Wales, 1990).

In cultures with little interest in art, even older children and adolescents produce simple forms. In the Jimi Valley—a remote region of Papua New Guinea with no indigenous pictorial art—many children do not go to school and therefore have little opportunity to develop drawing skills. When a Western researcher asked nonschooled Jimi 10- to 15-year-olds to draw a human figure for the first time, most produced nonrepresentational scribbles and shapes or simple "stick" or "contour" images resembling those of preschoolers (see Figure 8.10) (Martlew & Connolly, 1996). These forms seem to be a universal beginning in drawing. Once children realize that lines must evoke human features, they find solutions to figure drawing that vary somewhat from culture to culture but, overall, follow the sequence described earlier.

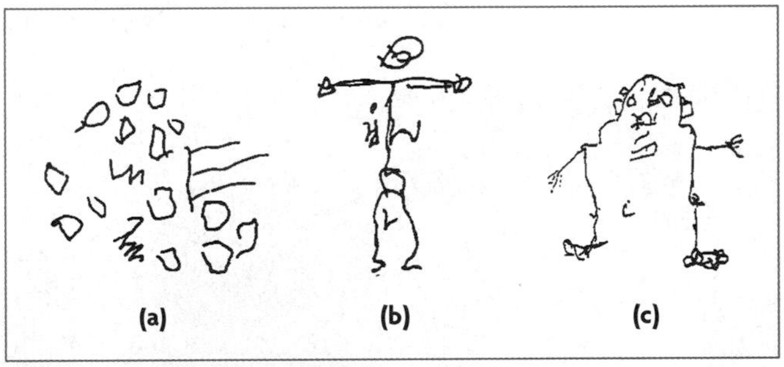

EARLY PRINTING ■ At first, preschoolers do not distinguish writing from drawing. When they try to write, they scribble, just as they do when they draw. As they experiment with lines and shapes, notice print in storybooks, and observe people writing, they attempt to print letters and, later, words. Around age 4, children's writing shows some distinctive features of print, such as separate forms arranged in a line on the page. But children often include picturelike devices in their writing—for example, using a circular shape to write "sun" (Levin & Bus, 2003). Applying their understanding of the symbolic function of drawings, 4-year-olds who are asked to write typically make a "drawing of print." Only gradually—between ages 4 and 6—do children realize that writing stands for language.

Preschoolers' first attempts to print often involve their name, generally using a single letter. "How do you make

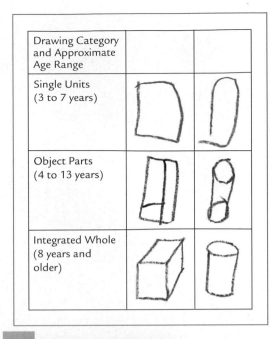

FIGURE 8.9

Development of children's drawings of geometric objects—a cube and a cylinder. As these examples show, drawings change from single units to representation of object parts. Then the parts are integrated into a realistic whole. (Adapted from Toomela, 1999.)

FIGURE 8.10

Drawings produced by nonschooled 10- to 15-year-old children of the Jimi Valley of Papua New Guinea when they were asked to draw a human figure for the first time. Many produced nonrepresentational scribbles and shapes (a), "stick" figures (b), or "contour" figures (c). Compared with the Western tadpole form, the Jimi "stick" and "contour" figures emphasize the hands and feet. Otherwise, the drawings of these older children resemble those of young preschoolers. (From M. Martlew & K. J. Connolly, 1996, "Human Figure Drawings by Schooled and Unschooled Children in Papua New Guinea," *Child Development, 67*, pp. 2750–2751. © The Society for Research in Child Development, Inc. Adapted by permission.)

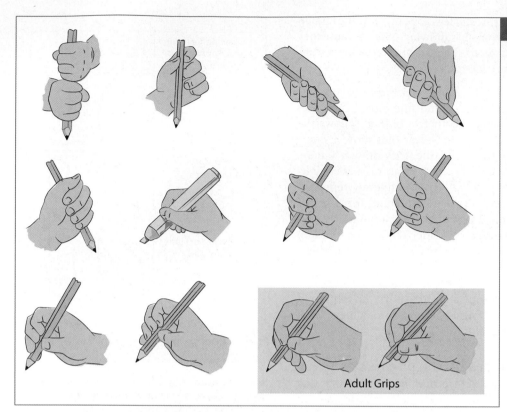

FIGURE 8.11

Variations in 3-year-olds' pencil grip. Through experimenting with different grips, preschoolers gradually discover an adult grip with one or two fingers on top of the pencil, which maximizes writing stability and efficiency. (Adapted from Greer & Lockman, 1998.)

Adult Grips

a *D?*" my older son, David, asked at age 3½. When I printed a large uppercase *D*, he tried to copy. "*D* for David," he said as he wrote, quite satisfied with his backward, imperfect creation. A year later, David added several letters, and around age 5, he wrote his name clearly enough that others could read it.

Between ages 3 and 5, children acquire skill in gripping a pencil. As Figure 8.11 shows, 3-year-olds display diverse grip patterns and pencil angles, varying their grip depending on the direction and location of the marks they want to make. By trying out different forms of pencil-holding, they discover the grip and angle that maximize stability and writing efficiency. By age 5, most children use an adult grip pattern and a fairly constant pencil angle across a range of drawing and writing conditions (Greer & Lockman, 1998).

In addition to gains in fine motor control, advances in perception contribute to the ability to print. Like many children, David continued to reverse letters until well into second grade. Once preschoolers distinguish writing from nonwriting around age 4, they make progress in identifying individual letters. Many preschoolers confuse letter pairs that are alike in shape with subtle distinctive features, such as *C* and *G*, *E* and *F*, and *M* and *W* (Bornstein & Arteberry, 1999; Gibson, 1970). Mirror-image letter pairs (*b* and *d*, *p* and *q*) are especially hard to discriminate. Until children start to read, they do not find it especially useful to notice the difference between these forms.

The ability to tune in to mirror images and to scan a printed line from left to right improves as children gain experience with written materials (Casey, 1986). The more parents and teachers assist preschoolers in their efforts to print, the more advanced children are in writing and in other aspects of literacy development (Aram & Levin, 2001, 2002). We will consider early childhood literacy in greater detail in Chapter 9.

Individual Differences in Motor Skills

Wide individual differences exist in the ages at which children reach motor milestones. A child with a tall, muscular body tends to move more quickly and to acquire certain skills earlier than a short, stocky youngster. And as in other domains, parents and teachers probably provide more encouragement to children with biologically based motor-skill advantages.

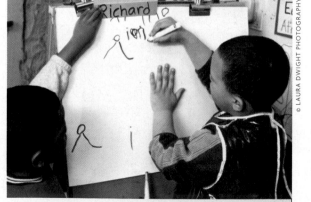

© LAURA DWIGHT PHOTOGRAPHY

This 4-year-old experiments with with gripping a marker as he tries to write his name while a classmate holds up his name card. Advances in fine motor control, perception, and experience with written materials contribute to gains in printing.

Sex differences in motor skills are evident in early childhood. Boys are ahead of girls in skills that emphasize force and power. By age 5, they can jump slightly farther, run slightly faster, and throw a ball about 5 feet farther. Girls have an edge in fine motor skills and in certain gross motor skills that require a combination of good balance and foot movement, such as hopping and skipping (Fischman, Moore, & Steele, 1992; Thomas & French, 1985). Boys' greater muscle mass and, in the case of throwing, slightly longer forearms, contribute to their skill advantages. And girls' greater overall physical maturity may be partly responsible for their better balance and precision of movement.

From an early age, boys and girls are usually channeled into different physical activities. Fathers are more likely to play catch with their sons than with their daughters. Baseballs and footballs are purchased for boys, jump ropes and sewing materials for girls. And though differences in physical capacity remain small until adolescence, sex differences in motor skills increase as children get older. This suggests that social pressures for boys to be active and physically skilled and for girls to play quietly at fine motor activities exaggerate small genetically based sex differences (Greendorfer, Lewko, & Rosengren, 1996). In support of this view, boys can throw a ball much farther than girls only when using their dominant hand. When they use their nondominant hand, the sex difference is minimal (Williams, Haywood, & Painter, 1996). Boys' superior throwing largely results from practice.

This 4-year-old girl, who gets plenty of modeling and practice at batting, throwing, and catching, is likely to outperform most of her agemates in those skills. Typically, girls receive far less encouragement than boys to engage in physical activities labeled "masculine."

Enhancing Early Childhood Motor Development

Many Western parents provide preschoolers with early training in gymnastics, tumbling, and other physical activities. These experiences offer excellent opportunities for exercise and social interaction. But aside from throwing (where direct instruction is helpful), formal lessons during the preschool years have little impact on motor development. Rather, children master the motor skills of early childhood naturally, as part of their everyday play.

Nevertheless, the physical environment in which informal play takes place can affect mastery of complex motor skills. The U.S. National Association for Sport and Physical Education (National Association of Sport and Physical Education, 2002) recommends that preschoolers engage in at least 60 minutes, and up to several hours, of unstructured physical activity every day. When children have play spaces and equipment appropriate for running, climbing, jumping, and throwing and are encouraged to use them, they respond eagerly to these challenges. But if balls are too large and heavy to be properly grasped and thrown, or jungle gyms, ladders, and horizontal bars are suitable for only the largest and strongest children, then preschoolers cannot easily acquire new motor skills. Playgrounds must offer a range of equipment to meet the diverse needs of individual children.

Similarly, fine motor development is supported by daily routines, such as pouring juice and dressing, and play that involves puzzles, construction sets, drawing, painting, sculpting, cutting, and pasting. Exposure to artwork of their own culture and others enhances children's awareness of the creative possibilities of artistic media. And opportunities to represent their own ideas and feelings, rather than coloring in predrawn forms, foster artistic development.

Finally, the social climate created by adults can enhance or dampen preschoolers' motor development. When parents and teachers criticize a child's performance, push specific motor skills, or promote a competitive attitude, they risk undermining children's self-confidence and, in turn, their motor progress (Berk, 2006a). Adult involvement in young children's motor activities should focus on "fun" rather than on winning or perfecting the "correct" technique.

This imaginative playground provides a rich variety of equipment suited to preschoolers' diverse individual needs. When play spaces are properly designed and equipped, young children respond eagerly to motor challenges and develop new skills through informal play.

Ask Yourself

Review Describe typical changes in children's drawings in early childhood, along with factors that contribute to those changes.

Review Explain how physical and social factors jointly contribute to sex differences in motor skills during early childhood.

Apply Mabel and Chad want to do everything they can to support their 3-year-old daughter's athletic development. What advice would you give them?

Connect Does preschoolers' developing skill at gripping a pencil fit with dynamic systems theory of motor development? Explain, returning to Chapter 5, page 189, if you need to review.

Summary

Body Growth

Describe changes in body size, proportions, and skeletal maturity during early childhood.

- Gains in body size taper off in early childhood. Body fat also declines, and children become longer and leaner. In various parts of the skeleton, new epiphyses emerge, where cartilage hardens into bone. Individual differences in body size and rate of physical growth are more apparent than in infancy and toddlerhood.

- By the end of the preschool years, children start to lose their primary teeth. Care of primary teeth is essential because diseased baby teeth can affect the health of permanent teeth. Childhood tooth decay remains common, especially among low-SES children.

What makes physical growth an asynchronous process?

- Body systems differ in their rates of growth. The **general growth curve** describes change in body size: rapid during infancy, slower in early and middle childhood, rapid again during adolescence. Exceptions to this trend include the genitals, the lymph tissue, and the brain.

Brain Development

Describe brain development in early childhood.

- During the preschool years, neural fibers in the brain continue to form synapses and myelinate. By this time, many cortical regions have overproduced synapses, and *synaptic pruning* occurs. To make room for the connective structures of active neurons, many surrounding neurons die, leading to reduced brain plasticity.

- For most children, the left hemisphere of the cerebral cortex develops ahead of the right hemisphere, supporting young children's rapidly expanding language skills.

- Hand preference, which reflects an individual's **dominant cerebral hemisphere**, strengthens during early childhood. Research on handedness supports the joint contribution of nature and nurture to brain lateralization.

- Although left-handedness is associated with developmental problems, the great majority of left-handed children have no such problems. Left- and mixed-handed youngsters are more likely to display outstanding verbal and mathematical talents.

- During early childhood, connections are established between brain structures. Fibers linking the **cerebellum** to the cerebral cortex grow and myelinate, enhancing motor coordination. The **reticular formation**, responsible for alertness and consciousness; the **hippocampus**, which plays a vital role in memory; and the **corpus callosum**, which connects the two cortical hemispheres, also form synapses and myelinate.

Influences on Physical Growth and Health

Explain how heredity influences physical growth.

- Heredity influences physical growth by controlling production and release of two vital hormones from the **pituitary gland: growth hormone (GH)**, which affects the development of almost all body tissues, and **thyroid-stimulating hormone (TSH)**, which affects brain growth and body size.

Describe the effects of emotional well-being, restful sleep, nutrition, and infectious disease on physical growth and health in early childhood.

- Emotional well-being continues to influence body growth and health in early childhood. Extreme emotional deprivation can lead to **psychosocial dwarfism.**

- Restful sleep contributes to body growth directly, through the release of GH during sleep, and indirectly, by contributing positively to family functioning. Bedtime routines are helpful for Western children, who—unlike children in many non-Western cultures—generally sleep alone. Most preschoolers awaken occasionally at night, and some may suffer from sleep disorders. A few experience sleepwalking or sleep terrors, which run in families, suggesting a genetic influence, but these problems can also be triggered by stress or extreme fatigue.

- As growth rate slows, preschoolers' appetites decline, and they often become picky eaters. Young children's social environments powerfully influence their food preferences. Modeling by others, repeated exposure to new foods, and a positive emotional climate at mealtimes can promote healthy, varied eating in young children.

- Many children in North America and in developing countries suffer from dietary deficiencies—most commonly, a lack of sufficient protein and essential vitamins and minerals. These deficiencies are associated with attention difficulties, academic and behavior problems, and greater susceptibility to infectious diseases. Disease also contributes to malnutrition, especially when intestinal infections cause persistent diarrhea. In developing countries, inexpensive oral rehydration therapy (ORT) can prevent most developmental impairments and deaths due to diarrhea.

- Immunization rates are lower in the United States than in other industrialized nations because many economically disadvantaged children lack access to necessary health care. Parental stress also contributes, as do widespread misconceptions about the dangers of immunization.

- Child-care attendance is associated with a rise in childhood illness, especially otitis media, or middle ear infection. Frequent ear infections predict delayed language progress, social isolation, and poorer academic performance after school entry—outcomes that can be prevented by high-quality child care and screening for otitis media.

What factors increase the risk of unintentional injuries, and how can childhood injuries be prevented?

- Unintentional injuries are the leading cause of childhood mortality. Injury victims are more likely to be boys; to be temperamentally irritable, inattentive, and negative; and to live in stressed, poverty-stricken, crowded family environments. Among developed nations, injury deaths are high in the United States and Canada. They are even higher in developing countries, where they may soon exceed disease as the leading cause of childhood deaths.

- Effective approaches to preventing childhood injuries include passing laws that promote child safety; creating safer home, travel, and play environments; relieving sources of family stress; improving public education; and changing parent and child behaviors.

Motor Development

Cite major milestones of gross and fine motor development in early childhood.

- During early childhood, children continue to integrate previously acquired motor skills into more complex dynamic systems of action. As the child's center of gravity shifts toward the trunk, balance improves, paving the way for new gross motor achievements. Preschoolers' gaits become smooth and rhythmic; they run, jump, hop, gallop; eventually skip, throw, and catch; and generally become better coordinated.

- Increasing control of the hands and fingers leads to dramatic improvements in fine motor skills. Preschoolers gradually dress themselves and use a fork and knife.

- By age 3, children's scribbles become pictures. As perception, language, memory, and fine motor capacities improve with age, children's drawings increase in complexity and realism. Children's drawings are also influenced by their culture's artistic traditions.

- Around age 4, children's writing shows some distinctive features of print, but only gradually do children realize that writing stands for language. Between 3 and 5 years, children experiment with pencil grip; by age 5, most use an adultlike grip that maximizes stability and writing efficiency.

- Advances in perception and exposure to written materials contribute to progress in discriminating individual letters. When parents and teachers support children's efforts to print, preschoolers are more advanced in writing and other aspects of literacy development.

Describe individual differences in preschoolers' motor skills and ways to enhance motor development in early childhood.

- Body build and opportunity for physical play affect early childhood motor development. Sex differences that favor boys in skills requiring force and power and girls in skills requiring good balance and fine movements are partly genetic, but social pressures exaggerate them.

- Children master the motor skills of early childhood through informal play experiences, with little benefit from exposure to formal training. Richly equipped play environments that accommodate a wide range of physical abilities are important. Emphasizing pleasure in motor activities is the best way to foster motor development during the preschool years.

Important Terms and Concepts

cerebellum (p. 298)
corpus callosum (p. 299)
dominant cerebral hemisphere (p. 297)
general growth curve (p. 296)

growth hormone (GH) (p. 301)
hippocampus (p. 299)
pituitary gland (p. 301)
psychosocial dwarfism (p. 302)

reticular formation (p. 298)
thyroid-stimulating hormone (TSH) (p. 302)

Chapter 9

On a trip to the beach, two preschoolers collaborate in make-believe play. Pretending is engrossing and enjoyable to preschoolers, who draw on their rich array of everyday experiences to create elaborate scenes and story lines. Make-believe contributes greatly to rapidly advancing cognitive and language skills in early childhood.

"The Beach"
Qi Hao
6 years, Singapore

Reprinted with permission from the International Museum of Children's Art, Oslo, Norway

Cognitive Development in Early Childhood

One rainy morning, as I observed in our laboratory preschool, Leslie, the children's teacher, joined me at the back of the room to watch for a moment herself. "Preschoolers' minds are such a curious blend of logic, fantasy, and faulty reasoning," Leslie reflected. "Every day, I'm startled by the maturity and originality of what they say and do. Yet at other times, their thinking seems limited and inflexible."

Leslie's comments sum up the puzzling contradictions of early childhood cognition. That day, for example, I found 3-year-old Sammy at the puzzle table, moments after a loud crash of thunder outside. Sammy looked up, startled, then said to Leslie, "A magic man turned on the thunder!" Leslie patiently explained that thunder is caused by lightning, not by a person turning it on or off. But Sammy persisted: "Then a magic lady did it."

In other respects, Sammy's thinking was surprisingly advanced. At snack time, he accurately counted, "One, two, three, four!" and then got four cartons of milk, one for each child at his table. Sammy's keen memory and ability to categorize were also evident. He could recite by heart *The Very Hungry Caterpillar*, a story he had heard many times. And he could name and classify dozens of animals.

But when his snack group included more than four children, Sammy's counting broke down. And some of his notions about quantity seemed as fantastic as his understanding of thunder. Across the snack table, Priti dumped out her raisins, which scattered in front of her. "How come you got lots, and I only got this little bit?" asked Sammy, not realizing that he had just as many; they were simply all bunched up in a tiny red box. While Priti was washing her hands after snack, Sammy put her remaining raisins in her cubby. When Priti returned and looked for her raisins, Sammy pronounced, "You know where they are!" He failed to grasp that Priti, who hadn't seen him move the raisins, would expect them to be where she had left them.

In this chapter, we explore early childhood cognition, drawing on three theories with which you are already familiar. To understand Sammy's reasoning, we begin with evidence highlighting the strengths and limitations of Piaget's and Vygotsky's ideas. Then we examine additional research inspired by the information-processing perspective. Next, we address factors that contribute to individual differences in mental development—the home environment, the quality of preschool and child care, and the many hours young children spend watching television and using computers. Our chapter concludes with the dramatic expansion of language in early childhood.

Piaget's Theory: The Preoperational Stage

As children move from the sensorimotor to the **preoperational stage**, which spans the years 2 to 7, the most obvious change is an extraordinary increase in mental representation. Recall that infants and toddlers have considerable ability to mentally represent their world. In early childhood, this capacity blossoms.

Advances in Mental Representation

Piaget acknowledged that language is our most flexible means of mental representation. By detaching thought from action, it permits far more efficient thinking than was possible earlier. When we think in words, we can deal with past, present, and future at once. We can also combine concepts in unique ways, imagining a hungry caterpillar eating bananas or monsters flying through the forest at night.

But Piaget did not regard language as the primary ingredient in childhood cognitive change. Instead, he believed that sensorimotor activity leads to internal images of experience, which children then label with words (Piaget, 1936/1952). In support of Piaget's view, recall from Chapter 6 that children's first words have a strong sensorimotor basis. And toddlers acquire an impressive range of cognitive categories long before they use words to label them (see pages 224–226). But as we will see, other theorists regard Piaget's account of the link between language and thought as incomplete.

Make-Believe Play

Make-believe play is another excellent example of the development of representation in early childhood. Piaget believed that through pretending, young children practice and strengthen newly acquired representational schemes. Drawing on his ideas, several investigators have traced changes in make-believe play during the preschool years.

DEVELOPMENT OF MAKE-BELIEVE PLAY ■ One day, Sammy's 18-month-old brother, Dwayne, visited the classroom. Dwayne wandered around, picked up a toy telephone receiver, said, "Hi, Mommy," and then dropped it. Next, he found a cup, pretended to drink, and then toddled off again. Meanwhile, Sammy joined Vance and Lynette in the block area for a space shuttle launch.

"That can be our control tower," Sammy suggested, pointing to a corner by a bookshelf. "Countdown!" he announced, speaking into his "walkie-talkie"—a small wooden block. "Five, six, two, four, one, blastoff!" Lynette made a doll push a pretend button, and the rocket was off!

Comparing Dwayne's pretend play with Sammy's, we see three important changes that reflect the preschool child's growing symbolic mastery:

■ *Play detaches from the real-life conditions associated with it.* In early pretending, toddlers use only realistic objects—a toy telephone to talk into or a cup to drink from. Their first pretend acts imitate adults' actions and are not yet flexible. Children younger than age 2, for example, will pretend to drink from a cup but refuse to pretend a cup is a hat (Tomasello, Striano, & Rochat, 1999). They have trouble using an object (cup) that already has an obvious use as a symbol of another object (hat).

   After age 2, children pretend with less realistic toys, such as a block for a telephone receiver. Gradually, they can flexibly imagine objects and events without support from the real world, as Sammy's imaginary control tower illustrates (O'Reilly, 1995; Striano, Tomasello, & Rochat, 2001).

■ *Play becomes less self-centered.* At first, make-believe is directed toward the self—for example, Dwayne pretends to feed only himself. Soon, children begin to direct pretend actions toward objects, as when the child feeds a doll. Early in the third year, they become detached participants, making a doll feed itself or pushing a button to launch a rocket. Make-believe becomes less self-centered as children realize that agents and recipients of pretend actions can be independent of themselves (McCune, 1993).

preoperational stage
Piaget's second stage, extending from about 2 to 7 years, in which rapid growth in representation takes place but thought is not yet logical.

■ *Play includes more complex combinations of schemes.* Dwayne can pretend to drink from a cup, but he does not yet combine drinking with pouring. Later, children combine schemes with those of peers in **sociodramatic play,** the make-believe with others that is under way by age 2½ and increases rapidly during the next few years. Already, Sammy and his classmates can coordinate several roles in an elaborate plot. By the end of early childhood, children have a sophisticated understanding of role relationships and story lines (Göncü, 1993).

In sociodramatic play. children display awareness that make-believe is a representational activity—an understanding that increases over early childhood (Lillard, 2003; Rakoczy, Tomasello, & Striano, 2004; Sobel, 2006). **TAKE A MOMENT...** Listen closely to preschoolers jointly creating an imaginary scene. You will hear them assign roles and negotiate make-believe plans: "*You pretend to be* the astronaut, *I'll act like* I'm operating the control tower!*" "Wait, *I gotta set up* the spaceship." In communicating about pretend, children think about their own and others' fanciful representations. This indicates that they have begun to reason about people's mental activities, a topic we will return to later in this chapter.

BENEFITS OF MAKE-BELIEVE PLAY ■ Today, Piaget's view of make-believe as mere practice of representational schemes is regarded as too limited. Play not only reflects but also contributes to children's cognitive and social skills. Sociodramatic play has been studied most thoroughly. In comparison to social nonpretend activities (such as drawing or putting puzzles together), during social pretend preschoolers' interactions last longer, show more involvement, draw more children into the activity, and are more cooperative (Creasey, Jarvis, & Berk, 1998).

It is not surprising, then, that preschoolers who spend more time in sociodramatic play are seen as more socially competent by their teachers (Connolly & Doyle, 1984). And many studies reveal that make-believe strengthens a variety of mental abilities, including sustained attention, memory, logical reasoning, language and literacy, imagination, creativity, and the ability to reflect on one's own thinking, control one's own behavior, and take another's perspective (Bergen & Mauer, 2000; Berk, 2006a; Elias & Berk, 2002; Kavanaugh & Engel, 1998; Lindsey & Colwell, 2003; Ruff & Capozzoli, 2003).

Between 25 and 45 percent of preschoolers and young school-age children spend much time in solitary make-believe, creating *imaginary companions*—special fantasized friends endowed with humanlike qualities. For example, one preschooler created Nutsy and Nutsy, a pair of boisterous birds living outside her bedroom window who often went along on family outings (Gleason, Sebanc, & Hartup, 2000; Taylor et al., 2004). Imaginary companions were once viewed as a sign of maladjustment, but research challenges this assumption. Children with an invisible playmate typically treat it with care and affection and say it offers caring, comfort, and good company, just as their real friendships do (Gleason & Hohmann, 2006; Hoff, 2005). Such children also display more complex and imaginative pretend play, are advanced in understanding others' viewpoints and emotions, and are more sociable with peers (Bouldin, 2006; Gleason, 2002; Taylor & Carlson, 1997).

Applying What We Know on page 324 lists some ways to enhance preschoolers' make-believe. Later we will return to the origins and consequences of make-believe from an alternative perspective—that of Vygotsky.

Symbol–Real World Relations

In a corner of the classroom, Leslie set up a dollhouse, replete with tiny furnishings. Sammy liked to arrange the furniture to match his real-world living room, kitchen, and bedroom. Representations of reality, like Sammy's, are powerful cognitive tools. When we understand that a photograph, model, or map corresponds to something specific in everyday life, we can use these tools to find out about objects and places we have not experienced.

These 3- and 4-year-olds coordinate several make-believe roles as they jointly care for a sick baby. Sociodramatic play contributes to cognitive, emotional, and social development.

sociodramatic play
Children's make-believe play with others.

Applying What We Know

Enhancing Make-Believe Play in Early Childhood

STRATEGY	DESCRIPTION
Provide sufficient space and play materials.	Generous space and materials allow for many play options and reduce conflict.
Supervise and encourage children's play without controlling it.	Respond to, guide, and elaborate on preschoolers' play themes when they indicate a need for assistance. Provide open-ended suggestions (for example, "Would the animals like a train ride?"), and talk with the child about the thoughts, motivations, and emotions of play characters. Refrain from directing the child's play; excessive adult control destroys the creativity and joy of make-believe.
Offer a variety of both realistic materials and materials without clear functions.	Children use realistic materials, such as trucks, dolls, tea sets, dress-up clothes, and toy scenes (house, farm, garage, airport) to act out everyday roles in their culture. Materials without clear functions (such as blocks, cardboard cylinders, paper bags, and sand) inspire fantastic role play, such as "pirate" and "creature from outer space."
Ensure that children have many rich, real-world experiences to inspire positive fantasy play.	Opportunities to participate in real-world activities with adults and to observe adult roles in the community provide children with rich social knowledge to integrate into make-believe. Restricting television viewing, especially programs with violent content, limits the degree to which violent themes and aggressive behavior become part of children's play. (See Chapter 10, pages 388–390.)
Help children solve social conflicts constructively.	Cooperation is essential for sociodramatic play. Guide children toward positive relationships with agemates by helping them resolve disagreements constructively. For example, ask, "What could you do if you want a turn?" If the child cannot think of possibilities, suggest some options, and assist the child in implementing them.

Sources: Berk, 2001a; Vandenberg, 1998.

When do children comprehend symbol–real world relations? In one study, 2½- and 3-year-olds watched an adult hide a small toy (Little Snoopy) in a scale model of a room, then were asked to retrieve it. Next, they had to find a larger toy (Big Snoopy) hidden in the room that the model represented. Not until age 3 could most children use the model as a guide to finding Big Snoopy in the real room (DeLoache, 1987). The 2½-year-olds did not realize that the model could be both *a toy room* and *a symbol of another room*. They had trouble with **dual representation**—viewing a symbolic object as both an object in its own right and a symbol. In support of this interpretation, when researchers made the model room less prominent as an object, by placing it behind a window and preventing children from touching it, more 2½-year-olds succeeded at the search task (DeLoache, 2000, 2002).

Recall that 1½- to 2-year-olds, when they pretend, cannot use an object with an obvious use (cup) to stand for another object (hat). Likewise, 2-year-olds do not yet grasp that a drawing—an object in its own right—represents real-world objects. When an adult held up a drawing indicating which of two objects preschoolers should drop down a chute, 3-year-olds used the drawing as a symbol to guide their behavior, but 2-year-olds did not (Callaghan, 1999).

How do children grasp the dual representation of symbolic objects? When adults point out similarities between models and real-world spaces, 2½-year-olds perform better on the find-Snoopy task (Peralta de Mendoza & Salsa, 2003). Also, insight into one type of symbol promotes mastery of others. For example, children regard photos as symbols early, around 1½ to 2 years, because a photo's primary purpose is to stand for something; it is not an interesting object in its own right (Preissler & Carey, 2004). And 3-year-olds who can use a model of a room to locate Big Snoopy readily transfer their understanding to a simple map (Marzolf & DeLoache, 1994).

In sum, exposing young children to diverse symbols—picture books, photographs, drawings, make-believe, and maps—helps them appreciate that one object can stand for another. With age, children come to understand a wide range of symbols that have little physical similarity to what they represent (Liben, 1999). As a result, doors open to vast realms of knowledge.

© ARIEL SKELLEY/CORBIS

Children who experience a variety of symbols come to understand that one object, such as the birdhouse this daughter and her father are making, can stand for another—a full-sized house that people live in.

Limitations of Preoperational Thought

Aside from gains in representation, Piaget described preschool children in terms of what they *cannot* understand (Beilin, 1992). As the term *pre*operational suggests, he compared them to older, more competent children who have reached the concrete operational stage. According to Piaget, young children are not capable of *operations*—mental actions that obey logical rules. Rather, their thinking is rigid, limited to one aspect of a situation at a time, and strongly influenced by the way things appear at the moment.

EGOCENTRISM ■ For Piaget, the most fundamental deficiency of preoperational thinking is **egocentrism**—failure to distinguish the symbolic viewpoints of others from one's own. He believed that when children first mentally represent the world, they tend to focus on their own viewpoint and assume that others perceive, think, and feel the same way they do.

Piaget's most convincing demonstration of egocentrism involves his *three-mountains problem*, described in Figure 9.1. He also regarded egocentrism as responsible for preoperational children's **animistic thinking**—the belief that inanimate objects have lifelike qualities, such as thoughts, wishes, feelings, and intentions (Piaget, 1926/1930). Recall Sammy's insistence that someone must have turned on the thunder. According to Piaget, because young children egocentrically assign human purposes to physical events, magical thinking is especially common during the preschool years.

Piaget argued that preschoolers' egocentric bias prevents them from *accommodating*, or reflecting on and revising their faulty reasoning in response to their physical and social worlds. To appreciate this shortcoming fully, let's consider some additional tasks that Piaget gave children.

INABILITY TO CONSERVE ■ Piaget's famous conservation tasks reveal several deficiencies of preoperational thinking. **Conservation** refers to the idea that certain physical characteristics of objects remain the same, even when their outward appearance changes. At snack time, Sammy and Priti had identical boxes of raisins, but when Priti spread her raisins out on the table, Sammy was convinced that she had more.

In another conservation task involving liquid, the child is shown two identical tall glasses of water and asked if they contain equal amounts. Once the child agrees, the water in one glass is poured into a short, wide container, changing the appearance of the water but not its amount. Then the child is asked whether the amount of water is the same or has changed. Preoperational children think the quantity has changed. They explain, "There is less now because the water is way down here" (that is, its level is so low) or "There is more because it is all spread out." Figure 9.2 on page 326 illustrates other conservation tasks that you can try with children.

The inability to conserve highlights several related aspects of preoperational children's thinking. First, their understanding is *centered*, or characterized by **centration.** They focus on one aspect of a situation, neglecting other important features. In conservation of liquid, the child *centers* on the height of the water, failing to realize that changes in width compensate for the changes in height. Second, children are easily distracted by the *perceptual appearance* of objects. Third, children treat the initial and final *states* of the water as unrelated events, ignoring the *dynamic transformation* (pouring of water) between them.

The most important illogical feature of preoperational thought is its **irreversibility**—an inability to mentally go through a series of steps in a problem and then reverse direction, returning to the starting point. *Reversibility* is part of every logical operation. After Priti spills

FIGURE 9.1

Piaget's three-mountains problem. Each mountain is distinguished by its color and by its summit. One has a red cross, another a small house, and the third a snow-capped peak. Children at the preoperational stage respond egocentrically. They cannot select a picture that shows the mountains from the doll's perspective. Instead, they simply choose the photo that reflects their own vantage point.

dual representation The ability to view a symbolic object as both an object in its own right and a symbol.

egocentrism Failure to distinguish the symbolic viewpoints of others from one's own.

animistic thinking The belief that inanimate objects have lifelike qualities, such as thoughts, wishes, feelings, and intentions.

conservation The understanding that certain physical characteristics of objects remain the same, even when their outward appearance changes.

centration The tendency to focus on one aspect of a situation, neglecting other important features.

irreversibility The inability to mentally go through a series of steps in a problem and then reverse direction, returning to the starting point.

FIGURE 9.2

Some Piagetian conservation tasks. Children at the preoperational stage cannot yet conserve. These tasks are mastered gradually over the concrete operational stage. Children in Western nations typically acquire conservation of number, mass, and liquid sometime between 6 and 7 years and of weight between 8 and 10 years.

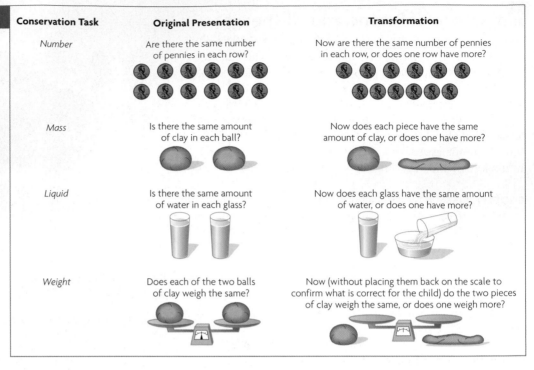

Conservation Task	Original Presentation	Transformation
Number	Are there the same number of pennies in each row?	Now are there the same number of pennies in each row, or does one row have more?
Mass	Is there the same amount of clay in each ball?	Now does each piece have the same amount of clay, or does one have more?
Liquid	Is there the same amount of water in each glass?	Now does each glass have the same amount of water, or does one have more?
Weight	Does each of the two balls of clay weigh the same?	Now (without placing them back on the scale to confirm what is correct for the child) do the two pieces of clay weigh the same, or does one weigh more?

her raisins, Sammy is unable to reverse by thinking, "I know Priti doesn't have more raisins than I do. If we put them back in that little box, her raisins and mine would look just the same."

LACK OF HIERARCHICAL CLASSIFICATION ■ Preoperational children have difficulty with **hierarchical classification**—the organization of objects into classes and subclasses on the basis of similarities and differences. Piaget's famous *class inclusion problem*, illustrated in Figure 9.3, demonstrates this limitation. Preoperational children center on the overriding feature, yellow. They do not think reversibly, moving from the whole class (flowers) to the parts (yellow and blue) and back again.

Follow-Up Research on Preoperational Thought

Over the past two decades, researchers have challenged Piaget's view of a cognitively deficient preschooler. Because many Piagetian problems contain unfamiliar elements or too many pieces of information for young children to handle at once, preschoolers' responses often do not reflect their true abilities. Piaget also missed many naturally occurring instances of effective reasoning by preschoolers. Let's look at some examples.

EGOCENTRIC, ANIMISTIC, AND MAGICAL THINKING ■ Do young children really believe that a person standing elsewhere in a room sees exactly what they see? When researchers change the nature of Piaget's three-mountains problem to include familiar objects and use methods other than picture selection (which is difficult even for 10-year-olds), 4-year-olds show clear awareness of others' vantage points (Borke, 1975; Newcombe & Huttenlocher, 1992).

Nonegocentric responses also appear in young children's conversations. For example, preschoolers adapt their speech to fit the needs of their listeners. Sammy uses shorter, simpler expressions when talking to his little brother Dwayne

FIGURE 9.3

A Piagetian class inclusion problem. Children are shown 16 flowers, 4 of which are blue and 12 of which are yellow. Asked, "Are there more yellow flowers or flowers?" the preoperational child responds, "More yellow flowers," failing to realize that both yellow and blue flowers are included in the category "flowers."

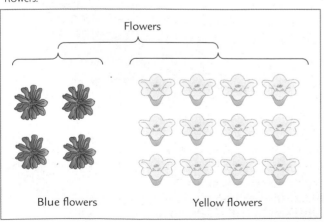

Flowers

Blue flowers   Yellow flowers

than when talking to agemates or adults (Gelman & Shatz, 1978). And in describing objects, children do not use such words as "big" and "little" in a rigid, egocentric fashion. Instead, they *adjust* their descriptions to allow for context. By age 3, children judge a 2-inch shoe as small when seen by itself (because it is much smaller than most shoes) but as big for a tiny 5-inch doll (Ebeling & Gelman, 1994).

In previous chapters, we saw that even toddlers have some appreciation of others' intentions and perspectives. And in his later writings, Piaget (1945/1951) did describe preschoolers' egocentrism as a tendency rather than an inability. As we revisit the topic of perspective taking, you will see that it develops gradually throughout childhood and adolescence.

Piaget also overestimated preschoolers' animistic beliefs. Beginning in infancy, children distinguish animate from inanimate, as indicated by babies' remarkable categorical distinctions among living and nonliving things (see Chapter 6, pages 224–226). By age 2½, children give psychological explanations—"He likes to" or "She wants to"—for people, and occasionally for animals, but rarely for objects (Hickling & Wellman, 2001). They do make errors when questioned about certain vehicles, such as trains and airplanes, which appear to be self-moving and have other lifelike features—for example, headlights that look like eyes (Gelman & Opfer, 2002). But their responses result from incomplete knowledge about objects, not from a belief that inanimate objects are alive.

Is this child convinced that the magician's trick is due to supernatural powers? Most 3- and 4-year-olds believe that magic accounts for events they cannot explain. But they deny that magic can alter their everyday experiences.

The same is true for other fantastic beliefs of the preschool years. Most 3- and 4-year-olds believe in the supernatural powers of fairies, goblins, and other enchanted creatures. They think that magic accounts for events they cannot explain, as in 3-year-old Sammy's magical account of thunder in the opening to this chapter (Rosengren & Hickling, 2000). But they deny that magic can alter their everyday experiences—for example, turn a picture into a real object (Subbotsky, 1994).

Between ages 4 and 8, as children gain familiarity with physical events and principles, their magical beliefs decline. They figure out who is really behind Santa Claus and the Tooth Fairy, and they realize that the antics of magicians are due to trickery (Subbotsky, 2004). But because children still entertain the possibility that something they imagine might materialize, they may react with anxiety to scary stories, TV shows, and nightmares. In one study, researchers had 4- to 6-year-olds imagine that a monster was inside one empty box and a puppy inside another. Almost all the children approached the "puppy" box, but many avoided putting their finger in the "monster" box, even though they knew that imagination cannot create reality (Harris et al., 1991).

Religion and culture play a role in how quickly children give up certain fantastic ideas. For example, Jewish children are more likely than their Christian agemates to express disbelief in Santa Claus and the Tooth Fairy. Having heard at home that Santa is imaginary, they seem to generalize this attitude to other mythical figures (Woolley, 1997). And cultural myths about wishing—for example, the custom of making a wish before blowing out birthday candles— probably underlie the conviction of most 3- to 6-year-olds that simply by wishing, you can sometimes make your desires come true (Woolley, 2000).

The importance of knowledge, experience, and culture can be seen in preschoolers' grasp of other natural concepts. Refer to the Social Issues: Education box on pages 328–329 to find out about young children's developing understanding of death.

ILLOGICAL THOUGHT ■ Many studies show that when preschoolers are given tasks that are simplified and made relevant to their everyday lives, they do not display the illogical characteristics that Piaget saw in the preoperational stage. For example, when a conservation-of-number task is scaled down to include only three items instead of six or seven, 3-year-olds perform well (Gelman, 1972). And when preschoolers are asked carefully worded questions about what happens to substances (such as sugar) after they are dissolved in water, they give accurate explanations. Most 3- to 5-year-olds know that the substance is conserved—that it continues

hierarchical classification The organization of objects into classes and subclasses on the basis of similarities and differences.

Social Issues: Education

Young Children's Understanding of Death

When 5-year-old Miriam arrived at preschool the day after her dog Pepper died, she didn't join the other children, as usual, but stayed close to Leslie, who noticed Miriam's discomfort. "What's wrong?" Leslie asked.

"Daddy said Pepper was so sick the vet had to put him to sleep." For a moment, Miriam looked hopeful. "When I get home, Pepper might be up."

Leslie answered directly: "No, Pepper won't get up again. He's not asleep. He's dead, and that means he can't sleep, eat, run, or play anymore."

Miriam wandered off. Later, she returned to Leslie and, sobbing, confessed, "I chased Pepper too hard."

Leslie put her arm around Miriam. "Pepper didn't die because you chased him," she explained. "He was very old and very sick."

Over the next few days, Miriam asked more questions: "When I go to sleep, will I die?" "Can a tummy ache make you die?" "Does Pepper feel better now?" "Will Mommy and Daddy die?"

Development of the Death Concept

An accurate understanding of death is based on five ideas: (1) *Permanence:* Once a living thing dies, it cannot be brought back to life. (2) *Inevitability:* All living things eventually die. (3) *Cessation:* All living functions, including thought, feeling, movement, and body processes, cease at death. (4) *Applicability:* Death applies only to living things. (5) *Causation:* Death is caused by a breakdown of bodily functioning.

To understand death, children must acquire some basic notions of biology—that animals and plants are living things containing certain body parts that are essential for maintaining life. They must also break down their global category of *not alive* into *dead, inanimate, unreal,* and *nonexistent* (Carey, 1999). Until children grasp these ideas, they interpret death in terms of familiar experiences—as a change in behavior. Like Miriam, they may believe that they caused the death of a relative or pet, that having a stomachache can cause someone to die, and that death is like sleep. When researchers asked 4- to 6-year-olds whether dead people need food, air, and water, whether they go to the bathroom, whether they sleep and dream, and whether a cut on their body would heal, more than half of those who had not yet started to acquire bio-logical understandings answered yes (Slaughter, Jaakkola, & Carey, 1999).

Most children master the components of the death concept by age 7. *Permanence* is the first and most easily understood idea. When Leslie explained that Pepper would not get up again, Miriam accepted this fact quickly, perhaps because she had seen it in other, less emotionally charged situations, such as the dead butterflies and beetles she picked up and inspected while playing outside. Appreciation of *inevitability* and *cessation* soon follow. At first, children think that certain people do not die—themselves, people like themselves (other children), and people with whom they have close emotional ties. Also, many preschoolers view dead things as retaining living capacities (Kenyon, 2001; Speece & Brent, 1996). *Applicability* and *causation,* the most difficult components to master, require a firm grasp of the biological concepts just noted.

Cultural Influences

Ethnic variations suggest that religious teachings affect children's understanding of death. In a

---

to exist, can be tasted, and makes the liquid heavier, even though it is invisible in the water (Au, Sidle, & Rollins, 1993; Rosen & Rozin, 1993).

Preschoolers' ability to reason about transformations is evident on other problems. They can engage in impressive *reasoning by analogy* about physical changes. When presented with the picture-matching problem "Playdough is to cut-up playdough as apple is to . . . ?," even 3-year-olds choose the correct answer from a set of alternatives, several of which (a bitten apple, a cut-up loaf of bread) share physical features with the correct choice (Goswami, 1996). These findings indicate that in familiar contexts, preschoolers can overcome appearances and think logically about cause and effect.

Furthermore, preschoolers have a remarkable understanding of diverse cause-and-effect relationships. For example, they know that the insides of animals differ from the insides of machines. Even without detailed biological or mechanical knowledge, they realize that animals' insides are responsible for certain cause–effect sequences (such as willing oneself to move) that are impossible for nonliving things (Gelman, 2003; Keil & Lockhart, 1999).

Finally, 3- and 4-year-olds use causal expressions, such as *if–then* and *because,* as accurately as adults do (McCabe & Peterson, 1988). They seem to use illogical reasoning only when they must grapple with unfamiliar topics, too much information, or contradictory facts, which they have trouble reconciling (Ruffman, 1999).

CATEGORIZATION ■ Despite their difficulty with Piagetian class inclusion tasks, preschoolers organize their everyday knowledge into nested categories at an early age. By the second half of the first year, children have formed a variety of global categories—furniture, animals, vehicles,

comparison of four ethnic groups in Israel, Druze and Muslim children's death concepts differed from those of Christian and Jewish children (Florian & Kravetz, 1985). The Druze emphasis on reincarnation and the greater religiosity of the Druze and Muslim groups may have led more of their children to deny permanence and cessation. Similarly, children of U.S. Southern Baptist families, who believe in an afterlife, are less likely to endorse permanence than are children from Unitarian families, who focus on achieving peace and justice in today's world (Candy-Gibbs, Sharp, & Petrun, 1985).

Experiences with death also influence understanding. Children growing up on Israeli kibbutzim (agricultural settlements) who have witnessed terrorist attacks, family members' departure on army tours, and parental anxiety about safety express a full grasp of the death concept by age 5 (Mahon, Goldberg, & Washington, 1999). Experiencing the death of a close relative or friend greatly accelerates appreciation of permanence and inevitability, even among children as young as age 3 (Reilly, Hasazi, & Bond, 1983).

Enhancing Children's Understanding

Parents often worry needlessly that discussing death candidly with children fuels their fears. But children with a good grasp of the facts of death have an easier time accepting it. Direct explanations, like Leslie's, that match the child's capacity to understand, work best. When adults use clichés or make misleading statements, children may take these literally and react with confusion. For example, after a parent said to her 5-year-old daughter, "Grandpa went on a long trip," the child wondered, "Why didn't he take me?" (Wolfelt, 1997). Sometimes children ask difficult questions: "Will I die? Will you die?" Parents can be truthful and comforting by taking advantage of children's sense of time. "Not for many, many years," they can say. "First I'm going to enjoy you as a grown-up and be a grandparent."

Another way to foster an accurate appreciation of death is to teach preschoolers about the biology of the human body. Three- to 5-year-olds given lessons in the role of the heart, kidneys, lungs, brain, digestion, bones, and muscles in sustaining life have more advanced death concepts than children not given such lessons (Slaughter & Lyons, 2003).

Adult–child discussions should also be culturally sensitive. Rather than presenting scientific evidence as negating religious beliefs, parents and teachers can assist children in blending the two sources of knowledge. As children get older, they often combine their apprecia-

As long as parents provide candid, age-appropriate explanations, experiencing the death of a pet can help children understand what happens when living things die. These parents comfort their children after the death of the family's dog by talking and reading about the experience.

tion of the death concept with religious and philosophical views, which offer solace during times of bereavement. Indeed, mystical explanations, such as being called by God and existing in a nonmaterial state, increase during adolescence as young people think more deeply about the nature of existence and grapple with religious and spiritual ideas (Cuddy-Casey & Orvaschel, 1997). Open, honest, and respectful communication about death contributes to cognitive development and emotional well-being.

plants, and kitchen utensils—each of which includes objects varying widely in perceptual features (Mandler, 2004a). The objects go together because of their common natural kind (animate versus inanimate), function, and behavior, challenging Piaget's assumption that young children's thinking is governed by the way things appear.

Indeed, 2- to 5-year-olds readily draw appropriate inferences using nonobservable characteristics shared by category members. For example, after being told that a bird has warm blood and that a stegosaurus (dinosaur) has cold blood, preschoolers infer that a pterodactyl (labeled a dinosaur) has cold blood, even though it closely resembles a bird (Gopnik & Nazzi, 2003). And when shown a set of three characters—two of whom look different but share an inner trait ("outgoing") and two of whom look similar but have different inner traits (one "shy," one "outgoing")—preschoolers rely on the trait category, not physical appearance, to predict similar preferred activities (Heyman & Gelman, 2000).

During the second and third years, and perhaps earlier, children's global categories differentiate. They form many *basic-level categories*—ones at an intermediate level of generality, such as "chairs," "tables," "dressers," and "beds." Performance on object-sorting tasks indicates that by the third or fourth year, children easily move back and forth between basic-level categories and *general categories,* such as "furniture" (Blewitt, 1994). They also break down the basic-level categories into *subcategories,* such as "rocking chairs" and "desk chairs." In fact, a case study of a highly verbal toddler with a strong interest in birds revealed that by age 2, he had constructed a hierarchical understanding of the bird domain that included such basic-level categories and subcategories as "waterbirds" ("ducks" and "swans"), "landbirds" ("roosters" and "turkeys"), and "other birds" ("bluebirds," "cardinals," and "seagulls") (Mervis, Pani, &

© TONY FREEMAN/PHOTOEDIT

Preschoolers form many categories based on nonobservational characteristics. Guided by knowledge that "dinosaurs have cold blood," this 4-year-old categorizes the pterodactyl (in the foreground) as a dinosaur rather than a bird, even though pterodactyls have wings and can fly.

Pani, 2003). The boy's category structure was not quite the same as that of many adults, but it was, indeed, hierarchical. And he used that knowledge to make many correct inferences about category membership—for example, that baby birds and their parents must be members of the same species (both "robins") even though they look strikingly different.

Preschoolers' rapidly expanding vocabularies and general knowledge support such impressive skill at categorizing. As they learn more about their world, they devise theories about underlying characteristics shared by category members, which help them identify new instances (Gelman & Kalish, 2006; Gelman & Koenig, 2003). For example, they realize that animals have an inborn potential for certain physical characteristics and behaviors that determine their identity. In categorizing, they look for causal links among these features. In one study, researchers invented two categories of animals—one with horns, armor, and a spiky tail; the other with wings, large ears, long toes, and a monkey-like tail (see Figure 9.4). Four-year-olds who were given a theory that identified an inner cause for the coexistence of the animals' features—animals in the first category "like to fight"; those in the second category "like to hide in trees"—easily classified new examples of animals. But 4-year-olds for whom animal features were merely pointed out or who were given a separate function for each feature could not remember the categories (Krascum & Andrews, 1998).

Finally, adults label and explain categories to young children—a major source of categorical learning. When adults use the word *bird* for hummingbirds, turkeys, and swans, they signal to children that something other than physical similarity binds these instances together (Gelman, 2003, 2006; Gelman & Kalish, 2006). Picture-book reading is an especially rich context for understanding categories. While looking at books with their preschoolers, parents provide information that guides children's inferences about the structure of categories: "Penguins live at the South Pole, swim, and catch fish" or "Fish breathe by taking water into their mouths."

In sum, although preschoolers' category systems are less complex than those of older children and adults, they already have the capacity to classify on the basis of nonobvious properties and in a hierarchical fashion. And preschoolers reason logically and causally in identifying the interrelated features that form the basis of a category and in classifying new members.

Categories of Animals   **New Instances**

"Likes to fight"

"Likes to hide in trees"

APPEARANCE VERSUS REALITY ■ As we have seen, preschoolers show some remarkably advanced reasoning when presented with familiar situations and simplified problems. What happens when they encounter objects that have two identities—a real one and an apparent one? Can they distinguish appearance from reality? In a series of studies, John Flavell and his colleagues presented children with objects that were disguised in various ways and asked what each "looks like" and what each "is really and truly." Preschoolers had difficulty. For example, when asked whether a candle that looks like a crayon "is really and truly" a crayon or whether a stone painted to look like an egg "is really and truly" an egg,

FIGURE 9.4

Categories of imaginary animals shown to preschoolers. When an adult provided a theory about the coexistence of animals' features—"likes to fight" and "likes to hide in trees"—4-year-olds easily classified new examples of animals with only one or two features. Without the theory, preschoolers could not remember the categories. Theories about underlying characteristics support the formation of many categories in early childhood. (From R. M. Krascum & S. Andrews, 1998, "The Effects of Theories on Children's Acquisition of Family-Resemblance Categories," *Child Development, 69,* p. 336. © The Society for Research in Child Development, Inc. Reprinted by permission.)

they often responded, "Yes!" Not until age 6 or 7 did children do well on these tasks (Flavell, Green, & Flavell, 1987).

Younger children's poor performance, however, is not due to a difficulty in distinguishing appearance from reality, as Piaget suggested. Rather, they have trouble with the language of these tasks (Deák, Ray, & Brenneman, 2003). When permitted to solve appearance–reality problems nonverbally, by selecting from an array of objects the one that "really" has a particular identity, most 3-year-olds perform well (Sapp, Lee, & Muir, 2000).

These findings suggest that preschoolers begin to grasp the appearance–reality distinction sometime during the third year. Note how it involves a capacity we discussed earlier: *dual representation,* the realization that an object can be one thing (a candle) while symbolizing another (a crayon). At first, however, children's understanding is fragile. After putting on a Halloween mask, young preschoolers may be frightened when they see themselves in a mirror. And not until the school years do children fully appreciate the unreality of much of what they see on TV. Performing well on verbal appearance–reality tasks signifies a more secure understanding and is related to further progress in representational ability (Bialystok & Senman, 2004).

This 3-year-old has begun to understand that an object can be one thing (in this case, a coin bank) while symbolizing something else (a pig). By age 6 or 7, his knowledge of the distinction between appearance and reality is likely to be solid and secure.

Evaluation of the Preoperational Stage

Table 9.1 on page 332 provides an overview of the cognitive attainments of early childhood just considered. **TAKE A MOMENT...** Compare them with Piaget's description of the preoperational child on pages 322–326. The evidence as a whole indicates that Piaget was partly wrong and partly right about young children's cognitive capacities. When given simplified tasks based on familiar experiences, preschoolers show the beginnings of logical operations. How can we make sense of the contradictions between Piaget's conclusions and the findings of recent research?

That preschoolers have some logical understanding suggests that they attain logical operations gradually. Over time, children rely on increasingly effective mental (as opposed to perceptual) approaches to solving problems. For example, children who cannot use counting to compare two sets of items do not conserve number. Rather, they rely on perceptual cues to compare the amounts in two sets of items (Rouselle, Palmers, & Noël, 2004; Sophian, 1995). Once preschoolers can count, they apply this skill to conservation-of-number tasks involving just a few items. As counting improves, they extend the strategy to problems with more items. By age 6, they understand that number remains the same after a transformation in the length and spacing of a set of items as long as nothing is added or taken away. Consequently, they no longer need to count to verify their answer (Halford & Andrews, 2006). Thus, children pass through several steps on the way to a full understanding of relationships among variables in conservation problems, although (as Piaget indicated) they do not fully grasp conservation until the early school years.

Evidence that preschool children can be trained to perform well on Piagetian problems also supports the idea that operational thought is not absent at one point in time and present at another (Roazzi & Bryant, 1997; Siegler, 1995; Siegler & Svetina, 2006). Children who possess some understanding would naturally benefit from training, unlike those with no understanding at all. The gradual development of logical operations poses a serious challenge to Piaget's assumption of abrupt change toward logical reasoning around age 6 or 7. Does a preoperational stage really exist? Some no longer think so. Recall from Chapter 6 that according to the information-processing perspective, children work out their understanding of each type of task separately. According to this view, their thought processes are basically the same at all ages—just present to a greater or lesser extent.

Other experts think that the stage concept is still valid, with modifications. For example, some *neo-Piagetian theorists* combine Piaget's stage approach with the information-processing emphasis on task-specific change (Case, 1998; Halford, 2002). They believe that Piaget's strict stage definition must be transformed into a less tightly knit concept, one in which a related set of competencies develops over an extended period, depending on brain development and specific

TABLE 9.1   Some Cognitive Attainments of the Preschool Years

APPROXIMATE AGE	COGNITIVE ATTAINMENTS
2–4 years 	Shows a dramatic increase in representational activity, as reflected in the development of language, make-believe play, understanding of symbol–real world relations (such as photos, drawings, and maps), and categorization
	Takes the perspective of others in simplified, familiar situations and in everyday, face-to-face communication
	Distinguishes animate beings from inanimate objects; denies that magic can alter everyday experiences
	Notices transformations, reverses thinking, and understands many cause-and-effect relationships in familiar contexts
	Categorizes objects on the basis of common natural kind, function, and behavior (not just perceptual features) and devises ideas about underlying characteristics that category members share
	Sorts familiar objects into hierarchically organized categories
	Distinguishes appearance from reality
4–7 years 	Becomes increasingly aware that make-believe (and other thought processes) are representational activities
	Replaces magical beliefs about fairies, goblins, and events that violate expectations with plausible explanations
	Solves verbal appearance–reality problems, signifying a more secure understanding

experiences. These investigators point to findings indicating that as long as the complexity of tasks and children's exposure to them are carefully controlled, children approach those tasks in similar, stage-consistent ways (Andrews & Halford, 2002; Case & Okamoto, 1996). For example, in drawing pictures, preschoolers depict objects separately, ignoring their spatial arrangement (return to the drawing on page 314 in Chapter 8 for an example). In understanding stories, they grasp a single story line but have trouble with a main plot plus one or more subplots.

This flexible stage notion recognizes the unique qualities of early childhood thinking. At the same time, it provides a better account of why, as Leslie put it, "Preschoolers' minds are such a blend of logic, fantasy, and faulty reasoning."

Piaget and Early Childhood Education

Three educational principles derived from Piaget's theory continue to have a major influence on teacher training and classroom practices, especially during early childhood:

- *Discovery learning.* In a Piagetian classroom, children are encouraged to discover for themselves through spontaneous interaction with the environment. Instead of presenting ready-made knowledge verbally, teachers provide a rich variety of activities designed to promote exploration and discovery, including art, puzzles, table games, dress-up clothing, building blocks, books, measuring tools, musical instruments.
- *Sensitivity to children's readiness to learn.* In a Piagetian classroom, teachers introduce activities that build on children's current thinking, challenging their incorrect ways of viewing the world. But they do not try to speed up development by imposing new skills before children indicate they are interested and ready.
- *Acceptance of individual differences.* Piaget's theory assumes that all children go through the same sequence of development, but at different rates. Therefore, teachers must plan

activities for individual children and small groups, not just for the whole class. In addition, teachers evaluate each child's educational progress in relation to the child's previous development, rather than on the basis of normative standards, or average performance of same-age peers.

Like his stages, educational applications of Piaget's theory have met with criticism. Perhaps the greatest challenge has to do with his insistence that young children learn primarily through acting on the environment (Brainerd, 2003). In the next section, we will see that children also use language-based routes to knowledge. Nevertheless, Piaget's influence on education has been powerful. He gave teachers new ways to observe, understand, and enhance young children's development and offered strong theoretical justification for child-oriented approaches to classroom teaching and learning.

Ask Yourself

Review   Select two of the following features of preoperational thought: egocentrism, a focus on perceptual appearances, difficulty reasoning about transformations, and lack of hierarchical classification. Cite findings that led Piaget to conclude that preschoolers are deficient in those ways. Present evidence indicating that preschoolers are more capable thinkers than Piaget assumed.

Apply   Three-year-old Will understands that his tricycle isn't alive and can't feel or move on its own. But at the beach, watching the sun dip below the horizon, Will exclaimed, "The sun is tired. It's going to sleep!" What explains this apparent contradiction in Will's reasoning?

Connect   Make-believe play promotes both cognitive and social development (see page 323). Explain why this is so.

Reflect   Did you have an imaginary companion as a young child? If so, what was your companion like, and why did you create it? Were your parents aware of your companion? What was their attitude toward it?

Vygotsky's Sociocultural Theory

Piaget's de-emphasis on language as an important source of cognitive development brought yet another challenge, this time from Vygotsky's sociocultural theory, which stresses the social context of cognitive development. In this theory, the child and the social environment collaborate to mold cognition in culturally adaptive ways. During early childhood, rapid growth in language broadens preschoolers' ability to participate in social dialogues with more knowledgeable individuals, who encourage them to master culturally important tasks. Soon children start to communicate with themselves in much the same way they converse with others. This greatly enhances the complexity of their thinking and their ability to control their own behavior. Let's see how it happens.

Children's Private Speech

Watch preschoolers as they go about their daily activities, and you will see that they frequently talk out loud to themselves. For example, as Sammy worked a puzzle one day, he said, "Where's the red piece? I need the red one. Now, a blue one. No, it doesn't fit. Try it here."

Piaget (1923/1926) called these utterances *egocentric speech,* reflecting his belief that young children have difficulty taking the perspectives of others. For this reason, he said, their talk is often "talk for self," in which they express thoughts in whatever form they happen to occur, regardless of whether a listener can understand. Piaget believed that cognitive development and

This 3-year-old makes a sculpture from playdough and plastic sticks with the aid of private speech. Research supports Vygotsky's theory that children use private speech to guide their own thinking and behavior.

certain social experiences eventually bring an end to egocentric speech. Specifically, through repeated disagreements with agemates, children see that others hold viewpoints different from their own. As a result, egocentric speech declines in favor of social speech, in which children adapt what they say to their listeners.

Vygotsky (1934/1987) disagreed strongly with Piaget's conclusions. Because language helps children think about mental activities and behavior and select courses of action, Vygotsky viewed it as the foundation for all higher cognitive processes, including controlled attention, deliberate memorization and recall, categorization, planning, problem solving, and self-reflection. In Vygotsky's view, children speak to themselves for self-guidance. As they get older and find tasks easier, their self-directed speech is internalized as silent, *inner speech*—the verbal dialogues we carry on with ourselves while thinking and acting in everyday situations.

Over the past three decades, almost all studies have supported Vygotsky's perspective (Berk & Harris, 2003). As a result, children's self-directed speech is now called **private speech** instead of egocentric speech. Research shows that children use more of it when tasks are challenging but within their *zone of proximal development,* or range of mastery (see page 227 in Chapter 6). For example, Figure 9.5 shows how 5- and 6-year-olds' private speech increased as researchers made a problem-solving task moderately difficult, then decreased as the researchers made the task very difficult. With age, as Vygotsky predicted, private speech goes underground, changing into whispers and silent lip movements (Patrick & Abravanel, 2000; Winsler & Naglieri, 2003). Furthermore, children who freely use self-guiding private speech during a challenging activity are more attentive and involved and show better task performance than their less talkative agemates (Al-Namlah, Fernyhough, & Meins, 2006; Berk & Spuhl, 1995; Fernyhough & Fradley, 2005; Winsler, Naglieri, & Manfra, 2006).

Finally, compared with their agemates, children with learning and behavior problems engage in private speech over a longer period of development (Berk, 2001b; Paladino, 2006; Winsler et al., 1999, 2007). They seem to use private speech to help compensate for impairments in attention and cognitive processing that make many tasks more difficult for them.

Social Origins of Early Childhood Cognition

Where does private speech come from? Recall from Chapter 6 that Vygotsky believed children's learning takes place within the *zone of proximal development*—a range of tasks too difficult for the child to do alone but possible with the help of others. Consider the joint activity of Sammy and his mother, who helps him put together a difficult puzzle:

Sammy: "I can't get this one in." [*Tries to insert a piece in the wrong place.*]

Mother: "Which piece might go down here?" [*Points to the bottom of the puzzle.*]

Sammy: "His shoes." [*Looks for a piece resembling the clown's shoes but tries the wrong one.*]

FIGURE 9.5

Relationship of private speech to task difficulty among 5- and 6-year-olds. Researchers increased the difficulty of a problem-solving task. Private speech rose as the task became moderately difficult, then declined as it became highly difficult. Children are more likely to use private speech for self-guidance when tasks are within their zone of proximal development, or range of mastery. (Adapted from Fernyhough & Fradley, 2005.)

Mother: "Well, what piece looks like this shape?" [*Pointing again to the bottom of the puzzle.*]

Sammy: "The brown one." [*Tries it, and it fits; then attempts another piece and looks at his mother.*]

Mother: "Try turning it just a little." [*Gestures to show him.*]

Sammy: "There!" [*Puts in several more pieces while his mother watches.*]

Sammy's mother keeps the puzzle within his zone of proximal development, at a manageable level of difficulty, by questioning, prompting, and suggesting strategies.

EFFECTIVE SOCIAL INTERACTION ■ To promote cognitive development, social interaction must have two vital features. The first is **intersubjectivity,** the process by which two participants who begin a task with different understandings arrive at a shared understanding (Newson & Newson, 1975). Intersubjectivity creates a common ground for communication, as each partner adjusts to the other's perspective. Adults try to promote it when they translate their own insights in ways that are within the child's grasp. As the child stretches to understand the adult, she is drawn into a more mature approach to the situation (Rogoff, 1998).

As this child works on a puzzle, her mother engages in scaffolding: breaking down the task into manageable units, suggesting and explaining strategies, and gradually turning over responsibility to the child.

The capacity for intersubjectivity is present early, in parent–infant mutual gaze, exchange of emotional signals, and imitation. Later, language facilitates it. As conversational skills improve, preschoolers increasingly seek others' help and direct that assistance to ensure that it is beneficial (Whitington & Ward, 1999). Between ages 3 and 5, children strive for intersubjectivity in dialogues with peers, as when they affirm a playmate's message, add new ideas, and make contributions to ongoing play to sustain it. They can also be heard saying, "I think [this way]. What do you think?"—evidence of a willingness to share viewpoints (Berk, 2001b). In these ways, children create zones of proximal development for one another.

A second important feature of social experience is **scaffolding**—adjusting the support offered during a teaching session to fit the child's current level of performance. When the child has little notion of how to proceed, the adult uses direct instruction, breaking down the task into manageable units, suggesting strategies, and offering rationales for using them. As the child's competence increases, effective scaffolders—like Sammy's mother—gradually and sensitively withdraw support, turning over responsibility to the child. Then children take the language of these dialogues, make it part of their private speech, and use this speech to organize their independent efforts.

Scaffolding captures the form of teaching interaction that occurs as children work on school or school-like tasks, such as puzzles, model building, picture matching, and (later) academic assignments. It may not apply to other contexts that are equally vital for cognitive development—for example, play or everyday activities, during which adults usually support children's efforts without deliberately teaching. To encompass children's diverse opportunities to learn through involvement with others, Barbara Rogoff (1998, 2003) suggests the term **guided participation,** a broader concept than scaffolding. It refers to shared endeavors between more expert and less expert participants, without specifying the precise features of communication. Consequently, it allows for variations across situations and cultures.

RESEARCH ON SOCIAL INTERACTION AND COGNITIVE DEVELOPMENT ■ What evidence supports Vygotsky's ideas on the social origins of cognitive development? In previous chapters, we reviewed evidence indicating that when adults establish intersubjectivity by being stimulating, responsive, and supportive, they foster many competencies—attention, language, complex play, and understanding of others' perspectives. Furthermore, children of effective scaffolders use more private speech and are more successful when attempting difficult tasks on their own

private speech Self-directed speech that children use to plan and guide their own behavior.

intersubjectivity The process whereby two participants who begin a task with different understandings arrive at a shared understanding.

scaffolding Adjusting the assistance offered during a teaching session to fit the child's current level of performance.

guided participation Shared endeavors between more expert and less expert participants, regardless of the precise features of communication.

(Berk & Spuhl, 1995; Conner & Cross, 2003). Adult cognitive support—teaching in small steps and offering strategies—predicts children's mature thinking. And adult emotional support—offering encouragement and transferring responsibility to the child—predicts children's effort (Neitzel & Stright, 2003). The result is a winning combination for school success.

Other research shows that although young children benefit from working on tasks with same-age peers, their planning and problem solving improve more when their partner is either an "expert" peer (especially capable at the task) or an adult (Radziszewska & Rogoff, 1988). And peer disagreement (emphasized by Piaget) seems to be less important for cognitive development than the extent to which children achieve intersubjectivity—resolve differences of opinion and cooperate (Kobayashi, 1994; Tudge, 1992).

Vygotsky and Early Childhood Education

Both Piagetian and Vygotskian classrooms provide opportunities for active participation and promote acceptance of individual differences. Yet a Vygotskian classroom goes beyond independent discovery. It promotes *assisted discovery*. Teachers guide children's learning with explanations, demonstrations, and verbal prompts, carefully tailoring their efforts to each child's zone of proximal development. Assisted discovery is aided by *peer collaboration*, as children with varying abilities work in groups, teaching and helping one another.

According to Vygotsky (1935/1978), make-believe play is the ideal social context for fostering cognitive development in early childhood—a unique, broadly influential zone of proximal development in which children try out a wide variety of challenging activities and acquire many competencies. Furthermore, as children create imaginary situations, they learn to follow internal ideas and social rules rather than their immediate impulses. For example, a child pretending to go to sleep follows the rules of bedtime behavior. A child imagining himself as a father and a doll as a child conforms to the rules of parental behavior.

Turn back to pages 322–323 to review findings that make-believe enhances a diverse array of cognitive and social skills. Pretending is also rich in private speech—a finding that supports its role in helping children bring action under the control of thought (Krafft & Berk, 1998). And preschoolers who spend more time engaged in sociodramatic play are better at taking personal responsibility for following classroom rules and at regulating emotion (Berk, Mann, & Ogan, 2006; Lemche et al., 2003). These findings support the role of make-believe in children's increasing self-control.

In this Vygotskian classroom, 4- and 5-year-olds benefit from peer collaboration as they work in groups, teaching and helping one another.

Evaluation of Vygotsky's Theory

In granting social experience a fundamental role in cognitive development, Vygotsky's theory underscores the vital role of teaching and helps us understand the wide cultural variation in children's cognitive skills. Nevertheless, it has not gone unchallenged. Verbal communication is not the only means—or even, in some cultures, the most important means—through which children's thinking develops. When Western parents scaffold their young children's mastery of challenging tasks, they assume much responsibility for children's motivation by frequently instructing and conversing with the child. Their communication resembles the teaching that takes place in school, where their children will spend years preparing for adult life. But in cultures that place less emphasis on schooling and literacy, parents often expect children to acquire new skills through keen observation and participation in community activities (Rogoff, 2003). Turn to the Cultural Influences box on the following page for research illustrating this difference.

Cultural Influences

Children in Village and Tribal Cultures Observe and Participate in Adult Work

In Western societies, children are largely excluded from participating in adult work, which generally takes place outside the home. The role of equipping children with the skills they need to become competent workers is assigned to school. In early childhood, middle-SES parents' interactions with children dwell on preparing children to succeed in school through child-focused activities—especially adult–child conversations and play that enhance language, literacy, and other school-related knowledge. In village and tribal cultures, children receive little or no schooling, spend their days in contact with or participating in adult work, and start to assume mature responsibilities in early childhood (Rogoff et al., 2003). Consequently, parents have little need to rely on conversation and play to teach children.

A study comparing 2- and 3-year-olds' daily lives in four cultures—two U.S. middle-SES suburbs, the Efe hunters and gatherers of the Republic of Congo, and a Mayan agricultural town in Guatemala—documented these differences (Morelli, Rogoff, & Angelillo, 2003). In the U.S. communities, young children had little access to adult work and spent much time involved in adult–child conversations and play that catered to children's interests and provided scholastic lessons. In contrast, the Efe and Mayan children rarely engaged in these child-focused activities. Instead, they spent their day in close proximity to adult work, which often took place in or near the Efe campsite or the Mayan family home. Compared to their American counterparts, Mayan and Efe children spent far more time observing adult work.

An ethnography of a remote Mayan village in Yucatan, Mexico, shows that when young children are legitimate onlookers and participants in a daily life structured around adult work, their competencies differ sharply from those of Western preschoolers (Gaskins, 1999). Yucatec Mayan adults are subsistence farmers. Men tend cornfields, aided by sons age 8 and older. Women oversee the household and yard; they prepare meals, wash clothes, and care for the livestock and garden, assisted by daughters and by sons not yet old enough to work in the fields. From the second year on, children join in these activities to the extent that they can. When not participating with adults, they are expected to be self-sufficient. Young children make many non-work decisions for themselves—how much to sleep and eat, what to wear, when to take their daily bath, and even when to start school. As a result, Yucatec Mayan preschoolers are highly competent at self-care. In contrast, their make-believe play is limited; when it occurs, it involves brief imitations of adult work. Otherwise, they watch others—for hours each day.

Yucatec Mayan parents rarely converse or play with preschoolers or scaffold their learning. Rather, when children imitate adult tasks, parents conclude that they are ready for more responsibility. Then they assign chores, selecting tasks the child can do with little help so that adult work is not disturbed. If a child cannot do a task, the adult takes over and the child observers, reengaging when able to contribute.

Expected to be autonomous and helpful, Yucatec Mayan children seldom display attention-getting behaviors or ask others for something interesting to do. From an early age, they can sit quietly for long periods with little fussing—through a lengthy religious service or a three-hour truck ride. And when an adult interrupts their activity and directs them to do a chore, they respond eagerly to a command that Western children frequently avoid or resent. By age 5, Yucatec Mayan children spontaneously take responsibility for tasks beyond those assigned.

© BERYL GOLDBERG

In Yucatec Mayan culture, adults rarely converse with children or scaffold their learning. And rather than engaging in make-believe, children join in the work of their community from an early age, spending many hours observing adults. This Mayan preschooler watches intently as her grandmother washes dishes. When the child begins to imitate adult tasks, she will be given additional responsibilities.

Vygotsky's theory has also been criticized for saying little about how basic motor, perceptual, attention, memory and problem-solving skills, discussed in Chapters 5 and 6, contribute to socially transmitted higher cognitive processes. For example, his theory does not address how these elementary capacities spark changes in children's social experiences, from which more advanced cognition springs (Moll, 1994). Piaget paid far more attention than Vygotsky to the development of basic cognitive processes. It is intriguing to speculate about the broader theory that might exist today had Piaget and Vygotsky—the two twentieth-century giants of cognitive development—had had a chance to meet and weave together their extraordinary accomplishments.

Ask Yourself

Review Describe characteristics of social interaction that support children's cognitive development. How does such interaction create a zone of proximal development?

Apply Tanisha sees her 5-year-old son Toby talking out loud to himself as he plays. She wonders whether she should discourage this behavior. Use Vygotsky's theory to explain why Toby talks to himself. How would you advise Tanisha?

Connect Explain how Piaget's and Vygotsky's theories complement each other. That is, what aspects of development does one emphasize that the other leaves out?

Reflect When do you use private speech? Does it serve a self-guiding function for you, as it does for children? Explain.

Information Processing

Return for a moment to the model of information processing discussed on pages 220–221 in Chapter 6. Recall that information processing focuses on *mental strategies* that children use to transform stimuli flowing into their mental systems. During early childhood, advances in representation and in children's ability to guide their own behavior lead to more efficient and flexible ways of attending, manipulating information, and solving problems. Preschoolers also become more aware of their own mental life and begin to acquire academically relevant knowledge important for school success.

Attention

As parents and teachers know, preschoolers—compared with school-age children—spend shorter times involved in tasks and are more easily distracted. But recall from Chapter 5 that sustained attention improves in toddlerhood, a trend that continues during early childhood.

A major reason is a steady gain in children's ability to inhibit impulses and keep their mind on a competing goal, supported by rapid growth of the frontal lobes of the cerebral cortex. Consider a task in which the child must tap once when the adult taps twice and tap twice when the adult taps once, or must say "night" to a picture of the sun and "day" to a picture of the moon with stars. Three- and 4-year-olds make many errors, but by age 6 to 7, children find such tasks easy (see Figure 9.6) (Diamond & Taylor, 1996; Kirkham, Cruess, & Diamond, 2003; Zelazo et al., 2003). Simultaneously, ERP and fMRI measures reveal a steady age-related increase in activation of the frontal lobes while children engage in activities requiring suppression of inappropriate responses (Bartgis, Lilly, & Thomas, 2003; Luna et al., 2001).

FIGURE 9.6

Gains between ages 3 and 7 in performance on tasks requiring children to inhibit an impulse and focus on a competing goal. In the tapping task, children had to tap once when the adult tapped twice and tap twice when the adult tapped once. In the day–night task, children had to say "night" to a picture of the sun and "day" to a picture of the moon with stars. (From A. Diamond, 2004, "Normal Development of the Prefrontal Cortex from Birth to Young Adulthood: Cognitive Functions, Anatomy, and Biochemistry," in D. T. Stuff & R. T. Knight, eds., *Principles of Frontal Lobe Function.* New York: Oxford University Press, p. 474. Reprinted by permission.)

The capacity to generate increasingly complex play goals (requiring concentration) and adult scaffolding of attention also contribute to development of attention (Ruff & Cappozoli, 2003). When parents help their preschoolers maintain a focus, by offering suggestions, questions, and comments about the child's current interest, the children are more mature, cognitively and socially, when reassessed a year or two later (Bono & Stifter, 2003; Landry et al., 2000). Many skills, including language, exploration, problem solving, social interaction, and cooperation, benefit from an improved ability to concentrate.

During early childhood, children also become better at **planning**—thinking out a sequence of acts ahead of time and allocating attention accordingly to reach a goal. For tasks that are familiar and not too complex, preschoolers sometimes generate and follow a plan. For example, by age 4, they search for a lost object in a play yard systematically and exhaustively, looking only in locations between where they last saw the object and where they discovered it missing (Wellman, Somerville, & Haake, 1979). But when asked to compare detailed pictures, preschoolers fail to search thoroughly. On complex tasks, they rarely decide what to do first and what to do next in an orderly fashion (Friedman & Scholnick, 1997; Ruff & Rothbart, 1996).

Children also learn from cultural tools that support planning—directions for playing games, patterns for construction, recipes for cooking—especially when they collaborate with more expert planners. When 4- to 7-year-olds were observed jointly constructing a toy with their mothers, the mothers provided basic information about the usefulness of plans and suggestions for implementing specific steps: "Do you want to look at the picture and see what goes where? What piece do you need first?" After working with their mothers, younger children more often referred to the plan when building on their own (Gauvain, 2004; Gauvain, de la Ossa, & Hurtado-Ortiz, 2001). When adults encourage planning in everyday activities, from loading the dishwasher to packing for a vacation, they help children plan more effectively.

While collaborating with his son in assembling a kite, a father points out the sequence of steps they must follow. Through joint planning in everyday activities, adults help preschoolers plan more effectively.

Memory

Unlike infants and toddlers, preschoolers have the language skills to describe what they remember, and they can follow directions on simple memory tasks. As a result, memory development becomes easier to study in early childhood.

RECOGNITION AND RECALL ▪ TAKE A MOMENT... Try showing a young child a set of 10 pictures or toys. Then mix them up with some unfamiliar items, and ask the child to point to the ones in the original set. You will find that preschoolers' *recognition* memory—ability to tell whether a stimulus is the same as or similar to one they have seen before—is remarkably good. It becomes even more accurate by the end of early childhood. In fact, 4- and 5-year-olds perform nearly perfectly.

Now keep the items out of view, and ask the child to name the ones she saw. This more demanding task requires *recall*—remembering in the absence of perceptual support. Young children's recall is much poorer than their recognition. At age 2, they can recall no more than one or two items, at age 4 only about three or four (Perlmutter, 1984).

Of course, recognition is much easier than recall for adults as well, but in comparison to adults, children's recall is quite deficient. Better recall in early childhood is strongly associated with language development, which greatly enhances long-lasting representations of past experiences (Simcock & Hayne, 2003). But even preschoolers with good language skills recall poorly because they are not skilled at using **memory strategies,** deliberate mental activities that improve our chances of remembering. For example, when you want to retain information, you might *rehearse,* or repeat the items over and over. Or you might *organize* it, intentionally grouping items that are alike so that you can easily retrieve them by thinking of their similar characteristics.

Preschoolers do show the beginnings of memory strategies. When circumstances permit, they arrange items in space to aid their memories. In one study, an adult placed either an

planning Thinking out a sequence of acts ahead of time and allocating attention accordingly to reach a goal.

memory strategies Deliberate mental activities that improve the likelihood of remembering.

A child remembers everyday experiences, like brushing his teeth, in terms of scripts—general descriptions of what occurs and when it occurs. Over time, children provide more elaborate scripts—for example, "You squeeze out the toothpaste and brush your teeth. You rinse your mouth and then your toothbrush."

episodic memory Memory for everyday experiences.

scripts General descriptions of what occurs and when it occurs in a particular situation, used to organize and interpret repeated events.

overlapping-waves theory The theory of problem solving that states that when given challenging problems, children try various strategies and gradually select those that are fastest and most accurate.

M&M or a wooden peg in each of 12 identical containers and handed them one by one to preschoolers, asking them to remember where the candy was hidden. By age 4, children put the candy containers in one place and the peg containers in another, a strategy that almost always led to perfect recall (DeLoache & Todd, 1988). But preschoolers do not yet rehearse or organize items (for example, all the vehicles together, all the animals together) when asked to remember. Even when they are trained to do so, their memory performance rarely improves, and they do not apply these strategies in new situations (Gathercole, Adams, & Hitch, 1994).

Why do young children seldom use memory strategies? One reason is that strategies tax their limited working memories. *Digit span* tasks, in which children try to repeat an adult-provided string of numbers, assess the capacity of working memory, which improves slowly, from an average of two digits at age 2½ to four digits at age 7 (Kail, 2003). With such limits, preschoolers have difficulty applying a strategy while simultaneously holding on to discrete pieces of information.

MEMORY FOR EVERYDAY EXPERIENCES ■ Think about differences between your recall of listlike information and your memory for everyday experiences—what researchers call **episodic memory.** In remembering lists, you recall isolated bits. In remembering everyday experiences, you recall complex, meaningful information. Between 3 and 6 years, children improve sharply in memory for relations among stimuli. For example, in a set of photos, they remember not just the animals they saw but the contexts in which they saw them—a bear emerging from a tunnel, a zebra tied to a tree on a city street (Sluzenski, Newcombe, & Kovacs, 2006). The capacity to *bind together stimuli* when encoding and retrieving them supports the development of an increasingly rich event memory during early childhood.

Memory for Familiar Events. Like adults, preschoolers remember familiar, repeated events—what you do when you go to child care or get ready for bed—in terms of **scripts,** general descriptions of what occurs and when it occurs in a particular situation. Young children's scripts begin as a structure of main acts. For example, when asked to tell what happens when you go to a restaurant, a 3-year-old might say, "You go in, get the food, eat, and then pay." Although children's first scripts contain only a few acts, as long as events in a situation take place in logical order, they are almost always recalled in correct sequence. Still, adults must work hard to obtain preschoolers' scripted reports, asking questions and prompting (Bauer, 1997, 2002a). With age, scripts become more spontaneous and elaborate, as in the following restaurant account given by a 5-year-old child: "You go in. You can sit at a booth or a table. Then you tell the waitress what you want. You eat. If you want dessert, you can have some. Then you pay and go home" (Hudson, Fivush, & Kuebli, 1992).

Scripts help children organize, interpret, and predict everyday experiences. Once formed, they can be used to predict what will happen on similar occasions in the future. Children use scripts to assist recall when listening to and telling stories. They also act out scripts in make-believe play as they pretend to put the baby to bed, go on a trip, or play school. And scripts support children's earliest efforts at planning as they represent sequences of actions that lead to desired goals (Hudson, Sosa, & Shapiro, 1997).

Memory for Unique Events. In Chapter 6 we considered a second type of episodic memory—*autobiographical memory,* or representations of personally meaningful, one-time events. As 3- to 6-year-olds' cognitive and conversational skills improve, their descriptions of special events become better organized, detailed, enriched with a personal perspective, and related to the larger context of their lives (Fivush, 2001). A young preschooler simply reports, "I went camping." Older preschoolers include specifics: where and when the event happened and who was present. And with age, preschoolers increasingly include subjective information—why, for example, an event was exciting, funny, sad, or made them feel proud or embarrassed ("I loved sleeping all night in the tent!")—that explains the event's personal significance (Fivush, 2001).

Adults use two styles for prompting children's autobiographical narratives. In the *elaborative style,* they follow the child's lead, discussing what the child wants to talk about, asking varied questions, adding information to the child's statements, and volunteering their own recollections and evaluations of events. For example, after a field trip to the zoo, Leslie asked, "What was the first thing we did? Why weren't the parrots in their cages? I thought the roaring lion was scary. What did you think?" In this way, she helped the children reestablish and reorganize their memory of the field trip. In contrast, adults who use the *repetitive style* keep repeating the same questions ("Do you remember the zoo? What did we do at the zoo? Which animals did you see at the zoo?"), regardless of the child's interest, and provide little additional information. Preschoolers who experience the elaborative style produce more organized and detailed personal stories when followed up one to two years later (Cleveland & Reese, 2005; Farrant & Reese, 2000).

As children converse with adults about the past, they not only improve their episodic memory but also create a shared history that strengthens close relationships and self-understanding. In line with these ideas, securely attached parents and preschoolers engage in more elaborate reminiscing, whereas parents who have insecure bonds with their preschoolers generally limit themselves to the repetitive style (Fivush & Reese, 2002). And children of elaborative-style parents describe themselves in more consistent ways (Bird & Reese, 2006). When, in past-event conversations, a child discovers that he finds swimming, running, climbing, getting together with friends, and going to the zoo fun, he can begin to connect these specific experiences into a general understanding of "what I enjoy." The result is a clearer image of himself.

In sum, the quality of the parent–child relationship affects the richness of children's autobiographical memories and, in turn, the extent to which children enter into the history of their families and communities and get to know themselves. As we conclude our consideration of early childhood memory, notice how adult support contributes to each aspect of preschoolers' memory development, in line with Vygotsky's ideas.

Problem Solving

How do preschoolers use their cognitive competencies to discover new problem-solving strategies? To find out, let's look in on 5-year-old Darryl as he added the marbles tucked into pairs of small bags that Leslie set out on a table.

As Darryl dealt with adding each pair, his strategies varied. Sometimes he guessed, without applying any strategy. At other times, he counted from one on his fingers. For example, for bags containing 2 + 4 marbles, his fingers popped up one by one as he exclaimed, "One, two, three, four, five, six!" On still other occasions, he started with the lower digit, 2, and "counted on" ("two, three, four, five, six"). Or he began with the higher digit, 4, and "counted on" ("four, five, six")—a strategy called *min* because it minimizes the work. Sometimes, he retrieved the answer from memory.

To study children's problem solving, Robert Siegler (1996, 2006) used the microgenetic research design (see Chapter 1, page 43), presenting children with many problems over an extended time. He found that children experiment with diverse strategies on many types of problems—basic math facts, numerical estimation, conservation, memory for lists of items, reading first words, spelling, even tic-tac-toe—follows the overlapping-waves pattern shown in Figure 9.7. According to **overlapping-waves theory,** when given challenging problems, children

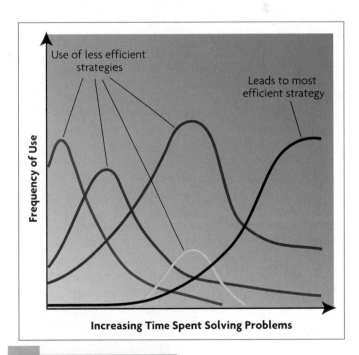

FIGURE 9.7

Overlapping-waves pattern of strategy use in problem solving. When given challenging problems, a child generates a variety of strategies, each represented by a wave. The waves overlap because the child tries several different strategies at the same time. Use of each strategy, depicted by the height of the wave, is constantly changing. As the child observes which strategies work best, which work less well, and which are ineffective, the one that results in the most rapid, accurate solutions wins out. (Adapted from R. S. Siegler, *Emerging Minds: The Process of Change in Children's Thinking,* copyright © 1996 by Oxford University Press, Inc. Used by permission of Oxford University Press, Inc.)

try out various strategies and observe which work best, which work less well, and which are ineffective. Gradually, they select strategies on the basis of two criteria: *accuracy* and *speed*— for basic addition, the *min* strategy. As children home in on effective strategies for solving the problems at hand, correct solutions become more strongly associated with problems, and children display the most efficient strategy—automatic retrieval of the answer.

How do children move from less to more efficient strategies? Often they discover a faster procedure by using a more time-consuming technique. For example, by repeatedly counting on fingers, Darryl began to recognize the number of fingers he held up (Siegler & Jenkins, 1989). Also, certain problems dramatize the need for a better strategy. When Darryl opened a pair of bags, one containing ten marbles and the other with only two, he realized that *min* would be best. Teaching children to reason logically with concepts relevant to the problems is also helpful (Canobi, Reeve, & Pattison, 1998; Siegler & Svetina, 2006). Once Darryl understood that he got the same result regardless of the order in which he combined two sets (3 + 6 = 9 and 6 + 3 = 9), he more often used *min* and arrived at correct answers. Finally, a large improvement in the accuracy of a newly discovered strategy over previous strategies generally leads to rapid adoption of the new approach (Siegler, 2006; Siegler & Booth, 2004).

Many factors, including practice, reasoning, tasks with new challenges, and adult assistance, contribute to improved problem solving. And experimenting with less mature strategies lets children see the limitations of those techniques. In sum, overlapping-waves theory emphasizes that trying many strategies is vital for developing new, more effective solution techniques. Even 2-year-olds solve problems, such as how to use a tool to obtain an out-of-reach toy, with an overlapping-waves pattern (Chen & Siegler, 2000). It characterizes problem solving across a wide range of ages. And in the tradition of the information-processing approach, the theory views development as occurring gradually, rather than in discontinuous stages.

The Young Child's Theory of Mind

As representation of the world, memory, and problem solving improve, children start to reflect on their own thought processes. They begin to construct a *theory of mind*, or coherent set of ideas about mental activities. This understanding is also called **metacognition**, or "thinking about thought" (the prefix *meta-* means "beyond" or "higher"). As adults, we have a complex appreciation of our inner mental worlds. For example, we can differentiate among believing, knowing, remembering, guessing, forgetting, and imagining, and we are aware of many factors that influence these cognitive activities. We rely on these understandings to interpret our own and others' behavior and to improve our performance on various tasks. How early are children aware of their mental lives, and how complete and accurate is their knowledge?

AWARENESS OF MENTAL LIFE ■ At the end of the first year, babies view people as intentional beings who can share and influence one another's mental states, a milestone that opens the door to new forms of communication—joint attention, social referencing, preverbal gestures, and spoken language (Tomasello & Rakoczy, 2003). As they approach age 2, children display a clearer grasp of others' emotions and desires, evident in their realization that others' perspectives can differ from their own ("Daddy *like* carrots. I no *like* carrots.").

As 2-year-olds' vocabularies expand, their first verbs include such words as *think, remember,* and *pretend.* By age 3, children realize that thinking takes place inside their heads and that a person can think about something without seeing, touching, or talking about it (Flavell, Green, & Flavell, 1995). But 2- to 3-year-olds, who have only a beginning grasp of the distinction between mental life and behavior, think that people always behave in ways consistent with their *desires*. They do not understand that less obvious, more interpretive mental states, such as *beliefs*, also affect behavior.

Between ages 3 and 4, children use *think* and *know* to refer to their own and others' thoughts and beliefs (Wellman, 2002). And from age 4 on, they realize that both *beliefs* and *desires* determine behavior. In one instance, Sammy put a blanket over his head and, pretending to be a ghost, pushed Dwayne, who fell and began to cry. "I couldn't see him! The blanket was over my face," Sammy pleaded, trying to alter his mother's *belief* about his motive and, thereby, ward off any *desire* on her part to punish him. From early to middle childhood, efforts to alter others' beliefs

metacognition Thinking about thought; awareness of mental activities.

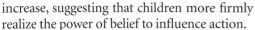

FIGURE 9.8

Example of a false-belief task. (a) An adult shows a child the contents of a Band-Aid box and of an unmarked box. The Band-Aids are in the unmarked container. (b) The adult introduces the child to a hand puppet named Pam and asks the child to predict where Pam would look for the Band-Aids and to explain Pam's behavior. The task reveals whether children understand that without having seen that the Band-Aids are in the unmarked container, Pam will hold a false belief.

(a)   (b)

increase, suggesting that children more firmly realize the power of belief to influence action.

Dramatic evidence for this new understanding comes from games that test whether they realize that *false beliefs*—ones that do not represent reality accurately—can guide people's behavior. **TAKE A MOMENT...** For example, show a child two small closed boxes, one a familiar Band-Aid box and the other a plain, unmarked box (see Figure 9.8). Then say, "Pick the box you think has the Band-Aids in it." Children usually pick the marked container. Next, open the boxes and show the child that, contrary to her own belief, the marked one is empty, and the unmarked one contains the Band-Aids. Finally, introduce the child to a hand puppet and explain, "Here's Pam. She has a cut, see? Where do you think she'll look for Band-Aids? Why would she look in there? Before you looked inside, did you think that the plain box contained the Band-Aids? Why?" (Bartsch & Wellman, 1995; Gopnik & Wellman, 1994). Only a handful of 3-year-olds can explain Pam's—and their own—false beliefs, but many 4-year-olds can.

Among children of diverse cultural and SES backgrounds, false-belief understanding strengthens between ages 4 and 6 (Callaghan et al., 2005; Wellman, Cross, & Watson, 2001). During that time, it becomes a powerful tool for reflecting on the thoughts and emotions of oneself and others and a good predictor of social skills (Harwood & Farrar, 2006; Jenkins & Astington, 2000; Watson et al., 1999). Understanding of false belief also predicts early reading ability, probably because it helps children comprehend story narratives (Astington & Pelletier, 2005). To follow a story line, children generally must link plot actions with characters' motives and beliefs.

FACTORS CONTRIBUTING TO PRESCHOOLERS' THEORY OF MIND ■ How do children manage to develop a theory of mind at such a young age? Language, cognitive abilities, make-believe play, and social interaction all contribute.

Language. Understanding the mind requires the ability to reflect on thoughts, which is made possible by language. A grasp of false belief requires language ability equivalent to that of an average 4-year-old (Jenkins & Astington, 1996). And children who spontaneously use, or are trained to use, complex sentences with mental-state words are more likely to pass false-belief tasks (de Villiers & de Villiers, 2000; Hale & Tager-Flusberg, 2003). The Quechua village people of the Peruvian highlands refer to mental states such as "think" and "believe" indirectly, because their language lacks mental-state terms. Quechua children have difficulty with false-belief tasks for years after children in industrialized nations have mastered them (Vinden, 1996). In contrast, Chinese languages have verb markers that can label the word "believe" as decidedly false. When adults use those markers within false-belief tasks, Chinese preschoolers perform better (Tardif et al., 2004).

Cognitive Abilities. The ability to inhibit inappropriate responses, think flexibly, and plan fosters mastery of false belief (Hughes, 1998; Sabbagh et al., 2006). Gains in inhibition predict false-belief understanding particularly strongly, perhaps because to do well on false-belief tasks, children must suppress a competing response—the tendency to assume that others share their own knowledge and beliefs (Birch & Bloom, 2003; Carlson, Moses, & Claxton, 2004).

Make-Believe Play. Make-believe offers a rich context for thinking about the mind. As children act out roles, they often create situations they know to be untrue in the real world and

Children with siblings—especially, older siblings—participate in more family talk about thoughts, beliefs, and emotions. Sibling interaction contributes to preschoolers' theory of mind, including their understanding of false belief.

then reason about their implications (Harris & Leevers, 2000). These experiences may increase children's awareness that belief influences behavior. In support of this idea, preschoolers who engage in extensive fantasy play are advanced in understanding false belief and other aspects of the mind (Astington & Jenkins, 1995). And the better 3- and 4-year-olds can reason about situations that contradict a real-world state of affairs, the more likely they are to pass false-belief tasks (Riggs & Peterson, 2000).

Social Interaction. Many social experiences promote understanding of the mind. In longitudinal research, mothers of securely attached babies were more likely to comment appropriately on their infants' mental states: "Do you remember Grandma?" "You really like that swing!" These mothers continued to describe their children, when they reached preschool age, in terms of mental characteristics: "She's got a mind of her own!" In several studies, such parental mental-state talk—about the child or about others—was positively associated with later performance on false-belief and other theory-of-mind tasks (Meins et al., 1998, 2003; Ruffman et al., 2006).

Also, preschoolers with siblings, especially those with older siblings, tend to be more aware of false belief. Children with older siblings are exposed to—and participate in—more family talk about thoughts, beliefs, and emotions (Jenkins et al., 2003; Peterson, 2001). Similarly, preschool friends who often engage in mental-state talk are advanced in understanding of false belief (Hughes & Dunn, 1998). Interacting with more mature members of society contributes as well. In a study of Greek preschoolers, daily contact with many adults and older children predicted mastery of false belief (Lewis et al., 1996). These encounters offer extra opportunities to observe different viewpoints and talk about inner states.

Core knowledge theorists (see Chapter 6, page 217) believe that to profit from the social experiences just described, children must be biologically prepared to develop a theory of mind. They claim that children with *autism,* for whom mastery of false belief is either greatly delayed or absent, are deficient in the brain mechanism that enables humans to detect mental states. See the Biology and Environment box on the following page to find out more about the biological basis of reasoning about the mind.

LIMITATIONS OF THE YOUNG CHILD'S THEORY OF MIND ■ Though surprisingly advanced, preschoolers' awareness of mental activities is far from complete. For example, 3- and 4-year-olds are unaware that people continue to think while they wait, look at pictures, listen to stories, or read books. They conclude that mental activity stops when there are no obvious cues to indicate a person is thinking. Preschoolers also do not realize that when two people view the same object, their trains of thought will differ because of variations in their knowledge and other characteristics (Eisbach, 2004; Flavell, Green, & Flavell, 1993, 1995; Flavell et al., 1997).

A major reason for these findings is that children younger than age 5 pay little attention to the *process* of thinking. When questioned about subtle distinctions between mental states, such as "know" and "forget," they express confusion (Lyon & Flavell, 1994). And they often say they have always known information they just learned (Taylor, Esbenson, & Bennett, 1994). Finally, they believe that all events must be directly observed to be known. They do not understand that *mental inferences* can be a source of knowledge (Miller, Hardin, & Montgomery, 2003).

These findings suggest that preschoolers view the mind as a passive container of information. Consequently, they greatly underestimate the amount of mental activity that people engage in and are poor at inferring what people know or are thinking about (Flavell, 1999; Wellman, 2002). In contrast, older children view the mind as an active, constructive agent that selects and interprets information—a change we will consider in Chapter 12.

Early Literacy and Mathematical Development

Researchers have begun to study how children's information-processing capacities affect the development of basic reading, writing, and mathematical skills that prepare them for school. The study of how preschoolers start to master these complex activities gives us additional information about their cognitive strengths and limitations—knowledge we can use to foster early literacy and mathematical development.

Biology and Environment

"Mindblindness" and Autism

Sidney stood at the water table in Leslie's classroom, repeatedly filling a plastic cup and dumping out its contents—dip-splash, dip-splash—until Leslie came over and redirected his actions. Without looking at Leslie's face, Sidney moved to a new repetitive pursuit: pouring water from one cup into another and back again. As other children entered the play space and conversed, Sidney hardly noticed. He rarely spoke, and when he did, he usually used words to get things he wanted, not to exchange ideas.

Sidney has *autism,* a term that means "absorbed in the self"—the most severe behavior disorder of childhood. Like other children with autism, by age 3 he displayed deficits in three core areas of functioning: First, he had only limited ability to engage in nonverbal behaviors required for successful social interaction, such as eye gaze, facial expressions, gestures, imitation, and give-and-take. Usually, he seemed aloof and uninterested in other people. Second, his language was delayed and stereotyped. He used words to echo what others said and to get things he wanted, not to exchange ideas. Third, he engaged in much less make-believe play than other children (Frith, 2003). And Sidney showed another typical feature of autism: His interests were narrow and overly intense. For example, one day he sat for more than an hour spinning a toy Ferris wheel.

Researchers agree that autism stems from abnormal brain functioning, usually due to genetic or prenatal environmental causes. From the first year on, children with the disorder have larger-than-average brains, perhaps because of massive overgrowth of synapses and lack of synaptic pruning, which accompanies normal development of cognitive, language, and communication skills (Courchesne, Carper, & Akshoomoff, 2003). Furthermore, fMRI studies reveal that autism is associated with reduced activity in areas of the cerebral cortex known to mediate emotional and social responsiveness and thinking about mental activities, including mirror neurons, discussed in Chapter 5 (see page 186) (Mundy, 2003; Théoret et al., 2005).

Growing evidence reveals that children with autism have a deficient theory of mind. Long after they reach the intellectual level of an average 4-year-old, they have great difficulty with false belief. Most find it hard to attribute mental states to themselves or others (Steele, Joseph, & Tager-Flusberg, 2003). Such words as *believe, think, know, feel,* and *pretend* are rarely part of their vocabularies.

As early as the second year, children with autism show deficits in social capacities believed to contribute to an understanding of mental life. Compared with other children, they less often establish joint attention, engage in social referencing, or imitate an adult's novel behaviors (Mundy & Stella, 2000). Furthermore, they are relatively insensitive to eye gaze as a cue to what a speaker is talking about. Instead, children with autism often assume that another person's language refers to what they themselves are looking at—a possible reason that they use many nonsensical expressions (Baron-Cohen, Baldwin, & Crowson, 1997).

Do these findings indicate that autism is due to an impairment in an innate, core brain function, which leaves the child "mindblind" and therefore unable to engage in human sociability? Some researchers think so (Baron-Cohen & Belmonte, 2005; Scholl & Leslie, 2000). But others point out that nonautistic, mentally retarded individuals also do poorly on tasks assessing mental understanding (Yirmiya et al., 1998). This suggests that some kind of general intellectual impairment may be involved.

One conjecture is that children with autism are impaired in *executive processing* (refer to the *central executive* in the information-processing model on page 220 in Chapter 6). This leaves them deficient in skills involved in flexible, goal-oriented thinking, including shifting attention to address relevant aspects of a situation, inhibiting irrelevant responses, applying strategies to hold information in working memory, and generating plans (Geurts et al., 2004; Joseph & Tager-Flusberg, 2004). Another possibility is that children with autism display a peculiar style of information processing, preferring to process the parts of stimuli over patterns and coherent wholes (Frith & Happé, 1994).

Performance of children with autism on diverse cognitive tasks supports both of these views. Deficits in thinking flexibly and in holistic processing of stimuli would each interfere with understanding the social world, since social interaction requires quick integration of information from various sources and evaluation of alternative possibilities.

It is not clear which of these hypotheses is correct. Some research suggests that impairments in social awareness, flexible thinking, processing coherent wholes, and verbal ability contribute independently to autism (Morgan, Maybery, & Durkin, 2003; Pellicano et al., 2006). Perhaps several biologically based cognitive deficits underlie the tragic social isolation of children like Sidney.

This child, who has autism, is hardly aware of his mother's voice or touch as she tries to direct his attention to the computer. Researchers agree that autism stems from abnormal brain functioning, and growing evidence indicates that children with autism have a deficient theory of mind.

As these preschoolers label items in a make-believe grocery story, they learn a great deal about written language—even before they read or write in conventional ways. When offered rich, informal literacy experiences, young children actively try to figure out how written symbols convey meaning.

LITERACY ■ One week, Leslie's students created a make-believe grocery store. They brought empty food boxes from home, placed them on shelves in the classroom, labeled items with prices, made shopping lists, and wrote checks at the cash register. A sign at the entrance announced the daily specials: "APLS BNS 5¢" ("apples bananas 5¢").

Such play reveals that preschoolers understand a great deal about written language long before they learn to read or write in conventional ways. This is not surprising: Children in industrialized nations live in a world filled with written symbols. Each day, they observe and participate in activities involving storybooks, calendars, lists, and signs. As part of these informal experiences, they try to figure out how written symbols convey meaning—active efforts known as **emergent literacy.**

Young preschoolers search for units of written language as they "read" memorized versions of stories and recognize familiar signs ("PIZZA"). But they do not yet understand the symbolic function of the elements of print (Bialystok & Martin, 2003). Many preschoolers think that a single letter stands for a whole word or that each letter in a person's signature represents a separate name. And in Chapter 8, we noted that initially, preschoolers do not distinguish between drawing and writing. Often they believe that letters (just like pictures) look like the meanings they represent. One child explained that the word *sun* begins with the letter *O* because that letter is shaped like the sun; he demonstrated by drawing an *O* and surrounding it with rays to produce a picture of the sun.

Children revise these ideas as their perceptual and cognitive capacities improve, as they encounter writing in many contexts, and as adults help them with written communication. Gradually preschoolers notice more features of written language and depict writing that varies in function, as in the "story" and "grocery list" in Figure 9.9.

Eventually children figure out that letters are parts of words and are linked to sounds in systematic ways, as seen in the invented spellings that are typical between ages 5 and 7. At first, children rely on sounds in the names of letters: "ADE LAFWTS KRMD NTU A LAVATR" ("80 elephants crammed into a[n] elevator"). Over time, they grasp sound–letter correspondences and learn that some letters have more than one common sound and that context affects their use ("*a*" is pronounced differently in "cat" than in "table") (McGee & Richgels, 2004).

Literacy development builds on a broad foundation of spoken language and knowledge about the world. Over time, children's language and literacy progress facilitate one another. **Phonological awareness**—the ability to reflect on and manipulate the sound structure of spoken language, as indicated by sensitivity to changes in sounds within words, to rhyming, and to incorrect pronunciation—is a strong predictor of emergent literacy and later reading and spelling achievement (Dickinson et al., 2003; Paris & Paris, 2006). When combined with sound–letter knowledge, it enables children to isolate speech segments and link them with their written symbols. Vocabulary and grammatical knowledge are also influential. And adult–child narrative conversations enhance diverse language skills essential for literacy progress.

The more informal literacy experiences young children have, the better their language and emergent literacy development and their later reading skills (Dickinson & McCabe, 2001; Speece et al., 2004). Pointing out letter–sound

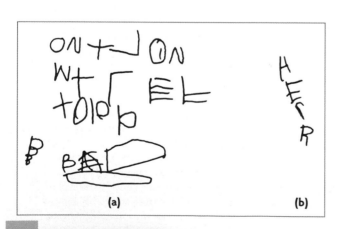

FIGURE 9.9

A story (a) and a grocery list (b) written by a 4-year-old child. This child's writing has many features of real print. It also reveals an awareness of different kinds of written expression. (From L. M. McGee & D. J. Richgels, 2004, *Literacy's Beginnings* [4th ed.]. Boston: Allyn and Bacon, p. 69. Reprinted by permission.)

Applying What We Know

Supporting Emergent Literacy in Early Childhood

STRATEGY	EXPLANATION
Provide literacy-rich home and preschool environments.	Homes and preschools with abundant reading and writing materials—including a wide variety of children's storybooks, some relevant to children's ethnic backgrounds—open the door to a wealth of language and literacy experiences.
Engage in interactive book reading.	When adults discuss story content, ask open-ended questions about story events, explain the meaning of words, and point out features of print, they promote language development, comprehension of story content, knowledge of story structure, and awareness of units of written language.
Provide outings to libraries, museums, parks, zoos, and other community settings.	Visits to child-oriented community settings enhance children's general knowledge and offer many opportunities to see how written language is used in everyday life. They also provide personally meaningful topics for narrative conversation, which promote many language skills essential for literacy development.
Point out letter–sound correspondences, play rhyming and other language-sound games, and read rhyming poems and stories.	Experiences that help children isolate the sounds in words foster *phonological awareness*—a powerful predictor of early childhood literacy knowledge and later reading and spelling achievement.
Support children's efforts at writing, especially narrative products.	Assisting children in their efforts to write—especially letters, stories, and other narratives—fosters many language and literacy skills.
Model literacy activities.	When children see adults engaged in reading and writing activities, they better understand the diverse, everyday functions of literacy skills and the knowledge and pleasure that literacy brings. As a result, children's motivation to become literate is strengthened.

Sources: Dickinson & McCabe, 2001; McGee & Richgels, 2004.

correspondences and playing language-sound games enhance children's awareness of the sound structure of language and how it is represented in print (Foy & Mann, 2003). *Interactive* reading, in which adults discuss storybook content with preschoolers, promotes many aspects of language and literacy development. Adult-supported writing activities that focus on narrative, such as preparing a letter or a story, also have wide-ranging benefits (Purcell-Gates, 1996; Wasik & Bond, 2001). In longitudinal research, each of these literacy experiences is linked to improved reading achievement in middle childhood (Senechal & LeFevre, 2002; Storch & Whitehurst, 2001).

Preschoolers from low-SES families have fewer home and preschool language and literacy learning opportunities—a major reason that they are behind in emergent literacy skills and in reading achievement throughout the school years (Foster et al., 2005; Serpell et al., 2002). In one study, researchers compared literacy experiences in publicly funded preschools for poverty-stricken children with those in private preschools serving higher-SES groups. The publicly funded programs were deficient in access to a rich array of books, in teacher talk about stories, in modeling the everyday uses of literacy, in classroom display of print information (such as the alphabet), in adult assistance with letter identification and writing, and in exposure to culturally relevant literacy materials. Children of poverty, the researchers concluded, "come away with little idea of what it means to be a literate person or what kind of power or responsibility literacy might confer" (McGill-Franzen, Lanford, & Adams, 2002, p. 460).

Providing low-SES parents with children's books, along with guidance in how to stimulate emergent literacy, greatly enhances literacy activities in the home (High et al., 2000). And in a program that "flooded" child-care centers with children's books and provided caregivers with training on how to get 3- and 4-year-olds to spend time with books, low-SES children showed much greater gains in emergent literacy than a control group (Neuman, 1999). Teachers who were given a tuition-free college course on effective early childhood literacy instruction readily applied what they learned, offering many more literacy activities in their classrooms (Dickinson & Sprague, 2001). For ways to support early childhood literacy development, refer to Applying What We Know above.

emergent literacy Young children's active efforts to construct literacy knowledge through informal experiences.

phonological awareness The ability to reflect on and manipulate the sound structure of spoken language, as indicated by sensitivity to changes in sounds within words, to rhyming, and to incorrect pronunciation.

Basic arithmetic knowledge emerges in children around the world when they are given many opportunities to count, compare quantities, and talk about number concepts.

MATHEMATICAL REASONING ■ Mathematical reasoning, like literacy, builds on informal knowledge. Between 14 and 16 months, toddlers display a beginning grasp of **ordinality,** or order relationships between quantities—for example, that 3 is more than 2, and 2 is more than 1. In the early preschool years, children attach verbal labels (*lots, little, big, small*) to amounts and sizes. Sometime in the third year, they begin to count. By the time children turn 3, they can count rows of about five objects, although they do not yet know what the words mean. For example, when asked for "one," they give one item, but when asked for "two," "three," "four," or "five," they usually give a larger, but incorrect, amount. Nevertheless, 2½- to 3½-year-olds realize that a number word refers to a unique quantity—that when a number label changes (for example, from "five" to "six"), the number of items should also change (Sarnecka & Gelman, 2004).

By age 3½ to 4, most children have mastered the meaning of numbers up to ten, count correctly, and grasp the vital principle of **cardinality**—that the last number in a counting sequence indicates the quantity of items in the set (Geary, 2006). In the preschool scene described in the opening of this chapter, Sammy showed an understanding of cardinality when he counted four children at his snack table and then retrieved four milk cartons. Mastery of cardinality increases the efficiency of counting. It also enables children to engage in *estimation*—for example, after watching several donuts being added to or removed from a plate of ten donuts, to predict how many donuts are on the plate, and to then count to check their prediction (Zur & Gelman, 2004).

Around age 4, children use counting to solve simple arithmetic problems. At first, their strategies are tied to the order of numbers presented; when given 2 + 4, they "count on" from 2 (Bryant & Nunes, 2002). But soon they experiment with other strategies and eventually arrive at the *min* strategy, a more efficient approach (see page 341). Around this time, children realize that subtraction cancels out addition. Knowing, for example, that 4 + 3 = 7, they infer without counting that 7 − 3 = 4 (Rasmussen, Ho, & Bisanz, 2003). Grasping this principle and other basic arithmetic rules greatly facilitates rapid computation and accurate solutions to more complex problems.

The arithmetic knowledge just described emerges universally around the world. But children construct these understandings sooner when adults provide many occasions for counting, comparing quantities, and talking about number concepts (Benigno & Ellis, 2004; Klibanoff et al., 2006). In a math intervention program for low-SES 4-year-olds, teachers included math activities in almost all classroom routines—for example, counting the number of steps needed to get from various locations in the classroom to the play yard. Compared with children in other classrooms, intervention children scored higher in math concepts and enjoyed math activities more (Arnold et al., 2002). Solid, secure early childhood math knowledge is essential for the wide variety of mathematical skills children will be taught once they enter school.

ordinality Relationships of order (more than and less than) between quantities.

cardinality The principle stating that the last number in a counting sequence indicates the quantity of items in the set.

Ask Yourself

Review   Describe a typical 4-year-old's understanding of mental activities, noting both strengths and limitations.

Apply   Lena, mother of 4-year-old Gregor, wonders why his preschool teacher provides extensive playtime in learning centers instead of formal lessons in literacy and math skills. Explain to Lena why adult-supported play is the best way for preschoolers to develop academically.

Connect   Cite evidence on preschoolers' development of memory, theory of mind, and literacy and mathematical understanding that is consistent with Vygotsky's sociocultural theory.

Reflect   Describe informal experiences important for literacy and math development that you experienced while growing up. How do you think those experiences contributed to your academic progress in school?

Individual Differences in Mental Development

Psychologists and educators typically measure how well preschoolers are developing mentally by giving them intelligence tests. Scores are computed in the same way as they are for infants and toddlers (return to Chapter 6, page 231, to review). But instead of emphasizing perceptual and motor responses, tests for preschoolers sample a wide range of mental abilities. Understanding the link between early childhood experiences and mental test performance highlights ways to intervene in support of children's cognitive development.

Early Childhood Intelligence Tests

Five-year-old Hal sat in a small, unfamiliar testing room while Sarah gave him an intelligence test. Some of Sarah's questions were *verbal*. For example, she showed him a picture of a shovel and said, "Tell me what this is"—an item measuring vocabulary. To test his memory, she asked Hal to repeat sentences and lists of numbers back to her. She probed his quantitative knowledge and problem solving by seeing if he could count and solve simple addition and subtraction problems. Finally, Sarah used *nonverbal* tasks to assess Hal's spatial reasoning: Hal copied designs with special blocks, figured out the pattern in a series of shapes, and indicated what a piece of paper folded and cut would look like when unfolded (Roid, 2003; Wechsler, 2002).

Sarah knew that Hal came from an economically disadvantaged family. When low-SES and certain ethnic minority preschoolers are bombarded with questions by an unfamiliar adult, they sometimes react with anxiety. Also, such children may not define the testing situation in terms of achievement. Instead, they may look for attention and approval from the adult and may settle for lower performance than their abilities allow. Sarah spent time playing with Hal before she began testing and encouraged him while the test was in progress. Under these conditions, low-SES preschoolers improve in performance (Bracken, 2000).

The questions Sarah asked Hal tap knowledge and skills that not all children have had an equal opportunity to learn. In Chapter 12, we will take up the hotly debated issue of *cultural bias* in mental testing. For now, keep in mind that intelligence tests do not sample all human abilities, and performance is affected by cultural and situational factors (Sternberg, 2003a). Nevertheless, test scores remain important: By age 6 to 7, they are good predictors of later IQ and academic achievement, which are related to vocational success in industrialized societies. Let's see how the environments in which children spend their days—home, preschool, and child care—affect mental test performance.

Home Environment and Mental Development

A special version of the *Home Observation for Measurement of the Environment (HOME)*, covered in Chapter 6, assesses aspects of 3- to 6-year-olds' home lives that foster intellectual growth (see Applying What We Know on page 350). Preschoolers who develop well intellectually have homes rich in educational toys and books. Their parents are warm and affectionate, stimulate language and academic knowledge, and arrange interesting outings. They also make reasonable demands for socially mature behavior—for example, that the child perform simple chores and behave courteously toward others. And these parents resolve conflicts with reason instead of physical force and punishment (Bradley & Caldwell, 1982; Espy, Molfese, & DiLalla, 2001; Roberts, Burchinal, & Durham, 1999).

As we saw in Chapter 2, these characteristics are less often seen in poverty-stricken families (Garrett, Ng'andu, & Ferron, 1994). When low-SES parents manage, despite daily stresses, to obtain high HOME scores, their preschoolers do substantially better on intelligence tests and measures of emergent literacy skills (Foster et al., 2005; Klebanov et al., 1998; Linver, Brooks-Gunn, & Kohen, 2002). And in a study of African-American 3- and 4-year-olds in low-income families, HOME cognitive stimulation and emotional support subscales predicted reading achievement four years later (Zaslow et al., 2006). These findings (along with others we will discuss in Chapter 12) indicate that the home plays a major role in the generally poorer intellectual performance of low-SES children, compared to their higher-SES peers.

Applying What We Know

Features of a High-Quality Home Life for Preschoolers: The HOME Early Childhood Subscales

HOME SUBSCALE	SAMPLE ITEMS
Cognitive stimulation through toys, games, and reading material	Home includes toys to learn colors, sizes, and shapes.
Language stimulation	Parent teaches child about animals through books, games, and puzzles.
	Parent converses with child at least twice during observer's visit.
Organization of the physical environment	All visible rooms are reasonably clean and minimally cluttered.
Emotional support	Parent spontaneously praises child's qualities or behavior twice during observer's visit.
	Parent caresses, kisses, or hugs child at least once during observer's visit.
Stimulation of academic behavior	Child is encouraged to learn colors.
Modeling and encouragement of social maturity	Parent introduces interviewer to child.
Opportunities for variety in daily stimulation	Family member takes child on one outing at least every other week (picnic, shopping).
Avoidance of physical punishment	Parent neither slaps nor spanks child during observer's visit.

Sources: Bradley, 1994; Bradley et al., 2001.

Preschool, Kindergarten, and Child Care

Children between ages 2 and 6 spend even more time away from their homes and parents than infants and toddlers do. Largely because of the rise in maternal employment, over the past several decades the number of young children enrolled in preschool or child care has steadily increased, reaching nearly 75 percent in the United States and in some Canadian provinces (Federal Interagency Forum on Child and Family Statistics, 2006a; Statistics Canada, 2005a). Figure 9.10 shows where preschoolers spend their days while their parents are at work.

A *preschool* is a program with planned educational experiences aimed at enhancing the development of 2- to 5-year-olds. In contrast, *child care* includes a variety of arrangements for supervising children of employed parents, ranging from care in the caregiver's or the child's home to some type of center-based program. The line between preschool and child care is fuzzy. As Figure 9.10 indicates, parents often select a preschool as a child-care option. Many preschools, as well as public school kindergartens, now offer full-day programs in response to the needs of employed parents (U.S. Department of Education, 2007).

With age, preschoolers tend to shift from home-based to center programs. But many children experience several types of arrangements at once (Federal Interagency Forum on Child and Family Statistics, 2006a; Statistics Canada, 2005a). In the United States, children of higher-income parents and children of very low-income parents are especially likely to be in preschools or child-care centers. Many low-income working parents rely on care by relatives because they are not eligible for public preschool or government-subsidized center child care (Bainbridge et al., 2005; Meyers et al., 2004).

Good child care means more than simply keeping children safe and adequately fed. It should provide the same high-quality educational experiences that an effective preschool does, the only difference being that children attend for an extended day.

TYPES OF PRESCHOOL AND KINDERGARTEN ■ Preschool and kindergarten programs range along a continuum from child-centered to teacher-directed. In **child-centered programs,** teachers provide activities from which children select, and most of the day is devoted to play. In contrast, in **academic programs,** teachers structure children's learning, teaching letters, numbers, colors, shapes, and other academic skills through formal lessons, often using repetition and drill.

Despite evidence that stressing formal academic training in early childhood undermines motivation and emotional well-being, preschool and kindergarten teachers have felt increased pressure to take this approach. Preschoolers and kindergartners who spend much time

child-centered programs
Preschools and kindergartens in which teachers provide activities from which children select, and most of the day is devoted to play.

academic programs
Preschools and kindergartens in which teachers structure children's learning, teaching academic skills through formal lessons, often using repetition and drill.

passively sitting and doing worksheets, as opposed to being actively engaged in learning centers, display more stress behaviors (such as wiggling and rocking), have less confidence in their abilities, prefer less challenging tasks, and are less advanced in motor, academic, language, and social skills at the end of the school year (Marcon, 1999a; Stipek et al., 1995). Follow-ups reveal lasting effects through elementary school in poorer study habits and lower achievement test scores (Burts et al., 1992; Hart et al., 1998, 2003). These outcomes are strongest for low-SES children, with whom teachers more often use an academic approach—a disturbing trend in view of its negative impact on motivation and learning (Stipek, 2004; Stipek & Byler, 1997). Another concern is that public preschool programs serving low-SES children are more likely to be staffed by teachers who lack a bachelor's degree, who communicate in less stimulating and encouraging ways, and whose classrooms are poorly equipped with educational materials (Clifford et al., 2005; Pianta et al., 2005).

A special type of child-centered approach is *Montessori education,* devised a century ago by Italian physician and child development researcher Maria Montessori, who originally applied her method to poverty-stricken children. Features of Montessori schooling include multiage classrooms, teaching materials specially designed to promote exploration and discovery, long time periods for individual and small-group learning in child-chosen activities, and equal emphasis on academic and social development (Lillard, 2007). In an evaluation of Montessori public preschools serving mostly urban minority children in Milwaukee, researchers compared students assigned by random lottery to Montessori classrooms with students not accepted and therefore placed in other classrooms (Lillard & Else-Quest, 2006). Five-year-olds who had completed two years of Montessori education outperformed controls on tests of literacy and math skills, cognitive flexibility, understanding of false belief, and concern with fairness in solving conflicts with peers. On the playground, Montessori children more often engaged in positive, joint play with classmates.

EARLY INTERVENTION FOR AT-RISK PRESCHOOLERS ■ In the 1960s, as part of the War on Poverty in the United States, many preschool intervention programs for low-SES children were initiated in an effort to address learning problems early, before formal schooling begins. The most extensive of these federal programs, **Project Head Start,** began in 1965 and currently includes more than 20,000 Head Start centers serving about 906,000 children (Head Start Bureau, 2006). In addition to providing a year or two of preschool and nutritional and health services for children, Head Start involves parents in policy councils, program planning, direct work with children in classrooms, and programs on parenting and child development. Parents also receive services addressing their own emotional, social, and vocational needs.

Similarly, Canada's **Aboriginal Head Start** program provides preschool education and nutritional and health services for children and encourages parent involvement. The program—initiated in 1995 for First Nations, Inuit, and Métis children younger than age 6, 60 percent of whom live in poverty—has about 120 sites and serves more than 3,900 children (Health Canada, 2004a).

Benefits of Preschool Intervention. More than two decades of research have established the long-term benefits of preschool intervention. The most extensive of these studies, combining data from seven interventions implemented by universities or research foundations, found

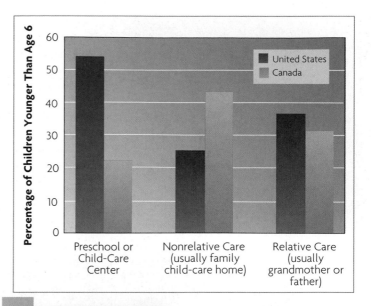

FIGURE 9.10

Who's minding North American young children? The percentages refer to settings in which infants and preschoolers spend most time during their parents' absence. In the United States, more children are in preschools or child-care centers than in family child-care homes; Canada shows the reverse trend. A great many children experience more than one type of child care, and with age, they tend to shift from home-based to center programs—facts not reflected in the figure. (Adapted from Statistics Canada, 2005a; Federal Interagency Forum on Child and Family Statistics, 2006a.)

Project Head Start The most extensive federally funded preschool intervention program in the United States, providing low-SES children with a year or two of preschool education, along with nutritional and medical services, and encouraging parent involvement in children's learning and development.

Aboriginal Head Start A Canadian federally funded preschool intervention program providing First Nations, Inuit, and Métis children younger than age 6 educational, nutritional, and health services and encouraging parent involvement in children's learning and development.

CP PHOTO/AARON HARRIS

These 4-year-olds benefit from an Aboriginal Head Start program in Nunavut, Canada. Like U.S. Head Start children, they receive rich, stimulating educational experiences and nutritional and health services, and their parents also participate. In the classroom, the children have many opportunities to engage in activities with special cultural meaning.

that children who attended programs scored higher than controls in IQ and academic achievement in the first two to three years of elementary school. After that, differences declined (Lazar & Darlington, 1982). But on real-life measures of school adjustment, children and adolescents who received intervention remained ahead. They were less likely to be placed in special education or retained in grade, and a greater number graduated from high school.

A separate report on one program, the High/Scope Perry Preschool Project, revealed benefits lasting into adulthood. Two years' exposure to cognitively enriching preschool was associated with increased employment and reduced pregnancy and delinquency rates in adolescence. At age 27, those who had attended preschool were more likely than no-preschool counterparts to have graduated from high school and college, have higher earnings, be married, and own their own home—and less likely to have been involved with the criminal justice system—advantages still evident in the most recent follow-up, at age 40 (see Figure 9.11) (Schweinhart et al., 2004; Weikart, 1998).

Do the effects on school adjustment of these well-designed and well-delivered programs generalize to Head Start and other community-based preschool interventions? Gains are similar, though not as strong. Head Start preschoolers, who are more economically disadvantaged than children in university-based programs, have more severe learning and behavior problems. And quality of services is more variable across community programs (NICHD Early Child Care Research Network, 2001). But interventions of documented high quality are associated with diverse, long-lasting favorable outcomes, including higher rates of high school graduation and college enrollment and lower rates of adolescent delinquency (Reynolds & Ou, 2004).

A consistent finding is that gains in IQ and achievement test scores from attending Head Start and other interventions quickly dissolve. These children typically enter inferior public schools in poverty-stricken neighborhoods, an experience that undermines the benefits of preschool education (Brooks-Gunn, 2003; Ramey, Ramey, & Lanzi, 2006). But in a program that began at age 4 and continued through third grade, achievement score gains were still apparent in junior high school (Reynolds & Temple, 1998). And recall from Chapter 6 that when intensive intervention persists from infancy through early childhood and children enter good-quality schools, IQ gains endure into adulthood (see page 235).

Still, the improved school adjustment that results from attending a one- or two-year Head Start program is impressive. Program effects on parents may contribute: The more involved parents are in Head Start, the better their child-rearing practices and the more stimulating their home learning environments. These factors are positively related to preschoolers' independence and task persistence in the classroom and to their year-end academic, language, and social skills (Marcon, 1999b; McLoyd, Aidens, & Burton, 2006; Parker et al., 1999).

Head Start and similar interventions are highly cost-effective when compared with the cost of providing special education, treating criminal behavior and delinquency, and supporting unemployed adults. Economists estimate that the lifetime return to society is more than $250,000 on an investment of $15,000 per preschool child—a total savings of many billions of dollars if every poverty-stricken preschooler in the United States and Canada were to be

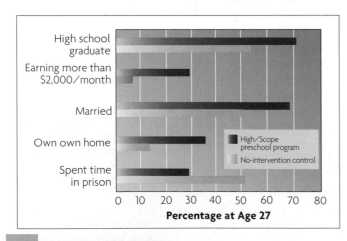

FIGURE 9.11

Some outcomes of the High/Scope Perry Preschool Project on follow-up at age 27. Although two years of a cognitively enriching preschool program did not eradicate the effects of growing up in poverty, children who received intervention were advantaged over no-intervention controls on all measures of life success when they reached adulthood. (Adapted from Schweinhart et al., 2004.)

enrolled (Heckman & Masterov, 2004). Because of funding shortages, however, many eligible children do not receive services.

CHILD CARE ■ We have seen that high-quality early intervention enhances the development of economically disadvantaged children. As noted in Chapter 6, however, much North American child care lacks quality. Regardless of family SES, preschoolers exposed to poor-quality child care score lower on measures of cognitive and social skills and display more behavior problems (Howes & James, 2002; Lamb & Ahnert, 2006; NICHD Early Child Care Research Network, 2003b, 2006). Psychological well-being also declines when children experience the instability of several child-care settings. The emotional and behavior problems of temperamentally difficult preschoolers worsen considerably (De Schipper, van IJzendoorn, & Tavecchio, 2004; De Schipper et al., 2004).

In contrast, good child care enhances cognitive, language, and social development, especially for low-SES children—effects that persist into the early school years (Lamb & Ahnert, 2006; NICHD Early Child Care Research Network, 2006; Peisner-Feinberg et al., 2001). In a study that followed 400 very low-income children over the preschool years, center-based care was more strongly associated with cognitive gains than were other child-care arrangements, probably because child-care centers are more likely than family child-care homes to provide a systematic educational program (Loeb et al., 2004). And in another investigation of more than 200 2- to 4-year-olds from very low-income families, the more time spent in high-quality child-care centers, the less likely children were to display emotional and behavior problems, even after many family characteristics were controlled (Votruba-Drzal, Coley, & Chase-Lansdale, 2004).

What are the ingredients of high-quality child care for preschoolers? Large-scale studies identify several important factors: group size (number of children in a single space), caregiver–child ratio, caregivers' educational preparation, and caregivers' personal commitment to learning about and caring for children. When these characteristics are favorable, adults are more verbally stimulating and sensitive to children's needs (Lamb & Ahnert, 2006). Applying What We Know on page 354 summarizes characteristics of high-quality early childhood programs, based on standards for developmentally appropriate practice devised by the U.S. National Association for the Education of Young Children. These standards offer a set of worthy goals as the United States and Canada strive to upgrade child-care and educational services for young children.

Ingredients of high-quality child care include small group size, generous caregiver–child ratios, richly equipped activity areas, and caregivers with good educational preparation in early childhood development or a related field. Child care that meets these criteria enhances development, especially for low-SES preschoolers.

Educational Media

Besides home and preschool, young children spend much time in another learning environment: electronic media, including both television and computers. In the United States, Canada, and other industrialized nations, nearly all homes have at least one television set, and most have two or more. About 85 percent of North American children live in homes with one or more computers, two-thirds of which have an Internet connection (Roberts, Foehr, & Rideout, 2005; Statistics Canada, 2004b).

EDUCATIONAL TELEVISION ■ Sammy's favorite TV program, *Sesame Street,* uses lively visual and sound effects to stress basic literacy and number concepts and presents engaging puppet and human characters to teach general knowledge, emotional and social understanding, and social skills. Today, more than two-thirds of North American preschoolers watch *Sesame Street,* and it is broadcast in more than 120 countries (Sesame Workshop, 2005).

The more children watch *Sesame Street,* the higher they score on tests that measure the program's academic goals (Fisch, Truglio, & Cole, 1999). One study reported a link between preschool viewing of *Sesame Street* and other similar educational programs and getting higher grades, reading more books, and placing more value on achievement in high school

Applying What We Know

Signs of Developmentally Appropriate Early Childhood Programs

PROGRAM CHARACTERISTIC	SIGNS OF QUALITY
Physical setting	Indoor environment is clean, in good repair, and well-ventilated. Classroom space is divided into richly equipped activity areas, including make-believe play, blocks, science, math, games and puzzles, books, art, and music. Fenced outdoor play space is equipped with swings, climbing equipment, tricycles, and sandbox.
Group size	In preschools and child-care centers, group size is no greater than 18 to 20 children with 2 teachers.
Caregiver–child ratio	In preschools and child-care centers, teacher is responsible for no more than 8 to 10 children. In family child care, caregiver is responsible for no more than 6 children.
Daily activities	Most of the time, children work individually or in small groups. Children select many of their own activities and learn through experiences relevant to their own lives. Teachers facilitate children's involvement, accept individual differences, and adjust expectations to children's developing capacities.
Interactions between adults and children	Teachers move among groups and individuals, asking questions, offering suggestions, and adding more complex ideas. Teachers use positive guidance techniques, such as modeling and encouraging expected behavior and redirecting children to more acceptable activities.
Teacher qualifications	Teachers have college-level specialized preparation in early childhood development, early childhood education, or a related field.
Relationships with parents	Parents are encouraged to observe and participate. Teachers talk frequently with parents about children's behavior and development.
Licensing and accreditation	Child-care setting, whether a center or a home, is licensed by the state or province. In the United States, voluntary accreditation by the National Academy of Early Childhood Programs, *www.naeyc.org/accreditation,* or the National Association for Family Child Care, *www.nafcc.org,* is evidence of an especially high-quality program. Canada is working on a voluntary accreditation system, under the leadership of the Canadian Child Care Federation, *www.cccf-fcsge.ca.*

Sources: Bredekamp & Copple, 1997; National Association for the Education of Young Children, 1998.

(Anderson et al., 2001). In recent years, *Sesame Street* has reduced its rapid-paced format in favor of leisurely episodes with a clear story line. Watching children's programs with slow-paced action and easy-to-follow narratives, such as *Mr. Rogers' Neighborhood* and *Barney and Friends,* leads to more elaborate make-believe play than viewing programs that present quick, disconnected bits of information (Singer & Singer, 2005).

Despite the spread of computers, television remains the dominant form of youth media. The average North American 2- to 6-year-old watches TV programs and videos from 1½ to 2 hours a day. In middle childhood, viewing time increases to an average of 3½ hours a day for U.S. children and 2½ hours a day for Canadian children, then declines slightly in adolescence (Rideout, Vandewater, & Wartella, 2003; Scharrer & Comstock, 2003; Statistics Canada, 2005g). Low-SES children watch more television, perhaps because few alternative forms of entertainment are available in their neighborhoods or are affordable for their parents. And if parents watch a lot of TV, their children do, too (Roberts, Foehr, & Rideout, 2005).

Does extensive TV viewing draw children away from worthwhile activities that are vital for cognitive development? The more preschool and school-age children watch prime-time television and cartoons, the less time they spend reading and interacting with others and the poorer their academic skills (Huston et al., 1999; Wright et al., 2001). Heavy viewing of entertainment TV, in contrast to educational television, detracts from children's school success and social experiences. Yet more than one-third of U.S. children age 6 and younger live in homes where the TV is on nearly constantly, and about one-third also have a TV in their bedroom (Rideout, Vandewater, & Wartella, 2003).

LEARNING WITH COMPUTERS ■ According to a survey of 1,000 U.S. parents, 70 percent of 4- to 6-year-olds have used a computer at one time or another, and more than one-fourth use one regularly, spending on average just over an hour a day at the keyboard (Rideout,

Vandewater, & Wartella, 2003). Children as young as age 3 can type simple keyboard commands and use a mouse to point and click.

Many early childhood classrooms include computer learning centers, which can offer rich educational benefits. Computer storybooks and other literacy programs encourage diverse language and emergent literacy skills (Hutinger et al., 1998). Kindergartners who use computers to draw or write produce more elaborate pictures and text, make fewer writing errors, and edit their work much as older children do. And combining everyday and computer experiences with math manipulatives is especially effective in promoting math concepts and skills (Clements & Sarama, 2003).

Simplified computer languages that children can use to make designs or build structures introduce them to programming skills. As long as adults support children's efforts, computer programming promotes improved problem solving and metacognition (awareness of thought processes) because children must plan and reflect on their thinking to get their programs to work. Furthermore, while programming, children are especially likely to help one another and to persist in the face of challenge (Nastasi & Clements, 1994; Resnick & Silverman, 2005). Small groups often gather around classroom computers, and children more often collaborate than in other pursuits (Svensson, 2000).

As with television, children spend most time using computers for entertainment, especially game-playing. Although parental reports suggest that only 3 percent of preschoolers play video games on a daily basis, that figure rises to 35 percent in middle childhood and adolescence, when—as we will see in Chapter 12—a large sex difference favoring boys emerges. Nevertheless, game consoles are among the bedroom furnishings of 10 percent of children age 6 and younger (Rideout, Vandewater, & Wartella, 2003; Roberts, Foehr, & Rideout, 2005). Video games designed for young children generally have specific educational goals, including literacy, math, colors, and relational concepts (Garrison & Christakis, 2005). But on the whole, TV and computer-game media are rife with gender stereotypes and violence. We will consider the impact of media on emotional and social development in the next chapter.

Ask Yourself

Review   What findings indicate that child-centered preschools and kindergartens are better suited than academic programs to fostering academic development?

Apply   Your senator has heard that IQ gains resulting from Head Start do not last, so he plans to vote against additional funding. Write a letter explaining why he should support Head Start.

Connect   Compare outcomes resulting from preschool intervention programs with those from interventions beginning in infancy (see pages 233–235 in Chapter 6). Which are more likely to lead to lasting cognitive gains? Explain.

Reflect   How much and what kinds of TV viewing and computer use did you engage in as a child? How do you think your home media environment influenced your development?

Language Development

Language is intimately related to virtually all the cognitive changes discussed in this chapter. Between ages 2 and 6, children make momentous advances in language. Their remarkable achievements, as well as their mistakes along the way, reveal their active, rule-oriented approach to mastering their native tongue.

To engage in effective verbal communication, these preschoolers must manage principles of sound, meaning, structure, and everyday use. How they accomplish this feat so rapidly raises some of the most puzzling questions about development.

Vocabulary

As Sammy neared age 2, he had a speaking vocabulary of 200 words. By age 6, he will have acquired around 10,000 words (Bloom, 1998). To accomplish this extraordinary feat, Sammy will learn an average of five new words each day (Anglin, 1993).

How do children build their vocabularies so quickly? Research shows that they can connect a new word with an underlying concept after only a brief encounter, a process called **fast mapping.** Even toddlers comprehend new labels remarkably quickly, but they need more repetitions of the word's use across several situations than preschoolers, who process speech-based information faster and are better able to categorize and recall it (Akhtar & Montague, 1999; Fernald, Perfors, & Marchman, 2006). During the preschool years, children become increasingly adept at fast-mapping two or more new words encountered in the same situation (Wilkinson, Ross, & Diamond, 2003).

TYPES OF WORDS ■ One day, Leslie announced to the children that they would soon take a field trip. That night, Sammy excitedly told his mother, "We're going on a field trip!" When she asked where the class would go, Sammy responded matter-of-factly, "To a field, of course." Sammy's error suggests that young children fast-map some words more easily than others.

Children in many Western and non-Western language communities learn labels for objects especially rapidly, perhaps because these usually refer to concepts that are easy to perceive (Bornstein & Cote, 2004; Gentner & Namy, 2004). Soon children add verbs *(go, run, broke)*, which require more complex understandings of relationships between objects and actions. Children who speak Chinese, Japanese, and Korean—languages in which nouns are often omitted from adult sentences, while verbs are stressed—acquire verbs especially quickly (Kim, McGregor, & Thompson, 2000; Tardif, Gelman, & Xu, 1999). Gradually, preschoolers add modifiers *(red, round, sad)*—first making general distinctions *(big–small)*, then more specific ones *(tall–short)* (Stevenson & Pollitt, 1987).

STRATEGIES FOR WORD LEARNING ■ Children figure out the meanings of words by contrasting them with words they already know and assigning the new label to a gap in their vocabulary (Clark, 1990). On learning a new noun, toddlers and preschoolers acquiring diverse languages tend to assume it refers to an object category at the basic level—an intermediate level of generality (see page 329). This preference helps young children narrow the range of possible meanings. Once they acquire a basic-level name *(dog)*, they add names at other hierarchical levels, both more general *(animal)* and more specific *(beagle, greyhound)* (Imai & Haryu, 2004; Waxman & Lidz, 2006).

How do children discover which concept each word picks out? This process is not yet fully understood. One speculation is that early in vocabulary growth, children adopt a **mutual exclusivity bias**—the assumption that words refer to entirely separate (nonoverlapping) categories (Markman, 1992). Two-year-olds seem to rely on mutual exclusivity when the objects named are perceptually distinct—for example, differ clearly in shape. After hearing the labels for two distinct novel objects (such as *clip* and *horn*), they assign each word correctly, to the whole object, not just a part of it (Waxman & Senghas, 1992).

Indeed, children's first several hundred nouns refer mostly to objects well-organized by shape. In a study in which toddlers repeatedly played with and heard names for novel objects of different shapes ("That's a *wif*") over a nine-week period, they soon formed the generalization that only similar-shaped objects have the same name (Smith et al., 2002a). Toddlers given this training added more than three times as many object names to their vocabularies outside the laboratory as did untrained controls. Because shape is a perceptual property relevant to most object categories for which they have already learned names, preschoolers continue to rely heavily on shape when first linking a new noun with its category of objects (Yoshida & Smith, 2003).

fast mapping Connecting a new word with an underlying concept after only a brief encounter.

mutual exclusivity bias Children's assumption in early vocabulary growth that words refer to entirely separate categories.

Mutual exclusivity and object shape are especially useful strategies when speakers provide few or no cues about a new word's meaning. But they cannot account for young children's response when objects have more than one name. By age 3, preschoolers' memory, categorization, and language skills have expanded, and they readily assign multiple labels to many objects (Deák, Yen, & Pettit, 2001). For example, they refer to a sticker of a gray goose as "sticker," "goose," and "gray." Children often call on other aspects of language for help in these instances. According to one proposal, preschoolers discover many word meanings by observing how words are used in *syntax,* or the structure of sentences—a hypothesis called **syntactic bootstrapping** (Gleitman et al., 2005; Hoff & Naigles, 2002). Consider an adult who says, "This is a *citron* one," while showing the child a yellow car. Two- and 3-year-olds conclude that a new word used as an adjective for a familiar object (car) refers to a property of that object (Hall & Graham, 1999; Imai & Haryu, 2004). As preschoolers hear the word in various sentence structures ("That lemon is bright *citron*"), they use syntactic information to refine the word's meaning and generalize it to other categories.

Young children rely on any useful information available to figure out the meanings of new words. This boy might be attending to how his mother uses the word *apple* in the structure of sentences. Or he might be noticing social cues—the direction of his mother's gaze and her actions on the object.

Young children also take advantage of the rich social information that adults frequently provide when they introduce new words. For example, they often draw on their expanding ability to infer others' intentions and perspectives (Akhtar & Tomasello, 2000). In one study, an adult performed an action on an object and then used a new label while looking back and forth between the child and the object, as if to invite the child to play. Two-year-olds concluded that the label referred to the action, not the object (Tomasello & Akhtar, 1995). And when an adult first designates the whole object ("See the bird") and then points to a part of it ("That's a beak"), 3-year-olds realize that *beak* is a certain part, not the whole bird (Saylor, Sabbagh, & Baldwin, 2002).

Adults also inform children directly about word meanings. Parents commonly highlight the meaning of adjectives by using the new label with several objects (a "red car," a "red truck")—information that helps children infer that the word refers to an object property (Hall, Burns, & Pawluski, 2003). And adults often explain which of two or more words to use, saying, "It looks like a car, but it's actually a truck," or "You can call it a sea creature, but it's better to say 'dolphin.'" Parents who provide such clarifying information have preschoolers whose vocabularies grow more quickly (Callanan & Sabbagh, 2004; Deák, 2000).

Furthermore, to fill in for words they have not yet learned, children as young as age 2 coin new words based on ones they already know. For example, Sammy called a gardener a "plant-man" and added the ending *-er* to create "crayoner" for a child using crayons (Clark, 1995). Preschoolers also extend language meanings through metaphor. For example, one 3-year-old described a stomachache as a "fire engine in my tummy" (Winner, 1988). Young preschoolers' metaphors involve concrete, sensory comparisons: "Clouds are pillows," "Leaves are dancers." As their vocabulary and general knowledge expand, they appreciate nonsensory comparisons: "Friends are like magnets" (Karadsheh, 1991). Metaphors permit young children to communicate in especially vivid and memorable ways.

EXPLAINING VOCABULARY DEVELOPMENT ■ Children acquire vocabulary so efficiently and accurately that some theorists believe that they are innately biased to induce word meanings using certain principles, such as mutual exclusivity and syntactic bootstrapping (Lidz, Gleitman, & Gleitman, 2004; Woodward & Markman, 1998). But critics observe that a small set of built-in, fixed principles is not sufficient to account for the varied, flexible manner in which children master vocabulary (Deák, 2000).

An alternative view is that word learning is governed by the same cognitive strategies that children apply to nonlinguistic information. These strategies become more effective as children's information processing, communication skills, vocabulary size, knowledge of categories, and mastery of syntax improve (Golinkoff & Hirsh-Pasek, 2006; Hollich, Hirsh-Pasek, &

syntactic bootstrapping
Discovering word meanings by observing how words are used in the structure of sentences.

Golinkoff, 2000). Preschoolers are most successful at figuring out new word meanings when several kinds of information are available (Saylor, Baldwin, & Sabbagh, 2005). Researchers have just begun to study the multiple cues that children use for different kinds of words and how they change with development.

Grammar

Grammar refers to the way we combine words into meaningful phrases and sentences. Between ages 2 and 3, English-speaking children use simple sentences that follow a subject–verb–object word order. Children learning other languages adopt the word orders of the adult speech to which they are exposed (Maratsos, 1998). This shows that they have a beginning grasp of the grammar of their language.

BASIC RULES ■ Studies of children acquiring diverse languages indicate that their first use of grammatical rules is piecemeal—limited to just a few verbs. As children listen for familiar verbs in adults' speech, they expand their own utterances containing those verbs, relying on adult speech as their model (Gathercole, Sebastián, & Soto, 1999; Lieven, Pine, & Baldwin, 1997). Sammy, for example, added the preposition *with* to the verb *open* ("You open with scissors") but not to the word *stick* ("He hit me stick").

To test preschoolers' ability to generate novel sentences that conform to basic English grammar, researchers had them use a new verb in the subject–verb–object form after hearing it in a different construction, such as passive: "Ernie is getting *gorped* by the dog." When children were asked what the dog was doing, the percentage who could respond, "He's *gorping* Ernie," rose steadily with age. But as Figure 9.12 on page 359 shows, not until age 3½ to 4 could the majority of children apply the fundamental subject–verb–object structure broadly, to newly acquired verbs (Tomasello, 2000, 2003, 2006).

As these examples suggest, once children form three-word sentences, they also make small additions and changes in words that enable speakers to express meanings flexibly and efficiently. For example, they add *-s* for plural *(cats)*, use prepositions *(in* and *on)*, and form various tenses of the verb *to be (is, are, were, has been, will)*. All English-speaking children master these grammatical markers in a regular sequence, starting with those that involve the simplest meanings and structures (Brown, 1973; de Villiers & de Villiers, 1973). For example, children master the plural form *-s* before they learn tenses of the verb *to be*.

Once children acquire these markers, they sometimes overextend the rules to words that are exceptions, a type of error called **overregularization**. Expressions like "My toy car *breaked*," "I *runned* faster than you," and "We each got two *feets*" appear between ages 2 and 3 and persist into middle childhood (Maratsos, 2000; Marcus, 1995). Children less often make this error on frequently used irregular verbs, such as the past tense of *go (went)* and *say (said)*, which they hear often enough to learn by rote. For rarely used verbs such as *grow* and *sing*, children alternate for months—or even several years—between overregularized forms *(growed, singed)* and correct forms, until the irregular form eventually wins out. Since children do not hear mature speakers use these forms, overregularization provides evidence that children apply grammatical rules creatively.

COMPLEX STRUCTURES ■ Gradually, preschoolers master more complex grammatical structures, although they make errors along the way. In first creating questions, 2- and 3-year-olds use many formulas: "Where's *X*?" "Can I *X*?" (Dabrowska, 2000; Tomasello, 1992). Question asking remains variable for the next couple of years. An analysis of one child's questions revealed that he inverted the subject and verb when asking certain questions but not others ("What she will do?" "Why he can go?"). The correct expressions were the ones he heard most often in his mother's speech (Rowland & Pine, 2000).

Similarly, children have trouble with some passive sentences. When told, "The car was pushed by the truck," young preschoolers often make a toy car push a truck. By age 5, they understand such expressions. But 3- to 6-year-olds almost always use abbreviated passives ("It got broken") rather than full passives ("The glass was broken by Mary"). Full mastery of the passive form is not complete until the end of middle childhood (Horgan, 1978; Lempert, 1990).

overregularization
Overextension of regular grammatical rules to words that are exceptions.

Nevertheless, preschoolers' grasp of grammar is remarkable. By age 4 to 5, they form embedded sentences ("I think *he will come*"), tag questions ("Dad's going to be home soon, *isn't he?*"), and indirect objects ("He showed *his friend* the present"). As the preschool years draw to a close, children use most of the grammatical constructions of their language competently (Tager-Flusberg, 2005).

EXPLAINING GRAMMATICAL DEVELOPMENT ■ Evidence that grammatical development is an extended process has raised questions about Chomsky's *language acquisition device (LAD)*, which assumes that children have innate knowledge of grammatical rules (see Chapter 6, page 237). Some experts believe that grammar is a product of general cognitive development—children's tendency to search the environment for consistencies and patterns of all sorts (Bloom, 1999; MacWhinney, 2005; Tomasello, 2003). Yet among these theorists, debate continues over just how children master grammar.

According to one view, young children rely on *semantics,* or word meanings, to figure out grammatical rules—an approach called **semantic bootstrapping.** For example, children might begin by grouping together words with "agent qualities" (things that cause actions) as *subjects* and words with "action qualities" as *verbs.* Then they merge these categories with observations of how words are used in sentences (Bates & MacWhinney, 1987; Braine, 1994). Others believe that children master grammar through direct observation of the structure of language: They notice which words appear in the same positions in sentences and are combined in the same way with other words. Over time, they group words into grammatical categories and use them appropriately in sentences (Bloom, 1999; Chang, Dell, & Bock, 2006; Tomasello, 2003).

Still other theorists agree with the essence of Chomsky's theory. One idea accepts semantic bootstrapping but proposes that the grammatical categories into which children group word meanings are innately given—present at the outset (Pinker, 1989, 1999). Critics, however, point out that toddlers' two-word utterances do not show a grasp of grammar (return to Chapter 6, page 243, to review). Another theory holds that children do not start with innate knowledge but, rather, have a *special language-making capacity*—a set of procedures for analyzing the language they hear, which supports the discovery of grammatical regularities. Research on children learning more than 40 different languages reveals common patterns, consistent with a basic set of strategies (Slobin, 1985, 1997). Yet controversy persists over whether a universal, built-in language-processing device exists or whether children who hear different languages devise unique strategies (de Villiers & de Villiers, 1999; Marchman & Thal, 2005).

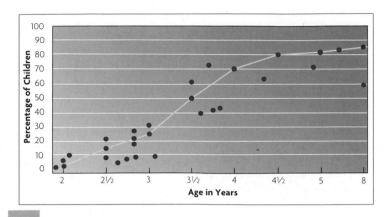

FIGURE 9.12

Percentage of children in different studies who could use a new verb in the subject–verb–object form after hearing it in another construction. Each dot in the graph represents the findings of one study. The ability to use the new verb—an indicator of the child's capacity to apply the subject–verb–object structure broadly—rose steadily with age. Children mastered this fundamental grammatical construction gradually. From M. Tomasello, 2000, "Do Young Children Have Adult Syntactic Competence?" *Cognition, 74,* p. 223. Reprinted by permission of Elsevier Science.

Conversation

Besides acquiring vocabulary and grammar, children must learn to engage in effective and appropriate communication—by taking turns, staying on the same topic, stating their messages clearly, and conforming to cultural rules for social interaction. This practical, social side of language is called **pragmatics,** and preschoolers make considerable headway in mastering it.

At the beginning of early childhood, children are skilled conversationalists. In face-to-face interaction, they take turns and respond appropriately to their partner's remarks (Pan & Snow, 1999). With age, the number of turns over which children can sustain interaction and their ability to maintain a topic over time increase, but even 2-year-olds converse effectively (Snow et al., 1996). These surprisingly advanced abilities probably grow out of early interactive experiences (see Chapter 6).

semantic bootstrapping Using word meanings to figure out grammatical rules.

pragmatics The practical, social side of language, concerned with how to engage in effective and appropriate communication.

Indeed, the presence of a sibling seems to be especially conducive to acquiring the pragmatics of language. Preschoolers closely monitor conversations between their twin or older siblings and parents, and they often try to join in. When they do, these verbal exchanges last longer, with each participant taking more turns (Barton & Strosberg, 1997; Barton & Tomasello, 1991). As they listen to these conversations, young language learners pick up important skills, such as use of personal pronouns ("I" versus "you"), which are more common in the early vocabularies of later-born than of firstborn siblings (Pine, 1995). Furthermore, older siblings' remarks to a younger brother or sister often focus on regulating interaction: "Do you like Kermit?" "OK, your turn" (Oshima-Takane & Robbins, 2003). This emphasis probably contributes to younger siblings' conversational skills.

By age 4, children adjust their speech to fit the age, sex, and social status of their listeners. For example, in acting out roles with hand puppets, they use more commands when playing socially dominant and male roles (teacher, doctor, father) but speak more politely and use more indirect requests when playing less dominant and female roles (student, patient, mother) (Andersen, 2000).

Preschoolers' conversational skills occasionally do break down. **TAKE A MOMENT...** Engage a preschooler in conversation on the telephone, jotting down what you and the child say. Here is an excerpt from one 4-year-old's phone conversation with his grandfather:

> *Grandfather:* "How old will you be?"
>
> *John:* "Dis many." [*Holding up four fingers*]
>
> *Grandfather:* "Huh?"
>
> *John:* "Dis many." [*Again holding up four fingers*] (Warren & Tate, 1992, pp. 259–260)

Young children's conversations appear less mature in highly demanding situations in which they cannot see their listeners' reactions or rely on typical conversational aids, such as gestures and objects to talk about. But when asked to tell a listener how to solve a simple puzzle, 3- to 6-year-olds give more specific directions over the phone than in person, indicating that they realize that more verbal description is necessary on the phone (Cameron & Lee, 1997). Between ages 4 and 8, both conversing and giving directions over the phone improve greatly. Telephone talk provides yet another example of how preschoolers' competencies depend on the demands of the situation.

Adults can support children's grammatical learning through indirect feedback, including recasts (restructuring inaccurate speech into correct form) and expansions (elaborating on children's speech). However, exposure to a rich language environment may be more important than these strategies, which are not seen in all cultures.

Supporting Language Learning in Early Childhood

How can adults foster preschoolers' language development? As in toddlerhood, interaction with more skilled speakers remains vital in early childhood. Conversational give-and-take with adults, either at home or in preschool, is consistently related to language progress (Hart & Risley, 1995; NICHD Early Child Care Research Network, 2000b). Furthermore, recall that language learning and literacy development are closely linked. Return to Applying What We Know on page 347, and notice how each strategy for supporting emergent literacy also fosters language progress.

Sensitive, caring adults use additional techniques that promote language skills. When children use words incorrectly or communicate unclearly, such adults give helpful, explicit feedback: "I can't tell which ball you want. Do you mean a large or small one or a red or green one?" But they do not overcorrect, especially when children make grammatical mistakes. Criticism discourages children from freely using language in ways that lead to new skills.

Instead, adults often provide indirect feedback about grammar by using two strategies, often in combination: **recasts**—restructuring inaccurate speech into correct form, and **expansions**—elaborating on children's speech, increasing its complexity (Bohannon & Stanowicz, 1988; Chouinard & Clark, 2003). For example, if a child says, "I gotted new red shoes," the parent might respond, "Yes, you got a pair of new red shoes."

However, some researchers question whether expansions and recasts are as important in children's mastery of grammar as mere exposure to a rich language environment. The techniques are not used in all cultures and do not consistently affect children's usage (Strapp & Federico, 2000; Valian, 1999). Rather than eliminating errors, perhaps expansions and recasts model grammatical alternatives and encourage children to experiment with them.

Do the findings just described remind you once again of Vygotsky's theory? In language, as in other aspects of intellectual growth, parents and teachers gently prompt young children to take the next developmental step forward. Children strive to master language because they want to connect with other people. Adults, in turn, respond to children's desire to become competent speakers by listening attentively, elaborating on what children say, modeling correct usage, and stimulating children to talk further. In the next chapter, we will see that this combination of warmth and encouragement of mature behavior is at the heart of early childhood emotional and social development as well.

> **recasts** Adult responses that restructure children's grammatically inaccurate speech into correct form.
>
> **expansions** Adult responses that elaborate on children's speech, increasing its complexity.

Ask Yourself

Review Provide a list of recommendations for supporting language development in early childhood, noting research that supports each.

Apply Sammy's mother explained to him that the family would take a vacation in Miami. The next morning, Sammy announced, "I gotted my bags packed. When are we going to Your-ami?" What explains Sammy's errors?

Connect Explain how children's strategies for word learning support the interactionist perspective on language development, described on pages 239–240 in Chapter 6.

Summary

Piaget's Theory: The Preoperational Stage

Describe advances in mental representation, and limitations of thinking, during the preoperational stage.

- Rapid advances in mental representation, notably language and make-believe play, mark the beginning of Piaget's **preoperational stage.** With age, make-believe becomes increasingly complex, evolving into **sociodramatic play.** Make-believe supports many aspects of cognitive and social development.

- **Dual representation** improves rapidly over the third year of life. Children realize that photographs, drawings, models, and simple maps correspond to circumstances in the real world. Adult teaching and experience with diverse symbols help preschoolers master many symbol–real world relations.

- Aside from representation, Piaget described preschoolers in terms of deficits rather than strengths. Preoperational children often fail to imagine the perspectives of others. Because this **egocentrism** prevents children from reflecting on their own thinking and accommodating, it contributes to **animistic thinking, centration,** and **irreversibility.** These difficulties cause preschoolers to fail **conservation** and **hierarchical classification** tasks.

What does follow-up research imply about the accuracy of Piaget's preoperational stage?

- When young children are given simplified problems relevant to their everyday lives, their performance appears more mature than Piaget assumed. Preschoolers recognize differing perspectives, distinguish animate from inanimate objects, and notice and reason about transformations and cause-and-effect relations. Their language reflects accurate causal reasoning and hierarchical classification. And they show impressive skill at categorizing on the basis of non-observable characteristics and notice distinctions between appearance and reality, revealing that their thinking is not dominated by perceptual appearances.

- These findings challenge Piaget's concept of stage. Rather than being absent in the preschool years, operational thinking develops gradually.

What educational principles can be derived from Piaget's theory?

■ A Piagetian classroom promotes discovery learning, sensitivity to children's readiness to learn, and acceptance of individual differences.

Vygotsky's Sociocultural Theory

Describe Vygotsky's perspective on the social origins and significance of children's private speech.

■ In contrast to Piaget, Vygotsky regarded language as the foundation for all higher cognitive processes. According to Vygotsky, **private speech,** or language used for self-guidance, emerges out of social communication as adults and more skilled peers help children master challenging tasks within the zone of proximal development. Eventually, private speech is internalized as inner, verbal thought.

■ **Intersubjectivity** and **scaffolding** are two features of social interaction that promote transfer of cognitive processes to children. The term **guided participation** recognizes situational and cultural variations in adult support of children's efforts.

© SW PRODUCTIONS/BRAND X PICTURES/JUPITER IMAGES

Describe applications of Vygotsky's theory to education, and evaluate his major ideas.

■ A Vygotskian classroom emphasizes assisted discovery, in which both teacher guidance and peer collaboration are vitally important. Make-believe play is a unique, broadly influential zone of proximal development in early childhood.

■ In granting social experience a central role in cognitive development, Vygotsky's theory helps us understand the wide cultural variation in cognitive skills. In some cultures, verbal communication is not the only means—or even the most important means—through which children learn.

■ Vygotsky said little about how basic cognitive and motor capacities, which develop in infancy, contribute to socially transmitted higher cognitive processes.

Information Processing

How do attention, memory, and problem solving change during early childhood?

■ Sustained attention increases sharply between ages 2½ and 3, due to growth of the frontal lobes of the cerebral cortex, the capacity to generate complex play goals, and adult scaffolding. **Planning** also improves. Nevertheless, compared with older children, pre-schoolers spend relatively short periods involved in tasks and are less systematic in planning.

■ Young children's recognition memory is remarkably accurate. But their recall of listlike information is much poorer than that of older children, largely because they use **memory strategies** less effectively.

■ **Episodic memory,** or memory for everyday experiences, is well developed in early childhood. Like adults, preschoolers remember recurring events as **scripts,** which become more elaborate with age.

■ As cognitive and conversational skills improve, children's autobiographical memories become better organized, detailed, and related to the larger context of their lives, especially when adults use an elaborative style to talk about the past.

■ According to **overlapping-waves theory,** children try out various strategies to solve challenging problems, gradually selecting those that result in rapid, accurate solutions. Practice with strategies, reasoning, tasks with new challenges, and adult assistance contribute to improved problem solving.

Describe the young child's theory of mind.

■ Preschoolers begin to construct a theory of mind, indicating that they are capable of **metacognition,** or thinking about thought. From age 4 on, they realize that both beliefs and desires can influence behavior and that people can hold false beliefs.

■ Factors contributing to young children's understanding of mental life include language and cognitive skills, make-believe play and reasoning about imaginary situations, and social interaction with older siblings, friends, and adults.

■ Preschoolers regard the mind as a passive container of information. As a result, they have difficulty inferring what people know or are thinking about.

Summarize children's literacy and mathematical knowledge during early childhood.

■ Young children's **emergent literacy** reveals that they understand a great deal about written language before they read and write in conventional ways. Preschoolers gradually revise incorrect ideas about the meaning of written symbols as their perceptual and cognitive capacities improve, as they encounter writing in many contexts, and as adults help them make sense of written information.

■ Literacy development builds on a foundation of spoken language and knowledge about the world. **Phonological awareness** is a strong predictor of emergent literacy and of later reading and spelling achievement. Adult–child narrative conversations and informal literacy experiences, such as interactive storybook reading, also contribute greatly to literacy development.

■ Mathematical reasoning also builds on informal knowledge. Toddlers' beginning grasp of **ordinality** serves as the basis for more complex under-standings. As children experiment with counting, they

© ELLEN B. SENISI/ THE IMAGE WORKS

discover additional mathematical principles, including **cardinality.** Gradually, counting becomes more flexible and efficient, and children use it to solve simple arithmetic problems. The more occasions adults provide for counting and comparing quantities, the sooner children construct basic numerical concepts.

Individual Differences in Mental Development

Describe the content of early childhood intelligence tests and the impact of home, preschool and kindergarten programs, child care, and educational media on mental development.

■ Intelligence tests in early childhood sample a range of verbal and nonverbal skills, including vocabulary, memory, quantitative knowledge, problem solving, and spatial reasoning. By age 6 to 7, scores are good predictors of later IQ and academic achievement.

■ Children growing up in warm, stimulating homes with parents who make reasonable demands for mature behavior score higher on mental tests. Home environment plays a major role in the poorer intellectual performance of low-SES children in comparison to their higher-SES peers.

■ Preschool and kindergarten programs include both **child-centered programs,** in which much learning occurs through play, and **academic programs,** in which teachers train children in academic skills, often using repetition and drill. Emphasizing formal academic instruction undermines young children's motivation and negatively influences later school achievement.

■ **Project Head Start** is the most extensive federally funded preschool program for low-income children in the United States. In Canada, **Aboriginal Head Start** serves First Nations, Inuit, and Métis preschoolers. High-quality preschool intervention results in immediate IQ and achievement gains and long-term improvements in school adjustment, educational attainment, and life success. The more parents are involved in Head Start, the higher their children's year-end academic, language, and social skills.

CP PHOTO/EUSTACIO HUMPHREY

■ Regardless of SES, poor-quality child care undermines preschoolers' cognitive and social skills, while good child care enhances cognitive, language, and social development, especially for low-SES children. Factors affecting quality of child care include group size, caregiver–child ratio, caregivers' educational preparation, and caregivers' personal commitment to learning about and caring for children.

■ Children pick up academic knowledge from educational television and computer software. TV shows with slow-paced action and easy-to-follow story lines help preschoolers comprehend program content. Heavy exposure to commercial entertainment TV, cartoons, and inappropriate computer games reduces time spent reading and interacting with others and is associated with poorer academic achievement after starting school.

Language Development

Trace the development of vocabulary, grammar, and conversational skills in early childhood.

■ Supported by **fast mapping,** preschoolers' vocabularies increase dramatically. Early in vocabulary growth, children seem to adopt a **mutual exclusivity bias** when objects differ perceptually—for example, in shape. Preschoolers also engage in **syntactic bootstrapping,** discovering a new word's meaning by observing how it is used in the structure of sentences. And they make use of adults' social cues and directly provided information. As their vocabulary and general knowledge improve, preschoolers extend language meanings through word coinages and metaphors.

■ Some researchers believe that children are innately biased to induce word meanings using certain principles. Others think that children use multiple cues for word learning, which is governed by the same cognitive strategies that children apply to nonlinguistic information.

■ Between ages 2 and 3, children adopt the word order of their language. As they gradually master grammatical constructions, they occasionally **overregularize,** applying the rules to words that are exceptions. By the end of the preschool years, children have acquired a wide variety of complex grammatical forms.

■ Some experts believe that grammar is a product of general cognitive development. According to one view, children engage in **semantic bootstrapping,** relying on word meanings to figure out grammatical rules. Others agree with the essence of Chomsky's theory that children's brains are innately tuned for acquiring grammar.

■ **Pragmatics** refers to the practical, social side of language. In face-to-face interaction with peers, young preschoolers are already skilled conversationalists. By age 4, they adapt their speech to their listeners in culturally accepted ways. Preschoolers' communicative skills appear less mature in highly demanding contexts—for example, over the telephone.

Cite factors that support language learning in early childhood.

■ Conversational give-and-take with more skilled speakers fosters preschoolers' language skills. Adults provide both explicit feedback on the clarity of children's utterances and indirect feedback about grammar through **recasts** and **expansions.** However, some researchers believe these strategies, which are not used in all cultures, are less important than mere exposure to a rich language environment.

Important Terms and Concepts

Chapter 10

This painting depicts warm, caring, early peer relationships. As Chapter 10 makes clear, preschoolers make great strides in understanding the thoughts and feelings of others, and they build on these skills as they form first friendships—special relationships marked by attachment and common interests.

"My World"
Viviana Astudillo
9 years, Canada

Emotional and Social Development in Early Childhood

As the children in Leslie's classroom moved through the preschool years, their personalities took on clearer definition. By age 3, they voiced firm likes and dislikes as well as new ideas about themselves. "Stop bothering me," Sammy said to Mark, who was reaching for Sammy's beanbag as Sammy aimed it toward the mouth of a large clown face. "See, I'm great at this game," Sammy announced with confidence, an attitude that kept him trying, even though he missed most of the throws.

The children's conversations also revealed their first notions about morality. Often they combined statements about right and wrong with forceful attempts to defend their own desires. "You're 'posed to share," stated Mark, grabbing the beanbag out of Sammy's hand.

"I was here first! Gimme it back," demanded Sammy, pushing Mark. The two boys struggled for the beanbag until Leslie intervened, provided an extra set of beanbags, and showed them how they could both play.

As the interaction between Sammy and Mark reveals, preschoolers have become complex social beings. Young children argue, grab, and push, but cooperative exchanges are far more frequent. Between ages 2 and 6, first friendships form, in which children converse, act out complementary roles, and learn that their own desires for companionship and toys are best met when they consider others' needs and interests.

The children's developing understanding of their social world was especially apparent in their growing attention to the dividing line between male and female. While Lynette and Karen cared for a sick baby doll in the housekeeping area, Sammy, Vance, and Mark transformed the block corner into a busy intersection. "Green light, go!" shouted police officer Sammy as Vance and Mark pushed large wooden cars and trucks across the floor. Already, the children preferred same-sex peers, and their play themes mirrored the gender stereotypes of their cultural community.

This chapter is devoted to the many facets of emotional and social development in early childhood. We begin with Erik Erikson's theory, which provides an overview of personality change in the preschool years. Then we consider children's concepts of themselves, their insights into their social and moral worlds, their gender typing, and their increasing ability to manage their emotional and social behaviors. Finally, we ask, What is effective child rearing? And we consider the complex conditions that support good parenting or lead it to break down, including the serious and widespread problems of child abuse and neglect.

This 3-year-old girl plays at washing clothes on the washing stone in her family's backyard in Ecuador. Children around the world act out highly visible occupations during play, developing a sense of initiative as they gain insight into what they can do in their culture.

Erikson's Theory: Initiative versus Guilt

Erikson (1950) described early childhood as a period of "vigorous unfolding." Once children have a sense of autonomy, they become less contrary than they were as toddlers. Their energies are freed for tackling the psychological conflict of the preschool years: **initiative versus guilt.** As the word *initiative* suggests, young children have a new sense of purposefulness. They are eager to tackle new tasks, join in activities with peers, and discover what they can do with the help of adults. They also make strides in conscience development.

Erikson regarded play as a means through which young children learn about themselves and their social world. Play permits preschoolers to try new skills with little risk of criticism and failure. It also creates a small social organization of children who must cooperate to achieve common goals. Around the world, children act out family scenes and highly visible occupations—police officer, doctor, and nurse in Western societies, rabbit hunter and potter among the Hopi Indians, hut builder and spear maker among the Baka of West Africa (Roopnarine et al., 1998).

Recall that Erikson's theory builds on Freud's psychosexual stages (see Chapter 1, page 15). In Freud's Oedipus and Electra conflicts, to avoid punishment and maintain the affection of parents, children form a *superego,* or conscience, by *identifying* with the same-sex parent. As a result, they adopt the moral and gender-role standards of their society. For Erikson, the negative outcome of early childhood is an overly strict superego, one that causes children to feel too much guilt because they have been threatened, criticized, and punished excessively by adults. When this happens, preschoolers' exuberant play and bold efforts to master new tasks break down.

Although Freud's ideas are no longer accepted as satisfactory explanations of conscience development, Erikson's image of initiative captures the diverse changes in young children's emotional and social lives. The preschool years are, indeed, a time when children develop a confident self-image, more effective control over their emotions, new social skills, the foundations of morality, and a clear sense of themselves as boy or girl. Now let's look closely at each of these aspects of development.

initiative versus guilt In Erikson's theory, the psychological conflict of early childhood, which is resolved positively through play experiences that foster a healthy sense of initiative and through the development of a superego, or conscience, that is not overly strict and/or guilt-ridden.

I-self The self as knower and actor, which is separate from the surrounding world, remains the same person over time, has a private inner life not accessible to others, and can control its own thoughts and actions.

me-self The self as an object of knowledge and evaluation, consisting of all physical, psychological, and social characteristics that make the self unique.

Self-Understanding

Virtually all investigators agree that the self has two distinct aspects, identified by American philosopher and psychologist William James (1890) more than a century ago:

- The **I-self,** or *self as knower and actor,* includes the realization that the self is separate from the surrounding world; remains the same person over time; has a private, inner life not accessible to others; and controls its own thoughts and actions.
- The **me-self,** or *self as object of knowledge and evaluation,* consists of all qualities that make the self unique—physical characteristics and possessions; psychological characteristics, including desires, attitudes, beliefs, and personality traits; and social characteristics, such as roles and relationships with others.

The I-self can be thought of as the active observer, the me-self as developing from the observing process (see Figure 10.1). Both aspects of the self emerge in the first two years, as babies become self-aware *(I-self)*, recognize the self's physical features, and start to categorize themselves on the basis of age, sex, and other characteristics *(me-self)*.

The development of language enables young children to talk about their own subjective experience of being. In Chapter 9, we noted that preschoolers acquire a vocabulary for talking about their inner mental lives and refine their understanding of mental states. As the I-self becomes more firmly established, children focus more intently on the me-self (Harter, 2003, 2006). They begin to develop a **self-concept,** the set of attributes, abilities, attitudes, and values that an individual believes defines who he or she is.

FIGURE 10.1

The I-self and the me-self. The I-self is a sense of self as knower and actor. It is the active observer. The me-self is a sense of self as object of knowledge and evaluation. It results from the observing process.

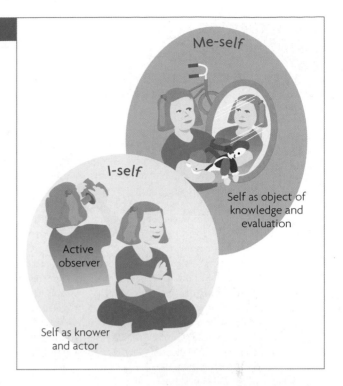

Me-self

Self as object of knowledge and evaluation

I-self

Active observer

Self as knower and actor

Foundations of Self-Concept

Ask a 3- to 5-year-old to tell you about him- or herself, and you are likely to hear something like this: "I'm Tommy. See, I got this new red T-shirt. I'm 4 years old. I can brush my teeth, and I can wash my hair all by myself. I have a new Tinkertoy set, and I made this big, big tower." Preschoolers' self-concepts are very concrete. Usually they mention observable characteristics, such as their name, physical appearance, possessions, and everyday behaviors (Harter, 2006; Watson, 1990).

By age 3½, children also describe themselves in terms of typical emotions and attitudes ("I'm happy when I play with my friends"; "I don't like being with grown-ups"), suggesting a beginning understanding of their unique psychological characteristics (Eder & Mangelsdorf, 1997). As further support for this budding grasp of personality, when given a trait label ("shy," "mean"), 4-year-olds infer appropriate motives and feelings. For example, they know that a shy person doesn't like to be with unfamiliar people (Heyman & Gelman, 1999). But preschoolers do not yet say, "I'm helpful" or "I'm shy." Direct references to personality traits must wait for greater cognitive maturity.

Because very young preschoolers' concepts of themselves are so bound up with specific possessions and actions, they spend much time asserting their rights to objects ("Mine!"), as Sammy did in the beanbag incident at the beginning of this chapter. The stronger children's self-definition, the more possessive they tend to be (Fasig, 2000; Levine, 1983). A firmer sense of self also enables children to cooperate in resolving disputes over objects, playing games, and solving simple problems (Brownell & Carriger, 1990; Caplan et al., 1991). When parents and teachers try to promote friendly peer interaction, they will be more successful if they accept the young child's possessiveness as a sign of self-assertion ("Yes, that's your toy") and encourage compromise ("But in a little while, would you give someone else a turn?"), rather than simply insisting on sharing.

Recall from Chapter 9 that adult–child conversations about the past contribute to the development of an autobiographical memory—a life-story narrative that is more coherent and enduring than the isolated, episodic memories of the first few years (see page 340). The richness of mothers' emotional communication about the past (evaluations of positive events, explanations of children's negative feelings and their resolution) helps children understand themselves: It predicts greater consistency in 5- and 6-year-olds' reports of their personal characteristics (Bird & Reese, 2006).

And as early as age 2, parents use these narratives to impart rules, standards for behavior, and evaluative information about the child: "You added the milk when we made the mashed potatoes. That's a very important job!" (Nelson, 2003). As the Cultural Influences box on page 368 reveals, these self-evaluative narratives are a major means through which caregivers imbue the young child's me-self with cultural values.

As they talk about personally significant events and as their cognitive skills advance, preschoolers gradually come to view the I-self as existing continuously in time. In Chapter 7, we noted that not until age 4 are children certain that a video image of themselves replayed shortly after it was filmed is still "me" (see page 284). Similarly, when researchers asked 3- to

These preschoolers work together to move a heavy recycling bin. A firmer sense of self enables children to cooperate in resolving disputes, playing games, and solving simple problems.

self-concept The set of attributes, abilities, attitudes, and values that an individual believes defines who he or she is.

Cultural Influences

Cultural Variations in Personal Storytelling: Implications for Early Self-Concept

Preschoolers of many cultural backgrounds participate in personal storytelling with their parents. Striking cultural differences exist in parents' selection and interpretation of events in these early narratives, affecting the way children come to view themselves.

In one study, researchers spent hundreds of hours over a two-year period studying the storytelling practices of six middle-SES Irish-American families in Chicago and six middle-SES Chinese families in Taiwan. From extensive videotapes of adults' conversations with 2½-year-olds, the investigators identified personal stories and coded them for content, quality of their endings, and evaluation of the child (Miller, Fung, & Mintz, 1996; Miller et al., 1997).

Parents in both cultures discussed pleasurable holidays and family excursions in similar ways and with similar frequency. But Chinese parents more often told long stories about the child's misdeeds—using impolite language, writing on the wall, or playing in an overly rowdy way. These narratives were conveyed with warmth and caring, stressed the impact of misbehavior on others ("You made Mama lose face"), and often ended with direct teaching of proper behavior ("Saying dirty words is not good"). By contrast, in the few instances

in which Irish-American stories referred to transgressions, parents downplayed their seriousness, attributing them to the child's spunk and assertiveness.

Early narratives about the child seem to launch preschoolers' self-concepts on culturally distinct paths. Influenced by Confucian traditions of strict discipline and social obligations, Chinese parents integrated these values into their personal stories, affirming the importance of not disgracing the family and explicitly conveying expectations in the story's conclusion. Although Irish-American parents disciplined their children, they rarely dwelt on misdeeds in storytelling. Rather, they cast the child's shortcomings in a positive light, perhaps to promote self-esteem.

Whereas most North Americans believe that favorable self-esteem is crucial for healthy development, Chinese adults generally regard it as unimportant or even negative—as impeding the child's willingness to listen and to be corrected (Miller et al., 2002). Consistent with this view, the Chinese parents did little to cultivate their child's individuality. Instead, they used storytelling to guide the child toward socially responsible behavior. Hence, by the end of the preschool years, the Chinese child's self-

image emphasizes membership in the collective and obligations to others ("I belong to the Lee family"; "I like to help my mom wash dishes"), whereas the North American child's is more autonomous, consisting largely of personal descriptions ("I do lots of puzzles" "I like hockey") (Wang, 2004).

As she gently but firmly conveys her expectations for proper behavior, this Chinese mother helps her son develop a view of himself that emphasizes social obligations rather than individuality.

This child's determined approach to loading the family dishwasher reflects a positive evaluation of her own competence. Her high self-esteem contributes to a sense of initiative as she masters new skills.

5-year-olds to imagine a future event (walking next to a waterfall) and to envision a future personal state by choosing from three items (a raincoat, money, a blanket) the one they would need to bring with them, performance—along with future-state justifications ("I'm gonna get wet")—increased sharply between ages 3 and 4 (Atance & Meltzoff, 2005).

Emergence of Self-Esteem

Another aspect of self-concept emerges in early childhood: **self-esteem,** our judgments about our own worth and the feelings associated with those judgments. These evaluations of our own competencies affect our emotional experiences, future behavior, and long-term psychological adjustment. **TAKE A MOMENT...** Make a list of your own self-judgments. Notice that, besides a global appraisal of your worth as a person, you have a variety of separate self-evaluations concerning different activities.

By age 4, preschoolers have several self-judgments—for example, about learning things well in school, making friends, getting along with parents, and treating others kindly (Marsh, Ellis, & Craven, 2002). But because they have difficulty distinguishing between their desired and their actual competence, preschoolers usually rate their own ability as extremely high and often underestimate task difficulty, as when Sammy asserted, despite his many misses, that he was great at beanbag throwing (Harter, 2003, 2006).

High self-esteem contributes greatly to preschoolers' initiative during a period in which they must master many new skills. By age 3, children whose parents patiently encourage while offering information about how to succeed are enthusiastic and highly motivated. In contrast, children with a history of parental criticism of their worth and performance give up easily when faced with a challenge and express shame and dependency after failing (Kelley, Brownell, & Campbell, 2000). When preschool nonpersisters use dolls to act out an adult's reaction to failure, they anticipate disapproval—saying, for example, "He's punished because he can't do the puzzle" (Burhans & Dweck, 1995). They are also likely to report that their parents berate them for making small mistakes (Heyman, Dweck, & Cain, 1992). To avoid promoting these self-defeating reactions, adults should adjust their expectations to children's capacities, scaffold children's attempts at difficult tasks (see Chapter 9, page 335), and accentuate the positive by pointing out effort and improvement in children's work or behavior.

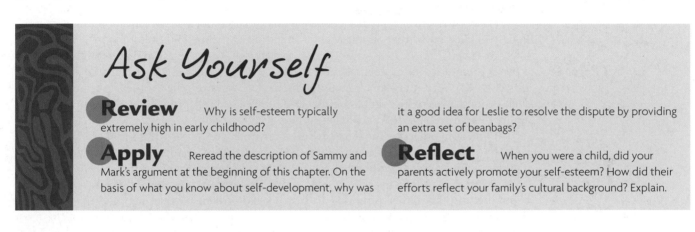

Ask Yourself

Review   Why is self-esteem typically extremely high in early childhood?

Apply   Reread the description of Sammy and Mark's argument at the beginning of this chapter. On the basis of what you know about self-development, why was

it a good idea for Leslie to resolve the dispute by providing an extra set of beanbags?

Reflect   When you were a child, did your parents actively promote your self-esteem? How did their efforts reflect your family's cultural background? Explain.

Emotional Development

Gains in representation, language, and self-concept support emotional development in early childhood. Between ages 2 and 6, children make strides in the emotional abilities that, collectively, researchers refer to as *emotional competence* (Halberstadt, Denham, & Dunsmore, 2001; Saarni et al., 2006). First, preschoolers gain in emotional understanding, becoming better able to talk about feelings and to respond appropriately to others' emotional signals. Second, they become better at emotional self-regulation—in particular, at coping with intense negative emotion. Finally, self-development contributes to a rise in *self-conscious emotions* and *empathy*, which contribute to children's developing sense of morality.

Parenting strongly influences preschoolers' emotional competence. Emotional competence, in turn, is vital for successful peer relationships and overall emotional health.

Understanding Emotion

Preschoolers' vocabulary for talking about emotion expands rapidly, and they use it skillfully to reflect on their own and others' behavior. Here are some excerpts from conversations in which 2-year-olds and 6-year-olds commented on emotionally charged experiences:

Two-year-old: [*After father shouted at child, she became angry, shouting back*] "I'm mad at you, Daddy. I'm going away. Good-bye."

Two-year-old: [*Commenting on another child who refused to nap and cried*] "Mom, Annie cry. Annie sad."

Six-year-old: [*In response to mother's comment, "It's hard to hear the baby crying"*] "Well, it's not as hard for me as it is for you." [*When mother asked why*] "Well, you like Johnny better than I do! I like him a little, and you like him a lot, so I think it's harder for you to hear him cry."

self-esteem The judgments individuals make about their own worth and the feelings associated with those judgments.

Six-year-old: [*Trying to comfort a small boy in church whose mother had gone up to communion*] "Aw, that's all right. She'll be right back. Don't be afraid. I'm here." (Bretherton et al., 1986, pp. 536, 540, 541)

COGNITIVE DEVELOPMENT AND EMOTIONAL UNDERSTANDING ■ As these examples show, early in the preschool years, children refer to causes, consequences, and behavioral signs of emotion, and over time their understanding becomes more accurate and complex (Stein & Levine, 1999). By age 4 to 5, they correctly judge the causes of many basic emotions ("He's happy because he's swinging very high"; "He's sad because he misses his mother"). Preschoolers' explanations tend to emphasize external factors over internal states—a balance that changes with age (Levine, 1995). In Chapter 9, we saw that after age 4, children appreciate that both desires and beliefs motivate behavior. Once these understandings are secure, children's grasp of how internal factors can trigger emotion expands.

Preschoolers can also predict what a playmate expressing a certain emotion might do next. Four-year-olds know that an angry child might hit someone and that a happy child is more likely to share (Russell, 1990). They realize that thinking and feeling are interconnected—that a person reminded of a previous sad experience is likely to feel sad (Lagattuta, Wellman, & Flavell, 1997). And they can come up with effective ways to relieve others' negative feelings, such as hugging to reduce sadness (Fabes et al., 1988). Overall, preschoolers have an impressive ability to interpret, predict, and change others' feelings.

At the same time, preschoolers have difficulty interpreting situations that offer conflicting cues about how a person is feeling. When shown a picture of a happy-faced child with a broken bicycle, 4- and 5-year-olds tended to rely only on the emotional expression: "He's happy because he likes to ride his bike." Older children more often reconciled the two cues: "He's happy because his father promised to help fix his broken bike" (Gnepp, 1983; Hoffner & Badzinski, 1989). As in their approach to Piagetian tasks, young children focus on the most obvious aspect of a complex emotional situation, neglecting other relevant information.

SOCIAL EXPERIENCE AND EMOTIONAL UNDERSTANDING ■ Social experience, along with cognitive development, contributes to gains in emotional understanding. The more mothers label emotions and explain them in conversing with preschoolers, the more "emotion words" children use in these discussions (Fivush & Haden, 2005). Maternal prompting of emotional thoughts ("What makes him afraid?") is a good predictor of 2-year-olds' emotion language. For older preschoolers, explanations ("He's sad because his dog ran away") are more important (Cervantes & Callanan, 1998). Does this remind you of the concept of *scaffolding*—that to be effective, adult teaching must adjust to children's increasing competence?

Preschoolers whose parents frequently acknowledge their children's emotional reactions and explicitly teach them about diverse emotions are better able to judge others' emotions when tested at later ages (Denham & Kochanoff, 2002). Discussions in which family members disagree are particularly helpful. In one study, mothers who explained feelings and negotiated and compromised during conflicts with their 2½-year-olds had children who, at age 3, were advanced in emotional understanding and used similar strategies to resolve disagreements (Laible & Thompson, 2002). Such dialogues seem to help children reflect on the causes and consequences of emotion while also modeling mature communication skills. Furthermore, preschoolers who are securely attached to their mothers better understand emotion. Attachment security is related to warmer and more elaborative parent–child narratives, including discussions of feelings that highlight the emotional significance of past events (Laible, 2004; Laible & Song, 2006; Raikes & Thompson, 2006). Parental warmth fosters children's participation, thereby enhancing the emotional knowledge they glean from these rich dialogues.

As preschoolers learn more about emotion from interacting with adults, they transfer this knowledge to other contexts, engaging in more emotion

© ELIZABETH CREWS

During the preschool years, children's understanding of the causes, consequences, and behavioral signs of emotion expands rapidly. This 4-year-old tries to figure out why his baby brother is crying. Perhaps the menu is not quite right.

talk with siblings and friends, especially during sociodramatic play (Brown, Donelan-McCall, & Dunn, 1996; Hughes & Dunn, 1998). Make-believe, in turn, contributes to emotional understanding, especially when children play with siblings (Youngblade & Dunn, 1995). The intense nature of the sibling relationship, combined with frequent acting out of feelings, makes pretending an excellent context for early learning about emotions. And when parents intervene in sibling disputes by reasoning and negotiating, preschoolers gain in sensitivity to their siblings' feelings (Perlman & Ross, 1997). They more often refer to their sibling's emotional perspective ("You get mad when I don't share") and engage in less fighting.

Knowledge about emotions helps children greatly in their efforts to get along with others. As early as 3 to 5 years of age, it is related to friendly, considerate behavior, willingness to make amends after harming another, and constructive responses to disputes with agemates (Brown & Dunn, 1996; Dunn, Brown, & Maguire, 1995; Garner & Estep, 2001). Also, the more preschoolers refer to feelings when interacting with playmates, the better liked they are by their peers (Fabes et al., 2001). Children seem to recognize that acknowledging others' emotions and explaining their own enhance the quality of relationships.

Emotional Self-Regulation

Language also contributes to preschoolers' improved *emotional self-regulation,* or ability to control the expression of emotion. By age 3 to 4, children verbalize a variety of strategies for adjusting their emotional arousal to a more comfortable level. For example, they know they can blunt emotions by restricting sensory input (covering their eyes or ears to block out a scary sight or sound), talking to themselves ("Mommy said she'll be back soon"), or changing their goals (deciding that you don't want to play anyway after being excluded from a game) (Thompson, 1990a).

As children use these strategies, emotional outbursts decline. *Effortful control*—in particular, inhibiting impulses and shifting attention—also continues to be vital in managing emotion in early childhood. Three-year-olds who can distract themselves when frustrated tend to become cooperative school-age children with few problem behaviors (Gilliom et al., 2002). By age 3, effortful control predicts children's skill at portraying an emotion they do not feel—for example, reacting cheerfully after receiving an undesirable gift (Kieras et al., 2005). These emotional "masks" are largely limited to the positive feelings of happiness and surprise. Children of all ages (and adults as well) find it harder to act sad, angry, or disgusted than pleased (Denham, 1998). To promote good social relations, most cultures teach children to communicate positive feelings and inhibit unpleasant ones.

Temperament affects the development of emotional self-regulation. Children who experience negative emotion intensely have greater difficulty inhibiting their feelings and shifting their focus of attention away from disturbing events. Beginning in early childhood, these children are more likely to be anxious and fearful or to respond with irritation to others' distress, react angrily or aggressively when frustrated, and get along poorly with teachers and peers (Chang et al., 2003; Denham et al., 2002; Eisenberg et al., 2005).

To avoid social difficulties, emotionally reactive children must develop effective emotion-regulation strategies (Rothbart & Bates, 2006). By watching parents manage their feelings, children pick up strategies for regulating their own. When parents rarely express positive emotion, dismiss children's feelings as unimportant, and have difficulty controlling their own anger, children have continuing problems in managing emotion that seriously interfere with psychological adjustment (Gilliom et al., 2002; Katz & Windecker-Nelson, 2004; Owens & Shaw, 2003). And because emotionally reactive children become increasingly difficult to rear, they are often targets of ineffective parenting, which compounds their poor self-regulation.

Adults' conversations with children also foster emotional self-regulation. Parents who prepare children for difficult experiences by describing what to expect and ways to handle anxiety offer coping strategies that children can apply. Preschoolers' vivid imaginations and incomplete grasp of the distinction between appearance and reality make fears common in early childhood. Consult Applying What We Know on page 372 for ways adults can help young children manage fears.

Applying What We Know

Helping Children Manage Common Fears of Early Childhood

FEAR	SUGGESTION
Monsters, ghosts, and darkness	Reduce exposure to frightening stories in books and on TV until the child is more certain of the distinction between appearance and reality. Make a thorough "search" of the child's room for monsters, showing him that none are there. Leave a night-light burning, sit by the child's bed until he falls asleep, and tuck in a favorite toy for protection.
Preschool or child care	If the child resists going to preschool but seems content once there, the fear is probably separation. Under these circumstances, provide a sense of warmth and caring while gently encouraging independence. If the child fears being at preschool, try to find out what is frightening—the teacher, the children, or a crowded, noisy environment. Provide extra support by accompanying the child and gradually lessening the amount of time you are present.
Animals	Do not force the child to approach a dog, cat, or other animal that arouses fear. Let the child move at her own pace. Demonstrate how to hold and pet the animal, showing the child that when treated gently, the animal reacts in a friendly way. If the child is larger than the animal, emphasize this: "You're so big. That kitty is probably afraid of you!"
Intense fears	If a child's fear is intense, persists for a long time, interferes with daily activities, and cannot be reduced in any of the ways just suggested, it has reached the level of a *phobia*. Sometimes phobias are linked to family problems, and counseling is needed to reduce them. At other times, phobias diminish without treatment as the child's capacity for emotional self-regulation improves.

Self-Conscious Emotions

One morning in Leslie's classroom, a group of children crowded around for a bread-baking activity. Leslie asked them to wait patiently while she got a baking pan. But Sammy reached over to feel the dough, and the bowl tumbled off the table. When Leslie returned, Sammy looked at her and then, feeling ashamed and guilty, covered his eyes with his hands. "I did something bad," he said.

As children's self-concepts develop, they become increasingly sensitive to praise and blame or (as Sammy did) to the possibility of such feedback. As a result, they more often experience *self-conscious emotions*—feelings that involve injury to or enhancement of their sense of self (see Chapter 7). By age 3, self-conscious emotions are clearly linked to self-evaluation (Lewis, 1995). But because preschoolers are still developing standards of excellence and conduct, they depend on adults to know when to feel self-conscious emotions. They are particularly sensitive to the messages of parents, teachers, and others who matter to them, often viewing their expectations as obligatory rules ("Dad said you're 'posed to take turns") (Stipek, 1995; Thompson, Meyer, & McGinley, 2006).

When parents repeatedly give feedback about the worth of the child and her performance ("That's a bad job! I thought you were a good girl"), children experience self-conscious emotions intensely—more shame after failure, more pride after success. In contrast, when parents focus on how to improve performance ("You did it this way; now try doing it that way"), they induce moderate, more adaptive levels of shame and pride and greater persistence on difficult tasks (Kelley, Brownell, & Campbell, 2000; Lewis, 1998).

Among Western children, beginning in early childhood, intense shame is associated with feelings of personal inadequacy ("I'm stupid"; "I'm a terrible person") and with maladjustment—withdrawal and depression as well as intense anger and aggression toward those who participated in the shame-evoking situation (Lindsay-Hartz, de Rivera, & Mascolo, 1995; Mills, 2005). In contrast, guilt—when it occurs in appropriate circumstances and is not accompanied by shame—is related to good adjustment. Guilt may help children resist harmful impulses, and it motivates a misbehaving child to repair the damage and behave more considerately (Ferguson et al., 1999; Tangney, 2001).

The consequences of shame for children's adjustment, however, may vary across cultures. As illustrated in the Cultural Influences box on page 368, people in Asian collectivist societies, who define themselves in relation to their social group, view shame as an adaptive reminder of an interdependent self and of the importance of others' judgments (Bedford, 2004).

prosocial, or altruistic, behavior Actions that benefit another person without any expected reward for the self.

sympathy Feelings of concern or sorrow for another's plight.

Empathy and Sympathy

Another emotional capacity that becomes more common in early childhood is *empathy*, which serves as an important motivator of **prosocial, or altruistic, behavior**—actions that benefit another person without any expected reward for the self (Eisenberg, Fabes, & Spinrad, 2006). Compared with toddlers, preschoolers rely more on words to communicate empathic feelings, a change that indicates a more reflective level of empathy (Bretherton et al., 1986). When a 4-year-old received a Christmas gift that she hadn't included on her list for Santa, she assumed it belonged to another little girl and pleaded with her parents, "We've got to give it back—Santa's made a big mistake. I think the girl's crying 'cause she didn't get her present!" As the ability to take the perspective of others improves, empathic responding increases.

In some children, empathy—*feeling with* another person and responding emotionally in a similar way—does not yield acts of kindness and helpfulness but, instead, escalates into *personal distress*. In trying to reduce these feelings, the child focuses on his own anxiety rather than on the person in need. As a result, empathy does not lead to **sympathy**—feelings of concern or sorrow for another's plight.

Temperament plays a role in whether empathy prompts sympathetic, prosocial behavior or a personally distressed, self-focused response. Children who are sociable, assertive, and good at regulating emotion are more likely than poor emotion regulators to display sympathy and prosocial behavior, helping, sharing, and comforting others in distress (Bengtson, 2005; Eisenberg et al., 1998; Valiente et al., 2004). Faced with someone in need, children who have difficulty regulating emotion react with facial and physiological distress—frowning, lip biting, a rise in heart rate, and a sharp increase in EEG brain-wave activity in the right cerebral hemisphere, which houses negative emotion—indications that they are overwhelmed by their feelings (Miller et al., 1996; Pickens, Field, & Nawrocki, 2001).

As with other aspects of emotional development, parenting affects empathy and sympathy. When parents are warm and encouraging and show a sensitive, empathic concern for their preschoolers' feelings, children are likely to react in a concerned way to the distress of others—relationships that persist into adolescence and young adulthood (Eisenberg & McNally, 1993; Koestner, Franz, & Weinberger, 1990; Strayer & Roberts, 2004). Besides modeling sympathy, parents can teach children the importance of kindness and can intervene when they display inappropriate emotion—strategies that predict high levels of sympathetic responding (Eisenberg 2003).

In contrast, angry, punitive parenting disrupts the development of empathy at an early age—particularly among children who are poor emotion regulators and who, therefore, respond to parental hostility with especially high personal distress (Valiente et al., 2004). In one study, physically abused preschoolers at a child-care center rarely expressed concern at a peer's unhappiness but, rather, reacted with fear, anger, and physical attacks (Klimes-Dougan & Kistner, 1990). The children's reactions resembled their parents' insensitive responses to the suffering of others.

© LAWRENCE MIGDALE/PIX

Outside the playhouse at preschool, a young boy comforts his friend. As children's language skills expand and their ability to take the perspective of others improves, empathy also increases, motivating prosocial, or altruistic, behavior.

Ask Yourself

Review What do preschoolers understand about emotion, and how do cognition and social experience contribute to their understanding?

Apply Four-year-old Tia had just gotten her face painted at a carnival. As she walked around with her mother, the heat of the afternoon caused her balloon to pop. When Tia started to cry, her mother said, "Oh, Tia, balloons aren't such a good idea when it's hot outside. We'll get another on a cooler day. If you cry, you'll mess up your beautiful face painting." What aspect of emotional development is Tia's mother trying to promote, and why is her intervention likely to help Tia?

Connect Cite ways that parenting contributes to preschoolers' self-esteem, emotional understanding, emotional self-regulation, self-conscious emotions, and empathy and sympathy. Do you see any patterns? Explain.

Peer Relations

As children become increasingly self-aware, more effective at communicating, and better at understanding the thoughts and feelings of others, their skill at interacting with peers improves rapidly. Peers provide young children with learning experiences they can get in no other way. Because peers interact on an equal footing, they must keep a conversation going, cooperate, and set goals in play. With peers, children form friendships—special relationships marked by attachment and common interests. Let's look at how peer interaction changes over the preschool years.

Advances in Peer Sociability

Mildred Parten (1932), one of the first to study peer sociability among 2- to 5-year-olds, noticed a dramatic rise with age in joint, interactive play. She concluded that social development proceeds in a three-step sequence. It begins with **nonsocial activity**—unoccupied, onlooker behavior and solitary play. Then it shifts to **parallel play**, a limited form of social participation in which a child plays near other children with similar materials but does not try to influence their behavior. At the highest level are two forms of true social interaction. In **associative play**, children engage in separate activities but exchange toys and comment on one another's behavior. Finally, in **cooperative play**, a more advanced type of interaction, children orient toward a common goal, such as acting out a make-believe theme.

FOLLOW-UP RESEARCH ON PEER SOCIABILITY ■ Longitudinal evidence indicates that these play forms emerge in the order Parten suggested but that later-appearing ones do not replace earlier ones in a developmental sequence (Rubin, Bukowski, & Parker, 2006). Rather, all types coexist during early childhood. **TAKE A MOMENT...** Watch preschool children move from one type of play to another in their classroom, and you will see that they often transition from onlooker to parallel to cooperative play and back again (Robinson et al., 2003). Preschoolers seem to use parallel play as a way station—a respite from the high demands of complex social interaction and a crossroad to new activities. And although nonsocial activity declines with age, it is still the most frequent form among 3- to 4-year-olds. Even among kindergartners it continues to occupy about one-third of children's free-play time. Also, both solitary and parallel play remain fairly stable from 3 to 6 years, accounting for as much of the young child's play as highly social, cooperative interaction (Rubin, Fein, & Vandenberg, 1983).

We now understand that it is the *type*, not the amount, of solitary and parallel play that changes during early childhood. In studies of preschoolers' play in Taiwan and the United States, researchers rated the *cognitive maturity* of nonsocial, parallel, and cooperative play by applying the categories shown in Table 10.1. Within each of Parten's play types, older children displayed more cognitively mature behavior than younger children (Pan, 1994; Rubin, Watson, & Jambor, 1978).

The 3-year-olds stringing beads (left) are engaged in parallel play. Cooperative play, like that of the two 5-year-olds fixing their classmate's hair (right), develops later than parallel play, but preschool children continue to move back and forth between the two types of sociability. Parallel play often serves as a respite from the demands of complex social interaction.

TABLE 10.1 Developmental Sequence of Cognitive Play Categories

PLAY CATEGORY	DESCRIPTION	EXAMPLES
Functional play	Simple, repetitive motor movements with or without objects. Especially common during the first 2 years of life.	Running around a room, rolling a car back and forth, kneading clay with no intent to make something
Constructive play	Creating or constructing something. Especially common between 3 and 6 years.	Making a house out of toy blocks, drawing a picture, putting together a puzzle
Make-believe play	Acting out everyday and imaginary roles. Especially common between 2 and 6 years.	Playing house, school, or police officer; acting out storybook or television characters

Source: Rubin, Fein, & Vandenberg, 1983.

Often parents wonder whether a preschooler who spends large amounts of time playing alone is developing normally. But only *certain types* of nonsocial activity—aimless wandering, hovering near peers, and functional play involving immature, repetitive motor action—are cause for concern. Children who behave reticently, by watching peers without playing, are usually temperamentally inhibited—high in social fearfulness. Their parents frequently overprotect them, criticize their social awkwardness, and unnecessarily control their play activities instead of patiently encouraging them to approach other children (Coplan et al., 2004; Rubin, Burgess, & Hastings, 2002). And preschoolers who engage in solitary, repetitive behavior (banging blocks, making a doll jump up and down) tend to be immature, impulsive children who find it difficult to regulate anger and aggression (Coplan et al., 2001). In the classroom, both reticent and impulsive children experience peer ostracism.

But most preschoolers with low rates of peer interaction are not socially anxious. They simply like to play by themselves, and their solitary activities are positive and constructive. Teachers encourage such play by setting out art materials, books, puzzles, and building toys. Children who spend much time at these activities are usually well-adjusted youngsters who, when they do play with peers, show socially skilled behavior (Rubin & Coplan, 1998). Still, a few preschoolers who engage in such age-appropriate solitary play (mostly boys) are rebuffed by peers. Perhaps because quiet play is inconsistent with the "masculine" gender role, boys who engage in it are at risk for negative reactions from both parents and peers and, eventually, for adjustment problems (Coplan et al., 2001, 2004).

As noted in Chapter 9, *sociodramatic play*—an advanced form of cooperative play—becomes especially common over the preschool years and supports cognitive, emotional, and social development (Göncü, Patt, & Kouba, 2004). In joint make-believe, preschoolers act out and respond to one another's pretend feelings. They also explore and gain control of fear-arousing experiences when they play doctor or pretend to search for monsters in a magical forest. As a result, they can better understand others' feelings and regulate their own (Smith, 2003). Finally, preschoolers spend much time negotiating roles and rules in play—arguing and then agreeing. To create and manage complex plots, they must resolve their disputes through negotiation and compromise. With age, preschoolers' conflicts center less on toys and other resources and more on differences of opinion—an indication of their expanding capacity to consider others' attitudes and ideas (Chen, Fein, & Tam, 2001; Hay, Payne, & Chadwick, 2004).

CULTURAL VARIATIONS ■ Peer sociability takes different forms in collectivist societies, which stress group harmony, than in individualistic cultures. For example, children in India generally play in large groups. Much of their behavior is imitative, occurs in unison, and involves close physical contact—a play style requiring high levels of cooperation. In a game called Bhatto Bhatto, children act out a script about a trip to the market, touching one another's elbows and hands as they pretend to cut and share a tasty vegetable (Roopnarine et al., 1994).

Furthermore, unlike North American preschoolers, who tend to reject reticent classmates, Chinese preschoolers are more willing to include a quiet, reserved child in play (Chen et al., 2006). In Chapter 7, we saw that until recently, collectivist values, which discourage self-

nonsocial activity Unoccupied, onlooker behavior and solitary play.

parallel play A limited form of social participation in which a child plays near other children with similar materials but does not try to influence their behavior.

associative play A form of true social interaction, in which children engage in separate activities but interact by exchanging toys and commenting on one another's behavior.

cooperative play A type of social interaction in which children orient toward a common goal, such as acting out a make-believe theme or working on a project together.

These cousins at a family birthday party in a village in central India play an intricate hand-clapping game, called "Chapte." The girls clap in unison to a jingle with eleven verses, which take them through their lifespan and conclude with their turning into ghosts. The girls end the game by mimicking a scary ghost's antics. Their play reflects the value their culture places on group harmony.

social problem solving Generating and applying strategies that prevent or resolve disagreements, leading to outcomes that are both acceptable to others and beneficial to the self.

assertion, led to positive evaluations of shyness in China (see page 267). Apparently, this benevolent attitude is still evident in the play behaviors of Chinese young children.

Cultural beliefs about the importance of play also affect early peer associations. Caregivers who view play as mere entertainment are less likely to provide props or to encourage pretend than those who value its cognitive and social benefits (Farver & Wimbarti, 1995). Preschool children of Korean-American parents, who emphasize task persistence as vital for learning, spend less time than Caucasian-American children in joint make-believe and more time unoccupied and in parallel play (Farver, Kim, & Lee, 1995).

Recall the description of children's daily lives in village and tribal cultures, described on page 337 in Chapter 9. Although Mayan parents do not promote children's play, Mayan children are socially competent (Gaskins, 2000). Perhaps Western-style sociodramatic play, with its elaborate materials and wide-ranging themes, is particularly important for social development in societies where the worlds of adults and children are distinct. It may be less crucial when children participate in adult activities from an early age.

First Friendships

As preschoolers interact, first friendships form that serve as important contexts for emotional and social development. **TAKE A MOMENT...** Jot down a description of what *friendship* means to you. You probably pictured a mutual relationship involving companionship, sharing, understanding of thoughts and feelings, and caring for and comforting one another in times of need. In addition, mature friendships endure over time and survive occasional conflicts.

Preschoolers understand something about the uniqueness of friendship. They say that a friend is someone "who likes you" and with whom you spend a lot of time playing. Yet their ideas about friendship are far from mature. Four- to 7-year-olds regard friendship as pleasurable play and sharing of toys. But friendship does not yet have a long-term, enduring quality based on mutual trust (Hartup & Abecassis, 2004; Selman, 1980). "Mark's my best friend," Sammy would declare on days when the boys got along well. But when a dispute arose, he would reverse himself: "Mark, you're not my friend!"

Nevertheless, interactions between young friends are unique. Preschoolers give twice as much reinforcement—greetings, praise, and compliance—to children they identify as friends, and they also receive more from them. Friends play together in more complex ways and are more cooperative and emotionally expressive—talking, laughing, and looking at each other more often than nonfriends do (Dunn, Cutting, & Fisher, 2002; Sebanc, 2003; Vaughn et al., 2001). And early childhood friendships offer social support: Children who begin kindergarten with friends in their class or readily make new friends adjust to school more favorably (Ladd, Birch, & Buhs, 1999; Ladd & Price, 1987). Perhaps the company of friends serves as a secure base from which to develop new relationships, enhancing children's feelings of comfort in the new classroom.

The ease with which kindergartners make new friends and are accepted by their classmates predicts cooperative participation in classroom activities and self-directed completion of learning tasks. These behaviors, in turn, are related to gains in achievement over the kindergarten year (Ladd, Birch, & Buhs, 1999; Ladd, Buhs, & Seid, 2000). Of course, kindergartners with friendly, prosocial behavioral styles make new friends easily, whereas those with weak emotional self-regulation skills and argumentative, aggressive, or peer-avoidant styles establish poor-quality relationships and make few friends. These negative social outcomes impair children's liking for school, classroom participation, and academic learning (Birch & Ladd, 1998).

The capacity to forge friendships enables kindergartners to integrate themselves into classroom environments in ways that foster both academic and social competence. In a longitudinal follow-up of more than 900 4-year-olds, children of average intelligence but with above-average social skills fared better in academic achievement in first grade than children of equal mental ability who were socially below average (Konold & Pianta, 2005). Because preschoolers' social maturity contributes to later school performance, a growing number of experts propose that readiness for kindergarten be assessed in terms of not just academic skills but also social skills, including capacity to form supportive bonds with teachers and peers, to participate actively and positively in interactions with classmates, and to behave prosocially (Ladd, Herald, & Kochel, 2006). Preschool interventions, too, should attend to these vital social prerequisites.

Social Problem Solving

As noted earlier, children, even those who are best friends, come into conflict—events that provide invaluable learning experiences in resolving disputes constructively. Preschoolers' disagreements only rarely result in hostile encounters. Although friends argue more than other peers do, they are also more likely to work out their differences through negotiation and to continue interacting (Hartup, 1999).

TAKE A MOMENT... At your next opportunity, observe preschoolers' play, noting disputes over objects ("That's mine!" "I had it first!"), entry into and control over play activities ("I'm on your team, Jerry." "No, you're not!"), and disagreements over facts, ideas, and beliefs ("I'm taller than he is." "No, you aren't!"). Children take these matters quite seriously. In Chapter 9 we noted that resolution of conflict, rather than conflict per se, promotes development. Social conflicts provide repeated occasions for **social problem solving**—generating and applying strategies that prevent or resolve disagreements, resulting in outcomes that are both acceptable to others and beneficial to the self. To engage in social problem solving, children must bring together diverse social understandings.

THE SOCIAL PROBLEM-SOLVING PROCESS ■ Nicki Crick and Kenneth Dodge (1994) organize the steps of social problem solving into the circular model shown in Figure 10.2. Notice

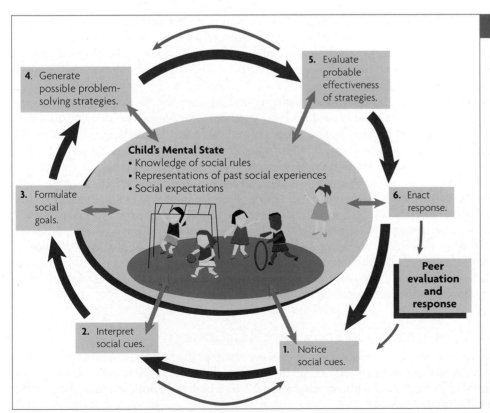

FIGURE 10.2

An information-processing model of social problem solving.

The model is circular because children often engage in several information-processing activities at once—for example, interpreting information as they notice it and continuing to consider the meaning of another's behavior while they generate and evaluate problem-solving strategies. The model also takes into account the impact of mental state on social information processing—in particular, children's knowledge of social rules, their representations of past social experiences, and their expectations for future experiences. Peer evaluations and responses to enacted strategies are also important factors in social problem solving. (Adapted from N. R. Crick & K. A. Dodge, 1994, "A Review and Reformulation of Social Information-Processing Mechanisms in Children's Social Adjustment," *Psychological Bulletin, 115,* 74–101, Figure 2 (adapted), p. 76. Copyright © 1994 by the American Psychological Association. Adapted by permission.)

Through resolving conflicts that arise during play, these children acquire social problem-solving skills, which will continue to improve over the preschool and early school years.

how this flowchart takes an *information-processing approach*, clarifying exactly what a child must do to grapple with and solve a social problem. It enables identification of processing deficits, so intervention can be tailored to meet individual needs.

Social problem solving profoundly affects peer relations. Children who get along well with agemates interpret social cues accurately, formulate goals (being helpful to peers) that enhance relationships, and have a repertoire of effective problem-solving strategies—for example, politely asking to play and requesting an explanation when they do not understand a peer's behavior. In contrast, children with peer difficulties often hold biased social expectations. Consequently, they attend selectively to social cues (such as hostile acts) and misinterpret others' behavior (view an unintentional jostle as hostile). Their social goals (satisfying an impulse, getting even with or avoiding a peer) often lead to strategies that damage relationships (Dodge, Coie, & Lynam, 2006; Youngstrom et al., 2000). They might barge into a play group without asking, use threats and physical force, or fearfully hover around peers' activities.

Children improve greatly in social problem solving over the preschool and early school years. Instead of grabbing, hitting, or insisting that another child obey, 5- to 7-year-olds tend to rely on friendly persuasion and compromise, to think of alternative strategies when an initial one does not work, and to resolve disagreements without adult intervention (Chen et al., 2001; Mayeux & Cillessen, 2003). Sometimes they suggest creating new, mutual goals, reflecting awareness that how they solve current problems will influence the future of the relationship (Yeates, Schultz, & Selman, 1991). By kindergarten, the accuracy and effectiveness of each component of social problem solving is related to socially competent behavior (Dodge et al., 1986).

TRAINING SOCIAL PROBLEM SOLVING ■ Intervening with children who have weak social problem-solving skills can enhance development in several ways. Besides improving peer relations, effective social problem solving offers children a sense of mastery in the face of stressful life events. It reduces the risk of adjustment difficulties in children from low-SES and troubled families (Goodman, Gravitt, & Kaslow, 1995).

In one widely applied social problem-solving training program, preschoolers and kindergartners discuss how to resolve social problems acted out with puppets in daily sessions over several months. In addition, teachers intervene as conflicts arise in the classroom, point out the consequences of children's behavior ("How do you think Johnny feels when you hit him?"), and help children think of alternative strategies ("Can you think of a different way to solve this problem so you both won't be mad?"). In several studies, trained children, in contrast to untrained controls, showed gains in ability to think about social problems and in teacher-rated adjustment that were still evident months after the program ended (Shure & Aberson, 2005).

Practice in enacting responses may strengthen these positive outcomes. Often preschoolers know how to solve a social problem effectively but do not apply their knowledge (Rudolph & Heller, 1997). And children who have repeatedly enacted maladaptive responses may need to rehearse alternatives to overcome their habitual behaviors and to spark more adaptive social information processing.

Parental Influences on Early Peer Relations

Children first acquire skills for interacting with peers within the family. Parents influence children's peer sociability both *directly,* through attempts to influence children's peer relations, and *indirectly,* through their child-rearing practices and play behaviors (Ladd & Pettit, 2002; Rubin et al., 2005).

DIRECT PARENTAL INFLUENCES ■ Outside preschool, child care, and kindergarten, young children depend on parents to help them establish rewarding peer associations. Preschoolers whose parents frequently arrange informal peer play activities tend to have larger peer networks and to be more socially skilled (Ladd, LeSieur, & Profilet, 1993). In providing play opportunities, parents show children how to initiate peer contacts and encourage them to be good "hosts" who consider their playmates' needs.

Parents also influence their children's peer interaction skills by offering guidance on how to act toward others. Their skillful suggestions for managing conflict, discouraging teasing, and entering a play group are associated with preschoolers' social competence and peer acceptance (Laird et al., 1994; Mize & Pettit, 1997; Parke et al., 2004).

INDIRECT PARENTAL INFLUENCES ■ Many parenting behaviors that are not directly aimed at promoting peer sociability nevertheless influence it. For example, secure attachments to parents are linked to more responsive, harmonious peer interactions; larger peer networks; and warmer, more supportive friendships during the preschool and school years (Coleman, 2003; Wood, Emmerson, & Cowan, 2004). The sensitive, emotionally expressive communication that contributes to attachment security may be responsible. In several studies, highly involved, emotionally positive parent–child conversations and play predicted prosocial behavior and positive peer relations in preschool children (Clark & Ladd, 2000; Lindsey & Mize, 2000).

Parents influence children's peer interaction skills by offering advice, guidance, and examples of how to behave. These boys receive a gentle lesson in how to greet a friend by shaking hands.

Parent–child play seems particularly effective for promoting peer interaction skills. During play, parents interact with their child on a "level playing field," much as peers do (Russell, Pettit, & Mize, 1998). Highly involved, emotionally positive, and cooperative play between parents and preschoolers is associated with more positive peer relations. And perhaps because parents play more with children of their own sex, mothers' play is more strongly linked to daughters' competence, fathers play to sons' competence (Lindsey & Mize, 2000; Pettit et al., 1998).

Some preschoolers already have great difficulty with peer relations. In Leslie's classroom, Robbie was one of them. Wherever he happened to be, comments like "Robbie ruined our block tower" and "Robbie hit me for no reason" could be heard. As we take up moral development in the next section, you will learn more about how parenting contributed to Robbie's peer problems.

Ask Yourself

Review   Among children who spend much time playing alone, what factors distinguish those who are likely to have adjustment difficulties from those who are well-adjusted and socially skilled?

Apply   Three-year-old Bart lives in the country, with no other preschoolers nearby. His parents wonder whether it is worth driving Bart into town once a week to play with his 3-year-old cousin. What advice would you give Bart's parents, and why?

Connect   Illustrate the influence of temperament on social problem solving by explaining how an impulsive child and a shy, inhibited child might respond at each social problem-solving step in Figure 10.2 on page 377.

Reflect   Think back to your first friendship. How old were you? Describe the quality of your relationship. What did your parents do, directly and indirectly, that might have influenced your earliest peer associations?

Foundations of Morality

Children's conversations and behavior provide many examples of their developing moral sense. By age 2, they use words to evaluate their own and others' actions: "I naughty. I wrote on the wall" or (after being hit by another child) "Connie not nice." They also react with distress to aggressive or potentially harmful behaviors (Kochanska, Casey, & Fukumoto, 1995). And we have seen that children of this age share toys, help others, and cooperate in games—early indicators of considerate, responsible, prosocial attitudes.

Adults everywhere take note of this budding capacity to distinguish right from wrong and to accommodate the needs of others. Some cultures have special terms for it. The Utku Indians of Hudson Bay say the child develops *ihuma* (reason). The Fijians believe that *vakayalo* (sense) appears. In response, parents hold children more responsible for their behavior (Dunn, 2005). By the end of early childhood, children can state many moral rules: "Don't take someone's things without asking." "Tell the truth!" In addition, they argue over matters of justice: "You sat there last time, so it's my turn." "It's not fair. He got more!"

All theories of moral development recognize that conscience begins to take shape in early childhood. And most agree that at first, the child's morality is *externally controlled* by adults. Gradually, it becomes regulated by *inner standards*. That is, truly moral individuals do not do the right thing just to conform to others' expectations. Rather, they have developed compassionate concerns and principles of good conduct, which they follow in many situations.

Each major theory of development emphasizes a different aspect of morality. Psychoanalytic theory stresses the *emotional side* of conscience development—in particular, identification and guilt as motivators of good conduct. Social learning theory focuses on how *moral behavior* is learned through reinforcement and modeling. Finally, the cognitive-developmental perspective emphasizes *thinking*—children's ability to reason about justice and fairness.

The Psychoanalytic Perspective

Recall that according to Freud, young children form a *superego,* or conscience, by *identifying* with the same-sex parent, whose moral standards they adopt. Children obey the superego to avoid *guilt,* a painful emotion that arises each time they are tempted to misbehave. Moral development, Freud believed, is largely complete by 5 to 6 years of age.

Today, most researchers disagree with Freud's view of conscience development. In his theory (see page 14), fear of punishment and loss of parental love motivate conscience formation and moral behavior (Tellings, 1999). Yet children whose parents frequently use threats, commands, or physical force tend to violate standards often and feel little guilt (Kochanska et al., 2002). And if a parent withdraws love—for example, refuses to speak to or states a dislike for the child—children often respond with high levels of self-blame, thinking, "I'm no good," or "Nobody loves me." Eventually, to protect themselves from overwhelming feelings of guilt, these children may deny the emotion and, as a result, also develop a weak conscience (Kochanska, 1991; Zahn-Waxler et al., 1990).

This teacher uses inductive discipline to explain to a child the impact of her transgression on others. Induction supports conscience development by indicating how the child should behave, encouraging empathy and sympathetic concern, and clarifying the reasons behind adult expectations.

THE POWER OF INDUCTIVE DISCIPLINE ■ In contrast, conscience formation is promoted by a type of discipline called **induction,** in which an adult helps make the child aware of feelings by pointing out the effects of the child's misbehavior on others, noting especially their distress and making clear that the child caused it. For example, the parent might say, "If you keep pushing him, he'll fall down and cry," or, "She's crying because you won't give back her doll" (Hoffman, 2000). When generally warm parents provide explanations that match the child's capacity to understand, while firmly insisting that the child listen and comply, induction is effective as early as age 2. Preschoolers whose parents use it are more likely to refrain from wrongdoing, confess and repair damages after misdeeds, and display prosocial behavior (Kerr et al., 2004; Zahn-Waxler, Radke-Yarrow, & King, 1979).

The success of induction may lie in its power to motivate children's active commitment to moral standards, in the following ways:

- Induction gives children information about how to behave that they can use in future situations.
- By emphasizing the impact of the child's actions on others, induction encourages empathy and sympathetic concern, which motivate prosocial behavior (Krevans & Gibbs, 1996).
- Giving children reasons for changing their behavior encourages them to adopt moral standards because those standards make sense.
- Children who consistently experience induction may form a *script* for the negative emotional consequences of harming others: Child causes harm, inductive message points out harm, child feels empathy for victim, child makes amends (Hoffman, 2000). The script deters future transgressions.

In contrast, discipline that relies too heavily on threats of punishment or love withdrawal makes children so anxious and frightened that they cannot think clearly enough to figure out what they should do. As a result, these practices do not get children to internalize moral rules and—as noted earlier—also interfere with empathy and prosocial responding (Eisenberg, Fabes, Spinrad, 2006). Nevertheless, warnings, disapproval, and commands are sometimes necessary to get an unruly child to listen to an inductive message.

THE CHILD'S CONTRIBUTION ■ Although good discipline is crucial, children's characteristics also affect the success of parenting techniques. Twin studies suggest a modest genetic contribution to empathy and prosocial behavior (Knafo & Plomin, 2006; Zahn-Waxler et al., 2001). Children who are more empathic, kind, and considerate require less power assertion and are more responsive to induction.

Temperament is also influential. Mild, patient tactics—requests, suggestions, and explanations—are sufficient to prompt guilt reactions and conscience development in anxious, fearful preschoolers (Kochanska et al., 2002). But with fearless, impulsive children, gentle discipline has little impact. Power assertion also works poorly, undermining the child's capacity for impulse control (Kochanska & Knaack, 2003). Instead, parents of impulsive children can foster conscience development by ensuring a secure attachment relationship and combining firm correction of misbehavior with induction (Fowles & Kochanska, 2000). When children are so low in anxiety that parental disapproval causes them little discomfort, a close parent–child bond provides an alternative foundation for morality. It motivates children to listen to parents as a means of preserving an affectionate, supportive relationship.

In sum, to foster early moral development, parents must tailor their disciplinary strategies to their child's personality. Does this remind you of *goodness of fit,* discussed in Chapter 7? Return to page 266 to review this idea.

THE ROLE OF GUILT ■ Although little support exists for Freudian ideas about conscience development, Freud was correct that guilt is an important motivator of moral action. By the end of toddlerhood, guilt reactions are evident, and preschoolers' assertions reveal that they have internalized the parent's moral voice: "Didn't you hear my mommy? We'd better not play with these toys" (Thompson, 2006).

Inducing *empathy-based* guilt (expressions of personal responsibility and regret, such as "I'm sorry I hurt him") by explaining that the child is causing someone distress and has disappointed the parent is a means of influencing children without using coercion. Guilt reactions are associated with stopping harmful actions, repairing damage caused by misdeeds, and engaging in future prosocial behavior (Baumeister, 1998). At the same time, parents must help

© MIKE/ZEFA/CORBIS

When children are low in anxiety, a secure attachment relationship motivates conscience development. This boy wants to follow parental rules to preserve an affectionate, co-operative relationship with his father.

induction A type of discipline in which an adult helps make the child aware of feelings by pointing out the effects of the child's misbehavior on others.

children deal with guilt feelings constructively—by guiding them to make up for immoral behavior rather than minimizing or excusing it (Bybee, Merisca, & Velasco, 1998).

But contrary to what Freud believed, guilt is not the only force that compels us to act morally. Nor is moral development complete by the end of early childhood. Rather, it is a gradual process extending into adulthood.

Social Learning Theory

According to social learning theory, morality does not have a unique course of development. Rather, moral behavior is acquired just like any other set of responses: through reinforcement and modeling.

IMPORTANCE OF MODELING ■ *Operant conditioning*—reinforcement for good behavior, in the form of approval, affection, and other rewards—is not enough for children to acquire moral responses. For a behavior to be reinforced, it must first occur spontaneously. Yet many prosocial acts—sharing, helping, comforting an unhappy playmate—occur so rarely at first that reinforcement cannot explain their rapid development in early childhood. Rather, social learning theorists believe that children learn to behave morally largely through *modeling*—by observing and imitating people who demonstrate appropriate behavior (Bandura, 1977; Grusec, 1988). Once children acquire a moral response, such as sharing or telling the truth, reinforcement in the form of praise for the act ("That was a very nice thing to do") and for the child's character ("You're a very kind and considerate boy") increases its frequency (Mills & Grusec, 1989).

Many studies show that having helpful or generous models increases young children's prosocial responses. And certain characteristics of the model affect children's willingness to imitate:

■ *Warmth and responsiveness.* Preschoolers are more likely to copy the prosocial actions of an adult who is warm and responsive than those of a cold, distant adult (Yarrow, Scott, & Waxler, 1973). Warmth seems to make children more attentive and receptive to the model and is itself an example of a prosocial response.

■ *Competence and power.* Children admire and therefore tend to imitate competent, powerful models—especially older peers and adults (Bandura, 1977).

■ *Consistency between assertions and behavior.* When models say one thing and do another—for example, announce that "it's important to help others" but rarely engage in helpful acts—children generally choose the most lenient standard of behavior that adults demonstrate (Mischel & Liebert, 1966).

Models are most influential in the early years. In one study, toddlers' eager, willing imitation of their mothers' behavior predicted moral conduct (not cheating in a game) and guilt following transgressions at age 3 (Forman, Aksan, & Kochanska, 2004). At the end of the preschool years, children who have had consistent exposure to caring adults tend to behave prosocially whether or not a model is present: They have internalized prosocial rules from repeated observations and encouragement by others (Mussen & Eisenberg-Berg, 1977).

EFFECTS OF PUNISHMENT ■ Many parents know that yelling at, slapping, and spanking children are ineffective disciplinary tactics. A sharp reprimand or physical force to restrain or move a child is justified when immediate obedience is necessary—for example, when a 3-year-old is about to run into the street. In fact, parents are most likely to use forceful methods under these conditions. But to foster long-term goals, such as acting kindly toward others, they tend to rely on warmth and reasoning (Kuczynski, 1984). And in response to serious transgressions, such as lying or stealing, they often combine power assertion with reasoning (Grusec & Goodnow, 1994).

When used frequently, however, punishment promotes only immediate compliance, not lasting changes in behavior. For example, Robbie's parents often punished by hitting, shouting, and criticizing. As soon as they were out of sight, Robbie usually engaged in the unacceptable behavior again. Many studies confirm that the more physical punishment children experience, the more likely they are to develop serious, lasting mental health problems. These include weak internalization of moral rules; depression, aggression, antisocial behavior, and poor academic performance in childhood and adolescence; and depression, alcohol abuse, criminality, and partner and child abuse in adulthood (Afifi et al., 2006; Gershoff, 2002a; Kochanska, Aksan, & Nichols, 2003; Lynch et al., 2006).

Harsh punishment has several undesirable side effects:

■ Parents often spank in response to children's aggression (Holden, Coleman, & Schmidt, 1995). Yet the punishment itself models aggression!

■ Harshly treated children react with anger, resentment, and a chronic sense of being personally threatened, which prompts a focus on the self's distress rather than a sympathetic orientation to others' needs.

■ Children who are frequently punished learn to avoid the punishing adult, who, as a result, has little opportunity to teach desirable behaviors.

■ By stopping children's misbehavior temporarily, harsh punishment gives adults immediate relief, reinforcing them for using coercive discipline. For this reason, a punitive adult is likely to punish with greater frequency over time, a course of action that can spiral into serious abuse.

■ Adults whose parents engaged in *corporal punishment*—the use of physical force to inflict pain but not injury—are more accepting of such discipline (Bower-Russa, Knutson, & Winebarger, 2001; Deater-Deckard et al., 2003). In this way, use of physical punishment may transfer to the next generation.

Parents with mental health problems—who are emotionally reactive, depressed, or aggressive—are more likely to be punitive and also to have hard-to-manage children, whose disobedience evokes more parental harshness (Belsky & Hsieh, 1998; Clark, Kochanska, & Ready, 2000; Kochanska, Aksan, & Nichols, 2003). These parent–child similarities suggest that heredity contributes to the link between punitive discipline and children's adjustment difficulties. But heredity is not a complete explanation. **TAKE A MOMENT...** Return to page 88 in Chapter 2 to review findings indicating that good parenting can shield children genetically at risk for aggression and antisocial activity from developing those behaviors.

Other research indicates that parental harshness predicts emotional and behavior problems in children of diverse temperaments (O'Connor et al., 1998). In view of these outcomes, the widespread use of corporal punishment by North American parents is cause for concern. A survey of a nationally representative sample of U.S. households revealed that although corporal punishment increases from infancy to age 5 and then declines, it is high at all ages (see Figure 10.3) (Straus & Stewart, 1999). And depending on the survey, 40 percent of Canadian parents of infants, and 50 to 70 percent of Canadian parents of preschoolers, admit to having disciplined with hitting or spanking (Durrant, Broberg, & Rose-Krasnor, 2000; Oldershaw, 2002). Furthermore, about one-fourth of physically punishing U.S. parents report having used a hard object, such as a brush or a belt (Gershoff, 2002b).

A prevailing North American belief is that corporal punishment, if implemented by caring parents, is harmless, perhaps even beneficial. But as the Cultural Influences box on page 384 reveals, this assumption is valid only under conditions of limited use in certain social contexts.

ALTERNATIVES TO HARSH PUNISHMENT ■ Alternatives to criticism, slaps, and spankings can reduce the side effects

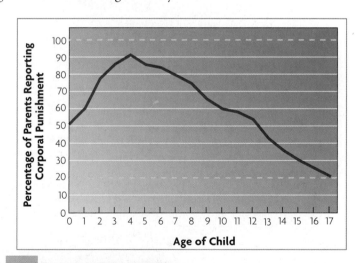

FIGURE 10.3

Prevalence of corporal punishment by child's age. Estimates are based on the percentage of parents in a nationally representative U.S. sample of nearly 1,000 reporting one or more instances of spanking, slapping, pinching, shaking, or hitting with a hard object in the past year. Physical punishment increases sharply during early childhood and then declines, but it is high at all ages. (From M. A. Straus & J. H. Stewart, 1999, "Corporal Punishment by American Parents: National Data on Prevalence, Chronicity, Severity, and Duration in Relation to Child and Family Characteristics," *Clinical Child and Family Psychology Review, 2,* p. 59. Adapted by permission of Kluwer Academic/Plenum Publishers and the author.)

Cultural Influences

Ethnic Differences in the Consequences of Physical Punishment

In an African-American community, six elders, all of whom had volunteered to serve as mentors for parents facing child-rearing challenges, met to discuss parenting issues at a social service agency. Their attitudes toward discipline were strikingly different from those of the white social workers who had brought them together. Each elder argued that successful child rearing required the use of appropriate physical tactics. At the same time, they voiced strong disapproval of screaming or cursing at children, calling such out-of-control parental behavior "abusive." Ruth, the oldest and most respected member of the group, characterized good parenting as a complex combination of warmth, teaching, talking nicely, and disciplining physically. She related how an older neighbor advised her to handle her own children when she was a young parent:

> She said to me says, don't scream . . . you talk to them real nice and sweet and when they do something ugly . . . she say you get a nice little switch and you won't have any trouble with them and from that day that's the way I raised 'em.

The others chimed in, emphasizing *mild* punishment. "Just tap 'em a little bit." "When you do things like [get too harsh] you're wronging yourself" (Mosby et al., 1999, pp. 511–512).

Use of physical punishment is highest among low-SES ethnic minority parents, who are more likely than middle-SES white parents to advocate slaps and spankings (Pinderhughes et al., 2000; Straus & Stewart, 1999). And although corporal punishment is linked to a wide array of negative child outcomes, exceptions do exist.

In one longitudinal study, researchers followed several hundred families for 12 years, collecting information from mothers on disciplinary strategies in early and middle childhood and from both mothers and their children on youth problem behaviors in adolescence. Even after many child and family characteristics were controlled, the findings were striking: In Caucasian-American families, physical punishment was positively associated with adolescent aggression and antisocial behavior. In African-American families, by contrast, the more mothers had disciplined physically in childhood, the less their teenagers displayed angry, acting-out behavior and got in trouble at school and with the police (Lansford et al., 2004).

African-American and Caucasian-American parents seem to mete out physical punishment differently. In black families, such discipline is culturally approved, generally mild, delivered in a context of parental warmth, and aimed at helping children become responsible adults. White parents, in contrast, typically consider physical punishment to be wrong, so when they resort to it, they are usually highly agitated and rejecting of the child (Dodge, McLoyd, & Lansford, 2006). As a result, black children may view spanking as a practice carried out with their best interests in mind, whereas white children may regard it as an "act of personal aggression" (Gunnoe & Mariner, 1997, p. 768).

In support of this view, when several thousand ethnically diverse children were followed from the preschool through the early school years, spanking was associated with a rise in behavior problems if parents were cold and rejecting but not if they were warm and supportive (McLoyd & Smith, 2002). These findings are not an endorsement of physical punishment. Other forms of discipline, including time out, withdrawal of privileges, and the positive strategies listed on page 385, are far more effective. But it is noteworthy that the meaning and impact of physical discipline varies sharply with cultural context.

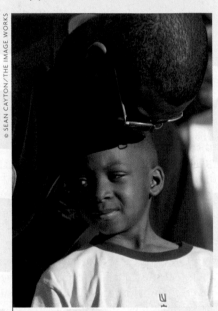

© SEAN CAYTON/THE IMAGE WORKS

To discipline children, many African-American parents use mild physical punishment. Because the practice is culturally approved and delivered in an overall context of parental warmth, African-American children may view spanking as something that is done with their best interests in mind, rather than as an act of personal aggression.

---

of punishment. A technique called **time out** involves removing children from the immediate setting—for example, by sending them to their rooms—until they are ready to act appropriately. When a child is out of control, a few minutes in time out can be enough to change behavior while also giving angry parents a cooling-off period. Another approach is *withdrawal of privileges*, such as playing outside or watching a favorite TV program. Like time out, removing privileges allows parents to avoid using harsh techniques that can easily intensify into violence.

When parents do decide to use punishment, they can increase its effectiveness in three ways:

■ *Consistency.* Permitting children to act inappropriately on some occasions but scolding them on others confuses children, and the unacceptable act persists (Acker & O'Leary, 1996).

time out A form of mild punishment in which children are removed from the immediate setting until they are ready to act appropriately.

Applying What We Know

Using Positive Discipline

STRATEGY	EXPLANATION
Use transgressions as opportunities to teach.	When a child engages in harmful or unsafe behavior, use induction, which motivates children to make amends and behave prosocially.
Reduce opportunities for misbehavior.	On a long car trip, bring back-seat activities that relieve children's restlessness. At the supermarket, converse with children and permit them to assist with shopping. As a result, children learn to occupy themselves constructively when options are limited.
Provide reasons for rules.	When children appreciate that rules are fair to all concerned, not arbitrary, they strive to follow the rules because they are reasonable and rational.
Arrange for children to participate in family routines and duties.	By joining with adults in preparing a meal, washing dishes, or raking leaves, children develop a sense of responsible participation in family and community life and acquire many practical skills.
When children are obstinate, try compromising and problem solving.	When a child refuses to obey, express understanding of the child's feelings ("I know it's not fun to clean up"), suggest a compromise ("You put those away, I'll take care of these"), and help the child think of ways to avoid the problem in the future. Responding firmly but kindly and respectfully increases the likelihood of willing cooperation.
Encourage mature behavior.	Express confidence in children's capacity to learn and appreciation for effort and cooperation, as in "You gave that your best!" "Thanks for helping!" Adult encouragement fosters pride and satisfaction in succeeding, thereby inspiring children to improve further.
Be sensitive to children's physical and emotional resources.	When children are tired, ill, or bored, they are likely to engage in attention-getting, disorganized, or otherwise improper behavior as a reaction to discomfort. In these instances, meeting the child's needs makes more sense than disciplining.

Sources: Berk, 2001a; Nelson, 1996.

■ *A warm parent–child relationship.* Children of involved, caring parents find the interruption in parental affection that accompanies punishment especially unpleasant. They want to regain parental warmth and approval as quickly as possible.

■ *Explanations.* Explanations help children recall the misdeed and relate it to expectations for future behavior. Consequently, providing reasons for mild punishment (such as time out) leads to far greater reduction in misbehavior than using punishment alone (Larzelere et al., 1996).

POSITIVE DISCIPLINE ■ The most effective forms of discipline encourage good conduct—by building a mutually respectful bond with the child, letting her know ahead of time how to act, and praising mature behavior (Zahn-Waxler & Robinson, 1995). When sensitivity, cooperation, and shared positive emotion are evident in joint activities between mothers and their toddlers or preschoolers, children show more favorable conscience development—expressing empathy after transgressions, behaving responsibly, playing fairly in games, and considering others' welfare (Kochanska, Forman, & Coy, 1999; Kochanska et al., 2005). Parent–child closeness leads children to heed parental demands because children feel a sense of commitment to the relationship. Note that this social-learning emphasis on positive emotion as a foundation for moral development is also consistent with psychoanalytic ideas.

Consult Applying What We Know above for ways to discipline positively. Parents who use these strategies focus on long-term social and life skills—cooperation, problem solving, and consideration for others. As a result, they greatly reduce the need for punishment.

The Cognitive-Developmental Perspective

The psychoanalytic and behaviorist approaches to morality focus on how children acquire ready-made standards of good conduct from adults. In contrast, the cognitive-developmental perspective regards children as *active thinkers* about social rules. As early as the preschool

Parents who engage in positive discipline encourage good conduct and reduce opportunities for misbehavior. This mother's calm, involved approach helps her child behave appropriately during a long wait at the airport.

years, children make moral judgments, deciding what is right or wrong on the basis of concepts they construct about justice and fairness (Gibbs, 2003; Piaget, 1932/1965; Turiel, 2006).

PRESCHOOLERS' MORAL UNDERSTANDING ■ Young children have some well-developed ideas about morality. As long as researchers emphasize people's intentions, 3-year-olds say that a person with bad intentions—someone who deliberately frightens, embarrasses, or otherwise hurts another—is more deserving of punishment than a well-intentioned person (Helwig, Zelazo, & Wilson, 2001; Jones & Thompson, 2001). Around age 4, children can tell the difference between truthfulness and lying. They approve of telling the truth and disapprove of lying, even when a lie remains undetected (Bussey, 1992).

Furthermore, preschoolers in diverse cultures distinguish **moral imperatives,** which protect people's rights and welfare, from two other types of action: **social conventions,** customs determined solely by consensus, such as table manners; and **matters of personal choice,** such as choice of friends and color of clothing, which do not violate rights and are up to the individual (Ardila-Rey & Killen, 2001; Nucci, 1996; Smetana, 2006). Interviews with 3- and 4-year-olds reveal that they consider moral violations (stealing an apple) as more wrong than violations of social conventions (eating ice cream with your fingers). They also say that moral violations would still be wrong even if an adult did not see them and no rules existed to prohibit them, because they harm others. And preschoolers' concern with personal choice, conveyed through statements like "I'm gonna wear *this* shirt," serves as the springboard for moral concepts of individual rights, which will expand greatly in middle childhood and adolescence (Killen & Smetana, 1999).

Within the moral domain, however, preschool and young school-age children tend to reason rigidly, making judgments based on salient features and consequences while neglecting other important information. For example, they are more likely than older children to claim that stealing and lying are always wrong, even when a person has a morally sound reason for engaging in these acts (Lourenco, 2003). And they view inflicting physical damage (breaking a peer's toy) as a more serious transgression than treating others unfairly (not sharing) (Nucci, 2002). An appreciation of fairness as equality and equal treatment must wait for greater cognitive maturity.

Still, preschoolers' ability to distinguish moral imperatives from social conventions is impressive. How do they do so? According to cognitive-developmental theorists, they *actively make sense* of their experiences. They observe that after a moral offense, peers respond with strong negative emotion, describe their own injury or loss, tell another child to stop, or retaliate (Arsenio & Fleiss, 1996). And an adult who intervenes is likely to call attention to the rights and feelings of the victim. In contrast, peers react less intensely to violations of social convention. And in these situations, adults tend to demand obedience without explanation or point to the importance of keeping order.

SOCIAL EXPERIENCE AND MORAL UNDERSTANDING ■ Although cognition and language support preschoolers' moral understanding, social experiences are vital. Disputes with siblings and peers over rights, possessions, and property allow preschoolers to work out their first ideas about justice and fairness (Killen & Nucci, 1995). Children also learn by observing the way adults handle rule violations and discuss moral issues. Children who are advanced in moral thinking tend to have parents who adapt their communications about fighting, honesty, and ownership to what their children can understand, tell stories with moral implications, encourage prosocial behavior, and gently stimulate the child to think further, without being hostile or critical (Janssens & Deković, 1997; Walker & Taylor, 1991a).

Preschoolers who verbally and physically assault others, often with little or no provocation, are already delayed in moral reasoning (Helwig & Turiel, 2004; Sanderson & Siegal, 1988). Without special help, such children show long-term disruptions in moral development.

The Other Side of Morality: Development of Aggression

Beginning in late infancy, all children display aggression from time to time, and as opportunities to interact with siblings and peers increase, aggressive outbursts occur more often (Tremblay, 2002). During the early preschool years, two general types of aggression emerge.

moral imperatives Standards that protect people's rights and welfare.

social conventions Customs such as table manners that are determined by consensus within a society.

matters of personal choice Concerns that do not violate rights and are up to each individual, such as choice of friends or color of clothing.

The most common is **instrumental aggression,** in which children want an object, privilege, or space and, in trying to get it, push, shout at, or otherwise attack a person who is in the way. The other type, **hostile aggression,** is meant to hurt another person.

Hostile aggression comes in at least three varieties:

- **Physical aggression** harms others through physical injury—pushing, hitting, kicking, or punching others, or destroying another's property.
- **Verbal aggression** harms others through threats of physical aggression, name-calling, or hostile teasing.
- **Relational aggression** damages another's peer relationships through social exclusion, malicious gossip, or friendship manipulation ("Go away, I'm not your friend!").

Although verbal aggression is always direct, physical and relational aggression can be either *direct* or *indirect.* For example, hitting injures a person directly, whereas destroying property indirectly inflicts physical harm. Similarly, saying, "Do what I say, or I won't be your friend," conveys relational aggression directly, while spreading rumors, refusing to talk to a peer, or manipulating friendship by saying behind someone's back, "Don't play with her; she's a nerd," does so indirectly.

In early childhood, verbal aggression gradually replaces physical aggression as language develops and adults and peers react negatively and strongly to physical attacks (Tremblay et al., 1999). And instrumental aggression declines as preschoolers' improved capacity to delay gratification enables them to avoid grabbing others' possessions. But hostile aggression rises over early and middle childhood (Tremblay, 2000). Older preschoolers are better able to recognize malicious intentions and, as a result, more often retaliate in hostile ways.

Beginning in the preschool years and throughout childhood and adolescence, boys in many cultures are more physically aggressive than girls (Broidy et al., 2003; Dodge, Coie, & Lynam, 2006). This sex difference is due in part to biology. Early temperamental traits on which boys and girls differ—specifically, irritability, fearlessness, and low effortful control—are moderately related to later childhood aggression (Eisenberg et al., 2001; Shaw et al., 2003). Male sex hormones, or androgens, are also linked to aggressive behavior, but the association is weak. Androgens (as we will see shortly) contribute to boys' greater physical activity, which may increase their opportunities for physically aggressive encounters (Book, Starzyk, & Quinsey, 2001; Collaer & Hines, 1995). At the same time, gender-role conformity is also important. As soon as 2-year-olds become dimly aware of gender stereotypes—that males and females are expected to behave differently—physical aggression drops off more sharply for girls than for boys (Fagot & Leinbach, 1989).

Although girls have a reputation for being verbally and relationally more aggressive than boys, in most studies the sex difference is small (Crick et al., 2004, 2006; Underwood, 2003). Beginning in the preschool years, girls concentrate most of their aggressive acts in the relational category. Boys inflict harm in more variable ways and, therefore, display overall rates of aggression that are much higher than girls'.

At the same time, girls more often use indirect relational tactics that—by disrupting intimate bonds especially important to girls—can be particularly mean. In contrast to physical attacks, which are usually brief, acts of indirect relational aggression may extend for hours, weeks, or even months (Nelson, Robinson, & Hart, 2005; Underwood, 2003). In one instance, a 6-year-old girl formed a "pretty-girls club" and—for nearly an entire school year—convinced its members to exclude several classmates by saying they were "dirty and smelly."

An occasional aggressive exchange between preschoolers is normal. As we have seen, children sometimes assert their sense of self through these encounters, which become important learning experiences as adults intervene and teach social problem solving (Vaughn et al., 2003). But some children—especially those who are emotionally negative, impulsive, and disobedient—are at risk for lasting difficulties. In longitudinal research conducted in Canada, New Zealand, and the United States, boys who were highly aggressive in kindergarten were

This preschool boy displays instrumental aggression as he grabs his classmate's toy. Instrumental aggression declines with age as children learn to compromise and share, and as their capacity to delay gratification improves.

instrumental aggression Aggression aimed at obtaining an object, privilege, or space with no deliberate intent to harm another person.

hostile aggression Aggression intended to harm another person.

physical aggression A form of hostile aggression that harms others through physical injury to individuals or their property.

verbal aggression A form of hostile aggression that harms others through threats of physical aggression, name-calling, or hostile teasing.

relational aggression A form of hostile aggression that damages another's peer relationships through social exclusion, malicious gossip, or friendship manipulation.

far more likely to engage in violent delinquency as adolescents (Brame, Nagin, & Tremblay, 2001; Nagin & Tremblay, 1999). A study of Canadian girls revealed a similar link between disruptive, disobedient behavior in childhood and conduct problems in adolescence (Coté et al., 2001). And for both boys and girls, childhood relational aggression predicts later internalizing and externalizing difficulties, including loneliness, anxiety, depression, and antisocial activity (Crick, 1996; Crick, Ostrov, & Werner, 2006). These negative outcomes, however, depend on child-rearing conditions.

THE FAMILY AS TRAINING GROUND FOR AGGRESSIVE BEHAVIOR ■ "I can't control him; he's impossible," Robbie's mother, Nadine, complained to Leslie one day. When Leslie asked if Robbie might be troubled by something happening at home, she discovered that his parents fought constantly. Their conflict led to high levels of family stress and a "spillover" of hostility into child rearing. The same parenting behaviors that undermine moral internalization—love withdrawal, power assertion, physical punishment, negative comments and emotions, and inconsistent discipline—are linked to aggression in diverse cultures, with most of these practices predicting both physical and relational forms (Bradford et al., 2003; Capaldi et al., 2002; Nelson et al., 1998, 2006; Rubin et al., 2003; Yang et al., 2003).

In families like Robbie's, parental anger and punitiveness quickly create a conflict-ridden family atmosphere and an "out-of-control" child. The pattern begins with forceful discipline, which occurs more often with stressful life experiences (such as economic hardship or an unhappy marriage), a parent with an unstable personality, or a temperamentally difficult child (Coie, Dodge, & Lynam, 2006). Typically, the parent threatens, criticizes, and punishes, and the child whines, yells, and refuses until the parent "gives in." At the end of each exchange, both parent and child get relief from stopping the unpleasant behavior of the other, so the behaviors repeat and escalate.

As these cycles become more frequent, they generate anxiety and irritability among other family members, who soon join in the hostile interactions. Compared with siblings in typical families, preschool siblings who have critical, punitive parents are more aggressive toward one another. Physically, verbally, and relationally destructive sibling conflict, in turn, quickly spreads to peer relationships (Garcia et al., 2000; Ostrov, Crick, & Stauffacher, 2006).

Boys are more likely than girls to be targets of harsh, inconsistent discipline because they are more active and impulsive and therefore harder to control. Children who are products of these family processes soon view the world from an antagonistic perspective, seeing hostile intent where it does not exist (Lochman & Dodge, 1998; Orbio de Castro et al., 2002). As a result, they make many unprovoked attacks and soon conclude that aggression "works" as a way of controlling others (Egan, Monson, & Perry, 1998).

Highly aggressive children tend to be rejected by peers, to fail in school, and (by adolescence) to seek out deviant peers. Together, these factors contribute to the long-term stability of aggression, evident in violence and other conduct problems. We will consider this life-course path of antisocial activity in Chapter 16.

VIOLENT MEDIA AND AGGRESSION ■ In the United States, 57 percent of American TV programs between 6 A.M. and 11 P.M. contain violent scenes, often in the form of repeated aggressive acts that go unpunished. Most TV violence does not show victims experiencing any serious harm, and few programs condemn violence or depict other ways of solving problems. Violent content is 9 percent above average in children's programming, and cartoons are the most violent (Center for Communication and Social Policy, 1998). Although Canadian broadcasters follow a code that sharply restricts televised violence, Canadians devote two-thirds of their viewing time to American channels (Statistics Canada, 2005g).

Children are especially likely to be influenced by television because, before age 8, they fail to understand a great deal of what they see on TV. For example, 2- and 3-year-olds say that people could reach into a TV and pick up the objects shown on the screen (Flavell et al., 1990). By age 4, children realize that TV is symbolic but still find it hard to separate true-to-life from fantasized television content. Not until age 7 do children fully grasp the unreality of TV fiction—that characters are following a

© MYRLEEN FERGUSON CATE/PHOTOEDIT

Parents can foster a positive approach to TV and computer use through active participation in young children's media exposure. This parent's warmth, involvement, and supervision encourage her child to enjoy educational media experiences.

script and do not retain their roles in real life (Wright et al., 1994). And because preschoolers and young school-age children have difficulty connecting separate scenes into a meaningful story line, they do not relate a TV character's actions to motives or consequences (Collins, 1983). A villain who gets what he wants by punching, shooting, and killing may not be a "bad guy" to a preschooler—even when the character is brought to justice in the end. These misunderstandings increase children's willingness to uncritically accept and imitate what they see on TV.

Reviewers of thousands of studies have concluded that TV violence increases the likelihood of hostile thoughts and emotions and of verbally, physically, and relationally aggressive behavior (Anderson et al., 2003; Comstock & Scharrer, 2006; Ostrov, Gentile, & Crick, 2006). And a growing number of studies show that playing violent video and computer games has similar effects (Anderson et al., 2003). The case is strengthened by the fact that research using a wide variety of research designs, methods, and participants yields similar findings.

Violent programming not only creates short-term difficulties in parent and peer relations but also has lasting, negative consequences. In several longitudinal studies, time spent watching TV in childhood and adolescence predicted aggressive behavior in early adulthood, after other factors linked to TV viewing (such as prior child and parent aggression, IQ, parental education, family income, and neighborhood crime) were controlled (see Figure 10.4) (Huesmann, 1986; Huesmann et al., 2003; Johnson et al., 2002). Aggressive children and adolescents have a greater appetite for violent TV and computer games. And boys devote more time to violent media than girls, in part because these TV shows and games cater to male audiences in their themes of conquest and adventure and their use of males as lead characters. But violent TV sparks hostile thoughts and behavior even in nonaggressive children; its impact is simply less intense (Bushman & Huesmann, 2001).

Furthermore, media violence "hardens" children to aggression, making them more willing to tolerate it in others. Viewers quickly habituate, responding with reduced arousal to real-world instances and tolerating more aggression in others (Anderson et al., 2003). Heavy viewers believe that there is much more violence in society than there actually is—an effect that is especially strong for children who perceive television violence to be relevant to their own lives (Donnerstein, Slaby, & Eron, 1994). As these responses indicate, exposure to violent media images modifies children's attitudes toward social reality so they increasingly match media images.

The ease with which television and computer games can manipulate the beliefs and behavior of children has resulted in strong public pressure to improve media content. In the United States, the First Amendment right to free speech has hampered efforts to regulate TV broadcasting. Instead, all programs must be rated for violent and sexual content, and all new TV sets are required to contain the V-chip, which allows parents to block undesired material.

Canada also mandates both the V-chip and program ratings. In addition, Canada's broadcasting code bans from children's shows realistic scenes of violence that minimize consequences and cartoons in which violence is the central theme. Further, violent programming intended for adults cannot be shown on Canadian channels before 9 P.M. (Canadian Broadcast Standards Council, 2003). Still, Canadian children have access to violent TV fare on U.S. channels.

At present, it is largely up to parents to regulate their children's exposure to media violence and other inappropriate content. Besides TV and computer games, the Internet poses risks: Some children begin accessing websites

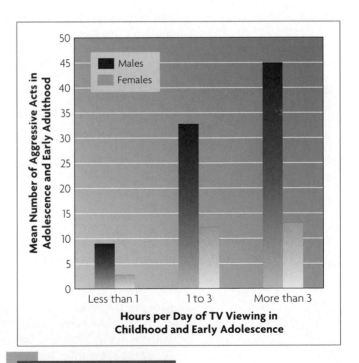

FIGURE 10.4

Relationship of television viewing in childhood and early adolescence to aggressive acts in adolescence and early adulthood. Interviews with more than 700 parents and youths revealed that the more TV watched in childhood and early adolescence, the greater the annual number of aggressive acts committed by the young person, as reported in follow-up interviews at ages 16 and 22. (Adapted from Johnson et al., 2002.)

Applying What We Know

Regulating TV and Computer Use

STRATEGY	EXPLANATION
Limit TV viewing and computer use.	Provide clear rules that limit what children can view—for example, an hour a day and only certain programs—and stick to the rules. Avoid using the TV or the computer as a baby-sitter. Do not place a TV or computer in the child's bedroom; doing so increases use by as much as 40 minutes per day among school-age children.
Refrain from using TV or computer time to reward or punish children.	When TV or computer access is used to reward or punish children, they become increasingly attracted to it.
Encourage child-appropriate TV and computer experiences.	Children who engage in TV and computer activities that are educational, prosocial, and age-appropriate gain in cognitive and social skills.
View TV with children, helping them understand what they see.	When adults express disapproval of on-screen behavior, raise questions about its realism, and encourage children to discuss it, they teach children to evaluate TV content rather than accepting it uncritically.
Link televised content to everyday learning experiences.	Building on TV programs in constructive ways enhances learning by encouraging children into active engagement with their surroundings. For example, a program on animals might spark a trip to the zoo, a visit to the library for books about animals, or new ways of observing and caring for the family pet.
Model good TV and computer practices.	Parental viewing patterns influence children's viewing patterns. Avoid excess television viewing, and exposure to violent media content, yourself.
Use a warm, rational approach to child rearing.	Children of warm parents who make reasonable demands for mature behavior prefer TV and computer experiences with educational and prosocial content and are less attracted to violent media fare.

Sources: Wiecha et al., 2001; Winn, 2002.

without parental supervision as early as age 4 (Varnhagen, 2007). As with TV and the V-chip, children's Internet access can be controlled with the use of filtering programs. But as children get older, they may simply go to other homes to engage in media activities forbidden by their own parents. Applying What We Know above lists strategies parents can use to protect children from undesirable TV and computer fare.

HELPING CHILDREN AND PARENTS CONTROL AGGRESSION ■ Treatment for aggressive children must begin early, before their antisocial behavior becomes well-practiced and difficult to change. Breaking the cycle of hostilities between family members and promoting effective ways of relating to others is crucial. The coercive cycles of punitive parents and aggressive children are so persistent that these children often are punished when they do behave appropriately (Strassberg, 1995).

Leslie suggested that Robbie's parents see a family therapist, who, after observing their inept practices, coached them in alternatives. They learned not to give in to Robbie, to pair commands with reasons, and to replace verbal insults and spankings with more effective punishments, such as time out and withdrawal of privileges. After several weeks of such training, children's aggression declines, and parents view their children more positively—benefits still evident one to four years later (Kazdin, 2003; Patterson & Fisher, 2002). The therapist also encouraged Robbie's parents to be warmer and to give him attention and approval for prosocial acts. Finally, she helped them with their marital problems. This, in addition to their improved ability to manage Robbie's behavior, greatly reduced tension and conflict in the household.

At the same time, Leslie began teaching Robbie more successful ways of relating to peers, had him practice these skills, and praised him whenever she noticed him using them. And as opportunities arose, she encouraged Robbie to talk about a playmate's feelings and to express his own. As Robbie practiced taking the perspective of others, empathizing, and feeling sympathetic concern, his angry lashing out at peers declined (Izard et al., 2004). Robbie participated in social problem-solving training as well (return to pages 377–378 to review). These interventions reduce conduct problems in preschool and school-age children and help them develop more rewarding relationships with teachers and peers (Kazdin, 2003; Webster-Stratton, Reid, & Hammond, 2001).

gender typing Any association of objects, activities, roles, or traits with one sex or the other in ways that conform to cultural stereotypes.

Finally, relieving stressors that stem from poverty and neighborhood disorganization and providing families with social supports help prevent childhood aggression (Boyle & Lipman, 2002). When parents better cope with difficulties in their own lives, interventions aimed at reducing children's aggression are even more effective (Kazdin & Whitley, 2003).

Ask Yourself

Review   What experiences help preschoolers distinguish between moral imperatives, social conventions, and matters of personal choice? Why are these distinctions important for moral development?

Apply   Alice and Wayne want their two young children to develop a strong, internalized conscience and to become generous, caring individuals. List some parenting practices that they should use and some they should avoid.

Connect   What must parents do to foster conscience development in fearless, impulsive children? Does this remind you of the concept of goodness of fit (see page 266 in Chapter 7)? Explain.

Reflect   Which types of punishment for a misbehaving preschooler do you endorse, and which types do you reject? Why?

Gender Typing

Gender typing refers to any association of objects, activities, roles, or traits with one sex or the other in ways that conform to cultural stereotypes (Liben & Bigler, 2002). In Leslie's classroom, girls spent more time in the housekeeping, art, and reading corners, while boys gathered more often in spaces devoted to blocks, woodworking, and active play. Already, the children acquired many gender-linked beliefs and preferences and tended to play with peers of their own sex.

The same theories that provide accounts of morality have been used to explain gender typing: *social learning theory*, with its emphasis on modeling and reinforcement, and *cognitive-developmental theory*, with its focus on children as active thinkers about their social world. As we will see, neither is adequate by itself. *Gender schema theory*, a third perspective that combines elements of both, has gained favor. In the following sections, we consider the early development of gender typing.

Gender-Stereotyped Beliefs and Behaviors

Even before children can label their own sex consistently, they have begun to acquire common associations with gender—men as rough and sharp, women as soft and round. In one study, 18-month-olds linked such items as fir trees, bears, and hammers with males, although they had not yet learned comparable feminine associations (Eichstedt et al., 2002). Recall from Chapter 7 that around age 2, children use such words as "boy," "girl," "lady," and "man" appropriately. As soon as gender categories are established, children sort out what they mean in terms of activities and behaviors.

Preschoolers associate toys, articles of clothing, tools, household items, games, occupations, colors (pink and blue), and behaviors (relational and physical aggression) with one sex or the other (Giles & Heyman, 2005; Poulin-Dubois et al., 2002; Ruble, Martin, & Berenbaum, 2006). And their actions reflect their beliefs—not only in play preferences but also in personality traits. We have seen that boys tend to be more active, impulsive, assertive, and overtly aggressive. Girls, in contrast, tend to be more fearful, dependent, compliant, considerate, emotionally sensitive, self-controlled, and skilled at understanding self-conscious emotions and inflicting indirect relational aggression (Bosacki & Moore, 2004; Else-Quest et al., 2006; Underwood, 2003).

Gender-stereotyped game and toy choices are present before age 2 and strengthen over the preschool years. Already, these 3-year-olds play in highly gender-stereotyped ways.

During early childhood, children's gender-stereotyped beliefs become stronger, operating more like blanket rules than as flexible guidelines. When children were asked whether gender stereotypes could be violated, half or more of 3- and 4-year-olds answered "no" to clothing, hairstyle, and play with certain toys (such as Barbie dolls and G.I. Joes). Although they were less insistent about other types of play and occupations, many said a girl can't play roughly or be a doctor (Blakemore, 2003).

The rigidity of preschoolers' gender stereotypes helps us understand some commonly observed everyday behaviors. When Leslie showed her class a picture of a Scottish bagpiper wearing a kilt, the children insisted, "Men don't wear skirts!" During free play, they often exclaimed that girls can't be police officers and boys don't take care of babies. These one-sided judgments are a joint product of gender stereotyping in the environment and young children's cognitive limitations—in particular, their difficulty coordinating conflicting sources of information (Trautner et al., 2005). Most preschoolers do not yet realize that characteristics *associated with* one's sex—activities, toys, occupations, hairstyle, and clothing—do not *determine* whether a person is male or female. They have trouble understanding that males and females can be different in terms of their bodies but similar in many other ways.

Biological Influences on Gender Typing

The sex differences in play and personality traits just described appear in many cultures around the world (Munroe & Romney, 2006; Whiting & Edwards, 1988a). Certain ones—male activity level and physical aggression, female emotional sensitivity, and a preference for same-sex playmates—are widespread among mammalian species (Beatty, 1992; de Waal, 1993). According to an evolutionary perspective, the adult life of our male ancestors was oriented toward competing for mates, that of our female ancestors toward rearing children. Therefore, males became genetically primed for dominance and females for intimacy and responsiveness. Evolutionary theorists claim that although family and cultural forces can influence the intensity of biologically based sex differences, leading some individuals to be more gender typed than others, experience cannot eradicate those aspects of gender typing that served adaptive functions in human history (Geary, 1999; Maccoby, 2002).

Experiments with animals reveal that prenatally administered androgens increase active play and suppress maternal caregiving in many mammals. Eleanor Maccoby (1998) argues that sex hormones also affect human play styles, leading to rough, noisy movements among boys and calm, gentle actions among girls. Then, as children interact with peers, they choose partners whose interests and behaviors are compatible with their own. Preschool girls increasingly seek out other girls and like to play in pairs because of a common preference for quieter activities involving cooperative roles. And boys come to prefer larger-group play with other boys, who share a desire to run, climb, play-fight, compete, and build up and knock down (Fabes, Martin, & Hanish, 2003). At age 4, children spend three times as much time with same-sex as with other-sex playmates. By age 6, this ratio has climbed to 11 to 1 (Martin & Fabes, 2001).

Even stronger support for the role of biology in human gender typing comes from research on girls exposed prenatally to high levels of androgens, due either to normal variation in hormone levels or to a genetic defect. In both instances, these girls showed more "masculine" behavior—a preference for trucks and blocks over dolls, for active over quiet play, and for boys as playmates—even when parents encouraged them to engage in gender-typical play (Pasterski et al., 2005; Hines et al., 2002). And additional evidence comes from a case study of a boy who experienced serious sexual-identity and adjustment problems because his biological makeup and sex of rearing were at odds. Refer to the Biology and Environment box on the following page to find out about David's development.

Environmental Influences on Gender Typing

A wealth of evidence reveals that environmental forces—at home, at school, and in the community—build on genetic influences to promote the vigorous gender typing of early childhood.

Biology and Environment

David: A Boy Who Was Reared as a Girl

As a married man and father in his mid-thirties, David Reimer talked freely about his everyday life—his problems at work and the challenges of child rearing. But when asked about his first 15 years, he distanced himself, speaking as if the child of his early life were another person. In essence, she was.

David—named Bruce at birth—underwent the first infant sex reassignment ever reported on a genetically and hormonally normal child. To find out about David's development, researchers intensively interviewed him and studied his medical and psychotherapy records (Colapinto, 2001; Diamond & Sigmundson, 1999).

When Bruce was 8 months old, his penis was accidentally severed during circumcision. Soon afterward, his desperate parents heard about psychologist John Money's success in assigning a sex to children born with ambiguous genitals. They traveled from their home in Canada to Johns Hopkins University in Baltimore, where, under Money's oversight, 22-month-old Bruce had surgery to remove his testicles and sculpt his genitals to look like those of a girl. The operation complete, Bruce's parents named their daughter Brenda.

Brenda's upbringing was tragic. From the outset, she resisted her parents' efforts to steer her in a "feminine" direction. Brian (Brenda's identical twin brother) recalled that Brenda looked like a delicate, pretty girl—until she moved or spoke. "She walked like a guy. She talked about guy things. . . . She played with my toys: Tinkertoys, dump trucks" (Colapinto, 2001, p. 57).

At school, Brenda's boyish behavior led classmates to taunt and tease her. When she played with girls, she tried organizing large-group, active games, but they weren't interested.

Friendless and uncomfortable as a girl, Brenda increasingly displayed behavior problems. During periodic medical follow-ups, she drew pictures of herself as a boy and refused additional surgery to create a vagina.

As adolescence approached, Brenda's parents moved her from school to school and therapist to therapist in an effort to help her fit in socially and accept a female identity—pressures that increased Brenda's anxiety and conflict with her parents. At puberty, when Brenda's shoulders broadened and her body added muscle, her parents insisted that she begin estrogen therapy to feminize her appearance. Soon she grew breasts and added fat around her waist and hips. Repelled by her feminizing shape, Brenda began overeating to hide it. Her classmates reacted to her confused appearance with stepped-up brutality.

At last, Brenda was transferred to a therapist who recognized her despair and encouraged her parents to tell her about her infancy. When Brenda was 14, her father explained the circumcision accident. David recalled reacting with relief. Deciding to return to his biological sex immediately, he chose for himself the name David, after the biblical lad who slew a giant and overcame adversity. David soon started injections of the androgen hormone testosterone to masculinize his body, and he underwent surgery to remove his breasts and to construct a penis. Although his adolescence continued to be troubled, in his twenties he fell in love with Jane, a single mother of three children, and married her.

David's case confirms the impact of genetic sex and prenatal hormones on a person's sense of self as male or female. His gender reassign-

Because of a tragic medical accident when he was a baby, David Reimer underwent the first sex reassignment on a genetically and hormonally normal baby: He was reared as a girl. His story illustrates the overwhelming impact of biology on gender identity. David is seen here at age 36, a married man and a father. Two years later, the troubled life that sprang from David's childhood ended tragically, in suicide.

ment failed because his male biology overwhelmingly demanded a consistent sexual identity. At the same time, his childhood highlights the importance of experience. David expressed outrage at adult encouragement of dependency in girls—after all, he had experienced it firsthand.

Although David tried to surmount his tragic childhood, the troubled life that sprang from it persisted. When he was in his mid-thirties, his twin brother, Brian, committed suicide. Then, after David had lost his job and had been swindled out of his life savings in a shady investment deal, his wife left him, taking the children with her. Grief-stricken, David sank into a deep depression. On May 4, 2004, at age 38, he shot himself.

THE FAMILY ■ Beginning at birth, parents perceive sons and daughters differently and hold different expectations for them (see Chapter 7). Many parents prefer that their children play with "gender-appropriate" toys. And they tend to describe achievement, competition, and control of emotion as important for sons and warmth, "ladylike" behavior, and closely supervised activities as important for daughters (Brody, 1999; Turner & Gervai, 1995).

These beliefs carry over into parenting practices. Parents give their sons toys that stress action and competition (such as guns, cars, tools, and footballs) and give their daughters toys that emphasize nurturance, cooperation, and physical attractiveness (dolls, tea sets, jewelry) (Leaper, 1994). Parents also actively reinforce independence in boys and dependency in girls. For example, parents react more positively when a son plays with cars and trucks, demands

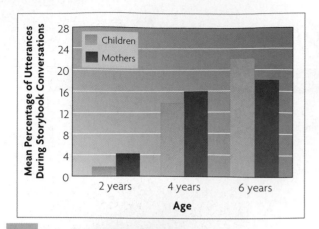

FIGURE 10.5

Mothers' and children's use of generic references to gender during storybook conversations. Generic utterances were broad in scope, in that they referred to many, or nearly all, males and females. Mothers' and children's use of generics increased dramatically between ages 2 and 6. At age 2, mothers produced more generics than children. By age 6, children produced more generics than mothers. (From S. A. Gelman, M. G. Taylor, & S. P. Nguyen, 2004, "Mother–Child Conversations about Gender," *Monographs of the Society for Research in Child Development, 69* [1, Serial No. 275], p. 46. © The Society for Research in Child Development, Inc. Adapted by permission.)

attention, runs and climbs, or tries to take toys from others. When interacting with daughters, they more often direct play activities, provide help, encourage participation in household tasks, and refer to emotions (Fagot & Hagan, 1991; Kuebli, Butler, & Fivush, 1995; Leaper et al., 1995). Gender-typed play contexts amplify these communication differences. For example, when playing housekeeping, mothers engage in high rates of supportive emotion talk with girls (Leaper, 2000).

Furthermore, parents provide children with indirect cues about gender categories and stereotypes through the language they use. In one study, researchers observed mothers talking about picture books with their 2- to 6-year-olds (Gelman, Taylor, & Nguyen, 2004). Mothers often labeled gender, even when they did not have to do so ("That's a boy." "Is that a she?"). And they frequently expressed *generic utterances,* referring to many, or nearly all, males and females: "Boys can be sailors." "Most girls don't like trucks." As Figure 10.5 shows, with age, both mothers and children produced an increasing number of these generic statements, which—even when they denied a stereotype ("Boys can be ballet dancers, too")—viewed individuals of the same gender as alike and ignored exceptions. Initially, mothers led the way in generic talk; at age 2, they introduced these sweeping generalizations nearly three times as often as children. By age 6, however, children were producing generics more often than mothers—a trend that suggests that children picked up many of these expressions from parental speech. Furthermore, 4- to 6-year-olds frequently made stereotyped generic statements, which their mothers often affirmed (*Child:* "Only boys can drive trucks." *Mother:* "OK.").

Parents who hold nonstereotyped values and consciously avoid behaving in these ways have less gender-typed children (Tenenbaum & Leaper, 2002; Turner & Gervai, 1995; Weisner & Wilson-Mitchell, 1990). Other family members may also reduce gender typing. For example, children with older, other-sex siblings have many more opportunities to imitate and participate in "cross-gender" activities and, as a result, are less gender typed in play preferences, attitudes, and personality traits (McHale et al., 2001; Rust et al., 2000).

Of the two sexes, boys are clearly the more gender-typed. Fathers, especially, apply more pressure for gender-role conformity to sons than to daughters. In Chapter 7 we saw that in infancy, fathers tend to engage in more physically stimulating play with their sons, whereas mothers usually play more quietly with infants of both sexes. In childhood, fathers more than mothers encourage "gender-appropriate" behavior, and they place more pressure to achieve on sons than on daughters (Gervai, Turner, & Hinde, 1995; Wood, Desmarais, & Gugula, 2002). Finally, fathers express far greater concern if a boy acts like a "sissy" than if a girl acts like a "tomboy."

TEACHERS ■ Teachers often act in ways that extend children's gender-role learning. Several times, Leslie caught herself emphasizing gender distinctions when she called out, "Will the girls line up on one side and the boys on the other?" or pleaded "Boys, I wish you'd quiet down like the girls!"

Like parents, preschool teachers give girls more encouragement to participate in adult-structured activities. Girls frequently cluster around the teacher, following directions, while boys are attracted to play areas where adults are minimally involved (Campbell, Shirley, & Candy, 2004; Powlishta, Serbin, & Moller, 1993). As a result, boys and girls engage in different social behaviors. Compliance and bids for help occur more often in adult-structured contexts; assertiveness, leadership, and creative use of materials appear more often in unstructured pursuits.

PEERS ■ Because most children associate nearly exclusively with peers of their own sex, the peer context is an especially potent source of gender-role learning. The more preschoolers play with same-sex partners, the more their behavior becomes gender-typed—in toy choices, activity level, aggression, and adult involvement (Martin & Fabes, 2001). By age 3, same-sex peers positively reinforce one another for gender-typed play by praising, imitating, or joining in. In contrast, when preschoolers engage in "cross-gender" activities—for example, when boys play with dolls or girls with cars and trucks—peers criticize them. Boys are especially intolerant of cross-gender play in other boys (Fagot, 1984). A boy who frequently crosses gender lines is likely to be ignored by other boys, even when he does engage in "masculine" activities!

Children also develop different styles of social influence in sex-segregated peer groups. To get their way in large-group play, boys often rely on commands, threats, and physical force. Girls' preference for playing in pairs leads to greater concern with a partner's needs, evident in girls' use of polite requests, persuasion, and acceptance. Girls soon find that these gentle tactics succeed with other girls but not with boys, who ignore their courteous overtures (Leaper, 1994; Leaper, Tenenbaum, & Shaffer, 1999). And boys' lack of responsiveness gives girls another reason to stop interacting with them.

These boys positively reinforce one another's gender-typed behavior. Preschoolers, especially boys, tend to be critical of peers who play with "cross-gender" toys or enjoy activities associated with the other sex.

Over time, children come to believe in the "correctness" of gender-segregated play, which further strengthens gender segregation and gender-stereotyped activities (Martin et al., 1999). As boys and girls separate, *in-group favoritism*—more positive evaluations of members of one's own gender—becomes another factor that sustains the separate social worlds of boys and girls, resulting in "two distinct subcultures" of shared knowledge, beliefs, interests, and behaviors (Maccoby, 2002). In sum, a *dynamic system* of forces—biological (see page 392), behavioral, and cognitive—work together to sustain gender segregation and the gender typing that occurs within it (Ruble, Martin, & Berenbaum, 2006).

THE BROADER SOCIAL ENVIRONMENT ■ Although children's everyday environments have changed to some degree, they continue to present many examples of gender typing—in men's and women's occupations, leisure activities, competencies, and achievements. For example, although today's TV programs include more career-oriented women than in the past, female characters continue to be young, attractive, caring, emotional, and victimized, and are seen in romantic and family contexts. In contrast, male characters are usually dominant and powerful (Signorielli, 2001). Gender stereotypes even pervade preschool educational software, which emphasize male characters exhibiting "masculine" traits (Sheldon, 2004). And stereotypes are especially prevalent in cartoons, music television (MTV), computer games, and other entertainment media for children and youths (Dietz, 1998).

As we will see next, children do more than imitate the many gender-linked responses they observe. They soon come to view themselves and their social surroundings through a "gender-biased lens"—a perspective that can seriously restrict their interests and learning opportunities.

Gender Identity

As adults, each of us has a **gender identity**—an image of oneself as relatively masculine or feminine in characteristics. By middle childhood, researchers can measure gender identity by asking children to rate themselves on personality traits. A child or adult with a "masculine" identity scores high on traditionally masculine items ("ambitious," "competitive," "self-sufficient") and low on traditionally feminine items ("affectionate," "cheerful," "soft-spoken"). Someone with a "feminine" identity does the reverse. And a substantial minority (especially females) have a gender identity called **androgyny,** scoring high on *both* masculine and feminine personality characteristics.

Gender identity is a good predictor of psychological adjustment. "Masculine" and androgynous children and adults have higher self-esteem than "feminine" individuals, perhaps because many typically feminine traits are not highly valued by society (Boldizar, 1991; Harter, 1998). Also, androgynous individuals are more adaptable—able to show masculine independence or feminine sensitivity, depending on the situation (Huyck, 1996). The existence of an androgynous identity demonstrates that children can acquire a mixture of positive qualities traditionally associated with each gender—an orientation that may best help them realize their potential.

gender identity An image of oneself as relatively masculine or feminine in characteristics.

androgyny The gender identity held by individuals who score high on both traditionally masculine and traditionally feminine personality characteristics.

EMERGENCE OF GENDER IDENTITY ■ How do children develop a gender identity? According to *social learning theory,* behavior comes before self-perceptions. Preschoolers first acquire gender-typed responses through modeling and reinforcement and only later organize these behaviors into gender-linked ideas about themselves. In contrast, *cognitive-developmental theory* maintains that self-perceptions come before behavior. Over the preschool years, children acquire a cognitive appreciation of the permanence of their sex, or **gender constancy**—the understanding that sex is biologically based and remains the same over time, even if clothing, hairstyle, and play activities change. Then children use this idea to guide their behavior (Kohlberg, 1966).

When asked such questions as "When you (a girl) grow up, could you ever be a daddy?" or "Could you be a boy if you wanted to?" 3- to 5-year-olds freely answer yes. And children younger than age 6 who watch an adult dressing a doll in "other-gender" clothing typically insist that the doll's sex has also changed (Chauhan et al., 2005; Fagot, 1985). Mastery of gender constancy occurs in a three-step sequence: *gender labeling* (correct naming of one's own and others' sex), *gender stability* (understanding that gender remains the same over time), and *gender consistency* (realization that gender is not altered by superficial changes in clothing or activities). Full attainment of gender constancy is strongly related to ability to pass Piagetian conservation and verbal appearance–reality tasks (see page 331 in Chapter 9) (De Lisi & Gallagher, 1991; Trautner, Gervai, & Nemeth, 2003).

In many cultures, young children do not have access to basic biological knowledge about gender because they rarely see members of the other sex naked. But giving children information about genital differences does not result in gender constancy. Preschoolers who have such knowledge usually say that changing a doll's clothing will not change its sex, but when asked to justify their response, they do not refer to sex as an innate, unchanging quality of people (Szkrybalo & Ruble, 1999). This suggests that cognitive immaturity, not social experience, is responsible for preschoolers' difficulty grasping the permanence of sex.

Is cognitive-developmental theory correct that gender constancy is responsible for children's gender-typed behavior? Evidence for this assumption is weak. "Gender-appropriate" behavior appears so early in the preschool years that its initial appearance must result from modeling and reinforcement, as social learning theory suggests. Researchers disagree on just how gender constancy influences gender-role development. But they do know that once children begin to reflect on gender roles, their gender-typed self-image and behavior strengthen. Yet another theory shows how this happens.

GENDER SCHEMA THEORY ■ **Gender schema theory** is an information-processing approach to gender typing that combines social learning and cognitive-developmental features. It explains how environmental pressures and children's cognitions work together to shape gender-role development (Martin & Halverson, 1987; Martin, Ruble, & Szkrybalo, 2002). At an early age, children pick up gender-stereotyped preferences and behaviors from others. At the same time, they organize experiences into *gender schemas,* or masculine and feminine categories, that they use to interpret their world. As soon as preschoolers can label their own gender, they select gender schemas consistent with it ("Only boys can be doctors" or "Cooking is a girl's job") and apply those categories to themselves. Their self-perceptions then become gender-typed and serve as additional schemas that children use to process information and guide their own behavior.

We have seen that individual differences exist in the extent to which children endorse gender-typed views. Figure 10.6 shows different cognitive pathways in children who often apply gender schemas to their experiences and those who rarely do (Liben & Bigler, 2002). Consider Billy, who encounters a doll. If Billy is a *gender-schematic child,* his *gender-salience filter* immediately makes gender highly relevant. Drawing on his prior learning, he asks himself, "Should boys play with dolls?" If he answers "yes," the toy interests him, he will approach it, explore it, and learn more about it. If he answers "no," he will respond by avoiding the "gender-inappropriate" toy. But if Billy is a *gender-aschematic child*—one who seldom views the world in gender-linked terms—he will simply ask himself, "Do I like this toy?" and respond on the basis of his interests.

To examine the consequences of gender-schematic processing, researchers showed 4- and 5-year-olds toys that were gender-neutral and that varied in attractiveness. An adult labeled

gender constancy The understanding that sex is biologically based, remaining the same over time even if clothing, hairstyle, and play activities change.

gender schema theory An information-processing approach to gender typing that explains how environmental pressures and children's cognitions work together to shape gender-role development.

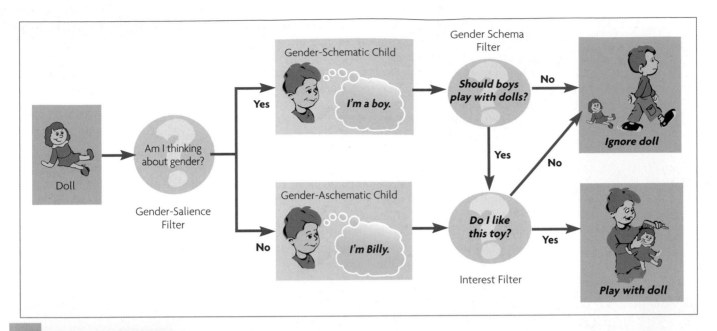

FIGURE 10.6

Cognitive pathways for gender-schematic and gender-aschematic children.   In *gender-schematic children,* the gender-salience filter immediately makes gender highly relevant: Billy sees a doll and thinks, "I'm a boy. Should boys play with dolls?" Drawing on his experiences, he answers "yes" or "no." If he answers "yes" and the doll interests him, he plays with the doll. If he answers "no," he avoids the "gender-inappropriate" toy. *Gender-aschematic children* rarely view the world in gender-linked terms. Billy simply asks, "Do I like this toy?" and responds on the basis of his interests.   (Reprinted by permission of Rebecca Bigler, University of Texas, Austin.)

some as boys' toys and others as girls' toys, leaving a third group unlabeled. Most children engaged in gender-schematic reasoning, preferring toys labeled for their gender and predicting that same-sex peers would also like those toys (Martin, Eisenbud, & Rose, 1995). Highly attractive toys, especially, lost their appeal when they were labeled as for the other gender. And because gender-schematic preschoolers typically conclude, "What I like, children of my own sex will also like," they often use their own preferences to add to their gender biases! For example, a girl who dislikes oysters may declare, "Only boys like oysters!" even though she has never actually been given information supporting such a stereotype (Liben & Bigler, 2002).

Gender-schematic thinking is so powerful that when children see others behaving in "gender-inconsistent" ways, they often cannot remember the behavior or they distort their memory to make it "gender-consistent"—for example, when shown a picture of a male nurse, remember him as a doctor (Liben & Signorella, 1993; Marin & Ruble, 2004). Over time, children learn much more about people, objects, and events that fit with their gender schemas than they do about "cross-gender" activities and behaviors. Of course, gender-schematic processing could not operate if society did not teach a wide variety of gender-linked associations.

Reducing Gender Stereotyping in Young Children

How can we help young children avoid rigid gender schemas that restrict their behavior and learning opportunities? No easy recipe exists. Biology clearly affects children's gender typing, channeling boys, on average, toward active, competitive play and girls toward quieter, more intimate interaction. But most aspects of gender typing are not built into human nature (Maccoby, 2000).

Because young children's cognitive limitations lead them to assume that cultural practices determine gender, parents and teachers are wise to try to delay preschoolers'

Parents and teachers can reduce preschoolers' gender stereotyping by modeling nonstereotyped behaviors and pointing out exceptions to stereotypes in their neighborhood and community. Perhaps because this boy has observed family members engaged in nonstereotyped activities, he enacts similar roles in his preschool classroom.

exposure to gender-stereotyped messages. Adults can begin by limiting traditional gender roles in their own behavior and by providing nontraditional alternatives for children—for example, taking turns making dinner, bathing children, and driving the family car. Parents can give their sons and daughters both trucks and dolls, both pink and blue clothing. Teachers can ensure that all children spend time in mixed-gender play activities and in both adult-structured and unstructured pursuits. Finally, adults can avoid language that conveys gender stereotypes, and they can shield children from media presentations that do so.

Once children notice the vast array of gender stereotypes in their society, parents and teachers can point out exceptions. For example, they can arrange for children to see men and women pursuing nontraditional careers and can explain that interests and skills, not sex, should determine a person's occupation. Research shows that such reasoning is highly effective in reducing children's tendency to view the world in a gender-biased fashion. By middle childhood, children who hold flexible beliefs about what boys and girls can do are more likely to notice instances of gender discrimination (Bigler & Liben, 1992; Brown & Bigler, 2004). And, as we will see in the next section, a rational approach to child rearing promotes healthy, adaptable functioning in many other areas as well.

Ask Yourself

Review Explain how the social environment and young children's cognitive limitations contribute to rigid gender stereotyping in early childhood.

Apply While looking at a book, 4-year-old Roger saw a picture of a boy cooking at a stove. Later, he recalled the person in the picture as a girl. Using gender schema theory, explain Roger's memory error.

Connect What other cognitive changes are associated with gender constancy? What do these attainments have in common?

Reflect Would you describe your own gender identity as "masculine," "feminine," or "androgynous"? What biological and social factors might have influenced your gender identity?

Child Rearing and Emotional and Social Development

In this and previous chapters, we have seen how parents can foster children's competence—by building a parent–child relationship based on affection and cooperation, by serving as models and reinforcers of mature behavior, by using reasoning and inductive discipline, and by guiding and encouraging mastery of new skills. Now let's put these practices together into an overall view of effective parenting.

Styles of Child Rearing

child-rearing styles
Combinations of parenting behaviors that occur over a wide range of situations, creating an enduring child-rearing climate.

Child-rearing styles are combinations of parenting behaviors that occur over a wide range of situations, creating an enduring child-rearing climate. In a landmark series of studies, Diana Baumrind gathered information on child rearing by watching parents interact with their preschoolers (Baumrind, 1971). Her findings, and those of others who have extended her work, reveal three features that consistently differentiate an effective style from less effective ones: (1) acceptance and involvement, (2) control, and (3) autonomy granting (Gray & Steinberg, 1999; Hart, Newell, & Olsen, 2003). Table 10.2 shows how child-rearing styles differ in these features. Let's discuss each style in turn.

TABLE 10.2   Features of Child-Rearing Styles

CHILD-REARING STYLE	ACCEPTANCE AND INVOLVEMENT	CONTROL	AUTONOMY GRANTING
Authoritative	Is warm, responsive, attentive, and sensitive to the child's needs	Makes reasonable demands for maturity and consistently enforces and explains them	Permits the child to make decisions in accord with readiness Encourages the child to express thoughts, feelings, and desires When parent and child disagree, engages in joint decision making when possible
Authoritarian	Is cold and rejecting and frequently degrades the child	Makes many demands coercively, using force and punishment; often uses psychological control, withdrawing love and intruding on the child's individuality	Makes decisions for the child Rarely listens to the child's point of view
Permissive	Is warm but overindulgent or inattentive	Makes few or no demands	Permits the child to make many decisions before the child is ready
Uninvolved	Is emotionally detached and withdrawn	Makes few or no demands	Is indifferent to the child's decision making and point of view

AUTHORITATIVE CHILD REARING ■ The **authoritative child-rearing style**—the most successful approach to child rearing—involves high acceptance and involvement, adaptive control techniques, and appropriate autonomy granting. Authoritative parents are warm, attentive, and sensitive to their child's needs. They establish an enjoyable, emotionally fulfilling parent–child relationship that draws the child into close connection. At the same time, authoritative parents exercise firm, reasonable control; they insist on mature behavior and give reasons for their expectations. Finally, authoritative parents engage in gradual, appropriate autonomy granting, allowing the child to make decisions in areas where he is ready to make choices (Kuczynski & Lollis, 2002; Russell, Mize, & Bissaker, 2004).

Throughout childhood and adolescence, authoritative parenting is linked to many aspects of competence—an upbeat mood, self-control, task persistence, cooperativeness, high self-esteem, social and moral maturity, and favorable school performance (Amato & Fowler, 2002; Aunola, Stattin, & Nurmi, 2000; Luster & McAdoo, 1996; Mackey, Arnold, & Pratt, 2001; Steinberg, Darling, & Fletcher, 1995).

AUTHORITARIAN CHILD REARING ■ The **authoritarian child-rearing style** is low in acceptance and involvement, high in coercive control, and low in autonomy granting. Authoritarian parents appear cold and rejecting; they frequently degrade their child by putting her down. To exert control, they yell, command, and criticize. "Do it because I said so!" is their attitude. They make decisions for their child and expect their child to accept their word unquestioningly. If the child resists, authoritarian parents resort to force and punishment.

Children of authoritarian parents are anxious, unhappy, and low in self-esteem and self-reliance. When frustrated, they tend to react with hostility. Boys, especially, show high rates of anger and defiance. Although girls also engage in acting-out behavior, they are more likely to be dependent, lacking interest in exploration, and overwhelmed by challenging tasks (Hart, Newell, & Olsen, 2003; Nix et al., 1999; Thompson, Hollis, & Richards, 2003).

In addition to unwarranted direct control, authoritarian parents engage in a more subtle type called **psychological control,** in which they intrude on and manipulate children's verbal expression, individuality, and attachments to parents. In an attempt to decide virtually everything for the child, these parents frequently interrupt or put down the child's ideas, decisions,

authoritative child-rearing style A child-rearing style that is high in acceptance and involvement, emphasizes firm control with explanations, and includes gradual, appropriate autonomy granting.

authoritarian child-rearing style A child-rearing style that is low in acceptance and involvement, is high in coercive control, and restricts rather than grants autonomy

psychological control Parental behaviors that intrude on and manipulate children's verbal expression, individuality, and attachments to parents.

and choice of friends. When they are dissatisfied, they withdraw love, making their affection contingent on the child's compliance. They also hold excessively high expectations that do not fit the child's developing capacities. Children subjected to psychological control exhibit adjustment problems involving both anxious, withdrawn and defiant, aggressive behaviors (Barber & Harmon, 2002; Silk et al., 2003).

PERMISSIVE CHILD REARING ■ The **permissive child-rearing style** is warm and accepting but uninvolved. Permissive parents are either overindulgent or inattentive. They make little effort to control their child's behavior. Instead of gradually granting autonomy, they allow children to make many decisions for themselves at an age when they are not yet capable of doing so. Their children can eat meals and go to bed when they feel like it and watch as much television as they want. They do not have to learn good manners or do household chores. Although some permissive parents truly believe in this approach, many others simply lack confidence in their ability to influence their child's behavior (Oyserman et al., 2005).

Children of permissive parents are impulsive, disobedient, and rebellious. Compared with children whose parents exert more control, they are also overly demanding and dependent on adults, and they show less persistence on tasks, poorer school achievement, and more antisocial behavior. The link between permissive parenting and dependent, nonachieving, rebellious behavior is especially strong for boys (Barber & Olsen, 1997; Baumrind, 1971).

UNINVOLVED CHILD REARING ■ The **uninvolved child-rearing style** combines low acceptance and involvement with little control and general indifference to autonomy granting. Often these parents are emotionally detached and depressed, so overwhelmed by life stress that they have little time and energy for children. At its extreme, uninvolved parenting is a form of child maltreatment called *neglect*. Especially when it begins early, it disrupts virtually all aspects of development (see Chapter 4, page 160). Even with less extreme parental disengagement, children and adolescents display many problems—poor emotional self-regulation, school achievement difficulties, and antisocial behavior (Aunola, Stattin, & Nurmi, 2000; Kurdek & Fine, 1994).

What Makes Authoritative Child Rearing Effective?

Like other correlational findings, the relationship between parenting and children's competence is open to interpretation. Perhaps parents of well-adjusted children are authoritative because their youngsters have especially cooperative dispositions. Children's characteristics do contribute to the ease with which parents can apply the authoritative style. An impulsive, noncompliant child makes it hard for parents to be warm, firm, and rational. But longitudinal research reveals that authoritative child rearing promotes maturity in children of diverse temperaments (Hart, Newell, & Olson, 2003; Olson et al., 2000; Rubin, Burgess, & Coplan, 2002). It seems to create an emotional context for positive parental influence in the following ways:

- Warm, involved parents who are secure in the standards they hold for their children provide models of caring concern as well as of confident, self-controlled behavior.
- Children are far more likely to comply with and internalize control that appears fair and reasonable, not arbitrary.
- Authoritative parents make demands and engage in autonomy granting that match children's ability to take responsibility for their own behavior. By letting children know that they are competent individuals who can do things for themselves, these parents foster high self-esteem and cognitive and social maturity.
- Supportive aspects of the authoritative style, including parental acceptance, involvement, and rational control, are a powerful source of *resilience*, protecting children from the negative effects of family stress and poverty (Beyers et al., 2003).

Over time, the relationship between parenting and children's attributes becomes increasingly bidirectional (Kuczynski, 2003). When parents intervene patiently but firmly, they promote favorable adjustment, setting the stage for a positive parent–child relationship.

permissive child-rearing style A child-rearing style that is high in acceptance but either overindulging or inattentive, low in control, and inappropriately lenient in autonomy granting.

uninvolved child-rearing style A child-rearing style that combines low acceptance and involvement with little control and indifference to autonomy granting.

Cultural Variations

Although authoritative parenting is broadly advantageous, ethnic minority parents often have distinct child-rearing beliefs and practices reflecting cultural values. Let's look at some examples.

Compared with Western parents, Chinese parents describe their parenting as more controlling. They are more directive in teaching and scheduling their children's time, as a way of fostering self-control and high achievement. Chinese parents may appear less warm than Western parents because they withhold praise, which, they believe, results in self-satisfied, poorly motivated children (Chao, 1994; Chen et al., 2001). High control reflects the Confucian belief in strict discipline, respect for elders, and socially desirable behavior, taught by deeply involved parents. Chinese parents report expressing affection and concern and using induction and other reasoning-oriented discipline as much as North American parents do, but they more often shame a misbehaving child, withdraw love, and use physical punishment (Jose et al., 2000; Schwalb et al., 2004; Wu et al., 2002). When these practices become excessive, resulting in an authoritarian style high in psychological or coercive control, Chinese children display the same negative outcomes seen in Western children: anxiety, depression, and aggressive behavior (Bradford et al., 2003; Nelson et al., 2005, 2006; Yang et al., 2003).

In Hispanic families, Asian Pacific Island families, and Caribbean families of African and East Indian origin, firm insistence on respect for parental authority is paired with high parental warmth—a combination suited to promoting competence and strong feelings of family loyalty (Harrison et al., 1994; Roopnarine & Evans, 2007). In one study, Mexican-American mothers living in poverty who adhered strongly to their cultural traditions tended to combine warmth with strict, even somewhat harsh control—a style that served a protective function, in that it was associated with reduced child and adolescent conduct problems (Hill, Bush, & Roosa, 2003). Although at one time viewed as coercive, contemporary Hispanic fathers typically spend much time with their children and are warm and sensitive (Cabrera & García Coll, 2004; Jambunathan, Burts, & Pierce, 2000). In Caribbean families that have immigrated to the United States, fathers' authoritativeness—but not mothers'—predicted preschoolers' literacy and math skills, probably because Caribbean fathers take a larger role in guiding their children's academic progress (Rooopnarine et al., 2006).

Although wide variation exists, low-SES African-American parents tend to expect immediate obedience. But like findings just reported for Mexican Americans, when African-American families live in depleted, crime-ridden neighborhoods and have few social supports, strict control may have a positive effect, preventing antisocial involvements. Other research suggests that black parents use firm control for broader reasons—to promote self-reliance, self-regulation, and a watchful attitude in risky surroundings, which protects children from becoming victims of crime (Brody & Flor, 1998). Consistent with this view, low-SES African-American parents who use more controlling strategies tend to have more cognitively and socially competent children (Brody, Stoneman, & Flor, 1996a, 1996b). And when using strict, "no-nonsense" discipline (including mild physical punishment), black parents typically combine it with warmth and reasoning.

These cultural variations remind us that child-rearing styles must be viewed in their larger context. As we have seen, many factors contribute to good parenting: personal characteristics of the child and parent, SES, access to extended family and community supports, cultural values and practices, and public policies.

As we turn now to the topic of child maltreatment, our discussion will underscore, once again, that effective child rearing is sustained not just by the desire of mothers and fathers to be good parents. Almost all want to be. Unfortunately, when vital supports for good parenting break down, children—as well as parents—can suffer terribly.

© BRAND X PICTURES/ALAMY

Some ethnic minority groups emphasize respect for parental authority together with high parental warmth. This combination promotes competence and strong family loyalty, and is also associated with fewer conduct problems in childhood and adolescence.

Child Maltreatment

Child maltreatment is as old as human history, but only recently has the problem been widely acknowledged and research aimed at understanding it. Perhaps public concern has increased because child maltreatment is especially common in large industrialized nations. In the most recently reported year, 872,000 American children (12 out of every 1,000) and 136,000 Canadian children (10 out of every 1,000) were identified as victims (Department of Justice Canada, 2006a; U.S. Department of Health and Human Services, 2006a). Because most cases go unreported, the true figures are much higher.

Child maltreatment takes the following forms:

- *Physical abuse:* Assaults, such as shaking, kicking, biting, punching, or stabbing, that inflict physical injury
- *Sexual abuse:* Fondling, intercourse, exhibitionism, commercial exploitation through prostitution or production of pornography, and other forms of sexual exploitation
- *Neglect:* Failure to provide for a child's basic needs for food, clothing, medical attention, education, or supervision
- *Emotional abuse:* Acts that could cause serious mental or behavior disorders, including social isolation, repeated unreasonable demands, ridicule, humiliation, intimidation, or terrorizing

Neglect accounts for 40 to 50 percent of reported cases, physical abuse for 30 percent, emotional abuse for 10 to 20 percent, and sexual abuse for 10 percent (U.S. Department of Health and Human Services, 2006a). But these figures are only approximate, as many children experience more than one form.

Parents commit more than 80 percent of abusive incidents. Other relatives account for about 7 percent. The remainder are perpetrated by parents' unmarried partners, school officials, camp counselors, and other adults. Mothers engage in neglect more often than fathers, whereas fathers engage in sexual abuse more often than mothers. Maternal and paternal rates of physical and emotional abuse are fairly similar. Infants and young preschoolers are at greatest risk for neglect, preschool and school-age children for physical, emotional, and sexual abuse. But each type occurs at every age (Trocomé & Wolfe, 2002; U.S. Department of Health and Human Services, 2006a). Because most sexual abuse victims are identified in middle childhood, we will pay special attention to this form of maltreatment in Chapter 13.

ORIGINS OF CHILD MALTREATMENT ■ Early findings suggested that child maltreatment was rooted in adult psychological disturbance (Kempe et al., 1962). But although child maltreatment is more common among disturbed parents, it soon became clear that a single "abusive personality type" does not exist. Parents who were abused as children do not necessarily become abusers (Buchanan, 1996; Simons et al., 1991). And sometimes even "normal" parents harm their children!

For help in understanding child maltreatment, researchers turned to *ecological systems theory* (see Chapters 1 and 2). They discovered that many interacting variables—at the family, community, and cultural levels—contribute. Table 10.3 summarizes factors associated with child maltreatment. The more risks present, the greater the likelihood that abuse or neglect will occur. Let's examine each set of influences in turn.

The Family. Within the family, children whose characteristics make them more of a challenge to rear are more likely to become targets of abuse. These include premature or very sick babies and children who are temperamentally difficult, are inattentive and overactive, or have other developmental problems. Child factors, however, only slightly increase the risk of abuse (Sidebotham et al., 2003). Whether such children are maltreated largely depends on parents' characteristics.

Maltreating parents are less skillful than other parents in handling discipline confrontations and getting children to cooperate in working toward common goals. They also suffer from biased thinking about their child. For example, they often evaluate transgressions as worse than they are, attribute their child's misdeeds to a bad disposition, and feel powerless in parenting—perspectives that lead them to move quickly toward physical force (Bugental & Happaney, 2004; Haskett et al., 2003).

Once abuse begins, it quickly becomes part of a self-sustaining relationship. The small irritations to which abusive parents react—a fussy baby, a preschooler who knocks over her

TABLE 10.3	Factors Related to Child Maltreatment
FACTOR	**DESCRIPTION**
Parent characteristics	Psychological disturbance; alcohol and drug abuse; history of abuse as a child; belief in harsh, physical discipline; desire to satisfy unmet emotional needs through the child; unreasonable expectations for child behavior; young age (most under 30); low educational level
Child characteristics	Premature or very sick baby; difficult temperament; inattentiveness and overactivity; other developmental problems
Family characteristics	Low income; poverty; homelessness; marital instability; social isolation; physical abuse of mother by husband or boyfriend; frequent moves; large families with closely spaced children; overcrowded living conditions; disorganized household; lack of steady employment; other signs of high life stress
Community	Characterized by social isolation; few parks, child-care centers, preschool programs, recreation centers, or churches to serve as family supports
Culture	Approval of physical force and violence as ways to solve problems

Sources: Wekerle & Wolfe, 2003; Whipple, 2006.

milk, or a child who will not mind immediately—soon become bigger ones. Then the harshness increases. By the preschool years, abusive and neglectful parents seldom interact with their children. When they do, they rarely express pleasure and affection; the communication is almost always negative (Wolfe, 2005).

Most parents have enough self-control not to respond to their children's misbehavior or developmental problems with abuse. Other factors combine with these conditions to prompt an extreme response. Unmanageable parental stress is strongly associated with maltreatment. Abusive parents respond to stressful situations with high emotional arousal. And such stressors as low income and education (less than a high school diploma), unemployment, young maternal age, alcohol and drug use, marital conflict, overcrowded living conditions, frequent moves, and extreme household disorganization are common in abusive homes (Wekerle & Wolfe, 2003). These conditions increase the chances that parents will be too overwhelmed to meet basic child-rearing responsibilities or will vent their frustrations by lashing out at their children.

The Community. The majority of abusive parents are isolated from both formal and informal social supports. This social isolation has at least two causes. First, because of their own life histories, many of these parents have learned to mistrust and avoid others. They do not have the skills necessary for establishing and maintaining positive relationships. Second, maltreating parents are more likely to live in unstable, run-down neighborhoods that provide few links between family and community, such as parks, child-care centers, preschool programs, recreation centers, and churches (Coulton, Korbin, & Su, 1999). For these reasons, they lack "lifelines" to others and have no one to turn to for help during stressful times.

The Larger Culture. Cultural values, laws, and customs profoundly affect the chances that child maltreatment will occur when parents feel overburdened. Societies that view violence as an appropriate way to solve problems set the stage for child abuse. Although the United States and Canada have laws to protect children from maltreatment, we have seen that parental use of corporal punishment is widespread. In many countries—including Austria, Croatia, Cyprus, Denmark, Finland, Germany, Israel, Italy, Latvia, Norway, and Sweden—physical punishment is outlawed, a measure that dampens both physical discipline and abuse (Bugental & Grusec, 2006).

Furthermore, every industrialized nation except the United States and Canada now prohibits corporal punishment in schools (Center for Effective Discipline, 2005). The U.S. Supreme Court has twice upheld the right of school officials to use physical discipline. Likewise, the Canadian federal criminal code permits corporal punishment of children by caregivers and teachers, as long as the physical force is "reasonable under the circumstances." This vague definition may encourage adults to assault children while providing a ready defense for those who do so (Justice for Children and Youth, 2003). Indeed, Canadian courts have deemed hard spankings, slaps to the head and face, and hitting of the buttocks and legs with belts and sticks to be consistent with the criminal code. Fortunately, some U.S. states and Canadian provinces have passed laws that ban corporal punishment.

CONSEQUENCES OF CHILD MALTREATMENT ■ The family circumstances of maltreated children impair the development of emotional self-regulation, empathy and sympathy, self-concept, social skills, and academic motivation. Over time, these youngsters show serious learning and adjustment problems: academic failure, severe depression, aggressive behavior, peer difficulties, substance abuse, and delinquency, including violent crime (Cicchetti & Toth, 2006; Shonk & Cicchetti, 2001; Wolfe et al., 2001).

How do these damaging consequences occur? Recall our earlier discussion of hostile cycles of parent–child interaction. For abused children, these are especially severe. Indeed, a family characteristic strongly associated with child abuse is spouse abuse (Cox, Kotch, & Everson, 2003). Clearly, the home lives of abused children overflow with opportunities to learn to use aggression as a way of solving problems.

Furthermore, demeaning parental messages, in which children are ridiculed, humiliated, rejected, or terrorized, result in low self-esteem, high anxiety, self-blame, depression, and efforts to escape from extreme psychological pain—at times severe enough to lead to attempted suicide in adolescence (Wolfe, 2005). At school, maltreated children present serious discipline problems. Their noncompliance, poor motivation, and cognitive immaturity interfere with academic achievement, further undermining their chances for life success (Wekerle & Wolfe, 2003).

Finally, the trauma of repeated abuse is associated with central nervous system damage, including abnormal EEG brain-wave activity, fMRI-detected reduced size and impaired functioning of the cerebral cortex and corpus callosum, and heightened production of stress hormones (Cicchetti, 2003; Kaufman & Charney, 2001; Teicher et al., 2004). These effects increase the chances that cognitive and emotional problems will endure.

By educating people about the needs of children and families, communities can simultaneously prevent child abuse and promote effective parenting. This poster, from the U.S. Department of Health and Human Services, reminds us that protecting children is the responsibility of each and every adult.

PREVENTING CHILD MALTREATMENT ■ Because child maltreatment is embedded in families, communities, and society as a whole, efforts to prevent it must be directed at each of these levels. Many approaches have been suggested, including teaching high-risk parents effective child-rearing strategies, providing direct experience with children in high school child development, and broad social programs aimed at bettering economic conditions for low-SES families.

We have seen that providing social supports to families is very effective in easing parental stress. This approach sharply reduces child maltreatment as well (Azar & Wolfe, 1998). Research indicates that a trusting relationship with another person is the most important factor in preventing mothers with childhood histories of abuse from repeating the cycle with their own youngsters (Egeland, Jacobvitz, & Sroufe, 1988). Parents Anonymous, a national organization that has as its main goal helping child-abusing parents learn constructive parenting practices, does so largely through social supports. Its local chapters offer self-help group meetings, daily phone calls, and regular home visits to relieve social isolation and teach responsible child-rearing skills.

Two-generation approaches to early intervention, aimed at strengthening both child and parent competencies, have also been tried. Healthy Families America, a program begun in Hawaii that has spread to 430 sites across the United States and Canada, identifies families at risk for maltreatment during pregnancy or at birth. Each receives three years of home visitation in which a trained worker helps parents manage crises, encourages effective child rearing, and puts parents in touch with community services to meet their own and their children's needs (PCA America, 2006). In an evaluation in which over 600 families were randomly assigned to intervention and control groups, Healthy Families home visitation alone reduced only neglect, not abuse (Duggan et al., 2004). But adding a *cognitive component* to home visitation dramatically increases its impact. When home visitors helped parents change nega- tive appraisals of their children—by countering inaccurate interpreta- tions (for example, that the baby is acting with malicious intent) and by working on solving child-rearing problems—physical punishment and abuse dropped sharply by the end of one year of intervention (see Figure 10.7) (Bugental et al., 2002).

Still, many experts believe that child maltreatment cannot be elimi- nated as long as violence is widespread and harsh physical punishment is regarded as acceptable. In addition, combating poverty and its diverse correlates—family stress and disorganization, inadequate food and medical care, teenage parenthood, low-birth-weight babies, and parental hopelessness—would protect many children.

Although more cases reach the courts than in decades past, child mal- treatment remains a crime that is difficult to prove. Usually, the only wit- nesses are the child victims or other loyal family members. And even when the evidence is strong, judges hesitate to impose the ultimate safeguard against further harm: permanently removing the child from the family. There are several reasons for their reluctance. First, in the United States and Canada, government intervention into family life is viewed as a last resort. Second, despite destructive family relationships, maltreated children and their parents usually are attached to one another. Usually, neither desires separation. Finally, U.S. and Canadian legal systems tend to regard children as parental property rather than as human beings in their own right, and this also has stood in the way of court-ordered protection.

Even with intensive treatment, some adults persist in their abusive acts. An estimated 1,500 American children and 100 Canadian children, most of them infants and preschoolers, die from maltreatment each year. About two-thirds suffered from beatings, drownings, suffocation, or *shaken baby syndrome,* in which shaking an infant or young child inflicts brain and neck injuries. And about one-third were severely ne- glected (Trocomé & Wolfe, 2002; U.S. Department of Health and Human Services, 2006a). When parents are unlikely to change their behavior, the drastic step of separating parent from child and legally terminating parental rights is the only justifiable course of action.

Child maltreatment is a distressing and horrifying topic—a sad note on which to end our discussion of a period of childhood that is so full of excitement, awakening, and discovery. But there is reason to be optimistic. Great strides have been made over the past several decades in understanding and preventing child maltreatment.

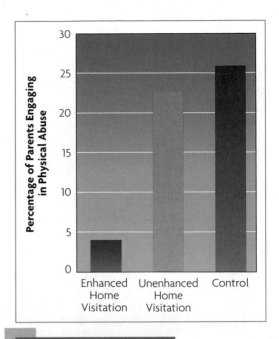

FIGURE 10.7

Impact of a home visitation program with a cognitive component on preventing physical abuse of young children. In an enhanced home visitation condition, home visitors not only provided social support, encouraged effective child rearing, and connected families with community resources but also helped at-risk parents change their negative appraisals of their babies and solve child-rearing problems. After one year of intervention, this cognitive component sharply reduced physical abuse of babies (hitting, shaking, beating, kicking, biting) compared with an unenhanced home visitation condition and a no-intervention control. (Adapted from Bugental et al., 2002.)

Ask Yourself

Review Summarize findings on ethnic variations in child-rearing styles. Is the concept of authoritative parenting useful for understanding effective parenting across cultures? Explain.

Apply Chandra heard a news report about 10 severely neglected children, living in squalor in an inner-city tenement. She wondered, "Why would parents mistreat their children so badly?" How would you answer Chandra?

Connect Which child-rearing style is most likely to be associated with use of inductive discipline, and why?

Reflect How would you classify your parents' child-rearing styles? What factors might have influenced their approach to parenting?

Summary

Erikson's Theory: Initiative versus Guilt

What personality changes take place during Erikson's stage of initiative versus guilt?

■ Preschoolers develop a new sense of purposefulness as they grapple with Erikson's psychological conflict of **initiative versus guilt.** A healthy sense of initiative depends on exploring the social world through play and experiencing supportive child rearing that fosters a secure (but not overly strict) conscience.

Self-Understanding

Describe preschoolers' self-concepts and the development of autobiographical memory and self-esteem.

■ As children gain self-awareness during the first two years, two aspects of the self develop: the **I-self,** or active observer, and the **me-self,** or self as object of knowledge and evaluation, from which children develop a **self-concept.** Preschoolers' self-concepts consist largely of observable characteristics and typical emotions and attitudes. Their increasing self-awareness underlies struggles with other children over objects as well as first efforts to cooperate.

■ Adult–child conversations about the past contribute to the development of autobiographical memory, a coherent narrative about the past. Gradually, children develop a sense of the I-self as existing continuously in time.

■ During early childhood, **self-esteem** differentiates into several self-judgments. Preschoolers' high self-esteem contributes to their mastery-oriented approach to the environment. Excessive adult criticism can undermine children's enthusiasm for learning and persistence at challenging tasks.

© ARIEL SKELLEY/GETTY IMAGES/BLEND IMAGES

Emotional Development

Identify changes in understanding and expressing emotion during early childhood, citing factors that influence those changes.

■ Preschoolers have an impressive understanding of the causes, consequences, and behavioral signs of basic emotions, which is supported by cognitive development, secure attachment, and conversations about feelings. By age 3 to 4, children are aware of various strategies for emotional self-regulation. Temperament, parental modeling, and parental communication about coping strategies influence preschoolers' capacity to handle negative emotion.

■ As their self-concepts become better developed, preschoolers experience self-conscious emotions more often. However, they depend on parental feedback to know when to feel pride, shame, or guilt.

■ Empathy also becomes more common in early childhood. The extent to which empathy leads to **sympathy** and results in **prosocial,** or **altruistic, behavior** depends on temperament and parenting.

Peer Relations

Describe peer sociability, friendship, and social problem solving in early childhood, along with cultural and parental influences on early peer relations.

■ During early childhood, peer interaction increases as children move from **nonsocial activity** to **parallel play** and then to **associative** and **cooperative play.** But as associative and cooperative play increase, both solitary and parallel play remain common.

■ Gains in sociodramatic play affect many aspects of emotional and social development and are especially important in societies where child and adult worlds are distinct. In collectivist societies, play generally occurs in large groups and is highly cooperative.

■ Preschoolers view friendship in concrete, activity-based terms. Their interactions with friends are especially positive and cooperative and serve as effective sources of social support as they enter kindergarten.

■ Conflicts with peers offer children occasions for **social problem solving,** which improves over the preschool and early school years. By kindergarten to second grade, each of its information-processing components is related to socially competent behavior. Training in social problem solving improves peer relations and psychological adjustment.

■ Parents influence early peer relations both directly, through attempts to influence their child's peer relations, and indirectly, through their child-rearing practices. Secure attachment, emotionally positive parent–child conversations, and cooperative parent–child play are linked to favorable peer interaction.

Foundations of Morality

What are the central features of psychoanalytic, social learning, and cognitive-developmental approaches to moral development?

■ The psychoanalytic perspective emphasizes the emotional side of moral development. Although Freud was correct that guilt is an important motivator of moral action, contrary to his theory, discipline that promotes fear of punishment and loss of parental love does not foster conscience development. **Induction** is far more effective in encouraging self-control and prosocial behavior.

■ Social learning theory focuses on how moral behavior is learned through reinforcement and modeling. Effective adult models of morality are warm and powerful, and they practice what they preach.

■ Frequent harsh punishment does not promote moral internalization and socially desirable behavior. Alternatives, such as **time out** and withdrawal of privileges, can help parents avoid the undesirable side effects of punishment. When parents do use punishment, they can increase its effectiveness by being consistent, maintaining a warm relationship with the child, and offering explanations. The most effective discipline encourages good conduct by building a mutually respectful bond with the child.

■ The cognitive-developmental perspective views children as active thinkers about social rules. By age 4, children consider intentions in making moral judgments and distinguish truthfulness from lying. Preschoolers also distinguish **moral imperatives** from **social conventions** and **matters of personal choice.** But they tend to reason rigidly about morality, focusing on salient features and consequences and neglecting other important information.

■ Through sibling and peer interaction, children work out their first ideas about justice and fairness. Parents who discuss moral issues with their children help them reason about morality.

Describe the development of aggression in early childhood, including family and media influences.

■ During early childhood, **instrumental aggression** declines while **hostile aggression** increases. Hostile aggression includes **physical aggression** (more common in boys), **verbal aggression,** and **relational aggression**.

■ Ineffective discipline and a conflict-ridden family atmosphere promote and sustain children's aggression. Media violence also triggers aggression. Young children's limited understanding of TV content increases their willingness to uncritically accept and imitate what they see.

■ Teaching parents effective child-rearing practices, providing children with social problem-solving training, intervening in marital problems, and shielding children from violent media reduce aggressive behavior.

Gender Typing

Discuss genetic and environmental influences on preschoolers' gender-stereotyped beliefs and behavior.

■ **Gender typing** is well under way in early childhood. Preschoolers acquire a wide range of gender-stereotyped beliefs, which operate as blanket rules rather than flexible guidelines for behavior.

■ Prenatal hormones contribute to boys' higher activity level and rowdier play, and to children's preference for same-sex playmates. At the same time, parents, same-sex older siblings, teachers, peers, and the broader social environment encourage many gender-typed responses. Parents apply more pressure for gender-role conformity to sons, and boys are more gender-typed than girls.

Describe and evaluate major theories that explain the emergence of gender identity.

■ Although most people have a traditional **gender identity,** some are **androgynous,** combining both masculine and feminine characteristics. Compared to a feminine identity, masculine and androgynous identities are linked to better psychological adjustment.

■ According to social learning theory, preschoolers first acquire gender-typed responses through modeling and reinforcement, then organize these into gender-linked ideas about themselves. Cognitive-developmental theory suggests that **gender constancy** must be mastered before children develop gender-typed behavior. However, gender-role behavior is acquired long before gender constancy.

■ **Gender schema theory** is an information-processing approach to gender typing that combines social learning and cognitive-developmental features to explain how gender role development occurs through the joint effects of environmental pressures and children's cognitions. As children acquire gender-stereotyped preferences and behaviors, they form masculine and feminine categories, or gender schemas, that they apply to themselves and their world.

Child Rearing and Emotional and Social Development

Describe the impact of child-rearing styles on children's development, and explain why authoritative parenting is effective.

■ Three features distinguish the major **child-rearing styles:** (1) acceptance and involvement, (2) control, and (3) autonomy granting. Compared with the **authoritarian, permissive,** and **uninvolved styles,** the **authoritative style** promotes cognitive, emotional, and social competence. Warmth, explanations, and reasonable demands for mature behavior account for the effectiveness of the authoritative style. **Psychological control** is associated with authoritarian parenting and contributes to adjustment problems.

■ Certain ethnic groups, including Chinese, Hispanic, Asian Pacific Island, and African-American, combine parental warmth with high levels of control. But when control becomes harsh and excessive, it impairs academic and social competence.

Discuss the multiple origins of child maltreatment, its consequences for development, and prevention strategies.

■ Child maltreatment is related to factors within the family, community, and larger culture. Maltreating parents use ineffective discipline and hold a negatively biased view of their child. Unmanageable parental stress and social isolation greatly increase the chances that abuse and neglect will occur. When a society approves of force and violence as a means for solving problems, child abuse is promoted.

■ Maltreated children are impaired in emotional self-regulation, empathy and sympathy, self-concept, social skills, and academic motivation. They are also likely to suffer central nervous system damage, which increases the chances that adjustment problems will endure. Successful prevention of child maltreatment requires efforts at the family, community, and societal levels.

Important Terms and Concepts

Milestones
Development in Early Childhood

2 years

LANGUAGE

- Vocabulary increases rapidly. (356)
- Coins new words based on known words. (357)
- Sentences follow basic word order of native language; adds grammatical markers piecemeal. (358)
- Displays effective conversational skills. (359)

EMOTIONAL/SOCIAL

- I-self becomes more firmly established, and focus shifts to the me-self. (336)
- Begins to develop self-concept and self-esteem. (367, 368–369)
- Throughout early childhood, emotional competence improves. (369)
- Understands causes, consequences, and behavioral signs of basic emotions. (370)
- Shows early indicators of developing moral sense—verbal evaluations of their own and others' actions and distress at harmful behaviors. (380)
- Instrumental aggression emerges. (387)
- Gender-stereotyped beliefs and behavior increase. (391)

3–4 years

PHYSICAL

- Rapid synaptic growth and myelination of neural fibers in the brain continue, especially in the frontal lobes. (296)
- May no longer need a daytime nap. (302)
- Running, jumping, hopping, throwing, and catching become more refined, with increasingly flexible upper body. (312)
- Galloping and one-foot skipping appear. (312)

PHYSICAL

- Throughout early childhood, height and weight increase more slowly than in toddlerhood. (293)
- Balance improves; walking becomes smooth and rhythmic; running emerges. (312)
- Jumps, hops, throws, and catches with rigid upper body. (312)
- Puts on and removes simple items of clothing. (313)
- Uses spoon effectively. (313)
- First drawings are gestural scribbles. (313)

COGNITIVE

- Make-believe becomes less dependent on realistic objects, less self-centered, and more complex; sociodramatic play increases. (322–323)
- Can take the perspective of others in simplified situations. (326–327)
- Recognition memory is well developed. (339)
- Shows awareness of the difference between inner mental and outer physical events. (342)
- Begins to count. (348)

- Pedals and steers tricycle. (312)
- Uses scissors. (312)
- Uses fork adeptly. (313)
- Draws first picture of a person, using tadpole image. (314)
- Distinguishes writing from nonwriting. (316)

COGNITIVE

- Masters dual representation. (324)
- Notices and reasons about conservation and transformations, can reverse thinking, and has a basic understanding of many cause-and-effect relationships. (328)
- Hierarchically organizes instances of familiar categories. (329–330)
- Distinguishes appearance from reality. (331)
- Uses private speech to guide behavior during challenging tasks. (334)
- Sustained attention and planning improve. (338–339)
- Uses scripts to recall familiar experiences. (340)
- Understands that both beliefs and desires determine behavior. (342)
- Shows awareness of some meaningful features of written language. (346)
- Knows meaning of numbers to ten, counts correctly, and grasps cardinality. (348)

LANGUAGE

- Extends language meanings through metaphor. (357)
- Applies basic subject–verb–object structure broadly, to new verbs. (358)
- Masters increasingly complex grammatical structures. (358)

- Occasionally overextends grammatical rules to exceptions. (358)
- Adjusts speech to fit the age, sex, and social status of listeners. (360)

EMOTIONAL/SOCIAL

- Adds typical emotions and attitudes to observable characteristics in self-concept. (367)
- Has several self-esteems, such as learning things in school, making friends, and getting along with parents. (368)
- Emotional self-regulation improves, with strategy use and effortful control. (371)
- Experiences self-conscious emotions more often. (372)
- Empathic responding increases. (373)
- Engages in interactive play (associative and cooperative) in addition to nonsocial activity and parallel play. (374)
- Instrumental aggression declines, while hostile aggression (verbal and relational) increases. (387)
- Forms first friendships. (376)
- Distinguishes moral imperatives from social-conventions and personal choices. (382)
- Preference for same-sex playmates strengthens. (394–395)

5–6 years

PHYSICAL

- Body is streamlined and longer-legged with proportions similar to adults'. (294)
- Starts to lose primary teeth. (294)
- Brain reaches 90 percent of its adult weight. (296)
- Gross motor skills increase in speed and endurance. (312)
- Gallops more smoothly and engages in true skipping. (312)
- Displays mature, flexible throwing and catching pattern. (312)

- Uses knife to cut soft foods. (313)
- Ties shoes. (313)
- Draws more complex pictures. (314)
- Uses an adult pencil grip, writes name, copies some numbers and simple words, and can discriminate letters of the alphabet. (315–316)

COGNITIVE

- Magical beliefs decline. (327)
- Ability to distinguish appearance from reality improves. (331)
- Attention and planning continue to improve. (338–339)
- Recognition, recall, scripted memory, and autobiographical memory improve. (339–340)
- Understanding of false belief strengthens. (343)
- Understands that letters and sounds are linked in systematic ways. (346)
- Experiments with strategies to solve simple arithmetic problems. (348)

LANGUAGE

- Vocabulary reaches about 10,000 words. (356)
- Uses most grammatical constructions competently. (359)

EMOTIONAL/SOCIAL

- Emotional understanding (ability to interpret, predict, and influence others' emotional reactions) improves. (370)
- Becomes better at social problem solving. (377–378)
- Has acquired many morally relevant rules and behaviors. (380–381)
- Gender-stereotyped beliefs and behavior continue to increase; preference for same-sex playmates increases further. (395)
- Understands gender constancy. (396)

Note: Numbers in parentheses indicate the page or pages on which each milestone is discussed.

Chapter 11

In this idyllic outdoor scene, players gather for an exciting game of soccer. Through child-organized games, children advance physically, cognitively, and socially. Chapter 11 takes up the diverse physical attainments of the school years.

Reprinted with permission from the International Child Art Foundation, Washington, D.C.

"Peace and Harmony"
George Margvelashvili
8 years, Tbilisi, Georgia

Physical Development in Middle Childhood

"**I**'m on my way, Mom!" hollered 10-year-old Joey as he stuffed the last bite of toast into his mouth, slung his book bag over his shoulder, dashed out the door, jumped on his bike, and headed down the street for school. Joey's 8-year-old sister Lizzie followed, kissing her mother goodbye and pedaling furiously until she caught up with Joey. Rena, the children's mother and one of my colleagues at the university, watched from the front porch as her son and daughter disappeared in the distance.

"They're branching out," Rena told me over lunch that day, as she described the children's expanding activities and relationships. Homework, household chores, soccer teams, music lessons, scouting, friends at school and in the neighborhood, and Joey's new paper route were all part of the children's routine. "It seems as if the basics are all there; I don't have to monitor Joey and Lizzie so constantly anymore. Being a parent is still very challenging, but it's more a matter of refinements—helping them become independent, competent, and productive individuals."

Joey and Lizzie have entered middle childhood—the years from 6 to 11. Around the world, children of this age are assigned new responsibilities. For children in industrialized nations, like Joey and Lizzie, middle childhood is often called the "school years" because its onset is marked by the start of formal schooling. In village and tribal cultures, the school may be a field or a jungle. But universally, mature members of society guide children of this age period toward real-world tasks that increasingly resemble those they will perform as adults.

This chapter focuses on physical growth in middle childhood—changes less spectacular than those seen in earlier years. By age 6, the brain has reached 90 percent of its adult weight, and the body continues to grow slowly. In this way, nature gives school-age children the mental powers to master challenging tasks as well as added time—before reaching physical maturity—to acquire the knowledge and skills they will need for life in a complex social world.

We begin by reviewing typical growth trends and special health concerns of middle childhood. Then we turn to rapid gains in motor abilities, which support practical everyday activities, athletic skills, and participation in organized games. We will see that each of these achievements is affected by and contributes to cognitive, emotional, and social development. Our discussion will echo a familiar theme—that all domains are interrelated.

Andy at 8 years

Andy at 6 years

Andy at 10½ years

Andy at 9 years

Amy at 8 years

Amy at 6 years

Amy at 9 years

Amy at 10½ years

FIGURE 11.1

Body growth during middle childhood.   Andy and Amy continued the slow, regular pattern of growth that they showed in early childhood (see Chapter 8, page 295). But around age 9, Amy began to grow at a faster rate than Andy. At age 10½, she was taller, heavier, and more mature-looking.

© MICHAEL NEWMAN/PHOTOEDIT

These young bowlers are similar in age but vary greatly in body size. They illustrate faster growth of the lower portion of the body in middle childhood, appearing longer-legged than they did as preschoolers.

Body Growth

Physical growth during the school years continues at the slow, regular pace of early childhood. At age 6, the average North American child weighs about 45 pounds and is 3½ feet tall. Over the next few years, children will add about 2 to 3 inches in height and 5 pounds in weight each year (see Figure 11.1). Between ages 6 and 8, girls are slightly shorter and lighter than boys. By age 9, this trend reverses. Already, Rena noticed, Lizzie was starting to catch up with Joey in physical size as she approached the dramatic adolescent growth spurt, which occurs two years earlier in girls than in boys.

Because the lower portion of the body is growing fastest, Joey and Lizzie appeared longer-legged than they had in early childhood. They grew out of their jeans more quickly than their jackets and frequently needed larger shoes. As in early childhood, girls have slightly more body fat and boys more muscle. After age 8, girls begin accumulating fat at a faster rate, and they will add even more during adolescence (Siervogel et al., 2000).

Worldwide Variations in Body Size

TAKE A MOMENT... Glance into any elementary school classroom, and you will see wide individual differences in body growth. Diversity in physical size is especially apparent when we travel to different nations. Worldwide, a 9-inch gap exists between the smallest and the largest 8-year-olds. The shortest children, found in South America, Asia, the Pacific Islands, and parts of Africa, include such ethnic groups as Colombian, Burmese, Thai, Vietnamese, Ethiopian, and Bantu. The tallest children, who reside in Australia, northern and central Europe, Canada, and the United States, come from Czech, Dutch, Latvian, Norwegian, Swiss, and African-American populations (Meredith, 1978; Ruff, 2002). These findings remind us that *growth norms* (age-related averages for height and weight) must be applied cautiously, especially in countries with high immigration rates and many ethnic minorities.

Body size is sometimes the result of evolutionary adaptations to a particular climate. These boys of the Sudan, who live on the hot African plains, have long, lean physiques, which permit the body to cool easily.

What accounts for these vast differences in physical size? Both heredity and environment are involved. Body size sometimes results from evolutionary adaptations to a particular climate. Long, lean physiques are typical in hot, tropical regions and short, stocky ones in cold, Arctic areas (Katzmarzyk & Leonard, 1998). Also, children who grow tallest usually reside in developed countries, where food is plentiful and infectious diseases are largely controlled. In contrast, small children tend to live in less developed regions, where poverty, hunger, and disease are common (Bogin, 2001). When families move from poor to wealthy nations, their children not only grow taller but also change to a longer-legged body shape. (Recall that during childhood, the legs are growing fastest). For example, U.S.-born school-age children of immigrant Guatemalan Mayan parents are, on average, $4\frac{1}{2}$ inches taller and nearly 3 inches longer-legged than their agemates in Guatemalan Mayan villages (Bogin et al., 2002).

Secular Trends in Physical Growth

Over the past 150 years, **secular trends in physical growth**—changes in body size from one generation to the next—have taken place in industrialized nations. Joey and Lizzie are taller and heavier than their parents and grandparents were as children. These trends have been found in Australia, Canada, Japan, New Zealand, the United States, and nearly all European nations (Ong, Ahmed, & Dunger, 2006). For example, measurements of more than 24,000 Bogalusa, Louisiana, schoolchildren between 1973 and 1992 revealed an average height gain of nearly $\frac{1}{3}$ inch per decade (Freedman et al., 2000). The secular gain appears early in life, increases over childhood and early adolescence, then declines as mature body size is reached. This pattern suggests that the larger size of today's children is mostly due to a faster rate of physical development.

Once again, improved health and nutrition are largely responsible for these growth gains. Secular trends are smaller for low-income children, who have poorer diets and are more likely to suffer from growth-stunting illnesses. And in regions of the world with widespread poverty, famine, and disease, either no secular change or a secular decrease in body size has occurred (Barnes-Josiah & Augustin, 1995; Cole, 2000). In most industrialized nations, the secular gain in height has slowed in recent decades. Weight gain, however, is continuing at a high rate. As we will see later, overweight and obesity have reached epic proportions.

Skeletal Growth

During middle childhood, the bones of the body lengthen and broaden. However, ligaments are not yet firmly attached to bones. This, combined with increasing muscle strength, gives children unusual flexibility of movement. School-age youngsters often seem like "physical contortionists," turning cartwheels and doing splits and handstands. As their bodies become stronger, many children experience a greater desire for physical exercise. Nighttime "growing pains"—stiffness and aches in the legs—are common as muscles adapt to an enlarging skeleton (Evans & Scutter, 2004).

secular trends in physical growth Changes in body size from one generation to the next.

Between ages 6 and 12, all 20 primary teeth are lost and replaced by permanent ones, with girls losing their teeth slightly earlier than boys. The first teeth to go are the lower and then upper front teeth, giving many first and second graders a "toothless" smile. For a while, the permanent teeth seem much too large. Gradually, growth of the facial bones, especially those of the jaw and chin, causes the child's face to lengthen and the mouth to widen, accommodating the newly erupting teeth.

Care of the teeth is essential during the school years because dental health affects the child's appearance, speech, and ability to chew properly. Parents need to remind children to brush their teeth thoroughly, and most children need help with flossing until about 9 years of age. More than 50 percent of North American school-age children have at least some tooth decay (World Health Organization, 2003, 2004). As in the preschool years, low-SES children have especially high levels (see Chapter 8). Children without health insurance are three times as likely to have unmet dental needs. As decay progresses, they experience pain, embarrassment at damaged teeth, distraction from play and learning, and school absences due to dental-related illnesses.

Malocclusion, a condition in which the upper and lower teeth do not meet properly, occurs in one-third of school-age children. In about 14 percent of cases, serious difficulties in biting and chewing result. Malocclusion can be caused by thumb and finger sucking after permanent teeth erupt. Children who were eager thumb suckers during infancy and early childhood may require gentle but persistent encouragement to give up the habit by school entry (Charchut, Allred, & Needleman, 2003). Another cause of malocclusion is crowding of permanent teeth. In some children, this problem clears up as the jaw grows. Others need braces, a common sight by the end of elementary school.

Brain Development

The weight of the brain increases by only 10 percent during middle childhood and adolescence. Nevertheless, considerable growth occurs in certain brain structures. Using fMRI, researchers can detect the volume of two general types of brain tissue: *white matter,* consisting largely of myelinated nerve fibers, and *gray matter,* consisting mostly of neurons and supportive material. White matter increases steadily throughout childhood and adolescence, especially in the frontal lobes of the cerebral cortex (responsible for consciousness, impulse control, integration of information, and strategic thinking), in the parietal lobes (supporting spatial abilities), and in the corpus callosum (leading to improved communication between the two cortical hemispheres) (Barnea-Goraly et al., 2005; Nelson, Thomas, & de Haan, 2006). As children acquire more complex abilities, stimulated neurons increase in synaptic connections, and their neural fibers become more elaborate and myelinated. At the same time, gray matter declines as a result of synaptic pruning (reduction of unused synapses) and death of surrounding neurons (Sowell et al., 2002). As a result, lateralization of the cerebral hemispheres increases.

Little information is available on how the brain develops in other ways. One idea is that much development takes place at the level of neurotransmitters, chemicals that permit neurons to communicate across synapses (see Chapter 5, page 168). Over time, neurons become increasingly selective, responding only to certain chemical messages. This change may contribute to the more efficient and flexible thinking and behavior of school-age children. Secretions of particular neurotransmitters are related to cognitive performance, social and emotional adjustment, and ability to withstand stress. When neurotransmitters are not present in appropriate balances, children may suffer serious developmental problems, such as inattention and overactivity, emotional disturbance, and epilepsy (an illness involving brain seizures and loss of motor control) (Brooks et al., 2006; Pearl et al., 2005; Weller, Kloos, & Weller, 2006).

Researchers also believe that brain functioning may change in middle childhood because of the influence of hormones. Around age 7 to 8, an increase in *androgens* (male sex hormones), secreted by the adrenal glands (located on top of the kidneys), occurs in children of both sexes. Androgens will rise further among boys at puberty, when the testes release them in large

In middle childhood, neural fibers in the brain become more elaborate and myelinated, especially in the frontal lobes of the cerebral cortex, contributing to strategic thinking and integration of information. These changes support more complex abilities, as demonstrated by these high-jumping gymnasts.

© DAVID HANDLEY/GETTY IMAGES/DORLING KINDERSLEY

amounts. Androgens affect brain organization and behavior in many animal species, and they do so in humans as well. Recall from Chapter 10 that androgens contribute to boys' higher activity level. They may also promote social dominance and play-fighting, topics we will take up at the end of this chapter (Azurmendi et al., 2006).

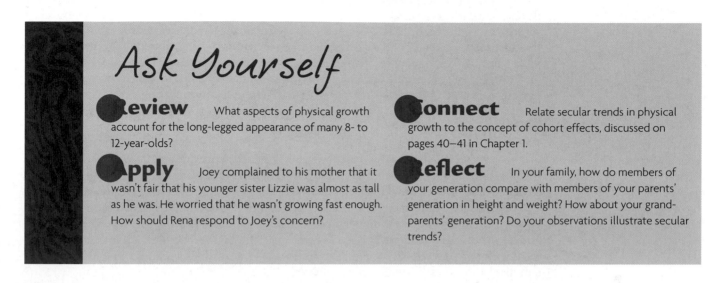

Ask Yourself

Review What aspects of physical growth account for the long-legged appearance of many 8- to 12-year-olds?

Apply Joey complained to his mother that it wasn't fair that his younger sister Lizzie was almost as tall as he was. He worried that he wasn't growing fast enough. How should Rena respond to Joey's concern?

Connect Relate secular trends in physical growth to the concept of cohort effects, discussed on pages 40–41 in Chapter 1.

Reflect In your family, how do members of your generation compare with members of your parents' generation in height and weight? How about your grandparents' generation? Do your observations illustrate secular trends?

Common Health Problems

Children from economically advantaged homes, like Joey and Lizzie, are at their healthiest in middle childhood, full of energy and play. The cumulative effects of good nutrition, combined with rapid development of the body's immune system, offer greater protection against disease. At the same time, growth in lung size permits more air to be exchanged with each breath, so children are better able to exercise vigorously without tiring.

Not surprisingly, poverty continues to be a powerful predictor of poor health during middle childhood. Recall that in the United States, economically disadvantaged children often lack health insurance and, if they are publicly insured, generally receive a lower standard of care (see Chapter 8, page 307). And a substantial number also lack such basic necessities as a comfortable home and regular meals.

Vision and Hearing

The most common vision problem in middle childhood is **myopia,** or nearsightedness. By the end of the school years, it affects nearly 25 percent of children—a rate that rises to 60 percent by early adulthood (Sperduto et al., 1996).

Kinship studies reveal that heredity contributes to myopia. Identical twins are more likely than fraternal twins to share the condition (Pacella et al., 1999). And compared to children with no myopic parents, those with one myopic parent have twice the risk, and those with two myopic parents two to five times the risk, of becoming myopic themselves. Worldwide, myopia occurs far more frequently in Asian than in Caucasian populations (Feldkámper & Schaeffel, 2003). Early biological trauma can also induce myopia. School-age children with low birth weights show an especially high rate, believed to result from immaturity of visual structures, slower eye growth, and a greater incidence of eye disease (O'Connor et al., 2002).

But myopia is also related to experience. When parents warn their children not to read in dim light or sit too close to the TV or computer screen, their concern ("You'll ruin your eyes!") is well-founded. Myopia progresses much more rapidly during the school year, when children spend more time reading and doing other close work, than during the summer months (Goss & Rainey, 1998). In diverse cultures, the more time children spend reading, writing, and using

malocclusion A condition in which the upper and lower teeth do not meet properly.

myopia Nearsightedness; inability to see distant objects clearly.

the computer, the more likely they are to be myopic (Mutti et al., 2002; Saw et al., 2002). Consequently, myopia is one of the few health conditions to increase with family income and education, and it has also increased in recent generations. Fortunately, myopia can easily be corrected with corrective lenses.

During middle childhood, the eustachian tube (the canal that runs from the inner ear to the throat) becomes longer, narrower, and more slanted, preventing fluid and bacteria from traveling so easily from the mouth to the ear. As a result, *otitis media* (middle ear infection) becomes less frequent than in infancy and early childhood (see Chapter 8). Still, about 3 to 4 percent of the school-age population, and as many as 20 percent of low-SES children, develop some hearing loss from repeated infections (Ryding et al., 2002). Regular screening for both vision and hearing permits defects to be corrected before they lead to serious learning difficulties.

Malnutrition

School-age children need a well-balanced, plentiful diet to provide energy for successful learning in school and increased physical activity. With their increasing focus on play, friendships, and new activities, many children spend little time at the table. Joey's hurried breakfast, described at the beginning of this chapter, is a common event in middle childhood. The percentage of children who eat dinner with their families drops sharply between ages 9 and 14, and family dinnertimes have waned in general over the past two decades. Yet eating an evening meal with parents leads to a diet higher in fruits and vegetables and lower in fried foods and soft drinks (Neumark-Sztainer et al., 2003).

School-age children report that they "feel better" and "focus better" after eating healthy foods and that they feel sluggish, "like a blob," after eating junk foods. But they also say that a major barrier to healthy eating is the ready availability of unhealthy options, especially in their homes. As one sixth grader commented, "When I get home from school, I think, 'I should eat some fruits,' but then I see the chips" (O'Dea, 2003, p. 498). Readily available, healthy between-meal snacks—such as cheese, fruit, raw vegetables, and peanut butter—can help meet school-age children's nutritional needs. Even mild nutritional deficits can affect cognitive functioning. Among school-age children from middle- to high-SES families, insufficient dietary iron and folate predicted slightly lower mental test performance (Arija et al., 2006).

As we have seen in earlier chapters, many poverty-stricken children in developing countries and in North America suffer from serious, prolonged malnutrition. By middle childhood, the effects are apparent in retarded physical growth, low IQ, poor motor coordination, and inattention. The negative impact of malnutrition on learning and behavior may intensify as children encounter new academic and social challenges at school. First, as in earlier years, growth-stunted school-age children respond with greater fear to stressful situations, as indicated by a sharper rise in heart rate and in saliva levels of the stress hormone cortisol (Fernald & Grantham-McGregor, 1998). Second, animal evidence reveals that a deficient diet alters the production of neurotransmitters in the brain—an effect that can disrupt all aspects of psychological functioning (Haller, 2005).

Unfortunately, malnutrition that persists from infancy or early childhood into the school years usually leads to permanent physical and mental damage (Grantham-McGregor, Walker, & Chang, 2000; Liu et al., 2003). Government-sponsored food programs from the early years through adolescence can prevent these effects. In studies of economically disadvantaged school-age children carried out in Egypt, Kenya, and Mexico, quality of food (protein, vitamin, and mineral content) strongly predicted favorable cognitive development (Sigman, 1995; Watkins & Pollitt, 1998).

obesity A greater-than-20-percent increase over healthy body weight, based on body mass index, a ratio of weight to height associated with body fat.

Obesity

Mona, a very heavy child in Lizzie's class, often stood on the sidelines during recess, watching the children's games. When she did play, she was slow and clumsy, an easy target for unkind comments: "Move it, Tubs!" Although Mona was a good student, the other children rejected her in the classroom as well. When they chose partners for special activities, Mona was among the last to be selected. Most afternoons, she walked home alone while her schoolmates gathered in groups, talking, laughing, and chasing. At home, Mona sought comfort in high-calorie snacks.

Today, about one-third of North American children and adolescents are overweight, half or more of them extremely so: Nearly 15 percent of Canadian and 17 percent of U.S. children and adolescents suffer from **obesity,** a greater-than-20-percent increase over healthy weight, based on *body mass index (BMI)*— a ratio of weight to height associated with body fat. (A BMI of 25 or more is generally considered overweight, a BMI of 30 or more obese.) During the past several decades, a rise in overweight and obesity has occurred in many Western nations, with dramatic escalations in Canada, Finland, Greece, Great Britain, Ireland, New Zealand, and especially the United States (Ogden et al., 2006; U.S. Department of Health and Human Services, 2006e; Willms, Tremblay, & Katzmarzyk, 2003). Smaller increases have occurred in other industrialized nations, including Australia, Germany, Israel, the Netherlands, and Sweden.

Obesity rates are also increasing rapidly in developing countries as urbanization shifts the population toward sedentary activities and diets high in meats and refined foods (World Press Review, 2004; Wrotniak et al., 2004). In China, for example,

These children are attending a weight-loss summer camp near Beijing. In China, lifestyle changes, together with long-standing cultural beliefs associating excess body fat with prosperity, have led to rising rates of childhood overweight and obesity, which currently affects 15 percent of school-age children and adolescents.

where obesity was nearly nonexistent a generation ago, today 15 percent of children and adolescents are overweight and 3 percent are obese—a fourfold increase over the past two decades, with boys affected more than girls (see Figure 11.2) (Wu, 2006). Childhood obesity in China is especially high in cities, where it has reached 8 percent (McLeod, 2007). In addition to lifestyle changes, a prevailing belief in Chinese culture that excess body fat represents prosperity and health—carried over from a half-century ago, when famine and malnutrition caused millions of deaths—has contributed to this alarming upsurge. High valuing of sons may induce Chinese parents to offer boys especially generous portions of meat, dairy products, and other energy-dense foods that were once scarce but now are widely available.

Overweight and obesity rise with age: Over 80 percent of affected children become overweight adults. Besides serious emotional and social difficulties, obese children are at risk for lifelong health problems. High blood pressure, high cholesterol levels, respiratory abnormalities, and insulin resistance begin to appear in the early school years—symptoms that are powerful predictors of heart disease and other circulatory difficulties, type 2 diabetes, gallbladder disease, sleep and digestive disorders, many forms of cancer, and early death (Calle et al., 2003; Krebs & Jacobson, 2003). Indeed, type 2 diabetes—in the past also known as "adult-onset" diabetes because it was rarely seen in childhood—is rising rapidly among overweight children, sometimes leading to early, severe complications, including stroke, kidney failure, and circulatory problems that heighten the risk of eventual blindness and leg amputation (Hannon, Rao, & Arslanian, 2005; National Diabetes Education Program, 2004). As you can see from Table 11.1 on page 418, childhood obesity is a complex physical disorder with multiple causes.

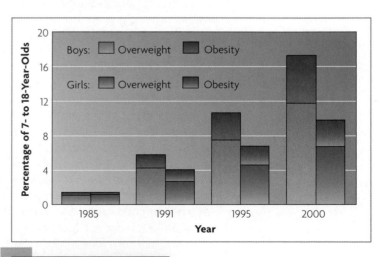

FIGURE 11.2

Increase in overweight and obesity among 7- to 18-year-olds in China from 1985 to 2000. The trend, though evident in both sexes, is much greater in boys. (From Y. Wu, 2006, "Overweight and Obesity in China," *British Medical Journal, 333,* p. 363. Reprinted by permission.)

CAUSES OF OBESITY ■ Not all children are equally at risk for excessive weight gain. Overweight children tend to have overweight parents, and concordance

TABLE 11.1	Factors Associated with Childhood Obesity
FACTOR	**DESCRIPTION**
Heredity	Obese children are likely to have at least one obese parent, and concordance for obesity is greater in identical than in fraternal twins.
Socioeconomic status	Obesity is more common in low-SES families.
Early growth pattern	Infants who gain weight rapidly are at greater risk for obesity, probably because their parents promote unhealthy eating habits (see Chapter 5).
Family eating habits	When parents purchase high-calorie fast foods, treats, and junk food, use them to reward their children, anxiously overfeed, or control their children's intake, their youngsters are more likely to be obese.
Responsiveness to food cues	Obese children often decide when to eat on the basis of external cues, such as taste, smell, sight, time of day, and food-related words, rather than hunger.
Physical activity	Obese children are less physically active than their normal-weight peers.
Television viewing	Children who spend many hours watching television are more likely to become obese.
Early malnutrition	Early, severe malnutrition that results in growth stunting increases the risk of later obesity.

for obesity is greater in identical than in fraternal twins. (Return to Chapter 2, page 84, to review the concept of concordance.) But heredity accounts for only a *tendency* to gain weight (Salbe et al., 2002). The importance of environment is seen in the consistent relationship between low SES and overweight and obesity in industrialized nations, especially among low-SES ethnic minorities, including African-American, Hispanic, Native-American, and Canadian-Aboriginal children and adults (Anand et al., 2001; Ogden et al., 2006). Among the factors responsible are lack of knowledge about healthy diet; a tendency to buy high-fat, low-cost foods; and family stress, which can prompt overeating.

A follow-up of more than 2,000 U.S. 3- to 12-year-olds revealed that children who got less nightly sleep were more likely to be overweight five years later (Snell, Adam, & Duncan, 2007). Reduced sleep may promote weight through several pathways—by increasing time available for eating, by leaving a child too fatigued for physical activity, or by disrupting the brain's regulation of hunger and metabolism.

Furthermore, children who were undernourished in their early years are at risk for later excessive weight gain. Studies in many poverty-stricken regions of the world reveal that growth-stunted children are more likely to be overweight than their nonstunted agemates (Branca & Ferrari, 2002). A malnourished body protects itself by establishing a low basal metabolism rate, which may endure after nutrition improves. Also, malnutrition may disrupt appetite control centers in the brain, causing the child to overeat when food becomes plentiful.

Parental feeding practices also contribute to childhood obesity. Overweight children are more likely to eat larger quantities of high-fat foods, perhaps because these foods are prominent in the diets offered by their parents, who also tend to be overweight. Some parents anxiously overfeed, interpreting almost all their child's discomforts as a desire for food. Others pressure their children to eat, a practice common among immigrant parents and grandparents, who as children themselves lived through deadly famines or periods of food deprivation due to poverty. Still other parents are overly controlling, restricting when, what, and how much their child eats and worrying that the child will gain too much weight (Birch, Fisher, & Davison, 2003; Spruijt-Metz et al., 2002). In each case, parents fail to help children learn to regulate their own food intake. Also, parents of obese children often use high-fat, sugary foods to reinforce other behaviors, which leads children to attach great value to the treat (Sherry et al., 2004).

Because of these experiences, obese children soon develop maladaptive eating habits. They are more responsive than normal-weight individuals to external stimuli associated with food—taste, sight, smell, time of day, and food-related words—and less responsive to internal hunger cues (Braet & Crombez, 2003; Jansen et al., 2003). They also eat faster and chew their food less thoroughly, a behavior pattern that appears as early as 18 months of age (Drabman et al., 1979).

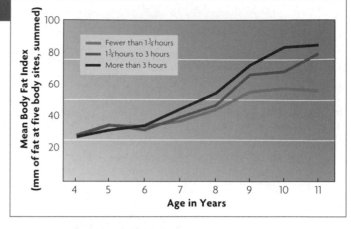

FIGURE 11.3

Relationship of television viewing to gains in body fat from ages 4 to 11. Researchers followed more than one hundred children from ages 4 to 11, collecting information on hours per day of television viewing and on body fat, measured in millimeters of skinfold thickness at five body sites (upper arms, shoulders, abdomen, trunk, and thighs). The more TV children watched, the greater the gain in body fat. At ages 10 to 11, the difference between children watching fewer than 1¾ hours and those watching more than 3 hours had become large. (Adapted from M. H. Proctor et al., 2003, "Television Viewing and Change in Body Fat from Preschool to Early Adolescence: The Framingham Children's Study," *International Journal of Obesity, 27*, p. 831, © Nature Publishing Group. Adapted by permission.)

Overweight children are less physically active than their normal-weight peers, and their parents are similarly inactive (Davison & Birch, 2002). This inactivity is both cause and consequence of excessive weight gain. Recent evidence reveals that the rise in childhood obesity is due in part to the many hours North American children spend watching television. In a study that tracked children's TV viewing from ages 4 to 11, the more TV children watched, the more body fat they added. Children who devoted more than 3 hours per day to TV accumulated 40 percent more fat than those devoting less than 1¾ hours (see Figure 11.3) (Proctor et al., 2003). Watching TV reduces time devoted to physical exercise, and TV ads encourage children to eat fattening, unhealthy snacks. As children get heavier, they increasingly replace active play with sedentary pursuits, including eating, and they gain more weight (Salbe et al., 2002a).

Finally, the broader food environment affects the incidence of obesity. The Pima Indians of Arizona, who recently changed from a traditional diet of plant foods to a high-fat, typically American diet, have one of the world's highest obesity rates. Compared with descendants of their ancestors living in the remote Sierra Madre region of Mexico, the Arizona Pima have body weights 50 percent greater. Half the population has diabetes (8 times the national average), with many in their twenties and thirties already disabled by the disease—blind, in wheelchairs, and on kidney dialysis (Gladwell, 1998). The Pima do have a genetic susceptibility to overweight, but it emerges only under Western dietary conditions. Refer to the Social Issues: Health box on pages 420–421 for societal changes that have led Americans to become the heaviest people in the world.

CONSEQUENCES OF OBESITY ■ Unfortunately, physical attractiveness is a powerful predictor of social acceptance. In Western societies, both children and adults rate obese youngsters as unlikable, stereotyping them as lazy, sloppy, dirty, ugly, stupid, and deceitful (Kilpatrick & Sanders, 1978; Tiggemann & Anesbury, 2000). In school, obese children are often socially isolated (Strauss & Pollack, 2003). By middle childhood, they report more emotional, social, and school difficulties and display more behavior problems than normal-weight peers. Because unhappiness and overeating contribute to each other, the child remains overweight (Mustillo et al., 2003; Zeller & Modi, 2006). Persistent obesity from childhood into adolescence predicts serious disorders, including defiance, aggression, and severe depression (Schwimmer, Burwinkle, & Varni, 2003). Also, as we will see in Chapter 14, overweight girls are more likely to reach puberty early, increasing their risk for early sexual activity and other adjustment problems.

The psychological consequences of obesity combine with continuing discrimination to result in reduced life chances. Overweight adults are less likely than their normal-weight agemates to be given financial aid for college, to be rented apartments, to find mates, and to be offered jobs. And they report frequent mistreatment by family members, peers, co-workers, and health-care professionals (Carr & Friedman, 2005; Rogge, Greenwald, & Golden, 2004).

TREATING OBESITY ■ Childhood obesity is difficult to treat because it is a family disorder. In Mona's case, the school nurse suggested that Mona and her obese mother enter a weight-loss program together. But Mona's mother, unhappily married for many years, had her own reasons for continuing to overeat. She rejected this idea, claiming that Mona would eventually decide to lose weight on her own. In one study, only one-fourth of overweight parents judged

© MARK RICHARDS/PHOTOEDIT

As they walk together, this father and son reinforce each other's efforts to lose weight and get in shape physically. The most effective interventions for childhood obesity focus on changing the whole family's behaviors.

Social Issues: Health

The Obesity Epidemic: How Americans Became the Heaviest People in the World

In the late 1980s, obesity in the United States stared to soar. The maps in Figure 11.4 show how quickly it engulfed the nation. Today nearly 40 percent of American school-age children and adolescents and 65 percent of adults are either overweight or obese (U.S. Department of Health and Human Services, 2007). The epidemic has spread to other Western nations, including Canada, where the respective figures are 30 and 59 percent (Starky, 2005). But no country matches the United States in prevalence of this life-threatening condition.

A Changing Food Environment and Lifestyle

Several societal factors have encouraged widespread rapid weight gain:

■ *Availability of cheap commercial fat and sugar.* The 1970s saw two massive changes in the U.S. food economy: (1) the discovery and mass production of high-fructose corn syrup, a sweetener six times as sweet as ordinary sugar, and therefore far less expensive; and (2) the importing from Malaysia of large quantities of palm oil, which is lower in cost than other vegetable oils and also tastier, because of its high saturated fat content. As food manufacturers relied on corn syrup and palm oil to make soft drinks and calorie-dense convenience foods, the production costs of these items dropped and their variety expanded. A new era of "cheap, abundant, and tasty calories had arrived" (Critser, 2003).

■ *Portion supersizing.* Fast-food chains discovered a successful strategy for attracting customers: increasing portion sizes substantially and prices just a little for foods that had become inexpensive to produce. Customers thronged to buy "value meals," jumbo burgers and burritos, pizza "by the foot," and 20-ounce Cokes (Critser, 2003). And research revealed that when presented with larger portions, individuals 2 years and older increased their intake, on average, by 25 to 30 percent (Fisher, Rolls, & Birch, 2003; Rolls, Morris, & Roe, 2002).

■ *Increasingly busy lives.* Between the 1970s and the 1990s, women entered the labor force in record numbers, and the average amount of time North Americans worked increased by 15 percent, or about 350 hours per year (Higgins & Duxbury, 2002; Schor, 2002). Number of hours employed mothers work increases risk of childhood obesity because as time for meal preparation shrinks, eating out increases (Anderson, Butcher, & Levine, 2003). In addition, North Americans have become frequent snackers, tempted by a growing assortment of high-calorie snack foods on supermarket shelves. During this period, number of calories Americans consumed away from home nearly doubled,

© DONNA DAY/GETTY IMAGES/STONE

A harmful food environment of cheap, calorie-dense convenience foods and supersize portions and an increasingly sedentary lifestyle have contributed to the obesity epidemic. Without intervention, this boy is at risk for many obesity-related illnesses. Already, he may have high blood pressure and high cholesterol, which are powerful predictors of heart disease, diabetes, various cancers, and other illnesses.

and dietary fat increased from 19 to 38 percent (Nielsen & Popkin, 2003). Overall, average daily food intake rose by almost 200 calories—enough to add an extra pound every 20 days (Nielsen & Popkin, 2003).

■ *Declining rates of physical activity.* As Americans spent more time working in sedentary jobs, they—and their children—exercised less. At home, TV had become their major leisure pursuit—consuming, on average, about 4 hours per day and linked to weight gain in adults and children alike (Gore et al., 2003).

their overweight children to have a weight problem (Jeffrey, 2004). Consistent with these findings, less than 20 percent of obese children get any treatment. Although many of them try to slim down in adolescence, they often go on crash diets that make matters worse. Temporary starvation leads to physical stress, discomfort, and fatigue. Soon the child returns to old eating patterns, and weight rebounds to a higher level. Then, to protect itself, the body burns calories more slowly and becomes more resistant to future weight loss.

When parents decide to seek treatment for an obese child, long-term changes in body weight do occur. The most effective interventions are family-based and focus on changing behaviors (Kitzmann & Beech, 2006). In one program, both parent and child revised their eating patterns, exercised daily, and reinforced each other with praise and points for progress, which they exchanged for special activities and times together. The more weight parents lost, the more

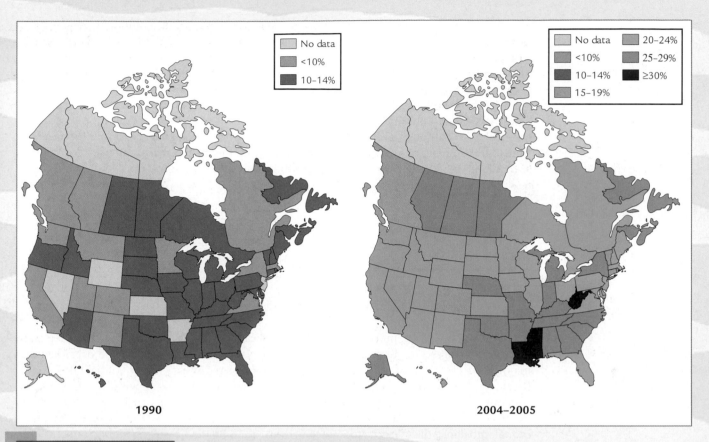

FIGURE 11.4

Obesity trends among Americans and Canadians, 1990 and 2004–2005. The darkening maps show that obesity has increased in both nations, with the United States more extremely affected. (From Health Canada, 2005c; Mokdad et al., 2001; U.S. Department of Health and Human Services, 2007.)

Combating the Obesity Epidemic

Obesity's toll on society is immense. It is responsible for $90 billion in health expenditures and 300,000 premature deaths per year in the United States alone (Manson et al., 2004). Besides individual treatment, societal efforts are needed to combat obesity. Suggestions include:

■ Government funding to support massive public education about healthy eating and physical activity
■ A high priority placed on building parks and recreation centers in low-income neighborhoods, where overweight and obesity are highest
■ Laws that mandate prominent posting of the calorie, sugar, and fat content of foods

sold in restaurants, movie theaters, and convenience stores
■ A special tax on foods high in calories, sugar, or fat
■ Incentives to schools and workplaces for promoting healthy eating and daily exercise and for offering weight-management programs

their children lost (Wrotniak et al., 2004). Follow-ups after 5 and 10 years showed that children maintained their weight loss more effectively than adults—a finding that underscores the importance of intervening at an early age (Epstein, Roemmich, & Raynor, 2001). Treatment programs that focus on both diet and lifestyle can yield substantial, long-lasting weight reduction among children and adolescents. But these interventions work best when parents' and children's weight problems are not severe (Eliakim et al., 2004; Nemet et al., 2005).

Getting obese children to exercise is challenging because they find being sedentary pleasurable. One successful technique is to reinforce them for spending less time inactive. Providing rewards (such as tickets to the zoo or a baseball game) for reducing sedentary time led to greater liking for physical activity and more weight loss among obese children than reinforcing them directly for exercising or punishing them (by loss of privileges) for remaining inactive

(Epstein, Saelens, & O'Brien, 1995; Epstein et al., 1997). Rewarding children for giving up inactivity seems to increase their sense of personal control over exercising—a factor linked to sustained physical activity.

Children consume one-third of their daily energy intake at school. Therefore, schools can help reduce obesity by serving healthier meals and ensuring regular physical activity. Because obesity is expected to rise further without broad prevention strategies, several U.S. states and cities have passed obesity-reduction legislation (Cotton et al., 2006). Among the measures taken are nutrition standards and limited vending machine access in schools, additional recess time in the elementary grades and physical education time in all grades, and obesity awareness and weight-reduction programs as part of school curricula.

Bedwetting

One Friday afternoon, Terry called Joey to see if he could sleep over, but Joey refused. "I can't," said Joey anxiously, without offering an explanation.

"Why not? We can take our sleeping bags out in the backyard. Come on, it'll be cool!"

"My mom won't let me," Joey responded, unconvincingly. "I mean, well, I think we're busy. We're doing something tonight."

"Gosh, Joey, this is the third time you've said no. See if I'll ask you again!" snapped Terry as he hung up the phone.

Joey is one of 10 percent of North American school-age children who suffer from **nocturnal enuresis,** or bedwetting during the night (Thiedke, 2003). In the overwhelming majority of cases, the problem has biological roots. Heredity is a major contributing factor: Parents with a history of bedwetting are far more likely to have a child with the problem, and concordance is greater among identical than fraternal twins (Norgaard et al., 1997). Most often, enuresis is caused by a failure of muscular responses that inhibit urination or by a hormonal imbalance that permits too much urine to accumulate during the night. Some children also have difficulty awakening to the sensation of a full bladder (Hjälmäs, 1998). Punishing a school-age child for wetting is only likely to make matters worse.

To treat enuresis, doctors often prescribe antidepressant drugs, which reduce the amount of urine produced. Although medication is a short-term solution for children attending camp or visiting a friend's house, once children stop taking it, they typically begin wetting again. Also, a small number show side effects, such as anxiety, loss of sleep, and personality changes (Diehr, 2003; Harari & Moulden, 2000). The most effective treatment is a urine alarm that wakes the child at the first sign of dampness and works according to conditioning principles. Success rates of about 60 to 70 percent occur after four to six months of treatment. Most children who relapse achieve dryness after trying the alarm a second time (Houts, 2003).

In a study of more than 3,300 U.S. school-age children with nocturnal enuresis, less than one-third had seen a health worker about the problem (Butler, Golding, & Heron, 2005). Yet treatment in middle childhood has immediate positive psychological consequences. It leads to gains in parents' evaluation of their child's behavior and in children's self-esteem (Longstaffe, Moffatt, & Whalen, 2000). Although many children outgrow enuresis without intervention, this generally takes years.

Illnesses

Children experience a somewhat higher rate of illness during the first two years of elementary school than later, because of exposure to sick children and an immune system that is still developing. On average, illness causes children to miss about 11 days of school per year, but most absences can be traced to a few students with chronic health problems (Moonie et al., 2006).

About 15 to 20 percent of North American children living at home have chronic diseases and conditions (including physical disabilities). By far the most common—accounting for about one-third of childhood chronic illness and the most frequent cause of school absence and childhood hospitalization—is **asthma,** in which the bronchial tubes (passages that connect the throat and lungs) are highly sensitive (Bonilla et al., 2005). In response to a variety of stimuli, such as cold weather, infection, exercise, allergies, and emotional stress, they fill with mucus and contract, leading to coughing, wheezing, and serious breathing difficulties.

nocturnal enuresis
Repeated bedwetting during the night.

asthma A chronic illness in which, in response to a variety of stimuli, highly sensitive bronchial tubes fill with mucus and contract, leading to episodes of coughing, wheezing, and serious breathing difficulties.

During the past 30 years, the number of children with asthma has more than doubled, and asthma-related deaths have also risen. Although heredity contributes to asthma, researchers believe that environmental factors are necessary to spark the illness. Boys, African-American children, and children who were born underweight, whose parents smoke, and who live in poverty are at greatest risk (Federico & Liu, 2003; Pearlman et al., 2006). The higher rate and greater severity of asthma among African-American and poverty-stricken youngsters may be the result of pollution in inner-city areas (which triggers allergic reactions), stressful home lives, and lack of access to good health care. Childhood obesity is also related to asthma in middle childhood, perhaps due to high levels of blood-circulating inflammatory substances associated with body fat (Saha, Riner, & Liu, 2005).

About 2 percent of North American children have more severe chronic illnesses, such as sickle cell anemia, cystic fibrosis, diabetes, arthritis, cancer, and acquired immune deficiency syndrome (AIDS). Painful medical treatments, physical discomfort, and changes in appearance often disrupt the sick child's daily life, making it difficult to concentrate in school and separating the child from peers. As the illness worsens, family stress increases (LeBlanc, Goldsmith, & Patel, 2003). For these reasons, chronically ill children are at risk for academic, emotional, and social difficulties. In adolescence, they are more likely than their agemates to suffer from low self-esteem and depression and report more often smoking cigarettes, using illegal drugs, and thinking about and attempting suicide (Erickson et al., 2005). Good family functioning and child well-being are closely linked for chronically ill children, just as they are for physically healthy children (Barakat & Kazak, 1999). Interventions that foster positive family relationships help parent and child cope with the disease and improve adjustment. These include the following:

■ Health education, in which parents and children learn about the illness and get training in how to manage it
■ Home visits by health professionals, who offer counseling and social support to enhance parents' and children's strategies for handling the stress of chronic illness
■ Schools that accommodate children's special health and education needs
■ Disease-specific summer camps, which teach children self-help skills and give parents time off from the demands of caring for an ill youngster
■ Parent and peer support groups
■ Individual and family therapy

These children are being treated for asthma in a pediatric emergency room. Heredity contributes to a susceptibility to asthma, but environmental factors trigger the illness. It occurs at higher rates in boys, African-American children, children living in poverty, those who were born underweight, those whose parents smoke, and those who are obese.

Unintentional Injuries

As we conclude our discussion of threats to children's health during the school years, let's return for a moment to the topic of unintentional injuries (discussed in detail in Chapter 8). As Figure 11.5 on page 424 shows, injury fatalities increase from middle childhood into adolescence, with rates for boys rising considerably above those for girls. Poverty and rural or inner-city residence—factors associated with dangerous environments and reduced parental monitoring of children—are also linked to high injury rates (Birken et al., 2006; Schwebel et al., 2004).

Motor vehicle accidents, involving children as passengers or pedestrians, continue to be the leading cause of injury, with bicycle accidents next in line (U.S. Department of Health and Human Services, 2006e). Pedestrian injuries most often result from midblock dart-outs, bicycle accidents from disobeying traffic signals and rules. When many stimuli impinge on them at once, young school-age children often fail to think before they act (Tuchfarber, Zins, & Jason, 1997). They need frequent reminders, supervision, and prohibitions against venturing into busy traffic on their own.

As children range farther from home, safety education becomes especially important. School-based programs with lasting effects use extensive modeling and rehearsal of safety practices, give children feedback about their performance along with praise and tangible rewards for acquiring safety skills, and provide occasional booster sessions (Zins et al., 1994). Parents, who often overestimate their child's safety knowledge and physical abilities, must be educated about children's age-related safety capacities (Schwebel & Bounds, 2003).

One vital safety measure is insisting that children wear protective helmets while bicycling, in-line skating, skateboarding, or using scooters. This simple precaution leads to an 85 percent reduction in risk of head injury, a leading cause of permanent physical disability and death in

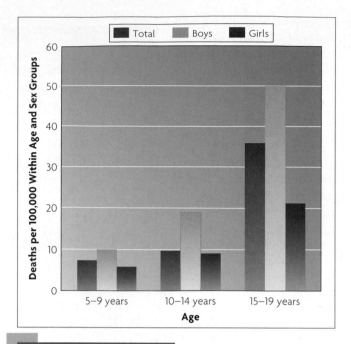

FIGURE 11.5

Rate of injury mortality in North America from middle childhood to adolescence. Injury fatalities increase with age, and the gap between boys and girls expands. Motor vehicle (passenger and pedestrian) accidents are the leading cause, with bicycle injuries next in line. American and Canadian injury rates are nearly identical. (From U.S. Department of Health and Human Services, 2005c.)

school-age children (Schieber & Sacks, 2001). Combining helmet use with other prevention strategies is especially effective. In the Harlem Hospital Injury Prevention Program, inner-city children received safety education in classrooms and in a simulated traffic environment. They also attended bicycle safety clinics, during which helmets were distributed. In addition, existing playgrounds were improved and new ones constructed to provide expanded off-street play areas. Finally, more community-sponsored, supervised recreational activities were offered. As a result, motor vehicle and bicycle injuries declined by 36 percent among school-age children (Durkin et al., 1999).

Not all children respond to efforts to increase their safety. By middle childhood, the greatest risk-takers tend to be those whose parents do not act as safety-conscious models, rarely supervise their children's activities, or use punitive or inconsistent discipline to enforce rules (Tuchfarber, Zins, & Jason, 1997). These child-rearing tactics, as we saw in Chapter 10, spark children's defiance, reduce their willingness to comply, and actually promote high-risk behavior (Rowe, Maughan, & Goodman, 2004).

Highly active, impulsive children, many of whom are boys, remain particularly susceptible to injury in middle childhood. Although they have just as much safety knowledge as their peers, they are far less likely to implement it. Parents tend to be particularly lax in intervening in the dangerous behaviors of such children (Mori & Peterson, 1995; Schwebel, Hodgens, & Sterling, 2006). Furthermore, compared with girls, boys judge risky play activities as less likely to result in injury, and they pay less attention to injury risk cues, such as a peer who looks hesitant or fearful (Morrongiello & Rennie, 1998). The greatest challenge for injury control programs is reaching these children, altering high-risk factors in their families, and reducing the dangers to which they are exposed.

These boys play a fast-paced pickup game of roller hockey. Unfortunately, their parents failed to insist that they wear helmets as well as arm and knee protection. A rough fall could result in a serious, life-threatening injury.

Health Education

Psychologists, educators, and pediatricians are intensely interested in finding ways to help school-age children understand their bodies, acquire mature conceptions of health and illness, and develop behaviors that foster good health throughout life. Successful health intervention requires information about children's current health-related knowledge. What can they understand? What reasoning processes do they use? What factors influence what they know? The Social Issues: Education box on the following page summarizes findings on children's concepts of health and illness in middle childhood.

The school-age period may be especially important for fostering healthy lifestyles because of the child's growing independence, increasing cognitive capacities, and rapidly developing self-concept, which includes a sense of physical well-being (Harter, 2006). During middle childhood, children can acquire a wide range of health information—about the structure and functioning of their bodies, about good nutrition, and about the causes and consequences of physical injuries and diseases. Yet most efforts to impart health concepts to

Social Issues: Education

Children's Understanding of Health and Illness

Lizzie lay on the living room sofa with a stuffy nose and sore throat, disappointed that she was missing her soccer team's final game and pizza party. "How'd I get this dumb cold anyhow?" she wondered aloud to Joey. "I probably got it by playing outside when it was freezing cold."

"No, no," Joey contradicted. "Viruses get into your blood and attack, just like an army."

"Gross. I didn't eat any viruses," responded Lizzie.

"You don't eat them, silly, you breathe them in. Somebody probably sneezed them all over you at school. That's how you got sick!"

Lizzie and Joey are at different developmental levels in their understanding of health and illness—due to cognitive development and exposure to biological knowledge. Researchers have asked preschool through high school students questions about the causes of health and of certain illnesses, such as colds, AIDS, and cancer.

During the preschool and early school years, children do not have much biological knowledge to bring to bear on their understanding of health and illness. For example, 3- to 8-year-olds, who know little about how their internal organs work, generally fall back on their rich knowledge of people's behavior to account for health and illness (Carey, 1995, 1999; Simons & Keil, 1995). Children of this age regard health as a matter of engaging in specific practices (eating the right foods, getting enough sleep and exercise, wearing warm clothing on cold days), and they regard illness as a matter of failing to follow these rules or coming too close to a sick person.

By age 9 or 10, when children can name many internal organs and view them as an interconnected system, they almost always explain health and illness biologically (Carey, 1999). Joey understands that illness can be caused by contagion—breathing in a harmful substance (a virus), which affects the operation of the body. He also realizes that we eat not just because food tastes good or to stay alive (younger children's explanations) but to build flesh, blood, muscle, and bone (Myant & Williams, 2005; Toyamo, 2000).

In early adolescence, explanations become more elaborate and precise. Eleven- to 14-year-olds recognize health as a long-term condition that depends on the interaction of body, mind,

and environment (Hergenrather & Rabinowitz, 1991). And their notions of illness involve clearly stated ideas about interference in normal biological processes: "You get a cold when your sinuses fill with mucus. Sometimes your lungs do, too, and you get a cough. Colds come from viruses. They get into the bloodstream and make your platelet count go down" (Bibace & Walsh, 1980; Myant & Williams, 2005).

Young school-age children can grasp basic biological ideas that are important for understanding disease. But whether or not they do so depends on the information in their environments. When given relevant facts and biological concepts, such as "gene," "germ," and "virus," even 5- and 6-year-olds use the concepts to organize the facts, and their understanding advances (Solomon & Johnson, 2000).

Without such knowledge, children readily generalize from their knowledge of familiar diseases to less familiar ones. As a result, they may conclude that risk factors for colds (sharing a Coke, sneezing on someone) can cause AIDS or that cancer (again, like a cold) is communicable through casual contact. These incorrect ideas can lead to unnecessary anxiety about getting a serious disease. In surveys of school-age children, about half incorrectly believed that everyone is at risk for AIDS. And more than half said they worry about getting AIDS or cancer (Chin et al., 1998; Holcomb, 1990).

Although misconceptions decline with age, culturally transmitted beliefs affect children's ideas. Once biological explanations of illness become well grounded, school-age children (like many adults) seem to combine them with other cultural ideas. For example, children in India, like those in the United States, favor biological explanations of illness. But

Indian children tend to suggest moral causes ("Maybe he's being punished by God for his bad behavior") influenced by Hindu notions of karma and retribution—that positive, caring actions lead to positive results, while negative, hurtful actions bring suffering (Raman & Gelman, 2004).

Unfortunately, when certain diseases take on powerfully negative cultural meanings—for example, cancer as a malignant, destructive evil or AIDS as a sign of moral decay—even adults with accurate biological knowledge expect bad things to happen from associating with affected people (Pryor & Reeder, 1993). Children quickly pick up these attitudes, which help explain the severe social rejection experienced by some youngsters with chronic diseases.

Education about the causes of various illnesses leads to an increasingly accurate appreciation of disease transmission and prevention during middle childhood and adolescence. To combat irrational fears and prejudices and foster compassion, teachers can give AIDS, cancer, and other debilitating and deadly illnesses "a human face" by bringing chronically ill people into the classroom or talking about the experiences of people who died of an illness.

Because this child understands that her grandfather's chronic illness is not contagious, she is able to visit and express her affection for him, without succumbing to irrational fears.

Applying What We Know

Strategies for Fostering Healthy Lifestyles in School-Age Children

STRATEGY	DESCRIPTION
Increase health-related knowledge and encourage healthy behaviors.	Provide health education that imparts knowledge about healthy lifestyles (including the health risks of overweight and obesity) and that includes modeling, role playing, rehearsal, and reinforcement of good health practices.
Involve parents in supporting health education.	Communicate with parents about health education goals in school, encouraging them to extend these efforts at home. Teach parents about unhealthy feeding practices and how to create healthy food environments at home. Promote proper parental supervision by providing information on children's age-related safety capacities.
Provide healthy environments in schools.	Ask school administrators to ensure that school breakfasts and lunches follow widely accepted dietary guidelines. Limit access to vending machines with junk food. Work for daily recess periods in elementary school and mandatory daily physical education at all grade levels.
Make voluntary screening for risk factors available as part of health education.	Offer periodic measures of height, weight, body mass, blood pressure, and adequacy of diet. Educate children about the meaning of each index, and encourage improvement.
Promote pleasurable physical activity.	Provide opportunities for regular, vigorous physical exercise through activities that de-emphasize competition and stress skill-building and personal and social enjoyment.
Teach children to be critical of media advertising.	Besides teaching children to be skeptical of TV ads for unhealthy foods, reduce advertising for such foods in schools.
Work for safer, healthier community environments for children.	Form community action groups to improve child safety, school nutrition, and play environments, and initiate community programs that foster healthy physical activity.

school-age children have little impact on behavior (Tinsley, 2003). Several related reasons underlie this gap between knowledge and practice:

- Health is seldom an important goal for children, who feel good most of the time. They are far more concerned about schoolwork, friends, and play.
- Children do not yet have an adultlike time perspective that relates past, present, and future. They cannot see the connection between engaging in preventive behaviors now and experiencing later health consequences.
- Much health information given to children is contradicted by other sources, such as television advertising (see Chapter 10) and the examples of adults and peers.

Teaching school-age children health-related facts, though important, must be supplemented by other efforts. As we have seen, a powerful means of fostering children's health is to reduce hazards, such as pollution, inadequate medical and dental care, and unhealthy diet. At the same time, because environments will never be totally free of health risks, parents and teachers must coach children in good health practices and must model and reinforce these behaviors. Refer to Applying What We Know above for ways to foster healthy lifestyles in school-age children.

Ask Yourself

Review Select one of the following health problems of middle childhood: myopia, obesity, bedwetting, asthma, or unintentional injuries. Explain how both genetic and environmental factors contribute to it.

Apply Nine-year-old Talia is afraid to hug and kiss her grandmother, who has cancer. What explains Talia's mistaken belief that the same behaviors that cause colds to spread might lead her to catch cancer? What would you do to change her thinking?

Connect Children who were undernourished in the early years are more likely to become overweight when their food environments improve. Explain how this finding illustrates the concept of epigenesis, described on pages 88–89 in Chapter 2.

Reflect List unintentional injuries that you experienced as a child. Were you injury-prone? Why or why not?

Motor Development and Play

TAKE A MOMENT... Visit a park on a pleasant weekend afternoon, and watch several pre-school and school-age children at play. You will see that gains in body size and muscle strength support improved motor coordination during middle childhood. And greater cognitive and social maturity enables older children to use their new motor skills in more complex ways. A major change in children's play takes place at this time.

Gross Motor Development

During the school years, running, jumping, hopping, and ball skills become more refined. At Joey and Lizzie's school one day, I watched during the third to sixth graders' recess. Children burst into sprints as they raced across the playground, jumped over rapidly twirling ropes, engaged in intricate hopscotch patterns, kicked and dribbled soccer balls, batted at balls pitched by their classmates, and balanced adeptly as they walked heel-to-toe across narrow ledges. Table 11.2 summarizes gross motor achievements between 6 and 12 years of age. These diverse skills reflect gains in four basic motor capacities:

- *Flexibility.* Compared with preschoolers, school-age children are physically more pliable and elastic, a difference that is evident as they swing bats, kick balls, jump over hurdles, and execute tumbling routines.
- *Balance.* Improved balance supports many athletic skills, including running, hopping, skipping, throwing, kicking, and the rapid changes of direction required in many team sports.

TABLE 11.2	**Changes in Gross Motor Skills During Middle Childhood**	
	SKILL	**DEVELOPMENTAL CHANGE**
	Running	Running speed increases from 12 feet per second at age 6 to over 18 feet per second at age 12.
	Other gait variations	Skipping improves. Sideways stepping appears around age 6 and becomes more continuous and fluid with age.
	Vertical jump	Height jumped increases from 4 inches at age 6 to 12 inches at age 12.
	Standing broad jump	Distance jumped increases from 3 feet at age 6 to over 5 feet at age 12.
	Precision jumping and hopping (on a mat divided into squares)	By age 7 children can accurately jump and hop from square to square, a performance that improves until age 9 and then levels off.
	Throwing	Throwing speed, distance, and accuracy increase for both sexes, but much more for boys than for girls. At age 6, a ball thrown by a boy travels 39 feet per second, one by a girl 29 feet per second. At age 12, a ball thrown by a boy travels 78 feet per second, one by a girl 56 feet per second.
	Catching	Ability to catch small balls thrown over greater distances improves with age.
	Kicking	Kicking speed and accuracy improve, with boys considerably ahead of girls. At age 6, a ball kicked by a boy travels 21 feet per second, one by a girl 13 feet per second. At age 12, a ball kicked by a boy travels 34 feet per second, one by a girl 26 feet per second.
	Batting	Batting motions become more effective with age, increasing in speed and accuracy and involving the entire body.
	Dribbling	Style of hand dribbling gradually changes, from awkward slapping of the ball to continuous, relaxed, even stroking.

Sources: Haywood & Getchell, 2001; Malina & Bouchard, 1991.

© BOB DAEMMRICH/PHOTOEDIT

© PETER HVIZDAK/THE IMAGE WORKS

■ *Agility.* Quicker and more accurate movements are evident in the fancy footwork of dance and cheerleading, as well as in the forward, backward, and sideways motions used to dodge opponents in tag and soccer.

■ *Force.* Older children can throw and kick a ball harder and propel themselves farther off the ground when running and jumping than they could at earlier ages (Haywood & Getchell, 2001).

Along with body growth, more efficient information processing plays a vital role in improved motor performance. Younger children often have difficulty with skills that require rapid responding, such as dribbling and batting. During middle childhood, the capacity to react only to relevant information increases. And steady gains in reaction time occur, with 11-year-olds responding twice as quickly as 5-year-olds (Band et al., 2000; Kail, 2003; Largo et al., 2001). These differences in speed of reaction have practical implications for physical education. Because 6- and 7-year-olds are seldom successful at batting a thrown ball, T-ball is more appropriate for them than baseball. Similarly, hand-ball, four-square, and kickball should precede instruction in tennis, basketball, and football.

This 10-year-old boy and his older sister, who live in Regina, Saskatchewan, go curling. Improved flexibility, balance, agility, and force, along with more efficient information processing, support the athletic skills needed to play this precision team sport, popular in Canada.

Fine Motor Development

Fine motor development also improves over the school years. On rainy afternoons, Joey and Lizzie experimented with yo-yos, built model airplanes, and wove potholders on small looms. Like many children, they took up musical instruments, which demand considerable fine motor control. And gains in fine motor skill are especially evident in children's writing and drawing.

By age 6, most children can print the alphabet, their first and last names, and the numbers from 1 to 10 with reasonable clarity. Their writing is large, however, because they make strokes using the entire arm rather than just the wrist and fingers. Children usually master uppercase letters first because their horizontal and vertical motions are easier to control than the small curves of the lowercase alphabet. Legibility of writing gradually increases as children produce more accurate letters with uniform height and spacing. These improvements prepare children for mastering cursive writing by third grade.

Children's drawings show dramatic gains in organization, detail, and representation of depth during middle childhood. By the end of the preschool years, children can accurately copy many two-dimensional shapes, and they integrate these into their drawings. Some depth cues have also begun to appear, such as making distant objects smaller than near ones (Braine et al., 1993). Yet recall from Chapter 8 that before age 8, children have trouble accurately copying a three-dimensional form, such as a cube or cylinder (see page 315). Around 9 to 10 years, the third dimension is clearly evident through overlapping objects, diagonal placement, and converging lines. Furthermore, as Figure 11.6 shows, school-age children not only depict objects in considerable detail but also relate them to one another as part of an organized whole (Case, 1998; Case & Okamoto, 1996).

Individual Differences in Motor Skills

As at younger ages, school-age children show marked individual differences in motor capacities that are influenced by both heredity and environment. Body build is one factor: Taller, more muscular children excel at many motor tasks. And children whose parents encourage physical exercise tend to enjoy it more and also to be more skilled.

Family income affects children's access to lessons needed to develop abilities in areas such as ballet, tennis, gymnastics, and instrumental music. For low-SES children, school and community provisions for nurturing athletics and other motor skills by making lessons, equipment,

FIGURE 11.6

Increase in organization, detail, and depth cues in school-age children's drawings. **TAKE A MOMENT...** Compare both drawings to the one by a 6-year-old on page 314. In the drawing on the left, an 8-year-old depicts her family—father, mother, and three children. Notice how all parts are depicted in relation to one another, and the human figures are given much more detail. (The artist is your author, as a third grader. In the drawing, Laura can be found between her older sister and younger brother.) Integration of depth cues increases dramatically over the school years, as shown in the drawing on the right, by a 10-year-old artist from Singapore. Here, depth is indicated by overlapping objects, diagonal placement, and converging lines, as well as by making distant objects smaller than near ones.

and opportunities for regular practice available and affordable are crucial. When these experiences combine with parental encouragement, many low-SES children become highly skilled.

Sex differences in motor skills that appeared during the preschool years extend into middle childhood and, in some instances, become more pronounced. Girls remain ahead in the fine motor area, including handwriting and drawing. They also continue to have an edge in skipping, jumping, and hopping, which depend on balance and agility. But boys outperform girls on all other skills listed in Table 11.2, especially throwing and kicking (Cratty, 1986; Haywood & Getchell, 2001).

School-age boys' genetic advantage in muscle mass is not large enough to account for their gross motor superiority. Rather, the social environment plays a larger role. Research confirms that parents hold higher expectations for boys' athletic performance, and children readily absorb these messages. From first through twelfth grades, girls are less positive than boys about the value of sports and their own sports ability—differences explained in part by parental beliefs (Fredricks & Eccles, 2002). In one study, boys more often stated that it was vital to their parents that they participate in athletics. These attitudes affected children's self-confidence and behavior. Girls saw themselves as having less talent at sports and, by sixth grade, devoted less time to athletics than their male classmates (Eccles & Harold, 1991). At the same time, girls and older school-age children regard boys' advantage in sports as unjust. They indicate, for example, that coaches should spend equal time with children of each sex and that female sports should command just as much media attention as male sports (Solomon & Bredemeier, 1999).

Clearly, steps must be taken to increase girls' participation, self-confidence, and sense of fair treatment in athletics. Educating parents about the minimal differences between school-age boys' and girls' physical capacities and sensitizing them to unfair biases against promotion of girls' athletic ability may help. And greater emphasis on skill training for girls, along with

Gains in perspective taking enable school-age children to play increasingly complex games with rules, like this high-spirited game of Twister. Through child-organized games, children experiment with different styles of cooperating, competing, winning, and losing.

increased attention to their athletic achievements, is likely to increase their involvement and performance. As a positive sign, compared with a generation ago, many more girls now participate in individual and team sports such as gymnastics and soccer (National Council of Youth Sports, 2005). Middle childhood is a crucial time to take these steps because during the school years, children start to discover what they are good at and make some definite skill commitments.

Child-Organized Games

The physical activities of school-age children reflect an important advance in quality of play: Games with rules become common. Children around the world engage in an enormous variety of informally organized games, including variants on popular sports such as soccer, baseball, and basketball, and such well-known games as tag, jacks, and hopscotch. They also have invented hundreds of other games, including red rover, statues, leapfrog, kick the can, and prisoner's base, which are passed on from one generation to the next (Kirchner, 2000).

Gains in perspective taking—in particular, the ability to understand the roles of several players in a game—permit this transition to rule-oriented games. These play experiences, in turn, contribute greatly to emotional and social development. Child-invented games usually rely on simple physical skills and a sizable element of luck. As a result, they rarely become contests of individual ability. Instead, they permit children to try out different styles of cooperating, competing, winning, and losing with little personal risk. Also, in their efforts to organize a game, children discover why rules are necessary and which ones work well. In fact, they often spend as much time working out the details of how a game should proceed as they do playing the game! As we will see in Chapter 13, these experiences help children form more mature concepts of fairness and justice.

Adult-Organized Youth Sports

Compared with past generations, school-age children today spend less time gathering informally on sidewalks and in playgrounds. In part, this change reflects parental concern about neighborhood safety, as well as competition for children's time from TV, video games, and the Internet. Another factor is the rise in adult-organized sports, such as Little League baseball and soccer and hockey leagues, which fill many hours that children used to devote to spontaneous play. About half of North American children—60 percent of boys and 40 percent of girls—participate in organized sports outside of school hours at some time between ages 5 and 14 (National Council of Youth Sports, 2005; Sport Canada, 2003).

For most children, joining community athletic teams is associated with increased self-esteem and social competence. And when young people continue to play on teams in adolescence, they are more likely to participate in sports and other physical fitness activities in early adulthood (McHale et al., 2005; Perkins et al., 2004). In some cases, through, the arguments of critics—that youth sports overemphasize competition and substitute adult control for children's natural experimentation with rules and strategies—are valid. Children who join teams so early that the necessary skills are beyond their capabilities soon lose interest. Coaches and parents who criticize rather than encourage can prompt intense anxiety in some children. And especially among boys—for whom competence at sports is linked to peer admiration—weaker performers generally experience social ostracism when coaches make winning the paramount goal (Stryer, Tofler, & Lapchick, 1998).

Parents, even more than coaches, influence children's athletic attitudes and abilities. At the extreme are parents who value sports so highly that they punish their child for making mistakes, insist that the child keep playing after injury, hold the child back in school to ensure a physical advantage, or even seek medical interventions to improve the child's performance.

rough-and-tumble play
A form of peer interaction involving friendly chasing and play-fighting that, in our evolutionary past, may have been important for the development of fighting skill.

Applying What We Know

Providing Developmentally Appropriate Organized Sports in Middle Childhood

Build on children's interests.	Permit children to select from among appropriate activities the ones that suit them best. Do not push children into sports they do not enjoy.
Teach age-appropriate skills.	For children younger than age 9, emphasize basic skills, such as kicking, throwing, and batting, and simplified games that grant all participants adequate playing time.
Emphasize enjoyment.	Permit children to progress at their own pace and to play for the fun of it, whether or not they become expert athletes.
Limit the frequency and length of practices.	Adjust practice time to children's attention spans and need for unstructured time with peers, with family, and for homework. Two practices a week, each no longer than 30 minutes for younger school-age children and 60 minutes for older school-age children, are sufficient.
Focus on personal and team improvement.	Emphasize effort, skill gains, and teamwork rather than winning. Avoid criticism for errors and defeat, which promotes anxiety and avoidance of athletics.
Discourage unhealthy competition.	Avoid all-star games and championship ceremonies that recognize individuals. Instead, acknowledge all participants.
Permit children to contribute to rules and strategies.	Involve children in decisions aimed at ensuring fair play and teamwork. To strengthen desirable responses, reinforce compliance rather than punishing noncompliance.

High parental pressure sets the stage for emotional difficulties and early athletic dropout, not elite performance (Marsh & Daigneault, 1999; Tofler, Knapp, & Drell, 1998).

In most organized youth sports, health and safety rules help ensure that injuries are infrequent and mild. The exception is football, which has a high rate of serious injury (Radelet et al., 2002). But frequent, intense practice in any sport can lead to painful "overuse" injuries and, in extreme cases, to stress-related fractures resulting in premature closure of the epiphyses of the long bones (Lord & Kozar, 1996). When parents and coaches emphasize effort, improvement, participation, and teamwork, young athletes enjoy sports more, exert greater effort to improve their skills, and perceive themselves as more competent at their chosen sport (Ullrich-French & Smith, 2006). See Applying What We Know above for ways to ensure that athletic leagues provide children with positive learning experiences.

Shadows of Our Evolutionary Past

TAKE A MOMENT... While watching children in your neighborhood park, notice how they occasionally wrestle, roll, hit, and run after one another, alternating roles while smiling and laughing. This friendly chasing and play-fighting is called **rough-and-tumble play.** It emerges in the preschool years and peaks in middle childhood, and children in many cultures engage in it with peers whom they like especially well. After a rough-and-tumble episode, children continue interacting rather than separating, as they do after an aggressive encounter (Pellegrini, 2004).

Children's rough-and-tumble play resembles the social behavior of many other young mammals. It seems to originate in parents' physical play with babies, especially fathers' play with sons (see page 278 in Chapter 7). And it is more common among boys, probably because prenatal exposure to androgens (male sex hormones) predisposes boys toward active play (see Chapter 10, page 392). Boys' rough-and-tumble largely consists of playful wrestling, restraining, and hitting, whereas girls tend to engage in running and chasing, with only brief physical contact (Boulton, 1996).

In middle childhood, rough-and-tumble accounts for as much as 10 percent of free-play behavior, before declining in adolescence. In our evolutionary past, it may have been important for the development

This father and his sons engage in rough-and-tumble play, which can be distinguished from aggression by its good-natured quality. In our evolutionary past, rough-and-tumble may have been important for promoting fighting skill and establishing dominance hierarchies.

of fighting skill (Boulton & Smith, 1992). Rough-and-tumble also may help children establish a **dominance hierarchy**—a stable ordering of group members that predicts who will win when conflict arises. Observations of arguments, threats, and physical attacks between children reveal a consistent lineup of winners and losers that becomes increasingly stable in middle childhood and adolescence, especially among boys. Many children seem to use these encounters to evaluate their own as well as others' strength in a safe venue before challenging a peer's dominance. Over time, children increasingly choose rough-and-tumble partners who resemble themselves in dominance status (Pellegrini & Smith, 1998).

As with nonhuman animals, dominance relations among children serve an adaptive function, limiting aggression among group members. Once a dominance hierarchy is established, hostility is rare. As children move closer to physical maturity and individual differences in strength become clearer, rough-and-tumble play declines. When it does occur, its meaning changes: Adolescent boys' rough-and-tumble is linked to aggression (Pellegrini, 2003). After becoming embroiled in a bout, players "cheat" and hurt their opponent. When asked to explain the episode, boys often respond that they are retaliating, apparently to reestablish dominance among their peers. Thus, a play behavior that limits aggression in childhood becomes a context for hostility in adolescence.

Physical Education

Physical activity supports many aspects of children's development—the health of their bodies, their sense of self-worth as physically active and capable beings, and the cognitive and social skills necessary for getting along with others. Yet to devote more time to academic instruction, North American elementary schools have cut back on recess, despite its contribution all domains of development (see the Social Issues: Education box on the following page). Similarly, only 20 percent of U.S. elementary students have daily physical education; the average American school-age child gets only 1 hour and 20 minutes of physical education a week. Although Canadian children fare better, averaging 2 hours per week, many Canadian schools have also reduced their physical education programs (Canadian Fitness and Lifestyle Research Institute, 2005a, 2005b; U.S. Department of Education, 2006a; U.S. Department of Health and Human Services, 2005d). In both nations, physical inactivity is pervasive. Among North American 5- to 17-year-olds, only about 40 percent of girls and 50 percent of boys are active enough for good health—that is, engage in at least 30 minutes of vigorous aerobic activity and 1 hour of walking per day.

Many experts believe that schools should not only offer more frequent physical education classes but also change the content of these programs. Training in competitive sports, often a high priority, is unlikely to reach the least physically fit youngsters, who avoid activities demanding a high level of skill. Instead, programs should emphasize enjoyable, informal games and individual exercise (walking, running, jumping, tumbling, and climbing)—pursuits especially likely to endure. Furthermore, children of varying skill levels are more likely to sustain physical activity when teachers focus on each child's personal progress and contribution to team accomplishment (Connor, 2003). Then physical education fosters a healthy sense of self while satisfying school-age children's need to participate with others.

Physically fit children take great pleasure in their rapidly developing motor skills. As a result, they seek out these activities, developing rewarding interests in physical exercise and becoming active adults who reap many benefits (Dennison et al., 1998; Tammelin et al., 2003). These include greater physical strength, resistance to many illnesses (from colds and flu to cancer, diabetes, and heart disease), enhanced psychological well-being, and a longer life.

© MARY KATE DENNY/PHOTOEDIT

Led by their physical education teacher, students participate in a jumping race. Many experts believe that physical education classes, instead of emphasizing competitive sports, should focus on informal games and each child's personal progress.

dominance hierarchy A stable ordering of group members that predicts who will win when conflict arises.

Social Issues: Education

School Recess—A Time to Play, A Time to Learn

When 7-year-old Whitney's family moved to a new city, she left a school with three daily recess periods for one with only one 15-minute break per day, which her second-grade teacher cancelled if any child misbehaved. Whitney, who had previously enjoyed school, complained daily of headaches and an upset stomach. Her mother, Jill, thought, "My child is stressing out because she can't move all day!" After Jill and other parents successfully appealed to the school board to add a second recess period, Whitney's symptoms vanished (Rauber, 2006).

In recent years, recess—along with its rich opportunities for child-organized play and peer interaction—has diminished or disappeared in many U.S. and Canadian elementary schools (Pellegrini, 2005; Pellegrini & Holmes, 2006). Under the assumption that extra time for academics will translate into achievement gains, 7 percent of U.S. schools no longer provide recess to students as young as second grade. And over half of schools that do have recess now schedule it just once a day (U.S. Department of Education, 2006a).

Yet rather than subtracting from classroom learning, recess periods boost it! Research dating back more than 100 years confirms that distributing cognitively demanding tasks over a longer time by introducing regular breaks, rather than consolidating intensive effort within one period, enhances attention and performance at all ages. Such breaks are particularly important for young children. In a series of studies, school-age children were more attentive in the classroom after recess than before it—an effect that was greater for second than fourth graders (Pellegrini, Huberty, & Jones, 1995).

In another investigation, kindergartners' and first graders' engagement in peer conversation and games during recess predicted improved later academic achievement, even after other factors that might explain the relationship (such as previous achievement) were controlled (Pellegrini, 1992; Pellegrini et al., 2002). Recall from Chapter 10 that children's social maturity contributes substantially to early academic competence. Recess is one of the few remaining contexts devoted to child-organized games that provide practice in vital social skills—cooperation, leadership, followership, and inhibition of aggression—under adult supervision rather than direction. As children transfer these skills to the classroom, they may participate in discussions, collaborate, follow rules, and enjoy academic pursuits more—factors that enhance motivation and achievement.

Finally, children are even more physically active during recess than in gym class (U.S. Department of Education, 2006a). School-age girls, especially, engage in more moderate-to-vigorous exercise during recess than at other times of the day (Mota et al., 2005). In sum, regular, unstructured recess fosters children's health and competence—physically, academically, and socially.

TORONTO STAR/FIRSTLIGHT

School-age children, especially girls, are even more physically active during recess than in gym class. The regular opportunities that recess affords for unstructured play and games promote physical, academic, and social competence.

Ask Yourself

Review Explain the adaptive value of rough-and-tumble play and dominance hierarchies.

Apply Nine-year-old Allison thinks she isn't good at sports, and she doesn't like physical education class. Suggest some strategies her teacher can use to improve her pleasure and involvement in physical activity.

Connect On Saturdays, 10-year-old Billy gathers with friends on the driveway of his house to play basketball. Besides improved ball skills, what else is he learning?

Reflect Did you participate in adult-organized sports as a child? If so, what kind of climate for learning did coaches and parents create? What impact do you think your experiences had on your development?

Summary

Body Growth

Describe changes in body size, proportions, and skeletal maturity during middle childhood.

■ School-age children's growth is slow and regular. On average, they add about 2 to 3 inches in height and 5 pounds in weight each year. By age 9, girls overtake boys in physical size.

■ Evolutionary adaptations to particular climates, food resources, and infectious diseases contribute to large individual and ethnic variations in physical growth. **Secular trends in physical growth** have occurred in industrialized nations. Because of improved health and nutrition, many children are growing larger and reaching physical maturity earlier than their ancestors.

■ During middle childhood, bones continue to lengthen and broaden. All 20 primary teeth are replaced by permanent ones. Tooth decay affects over half of North American school-age children, with especially high levels among low-SES children. One-third of school-age children suffer from **malocclusion,** making braces common by the end of elementary school.

Describe brain development in middle childhood.

■ Only a small gain in brain size occurs during middle childhood. White matter (myelinated nerve fibers) increases steadily, especially in the frontal lobes of the cerebral cortex, the parietal lobes, and the corpus callosum. In contrast, gray matter (neurons and supportive material) declines as a result of synaptic pruning, and lateralization of the cerebral hemispheres increases. Brain development during the school years is believed to involve neurotransmitter and hormonal influences.

Common Health Problems

Describe the overall status of children's health during middle childhood.

■ School-age children from economically advantaged homes are at their healthiest, benefiting from the cumulative effects of good nutrition and rapid development of the body's immune system. At the same time, a variety of health problems do occur, many of which are more common among low-SES children.

■ The most common vision problem, **myopia,** is influenced by heredity, early biological trauma, and time spent reading and doing other close work. It is one of the few health conditions that increase with family education and income. Although ear infections decline during the school years, many low-SES children experience some hearing loss because of chronic, untreated otitis media.

Describe the causes and consequences of serious nutritional problems in middle childhood, giving special attention to obesity.

■ Poverty-stricken children in developing countries and in North America continue to suffer from malnutrition. Malnutrition that persists for many years usually results in permanent physical and mental damage. Severely malnourished, growth-stunted children display a heightened stress response, altered production of neurotransmitters in the brain, and greater vulnerability to obesity after their diets improve.

■ Overweight and **obesity** have increased dramatically in both industrialized and developing nations, especially in the United States. Although heredity accounts for a tendency to gain weight, parental feeding practices, maladaptive eating habits, lack of exercise, and Western high-fat diets are more powerful influences. Obese children are often socially rejected, are more likely to report feeling depressed, and display more behavior problems than their normal-weight peers.

■ Family-based interventions in which parents and children revise eating patterns, engage in regular daily exercise, and reinforce one another's progress are the most effective approaches to treating childhood obesity. Rewarding obese children for reducing sedentary time is effective in getting them to enjoy and engage in more physical activity. Schools can help by ensuring regular physical activity and serving healthier meals.

What factors contribute to nocturnal enuresis and to asthma, and how can these health problems be reduced?

■ Heredity is responsible for most cases of **nocturnal enuresis,** through a failure of muscular responses that inhibit urination or a hormonal imbalance that permits too much urine to accumulate. The most effective treatment is a urine alarm that works according to conditioning principles.

■ Over the past 30 years, the number of children with **asthma** has more than doubled. This chronic disease, the most frequent cause of school absence and childhood hospitalization, occurs more often among African-American and poverty-stricken children, perhaps because of inner-city pollution, stressful home lives, and lack of access to good health care. Childhood obesity is also a factor. Children with severe chronic illnesses are at risk for academic, emotional, and social difficulties. Interventions that

foster positive family interactions and help parent and child cope with the disease improve adjustment.

Describe changes in the occurrence of unintentional injuries during middle childhood, and cite effective interventions.

■ The rate of unintentional injury increases from middle childhood into adolescence. Motor vehicle accidents (with children as passengers or pedestrians) and bicycle accidents are the leading causes. Highly active, impulsive children, especially boys, often do not implement their safety knowledge and are particularly susceptible to injury.

■ Effective school-based safety education programs use modeling and rehearsal of safety practices, reward children for good performance, and provide occasional booster sessions. Parents also must be educated about children's age-related safety capacities. One vital safety measure is insisting that children wear protective bicycle helmets, which dramatically reduces the risk of serious head injury.

Health Education

What can parents and teachers do to encourage good health practices in school-age children?

■ Besides providing health-related information, adults must reduce health hazards in children's environments, coach children in good health practices, and model and reinforce these behaviors.

Motor Development and Play

Cite major changes in gross and fine motor development during middle childhood.

■ Gradual increases in body size and muscle strength support refinements in many gross motor skills. Gains in flexibility, balance, agility, and force occur. In addition, improvements in responding only to relevant information and in reaction time contribute to athletic performance.

■ Fine motor development also improves. Handwriting becomes more legible, and children's drawings show dramatic increases in organization, detail, and representation of depth.

Describe individual differences in motor performance during middle childhood.

■ Wide individual differences in children's motor capacities are influenced by both heredity and environment, including such factors as body build, parental encouragement, and opportunities to take lessons. Gender stereotypes, which affect parental

expectations for children's athletic performance, largely account for school-age boys' superiority on a wide range of gross motor skills. Greater emphasis on skill training for girls and attention to their athletic achievements can help increase their involvement and performance.

What qualities of children's play are evident in middle childhood?

■ Organized games with rules become common during the school years. Children's informally organized games support many aspects of emotional and social development. Expansion of adult-organized youth sports programs is associated with increased self-esteem and social competence in most players, but for some

children, adult overemphasis on competition and winning promotes undue anxiety and avoidance of sports. Promoting effort, improvement, participation, and teamwork makes organized sports enjoyable and beneficial for self-esteem.

■ Some features of children's physical activity reflect our evolutionary past. **Rough-and-tumble play** may once have been important for the development of fighting skill and may help children establish a **dominance hierarchy.** In middle childhood, dominance hierarchies become increasingly stable, especially among boys, and serve the adaptive function of limiting aggression among group members.

What steps can schools take to promote physical fitness in middle childhood?

■ In addition to providing an opportunity for physical activity, school recess is a rich context for child-organized games and social interaction. Regular, unstructured recess promotes both physical and social skills and boosts academic achievement.

■ Physical education classes help ensure that all children have access to the physical, cognitive, and social benefits of exercise and play. Daily classes emphasizing informal games that most children can perform well translate into lifelong psychological and physical health benefits.

Important Terms and Concepts

asthma (p. 422)
dominance hierarchy (p. 432)
malocclusion (p. 414)

myopia (p. 415)
nocturnal enuresis (p. 422)
obesity (p. 417)

rough-and-tumble play (p. 431)
secular trends in physical growth
  (p. 413)

Chapter 12

Middle childhood is a period of rapidly developing attention, memory, categorization, reasoning, and problem solving. This 11-year-old uses his advancing cognitive skills to depict not only the landscape he is painting but also himself as the painter, with friends looking on.

Reprinted with permission from the International Museum of Children's Art, Oslo, Norway

"I'm an artist"
Maung Ye Myint
11 years, Myanmar

Cognitive Development in Middle Childhood

"Finally!" 6-year-old Lizzie exclaimed the day she entered first grade. "Now I get to go to real school just like Joey!" Lizzie walked into her classroom confidently, pencils, crayons, and writing pad in hand, ready for a more disciplined approach to learning than she had experienced in early childhood. As a preschooler, Lizzie had loved playing school, giving assignments as the "teacher" and pretending to read and write as the "student." Now she was eager to master the tasks that had sparked her imagination as a 4- and 5-year-old.

Lizzie entered a whole new world of challenging mental activities. In a single morning, she and her classmates wrote in journals, met in reading groups, worked on addition and subtraction, and sorted leaves gathered for a science project. As Lizzie and Joey moved through the elementary school grades, they tackled increasingly complex tasks and gradually became more accomplished at reading, writing, math skills, and general knowledge of the world.

We begin by returning to research inspired by Piaget's theory and the information-processing approach. Together, they provide an overview of cognitive changes during the school years. Then we look at expanding definitions of intelligence that help us appreciate individual differences in mental development. We also examine the genetic and environmental roots of IQ scores, which often influence important educational decisions. Our discussion continues with language, which blossoms further during middle childhood. Finally, we consider the importance of schools in children's learning and development.

Piaget's Theory: The Concrete Operational Stage

When Lizzie visited my child development class as a 4-year-old, Piaget's conservation problems confused her (see Chapter 9, page 326). For example, when water was poured from a tall, narrow container into a short, wide one, she insisted that the amount of water had changed. But when Lizzie returned at age 8, she found these tasks easy. "Of course it's the same!" she exclaimed. "The water's shorter, but it's also wider. Pour it back," she instructed the college student who was interviewing her. "You'll see, it's the same amount!"

An improved ability to categorize underlies children's interest in collecting objects during middle childhood. These older school-age children sort baseball cards into an elaborate structure of categories and subcategories.

concrete operational stage Piaget's third stage, extending from about 7 to 11 years, in which thought becomes logical, flexible, and organized in its application to concrete information.

decentration The ability to focus on several aspects of a problem at once and relate them.

reversibility The ability to go through a series of steps in a problem and then mentally reverse direction, returning to the starting point.

seriation The ability to order items along a quantitative dimension, such as length or weight.

transitive inference The ability to seriate—or order items along a quantitative dimension—mentally.

cognitive maps Mental representations of familiar, large-scale spaces, such as school or neighborhood.

Achievements of the Concrete Operational Stage

Lizzie has entered Piaget's **concrete operational stage,** which extends from about 7 to 11 years. Thought is now more logical, flexible, and organized than it was during early childhood.

CONSERVATION ■ The ability to pass *conservation tasks* provides clear evidence of *operations*—mental actions that obey logical rules. Notice how Lizzie is capable of **decentration,** focusing on several aspects of a problem and relating them, rather than centering on just one. She also demonstrates **reversibility,** the capacity to think through a series of steps and then mentally reverse direction, returning to the starting point. Recall from Chapter 9 (page 325) that reversibility is part of every logical operation. It is solidly achieved in middle childhood.

CLASSIFICATION ■ Between ages 7 and 10, children pass Piaget's *class inclusion problem* (see page 326). This indicates that they are more aware of classification hierarchies and can focus on relations between a general category and two specific categories at the same time—that is, three relations at once (Hodges & French, 1988; Ni, 1998). You can see this in children's play activities. Collections—stamps, coins, baseball cards, rocks, bottle caps—become common in middle childhood. At age 10, Joey spent hours sorting and resorting his baseball cards, grouping them first by league and team, then by playing position and batting average. He could separate the players into a variety of classes and subclasses and easily rearrange them.

SERIATION ■ The ability to order items along a quantitative dimension, such as length or weight, is called **seriation.** To test for it, Piaget asked children to arrange sticks of different lengths from shortest to longest. Older preschoolers can put the sticks in a row to create the series, but they do so haphazardly, making many errors. In contrast, 6- to 7-year-olds create the series efficiently, moving in an orderly sequence from the smallest stick, to the next largest, and so on.

The concrete operational child can also seriate mentally, an ability called **transitive inference.** In a well-known transitive inference problem, Piaget showed children pairings of sticks of different colors. From observing that stick *A* is longer than stick *B* and that stick *B* is longer than stick *C*, children must make the mental inference that *A* is longer than *C*. Like Piaget's class inclusion task, transitive inference requires children to integrate three relations at once—in this instance, *A*–*B*, *B*–*C*, and *A*–*C*. When researchers take steps to ensure that children remember the premises (*A*–*B* and *B*–*C*), 7- to 8-year-olds can grasp transitive inference (Andrews & Halford, 1998; Wright & Dowker, 2002).

SPATIAL REASONING ■ Piaget found that children improve greatly in spatial reasoning over the school years. Let's take two related examples: understanding of directions and maps.

Directions. When asked to name an object to the left or right of another person, 5- and 6-year-olds answer incorrectly; they apply their own frame of reference. Between 7 and 8 years, children start to perform *mental rotations,* aligning the self's frame to match that of a person in a different orientation. As a result, they can identify left and right for positions they do not occupy (Roberts & Aman, 1993). Around 8 to 10 years, children can give clear, well-organized directions for getting from one place to another by using a "mental walk" strategy in which they imagine another person's movements along a route (Gauvain & Rogoff, 1989b). Six-year-olds give more organized directions after they walk the route themselves or are specially prompted. Otherwise, they focus on the end point without describing exactly how to get there (Plumert et al., 1994).

Maps. Children's mental representations of familiar, large-scale spaces, such as their school or neighborhood, are called **cognitive maps.** Drawing a map of a large-scale space requires considerable perspective-taking skill because the entire space cannot be seen at once. Instead, children must infer its overall layout by relating its separate parts.

Preschoolers and young school-age children include *landmarks* on the maps they draw, but their arrangement is not always accurate. They do better when asked to place stickers showing the location of desks and people on a map of their classroom. But if the map is rotated

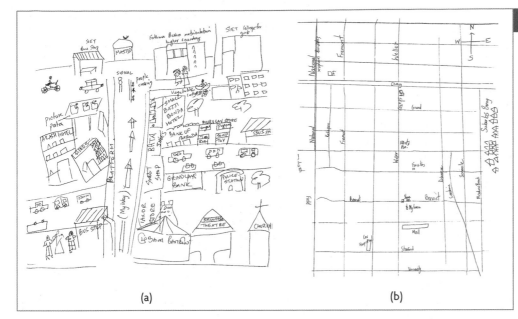

FIGURE 12.1

Maps drawn by older school-age children from India and the United States.
(a) The Indian child depicted many landmarks and features of social life in a small area near her home. (b) The U.S. child drew a more extended space and highlighted main streets and key directions but included few landmarks and people. (From G. Parameswaran, 2003, "Experimenter Instructions as a Mediator in the Effects of Culture on Mapping One's Neighborhood," *Journal of Environmental Psychology, 23,* pp. 415–416. © 2003 Elsevier Ltd. Reprinted by permission.)

(a)   (b)

to a position other than the orientation of the classroom, they have difficulty placing the stickers (Liben & Downs, 1993).

In the early school grades, children's maps become more coherent. They draw landmarks along an *organized route of travel*—an attainment that resembles their improved direction giving. By the end of middle childhood, children *combine landmarks and routes into an overall view of space.* And they readily draw and read maps, even when the map's orientation and the space it represents do not match (Liben, 1999). Ten- to 12-year-olds also grasp the notion of *scale*—the proportional relation between a space and its map representation (Liben, 2006).

Cultural frameworks influence children's map making. In many non-Western communities, people rarely use maps for way-finding but rely on information from neighbors, street vendors, and shopkeepers. Also, non-Western children ride in cars less often and walk more often than their Western agemates, thereby gaining intimate neighborhood knowledge. When a researcher had older school-age children in small cities in India and in the United States draw maps of their neighborhoods, the Indian children represented a rich array of landmarks and aspects of social life, such as people and vehicles, in a small area surrounding their home. The American children, in contrast, drew a more formal, extended space, highlighting main streets and key directions (north–south, east–west) but including few landmarks (see Figure 12.1). (Parameswaran, 2003). Although the American children's maps scored higher in cognitive maturity, this difference reflected cultural interpretations of the task: When asked to create a map to "help people find their way," the Indian children drew spaces as far-reaching and organized as the American children's.

This fourth grader, who is constructing a map that depicts the overall layout of her neighborhood, represents landmarks and routes of travel as interrelated.

Limitations of Concrete Operational Thought

As suggested by the name of this stage, concrete operational thinking suffers from one important limitation: Children think in an organized, logical fashion only when dealing with concrete information they can perceive directly. Their mental operations work poorly with abstract ideas—ones not apparent in the real world. Children's solutions to transitive inference problems provide a good illustration. When shown pairs of sticks of unequal length, Lizzie easily engaged in transitive inference. But she had great difficulty with a hypothetical version of this task: "Susan is taller than Sally, and Sally is taller than Mary. Who is the tallest?" Not until age 11 or 12 can children solve this problem.

That logical thought is at first tied to immediate situations helps account for school-age children's step-by-step mastery of concrete operational tasks. For example, they usually grasp conservation of number, followed by length, liquid, and mass, followed by weight. This *continuum of acquisition* (or gradual mastery) of logical concepts is another indication of the limitations of concrete operational thinking (Fischer & Bidell, 1991). School-age children do not come up with general logical principles and then apply them to all relevant situations. Instead, they seem to work out the logic of each problem separately.

Follow-Up Research on Concrete Operational Thought

According to Piaget, brain development combined with experience in a rich and varied external world should lead children everywhere to reach the concrete operational stage. Yet recent evidence indicates that specific cultural and school practices have much to do with mastery of Piagetian tasks (Rogoff, 2003; Rogoff & Chavajay, 1995). And information-processing research helps explain the gradual mastery of logical concepts in middle childhood.

IMPACT OF CULTURE AND SCHOOLING ■ In tribal and village societies, conservation is often delayed. For example, among the Hausa of Nigeria, who live in small agricultural settlements and rarely send their children to school, even basic conservation tasks—number, length, and liquid—are not understood until age 11 or later (Fahrmeier, 1978). This suggests that taking part in relevant everyday activities helps children master conservation and other Piagetian problems. Joey and Lizzie, for example, think of fairness in terms of equal distribution—a value emphasized in their culture. They frequently divide materials, such as Halloween treats or lemonade, equally among their friends. Because they often see the same quantity arranged in different ways, they grasp conservation early.

The very experience of going to school seems to promote mastery of Piagetian tasks. When children of the same age are tested, those who have been in school longer do better on transitive inference problems (Artman & Cahan, 1993). Opportunities to seriate objects, to learn about order relations, and to remember the parts of a complex problem are probably responsible.

Yet certain informal, nonschool experiences can also foster operational thought. Brazilian 6- to 9-year-old street vendors, who seldom attend school, do poorly on Piagetian class inclusion tasks. But they perform much better than economically advantaged schoolchildren on versions relevant to street vending—for example, "If you have 4 units of mint chewing gum and 2 units of grape chewing gum, is it better to sell me the mint gum or [all] the gum?" (Ceci & Roazzi, 1994). Similarly, around age 7 to 8, Zinacanteco Indian girls of southern Mexico, who learn to weave elaborately designed fabrics as an alternative to schooling, engage in mental transformations to figure out how a warp strung on will turn out as woven cloth—reasoning expected at the concrete operational stage. North American children of the same age, who do much better than Zinacanteco children on Piagetian tasks, have great difficulty with these weaving problems (Maynard & Greenfield, 2003).

On the basis of such findings, some investigators have concluded that the forms of logic required by Piagetian tasks do not emerge spontaneously in children but, rather, are heavily influenced by training, context, and cultural conditions. Does this view remind you of Vygotsky's sociocultural theory, which we discussed in earlier chapters?

AN INFORMATION-PROCESSING VIEW OF CONCRETE OPERATIONAL THOUGHT ■ In Chapter 9 we showed that the beginnings of logical thinking are evident during the preschool years on simplified and familiar tasks. The gradual mastery of logical concepts in middle childhood raises a familiar question about Piaget's theory: Is an abrupt stagewise transition to logical thought the best way to describe cognitive development in middle childhood?

© LAUREN GREENFIELD/VII PHOTO

This Zinacanteco Indian girl of southern Mexico learns the centuries-old practice of backstrap weaving. Although North American children perform better on Piaget's tasks, Zinacanteco children are far more adept at the complex mental transformations required to figure out how warp strung on a loom will turn out as woven cloth.

Some *neo-Piagetian theorists* argue that the development of operational thinking can best be understood in terms of gains in information-processing speed rather than a sudden shift to a new stage (Halford & Andrews, 2006). For example, Robbie Case (1996, 1998) proposed that, with practice, cognitive schemes demand less attention and become more automatic. This frees up space in *working memory* (see Chapter 6, page 220) so children can focus on combining old schemes and generating new ones. For instance, the child who sees water poured from one container to another recognizes that the height of the liquid changes. As this understanding becomes routine, the child notices that the width of the water changes as well. Soon children coordinate these observations, and they grasp conservation of liquid. Then, as this logical idea becomes well-practiced, the child transfers it to more demanding situations, such as weight.

Once the schemes of a Piagetian stage are sufficiently automatic, enough working memory is available for the child to integrate them into an improved representation. As a result, children acquire *central conceptual structures*—networks of concepts and relations that permit them to think more effectively in a wide range of situations (Case, 1996, 1998). The central conceptual structures that emerge from integrating concrete operational schemes are broadly applicable principles that result in increasingly complex, systematic reasoning, which we will discuss in Chapter 15 in the context of formal operational thought.

Some neo-Piagetian theorists explain the development of operational thinking in information-processing terms. As these children coordinate their observations of changes in the liquid's height and width, they master conservation of liquid. Once this logical idea becomes automatic, they start to form a more general representation of conservation that applies to a wider range of situations.

Case and his colleagues—along with other information processing researchers—have examined children's performance on a wide variety of tasks, including solving arithmetic word problems, understanding stories, drawing pictures, sight-reading music, handling money, and interpreting social situations. In each task, preschoolers typically focus on only one dimension. In understanding stories, for example, they grasp only a single story line. In drawing pictures, they depict objects separately. By the early school years, children coordinate two dimensions—two story lines in a single plot and drawings that show both the features of objects and their relationships. Around 9 to 11 years, children integrate multiple dimensions (Case, 1998; Halford & Andrews, 2006). They tell coherent stories with a main plot and several subplots. And their drawings follow a set of rules for representing perspective and, therefore, include several points of reference, such as near, midway, and far.

Case's theory helps explain why many understandings appear in specific situations at different times rather than being mastered all at once. First, different forms of the same logical insight, such as the various conservation tasks, vary in their processing demands, with those acquired later requiring more space in working memory. Second, children's experiences vary widely. A child who often listens to and tells stories but rarely draws pictures displays more advanced central conceptual structures in storytelling. Compared with Piaget's, Case's theory better accounts for unevenness in cognitive development. When tasks make similar processing demands, such as Piaget's class inclusion and transitive inference problems (each of which requires children to consider three relations at once), children with relevant experiences master those tasks at about the same time (Halford, Wilson, & Phillips, 1998).

As noted in Chapter 9, young children can be trained to solve many Piagetian problems. Many such tasks can be solved either empirically or logically. In the class inclusion problem shown on page 326 in Chapter 9, children can count the yellow flowers and all the flowers (yellow plus blue) to see that there are more *flowers* than *yellow flowers*—an empirical approach. Or they can reason, "There are more flowers than yellow flowers because yellow flowers are just a type of flower"—a logical approach. Younger children, in contrast to older children and adults, often rely on cumbersome empirical strategies, perhaps because they do not realize that certain problems can be solved logically. When 5-year-olds were given logical explanations after failing at class-inclusion tasks, they improved rapidly in performance (Siegler & Svetina, 2006). Indeed, children who spontaneously try to use logic on conservation tasks, though reaching the wrong conclusion, are more responsive than their peers to training that provides logical insights (Murray & Zhang, 2005). Relying on logical strategies enhances both accuracy and speed of thinking.

Evaluation of the Concrete Operational Stage

Piaget was correct that school-age children approach many problems in more organized, rational ways than preschoolers. But disagreement continues over whether this difference occurs because of *continuous* improvement in logical skills or *discontinuous* restructuring of children's thinking (as Piaget's stage idea assumes). Many researchers think that both types of change may be involved (Carey, 1999; Case, 1998; Demetriou et al., 2002; Fischer & Bidell, 1998; Halford, 2002). During the school years, children apply logical schemes to many more tasks. In the process, their thought seems to change qualitatively—toward a more comprehensive grasp of the underlying principles of logical thought.

Piaget himself seems to have recognized this possibility in evidence for gradual mastery of conservation and other tasks. So perhaps some blend of Piagetian and information-processing ideas holds the greatest promise for explaining cognitive development in middle childhood.

Ask Yourself

Review   Children's performance on conservation tasks illustrates a continuum of acquisition of logical concepts. Review the preceding sections, and list additional examples of gradual development of operational reasoning.

Apply   Nine-year-old Adrienne spends many hours helping her father build furniture in his woodworking shop. How might this experience facilitate Adrienne's advanced performance on Piagetian seriation problems?

Connect   Examine the following children's drawings: the first by a 6-year-old (on the right in Figure 8.8 on page 314), the second by an 8-year-old (on the left in Figure 11.6 on page 429), and the third by a 10-year-old (on the right in Figure 11.6 on page 429). Explain how the drawings illustrate Case's information-processing view of the development of operational thought.

Reflect   Which aspects of Piaget's description of the concrete operational child do you accept? Which do you doubt? Explain, citing research evidence.

Information Processing

In contrast to Piaget's focus on overall cognitive change, the information-processing perspective examines separate aspects of thinking. Attention and memory, which underlie every act of cognition, are central concerns in middle childhood, just as they were during infancy and the preschool years. Researchers are also interested in how children's growing knowledge of the world and awareness of their own mental activities affect these basic components of thinking. Finally, increased understanding of how children process information is being applied to their academic learning—in particular, to reading and mathematics.

Researchers believe that brain development contributes to the following basic changes in information processing that facilitate the diverse aspects of thinking we are about to consider:

■ *Gains in information-processing speed and capacity.* Time needed to process information on a wide variety of cognitive tasks declines rapidly between ages 6 and 12 in children from several cultures (Kail & Park, 1992, 1994). This suggests a biologically based, age-related gain in speed of thinking, possibly due to myelination and synaptic pruning in the brain (Kail, 2000). Some researchers believe this greater efficiency contributes to more complex, effective thinking because a faster thinker can hold on to and operate on more information in working memory (Halford & Andrews, 2006; Luna et al., 2004). Indeed, *digit span,* which assesses the basic capacity of working memory (see Chapter 9, page 340), increases from about 4 digits at age 7 to 7 digits at age 12 (Kail, 2003).

■ *Gains in inhibition.* As indicated in earlier chapters, inhibition—the ability to control internal and external distracting stimuli—improves from infancy on. But additional strides occur in middle childhood as the frontal lobes of the cerebral cortex develop further (Luna et al., 2004; Nelson, Thomas, & de Haan, 2006). EEG brain-wave and fMRI measures reveal a steady, age-related increase in activation of diverse cortical regions, especially the frontal lobes, in children and adolescents working on tasks that require suppression of inappropriate responses (Bartgis, Lilly, & Thomas, 2003; Luna et al., 2001). Individuals skilled at inhibition can prevent their minds from straying to irrelevant thoughts, an ability that supports many information-processing skills by preserving space in working memory for the task at hand (Dempster & Corkill, 1999; Klenberg, Korkman, & Lahti-Nuuttila, 2001).

Besides brain development, strategy use contributes to more effective information processing. As we have already seen, school-age children think far more strategically than preschoolers. At the same time, neurological change supports gains in strategy use.

Fourth graders and their teacher collaborate in a quilt-making project. As a result of adult guidance and encouragement to plan, these children will become increasingly skilled at solving problems involving multiple steps in a deliberate, orderly fashion.

Attention

During middle childhood, attention changes in three ways. It becomes more selective, adaptable, and planful.

SELECTIVITY AND ADAPTABILITY ■ As Joey and Lizzie moved through elementary school, they became better at deliberately attending to just those aspects of a situation that were relevant to their task goals. Researchers study this increasing selectivity of attention by introducing irrelevant stimuli into a task and seeing how well children attend to its central elements. For example, they might present a stream of numbers on a computer screen and ask children to press a button whenever a particular two-digit sequence (such as "1" followed by "9") appears. Findings show that selective attention improves sharply between ages 6 and 10, with gains continuing into adulthood (Goldberg, Maurer, & Lewis, 2001; Gomez-Perez & Ostrosky-Solis, 2006; Lin, Hsiao, & Chen, 1999).

Older children also flexibly adapt their attention to situational requirements. For example, when sorting cards with pictures that vary in both color and shape, children age 5 and older can switch their basis of sorting from color to shape when asked; younger children typically persist in sorting in just one way (Brooks et al., 2003; Zelazo, Frye, & Rapus, 1996). And when studying for a spelling test, 10-year-old Joey was much more likely than Lizzie to devote most attention to the words he knew least well (Masur, McIntyre, & Flavell, 1973).

How do children acquire selective, adaptable attentional strategies? Children's performance on many tasks reveals a predictable, four-step sequence:

1. **Production deficiency.** Preschoolers rarely engage in attentional strategies. In other words, they fail to *produce* strategies when they could be helpful.
2. **Control deficiency.** Young elementary school children sometimes produce strategies, but not consistently. They fail to *control*, or execute, strategies effectively.
3. **Utilization deficiency.** Slightly later, children execute strategies consistently, but their performance does not improve.
4. **Effective strategy use.** By the mid-elementary school years, children use strategies consistently, and performance improves (Miller, 2000).

As we will soon see, these phases also characterize children's use of memory strategies. Why, when children first use a strategy, does it not work well? A likely reason is that applying a new strategy takes so much effort and attention that little remains to perform other parts of the task well (Woody-Dorning & Miller, 2001).

PLANNING ■ School-age children's attentional strategies also become increasingly planful. They scan detailed pictures and written materials for similarities and differences more thoroughly

production deficiency The failure to produce a mental strategy when it could be helpful.

control deficiency The inability to control, or execute, a mental strategy consistently.

utilization deficiency The inability to improve performance despite consistent use of a mental strategy.

effective strategy use Consistent use of a mental strategy, leading to improvement in performance.

Biology and Environment

Children with Attention-Deficit Hyperactivity Disorder

While the other fifth graders worked quietly at their desks, Calvin squirmed in his seat, dropped his pencil, looked out the window, fiddled with his shoelaces, and talked out. "Hey Joey," he yelled over the heads of several classmates, "wanna play ball after school?" But Joey and the other children weren't eager to play with Calvin. On the playground, Calvin was physically awkward and a poor listener who failed to follow the rules of the game. He had trouble taking turns at bat. In the outfield, he tossed his mitt in the air and looked elsewhere when the ball came his way. Calvin's desk at school and his room at home were chaotic messes. He often lost pencils, books, and other materials he needed to complete his work, and he had difficulty remembering assignments and when they were due.

Symptoms of ADHD

Calvin is one of 3 to 6 percent of school-age children with **attention-deficit hyperactivity disorder (ADHD),** which involves inattention, impulsivity, and excessive motor activity resulting in academic and social problems (American Psychiatric Association, 1994; Barkley, 2006). Boys are diagnosed about four times as often as

girls. However, many girls with ADHD seem to be overlooked, either because their symptoms are less flagrant or because of a gender bias: A difficult, disruptive boy is more likely to be referred for treatment (Abikoff et al., 2002; Biederman et al., 2005).

Children with ADHD cannot stay focused on a task that requires mental effort for more than a few minutes. In addition, they often act impulsively, ignoring social rules and lashing out with hostility when frustrated. Many (but not all) are *hyperactive*. Their excessive motor activity is exhausting for parents and teachers and so irritating to other children that they are quickly rejected. For a child to be diagnosed with ADHD, these symptoms must have appeared before age 7 as a persistent problem.

Because of their difficulty concentrating, ADHD children score 7 to 15 points lower than other children on intelligence tests (Barkley, 2002b). Researchers agree that deficient executive processing (see page 221 in Chapter 6) underlies ADHD symptoms. According to one view, children with ADHD are impaired in capacity to inhibit action in favor of thought—a basic difficulty that results in wide-ranging

inadequacies in strategic thinking and, therefore, in poor self-regulation (Barkley, 2001). Another hypothesis is that ADHD is the direct result of a cluster of executive processing problems that interfere with ability to guide one's own behavior (Brown, 2005, 2006). Research confirms that children with ADHD do poorly on tasks requiring sustained attention, find it hard to ignore irrelevant information, have difficulty with memory, planning, reasoning, and problem solving in academic and social situations, and often fail to manage frustration and intense emotion (Barkley, 2003, 2006).

Origins of ADHD

ADHD runs in families and is highly heritable. Identical twins share it more often than fraternal twins (Rasmussen et al., 2004; Rietvelt et al., 2004). Children with ADHD show abnormal brain functioning, including reduced electrical and blood-flow activity in the frontal lobes of the cerebral cortex and in other areas involved in attention, inhibition of behavior, and other aspects of motor control (Castellanos et al., 2003; Sowell et al., 2002). Also, the brains of children with ADHD grow more slowly and are

than preschoolers (Vurpillot, 1968). And on tasks with many parts, they make decisions about what to do first and what to do next in an orderly fashion. In one study, 5- to 9-year-olds were given lists of items to obtain from a play grocery store. Older children more often took time to scan the store before shopping. They also paused more often to look for each item before moving to get it. Consequently, they followed shorter routes through the aisles (Gauvain & Rogoff, 1989a; Szepkouski, Gauvain, & Carberry, 1994).

The development of planning illustrates how attention becomes coordinated with other cognitive processes. To solve problems involving multiple steps, children must postpone action in favor of weighing alternatives, organizing task materials (such as items on a grocery list), and remembering the steps of their plan so they can attend to each one in sequence. Along the way, they must monitor how well the plan works and revise it if necessary. Clearly, planning places heavy demands on working-memory capacity.

As Chapter 9 revealed, children learn much about planning by collaborating with more expert planners. With age, children take on more responsibility in these joint endeavors, such as organizing task materials and suggesting planning strategies. In one study of parent–child interactions, discussions involving planning at ages 4 and 9 predicted planning competence in adolescence (Gauvain & Huard, 1999). The demands of school tasks—and teachers' explanations of how to plan—also contribute to gains in planning.

The attentional strategies just considered are crucial for success in school. Unfortunately, some children have great difficulty paying attention. See the Biology and Environment box above for a discussion of the serious learning and behavior problems of children with attention-deficit hyperactivity disorder.

attention-deficit hyperactivity disorder A childhood disorder involving inattention, impulsivity, and excessive motor activity, often resulting in academic failure and social problems.

about 3 percent smaller in overall volume than those of those unaffected agemates (Castellanos et al., 2002; Durston et al., 2004). Several genes that affect neural communication have been implicated in the disorder (Biederman & Spencer, 2000; Quist & Kennedy, 2001).

At the same time, ADHD is associated with environmental factors. Prenatal teratogens—particularly those involving long-term exposure, such as illegal drugs, alcohol, and tobacco—are linked to inattention and hyperactivity (Milberger et al., 1997). Furthermore, children with ADHD are more likely to come from homes with unhappy marriages and high family stress (Bernier & Siegel, 1994). But a stressful home life rarely causes ADHD. Rather, these children's behaviors can contribute to family problems, which intensify the child's preexisting difficulties.

Treating ADHD

Calvin's doctor eventually prescribed stimulant medication, the most common treatment for ADHD. As long as dosage is carefully regulated, these drugs reduce symptoms in 70 percent of children who take them, with benefits for academic performance and peer relations (Greenhill, Halperin, & Abikoff, 1999). Stimulant medication seems to increase activity in the frontal lobes, thereby improving the child's capacity to sustain attention and to inhibit off-task and self-stimulating behavior.

In 2006, an advisory panel convened by the U.S. Food and Drug Administration warned that stimulants might impair heart functioning, even

causing sudden death in a few individuals, and advocated warning labels describing these potential risks. Debate over the safety of medication for ADHD is likely to intensify. In any case, medication is not enough. Drugs cannot teach children to compensate for inattention and impulsivity. The most effective treatment approach combines medication with interventions that model and reinforce appropriate academic and social behavior (American Academy of Pediatrics, 2005c; Smith, Barkley, & Shapiro, 2006). Family intervention is also important. Inattentive, overactive children strain the patience of parents, who are likely to react punitively and inconsistently—a child-rearing style that strengthens inappropriate behavior. Breaking this cycle through training parents in effective child-rearing skills is as important for ADHD children as it is for the defiant, aggressive youngsters discussed in Chapter 10. In fact, in 45 to 65 percent of cases, these two sets of behavior problems occur together (Barkley, 2002a).

Some media reports suggest that the number of North American children diagnosed with ADHD has increased greatly. But two large surveys yielded similar overall prevalence rates 20 years ago and today. Nevertheless, the incidence of ADHD is much higher in some communities than others. At times, children are overdiagnosed and unnecessarily medicated because their parents and teachers are impatient with inattentive, active behavior within normal range. In Hong Kong, where academic success is particularly prized, children are

diagnosed at more than twice the rate seen in North America. At other times, children are underdiagnosed and do not receive the treatment they need, as occurs in Great Britain, where doctors are hesitant to label a child with ADHD or to prescribe medication (Taylor, 2004).

ADHD is usually a lifelong disorder. Affected individuals are at risk for persistent antisocial behavior, depression, alcohol and drug abuse, and other problems (Kessler et al., 2005, 2006). Adults with ADHD continue to need help—in structuring their environments, regulating negative emotion, selecting appropriate careers, and understanding their condition as a biological deficit rather than a character flaw.

This girl frequently engages in disruptive behavior at school. Children with ADHD have great difficulty staying on task and often act impulsively, ignoring social rules.

Memory Strategies

As attention improves, so do *memory strategies,* the deliberate mental activities we use to store and retain information. During the school years, these techniques for holding information in working memory and transferring it to our long-term knowledge base take a giant leap forward (Schneider, 2002).

REHEARSAL AND ORGANIZATION ■ When Lizzie had a list of things to learn, such as a phone number, the capitals of the United States, or the names of geometric shapes, she immediately used **rehearsal**—repeating the information to herself. This memory strategy first appears in the early grade school years. Soon after, a second strategy becomes common: **organization**—grouping related items (for example, all state capitals in the same part of the country), an approach that improves recall dramatically.

Perfecting memory strategies requires time and effort. For example, 8-year-old Lizzie rehearsed in a piecemeal fashion. After being given the word *cat* in a list of items, she said, "Cat, cat, cat." But 10-year-old Joey combined previous words with each new item, saying, "Desk, man, yard, cat, cat"—an approach that greatly increases retention (Kunzinger, 1985). In longitudinal research, younger children organized inconsistently (a *control deficiency*) and, when they did organize, showed little or no memory benefit (a *utilization deficiency*). In contrast, between ages 8 and 10, after realizing how effective organization is, many children suddenly began using it consistently, and their recall improved immediately (Schlagmüller & Schneider,

rehearsal A memory strategy that involves repeating information to oneself.

organization A memory strategy that involves grouping related items, which dramatically improves recall.

2002; Weinert & Schneider, 1999). With experience, children organize more skillfully, grouping items into fewer categories. And they apply the strategy to a wider range of memory tasks, including ones with less clearly related materials (Bjorklund et al., 1994).

Furthermore, as children gain in processing capacity and familiarity with strategies, they are more likely to use several memory strategies at once—rehearsing, organizing, and stating category names. And the more strategies they apply simultaneously, the better they remember (Coyle & Bjorklund, 1997; DeMarie et al., 2004). Although younger children's use of multiple strategies has little impact on performance (a *utilization deficiency*), their tendency to experiment is adaptive. By generating a variety of strategies, they discover which ones work best and how to combine them effectively. For example, second to fourth graders know that organizing the items first, next rehearsing category names, and finally rehearsing individual items is a good way to study lists (Hock, Park, & Bjorklund, 1998). Recall from *overlapping-waves theory*, discussed in Chapter 9, that children experiment with strategies when faced with many cognitive challenges.

ELABORATION ■ By the end of middle childhood, children start to use **elaboration**—creating a relationship, or shared meaning, between two or more pieces of information that are not members of the same category. For example, if you needed to learn the words *fish* and *pipe*, you might generate a verbal statement or a mental image: "The fish is smoking a pipe." This highly effective memory technique, which requires considerable effort and space in working memory, becomes increasingly common in adolescence and early adulthood (Schneider & Pressley, 1997).

Because organization and elaboration combine items into *meaningful chunks*, they permit children to hold on to much more information. In addition, when children link a new item to information they already know, they can *retrieve* it easily by thinking of other items associated with it. As we will see, this also contributes to improved memory during the school years.

The Knowledge Base and Memory Performance

During middle childhood, the long-term knowledge base grows larger and becomes organized into increasingly elaborate, hierarchically structured networks. This rapid growth of knowledge helps children use strategies and remember (Schneider, 2002). In other words, knowing more about a topic makes new information more meaningful and familiar so it is easier to store and retrieve.

To test this idea, researchers classified fourth graders as "experts" or "novices" in soccer knowledge, then gave both groups lists of new soccer and nonsoccer items to learn. Experts remembered far more items on the soccer list (but not on the nonsoccer list) than nonexperts. And during recall, the experts' listing of items was better-organized, as indicated by clustering of items into categories (Schneider & Bjorklund, 1992). These findings suggest that highly knowledgeable children organize information in their area of expertise with little or no effort—by rapidly associating new items with the large number they already know. Consequently, experts can devote more working-memory resources to using recalled information to reason and solve problems (Bjorklund & Douglas, 1997).

Though powerfully influential, knowledge is not the only important factor in children's strategic memory processing. Children who are expert in an area are usually highly motivated. As a result, they not only acquire knowledge more quickly but also *actively use what they know* to add more. In contrast, academically unsuccessful children often fail to ask how previously stored information can clarify new material. This, in turn, interferes with the development of a broad knowledge base (Schneider & Bjorklund, 1998). By the end of the school years, then, extensive knowledge and use of memory strategies support one another.

Culture, Schooling, and Memory Strategies

Rehearsal, organization, and elaboration are techniques that people usually use when they need to remember information for its own sake. On many other occasions, memory occurs as a natural byproduct of participation in daily activities (Rogoff, 2003). For example, Joey can spout a wealth of facts about baseball teams and players—information he picked up from

elaboration A memory strategy that involves creating a relationship, or shared meaning, between two or more pieces of information that are not members of the same category.

watching ball games, discussing the game, and trading baseball cards with his friends. And without prior rehearsal, he can recount the story line of an exciting movie or novel—narrative material that is already meaningfully organized.

A repeated finding is that people in non-Western cultures who have no formal schooling do not use or benefit from instruction in memory strategies (Rogoff & Chavajay, 1995). Tasks that require children to recall isolated bits of information, which are common in classrooms, motivate children to use memory strategies. In fact, Western children get so much practice with this type of learning that they do not refine techniques that rely on spatial location and arrangement of objects—cues that are readily available in everyday life. Australian Aboriginal and Guatemalan Mayan children are considerably better at these memory skills (Kearins, 1981; Rogoff, 1986). The development of memory strategies, then, is not just a matter of a more competent information-processing system. It also depends on task demands and cultural circumstances.

A father in Kabul, Afghanistan, draws water from a well, and his son distributes it among ceramic pitchers. As the boy engages in this meaningful work, he demonstrates keen memory for relevant information— how to pour without spilling, how much water each pitcher can hold. Nevertheless, he may not perform well on a list-memory task of the kind often given in schools.

The School-Age Child's Theory of Mind

During middle childhood, children's *theory of mind*, or set of beliefs about mental activities, becomes much more elaborate and refined. Recall from Chapter 9 that this awareness of thought is often called *metacognition*. School-age children's improved ability to reflect on their own mental life is another reason that their thinking and problem solving advance.

KNOWLEDGE OF COGNITIVE CAPACITIES ■ Unlike preschoolers, who view the mind as a passive container of information, older children regard it as an active, constructive agent, capable of selecting and transforming information (Kuhn, 2000a). Consequently, they better understand the process of thinking and the impact of psychological factors on performance.

Six- and 7-year-olds, for example, realize that doing well on a task depends on focusing attention—concentrating, wanting to do it, and not being distracted by anything else (Miller & Bigi, 1979). And by age 10, children realize that if you "remember," "know," or "understand," you are more certain of your knowledge than if you simply "guessed," "estimated," or "compared." They also grasp relationships between mental activities—for example, that remembering is crucial for understanding and that understanding strengthens memory (Schwanenflugel, Henderson, & Fabricius, 1998).

Furthermore, during the early school years, children's understanding of sources of knowledge expands. They realize that people can extend their knowledge not only by directly observing events and talking to others but also by making *mental inferences* (Carpendale & Chandler, 1996; Miller, Hardin, & Montgomery, 2003). This grasp of inference enables knowledge of false belief to expand. In several studies, researchers told children complex stories involving one character's belief about a second character's belief. Then the children answered questions about what the first character thought the second character would do (see Figure 12.2 on page 448). By age 7, children were aware that people form beliefs about other people's beliefs and that these *second-order beliefs* can also be wrong! Once children appreciate *second-order false belief,* they are better able to pinpoint the reasons that another person arrived at a certain belief (Astington, Pelletier, & Homer, 2002; Harris, 2006). This assists them greatly in understanding others' perspectives.

School-age children's capacity for more complex thinking contributes greatly to their more reflective, process-oriented view of the mind. But experiences that foster awareness of mental activities are also involved. In a study of rural children of Cameroon, Africa, those who attended school performed much better on theory-of-mind tasks (Vinden, 2002). In school, teachers often call attention to the workings of the mind when they remind children to pay attention, remember mental steps, and evaluate their reasoning. And as children engage in reading, writing, and math, they often use *private speech,* at first speaking aloud and later silently to themselves. As they "hear themselves think," they probably detect many aspects of mental life (Flavell, Green, & Flavell, 1995).

KNOWLEDGE OF STRATEGIES ■ Consistent with their more active view of the mind, school-age children are far more conscious of mental strategies than are preschoolers. For example, when shown video clips of two children using different recall strategies and asked which one is

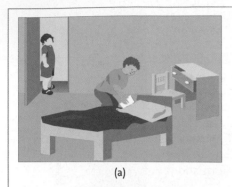 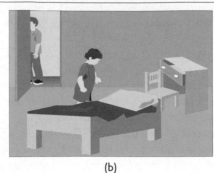 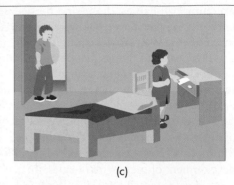

(a)

Jason has a letter from a friend. Lisa wants to read the letter, but Jason doesn't want her to. Jason puts the letter under his pillow.

(b)

Jason leaves the room to help his mother.

(c)

While Jason is gone, Lisa takes the letter and reads it. Jason returns and watches Lisa, but Lisa doesn't see Jason. Then Lisa puts the letter in Jason's desk.

FIGURE 12.2

A second-order false belief task.   After relating the story in the sequence of pictures, the researcher asks a second-order false-belief question: "Where does Lisa think Jason will look for the letter? Why?" Around age 7, children answer correctly—that Lisa thinks Jason will look under his pillow because Lisa doesn't know that Jason saw her put the letter in the desk.   (Adapted from Astington, Pelletier, & Homer, 2002.)

likely to produce better memory, kindergarten and young elementary school children knew that rehearsing or organizing is better than looking or naming. Older children were aware of more subtle differences—that organizing is better than rehearsing (Justice, 1986; Schneider, 1986). And between third and fifth grade, children develop a much better appreciation of how and why strategies work (Alexander et al., 2003).

Once children become conscious of the many factors that influence mental activity, they combine them into a more effective understanding. By the end of middle childhood, children take account of *interactions* among multiple variables—how age and motivation of the learner, effective use of strategies, and nature and difficulty of the task together affect cognitive performance (Wellman, 1990). In this way, metacognition broadens into a more complex theory.

Cognitive Self-Regulation

Although metacognition expands, school-age children often have difficulty putting what they know about thinking into action. They are not yet good at **cognitive self-regulation,** the process of continuously monitoring progress toward a goal, checking outcomes, and redirecting unsuccessful efforts. For example, Lizzie is aware that she should attend closely to her teacher's directions, group items when memorizing, reread a complicated paragraph to make sure she understands it, and relate new information to what she already knows. But she does not always engage in these activities.

To study cognitive self-regulation, researchers sometimes look at the impact of children's awareness of memory strategies on how well they remember. By second grade, the more children know about memory strategies, the more they recall—a relationship that strengthens over middle childhood (Pierce & Lange, 2000). Furthermore, children who can explain why a memory strategy works use it more effectively, which results in better memory performance (Justice et al., 1997). And when children apply a useful strategy consistently, their knowledge of strategies strengthens, resulting in a bidirectional relationship between metacognition and strategic processing that enhances self-regulation (Schlagmüller & Schneider, 2002).

Why does cognitive self-regulation develop gradually? Monitoring learning outcomes is cognitively demanding, requiring constant evaluation of effort and progress. By adolescence, self-regulation is a strong predictor of academic success (Joyner & Kurtz-Costes, 1997). Students who do well in school know when their learning is going well and when it is not. If they

cognitive self-regulation
The process of continuously monitoring progress toward a goal, checking outcomes, and redirecting unsuccessful efforts.

encounter obstacles—poor study conditions, a confusing text passage, or an unclear class presentation—they take steps to organize the learning environment, review the material, or seek other sources of support. This active, purposeful approach contrasts sharply with the passive orientation of students who achieve poorly (Zimmerman & Risemberg, 1997).

Parents and teachers can foster self-regulation. In one study, researchers observed parents instructing their children on a problem-solving task during the summer before third grade. Parents who patiently pointed out important features of the task and suggested strategies had children who, in the classroom, more often discussed ways to approach problems and monitored their own performance (Stright et al., 2002). Explaining the effectiveness of strategies is particularly helpful. When adults tell children not just what to do but also why to do it, they provide a rationale for future action.

Children who acquire effective self-regulatory skills develop a sense of *academic self-efficacy*—confidence in their own ability, which supports future self-regulation (Schunk & Pajares, 2005). Unfortunately, some children receive messages from parents and teachers that seriously undermine their academic self-esteem and self-regulatory skills. We will consider these *learned-helpless* youngsters, along with ways to help them, in Chapter 13.

This student's capacity for cognitive self-regulation is evident as she does a home-work assignment. Will she reread complex material and relate new information to existing knowledge? Her parents and teachers can foster her self-regulatory skills by suggesting strategies and explaining why they are effective.

Applications of Information Processing to Academic Learning

Joey entered first grade able to recognize only a handful of written words. By fifth grade, he was a proficient reader. Similarly, at age 6, Joey had an informally acquired knowledge of number concepts. By age 10, he could add, subtract, multiply, and divide with ease, and he had begun to master fractions and percentages. Fundamental discoveries about the development of information processing have been applied to children's learning of reading and mathematics. Researchers are identifying the cognitive ingredients of skilled performance, tracing their development, and distinguishing good from poor learners by pinpointing differences in cognitive skills. They hope, as a result, to design teaching methods that will improve children's learning.

READING ■ Reading makes use of use many skills at once, taxing all aspects of our information-processing systems. We must perceive single letters and letter combinations, translate them into speech sounds, recognize the visual appearance of many common words, hold chunks of text in working memory while interpreting their meaning, and combine the meanings of various parts of a text passage into an understandable whole. In fact, reading is so demanding that most or all of these skills must be done automatically. If one or more are poorly developed, they will compete for resources in our limited working memories, and reading performance will decline.

As children make the transition from emergent literacy to conventional reading, language development continues to facilitate their progress. Recall from Chapter 9 that *phonological awareness*—the ability to reflect on and manipulate the sound structure of spoken language—strongly predicts early reading and spelling achievement. Other information-processing skills also contribute to reading proficiency. Gains in processing speed enable children to rapidly convert visual symbols into sounds (McBride-Chang & Kail, 2002). Visual scanning and discrimination play important roles and improve with reading experience (Rayner, Pollatsek, & Starr, 2003). Performing all these skills efficiently releases working memory for higher-level activities involved in comprehending the text's meaning.

Until recently, researchers were involved in an intense debate over how to teach beginning reading. Those who took a **whole-language approach** argued that reading should be taught in a way that parallels natural language learning. From the beginning, children should be exposed to text in its complete form—stories, poems, letters, posters, and lists—so that they can appreciate the communicative function of written language. According to this view, as long as reading is kept meaningful, children will be motivated to discover the specific skills they need (Watson, 1989). Other experts advocated a **phonics approach,** believing that children should first be coached on *phonics*—the basic rules for translating written symbols into sounds. Only after mastering these skills should they get complex reading material (Rayner & Pollatsek, 1989).

whole-language approach An approach to beginning reading instruction that parallels children's natural language learning through the use of reading materials that are whole and meaningful.

phonics approach An approach to beginning reading instruction that emphasizes coaching children on phonics, the basic rules for translating written symbols into sounds.

Effective reading instruction involves balancing basic-skills and whole-language teaching. This first-grade teacher works with a small group on identifying, pronouncing, and writing words that being with "fr." Teaching of phonics is embedded in interesting stories and challenging writing tasks.

Many studies show that, in fact, children learn best with a mixture of both approaches. In kindergarten, first, and second grades, teaching that includes phonics boosts reading scores, especially for children who lag behind in reading progress (Berninger et al., 2003; Xue & Meisels, 2004). And when teachers combine real reading and writing with teaching of phonics and engage in other excellent teaching practices—encouraging children to tackle reading challenges and integrating reading into all school subjects—first graders show far greater literacy progress (Pressley et al., 2002).

Why might combining phonics with whole language work best? Learning the relationships between letters and sounds enables children to *decode,* or decipher, words they have never seen before. Children who enter school low in phonological awareness make far better reading progress when given training in phonics. Soon they detect new letter–sound relations while reading on their own (Goswami, 2000). It is not surprising, then, that phonics training promotes children's belief that they can succeed at challenging reading tasks (Tunmer & Chapman, 2002).

Yet if practicing basic skills is overemphasized, children may lose sight of the goal of reading—understanding. Children who read aloud fluently without registering meaning know little about effective reading strategies—for example, that they must read more carefully if they will be tested than if they are reading for pleasure or that explaining a passage in their own words is a good way to assess comprehension. Providing instruction aimed at increasing knowledge and use of reading strategies enhances reading performance from third grade on (Paris & Paris, 2006; Van Keer, 2004).

Table 12.1 charts the general sequence of reading development. Notice the major shift, around age 7 to 8, from "learning to read" to "reading to learn" (Ely, 2005). As decoding and comprehension skills reach a high level of efficiency, older readers become actively engaged with the text. They adjust the way they read to fit their current purpose—sometimes seeking new facts and ideas, sometimes questioning, agreeing with, or disagreeing with the writer's viewpoint.

MATHEMATICS ■ Mathematics teaching in elementary school builds on and greatly enriches children's informal knowledge of number concepts and counting. Written notation systems and formal computational techniques enhance children's ability to represent numbers and

TABLE 12.1   Sequence of Reading Development

GRADE/AGE	DEVELOPMENT	METHOD OF LEARNING
Preschool and kindergarten 2–6 years	"Pretends" to read; recognizes some familiar signs ("ON," "OFF," "PIZZA"); "pretends" to write; prints own name and other words	Informal literacy experiences through literacy-rich physical environments, literacy-related play, and storybook reading (see Chapter 9, page 347)
Grades 1 and 2 6–7 years	Masters letter–sound correspondences; sounds out one-syllable words; reads simple stories; reads about 600 words	Direct teaching, through exposure to many types of texts and the basic rules of decoding written symbols into sounds
Grades 2 and 3 7–8 years	Reads simple stories more fluently; masters basic decoding rules; reads about 3,000 words	Same as above
Grades 4 to 9 9–14 years	Reads to learn new knowledge, usually without questioning the reading material	Reading and studying; participating in classroom discussion; completing written assignments
Grades 10 to 12 15–17 years	Reads more widely, tapping materials with diverse viewpoints	Reading more widely; writing papers
College 18 years and older	Reads with a self-defined purpose; decoding and comprehension skills reach a high level of efficiency	Reading even more widely; writing more sophisticated papers

Source: Chall, 1983.

compute. Over the early elementary school years, children acquire basic math facts through a combination of frequent practice, reasoning about number concepts, and teaching that conveys effective strategies. (Return to Chapter 9, pages 341–342, for research supporting the importance of both extended practice and a grasp of concepts.) Eventually children retrieve answers automatically and apply this basic knowledge to more complex problems.

Arguments about how to teach math resemble those in reading, pitting drill in computing against "number sense," or understanding. Again, a blend of these two approaches is most beneficial. In learning basic math, poorly performing students use cumbersome techniques (such as counting all items in an addition problem) or try to retrieve answers from memory too soon. They have not sufficiently experimented with strategies to see which are most effective and to reorganize their observations in logical ways—for example, noticing that multiplication problems involving 2 (2×8) are equivalent to addition doubles ($8 + 8$). On tasks assessing their grasp of math concepts, their performance is weak (Canobi, 2004; Canobi, Reeve, & Pattison, 2003). This suggests that encouraging students to apply strategies and making sure they know why certain strategies work well are essential for solid mastery of basic math.

A similar picture emerges for more complex skills, such as carrying in addition, borrowing in subtraction, and operating with decimals and frac-

Children develop math skills through a combination of frequent practice and reasoning about number concepts. The most effective teaching combines both approaches.

tions. Children taught by rote cannot apply the procedure to new problems. Instead, they persistently make mistakes, following a "math rule" that they recall incorrectly because they do not understand it (Carpenter et al., 1999). Look at the following subtraction errors:

$$
\begin{array}{r}
427 \\
-138 \\
\hline
311
\end{array}
\qquad\qquad
\begin{array}{r}
7002 \\
-5445 \\
\hline
1447
\end{array}
$$

In the first problem, the child consistently subtracts a smaller from a larger digit, regardless of which is on top. In the second, the child skips columns with zeros in a borrowing operation and, whenever there is a zero on top, writes the bottom digit as the answer.

Children who are given rich opportunities to experiment with problem solving, to appreciate the reasons behind strategies, and to evaluate solution techniques seldom make such errors. In one study, second graders who were taught in these ways not only mastered correct procedures but invented their own successful strategies, some of which were superior to standard, school-taught methods! Consider this solution:

$$
\begin{array}{cccc}
3 & 15 & 14 & 12 \\
\cancel{4} & \cancel{6} & \cancel{5} & \cancel{2} \\
-1 & 9 & 6 & 8 \\
\hline
2 & 6 & 8 & 4
\end{array}
$$

In subtracting, the child performed all trades first, flexibly moving either from right to left or from left to right, and then subtracted all four columns—a highly efficient, accurate approach (Fuson & Burghard, 2003).

In a German study, the more teachers emphasized conceptual knowledge, by having children actively construct meanings in word problems before practicing computation and memorizing math facts, the more children gained in math achievement from second to third grade (Staub & Stern, 2002). Children taught in this way draw on their solid knowledge of relationships between operations (for example, that the inverse of division is multiplication) to generate efficient, flexible procedures: To solve the division problem 360/9, they might multiply $9 \times 40 = 360$. And because such children have been encouraged to estimate answers, if they go down the wrong track in computation, they are usually self-correcting. Furthermore, they appreciate connections between math operations and problem contexts. They can solve a word problem ("If Jesse spent $3.45 for bananas, $2.62 for bread, and $3.55 for peanut butter. Can he pay for it all with a $10 bill?") quickly through estimation instead of exact calculation (De Corte & Verschaffel, 2006).

In Asian countries, students receive a variety of supports for acquiring mathematical knowledge and often excel at both math reasoning and computation. Use of the metric system, which presents ones, tens, hundreds, and thousands values in all areas of measurement, helps Asian children grasp place value. The consistent structure of number words in Asian languages (*ten-two* for 12, *ten-three* for 13) also makes this idea clear (Miura & Okamoto, 2003). And Asian number words are shorter and more quickly pronounced, so more digits can be held in working memory at once, increasing the speed of thinking (Geary et al., 1996). Finally, in early math lessons, particularly abacus instruction, many Chinese and Japanese children learn to use the number 5 as an anchor, which facilitates efficient computation (Kuriyama & Yoshida, 1995). As we will see later in this chapter, compared with lessons in North America, those in Asian classrooms devote more time to exploring math concepts and less to drill and repetition.

Ask Yourself

Review   Cite evidence indicating that school-age children view the mind as an active, constructive agent.

Apply   After viewing a slide show about endangered species, second and fifth graders in Lizzie and Joey's school were told to remember as many animal names as they could. Explain why the fifth graders recalled much more than the second graders.

Apply   Lizzie knows that if you have difficulty learning part of a task, you should devote extra attention to that part. But she plays each of her piano pieces from beginning to end instead of spending more time on the hard parts. Explain why Lizzie does not engage in cognitive self-regulation.

Reflect   In your own elementary school math education, how much emphasis was placed on computational drill and how much on understanding concepts? How do you think that balance affected your interest and performance in math?

Individual Differences in Mental Development

In middle childhood, educators rely heavily on intelligence tests for assessing individual differences in mental development. Around age 6, IQ becomes more stable than it was at earlier ages, and it correlates moderately well with academic achievement, typically around .50 to .60. And children with higher IQs are more likely when they grow up to attain higher levels of education and enter more prestigious occupations (Brody, 1997).

Because IQ predicts school performance, it often plays a major role in educational decisions. Do intelligence tests accurately assess ability to profit from academic instruction? Let's look closely at this controversial issue.

Defining and Measuring Intelligence

Virtually all intelligence tests provide an overall score (the IQ), which represents *general intelligence* or reasoning ability, along with an array of separate scores measuring specific mental abilities. But intelligence is a collection of many capacities, not all of which are included on currently available tests (Sternberg et al., 2000). Test designers use a complicated statistical technique called *factor analysis* to identify the various abilities that intelligence tests measure. It identifies which sets of test items cluster together, meaning that test-takers who do well on

FIGURE 12.3

Test items like those on commonly used intelligence tests for children. The verbal items emphasize culturally loaded, fact-oriented information. The perceptual- and spatial-reasoning, working-memory, and processing-speed items emphasize aspects of information processing and are assumed to assess more biologically based skills.

TYPICAL VERBAL ITEMS

Vocabulary	Tell me what *carpet* means.
General Information	What day of the week comes right after Thursday?
Verbal Comprehension	Why do we need police officers?
Similarities	How are a ship and a train alike?
Arithmetic	If a $60 jacket is 25% off, how much does it cost?

TYPICAL PERCEPTUAL- AND SPATIAL-REASONING ITEMS

Block Design Make these blocks look just like the picture.

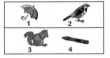

Picture Concepts Choose one object from each row to make a group of objects that goes together.

Spatial Visualization Which of the boxes on the right can be made from the pattern on the left?

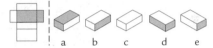

TYPICAL WORKING-MEMORY ITEMS

Digit Span Repeat these digits in the same order. Now repeat these digits (a similar series) backward.
2, 6, 4, 7, 1, 8

Letter–Number Sequencing Repeat these numbers and letters, first giving the numbers, then the letters, each in correct sequence.
8 G 4 B 5 N 2

TYPICAL PROCESSING-SPEED ITEM

Symbol Search If the shape on the left is the same as any of those on the right, mark YES. If the shape is not the same, mark NO. Work as quickly as you can without making mistakes.

---

one item in the cluster tend to do well on the others. Distinct clusters are called *factors,* each of which represents an ability. See Figure 12.3 for items typically included in intelligence tests for children.

The intelligence tests given from time to time in classrooms are *group-administered tests.* They permit large numbers of students to be tested at once and are useful for instructional planning and for identifying children who require more extensive evaluation with *individually administered tests.* Unlike group tests, which teachers can give with minimal training, individually administered tests demand that considerable training and experience to give well. The examiner not only considers the child's answers but also observes the child's behavior, noting such reactions as attention to and interest in the tasks and wariness of the adult. These observations provide insight into whether the test score accurately reflects the child's abilities. Two individual tests—the Stanford-Binet and the Wechsler—are often used to identify highly intelligent children and to diagnose children with learning problems.

The modern descendent of Alfred Binet's first successful intelligence test is the *Stanford-Binet Intelligence Scales, Fifth Edition,* for individuals from age 2 to adulthood. In addition to general intelligence, it assesses five intellectual factors: general knowledge, quantitative reasoning, visual–spatial processing, working memory, and basic information processing (such as speed of analyzing information). Each factor includes both a verbal mode and a nonverbal mode of testing, yielding 10 subtests in all (Roid, 2003). The nonverbal subtests do not require spoken language and are especially useful when assessing individuals with limited English, hearing impairments, or communication disorders. The knowledge and quantitative reasoning factors emphasize culturally loaded, fact-oriented information, such as vocabulary and arithmetic problems. In contrast, the basic information processing, visual–spatial processing, and working-memory factors are assumed to be less culturally biased because they require little specific information (see the spatial visualization item in Figure 12.3).

The *Wechsler Intelligence Scale for Children–IV (WISC–IV)* is the fourth edition of a widely used test for 6- through 16-year-olds. A downward extension of it, the *Wechsler Preschool and Primary Scale of Intelligence–Revised (WPPSI–III),* is appropriate for children 2 years 6 months through 7 years 3 months (Wechsler, 2002, 2003). The Wechsler tests offered both a measure of general intelligence and a variety of factor scores long before the Stanford-Binet. As a result, many psychologists and educators came to prefer them. The WISC–IV has four broad intellectual factors: verbal reasoning, perceptual (or visual–spatial) reasoning, working memory, and processing speed. Each factor is made up of two or three subtests, yielding 10 separate scores in all. The WISC-IV was designed to downplay culture-dependent information, which is emphasized on only one factor (verbal reasoning). The remaining three factors emphasize information processing. According to the test designers, the result is the most "culture-fair" intelligence test available (Williams, Weis, & Rolfhus, 2003).

The WISC was the first test to be standardized on children representing the total population of the United States, including ethnic minorities. Previous editions have been adapted for children in Canada, where both English and French versions are available (Sarrazin, 1999; Wechsler, 1996).

Recent Efforts to Define Intelligence

As we have seen, mental tests now tap important aspects of information processing. In line with this trend, some researchers are combining the factor-analytic approach to defining intelligence with the information-processing approach. They believe that factors on intelligence tests have limited usefulness unless we can identify the cognitive processes responsible for those factors. Once we understand the underlying basis for IQ, we will know much more about why a particular child does well or poorly. These researchers conduct *componential analyses* of children's test scores. This means that they look for relationships between aspects (or components) of information processing and children's IQs.

Many studies reveal a moderate relationship between processing speed, measured in terms of reaction time on diverse cognitive tasks, and IQ (Deary, 2001; Li et al., 2004). Individuals whose nervous systems function more efficiently, permitting them to take in more information and manipulate it quickly, appear to have an edge in intellectual skills. In support of this interpretation, fast, strong ERPs (EEG brain waves in response to stimulation) predict both speedy cognitive processing and higher mental test scores (Rijsdijk & Boomsma, 1997; Schmid, Tirsch, & Scherb, 2002). And measures of working-memory capacity (such as digit span) correlate well with IQ in both school-age children and adults (Conway, Kane, & Engle, 2003; de Ribaupierre & Lecerf, 2006).

But other factors, including flexible attention, memory, and reasoning strategies, are as important as efficient thinking in predicting IQ, and they explain some of the association between response speed and good test performance (Lohman, 2000; Miller & Vernon, 1992). Children who apply strategies effectively acquire more knowledge and can retrieve it rapidly—advantages that carry over to test performance. Similarly, recall from page 443 that working-memory capacity depends in part on effective inhibition—keeping irrelevant information from intruding on the task at hand. Inhibition, selective attention, and sustained attention are among a wide array of attentional strategies that are good predictors of IQ (Schweizer, Moosbrugger, & Goldhammer, 2006).

The componential approach has one major shortcoming: It regards intelligence as entirely due to causes within the child. Throughout this book, we have seen how cultural and situational factors also affect children's thinking. Robert Sternberg has expanded the componential approach into a comprehensive theory that regards intelligence as a product of inner and outer forces.

STERNBERG'S TRIARCHIC THEORY ■ As Figure 12.4 shows, Sternberg's (2001, 2002b, 2005) **triarchic theory of successful intelligence** is made up of three broad, interacting intelligences: (1) *analytical intelligence*, or information-processing skills; (2) *creative intelligence*, the capacity to solve novel problems; and (3) *practical intelligence*, application of intellectual skills in everyday situations. Intelligent behavior involves balancing all three intelligences to achieve success in life according to one's personal goals and the requirements of one's cultural community.

triarchic theory of successful intelligence Sternberg's theory, which identifies three broad, interacting intelligences—analytical, creative, and practical—that must be balanced to achieve success according to one's personal goals and the requirements of one's cultural community.

Analytical Intelligence. *Analytical intelligence* consists of the information-processing components that underlie all intelligent acts: applying strategies, acquiring task-relevant and metacognitive knowledge, and engaging in self-regulation. But on mental tests, processing skills are used in only a few of their potential ways, resulting in a far too narrow view of intelligent behavior. As we have seen, children in tribal and village societies do not necessarily perform well on measures of "school" knowledge but thrive when processing information in out-of-school situations that most Westerners would find highly challenging.

Creative Intelligence. In any context, success depends not only on processing familiar information but also on generating useful solutions to new problems. People who are *creative* think

FIGURE 12.4

Sternberg's triarchic theory of successful intelligence.
People who behave intelligently balance three interrelated intelligences—analytical, creative, and practical—to achieve success in life, defined by their personal goals and the requirements of their cultural communities.

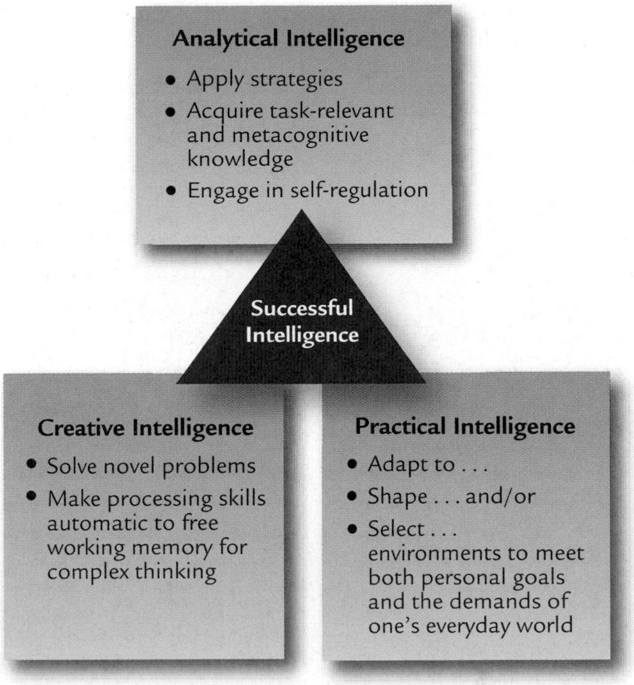

Analytical Intelligence
- Apply strategies
- Acquire task-relevant and metacognitive knowledge
- Engage in self-regulation

Successful Intelligence

Creative Intelligence
- Solve novel problems
- Make processing skills automatic to free working memory for complex thinking

Practical Intelligence
- Adapt to . . .
- Shape . . . and/or
- Select . . . environments to meet both personal goals and the demands of one's everyday world

more skillfully than others when faced with novelty. Given a new task, they apply their information-processing skills in exceptionally effective ways, rapidly making these skills automatic so that working memory is freed for more complex aspects of the situation. Consequently, they quickly move to high-level performance. Although all of us are capable of some creativity, only a few individuals excel at generating novel solutions.

Practical Intelligence. Finally, intelligence is a *practical,* goal-oriented activity aimed at one or more of the following purposes: *adapting to, shaping,* or *selecting environments.* Intelligent people skillfully *adapt* their thinking to fit with both their desires and the demands of their everyday worlds. When they cannot adapt to a situation, they try to *shape,* or change, it to meet their needs. If they cannot shape it, they *select* new contexts that better match their skills, values, or goals. Practical intelligence reminds us that intelligent behavior is never culture-free. Because of their backgrounds, some children do well at the behaviors required for success on intelligence tests and adapt easily to the testing conditions and tasks. Others, with different life histories, may misinterpret or reject the testing context. Yet such children often display sophisticated abilities in daily life—for example, telling stories, engaging in complex artistic activities, or interacting skillfully with other people.

The triarchic theory emphasizes the complexity of intelligent behavior and the limitations of current intelligence tests in assessing that complexity. For example, out-of-school, practical forms of intelligence are vital for life success and help explain why cultures vary widely in the behaviors they regard as intelligent (Sternberg et al., 2000). When researchers asked ethnically diverse parents for their idea of an intelligent first grader, Caucasian Americans mentioned cognitive traits. In contrast, ethnic minorities (Cambodian, Filipino, Vietnamese, and Mexican immigrants) saw noncognitive capacities—motivation, self-management, and social skills—as particularly important (Okagaki & Sternberg, 1993). According to Sternberg, mental tests can easily underestimate, and even overlook, the intellectual strengths of some children, especially ethnic minorities.

GARDNER'S THEORY OF MULTIPLE INTELLIGENCES ■ In yet another view of how information-processing skills underlie intelligence behavior, Howard Gardner's (1983, 1993, 2000) **theory of multiple intelligences** defines intelligence in terms of distinct sets of processing operations that permit individuals to engage in a wide range of culturally valued activities. Dismissing the idea of general intelligence, Gardner proposes at least eight independent intelligences (see Table 12.2 on page 456).

Gardner believes that each intelligence has a unique biological basis, a distinct course of development, and different expert, or "end-state," performances. At the same time, he emphasizes that a lengthy process of education is required to transform any raw potential into a mature social role (Connell, Sheridan, & Gardner, 2003). Cultural values and learning opportunities affect the extent to which a child's intellectual strengths are realized and the way they are expressed.

Gardner's list of abilities has yet to be firmly grounded in research. Neurological evidence for the independence of his abilities is weak. Some exceptionally gifted individuals have abilities

theory of multiple intelligences Gardner's theory, which proposes at least eight independent intelligences on the basis of distinct sets of processing operations that permit individuals to engage in a wide range of culturally valued activities.

TABLE 12.2 Gardner's Multiple Intelligences

INTELLIGENCE	PROCESSING OPERATIONS	END-STATE PERFORMANCE POSSIBILITIES
Linguistic	Sensitivity to the sounds, rhythms, and meaning of words and the functions of language	Poet, journalist
Logico-mathematical	Sensitivity to, and capacity to detect, logical or numerical patterns; ability to handle long chains of logical reasoning	Mathematician
Musical	Ability to produce and appreciate pitch, rhythm (or melody), and aesthetic quality of the forms of musical expressiveness	Instrumentalist, composer
Spatial	Ability to perceive the visual-spatial world accurately, to perform transformations on those perceptions, and to re-create aspects of visual experience in the absence of relevant stimuli	Sculptor, navigator
Bodily-kinesthetic	Ability to use the body skillfully for expressive as well as goal-directed purposes; ability to handle objects skillfully	Dancer, athlete
Naturalist	Ability to recognize and classify all varieties of animals, minerals, and plants	Biologist
Interpersonal	Ability to detect and respond appropriately to the moods, temperaments, motivations, and intentions of others	Therapist, salesperson
Intrapersonal	Ability to discriminate complex inner feelings and to use them to guide one's own behavior; knowledge of one's own strengths, weaknesses, desires, and intelligences	Person with detailed, accurate self-knowledge

Sources: Gardner, 1993, 1998, 2000.

According to Gardner, children are capable of at least eight distinct intelligences. As this 10-year-old notes characteristics of different trees on a school field trip, he enriches his naturalist intelligence.

that are broad rather than limited to a particular domain (Goldsmith, 2000). And research with mental tests suggests that several of Gardner's intelligences (linguistic, logico-mathematical, and spatial) have at least some features in common.

Nevertheless, Gardner calls attention to several intelligences not tapped by IQ scores. For example, his interpersonal and intrapersonal intelligences include a set of capacities for dealing with people and understanding oneself that has become known as *emotional intelligence*. As the Social Issues: Education box on the following page indicates, researchers are attempting to define, measure, and foster the abilities that make up emotional intelligence, which is vital for a satisfying, successful life.

TAKE A MOMENT... Review the *core knowledge perspective,* discussed on page 217 in Chapter 6, and compare it with Gardner's view. Gardner also accepts the existence of innately specified, core domains of thought, present at birth or emerging early in life. Then, as children respond to the demands of their culture, they transform those intelligences to fit the activities they are called on to perform. Gardner's multiple intelligences have been helpful in efforts to understand and nurture children's special talents, a topic we will take up at the end of this chapter.

Explaining Individual and Group Differences in IQ

When we compare individuals in terms of academic achievement, years of education, and the status of their occupations, it is clear that certain sectors of the population are advantaged over others. In trying to explain these differences, researchers have compared the IQ scores of ethnic and SES groups. North American black children and adolescents score, on average, 12 to 13 IQ points below American white

Social Issues: Education

Emotional Intelligence

During recess, Muriel handed a birthday party invitation to every fifth-grade girl except Claire, who looked on sadly as her classmates chattered about the party. But one of Muriel's friends, Jessica, appeared troubled. Pulling Jessica aside, she exclaimed, "Why'd you do that? You hurt Claire's feelings—you embarrassed her! If you bring invitations to school, you've got to give everybody one!" And after school, Jessica offered these comforting words to Claire: "If you aren't invited, I'm not going, either!"

Jessica's IQ is only slightly above average, but she excels at *emotional intelligence*—a term that has captured public attention because of popular books suggesting that it is an overlooked set of skills essential for acting wisely in social situations (Goleman, 1995, 1998). According to one influential definition, **emotional intelligence** refers to a set of emotional abilities that enable individuals to process and adapt to emotional information (Salovey & Pizzaro, 2003). To measure it, researchers have devised items that tap various aspects of emotional competence. One test requires people to identify and rate the strength of emotions expressed in photographs of faces (perceiving emotions), to reason about emotions in social situations (understanding emotions), and to evaluate the effectiveness of strategies for controlling negative emotions (regulating emotions). Factor analyses of the scores of hundreds of test-takers identified several emotional capacities as well as a higher-order general factor (Mayer, Salovey, & Caruso, 2003).

Emotional intelligence is modestly related to IQ. It also is positively associated with self-esteem, empathy, prosocial behavior, and life satisfaction and negatively related to aggressive behavior (Bohnert, Crnic, & Lim, 2003; Law et al, 2004; Wilhelm, 2005). In adulthood, emotional intelligence predicts many aspects of success, including leadership, workgroup cooperation, and job performance (Abraham, 2005). Only a few assessments of emotional intelligence are available for children. These require careful training of teachers in observing and recording children's emotional skills during everyday activities, gathering information from parents, and taking into account children's ethnic backgrounds (Denham, 2005; Denham & Burton, 2003). As more and better measures are devised, they may help identify children with weak emotional and social competencies who would profit from intervention (Denham, 2006). But some researchers worry that emotional ability scores will lead psychologists and educators to make simplistic comparisons among children and to lose sight of the fact that the adaptiveness of emotional and social behavior often varies across situations (Saarni, 2000).

The concepts of social and emotional intelligence have increased teachers' awareness that providing experiences that meet students' social and emotional needs can improve their adjustment. Lessons that teach emotional understanding, respect and caring for others, strategies for regulating emotion, and resistance to unfavorable peer pressure—using active learning techniques that provide skill practice both in and out of the classroom—are becoming more common (Goetz et al., 2005).

The child on the left displays high emotional intelligence as she accurately interprets her friend's sadness and offers comfort. Because emotional intelligence is positively associated with self-esteem and prosocial behavior, teachers are increasingly providing lessons aimed at promoting emotional and social skills.

---

children. Although the difference has been shrinking over the past several decades, a substantial gap remains (Dickens & Flynn, 2006; Hedges & Nowell, 1998; Rushton & Jensen, 2006). Hispanic children fall midway between black and white children (Ceci, Rosenblum, & Kumpf, 1998).

The gap between middle-SES and low-SES children—about 9 points—accounts for some, but not all, of ethnic IQ differences. For example, when black children and white children are matched on family income, the black–white gap is reduced by a third to a half (Brooks-Gunn et al., 2003; Smith, Duncan, & Lee, 2003). Of course, considerable IQ variation exists *within* each ethnic and SES group. Still, these group differences are large enough and of serious enough consequence that they cannot be ignored.

In the 1970s, the IQ nature–nurture controversy escalated after psychologist Arthur Jensen (1969) published a controversial article entitled, "How Much Can We Boost IQ and Scholastic Achievement?" Jensen's answer was "not much." He claimed—and still maintains—that heredity is largely responsible for individual, ethnic, and SES variations in intelligence (Jensen, 1998, 2001, Rushton & Jensen, 2005). Jensen's work prompted an outpouring of responses and research studies. Richard Herrnstein and Charles Murray rekindled the controversy with *The Bell Curve* (1994).

emotional intelligence A set of emotional abilities that enable individuals to process and adapt to emotional information.

Among these Canadian students, differences in IQ scores may correlate with ethnicity and SES. Research aimed at uncovering the reasons for these associations has generated heated controversy.

Like Jensen, they argued that heredity contributes substantially to individual and SES differences in IQ, and they implied that heredity plays a sizable role in the black–white IQ gap. Let's look closely at some important evidence.

NATURE VERSUS NURTURE ■ In Chapter 2 we introduced the *heritability estimate.* Recall that heritabilities are obtained from *kinship studies,* which compare family members. The most powerful evidence on the role of heredity in IQ involves twin comparisons. The IQ scores of identical twins (who share all their genes) are more similar than those of fraternal twins (who are genetically no more alike than ordinary siblings). On the basis of this and other kinship evidence, researchers estimate that about half the differences in IQ among children can be traced to their genetic makeup.

Recall, however, that heritabilities risk overestimating genetic influences and underestimating environmental influences. These measures offer convincing evidence that genes contribute to IQ, but disagreement persists over how large a role heredity plays (Grigorenko, 2000; Plomin, 2003). And heritability estimates do not reveal the complex processes through which genes and experiences influence intelligence as children develop.

Adoption studies offer a wider range of information than heritabilities. In one investigation, children of two extreme groups of biological mothers—those with IQs below 95 and those with IQs above 120—were adopted at birth by parents who were well above average in income and education. During the school years, children of the low-IQ biological mothers scored above average in IQ, indicating that test performance can be greatly improved by an advantaged home life! But they did not do as well as children of high-IQ biological mothers placed in similar adoptive families (Loehlin, Horn, & Willerman, 1997). Adoption research confirms that heredity and environment contribute jointly to IQ.

Some intriguing adoption research sheds light on the black–white IQ gap. In two studies, African-American children adopted into economically well-off white homes during the first year of life scored high on intelligence tests, attaining mean IQs of 110 and 117 by middle childhood—20 to 30 points higher than the typical scores of children growing up in low-income black communities (Moore, 1986; Scarr & Weinberg, 1983). The IQs of black adoptees declined in adolescence, perhaps because of the challenges minority teenagers face in forming an ethnic identity that blends birth and rearing backgrounds (DeBerry, Scarr, & Weinberg, 1996; Waldman, Weinberg, & Scarr, 1994). Still, the black adoptees remained above the IQ average for low-SES African Americans. The IQ gains of black children "reared in the culture of the tests and schools" are consistent with a wealth of evidence that poverty severely depresses the intelligence of ethnic minority children (Nisbett, 1998).

Furthermore, a dramatic *secular trend* in mental test performance—a generational rise in average IQ in both industrialized nations and the developing world—supports the role of environmental factors, such as improved nutrition and education, technological advances, and an increase in cognitively demanding leisure activities (Flynn, 1999, 2003). The greatest gains have occurred on tests of spatial reasoning—tasks often assumed to be "culture fair" and, therefore, more genetically based. These show, on average, an increase of 18 points per generation (30 years). The existence of a large, environmentally induced secular trend that exceeds the black–white IQ gap presents another major challenge to the assumption that black–white and other ethnic variations in IQ are mostly genetic (Dickens & Flynn, 2001).

CULTURAL INFLUENCES ■ A controversial question raised about ethnic differences in IQ has to do with whether they result from *test bias.* If a test samples knowledge and skills that not all groups of children have had equal opportunity to learn, or if the testing situation impairs the performance of some groups but not others, the resulting score is a biased, or unfair, measure.

Some experts reject the idea that intelligence tests are biased, claiming that they are intended to represent success in the common culture. According to this view, because IQ predicts academic achievement equally well for majority and minority children, IQ tests are fair to both groups (Brown, Reynolds, & Whitaker, 1999; Jensen, 2002). Others take a broader view of test bias. They believe that lack of exposure to certain communication styles and knowledge, and negative stereotypes about the test-taker's ethnic group, can undermine children's performance (Ceci & Williams, 1997; Sternberg, 2005).

Communication Styles. Ethnic minority families often foster unique language skills that do not match the expectations of most classrooms and testing situations. In one study, a researcher spent many hours observing in low-SES black homes in a southeastern U.S. city (Heath, 1990). She found that African-American parents rarely asked their children the types of knowledge-training questions typical of middle-SES white parents ("What color is it?" "What's this story about?"), which resemble the questioning style of tests and classrooms. Instead, the black parents asked only "real" questions, ones that they themselves could not answer. Often these were analogy questions ("What's that like?") or story-starter questions ("Didja hear Miss Sally this morning?") that called for elaborate responses about personal experiences and had no "right" answer.

This mother of the Yakut people of Siberia, Russia, works collaboratively with her daughter on a food preparation task, smoothly coordinating actions until the dish is complete. Ethnic minority parents with little education often communicate this way. Because their children are not accustomed to the hierarchical style of communication typical of classrooms, they may do poorly on tests and assignments.

These experiences lead low-SES black children to develop complex verbal skills at home, such as storytelling and exchanging quick-witted remarks. But their language emphasizes emotional and social concerns rather than facts about the world. Not surprisingly, black children may be confused by the "objective" questions they encounter on tests and in classrooms.

Furthermore, many ethnic minority parents without extensive schooling prefer a *collaborative style of communication* when completing tasks with children. They work together in a coordinated, fluid way, each focused on the same aspect of the problem. This pattern of adult–child engagement has been observed in Native American, Canadian Inuit, Hispanic, and Guatemalan Mayan cultures (Chavajay & Rogoff, 2002; Crago, Annahatak, & Ningiuruvik, 1993; Delgado-Gaitan, 1994). With increasing education, parents establish a *hierarchical style of communication,* more like that of classrooms and tests. The parent directs each child to carry out an aspect of the task, and children work independently (Greenfield, Suzuki, & Rothstein-Fish, 2006). This sharp discontinuity between home and school communication practices may contribute to low-SES minority children's lower IQ and school performance.

Test Content. Many researchers argue that IQ scores are affected by specific information acquired as part of majority-culture upbringing. Consistent with this view, low-SES African-American children often miss vocabulary words on mental tests that have alternative meanings in their cultural community—for example, interpreting the word *frame* to mean "physique" or *wrapping* as "rapping," a popular style of music (Champion, 2003a).

Unfortunately, attempts to change tests by eliminating verbal, fact-oriented items have not raised the scores of ethnic minority children much (Reynolds & Kaiser, 1990). Yet even non-verbal tasks, such as spatial reasoning items, depend on learning opportunities. For example, using small blocks to duplicate designs and playing video games that require fast responding and mental rotation of visual images increase success on spatial test items (Dirks, 1982; Maynard, Subrahmanyam, & Greenfield, 2005). Low-income minority children, who often grow up in more "people-oriented" than "object-oriented" homes, may lack opportunities to use games and objects that promote certain intellectual skills.

Furthermore, the sheer amount of time a child spends in school predicts IQ. When children of the same age who are in different grades are compared, those who have been in school longer score higher on intelligence tests. Similarly, dropping out of school causes IQ to decline. The earlier young people leave school, the greater their loss of IQ points (Ceci, 1991, 1999). Taken together, these findings indicate that children's exposure to the factual knowledge and ways of thinking valued in classrooms has a sizable impact on their intelligence test performance.

Stereotypes. **TAKE A MOMENT...** Imagine trying to succeed at an activity when the prevailing attitude is that members of your group are incompetent. What might you be feeling and saying to yourself? **Stereotype threat**—the fear of being judged on the basis of a negative

stereotype threat The fear of being judged on the basis of a negative stereotype, which can trigger anxiety that interferes with performance.

FIGURE 12.5

Effect of stereotype threat on performance. Among African-American and Hispanic-American children who were aware of ethnic stereotypes, being told that verbal tasks were a "test of how good children are at school problems" led to far worse performance than being told that tasks "were not a test." These statements had little impact on the performance of Caucasian-American children. (Adapted from McKown & Weinstein, 2003.)

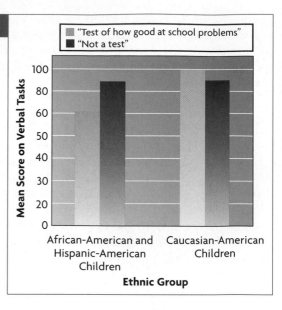

During middle childhood, minority children become increasingly aware of stereotypes. A teacher's casual remark ("This is a test," or "This will tell me how good you are at schoolwork") can induce stereotype threat, which undermines academic performance in African-American and Hispanic children.

dynamic assessment An approach to testing in which an adult introduces purposeful teaching into the testing situation to find out what the child can attain with social support.

stereotype—can trigger anxiety that interferes with performance (Steele, 1997). Mounting evidence confirms that stereotype threat undermines test taking in children and adults. For example, researchers gave African-American, Hispanic-American, and Caucasian 6- to 10-year-olds verbal tasks. Some children were told that the tasks were "not a test." Others were told that they were "a test of how good children are at school problems"— a statement designed to induce stereotype threat in the ethnic minority children. Among children who were aware of ethnic stereotypes (such as "black people aren't smart"), African Americans and Hispanics performed far worse in the "test" condition than in the "not a test" condition. Caucasian children, in contrast, performed similarly in both conditions (see Figure 12.5) (McKown & Weinstein, 2003).

Over middle childhood, children become increasingly conscious of ethnic stereotypes, and those from stigmatized groups are especially mindful of them. By junior high school, many low-SES, minority students start to devalue doing well in school, saying it is not important to them (Major et al., 1998; Osborne, 1994). Self-protective disengagement, sparked by stereotype threat, may be responsible. This undermining of motivation can have serious long-term consequences. Research shows that self-discipline—effort and delay of gratification—predicts school performance at least as well as, and sometimes better than, IQ does (Duckworth & Seligman, 2005).

Reducing Cultural Bias in Testing

Although not all experts agree, many acknowledge that IQ scores can underestimate the intelligence of children from ethnic minority groups. A special concern exists about incorrectly labeling minority children as slow learners and assigning them to remedial classes, which are far less stimulating than regular school experiences. Because of this danger, test scores need to be combined with assessments of children's adaptive behavior—their ability to cope with the demands of their everyday environments. The child who does poorly on an IQ test yet plays a complex game on the playground, figures out how to rewire a broken TV, or cares for younger siblings responsibly is unlikely to be mentally deficient.

In addition, culturally relevant testing procedures enhance minority children's performance. In an approach called **dynamic assessment,** an innovation consistent with Vygotsky's zone of proximal development, the adult introduces purposeful teaching into the testing situation to find out what the child can attain with social support (Lidz, 2001; Sternberg & Grigorenko, 2002). Dynamic assessment often follows a pretest–intervene–retest procedure. While intervening, the adult seeks the teaching style best suited to the child and communicates strategies that the child can apply in new situations.

Research consistently shows that "static" assessments, such as IQ scores, frequently underestimate how well children do on test items after adult assistance. Children's receptivity to teaching and their capacity to transfer what they have learned to novel problems add considerably to the prediction of future performance (Sternberg & Grigorenko, 2002; Tzuriel, 2001). In

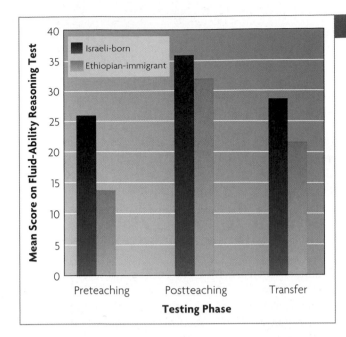

FIGURE 12.6

Influence of dynamic assessment on mental test scores of Ethiopian-immigrant and Israeli-born 6- and 7-year-olds. Each child completed test items in a preteaching phase, a postteaching phase, and a transfer phase, in which they had to generalize their learning to new problems. After dynamic assessment, Ethiopian and Israeli children's scores were nearly equal. Ethiopian children also transferred their learning to new test items, performing much better in the transfer phase than in the preteaching phase. (Adapted from Tzuriel & Kaufman, 1999.)

one study, Ethiopian 6- and 7-year-olds who had recently immigrated to Israel scored well below their Israeli-born agemates on spatial reasoning tasks. The Ethiopian children had little experience with this type of thinking. After several dynamic assessment sessions in which the adult suggested effective strategies, the Ethiopian children's scores rose sharply, nearly equaling those of Israeli-born children (see Figure 12.6). They also transferred their learning to new test items (Tzuriel & Kaufman, 1999).

Dynamic assessment is time-consuming and requires extensive knowledge of minority children's cultural values and practices. As yet the approach has not been more effective than traditional tests in predicting academic achievement (Grigorenko & Sternberg, 1998). Better correspondence may emerge in classrooms where teaching interactions resemble the dynamic assessment approach—namely, individualized assistance on tasks carefully selected to help the child move beyond her current level of development.

In view of its many problems, should intelligence testing in schools be suspended? Most experts regard this solution as unacceptable. Without testing, important educational decisions would be based only on subjective impressions—a policy that could increase the discriminatory placement of minority children. Intelligence tests are useful when interpreted carefully by examiners who are sensitive to cultural influences on test performance. And despite their limitations, IQ scores continue to be valid measures of school learning potential for the majority of Western children.

Ask Yourself

Review   Using Sternberg's triarchic theory and Gardner's theory of multiple intelligences, explain the limitations of current mental tests in assessing the diversity of human intelligence.

Apply   Lonnie, an African-American fourth grader, does well on homework assignments. But when his teacher announces, "It's time for a test to see how much you've learned," Lonnie usually does poorly. How might stereotype threat explain this inconsistency?

Connect   Explain how dynamic assessment is consistent with Vygotsky's zone of proximal development and with scaffolding (see Chapter 9, pages 334–335).

Reflect   Do you think that intelligence tests are culturally biased? What evidence and observations influenced your conclusion?

Language Development

Vocabulary, grammar, and pragmatics continue to develop in middle childhood, though less obviously than at earlier ages. In addition, children's attitude toward language undergoes a fundamental shift. They develop **metalinguistic awareness,** the ability to think about language as a system.

Schooling contributes greatly to these language competencies. Reflecting on language is extremely common during reading instruction. And fluent reading is a major new source of language learning (Ravid & Tolchinsky, 2002). In the following sections, we will see how an improved ability to reflect on language grows out of literacy and supports many complex language skills.

Vocabulary

During the elementary school years, vocabulary increases fourfold, eventually exceeding 40,000 words. On average, children learn about 20 new words each day—a rate of growth greater than in early childhood. In addition to the word-learning strategies discussed in Chapter 9, school-age children enlarge their vocabularies by analyzing the structure of complex words. From *happy* and *decide,* they quickly derive the meanings of *happiness* and *decision* (Anglin, 1993). They also figure out many more word meanings from context (Nagy & Scott, 2000).

As at earlier ages, children benefit from conversations with more expert speakers, especially when their partners use and explain complex words (Weizman & Snow, 2001). But because written language contains a far more diverse and complex vocabulary than spoken language, reading contributes enormously to vocabulary growth. Children who engage in as little as 21 minutes of independent reading per day are exposed to nearly 2 million words per year (Cunningham & Stanovich, 1998).

As their knowledge becomes better organized, school-age children think about and use words more precisely, as reflected in their word definitions. Five- and 6-year-olds offer concrete descriptions referring to functions or appearance—for example, *knife:* "when you're cutting carrots"; *bicycle:* "it's got wheels, a chain, and handlebars." By the end of elementary school, synonyms and explanations of categorical relationships appear—for example, *knife:* "something you could cut with. A saw is like a knife. It could also be a weapon" (Wehren, DeLisi, & Arnold, 1981). This advance reflects older children's ability to deal with word meanings on an entirely verbal plane. They can add new words to their vocabulary simply by being given a definition.

The school-age child's more reflective and analytical approach to language permits appreciation of the multiple meanings of words. For example, children now realize that many words, such as *cool* or *neat,* have psychological as well as physical meanings: "Cool shirt!" or "That movie was really neat!" This grasp of double meanings permits 8- to 10-year-olds to comprehend subtle metaphors, such as "sharp as a tack" and "spilling the beans" (Nippold, Taylor, & Baker, 1996; Wellman & Hickling, 1994). It also leads to a change in children's humor. Riddles and puns that alternate between different meanings of a key word are common: "Hey, did you take a bath?" "Why, is one missing?"

Grammar

During the school years, mastery of complex grammatical constructions improves. For example, English-speaking children use the passive voice more frequently, and they more often extend it from an abbreviated structure ("It broke") into full statements ("The glass was broken by Mary") (Israel, Johnson, & Brooks, 2000; Tomasello, 2006). Older children also apply their grasp of the passive voice to a wider range of nouns and verbs. Preschoolers comprehend the passive best when the subject of the sentence is an animate being and the verb is an action word, as in "The boy is *kissed* by the girl." School-age children extend the passive to inanimate

© CORBIS

How might this older school-age child and adolescent define the word *bicycle* compared with a younger child? Rather than merely listing the object's concrete features ("it's got wheels, a chain, and handlebars"), they are likely to point out categorical relationships ("a vehicle with two wheels and no motor").

metalinguistic awareness The ability to think about language as a system.

subjects *(drum, hat)* and include experiential verbs *(like, know)* (Lempert, 1989; Pinker, Johnson, & Frost, 1987). Although the passive form is challenging, language input makes a difference. When adults speak a language that emphasizes full passives, such as Inuktitut (spoken by the Inuit people of Arctic Canada), children produce them earlier (Allen & Crago, 1996).

Another grammatical achievement of middle childhood is advanced understanding of infinitive phrases—the difference between "John is eager to please" and "John is easy to please" (Chomsky, 1969). Like gains in vocabulary, appreciation of these subtle grammatical distinctions is supported by improved ability to analyze and reflect on language.

Pragmatics

The school years also bring dramatic gains in *pragmatics,* the communicative side of language. Opportunities to communicate in many situations with a variety of people help children refine these skills.

COMMUNICATING CLEARLY ■ In middle childhood, children can adapt to the needs of listeners in challenging communicative situations, such as describing one object among a group of very similar objects. Whereas preschoolers tend to give ambiguous descriptions ("the red one"), school-age children are precise: "the round red one with stripes on it" (Deutsch & Pechmann, 1982). Because peers challenge unclear messages that adults accept, peer interaction probably contributes greatly to this aspect of conversational competence.

Gains in the ability to evaluate the clarity of others' messages occur as well, and children become better at resolving inconsistencies. Consider the instruction, "Put the frog on the book in the box." Preschoolers cannot make sense of the ambiguity, even though they use similar embedded phrases in their own speech. They respond by attending only to the first prepositional phrase ("on the book") and place a toy frog on a book. School-age children, in contrast, can attend to and integrate two competing representations ("on the book" and "in the box"). They quickly figure out the speaker's meaning and pick up a toy frog resting on a book and place it in a box (Hurewitz et al., 2000). School-age children are also more sensitive to distinctions between what people say and what they mean (Lee, Torrance, & Olson, 2001). Lizzie, for example, knew that when her mother said, "The garbage is beginning to smell," she really meant, "Take that garbage out!"

NARRATIVES ■ As a result of improved memory, ability to take a listener's perspective, and conversations with adults about past experiences, children's narratives increase in organization, detail, and expressiveness. A typical 4- or 5-year-old's narrative states what happened: "We went to the lake. We fished and waited. Paul caught a huge catfish!" Six- and 7-year-olds add orienting information (time, place, participants) and connectives ("next," "then," "so," "finally") that lend coherence to the story. Gradually, narratives lengthen into a *classic form* in which events not only build to a high point but resolve: "After Paul reeled in the catfish, Dad cleaned and cooked it. Then we ate it all up!" Evaluative comments also increase, becoming common by age 8 to 9: "The catfish tasted great. Paul was so proud!" (Bliss, McCabe, & Miranda, 1998; Ely, 2005).

Because children pick up the narrative styles of significant adults in their lives, their narratives vary widely across cultures. Most North American school-age children use a *topic-focused style,* describing an experience from beginning to end. In contrast, African-American children often use a *topic-associating style,* blending several similar experiences. One 9-year-old related having a tooth pulled, then described seeing her sister's tooth pulled, next told how she had removed one of her baby teeth, and concluded, "I'm a pullin-teeth expert . . . call me, and I'll be over" (McCabe, 1997, p. 164). Consequently, African-American children's narratives are usually longer and more complex than those of white children (Champion, 2003b).

The ability to generate clear oral narratives enhances reading comprehension and prepares children for producing longer, more explicit written narratives. In families who regularly eat meals together, children are advanced in language and literacy

A boy tells a story to an elderly relative wearing the traditional Bedouin costume of the nomadic Al Murrah tribe in Saudi Arabia. Children's narratives vary widely across cultures, reflecting the styles of significant adults in their lives.

development, perhaps because mealtimes offer many opportunities to relate personal stories (Beals, 2001).

Learning Two Languages at a Time

Joey and Lizzie speak only one language—English, their native tongue. Yet throughout the world, many children grow up *bilingual,* learning two languages and sometimes more than two. Recall from Chapter 1 that both the United States and Canada have large immigrant populations. An estimated 15 percent of American children—6 million in all—speak a language other than English at home (U.S. Census Bureau, 2007b). Similarly, 12 percent of Canadian children—nearly 700,000—speak a native language that is neither English nor French, the country's two official languages. In the French-speaking province of Québec, 41 percent of the population are French–English bilinguals. In the remaining English-speaking provinces, the French–English bilingualism rate is about 10 percent (Statistics Canada, 2003b).

BILINGUAL DEVELOPMENT ■ Children can become bilingual in two ways: (1) by acquiring both languages at the same time in early childhood or (2) by learning a second language after mastering the first. Children of bilingual parents who teach them both languages in infancy and early childhood show no special problems with language development. From the start, they separate the language systems, distinguishing their sounds, mastering equivalent words in each, and attaining early language milestones according to a typical timetable (Bosch & Sebastian-Galles, 2001; Holowka, Brosseau-Lapré, & Petitto, 2002; Conboy & Thal, 2006). Preschoolers acquire normal native ability in the language of their surrounding community and good-to-native ability in the second language, depending on their exposure to it (Genesee, 2001). When school-age children acquire a second language after they already speak a first, they generally take 3 to 5 years to become as fluent in the second language as native-speaking agemates (Hakuta, 1999).

Like many bilingual adults, bilingual children sometimes engage in *code switching*—producing an utterance in one language that contains one or more "guest" words from the other. In doing so, they do not violate the grammar of either language. Children may engage in code switching because they lack the vocabulary to convey a particular thought in one language, so they use the other. But the children who code-switch the most are those whose parents often do so. Bilingual adults frequently code-switch to express cultural identity, and children may follow suit—as when a Korean child speaking English switches to Korean on mentioning her piano teacher, as a sign of respect for authority (Chung, 2006). Opportunities to listen to code switching may facilitate bilingual development (Gawlitzek-Maiwald & Tracy, 1996). For example, a child accustomed to hearing French sentences with English guest words may rely on sentence-level cues to figure out English word meanings.

Recall from Chapter 6 that, just as with first-language development, a sensitive period for second-language development exists. Although mastery must begin sometime in childhood for full development to occur, a precise age cutoff for a decline in second-language learning has not been established. Rather, a continuous age-related decrease from childhood to adulthood occurs (Hakuta, Bialystok, & Wiley, 2003). Children who become fluent in two languages develop denser gray matter (neurons and connective fibers) in areas of the left hemisphere devoted to language (Mechelli et al., 2004). They are advanced in cognitive development, outperforming others on tests of selective attention, analytical reasoning, concept formation, and cognitive flexibility (Bialystok, 2001; Bialystok & Martin, 2004). They also are advanced in certain aspects of metalinguistic awareness, such as detection of errors in grammar and meaning. And children transfer their phonological awareness skills in one language to the other, especially if the two languages share phonological features and letter–sound correspondences, as Spanish and English do (Bialystok, McBride-Chang, & Luk, 2005; Snow & Kang, 2006). These capacities, as noted earlier, enhance reading achievement.

BILINGUAL EDUCATION ■ The advantages of bilingualism provide strong justification for bilingual education programs in schools. In Canada, about 7 percent of elementary school students are enrolled in *language immersion programs,* in which English-speaking children are taught entirely in French for several years. The Canadian language immersion strategy succeeds in developing children who are proficient in both languages and who, by grade 6, achieve as well as their counterparts in the regular English program (Harley & Jean, 1999; Holobow, Genesee, & Lambert, 1991; Turnbull, Hart, & Lapkin, 2003). Canadian schools are also encouraged to provide programs that maintain the languages and cultures of immigrants and to promote First Nations languages. Although such programs are in short supply, funding for them is increasing.

In the United States, fierce disagreement exists over the question of how best to educate ethnic minority children with limited English proficiency. Some believe that time spent communicating in the child's native tongue detracts from English language achievement, which is crucial for success in the worlds of school and work. Other educators, committed to developing minority children's native language while fostering mastery of English, note that providing instruction in the native tongue lets minority children know that their heritage is respected. It also prevents *semilingualism*—inadequate proficiency in both languages. Minority children who gradually lose their first language as a result of being taught the second end up limited in both languages for a time, a circumstance that leads to serious academic difficulties (Ovando & Collier, 1998). Semilingualism is believed to contribute to the high rates of school failure and dropout among low-SES Hispanic youngsters, who make up nearly 50 percent of the U.S. language-minority population.

At present, public opinion and educational practice favor English-only instruction. Many U.S. states have passed laws declaring English to be their official language, creating conditions in which schools have no obligation to teach minority students in languages other than English. Yet in classrooms where both languages are integrated into the curriculum, minority children are more involved in learning, participate more actively in class discussions, and acquire the second language more easily. In contrast, when teachers speak only in a language that children can barely understand, minority children display frustration, boredom, and withdrawal (Crawford, 1997).

Supporters of U.S. English-only education often point to the success of Canadian language immersion programs, in which classroom lessons are conducted in the second language. But Canadian parents enroll their children in immersion classrooms voluntarily, and both French and English are majority languages that are equally valued in Canada. Furthermore, teaching in the child's native language is merely delayed, not ruled out. For American non-English-speaking minority children, whose native languages are not valued by the larger society, a different strategy seems necessary: one that promotes children's native-language skills while they learn English (Cloud, Genesee & Hamayan, 2000).

This English–Spanish bilingual classroom serves low-SES third graders who are recent immigrants to the United States. Because both their first and second languages are integrated into the curriculum, the children are more involved in learning, participate more actively in class, and acquire the second language more easily.

Ask Yourself

Review Cite examples of how language awareness fosters school-age children's language progress.

Apply Ten-year-old Shana arrived home from soccer practice and remarked, "I'm wiped out!" Megan, her 5-year-old sister, looked puzzled and asked, "What did'ya wipe out, Shana?" Explain Shana's and Megan's different understandings of this expression.

Reflect Did you acquire a second language at home or study one in school? If so, when did you begin, and how proficient are you in the second language? Considering research on bilingualism, what changes would you make in your second-language learning, and why?

Children's Learning in School

Evidence cited throughout this chapter indicates that schools are vital forces in children's cognitive development. How do schools exert such a powerful influence? Research looking at schools as complex social systems—class size, educational philosophies, teacher–student relationships, and larger cultural context—provides important insights. As you read about these topics, refer to Applying What We Know below, which summarizes characteristics of high-quality education in elementary school.

Class Size

As each school year began, Rena telephoned the principal's office to ask, "How large will Joey's and Lizzie's classes be?" Her concern is well-founded. In a large field experiment, more than 6,000 Tennessee kindergartners were randomly assigned to three class types: "small" (13 to 17 students), "regular" (22 to 25 students) with only a teacher, and regular with a teacher plus a full-time teacher's aide. These arrangements continued into third grade. Small-class students— especially minority children—scored higher in reading and math achievement each year (Mosteller, 1995). Placing teacher's aides in regular-size classes had no impact. Rather, experiencing small classes from kindergarten through third grade predicted substantially higher achievement from fourth through ninth grades, after children had returned to regular-size classes. It also predicted greater likelihood of graduating from high school, particularly for low-income students (Finn, Gerber, & Boyd-Zaharias, 2005; Nye, Hedges, & Konstantopoulos, 2001).

Why is small class size beneficial? With fewer children, teachers spend less time disciplining and more time teaching and giving individual attention. Also, children who learn in smaller groups show better concentration, higher-quality class participation, and more favorable attitudes toward school (Blatchford et al., 2003; Finn, Pannozzo, & Achilles, 2003).

Applying What We Know

Signs of High-Quality Education in Elementary School

CLASSROOM CHARACTERISTICS	SIGNS OF QUALITY
Class size	Optimum class size is no larger than 18 children.
Physical setting	Space is divided into richly equipped activity centers—for reading, writing, playing math or language games, exploring science, working on construction projects, using computers, and engaging in other academic pursuits. Spaces are used flexibly for individual and small-group activities and whole-class gatherings.
Curriculum	The curriculum helps children both achieve academic standards and make sense of their learning in all subjects, including literacy, mathematics, social studies, art, music, health, and physical education. Subjects are integrated so that children apply knowledge in one area to others. The curriculum is implemented through activities responsive to children's interests, ideas, and everyday lives, including their cultural backgrounds.
Daily activities	Teachers provide challenging activities that include opportunities for small-group and independent work. Groupings vary in size and makeup of children, depending on the activity and on children's learning needs. Teachers encourage cooperative learning and guide children in attaining it.
Interactions between teachers and children	Teachers foster each child's progress, including children with academic difficulties and children capable of advanced performance. Teachers use intellectually engaging strategies, including posing problems, asking thought-provoking questions, discussing ideas, and adding complexity to tasks. They also demonstrate, explain, coach, and assist in other ways, depending on each child's learning needs.
Evaluations of progress	Teachers regularly evaluate children's progress through written observations and work samples, which they use to enhance and individualize teaching. They help children reflect on their work and decide how to improve it. They also seek information and perspectives from parents on how well children are learning and include parents' views in evaluations.
Relationship with parents	Teachers forge partnerships with parents. They hold periodic conferences and encourage parents to visit the classroom anytime, to observe and volunteer.

Source: Bredekamp & Copple, 1997.

Educational Philosophies

Each teacher brings to the classroom an educational philosophy that plays a major role in children's learning. Two philosophical approaches have received the most research attention. They differ in what children are taught, in the way they are believed to learn, and in how their progress is evaluated.

TRADITIONAL VERSUS CONSTRUCTIVIST CLASSROOMS ■ In a **traditional classroom,** the teacher is the sole authority for knowledge, rules, and decision making and does most of the talking. Students are relatively passive—listening, responding when called on, and completing teacher-assigned tasks. Their progress is evaluated by how well they keep pace with a uniform set of standards for their grade.

A **constructivist classroom,** in contrast, encourages students to *construct* their own knowledge. Although constructivist approaches vary, many are grounded in Piaget's theory, which views children as active agents who reflect on and coordinate their own thoughts, rather than absorbing those of others. A glance inside a constructivist classroom reveals richly equipped learning centers, small groups and individuals solving problems they choose themselves, and a teacher who guides and supports in response to children's needs. Students are evaluated by considering their progress in relation to their own prior development.

In North America, the pendulum has swung back and forth between these two views. In the 1960s and early 1970s, constructivist classrooms gained in popularity. Then, as concern arose over the academic progress of children and youths, a "back-to-basics" movement arose. Classrooms returned to traditional instruction—a style still prevalent today.

Although older elementary school children in traditional classrooms have a slight edge in achievement test scores, constructivist settings are associated with many other benefits—gains in critical thinking, greater social and moral maturity, and more positive attitudes toward school (DeVries, 2001; Rathunde & Csikszentmihalyi, 2005; Walberg, 1986). And as noted in Chapter 9, when teacher-directed instruction is emphasized in preschool and kindergarten, it actually undermines academic motivation and achievement, especially among low-SES children. The heavy emphasis on knowledge absorption in many kindergarten and primary classrooms has contributed to a growing trend among parents to delay their child's school entry. Traditional teaching practices may also increase the incidence of grade retention. For research on these practices, refer to the Social Issues: Education box on page 468.

NEW PHILOSOPHICAL DIRECTIONS ■ New approaches to education, grounded in Vygotsky's sociocultural theory, capitalize on the rich social context of the classroom to spur children's learning. In these **social-constructivist classrooms,** children participate in a wide range of challenging activities with teachers and peers, with whom they jointly construct understandings. As children *appropriate* (take for themselves) the knowledge and strategies generated through working together, they become competent, contributing members of their classroom community and advance in cognitive and social development (Bodrova & Leong, 2006; Palincsar, 2003). Vygotsky's emphasis on the social origins of complex mental activities has inspired the following educational themes:

■ *Teachers and children as partners in learning.* A classroom rich in both teacher–child and child–child collaboration transfers culturally valued ways of thinking to children.

■ *Experience with many types of symbolic communication in meaningful activities.* As children master reading, writing, and mathematics, they become aware of their culture's communication systems, reflect on their own thinking, and bring it under voluntary control. **TAKE A MOMENT...** Can you identify research presented earlier in this chapter that supports this theme?

■ *Teaching adapted to each child's zone of proximal development.* Assistance that both responds to current understandings and encourages children to take the next step helps ensure that each child makes the best progress possible.

Let's look at two examples of a growing number of programs that have translated these ideas into action.

traditional classroom An elementary school classroom in which the teacher is the sole authority for knowledge, rules, and decision making and students are relatively passive learners who are evaluated in relation to a uniform set of standards.

constructivist classroom A classroom in which students are active learners who are encouraged to construct their own knowledge, the teacher guides and supports in response to children's needs, and students are evaluated by considering their progress in relation to their own prior development.

social-constructivist classroom A classroom in which children participate in a wide range of challenging activities with teachers and peers, with whom they jointly construct understandings.

Social Issues: Education

School Readiness and Grade Retention

While waiting to pick up their sons from pre-school, Susan and Vicky struck up a conversation about kindergarten enrollment. "Freddy will be 5 in August," Susan announced. "He's a month older than the cutoff date."

"But he'll be one of the youngest in the class," Vicky countered. "Better check into what kids have to do in kindergarten these days. Have you asked his teacher what she thinks?"

"Well," Vicky admitted. "She did say Freddy was a bit young."

Since the 1980s, more parents have been delaying their children's kindergarten entry, a trend that has accelerated recently as academic expectations of kindergartners have increased. Aware that boys lag behind girls in development, parents most often hold out sons whose birth dates are close to the cutoff for enrolling in kindergarten. Is delaying kindergarten entry beneficial? Although some teachers and principals recommend it, research has not revealed any advantages. Younger children make just as much academic progress as older children in the same grade (Cameron & Wilson, 1990; Graue & DiPerna, 2000). And younger first graders reap academic gains from on-time enrollment, outperforming same-age children a year behind them in school (Stipek & Byler, 2001). Furthermore, delaying kindergarten entry does not seem to prevent or solve emotional and social difficulties. To the contrary, students who are older than the typical age for their grade show high rates of behavior problems—considerably higher than students who are young for their grade (Stipek, 2002).

A related dilemma concerns whether to retain a student for a second year in kindergarten or in one of the primary grades. A wealth of research reveals no learning benefits and suggests negative consequences for motivation, self-esteem, peer relations, school attitudes, and achievement (Hong & Raudenbush, 2005; Jimerson et al., 2006; Silberglitt et al., 2006). In a Canadian study, students retained between kindergarten and second grade—regardless of the academic and social characteristics they brought to the situation—showed worsening academic performance, anxiety, and (among boys) disruptiveness throughout elementary school. These unfavorable trends did not characterize nonretained students (Pagani et al., 2001).

As an alternative to kindergarten retention, some school districts place poorly performing kindergarten children in a "transition" class—a waystation between kindergarten and first grade. Transition classes, however, are a form of homogeneous grouping. As with other "low groups," teachers may have reduced expectations and may teach transition children in a less stimulating fashion than other children (Dornbusch, Glasgow, & Lin, 1996).

Each of the options just considered is based on the view that readiness for school results largely from biological maturation. An alternative perspective, based on Vygotsky's sociocultural theory, is that children acquire the knowledge, skills, and attitudes for school success through assistance from parents and teachers. The U.S. National Association for the Education of Young Children recommends that all children of legal age start kindergarten and be granted classroom experiences that foster their individual progress. Research shows that school readiness is not something to wait for; it can be cultivated.

Saying good-bye on the first day of school, this father may wonder how ready his son is for classroom learning. Yet delaying kindergarten entry for a year has no demonstrated benefits for academic or social development.

Reciprocal Teaching. Originally designed to improve reading comprehension in poorly achieving students, this Vygotsky-inspired teaching method has been extended to other subjects and all schoolchildren (Palincsar & Herrenkohl, 1999). In **reciprocal teaching,** a teacher and two to four students form a cooperative group and take turns leading dialogues on the content of a text passage. Within the dialogues, group members apply four cognitive strategies: questioning, summarizing, clarifying, and predicting.

The dialogue leader (at first a teacher, later a student) begins by *asking questions* about the content of the text passage. Students offer answers, raise additional questions, and, in case of disagreement, reread the original text. Next, the leader *summarizes* the passage, and children discuss the summary and *clarify* unfamiliar ideas. Finally, the leader encourages students to *predict* upcoming content based on clues in the passage.

reciprocal teaching A teaching method in which a teacher and two to four students form a cooperative group, within which dialogues occur that create a zone of proximal development.

Elementary and middle school students exposed to reciprocal teaching show impressive gains in reading comprehension compared to controls taught in other ways (Lederer, 2000; Rosenshine & Meister, 1994; Takala, 2006). Notice how reciprocal teaching creates a zone of proximal development in which children gradually learn to scaffold one another's progress and assume more responsibility for comprehending text passages (Gillies, 2003). Also, by collaborating with others, children forge group expectations for high-level thinking, more often apply their metacognitive knowledge, and acquire skills vital for learning and success in everyday life.

Communities of Learners. Recognizing that collaboration requires a supportive context, another Vygotsky-based innovation makes it a school-wide value. Classrooms are transformed into **communities of learners** where teachers guide the overall process of learning, but otherwise, no distinction is made between adult and child contributors: all participate in joint endeavors and have the authority to define and resolve problems. This approach is based on the assumption that different people have different expertises that can benefit the community and that students may become experts to whom others may turn (Engle & Conant, 2002). Classroom activities often consist of long-term projects that address complex, real-world issues. In working toward project goals, children and teachers draw on the expertises of one another and of others within and outside the school.

In reciprocal teaching, a Vygotsky-inspired educational innovation, a teacher and two to four students form a cooperative learning group to discuss a text passage. Elementary and middle school students who participate show impressive gains in reading comprehension.

In one classroom, students studied animal–habitat relationships in order to design an animal of the future, suited to environmental changes. The class formed small research groups, each of which selected a subtopic—for example, defense against predators, protection from the elements, reproduction, or food getting. Each group member assumed responsibility for part of the subtopic, consulting diverse experts and preparing teaching materials. Then group members taught one another, assembled their contributions, and brought them to the community as a whole so the knowledge gathered could be used to solve the problem (Brown, 1997; Stone, 2005). The result was a multifaceted understanding of the topic that would have been too difficult and time-consuming for any learner to accomplish alone.

In communities of learners, collaboration is created from within by teachers and children and supported from without by the culture of the school (Sullivan & Glanz, 2006). As a result, the approach broadens Vygotsky's concept of the zone of proximal development, from a child in collaboration with a more expert partner (adult or peer) to multiple, interrelated zones.

Teacher–Student Interaction

Elementary and secondary school students describe good teachers as caring, helpful, and stimulating—behaviors associated with gains in motivation, achievement, and positive peer relations (Daniels, Kalkman, & McCombs, 2001; Hughes & Kwok, 2006; Hughes, Zhang, & Hill, 2006). But too many North American teachers emphasize repetitive drill over higher-level thinking, such as grappling with ideas and applying knowledge to new situations (Sacks, 2005). In a longitudinal investigation of more than 5,000 seventh graders, those in more stimulating, academically demanding classrooms showed better attendance and larger gains in math achievement over the following two years (Phillips, 1997).

Of course, teachers do not interact in the same way with all children. Well-behaved, high-achieving students typically get more support and praise, whereas unruly students have more conflicts with teachers and receive more criticism from them (Henricsson & Rydell, 2004). Caring teacher–student relationships have an especially strong impact on the achievement and social behavior of low-SES minority students and other children at risk for learning difficulties

communities of learners Classrooms in which both teachers and students have the authority to define and resolve problems, drawing on the expertise of one another and of others as they work toward project goals, which often address complex, real-world issues.

(Baker, 2006; Crosno, Kirkpatrick, & Elder, 2004). But overall, higher-SES students—who tend to be higher-achieving and to have fewer learning and behavior problems—have more sensitive and supportive relationships with teachers (Pianta, Hamre, & Stuhlman, 2003).

Unfortunately, once teachers' attitudes toward students are established, they can become more extreme than is warranted by children's behavior. Of special concern are **educational self-fulfilling prophecies:** Children may adopt teachers' positive or negative views and start to live up to them. As early as first grade, teachers' beliefs in children's ability to learn predict students' year-end achievement progress. This effect is particularly strong when teachers emphasize competition and publicly compare children, regularly favoring the best students (Kuklinski & Weinstein, 2001; Weinstein, 2002).

Teacher expectations have a greater impact on low-achieving than high-achieving students (Madom, Jussim, & Eccles, 1997). High achievers have less room to improve when teachers think well of them, and when a teacher is critical, they can fall back on their history of success. Low-achieving students' sensitivity to self-fulfilling prophecies can be beneficial when teachers believe in them. But biased teacher judgments are usually slanted in a negative direction. In one study, African-American children were especially responsive to negative teacher expectations in reading, and girls were especially responsive to negative teacher expectations in math (McKown & Weinstein, 2002). Recall our discussion of *stereotype threat*. A child in the position of confirming a negative stereotype may respond with intense anxiety and reduced motivation, increasing the likelihood of a negative self-fulfilling prophecy.

Grouping Practices

In many schools, students are assigned to *homogeneous* groups or classes, in which children of similar ability levels are taught together. Homogeneous grouping can be a potent source of self-fulfilling prophecies. Low-group students get more drill on basic facts and skills, engage in less discussion, and progress at a slower learning pace. Gradually, they may be viewed by themselves and others as "not smart" and decline in self-esteem and motivation (Chorzempa & Graham, 2006; Trautwein et al., 2006). Not surprisingly, homogeneous grouping widens the gap between high and low achievers (Dornbusch, Glasgow, & Lin, 1996; Ross & Harrison, 2006).

Partly because of this finding, some schools have increased the *heterogeneity* of student groups by combining two or three adjacent grades. In *multigrade classrooms,* academic achievement, self-esteem, and attitudes toward school are usually more favorable than in the single-grade arrangement, perhaps because multigrade classrooms often decrease competition and increase harmony (Lloyd, 1999; Ong, Allison, & Haladyna, 2000). The opportunity that mixed-age grouping affords for peer tutoring may also contribute to its favorable outcomes. When older or more expert students teach younger or less expert students, both tutors and tutees benefit in achievement and self-esteem, with stronger effects for low-income, minority students and students in grades 1 to 3 than grades 4 to 6 (Ginsburg-Block, Rohrbeck, & Fantuzzo, 2006; Renninger, 1998).

However, small, heterogeneous groups of students working together often engage in poorer-quality interaction (less accurate explanations and answers) than homogeneous groups of above-average students (Webb, Nemer, & Chizhik, 1998). For collaboration between heterogeneous peers to succeed, children need extensive training and guidance in **cooperative learning**— resolving differences of opinion, sharing responsibility, considering one another's ideas, and working toward common goals. When teachers explain, model, and have children role-play how to work together effectively, cooperative learning among heterogeneous peers results in greater enjoyment of learning and achievement gains across a wide range of school subjects (Gillies, 2003; Terwel et al., 2001). And children readily cooperate in future group activities, building on others' ideas and offering assistance (Gillies, 2002).

These second and third graders learn together during a visit to their school library. Compared to children in single-grade classrooms, children in multigrade classrooms are usually advantaged in academic achievement, self-esteem, and attitudes toward school.

© GUY CALI/THE STOCK CONNECTION

Computers and Academic Learning

In Joey and Lizzie's classrooms, several computers sat on desks in quiet corners. Virtually all U.S. and Canadian public schools have integrated computers into their instructional programs and can access the Internet—trends also apparent in other industrialized nations. And about 85 percent of North American school-age children and adolescents live in homes with one or more computers, two-thirds of which have an Internet connection, usually a high-speed link (Statistics Canada, 2004a; U.S. Census Bureau, 2007b). Although higher-SES homes are more likely to have computers, over 70 percent of lower-SES families now have them.

These fifth graders download video from a camera to a computer as part of a class project. Schools must take special steps to ensure that girls have rich opportunities to master the varied aspects of computer technology.

Using computers can have rich educational benefits. Educational software permits children to practice basic skills and, in some instances, to solve problems and acquire new knowledge. When children in the early grades use basic-skills programs for several months, they gain in reading and math achievement—benefits that are greatest for students with learning difficulties (Fletcher-Flinn & Gravatt, 1995; Hughes & Filbert, 2000).

Children who use the computer for word processing can write freely, experimenting with letters and words without having to struggle with handwriting. In addition, they can revise the text's meaning and style as well as check their spelling. As a result, they worry less about making mistakes, and their written products tend to be longer and of higher quality (Clements & Sarama, 2003). And as in early childhood, computer programming projects promote problem solving and metacognition and are common classroom contexts for peer collaboration (see page 355 in Chapter 9).

As children get older, they increasingly use the computer for schoolwork, mostly to search the Web for information and to prepare written assignments. But a survey of a nationally representative sample of more than 2,000 U.S. 8- to 18-year-olds revealed that children and adolescents, on average, used the computer only a half-hour a day for schoolwork and an hour for pleasure—surfing the Web, communicating by e-mail or instant messaging, and accessing music, video, and computer games. More than half report being "media multitaskers" who engage in two or more media activities some or most of the time—having several computer activities going, using the computer while watching TV or listening to music, or doing all three at once (Roberts, Foehr, & Rideout, 2005; Media Awareness Network, 2001). Media multitasking greatly increases media exposure, but its impact on learning and behavior is not yet known.

By the end of elementary school, boys spend more time with computers than girls, both at home and in school, and use computers somewhat differently. Boys, for example, more often connect to the Internet to download games and music, trade and sell things, and create Web pages. Girls emphasize information gathering, e-mail, and instant messaging (La Ferle, Edwards, & Lee, 2000; Lenhart, Rainie, & Lewis, 2001). In a Canadian survey of a nationally representative sample of 1,200 15- and 16-year-olds, boys engaged in more computer activities overall, including writing programs, analyzing data, and using spreadsheets and graphics programs. And many more boys than girls rated their computer skills as "excellent" (Looker & Thiessen, 2003). Similarly, time spent with computers and confidence in using them rise with SES (Subrahmanyam et al., 2001). These findings indicate a need to ensure that girls and low-SES students have added opportunities to benefit from the cognitively enriching aspects of computer technology.

Most parents say they purchased a computer to enrich their child's education; about one-third of North American school-age children and adolescents have a computer in their bedroom. At the same time, parents express great concern about the influence of violent computer games (see page 389 in Chapter 10) and the Internet. Yet only a minority of children and youths—about 30 percent in the United States and 40 percent in Canada—say their parents have rules about computer use and know what sites they visit on the Web (Media Awareness Network, 2001; Roberts, Foehr, & Rideout, 2005).

educational self-fulfilling prophecies Teachers' positive or negative views of individual children, who tend to adopt and start to live up to these views.

cooperative learning Collaboration on a task by a small group of students who resolve differences of opinion, share responsibility, consider one another's ideas, and work toward common goals.

© PAUL CONKLIN/PHOTOEDIT

The girl in the blue shirt, who has mild mental retardation, is fully included in this regular classroom. She is likely to do well if she receives support from a special education teacher and if her classroom teacher minimizes comparisons with classmates and encourages cooperative learning—as in this card game.

Teaching Children with Special Needs

We have seen that effective teachers flexibly adjust their teaching strategies to accommodate students with a wide range of abilities and characteristics. But such adjustments are increasingly difficult at the very low and high ends of the ability distribution. How do schools serve children with special learning needs?

CHILDREN WITH LEARNING DIFFICULTIES ■ U.S. and Canadian legislation mandates that schools place children who require special supports for learning in the "least restrictive" (as close to normal as possible) environments that meet their educational needs. In **inclusive classrooms,** students with learning difficulties learn alongside typical students in the regular educational setting for part or all of the school day—a practice designed to prepare them for participation in society and to combat prejudices against individuals with disabilities that lead to social exclusion (Kugelmass & Ainscow, 2004). Largely as the result of parental pressures, an increasing number of students experience *full inclusion*—full-time placement in regular classrooms.

Some students in inclusive classrooms have *mild mental retardation:* Their IQs fall between 55 and 70, and they also show problems in adaptive behavior, or skills of everyday living (American Psychiatric Association, 1994). But the largest number—5 to 10 percent of school-age children—have **learning disabilities,** great difficulty with one or more aspects of learning, usually reading. As a result, their achievement is considerably behind what would be expected on the basis of their IQ. But sometimes, the deficit expresses itself in other ways—as in severe inattention, which depresses both IQ and achievement test scores. The problems of students with learning disabilities cannot be traced to any obvious physical or emotional difficulty or to environmental disadvantage. Instead, subtle deficits in brain functioning are involved (Berninger, 2006). Some disorders run in families, and in certain cases, specific genes have been identified that contribute to the problem (Miller, Sanchez, & Hynd, 2003; Raskind et al., 2005). In many instances, the cause is unknown.

Does placement of these children in regular classes provide appropriate academic experiences as well as integrated participation in classroom life? Although some included students benefit academically, many do not. Achievement gains depend on both the severity of the disability and the support services available (Klingner et al., 1998). Furthermore, children with disabilities often are rejected by regular-classroom peers. Students with mental retardation are overwhelmed by the social skills of their classmates; they cannot interact adeptly in a conversation or game. And the processing deficits of some learning-disabled students lead to problems in social awareness and responsiveness (Kelly & Norwich, 2004; Sridhar & Vaughn, 2001).

Does this mean that students with special needs cannot be served in regular classrooms? Not necessarily. Often these children do best when they receive instruction in a resource room for part of the day and in the regular classroom for the remainder—an arrangement that the majority of school-age children with learning disabilities say they prefer (Vaughn & Klingner, 1998; Weiner & Tardif, 2004). In the resource room, a special education teacher works with students on an individual and small-group basis. Then, depending on their progress, children join regular classmates for different subjects and amounts of time.

Special steps must be taken to promote positive peer relations in inclusive classrooms. Cooperative learning and peer-tutoring experiences in which teachers guide children with learning difficulties and their classmates in working together lead to friendly interaction, improved peer acceptance, and achievement gains (Fuchs et al., 2002a, 2002b). Teachers also can prepare their class for the arrival of a student with special needs. Under these conditions, inclusion may foster emotional sensitivity and prosocial behavior among regular classmates.

GIFTED CHILDREN ■ In Joey and Lizzie's school, some children were **gifted,** displaying exceptional intellectual strengths. In every grade were one or two students with IQ scores above 130,

inclusive classrooms Classrooms in which students with learning difficulties learn alongside typical students in a regular educational setting.

learning disabilities Specific learning disorders that lead children to achieve poorly in school.

gifted Displaying exceptional intellectual strengths, including high IQ, creativity, and talent.

FIGURE 12.7

Responses of an 8-year-old who scored high on a figural measure of divergent thinking. This child was asked to make as many pictures as she could from the circles on the page. The titles she gave her drawings, from left to right, are as follows: "Dracula," "one-eyed monster," "pumpkin," "Hula-Hoop," "poster," "wheelchair," "earth," "stop-light," "planet," "movie camera," "sad face," "picture," "beach ball," "the letter O," "car," "glasses." Tests of divergent thinking tap only one of the complex cognitive contributions to creativity. (Reprinted by permission of Laura Berk.)

the standard definition of giftedness based on intelligence test performance (Gardner, 1998). High-IQ children, as we have seen, are particularly quick at academic work. They have keen memories and an exceptional capacity to solve challenging academic problems.

Yet earlier in this chapter, we noted that intelligence tests do not sample the entire range of human mental skills. Recognition of this fact has led to an expanded conception of giftedness in schools.

Creativity and Talent. **Creativity** is the ability to produce work that is *original* yet *appropriate*—something that others have not thought of but that is useful in some way. A child with high potential for creativity can be designated as gifted. Because most children are not mature enough to produce useful creative works, researchers have devised tests to assess their capacity for creative thought. These tests tap **divergent thinking**—the generation of multiple and unusual possibilities when faced with a task or problem. Divergent thinking contrasts sharply with **convergent thinking,** which involves arriving at a single correct answer and is emphasized on intelligence tests (Guilford, 1985).

Because highly creative children (like high-IQ children) are often better at some types of tasks than others, a variety of tests of divergent thinking are available (Runco, 1992; Torrance, 1988). A verbal measure might ask children to name uses for common objects (such as a newspaper). A figural measure might ask them to come up with drawings based on a circular motif (see Figure 12.7). A "real-world problem" measure requires students to suggest solutions to everyday problems. Responses to all these tests can be scored for the number of ideas generated and their originality.

Yet critics point out that these measures are poor predictors of creative accomplishment because they tap only one of the complex cognitive aspects of creativity. Also involved are defining new and important problems, evaluating divergent ideas and choosing the most promising, and calling on relevant knowledge to understand and solve problems (Sternberg, 2003b; Sternberg & Lubart, 1996).

Consider these additional ingredients, and you will see why people usually demonstrate expertise and creativity in only one or a few related areas. Even individuals designated as gifted by virtue of their high IQ often show uneven ability across academic subjects. Partly for this reason, definitions of giftedness have been extended to include **talent**—outstanding performance in a specific field. Case studies reveal that excellence in such endeavors as creative writing, mathematics, science, music, visual arts, athletics, and leadership have roots in specialized skills that first appear in childhood (Moran & Gardner, 2006; Winner, 2003). Highly talented children are biologically prepared to master their domain of interest—and display a passion for doing so.

But talent must be nurtured. Studies of the backgrounds of talented children and highly accomplished adults often reveal parents who are warm and sensitive, provide a stimulating

creativity The ability to produce work that is original yet appropriate—something that others have not thought of but that is useful in some way.

divergent thinking Thinking that involves generating multiple and unusual possibilities when faced with a task or problem; associated with creativity.

convergent thinking Thinking that involves arriving at a single correct answer to a problem; emphasized on intelligence tests.

talent Outstanding performance in a specific field.

home life, are devoted to developing their child's abilities, and provide models of hard work and high achievement. Rather than being driving and overambitious, these parents are reasonably demanding (Winner, 1996, 2000). They arrange for caring teachers while the child is young and for more rigorous master teachers as the child's talent develops.

Extreme giftedness often results in social isolation. Many gifted children and adolescents spend much time alone, partly because their highly driven, nonconforming, and independent styles leave them out of step with peers and partly because they enjoy solitude, which is necessary to develop their talents. Still, gifted children desire gratifying peer relationships, and some—more often girls than boys—try to hide their abilities to become better-liked. Compared with their ordinary agemates, gifted youths, especially girls, report more emotional and social difficulties, including low self-esteem and depression (Reis, 2004; Winner, 2000).

Finally, whereas many talented youths become experts in their fields and solve problems in new ways, few become highly creative. Rapidly mastering an existing field and thinking flexibly within it require different skills than innovating in that field. Gifted individuals who are restless with the status quo and daring about changing it are rare. And before these individuals become creative masters, they typically spend a decade or more becoming proficient in their field of interest (Csikszentmihalyi, 1999; Moran & Gardner, 2006). The world, however, needs both experts and creators.

Eight-year-old piano prodigy Harris Wang performs in Edmonton, Alberta, in 2004. Parents of highly talented children can best promote their talents by offering warmth, sensitivity, and stimulation and arranging for master teachers as the child's talent develops. But parents should avoid being driving or overambitious.

Educating the Gifted. Gifted children thrive in learning environments that permit them to choose topics for extended projects, take intellectual risks, reflect on ideas, and interact with like-minded peers. When not sufficiently challenged, they sometimes lose their drive to excel. And when parents and teachers push them too hard, by adolescence they are likely to ask, "Who am I doing this for?" If the answer is not "myself," they may decide not to pursue their gift (Winner, 1997, 2000, p. 166).

Although many schools offer programs for the gifted, debate about their effectiveness usually focuses on factors irrelevant to giftedness—whether to provide enrichment in regular classrooms, to pull children out for special instruction (the most common practice), or to advance brighter students to a higher grade. Overall, gifted children fare well academically and socially within each of these models (Moon & Feldhusen, 1994). At the same time, interventions aimed at protecting students' self-esteem are crucial in selective educational settings. In a study of more than 100,000 students in 26 countries, the more selective the high school, the lower students' academic self-esteem (Marsh & Hau, 2003). A top student in elementary school who enters a selective secondary school may suddenly find herself average or below average, with potentially detrimental effects on motivation and achievement.

Gardner's theory of multiple intelligences has inspired several model programs that provide enrichment to all students in diverse subjects, so any child capable of high-level performance can manifest it. Meaningful activities, each tapping a specific intelligence or set of intelligences, serve as contexts for assessing strengths and weaknesses and, on that basis, teaching new knowledge and original thinking (Gardner, 1993, 2000). For example, linguistic intelligence might be fostered through storytelling or playwriting; spatial intelligence through drawing, sculpting, or taking apart and reassembling objects; and kinesthetic intelligence through dance or pantomime.

Evidence is still needed on how well these programs nurture children's talents. But so far, they have succeeded in one way—by highlighting the strengths of some students who previously had been considered unexceptional or even at risk for school failure (Kornhaber, 2004). Consequently, they may be especially useful in identifying talented low-SES, ethnic minority children, who are often underrepresented in programs for the gifted.

How Well-Educated Are North American Children?

Our discussion of schooling has largely focused on how teachers can support the education of children. Yet many factors—both within and outside schools—affect children's learning. Societal

FIGURE 12.8

Average mathematics scores of 15-year-olds by country.
The Programme for International Student Assessment assessed achievement in many nations around the world. Japan, Korea, and Canada were among the top performers in mathematics, whereas the United States performed below the international average. Similar outcomes occurred in reading and science. (Adapted from Programme for International Student Assessment, 2005.)

	Country	Average Math Achievement Score
High-Performing Nations	Hong Kong	550
	Finland	544
	Korea, Republic of	542
	Netherlands	538
	Japan	534
	Canada	**532**
	Belgium	529
	United Kingdom	529
	Switzerland	527
	Australia	524
	New Zealand	523
Intermediate-Performing Nations	Czech Republic	516
	Iceland	515
	Denmark	514
	France	511
	Sweden	509
	Austria	505
	Germany	503
International Average = 500	Ireland	503
	Norway	495
	Luxembourg	493
	Hungary	490
	Poland	490
	Spain	485
	United States	**483**
Low-Performing Nations	Italy	466
	Portugal	466
	Greece	445
	Mexico	385

values, school resources, quality of teaching, and parental encouragement all play important roles. Nowhere are these multiple influences more apparent than when schooling is examined in cross-cultural perspective.

In international studies of reading, mathematics, and science achievement, young people in Hong Kong, Korea, and Japan are consistently top performers. Among Western nations, Canada is also in the top tier, but U.S. students typically perform at the international average, and sometimes below it (see Figure 12.8) (Programme for International Student Assessment, 2003, 2005).

Why do U.S. children fall behind in academic accomplishments? According to international comparisons, instruction in the United States is less challenging and focused than in other countries. In the Programme for International Student Assessment, which assessed the academic achievement of 15-year-olds in many countries, students were asked about their study habits. Compared with students in the top-achieving nations listed in Figure 12.8, many more U.S. students reported studying by memorizing rather than relating information to previously acquired knowledge. And achievement varies much more among U.S. schools, suggesting that the United States is less equitable in the quality of education it provides (Programme for International Student Assessment, 2005).

Researchers have conducted in-depth research on learning environments in Asian nations, such as Japan, Korea, and Taiwan, to clarify factors that support high achievement. Except for the influence of language on early counting skills (see page 452), Asian students do not start school with cognitive advantages over their North American peers. Rather, a variety of social forces combine to foster a much stronger commitment to learning in Asian families and schools:

- *Cultural valuing of academic achievement.* Compared to Western countries, Japan, Korea, and Taiwan invest more in education, including higher salaries for teachers. In these countries, where natural resources are limited, progress in science and technology is essential for economic well-being (United Nations Development Programme, 2002).

- *Emphasis on effort.* North American parents and teachers tend to regard native ability as the key to academic success. In contrast, Japanese, Korean, and Taiwanese parents and teachers believe that all children can succeed academically with enough effort. Asian parents devote many more hours to helping their children with homework (Stevenson, Lee, & Mu, 2000). Furthermore, Asian youths, influenced by collectivist values, typically view striving to achieve as a moral obligation—part of their responsibility to family and community. North American young people view working hard in individualistic terms—as a personal choice (Bempechat & Drago-Severson, 1999).

- *High-quality education for all.* Ability grouping does not exist in Japanese, Korean, and Taiwanese elementary schools. All students receive the same nationally mandated, high-quality instruction. Academic lessons are particularly well-organized and presented in ways that capture children's attention and encourage high-level thinking (Grow-Maienza, Hahn, & Joo, 2001). Topics in mathematics are treated in greater depth, with

Compared with their American counterparts, Japanese children have a longer school day, which permits frequent alternation of academic instruction with pleasurable activity—an approach that fosters learning. During a break from academic subjects, these Japanese students enjoy a calligraphy class.

less repetition of previously taught material. And Japanese elementary school teachers are three times as likely as U.S. teachers to work outside class with students who need extra help (Woodward & Ono, 2004).

■ *More time devoted to instruction.* In Japan, Hong Kong, and Taiwan, the school year is more than 50 days longer than in the United States and about 30 days longer than in Canada (World Education Services, 2007). And on a day-to-day basis, Asian teachers devote more time to academic pursuits (Stevenson, Lee, & Mu, 2000). But Asian schools are not regimented places. An 8-hour school day allows time for extra recesses as well as field trips and extracurricular activities (Stevenson, 1994). Frequent breaks may increase Asian children's capacity to learn (see page 433 in Chapter 11).

The Asian examples underscore the need for families, schools, and the larger society to work together to upgrade education. Currently, the United States is investing more tax dollars in elementary and secondary education and strengthening teacher preparation. In addition, many schools are taking steps to increase parent involvement. Children whose parents create stimulating learning environments at home, monitor their child's academic progress, help with homework, and communicate often with teachers consistently show superior achievement (Christenson & Sheridan, 2001). The results of these efforts can be seen in recent national assessments of educational progress (U.S. Department of Education, 2003, 2005b). After two decades of decline, American students' overall academic achievement has risen, although not enough to enhance their standing internationally.

Ask Yourself

Review   List some teaching practices that foster children's academic achievement and some that undermine it. Provide a brief explanation for each practice.

Apply   Sandy, a parent of a third grader, wonders whether she should support her school board's decision to teach first, second, and third graders together, in mixed-age classrooms. How would you advise Sandy, and why?

Connect   Review research on child-rearing styles on pages 398–400 in Chapter 10. What style do gifted children who realize their potential typically experience? Explain.

Reflect   What grouping practices were used in your elementary education—homogeneous, heterogeneous, or a combination? What impact do you think those practices had on your motivation and achievement?

Summary

Piaget's Theory: The Concrete Operational Stage

What are the major characteristics of concrete operational thought?

■ During the **concrete operational stage,** children can reason logically about concrete, tangible information. Mastery of conservation indicates that children are capable of mental actions that obey logical rules, including **decentration** and **reversibility.** They are more aware of classification hierarchies and capable of **seriation,** including **transitive inference,** or seriating mentally.

■ Spatial reasoning also improves, as revealed by school-age children's ability to give directions and their understanding of **cognitive maps.** Children's approach to map-making is influenced by cultural frameworks as well as cognitive maturity.

© DAVID YOUNG-WOLFF/PHOTOEDIT

Discuss recent research on concrete operational thought.

■ Specific cultural practices, especially those associated with schooling, promote mastery of Piagetian tasks. In cultures where children seldom attend school, certain informal, nonschool experiences foster operational thought in everyday situations.

■ Information-processing research helps explain the gradual mastery of logical thinking in middle childhood. Case's neo-Piagetian theory proposes that with practice, cognitive schemes demand less attention and become more automatic, freeing up space in working memory for combining old schemes and generating new ones. Eventually, children consolidate schemes into central conceptual structures, highly efficient networks of concepts and relationships that permit them to think more effectively in a wide range of situations.

■ On diverse tasks, children move from a focus on only one dimension to coordinating two dimensions to integrating multiple dimensions. Because different forms of the same logical insight vary in their processing demands and children's experiences vary widely, many understandings appear in specific situations at different times rather than being mastered all at once.

Information Processing

Cite basic changes in information processing, and describe the development of attention and memory in middle childhood.

■ Brain development contributes to gains in information-processing speed and capacity during the school years. Gains in inhibition also occur, supporting information processing by preserving space in working memory for the task at hand.

■ During middle childhood, attention becomes more selective and adaptable. Attention (and memory) strategies develop in a four-step sequence: (1) **production deficiency** (failure to use the strategy); (2) **control deficiency** (failure to execute the strategy consistently); (3) **utilization deficiency** (consistent use of the strategy, but without improvement in performance); and finally (4) **effective strategy use.**

■ School-age children also become better at planning. On tasks requiring systematic visual search or the coordination of many acts, they are more likely to decide in advance how to proceed.

■ Deficits in executive processing and inhibition may underlie the serious attentional and impulse-control difficulties of children with **attention-deficit hyperactivity disorder (ADHD).** ADHD leads to serious academic and social problems.

■ Memory strategies improve during the school years. **Rehearsal** appears first, followed by **organization** and then **elaboration.** With age, children use several memory strategies at once.

■ Development of the long-term knowledge base facilitates strategic memory processing. Children's motivation to use what they know also contributes to memory development. Memory strategies are promoted by learning activities in school and are not used by children in non-Western cultures who have no formal schooling.

Describe the school-age child's theory of mind and capacity to engage in self-regulation.

■ Metacognition expands over middle childhood as children better understand the process of thinking and the factors that influence it. School-age children regard the mind as an active, constructive agent. Their understanding of sources of knowledge expands. They realize that people can extend their knowledge by making mental inferences, and they grasp second-order false belief, which is helpful in understanding others' perspectives. They also appreciate the benefits of mental strategies.

■ School-age children gradually improve at **cognitive self-regulation**—putting what they know about thinking into action. Giving children instructions for monitoring their cognitive activity improves self-regulatory skills and task performance.

Discuss current perspectives on teaching reading and mathematics to elementary school children.

■ Skilled reading draws on all aspects of the information-processing system. Research shows that a combination of **whole-language** and **phonics approaches** is most effective for teaching beginning reading. Whole language keeps reading meaningful, while phonics enables children to decode new words.

■ As with reading, instruction that combines practice in basic skills with conceptual understanding is best in mathematics. Students acquire both math facts and complex math skills through extensive opportunities to experiment with strategies and reason about number concepts. Conceptual knowledge greatly aids complex math computation. Teaching by rote, by contrast, is associated with computational error and inability to apply procedures to new problems.

Individual Differences in Mental Development

Describe major approaches to defining intelligence.

■ During the school years, IQ becomes more stable and correlates well with academic achievement. Most intelligence tests yield an overall score as well as scores for separate intellectual factors. The Stanford-Binet Intelligence Scales, Fifth Edition, and the Wechsler Intelligence Scale for Children–IV (WISC–IV) are widely used individually administered intelligence tests.

■ To search for the precise mental processes underlying mental ability factors, researchers are combining the factor-analytic approach with the information-processing approach. Findings reveal that speed of processing is related to IQ, as are flexible attention, memory, and reasoning strategies.

■ Sternberg's **triarchic theory of successful intelligence** extends these efforts. It views intelligence as a complex interaction of analytical intelligence (information-processing skills), creative intelligence (ability to solve novel problems), and practical intelligence (application of intellectual skills in everyday situations). The practical intelligence of many ethnic minority children is not tapped by mental tests.

■ Gardner's **theory of multiple intelligences** identifies at least eight independent mental abilities, each with a unique biological basis and a distinct course of development. Gardner's theory has been helpful in understanding and nurturing children's talents. It has also stimulated efforts to define, measure, and foster **emotional intelligence**.

© MICHAEL NEWMAN/PHOTOEDIT

Describe evidence indicating that both heredity and environment contribute to intelligence.

■ Heritability estimates and adoption research reveal that intelligence is a product of both heredity and environment. Studies of African-American children adopted into economically well-off white homes indicate that the black–white IQ gap is substantially determined by environment. A dramatic generational increase in IQ also supports the role of environmental factors.

■ IQ scores are affected by culturally influenced communication styles, exposure to specific information that is part of majority-culture upbringing, and the sheer amount of time a child spends in school. **Stereotype threat** can trigger anxiety that impairs children's test performance.

■ Because of cultural bias in intelligence testing, IQ scores can underestimate minority children's intelligence. By introducing purposeful teaching into the testing situation, **dynamic assessment** narrows the gap between a child's actual and potential performance.

Language Development

Describe changes in metalinguistic awareness, vocabulary, grammar, and pragmatics during middle childhood.

■ Schooling, especially reading, contributes greatly to **metalinguistic awareness** and other complex language competencies. Vocabulary continues to grow rapidly, and children have a more precise and flexible understanding of word meanings. Grasp of complex grammatical constructions also improves.

■ School-age children also gain in pragmatics. They adapt to listeners' needs in challenging communicative situations, better evaluate the clarity of others' messages, and refine their conversational strategies.

What are the advantages of bilingualism in childhood?

■ Children who learn two languages in early childhood separate the two language systems from the start and acquire each according to a typical timetable. When school-age children acquire a second language after mastering the first, they take 3 to 5 years to attain the competence of native-speaking agemates. Bilingual children are advanced in cognitive development and metalinguistic awareness. They transfer their phonological awareness skills in one language to the other, which enhances reading achievement.

■ In Canada, language immersion programs succeed in developing children who are proficient in both English and French. Bilingual education that combines instruction in the native language and in English supports American non-English-speaking minority children's academic learning.

Children's Learning in School

Describe the impact of class size and educational philosophies on children's motivation and academic achievement.

■ As class size declines, academic achievement improves. Older students in **traditional classrooms** have a slight edge in academic achievement. Those in **constructivist classrooms** tend to be critical thinkers who are advanced in social and maturity and have more positive attitudes toward school.

■ Vygotsky's sociocultural theory has inspired **social-constructivist classrooms,** which use the rich social context of the classroom to promote children's learning. Vygotsky-inspired teaching methods include **reciprocal teaching** and **communities of learners.** In each, learning experiences involve teacher–child and child–child collaboration, children acquire literacy skills through meaningful activities, and teaching adapts to each child's zone of proximal development.

Discuss the role of teacher–student interaction and grouping practices in academic achievement.

■ Teaching that encourages high-level thinking and that creates a warm, stimulating, demanding academic climate fosters children's interest, involvement, and academic achievement. **Educational self-fulfilling prophecies,** which are most likely to occur in classrooms that emphasize competition and public evaluation, have a greater impact on low achievers.

■ Homogeneous grouping by ability is linked to poorer-quality instruction and a drop in self-esteem and achievement for children in low-ability groups. In contrast, heterogeneous grouping, including multigrade classrooms, promotes academic achievement, self-esteem, and positive school attitudes. For collaboration between heterogeneous peers to lead to achievement gains, children need extensive training and guidance in **cooperative learning.**

Describe educational benefits of computer use as well as concerns about computers.

■ Educational software that permits children to practice basic skills and solve problems results in achievement gains. Word processing frees children to write longer, higher-quality text. Computer programming promotes a variety of complex cognitive skills. However, gender and SES differences exist in time spent with computers and confidence in using them.

Under what conditions is placement of mildly mentally retarded and learning disabled children in regular classrooms successful?

■ U.S. and Canadian legislation has led to increasing use of **inclusive classrooms,** where students with learning difficulties (both those with mild mental retardation and a larger number who have **learning disabilities**) learn alongside typical students, often through full inclusion. The success of regular classroom placement depends on tailoring learning experiences to children's academic needs and promoting positive peer relations.

Describe the characteristics of gifted children and current efforts to meet their educational needs.

■ **Giftedness** includes high IQ, **creativity,** and **talent.** Tests of creativity that tap **divergent thinking** rather than **convergent thinking** focus on only one of the complex cognitive ingredients of creativity. People usually demonstrate expertise and creativity in only one or a few related areas.

■ Highly talented children are biologically prepared to master their domain of interest and have parents and teachers who nurture their extraordinary ability. Extreme giftedness often results in social isolation. Gifted girls, especially, report more emotional and social difficulties. Gifted children are best served by educational programs that build on their special strengths.

How well are North American children achieving compared with children in other industrialized nations?

■ In international studies, young people in Asian nations are consistently top performers. Canadian students generally score high, whereas U.S. students typically display average or below-average performance. A strong cultural commitment to learning in families and schools underlies the high academic success of Asian students.

Important Terms and Concepts

Chapter 13

School-age children become increasingly capable of viewing themselves and their social surroundings from diverse perspectives. The artist's depiction of a trip to a farm reveals a growing understanding of the variety of roles people can play—from feeding the cows to photographing the scene.

Reprinted with permission from the International Child Art Foundation, Washington, D.C.

"Family Trip to a Farm"
Chen Shiang
11 years, Taiwan

Emotional and Social Development in Middle Childhood

Late one afternoon, Rena heard her son Joey burst through the front door, run upstairs, and phone his best friend Terry. "Terry, gotta talk to you," Joey pleaded breathlessly. "Everything was going great until I got that word—*porcupine*," Joey went on, referring to the fifth-grade spelling bee at school that day. "Just my luck! *P-o-r-k,* that's how I spelled it! I can't believe it. Maybe I'm not so good at social studies," Joey confided, "but I *know* I'm better at spelling than that stuck-up Belinda Brown. I knocked myself out studying those spelling lists. Then *she* got all the easy words. If I *had* to lose, why couldn't it at least be to a nice person?"

Joey's conversation reflects his new emotional and social capacities. By entering the spelling bee, he shows *industriousness,* the energetic pursuit of meaningful achievement in his culture—a major change of middle childhood. Joey's social understanding has also expanded. He can size up strengths, weaknesses, and personality characteristics. Furthermore, friendship means something different to Joey than it did earlier—he counts on his best friend, Terry, for understanding and emotional support.

We begin this chapter by returning to Erikson's theory for an overview of the personality changes of middle childhood. Then we look at children's views of themselves and of others and at their peer relationships. Each increases in complexity as children reason more effectively and spend more time in school and with agemates. Despite changing parent–child relationships, the family remains powerfully influential in middle childhood. Today, family lifestyles are more diverse than ever before. Through Joey's and Lizzie's experiences with parental divorce, we will see that family functioning is far more important than family structure in ensuring children's well-being. Finally, we look at some common emotional problems of middle childhood.

Erikson's Theory: Industry versus Inferiority

According to Erikson (1950), children whose experiences have been positive enter middle childhood prepared to redirect their energies from the make-believe of early childhood into realistic accomplishment. Erikson believed that the combination of

The industriousness of middle childhood involves mastery of useful skills and tasks. As these young musicians participate in their school orchestra, they become more aware of one another's unique capacities and come to view themselves as responsible, capable, and cooperative.

adult expectations and children's drive toward mastery sets the stage for the psychological conflict of middle childhood: **industry versus inferiority,** which is resolved positively when experiences lead children to develop a sense of competence at useful skills and tasks.

In cultures everywhere, adults respond to children's improved physical and cognitive capacities by making new demands, and children are ready to benefit from these challenges. Among the Baka hunters and gatherers of Cameroon, 5- to 7-year-olds fetch and carry water, bathe and mind younger siblings, and accompany adults on food-gathering missions. In a miniature village behind the main camp, children practice hut building, spear shaping, and fire making (Avis & Harris, 1991). The Ngoni of Malawi, Central Africa, believe that when children shed their first teeth, they are mature enough for intensive skill training. Six and 7-year-old boys move out of family huts into dormitories, where they enter a system of male domination and instruction. And all children of this age are expected to show independence and are held accountable for irresponsible and disrespectful behavior (Rogoff, 1996).

In industrialized nations, the transition to middle childhood is marked by the beginning of formal schooling. With it comes literacy training, which prepares children for a vast array of specialized careers. In school, children discover their own and others' unique capacities, learn the value of division of labor, and develop a sense of moral commitment and responsibility. The danger at this stage is *inferiority,* reflected in the pessimism of children who have little confidence in their ability to do things well. This sense of inadequacy can develop when family life has not prepared children for school life or when experiences with teachers and peers destroy children's feelings of competence and mastery with negative responses.

Erikson's sense of industry combines several developments of middle childhood: a positive but realistic self-concept, pride in accomplishment, moral responsibility, and cooperative participation with agemates. How do these aspects of self and social relationships change over the school years?

Self-Understanding

In middle childhood, children become able to describe themselves in terms of psychological traits, to compare their own characteristics with those of their peers, and to speculate about the causes of their strengths and weaknesses. These transformations in self-understanding have a major impact on children's self-esteem.

Self-Concept

During the school years, children refine their *me-self,* or self-concept, organizing their observations of behaviors and internal states into general dispositions, with a major change taking place between ages 8 and 11. Consider this 11-year-old's self-description:

industry versus inferiority
In Erikson's theory, the psychological conflict of middle childhood, which is resolved positively when experiences lead children to develop a sense of competence at useful skills and tasks.

My name is A. I'm a human being. I'm a girl. I'm a truthful person. I'm not pretty. I do so-so in my studies. I'm a very good cellist. I'm a very good pianist. I'm a little bit tall for my age. I like several boys. I like several girls. I'm old-fashioned. I play tennis. I am a very good swimmer. I try to be helpful. I'm always ready to be friends with anybody. Mostly I'm good, but I lose my temper. I'm not well liked by some girls and boys. I don't know if I'm liked by boys or not. (Montemayor & Eisen, 1977, pp. 317–318)

Instead of specific behaviors, this child emphasizes competencies: "I'm a very good cellist" (Damon & Hart, 1988). She also clearly describes her personality, mentioning both positive and negative traits: "truthful" but short-tempered, a "good cellist [and] pianist" but only "so-so in my studies." Older school-age children are far less likely than younger children to describe themselves in extreme, all-or-none ways (Harter, 2003, 2006).

These qualified self-descriptions result from another change in self-concept that occurs in middle childhood: Children make **social comparisons,** judging their own appearance, abilities, and behavior in relation to those of others. In talking about the spelling bee, Joey compared his abilities to those of his peers, noting that he was "better at spelling" but "not so good at social studies." Whereas 4- to 6-year-olds can compare their own performance to that of a single peer, older children can compare multiple individuals, including themselves. Consequently, they conclude that they are "very good" at some things, "so-so" at others, and "not good" at still others (Butler, 1998; Harter, 2006).

Cognitive, Social, and Cultural Influences on Self-Concept

What factors are responsible for these revisions in self-concept? Cognitive development certainly affects the changing *structure* of the self. School-age children, as we saw in Chapter 12, can better coordinate several aspects of a situation when they reason about their physical world. Similarly, in the social realm, they combine typical experiences and behaviors into stable psychological dispositions, blend positive and negative characteristics, and compare their own characteristics with those of many peers (Harter, 2003, 2006). In middle childhood, children also gain a clearer understanding that traits are linked to specific desires (a "generous" person *wants* to share) and, therefore, are causes of behavior (Yuill & Pearson, 1998).

The changing *content* of self-concept is a product of both cognitive capacities and feedback from others. Sociologist George Herbert Mead (1934) described the self as a blend of what important people in our lives think of us. He proposed that a well-organized, psychological self emerges when the child's *I-self* adopts a view of the *me-self* that resembles others' attitudes toward the child. Mead's ideas indicate that *perspective-taking* skills—in particular, an improved ability to infer what other people are thinking—are crucial for developing a self-concept based on personality traits. School-age children become better at "reading" others' messages and incorporating these into their self-definitions. As they internalize others' expectations, children form an *ideal self* that they use to evaluate their *real self.* As we will see, a large discrepancy between the two can greatly undermine self-esteem, leading to sadness, hopelessness, and depression.

Parental support for self-development continues to be vitally important. School-age children with a history of elaborative parent–child conversations about past experiences construct a rich, positive narrative about the self and thus have more complex, favorable, and coherent self-concepts (Harter, 2006). In middle childhood, children also look to more people beyond the family for information about themselves as they enter a wider range of settings in school and community. And self-descriptions now include frequent reference to social groups: "I'm a Boy Scout, a paper boy, and a Prairie City soccer player," said Joey when asked to describe himself. Gradually, as children move into adolescence, their sources of self-definition become more selective. Although parents remain influential, self-concept is increasingly vested in feedback from close friends (Oosterwegel & Openheimer, 1993).

Keep in mind, however, that the content of self-concept varies from culture to culture. In earlier chapters, we noted that Asian parents stress harmonious interdependence, whereas Western parents emphasize separateness and self-assertion. Consequently, in China and Japan, the self is defined in relation to the social group. In the United States, the self usually becomes the "property" of a self-contained individual (Markus & Kitayama, 1991). When asked to recall personally significant past experiences (their last birthday, a time their parent scolded them), U.S. school-age children gave longer accounts including more personal preferences, interests, skills, and opinions. Chinese children, in contrast, more often referred to social interactions and to others rather than themselves. Similarly, in their self-descriptions, American children listed more personal attributes ("I'm kind," "I like hockey"), Chinese children more collectivist attributes involving group membership and relationships with others ("I'm in second grade," "My friends are crazy about me") (Wang, 2004).

social comparisons
Children's assessments of their own appearance, abilities, and behavior in relation to those of others.

Strong collectivist values also exist in many subcultures in Western nations. In one study, Puerto Rican children in a small fishing village described themselves as "polite," "respectful," and "obedient" more often than American small-town children; they justified these social traits by noting others' positive reactions to them (Damon & Hart, 1988).

Self-Esteem

Recall that most preschoolers have extremely high self-esteem. But as children enter school and receive much more feedback about how well they perform compared with their peers, grades on papers, tests, and report cards, along with the comments of adults and other children, are integrated into their self-evaluations. As a result, self-esteem differentiates and also adjusts to a more realistic level.

A HIERARCHICALLY STRUCTURED SELF-ESTEEM ■ Researchers have asked children to indicate the extent to which statements, such as "I'm good at reading" or "I'm usually the one chosen for games" are true of themselves. By age 6 to 7, children in diverse Western cultures have formed at least four broad self-evaluations: academic competence, social competence, physical/athletic competence, and physical appearance. Within these are more refined categories that become increasingly distinct with age (Marsh, 1990; Marsh & Ayotte, 2003; Van den Bergh & De Rycke, 2003). Furthermore, the capacity to view the self in terms of stable dispositions permits school-age children to combine their separate self-evaluations into a general psychological image of themselves—an overall sense of self-esteem (Harter, 2003, 2006). As a result, by the mid-elementary school years, self-esteem takes on the hierarchical structure shown in Figure 13.1.

Separate self-esteems, however, do not contribute equally to general self-esteem. Children attach greater importance to certain self-judgments and give them more weight in the total

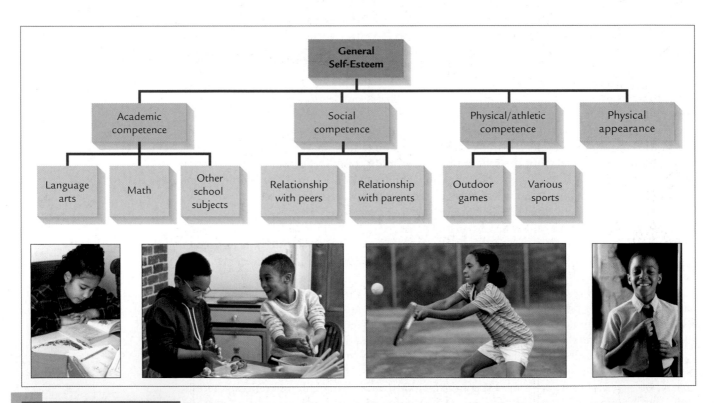

FIGURE 13.1

Hierarchical structure of self-esteem in the mid-elementary school years. From their experiences in different settings, children form at least four separate self-esteems: academic competence, social competence, physical/athletic competence, and physical appearance. These differentiate into additional self-evaluations and combine to form a general sense of self-esteem. (Photo credits: far left: © 2004 Laura Dwight Photography, All Rights Reserved; middle left: © George Disario/CORBIS; middle right: © Mitch Wojnarowicz/The Image Works; far right: Charles Gupton/Stock Boston, LLC.)

picture. Although individual differences exist, during childhood and adolescence perceived physical appearance correlates more strongly with overall self-worth than does any other self-esteem factor (Klomsten, Skaalvik, & Espnes, 2004; Shapka & Keating, 2005). Emphasis on appearance—in the media, among peers, and in society—has major implications for satisfaction with the self. As early as age 6, for example, many girls have a strong desire to be thin (Dohnt & Tiggemann, 2005; Poudevigne et al., 2003). In one study, the more 5- to 8-year-old girls talked with friends about they way people look, watched TV shows focusing on physical appearance, and perceived their friends as valuing thinness, the greater their dissatisfaction with their physical self and the lower their overall self-esteem a year later (Dohnt & Tiggemann, 2006).

CHANGES IN LEVEL OF SELF-ESTEEM ■ As children evaluate themselves in various areas, they lose the sunny optimism of early childhood. Self-esteem declines during the first few years of elementary school (Marsh, Craven, & Debus, 1998; Wigfield et al., 1997). This decline occurs as children receive more competence-related feedback, as their performances are increasingly judged in relation to those of others, and as they become cognitively capable of social comparison.

To protect their self-worth, children eventually balance social comparisons with personal achievement goals (Ruble & Flett, 1988). Perhaps for this reason, the drop in self-esteem in the early school years usually is not harmful. Then, from fourth grade on, self-esteem rises for the majority of young people, who feel especially good about their peer relationships and athletic capabilities (Cole et al., 2001; Twenge & Campbell, 2001). And as they evaluate their various strengths and weaknesses, individual differences in self-esteem become increasingly stable from childhood to adolescence (Trzesniewski, Donnellan & Robins, 2003).

Influences on Self-Esteem

From middle childhood on, positive relationships exist between self-esteem, valuing of various activities, and success at those activities—relationships that strengthen with age. For example, academic self-esteem predicts how important, useful, and enjoyable children judge school subjects to be, their willingness to try hard, and their achievement in those subjects (Jacobs et al., 2002; Valentine, DuBois, & Cooper, 2004). And children with high social self-esteem are better-liked by their classmates (Harter, 1999; Jacobs et al., 2002). Furthermore, across age, sex, SES, and ethnic groups, individuals who are high in self-esteem tend to be well-adjusted, sociable, and conscientious. In contrast, a profile of low self-esteem in all areas is linked to anxiety, depression, and antisocial behavior (DuBois et al., 1999; Kim & Cicchetti, 2006; Robins et al., 2001).

CULTURE ■ Cultural forces profoundly affect self-esteem. An especially strong emphasis on social comparison in school may explain why Chinese, Japanese, and Korean children, despite their higher academic achievement, score lower in self-esteem than North American children—a difference that widens with age (Harter, 2006; Hawkins, 1994; Twenge & Crocker, 2002). In Asian classrooms, competition is tough, and achievement pressure is high. At the same time, because their culture values modesty and social harmony, Asian children less often call on social comparisons to promote their own self-esteem. Rather, they tend to be reserved about judging themselves positively but generous in their praise of others (Falbo et al., 1997). In addition, certain self-evaluations important to Asian children—willingness to help others, respect for parental and teacher authority—are not included on self-esteem questionnaires for North American children (Meredith, Wang, & Zheng, 1993).

Furthermore, parents' gender-stereotyped beliefs predict sex differences in children's self-evaluations of competence in and liking for various school subjects. Girls are advantaged in language-arts

This grandmother puts the final touches on the Mardi Gras costumes her grandchildren will wear in a Martin Luther King, Jr., parade in Miami, Florida. Warm extended families may be responsible for African-American children's higher self-esteem relative to their Caucasian agemates.

self-esteem and boys in math, science, and physical/athletic self-esteem, even when children of equal skill level are compared (Fredricks & Eccles, 2002; Jacobs et al., 2002; Tenenbaum & Leaper, 2003). But although only a slight difference exists between boys and girls in overall self-esteem, a widely held assumption persists that boys' overall sense of self-esteem is much higher than girls' (Cole et al., 2001; Marsh & Ayotte, 2003; Young & Mroczek, 2003). Girls may think less well of themselves because they internalize this negative cultural message.

Compared with their Caucasian agemates, African-American children tend to have slightly higher self-esteem, perhaps because of warm extended families and a stronger sense of ethnic pride (Gray-Little & Hafdahl, 2000). Finally, children and adolescents who attend schools or live in ethnic neighborhoods where their SES and ethnic groups are well-represented feel a stronger sense of belonging and have fewer self-esteem problems (Gray-Little & Carels, 1997).

CHILD REARING ■ Children whose parents use an *authoritative* child-rearing style (see Chapter 10) feel especially good about themselves (Carolson, Uppal, & Prosser, 2000; Feiring & Taska, 1996). Warm, positive parenting lets children know that they are accepted as competent and worthwhile. And firm but appropriate expectations, backed with explanations, help children make sensible choices and evaluate their own behavior against reasonable standards.

Controlling parents—those who too often help or make decisions for their child—communicate a sense of inadequacy to children that is linked to low self-esteem. Having parents who are repeatedly disapproving and insulting is also linked to low self-esteem, as are repeated disapproval and parental insults (Kernis, 2002; Pomerantz & Eaton, 2000). Children subjected to such parenting need constant reassurance, and their self-worth fluctuates with every evaluative remark from others. Many become adolescents who rely heavily on peers rather than adults to affirm their self-esteem—a risk factor for adjustment difficulties, including aggression, antisocial behavior, and delinquency (Donellan et al., 2005).

In contrast, overly indulgent parenting is linked to unrealistically high self-esteem, which also undermines development. These children tend to lash out at challenges to their overblown self-images and are also likely to have adjustment problems, including meanness and aggression (Hughes, Cavell, & Grossman, 1997).

North American cultural values have increasingly emphasized a focus on the self that may lead parents to indulge children and boost their self-esteem too much. The self-esteem of American young people has risen sharply over the past few decades—a period in which much popular parenting literature advised promoting children's self-esteem (Twenge & Campbell, 2001). Yet compared with previous generations, American youths are achieving less well and displaying more antisocial behavior and other adjustment problems (Berk, 2005). Research confirms that children do not benefit from compliments ("You're terrific") that have no basis in real attainment (Damon, 1995). Rather, the best way to foster a positive, secure self-image is to encourage children to strive for worthwhile goals. Over time, a bidirectional relationship emerges: Achievement fosters self-esteem, which, in turn, promotes good performance (Guay, Marsh, & Boivin, 2003).

What can adults do to encourage—and to avoid undermining—this mutually supportive relationship between motivation and self-esteem? Some answers come from research on the precise content of adults' messages to children in achievement situations.

ACHIEVEMENT-RELATED ATTRIBUTIONS ■ **Attributions** are our common, everyday explanations for the causes of behavior—our answers to the question, "Why did I [or another person] do that?" Notice how Joey, in talking about the spelling bee at the beginning of this chapter, attributes his disappointing performance to *luck* (Belinda got all the easy words) and his usual success to *ability* (he *knows* he's a better speller than Belinda). Joey also appreciates that *effort* matters: "I knocked myself out studying those spelling lists."

The combination of improved reasoning skills and frequent evaluative feedback permits 10- to 12-year-olds to recognize and separate all these variables in explaining performance (Dweck, 2002). Yet children differ greatly in how they account for their successes and failures. Those who are high in academic self-esteem make **mastery-oriented attributions,** crediting

attributions Common, everyday explanations of the causes of behavior.

mastery-oriented attributions Attributions that credit success to ability, which can be improved by trying hard, and failure to insufficient effort.

their successes to ability—a characteristic they can improve through trying hard and can count on when faced with new challenges. This *incremental view of ability*—that it can increase—influences the way mastery-oriented children interpret negative events. They attribute failure to factors that can be changed and controlled, such as insufficient effort or a difficult task (Heyman & Dweck, 1998). So whether these children succeed or fail, they take an industrious, persistent approach to learning.

In contrast, children who develop **learned helplessness** attribute their failures, not their successes, to ability. When they succeed, they are likely to conclude that external factors, such as luck, are responsible. Unlike their mastery-oriented counterparts, they hold a *fixed view of ability*—that it cannot be improved by trying hard (Cain & Dweck, 1995). When a task is difficult, these children experience an anxious loss of control—in Erikson's terms, a pervasive sense of inferiority. They give up without really trying.

Children's attributions affect their goals. Mastery-oriented children focus on *learning goals*—increasing ability through effort and seeking information on how to do so. In contrast, learned-helpless children focus on *performance goals*—obtaining positive and avoiding negative evaluations of their fragile sense of ability. Over time, the ability of learned-helpless children no longer predicts how well they do. In one study, the more fourth to sixth graders held self-critical attributions, the lower they rated their competence, the less they knew about effective study strategies, the more they avoided challenge, and the poorer their academic performance. These outcomes strengthened their fixed view of ability (Pomerantz & Saxon, 2001). Because learned-helpless children fail to connect effort with success, they do not develop the metacognitive and self-regulatory skills necessary for high achievement (see Chapter 12). Lack of effective learning strategies, reduced persistence, and a sense of loss of control sustain one another in a vicious cycle (Heyman & Dweck, 1998).

Repeated negative evaluations of their ability can cause children to develop learned helplessness—the belief that failure is due to inability. Faced with a challenging task, this learned-helpless child concludes that he cannot succeed by trying hard. He is overwhelmed by negative thoughts and anxiety.

INFLUENCES ON ACHIEVEMENT-RELATED ATTRIBUTIONS ■ What accounts for the very different attributions of mastery-oriented and learned-helpless children? Adult communication plays a key role. When parents hold a fixed view of ability, their perceptions of children's academic competence tend to act as self-fulfilling prophecies (see page 470 in Chapter 12). Their children's self-evaluations and school grades conform more closely to parental ability judgments than do those of children whose parents deny that ability is fixed (Pomerantz & Dong, 2006). Parents who believe that little can be done to improve ability may ignore information that is inconsistent with their perceptions, giving their child little opportunity to counteract a negative parental evaluation.

Indeed, children with a learned-helpless style often have parents who believe that their child is not very capable and must work much harder than others to succeed. When the child fails, the parent might say, "You can't do that, can you? It's OK if you quit" (Hokoda & Fincham, 1995). When the child succeeds, the parent might offer feedback that evaluates the child's traits ("You're so smart"). Trait statements—even when positive—encourage children to adopt a fixed view of ability, which leads them to question their competence in the face of setbacks and to retreat from challenge (Mueller & Dweck, 1998).

Teachers' messages also affect children's attributions. Teachers who are caring and helpful and who emphasize learning over getting good grades tend to have mastery-oriented students (Anderman et al., 2001). In a study of 1,600 third to eighth graders, students who viewed their teachers as providing positive, supportive learning conditions worked harder and participated more in class—factors that predicted high achievement, which sustained children's belief in the role of effort. In contrast, students with unsupportive teachers regarded their performance as externally controlled (by their teachers or by luck). This attitude predicted withdrawal from learning activities and declining achievement—outcomes that led children to doubt their ability (Skinner, Zimmer-Gembeck, & Connell, 1998).

learned helplessness The view that success is due to external factors, such as luck, while failure is due to ability, which cannot be improved by trying hard.

These schoolchildren, who live on an Israeli kibbutz, are protected from learned helplessness by classrooms that emphasize mastery and interpersonal harmony over ability and competition. Their teacher takes steps to instill in each child the belief that he or she can succeed.

For some children, performance is especially likely to be undermined by adult feedback. Despite their higher achievement, girls more often than boys attribute poor performance to lack of ability. Girls tend to receive messages from teachers and parents that their ability is at fault when they do not do well, and negative stereotypes (for example, that girls are weak at math) undermine their interest and performance (Bleeker & Jacobs, 2004; Cole et al., 1999). And as Chapter 12 revealed, low-SES, ethnic-minority students often receive less favorable feedback from teachers, especially when assigned to homogeneous groups of poorly achieving students—conditions that result in a drop in academic self-esteem and achievement. Furthermore, when ethnic-minority children observe that adults in their own family are not rewarded by society for their achievement efforts, they may try less hard themselves (Harris & Graham, 2007; Ogbu, 1997).

Finally, cultural values affect the likelihood that children will develop learned helplessness. Recall from Chapter 12 that compared with North Americans, Asian parents and teachers believe that success depends much more on effort than on ability and that trying hard is a moral responsibility—messages they transmit to children (Grant & Dweck, 2001; Tuss, Zimmer, & Ho, 1995). And Israeli children growing up on *kibbutzim* (cooperative agricultural settlements) are shielded from learned helplessness by classrooms that emphasize mastery and interpersonal harmony rather than ability and competition (Butler & Ruzany, 1993).

PROMOTING MASTERY-ORIENTED ATTRIBUTIONS ■ Attribution research suggests that well-intended messages from adults sometimes undermine children's competence. An intervention called **attribution retraining** encourages learned-helpless children to believe they can overcome failure by exerting more effort. Children are given tasks difficult enough that they will experience some failure, followed by repeated feedback that helps them revise their attributions: "You can do it if you try harder." After they succeed, children are given additional feedback—"You're really good at this" or "You really tried hard on that one"—so that they view their success as due to both ability and effort, not to chance. Another approach is to encourage low-effort children to focus less on grades and more on mastering a task for its own sake (Hilt, 2004; Horner & Gaither, 2004). Instruction in effective strategies and self-regulation is also vital, to compensate for development lost in this area and to ensure that renewed effort will pay off (Borkowski & Muthukrishna, 1995; Wigfield et al., 2006).

Attribution retraining works best when it is begun in middle childhood, before children's views of themselves become hard to change. An even better approach is to prevent learned helplessness, using strategies summarized in Applying What We Know on the following page.

Ask Yourself

Review   How does level of self-esteem change in middle childhood, and what accounts for these changes?

Apply   Should parents try to promote children's self-esteem by telling them they're "smart" or "wonderful"? Is it harmful for children not to feel good about everything they do? Why or why not?

Connect   What cognitive changes, described in Chapter 12 (pages 437–438), support the transition to a self-concept emphasizing competencies, personality traits, and social comparisons?

Reflect   Recall your own attributions for academic successes and failures when you were in elementary school. What are those attributions like now? What messages from others may have contributed to your attributions?

Applying What We Know

Fostering a Mastery-Oriented Approach to Learning

Provision of tasks	Select tasks that are meaningful, responsive to a diversity of student interests, and appropriately matched to current competence so the child is challenged but not overwhelmed.
Parent and teacher encouragement	Communicate warmth, confidence in the child's abilities, the value of achievement, and the importance of effort in success.
	Model high effort in overcoming failure.
	(For teachers) Communicate often with parents, suggesting ways to foster children's effort and progress.
	(For parents) Monitor schoolwork; provide scaffolded assistance that promotes knowledge of effective strategies and self-regulation.
Performance evaluations	Make evaluations private; avoid publicizing success or failure through wall posters, stars, privileges to "smart" children, and prizes for "best" performance.
	Stress individual progress and self-improvement.
School environment	Offer small classes, which permit teachers to provide individualized support for mastery.
	Provide for cooperative learning and peer tutoring, in which children assist one another; avoid ability grouping, which makes evaluations of children's progress public.
	Accommodate individual and cultural differences in styles of learning.
	Create an atmosphere that sends a clear message that all pupils can learn.

Sources: Hilt, 2004; Wigfield et al., 2006.

Emotional Development

Greater self-awareness and social sensitivity support emotional development in middle childhood. Gains take place in children's experience of self-conscious emotions, understanding of emotional states, and emotional self-regulation.

Self-Conscious Emotions

As children integrate social expectations into their self-concepts, self-conscious emotions of pride and guilt become clearly governed by personal responsibility. Unlike preschoolers, school-age children experience these feelings—pride in a new accomplishment or guilt about a transgression—even when no adult is present (Harter & Whitesell, 1989). Also, children no longer report guilt for any mishap, as they did earlier, but only for intentional wrongdoing, such as ignoring responsibilities, cheating, or lying (Ferguson, Stegge, & Damhuis, 1991). These changes reflect the older child's more mature sense of morality, a topic we will take up later in this chapter.

When school-age children feel pride or guilt, they view specific aspects of the self as leading to success or failure: "I tried hard on that difficult task, and it paid off" (pride) or "I made a mistake, and now I have to deal with it" (guilt). They tend to feel shame when their violation of a standard is not under their control (Lewis & Ramsay, 2002; Saarni et al., 2006). For example, Lizzie felt ashamed when she dropped a spoonful of spaghetti and had a large spot on her shirt for the rest of the school day. But as children develop an overall sense of self-esteem, they may also experience shame after a controllable breach of standards if someone blames them for it (Harter, 1999, 2006; Mascolo & Fischer, 1995). For example, the child who does poorly on a test and whose teacher or parent reprimands him ("Everyone else can do it! Why can't you?") may hang his head in shame while repeating to himself, "I'm stupid! I'm a terrible kid!"

Pride motivates children to take on further challenges. And guilt prompts them to make amends and strive for self-improvement. But profound feelings of shame (as noted in

attribution retraining An intervention that uses adult feedback to encourage learned-helpless children to believe that they can overcome failure through effort.

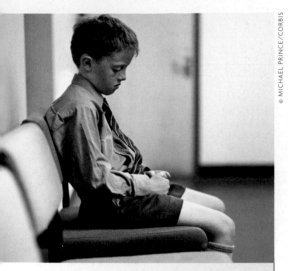

School-age children experience emotions that are governed by their developing sense of personal responsibility. If this child reacts with guilt to wrongdoing, he is likely to make amends. But if parents and teachers blame and criticize, he may experience intense shame, which can induce a sharp drop in self-esteem accompanied by depression or anger.

problem-centered coping An approach to coping with stress in which the individual appraises the situation as changeable, identifies the difficulty, and decides what to do about it.

emotion-centered coping An approach to coping with stress that is internal, private, and aimed at controlling distress when little can be done to change an outcome.

perspective taking The capacity to imagine what other people are thinking and feeling.

Chapter 10) are particularly destructive. A sharp, shame-induced drop in self-esteem can trigger withdrawal and depression or intense anger at those who participated in the shame-evoking situation (Lindsay-Hartz, de Rivera, & Mascolo, 1995; Mills, 2005).

Emotional Understanding

School-age children's understanding of mental activity means that, unlike preschoolers, they are likely to explain emotion by referring to internal states, such as happy or sad thoughts, rather than to external events (Flavell, Flavell, & Green, 2001). Also, around age 8, children become aware that they can experience more than one emotion at a time, each of which may be positive or negative and may differ in intensity (Pons et al., 2003). For example, recalling the birthday present he received from his grandmother, Joey reflected, "I was very happy I got something but a little sad that I didn't get just what I wanted."

Appreciating mixed emotions helps children realize that people's expressions may not reflect their true feelings (Saarni, 1999). It also fosters awareness of self-conscious emotions. For example, 8- and 9-year-olds understand that pride combines two sources of happiness—joy in accomplishment and joy that a significant person recognized that accomplishment (Harter, 1999). Furthermore, children of this age can reconcile contradictory facial and situational cues in figuring out another's emotions. And they can use information about "what might have happened" to predict how people will feel in a new situation—realizing, for example, that someone will feel better (a sense of relief) when an actual outcome was more favorable than what could have occurred (Guttentag & Ferrell, 2004).

As with self-understanding, gains in emotional understanding are supported by cognitive development and social experiences, especially adults' sensitivity to children's feelings and willingness to discuss emotions. Together, these factors contribute to a rise in empathy as well. As children move closer to adolescence, advances in perspective taking permit an empathic response not just to people's immediate distress but also to their general life condition (Hoffman, 2000). As at early ages, emotional understanding and empathy are linked to favorable social relationships and prosocial behavior (Schultz et al., 2001). As Joey and Lizzie imagined how people who are chronically ill or hungry feel and evoked those emotions in themselves, they gave part of their allowance to charity and joined in fund-raising projects through school, church, and scouting.

Emotional Self-Regulation

Rapid gains in emotional self-regulation occur in middle childhood. As children engage in social comparison and care more about peer approval, they must learn to manage negative emotion that threatens their self-esteem.

By age 10, most children shift adaptively between two general strategies for managing emotion. In **problem-centered coping,** they appraise the situation as changeable, identify the difficulty, and decide what to do about it. If problem solving does not work, they engage in **emotion-centered coping,** which is internal, private, and aimed at controlling distress when little can be done about an outcome (Kliewer, Fearnow, & Miller, 1996; Lazarus & Lazarus, 1994). For example, when faced with an anxiety-provoking test or an angry friend, older school-age children view problem solving and seeking social support as the best strategies. But when outcomes are beyond their control—for example, after receiving a bad grade—they opt for distraction or try to redefine the situation in ways that help them accept it: "Things could be worse. There'll be another test." Compared with preschoolers, school-age children more often use these internal strategies to regulate emotion, a change due to their improved ability to appraise situations and reflect on thoughts and feelings (Brenner & Salovey, 1997).

Cognitive development and a wider range of social experiences permit children to flexibly vary their coping strategies. And from interacting with parents, teachers, and peers, children become more knowledgeable about socially approved ways to display negative emotion. With age, they increasingly prefer verbal strategies ("Please stop pushing and wait your turn") to crying, sulking, or aggression (Shipman et al., 2003). Young school-age children justify these more mature displays of emotion by mentioning avoidance of punishment or disapproval, but by third grade, they emphasize concern for others' feelings. Children with this awareness are rated as especially helpful, cooperative, and socially responsive (Garner, 1996; McDowell & Parke, 2000).

When emotional self-regulation has developed well, school-age children acquire a sense of *emotional self-efficacy*—a feeling of being in control of their emotional experience (Saarni, 2000). This fosters a favorable self-image and an optimistic outlook, which helps them face future emotional challenges. As at younger ages, school-age children whose parents respond sensitively and helpfully when the child is distressed are emotionally well-regulated—generally upbeat in mood and also empathic and prosocial. In contrast, poorly regulated children often experience hostile, dismissive parental reactions to distress. These children are overwhelmed by negative emotion, a response that interferes with empathy and prosocial behavior (Davidov & Grusec, 2006; Zeman, Shipman, & Suveg, 2002).

Finally, culture influences emotional self-regulation. In a striking illustration, researchers studied children in two collectivist subcultures in rural Nepal. In response to stories about emotionally charged situations (such as peer aggression or unjust parental punishment), Hindu children more often said they would feel angry but would try to mask their feelings. Buddhist children, in contrast, interpreted the situation so they did not experience anger. Saying they would feel just OK, they explained, "Why be angry? The event already happened." In line with this difference, Hindu mothers reported that they often teach their children how to control their emotional behavior, whereas Buddhist mothers pointed to the value their religion places on a calm, peaceful disposition (Cole & Tamang, 1998; Cole, Tamang, & Shrestha, 2006). In comparison to both Nepalese groups, U.S. children preferred conveying anger verbally in these situations—for example, to an unjust punishment, they answered, "If I say I'm angry, he'll stop hurting me!" (Cole, Bruschi, & Tamang, 2002). Notice how this response fits with the Western individualistic emphasis on personal rights and self-expression.

Understanding Others: Perspective Taking

We have seen that middle childhood brings major advances in **perspective taking,** the capacity to imagine what other people are thinking and feeling. These changes support self-concept and self-esteem, understanding of others, and a wide variety of social skills. Robert Selman's five-stage sequence describes changes in perspective-taking skill, based on children's and adolescents' responses to social dilemmas in which characters have differing information and opinions about an event.

As Table 13.1 on page 492 indicates, at first, children have only a limited idea of what other people might be thinking and feeling. Over time, they become more aware that people can interpret the same event quite differently. Soon they can "step into another person's shoes" and reflect on how that person might regard their own thoughts, feelings, and behavior, as when they make statements like this: "I *thought you would think* I was just kidding when I said that." (Note the similarity between this level of perspective taking and second-order false belief, described on page 447 in Chapter 12.) Finally, older children and adolescents can evaluate two people's perspectives simultaneously, at first from the vantage point of a disinterested spectator and later by referring to societal values, as the following explanation illustrates: "I know why Joey hid the stray kitten in the basement, even though his mom was against keeping it. He believes in not hurting animals. If you put the kitten outside or give it to the pound, it might die."

These children are conducting a fundraiser to help the thousands of pets who were injured or left homeless by Hurricane Katrina in 2005. Their efforts are an adaptive strategy for managing the intense fear they may have felt after witnessing on television the destructive effects of the hurricane.

TABLE 13.1	Selman's Stages of Perspective Taking	
STAGE	**APPROXIMATE AGE RANGE**	**DESCRIPTION**
Level 0: Undifferentiated perspective taking	3–6	Children recognize that self and other can have different thoughts and feelings, but they frequently confuse the two.
Level 1: Social-informational perspective taking	4–9	Children understand that different perspectives may result because people have access to different information.
Level 2: Self-reflective perspective taking	7–12	Children can "step into another person's shoes" and view their own thoughts, feelings, and behavior from the other person's perspective. They also recognize that others can do the same.
Level 3: Third-party perspective taking	10–15	Children can step outside a two-person situation and imagine how the self and other are viewed from the point of view of a third, impartial party.
Level 4: Societal perspective taking	14–adult	Individuals understand that third-party perspective taking can be influenced by one or more systems of larger societal values.

Sources: Selman, 1976; Selman & Byrne, 1974.

Experiences in which adults and peers explain their viewpoints contribute greatly to children's perspective taking. Good perspective takers, in turn, are more likely to display empathy and sympathy and to handle difficult social situations effectively—among the reasons they are better-liked by peers (FitzGerald & White, 2003). Children with poor social skills, especially the angry, aggressive styles we discussed in Chapter 10, have great difficulty imagining others' thoughts and feelings. They often mistreat adults and peers without feeling the guilt and remorse prompted by awareness of another's viewpoint. Interventions that provide coaching and practice in perspective taking reduce antisocial behavior and increase empathy and pro-social responding (Chalmers & Townsend, 1990).

Moral Development

Recall from Chapter 10 that preschoolers pick up many morally relevant behaviors through modeling and reinforcement. By middle childhood, they have had time to internalize rules for good conduct: "It's good to help others in trouble" or "It's wrong to take something that doesn't belong to you." This change leads children to become considerably more independent and trustworthy.

In Chapter 10, we also saw that children do not just copy their morality from others. As the cognitive-developmental approach emphasizes, they actively think about right and wrong. An expanding social world and gains in reasoning and perspective taking lead moral understanding to advance greatly in middle childhood.

Learning about Justice Through Sharing

In everyday life, children frequently experience situations involving **distributive justice**—beliefs about how to divide material goods fairly. Heated debate arises over how much weekly allowance is appropriate for siblings of different ages, who should sit where on a long car trip, or how six hungry playmates should share an eight-slice pizza. William Damon (1977, 1988) has traced children's changing concepts of distributive justice over early and middle childhood.

Even 4-year-olds recognize the importance of sharing, but their reasons are often self-serving: "I shared because if I didn't, she wouldn't play with me." As children enter middle

distributive justice Beliefs about how to divide material goods fairly.

childhood, they express more mature notions of distributive justice. Their basis of reasoning follows a three-step sequence:

1. *Strict equality* (5 to 6 years). Children in the early school grades are intent on making sure that each person gets the same amount of a treasured resource, such as money, turns in a game, or a delicious treat.
2. *Merit* (6 to 7 years). A short time later, children say extra rewards should go to someone who has worked especially hard or otherwise performed in an exceptional way.
3. *Equity and benevolence* (8 to 9 years). Finally, children recognize that special consideration should be given to those at a disadvantage—for example, that a child who cannot produce as much or who does not get any allowance should be given more. Older children also adapt their basis of fairness to fit the situation, relying more on equality when interacting with strangers and more on benevolence when interacting with friends (McGillicuddy-De Lisi, Watkins, & Vinchur, 1994).

According to Damon (1988), the give-and-take of peer interaction makes children more sensitive to others' perspectives, and this supports their developing ideas of justice (Kruger, 1993). Advanced distributive justice reasoning, in turn, is associated with a greater willingness to help, share, and cooperate (Blotner & Bearison, 1984; McNamee & Peterson, 1986).

Children's ideas about distributive justice—how to divide material goods fairly—develop gradually in middle childhood. The child on the right understands that fairness should include benevolence. He shares with two younger children who do not have access to a special treat.

Moral and Social-Conventional Understanding

During the school years, children construct a flexible appreciation of moral rules. By age 7 to 8, they no longer say truth telling is always good and lying is always bad but also consider prosocial and antisocial intentions. They evaluate very negatively certain types of truthfulness, such as bluntly telling a classmate that you don't like her drawing (Bussey, 1999). And although both Chinese and Canadian schoolchildren consider lying about antisocial acts "very naughty," Chinese children—influenced by collectivist values—are more likely than their North American agemates to rate lying favorably when the intention is modesty, as when a student who has thoughtfully picked up litter from the playground says, "I didn't do it" (Lee et al., 1997).

As children construct more advanced ideas about justice, taking into account an increasing number of variables, they clarify and link moral rules and social conventions. School-age children, for example, distinguish social conventions with a clear *purpose* (not running in school hallways to prevent injuries) from ones with no obvious justification (crossing a "forbidden" line on the playground). They regard violations of purposeful conventions as closer to moral transgressions (Buchanan-Barrow & Barrett, 1998). They also realize that people's *intentions* and the *context* of their actions affect the moral implications of violating a social convention. In a Canadian study, 8- to 10-year-olds judged that because of a flag's symbolic value, burning it to express disapproval of a country or to start a cooking fire is worse than burning it accidentally. They also stated that public flag burning is worse than private flag burning because it inflicts emotional harm on others. But they recognized that flag burning is a form of freedom of expression, and most agreed that it would be acceptable in a country that treated its citizens unfairly (Helwig & Prencipe, 1999).

In middle childhood, children also realize that people whose *knowledge* differs may not be equally responsible for moral transgressions. Many 7-year-olds tolerate a teacher's decision to give more snack to girls than to boys because she thinks (incorrectly) that girls need more food. But when a teacher gives girls more snack because she holds an *immoral belief* ("it's all right to be nicer to girls than boys"), almost all children judge her actions negatively (Wainryb & Ford, 1998).

CP PHOTO/PETERBOROUGH EXAMINER/CLIFFORD SKARSTEDT

These Canadian schoolchildren, who are celebrating the fortieth anniversary of their country's maple-leaf flag, are aware that the social convention of respecting the flag has moral implications. They realize that any public flag-burning would harm others emotionally. At the same time, they acknowledge that destroying a flag is a form of freedom of expression that is warranted in a country that treats its citizens unfairly.

Understanding Individual Rights

When children do challenge adult authority, they typically do so within the personal domain. As their grasp of moral imperatives and social conventions strengthens, so does their conviction that certain choices, such as hairstyle, friends, and leisure activities, are up to the individual (Nucci, 2002).

Notions of personal choice, in turn, enhance children's moral understanding. As early as age 6, children view freedom of speech and religion as individual rights, even if laws exist that deny those rights (Helwig & Turiel, 2002). And they regard laws that discriminate against individuals—for example, denying certain people access to medical care or education—as wrong and worthy of violating (Helwig & Jasiobedzka, 2001). In justifying their responses, children appeal to personal privileges and, as they move into adolescence, to democratic ideals, such as the importance of individual rights for a fair society.

At the same time, older school-age children place limits on individual choice. While they believe nonacademic matters (such as where to go on field trips) are best decided democratically, they regard the academic curriculum as the province of teachers, based on teachers' superior ability to make such choices (Helwig & Kim, 1999). And when issues of fairness are brought to their attention, fourth graders faced with conflicting moral and personal concerns—such as whether or not to be friends with a classmate of a different ethnicity or gender—typically decide in favor of fairness (Killen et al., 2002). Partly for this reason, prejudice generally declines in middle childhood.

Culture and Moral Understanding

Children and adolescents in diverse Western and non-Western cultures use similar criteria to reason about moral, social-conventional, and personal concerns (Neff & Helwig, 2002; Nucci, 2002). For example, Chinese young people, whose culture places a high value on respect for and deference to adult authority, nevertheless say that adults have no right to interfere in children's personal matters, such as how they spend free time (Helwig et al., 2003).

Furthermore, North American and Korean children alike claim that a child with no position of authority should be obeyed when she gives a fair and caring directive, such as to share candy or to return lost money to its owner. And although they recognize a parent's right to set social conventions at home and a teacher's right to do so at school, they evaluate negatively an adult's order to engage in immoral acts (Kim, 1998; Kim & Turiel, 1996). In sum, children everywhere seem to realize that higher principles, independent of rule and authority, must prevail when people's personal rights and welfare are at stake.

As children extend their grasp of moral imperatives, they also contemplate religious and spiritual concepts. Refer to the Cultural Influences box on the following page for current evidence on how children understand the existence of God, the core idea in the vast majority of the world's religions.

Understanding Diversity and Inequality

By the early school years, children associate power and privilege with white people and inferior status with people of color. They do not necessarily acquire these views directly from parents or friends. In one study, although white school-age children assumed that parents' and friends' racial attitudes would resemble their own, no similarities in attitudes emerged (Aboud & Doyle, 1996). Perhaps white parents are reluctant to discuss their racial and ethnic views with children, and friends also say little. Given limited or ambiguous information, children may fill in the gaps with information they encounter in the media and elsewhere in their environments and then rely on their own attitudes as the basis for inferring others'.

Cultural Influences

Children's Understanding of God

Here is how several 6- to 9-year-olds responded to the question: "What is God?"

- "You can pray anytime you feel like it, and they [Jesus and God] are sure to hear you because they got it worked out so one of them is on duty at all times."

- "God hears everything, not just prayers, so there must be an awful lot of noise in his ears, unless he has thought of a way to turn it off."

- "God is a spirit who can go anywhere." *What is a spirit?* "It's a ghost, like in the movies." (From Briggs, 2000; Gandy, 2004.)

Ideas about God differ radically from ideas about ordinary experiences because they violate real-world assumptions. Recall from Chapter 9 that between ages 4 and 8, children distinguish magical beings (such as Santa Claus and the Tooth Fairy) from reality (see page 327). At the same time, they embrace other beliefs that are part of their culturally transmitted religion. To avoid confusion, they must isolate their concepts of God from their grasp of human agents, placing God in a separate religious realm governed by superhuman rules (Woolley, 2000). This is a challenging task for preschool and school-age children.

Previous research, strongly influenced by Piaget's theory, led to a uniform conclusion: Children assign *anthropomorphic* (human) characteristics to God, whom they view as a parentlike figure residing in the sky. Not until adolescence does this concrete image of God as "big person" give way to an abstract, mystical view of God as formless, all-knowing (omniscient), all-powerful (omnipotent), and transcending the limits of time.

Consider the responses of children just given, which contain both concrete human images (God as being "on duty in the sky" or as

overwhelmed by the "noise in his ears") and a variety of superhuman properties ("a spirit who can go anywhere"). Recent evidence reveals that even preschoolers are not limited to human, parental images of God. The procedures typically used to investigate children's religious knowledge—asking them to respond to open-ended questions—are so cognitively demanding that children often fall back on their highly detailed notions of humans to fill in for their sketchier thoughts about God.

When researchers make tasks less demanding, children recognize that God has supernatural powers not available to humans, such as seeing and hearing everything (Richert & Barrett, 2005). For example, in research in the United States and in a Mexican Mayan village, most 5- to 6-year-olds given a typical false-belief task indicated that their parents might hold a false belief, but God would not (Knight et al., 2004). Children of this age also say that God—but not a humanlike puppet—can see an object in a darkened box (Barrett, Richert, & Driesenga, 2001). And with respect to God's omnipotence, even preschoolers state with certainty that God, but not humans, gives life to all natural things (animals, plants, and trees) (Petrovich, 1997).

Indeed, the most striking feature of children's concepts of God is their mix of tangible and intangible features. In this respect, their religious thinking is far more similar to adults' than previously thought. That children's representations of God are not restricted to a "big person" image suggests that religious education strongly influences their thinking. Indeed, wide cultural variation in children's and adults' ideas exists (Barrett, 2002; Barrett & Van Orman, 1996). In studies in which school-age children drew pictures of God, Mormons, Lutherans, Mennonites, and Catholics, in line with the teachings of their denominations, more often represented God as humanlike than did Unitarians and Jews (Pitts,

1976; Tamminen, 1991). Further, children say some things about God that seem strange or amusing because their culturally relevant knowledge is often incomplete. During the school years, they frequently ask thoughtful questions about God aimed at broadening their understanding: "Does God have parents?" or "Why doesn't God stop bad things from happening?"

Finally, some children are aware that visions of God can provide emotional comfort and guidance, as these comments reveal: "He comes down and helps you when you're sad or lonely or can't get to sleep at night." "In case you forget, he reminds you to act nice" (Berk, 2004). As we will see in Chapter 16, by adolescence (and perhaps before), religiosity is linked to psychological well-being and to prosocial attitudes and behavior.

Cognitive development, religious education, and culture combine to influence children's understanding of God. Like adults, these children—who are greeting their priest on Sunday morning—probably view God as having both humanlike and supernatural powers.

IN-GROUP AND OUT-GROUP BIASES: DEVELOPMENT OF PREJUDICE ■ Studies in diverse Western nations confirm that by age 5 to 7, white children generally evaluate their own racial group favorably and other racial groups less favorably or negatively—biases that also characterize many adults. *In-group favoritism* emerges first and strengthens until age 7 to 8. Children simply prefer their own group, generalizing from self to similar others (Bennett et al., 2004; Cameron et al., 2001). *Out-group prejudice* requires a more challenging social comparison between in-group and out-group. But it does not take long for white children to acquire negative attitudes toward ethnic minority out-groups, especially when they have little direct

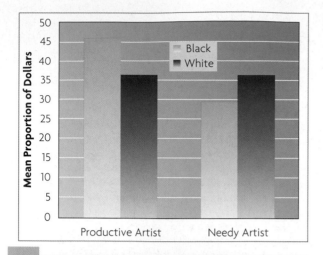

FIGURE 13.2

White fourth graders' racially biased use of equity and benevolence in a distributive justice task.
When dividing money earned from selling children's art among three child artists—two white and one black—the fourth graders gave more money to a productive black artist (who countered a stereotype) than a productive white artist, and less money to a needy black artist (who conformed to a stereotype) than a needy white artist. In both instances, the fourth graders seemed to engage in subtle, unintentional prejudice. (Adapted from A. V. McGillicuddy-De Lisi, M. Daly, & A. Neal, 2006, "Children's Distributive Justice Judgments: Aversive Racism in Euro-American Children?" *Child Development, 77,* p. 1072. Copyright © Society for Research in Child Development. Reprinted by permission.)

experience with them. When white Canadian 4- to 7-year-olds living in a white community and attending nearly all-white schools sorted positive and negative adjectives into boxes labeled as belonging to a white child and a black child, out-group prejudice emerged at age 5 (Aboud, 2003).

Unfortunately, many ethnic-minority children show a reverse pattern: *out-group favoritism,* in which they assign positive characteristics to the privileged white majority and negative characteristics to their own group. In one study, researchers asked African-American 5- to 7-year-olds to recall information in stories either consistent or inconsistent with stereotypes of blacks. The children recalled more stereotyped traits, especially if they agreed with negative cultural views of African Americans (Averhart & Bigler, 1997). Similarly, Native Canadian children recall more positive attributes about white Canadians and more negative attributes about Native Canadians (Corenblum, 2003).

But recall that with age, children pay more attention to inner traits. The capacity to classify the social world in multiple ways enables school-age children to understand that people can be both "the same" and "different"—those who look different need not think, feel, or act differently (Aboud & Amato, 2001). Consequently, voicing of negative attitudes toward minorities declines. After age 7 or 8, both majority and minority children express in-group favoritism, and white children's prejudice against out-group members often weakens (Ruble et al., 2004). Most school-age children and adolescents are also quick to verbalize that it is wrong to exclude others from peer-group and learning activities on the basis of skin color—discrimination they evaluate as unfair (Killen et al., 2002).

Yet even in children aware of the immorality of discrimination, prejudice may operate subtly, unintentionally, and without awareness—as it does in many white adults (Dovidio et al., 2004; Dunham, Baron, & Banaji, 2006). Consider a study in which white second and fourth graders were given a distributive-justice task in which they had to divide money earned from selling children's art among three child artists— two white and one black. In each version of the task, one artist was labeled as "productive" (making more art works), one as "the oldest," and one as "poor and needing money for lunch." Most fourth graders— who (unlike second graders) are able to use equity and benevolence as the basis for distributive justice—failed to apply these principles in an even-handed way. They gave more money to a productive black artist (who countered the racial stereotype of "low achiever") than to a productive white artist, and less money to a needy black artist (who conformed to the racial stereotype of "poor") than to a needy white artist (see Figure 13.2) (McGillicuddy-De Lisi, Daly, & Neal, 2006).

The extent to which children hold racial and ethnic biases varies, depending on the following personal and situational factors:

Children who collaborate with members of other racial and ethnic groups are more likely to develop positive attitudes toward those who differ from themselves. These boys have many opportunities to work toward common goals at a summer camp.

- *A fixed view of personality traits.* Children who believe that people's personality traits are fixed rather than changeable often judge others as either "good" or "bad." Ignoring motives and circumstances, they readily form prejudices on the basis of limited information. For example, they might infer that "a new child at school who tells a lie to get other kids to like her" is simply a bad person (Levy & Dweck, 1999).
- *Overly high self-esteem.* Children (and adults) with very high self-esteem are more likely to hold racial and ethnic prejudices

(Baumeister et al., 2003; Bigler, Brown, & Markell, 2001). These individuals seem to belittle disadvantaged individuals or groups to justify their own extremely favorable self-evaluation.

■ *A social world in which people are sorted into groups.* The more adults highlight group distinctions for children, the more likely white children are to display prejudice.

REDUCING PREJUDICE ■ These findings offer guidance in how to reduce racial and ethnic prejudices. One promising approach involves inducing children to view others' traits as changeable, by discussing with them the many possible influences on those traits. The more school-age children and adolescents believe that people can change their personalities, the more they report liking and perceiving themselves as similar to members of disadvantaged out-groups, and the more willing they are to help the needy in their communities (Karafantis & Levy, 2004). Volunteering, in turn, may promote a changeable view of others by inducing children to imagine themselves in the place of the underprivileged and thus to appreciate the social conditions leading to disadvantage.

Intergroup contact, in which racially and ethnically different children become personally acquainted by collaborating on projects, is another way to reduce prejudice. Long-term contact in schools and communities seems most effective. In support of this view, white 5- and 6-year-olds attending a racially mixed school used their everyday experiences to form generally positive out-group attitudes (Aboud, 2003). Classrooms that expose children to diversity early and encourage them to value it prevent them from forming negative biases that are hard to undo.

Ask Yourself

Review   How does emotional self-regulation improve in middle childhood? What implications do these changes have for children's self-esteem?

Apply   Ten-year-old Marla says her classmate Bernadette will never get good grades because she's lazy. Jane believes that Bernadette tries but can't concentrate because her parents are divorcing. Why is Marla more likely than Jane to develop prejudices?

Connect   Cite examples of how older children's capacity to take more information into account enhances their emotional understanding, perspective taking, and moral understanding.

Reflect   Describe several efforts by schools, religious institutions, and youth organizations in your community to combat racial and ethnic prejudices in children. What would you do to increase the effectiveness of these efforts?

Peer Relations

In middle childhood, the society of peers becomes an increasingly important context for development. Peer contact, as we have seen, contributes to perspective taking and understanding of self and others. These developments, in turn, enhance peer interaction. Compared with preschoolers, school-age children resolve conflicts more effectively, using persuasion and compromise (Mayeux & Cillessen, 2003). Sharing, helping, and other prosocial acts also increase. In line with these changes, aggression declines, especially physical attacks (Tremblay, 2000). As we will see, other types of hostile aggression continue as school-age children form peer groups.

Peer Groups

TAKE A MOMENT... Watch children in the schoolyard or neighborhood, and notice how groups of three to a dozen or more often gather. In what ways are members of the same group noticeably alike?

Peer groups first form in middle childhood. These girls have probably established a social structure of leaders and followers as they gather for joint activities. Their relaxed body language and similar way of dressing suggest their strong sense of group belonging.

By the end of middle childhood, children display a strong desire for group belonging. They form **peer groups,** collectives that generate unique values and standards for behavior and a social structure of leaders and followers. Peer groups organize on the basis of proximity (being in the same classroom) and similarity in sex, ethnicity, academic achievement, popularity, and aggression (Rubin, Bukowski, & Parker, 2006). When groups are tracked for 3 to 6 weeks, membership changes very little. When they are followed for a year or longer, substantial change can occur, depending on whether children are reshuffled into different classrooms. For children who remain together, 50 to 70 percent of groups consist mostly of the same children from year to year (Cairns, Xie, & Leung, 1998).

The practices of these informal groups lead to a "peer culture" that typically involves a specialized vocabulary, dress code, and place to "hang out." Joey and three other boys formed a club whose "uniform" was T-shirts, jeans, and sneakers. They met at recess and on Saturdays in the tree house in Joey's backyard. Calling themselves "the pack," the boys devised a secret handshake and chose Joey as their leader. Their activities included improving the clubhouse, trading baseball cards, playing basketball and video games, and—just as important—keeping unwanted peers and adults out!

As children develop these exclusive associations, the codes of dress and behavior that grow out of them become more broadly influential. At school, children who deviate are often rebuffed. "Kissing up" to teachers, wearing the wrong clothes, or tattling on classmates can be grounds for critical glances and comments. These customs bind peers together, creating a sense of group identity. Within the group, children acquire many social skills—cooperation, leadership, followership, and loyalty to collective goals. Through these experiences, children experiment with and learn about social organizations.

As with other aspects of social reasoning, children evaluate a group's decision to exclude a peer in complex ways. Most view exclusion as wrong, even when they see themselves as different from the excluded child. And with age, children are less likely to endorse excluding someone because of unconventional appearance or behavior. Girls, especially, regard exclusion as unjust, perhaps because they experience it more often than boys (Killen, Crystal, & Watanabe, 2002). But when a peer threatens group functioning, by acting disruptively or by lacking skills to participate in a valued group activity (such as sports), both boys and girls say that exclusion is justified—a perspective that strengthens with age (Killen & Stangor, 2001).

Despite these sophisticated understandings, children do exclude unjustly, often using relationally aggressive tactics. Peer groups—at the instigation of their leaders, who can be skillfully aggressive—frequently oust no longer "respected" children. These cast-outs are profoundly wounded, and many find new group ties hard to establish. Some, whose own previous hostility toward outsiders reduces their chances of being included elsewhere, turn to other low-status peers with poor social skills (Werner & Crick, 2004). Socially anxious children, when ousted, often become increasingly peer-avoidant and thus more isolated (Gazelle & Rudolph, 2004). In either case, opportunities to acquire socially competent behavior diminish. As excluded children's class participation declines, their academic achievement suffers (Buhs, Ladd, & Herald, 2006). And some aggressive children—especially popular boys—link up with popular, nonaggressive agemates (Bagwell et al., 2000; Farmer et al., 2002). In these groups, mild-mannered children may accept and even support the antisocial acts of their dominant, antisocial associates, who pick fights with other groups or bully weaker children. Consequently, teachers and counselors must target both antisocial and mixed peer groups to reduce peer aggression.

School-age children's desire for group belonging can also be satisfied through formal group ties such as scouting, 4-H, and religious youth groups, where adult involvement holds in check the negative behaviors associated with children's informal peer groups. And through working on joint projects and helping in their communities, children gain in social and moral maturity (Vandell & Shumow, 1999).

peer groups Social units of peers who generate unique values and standards for behavior and a social structure of leaders and followers.

Friendships

Whereas peer groups provide children with insight into larger social structures, one-to-one friendships contribute to the development of trust and sensitivity. During the school years, friendship becomes more complex and psychologically based. Consider the following 8-year-old's ideas:

> *Why is Shelly your best friend?* Because she helps me when I'm sad, and she shares. . . . *What makes Shelly so special?* I've known her longer, I sit next to her and got to know her better. . . . *How come you like Shelly better than anyone else?* She's done the most for me. She never disagrees, she never eats in front of me, she never walks away when I'm crying, and she helps me on my homework. . . . *How do you get someone to like you?* . . . If you're nice to [your friends], they'll be nice to you. (Damon, 1988, pp. 80–81)

As these responses show, friendship has become a mutually agreed-on relationship in which children like each other's personal qualities and respond to one another's needs and desires. And once a friendship forms, *trust* becomes its defining feature. School-age children state that a good friendship is based on acts of kindness, signifying that each person can be counted on to support the other. Consequently, older children regard violations of trust, such as not helping when others need help, breaking promises, and gossiping behind the other's back, as serious breaches of friendship (Hartup & Abecassis, 2004; Selman, 1980). School-age children whom peers consider "trustworthy" have more friends and more easily make new friends (Rotenberg et al., 2004).

Because of these features, school-age children's friendships are more selective. Whereas preschoolers say they have lots of friends, by age 8 or 9, children name only a handful of good friends. Girls, who demand greater closeness than boys, are more exclusive in their friendships (Markovits, Benenson, & Dolensky, 2001).

In addition, children tend to select friends similar to themselves in age, sex, race, ethnicity, and SES. Friends also resemble one another in personality (sociability, inattention/hyperactivity, aggression, depression), peer popularity, academic achievement, and prosocial behavior (Hartup, 1999; Mariano & Harton, 2005). Note, however, that school and neighborhood characteristics also affect friendship choices. For example, in integrated schools, students are more optimistic about forming cross-race friendships on the basis of common interests, and they report having more cross-race friends (McGlothlin & Killen, 2005; Slavin & Cooper, 1999).

Over middle childhood, high-quality friendships remain fairly stable, usually lasting for several years (Berndt, 2004). Through them, children learn the importance of emotional commitment. They come to realize that close relationships can survive disagreements if both parties are secure in their liking for one another and resolve conflicts in ways that meet both partners' needs (Rose & Asher, 1999). As a result, friendship provides an important context in which children learn to tolerate criticism and resolve disputes.

Yet the impact of friendships on children's development depends on the nature of their friends. Children who bring kindness and compassion to their friendships strengthen each other's prosocial tendencies. But relationships between aggressive children often magnify antisocial acts. Aggressive girls' friendships are high in exchange of private feelings but also full of jealousy, conflict, and betrayal (Grotpeter & Crick, 1996; Werner & Crick, 2004). Among aggressive boys, friendships involve frequent expressions of anger, coercive statements, physical attacks, and enticements to rule-breaking behavior (Bagwell & Coie, 2004; Crick & Nelson, 2002; Dishion, Andrews, & Crosby, 1995). These findings indicate that the social problems of aggressive children operate within their closest peer ties. As we will see next, these children often acquire negative reputations in the wider world of peers.

During middle childhood, concepts of friendship become more psychologically based. These boys share their enjoyment of cooking, but they want to spend time together because they like each other's personal qualities.

© JUSTIN GUARIGLIA/THE IMAGE WORKS

These schoolgirls of Beijing, China, gather around a popular classmate. Popular children, whom many peers say they "like very much," are often *prosocial* youngsters who are academically successful, socially sensitive, and cooperative. But some popular girls are *antisocial*—admired for their skill at controlling peer relationships through relational aggression. Over time, their popularity declines, and they are at risk for rejection.

Peer Acceptance

Peer acceptance refers to likability—the extent to which a child is viewed by a group of agemates, such as classmates, as a worthy social partner. Unlike friendship, likability is not a mutual relationship but a one-sided perspective, involving the group's view of an individual. Nevertheless, certain social skills that contribute to friendship also enhance peer acceptance. Better-accepted children tend to have more friends and more positive relationships with friends (Gest, Graham-Bermann, & Hartup, 2001).

To assess peer acceptance, researchers usually use self-reports that measure *social preferences*—for example, asking children to identify classmates whom they "like very much" or "like very little." Another approach assesses *social prominence*—children's judgments of whom most of their classmates admire. Only moderate correspondence exists between the classmates children identify as prominent (looked up to by many others) and those they say they personally prefer (LaFontana & Cillessen, 1999).

Children's self-reports yield four general categories of peer acceptance:

- **Popular children,** who get many positive votes
- **Rejected children,** who are actively disliked
- **Controversial children,** who receive many votes, both positive and negative
- **Neglected children,** who are seldom mentioned, either positively or negatively

About two-thirds of students in a typical elementary school classroom fit one of these categories (Coie, Dodge, & Coppotelli, 1982). The remaining one-third, who do not receive extreme scores, are considered *average* in peer acceptance.

Peer acceptance is a powerful predictor of current as well as later psychological adjustment. Rejected children, especially, are unhappy, alienated, poorly achieving children with low self-esteem. Both teachers and parents rate them as having a wide range of emotional and social problems. Peer rejection in middle childhood is also strongly associated with poor school performance, absenteeism, dropping out, antisocial behavior, and delinquency in adolescence and with criminality in emerging adulthood (Bagwell, Newcomb, & Bukowski, 1998; Laird et al., 2001; Parker et al., 1995).

However, earlier influences—children's characteristics combined with parenting practices—may largely explain the link between peer acceptance and adjustment. School-age children with peer-relationship problems are more likely to have experienced family stress due to low income, insensitive child rearing, and coercive discipline (Cowan & Cowan, 2004). Nevertheless, as we will see, rejected children evoke reactions from peers that contribute to their unfavorable development.

peer acceptance The extent to which a child is viewed by a group of agemates as a worthy social partner.

popular children Children who get many positive votes on assessments of peer acceptance.

rejected children Children who are actively disliked and get many negative votes on assessments of peer acceptance.

controversial children Children who get many votes, both positive and negative, on assessments of peer acceptance.

DETERMINANTS OF PEER ACCEPTANCE ■ Why is one child liked while another is rejected? A wealth of research reveals that social behavior plays a powerful role.

Popular Children. Many popular children are kind and considerate. These **popular-prosocial children** usually combine academic and social competence. They perform well in school, communicate with peers in sensitive, friendly, and cooperative ways, and solve social problems constructively (Cillessen & Bellmore, 2004).

But other popular children are admired for their socially adept yet belligerent behavior. This smaller subtype, **popular-antisocial children,** includes "tough" boys—who have athletic skill but are poor students who cause trouble and defy adult authority—and relationally aggressive boys and girls who enhance their own status by ignoring, excluding, and spreading rumors about other children (Cillessen & Mayeux, 2004; Rodkin et al., 2000; Rose, Swenson, & Waller, 2004). Despite their aggressiveness, peers view these youths as "cool," perhaps because of their athletic ability and sophisticated though devious social skills. Although peer admiration gives them some protection against lasting adjustment difficulties, their antisocial acts require intervention (Prinstein & La Greca, 2004; Rodkin et al., 2006). With age, peers like these high-status, aggressive youths less and less, and may eventually reject them.

Rejected Children. Rejected children display a wide range of negative social behaviors. The largest subtype, **rejected-aggressive children,** show high rates of conflict, physical and relational aggression, and hyperactive, inattentive, and impulsive behavior. They are more belligerent than popular-aggressive children and are also deficient in perspective taking and emotion regulation. For example, they tend to misinterpret the innocent behaviors of peers as hostile and to blame others for their social difficulties (Coie & Dodge, 1998; Crick, Casas, & Nelson, 2002; Hoza et al., 2005).

In contrast, **rejected-withdrawn children** are passive and socially awkward. These timid children are overwhelmed by social anxiety, hold negative expectations for how peers will treat them, and worry about being scorned and attacked. Like their aggressive counterparts, they typically feel like retaliating rather than compromising in conflicts with peers, although they less often act on those feelings (Hart et al., 2000; Ladd & Burgess, 1999; Troop-Gordon & Asher, 2005).

Rejected children are excluded by peers as early as kindergarten. Rejection, in turn, further impairs these children's biased social information processing, heightening their hostility (Dodge et al., 2003). Soon rejected children's classroom participation declines, their feelings of loneliness rise, their academic achievement falters, and they want to avoid school (Buhs & Ladd, 2001). Most have few friends, and some have none—a circumstance that is linked to low self-esteem, mistrust of peers, and severe adjustment difficulties (Ladd & Troop-Gordon, 2003).

Both rejected-aggressive and rejected-withdrawn children are at risk for peer harassment. But as the Biology and Environment box on page 502 reveals, rejected-withdrawn children are especially likely to be targeted by bullies because of their inept, submissive style of interaction (Sandstrom & Cillessen, 2003).

Controversial and Neglected Children. Consistent with the mixed peer opinion they engender, controversial children display a blend of positive and negative social behaviors. They are hostile and disruptive, but they also engage in high rates of positive, prosocial acts. Though some peers dislike them, they have qualities that protect them from exclusion. They have as many friends as popular children and are happy with their peer relationships (Newcomb, Bukowski, & Pattee, 1993). But like their popular-antisocial counterparts, they often bully agemates to get their way and engage in calculated relational aggression to sustain their social dominance (DeRosier & Thomas, 2003). The social status of controversial children often changes over time as agemates react to their mixed behavior.

Perhaps the most surprising finding is that neglected children, once thought to be in need of treatment, are usually well-adjusted. Although they engage in low rates of interaction, most are just as socially skilled as average children. They do not report feeling unhappy about their social life, and when they want to, they can break away from their usual pattern of playing alone (Harrist et al., 1997; Ladd & Burgess, 1999). Probably for this reason, neglected status (like controversial status) is usually temporary. Neglected children remind us that an outgoing, gregarious personality style is not the only path to emotional well-being.

HELPING REJECTED CHILDREN ■ A variety of interventions exist to improve the peer relations and psychological adjustment of rejected children. Most involve coaching, modeling, and reinforcing positive social skills, such as how to initiate interaction with a peer, cooperate in play, and respond to another child with friendly emotion and approval. Several of these programs have produced gains in social competence and peer acceptance still present from several weeks to a year later (Asher & Rose, 1997). Combining social-skills training with other treatments

neglected children
Children who are seldom mentioned, either positively or negatively, on assessments of peer acceptance.

popular-prosocial children
A subtype of popular children who combine academic and social competence.

popular-antisocial children
A subtype of popular children consisting of "tough," athletically skilled but defiant, trouble-causing boys and of relationally aggressive boys and girls who are admired for their sophisticated but devious social skills.

rejected-aggressive children A subtype of rejected children who show high rates of conflict, physical and relational aggression, and hyperactive, inattentive, and impulsive behavior.

rejected-withdrawn children A subtype of rejected children who are passive, socially awkward, and overwhelmed by social anxiety.

Biology and Environment

Bullies and Their Victims

Follow the activities of aggressive children over a school day, and you will see that they reserve their hostilities for certain peers. A particularly destructive form of interaction is **peer victimization,** in which certain children become frequent targets of verbal and physical attacks or other forms of abuse. What sustains these repeated assault–retreat cycles between pairs of children?

Research indicates that about 10 to 20 percent of children are bullies, while 15 to 30 percent are repeatedly victimized. Most bullies are boys who use both physical and verbal attacks, but girls sometimes bombard a vulnerable classmate with verbal hostility (Pepler et al., 2004; Rigby, 2004). A substantial number of bullies are high-status youngsters. Some are liked for their leadership or athletic abilities, but most are disliked—or eventually become so—because of their cruelty (Vaillancourt, Hymel, & McDougall, 2003). Nevertheless, peers rarely

Children who are victimized by bullies tend to be physically weak, rejected by peers, and afraid to defend themselves—characteristics that make them easy targets. Most bullies are boys who use both physical and relational aggression, but some girls are bullies, too, bombarding their victims with relational hostility.

help victims of bullying, and about 20 to 30 percent of onlookers actually encourage bullies, even joining in (Salmivalli & Voeten, 2004).

Chronic victims are passive when active behavior is expected. On the playground, they hang around chatting or wander on their own. When bullied, they reinforce perpetrators by giving in to their demands, crying, and assuming defensive postures (Boulton, 1999). Biologically based traits—an inhibited temperament and a frail physical appearance—contribute to victimization. But victims also have histories of resistant attachment, overly controlling child rearing, and maternal overprotection—parenting behaviors that prompt anxiety, low self-esteem, and dependency, resulting in a fearful demeanor that marks these children as vulnerable (Snyder et al., 2003). Victimization leads to adjustment difficulties that may include depression, loneliness, low self-esteem, poor school performance, disruptive behavior, and school avoidance (Kochenderfer-Ladd & Wardrop, 2001; Paul & Cillessen, 2003).

In a recent survey of several hundred middle-school students, about one in four said they had experienced "cyberbullying"—bullying through e-mail or other electronic tools. And about half the students reported knowing someone who was being cyberbullied. As with other forms of bullying, boys were more likely than girls to be cyberbullies, and almost half of cyberbullies engaged in this type of harassment more than three times. Most victims and bystanders did not report the incidents to adults (Li, 2006).

Aggression and victimization are not polar opposites. One-third to one-half of victims are also aggressive, picking fights or retaliating with relational aggression. Occasionally, they strike back at powerful bullies, who respond by abusing them again—a cycle that sustains their victim status (Kochenderfer-Ladd, 2003). Among rejected children, bully/victims are the most despised. They often have histories of extremely maladaptive parenting, including child abuse.

This combination of highly negative home and peer experiences places them at severe risk for maladjustment (Schwartz, Proctor, & Chien, 2001).

Interventions that change victimized children's negative opinions of themselves and that teach them to respond in nonreinforcing ways to their attackers are helpful. Another way to assist victimized children is to help them acquire the social skills needed to form and maintain a gratifying friendship. When children have a close friend to whom they can turn for help, bullying episodes usually end quickly. Anxious, withdrawn children with a prosocial best friend have fewer adjustment problems than victims with no close friends (Bollmer et al., 2005; Fox & Boulton, 2006).

Although changing the behavior of victimized children can help, this does not mean they are to blame. The best way to reduce bullying is to change youth environments (including school, sports programs, recreation centers, and neighborhoods), promoting prosocial attitudes and behaviors and enlisting young people's cooperation. Effective approaches include developing school and community codes against bullying, teaching child bystanders to intervene, enlisting parents' assistance in changing bullies' behaviors, and (if necessary) moving socially prominent bullies to another class or school (Leadbeater & Hoglund, 2006; Smith, Ananiadou, & Cowie, 2003).

In Canada, government leaders, national organizations, community groups, and schools are collaborating in the Canadian Initiative for the Prevention of Bullying, www.bullying.org, which aims to create nationwide safe, respectful environments for children and adolescents. The U.S. Department of Health and Human Services has launched a media campaign, Stop Bullying Now, www.stopbullyingnow.hrsa.gov, which raises awareness of the harmfulness of bullying through TV and radio public service announcements and provides parents, teachers, and students with information on prevention.

increases their effectiveness. Rejected children are often poor students, and their low academic self-esteem magnifies their negative reactions to teachers and classmates. Intensive academic tutoring improves school achievement and social acceptance (O'Neil et al., 1997).

Still another approach focuses on training in perspective taking and social problem solving. Many rejected-aggressive children are unaware of their poor social skills and do not take responsibility for their social failures (Mrug, Hoza, & Gerdes, 2001). Rejected-withdrawn children, on the other hand, are likely to develop a *learned-helpless* approach to peer acceptance—concluding, after repeated rebuffs, that they will never be liked (Wichmann, Coplan, & Daniels, 2004). Both types of rejected children need help attributing their peer difficulties to internal, changeable causes.

Finally, because rejected children's socially incompetent behaviors often originate in harsh, intrusive, authoritarian parenting, interventions that focus on the child alone may not be sufficient (Rubin, Bukowski, & Parker, 2006). If parent–child interaction does not change, children may soon return to their old behavior patterns.

Gender Typing

Children's understanding of gender roles broadens in middle childhood, and their gender identities (views of themselves as relatively masculine or feminine) change as well. We will see that development differs for boys and girls, and it can vary considerably across cultures.

Gender-Stereotyped Beliefs

By age 5, gender stereotyping of activities and occupations is well-established. During the school years, knowledge of stereotypes increases in the less obvious areas of personality traits and achievement.

PERSONALITY TRAITS ■ Research in many cultures reveals that stereotyping of personality traits increases steadily, resembling that of adults around age 11 (Best, 2001; Heyman & Legare, 2004). For example, children regard "tough," "aggressive," "rational," and "dominant" as masculine and "gentle," "sympathetic," and "dependent" as feminine (Serbin, Powlishta, & Gulko, 1993).

Children derive these distinctions from observing sex differences in behavior as well as from adult treatment. Adults, for example, tend to demand greater independence from boys. When helping a child with a task, parents (especially fathers) behave in a more mastery-oriented fashion with sons, setting higher standards, explaining concepts, and pointing out important features of tasks—particularly during gender-typed pursuits, such as science activities (Tenenbaum & Leaper, 2003; Tenenbaum et al., 2005). Furthermore, parents less often encourage girls to make their own decisions. And both parents and teachers more often praise boys for knowledge and accomplishment, girls for obedience (Good & Brophy, 2003; Leaper, Anderson, & Sanders, 1998; Pomerantz & Ruble, 1998).

ACHIEVEMENT AREAS ■ Shortly after entering elementary school, school-age children quickly figure out which academic subjects and skill areas are "masculine" and which are "feminine." They often regard reading, spelling, art, and music as more for girls and mathematics, science, athletics, and mechanical skills as more for boys (Eccles, Jacobs, & Harold, 1990; Jacobs & Weisz, 1994). These stereotypes—and the attitudes and behaviors of parents and teachers that promote them—influence children's preferences for certain subjects and, in turn, how well they do at them. As we saw in our discussion of self-esteem, boys feel more competent than girls at math, science, and athletics, and girls feel more competent than boys at language arts—even when children of equal skill level are compared (Bhanot & Jovanovic, 2005; Freedman-Doan et al., 2000; Hong, Veach, & Lawrenz, 2003).

Adults' gender-typed judgments of children's competence can have lasting consequences. In one study, mothers' early perceptions of their children's competence at math continued to

peer victimization A destructive form of peer interaction in which certain children become frequent targets of verbal and physical attacks or other forms of abuse.

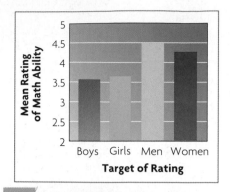

FIGURE 13.3

School-age girls' ratings of the math ability of children and adults. The girls regarded children of each gender as equally good at math. Their ratings of adults, however, reverted to the stereotype that men were better at math than women. (Adapted from Steele, 2003.)

predict daughters' self-perceptions and also career choices in their mid-twenties. Young women whose mothers had regarded them as highly capable at math were far more likely to choose a physical science career (Bleeker & Jacobs, 2004). Yet mothers rarely made such optimistic judgments about girls.

Furthermore, girls often adopt a more general stereotype of males as smarter than females, which they apply to themselves. In a study of over 2,000 second to sixth graders from diverse cultures (Eastern and Western Europe, Japan, Russia, and the United States), girls consistently had higher school grades than boys. Yet despite being aware of their better performance, girls did not report stronger beliefs in their own ability but, compared with boys, discounted their talent (Stetsenko et al., 2000). Apparently, gender stereotyping of mental ability occurs in many parts of the world.

One encouraging sign is that some children's gender-stereotyped beliefs about achievement may be changing. In a recent investigation, U.S. elementary school girls from economically advantaged homes regarded children of each gender as equally good at math. But when the girls were asked about adults, their judgments reverted to the stereotype—that men were better than women (see Figure 13.3). Boys, in contrast, held stereotyped views of math ability for both children and adults (Steele, 2003).

TOWARD GREATER FLEXIBILITY ■ Clearly school-age children are knowledgeable about a wide variety of gender stereotypes. At the same time, they develop a more flexible, open-minded view of what males and females *can do,* a trend that continues into adolescence. As they develop the capacity to integrate conflicting social cues, children realize that a person's sex is not a certain predictor of his or her personality traits, activities, and behaviors (Trautner et al., 2005). By the end of the school years, children regard gender typing as socially rather than biologically influenced (Taylor, 1996). Nevertheless, acknowledging that people *can* cross gender lines does not mean that children always *approve* of doing so. They take a harsh view of certain violations—boys playing with dolls and wearing girls' clothing, girls acting noisily and roughly. They are especially intolerant when boys engage in these "cross-gender" acts, which children regard as nearly as bad as moral transgressions (Blakemore, 2003; Levy, Taylor, & Gelman, 1995).

Gender Identity and Behavior

Boys' and girls' gender identities follow different paths in middle childhood. From third to sixth grade, boys tend to strengthen their identification with "masculine" personality traits, whereas girls' identification with "feminine" traits declines. Girls begin to describe themselves as having some "other-gender" characteristics (Serbin, Powlishta, & Gulko, 1993). This difference is also evident in children's activities. Boys usually stick to "masculine" pursuits, while girls experiment with a wider range of options. Besides cooking, sewing, and baby-sitting, they join organized sports teams and work on science projects. And girls, more often than boys, consider future work roles stereotyped for the other gender, such as firefighter and astronomer (Liben & Bigler, 2002).

These changes reflect a mixture of cognitive and social forces. School-age children of both sexes are aware that society attaches greater prestige to "masculine" characteristics. For example, they rate "masculine" occupations as having higher status than "feminine" occupations (Liben, Bigler, & Krogh, 2001). Messages from adults and peers are also influential. In Chapter 10, we saw that parents (especially fathers) are far less tolerant when sons, as opposed to daughters, cross gender lines. Similarly, a tomboyish girl can make her way into boys' activities without losing the approval of her female peers, but a boy who hangs out with girls is likely to be ridiculed and rejected.

As school-age children characterize themselves in terms of general dispositions, their gender identity expands to include the following self-evaluations, which greatly affect their adjustment:

■ *Gender typicality*—the degree to which the child feels similar to others of the same gender. Although children need not be highly gender typed to view themselves as gender-typical, their psychological well-being depends, to some degree, on feeling that they "fit in" with their same-sex peers.

During middle childhood, girls feel freer than boys to experiment with "cross-gender" activities. This 9-year-old perfects her wood-carving skills.

FIGURE 13.4

Percentage of children and adolescents saying "It's OK" to exclude an agemate from a peer-group activity on the basis of gender and ethnicity. When asked about excluding an other-sex or other-ethnicity peer from a peer-group activity (a music club in which members trade CDs), many more young people said that it is OK to do so on the basis of gender than on the basis of ethnicity. Willingness to exclude on the basis of gender increased with age, with many participants justifying their decision by pointing to sex differences in interests and communication styles. (Adapted from Killen et al., 2002.)

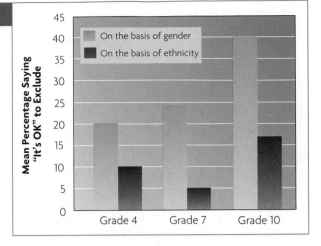

- *Gender contentedness*—the degree to which the child feels comfortable with his or her gender assignment, which also promotes happiness and satisfaction with oneself.
- *Felt pressure to conform to gender roles*—the degree to which the child feels parents and peers disapprove of his or her gender-related traits. Because such pressure reduces the likelihood that children will explore options related to their interests and talents, children who feel strong gender-typed pressure are often distressed.

In a longitudinal study of third through seventh graders, *gender-typical* and *gender-contented* children gained in self-esteem over the following year. In contrast, children who were *gender-atypical* and *gender-discontented* declined in self-worth. Furthermore, gender-atypical children who reported intense pressure to conform to gender roles experienced serious difficulties—withdrawal, sadness, disappointment, and anxiety (Yunger, Carver, & Perry, 2004).

Clearly, how children feel about themselves in relation to their gender group becomes vitally important in middle childhood and adolescence, and those who experience rejection because of their gender-atypical traits suffer profoundly. **TAKE A MOMENT...** Return to the case of David, the boy who was reared as a girl, on page 393 in Chapter 10, and note how his dissatisfaction with his gender assignment, together with severe peer condemnation, severely impaired his adjustment.

Peers, Gender Typing, and Culture

In many cultures, sex-segregated peer associations strengthen during middle childhood and continue to contribute powerfully to gender-role learning (see page 395 in Chapter 10). As with ethnicity, the majority of children regard excluding an agemate from peer group activities on the basis of gender as unfair. But between fourth and seventh grade, more young people—especially boys—say it is OK to exclude on the basis of gender than on ethnicity (see Figure 13.4). When asked to explain, they point to concerns about group functioning related to sex differences in interests and communication styles—boys' preference for active pursuits and commanding, forceful behavior, girls' preference for quiet activities, politeness, and compromise (Killen et al., 2002, p. 56).

Although sex segregation is pervasive, interaction patterns vary with culture. African-American and Hispanic-American lower-SES girls, for example, are more assertive and independent in their interactions with one another and with boys than are Caucasian-American girls (Goodwin, 1998). A comparison of Chinese and U.S. girls' play revealed similar differences: Chinese girls used more commands, complaints, and critical statements when interacting with both same- and other-sex peers. And Chinese boys frequently combined commands with justifying and appeasing statements that reduced the roughness of their communication: "Better not open that. It might spill." "I'll do it. I'm here to help you!" (Kyratzis & Guo, 2001).

In collectivist societies, where group cohesion is highly valued, children may not feel a need to work as hard at maintaining same-sex peer relations through traditional interaction patterns. In addition to reducing children's ethnic prejudices (see pages 496–497), ethnically integrated classrooms might reduce gender-typed peer communication as some children's interaction styles influence those of others.

Ask Yourself

Review   Describe changes in friendship during middle childhood.

Apply   What changes in parent–child relationships are probably necessary to help rejected children?

Connect   Return to Chapter 10, page 395, and review the concept of androgyny. Which of the two sexes is more androgynous in middle childhood, and why? (pp. 504–505)

Reflect   As a school-age child, did you have classmates you would classify as popular-aggressive? What were they like, and why do you think peers admired them?

Family Influences

As children move into school, peer, and community contexts, the parent–child relationship changes. We will see that gradual lessening of direct control supports development as long as parental warmth and involvement are sustained. Our discussion will also reveal that families in industrialized nations have become more diverse. Today, there are fewer births per family unit, more lesbian and gay parents who are open about their sexual orientation, and more never-married parents. Further, high rates of divorce, remarriage, and maternal employment have reshaped the family system. **TAKE A MOMENT...** As you consider this array of family forms, note how children's well-being, in each instance, depends on the quality of family interaction, which is sustained by supportive ties to kin and community and by favorable public policies.

Parent–Child Relationships

In middle childhood, the amount of time children spend with parents declines dramatically. Children's growing independence means that parents must deal with new issues. "I've struggled with how many chores to assign, how much allowance to give, whether their friends are good influences, and what to do about problems at school," Rena remarked. "And then there's the challenge of keeping track of them when they're out—or even when they're home and I'm not there to see what's going on."

Despite these new concerns, child rearing becomes easier for parents who established an authoritative style during the early years. Reasoning is more effective with school-age children because of their greater capacity for logical thinking and their increased respect for parents' expert knowledge (Collins, Madsen, & Susman-Stillman, 2002). When parents communicate openly with children and engage in joint decision making when possible, children are more likely to listen to parents' perspectives in situations where compliance is vital (Kuczynski & Lollis, 2002; Russell, Mize, & Bissaker, 2004).

As children demonstrate that they can manage daily activities and responsibilities, effective parents gradually shift control from adult to child. They do not let go entirely but, rather, engage in **coregulation,** a form of supervision in which they exercise general oversight while letting children take charge of moment-by-moment decision making. Coregulation grows out of a warm, cooperative relationship between parent and child based on give-and-take and mutual respect. Parents must guide and monitor from a distance and effectively communicate expectations when they are with their children. And children must inform parents of their whereabouts, activities, and problems so parents can intervene when necessary (Maccoby, 1984). Coregulation supports and protects children while preparing them for adolescence, when they will make many important decisions themselves.

coregulation A form of supervision in which parents exercise general oversight while letting children take charge of moment-by-moment decision making.

As at younger ages, mothers spend more time than fathers with school-age children and know more about children's everyday activities, although fathers often are highly involved. Both parents, however, tend to devote more time to children of their own sex (Crouter et al., 1999; Lamb & Lewis, 2004). In parents' separate activities with children, mothers are more concerned with caregiving and ensuring that children meet responsibilities for homework, after-school lessons, and chores. Fathers, especially those with sons, focus on achievement-related and recreational pursuits (Collins & Russell, 1991). But when both parents are present, fathers engage in as much caregiving as mothers.

Although school-age children often press for greater independence, they also know how much they need their parents' support. In one study, fifth and sixth graders described parents as the most influential people in their lives, often turning to them for affection, advice, enhancement of self-worth, and assistance with everyday problems (Furman & Buhrmester, 1992). And in a longitudinal survey of more than 13,000 nationally representative U.S. parents, those who were warm and involved, monitored their child's activities, and avoided coercive discipline were more likely to have academically and socially competent children. Using these authoritative strategies in middle childhood predicted reduced engagement in antisocial behavior when children reached adolescence (Amato & Fowler, 2002).

Siblings

In addition to parents and friends, siblings are important sources of support for school-age children. Yet sibling rivalry tends to increase in middle childhood. As children participate in a wider range of activities, parents often compare siblings' traits and accomplishments. The child who gets less parental affection, more disapproval, or fewer material resources is likely to be resentful and show poorer adjustment over time (Dunn, 2004; Tamrouti-Makkink et al., 2004).

For same-sex siblings who are close in age, parental comparisons are more frequent, resulting in more quarreling, antagonism, and adjustment difficulties. This effect is particularly strong when parents are under stress as a result of financial worries, marital conflict, or single parenthood (Jenkins, Rasbash, & O'Connor, 2003). Parents whose energies are drained become less careful about being fair. Children react especially intensely when fathers prefer one child. Perhaps because fathers, overall, spend less time with children than mothers, their favoritism is more noticeable and triggers greater anger (Brody, Stoneman, & McCoy, 1992).

To reduce this rivalry, siblings often strive to be different from one another. For example, two brothers I know deliberately selected different athletic pursuits and musical instruments. If the older one did especially well at an activity, the younger one did not want to try it. Parents can limit these effects by making an effort not to compare children, but some feedback about their competencies is inevitable. As siblings attempt to win recognition for their own uniqueness, they shape important aspects of each other's development.

Although conflict rises, most school-age siblings rely on one another for companionship and assistance. When researchers asked siblings about shared daily activities, children mentioned that older siblings often helped younger siblings with academic and peer challenges. And both offered one another help with family issues (Tucker, McHale, & Crouter, 2001). But for siblings to reap these benefits, parental encouragement of warm sibling ties is vitally important. The warmer their relationship, the more siblings resolve disagreements constructively and turn to one another for emotional support (Howe et al., 2001; Ram & Ross, 2001).

Finally, when siblings feel affection for one another, the older sibling's academic and social competence tends to "rub off on" the younger sibling, fostering higher achievement and more positive peer relations (Brody & Murry, 2001; Lamarche et al., 2006). At the same time, older siblings with conflict-ridden peer relations tend to transmit their physically or relationally aggressive styles to their younger brothers and sisters (Ostrov, Crick, & Stauffacher, 2006).

Although sibling rivalry tends to increase in middle childhood, siblings also provide one another with emotional support and help with difficult tasks.

Only Children

Although sibling relationships bring many benefits, they are not essential for normal development. Contrary to popular belief, only children are not spoiled. In some respects, they are even advantaged. North American children growing up in one-child families are higher in self-esteem and achievement motivation, do better in school, and attain higher levels of education (Falbo, 1992). One reason may be that only children have somewhat closer relationships with parents, who may exert more pressure for mastery and accomplishment. Furthermore, only children have just as many close, high-quality friends as children with siblings. They do tend to be less well accepted in the peer group, perhaps because they have not had opportunities to learn effective conflict-resolution strategies from sibling interactions (Kitzmann, Cohen, & Lockwood, 2002).

Favorable development also characterizes only children in China, where a one-child family policy has been strictly enforced in urban areas for two decades to control overpopulation. Compared with agemates who have siblings, Chinese only children are advanced in cognitive development and academic achievement (Falbo & Poston, 1993; Jiao, Ji, & Jing, 1996). They also feel more emotionally secure, perhaps because government disapproval promotes tension in families with more than one child (Yang et al., 1995). Chinese mothers usually ensure that their children have regular contact with first cousins (who are considered siblings). Perhaps as a result, Chinese only children do not differ from agemates with siblings in social skills and peer acceptance (Hart, Newell, & Olsen, 2003). The next generation of Chinese only children, however, will have no first cousins.

Gay and Lesbian Families

Several million American and tens of thousands of Canadian gay men and lesbians are parents, most through previous heterosexual marriages, some through adoption, and a growing number through reproductive technologies (Ambert, 2005; Patterson, 2002). In the past, because of laws assuming that homosexuals could not be adequate parents, those who divorced a heterosexual partner lost custody of their children. Today, some states and the nation of Canada hold that sexual orientation in itself is irrelevant to custody. A few U.S. states, however, ban gay and lesbian adoptions (Laird, 2003).

Most research on homosexual parents and children is limited to volunteer samples. Findings of these investigations indicate that gay and lesbian parents are as committed to and effective at child rearing as heterosexual parents (Tasker, 2005). Also, whether born to or adopted by their parents or conceived through donor insemination, children in gay and lesbian families did not differ from the children of heterosexuals in mental health, peer relations, and gender identity (Allen & Burrell, 1996; Flaks et al., 1995; Golombok & Tasker, 1996). Two additional studies, which surmounted the potential bias associated with volunteer samples by including all lesbian-mother families who had conceived children at a fertility clinic, also reported that children were developing favorably (Brewaeys et al., 1997; Chan, Raboy, & Patterson, 1998). Likewise, among participants drawn from a representative sample of British mothers and their 7-year-olds, children reared in lesbian-mother families did not differ from children reared in heterosexual families in adjustment and gender-role preferences (Golombok et al., 2003).

Virtually all studies have concluded that children of gay and lesbian parents do not differ from other children in sexual orientation: The large majority are heterosexual (Tasker, 2005). But some evidence suggests that more adolescents from homosexual families experiment for a time with partners of both sexes, perhaps as a result of being reared in families and communities highly tolerant of nonconformity and difference (Bos, van Balen, & van den Boom, 2004; Stacey & Biblarz, 2001).

A major concern of gay and lesbian parents is that their children will be stigmatized by their parents' sexual orientation. Most studies indicate that incidents of teasing or bullying are rare because parents and children carefully manage the information they reveal to others (Tasker, 2005). But in an Australian study, even though most third to tenth graders were guarded about discussing their parents' relationship with peers, nearly half reported harassment (Ray & Gregory, 2001). Overall, children of gay and lesbian parents can be distinguished from other children mainly by issues related to living in a nonsupportive society.

CREATAS IMAGES/JUPITER IMAGES

Gay and lesbian parents are as committed to and as effective at child rearing as heterosexual parents. Their children are well adjusted, and the large majority develop a heterosexual orientation.

Never-Married Single-Parent Families

About 10 percent of American children and 5 percent of Canadian children live with a single parent who has never married and does not have a partner. Of these parents, about 90 percent are mothers, 10 percent fathers (Ambert, 2006; U.S. Census Bureau, 2007b). In recent years, more single women over age 30 in high-status occupations have become parents. However, they are still few in number, and little is known about their children's development.

In the United States, the largest group of never-married parents is African-American young women. Over 60 percent of births to black mothers in their twenties are to women without a partner, compared with 13 percent of births to white women (U.S. Census Bureau, 2007b). African-American women postpone marriage more and childbirth less than women in other American ethnic groups. Job loss, persisting unemployment, and consequent lack of opportunities for many black men to provide economically for their families have contributed to the number of African-American never-married, single-mother families.

Never-married black mothers tap the extended family, especially their own mothers and sometimes male relatives, for help in rearing their children (Gasden, 1999; Jayakody & Kalil, 2002). For about one-third, marriage—not necessarily to the child's biological father—occurs within nine years after birth of the first child (Wu, Bumpass, & Musick, 2001). These couples function much like other first-marriage parents. Their children often are unaware that the father is a stepfather, and parents do not report the child-rearing difficulties typical of blended families (Ganong & Coleman, 1994).

Still, never-married parenthood generally increases financial hardship for low-SES women. Nearly 50 percent of white mothers and 60 percent of black mothers have a second child while unmarried. And they are far less likely than divorced mothers to receive paternal child support payments (Lipman et al., 2002; Wu, Bumpass, & Musick, 2001). Consequently, many children in single-mother homes display adjustment problems associated with economic hardship and living in run-down neighborhoods (Kotchick, Dorsey, & Heller, 2005). Furthermore, children of never-married mothers who lack a father's warmth and involvement achieve less well in school and engage in more antisocial behavior than children in low-SES, first-marriage families (Coley, 1998). But marriage to the child's biological father benefits children only when the father is a reliable source of economic and emotional support. For example, when a mother pairs up with an antisocial father, her child is at far greater risk for conduct problems than if she had reared the child alone (Jaffee et al., 2003). Overall, strengthening social support, education, and employment opportunities for low-income parents would greatly enhance the well-being of unmarried mothers and their children.

Divorce

Children's interactions with parents and siblings are affected by other aspects of family life. Joey and Lizzie's relationship, Rena told me, had been particularly negative only a few years before. Joey pushed, hit, taunted, and called Lizzie names. Lizzie tried to retaliate but, overwhelmed by Joey's physical advantage, usually ended up running in tears to her mother. Joey and Lizzie's fighting coincided with their parents' growing marital unhappiness. When Joey was 8 and Lizzie 5, their father, Drake, moved out.

The children were not alone in experiencing this traumatic event. Between 1960 and 1985, divorce rates in Western nations rose dramatically before stabilizing in most countries. The United States has the highest divorce rate in the world, Canada the sixth highest (see Figure 13.5). Of the 45 percent of American

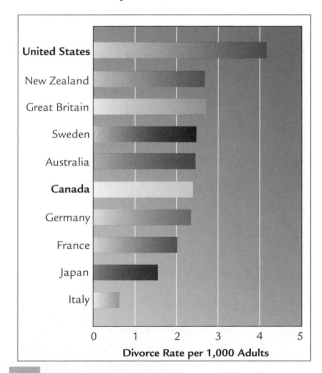

FIGURE 13.5

Divorce rates in 10 industrialized nations. The U.S. divorce rate is the highest in the industrialized world, far exceeding divorce rates in other countries. The Canadian divorce rate is the sixth highest. (Adapted from U.S. Census Bureau, 2007b; United Nations, 2002.)

and 30 percent of Canadian marriages that end in divorce, half involve children. At any given time, one-fourth of American and one-fifth of Canadian children live in single-parent households. Although most reside with their mothers, the percentage in father-headed households has increased steadily, to about 12 percent in both nations (Federal Interagency Forum on Child and Family Statistics, 2006b; Statistics Canada, 2005c).

Children of divorce spend an average of five years in a single-parent home—almost a third of childhood. For many, divorce leads to new family relationships. About two-thirds of divorced parents marry again. Half their children eventually experience a third major change—the end of their parent's second marriage (Hetherington & Kelly, 2002).

These figures reveal that divorce is not a single event in the lives of parents and children. Instead, it is a transition that leads to a variety of new living arrangements, accompanied by changes in housing, income, and family roles and responsibilities. Since the 1960s, many studies have reported that marital breakup is stressful for children. But research also reveals great individual differences (Hetherington, 2002). How well children fare depends on many factors: the custodial parent's psychological health, the child's characteristics, and social supports within the family and surrounding community.

IMMEDIATE CONSEQUENCES ■ "Things were worst during the period when Drake and I decided to separate," Rena reflected. "We fought over division of our belongings and the custody of the children, and the kids suffered. Sobbing, Lizzie told me she was 'sorry she made Daddy go away.' Joey kicked and threw things at home and didn't do his work at school. In the midst of everything, I could hardly deal with their problems. We had to sell the house; I couldn't afford it alone. And I needed a better-paying job."

Rena's description captures conditions in many newly divorced households. Family conflict often rises as parents try to settle disputes over children and possessions. Once one parent moves out, additional events threaten supportive interactions between parents and children. Mother-headed households typically experience a sharp drop in income. In the United States and Canada, the majority of divorced mothers with young children live in poverty, getting less than the full amount of child support from the absent father or none at all (Ambert, 2006; Children's Defense Fund, 2006). They often have to move to lower-cost housing, reducing supportive ties to neighbors and friends.

The transition from marriage to divorce typically leads to high maternal stress, depression, and anxiety and to a disorganized family situation (Hope, Power, & Rodgers, 1999). "Meals and bedtimes were at all hours, the house didn't get cleaned, and I stopped taking Joey and Lizzie on weekend outings," said Rena. As children react with distress and anger to their less secure home lives, discipline may become harsh and inconsistent. Contact with noncustodial fathers often decreases over time (Hetherington & Kelly, 2003). Fathers who see their children only occasionally are inclined to be permissive and indulgent, making the mother's task of managing the child even more difficult.

In view of these changes, it is not surprising that about 20 to 25 percent of children in divorced families display severe problems, compared with about 10 percent in nondivorced families. The more parents argue and fail to provide children with warmth, involvement, and consistent guidance, the poorer children's adjustment (Martinez & Forgatch, 2002; Pruett et al., 2003; Strohschein, 2005). At the same time, reactions vary with children's age, temperament, and sex.

Children's Age. Five-year-old Lizzie's fear that she caused her father to leave home is not unusual. The cognitive immaturity of preschool and early school-age children makes it difficult for them to grasp the reasons behind their parents' separation. Younger children often blame themselves and take the marital breakup as a sign that both parents may abandon them (Lansford et al., 2006). Hence, they are more likely to display both anxious, fearful and angry, defiant reactions than older children and adolescents, who can better understand the reasons for their parents' divorce.

Still, many school-age and adolescent youngsters also react strongly, escaping into undesirable peer activities, such as running away, truancy, early sexual activity, and delinquency, particularly when parental conflict is high and supervision is low (Hetherington & Stanley-Hagan, 1999). And as academic pressures in school rise and preoccupied divorcing parents reduce their involvement and support, poor school achievement is common (Lansford et al., 2006). But some older children—especially the oldest child in the family—display more mature behavior, willingly taking on extra family and household tasks, care and protection of younger siblings, and emotional support of a depressed, anxious mother. But if these demands are too great, these children may eventually become resentful, withdraw from the family, and engage in angry, acting-out behavior (Hetherington, 1999a).

Children's Temperament and Sex. Exposure to stressful life events and inadequate parenting magnifies the problems of temperamentally difficult children (Lengua et al., 2000). Easy children, who are less often targets of parental anger, also cope better with adversity.

These findings help us understand sex differences in response to divorce. Girls sometimes respond as Lizzie did, with internalizing reactions—crying, self-criticism, and withdrawal—or, more often, with demanding, attention-getting behavior. But in mother-custody families, boys are at slightly greater risk for serious adjustment problems (Amato, 2001). Recall from Chapter 10 that boys are more active and noncompliant—behaviors that increase with exposure to parental conflict and inconsistent discipline. Research reveals that long before the marital breakup, sons of divorcing couples display higher rates of impulsivity, defiance, and aggression—behaviors that may have been caused by their parents' marital problems while also contributing to them (Hetherington, 1999a; Shaw, Winslow, & Flanagan, 1999; Strohschein, 2005). As a result, many boys enter the period of turmoil surrounding divorce with reduced capacity to cope with family stress.

Perhaps because their behavior is more unruly, boys of divorcing parents receive less emotional support from mothers, teachers, and peers. And as Joey's behavior toward Lizzie illustrates, the coercive cycles of interaction between distressed children and their divorced mothers soon spread to sibling relations (Hetherington & Kelly, 2002; Sheehan et al., 2004). After divorce, children who are challenging to rear generally get worse.

LONG-TERM CONSEQUENCES ■ Rena eventually found better-paying work and gained control over the daily operation of the household. Her own feelings of anger and rejection also declined. And after several meetings with a counselor, Rena and Drake realized the harmful impact of their quarreling on Joey and Lizzie. Drake visited regularly and handled Joey's disruptiveness with firmness and consistency. Soon Joey's school performance improved, his behavior problems subsided, and both children seemed calmer and happier.

Most children show improved adjustment by two years after divorce. Yet overall, children and adolescents of divorced parents continue to score slightly lower than children of continuously married parents in academic achievement, self-esteem, social competence, and emotional and behavioral adjustment (Amato, 2001). Children with difficult temperaments are more likely to drop out of school, to be depressed, and to engage in antisocial behavior in adolescence. And divorce is linked to problems with sexuality and development of intimate ties. Young people who experienced parental divorce—especially more than once—display higher rates of early sexual activity and adolescent parenthood (Wolfinger, 2000). Some experience other lasting difficulties—reduced educational attainment, troubled romantic relationships and marriages, divorce in adulthood, and poor parent–child relationships (Amato, 2006; Amato & Cheadle, 2005; Wallerstein & Lewis, 2004). Thus, divorce can have consequences for subsequent generations.

The overriding factor in positive adjustment following divorce is effective parenting—how well the custodial parent handles stress and shields the child from family conflict and the extent to which each parent uses authoritative child rearing (Leon, 2003; Wolchik et al., 2000). Where the custodial parent is the mother, contact with fathers is especially important. The more paternal contact and the warmer the father–child relationship, the less children react with defiance and aggression (Dunn et al., 2004). For girls, a good father–child relationship protects against early sexual activity and unhappy romantic involvements. For boys, it seems to affect overall psychological well-being. In fact, several studies indicate

© GARETH BROWN/CORBIS

Effective parenting is the most important factor in children's positive adjustment following divorce. Usually, the custodial parent is the mother, but contact with fathers is also important. And some evidence indicates that sons do better when the father is the custodial parent.

that outcomes for sons are better when the father is the custodial parent (Clarke-Stewart & Hayward, 1996; McLanahan, 1999). Fathers' greater economic security and image of authority seem to help them engage in effective parenting with sons. And boys in father-custody families may benefit from greater involvement of both parents because noncustodial mothers participate more in their children's lives than noncustodial fathers.

Although divorce is painful for children, remaining in an intact but high-conflict family is much worse than making the transition to a low-conflict, single-parent household (Greene et al., 2003; Strohschein, 2005). However, more parents today are divorcing because they are moderately (rather than extremely) dissatisfied with their relationship. Research suggests that children in these low-discord homes are especially puzzled and upset. Perhaps these youngsters' inability to understand the marital breakup and grief over the loss of a seemingly happy home life explain why the adjustment problems of children of divorce have intensified over time (Amato, 2001; Reifman et al., 2001).

Regardless of the extent of parents' friction, those who set aside their disagreements and support each other in their child-rearing roles greatly improve their children's chances of growing up competent, stable, and happy. Caring extended-family members, teachers, siblings, and friends also reduce the likelihood that divorce will result in long-term difficulties (Hetherington, 2003; Lussier et al., 2002).

DIVORCE MEDIATION, JOINT CUSTODY, AND CHILD SUPPORT ■ Awareness that divorce is highly stressful for children and families has led to community-based services aimed at helping them through this difficult time. One such service is **divorce mediation,** a series of meetings between divorcing adults and a trained professional aimed at reducing family conflict, including legal battles over property division and child custody. Research reveals that mediation increases out-of-court settlements, cooperation and involvement of both parents in child rearing, and parents' and children's feelings of well-being (Emery, Sbarra, & Grover, 2005). In one study, parents who had resolved disputes through mediation were still more involved in their children's lives 12 years later (Emery et al., 2001).

To further encourage parents to resolve their disputes, parent education programs are becoming common. During several sessions, professionals teach parents about the impact of constructive conflict resolution and of mutual support in child rearing. Because of its demonstrated impact on parental cooperation, parent education prior to filing for divorce is increasingly becoming mandatory across Canada (Department of Justice Canada, 2006b). In many U.S. states, the court may require parents to attend a program.

An increasingly common child custody option is **joint custody,** which grants each parent an equal say in important decisions about the child's upbringing, encouraging both to remain involved in their children's lives. In most instances, children reside with one parent and see the other on a fixed schedule, much like the typical sole-custody situation. But in other cases, parents share physical custody, and children move between homes and sometimes between schools and peer groups. These transitions can be especially hard on some children. Joint-custody parents report little conflict—fortunately so, since the success of the arrangement depends on parental cooperation. And their children, regardless of living arrangements, tend to be better-adjusted than children in sole maternal-custody homes (Bauserman, 2002).

Finally, many single-parent families depend on child support from the absent parent to relieve financial strain. All U.S. states and Canadian provinces have procedures for withholding wages from parents who fail to make these payments. Although child support is usually not enough to lift a single-parent family out of poverty, it can ease its burdens substantially. Noncustodial fathers who have generous visitation schedules and who often see their children are more likely to pay child support regularly (Amato & Sobolewski, 2004). Applying What We Know on the following page summarizes ways to help children adjust to their parents' divorce.

Blended Families

"If you get married to Wendell and Daddy gets married to Carol," Lizzie wondered aloud to Rena, "then I'll have two sisters and one more brother. And let's see, how many grandmothers and grandfathers? A lot!" exclaimed Lizzie.

divorce mediation A series of meetings between divorcing adults and a trained professional aimed at reducing family conflict.

joint custody A legal arrangement that grants divorced parents equal say in important decisions about their children's upbringing.

blended, or reconstituted, **family** A family structure formed through cohabitation or remarriage that includes parent, child, and steprelatives.

Applying What We Know

Helping Children Adjust to Their Parents' Divorce

SUGGESTION	EXPLANATION
Shield children from conflict.	Witnessing intense parental conflict is very damaging to children. If one parent insists on expressing hostility, children fare better if the other parent does not respond in kind.
Provide children with as much continuity, familiarity, and predictability as possible.	Children adjust better during the period surrounding divorce when their lives have some stability—for example, the same school, bedroom, baby-sitter, playmates, and daily schedule.
Explain the divorce and tell children what to expect.	Children are more likely to develop fears of abandonment if they are not prepared for their parents' separation. They should be told that their mother and father will not be living together anymore, which parent will be moving out, and when they will be able to see that parent. If possible, mother and father should explain the divorce together. Parents should provide a reason for the divorce that the child can understand and assure the child that he is not to blame.
Emphasize the permanence of the divorce.	Fantasies of parents getting back together can prevent children from accepting the reality of their current life. Children should be told that the divorce is final and that they cannot change this fact.
Respond sympathetically to children's feelings.	Children need a supportive and understanding response to their feelings of sadness, fear, and anger. For children to adjust well, their painful emotions must be acknowledged, not denied or avoided.
Engage in authoritative parenting.	Provide children with affection and acceptance as well as reasonable demands for mature behavior and consistent, rational discipline. Parents who engage in authoritative parenting greatly reduce their children's risk of maladjustment following divorce.
Promote a continuing relationship with both parents.	When parents disentangle their lingering hostility toward the former spouse from the child's need for a continuing relationship with the other parent, children adjust well. Grandparents and other extended-family members can help by not taking sides.

Source: Teyber, 2001.

Life in a single-parent family is often temporary. About 60 percent of divorced parents remarry within a few years. Others cohabit, or share a sexual relationship and a residence with a partner outside of marriage. Parent, stepparent, and children form a new family structure called a **blended,** or **reconstituted, family.** For some children, this expanded family network is positive, bringing greater adult attention. But most have more problems than children in stable, first-marriage families. Switching to stepparents' new rules and expectations can be stressful, and children often regard steprelatives as "intruders." But how well they adapt is, again, related to the quality of family functioning (Hetherington & Kelly, 2002). This depends on which parent forms a new relationship, the child's age and sex, and the complexity of blended-family relationships. As we will see, older children and girls seem to have the hardest time.

MOTHER–STEPFATHER FAMILIES ■ Since mothers generally retain custody of children, the most common form of blended family is a mother–stepfather arrangement. Boys tend to adjust quickly, welcoming a stepfather who is warm, who refrains from exerting his authority too quickly, and who offers relief from coercive cycles of mother–son interaction. Mothers' friction with sons also declines as a result of greater economic security, another adult to share household tasks, and an end to loneliness (Visher, Visher, & Pasley, 2003). Stepfathers who marry rather than cohabit are more involved in parenting, perhaps because men who choose to marry a mother with children are more interested in and skilled at child rearing (Hofferth & Anderson, 2003). Girls, however, often have difficulty with their custodial mother's remarriage. Stepfathers disrupt the close ties many girls have established with their mothers, and girls often react with sulky, resistant behavior (Bray, 1999).

Note, however, that age affects these findings. Older school-age children and adolescents of both sexes display more irresponsible, acting-out behavior than their peers not in stepfamilies (Hetherington & Stanley-Hagan,

© ROYALTY-FREE/CORBIS

Adapting to life in a blended family is stressful for children. When stepparents build warm relationships with children before moving into their parenting role and form a cooperative "parenting coalition" with their partner, they provide consistency in child rearing, limit loyalty conflicts, and ease children's adjustment.

2000). Some parents are warmer and more involved with their biological children than with their stepchildren. Older children are more likely to notice and challenge unfair treatment. And adolescents often view the new stepparent as a threat to their freedom, especially if they experienced little parental monitoring in the single-parent family. But when teenagers have affectionate, cooperative relationships with their mothers, many eventually develop good relationships with their stepfathers—a circumstance linked to more favorable adolescent well-being (Yuan & Hamilton, 2006).

FATHER–STEPMOTHER FAMILIES ■ Remarriage of noncustodial fathers often leads to reduced contact with their biological children, as these fathers tend to withdraw from their "previous" families (Dunn, 2002). When fathers have custody, children typically react negatively to remarriage. One reason is that children living with fathers often start out with more problems. Perhaps the biological mother could no longer handle the difficult child (usually a boy), so the father and his new partner are faced with a youngster who has behavior problems. In other instances, the father has custody because of a very close relationship with the child, and his remarriage disrupts this bond (Buchanan, Maccoby, & Dornbusch, 1996).

Girls, especially, have a hard time getting along with their stepmothers, either because the remarriage threatens the girl's bond with her father or because she becomes entangled in loyalty conflicts between the two mother figures. But the longer girls live in father–stepmother households, the more positive their interaction with stepmothers becomes (Hetherington & Jodl, 1994). With time and patience most girls eventually benefit from the support of a second mother figure.

SUPPORT FOR BLENDED FAMILIES ■ Family life education and counseling can help parents and children in blended families adapt to the complexities of their new circumstances. Effective approaches encourage stepparents to move into their new roles gradually by first building a friendly relationship with the child. Only when a warm bond has formed between stepparents and stepchildren is more active parenting possible (Visher, Visher, & Pasley, 2003). In addition, counselors can offer couples help in forming a "parenting coalition" to limit loyalty conflicts and provide consistency in child rearing. This allows children to benefit from the increased diversity that stepparent relationships bring to their lives.

Unfortunately, the divorce rate for second marriages is even higher than that for first marriages. Parents with antisocial tendencies and poor child-rearing skills are particularly likely to have several divorces and remarriages. The more marital transitions children experience, the greater their difficulties (Dunn, 2002). These families usually require prolonged, intensive therapy.

Maternal Employment and Dual-Earner Families

Today, North American single and married mothers are in the labor force in nearly equal proportions, and more than three-fourths of those with school-age children are employed (Statistics Canada, 2005a; U.S. Census Bureau, 2007b). In Chapter 7, we saw that the impact of maternal employment on early development depends on the quality of child care and the continuing parent–child relationship. The same is true in later years.

MATERNAL EMPLOYMENT AND CHILD DEVELOPMENT ■ When mothers enjoy their work and remain committed to parenting, children show favorable adjustment—higher self-esteem, more positive family and peer relations, less gender-stereotyped beliefs, and better grades in school. Girls, especially, profit from the image of female competence. Regardless of SES, daughters of employed mothers perceive women's roles as involving more freedom of choice and satisfaction and are more achievement- and career-oriented (Hoffman, 2000).

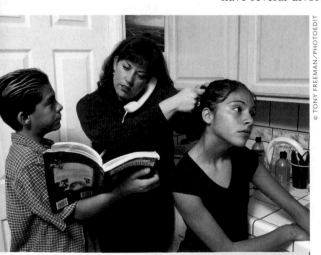

© TONY FREEMAN/PHOTOEDIT

Employed mothers who enjoy their work while remaining committed to parenting tend to have children who show higher self-esteem, more positive family and peer relations, less gender-stereotyped beliefs, and better school performance.

These benefits reflect parenting practices. Employed mothers who value their parenting role are more likely to use authoritative child rearing and coregulation. Also, children in dual-earner households devote more daily hours to doing homework under parental guidance and participate more in household chores. And maternal employment leads fathers to take on greater child-rearing responsibilities, with a small but increasing number staying home full-time (Gottfried, Gottfried, & Bathurst, 2002; Hoffman & Youngblade, 1999). Paternal involvement is associated with higher intelligence and achievement, more mature social behavior, and a flexible view of gender roles in childhood and adolescence, and with generally better mental health in adulthood (Coltrane, 1996; Pleck & Masciadrelli, 2004).

But when employment places heavy demands on the mother's schedule or is stressful for other reasons, children are at risk for ineffective parenting (Brooks-Gunn, Han, & Waldfogel, 2002; Costigan, Cox, & Cauce, 2003). Negative consequences are magnified when low-SES mothers spend long days at low-paying, physically exhausting jobs—conditions linked to maternal depression and to harsh, inconsistent discipline (Raver, 2003). In contrast, part-time employment and flexible work schedules have benefits for children of all ages. By preventing work–family role conflict, these arrangements help parents meet children's needs (Frederiksen-Goldsen & Sharlach, 2000).

SUPPORT FOR EMPLOYED PARENTS AND THEIR FAMILIES ■ In dual-earner families, the father's willingness to share responsibilities is a crucial factor. If he is uninvolved, the mother carries a double load, at home and at work, leading to fatigue, distress, and little time and energy for children.

Employed mothers and dual-earner parents need assistance from employers and communities in their child-rearing roles. Part-time employment, flexible schedules, job sharing, and paid leave when children are ill help parents juggle the demands of work and child rearing. Equal pay and employment opportunities for women are also important. Because these policies enhance financial status and morale, they improve the way mothers feel and behave when they arrive home at the end of the working day.

CHILD CARE FOR SCHOOL-AGE CHILDREN ■ High-quality child care is vital for parents' peace of mind and children's well-being, even during middle childhood. An estimated 2.4 million 5- to 13-year-olds in the United States and several hundred thousand in Canada are **self-care children,** who regularly look after themselves during after-school hours. Self-care increases with age, from 3 percent of 5- to 7-year-olds to 33 percent of 11- to 13-year-olds. It also rises with SES, perhaps because of the greater safety of higher-income suburban neighborhoods. But when lower-SES parents must use self-care because they lack alternatives, their children spend more hours on their own (Casper & Smith, 2002).

Some studies report that self-care children suffer from low self-esteem, antisocial behavior, poor academic achievement, and fearfulness. Others show no such effects. Children's maturity and the way they spend their time seem to explain these contradictions. Among younger school-age children, those who spend more hours alone have more adjustment difficulties (Vandell & Posner, 1999). As children become old enough to look after themselves, those who have a history of authoritative child rearing, are monitored by parental telephone calls, and have regular after-school chores appear responsible and well-adjusted. In contrast, children left to their own devices are more likely to bend to peer pressures and engage in antisocial behavior (Coley, Morris, & Hernandez, 2004; Steinberg, 1986).

Before age 8 or 9, most children need supervision because they are not yet competent to handle emergencies (Galambos & Maggs, 1991). But throughout middle childhood and early adolescence, attending after-school programs with well-trained staffs, generous adult–child ratios, and positive adult–child communication is linked to better social skills and emotional adjustment (Pierce, Hamm, & Vandell, 1999). And as early as kindergarten, consistent participation in after-school enrichment activities (sports, music and art lessons, and clubs)

© AMY ETRA/PHOTOEDIT

In this high-quality after-school program in Los Angeles, a community volunteer assists children with learning and completing homework. Children who attend such programs have better work habits and school grades and fewer behavior problems.

self-care children Children who regularly look after themselves during after-school hours.

predicts higher academic achievement the following year, after many factors (including prior achievement) are controlled (NICHD Early Child Care Research Network, 2004a).

Low-SES children and children whose parents work long hours are less likely to be enrolled in such activities. But when lessons and scouting are included in "after-care" programs, low-SES children show special benefits, including better work habits, higher school grades, and fewer behavior problems (Posner & Vandell, 1994; Vandell, 1999). Unfortunately, good after-care is in especially short supply in inner-city neighborhoods. A special need exists for well-planned programs in these areas—ones that provide safe environments, enjoyable, skill-building activities, and warm relationships with adults.

Ask Yourself

Review   Describe and explain changes in sibling relationships during middle childhood. What can parents do to promote positive sibling ties?

Apply   Steve and Marissa are in the midst of an acrimonious divorce. Their 9-year-old son Dennis has become hostile and defiant. How can Steve and Marissa help Dennis adjust?

Connect   How does each level in Bronfenbrenner's ecological systems theory—microsystem, mesosystem, exosystem, and macrosystem—contribute to the effects of maternal employment on children's development?

Reflect   What after-school child-care arrangements did you experience in elementary school? How do you think they influenced your development?

Some Common Problems of Development

We have considered a variety of stressful experiences that place children at risk for future problems. Next, we address two more areas of concern: school-age children's fears and anxieties and the devastating consequences of child sexual abuse. Finally, we sum up factors that help school-age children cope effectively with stress.

Fears and Anxieties

Although fears of the dark, thunder and lightning, animals, and supernatural beings persist into middle childhood, older children's anxieties are also directed toward new concerns. As children begin to understand the realities of the wider world, the possibility of personal harm (being robbed, stabbed, or shot) and media events (war and disasters) often trouble them. Other common worries include academic failure, separation from parents, parents' health, physical injuries, the possibility of dying, and peer rejection (Muris et al., 2000; Weems & Costa, 2005). Because children often mull over frightening thoughts at bedtime, nighttime fears actually increase between ages 7 and 9 (Muris et al., 2001).

Children in Western nations mention exposure to negative information, especially on television, as the most common source of their fears, followed by direct exposure to frightening events (Muris et al., 2001). But as with computer use and Web access (see page 471 in Chapter 12), only a minority of North American parents have rules about what TV programs their school-age children and young teenagers can watch (Media Awareness Network, 2001; Roberts, Foehr, & Rideout, 2005).

As long as fears are not too intense, most children handle them constructively, using the more sophisticated emotional self-regulation strategies that develop in middle childhood. Consequently, fears decline at the end of middle childhood, especially for girls, who express

phobia An intense, unmanageable fear that leads to persistent avoidance of the feared situation.

more fears than boys at all ages (Gullone, 2000). But about 5 percent of school-age children develop an intense, unmanageable fear, called a **phobia.** Children with inhibited temperaments are at high risk, displaying phobias five to six times as often than other children (Ollendick, King, & Muris, 2002).

For example, in *school phobia,* children feel severe apprehension about attending school, often accompanied by physical complaints (dizziness, nausea, stomachaches, and vomiting). About one-third of children with school phobia are 5- to 7-year-olds for whom the real fear is separation from their mother. Family therapy and behavior modification procedures that reinforce the child for going to school help these children, whose difficulty can often be traced to parental overprotection (Elliott, 1999).

Most cases of school phobia appear later, around age 11 to 13, during the transition from middle childhood to adolescence. These youngsters usually find a particular aspect of school experience frightening—an overcritical teacher, a school bully, or excessive parental pressure to achieve. Treating this form of school phobia may require a change in school environment or parenting practices. Firm insistence that the child return to school, along with training in how to cope with difficult situations, is also helpful (Csoti, 2003).

Severe childhood anxieties may also arise from harsh living conditions. In inner-city ghettos and in war-torn areas of the world, a great many children live in the midst of constant danger, chaos, and deprivation. As the Cultural Influences box on page 518 reveals, these youngsters are at risk for long-term emotional distress and behavior problems. Finally, as we saw in our discussion of child abuse in Chapter 10, too often violence and other destructive acts become part of adult–child relationships. During middle childhood, child sexual abuse increases.

Child Sexual Abuse

Until recently, child sexual abuse was considered rare, and adults often dismissed children's claims of abuse. In the 1970s, efforts by professionals and media attention led to recognition of child sexual abuse as a serious and widespread problem. About 90,000 cases in the United States and 5,000 cases in Canada were confirmed in the most recently reported year (Department of Justice Canada, 2006a; U.S. Department of Health and Human Services, 2006a).

CHARACTERISTICS OF ABUSERS AND VICTIMS ■ Sexual abuse is committed against children of both sexes, but more often against girls. Most cases are reported in middle childhood, but sexual abuse also occurs at younger and older ages. For some victims, the abuse begins early in life and continues for many years (Hoch-Espada, Ryan, & Deblinger, 2006; Trickett & Putnam, 1998).

Typically, the abuser is a male, either a parent or someone the parent knows well—a father, stepfather, or live-in boyfriend or, somewhat less often, an uncle or older brother. But in about 25 percent of cases, mothers are the offenders, more often with sons (Boroughs, 2004). If the abuser is a nonrelative, the person is usually someone the child has come to know and trust. However, the Internet and mobile phones have become avenues through which other adults commit sexual abuse—for example, by exposing children and adolescents to pornography and online sex as a way of "grooming" them for sexual acts offline (Gardner, 2005).

Abusers make their victims comply in a variety of distasteful ways, including deception, bribery, verbal intimidation, and physical force. You may wonder how any adult—especially a parent or close relative—could possibly violate a child sexually. Many offenders deny their own responsibility, blaming the abuse on the willing participation of a seductive youngster. Yet children are not capable of making a deliberate, informed decision to enter into a sexual relationship! Even older children and adolescents are not free to say yes or no. Rather, the responsibility lies with abusers, who

COURTESY OF DUNEBROOK—PREVENT CHILD ABUSE LA PORTE COUNTY

So there really was a monster in her bedroom.

For many kids, there's a real reason to be afraid of the dark. Each year in Indiana, there are thousands of substantiated cases of sexual abuse. (Not to mention the number that goes unreported.) The trauma can be devastating for the child and for the family. So listen closely to the children around you. If you hear something that you don't want to believe, perhaps you should. For information on child abuse prevention, contact: Dunebrook Prevent Child Abuse LaPorte County, 7451 Johnson Road, Michigan City, IN 46360. **1-800-897-0007.** Or visit www.dunebrook.org.

This public service announcement reminds adults that child sexual abuse, until recently regarded as a product of children's vivid imaginations, is a devastating reality.

Cultural Influences

The Impact of Ethnic and Political Violence on Children

Today, half of all casualties of worldwide conflict are children. Around the world, many children live with armed conflict, terrorism, and other acts of violence stemming from ethnic and political tensions. Some children may participate in fighting, either because they are forced or because they want to please adults. Others are kidnapped, assaulted, and tortured. Those who are bystanders often come under direct fire and may be killed or physically maimed. And many watch in horror as family members, friends, and neighbors flee, are wounded, or die. In the past decade, wars have left 4 to 5 million children physically disabled, 20 million homeless, and more than 1 million separated from their parents (UNICEF, 2005b).

When war and social crises are temporary, most children can be comforted and do not show long-term emotional difficulties. But chronic danger requires children to make substantial adjustments that can seriously impair their psychological functioning. Many children of war lose their sense of safety, become desensitized to violence, are haunted by terrifying intrusive memories, struggle with moral reasoning, and adopt a pessimistic view of the future. Anxiety and depression increase, as do aggression and antisocial behavior (Joshi et al.,

2006; Klingman, 2006). These outcomes appear to be culturally universal, appearing among children from every war zone studied—from Bosnia, Angola, Rwanda, and the Sudan to the West Bank, Afghanistan, and Iraq (Barenbaum, Ruchkin, & Schwab-Stone, 2004).

Parental affection and reassurance are the best protection against lasting problems. When parents offer security, discuss traumatic experiences with children sympathetically, and serve as role models of calm emotional strength, most children can withstand even extreme war-related violence (Smith et al., 2001; Wiseman & Barber, 2004). Children who are separated from parents must rely on help from their communities. Preschool and school-age orphans in Eritrea who were placed in residential settings where they could form close emotional ties with at least one adult showed less emotional stress five years later than orphans placed in impersonal settings (Wolff & Fesseha, 1999). Education and recreation programs are powerful safeguards, too, providing children with a sense of consistency in their lives along with teacher and peer supports.

With the September 11, 2001, terrorist attacks on the World Trade Center and the Pentagon, some American children experienced extreme

wartime violence firsthand. Children in Public School 31 in Brooklyn, New York, for example, stared out windows as planes rushed toward the towers and were engulfed in flames and watched the towers crumble. Many worried about the safety of family members, and some lost them. In the aftermath, most expressed intense fears—for example, that terrorists were in their neighborhoods and that planes flying overhead might smash into nearby buildings.

Unlike many war-traumatized children in the developing world, Public School 31 students received immediate intervention—a "trauma curriculum" in which they expressed their emotions through writing, drawing, and discussion and participated in experiences aimed at restoring trust and tolerance (Lagnado, 2001). Older children learned about the feelings of their Muslim classmates, the dire condition of children in Afghanistan, and ways to help victims as a means of overcoming a sense of helplessness.

When wartime drains families and communities of resources, international organizations must step in and help children. Efforts to preserve children's physical, psychological, and educational well-being may be the best way to stop the transmission of violence to the next generation.

These traumatized victims of air raids in Kabul, Afghanistan, witnessed the destruction of their neighborhoods and the maimings and deaths of family members and friends. The children draw pictures during a therapy session at a mental health hospital. One 7-year-old depicts several of his schoolmates who died. Without special support from caring adults, the children are likely to have lasting emotional problems.

tend to have characteristics that predispose them toward sexual exploitation of children. They have great difficulty controlling their impulses and may suffer from psychological disorders, including alcohol or drug addiction. Often they pick out children who are unlikely to defend themselves or to be believed—those who are physically weak, emotionally deprived, socially isolated, or affected by disabilities such as blindness, deafness, or mental retardation (Bolen, 2001).

Reported cases of child sexual abuse are linked to poverty, marital instability, and resulting weakening of family ties. Children who live in homes with a constantly changing cast of characters—repeated marriages, separations, and new partners—are especially vulnerable. But children in economically advantaged, stable homes are also victims, although their abuse is more likely to escape detection (Putnam, 2003).

CONSEQUENCES OF SEXUAL ABUSE ■ The adjustment problems of child sexual abuse victims—including depression, low self-esteem, mistrust of adults, and anger and hostility—are often severe and can persist for years after the abusive episodes. Younger children frequently react with sleep difficulties, loss of appetite, and generalized fearfulness. Adolescents may run away and show suicidal reactions, substance abuse, and delinquency. At all ages, persistent abuse accompanied by force, violence, and a close relationship to the perpetrator (incest) has a more severe impact (Feiring, Taska, & Lewis, 1999; Tricket et al., 2001). And repeated sexual abuse, like physical abuse, is associated with central nervous system damage (see Chapter 10, page 404)—an outcome that increases the risk of lasting psychological disorders.

Sexually abused children frequently display precocious sexual knowledge and behavior. They have learned from their abusers that sexual overtures are acceptable ways to get attention and rewards. In adolescence, abused young people often become promiscuous, and as adults, they show increased arrest rates for sex crimes (mostly against children) and prostitution (Salter et al., 2003; Whipple, 2006). Furthermore, women who were sexually abused are likely to choose partners who abuse them and their children. As mothers, they often engage in irresponsible and coercive parenting, including child abuse and neglect (Pianta, Egeland, & Erickson, 1989). In these ways, the harmful impact of sexual abuse is transmitted to the next generation.

PREVENTION AND TREATMENT ■ Treating child sexual abuse is difficult. The reactions of family members—anxiety about harm to the child, anger toward the abuser, and sometimes hostility toward the victim for telling—can increase children's distress. Because sexual abuse typically appears in the midst of other serious family problems, long-term therapy with children and families is usually needed (Olafson & Boat, 2000). The best way to reduce the suffering of victims is to prevent sexual abuse from continuing. Today, courts are prosecuting abusers more vigorously and taking children's testimony more seriously (see the Social Issues: Health box on page 520).

Educational programs that teach children to recognize inappropriate sexual advances and whom to turn to for help reduce the risk of abuse (Hebert & Tourigny, 2004). Yet because of controversies over educating children about sexual abuse, few schools offer these interventions. New Zealand is the only country with a national, school-based prevention program targeting sexual abuse. In Keeping Ourselves Safe, children and adolescents learn that abusers are generally not strangers. Parent involvement ensures that home and school work together in teaching children self-protection skills. Evaluations reveal that virtually all New Zealand parents and children support the program and that it has helped many children avoid or report abuse (Briggs, 2002).

Fostering Resilience in Middle Childhood

Throughout middle childhood—and other phases of development as well—children are confronted with challenging and sometimes threatening situations that require them to cope with psychological stress. In this

COURTESY OF THE NEW ZEALAND POLICE

In Keeping Ourselves Safe, New Zealand's national, school-based child abuse prevention program, teachers and police officers collaborate in teaching children to recognize abusive adult behaviors so they can take steps to protect themselves. Parents are informed about children's classroom learning experiences and encouraged to support and extend them at home.

Social Issues: Health

Children's Eyewitness Testimony

Increasingly, children are being called on to testify in court cases involving child abuse and neglect, child custody, and other matters. Providing information on such topics can be difficult and traumatic. Almost always, children must report on highly stressful events, and they may have to speak against a parent or other relative to whom they feel loyal. In some family disputes, they may fear punishment for telling the truth. In addition, child witnesses are faced with an unfamiliar situation—at the very least an interview in the judge's chambers and at most an open courtroom with judge, jury, spectators, and the possibility of unsympathetic cross-examination. Not surprisingly, these conditions can compromise the accuracy of children's recall.

Age Differences

Until recently, children younger than age 5 were rarely asked to testify, and not until age 10 were they assumed fully competent to do so. Yet as a result of societal reactions to rising rates of child abuse and difficulties in prosecuting perpetrators, legal requirements for child testimony have been relaxed in the United States and Canada (Sandler, 2006). Children as young as age 3 frequently serve as witnesses.

School-age children are better able than preschoolers to give detailed descriptions of past experiences and make accurate inferences about others' motives and intentions. In addition, older children are generally more resistant than preschoolers to misleading questions that attorneys may ask when probing for more information or trying to influence the child's response (Roebers & Schneider, 2001). But when properly questioned, even 3-year-olds can recall personally relevant events accurately, including highly stressful ones (Peterson & Rideout, 1998).

Suggestibility

Court testimony, however, often involves repeated interviews. When adults lead witnesses by suggesting incorrect "facts" ("He touched you there, didn't he?"), repeatedly interrupt their denials, reinforce them for giving desired answers, or use a confrontational questioning style, they increase the likelihood of incorrect reporting by children and adolescents alike (Bruck & Ceci, 2004; Owen-Kostelnik, Reppucci, & Meyer, 2006).

In one study, 4- to 7-year-olds were asked to recall details about a visitor who had come to their classroom a week earlier. Half the children received a low-pressure interview containing leading questions that implied abuse ("He took your clothes off, didn't he?"). The other half receive a high-pressure interview in which an adult told the child that her friends had said "yes" to the leading questions, praised the child for agreeing ("You're doing great"), and, if the child did not agree, asked the question again. Children were far more likely to give false information—even to fabricate quite fantastic events—in the high-pressure condition (Finnilä et al., 2003).

By the time children appear in court, weeks, months, or even years have passed since the target events. When a long delay is combined with biased interviewing and with stereotyping of the accused ("He's in jail because he's been bad"), children can easily be misled into giving false information (Ceci, Fitneva, & Gilstrap, 2003).

Special interviewing methods have been devised to ease children's task in providing testimony. In many sexual abuse cases, anatomically correct dolls are used to prompt children's recall. Although this method helps older children provide more detail about experienced events, it also increases the suggestibility of preschoolers, who report physical and sexual contact that never happened (Goodman et al., 1999).

Interventions

Adults must prepare child witnesses so that they understand the courtroom process and know what to expect. In some places, "court schools" take children through the setting and give them an opportunity to role-play court activities. Practice interviews—in which children learn to provide the most accurate, detailed information possible and to admit not knowing rather than agreeing or guessing—are helpful (Saywitz, Goodman, & Lyon, 2002).

At the same time, legal professionals must use interviewing procedures that increase children's accurate reporting. Unbiased, open-ended questions that prompt children to disclose details—"Tell me what happened" or "You said there was a man; tell me about the man"—reduce suggestibility (Holliday, 2003). Also, a warm, supportive interview tone fosters accurate recall, perhaps by easing children's anxiety so they feel freer to disagree with an interviewer's false suggestions (Ceci, Bruck, & Battin, 2000).

If children are likely to experience emotional trauma or later punishment (as in a family dispute), courtroom procedures can be adapted to protect them. For example, children can testify over closed-circuit TV so they do not have to face an abuser. When it is not wise for a child to participate directly, expert witnesses can provide testimony that reports on the child's psychological condition and includes important elements of the child's story.

This 9-year-old, accompanied by her mother and the defense attorney, is arriving at court to testify for the defense in the 2005 Michael Jackson child molestation trial. As her expression suggests, the prospect of testifying in this court case is difficult. But as long as attorneys refrain from using biased interviewing tactics, school-age children are able to provide accurate, detailed descriptions of past experiences.

Applying What We Know

Resources That Foster Resilience in Middle Childhood

TYPE OF RESOURCE	DESCRIPTION
Personal	• Easygoing, sociable temperament
	• Above-average intelligence
	• Favorable self-esteem
	• Persistence in the face of challenge and pleasure in mastery
	• Good emotional self-regulation and flexible coping strategies
Family	• Warm, trusting relationship with at least one parent
	• Authoritative child-rearing style
	• Positive discipline, avoidance of coercive tactics
	• Warm, supportive sibling relationships
School	• Teachers who are warm, helpful, and stimulating, who encourage students to collaborate, and who emphasize effort and self-improvement
	• Lessons in tolerance and respect and codes against bullying, which promote positive peer relationships and gratifying friendships
	• Extracurricular activities, including sports and social service pursuits, that strengthen physical, cognitive, and social skills
	• High-quality after-school programs that protect children's safety and offer stimulating, skill-building activities
Community	• An adult—such as an extended-family member, teacher, or neighbor—who provides warmth and social support and is a positive coping model
	• Stability of neighborhood residents and services—safe outdoor play areas, community centers, and religious organizations—that relieve parental stress and encourage families and neighbors to share leisure time
	• Youth groups—scouting, clubs, religious youth groups, and other organized activities—that promote positive peer relationships and prosocial behavior

Note: One or a few resources may be sufficient to foster resilience, since each resource strengthens others.
Sources: Conger & Conger, 2002; Seccombe, 2002; Wright & Masten, 2005.

trio of chapters, we have considered such topics as chronic illness, learning disabilities, achievement expectations, divorce, harsh living conditions and wartime trauma, and sexual abuse. Each taxes children's coping resources, creating serious risks for development.

Nevertheless, only a modest relationship exists between stressful life experiences and psychological disturbance in childhood (Masten & Reed, 2002). In our discussion in Chapter 4 of the long-term consequences of birth complications, we noted that some children overcome the combined effects of birth trauma, poverty, and a troubled family life. The same is true for school difficulties, family transitions, children of war, and child maltreatment. Refer to Applying What We Know above for an overview of factors that promote *resilience*—the capacity to overcome adversity—during middle childhood.

Often just one or a few of these ingredients account for why one child is "stress-resilient" and another is not. Usually, however, personal and environmental factors are interconnected: Each resource favoring resilience strengthens others. For example, safe, stable neighborhoods with family-friendly community services reduce parents' daily hassles and stress, thereby promoting good parenting (Pinderhughes et al., 2001). In contrast, unfavorable home and neighborhood experiences increase the chances that children will act in ways that expose them to further hardship. And when negative conditions pile up, such as marital discord, poverty, crowded living conditions, neighborhood violence, and abuse and neglect, the rate of maladjustment multiplies (Wright & Masten, 2005).

Of great concern are children's violent acts. Violence committed in schools and communities by U.S. children and adolescents with troubled lives has at times reached the level of atrocities—maimings and murders of adults and peers. Because children spend a great deal

Often one resource that fosters resilience strengthens others. This child, who is enjoying a game of checkers with her father at a recreation center, benefits from high-quality neighborhood services, which relieve parental stress and encourage parents and children to share leisure time.

of time in school, the quality of their relationships with teachers and classmates strongly influences their development, academically and socially (Elias, Parker, & Rosenblatt, 2005).

Several highly effective school-based *social and emotional learning programs* reduce violence (including bullying and gang involvement) and other antisocial acts and increase academic motivation by fostering social competence and supportive relationships. Among these is the Resolving Conflict Creatively Program (RCCP), used in more than 400 schools throughout the United States, serving 175,000 students (Lantieri, 2003). RCCP provides children and adolescents with up to 51 hour-long lessons in emotional and social understanding and skills. Topics include expressing feelings, regulating anger, resolving social conflicts, cooperating, appreciating diversity, identifying and standing up against prejudice and bullying, and making decisions based on long- rather than short-term goals. Compared with students receiving few or no lessons, second to sixth graders receiving substantial RCCP instruction less often misinterpreted others' acts as hostile, less often behaved aggressively, more often engaged in prosocial behavior, and more often gained in academic achievement. Two years of intervention, as opposed to just one, strengthened these outcomes (Brown et al., 2004). In unsafe neighborhoods, the program transforms schools into places of safety and mutual respect, where learning can occur.

RCCP and other similar programs recognize that resilience is not a preexisting attribute but rather a capacity that *develops,* enabling children to use internal and external resources to cope with adversity (Roberts & Masten, 2004; Yates, Egeland, & Sroufe, 2003). Throughout our discussion, we have seen how families, schools, communities, and society as a whole can enhance or undermine the school-age child's developing sense of competence. As the next three chapters reveal, young people whose childhood experiences helped them learn to control impulses, overcome obstacles, strive for self-direction, and respond considerately and sympathetically to others meet the challenges of the next period—adolescence—quite well.

Ask Yourself

Review   When children must testify in court cases, what factors increase the chances of accurate reporting?

Apply   Claire told her 6-year-old daughter to be very careful never to talk to or take candy from strangers. Why will Claire's warning not protect her daughter from sexual abuse?

Connect   Explain how factors that promote resilience, listed on page 521, contribute to favorable adjustment following divorce.

Reflect   Describe a challenging time during your childhood. What aspects of the experience increased stress? What resources helped you cope with adversity?

Summary

Erikson's Theory: Industry versus Inferiority

What personality changes take place during Erikson's stage of industry versus inferiority?

■ According to Erikson, children who successfully resolve the psychological conflict of **industry versus inferiority** develop a sense of competence at useful skills and tasks, learn the value of division of labor, and develop a sense of moral commitment and responsibility.

Self-Understanding

Describe school-age children's self-concept and self-esteem, and discuss factors that affect their achievement-related attributions.

■ During middle childhood, children's self-concepts include personality traits (both positive and negative), competencies, and **social comparisons.** Separate self-esteems become increasingly distinct and hierarchically organized. Over the early school years, self-esteem declines as children get more competence-related feedback and compare their performance to that of others.

■ Cultural forces affect self-esteem. An especially strong emphasis on social comparison in school may underlie Asian children's lower self-esteem in comparison to that of North American children. Warm extended families and strong ethnic pride may contribute to the slight self-esteem advantage of Africa-American over Caucasian children.

© JEFF GREENBERG/PHOTOEDIT

■ Parental support for self-development affects self-esteem. Parents' gender-stereotyped beliefs predict sex differences in children's self-evaluations of competence in various areas. The authoritative child-rearing style is linked to favorable self-esteem.

■ Research on achievement-related **attributions** has identified adult messages that affect children's academic self-esteem. Children with **mastery-oriented attributions** hold an incremental view of ability, believing that it can be improved by trying hard, and attribute failure to insufficient effort. In contrast, children with **learned helplessness** attribute their successes to luck and hold a fixed view of ability, believing that it cannot be changed and that their failures are due to lack of ability.

■ Parents' and teachers' feedback about ability plays a large role in whether children develop a mastery-oriented approach as opposed to learned helplessness. Supportive teachers and cultural valuing of effort increase the likelihood of a mastery-oriented approach.

■ **Attribution retraining** encourages learned-helpless children to believe they can overcome failure by exerting more effort. Teaching children to focus less on grades and more on mastery for its own sake also leads to gains in students' academic self-esteem and motivation.

Emotional Development

Cite changes in the expression and understanding of emotion in middle childhood.

■ In middle childhood, self-conscious emotions of pride and guilt become clearly governed by personal responsibility. Experiencing intense shame can shatter children's overall sense of self-esteem.

■ School-age children recognize that people can experience more than one emotion at a time and that emotional expressions may not reflect people's true feelings. They also attend to both facial and situational cues and to information about a person's past experiences in interpreting their feelings. Gains in perspective taking and emotional understanding lead empathy to increase in middle childhood.

■ By the end of middle childhood, most children have an adaptive set of techniques for regulating emotion. They shift between **problem-centered coping** and **emotion-centered coping,** depending on the situation. Emotionally well-regulated children are optimistic, prosocial, and well-liked by peers.

Understanding Others: Perspective Taking

How does perspective taking change in middle childhood?

■ **Perspective taking** improves greatly over the school years, as described by Selman's five-stage sequence. Cognitive maturity and experiences in which adults and peers encourage children to take another's viewpoint support school-age children's perspective-taking skill. Good perspective takers show more empathy, sympathy, and positive social skills.

Moral Development

Describe changes in moral understanding during middle childhood, including children's understanding of diversity and inequality.

■ By middle childhood, children follow internalized standards, so their need for adult oversight, modeling, and reinforcement declines. School-age children's concepts of **distributive justice** change, from equality to merit to equity and benevolence.

■ As children develop more advanced ideas about justice, they clarify and link moral rules and social conventions. In judging the seriousness of transgressions, they take into account the purpose of the rule; people's intentions, knowledge, and beliefs; and the context of their actions.

■ Stronger convictions about personal choice strengthen children's appreciation of individual rights, such as freedom of speech and religion. But when moral and personal concerns conflict, older school-age children typically emphasize fairness. Children in diverse cultures use similar criteria to reason about moral, social-conventional, and personal concerns.

■ Children of all races pick up prevailing societal attitudes about race and ethnicity. With age, children pay more attention to inner traits and realize that people can be both "the same" and "different," and children's prejudice declines. Still, among white children, prejudice continues to operate subtly and without awareness.

■ Children most likely to hold racial and ethnic biases are those who believe that personality traits are fixed, who have inflated self-esteem, and who live among adults who highlight group differences. Promising approaches to reducing prejudice include inducing children to view others' traits as changeable and arranging intergroup contact in schools and communities.

Peer Relations

How do peer sociability and friendship change in middle childhood?

■ In middle childhood, peer interaction becomes more prosocial, and physical aggression declines. By the end of the school years, children organize themselves into **peer groups.** Although most children regard exclusion as wrong, they often exclude children who deviate from group codes of dress and behavior and who are no longer "respected." Formal groups under adult guidance can hold these negative behaviors in check.

■ Friendships develop into mutual relationships based on trust and become more selective. Children tend to select friends who resemble themselves in age, sex, race, ethnicity, SES, personality, popularity, academic achievement, and prosocial behavior. Girls form closer, more exclusive friendships than boys.

Describe major categories of peer acceptance and ways to help rejected children.

■ Researchers use self-reports to distinguish four types of **peer acceptance:** (1) **popular children,** who are liked by many agemates; (2) **rejected children,** who are actively disliked; (3) **controversial children,** who are liked by some and disliked by others; and (4) **neglected children,** who arouse little reaction, positive or negative, but are usually well-adjusted.

© JUSTIN GUARIGLIA / THE IMAGE WORKS

■ **Popular-prosocial children** are academically and socially competent, while **popular-antisocial children** include athletically skilled boys who are poor students and defiant of adult authority and relationally aggressive boys and girls, admired for their sophisticated but devious social skills. **Rejected-aggressive children** are especially high in conflict and hostility, while **rejected-withdrawn children** are passive, socially awkward, and frequent targets of **peer victimization.** Both types of rejected children often experience lasting adjustment difficulties.

■ Coaching in social skills, academic tutoring, and training in perspective taking and social problem solving have been used

to help rejected youngsters. Teaching children to attribute peer difficulties to internal, changeable causes is also important. To produce lasting change, intervening in parent–child interaction is often necessary.

Gender Typing

What changes in gender-stereotyped beliefs and gender identity take place during middle childhood?

■ School-age children extend their awareness of gender stereotypes to personality traits and academic subjects. As a result, girls often discount their academic ability. Children also develop a more flexible, open-minded view of what males and females can do. But they judge certain violations of appearance and behavior harshly and are especially intolerant when boys engage in these "cross-gender" acts.

■ Boys strengthen their identification with the masculine role, whereas girls feel free to experiment with "cross-gender" activities. School-age children's gender identities also expand to include self-evaluations of gender typicality, gender contentedness, and felt pressure to conform to gender roles—each of which affects psychological well-being.

Family Influences

How do parent–child communication and sibling relationships change in middle childhood?

■ Effective parents of school-age children engage in **coregulation,** exerting general oversight while letting children take charge of moment-by-moment decision making. Coregulation depends on a cooperative relationship between parent and child.

■ Sibling rivalry tends to increase as children participate in a wider range of activities and as parents compare their traits and accomplishments. Siblings often try to reduce this rivalry by striving to be different from one another. When siblings maintain warm bonds, they resolve disagreements constructively and provide one another with emotional support.

■ Compared to children with siblings, only children have higher self-esteem, do better in school, and attain higher levels of education. But although only children form close, high-quality friendships, they are less well accepted in the peer group, perhaps because they have had fewer opportunities to resolve conflicts through sibling interactions.

How do children fare in gay and lesbian families and in single-parent, never-married families?

■ Gay and lesbian parents are as committed to and effective at child rearing as heterosexuals. Their children do not differ from the children of heterosexual parents in adjustment and gender-role preferences.

■ The largest group of never-married parents is African-American young women, who postpone marriage more and childbirth less than all other American ethnic groups. Never-married parenthood generally increases economic hardship for low-SES mothers and their children. Children of never-married mothers who lack a father's warmth and involvement achieve less well in school and engage in more antisocial behavior than children in low-SES, first-marriage families.

What factors influence children's adjustment to divorce and blended family arrangements?

- Although all children experience painful emotional reactions during the period surrounding divorce, children with difficult temperaments and boys in mother-custody homes have more adjustment problems. Over time, children of divorce show improved functioning, but they continue to score slightly lower than children of continuously married parents on a variety of adjustment indicators. Problems with adolescent sexuality, early parenthood, and development of intimate ties surface at later ages.

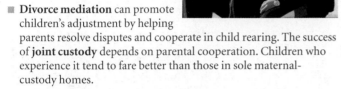

- The overriding factor in positive adjustment following divorce is effective parenting. Contact with noncustodial fathers is important for children of both sexes, and father custody is associated with better outcomes for sons.

- **Divorce mediation** can promote children's adjustment by helping parents resolve disputes and cooperate in child rearing. The success of **joint custody** depends on parental cooperation. Children who experience it tend to fare better than those in sole maternal-custody homes.

- When divorced parents enter new relationships through cohabitation or remarriage, children must adapt to a **blended, or reconstituted, family.** How well they fare depends on which parent remarries and on the age and sex of the child. Girls, older school-age children and adolescents, and children in father–stepmother families have more adjustment problems. Stepparents who move into their roles gradually and couples who form a "parenting coalition" help children adjust.

How do maternal employment and life in dual-earner families affect children's development?

- When mothers enjoy their work and remain committed to parenting, maternal employment is associated with favorable consequences for children, including higher self-esteem, more positive family and peer relations, less gender-stereotyped beliefs, and better grades in school. But when employment is stressful because of time demands or other factors, children are at risk for ineffective parenting and adjustment difficulties.

- In dual-earner families, the father's willingness to share child rearing is crucial for mothers' and children's well-being. Workplace sup-

ports, such as part-time employment and flexible work schedules, help parents meet the demands of work and child rearing.

- **Self-care children** who are old enough to look after themselves, are monitored from a distance, and have a history of authoritative parenting appear responsible and well adjusted. In contrast, children left to their own devices are at risk for antisocial behavior. Children in high-quality after-school programs reap academic and social benefits.

Some Common Problems of Development

Cite common fears and anxieties in middle childhood.

- School-age children's fears are directed toward new concerns, including physical harm, media events, academic failure, parents' health, the possibility of dying, and peer rejection. Children with inhibited temperaments are at high risk for developing **phobias,** or intense, unmanageable fears, including school phobia. Severe anxiety can also result from exposure to harsh living conditions, such as constant violence.

Discuss factors related to child sexual abuse, its consequences for children's development, and its prevention and treatment.

- Child sexual abuse is most commonly committed by male family members, more often against girls than against boys. Abusers have characteristics that predispose them toward sexual exploitation of children. Reported cases are linked to poverty and marital instability, but children in economically advantaged, stable homes are also victims. Adjustment problems of abused children often are severe and include depression, low self-esteem, mistrust of adults, anger and hostility, suicidal reactions, and inappropriate sexual behavior.

- Because sexual abuse is related to other serious family problems, long-term therapy with children and families is usually necessary. Today, courts are prosecuting abusers more vigorously and taking children's testimony more seriously. Educational programs that teach children to recognize inappropriate sexual advances and whom to turn to for help reduce the risk of sexual abuse.

Cite factors that foster resilience in middle childhood.

- Overall, a modest relationship exists between stressful life experiences and psychological disturbance in childhood. Children's personal characteristics, a warm family life that includes authoritative parenting, and social supports at school and in the community are related to resilience in the face of stress. Resilience is not a preexisting attribute but, rather, a capacity that develops through childhood experiences.

Important Terms and Concepts

Milestones
Development in Middle Childhood

6–8 years

PHYSICAL

- Slow gains in height and weight continue until adolescent growth spurt. (412)
- Permanent teeth gradually replace primary teeth. (414)
- Lateralization of the cerebral hemispheres increases; brain plasticity declines. (414)
- Writing becomes smaller and more legible; cursive writing is mastered. (428)
- Drawings become more organized and detailed and include some depth cues. (428)
- Games with rules and rough-and-tumble play become common. (430–431)
- Dominance hierarchies become more stable, especially among boys. (432)

COGNITIVE

- Thought becomes more logical, as shown by the ability to pass Piagetian conservation, class inclusion, and seriation problems. (437–438)
- Spatial reasoning improves, as illustrated by the ability to give clear, well-organized directions and draw coherent cognitive maps. (438–439)
- Attention becomes more selective, adaptable, and planful. (443)
- Uses memory strategies of rehearsal and then organization. (445–446)
- Views the mind as an active, constructive agent, capable of transforming information. (447)

- Awareness of memory strategies and the impact of psychological factors (such as focusing attention) on task performance improves. (447–448)
- Appreciates second-order false beliefs. (447–448)
- By the end of this period, makes the transition from "learning to read" to "reading to learn." (450)
- Uses informal knowledge of number concepts and counting to master more complex mathematical skills. (450–451)`

LANGUAGE

- Vocabulary increases rapidly throughout middle childhood, eventually exceeding 40,000 words. (462)
- Word definitions are concrete, referring to functions and appearance. (462)
- Narratives gradually increase in organization, detail, and expressiveness. (463)
- Metalinguistic awareness improves. (462–464)

EMOTIONAL/SOCIAL

- Self-concept begins to include personality traits and social comparisons. (482–483)
- Self-esteem differentiates, is hierarchically organized, and declines to a more realistic level. (484–485)
- Self-conscious emotions of pride and guilt are governed by personal responsibility. (489)
- Explains emotion by referring to internal states. (490)
- Recognizes that individuals can experience more than one emotion at a time. (490)

- Attends to more cues (facial, situational, and past experiences) in interpreting another's feelings. (490)
- Understands that people may have different perspectives because they have access to different information. (491–492)
- Becomes more independent, trustworthy, and responsible. (492)
- Distributive justice reasoning changes from equality to merit to equity and benevolence. (492, 496)
- Peer interaction becomes more prosocial, and physical aggression declines. (497)

9–11 years

PHYSICAL

- Adolescent growth spurt begins two years earlier in girls than in boys. (412)
- Brain weight increases by 10 percent during middle childhood and adolescence. (414)
- Executes gross motor skills of running, jumping, throwing, catching, kicking, batting, and dribbling more quickly and with better coordination. (427–428)
- Reaction time improves, contributing to motor skill development. (428)
- Representation of depth in drawings expands. (428)

COGNITIVE

- Spatial reasoning improves further, as illustrated by direction-giving and map-drawing. (438)
- Continues to master Piagetian tasks in a step-by-step fashion. (439)
- Selective attention and planning improve further. (443)
- Uses memory strategies of rehearsal and organization more effectively. (445–446)
- Applies several memory strategies at once and begins to use elaboration. (446)
- Long-term knowledge base grows larger and becomes better organized. (446)
- Cognitive self-regulation improves. (448–449)

LANGUAGE

- Word definitions emphasize synonyms and categorical relations. (462)
- Grasps double meanings of words, as reflected in comprehension of metaphors and humor. (462)
- Continues to master complex grammatical constructions. (462–463)

- Adapts messages to the needs of listeners in challenging communicative situations. (463)
- Develops more refined conversational strategies. (463)
- Narratives increase in organization, detail, and expressiveness. (463)

EMOTIONAL/SOCIAL

- Me-self is more refined; self-concept includes positive and negative personality traits. (483)
- Self-esteem tends to rise. (485)
- Distinguishes ability, effort, and luck in attributions for success and failure. (486–487)
- Empathic responding extends to general life conditions. (490)

- Shifts adaptively between problem-centered and emotion-centered strategies in regulating emotion. (490–491)
- Can "step into another's shoes" and view the self from that person's perspective; later, can view the relationship between self and other from the perspective of a third, impartial party. (491)

- Clarifies and links moral rules and social conventions. (493)
- Understanding of individual rights expands. (494)

- Peer groups emerge. (498)
- Friendships become more selective and are based on mutual trust. (499)
- Becomes aware of more gender stereotypes, including personality traits and achievement, but has a flexible appreciation of what males and females can do. (503–504)
- Gender identity expands to include self-evaluations of typicality, contentedness, and pressure to conform. (504–505)
- Sibling rivalry tends to increase. (507)

Note: Numbers in parentheses indicate the page or pages on which each milestone is discussed.

Chapter 14

As Chapter 14 indicates, puberty is both an exhilarating and apprehensive time. In all societies, as young people's bodies mature, they are expected to give up childish ways for greater responsibility. Here, a teenage artist portrays two painters entering the world of adult work.

Reprinted with permission from the International Museum of Children's Art, Oslo, Norway

"Two Painters"
Ishmael Mensah
13 years, Ghana

Physical Development in Adolescence

adolescence The transition between childhood and adulthood.

puberty A flood of biological events leading to an adult-size body and sexual maturity.

O n Sabrina's eleventh birthday, her friend Joyce gave her a surprise party, but Sabrina seemed somber during the celebration. Although Sabrina and Joyce had been close friends since third grade, their relationship was faltering. Sabrina was a head taller and some 20 pounds heavier than most of the other girls in her sixth-grade class. Her breasts were well-developed, her hips and thighs had broadened, and she had begun to menstruate. In contrast, Joyce still had the short, lean, flat-chested body of a school-age child.

Ducking into the bathroom while Joyce and the other girls set the table for cake and ice cream, Sabrina looked herself over in the mirror and frowned. "I feel so big and heavy," she whispered. At church youth group on Sunday evenings, Sabrina broke away from Joyce and spent time with the eighth-grade girls. Around them, she didn't feel so large and awkward.

Once every two weeks, parents gathered at Sabrina's and Joyce's school for discussions about child-rearing concerns. Sabrina's Italian-American parents, Franca and Antonio, attended whenever they could. "How you know they are becoming teenagers is this," volunteered Antonio. "The bedroom door is closed, and they want to be alone. Also, they contradict and disagree. I tell Sabrina, 'You have to go to Aunt Gina's on Saturday for dinner with the family.' The next thing I know, she's arguing with me."

Sabrina has entered **adolescence**, the transition between childhood and adulthood. In industrialized societies, the skills young people must master are so complex and the choices confronting them so diverse that adolescence is greatly extended. But around the world, the basic tasks of this period are much the same. Sabrina must accept her full-grown body, acquire adult ways of thinking, attain greater independence from her family, develop more mature ways of relating to peers of both sexes, and begin to construct an identity—a secure sense of who she is in terms of sexual, vocational, moral, ethnic, religious, and other life values and goals.

The beginning of adolescence is marked by **puberty**, a flood of biological events leading to an adult-size body and sexual maturity. As Sabrina's reactions suggest, entry into adolescence can be an especially trying time for some young people. In this chapter, we trace the events of puberty and take up a variety of health concerns—physical exercise, nutrition, sexual activity, substance abuse, and other problems affecting teenagers who encounter difficulties on the path to maturity. But before we delve into these specifics, let's consider how views of adolescence have changed over the past century.

Conceptions of Adolescence

Why is Sabrina self-conscious, argumentative, and in retreat from family activities? Historically, theorists explained the impact of puberty on psychological development by resorting to extremes—either a biological or a social explanation. Today, researchers realize that both biological and social forces jointly contribute to adolescent psychological change.

The Biological Perspective

TAKE A MOMENT... Ask several parents of young children what they expect their sons and daughters to be like as teenagers. You will probably get answers like these: "Rebellious and irresponsible," "Full of rages and tempers" (Buchanan & Holmbeck, 1998). This widespread view dates back to the ideas of eighteenth-century philosopher Jean-Jacques Rousseau (see Chapter 1), who believed that the biological upheaval of puberty triggered heightened emotionality, conflict, and defiance of adults.

In the early twentieth century, major theorists picked up this storm-and-stress perspective. The most influential, G. Stanley Hall, based his ideas about development on Darwin's theory of evolution. Hall (1904) described adolescence as a cascade of instinctual passions, a phase of growth so turbulent that it resembled the era in which humans evolved from savages into civilized beings. Similarly, Anna Freud (1969), who expanded the focus on adolescence of her father Sigmund Freud's theory, viewed the teenage years as a biologically based, universal "developmental disturbance." In Freud's *genital stage*, sexual impulses reawaken, triggering psychological conflict and volatile behavior. As adolescents find intimate partners, inner forces achieve a new, more mature harmony, and the stage concludes with marriage, birth, and child rearing. In this way, young people fulfill their biological destiny: sexual reproduction and survival of the species.

The Social Perspective

Contemporary research suggests that the storm-and-stress notion of adolescence is greatly exaggerated. Certain problems, such as eating disorders, depression, suicide, and lawbreaking, do occur more often in adolescence than earlier (Farrington, 2004; Graber, 2004). But the overall rate of serious psychological disturbance rises only slightly (by about 2 percent) from childhood to adolescence, when it is the same as in the adult population—about 20 percent (Costello & Angold, 1995). Although some teenagers encounter serious difficulties, emotional turbulence is not routine.

The first researcher to point out the wide variability in adolescent adjustment was anthropologist Margaret Mead (1928). She returned from the Pacific islands of Samoa with a startling conclusion: Because of the culture's relaxed social relationships and openness toward sexuality, adolescence "is perhaps the pleasantest time the Samoan girl (or boy) will ever know" (p. 308). Mead offered an alternative view in which the social environment is entirely responsible for the range of teenage experiences, from erratic and agitated to calm and stress-free. Later researchers found that Samoan adolescence was not as untroubled as Mead had assumed (Freeman, 1983). Still, she showed that to understand adolescent development, researchers must pay greater attention to social and cultural influences.

A Balanced Point of View

Today we know that biological, psychological, and social forces combine to influence adolescent development (Magnusson, 1999; Susman & Rogol, 2004). Biological changes are universal—found in all primates and all cultures. These internal stresses and the social expectations accompanying them—that the young person give up childish ways, develop new interpersonal relationships, and take on greater responsibility—are likely to prompt moments of uncertainty, self-doubt, and disappointment in all teenagers. Adolescents' prior and current experiences affect their success in surmounting these challenges.

At the same time, the length of adolescence and the number of hurdles a young person must overcome differ from one culture to the next. Most tribal and village societies have only a brief intervening phase between childhood and full assumption of adult roles (Schlegel & Barry, 1991; Weisfeld, 1997). In industrialized nations, where successful participation in economic life requires many years of education, young people face extra years of dependence on parents and postponement of sexual gratification as they prepare for a productive work life. As a result, adolescence is greatly extended—so much so that researchers commonly divide it into three phases:

1. *Early adolescence* (11–12 to 14 years): This is a period of rapid pubertal change.
2. *Middle adolescence* (14 to 16 years): Pubertal changes are now nearly complete.
3. *Late adolescence* (16 to 18 years): The young person achieves full adult appearance and anticipates assumption of adult roles.

The more the social environment supports young people in achieving adult responsibilities, the better they adjust. For all the biological tensions and uncertainties about the future that teenagers feel, most negotiate this period successfully. With this in mind, let's look closely at puberty, the dawning of adolescent development.

Puberty: The Physical Transition to Adulthood

The changes of puberty are dramatic. Within a few years, the body of the school-age child is transformed into that of a full-grown adult. Genetically influenced hormonal processes regulate pubertal growth. Girls, who have been advanced in physical maturity since the prenatal period, reach puberty, on average, two years earlier than boys.

Hormonal Changes

The complex hormonal changes that underlie puberty take place gradually and are under way by age 8 or 9 (see Figure 14.1 on page 532). Recall from Chapter 8 that the *pituitary gland,* located at the base of the brain, releases *growth hormone (GH)* and stimulates other glands to produce hormones that act on body tissues, causing them to mature. Secretions of GH and *thyroxine* (a hormone released by the thyroid gland) increase, leading to tremendous gains in body size and to attainment of skeletal maturity.

Sexual maturation is controlled by the sex hormones. Although we think of *estrogens* as female hormones and *androgens* as male hormones, both types are present in each sex but in different amounts. The boy's testes release large quantities of the androgen *testosterone,* which leads to muscle growth, body and facial hair, and other male sex characteristics. Androgens (especially testosterone for boys) exert a GH-enhancing effect, contributing greatly to gains in body size. The testes secrete small amounts of estrogen as well—the reason that 50 percent of boys experience temporary breast enlargement. In both sexes, estrogens also increase GH secretion, adding to the growth spurt and, in combination with androgens, stimulating gains in bone density, which continue into early adulthood (Delemarre-van de Waal, van Coeverden, & Rotteveel, 2001; Styne, 2003).

Estrogens released by girls' ovaries cause the breasts, uterus, and vagina to mature, the body to take on feminine proportions, and fat to accumulate. Estrogens also contribute to regulation of the menstrual cycle. *Adrenal androgens,* released from the adrenal glands on top of each kidney, influence girls'

Sex differences in pubertal growth are obvious among these sixth graders. Although all are the same age, the girl is taller and more mature looking than the boys.

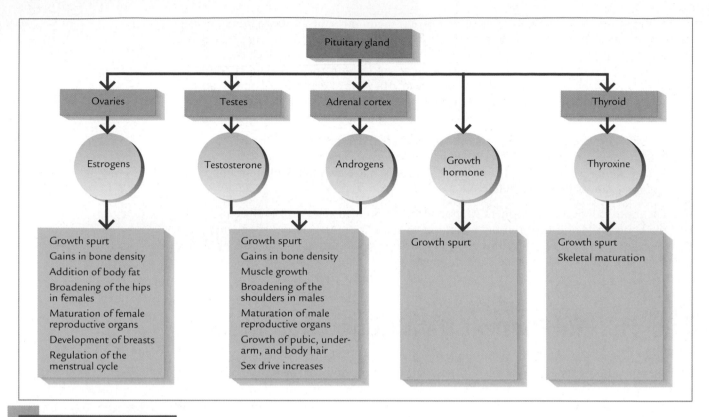

FIGURE 14.1

Hormonal influences on the body at puberty. The pituitary gland releases hormones that either induce growth directly or stimulate other endocrine glands to release growth-inducing hormones.

height spurt and stimulate growth of underarm and pubic hair. They have little impact on boys, whose physical characteristics are mainly influenced by androgen and estrogen secretions from the testes.

As you can see, pubertal changes are of two broad types: (1) overall body growth, and (2) maturation of sexual characteristics. We have seen that the hormones responsible for sexual maturity also affect body growth; boys and girls differ in both aspects. In fact, puberty is the time of greatest sexual differentiation since prenatal life.

Body Growth

The first outward sign of puberty is the rapid gain in height and weight known as the **growth spurt.** On average, it is under way for North American and European girls shortly after age 10, for boys around age 12½. Because estrogens trigger and then restrain GH secretion more readily than androgens, the typical girl is taller and heavier during early adolescence (Archibald, Graber, & Brooks-Gunn, 2006; Bogin, 2001). At age 14, however, she is surpassed by the typical boy, whose adolescent growth spurt has now started, whereas hers is almost finished. Growth in body size is complete for most girls by age 16 and for boys by age 17½, when the epiphyses at the ends of the long bones close completely (see Chapter 8, page 294).

Altogether, adolescents add 10 to 11 inches in height and 50 to 75 pounds—nearly 50 percent of adult body weight. But even more striking is the swiftness of these changes. When growing at their peak, boys add more than 4 inches and 26 pounds in a single year, girls about 3.5 inches and 20 pounds (Rogol, Roemmich, & Clark, 2002). Figure 14.2 illustrates pubertal changes in general body growth.

growth spurt A rapid gain in height and weight that is the first outward sign of puberty.

BODY PROPORTIONS ■ During puberty, the cephalocaudal trend of infancy and childhood reverses. The hands, legs, and feet accelerate first, followed by the torso, which accounts for most

COURTESY PHOTO

Andy at 15 years

Andy at 11 years

Amy at 12 years

Andy at 12 years

Amy at 13 years

Amy at 15 years

FIGURE 14.2

Body growth during adolescence.
Because the pubertal growth spurt takes place earlier for girls than for boys, Amy reached her adult body size earlier than Andy. Rapid pubertal growth is accompanied by large sex differences in body proportions that were not present in middle childhood (see Chapter 11, page 412).

of the adolescent height gain (Sheehy et al., 1999). This pattern helps explain why early adolescents often appear awkward and out of proportion—long-legged and with giant feet and hands.

Large sex differences in body proportions also appear, caused by the action of sex hormones on the skeleton. Boys' shoulders broaden relative to the hips, whereas girls' hips broaden relative to the shoulders and waist. Of course, boys also end up considerably larger than girls, and their legs are longer in relation to the rest of the body. The major reason is that boys have two extra years of preadolescent growth, when the legs are growing the fastest.

MUSCLE–FAT MAKEUP AND OTHER INTERNAL CHANGES ■ Sabrina worried about her weight because compared with her later-developing girlfriends, she had accumulated much more fat. Around age 8, girls start to add more fat than boys on their arms, legs, and trunk, a trend that accelerates between ages 11 and 16. In contrast, arm and leg fat decreases in adolescent boys. Although both sexes gain in muscle, this increase is 150 percent greater in boys, who develop larger skeletal muscles, hearts, and lung capacity (Rogol, Roemmich, & Clark, 2002). Also, the number of red blood cells—and therefore the ability to carry oxygen from the lungs to the muscles—increases in boys but not in girls. Altogether, boys gain far more muscle strength than girls, a difference that contributes to boys' superior athletic performance during the teenage years (Ramos et al., 1998).

Motor Development and Physical Activity

Puberty brings steady improvement in gross motor performance, but the pattern of change differs for boys and girls. Girls' gains are slow and gradual, leveling off by age 14. In contrast, boys show a dramatic spurt in strength, speed, and endurance that continues through the

These exuberant young baseball players celebrate each other's hard-won athletic accomplishments. However, some adolescent boys become so obsessed with physical prowess that they turn to performance-enhancing drugs, ignoring their dangerous side effects.

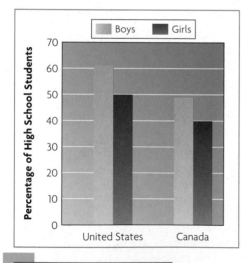

FIGURE 14.3

Involvement of American and Canadian high school students in school sports outside physical education classes. In both nations, more boys than girls participate. Nevertheless, girls' participation has increased greatly over the past several decades. (From Canadian Fitness and Lifestyle Research Institute, 2005; National Federation of State High School Associations, 2006.)

teenage years. The gender gap in physical skill widens with age. By mid-adolescence, few girls perform as well as the average boy in running speed, broad jump, or throwing distance. And practically no boys score as low as the average girl (Haywood & Getchell, 2004; Malina & Bouchard, 1991).

Because boys and girls are no longer well-matched physically, gender-segregated physical education usually begins in middle or junior high school. At the same time, athletic options for both sexes expand. Many new sports are added to the curriculum—track and field, wrestling, tackle football, weight lifting, floor hockey, archery, tennis, and golf, to name just a few.

Among adolescent boys, athletic competence is strongly related to peer admiration and self-esteem. Some adolescents become so obsessed with physical prowess that they turn to performance-enhancing drugs, with rates of use rising sharply with age. In recent large-scale surveys, about 8 percent of North American high school seniors, mostly boys, reported using creatine, an over-the-counter substance that increases the speed with which energy is supplied to muscle. Although creatine enhances short-term muscle power, it is associated with muscle cramping, intestinal discomfort, rashes, anxiety, fatigue, and (more seriously) muscle tissue disease, brain seizures, and heart irregularities. Furthermore, 4 percent of seniors, again mostly boys, have taken anabolic steroids or a related substance, androstenedione—powerful prescription medications that boost muscle mass and strength (Focus on the Family Canada, 2004; Johnston et al., 2006). Teenagers usually obtain steroids illegally, ignoring their side effects, which range from acne, excess body hair, and high blood pressure to mood swings, aggressive behavior, and damage to the liver, circulatory system, and reproductive organs (American Academy of Pediatrics, 2005b). Coaches and health professionals should inform teenagers of the dangers of using performance-enhancing substances.

In 1972, the U.S. federal government required schools receiving public funds to provide equal opportunities for males and females in all educational programs, including athletics. Since then, high school girls' sports participation has increased greatly in both the United States and Canada, although it still falls short of boys' (see Figure 14.3). In Chapter 11, we saw that from an early age, girls get less encouragement and recognition for athletic achievement, a pattern that persists into the teenage years. Recall that only about 40 percent of North American girls and 50 percent of boys are active enough for good health (see page 432). And activity rates of U.S. and Canadian youths decline over the teenage years (Faulkner & Goodman, 2007; U.S. Department of Health and Human Services, 2006j).

Besides improving motor performance, sports and exercise influence cognitive and social development. Interschool and intramural athletics provide important lessons in teamwork, problem solving, assertiveness, and competition. And regular, sustained physical activity is associated with lifelong health benefits, including enhanced functioning of the immune system, cardiovascular health, and improved psychological well-being (Newcombe & Boyle, 1995). Yet in high school, only 55 percent of U.S. and 65 percent of Canadian students are enrolled in physical education, and only about one-third of students attend a physical education class daily (Canadian Fitness & Lifestyle Research Institute, 2005b; U.S. Department of Health and Human Services, 2006j). Attendance drops off with each grade, especially for girls.

Required daily physical education, aimed at helping all teenagers find pleasure in sports and exercise, is a vital means of promoting adolescent physical and psychological well-being. In a longitudinal study, participating in team or individual sports at age 14 at least once a week for girls and twice a week for boys predicted high rates of physical activity at age 31. Endurance sports, such as running and cycling—activities that can easily be performed

TABLE 14.1   Average Age and Age Range of Major Pubertal Changes in North American Boys and Girls

GIRLS	AVERAGE	RANGE	BOYS	AVERAGE	RANGE
Breasts begin to "bud"	10	(8–13)	Testes begin to enlarge	11.5	(9.5–13.5)
Height spurt begins	10	(8–13)	Pubic hair appears	12	(10–15)
Pubic hair appears	10.5	(8–14)	Penis begins to enlarge	12	(10.5–14.5)
Peak strength spurt	11.6	(9.5–14)	Height spurt begins	12.5	(10.5–16)
Peak height spurt	11.7	(10–13.5)	Spermarche (first ejaculation) occurs	13.5	(12–16)
Menarche (first menstruation) occurs	12.5	(10.5–14)	Peak height spurt	14	(12.5–15.5)
Peak weight spurt	12.7	(10–14)	Peak weight spurt	14	(12.5–15.5)
Adult stature reached	13	(10–16)	Facial hair begins to grow	14	(12.5–15.5)
Breast growth completed	14	(10–16)	Voice begins to deepen	14	(12.5–15.5)
Pubic hair growth completed	14.5	(14–15)	Penis and testes growth completed	14.5	(12.5–16)
			Peak strength spurt	15.3	(13–17)
			Adult stature reached	15.5	(13.5–17.5)
			Pubic hair growth completed	15.5	(14–17)

Sources: Chumlea et al., 2003; Rogol, Roemmich, & Clark, 2002; Wu, Mendola, & Buck, 2002.

on one's own time, without expensive equipment or special facilities—were especially likely to carry over into adulthood (Tammelin et al., 2003). Also, adolescent exertion during exercise, defined as sweating and breathing heavily, is one of the best predictors of adult physical exercise, perhaps because it fosters high *physical self-efficacy*—belief in one's ability to sustain an exercise program (Motl et al., 2002; Telama et al., 2005).

Sexual Maturation

Accompanying the rapid increase in body size are changes in physical features related to sexual functioning. Some, called **primary sexual characteristics,** involve the reproductive organs directly (ovaries, uterus, and vagina in females; penis, scrotum, and testes in males). Others, called **secondary sexual characteristics,** are visible on the outside of the body and serve as additional signs of sexual maturity (for example, breast development in females and the appearance of underarm and pubic hair in both sexes). As Table 14.1 shows, these characteristics develop in a fairly standard sequence, although the ages at which each begins and is completed vary greatly. Typically, pubertal development takes about 4 years, but some adolescents complete it in 2 years, whereas others take 5 to 6 years.

SEXUAL MATURATION IN GIRLS ■ The scientific name for first menstruation is **menarche,** from the Greek word *arche,* meaning "beginning." Although most people view menarche as the major sign of puberty in girls, it actually occurs late in the sequence of pubertal events. Female puberty begins with the budding of the breasts, the growth spurt, and the appearance of pubic hair. Typically, menarche occurs around age 12½ for North American girls, 13 for Western Europeans. But the age range is wide, extending from 10½ to 15½ years. Following menarche, breast and pubic hair growth are completed, and underarm hair appears. Most girls take 3 to 4 years to complete this sequence, but some do so in 2 years, whereas others take 5 to 6 years (Archibald, Graber, & Brooks-Gunn, 2006).

Notice in Table 14.1 that nature delays sexual maturity until the girl's body is large enough for childbearing; menarche takes place after the peak of the height spurt. As an extra measure of

primary sexual characteristics Characteristics of the reproductive organs— ovaries, uterus, and vagina in females; penis, scrotum, and testes in males.

secondary sexual characteristics Features visible on the outside of the body that serve as signs of sexual maturity, including breast development in females and the appearance of underarm and pubic hair in both sexes.

menarche Scientific name for first menstruation, from the Greek word *arche,* meaning "beginning."

security, for 12 to 18 months following menarche, the menstrual cycle often occurs without an ovum being released from the ovaries (Bogin, 2001). However, this temporary period of sterility does not occur in all girls, and it cannot be counted on for protection against pregnancy.

SEXUAL MATURATION IN BOYS ■ The first sign of puberty in boys is the enlargement of the testes (glands that manufacture sperm), accompanied by changes in the texture and color of the scrotum. Soon after, pubic hair emerges, and the penis begins to enlarge (Rogol, Roemmich, & Clark, 2002).

Refer again to Table 14.1, and you will see that the growth spurt occurs much later in the sequence of pubertal events for boys than for girls. Also, boys' height gain is more intense and longer-lasting. When it reaches its peak (about age 14), enlargement of the testes and penis is nearly complete, and underarm hair appears soon after. Facial and body hair also emerge just after the peak in body growth and increase gradually for several years. Another landmark of male physical maturity is the deepening of the voice as the larynx enlarges and the vocal cords lengthen. (Girls' voices also deepen slightly.) Voice change usually takes place at the peak of the male growth spurt and often is not complete until puberty is over (Archibald, Graber, & Brooks-Gunn, 2006). When it first occurs, boys' newly acquired baritone occasionally breaks into a high-pitched sound.

While the penis is growing, the prostate gland and seminal vesicles (which together produce semen, the fluid containing sperm) enlarge. Then, around age 13½, **spermarche,** or first ejaculation, occurs (Rogol, Roemmich, & Clark, 2002). For a while, the semen contains few living sperm. So, like girls, boys have an initial period of reduced fertility.

Individual Differences in Pubertal Growth

Heredity contributes substantially to the timing of pubertal changes. Identical twins are more similar than fraternal twins in attainment of most pubertal milestones, including growth spurt, menarche, breast development, body hair, and voice change (Eaves et al., 2004; Mustanski et al., 2004). Nutrition and exercise also make a difference. In females, a sharp rise in body weight and fat may trigger sexual maturation. Fat cells release a protein called *leptin,* which is believed to signal the brain that the girl's energy stores are sufficient for puberty—a likely reason that breast and pubic hair growth and menarche occur earlier for heavier and, especially, obese girls. In contrast, girls who begin rigorous athletic training at young ages or who eat very little (both of which reduce the percentage of body fat) usually experience later puberty (Anderson, Dallal, & Must, 2003; Delemarre-van de Waal, 2002; Slyper, 2005).

Variations in pubertal growth also exist between regions of the world and between SES and ethnic groups. Physical health plays a major role. In poverty-stricken regions where malnutrition and infectious disease are common, menarche is greatly delayed, occurring as late as age 14 to 16 in many parts of Africa. Within developing countries, girls from higher-income families typically reach menarche 6 to 18 months earlier than those living in economically disadvantaged homes (Parent et al., 2003).

But in industrialized nations where food is abundant, the joint roles of heredity and environment in pubertal growth are apparent. For example, breast and pubic hair growth begin, on average, around age 9 in African-American girls—a year earlier than in Caucasian-American girls. And African-American girls reach menarche about 6 months earlier, around age 12. Although widespread overweight and obesity in the black population contribute, a genetically influenced faster rate of physical maturation also seems to be involved. Black girls usually reach menarche before white girls of the same age and body weight (Anderson, Dallal, & Must, 2003; Freedman et al., 2002; Chumlea et al., 2003).

Early family experiences may also contribute to the timing of puberty. One theory suggests that humans have evolved to be sensitive to the emotional quality of their childhood environments. When children's safety and security are at risk, it is adaptive for them to reproduce early. A growing number of studies indicate that girls exposed to family conflict and both boys and girls exposed to parental separation tend to reach puberty early. In contrast, girls with warm, stable family ties reach menarche relatively late (Bogaert, 2005; Tremblay & Frigon, 2005; Ellis,

spermarche Scientific name for first ejaculation.

FIGURE 14.4

Secular trend in age at menarche in six industrialized nations.   Age of menarche declined from 1900 to 1970. Thereafter, a few countries showed a modest, continuing decline due to rising rates of overweight and obesity. Others leveled off or underwent a slight reversal.   (From S. M. P. F. de Muinck Keizer-Schrama & D. Mul, 2001, "Trends in Pubertal Development in Europe," *Human Reproduction Update, 7,* p. 289. Reprinted by permission.)

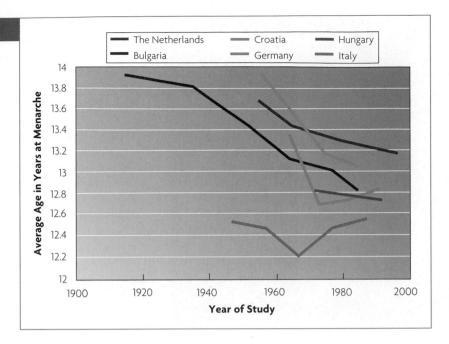

2004; Mustanski et al., 2004; Romans et al., 2003). But critics of this theory claim that the process through which parental behavior affects timing of menarche is unclear. According to an alternative explanation, mothers who reached puberty early are more likely to bear children earlier, which increases risk of marital conflict and separation. At the same time, the children of these mothers may inherit a genetic tendency toward early puberty.

The Secular Trend

In Chapter 11 we saw that children in industrialized nations grow faster and larger than in past generations. Similarly, age of menarche declined steadily—by about 3 to 4 months per decade—from 1900 to 1970, a period in which nutrition, health care, sanitation, and control of infectious disease improved greatly (see Figure 14.4). Boys, too, have reached puberty earlier in recent decades (Karpati et al., 2002). This *secular trend* in pubertal timing lends added support to the role of physical well-being in adolescent growth.

As noted in Chapter 11, the secular gain in height has slowed. And the trend toward earlier menarche has stopped or undergone a slight reversal in most industrialized nations. But in North America and a few European countries, soaring rates of overweight and obesity may be responsible for a modest, continuing trend toward earlier menarche (Kaplowitz, 2006; Parent et al., 2003). A worrisome consequence is that girls who reach sexual maturity at age 10 or 11 will feel pressure to act much older than they are. As we will see shortly, early-maturing girls are at risk for unfavorable peer involvements, including sexual activity.

Brain Development

The physical transformations of adolescence include major changes in the brain. In Chapter 11, we noted that during middle childhood and adolescence, *white matter* (myelinated nerve fibers) increases while *gray matter* (neurons and supportive material) declines, especially in the frontal and parietal lobes of the cerebral cortex and in the corpus callosum (see page 414 to review). Brain-imaging research reveals continued pruning of unused synapses in the cerebral cortex, especially in the frontal lobes—the "governor" of thought and action. In addition, growth and myelination of stimulated neural fibers accelerate, contributing to a slight increase in brain weight and strengthening connections among various brain regions. In particular, linkages between the two cerebral hemispheres through the corpus callosum and between the frontal lobes and other brain areas expand and attain rapid communication (Blakemore & Choudhury, 2006; Keating, 2004; Lenroot & Giedd, 2006). This sculpting of the adolescent brain supports diverse cognitive skills, including improved processing speed, attention, memory, planning, capacity to integrate information, and self-regulation.

In addition, sensitivity of neurons to certain chemical messages changes. In humans and other mammals, neurons become more responsive to excitatory neurotransmitters during

Because neurons become more sensitive to certain neurotransmitters during adolescence, young people react more strongly to stressful and pleasurable events than they did as children. You can see this intensity in the elation of these teenagers, completely engaged in the delights of summer.

puberty. As a result, adolescents react more strongly to stressful events, and they also experience pleasurable stimuli more intensely (Dahl, 2004; Spear, 2004). These changes probably contribute to the drive for novel experiences, including drug taking, during this period, especially among teenagers who are highly stressed and engage in reward seeking to counteract chronic emotional pain. Alterations in neurotransmitter activity may also be involved in adolescents' increased susceptibility to certain disorders, such as depression and eating disturbances.

To what extent are the hormonal changes of puberty responsible for adolescent brain growth and reorganization? Researchers do not yet have a ready answer. But their investigations of the transformations that occur—much greater than previously thought—enhance our understanding of both the cognitive advances and the troubling behaviors of adolescence, along with teenagers' need for plenty of adult patience, oversight, and guidance.

Changing States of Arousal

At puberty, revisions occur in the way the brain regulates the timing of sleep, perhaps because of increased neural sensitivity to evening light. As a result, adolescents go to bed much later than they did as children. Yet they need almost as much sleep as they did in middle childhood— about nine hours. When they must get up early for school, their sleep needs are not satisfied.

This sleep "phase delay" strengthens with pubertal growth. But today's teenagers often have evening social activities and part-time jobs, as well as TVs, computers, and phones in their bedrooms. As a result, they get much less sleep than teenagers of previous generations (Carskadon, Acebo, & Jenni, 2004; Carskadon et al., 2002). Sleep-deprived adolescents perform especially poorly on cognitive tasks during morning hours. And they are more likely to achieve less well in school, suffer from depressed mood, and engage in high-risk behaviors, including drinking and reckless driving (Dahl & Lewin, 2002; Hansen et al., 2005). Although most teenagers say they enjoy staying up late, they also complain of daytime sleepiness and engage in sleep rebound on weekends, when they wake up later. This sustains the pattern by leading to difficulty falling asleep on subsequent evenings (Laberge et al., 2001). Later school start times ease sleep loss but do not eliminate it. Because of the dangers of sleep deprivation, educating teenagers' about the importance of sleep is vital.

Ask Yourself

Review Many people believe that adolescents are rebellious because of the rising sexual passions of puberty. Where did this belief originate? Why is it incorrect?

Review What changes in the brain contribute to cognitive advances during adolescence? What changes promote increased sensation seeking, especially among highly stressed teenagers?

Apply When he was younger, Jonah used to go to bed early, but now, at 16, he routinely stays up until 2:00 A.M. He is often late for school and sometimes dozes in class. Why might Jonah's sleep habits have changed, and what can his parents and his school do to help?

Reflect Do you currently engage in regular sports or exercise? If so, what activities do you enjoy, and why? How did your experiences during adolescence influence your current involvement in physical activity?

The Psychological Impact of Pubertal Events

TAKE A MOMENT... Think back to your late elementary school and junior high days. As you reached puberty, how did your feelings about yourself and your relationships with others change? Research reveals that pubertal events affect the adolescent's self-image, mood, and interaction with parents and peers. Some of these outcomes are a response to dramatic physical change, regardless of when it occurs. Others have to do with pubertal timing.

Reactions to Pubertal Changes

Two generations ago, menarche was often traumatic. Today, girls commonly react with "surprise," undoubtedly due to the sudden onset of the event. Otherwise, they typically report a mixture of positive and negative emotions. Yet wide individual differences exist that depend on prior knowledge and support from family members, which in turn are influenced by cultural attitudes toward puberty and sexuality.

For girls who have no advance information, menarche can be shocking and disturbing. In the 1950s, up to 50 percent received no prior warning, and of those who did, many were given negative, "grin-and-bear-it" messages (Costos, Ackerman, & Paradis, 2002; Shainess, 1961). Today, few are uninformed, a shift that is probably due to more widespread health education classes and parents' greater willingness to discuss pubertal changes (Omar, McElderry, & Zakharia, 2003). Almost all girls get some information from their mothers. And some evidence suggests that compared with Caucasian-American families, African-American families may better prepare girls for menarche, treat it as an important milestone, and express less conflict over girls reaching sexual maturity—factors that lead African-American girls to react more favorably (Martin, 1996; Scott et al., 1989).

Like girls' reactions to menarche, boys' responses to spermarche reflect mixed feelings. Virtually all boys know about ejaculation ahead of time, but many say that no one spoke to them prior to or during puberty about physical changes (Omar, McElderry, & Zakharia, 2003). Usually they get their information from their own reading. Even boys who had advance information often say that their first ejaculation occurred earlier than they expected and that they were unprepared for it. As with girls, boys who feel better prepared tend to react more positively (Stein & Reiser, 1994). But whereas almost all girls eventually tell a friend that they are menstruating, far fewer boys tell anyone about spermarche (Downs & Fuller, 1991). Overall, boys get much less social support than girls for the changes of puberty. This suggests that boys might benefit, especially, from opportunities to ask questions and discuss feelings with a sympathetic parent or health professional.

Many tribal and village societies celebrate physical maturity with an *initiation ceremony,* a ritualized announcement to the community that marks an important change in privilege and responsibility. Consequently, young people know that reaching puberty is valued in their culture. In contrast, Western societies grant little formal recognition to movement from childhood to adolescence or from adolescence to adulthood. Certain ethnic and religious ceremonies, such as the Jewish bar or bat mitzvah and the *quinceañera* in Hispanic communities (celebrating a 15-year-old girl's sexual maturity and marriage availability), resemble initiation ceremonies. But although they carry a meaningful social message within the young person's ethnic group, they do not result in a significant change in social status in the larger society.

In Hispanic communities, the *quinceañera,* celebrated at age 15, is a rite of passage honoring a girl's journey from childhood to maturity. It usually begins with a mass in which the priest blesses gifts presented to the girl.

Instead, Western adolescents are granted partial adult status at many different ages—for example, ages for starting employment, for driving, for leaving high school, for voting, and for drinking. And in some contexts (at home and at school), they may still be regarded as children. The absence of a single widely accepted marker of physical and social maturity makes the process of becoming an adult more confusing.

Pubertal Change, Emotion, and Social Behavior

A common belief is that puberty has something to do with adolescent moodiness and the desire for greater physical and psychological separation from parents. What does research say about these relationships?

ADOLESCENT MOODINESS ■ Although research reveals that higher hormone levels are linked to greater moodiness, these relationships are not strong (Buchanan, Eccles, & Becker, 1992). What else might contribute to the common observation that adolescents are moody? In several studies, the moods of children, adolescents, and adults were monitored by having them carry electronic pagers. Over a one-week period, they were beeped at random intervals and asked to write down what they were doing, whom they were with, and how they felt.

As expected, adolescents reported less favorable moods than school-age children and adults (Larson et al., 2002; Larson & Lampman-Petraitis, 1989). But negative moods were linked to a greater number of negative life events, such as difficulties with parents, disciplinary actions at school, and breaking up with a boyfriend or girlfriend. Negative events increased steadily from childhood to adolescence, and teenagers also seemed to react to them with greater emotion than children (Larson & Ham, 1993). (Recall that stress reactivity is heightened by changes in brain neurotransmitter activity during adolescence.)

Compared with the moods of older adolescents and adults, those of younger adolescents (ages 12 to 16) were less stable, often shifting from cheerful to sad and back again. These mood swings were strongly related to situational changes. High points of adolescents' days were times spent with friends and in self-chosen leisure activities. Low points tended to occur in adult-structured settings—class, job, and religious services. Furthermore, teenagers' emotional highs coincided with Friday and Saturday evenings, especially in high school (see Figure 14.5). Going out with friends and romantic partners increases so dramatically during adolescence that it becomes a "cultural script" for what is *supposed* to happen. Teenagers who spend weekend evenings at home often feel profoundly lonely (Larson & Richards, 1998).

Fortunately, teenagers' frequent reports of negative mood level off around tenth grade, when their emotions also become more stable. After age 18, young people typically experience minor fluctuations around a mildly positive state (Larson et al., 2002; Diener et al., 1999; Holsen, Kraft, & Vitterso, 2000). In sum, biological, psychological, and social forces combine to make adolescence a time of deeper valleys and higher peaks in emotional experience than the periods that surround it—a conclusion that is consistent with the balanced view presented earlier in this chapter.

PARENT–CHILD RELATIONSHIPS ■ Sabrina's father noticed that as his children entered adolescence, they kept their bedroom doors closed, resisted spending time with the family, and became more argumentative. Sabrina and her mother squabbled over Sabrina's messy room ("It's *my* room, Mom. You don't have to live in it!") and her clothing purchases ("Sabrina, if you *buy* it, then *wear* it. Otherwise, you're just wasting money!"). And Sabrina resisted the family's regular weekend visit to Aunt Gina's

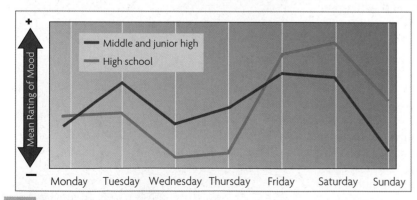

FIGURE 14.5

Younger and older adolescents' emotional experiences across the week. Adolescents' reports revealed that emotional high points are on Fridays and Saturdays. Mood drops on Sunday, before returning to school, and during the week, as students spend much time in adult-structured settings in school. (From R. Larson & M. Richards, 1998, "Waiting for the Weekend: Friday and Saturday Night as the Emotional Climax of the Week." In A. C. Crouter & R. Larson [Eds.], *Temporal Rhythms in Adolescence: Clocks, Calendars, and the Coordination of Daily Life.* San Francisco: Jossey-Bass, p. 41. Reprinted by permission.)

("Why do I have to go *every* week?"). Research in cultures as diverse as the United States and Turkey show that puberty is related to a rise in parent–child conflict. During this time, both parents and teenagers report feeling less close to one another (Gure, Ucanok, & Sayil, 2006; Laursen, Coy, & Collins, 1998; Steinberg & Morris, 2001). Frequency of arguing is surprisingly similar across North American subcultures, occurring as often in families of European descent as in immigrant Asian and Hispanic families whose traditions emphasize respect for parental authority (Fuligni, 1998).

Why should a youngster's more adultlike appearance trigger these disputes? According to an evolutionary view, the association may have adaptive value. Among nonhuman primates, the young typically leave the family group around the time of puberty. The same is true in many nonindustrialized cultures (Caine, 1986; Schlegel & Barry, 1991). Departure of young people discourages sexual relations between close blood relatives. But because they are still economically dependent on parents, adolescents in industrialized nations cannot leave the family. Consequently, a modern substitute seems to have emerged: psychological distancing.

As children become physically mature, they demand to be treated in adultlike ways. And as we will see in later chapters, adolescents' new powers of reasoning may also contribute to a rise in family tensions. Parent–adolescent disagreements focus largely on mundane, day-to-day matters—driving, dating partners, curfews, and the like (Adams & Laursen, 2001). But beneath these disputes lie serious concerns: parental efforts to protect teenagers from substance use, auto accidents, and early sex. The larger the gap between parents' and adolescents' views of teenagers' readiness for new responsibilities, the more quarreling (Deković, Noom, & Meeus, 1997).

Parent–daughter conflict tends to be more intense than conflict with sons, perhaps because parents place more restrictions on girls (Allison & Schultz, 2004). But most disputes are mild, and by late adolescence, only a small minority of families experience continuing friction. Parents and teenagers display both conflict and affection, and they usually agree on important values, such as honesty and the importance of education. Although separation from parents is adaptive, both generations benefit from warm, protective family bonds throughout the lifespan.

Puberty brings an increase in parent–child conflict—psychological distancing that may, in part, be a modern substitute for physical departure from the family. Unlike nonhuman primates and young people in many nonindustrialized cultures, adolescents in industrialized societies remain economically dependent on and live with parents long after they reach puberty.

Pubertal Timing

"All our children were early maturers," said Franca during the parents' discussion group. "The three boys were tall by age 12 or 13, but it was easier for them. They felt big and important. Sabrina was skinny as a little girl, but now she says she is too fat and needs to diet. She thinks about boys and doesn't concentrate on her schoolwork."

Findings of several studies match the experiences of Sabrina and her brothers. Both adults and peers viewed early-maturing boys as relaxed, independent, self-confident, and physically attractive. Popular with agemates, they tended to hold leadership positions in school and to be athletic stars. In contrast, late-maturing boys were viewed by both adults and peers as anxious, overly talkative, and attention-seeking (Brooks-Gunn, 1988; Clausen, 1975). However, early-maturing boys, though viewed as well-adjusted, report more psychological stress and problem behaviors (sexual activity, smoking, drinking, delinquency) than their later-maturing agemates (Ge, Conger, & Elder, 2001; Huddleston & Ge, 2003).

In contrast, early-maturing girls were unpopular, withdrawn, lacking in self-confidence, anxious, and prone to depression, and they held few leadership positions (Ge, Conger, & Elder, 1996; Graber et al., 1997; Graber, Brooks-Gunn, & Warren, 2006; Jones & Mussen, 1958). They were more involved in deviant behavior (getting drunk, participating in early sexual activity) and achieved less well in school (Caspi et al., 1993; Dick et al., 2000). In contrast, their later-maturing counterparts were regarded as physically attractive, lively, sociable, and leaders at school. In a one study of several hundred eighth graders, however, negative effects of early pubertal timing were not evident among African-American girls, whose families, and perhaps friends, tend to be more unconditionally welcoming of menarche (see page 539) (Michael & Eccles, 2003).

Two factors largely account for these trends just described: (1) how closely the adolescent's body matches cultural ideals of physical attractiveness and (2) how well young people fit in physically with their agemates.

THE ROLE OF PHYSICAL ATTRACTIVENESS ■ **TAKE A MOMENT...** Flip through the pages of your favorite popular magazine. You will see evidence of our society's view of an attractive female as thin and long-legged and of a good-looking male as tall, broad-shouldered, and muscular. The female image is a girlish shape that favors the late developer. The male image fits the early-maturing boy.

Consistent with these preferences, early-maturing Caucasian girls tend to report a less positive **body image**—conception of and attitude toward their physical appearance—than their on-time and late-maturing agemates. Compared with African-American and Hispanic girls, Caucasian girls are more likely to have internalized the cultural ideal of female attractiveness and desire to be thinner (Rosen, 2003; Stice, Presnell, & Bearman, 2001; Williams & Currie, 2000). Although findings are less consistent among boys, early, rapid maturers are more likely to be satisfied with their physical characteristics (Alsaker, 1995; Sinkkonen, Anttila, & Siimes, 1998). These conclusions affect young people's self-esteem and psychological well-being. But the negative effects of pubertal timing on body image and—as we will see next—emotional adjustment are greatly amplified when accompanied by other stressors (Stice, 2003).

THE IMPORTANCE OF FITTING IN WITH PEERS ■ Physical status in relation to peers also explains differences in adjustment between early and late maturers. From this perspective, early-maturing girls and late-maturing boys have difficulty because they fall at the extremes of physical development. Recall that Sabrina felt "out of place" when with her agemates. She was not just larger than the girls; she also towered over the boys. Not surprisingly, adolescents feel most comfortable with peers who match their own level of biological maturity (Stattin & Magnusson, 1990).

Because few agemates of the same pubertal status are available, early-maturing adolescents of both sexes seek out older companions, sometimes with unfavorable consequences. Older peers often encourage them into activities they are not yet ready to handle emotionally, including sexual activity, drug and alcohol use, and minor delinquent acts. For example, the eighth graders Sabrina met at church introduced her to several high school boys, who were unconcerned that she was only a sixth grader! And Sabrina welcomed their attentions, which gratified her desire to feel socially accepted and physically attractive. Perhaps because of involvements like these, early maturers of both sexes more often report feeling emotionally stressed and show declines in academic performance (Graber, 2003; Kaltiala-Heino, Kosunen, & Rimpelä, 2003).

Research confirms that the young person's context greatly increases the likelihood that early pubertal timing will lead to negative outcomes. For example, in a study of several hundred ethnically diverse urban teenage girls, early maturers engaged in more antisocial acts only if they lived in neighborhoods with high concentrations of poverty, inadequate housing, and poor schools (Obeidallah et al., 2004). Early maturers in economically disadvantaged neighborhoods are especially vulnerable to establishing ties with deviant peers, which heightens their defiant, hostile behavior. And because families in such neighborhoods tend to be exposed to chronic, severe stressors and to have few social supports, these early maturers are also more likely to experience harsh, inconsistent parenting (see page 76 in Chapter 2). Parental coercion and inconsistency, in turn, predict both deviant peer associations and externalizing problems (Conger et al., 2002; Ge et al., 2002).

© ETHEL WOLVOVITZ/THE IMAGE WORKS

These three boys in Brooklyn, New York, are close to the same age but differ in pubertal timing. The early-maturing boy (center) is likely to be popular, self-confident, and athletic, with a positive body image, compared to his later-maturing companions.

LONG-TERM CONSEQUENCES ■ Do the effects of pubertal timing persist? Follow-ups reveal that early-maturing girls, especially, are prone to lasting difficulties. In one study, early-maturing boys' depression subsided by age 13, but depressed early-maturing girls tended to remain depressed (Ge et al., 2003). In another study, which followed young people from ages 14 to 24, early-maturing boys again showed good adjustment. Early-maturing girls, however, reported poorer-quality relationships with family and friends, smaller social networks, and lower life satisfaction into early adulthood than did their on-time counterparts (Graber et al., 2004). Similarly, in a Swedish investigation, achievement and substance-use difficulties of early-maturing girls lingered, in the form of greater alcohol abuse and lower educational attainment than their agemates (Andersson & Magnusson, 1990; Stattin & Magnusson, 1990).

Impaired social relationships may underlie these long-term negative outcomes (Graber, 2003). Recall that childhood family stress tends to be associated with early menarche (see page 536). Consequently, many early-maturing girls may enter adolescence with emotional and social difficulties. As the stresses of puberty interfere with school performance and lead to unfavorable peer pressures, poor adjustment extends and deepens. Clearly, interventions that target at-risk early-maturing youngsters are needed. These include educating parents and teachers and providing adolescents with counseling and social supports so they will be better prepared to handle the emotional and social challenges of this transition.

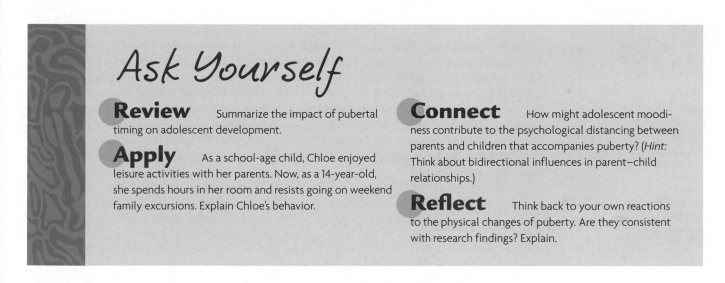

Ask Yourself

Review Summarize the impact of pubertal timing on adolescent development.

Apply As a school-age child, Chloe enjoyed leisure activities with her parents. Now, as a 14-year-old, she spends hours in her room and resists going on weekend family excursions. Explain Chloe's behavior.

Connect How might adolescent moodiness contribute to the psychological distancing between parents and children that accompanies puberty? (*Hint:* Think about bidirectional influences in parent–child relationships.)

Reflect Think back to your own reactions to the physical changes of puberty. Are they consistent with research findings? Explain.

Health Issues

The arrival of puberty is accompanied by new health issues related to the young person's striving to meet physical and psychological needs. As adolescents attain greater autonomy, their personal decision making becomes important, in health as well as in other areas. Yet none of the health concerns we are about to discuss can be traced to a single cause. Rather, biological, psychological, family, peer, and cultural factors jointly contribute.

Nutritional Needs

When their sons reached puberty, Franca and Antonio reported a "vacuum cleaner effect" in the kitchen as the boys routinely emptied the refrigerator. Rapid body growth leads to a dramatic rise in food intake. During the growth spurt, boys require about 2,700 calories a day and much more protein than they did earlier, girls about 2,200 calories but somewhat less protein than boys because of their smaller size and muscle mass (Cortese & Smith, 2003).

body image A person's conception of and attitude toward his or her physical appearance.

AP IMAGES/STUART RAMSON

Cultural admiration of extreme female thinness, evident in the fashion industry, has accompanied the rise in anorexia nervosa over the past half century. This emaciated model encourages young girls to feel dissatisfied with average body weight.

This increase in nutritional requirements comes at a time when the diets of many young people are the poorest. Of all age groups, adolescents are the most likely to skip breakfast (a practice linked to overweight and obesity), consume empty calories, and eat on the run (Stockman et al., 2005; Videon & Manning, 2003). Fast-food restaurants, where teenagers like to gather, have started to offer some healthy menu options. But adolescents need guidance in choosing these alternatives. Fast-food eating and school food purchases from snack bars and vending machines are associated with consumption of high-fat foods and soft drinks, indicating that teenagers often make unhealthy food selections (Bowman et al., 2004; Kubik et al., 2003).

The most common nutritional problem of adolescence is iron deficiency, as iron requirements increase to a maximum during the growth spurt and remain high among girls because of iron loss during menstruation. A tired, irritable teenager may be suffering from anemia rather than unhappiness and should have a medical checkup. Most adolescents do not get enough calcium, and they are also deficient in riboflavin (vitamin B$_2$) and magnesium, both of which support metabolism (Cavadini, Siega-Riz, & Popkin, 2000). And contrary to what many parents believe, obese children rarely outgrow their weight problem as teenagers (Berkowitz & Stunkard, 2002).

Frequency of family meals is strongly associated with healthy eating in teenagers—greater intake of fruits, vegetables, grains, and calcium-rich foods and reduced soft drink consumption (Neumark-Sztainer et al., 2003). But compared to families with younger children, those with adolescents eat fewer meals together. In addition to their other benefits (see page 73 in Chapter 2 and page 463 in Chapter 12), family meals can greatly improve teenagers' diets.

Adolescents—especially girls concerned about their weight—tend to be attracted to fad diets. Unfortunately, most are too limited in nutrients and calories to be healthy for fast-growing, active teenagers (Donatelle, 2004). Adolescence is also a time when many young people choose to become vegetarians. As they formulate a philosophy of life, some find the killing of animals distasteful, while others claim that meats are sources of impurities and toxins. Vegetarian adolescents are far more likely than their nonvegetarian counterparts to have healthy eating habits (Perry et al., 2002). Still, because some vegetarian diets are deficient in certain nutrients, when a young person wants to try a special diet, parents should encourage consultation with a doctor or a dietitian.

Serious Eating Disturbances

Sabrina's desire to lose weight worried Franca. She explained to her daughter that Sabrina was really quite average in build for an adolescent girl and reminded her that her Italian ancestors had considered a plump female body more beautiful than a thin one. Girls who reach puberty early, who are very dissatisfied with their body image, and who grow up in homes where concern with weight and thinness is high are at risk for serious eating problems. Severe dieting is the strongest predictor of the onset of an eating disorder in adolescence (Patton et al., 1999). The two most serious are anorexia nervosa and bulimia.

anorexia nervosa An eating disorder in which young people, mainly girls, starve themselves because of a compulsive fear of getting fat.

bulimia nervosa An eating disorder in which young people engage in strict dieting and excessive exercise accompanied by binge eating, often followed by deliberate vomiting and purging with laxatives.

ANOREXIA NERVOSA ■ **Anorexia nervosa** is a tragic eating disturbance in which young people starve themselves because of a compulsive fear of getting fat. About 1 percent of North American and Western European teenage girls are affected. During the past half-century, cases have increased sharply, fueled by cultural admiration of female thinness. Anorexia nervosa is equally common in all SES groups, but Asian-American, Caucasian-American, and Hispanic girls are at greater risk than African-American girls, who tend to be more satisfied with their size and shape (Fairburn & Harrison, 2003; Granillo, Jones-Rodriguez, & Carvajal, 2005; Steinhausen, 2006). Boys account for about 10 percent of cases of anorexia; about half of these are homosexual or bisexual young people who are uncomfortable with a strong, muscular appearance (Robb & Dadson, 2002).

Anorexics have an extremely distorted body image. Even after they have become severely underweight, they see themselves as too heavy. Most go on self-imposed diets so strict that they struggle to avoid eating in response to hunger. To enhance weight loss, they exercise strenuously.

In their attempt to reach "perfect" slimness, anorexics lose between 25 and 50 percent of their body weight. Because a normal menstrual cycle requires about 15 percent body fat, either menarche does not occur or menstrual periods stop. Malnutrition causes pale skin, brittle discolored nails, fine dark hairs all over the body, and extreme sensitivity to cold. If it continues, the heart muscle can shrink, the kidneys can fail, and irreversible brain damage and loss of bone mass can occur. About 6 percent of anorexics die of the disorder, as a result of either physical complications or suicide (Katzman, 2005).

Forces within the person, the family, and the larger culture give rise to anorexia nervosa. Identical twins share the disorder more often than fraternal twins, indicating a genetic influence. Abnormalities in neurotransmitters in the brain, linked to anxiety and impulse control, may make some individuals more susceptible (Holtkamp et al., 2005; Kaye et al., 2005). And problem eating behavior in early childhood—persistently refusing to eat or eating very little—is linked to anorexia in adolescence (Rosen, 2003). Many anorexics have unrealistically high standards for their own behavior and performance, are emotionally inhibited, and avoid intimate ties outside the family. Consequently, these girls are often excellent students who are responsible and well-behaved. But as we have also seen, the societal image of "thin is beautiful" contributes to the poor body image of many girls—especially early-maturing girls, who are at greatest risk for anorexia nervosa (Tyrka, Graber, & Brooks-Gunn, 2000).

In addition, parent–adolescent interactions reveal problems related to adolescent autonomy. Often the mothers of these girls have high expectations for physical appearance, achievement, and social acceptance and are overprotective and controlling. Fathers tend to be emotionally distant. These parental attitudes and behavior may contribute to anorexic girls' fierce pursuit of perfection in achievement, respectable behavior, and thinness (Bruch, 2001). Nevertheless, it remains unclear whether maladaptive parent–child relationships precede the disorder, emerge as a response to it, or both. In a longitudinal study in which 12- to 16-year-old girls were followed for four years, unhealthy eating behaviors led to conflict-ridden interactions with parents, not the reverse (Archibald et al., 2002).

Because anorexic girls commonly deny or minimize the seriousness of their disorder, treating it is difficult (Couturier & Lock, 2006). Hospitalization often is necessary to prevent life-threatening malnutrition. The most successful treatment is family therapy and medication to reduce anxiety and neurotransmitter imbalances (Fairburn, 2005; Patel, Pratt, & Greydanus, 2003; Treasure & Schmidt, 2005). As a supplementary approach, behavior modification—in which hospitalized anorexics are rewarded with praise, social contact, and opportunities for exercise when they eat and gain weight—is helpful. Still, less than 50 percent of anorexics fully recover (Seinhausen, 2002). For many, eating problems continue in less extreme form. About 10 percent show signs of a less severe, but nevertheless debilitating, disorder: bulimia nervosa. And the chronic anxiety associated with both eating disturbances increases girls' risk for major depression in both adolescence and adulthood (Godart et al., 2006).

BULIMIA NERVOSA ■ When Sabrina's 16-year-old brother, Louis, brought his girlfriend Cassie to the house, Sabrina admired her good figure. "What willpower!" Sabrina thought. "Cassie hardly touches food. But what in the world is wrong with her teeth?"

Willpower was not the secret to Cassie's slender shape. When it came to food, she actually had great difficulty controlling herself. Cassie suffered from **bulimia nervosa,** an eating disorder in which young people (again, mainly girls, but gay and bisexual boys are also vulnerable) engage in strict dieting and excessive exercise accompanied by binge eating, often followed by deliberate vomiting and purging with laxatives (Herzog, Eddy, & Beresin, 2006; Wichstrøm, 2006). When she was alone, Cassie often felt anxious and unhappy. She responded with eating rampages, consuming thousands of calories in an hour or two, followed by vomiting that eroded the enamel on her teeth. In some cases, bulimia can lead to life-threatening damage to the throat and stomach.

Bulimia is more common than anorexia nervosa. About 2 to 4 percent of teenage girls are affected; only 5 percent have previously been anorexic. Twin studies show that bulimia, like anorexia, is influenced by heredity (Klump, Kaye, & Strober, 2001). Overweight and early menarche increase the risk. Some bulimics, like anorexics, are perfectionists. Others lack self-control not just in eating but also in other areas of their lives, engaging in petty shoplifting

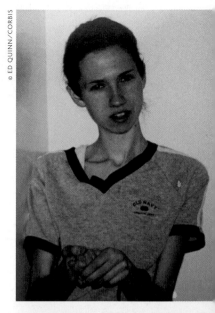

Gennifer, an anorexia nervosa patient, is shown in the top photo in the hospital where she received life-saving treatment for malnutrition. After prolonged family therapy, she recovered and, in the bottom photo, appears at home, two years after her hospital stay.

and alcohol abuse. And although bulimics share with anorexics pathological anxiety about gaining weight, they may have experienced their parents as disengaged and emotionally unavailable rather than controlling (Fairburn & Harrison, 2003).

Unlike anorexics, bulimics usually feel guilty about their abnormal eating habits and are desperate to get help. As a result, bulimia is usually easier to treat than anorexia, through support groups, nutrition education, training in changing eating habits, and the use of anti-anxiety, antidepressant, and appetite-control medication.

Injuries

As noted in Chapter 11, the total rate of unintentional injuries increases during adolescence (see page 423), the result of risk taking fueled by sensation seeking and a tendency to act without forethought. Automobile accidents are the leading killer of North American teenagers, accounting for more than 40 percent of deaths between ages 15 and 19 (Health Canada, 2005b; U.S. Department of Health and Human Services, 2006j). Many result from driving at high speeds, using alcohol, and not wearing seat belts. Parents must set firm limits on their teenager's car use, particularly with respect to drinking and fastening seat belts. These efforts are more likely to succeed in families with a history of good parent–child communication, a powerful preventive of adolescent injury (Sleet & Mercy, 2003).

In the United States, firearms cause the majority of other fatal injuries. Although violence-related behaviors among high school students have declined in the past decade, 19 percent report having carried a weapon within the past month—5 percent, a gun (U.S. Department of Health and Human Services, 2006j). The rate of disability and death resulting from firearms—mostly homicidal but occasionally accidental—is especially high in poverty-stricken inner-city neighborhoods. In response, many schools have installed metal detectors and security guards. Unfortunately, these environmental changes increase teenagers' fear of crime but have little impact on violence (Gagnon & Leone, 2002). School-based violence prevention programs (see Chapter 13, page 522) help reduce assaults. Banning handguns is an especially powerful tactic. In nations with strict gun registration, safety, and control policies, including prohibition of handguns, the firearm death rate among 15- to 19-year-olds is, on average, one-fourth the U.S. rate (see Figure 14.6) (Canadian Paediatric Society, 2005; U.S. Department of Health and Human Services, 2006j).

A third type of adolescent injury is sports-related. More than one-fifth of students involved in sports experience injuries that require medical treatment (Health Canada, 2005b; U.S. Department of Health and Human Services, 2006j). Most are muscle strains and bruises, but occasionally, severe injuries occur. These generally result from contact and collision with others in basketball, football, ice hockey, and soccer and from physical fights between players (Cheng et al., 2000).

Teenagers who overestimate their sports ability are more likely to be reckless and, as a result, to be injured during games (Kontos, 2004). And coaches, in their drive to win, sometimes make unreasonable demands of players that can lead to injury. In one observational study, coaches of girls' softball tended to ignore players' complaints of pain from injury, encouraging them to "tough it out"—and highly committed players more often did so (Malcom, 2006). Young adolescents are especially vulnerable. Many coaches match competitors on the basis of age and weight without considering pubertal maturity, which yields massive gains in boys' muscle strength (Malina & Beunen, 1996). The safest athletic activities during the pubertal growth period are limited-contact team sports, such as basketball, softball, and volleyball, and individual sports, such as track, swimming, and tennis.

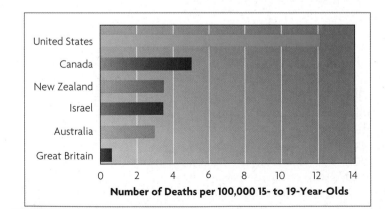

FIGURE 14.6

Firearm death rates among 15- to 19-year-olds in six industrialized nations. Death rates are far higher in the United States than in nations with strict gun control policies, including banning of handguns. (From Fingerhut & Christoffel, 2002; U.S. Department of Health and Human Services, 2006j.)

Sexual Activity

Louis and Cassie hadn't planned to have intercourse—it "just happened." But before and after, a lot of things passed through their minds. Cassie had been dating Louis for three months, and she began to wonder, "Will he think I'm normal if I don't have sex with him? If he wants to and I say no, will I lose him?" Both young people knew their parents wouldn't approve. In fact, when Franca and Antonio noticed how attached Louis was to Cassie, they talked to him about the importance of waiting and the dangers of pregnancy. But that Friday evening, Louis and Cassie's feelings for each other seemed overwhelming. As things went further and further, Louis thought, "If I don't make a move, will she think I'm a wimp?"

With the arrival of puberty, hormonal changes—in particular, the production of androgens in young people of both sexes—lead to an increase in sex drive (Halpern, Udry, & Suchindran, 1997). As Louis and Cassie's inner thoughts reveal, adolescents become very concerned about how to manage sexuality in social relationships. New cognitive capacities involving perspective taking and self-reflection affect their efforts to do so. Yet like the eating behaviors we have just discussed, adolescent sexuality is heavily influenced by the young person's social context.

THE IMPACT OF CULTURE ■ TAKE A MOMENT... When did you first learn "the facts of life"—and how? Was sex discussed openly in your family, or was the subject treated with secrecy? Exposure to sex, education about it, and efforts to limit the sexual curiosity of children and adolescents vary widely around the world. At one extreme are a number of Middle Eastern peoples, who murder girls if they lose their virginity before marriage. At the other extreme are several Asian and Pacific Island groups with highly permissive sexual attitudes and practices. For example, among the Trobriand Islanders of Papua New Guinea, older companions provide children with instruction in sexual practices, and adolescents are expected to engage in sexual experimentation with a variety of partners (Weiner, 1988).

Despite the prevailing image of a sexually free adolescent, sexual attitudes in North America are relatively restrictive. Typically, parents give their children little or no information about sex, discourage sex play, and rarely talk about sex in their presence. When young people become interested in sex, only about half report getting information from parents about intercourse, pregnancy prevention, and sexually transmitted disease (see the Social Issues: Education box on pages 548–549).

Rather, the majority learn about sex from friends, books, magazines, movies, TV, and the Internet (Jaccard, Dodge, & Dittus, 2002; Sutton et al., 2002). On prime-time TV shows, which adolescents watch more than other TV offerings, 80 percent of programs contain sexual content. Most depict partners as spontaneous and passionate, taking no steps to avoid pregnancy or sexually transmitted disease, and experiencing no negative consequences (Roberts, Henriksen, & Foehr, 2004).

The Internet is an especially hazardous "sex educator." In a survey of 1,500 U.S. 10- to 17-year-olds, 42 percent said they had viewed online pornographic websites (images of naked people or people having sex) while surfing the Internet in the past 12 months. Of these, 66 percent indicated they had encountered the images accidentally and did not want to view them. Most were 13- to 17-year-olds, but 16 percent of 10- to 11-year-olds experienced these unwanted encounters. And youths who felt depressed, had been victimized by peers, or were involved in delinquent activities had more encounters with Internet pornography, which may have intensified their adjustment problems (Wolak, Mitchell, & Finkelhor, 2007). In other studies of middle and high school students, reports of media (including Internet) exposure to sexual content predicted both current sexual activity and intentions to be sexually active in the future (Pardun et al., 2005; Ward & Friedman, 2006).

© JEFF GREENBERG/PHOTOEDIT

North American teenagers receive contradictory and confusing messages from the social environment about their readiness for sex. A considerable number do not use contraception consistently and are at risk for unintended pregnancy and sexually transmitted disease.

Social Issues: Education

Parents and Teenagers (Don't) Talk about Sex

When a researcher asked a father of two girls and a boy to reflect on communication about sexual issues in his family, he replied,

> I've never had to talk to my children . . . about these issues because . . . my wife's already done it. . . . I feel almost guilty for not partaking. The other thing, of course, is I don't know how—it's not an excuse, it's

a fact. I don't know how comfortable they would be, me trying to talk to them about these topics. . . . So I guess it's a bit of a coward's way out, to save embarrassment by both parties. . . . (Kirkman, Rosenthal, & Feldman, 2002, p. 60)

In families varying widely in SES and ethnicity, warm communication, in which parents provide information on sex and contraception and convey their values, is associated with teenagers' adoption of parents' views and with reduced teenage sexual risk taking (Fasula & Miller, 2006; Jaccard, Dodge, & Dittus, 2003; Miller, Forehand, & Kotchick, 1999). But many parents fail to discuss sex, birth control, and negative consequences of pregnancy with their teenagers. On average, only 50 percent of adolescents report such conversations (Jaccard, Dodge, & Dittus, 2002).

As this father's remarks suggest, parents steer clear of meaningful discussions with teenagers about sex out of fear of embarrassment. They

© KATE MITCHELL/ZEFA/CORBIS

This mother's quiet, patient approach gives her daughter a chance to ask questions and express opinions about sexual issues without becoming uncomfortable or feeling judged. Warm communication about sexuality is associated with teenagers' adoption of their parents' views and with a reduction in sexual risk taking.

also express concern that the adolescent will not take them seriously. And because teenagers frequently tell parents they already know everything they need to know, many parents conclude that talking about sex is unnecessary (Jaccard, Dittus, & Gordon, 2000). But adolescents' perceptions of their knowledge are only weakly related to their actual knowledge (Radecki & Jaccard, 1995).

When parents do initiate discussions, teenagers may be reluctant to participate. They complain that parents do not treat them as equals, know little about contemporary teenage lifestyles, and are not sufficiently open, supportive, and understanding. Perhaps because of their better communication skills, mothers talk to adolescents about sex and birth control more than fathers do. But mothers more often dominate conversations about sexual than about everyday matters, especially when talking to sons (Lefkowitz et al., 2002). When parents dominate, teenagers withdraw, reporting fewer sexual discussions and less knowledge (Lefkowitz, Sigman, & Au, 2000). Overall, balanced, mutual interaction and thorough consideration of sexual topics occur more often with daughters than with sons (Raffaelli, Bogenschneider, & Flood, 1998; Raffaelli & Green, 2003).

Cultural variations exist in parental communication about sex. For example, when Hispanic women who had grown up in U.S. Spanish-speaking

---

Consider the contradictory messages delivered by these sources. On one hand, adults emphasize that sex at a young age and outside marriage is wrong. On the other hand, the social environment extols sexual excitement, experimentation, and promiscuousness. North American teenagers are left bewildered, poorly informed about sexual facts, and with little sound advice on how to conduct their sex lives responsibly.

ADOLESCENT SEXUAL ATTITUDES AND BEHAVIOR ■ Although differences between subcultural groups exist, the sexual attitudes of North American adolescents and adults have become more liberal over the past 40 years. Compared with a generation ago, more people believe that sexual intercourse before marriage is all right, as long as two people are emotionally committed to each other (Michael et al., 1994). Recently, a slight swing back in the direction of conservative sexual beliefs has occurred, largely due to the risk of sexually transmitted disease, especially AIDS, and to teenage sexual abstinence programs sponsored by schools and religious organizations (Ali & Scelfo, 2002; Cope-Farrar & Kunkel, 2002).

Trends in adolescents' sexual behavior are quite consistent with these attitudes. Rates of extramarital sex among American and Canadian young people rose for several decades but have declined since 1990 (Boyce et al., 2003; U.S. Department of Health and Human Services, 2006j). Nevertheless, as Figure 14.7 on page 550 reveals, a substantial percentage of young people are sexually active quite early, by ninth grade or before. Boys tend to have their first intercourse earlier than girls.

families were asked to recall what their parents had told them about sex as teenagers, only a minority recalled talking about physical changes, intercourse, and pregnancy. Rather, parental messages usually took the form of strict limits on dating age, behavior, and place. Teresa, from a Mexican-American family, said, "You would be outside the house [where you could be observed]... your parents would tell you... no kissing or holding hands or nothing, actually it was just talking... until you decided whether you wanted to get married and then... the guy would have to... ask for your hand in marriage"

(Raffaelli & Ontai, 2001, p. 301). The gap between parental expectations and U.S. cultural dating practices often became a source of conflict. Many women reported having engaged in "sneak dating," but they were ill-prepared to manage their own sexual behavior. Over half did not use birth control the first time they had sex, and nearly a third had an unplanned pregnancy.

In sum, parent-based sex education has many advantages. Parents can discuss topics in ways consistent with their own values and, unlike school classes, can tailor their delivery of information to their youngster's personality and cur-

rent life circumstances. But parents need help communicating effectively about sexual issues. In one study, mothers who received training in talking with teenagers about sex, compared with a no-training control group, engaged in more give-and-take, asked more open-ended questions, were less judgmental, and discussed dating and sexuality more extensively. And their teenagers reported increased comfort with conversations and more consideration of birth control (Lefkowitz, Sigman, & Au, 2000). Refer to Applying What We Know for qualities of successful communication.

Applying What We Know

Communicating with Adolescents about Sexual Issues

STRATEGY	EXPLANATION
Foster open communication.	Let the teenager know you are a willing and trustworthy resource by stating that you are available when questions arise and will answer fully and accurately.
Use correct terms for body parts.	Correct vocabulary provides the young person with a basis for future discussion and also indicates that sex is not a secretive topic.
Use effective discussion techniques.	Listen, encourage the adolescent to participate, ask open-ended rather than yes/no questions, and give supportive responses. Avoid dominating and lecturing, which cause teenagers to withdraw. If questions arise that you cannot answer, collaborate with the teenager to gather further information.
Reflect before speaking.	When the adolescent asks questions or offers opinions about sex, remain nonjudgmental. If you differ with the teenager's views, convey your perspective in a nonthreatening manner, emphasizing that although you disagree, you are not attacking his or her character. Trying to dictate the young person's behavior generally results in alienation.
Keep conversations going.	Many parents regard their job as finished once they have had the "big talk" in early adolescence. But young people are more likely to be influenced by an accumulation of smaller discussions. If open communication is sustained, the teenager is more likely to return with thoughts and questions.

Source: Berkowitz, 2004.

As Figure 14.7 on page 550 suggests, American youths, compared with their Canadian and Western European counterparts, begin sexual activity at younger ages (Boyce et al., 2003; U.S. Department of Health and Human Services, 2006j). Because early intercourse is linked to briefer and more sporadic sexual relationships, U.S. teenagers are also more likely to have multiple sexual partners. For example, about 12 percent of adolescent boys in the United States, compared to 8 percent in Canada, have had relations with three or more partners in the past year (Alan Guttmacher Institute, 2004). These teenagers, however, are in the minority; most have had only one or two partners by the end of high school.

CHARACTERISTICS OF SEXUALLY ACTIVE ADOLESCENTS ■ Early and frequent teenage sexual activity is linked to personal, family, peer, and educational characteristics. These include childhood impulsivity and weak self-regulation, early pubertal timing, parental divorce, single-parent and stepfamily homes, large family size, little or no religious involvement, weak parental monitoring, disrupted parent–child communication, sexually active friends and older siblings, poor school performance, lower educational aspirations, and tendency to engage in norm-violating acts, including alcohol and drug use and delinquency (Crockett, Raffaelli, & Shen, 2006; Howard & Wang, 2004; Silver & Bauman, 2006).

Because many of these factors are associated with growing up in a low-income family, it is not surprising that early sexual activity is more common among young people from economically

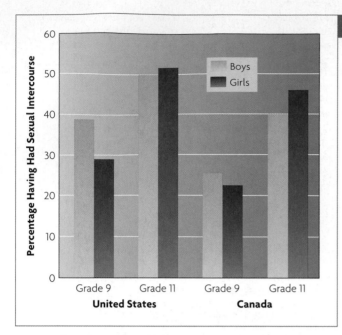

FIGURE 14.7

Adolescents in the United States and Canada reporting ever having had sexual intercourse. Boys tend to have their first intercourse earlier than girls, and U.S. adolescents, compared with Canadian adolescents, begin sexual activity at younger ages. (Adapted from Boyce et al., 2003; U.S. Department of Health and Human Services, 2006j.)

disadvantaged homes. Living in a hazardous neighborhood—one high in physical deterioration, crime, and violence—also increases the likelihood that teenagers will be sexually active (Ge et al., 2002). In such neighborhoods, social ties are weak, adults exert little oversight and control over adolescents' activities, and negative peer influences are widespread. In fact, the high rate of sexual activity among African-American teenagers—67 percent report having had sexual intercourse, compared with 47 percent of all American young people—is largely accounted for by widespread poverty in the black population (Darroch, Frost, & Singh, 2001; U.S. Department of Health and Human Services, 2006j).

Early and prolonged father absence predicts higher rates of intercourse and pregnancy among adolescent girls, after many family background and personal characteristics are controlled (Ellis et al., 2003). Perhaps father absence exposes young people to the dating and sexual behaviors of their mothers, who serve as models for their physically maturing children. An alternative, evolutionary account proposes that fathers' investment in parenting encourages daughters to delay sexual activity in favor of seeking a similarly committed male partner to ensure their own and their offspring's well-being. Because father-absent girls view male commitment as uncertain, they may readily enter into casual sexual relationships.

FIGURE 14.8

Adolescent contraceptive use in five industrialized nations.

Sexually active U.S. teenagers are less likely to use contraception consistently than teenagers in other industrialized nations. Canadian adolescents, as well, fall below adolescents in Western Europe in contraceptive use. (Adapted from Darroch, Frost, & Singh, 2001; U.S. Department of Health and Human Services, 2006j.)

CONTRACEPTIVE USE ■ Although adolescent contraceptive use has increased in recent years, 20 percent of sexually active teenagers in the United States and 13 percent in Canada are at risk for unintended pregnancy because they do not use contraception consistently (see Figure 14.8) (Alan Guttmacher Institute, 2002a, 2005; Manlove, Ryan, & Franzetta, 2003). Why do so many fail to take precautions? As we will see when we take up adolescent cognitive development in Chapter 15, adolescents can consider many possibilities when faced with a problem, but they often fail to apply this reasoning to everyday situations. When asked to explain why they did not use contraception, they often give answers like these: "I was waiting until I had a steady boyfriend," or "I wasn't planning to have sex."

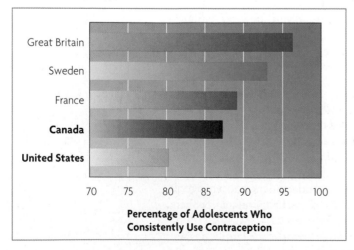

Percentage of Adolescents Who Consistently Use Contraception

One reason for these responses is that advances in perspective taking lead teenagers, for a time, to be extremely concerned about others' opinion of them. Recall how Cassie and Louis each worried about what the other would think if they decided not to have sex. Furthermore, in the midst of everyday social pressures, adolescents often overlook the consequences of engaging in risky behaviors (Beyth-Marom & Fischhoff, 1997). And many teenagers—especially those from troubled, low-income families—do not have realistic expectations about the impact of early parenthood on their current and future lives (Stevens-Simon, Sheeder, & Harter, 2005).

As these findings suggest, the social environment also contributes to adolescents' reluctance to use contraception. Those without the rewards of meaningful education and work are especially likely to engage in irresponsible sex, sometimes within exploitative relationships. About 11 percent of North American girls and 4 percent of boys say they were physically forced to have intercourse. And among girls who voluntarily had sex, one-fourth indicate that they really did not want to do so (Boyce et al., 2003; U.S. Department of Health and Human Services, 2006j).

In contrast, teenagers who report good relationships with parents and who talk openly with them about sex and contraception are more likely to use birth control (Kirby, 2002a; Henrich et al., 2006). But few adolescents believe their parents would be understanding and supportive. School sex education classes, as well, often leave teenagers with incomplete or incorrect knowledge. Some young people do not know where to get birth control counseling and devices. When they do, they often worry that a doctor or family planning clinic might not keep their visits confidential. About 20 percent of adolescents using health services say that if their parents were notified, they would still have sex, but without contraception (Jones et al., 2005).

SEXUAL ORIENTATION ■ Up to this point, our discussion has focused only on heterosexual behavior. About 2 to 3 percent of young people identify as lesbian, gay, or bisexual (Bailey, Dunne, & Martin, 2000; Savin-Williams & Diamond, 2004). An as-yet-unknown number who experience same-sex attraction have not come out to friends or family (see the Biology and Environment box on page 552–553). Adolescence is an equally crucial time for the sexual development of these young people, and societal attitudes, once again, loom large in how well they fare.

Heredity makes an important contribution to homosexuality: Identical twins of both sexes are much more likely than fraternal twins to share a homosexual orientation. The same is true for biological as opposed to adoptive relatives (Kendler et al., 2000; Kirk et al., 2000). Furthermore, male homosexuality tends to be more common on the maternal than on the paternal side of families. This suggests that it might be X-linked (see Chapter 2). Indeed, one gene-mapping study found that among 40 pairs of homosexual brothers, 33 (82 percent) had an identical segment of DNA on the X chromosome. One or several genes in that region might predispose males to become homosexual (Hamer et al., 1993).

How might heredity lead to homosexuality? According to some researchers, certain genes affect the level or impact of prenatal sex hormones, which modify brain structures in ways that induce homosexual feelings and behavior (Bailey et al., 1995; LeVay, 1993). In Chapter 10, we saw how prenatal androgens influence children's gender-typical play behaviors (see page 392). Consistent with early hormonal influences, childhood gender nonconformity—boys' preference for quiet, "feminine" play and girls' preference for active, "masculine" pursuits—is strongly linked to homosexuality.

Keep in mind, however, that both genetic and environmental factors can alter prenatal hormones. Girls exposed prenatally to very high levels of androgens or estrogens—either because of a genetic defect or from drugs given to the mother to prevent miscarriage—are more likely to become homosexual or bisexual (Meyer-Bahlburg et al., 1995). Furthermore, homosexual men tend to be later in birth order and to have a higher-than-average number of older brothers (Blanchard & Bogaert, 2004). One possibility is that mothers with several male children sometimes produce antibodies to androgens, which reduce the prenatal impact of male sex hormones on the brains of later-born boys.

Stereotypes and misconceptions about homosexuality continue to be widespread. For example, contrary to common belief, most homosexual adolescents are not "gender-deviant" in dress or behavior. Furthermore, attraction to members of the same sex is not limited to gay and lesbian teenagers. About 50 to 60 percent of adolescents who report having engaged in homosexual acts identify as heterosexual (Savin-Williams & Diamond, 2004).

Although definitive conclusions must await further research, the evidence to date suggests that genetic and prenatal biological influences are largely responsible for homosexuality. In our evolutionary past, homosexuality may have served the adaptive function of reducing aggressive competition for other-sex mates, thereby promoting the survival of group members (Rahman & Wilson, 2003).

Biology and Environment

Gay, Lesbian, and Bisexual Youths: Coming Out to Oneself and Others

Cultures vary as much in their acceptance of homosexuality as in their approval of extramarital sex. In North America, homosexuals are stigmatized, as shown by the degrading language often used to describe them. This makes forming a sexual identity a much greater challenge for gay, lesbian, and bisexual youths than for their heterosexual counterparts.

Wide variations in sexual identity formation exist, depending on personal, family, and community factors. Yet interviews with gay and lesbian adolescents and adults reveal that many (though not all) move through a three-phase sequence in coming out to themselves and others.

Feeling Different

Many gay men and lesbians say they felt different from other children when they were young. Typically, this first sense of their biologically determined sexual orientation appears between ages 6 and 12, in play interests more like those of the other gender (Rahman & Wilson, 2003). Boys may find that they are less interested in sports, drawn to quieter activities, and more emotionally sensitive than other boys; girls that they are more athletic and active than other girls.

By age 10, many of these children start to engage in *sexual questioning*—wondering why the typical heterosexual orientation does not apply to them. Often, they experience their sense of being different as deeply distressing. They worry, for example, about "being normal" and being "found out" by family members and friends. Compared with children confident of their homosexuality, sexual-questioning children report greater anxiety about peer relationships, greater dissatisfaction with their biological gender, and greater gender nonconformity in personal traits and activities over time (Carver, Egan, & Perry, 2004).

Confusion

With the arrival of puberty, feeling different clearly encompasses feeling sexually different. In research on ethnically diverse gay, lesbian, and bisexual youths, awareness of a same-sex physical attraction occurred, on average, between ages 11 and 12 for boys and 14 and 15 for girls, perhaps because adolescent social pressures toward heterosexuality are particularly intense for girls (D'Augelli, 2006; Diamond, 1998).

Realizing that homosexuality has personal relevance generally sparks additional confusion. A few adolescents resolve their discomfort by crystallizing a gay, lesbian, or bisexual identity quickly, with a flash of insight into their sense of being different. But most experience an inner struggle and deep sense of isolation—outcomes intensified by a lack of role models and social support (D'Augelli, 2002).

Some throw themselves into activities they have come to associate with heterosexuality. Boys may go out for athletic teams; girls may drop softball and basketball in favor of dance. And homosexual youths typically try heterosexual dating, sometimes to hide their sexual orientation and at other times to develop intimacy skills that they later apply to same-sex relationships (Dubé, Savin-Williams, & Diamond, 2001). Those who are extremely troubled and guilt-ridden may escape into alcohol, drugs, and suicidal thinking. Suicide attempts are unusually high among gay, lesbian, and bisexual young people (McDaniel, Purcell, & D'Augelli, 2001; Morrow, 2006).

Self-Acceptance

By the end of adolescence, the majority of gay, lesbian, and bisexual teenagers accept their sexual identity. But they face another crossroad: whether to tell others. Powerful stigma against their sexual orientation leads some to decide

Sexually Transmitted Diseases

Sexually active adolescents, both homosexual and heterosexual, are at risk for sexually transmitted diseases (STDs) (see Table 14.2 on page 554). Adolescents have the highest rates of STDs of all age groups. Despite a recent decline in STDs in the United States, one out of six sexually active teenagers contracts one of these illnesses each year—a rate three times as high as that of Canada. Canada, however, exceeds many other Western nations in incidence of the most common STDs, such as chlamydia and herpes (Maticka-Tyndale, 2001; Weinstock, Berman, & Cates, 2004). When STDs are left untreated, sterility and life-threatening complications can result. Teenagers in greatest danger of contracting STDs are the same ones most likely to engage in irresponsible sexual behavior—poverty-stricken young people who feel a sense of hopelessness about their lives (Niccolai et al., 2004).

By far the most serious STD is AIDS. In contrast to Canada, where the incidence of AIDS among people under age 30 is low, one-fifth of U.S. AIDS cases occur in young people between ages 20 and 29. Since AIDS symptoms typically take 8 to 10 years to emerge in a person infected with the HIV virus, nearly all these cases originated in adolescence. Drug-abusing teenagers who share needles and male adolescents who have sex with HIV-positive same-sex partners account for most cases, but heterosexual spread of the disease remains high, especially

that no disclosure is possible, so they self-define as gay but otherwise "pass" as heterosexual (Savin-Williams, 2001). When homosexual youths do come out, they often are targets of intense hostility. In a study of over 500 gay, lesbian, and bisexual youths in Canada, New Zealand, and the United States, 75 percent reported being verbally abused, and 15 percent being physically attacked, because of their sexual orientation (D'Augelli, 2002).

Nevertheless, many young people eventually acknowledge their sexual orientation publicly, usually by telling trusted friends first. Once teenagers establish a same-sex sexual or romantic relationship, many come out to parents—generally to their mother first, either because she asks or because youths feel closer to her. Few parents respond with severe rejection; most are positive or slightly negative and disbelieving (Savin-Williams & Ream, 2003a). This is an encouraging outcome because parental understanding is the strongest predictor of favorable adjustment among homosexual youths—including reduced *internalized homophobia*, or societal prejudice turned against the self (D'Augelli, Grossman, & Starks, 2005; Savin-Williams, 2003).

When people react positively, coming out strengthens the young person's view of homosexuality as a valid, meaningful, and fulfilling identity. Contact with other gays and lesbians is important for reaching this phase, and changes in society permit many adolescents in urban areas to attain it earlier than they did a decade or two ago. Gay and lesbian communities exist in large cities, along with specialized interest

© MARILYN HUMPHRIES/THE IMAGE WORKS

Boston-area teenagers march in the annual Gay/Straight Youth Pride March. When family members and peers react with acceptance, coming out strengthens young people's view of homosexuality as a valid, meaningful, and fulfilling identity.

groups, social clubs, religious groups, newspapers, and periodicals. Small towns and rural areas remain difficult places to meet other homosexuals and to find a supportive environment. Teenagers in these locales have a special need for caring adults and peers who can help them find self- and social acceptance.

Gay and lesbian youths who succeed in coming out to themselves and others integrate their sexual orientation into a broader sense of identity, a process we will address in Chapter 16. As a result, they no longer need to focus so heavily on their homosexual self, and energy is freed for other aspects of psychological growth. In sum, coming out can foster many aspects of adolescent development, including self-esteem, psychological well-being, and relationships with family and friends.

among teenagers with more than one partner in the previous 18 months (Kelley et al., 2003). It is at least twice as easy for a male to infect a female with any STD, including AIDS, as for a female to infect a male. Currently, females account for about 37 percent of new U.S. AIDS cases among adolescents and young adults (Rangel et al., 2006).

As a result of school courses and media campaigns, about 60 percent of middle-school students and 90 percent of high school students are aware of basic facts about AIDS. But some hold false beliefs that put them at risk—for example, that birth control pills provide some protection. And most have limited understanding of other STDs and their consequences, underestimate their own susceptibility, and are poorly informed about how to protect themselves (Coholl et al., 2001; Ethier et al., 2003).

Furthermore, high school students report engaging in oral sex much more often than intercourse, and they also report more oral sex partners. Although oral sex is a significant mode of transmission of several STDs, including chlamydia, gonorrhea, herpes, and perhaps AIDS, only a small minority of teenagers say they consistently use STD protection while engaged in it, and nearly three-fourths never take any precautions (Boyce et al., 2003; Prinstein, Meade, & Cohen, 2003).

Concerted efforts are needed to educate young people about the full range of STDs and risky sexual behaviors. Applying What We Know on page 555 lists strategies for STD prevention.

TABLE 14.2   Most Common Sexually Transmitted Diseases of Adolescence

DISEASE	REPORTED CASES AMONG 15- TO 19-YEAR-OLDS (RATE PER 100,000)		CAUSE	SYMPTOMS AND CONSEQUENCES	TREATMENT
	U.S.	**Canada**			
AIDS	20[a]	0.2[a]	Virus	Fever, weight loss, severe fatigue, swollen glands, and diarrhea. As the immune system weakens, severe pneumonias and cancers, especially on the skin, appear. Death due to other diseases usually occurs.	No cure; experimental drugs prolong life
Chlamydia	2,797	847	Bacteria	Discharge from the penis in males; painful itching, burning vaginal discharge, and dull pelvic pain in females. Often no symptoms. If left untreated, can lead to inflammation of the pelvic region, infertility, and sterility.	Antibiotic drugs
Cytomegalovirus	Unknown[b]		Virus of the herpes family	No symptoms in most cases. Sometimes a mild flulike reaction. In pregnant women, can spread to the embryo or fetus and cause miscarriage or serious birth defects (see page 115).	None; usually disappears on its own
Gonorrhea	438	91	Bacteria	Discharge from the penis or vagina, painful urination. Sometimes no symptoms. If left untreated, can spread to other regions of the body, resulting in such complications as infertility, sterility, blood poisoning, arthritis, and inflammation of the heart.	Antibiotic drugs
Herpes simplex 2 (genital herpes)	167	55	Virus	Fluid-filled blisters on the genitals, high fever, severe headache, and muscle aches and tenderness. No symptoms in a few people. In a pregnant woman, can spread to the embryo or fetus and cause birth defects (see page 115).	No cure; can be controlled with drug treatment
Human papillomavirus	16,000	No data	Virus	Causes genital warts that typically grow near the vaginal opening in females, on the penis or scrotum in males, which may be accompanied by severe itching. Can cause cellular changes that lead to cervical, vaginal, anal, and less commonly penile and oral cancers. A vaccine is available that prevents uninfected people from contracting the disease.	Removal of warts, but virus persists
Syphilis	2.1	0.7	Bacteria	Painless chancre (sore) at site of entry of germ and swollen glands, followed by rash, patchy hair loss, and sore throat within 1 week to 6 months. These symptoms disappear without treatment. Latent syphilis varies from no symptoms to damage to the brain, heart, and other organs after 5 to 20 years. In pregnant women, can spread to the embryo and fetus and cause birth defects.	Antibiotic drugs

[a]This figure includes both adolescents and young adults. For most U.S. cases, the virus is contracted in adolescence, and symptoms appear in early adulthood.

[b]Cytomegalovirus is the most common STD. Because there are no symptoms in most cases, its precise rate of occurrence is unknown. Half of the population or more may have had the virus sometime during their lives.

Sources: Health Canada, 2006d; U.S. Centers for Disease Control and Prevention, 2006.

Applying What We Know

Preventing Sexually Transmitted Diseases

STRATEGY	DESCRIPTION
Know your partner well.	Take time to get to get to know your partner. Find out whether your partner has had sex with many people or has used injectable drugs.
Maintain mutual faithfulness.	This strategy works only when neither partner has an STD at the start of the relationship.
Do not use drugs.	Using a needle, syringe, or drug liquid previously used by others can spread STDs. Alcohol, marijuana, or other illegal substances impair judgment, reducing your capacity to think clearly about the consequences of behavior.
Always use a latex condom and vaginal contraceptive when having sex with a nonmarital partner.	Latex condoms give good (but not perfect) protection against STDs by reducing the passage of bacteria and viruses. Vaginal contraceptives containing nonoxynol-9 can kill several kinds of STD microbes. They increase protection when combined with condom use.
Do not have sex with a person you know has an STD.	Even if you are protected by a condom, you still risk contracting STDs. In the case of the AIDS virus, you risk your life. If either partner has engaged in behavior that might have risked HIV infection, a blood test to detect infection must be administered and repeated at least six months after that behavior, since it takes time for the body to develop antibodies.
If you get an STD, inform all recent sexual partners.	Notifying people you may have exposed to an STD permits them to get treatment before spreading the disease to others.

Adolescent Pregnancy and Parenthood

Cassie was lucky not to get pregnant after having sex with Louis, but some of her high school classmates weren't so fortunate. Cassie had heard about Veronica, who missed several periods, pretended nothing was wrong, and didn't go to a doctor until a month before she gave birth. Veronica lived at home until she became pregnant a second time. When her parents told her they didn't have room for a second baby, Veronica dropped out of school and moved in with her 17-year-old boyfriend, Todd, who worked in a fast-food restaurant. A few months later, Todd left Veronica because he couldn't stand being tied down with the babies. Veronica had to apply for public aid to support herself and the two infants.

An estimated 750,000 to 850,000 teenage girls in the United States—20 percent of those who have sexual intercourse—become pregnant annually, about 25,000 of them younger than age 15. Despite a steady decline since 1991, the U.S. adolescent pregnancy rate is higher than that of most other industrialized countries (see Figure 14.9). Although the Canadian rate is about half the U.S. rate, teenage pregnancy in Canada remains a problem. Three factors heighten the incidence of adolescent pregnancy: (1) Effective sex education reaches too few teenagers, (2) convenient, low-cost contraceptive services for adolescents are scarce, and (3) many families live in poverty, which encourages young people to take risks without considering the future implications of their behavior.

Because 40 percent of U.S. and 50 percent of Canadian teenage pregnancies end in abortion, the number of North American teenage births is actually lower than it was 35 years ago (Maticka-Tyndale, 2001; U.S. Department of Health and Human Services, 2005a). But teenage parenthood is a much greater problem today because modern adolescents are far less likely to marry before childbirth. In 1960, only 15 percent of teenage births were to unmarried females,

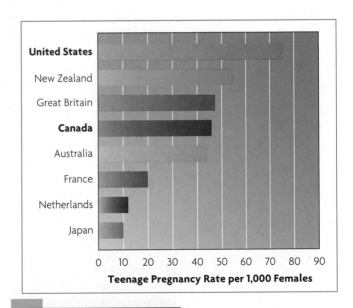

FIGURE 14.9

Pregnancy rates among 15- to 19-year-olds in eight industrialized nations. U.S. teenagers have the highest pregnancy rate. The pregnancy rate in Canada is about half the U.S. rate but much higher than that in Western European nations and Japan. (Adapted from Alan Guttmacher Institute, 2001, 2006.)

compared with 85 percent today. Increased social acceptance of single motherhood, along with the belief of many teenage girls that a baby might fill a void in their lives, means that only a small number of girls give up their infants for adoption.

CORRELATES AND CONSEQUENCES OF ADOLESCENT PARENTHOOD ■ Becoming a parent is challenging and stressful for anyone, but especially for adolescents. Teenage parents have not yet established a clear sense of direction for their own lives. Longitudinal research tracking girls from birth through adolescence reveals that life conditions and personal attributes jointly contribute to adolescent childbearing and also interfere with teenage mothers' capacity to parent effectively (Jaffee et al., 2001).

As we have seen, adolescent sexual activity is linked to economic disadvantage. Teenage mothers are many times more likely to be poor than their agemates who postpone childbearing. Their backgrounds often include low parental warmth and involvement, domestic violence and child abuse, repeated parental divorce and remarriage, adult models of unmarried parenthood, and residence in neighborhoods where other adolescents also display these risks. In terms of personal characteristics, girls at risk for early pregnancy do poorly in school, engage in alcohol and drug use, have a childhood history of aggressive and antisocial behavior, associate with deviant peers, and experience high rates of depression (Elfenbein & Felice, 2003: Hillis et al., 2004; Luster & Haddow, 2005). A high percentage of out-of-wedlock births are to low-income minority teenagers—African-American, Native-American, Hispanic, and Canadian-Aboriginal. Many of these young people, after unrewarding school experiences, turn to early parenthood as a way to move into adulthood when educational and career avenues are unavailable.

The lives of pregnant teenagers are troubled in many ways. After the baby is born, their circumstances often worsen in at least three respects:

■ *Educational attainment.* Giving birth before age 18 reduces the likelihood of finishing high school. Only about 70 percent of U.S. adolescent mothers graduate, compared with 95 percent of girls who wait to become parents (U.S. Department of Education, 2005a).

■ *Marital patterns.* Teenage motherhood reduces the chances of marriage. When these mothers do marry, they are more likely to divorce than their peers who delay childbearing (Moore et al., 1993). Consequently, teenage mothers spend more of their parenting years as single parents. About 35 percent become pregnant again within two years, and about half of these go on to deliver a second child (Child Trends, 2005).

■ *Economic circumstances.* Because of low educational attainment, marital instability, and poverty, many teenage mothers are on welfare. If they are employed, their limited education restricts them to unsatisfying, low-paid jobs. Many adolescent fathers, too, are unemployed or work at unskilled jobs, usually earning too little to provide their children with basic necessities (Bunting & McAuley, 2004). And an estimated 50 percent have committed illegal offenses resulting in imprisonment (Elfenbein & Felice, 2003).

Because many pregnant teenage girls have inadequate diets, smoke, use alcohol and other drugs, and do not receive early prenatal care, their babies often experience prenatal and birth complications—especially low birth weight (Dell, 2001). And compared with adult mothers, adolescent mothers know less about child development, have unrealistically high expectations of their infants, perceive their babies as more difficult, interact less effectively with them, and more often engage in child abuse (Moore & Florsheim, 2001; Pomerleau, Scuccimarri, & Malcuit, 2003). Their children tend to score low on intelligence tests, achieve poorly in school, and engage in disruptive social behavior.

Furthermore, teenage parents tend to pass on their personal attributes as well as create unfavorable child-rearing conditions. Consequently, their offspring are at risk for irresponsible sexual activity when they reach puberty. As the Social Issues: Health box on the following page indicates, adolescent parenthood frequently is repeated in the next generation (Brooks-Gunn, Schley, & Hardy, 2002). Even when children born to teenage parents do not become early childbearers, their development is often compromised, in terms of increased rates of antisocial behavior and drug use and reduced likelihood of high school graduation, financial independence

Social Issues: Health

Like Parent, Like Child: Intergenerational Continuity in Adolescent Parenthood

Does adolescent parenthood increase the chances of teenage childbearing in the next generation? To find out, researchers have conducted several unique studies of mothers (first generation)—some who gave birth as teenagers and some who postponed parenting—and their children (second generation), who were followed longitudinally for several decades (Barber, 2001b; Campa & Eckenrode, 2006; Hardy et al., 1998; Manlove, 1997).

First-generation mothers' age at first childbirth strongly predicted the age at which second-generation young people—both daughters and sons—became parents. Yet becoming a second-generation teenage parent is not simply a matter of having been born to an adolescent mother. Rather, adolescent parenthood is linked to a set of related, unfavorable family conditions and personal characteristics, which negatively influence development over an extended time and, therefore, often transfer to the next generation:

■ *Home environmental quality and parenting skills.* The long-term poverty and unstable marital patterns linked to adolescent parenthood reduce the quality of the home environment—in terms of organization, play and learning materials, and parental warmth, encouragement, verbal stimulation, and acceptance of the child (as opposed to punitiveness and abuse). Compared with daughters in other families, the daughters of unmarried adolescent

mothers live in families that obtain lower early childhood HOME scores (see page 349 in Chapter 9), even after mothers' prebirth SES is controlled (Campa & Eckenrode, 2006). Low HOME scores, in turn, are associated with poorer language and IQ scores, which in turn contribute to the poor school performance and decision making associated with early sexual activity, laxity in use of contraceptives, and adolescent childbearing.

■ *Intelligence and education.* Younger mothers' cognitive deficits and reduced educational attainment contribute to the likelihood their children will experience long-term, poor-quality home environments and, thus, in adolescence will engage in the maladaptive behaviors just mentioned (Barber, 2001; Hardy et al., 1998).

■ *Father absence.* In several studies, intergenerational continuity in adolescent parenthood—especially for daughters—was far greater when teenage mothers remained unmarried (Barber, 2001b; Campa & Eckenrode, 2006). Marriage may limit the negative impact of teenage childbearing on development by strengthening parental financial resources and involvement and reducing family stress. It may be particularly protective for girls because unmarried fathers are less likely to remain in regular contact with daughters than with sons. Recall from Chapter 13 that a warm, involved noncustodial father

is linked to reduced early sexual activity in girls (see page 511).

In sum, a life course of adversity—poverty, depleted and disorganized home environments, poor parenting, father absence, intellectual deficits, poor academic performance, and limited educational opportunities—contribute to intergenerational continuity in adolescent pregnancy and parenthood.

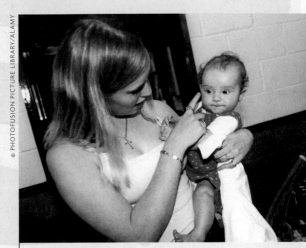

Will the daughter of this teenage mother become an adolescent parent herself? Negative family conditions and personal characteristics associated with early childbearing increase the likelihood that teenage parenthood will recur in the next generation.

in adulthood, and long-term physical and mental health (Moore, Morrison, & Green, 1997; Pogarsky, Thornberry, & Lizotte, 2006).

Still, how well adolescent parents and their children fare varies a great deal. If the teenager finishes high school and secures gainful employment, avoids additional births, and finds a stable marriage partner, long-term disruptions in her own and her child's development will be less severe.

PREVENTION STRATEGIES ■ Preventing teenage pregnancy means addressing the many factors underlying early sexual activity and lack of contraceptive use. Too often, sex education courses are given late (after sexual activity has begun), last only a few sessions, and are limited to a catalogue of facts about anatomy and reproduction. Sex education that goes beyond this minimum does not encourage early sex, as some opponents claim (Kirby, 2002c). It does improve awareness of sexual facts—knowledge that is necessary for responsible behavior.

Knowledge, however, is not enough. Sex education must also help teenagers build a bridge between what they know and what they do. Today, more effective sex education programs have emerged with the following key elements:

■ They teach behaviors for handling sexual situations—including refusal skills for avoiding risky sexual behaviors and communication skills for improving contraceptive use—and offer role-playing and other activities in which young people practice those behaviors.
■ They deliver clear, accurate messages that are appropriate for the culture and sexual experiences of participating adolescents.
■ They last long enough to have an impact.
■ They provide specific information about contraceptives and ready access to them.

Many studies show that sex education that includes these components can delay the initiation of sexual activity, increase contraceptive use, and reduce pregnancy rates (Kirby, 2002b; Manlove et al., 2006).

Proposals to increase access to contraceptives are the most controversial aspect of adolescent pregnancy prevention. Many adults argue that placing birth control pills or condoms in the hands of teenagers is equivalent to saying that early sex is OK. Yet sex education programs focusing on abstinence have little or no impact on delaying teenage sexual activity or on preventing pregnancy (Aten et al., 2002; Bennett & Assefi, 2005; DiCenso et al., 2002). And in Canada and Western Europe, where community and school-based clinics offer contraceptives and where universal health insurance helps pay for them, teenage sexual activity is not higher than in North America—but pregnancy, childbirth, and abortion rates are much lower (Alan Guttmacher Institute, 2001). Mass media campaigns such as radio and TV messages promoting contraceptive use—used widely in Europe, India, Africa, and South America—are associated with a reduction in early sexual activity and with an increase in teenagers' use of birth control (Keller & Brown, 2002).

Efforts to prevent adolescent pregnancy and parenthood must go beyond improving sex education and access to contraception; they must build academic and social competence. In one study, researchers randomly assigned at-risk high school students to either a year-long community service class, called Teen Outreach, or regular classroom experiences in health or social studies. In Teen Outreach, adolescents participated in at least 20 hours per week of volunteer work tailored to their interests. They returned to school for discussions that focused on enhancing their community service skills and ability to cope with everyday challenges. At the end of the school year, pregnancy, school failure, and school suspension were substantially lower in the group enrolled in Teen Outreach, which fostered social skills, connectedness to community, and self-respect (Allen et al., 1997).

Finally, school involvement is linked to delayed initiation of sexual activity and to reduced teenage pregnancy and childbearing, perhaps because it increases interaction with and attachment to adults who discourage risk taking, and it strengthens belief in a promising future (Lammers et al., 2000). We will take up factors that promote adolescents' commitment to school in Chapter 15.

INTERVENING WITH ADOLESCENT PARENTS ■ The most difficult and costly way to deal with adolescent parenthood is to wait until it has happened. Young parents need health care, encouragement to stay in school, job training, instruction in parenting and life-management skills, and high-quality child care. School programs that provide these services reduce the incidence of low-birth-weight babies, increase educational success, and prevent additional childbearing (Barnet et al., 2004; Seitz & Apfel, 2005).

Adolescent mothers also benefit from relationships with family members and other adults who are sensitive to their developmental needs. Older teenage mothers display more effective parenting when they establish their own residence with the help of relatives—an arrangement that grants the teenager a balance of autonomy and support (East & Felice, 1996). In one study, African-American teenage mothers who had a long-term "mentor" relationship—an aunt, neighbor, or teacher who provided emotional support and guidance—were far more likely than those without a mentor to stay in school and graduate (Klaw, Rhodes, & Fitzgerald, 2003).

© JEFF GREENBERG/PHOTOEDIT

This youth community clean-up program in the Miami, Florida, neighborhood of Little Haiti helps teenagers acquire new competencies and a sense of community involvement that reduce the likelihood of adolescent pregnancy and school failure.

Programs focusing on fathers are attempting to increase their emotional and financial commitment to the baby. Although nearly half of young fathers visit their children during the first few years after birth, contact usually diminishes. By the time the child reaches school age, fewer than one-fourth have regular paternal contact. As with teenage mothers, support from family members helps fathers say involved (Bunting & McAuley, 2004). Teenage mothers who receive financial and child-care assistance and emotional support from the child's father are less distressed and more likely to sustain a relationship with him (Cutrona et al., 1998; Gee & Rhodes, 2003). And infants with lasting ties to their teenage fathers receive warmer, more stimulating caregiving and show better long-term adjustment (Furstenberg & Harris, 1993).

Laws that enforce child support payments are aimed at increasing paternal responsibility. But unless these efforts are accompanied by assistance in finding adequate employment, teenage fathers may flee to evade arrest instead of becoming involved with their children. Fatherhood interventions that begin early, before the relationship with the adolescent mother withers or terminates, are more likely to succeed (McLanahan & Carlson, 2002).

Although early parenthood imposes lasting hardships on both adolescent parents and their newborn babies, the presence of a caring father and a stable partnership between the parents can improve outcomes for young families.

Substance Use and Abuse

At age 14, Louis waited until he was alone at home, took some cigarettes out of his uncle's pack, and smoked them. At an unchaperoned party, he and Cassie drank several cans of beer and lit up marijuana joints. Louis got little physical charge out of these experiences. He was a good student, was well-liked by peers, and got along well with his parents. He had no need for drugs as an escape valve from daily life. But he knew of others for whom things were different—teenagers who started with alcohol and cigarettes, moved on to harder substances, and eventually were hooked.

In industrialized nations, teenage alcohol and drug use is pervasive, rising steadily over adolescence. According to the most recent, nationally representative survey of U.S. high school students, by tenth grade, 40 percent of U.S. young people have tried smoking, 63 percent drinking, and 38 percent at least one illegal drug (usually marijuana). At the end of high school, 17 percent smoke cigarettes regularly, 28 percent have engaged in heavy drinking during the past two weeks, and 40 percent have experimented with illegal drugs. About 20 percent have tried at least one highly addictive and toxic substance, such as amphetamines, cocaine, phencyclidine (PCP), Ecstasy (MDMA), inhalants, heroin, sedatives (including barbiturates), or OxyContin (a narcotic painkiller). Canadian rates of teenage alcohol and drug use are similar. Generally, boys have higher rates of drug taking than girls, except for cigarette smoking, where the genders have been roughly equivalent since 1980 (Johnson et al., 2006; Statistics Canada, 2003c).

These figures represent a substantial decline in overall drug use since the mid-1990s, probably resulting from greater parent, school, and media focus on the hazards of drug taking. But use of several drugs—inhalants, sedatives, and OxyContin—has risen in recent years (Johnson et al., 2006). Unfortunately, claims about the "benefits" of new drugs spread faster than information about their dangers, a process greatly aided by the Internet. Furthermore, after falling from popularity, certain drugs (such as LSD, PCP, and Ecstasy) have made a comeback as adolescents' knowledge of their risks faded.

Why do so many young people subject themselves to the health risks of these substances? In part, drug taking reflects the sensation seeking of these years. But teenagers also live in drug-dependent cultural contexts. They see adults using caffeine to wake up in the morning, cigarettes to cope with daily hassles, a drink to calm down in the evening, and other remedies to relieve stress, depression, and physical illness. And compared to a decade or two ago, today doctors more often prescribe—and parents frequently seek—medication to treat their children's problems (Brody, 2006). When these young people reach adolescence, they may readily "self-medicate" in the face of stress. Furthermore, an increasing number of cigarette and alcohol ads are designed to appeal to teenagers. Over 90 percent of teenagers are aware of such advertising, and most say the ads influence their behavior (Alcohol Concern, 2004).

The majority of teenagers who dabble in alcohol, tobacco, and marijuana are not headed for a life of decadence and addiction. Rather, these *minimal experimenters* are usually psychologically

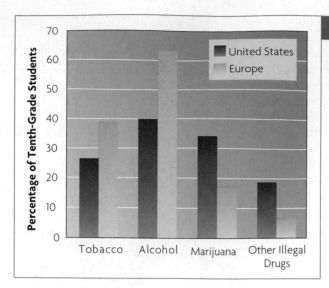

FIGURE 14.10

Tenth-grade students in the United States and Europe who have used various substances. Rates for tobacco and alcohol are based on any use in the past 30 days. Rates for marijuana and other illegal drugs are based on any lifetime use. Tobacco use and alcohol use are greater for European adolescents, whereas illegal drug use is greater for U.S. adolescents. (Adapted from Hibell, 2001; Johnson et al., 2006.)

healthy, sociable, curious young people (Shedler & Block, 1990). As Figure 14.10 shows, tobacco and alcohol use is somewhat greater among European than among American adolescents, perhaps because European adults more often smoke and drink. In contrast, illegal drug use is far more prevalent among American teenagers (Hibell, 2001). A greater percentage of American young people live in poverty, which is linked to family and peer contexts that promote illegal drug use. At the same time, use of diverse drugs is lower among African Americans than among Hispanic and Caucasian Americans; Native-American and Canadian-Aboriginal youths rank highest in drug taking (van der Woerd & Cox, 2001; Wallace et al., 2003). Researchers have yet to explain these variations.

Regardless of type of drug, adolescent experimentation should not be taken lightly. Because most drugs impair perception and thought processes, a single heavy dose can lead to permanent injury or death. And a worrisome minority of teenagers move from substance *use* to *abuse*—taking drugs regularly, requiring increasing amounts to achieve the same effect, moving to harder substances, and using enough to impair their ability to meet school, work, and other responsibilities. Three percent of high school seniors are daily drinkers, and 5 percent have taken illegal drugs on a daily basis over the past month (Johnson et al., 2006).

Of all teenage drug habits, cigarette smoking has received the least attention because its short-term effects are minimal. Yet in the long run, it is one of the deadliest substances—an established cause of heart and lung disease and cancer. Habitual cigarette use usually begins in early adolescence; 9 percent of U.S. eighth graders say they smoked in the last month, and 4 percent report doing so daily. Of the nearly 7 percent of high school students who smoke half a pack or more a day, 50 percent indicate that they tried to quit but could not (Johnson et al., 2006).

CORRELATES AND CONSEQUENCES OF ADOLESCENT SUBSTANCE ABUSE ■ In contrast to experimenters, drug abusers are seriously troubled young people who are impulsive, deficient in cognitive and emotional self-regulation, and inclined to express their unhappiness through antisocial acts. Longitudinal evidence reveals that their impulsive, disruptive, hostile styles often are evident during the preschool years. And compared with other young people, their drug taking starts earlier and may have genetic roots (Chassin et al., 2004; Ellickson et al., 2005; Kassel et al., 2005). But a wide range of environmental factors also promote it. These include low SES, family mental health problems, parental and older sibling drug abuse, lack of parental warmth and involvement, physical and sexual abuse, and poor school performance. Especially among teenagers with family difficulties, peer encouragement—friends who use and provide access to drugs—increases substance abuse and other antisocial behaviors (Goldstein, Davis-Kean, & Eccles, 2005; Prinstein, Boergers, & Spirito, 2001).

Adolescent substance abuse often has lifelong consequences. When teenagers depend on alcohol and hard drugs to deal with daily stresses, they fail to learn responsible decision-making skills and alternative coping techniques. These young people show serious adjustment problems, including chronic anxiety, depression, and antisocial behavior, that are both cause and consequence of heavy drug taking (Kassel et al., 2005; Simons-Morton & Haynie, 2003). They often enter into marriage, childbearing, and the work world prematurely and fail at them—painful outcomes that encourage further addictive behavior.

PREVENTION AND TREATMENT ■ School and community programs that reduce drug experimentation typically combine several features:

- They promote effective parenting, including monitoring of teenagers' activities.
- They teach skills for resisting peer pressure.
- They reduce the social acceptability of drug taking by emphasizing health and safety risks.
- They get students to commit to not using drugs (Cuijpers, 2002; Griffin et al., 2003).

But because some drug taking seems inevitable, interventions that prevent teenagers from harming themselves and others when they do experiment are essential. Many communities offer weekend on-call transportation services that any young person can contact for a safe ride home, with no questions asked. Providing appealing substitute activities, such as drug-free video arcades, dances, and sports activities, is also helpful.

Drug Free Youth in Town (DFYIT) is a youth substance abuse and leadership training program, in which high school students trained as peer-to-peer educators teach middle school students drug prevention and life skills. Participants acquire strategies for resisting peer pressure and engage in enjoyable, drug-free social and community service activities.

Because drug abuse, as we have seen, has different roots than occasional use, different preventive strategies are required. One approach is to work with parents early, reducing family adversity and improving parenting skills, before children are old enough to become involved with drugs (Kumpfer & Alvarado, 2003; Velleman, Templeton, & Copello, 2005). Addicted mothers may be especially responsive to such interventions because many seek treatment out of concern for the well-being of their children (Luthar, Cushing, & McMahon, 1997). Programs that teach at-risk teenagers effective strategies for handling life stressors and that build competence through community service reduce alcohol and drug use, just as they reduce teenage pregnancy.

When an adolescent becomes a drug abuser, family and individual therapy are generally needed to treat negative parent–child relationships, impulsivity, low self-esteem, anxiety, and depression. Academic and vocational training to improve life success and satisfaction makes a difference as well. But even comprehensive programs have alarmingly high relapse rates—from 35 to 85 percent (Brown & Ramo, 2005; Cornelius et al., 2003; Waldron, Turner, & Ozechowski, 2005). One recommendation is to start treatment gradually, beginning with support-group sessions that focus on reducing drug taking. Within the group, interveners can address drug-abusing teenagers' low motivation to change and resistance to adult referral, which they often view as an infringement on their personal freedom. Such brief interventions lessen drug taking in the short term (Myers et al., 2001). Modest improvement may boost the young person's sense of self-efficacy for behavior change and, as a result, increase motivation to make longer-lasting changes through intensive treatment.

Ask Yourself

Review   Compare risk factors for anorexia nervosa and bulimia nervosa. How do treatments and outcomes differ for the two disorders?

Apply   Return to page 555 to review Veronica's life circumstances after she became a teenage mother. Why are Veronica and her children likely to experience long-term hardships?

Connect   What unfavorable life experiences do teenagers who engage in early and frequent sexual activity have in common with those who abuse drugs?

Reflect   Describe your experiences with peer pressures to experiment with alcohol and drugs. What factors influenced your response?

Summary

Conceptions of Adolescence

How have conceptions of adolescence changed over the twentieth century?

■ Early biologically oriented theories viewed **puberty** as a period of inevitable storm and stress resulting from biological upheaval. An alternative perspective regarded the social and cultural environment as entirely responsible for the variability in adolescent adjustment.

■ Current research shows that **adolescence** is neither biologically nor socially determined but a joint product of biological, psychological, and social forces. In cultures that require many years of education for successful participation in the work life of the community, adolescence is greatly extended.

Puberty: The Physical Transition to Adulthood

Describe body growth, motor performance, and sexual maturation during puberty.

■ Hormonal changes under way in middle childhood initiate puberty, which arrives, on average, two years earlier for girls than for boys. The first outward sign of puberty is the rapid gain in height and weight known as the **growth spurt**. In early adolescence, the cephalocaudal trend of body growth reverses. Most height gain results from lengthening of the torso. As the body enlarges, girls' hips and boys' shoulders broaden. Girls add more fat, boys more muscle. Because athletic competence is related to peer admiration, some adolescents, mostly boys, use steroids and other dangerous performance-enhancing drugs to boost muscle power.

■ Puberty brings slow, gradual improvements in gross motor performance for girls, dramatic gains for boys. Although girls' involvement in high school sports has increased, they still receive less athletic encouragement than boys. The number of North American adolescents participating in regular physical activity and physical education declines over the teenage years.

■ Sex hormones regulate changes in **primary** and **secondary sexual characteristics**. **Menarche** occurs late in the girl's sequence of pubertal events, following the rapid increase in body size. After menarche, growth of the breasts and of pubic and underarm hair are completed. In boys, as the sex organs and body enlarge and pubic and underarm hair appear, **spermarche** takes place. This is followed by growth of facial and body hair and deepening of the voice.

What factors influence the timing of puberty?

■ Heredity, nutrition, and overall health contribute to the timing of puberty. Obese girls reach menarche early, whereas girls involved in rigorous athletic training experience it later. Menarche is delayed in poverty-stricken regions of the world with widespread malnutrition and infectious disease. In industrialized nations, both heredity and environment contribute to ethnic variations—for example, earlier age of menarche in African-American than in Caucasian-American girls.

■ Girls in conflict-ridden families tend to reach menarche earlier. Both genetic and environmental explanations for this trend exist. Also, improved physical well-being has led to a secular trend toward earlier menarche in industrialized nations. In most countries, the trend either has stopped or has undergone a slight reversal, but in North America and a few European countries, overweight and obesity may account for a modest continuation.

Describe brain development and changes in the organization of sleep and wakefulness during adolescence.

■ During puberty, synaptic pruning continues, especially in the frontal lobes, while myelination of neural fibers accelerates and connections among various brain regions strengthen, resulting in more efficient brain functioning. In addition, neurons become more responsive to excitatory neurotransmitters, increasing reactivity to stressful events and pleasurable stimuli.

■ Because of changes in the way the brain regulates timing of sleep, adolescents tend to go to bed much later than they did as children, a pattern that strengthens with pubertal growth. Sleep deprivation is associated with poor school performance, depressed mood, and high-risk behaviors.

The Psychological Impact of Pubertal Events

What factors influence adolescents' reactions to the physical changes of puberty?

■ Girls generally react to menarche with surprise and mixed emotions, but whether their feelings are primarily positive or negative depends on advance information and support from family members. Boys usually know in advance about spermarche but receive less support for the physical changes of puberty than girls.

■ Tribal and village societies often celebrate puberty with an *initiation ceremony*. Customs such as the Jewish bar or bat mitzvah and the Hispanic *quinceañera* resemble initiation ceremonies, but in general, the absence of a widely accepted marker for physical and social maturity in Western industrialized societies makes the process of becoming an adult more confusing.

■ Besides higher hormone levels, negative life events and adult-structured situations are associated with adolescents' negative moods. In contrast, teenagers feel upbeat when with friends and in self-chosen leisure activities, making weekend evenings emotional high points.

■ Puberty is accompanied by psychological distancing between parent and child. The reaction may be a modern substitute for physical departure from the family, which typically occurs at sexual maturity in primate species. Parent–adolescent conflict also reflects parents' efforts to protect teenagers from such risks as substance use, auto accidents, and early sex.

Describe the impact of maturational timing on adolescent adjustment, noting sex differences.

■ Early-maturing boys and late-maturing girls, whose appearance closely matches cultural standards of physical attractiveness, have a more positive **body image** and usually adjust well in adolescence. In contrast, early-maturing girls and late-maturing boys, who fit in least well physically with peers, tend to experience emotional and social difficulties. Especially for early-maturing girls, negative consequences often persist.

Health Issues

Describe nutritional needs, and cite factors related to serious eating disturbances during adolescence.

■ As the body grows, nutritional requirements increase, at a time when the eating habits of young people are the poorest. Many adolescents suffer from iron, calcium, riboflavin, and magnesium deficiencies. Frequency of family meals is associated with healthy eating in teenagers.

■ Girls who reach puberty early, who are very dissatisfied with their body images, and who grow up in homes where thinness is emphasized are at risk for serious eating disturbances. Heredity, family influences, and forces in the larger culture combine to give rise to these disorders. **Anorexia nervosa** tends to affect girls with perfectionist personalities, overprotective and controlling mothers, and emotionally distant fathers. The impulsive eating and purging of **bulimia nervosa** is associated with disengaged parenting. Some bulimics, like anorexics, are perfectionists; others lack self-control in eating and in other areas of their lives.

AP IMAGES/STUART RAMSON

Cite common unintentional injuries in adolescence.

■ Motor vehicle collisions are the leading cause of adolescent injury and death. In the United States, firearms cause the majority of other fatal injuries. Sports-related injuries are also common.

Discuss social and cultural influences on adolescent sexual attitudes and behavior.

■ The hormonal changes of puberty lead to an increase in sex drive, but social factors affect how teenagers manage their sexuality. Compared with most other cultures, North America is fairly restrictive in typical attitudes toward adolescent sex. Young people receive contradictory messages from the larger social environment. Sexual attitudes and behavior of adolescents have become more liberal, with a slight swing back recently toward more conservative beliefs.

■ Early and frequent sexual activity is linked to a variety of factors associated with economic disadvantage. Early and prolonged father absence may contribute uniquely to early sexual activity.

■ Many sexually active teenagers do not practice contraception regularly. Adolescent cognitive processes, lack of rewards through meaningful education and work, and weak social supports for responsible sexual behavior underlie the failure of many young people to protect themselves against pregnancy.

Describe factors involved in the development of homosexuality.

■ About 2 to 3 percent of young people identify as lesbian, gay, or bisexual. A still-unknown number experience same-sex attraction but have not come out to friends or family. Biological factors, including heredity and prenatal hormone levels, play an important role in homosexuality. Gay and lesbian teenagers face special challenges in establishing a positive sexual identity.

Discuss factors related to sexually transmitted disease and to teenage pregnancy and parenthood.

■ Early sexual activity, combined with inconsistent contraceptive use, results in high rates of sexually transmitted diseases (STDs) among U.S. and (to a lesser extent) Canadian teenagers. Many young adults with AIDS contracted HIV as adolescents. An important goal of sex education is prevention of STDs.

■ Adolescent pregnancy and parenthood rates are higher in the United States than in many industrialized nations. Although less prevalent than in the United States, teenage pregnancy in Canada is still a problem. A combination of unfavorable life conditions jointly contribute, including economic disadvantage and personal attributes. Adolescent parenthood is associated with high school dropout, reduced chances of marriage, greater likelihood of divorce, and poverty—circumstances that jeopardize the well-being of both adolescent and newborn child. Adolescent parenthood frequently is repeated in the next generation.

■ Improved sex education, access to contraceptives, and programs that build social competence help prevent early pregnancy. Adolescent parents benefit from health care and school programs that provide job training and child care. Young mothers fare better when they have access to family relationships that are sensitive to their developmental needs. When teenage fathers stay involved, teenage mothers are less distressed and children develop more favorably.

What personal and social factors are related to adolescent substance use and abuse?

■ Teenage alcohol and drug use is widespread in industrialized nations, although overall drug use has declined since the mid-1990s in the United States and Canada. Most young people are minimal experimenters, who dabble in drug use out of curiosity. But those who move from use to abuse have serious personal, family, school, and peer problems. Programs that work with parents early to reduce family adversity and improve parenting skills and that build teenagers' competence help prevent substance abuse.

Important Terms and Concepts

Chapter 15

This depiction of a multimedia and interplanetary world offers vivid insight into adolescents' capacity to imagine many possibilities, as well as their exhilaration at the options that lie before them. Chapter 15 delves into the increasingly complex reasoning powers of this transitional period between childhood and adulthood.

Reprinted with permission from the International Child Art Foundation, Washington, D.C.

"Our World"
Muthumudalige Emashi Nilupuli Perera
11 years, Sri Lanka

Cognitive Development in Adolescence

One mid-December evening, a knock at the front door announced the arrival of Franca and Antonio's oldest son Jules, home for vacation after the fall semester of his sophomore year at college. The family gathered around the kitchen table. "How did it all go, Jules?" asked Antonio as he passed out slices of apple pie.

"Well, physics and philosophy were awesome," Jules responded with enthusiasm. "The last few weeks, our physics prof introduced us to Einstein's theory of relativity. Boggles my mind, it's so incredibly counterintuitive."

"Counter-what?" asked 11-year-old Sabrina.

"Counterintuitive. Unlike what you'd normally expect," explained Jules. "Imagine you're on a train, going unbelievably fast, like 160,000 miles a second. The faster you go, approaching the speed of light, the slower time passes and the denser and heavier things get relative to on the ground. The theory revolutionized the way we think about time, space, matter—the entire universe."

Sabrina wrinkled her forehead, unable to comprehend Jules's otherworldly reasoning. "Time slows down when I'm bored, like right now, not on a train when I'm going somewhere exciting. No speeding train ever made me heavier, but this apple pie will if I eat any more of it," Sabrina announced, leaving the table.

Sixteen-year-old Louis reacted differently. "Totally cool, Jules. So what'd you do in philosophy?"

"It was a course in philosophy of technology. We studied the ethics of futuristic methods in human reproduction. For example, we argued the pros and cons of a world in which all embryos develop in artificial wombs."

"What do you mean?" asked Louis. "You order your kid at the lab?"

"That's right. I wrote my term paper on it. I had to evaluate it in terms of principles of justice and freedom. I can see some advantages but also lots of dangers. . . ."

As this conversation illustrates, adolescence brings with it vastly expanded powers of reasoning. At age 11, Sabrina finds it difficult to move beyond her own firsthand experiences to a world of possibilities. Over the next few years, her thinking will take on the complex qualities that characterize the cognition of her older brothers. Jules considers multiple variables simultaneously and thinks about situations that are not easily detected in the real world or that do not exist at all. As a result, he can grasp advanced scientific and mathematical principles, grapple with social and political issues, and delve deeply into the meaning of a poem or story. Compared with school-age children's thinking, adolescent thought is more enlightened, imaginative, and rational.

The first part of this chapter traces these extraordinary changes. Systematic research on adolescent cognitive development began with testing of Piaget's ideas (Keating, 2004). Recently, information-processing research has greatly enhanced our understanding. Next, we turn to research findings that have attracted a great deal of public attention: sex differences in mental abilities. We also discuss gains in language that reflect and also contribute to the advanced thinking of the teenage years. The middle portion of this chapter is devoted to the primary setting in which adolescent thought takes shape: the school. We conclude with a consideration of vocational development.

Piaget's Theory: The Formal Operational Stage

According to Piaget, around age 11 young people enter the **formal operational stage,** in which they develop the capacity for abstract, systematic, scientific thinking. Whereas concrete operational children can "operate on reality," formal operational adolescents can "operate on operations." In other words, they no longer require concrete things or events as objects of thought. Instead, they can come up with new, more general logical rules through internal reflection (Inhelder & Piaget, 1955/1958). Let's look at two major features of the formal operational stage.

FIGURE 15.1

Piaget's pendulum problem. Adolescents who engage in hypothetico-deductive reasoning think of variables that might possibly affect the speed with which a pendulum swings through its arc. Then they isolate and test each variable, as well as testing the variables in combination. Eventually they deduce that the weight of the object, the height from which it is released, and how forcefully it is pushed have no effect on the speed with which the pendulum swings through its arc. Only string length makes a difference.

Hypothetico-Deductive Reasoning

Piaget believed that at adolescence, young people first become capable of **hypothetico-deductive reasoning.** When faced with a problem, they start with a *hypothesis,* or prediction about variables that might affect an outcome. From that hypothesis, they *deduce* logical, testable inferences, then systematically isolate and combine variables to see which of these inferences are confirmed in the real world. Notice how this form of problem solving begins with possibility and proceeds to reality. In contrast, concrete operational children start with reality—with the most obvious predictions about a situation. When these are not confirmed, they usually cannot think of alternatives and fail to solve the problem.

Adolescents' performance on Piaget's famous *pendulum problem* illustrates their new approach. Suppose we present several school-age children and adolescents with strings of different lengths, objects of different weights to attach to the strings, and a bar from which to hang the strings (see Figure 15.1). Then we ask each of them to figure out what influences the speed with which a pendulum swings through its arc.

Formal operational adolescents hypothesize that four variables might be influential: (1) the length of the string, (2) the weight of the object hung on it, (3) how high the object is raised before it is released, and (4) how forcefully the object is pushed. By varying one factor at a time while holding the other three constant, they try out each possibility and, if necessary, also test the variables in combination. Eventually they discover that only string length makes a difference.

In contrast, concrete operational children cannot separate the effects of each variable. They may test for the effect of string length without holding weight constant—comparing, for example, a short, light pendulum with a long, heavy one. Also, they typically fail to notice variables that are not immediately suggested by the concrete materials of the task—for example, how high the object is raised or how forcefully it is released.

Propositional Thought

A second important characteristic of Piaget's formal operational stage is **propositional thought**—adolescents' ability to evaluate the logic of propositions (verbal statements) without referring to real-world circumstances. In contrast, children can evaluate the logic of statements only by considering them against concrete evidence in the real world.

In a study of propositional reasoning, researchers showed children and adolescents a pile of poker chips and asked whether statements about the chips were true, false, or uncertain (Osherson & Markman, 1975). In one condition, the adult hid a chip in her hand and presented the following propositions:

"*Either* the chip in my hand is green *or* it is not green."

"The chip in my hand is green *and* it is not green."

In another condition, the experimenter held either a red or a green chip in full view and made the same statements.

School-age children focused on the concrete properties of the poker chips. When the chip was hidden from view, they replied that they were uncertain about both statements. When it was visible, they judged both statements to be true if the chip was green and false if it was red. In contrast, adolescents analyzed the logic of the statements. They understood that the "either–or" statement is always true while the "and" statement is always false, regardless of the poker chip's color.

Although Piaget did not view language as playing a central role in cognitive development (see Chapter 9), he acknowledged its importance in adolescence. Formal operations require language-based and other symbolic systems that do not stand for real things, such as those in higher mathematics. Secondary school students use such systems in algebra and geometry. Formal operational thought also involves verbal reasoning about abstract concepts. Jules showed that he could think in this way when he pondered the relationships between time, space, and matter in physics and wondered about justice and freedom in philosophy.

In Piaget's formal operational stage, adolescents engage in propositional thought. As these students discuss problems in a science class, they show that they can reason logically with symbols that do not necessarily represent objects in the real world.

Follow-Up Research on Formal Operational Thought

Research on formal operational thought poses questions similar to those we discussed with respect to Piaget's earlier stages: Does formal operational thinking appear earlier than Piaget expected? And do all individuals reach formal operations during their teenage years?

ARE CHILDREN CAPABLE OF HYPOTHETICO-DEDUCTIVE AND PROPOSITIONAL THINKING?
■ School-age children show the glimmerings of hypothetico-deductive reasoning, although they are less competent at it than adolescents. For example, in simplified situations—ones involving no more than two possible causal variables—6-year-olds understand that hypotheses must be confirmed by appropriate evidence. They also realize that once it is supported, a hypothesis shapes predictions about what might happen in the future (Ruffman et al., 1993). But school-age children cannot sort out evidence that bears on three or more variables at once. And as we will see when we take up information-processing research on scientific reasoning, children have difficulty explaining why a pattern of observations supports a hypothesis, even when they recognize the connection between the two.

With respect to propositional thought, when a simple set of premises defies real-world knowledge ("All cats bark. Rex is a cat. Does Rex bark?"), 4- to 6-year-olds can reason logically in make-believe play. In justifying their answer, they are likely to say, "We can pretend cats bark!" (Dias & Harris, 1988, 1990). But in an entirely verbal mode, children have great difficulty reasoning from premises that contradict reality or their own beliefs.

Consider the following set of statements: "If dogs are bigger than elephants, and elephants are bigger than mice, then dogs are bigger than mice." Children younger than 10 judge this

formal operational stage Piagetian stage beginning around age 11, in which young people develop the capacity for abstract, systematic, scientific thinking.

hypothetico-deductive reasoning A formal operational problem-solving strategy that begins with a hypothesis, from which logical inferences can be deduced and then tested by systematically isolating and combining variables.

propositional thought A type of formal operational reasoning involving the ability to evaluate the logic of propositions without referring to real-world circumstances.

reasoning to be false, since not all of the relations specified occur in real life (Moshman & Franks, 1986; Pillow, 2002). They automatically think of well-learned knowledge ("Elephants are larger than dogs") that casts doubt on the truthfulness of the premises. Children find it more difficult than adolescents to inhibit activation of such knowledge (Klaczynski, Schuneman, & Daniel, 2004; Simoneau & Markovits, 2003). Partly for this reason, they fail to grasp the **logical necessity** of propositional reasoning—that the accuracy of conclusions drawn from premises rests on the rules of logic, not on real-world confirmation.

Furthermore, in reasoning with propositions, school-age children do not think carefully about the major premise and, therefore, violate the most basic rules of logic (Markovits, Schleifer, & Fortier, 1989). For example, when given the following problem, they almost always draw an incorrect conclusion:

Major premise: If Susan hits a tambourine, then she will make a noise.

Second premise: Suppose that Susan does not hit a tambourine.

Question: Did Susan make a noise?

Wrong conclusion: No, Susan did not make a noise.

Notice that the major premise did *not* state that Susan can make noise *if, and only if,* she hits a tambourine. Adolescents generally detect that Susan could make a noise in other ways, partly because they are better at searching their knowledge for examples that contradict wrong conclusions (Klaczynski & Narasimham, 1998b; Markovits & Barrouillet, 2002).

As with hypothetico-deductive reasoning, in early adolescence, young people become better at analyzing the *logic* of a series of propositions, regardless of their *content*. And as they get older, they handle problems requiring more complex sets of mental operations. Further, in justifying their reasoning, they move from giving a concrete example ("She could have hit a drum instead of a tambourine") to explaining the logical rules on which it is based ("We can be certain that Susan did not hit a tambourine. But we cannot be certain that Susan did not make a noise; she might have done so in many other ways") (Müller, Overton, & Reene, 2001; Venet & Markovits, 2001). But these capacities do not appear suddenly around the time of puberty. Rather, gains occur gradually from childhood on—findings that call into question the emergence of a discrete new stage of cognitive development at adolescence (Keating, 2004; Kuhn & Franklin, 2006; Moshman, 2005).

DO ALL INDIVIDUALS REACH THE FORMAL OPERATIONAL STAGE? ■ **TAKE A MOMENT...** Try giving one or two of the formal operational tasks just described to your friends. How well do they do? Even many well-educated adults fail hypothetico-deductive tasks and have trouble reasoning with sets of propositions that contradict real-world facts (Keating, 1979; Markovits & Vachon, 1990)!

Why are so many adults not fully formal operational? One reason is that people are most likely to think abstractly and systematically on tasks in which they have had extensive guidance and practice in using such reasoning. This conclusion is supported by evidence that taking college courses leads to improvements in formal reasoning related to course content (Lehman & Nisbett, 1990). The physics student grasps Piaget's pendulum problem with ease. The English enthusiast excels at analyzing the themes of a Shakespeare play, whereas the history buff skillfully evaluates the causes and consequences of the Vietnam War. Consider these findings, and you will see that formal operations, like the concrete reasoning that preceded it, does not emerge in all contexts at once—it is specific to situation and task (Keating, 1990, 2004).

In tribal and village societies, formal operational tasks usually are not mastered at all (Cole, 1990). When asked to engage in propositional thought, people in nonliterate societies often refuse. Take this hypothetical proposition: "In the North, where there is snow, all bears are white. Novaya Zemlya is in the Far North, and it always has snow. What color are the bears there?" In response, a Central Asian peasant explains that he must see the event to discern its logical implications. The peasant insists on firsthand knowledge, whereas the interviewer asserts that truth can be based on ideas alone. Yet the peasant uses propositions to defend his point of view: "*If* a man . . . had seen a white bear and had told about it, [*then*] he could be believed, *but* I've never seen one and *hence* I can't say" (Luria 1976, pp. 108–109). Although he rarely displays it in everyday life, the peasant is clearly capable of formal operational thought!

logical necessity The idea that the accuracy of conclusions drawn from premises rests on the rules of logic, not on real-world confirmation.

Piaget acknowledged that without the opportunity to solve hypothetical problems, people in some societies might not display formal operations. Still, these findings raise further questions about Piaget's stage sequence. Does the formal operational stage result largely from children's and adolescents' independent efforts to make sense of their world, as Piaget claimed? Or is it a culturally transmitted way of thinking that is specific to literate societies and taught in school?

In an Israeli study of seventh to ninth graders, after controlling participants' age, researchers found that years of schooling fully accounted for early adolescent gains in propositional thought (Artman, Cahan, & Avni-Babad, 2006). School tasks, the investigators speculated, provide crucial experience in setting aside the "if . . . then" logic of everyday conversations that is often used to convey intentions, promises, and threats ("If you don't do your chores, then you won't get your allowance") but that conflicts with the logic of laboratory and academic reasoning tasks. In school, adolescents gradually learn that the real world and the verbal-hypothetical world require different approaches to reasoning. These and other similar findings have prompted many investigators to adopt an information-processing view.

These adolescents of Irian Jaya Province in Indonesia live in highland rainforests, where their people have little contact with the outside world. Although the boys would probably have great difficulty with Piaget's formal operational tasks, they show their capacity for complex reasoning in familiar situations as they deftly build a tree house, mentally coordinating multiple variables to ensure that the structure is stable and sturdy.

An Information-Processing View of Adolescent Cognitive Development

Information-processing theorists refer to a variety of specific mechanisms, supported by brain development and experience, that underlie cognitive change in adolescence. Each was discussed in previous chapters (Case, 1998; Kuhn & Franklin, 2006; Luna et al., 2004). Now let's draw them together:

- *Attention* becomes more selective (focused on relevant information) and better adapted to the changing demands of tasks.
- *Inhibition*—both of irrelevant stimuli and of well-learned responses in situations where they are inappropriate—improves, supporting gains in attention and reasoning.
- *Strategies* become more effective, improving storage, representation, and retrieval of information.
- *Knowledge* increases, easing strategy use.
- *Metacognition* (awareness of thought) expands, leading to new insights into effective strategies for acquiring information and solving problems.
- *Cognitive self-regulation* improves, yielding better moment-by-moment monitoring, evaluation, and redirection of thinking.
- *Speed of thinking* and *processing capacity* increase. As a result, more information can be held at once in working memory and combined into increasingly complex, efficient representations, "opening possibilities for growth" in the capacities just listed and also improving as a result of gains in those capacities (Demetriou et al., 2002, p. 97).

As we look at influential findings from an information-processing perspective, we will see some of these mechanisms of change in action. And we will discover that researchers regard one of them—*metacognition*—as central to adolescent cognitive development.

Scientific Reasoning: Coordinating Theory with Evidence

During a free moment in physical education class, Sabrina wondered why more of her tennis serves and returns passed the net and dropped in her opponent's court when she used a particular brand of balls. "Is it something about their color or size?" she asked herself. "Hmm . . . or could it be their surface texture? That might affect their bounce."

Good serve

Bad serve

FIGURE 15.2

Which features of these sports balls—size, color, surface texture, or presence or absence of ridges—influence the quality of a player's serve? This set of evidence suggests that color might be important, since light-colored balls are largely in the good-serve basket and dark-colored balls in the bad-serve basket. But the same is true for texture! The good-serve basket has mostly smooth balls, the bad-serve basket rough balls. Since all light-colored balls are smooth and all dark-colored balls are rough, we cannot tell whether color or texture makes a difference. But we can conclude that size and presence or absence of ridges are not important, because these features are equally represented in the good-serve and bad-serve baskets. (Adapted from Kuhn, Amsel, & O'Loughlin, 1988.)

The heart of scientific reasoning is coordinating theories with evidence. A scientist can clearly describe the theory he or she favors, knows what evidence is needed to support it and what would refute it, and can explain how pitting evidence against theories led to the acceptance of one theory as opposed to others. What evidence would Sabrina need to confirm her theory about the tennis balls?

Deanna Kuhn (2002) has conducted extensive research into the development of scientific reasoning, using problems that resemble Piaget's tasks, in that several variables might affect an outcome. In one series of studies, third, sixth, and ninth graders and adults were provided evidence, sometimes consistent with and sometimes conflicting with theories. Then they were questioned about the accuracy of each theory.

For example, participants were given a problem much like the one Sabrina posed. They were asked to theorize about which of several features of sports balls—size (large or small), color (light or dark), surface texture (rough or smooth), or presence or absence of ridges on the surface—influences the quality of a player's serve. Next, they were told about the theory of Mr. (or Ms.) S, who believes the ball's size is important, and the theory of Mr. (or Ms.) C, who thinks color makes a difference. Finally, the interviewer presented evidence by placing balls with certain characteristics in two baskets labeled "good serve" and "bad serve" (see Figure 15.2).

Kuhn found that the capacity to reason like a scientist improved with age. The youngest participants often ignored conflicting evidence or distorted it in ways consistent with their theory. When one third grader, who judged that size was causal (that large balls produced good serves and small balls produced bad serves), was shown incomplete evidence (a single large, light-colored ball in the good-serve basket and no balls in the bad-serve basket), he insisted on the accuracy of Mr. S's theory (which was also his own). Asked to explain, he stated flatly, "Because this ball is big . . . the color doesn't really matter" (Kuhn, 1989, p. 677).

These findings, and others like them, reveal that instead of viewing evidence as separate from and bearing on a theory, children often blend the two into a single representation of "the way things are." The ability to distinguish theory from evidence and to use logical rules to examine their relationship in complex, multivariable situations improves steadily from childhood into adolescence and adulthood (Kuhn & Dean, 2004; Kuhn & Pearsall, 2000).

How Scientific Reasoning Develops

What factors support adolescents' skill at coordinating theory with evidence? Greater working memory capacity, permitting a theory and the effects of several variables to be compared at once, is vital. In addition, adolescents benefit from exposure to increasingly complex problems and instruction that highlights critical features of tasks and effective strategies. Consequently, scientific reasoning is strongly influenced by years of schooling, whether individuals grapple with traditional scientific tasks (like the sports ball problem or Piaget's pendulum task) or engage in informal reasoning—for example, justify a theory about what causes children to fail in school (Kuhn, 1993).

Researchers believe that sophisticated *metacognitive understanding* is at the heart of scientific reasoning (Kuhn, 1999; Moshman, 1999). Microgenetic research (see Chapter 1, page 43) shows that when adolescents regularly pit theory against evidence over many weeks, they experiment with various strategies, reflect on and revise them, and gradually become aware of the nature of logic. Over time, they apply their appreciation of logic to an increasingly wide range of situations. The ability to *think about* theories, *deliberately isolate* variables, and *actively seek* disconfirming evidence is rarely present before adolescence (Kuhn, 2000b; Moshman, 1998).

But adolescents and adults vary widely in scientific reasoning skills. Many continue to show a self-serving bias, applying logic more effectively to ideas they doubt than to ideas they favor (Klaczynski, 1997; Klaczynski & Narasimham, 1998a). Reasoning scientifically requires the metacognitive capacity to evaluate one's objectivity—a disposition to be fair-minded rather than self-serving (Moshman, 1999). As we will see in Chapter 16, this flexible, open-minded approach is both a cognitive attainment and a personality trait—one that assists young people greatly in forming an identity and developing morally.

Adolescents develop scientific reasoning skills in a similar step-by-step fashion on different types of tasks. In a series of studies, 10- to 20-year olds were given sets of problems graded in difficulty. For example, one set consisted of quantitative-relational tasks like the pendulum problem in Figure 15.1. Another set contained verbal propositional tasks like the tambourine problem on page 568. And in still another set were causal-experimental tasks like the sports ball problem in Figure 15.2 (Demetriou et al., 1993, 1996, 2002).

In each type of task, adolescents mastered component skills in sequential order by expanding their metacognitive awareness. For example, on causal-experimental tasks, they first became aware of the many variables that—separately and in combination—could influence an outcome. This enabled them to formulate and test hypotheses. Over time, adolescents combined separate skills into a smoothly functioning system, constructing a general model that they could apply to many instances of a given type of problem. In the researchers' words, young people seem to form a "hypercognitive system," or supersystem, that understands, organizes, and influences other aspects of cognition (Demetriou & Kazi, 2001).

TAKE A MOMENT... Return to Chapter 12, page 441, and review Robbie Case's information-processing view of development during Piaget's concrete operational stage. Does Case's concept of *central conceptual structures* remind you of the metacognitive advances just described? Piaget also underscored the role of metacognition in formal operational thought when he spoke of "operating on operations" (see page 566). However, information-processing findings confirm that scientific reasoning is not the result of an abrupt, stagewise change. Instead, it develops out of many experiences that require children and adolescents to match theory against evidence and reflect on and evaluate their thinking.

High school students attending an engineering summer camp at the University of Texas attempt to design a catapult for shooting water balloons. Extensive experience coordinating theory with evidence in complex problems results in gains in scientific reasoning as teenagers reflect on their strategies and revise them.

Consequences of Adolescent Cognitive Changes

The development of increasingly complex, effective thinking leads to dramatic revisions in the way adolescents see themselves, others, and the world in general. But just as adolescents are occasionally awkward in the use of their transformed bodies, they are initially faltering in their abstract thinking. Although teenagers' self-concern, idealism, criticism, and indecisiveness often perplex and worry adults, they usually are beneficial in the long run. Applying What We Know on page 572 suggests ways to handle the everyday consequences of teenagers' newfound cognitive capacities.

Self-Consciousness and Self-Focusing

Adolescents' ability to reflect on their own thoughts, combined with the physical and psychological changes they are undergoing, means that they think more about themselves. Piaget believed that a new form of egocentrism arises, in which adolescents again have difficulty distinguishing their own and others' perspectives (Inhelder & Piaget, 1955/1958). Followers of Piaget suggest that two distorted images of the relationship between self and other appear.

Applying What We Know

Handling Consequences of Teenagers' New Cognitive Capacities

ABSTRACT THOUGHT EXPRESSED AS . . .	SUGGESTION
Sensitivity to public criticism	Refrain from finding fault with the adolescent in front of others. If the matter is important, wait until you can speak to the teenager alone.
Exaggerated sense of personal uniqueness	Acknowledge the adolescent's unique characteristics. At opportune times, point out how you felt similarly as a young teenager, encouraging a more balanced perspective.
Idealism and criticism	Respond patiently to the adolescent's grand expectations and critical remarks. Point out positive features of targets, helping the teenager see that all worlds and people are blends of virtues and imperfections.
Difficulty making everyday decisions	Refrain from deciding for the adolescent. Model effective decision making, and offer diplomatic suggestions about the pros and cons of alternatives, the likelihood of various outcomes, and learning from poor choices.

The first is called the **imaginary audience,** adolescents' belief that they are the focus of everyone else's attention and concern (Elkind & Bowen, 1979). As a result, they become extremely self-conscious, often going to great lengths to avoid embarrassment. When Sabrina woke up one Sunday morning with a large pimple on her chin, her first thought was, "I can't possibly go to church! Everyone will notice how ugly I look." The imaginary audience helps explain the long hours adolescents spend inspecting every detail of their appearance, as well as their extreme sensitivity to public criticism. To teenagers, who believe that everyone is monitoring their performance, a critical remark from a parent or teacher can be mortifying.

A second cognitive distortion is the **personal fable.** Because teenagers are sure that others are observing and thinking about them, they develop an inflated opinion of their own importance. They feel that they are special and unique. Many adolescents view themselves as reaching great heights of glory as well as sinking to unusual depths of despair—experiences that others could not possibly understand (Elkind, 1994). As one teenager wrote in her diary, "My parents' lives are so ordinary, so stuck in a rut. Mine will be different. I'll realize my hopes and ambitions." When combined with a sensation-seeking personality, the personal fable seems to contribute to adolescent risk taking by reducing teenagers' sense of vulnerability. In one study, young people with high personal-fable and sensation-seeking scores took more sexual risks, more often used drugs, and committed more delinquent acts than their agemates (Greene et al., 2000).

© DAVID YOUNG-WOLFF/PHOTOEDIT

These adolescents are acting for the camera. But even at other times, the imaginary audience leads them to think that they are the focus of everyone's attention. In addition to reflecting their self-consciousness, young teenagers' concern with others' opinions is also prompted by a growing awareness that those evaluations have important *real* consequences.

The imaginary audience and personal fable are strongest during early adolescence, then gradually decline (Lapsley et al., 1988). Yet these distorted visions of the self do not result from egocentrism, as Piaget suggested. Rather, they are an outgrowth of gains in perspective taking, which cause young teenagers to be more concerned with what others think (Vartanian & Powlishta, 1996). When asked why they worry about the opinions of others, adolescents responded that they do so because others' evaluations have important *real* consequences—for self-esteem, peer acceptance, and social support (Bell & Bromnick, 2003). Teenagers also have emotional reasons for clinging to the idea that others are concerned with their appearance and behavior. Doing so helps them maintain a hold on important relationships as they struggle to separate from parents and establish an independent sense of self (Vartanian, 1997).

Idealism and Criticism

Adolescents' capacity to think about possibilities opens up the world of the ideal and the notion of perfection. Teenagers can imagine alternative family, religious, political, and moral systems, and they want to explore them. Doing so is part of investigating new realms of experience, developing larger social commitments, and defining their own values and preferences.

Teenagers' idealism leads them to construct grand visions of a perfect world with no injustice, discrimination, or tasteless behavior. Adults, with their longer life experience, have a more realistic outlook. The disparity between adults' and teenagers' worldviews, often called the "generation gap," creates tension between parent and child. Aware of the perfect family against which their real parents and siblings do not measure up, adolescents become fault-finding critics.

Overall, however, teenage idealism and criticism are advantageous. Once adolescents come to see other people as having both strengths and weaknesses, they have a much greater capacity to work constructively for social change and to form positive and lasting relationships (Elkind, 1994). Parents can help teenagers forge a better balance between the ideal and the real by tolerating their criticism while reminding them that all people are blends of virtues and imperfections.

Planning and Decision Making

Because they think more analytically, adolescents handle cognitive tasks more effectively than they did when younger. Given a homework assignment, they are far better at *cognitive self-regulation*—planning what to do first and what to do next, monitoring progress toward a goal, and redirecting actions that prove unsuccessful. For this reason, study skills improve from middle childhood into adolescence.

In addition, adolescents are better at a form of self-regulation called *comprehension monitoring*—continually evaluating how well they understand while reading or listening. With age, teenagers more often notice when a passage does not make sense. Rather than moving ahead, they slow down and look back to see if they have missed important information (Hacker, 1997). Their greater sensitivity to text errors means that they are more likely to revise their written work.

But when it comes to planning and decision making in everyday life, teenagers often do not think rationally: (1) identifying the pros and cons of each alternative, (2) assessing the likelihood of various possible outcomes, (3) evaluating their choice in terms of whether their goals were met, and, if not, (4) learning from the mistake and making a better future decision. In one study of decision making, researchers gave adolescents and adults hypothetical dilemmas—whether to have cosmetic surgery, whether to participate in an experimental study of a new acne medication, which parent to live with after divorce—and asked them to explain how they would decide. Adults outperformed adolescents, especially the younger ones, more often considering alternatives, weighing the benefits and risks of each, and suggesting advice-seeking, especially in areas (such as medical decisions) where they had little experience (Halpern-Felsher & Cauffman, 2001). Other evidence shows that adolescents are less likely than adults to learn from feedback by revising their decision-making strategies (Byrnes, 2002).

Furthermore, in making decisions, adolescents, more often than adults (who also have difficulty), fall back on well-learned intuitive judgments (Jacobs & Klaczynski, 2002). Consider a hypothetical problem in which you have to choose, on the basis of two arguments, between taking a traditional lecture class and taking a computer-based class. One argument contains large-sample information: course evaluations from 150 students, 85 percent of whom liked the computer class. The other argument contains small-sample personal reports: complaints of two honor-roll students who both hated the computer class and enjoyed the traditional class. Many adolescents knew that selecting the large-sample argument was "more intelligent." Even so, most based their choice on the small-sample argument, which resembled the informal opinions they depend on in everyday life (Klaczynski, 2001).

Why is decision making so challenging for adolescents? As "first-timers" at many experiences, they do not have enough knowledge to consider the pros and cons of many options and to predict how they might react after selecting one over the others. They also face many more

imaginary audience Adolescents' belief that they are the focus of others' attention and concern.

personal fable Adolescents' inflated opinion of their own importance—the belief that they are special and unique and that others cannot possibly understand their thoughts and feelings.

© BOB DAEMMRICH/THE IMAGE WORKS

These high school students attending a college fair will face many choices over the next few years. In unfamiliar situations, teenagers are more likely than adults to fall back on intuitive judgments rather than using sound decision-making strategies.

complex situations involving competing goals—for example, how to maintain peer approval while avoiding getting drunk at a party. In the heat of the moment and in unfamiliar situations, when making a good decision requires them to inhibit "feel-good" behavior (smoking, overeating, unsafe sex), adolescents are far more likely than adults to emphasize short-term over long-term goals (Amsel et al., 2005; Boyer, 2006; Reyna & Farley, 2006). And after engaging in such behavior without negative consequences, teenagers rate its benefits higher and its risks lower than peers who have not tried it (Halpern-Felsher et al., 2004).

Furthermore, adolescents often feel overwhelmed by their expanding range of options—abundant choices of school courses, extracurricular activities, social events, and material goods. As a result, their efforts to choose frequently break down, and they resort to habit, act on impulse, or postpone decision making. Louis, for example, procrastinated over his college plans. When Franca mentioned that he was about to miss the deadline for taking entrance tests, he agonized over the forms, unable to decide when to take the exam.

When teenagers were younger, adults usually limited the decisions they had to make. Adolescents, in contrast, face an increasing number of decisions that have far-reaching consequences. School and community interventions that teach effective decision-making skills can help adolescents apply their capacity for metacognition, more often thinking about and monitoring the decision process (Jacobs & Klaczynski, 2002). But because engaging in risk taking without experiencing harmful outcomes can heighten adolescents' sense of invulnerability, they also need supervision and protection from high-risk experiences until their decision making improves.

Ask Yourself

Review   Describe research findings that challenge Piaget's notion of a new, discrete stage of cognitive development at adolescence.

Apply   Thirteen-year-old Rosie had a crush on a boy who failed to return her affections. When her mother assured her that there would be other boys, Rosie snapped, "Mom! You don't know what it's like to be in love!" Which cognitive distortion of adolescence does Rosie's thinking illustrate? Explain.

Connect   How does evidence on adolescent decision making help us understand teenagers' risk taking in sexual activity and drug use?

Reflect   Do you recall engaging in idealistic thinking or poor decision making as a teenager? Cite examples. How has your thinking changed?

Sex Differences in Mental Abilities

Sex differences in intellectual performance have sparked almost as much controversy as the ethnic and SES differences in IQ considered in Chapter 12. Although boys and girls do not differ in general intelligence, they do vary in specific mental abilities.

Verbal Abilities

Throughout the school years, girls attain higher scores in reading and writing achievement and account for a lower percentage of children referred for remedial reading instruction. Girls continue to score slightly higher on tests of verbal ability in adolescence (Halpern, 2000, 2004).

But a special concern is that girls' advantage in reading and writing achievement increases over adolescence, with boys doing especially poorly in writing—trends evident in the United States, Canada, and other industrialized nations (OECD, 2005; Statistics Canada, 2006b; U.S. Department of Education, 2006e, 2006g). These differences in literacy skills are believed to be major contributors to a widening gender gap in college enrollments. Whereas 30 years ago, males accounted for 60 percent of North American undergraduates, today they are in the minority, at 42 percent (Statistics Canada, 2005h; U.S. Department of Education, 2006b).

Recall from Chapter 6 that girls show a biological advantage in earlier development of the left hemisphere of the cerebral cortex, where language is localized. Girls also receive more maternal verbal stimulation from the preschool years through adolescence (Peterson & Roberts, 2003). Furthermore, in Chapter 13 we noted that children view language arts as a "feminine" subject. And as a result of the high-stakes testing movement, students spend more time at their desks being taught in a regimented, uniform way—an approach particularly at odds with boys' higher activity level, assertiveness, and incidence of learning problems.

Finally, high rates of divorce and out-of-wedlock births mean that more children today grow up without a father who models and encourages good work habits and skill at reading and writing. Both maternal and paternal involvement contributes to the achievement and educational attainment of adolescents of both genders (Flouri & Buchanan, 2004). But some research suggests that high-achieving African-American boys are particularly likely to come from homes where fathers are warm, verbally communicative, and demanding of achievement (Grief, Hrabowski, & Maton, 1998). Clearly, reversing boys' weakening literacy skills is a high priority—one that requires a concerted effort on the part of families, schools, and supportive communities.

Mathematical Abilities

Sex differences in mathematical abilities are apparent by first grade. Girls more often depend on concrete manipulatives to solve basic math problems, whereas boys more often mentally represent numbers and rapidly retrieve answers from memory (Fennema et al., 1998). Girls' better verbal skills and careful approach to problem solving contribute to an advantage in arithmetic computation in the early grades. But boys start to outperform girls around early adolescence, when math concepts become more abstract and spatial. The difference is especially evident on tests of complex reasoning and geometry (Bielinski & Davison, 1998). It also extends to science achievement, where boys' advantage increases as problems become more difficult (Penner, 2003).

When all adolescents are considered, this male advantage is evident in virtually every country where males and females have equal access to secondary education. At the same time, the gap is small, and it has diminished over the past 30 years (Halpern, Wai, & Saw, 2005; U.S. Department of Education, 2006c). Among the most capable students, however, the gender gap is greater. In widely publicized research on more than 100,000 bright seventh and eighth graders invited to take the Scholastic Aptitude Test (SAT), boys outscored girls on the mathematics subtest year after year. Yet even this disparity has been shrinking. A quarter-century ago, 13 times as many boys as girls scored over 700 (out of a possible 800) on the math portion of the SAT; today, the ratio is 2.8 to 1 (Benbow & Stanley, 1983; Monastersky, 2005).

Some researchers believe that heredity contributes substantially to the gender gap in math, especially to the tendency for more boys to be extremely talented. Accumulating evidence indicates that boys' advantage originates in two skill areas. First, boys' more rapid numerical memory permits them to devote more energy to complex mental operations. Second, boys' superior spatial reasoning enhances their mathematical problem solving (Geary et al., 2000). See the Biology and Environment box on page 576 for further consideration of this issue.

Social pressures are also highly influential. In the early school grades—long before sex differences in math achievement appear—both boys and girls view math as a "masculine" subject. Also, many parents think that boys are better at it—an attitude that encourages girls to view themselves as having to work harder at math to do well, to blame their errors on lack of ability, and to regard math as less useful for their future lives. These beliefs reduce girls' self-efficacy at doing math, which undermines their performance on math achievement tests and their willingness to consider math- or science-related careers in college (Bhanot & Jovanovic,

Biology and Environment

Sex Differences in Spatial Abilities

Spatial abilities are a key focus of researchers' efforts to explain sex differences in mathematical reasoning. The gender gap favoring males is large for *mental rotation tasks*, in which individuals must rotate a three-dimensional figure rapidly and accurately inside their heads (see Figure 15.3). Males also do considerably better on *spatial perception tasks*, in which people must determine spatial relationships by considering the orientation of the surrounding environment. Sex differences on *spatial visualization tasks*, involving analysis of complex visual forms, are weak or nonexistent. Because many strategies can be used to solve these tasks, both sexes may come up with effective procedures (Collaer & Hill, 2006; Voyer, Voyer, & Bryden, 1995).

Sex differences in spatial abilities emerge in early childhood and persist throughout the lifespan (Levine et al., 1999). The pattern is consistent enough to suggest a biological explanation. One hypothesis is that heredity, perhaps through

FIGURE 15.3

Types of spatial tasks. Large sex differences favoring males appear on mental rotation, and males do considerably better than females on spatial perception. In contrast, sex differences on spatial visualization are weak or nonexistent. (From M. C. Linn & A. C. Petersen, 1985, "Emergence and Characterization of Sex Differences in Spatial Ability: A Meta-Analysis," *Child Development, 56,* pp. 1482, 1483, 1485. © The Society for Research in Child Development, Inc. Reprinted by permission.)

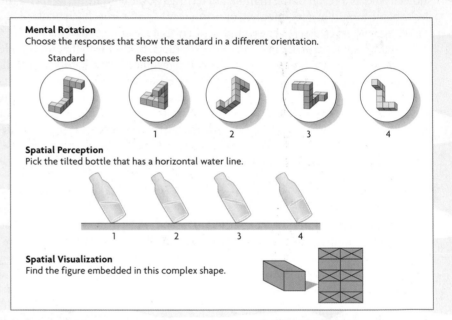

Mental Rotation
Choose the responses that show the standard in a different orientation.

Standard   Responses

1   2   3   4

Spatial Perception
Pick the tilted bottle that has a horizontal water line.

1   2   3   4

Spatial Visualization
Find the figure embedded in this complex shape.

2005; Bleeker & Jacobs, 2004; Kenney-Benson et al., 2006). Furthermore, *stereotype threat*—the fear of being judged on the basis of a negative stereotype (see page 459 in Chapter 12)—causes females to do worse than their abilities allow on difficult math problems (Ben-Zeev et al., 2005; Steele, 1997). As a result of all these influences, girls—even those who are highly talented—are less likely to develop effective math reasoning skills.

A positive sign is that today, boys and girls reach advanced levels of high school math and science study in equal proportions—a crucial factor in reducing sex differences in knowledge and skill (Gallagher & Kaufman, 2005). But, as noted in Chapter 12, boys spend more time than girls with computers, and they tend to use them differently: Girls focus on e-mail, instant messaging, and gathering information for homework assignments; boys more often write computer programs, analyze data, and use graphics software. As a result, boys acquire more specialized computer knowledge (Freeman, 2004; Looker & Thiessen, 2003).

Clearly, extra steps must be taken to promote girls' interest in and confidence at math and science. Daughters whose parents hold nonstereotyped beliefs are less likely to avoid math and science and more likely to achieve well (Updegraff, McHale, & Crouter, 1996). And a math curriculum beginning in kindergarten that teaches children how to apply effective spatial strategies—drawing diagrams, mentally manipulating visual images, searching for numerical patterns, and graphing—is vital (Nuttal, Casey, & Pezaris, 2005). Because girls are biased toward verbal processing, they may not realize their math and science potential unless they are specifically taught how to think spatially. Exposure to successful women as role models is likely to improve girls' belief in their own capacity to succeed.

This seventh-grade girl won a gold medal in her age category in the 2003 Canada-Wide Science Fair for her project examining the hazards of cell phone use while driving. An excellent math curriculum, including emphasis on spatial strategies and confidence-building experiences, may have contributed to her outstanding performance, which involved sophisticated data analysis and graphing.

of males became adapted for hunting, which required generating mental representations of large-scale spaces to find one's way (Choi & Silverman, 2003; Jones, Braithwaite, & Healy, 2003).

Experience also contributes to males' superior spatial performance. Children who engage in manipulative activities, such as block play, model building, and carpentry, do better on spatial tasks (Baenninger & Newcombe, 1995). Furthermore, playing video games that require rapid mental rotation of visual images enhances spatial scores (Subrahmanyam & Greenfield, 1996; Terlecki & Newcombe, 2005). Boys spend far more time than girls at these pursuits.

Research confirms that superior spatial skills contribute to the greater ease with which males solve complex math problems. In studies of middle and high school students, both spatial ability and self-efficacy at doing math were related to performance on complex math problems, with spatial skills being the stronger predictor (Casey, Nuttal, & Pezaris, 1997, 2001). Boys are advantaged in both spatial abilities and math self-confidence. Still spatial skills respond readily to training, with improvements in performance often larger than the sex differences themselves. But because boys and girls show similar training effects, sex differences remain (Newcombe & Huttenlocher, 2006). In sum, biology and environment *jointly* explain variations in spatial and math performance—both within and between the sexes.

superior performance on spatial rotation tasks (Berenbaum, 2001; Halpern & Collaer, 2005). And in some studies, spatial performance varies with daily and annual androgen levels in both men and women (Temple & Carney, 1995; Van Goozen et al., 1995).

prenatal exposure to androgen hormones, enhances right-hemispheric functioning, giving males a spatial advantage. (Recall that for most people, spatial skills are housed in the right hemisphere of the cerebral cortex.) In support of this idea, girls and women whose prenatal androgen levels were abnormally high show

Why might a biologically based gender difference in spatial abilities exist? Evolutionary theorists point out that mental rotation skill predicts rapid, accurate map drawing and interpretation, areas in which boys and men do better than girls and women. Over the course of human evolution, the cognitive abilities

Language Development

Although language development is largely complete by the end of childhood, subtle but important changes take place in adolescence. These gains are largely influenced by adolescents' improved capacity for reflective thought and abstraction, which enhances their *metalinguistic awareness,* or ability to think about language as a system.

Vocabulary and Grammar

Adolescents add a wide variety of abstract words to their vocabularies. In the conversation at the beginning of this chapter, note Jules's use of "counterintuitive," "revolutionized," "philosophy," and "reproduction." As a 9- or 10-year-old, he rarely used such words, and he had difficulty grasping their meaning. From high school to college, definitions of abstract words improve greatly in clarity and accuracy (Nippold, 1999). For example, in explaining the meaning of *burden,* Louis said, "It's like a heavy weight on your shoulders. The word can be used literally, or it can be used figuratively, to mean an unpleasant responsibility or a long-term problem."

Adolescents also master irony and sarcasm (Winner, 1988). "Don't have a major brain explosion," Louis commented to Sabrina when she complained about having to work on an essay for school. And when Franca prepared a dish for dinner that Louis disliked, he quipped,

Greater skill at reflecting on the features of language enables adolescents to vary their language style to fit a wide range of situations. These high school students use a very different style for text messaging with friends than for a school presentation or a conference with their teacher.

"Oh boy, my favorite!" Young children sometimes realize that a sarcastic remark is insincere if it is said in a very exaggerated, mocking tone of voice. But adolescents and adults need only notice the discrepancy between the statement and its context to grasp the intended meaning (Capelli, Nakagawa, & Madden, 1990).

Similarly, grasp of figurative language, in the form of proverbs, improves greatly in adolescence. Proverbs that express subtle attitudes are among the most challenging. They can be used to comment ("Blood is thicker than water"), interpret ("His bark is worse than his bite"), advise ("Humility often gains more than pride"), warn ("Of idleness comes no goodness"), and encourage ("Every cloud has a silver lining") (Nippold, 2000). Reading proficiency fosters understanding of proverbs (Nippold, Allen, & Kirsch, 2001). And a better grasp of figurative language enables teenagers to appreciate adult literary works.

Furthermore, adolescents use more elaborate grammatical constructions—longer sentences that consist of a greater number of subordinate clauses. Persuasive speaking and writing, which draw on adolescents' advanced perspective-taking skill, illustrate this change. With age, this challenging form of communication contains many more connecting words, such as "although," "moreover," and "on the other hand" (Crowhurst, 1990).

Finally, teenagers more effectively analyze and correct their grammar. Although out of favor since the 1970s, overt grammar instruction in U.S. schools is making a comeback, prompted by the mediocre writing skills of many adolescents. In the most recent national assessment of educational progress, only about one-fourth of U.S. high school seniors scored at a "proficient" level or above in writing achievement (U.S. Department of Education, 2006g). But traditional grammar instruction (such as diagramming sentences) has no impact on students' writing skills (Andrews et al., 2006). Rather, grammatically accurate written expression is best learned in the context of writing. And writing improves when teachers show students how to write for different purposes, give them many opportunities to write, and help them critique and improve their compositions (Medina, 2006).

Pragmatics

One obvious gain in adolescents' communication skills is an improved capacity to vary language style to fit the situation. This change results in part from opportunities to enter many more situations. To succeed on the debate team, Louis had to speak in a rapid-fire, well-organized, persuasive manner. In theater class, he worked on reciting memorized lines as if they were natural. At work, his boss insisted that he respond to customers cheerfully and courteously. Greater skill at reflecting on the features of language and engaging in cognitive self-regulation also supports effective use of language styles (Obler, 2005). Teenagers are far more likely than school-age children to practice what they want to say in an expected situation, review what they did say, and figure out how they could say it better.

TAKE A MOMENT... Listen to adolescents conversing, and note their use of slang—another illustration of their mastery of language styles. Adolescents' communication by computer—especially instant messaging, teenagers' preferred means of online interaction—is also rich in slang. "Cyber slang," devised to facilitate communication while protecting its privacy, has become a familiar part of popular culture—for example, "gg" (gotta go), "mwah" (kiss), "lol" (laugh out loud), "brb" (be right back), "yt" (you there?), "pos" (parents over shoulder). Teenagers use slang as a sign of group belonging and as a way to distinguish themselves from adults. Doing so is part of separating from parents and seeking a temporary self-definition in the peer group. We will discuss these developments in Chapter 16.

Learning in School

In complex societies, adolescence coincides with entry into secondary school. Most young people move into either a middle or a junior high school, then into a high school. With each change, academic achievement becomes more serious, affecting higher education options and job opportunities. In the following sections, we take up various aspects of secondary school life.

School Transitions

When Sabrina started junior high, she left a small, intimate, self-contained sixth-grade class-room for a much larger school. "I don't know most of the kids in my classes, and my teachers don't know me," she complained to her mother at the end of the first week. "Besides, I don't have enough time to move from one class to the next, and there's too much homework. I get assignments in all my classes at once." Bursting into tears, she shouted, "I can't do all this!"

IMPACT OF SCHOOL TRANSITIONS ■ As Sabrina's reactions suggest, school transitions can create adjustment problems. With each school change—from elementary to middle or junior high and then to high school—adolescents' grades decline. The drop is partly due to tighter academic standards. At the same time, the transition to secondary school often brings with it less personal attention, more whole-class instruction, and less chance to participate in classroom decision making (Seidman, Aber, & French, 2004). In view of these changes, it is not surprising that students rate their middle or junior high school learning experiences less favorably than their elementary school experiences (Wigfield & Eccles, 1994). They also report that their teachers care less about them, are less friendly, offer less support, grade less fairly, and stress competition more. Consequently, many young people feel less academically competent, and their liking for school and motivation decline (Barber & Olsen, 2004; Gutman & Midgley, 2000; Otis, Grouzet, & Pelletier, 2005).

Inevitably, students must readjust their feelings of self-confidence and self-worth as academic expectations are revised and students enter a more complex social world. A study following more than 300 students from sixth to tenth grade revealed that grade point average declined and feelings of anonymity increased after each school change—to junior high and then to high school. But the earlier school transition had a more negative impact, especially on girls' self-esteem, which dropped sharply after transition to junior high school and then only gradually rebounded. Girls fared poorer, the researchers conjectured, because movement to junior high tended to coincide with other life changes: the onset of puberty and dating. Adolescents who face added strains, such as family disruption, poverty, low parental involvement, high parental conflict, or learned helplessness on academic tasks, are at greatest risk for self-esteem, motivational, and academic difficulties (de Bruyn, 2005; Rudolph et al., 2001; Seidman et al., 2003).

Distressed young people whose school performance either remains low or drops sharply after school transition often show a persisting pattern of poor self-esteem, motivation, and achievement. In another study, researchers compared "multiple-problem" youths (those having both academic and mental health problems), youths having difficulties in just one area (either academic or mental health), and well-adjusted youths (those doing well in both areas) across the transition to high school. Although all groups declined in grade point average, well-adjusted students continued to get high marks and multiple-problem youths low marks, with the others falling in between. And as Figure 15.4 shows, the multiple-problem youths showed a far greater rise in truancy and out-of-school problem behaviors, such as doing something dangerous for the thrill of it, damaging public property, or getting drunk (Roeser, Eccles, & Freedman-Doan, 1999).

Adolescents with academic and emotional difficulties often turn to similarly alienated peers for the support they lack in other spheres of life (Rubin, Bukowski, & Parker, 2006). For these vulnerable youths, the transition to high school may initiate a downward spiral in school involvement and performance that eventually leads to failure and dropping out.

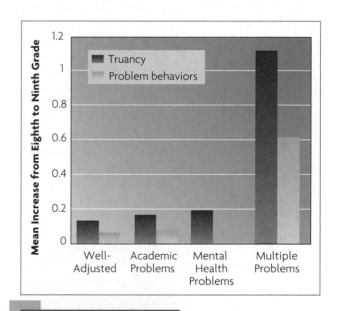

FIGURE 15.4

Increase in truancy and out-of-school problem behaviors across the transition to high school in four groups of students. Well-adjusted students, students with only academic problems, and students with only mental health problems showed little change. (Good students with mental health problems actually declined in problem behaviors, so no yellow bar is shown for them.) In contrast, multiple-problem students—with both academic and mental health difficulties—increased sharply in truancy and problem behaviors after changing schools from eighth to ninth grade. (Adapted from Roeser, Eccles, & Freedman-Doan, 1999.)

AP IMAGES/THE EXAMINER, PAUL BEAVER

Arriving at their new middle school on the first day of classes, this boy, and the line of students behind him, must figure out their schedules and find their classrooms. Moving from a small, self-contained elementary school classroom to a large, impersonal secondary school is stressful for adolescents.

HELPING ADOLESCENTS ADJUST TO SCHOOL TRANSITIONS ■ As these findings reveal, school transitions often lead to environmental changes that fit poorly with adolescents' developmental needs (Eccles, 2004). They disrupt close relationships with teachers at a time when adolescents need adult support. They emphasize competition during a period of heightened self-focusing. They reduce decision making and choice as the desire for autonomy is increasing. And they interfere with peer networks as young people become more concerned with peer acceptance.

Enhanced support from parents, teachers, and peers eases the strain of school transition. Parental involvement, monitoring, and gradual autonomy granting are associated with better adjustment after entering middle or junior high school (Grolnick et al., 2000). Adolescents with close friends adapt more successfully because they are more likely to sustain these friendships across the transition, which increases social integration and academic motivation in the new school (Aikins, Bierman, & Parker, 2005). Forming smaller units within large schools promotes closer relations with both teachers and peers along with greater extracurricular involvement (Seidman, Aber, & French, 2004).

Other, less extensive changes are also effective. In the first year after a school transition, homerooms can be provided in which teachers offer academic and personal counseling and work closely with parents to promote favorable adjustment. Students can also be assigned to classes with several familiar peers or a constant group of new peers—arrangements that strengthen emotional security and social support. In schools that intervened in these ways, students were less likely to decline in academic performance and to display other adjustment problems, including low self-esteem, depression, substance abuse, delinquency, and dropping out (Felner et al., 2002).

Finally, teenagers' perceptions of the sensitivity and flexibility of their school learning environments contribute substantially to successful school transitions. When schools minimize competition and differential treatment based on ability, students in middle or junior high school are less likely to feel angry and depressed, to be truant, or to show declines in self-esteem, academic values, and achievement (Roeser, Eccles, & Sameroff, 2000).

Academic Achievement

Adolescent achievement is the result of a long history of cumulative effects. Early on, positive educational environments, both family and school, lead to personal traits that support achievement—intelligence, confidence in one's own abilities, the desire to succeed, and high educational aspirations. Yet improving an unfavorable environment can foster resilience among poorly performing young people. See Applying What We Know on the following page for a summary of environmental factors that enhance achievement during the teenage years.

CHILD-REARING STYLES ■ Authoritative parenting (which combines warmth with firm, reasonable demands for maturity) is linked to achievement in adolescence, just as it predicts mastery-oriented behavior during the childhood years. The authoritative style is linked to higher grades for young people varying widely in SES. In contrast, authoritarian and permissive styles are associated with lower grades (Collins & Steinberg, 2006; Vazsonyi, Hibbert, & Snider, 2003). Of all parenting approaches, an uninvolved style (low in both warmth and maturity demands) predicts the poorest grades and worsening school performance over time (Glasgow et al., 1997; Kaisa, Stattin, & Nurmi, 2000).

The link between authoritative parenting and adolescents' academic competence has been confirmed in countries with diverse value systems, including Argentina, Australia, China, Hong Kong, the Netherlands, Pakistan, and Scotland (de Bruyn, Deković, & Meijnen, 2003; Steinberg, 2001). Still, some variations in parental control are adaptive. Recall from Chapter 10 that Chinese and African-American parents are unusually demanding (see page 401). For Chinese parents, high control represents deep parental commitment, stemming from Confucian values. For

Applying What We Know

Factors That Support High Achievement in Adolescence

FACTOR	DESCRIPTION
Child-rearing practices	Authoritative parenting
	Joint parent–adolescent decision making
	Parent involvement in the adolescent's education
Peer influences	Peer valuing of and support for high achievement
School characteristics	Teachers who are warm and supportive, develop personal relationships with parents, and show them how to foster their child's learning
	Learning activities that encourage high-level thinking
	Active student participation in learning activities and classroom decision making
Employment schedule	Job commitment limited to less than 15 hours per week
	High-quality vocational education for non-college-bound adolescents

African-American parents, dangerous living conditions may require greater strictness to foster children's competence. Consistent with these trends, highly controlling (but noncoercive) parenting is linked to better grades among first-generation Chinese immigrant youths and African-American teenagers (Chao, 2001; Glasgow et al., 1997).

Why does combining warmth with moderate to high control promote school success? In Chapter 10, we noted that authoritative parents adjust their expectations to children's capacity to take responsibility for their own behavior. Adolescents whose parents engage in joint decision making, gradually permitting more autonomy with age, achieve especially well (Dornbusch et al., 1990; Spera, 2005). Warmth, open discussion, firmness, and monitoring of the adolescents' whereabouts and activities make young people feel cared about and valued, encourage reflective thinking and self-regulation, and increase awareness of the importance of doing well in school. These factors, in turn, are related to mastery-oriented attributions, effort, achievement, and high educational expectations (Aunola, Stattin, & Nurmi, 2000; Gregory & Weinstein, 2004; Trusty, 1999).

PARENT–SCHOOL PARTNERSHIPS ■ High-achieving students typically have parents who keep tabs on their child's progress, communicate with teachers, and make sure their child is enrolled in challenging, well-taught classes. These efforts are just as important during middle and high school as they were earlier (Hill & Taylor, 2004). In a nationally representative sample of more than 15,000 American adolescents, parents' school involvement in eighth grade strongly predicted students' grade point average in tenth grade, beyond the influence of SES and previous academic achievement. This relationship held for each ethnic group included—black, white, Native American, and Asian (Keith et al., 1998). Parents who are in frequent contact with the school send a message to their child about the value of education, promote wise educational decisions, and model constructive solutions to academic problems. Involved parents can also prevent school personnel from placing a bright student who is not working up to potential in unstimulating classes.

Parents living in low-income, high-risk neighborhoods face daily stresses that strain relationships with their teenagers and reduce their energy for school involvement—factors consistently linked to poor academic performance (Bowen, Bowen, & Ware, 2002). Yet stronger home–school links could relieve some of this stress. Schools can build parent–school

By keeping tabs on his son's progress in school, the father sends his child a message about the importance of education and teaches skills for solving academic problems.

partnerships by strengthening personal relationships between teachers and parents, showing parents how to support their child's education at home, building bridges between minority home cultures and the culture of the school, tapping parents' talents to increase the quality of school programs, and including parents in school governance so they remain invested in school goals (Epstein, 2001).

PEER INFLUENCES ■ Peers also play an important role in achievement during adolescence, in a way that relates to both family and school. Teenagers whose parents value achievement generally choose friends who share those values (Berndt & Keefe, 1995). For example, when Sabrina began to make new friends in junior high, she often studied with her girlfriends and called them to check answers to homework assignments. Each girl wanted to do well and reinforced the same desire in the others. In a study that followed seventh graders during their first year after school transition, students in high-achieving peer groups declined less in academic performance than students in other groups. And those in groups whose members disliked school showed an especially large drop in school enjoyment (Ryan, 2001).

Ethnic variations exist in the strength of peer support for achievement and in peer-group valuing of school success. In an investigation of more than 5,000 U.S. high school students, integration into the school peer network predicted higher grades among Caucasians and Hispanics but not among Asians and African Americans (Faircloth & Hamm, 2005). Asian cultural values stress respect for family and teacher expectations over close peer ties (Chen, 2005; Ping & Berryman, 1996). And African-American minority adolescents readily observe that their ethnic group is worse off than the white majority in educational attainment, jobs, income, housing, and political power. Also, when African-American students are targets of discriminatory treatment because of cultural stereotypes that they are "not intelligent" held by teachers and white peers, they react with anger, anxiety, self-doubts about succeeding academically, declines in achievement, association with peers who are not interested in school, and increases in problem behaviors (Wong, Eccles, & Sameroff, 2003). Under these conditions, even middle-SES black teenagers may react against working hard, convinced that doing well in school will have little future payoff (Ogbu, 2003).

Yet not all economically disadvantaged African-American and other minority students respond this way. Case studies of inner-city, poverty-stricken African-American adolescents who were high-achieving and optimistic about their futures revealed that they were intensely aware of oppression but believed in striving to alter their social position (O'Connor, 1997). How did they develop this sense of agency? Parents, relatives, and teachers had convinced them through discussion and example that injustice should not be tolerated and that together, African Americans could overcome it—a perspective that encouraged academic motivation even in the face of peer pressures against doing well academically.

Schools that build close networks of support with teachers and other students are also powerful. One high school with a largely low-income ethnic-minority student body (65 percent African American) reorganized into "career academies"—learning communities within the school, each offering a different career-related curriculum (for example, one focused on health, medicine, and life sciences, another on computer technology). The smaller-school climate and focus on a common theme helped create a peer culture that fostered a sense of belonging, valuing of school engagement, mutual support, collaboration on projects, and academic success. Consequently, high school graduation and college enrollment rates rose from a small minority to over 90 percent (Conchas, 2006). One African-American student explained:

> I mean, we develop relationships where . . . they inspire me to do my work . . . I mean, it's just like they're just there, it's an inspiration. When I have one of those days when I just don't feel like doing no work, if I see them doing their work, I start working. I think to myself, "Man, I'm slipping in this class. I need to take you up and start doing my work." (p. 50)

SCHOOL CHARACTERISTICS ■ All adolescents need school environments that are responsive to their expanding powers of reasoning and emotional and social needs. Without appropriate learning experiences, their cognitive potential is unlikely to be realized.

Classroom Learning Experiences. As noted earlier, in large, departmentalized secondary schools, many adolescents report that their classes lack warmth and supportiveness—a circumstance that dampens their motivation. One study tracked changes in students' academic orientation in math classes from seventh to eighth grade. Those who entered classrooms high in teacher support, encouragement of student interaction about academic work, and promotion of mutual respect among classmates gained in academic motivation and cognitive self-regulation (reflected in whether they understood concepts and in their willingness to check their work). In contrast, declines in motivation and self-regulation occurred among students who moved to classrooms emphasizing competition and public comparison of students (Ryan & Patrick, 2001). In other investigations, adolescents who perceived their relationships with teachers as warm, trusting, and cooperative and who viewed classroom control as shared between teacher and students showed better attendance and achievement (Eshel & Kohavi, 2003; Schulte et al., 2003).

This high school teacher's warm, personalized way of relating to students encourages both academic motivation and cognitive self-regulation in his classroom.

As these findings indicate, adolescents, like children, need close relationships with teachers. As they develop an identity beyond the family, they seek adult models other than their parents. And just as they profit from appropriate granting of autonomy at home, they also benefit from increasing opportunities to exercise autonomy in the classroom through discussion and choice of learning activities.

Of course, an important benefit of separate classes in each subject is that adolescents can be taught by experts, who are more likely to encourage high-level thinking, teach effective learning strategies, and emphasize content relevant to students' experiences—factors that promote interest, effort, and achievement (Eccles, 2004). But secondary school classrooms do not consistently provide interesting, challenging teaching. Because of the uneven quality of instruction, many seniors graduate from high school deficient in basic academic skills. Although the achievement gap separating African-American, Hispanic, Native-American, and Canadian-Aboriginal students from white students has declined since the 1970s, mastery of reading, writing, mathematics, and science by low-SES ethnic minority students remains disappointing (Statistics Canada, 2006b; U.S. Department of Education, 2006f, 2006d). Too often these young people attend underfunded schools with run-down buildings, outdated equipment, and textbook shortages. In some, crime and discipline problems receive more attention than teaching and learning.

To upgrade the academic achievement of poorly performing students, a *high-stakes testing* movement has arisen, which makes progress through the school system contingent on passing achievement tests. But as the Social Issues: Education box on page 584 points out, high-stakes testing narrows the focus of classroom instruction to preparing for tests, and in some school districts, may widen group differences in educational attainment. Another source of educational inequity is the placement of many low-SES, minority students in low academic tracks, which compounds their learning difficulties.

Tracking. Ability grouping, as we saw in Chapter 12, is detrimental during the elementary school years. At least into middle or junior high school, mixed-ability classes are desirable. They effectively support the motivation and achievement of students who vary widely in academic progress (Gillies, 2003; Gillies & Ashman, 1996) (also see Chapter 12, page 470).

By high school, some grouping is unavoidable because certain aspects of education must dovetail with the young person's future educational and vocational plans. In the United States and Canada, high school students are counseled into college preparatory, vocational, or general education tracks. Unfortunately, the system perpetuates educational inequalities of earlier years. Low-SES minority students are assigned in large numbers to noncollege tracks.

Longitudinal research following thousands of U.S. students from eighth to twelfth grade revealed that assignment to a college track accelerates academic progress, whereas assignment to a vocational or general education track decelerates it (Hallinan & Kubitschek, 1999). Even in secondary schools that do not have a formal tracking program, low-SES minority students tend to be assigned to lower course levels in most or all of their academic subjects, resulting in *de facto* (unofficial) *tracking* that sorts students by SES and ethnicity (Lucas & Behrends, 2002).

Social Issues: Education

High-Stakes Testing

To better hold schools accountable for educating students, during the past two decades many U.S. states and Canadian provinces mandated that students pass exams for high school graduation. As these high-stakes achievement tests spread, schools stepped up their testing programs, extending them downward to elementary school. Some U.S. states and school districts also made grade promotion (in New York City, as early as the third grade) and secondary school academic course credits contingent on test scores (Gootman, 2005).

The U.S. No Child Left Behind Act, authorized by Congress in 2002, broadens high-stakes testing to the identification of "passing" and "failing" schools. The law mandates that each state evaluate every public school's performance through annual achievement testing and publicize the results. Schools that consistently perform poorly (have a high percentage of failing students) must give parents options for upgrading their children's education, such as transfers to

nearby, higher-performing schools or enrollment in remedial classes. In some states, schoolwide rewards for high scores and penalties for low scores are in place. These include, on the positive side, official praise and financial bonuses to school staff and, on the negative side, withdrawal of accreditation, state takeover, and closure.

Proponents of high-stakes testing believe that it will introduce greater rigor into classroom teaching, improve student motivation and achievement, and either turn around poor-performing schools or protect students from being trapped in them. But accumulating evidence indicates that high-stakes testing often undermines, rather than upgrades, the quality of education.

For example, in a Canadian study, researchers examined the impact of requiring students to pass British Columbia's high-school exit exam on eighth-, tenth-, and twelfth-grade science teaching. Observing classes and interviewing teachers, they found that twelfth-grade teachers narrowed the scope of what they taught to strings of facts to be memorized for the test. As a result, eighth and tenth graders, in some respects, were doing more advanced work than twelfth graders—conducting more experiments, exploring topics in greater depth, and engaging in more critical thinking (Wideen et al., 1997).

Many teachers also express concern that high-states testing promotes a one-size-fits-all education that is insensitive to student diversity. And because high-stakes testing has as its main goal upgrading the test performance of poorly performing students, the educational needs of gifted and talented students are neglected (Mondoza, 2006).

An additional concern is that high-stakes testing promotes fear—a poor motivator for upgrading teaching and learning. Principals and teachers worry about losing funding and their jobs if students do poorly. And many students

who get passing grades, even high grades, fail exams because a time-limited test with several dozen multiple-choice questions can tap only a small sampling of the skills covered in the classroom (Sacks, 1999). Students most likely to score poorly are minority youths living in poverty. When they are punished with course failure and grade retention, their self-esteem and motivation drop sharply, and they are likely to drop out (Kornhaber, Orfield, & Kurlaender, 2001). A Massachusetts study demonstrated that relying solely on test scores while ignoring teacher-assigned grades (which take into account effort and a broad range of skills) amplifies achievement gaps between white and black students and between boys and girls in math and science (Brennan et al., 2001).

The trend toward teaching to tests induced by high-stakes testing contrasts sharply with the emphasis on teaching for deeper understanding in countries that rank at the top in cross-cultural comparisons of academic achievement (see Chapter 12, pages 475–476). Even after hundreds of hours of class time devoted to test preparation, thousands of North American students fail school-exit exams and do not graduate. As just one example, in the Canadian province of Ontario, more than 60,000 high school seniors—most of them low-SES minorities, recent immigrants not yet proficient in English, or students with learning problems—were in danger of not graduating in 2006 because they had failed the grade 10 literacy exam (OSSTF, 2006). Although most try the test again, some fail repeatedly, with potentially dire consequences for the course of their lives.

Clearly, many issues remain for lawmakers and educators to resolve about the use of high-stakes tests. These include their ethnic and gender fairness and their questionable power to spark school reforms that make students better learners.

High-stakes testing often negatively affects educational quality and student learning. Pressure on teachers to "teach to the test" narrows the focus of the curriculum. And students who fail courses or are retained in grade because of poor test performance are likely to lose motivation and drop out of school.

Once a student is assigned to a low track of courses, breaking out is difficult. Track or course enrollment is generally based on past performance, which is limited by history of placement. Interviews with African-American students in one high school revealed that many thought their previous performance did not reflect their ability. Yet teachers and counselors, overburdened with other responsibilities, had little time to reconsider individual cases (Ogbu, 2003).

Compared to students in higher tracks, students in low tracks exert substantially less effort—a difference due in part to less stimulating experiences in their classes (Carbonaro, 2005). When capable students (as indicated by their achievement test scores) end up in low tracks, they "sink" to the performance level of their trackmates. Furthermore, teachers of non-college-track classes are less likely to communicate with parents about what they can do to support their adolescent's learning. Many minority parents, in turn, do not understand the tracking system, are unaware of their child's low placement, and therefore do not intervene on behalf of their child (Dornbusch & Glasgow, 1997).

High school students are separated into academic and vocational tracks in virtually all industrialized nations. In China, Japan, and most Western European countries, students take a national examination to determine their track placement in high school. The outcome usually fixes future possibilities for the young person. In North America, educational decisions are more fluid. Students who are not assigned to a college preparatory track or who do poorly in high school can still get a college education. In the end, however, many young people do not benefit from this more open system. By the adolescent years, SES differences in quality of education and academic achievement are greater in the United States than in most other industrialized countries (Marks, Cresswell, & Ainley, 2006). And both the United States and Canada have a higher percentage of young people who regard themselves as educational failures and drop out of high school (see Figure 15.5).

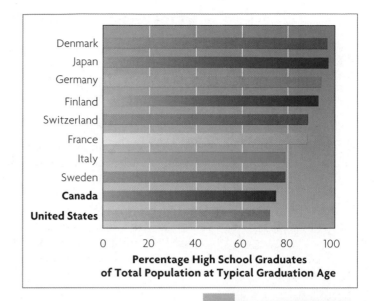

FIGURE 15.5

High school graduation rates in ten industrialized nations. The United States and Canada rank below many other developed countries. (OECD, 2005.)

Dropping Out

Across the aisle from Louis in math class sat Norman, who daydreamed, crumpled his notes into his pocket, and rarely did his homework. On test days, he twirled a rabbit's foot for good luck but left most of the questions blank. Louis had been in school with Norman since fourth grade, but the two boys had little to do with each other. To Louis, who was quick at schoolwork, Norman seemed to live in another world. Once or twice each week, Norman cut class; one spring day, he stopped coming altogether.

Norman is one of about 10 percent of U.S. and Canadian young people who leave high school without a diploma (Statistics Canada, 2005d; U.S. Department of Education, 2006b). The dropout rate is higher among boys than girls, and it is particularly high among low-SES ethnic minority youths, especially Hispanic and Canadian Aboriginal teenagers (see Figure 15.6). The decision to leave school has dire consequences. Youths without upper secondary education have much lower literacy scores than high school graduates; they lack the skills valued by employers in today's knowledge-based economy. Consequently, employment rates are much lower for U.S. and Canadian dropouts than for high school graduates. Even when they are employed, dropouts are far more likely to remain in menial, low-paid jobs and to be out of work from time to time.

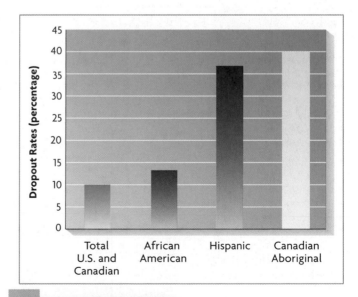

FIGURE 15.6

High school dropout rates by ethnicity, United States and Canada. Because many African-American, Hispanic, and Canadian Aboriginal teenagers come from low-income and poverty-stricken families, their dropout rates are above the national average. Rates for Hispanic and Canadian-Aboriginal youths are especially high. (*Sources:* Statistics Canada, 2005d; U.S. Department of Education, 2006b.)

FACTORS RELATED TO DROPPING OUT ■ Table 15.1 lists the diverse factors related to leaving school early. The more that are present, the greater the risk of dropping out. Many dropouts show a persistent pattern of disruptive behavior and poor achievement (Vitaro et al., 2001). But others, like Norman, have few behavior problems; they simply experience academic difficulties and quietly disengage from school (Janosz et al., 2000; Newcomb et al., 2002). The pathway to dropping out starts early. Risk factors in first grade predict later dropout nearly as well as risk factors in secondary school (Entwisle, Alexander, & Olson, 2005).

Norman had a long history of marginal-to-failing school grades and low academic self-esteem. He gave up on tasks that presented the least bit of challenge and counted on luck—his rabbit's foot—to get by. As Norman got older, he attended class less regularly, paid little attention when he was there, and rarely did his homework. He didn't join any school clubs or participate in athletics. Because he was so uninvolved, few teachers or students got to know him well. By the day Norman left, he felt alienated from all aspects of school life.

As with other dropouts, Norman's family background contributed to his problems. Compared with other students, even those with the same grade profile, dropouts are more likely to have parents who are less involved in their youngster's education. Many did not finish high school themselves and are unemployed or coping with the aftermath of divorce. When their youngsters bring home poor report cards, these parents are more likely than others to respond with punishment and anger, causing adolescents to rebel further against academic work (Garnier, Stein, & Jacobs, 1997).

Academically marginal students who drop out often have school experiences that undermine their chances for success—large, impersonal schools and classes, unsupportive teachers, and few opportunities for active participation (Croninger & Lee, 2001; Hardre & Reeve, 2003; Lee & Burkam, 2003). Recent reports indicate that over 60 percent of adolescents in some inner-city high schools do not graduate. Students in general education and vocational tracks, where teaching tends to be the least stimulating, are three times more likely to drop out than those in a college preparatory track (U.S. Department of Education, 2006b).

TABLE 15.1 Factors Related to Dropping Out of High School

STUDENT CHARACTERISTICS	FAMILY CHARACTERISTICS	SCHOOL AND COMMUNITY CHARACTERISTICS
Poor school attendance	Parents who do not support or emphasize achievement	Large, unstimulating classes
Inattentiveness in class	Parents who were high school dropouts	Lack of opportunity to form personal relationships with teachers
School discipline problems, especially aggressive behavior	Parents who are uninvolved in the adolescent's education	Curriculum irrelevant to student interests and needs
Inability to get along with teachers	Parents who react with anger and punishment to the adolescent's low grades	School authority structure that emphasizes the teacher and discourages student input
1 to 2 years behind in grade level	Single-parent household	Large student body
Low academic achievement	Low income	School located in low-SES racially or ethnically segregated neighborhood
A sharp drop in achievement after school transition	Frequent school changes	Availability of work that requires only on-the-job training
Dislike of school		
Enrollment in a general education or vocational track		
Low educational aspirations		
Low self-esteem, especially academic self-esteem		
Friendships with peers who have left school		
Low involvement in extracurricular activities		
Drug use		
Law-breaking behavior		
Adolescent parenthood		

Sources: Lee & Burkam, 2003; Stearns & Glennie, 2006.

The high dropout rates among urban minority teenagers are also influenced by young people's observations and experiences of discrimination, which strengthen their conviction that finishing school will not bring them greater vocational and financial rewards (Harwood et al., 2002; Valdés, 1997). When work requiring only on-the-job training becomes available in their communities, these teenagers (more often boys), despite being within a year or two of graduating, often opt out of school for employment (Beekhoven & Dekkers, 2005; Stearns & Glennie, 2006). And more often in ethnic-minority families, young people (especially girls) must take on family responsibilities, including care of elders and siblings, which prompts school leaving.

PREVENTION STRATEGIES ■ The most powerful way to prevent school dropout is to address the academic and social problems of at-risk students beginning in elementary school, and to involve their parents (Prevatt & Kelly, 2003). In addition, programs have been developed for adolescents. Among the diverse strategies available, several common themes are related to success:

- *Remedial instruction and counseling that offer personalized attention.* Most potential dropouts need intensive remedial instruction in small classes that permit warm, caring teacher–student relationships to form. To overcome the negative psychological effects of repeated school failure, academic assistance must be combined with social support (Christenson & Thurlow, 2004). One successful approach is to match at-risk students with retired adults, who serve as tutors, mentors, and role models in addressing academic and vocational needs (Prevatt, 2003).
- *High-quality vocational education.* For many marginal students, the real-life nature of vocational education is more comfortable and effective than purely academic work. To work well, vocational training must carefully integrate academic and job-related instruction so students can see the relevance of what happens in the classroom to their future goals (Harvey, 2001).
- *Efforts to address the many factors in students' lives related to leaving school early.* Programs that strengthen parent involvement, offer flexible work–study arrangements, and provide on-site child care for teenage mothers can make staying in school easier for at-risk adolescents.
- *Participation in extracurricular activities.* Another way of helping marginal students is to draw them into the community life of the school (Mahoney & Stattin, 2000). The most powerful influence on extracurricular involvement is small school size. In smaller high schools (500 to 700 students or less), a greater proportion of the student body is needed to staff and operate activities. Potential dropouts are far more likely to participate, feel needed, gain recognition, and remain until graduation. Consult the Social Issues: Education box on page 588 for research indicating that extracurricular participation has a lasting favorable impact on development.

The most effective interventions for preventing school dropout offer personalized attention and social support along with remedial assistance. One such approach pairs at-risk students with retired adults, who serve as tutors, mentors, and role models.

As we conclude our discussion of academic achievement, let's place the school dropout problem in historical perspective. Over the second half of the twentieth century, the percentage of U.S. and Canadian adolescents completing high school by age 24 rose steadily, from less than 50 percent to nearly 90 percent. During this same period, college attendance also increased. Today, nearly 42 percent of American and 58 percent of Canadian young people earn college degrees. Despite the worrisome decline in male college enrollment noted earlier, U.S. and Canadian higher education rates continue to rank among the highest in the world (OECD, 2005).

Finally, although many dropouts get caught in a vicious cycle in which their lack of self-confidence and skills prevents them from seeking further education and training, about one-third return to finish their secondary education within a few years. And some extend their schooling further (U.S. Department of Education, 2006b). As the end of adolescence approaches, many young people realize how essential education is for a rewarding job and a satisfying adult life.

Social Issues: Education

Extracurricular Activities: Contexts for Positive Youth Development

The weekend before graduation, Terrell—a senior at an inner-city high school—attended a cast party celebrating the drama club's final performance of the year. That evening, Terrell had played a leading role in a production written and directed by club members. As Mrs. Meyer, the club's adviser, congratulated Terrell, he responded, "I loved this club. When I joined, I wasn't good at English and math and all that stuff, and I thought I couldn't do anything. Working on the sets and acting were great—finding out that I could do these things well. Before, I wasn't secure with myself. Now I've got this boost of confidence."

Many studies show that high school extracurricular activities focusing on the arts, community service, and vocational development promote diverse academic and social skills and have a lasting positive impact on adjustment. Outcomes include improved academic performance, reduced antisocial behavior, more favorable self-esteem and initiative, and greater peer acceptance and concern for others, with engagement in a greater number of activities having a stronger impact (Fredricks & Eccles, 2005, 2006). The benefits of extracurricular involvement extend into adult life. Young people who were more involved in high school clubs and organizations achieve more in their occupations and engaged in more community service in their twenties and thirties, after other factors that might explain the association (including SES, IQ, and academic performance) were controlled (Berk, 1992; Obradović & Masten, 2007).

How do extracurricular activities produce such wide-ranging benefits? Not just by giving young people something fun to do during leisure hours. In a Swedish study, adolescents who spent many afternoons and evenings in youth recreation centers offering such unstructured pastimes as pool, Ping Pong, video games, and TV showed repeated and persisting antisocial behavior (Mahoney, Stattin, & Magnusson, 2001). In contrast, activities with a positive impact on development are highly structured, goal-oriented pursuits that require teenagers to take on challenging roles and responsibilities. In addition, such activities include caring and supportive interactions with peers and adults, who impose high expectations, help with problems, and serve as mentors (Fredricks & Eccles, 2006; Roth et al., 1998). Youths with academic, emotional, and social problems are especially likely to benefit from extracurricular participation. In a study of teenagers experiencing uninvolved parenting, those with extracurricular pursuits showed far lower levels of depressed mood. This outcome was strongest for adolescents reporting a trusting relationship with an activity adviser who validated their skills and strengthened their motivation to do their best (Mahoney, Schweder, & Stattin, 2002). Furthermore, participation sometimes strengthens connectedness between parent and teenager, as family members attend performances and exhibits or otherwise see the fruits of the young person's efforts (Mahoney & Magnusson, 2001).

Students seem to recognize the power of their extracurricular experiences to foster a smooth transition to adulthood. They report enjoyment, increased confidence, valuable relationships with adults, new friendships, and gains in setting goals, managing time, and working with others (Dworkin, Larson, & Hansen, 1993). Unfortunately, extracurricular activities are among the first aspects of school life to be cut during funding shortages. Yet a wealth of evidence indicates that these pursuits should be expanded, with special attempts made to reach academically and socially marginal young people. One example is TRUCE (The Renaissance University for Community Education), a program in the Harlem neighborhood of New York City that serves ethnic-minority teenagers through a variety of extracurricular pursuits—for example, publishing a widely circulated community newspaper and producing a TV show for a local cable channel. TRUCE's effects included improved academic achievement, reduced dropout rates, and enhanced leadership skills in participating teenagers.

These high school students are rehearsing for a school play. Extracurricular activities build many competencies, including academic performance, self-esteem, peer acceptance, and concern for others. Benefits extend into adult life, enhancing occupational achievement and community service.

Ask Yourself

Review   List ways parents can promote their adolescent's academic achievement, and explain why each is effective.

Apply   Tanisha is finishing sixth grade. She could either continue in her current school through eighth grade or switch to a much larger junior high school. What would you suggest she do, and why?

Connect   How are educational practices that prevent school dropout similar to those that improve learning for adolescents in general?

Reflect   Describe your own experiences in making the transition to middle or junior high school and then to high school. What did you find stressful? What helped you adjust?

Vocational Development

As the end of adolescence approaches, young people face a major life decision: the choice of a suitable work role. As we will see in Chapters 16 and 17, selecting a vocation is central to the development of a solid, secure identity. This is not surprising, since economic independence and career progress are hallmarks of adulthood in industrialized societies.

Being a productive worker calls for many of the same qualities needed to be an active citizen and a nurturant family member—good judgment, responsibility, dedication, and cooperation. What influences young people's decisions about careers? What is the transition from school to work like, and what factors make it easy or difficult?

Selecting a Vocation

In societies with an abundance of career possibilities, occupational choice is a gradual process, beginning long before adolescence and often extending into the mid-twenties. Major theorists view the young person as moving through several periods of vocational development (Gottfredson, 2005; Super, 1980, 1984):

1. The **fantasy period:** In early and middle childhood, children gain insight into career options by fantasizing about them. Their preferences, guided largely by familiarity, glamour, and excitement, usually bear little relation to the decisions they will eventually make.
2. The **tentative period:** Between ages 11 and 16, adolescents think about careers in more complex ways, at first in terms of their *interests,* and soon—as they become more aware of personal and educational requirements for different vocations—in terms of their *abilities* and *values.* "I like business and selling things," 16-year-old Louis said as he neared high school graduation. "But I'm also good with people, and I'd like to do something to help others. So maybe counseling or social work would suit my needs."
3. The **realistic period:** By the late teens and early twenties, with the economic and practical realities of adulthood just around the corner, young people start to narrow their options. A first step is often further *exploration*—gathering more information about possibilities that blend with their personal characteristics. In the final phase, *crystallization,* they focus on a general vocational category, within which they experiment for a time before settling on a single occupation. As a college sophomore, Jules pursued his interest in science, but he is not sure whether he prefers chemistry, math, or physics. Within the next few months, he will choose a major. Then he will consider whether he wants to work for a company following graduation or study further to become a doctor or research scientist.

Factors Influencing Vocational Choice

Most, but not all, young people follow this pattern of vocational development. A few know from an early age just what they want to be and pursue a direct path to a career goal. Some decide later or change their minds, and still others remain undecided for an extended period. College gives students time to explore various options. In contrast, the life conditions of many low-SES youths restrict their range of choices.

Making an occupational choice is not just a rational process in which young people weigh abilities, interests, and values against career options. Like other developmental milestones, it is the result of a dynamic interaction between person and environment (Van Esbroeck, Tibos, & Zaman, 2005). A great many influences feed into the decision.

PERSONALITY ■ People are attracted to occupations that complement their personalities. John Holland (1985, 1997) has identified six personality types that affect vocational choice:

■ The *investigative person,* who enjoys working with ideas, is likely to select a scientific occupation (for example, anthropologist, physicist, or engineer).

fantasy period The period of vocational development in which young children fantasize about career options through make-believe play.

tentative period The period of vocational development in which adolescents start to think about careers in more complex ways, evaluating vocational options in terms of their interests, abilities, and values.

realistic period The period of vocational development in which adolescents focus on a general vocational category and, within it, experiment for a time before settling on a single occupation.

- The *social person,* who likes interacting with people, gravitates toward human services (counseling, social work, or teaching).
- The *realistic person,* who prefers real-world problems and work with objects, tends to choose a mechanical occupation (construction, plumbing, or surveying).
- The *artistic person,* who is emotional and high in need for individual expression, looks toward an artistic field (writing, music, or the visual arts).
- The *conventional person,* who likes well-structured tasks and values material possessions and social status, has traits well-suited to certain business fields (accounting, banking, or quality control).
- The *enterprising person,* who is adventurous, persuasive, and a strong leader, is drawn to sales and supervisory positions or to politics.

TAKE A MOMENT... Does one of these personality types describe you? Or do you have aspects of more than one type? Research confirms a relationship between personality and vocational choice in diverse cultures, but it is only moderate. Many people are blends of several personality types and can do well at more than one kind of occupation (Holland, 1997; Spokane & Cruza-Guet, 2005). Louis, for example, is both enterprising and social—dispositions that led him to consider both business and human services. Furthermore, career decisions are made in the context of family influences, educational opportunities, current life circumstances, and societal conditions.

FAMILY INFLUENCES ■ Young people's vocational aspirations correlate strongly with their parents' jobs. Teenagers from higher-SES homes are more likely to select high-status, white-collar occupations, such as doctor, lawyer, scientist, or engineer. In contrast, those with lower-SES backgrounds tend to choose less prestigious, blue-collar careers—for example, plumber, construction worker, food service employee, or secretary. Parent–child vocational similarity is partly a function of similarity in personality, intellectual abilities, and—especially—educational attainment (Ellis & Bonin, 2003; Schoon & Parsons, 2002). More today than in the past, number of years of schooling completed is a powerful predictor of occupational status.

Other factors also promote family resemblance in occupational choice. Higher-SES parents are more likely to give their children important information about the worlds of education and work and to have connections with people who can help the young person obtain a high-status position (Kalil, Levine, & Ziol-Guest, 2005). In a study of African-American mothers' influence on their adolescent daughters' academic and career goals, college-educated mothers engaged in a wider range of strategies to promote their daughters' progress, including gathering information on colleges and areas of study and identifying knowledgeable professionals who could help (Kerpelman, Shoffner, & Ross-Griffin, 2002). Parenting practices also shape work-related preferences. Recall from Chapter 2 (page 71) that higher-SES parents tend to promote curiosity and self-direction, which are required in many high-status careers. Lower-SES parents, in contrast, are more likely to emphasize conformity and obedience. Eventually, young people may choose careers that dovetail with these differences.

Still, parents can foster higher aspirations. Parental pressure to do well in school and encouragement toward high-status occupations predict vocational attainment beyond SES (Bryant, Zvonkovic, & Reynolds, 2006).

TEACHERS ■ Young people preparing for or engaged in careers requiring extensive education often report that teachers influenced their choice (Bright et al., 2005; Reddin, 1997). Jules regarded his high school chemistry teacher as the most important influence on his scientific career goal. "Mr. Garvin showed me how to think about chemistry—and science in general. If I hadn't taken his class my junior year, I probably wouldn't have considered a career in science."

This 13-year-old helps in his parents' business—a lobster fishery in Maine. Because of similarity in personality, intellectual abilities, and—especially— educational attainment, adolescents' vocational aspirations frequently resemble the jobs of their parents.

© JUDY GRIESEDIECK/CORBIS

College-bound adolescents tend to have closer relationships with teachers than do other students—relationships that are especially likely to foster high career aspirations in young women (Wigfield et al., 2002). In contrast, students with academic and behavior problems generally have neither family nor teacher supports. Consequently, many feel discouraged about their career options, perceive barriers to attaining their goals, withdraw from making choices, and display large discrepancies between their vocational aspirations and expectations (Rojewski & Hill, 1998). The power of teachers in offering encouragement and acting as role models can serve as an important source of resilience for these young people.

GENDER STEREOTYPES ■ Over the past three decades, young women have expressed increasing interest in occupations largely held by men (Gottfredson, 2005). Changes in gender-role attitudes, along with a dramatic rise in numbers of employed mothers, who serve as career-oriented models for their daughters, are common explanations for girls' attraction to nontraditional careers.

TABLE 15.2	Percentage of Women in Various Professions in the United States, 1983 and 2006	
PROFESSION	1983	2006
Engineer	5.8	9.2
Lawyer	15.8	29.4
Doctor	15.8	29.4
Business executive	32.4	36.7[a]
Author, artist, entertainer	42.7	47.8
Social worker	64.3	77.7
Elementary or middle school teacher	93.5	81.3
Secondary school teacher	62.2	55.3
College or university professor	36.3	46.0
Librarian, museum curator	84.4	83.2
Registered nurse	95.8	92.2
Psychologist	57.1	66.7

Source: U.S. Census Bureau, 2007b.

[a]This percentage includes executives and managers at all levels. As of 2006, women make up only 23 percent of chief executive officers at large corporations, although that figure represents a sixfold increase in the past two decades.

But women's progress in entering and excelling at male-dominated professions has been slow. As Table 15.2 shows, although the percentage of women engineers, lawyers, doctors, and business executives increased between 1983 and 2006 in the United States, it still falls far short of equal representation. Women remain concentrated in less-well-paid, traditionally feminine professions such as writing, social work, education, and nursing (U.S. Census Bureau, 2007). In virtually all fields, women's achievements lag behind those of men, who write more books, make more discoveries, hold more positions of leadership, and produce more works of art.

Ability cannot account for these dramatic sex differences. As we have seen, girls are advantaged in reading and writing achievement, and the gender gap favoring boys in math is small. Rather, gender-stereotyped messages play a key role. Although girls earn higher grades than boys, they reach secondary school less confident of their abilities and are more likely to underestimate their achievement (Wigfield et al., 2002). In college, the career aspirations of many academically talented women decline as they question their capacity and opportunities to succeed in male-dominated fields (Wigfield et al., 2006).

These findings reveal a pressing need for programs that sensitize parents, teachers, and school counselors to the special problems girls face in developing and maintaining high career aspirations. Girls' ambitions rise in response to parents' and teachers' confidence-building messages and career guidance that encourages students to set goals that match their abilities, interests, and values. Models of high-achieving women are also important (Wall, Covell, & MacIntyre, 1999; Zeldin & Pajares, 2000).

Vocational Preparation of Non-College-Bound Adolescents

Franca and Antonio's middle son, 18-year-old Martin—who is a year younger than Jules and two years older than Louis—graduated from high school in a vocational track. Like approximately one-third of young people with a high school diploma, he had no plans to go to college. While in school, Martin held a part-time job selling candy at the local shopping mall. He

© ROBIN NELSON/PHOTOEDIT

Teenagers' employment opportunities are generally limited to menial tasks that do little to extend their knowledge or skills. Students with a heavy time commitment to such jobs are less likely to participate in extracurricular activities and more likely to drop out of school.

High school students on site in a home-construction course learn energy-efficient building techniques from an expert. The success of apprenticeship programs in several European countries suggests that similar programs would improve the transition from school to work in the United States and Canada.

AP IMAGES/ROBERT E. KLEIN

hoped to work in data processing after graduation, but six months later he was still a clerk at the candy store. Although Martin had filled out many job applications, he got no interviews or offers. He soon despaired of discovering any relationship between his schooling and a career.

Martin's inability to find a job other than the one he had held as a student is typical for North American non-college-bound high school graduates. Although they are more likely to find employment than youths who drop out, they have fewer work opportunities than high school graduates of several decades ago. About 15 percent of Canadian and 20 percent of U.S. recent high school graduates who do not continue their education are unemployed (Statistics Canada, 2004c; U.S. Department of Education, 2006b). When they do find work, most are limited to temporary, low-paid, unskilled jobs. In addition, they have few alternatives for vocational counseling and job placement as they transition from school to work (Shanahan, Mortimer, & Krüger, 2002).

North American employers regard recent high school graduates as poorly prepared for skilled business and industrial occupations and manual trades. And there is some truth to this impression. In high school, nearly half of North American adolescents are employed—a greater percentage than in other developed countries (Bowlby & McMullen, 2002; Children's Defense Fund, 2006). But most are middle-SES students in pursuit of spending money rather than vocational exploration and training. Low-income teenagers who need to contribute to family income find it harder to get jobs (U.S. Department of Education, 2006b).

Furthermore, the jobs that adolescents hold are largely limited to low-level, repetitive tasks that provide little contact with adult supervisors. A heavy commitment to such jobs is harmful. The more hours students work, the poorer their school attendance, the lower their grades, the less likely they are to participate in extracurricular activities, and the more likely they are to drop out (Marsh & Kleitman, 2005). Students who spend many hours at such jobs also tend to feel more distant from their parents and report more drug and alcohol use and delinquent acts (Kouvonen & Kivivuori, 2001; Staff & Uggen, 2003).

When work experiences are specially designed to meet educational and vocational goals, outcomes are different. Participation in work–study programs or other jobs that provide academic and vocational learning opportunities is related to positive school and work attitudes, improved achievement, and reduced delinquency (Hamilton & Hamilton, 2000; Staff & Uggen, 2003). Yet high-quality vocational preparation for non-college-bound North American adolescents is scarce. Unlike some European nations, the United States and Canada have no widespread training systems to prepare youths for skilled business and industrial occupations and manual trades (Heinz, 1999a).

In Germany, adolescents who do not go to a *Gymnasium* (college-preparatory high school) have access to one of the world's most successful work–study apprenticeship systems for entering business and industry. About two-thirds of German youths participate. After completing full-time schooling at age 15 or 16, they spend the remaining two years of compulsory education in the *Berufsschule*, which offers part-time vocational courses that they combine with an apprenticeship that is jointly planned by educators and employers. Students train in work settings for more than 400 blue- and white-collar occupations. Apprentices who complete the program and pass a qualifying examination are certified as skilled workers and earn union-set wages. Businesses provide financial support because they know that the program guarantees a competent, dedicated work force (Heinz, 1999b; Kerckhoff, 2002). Many apprentices are hired into well-paid jobs by the firms that trained them.

The success of the German system—and of similar systems in Austria, Denmark, Switzerland, and several Eastern European countries—suggests that a national apprenticeship program would improve the transition from high school to work for North American non-college-bound young people. The many benefits of bringing together the worlds of schooling and work include helping non-college-bound young people establish productive lives right after graduation, motivating at-risk youths to stay in school, and contributing to the nation's economic growth. Nevertheless, implementing an apprenticeship system poses major challenges: overcoming the reluctance of employers to assume part of the responsibility for vocational training, ensuring cooperation between schools and businesses, and preventing low-SES youths from being concentrated in the lowest-skilled apprenticeship placements, an obstacle that Germany itself has not yet fully overcome (Hamilton & Hamilton, 2000). Currently, small-scale school-to-work projects in the United States and Canada are attempting to solve these problems and build bridges between learning and working.

Although vocational development is a lifelong process, adolescence is a crucial period for defining occupational goals. Young people who are well-prepared for an economically and personally satisfying work life are much more likely to become productive citizens, devoted family members, and contented adults. The support of families, schools, businesses, communities, and society as a whole can contribute greatly to a positive outcome.

Ask Yourself

Review   What steps can schools take to help ensure that adolescents' occupational choices match their interests, personality dispositions, and abilities?

Apply   Diane, a high school senior, knows that she wants to "work with people" but doesn't yet have a specific career in mind. Her father is a history professor, her mother a social worker. What steps can Diane's parents take to broaden her awareness of the world of work and help her focus on an occupational goal?

Connect   What have you learned in previous chapters about development of gender stereotypes that helps explain why women's progress in entering and excelling at male-dominated professions has been slow? (*Hint:* See Chapter 13, pages 503–504.)

Reflect   Describe your progress in choosing a vocation. What personal and environmental factors have been influential?

Summary

Piaget's Theory: The Formal Operational Stage

What are the major characteristics of formal operational thought?

■ During Piaget's **formal operational stage,** adolescents become capable of **hypothetico-deductive reasoning:** When faced with a problem, they start with a hypothesis about variables that might affect an outcome, deduce logical, testable inferences, and systematically isolate and combine variables to see which inferences are confirmed.

■ **Propositional thought** also develops. Young people can evaluate the logic of verbal statements without referring to real-world circumstances.

Discuss recent research on formal operational thought and its implications for the accuracy of Piaget's formal operational stage.

■ School-age children display the beginnings of hypothetico-deductive reasoning but are less cognitively competent than adolescents. They cannot sort out evidence that bears on three or more variables at once, and they do not grasp the **logical necessity** of propositional reasoning. Also, adolescents are better than school-age children at representing major premises precisely and at thinking of examples that contradict wrong conclusions.

■ Adolescents and adults are most likely to think abstractly and systematically in situations in which they have had extensive guidance and practice in using such reasoning. In tribal and village societies, formal operational tasks usually are not mastered at all.

These findings indicate that Piaget's highest stage is affected by specific learning opportunities typically encountered in school.

An Information-Processing View of Adolescent Cognitive Development

How do information-processing researchers account for the development of abstract thought?

■ Information-processing researchers believe that a variety of specific mechanisms, supported by both brain development and experience, underlie adolescent cognitive change. These include gains in attention, inhibition, and knowledge; more effective strategies; expansion of metacognition; and increases in cognitive self-regulation, speed of thinking, and processing capacity.

■ Research on scientific reasoning reveals that the ability to coordinate theory with evidence improves from childhood to adolescence, as young people solve increasingly complex problems and reflect on their thinking, acquiring more  sophisticated metacognitive understanding. Nevertheless, adolescents and adults continue to show a self-serving bias, applying logic more effectively to ideas they doubt than to ideas they favor.

■ Adolescents develop scientific reasoning skills in a similar, step-by-step fashion on different types of tasks, constructing general models they can apply to many instances of a given type of problem. Formal operational thought develops gradually, not as the result of an abrupt, stagewise change.

Consequences of Adolescent Cognitive Changes

Describe typical reactions of adolescents that result from their advancing cognition.

■ As adolescents reflect on their own thoughts, two distorted images of the relationship between self and other appear: the **imaginary audience** and the **personal fable**. Both are an outgrowth of gains in perspective taking and teenagers' recognition that others' opinions of them have important, real consequences.

■ Teenagers' capacity to think about possibilities prompts idealistic visions at odds with everyday reality. Consequently, they often become fault-finding critics.

■ Adolescents show gains in cognitive self-regulation and comprehension monitoring on academic tasks. But they are less competent than adults at planning and decision making in everyday life, where they tend to fall back on intuitive judgments and emphasize short-term over long-term goals.

Sex Differences in Mental Abilities

Describe sex differences in mental abilities at adolescence, along with factors that influence them.

■ During adolescence, girls score slightly better than boys on tests of verbal ability, and their advantage in reading and writing

achievement increases. Earlier development of the left hemisphere of the cerebral cortex and greater maternal verbal stimulation probably contribute to girls' better verbal performance. And gender stereotyping of language arts as "feminine" and regimented teaching may weaken boys' literacy skills.

■ Boys exceed girls in complex mathematical reasoning. Overall, the gender difference is small, but among the most capable students, it is greater. Boys' biologically based superior spatial skills enhance their mathematical problem solving. At the same time, childhood manipulative play activities, gender stereotyping of math as "masculine," self-confidence and interest in doing math, and specialized computer knowledge contribute to boys' spatial and math advantages.

Language Development

Describe changes in vocabulary, grammar, and pragmatics during adolescence.

■ Adolescents add many abstract words to their vocabulary and define these words with greater clarity and accuracy. The capacity to think flexibly about word meanings permits adolescents to better understand irony, sarcasm, and figurative language.

■ Adolescents use more elaborate grammatical constructions and more effectively analyze and correct their grammar. They also show an improved capacity to vary their language style to fit the situation—a change supported by opportunities to enter more situations, the ability to reflect on the features of language, and gains in cognitive self-regulation.

Learning in School

Discuss the impact of school transitions on adolescent adjustment.

■ School transitions can be stressful. As school environments become larger and more impersonal, grades and feelings of competence decline. Girls experience more adjustment difficulties after the transition from elementary to middle or junior high school, a time when other life changes (puberty and the beginning of dating) are also occurring. Teenagers coping with added stresses, especially those with both academic and emotional difficulties, are at greatest risk for reduced self-esteem, achievement declines, and problem behaviors following school transition.

Discuss family, peer, and school influences on academic achievement during adolescence.

■ Authoritative parenting and parents' school involvement promote high achievement. Teenagers whose parents value achievement are likely to choose friends from similar families. The surrounding social order affects peer cultures of minority youths, who may react against working hard in school because they see little future payoff.

■ Warm, supportive classroom environments that encourage student interaction about academic work, mutual respect among classmates, and high-level thinking enable adolescents to reach their cognitive potential. But many secondary school classrooms do not consistently provide interesting, challenging teaching.

■ By high school, separate educational tracks that dovetail with adolescents' future plans are necessary. Unfortunately, high school tracking in the United States and Canada usually extends the educational inequalities of earlier years. Low-SES students are at risk for unfair placement in noncollege tracks, reduced parental involvement in their education, less stimulating teaching, and resulting declines in school performance.

What factors are related to dropping out of school?

■ About 10 percent of American and Canadian young people, many of them low-SES minority youths, leave high school without a diploma. Dropping out is the result of a long, gradual process of disengagement from school that is influenced by both family and school factors, including poor grades, dislike of school, antisocial behavior, lack of parental support for achievement, unstimulating teaching, and experiences with discrimination.

Vocational Development

Trace the development of vocational choice, and describe the factors that influence adolescents' vocational decisions.

■ Vocational development typically moves through a **fantasy period,** in which children explore career options through play; a **tentative period,** in which teenagers weigh careers against their interests, abilities, and values; and a **realistic period,** in which older adolescents and emerging adults settle on a vocational category and, finally, a specific career.

■ People are attracted to occupations that complement their personalities. However, personality is only moderately related to vocational choice, since individual and contextual factors combine to influence adolescents' decisions.

■ Adolescents' vocational aspirations correlate strongly with the jobs of their parents. The resemblance is partly due to resemblance in personality, intellectual abilities, and—especially—educational

attainment, a powerful predictor of occupational status. In addition, higher-SES parents are more likely to give their children information about the world of work and to identify knowledgeable people who can assist them. Close relationships with teachers, which are more available to college-bound adolescents than to others, are linked to higher career aspirations.

■ Today, although more girls express interest in male-dominated occupations, gender-stereotyped messages prevent many of them from reaching their career potential. Girls' career aspirations rise in response to confidence-building messages from parents, teachers, and school counselors.

What problems do non-college-bound North American youths face in making the transition from school to work?

■ Unlike some European nations, the United States and Canada have no widespread vocational training systems to help non-college-bound adolescents prepare for challenging, well-paid careers in business, industry, and manual trades. The jobs available to teenagers are largely limited to low-level, repetitive tasks that provide little contact with adult supervisors. Spending too many hours in these work settings undermines school performance and work-related attitudes.

■ In contrast, work–study programs designed to meet both educational and vocational goals foster a positive orientation toward academic achievement and work. Youth apprenticeships that coordinate on-the-job training with classroom instruction would improve the transition from school to work for North American non-college-bound young people.

Important Terms and Concepts

Chapter 16

"Up-date"
Lunyova Maria
15 years, Russia

Within a framework of stylized clock hands and gears, a young woman—perhaps the artist herself—strides boldly into the future. Her straight-ahead gaze reflects adolescents' optimism and idealism as they begin to construct an identity based on their talents and aspirations.

Reprinted with permission from the International Museum of Children's Art, Oslo, Norway

Emotional and Social Development in Adolescence

Louis sat on the grassy hillside overlooking the high school, waiting for his best friend Darryl to arrive from his fourth-period class. The two boys often met at noon-time and had lunch together. Watching as hundreds of students poured onto the school grounds, Louis reflected on what he had learned in government class that day: "Suppose I *had* been born in the People's Republic of China. I'd be sitting here, speaking a different language, being called by a different name, and thinking about the world in different ways. Wow," Louis pondered. "I am who I am through some quirk of fate."

Louis awoke from his thoughts with a start to see Darryl standing in front of him. "Hey, dreamer! I've been shouting and waving from the bottom of the hill for five minutes. How come you're so spaced out lately, Louis?"

"Oh, just wondering about stuff—like what I want, what I believe in. My older brother Jules—I envy him. He seems to know more about where he's going. Most of the time, I'm up in the air about it. You ever feel that way?"

"Yeah, a lot," Darryl admitted, looking at Louis seriously. "I wonder, what am I really like? Who will I become?"

Louis and Darryl's introspective remarks are signs of a major reorganization of the self at adolescence: the development of identity. Both young people are attempting to formulate who they are—their personal values and the directions they will pursue in life. The restructuring of the self that begins in adolescence is profound. Rapid physical changes prompt teenagers to reconsider what they are like as people. And the capacity to think hypothetically enables adolescents to project themselves into the distant future. They start to realize the significance of their choice of values, beliefs, and goals for their later lives.

We begin this chapter with Erikson's account of identity development and the research it has stimulated on teenagers' thoughts and feelings about themselves. The quest for identity extends to many aspects of development. We will see how a sense of cultural belonging, moral understanding, and masculine and feminine self-images are refined in adolescence. And as parent–child relationships are revised and young people become increasingly independent of the family, friendships and peer networks become crucial contexts for bridging the gap between childhood and adulthood. Our chapter concludes with a discussion of several serious adjustment problems of adolescence: depression, suicide, and delinquency.

Questioning family values and exploring alternatives are central to identity development. With her bright-pink hair, this teenager has found one way to express her individuality. While leaning on the security of this temporary identity, she may be sorting through a daunting array of life possibilities.

identity A well-organized conception of the self that defines who one is, what one values, and what directions one wants to pursue in life.

identity versus role confusion In Erikson's theory, the psychological conflict of adolescence, which is resolved positively when adolescents attain an identity after successful outcomes of earlier stages.

Erikson's Theory: Identity versus Role Confusion

Erikson (1950, 1968) was the first to recognize **identity** as the major personality achievement of adolescence and as a crucial step toward becoming a productive, happy adult. Constructing an identity involves defining who you are, what you value, and the directions you choose to pursue in life. One expert described it as an explicit theory of oneself as a rational agent—one who acts on the basis of reason, takes responsibility for those actions, and can explain them (Moshman, 2005). This search for what is true and real about the self drives many choices—vocation, interpersonal relationships, community involvement, ethnic-group membership, and expression of one's sexual orientation, as well as moral, political, and religious ideals.

Erikson called the psychological conflict of adolescence **identity versus role confusion.** Successful outcomes of earlier stages pave the way to its positive resolution. Young people who reach adolescence with a weak sense of *trust* have trouble finding ideals to have faith in. Those with little *autonomy* or *initiative* do not engage in the active exploration required to choose among alternatives. And those who lack a sense of *industry* fail to select a vocation that matches their interests and skills.

Although the seeds of identity formation are planted early, not until late adolescence and emerging adulthood do young people become absorbed in this task. According to Erikson, in complex societies, young people often experience an *identity crisis*—a temporary period of confusion and distress as they experiment with alternatives before settling on values and goals. Those who go through a process of inner soul-searching eventually arrive at a mature identity. They sift through characteristics that defined the self in childhood and combine them with emerging traits, capacities, and commitments. Then they mold these into a solid inner core that provides a sense of stability as they move through various roles in daily life. Once formed, identity continues to be refined throughout life as people reevaluate earlier commitments and choices.

Current theorists agree with Erikson that questioning of values, plans, and priorities is necessary for a mature identity, but they no longer describe this process as a "crisis" (Grotevant, 1998; Kroger, 2005). For some young people, identity development is traumatic and disturbing, but the typical experience is, rather, one of *exploration* followed by *commitment.* As young people try out life possibilities, they gather important information about themselves and their environment and sort through that information for the purpose of making enduring decisions. In the process, they forge an organized self-structure (Arnett, 2000a; Moshman, 2005).

Erikson described the negative outcome of adolescence as *role confusion.* If young people's earlier conflicts were resolved negatively or if society limits their choices to ones that do not match their abilities and desires, they may appear shallow, directionless, and unprepared for the psychological challenges of adulthood. For example, individuals who lack a firm sense of self (an identity) to which they can return will find it difficult to risk *intimacy*—the self-sharing involved in Erikson's early adulthood stage.

Does research support Erikson's ideas about identity development? In the following sections, we will see that young people go about the task of defining the self in ways that closely match Erikson's description.

Self-Understanding

During adolescence, cognitive changes transform the young person's vision of the self into a more complex, well-organized, and consistent picture. Compared with younger children, adolescents have more or less positive feelings about an increasing variety of aspects of the self. Over time, they form a balanced, integrated representation of their strengths and limitations (Harter, 2003, 2006). Changes in self-concept and self-esteem set the stage for development of a unified personal identity.

Changes in Self-Concept

Recall from Chapter 13 that by the end of middle childhood, children can describe themselves in terms of personality traits. In early adolescence, the self differentiates further. Gradually, teenagers include mention a wider array of traits, which vary with social context—for example, self with mother, father, close friends, romantic partner, and as student, athlete, and employee. As one young teenager commented:

> I'm an extrovert with my friends: I'm talkative, pretty rowdy, and funny. . . . With my parents, I'm more likely to be depressed. I feel sad as well as mad and also hopeless about ever pleasing them. . . . At school, I'm pretty intelligent. I know that because I'm smart when it comes to how I do in classes. I'm curious about learning new things, and I'm also creative when it comes to solving problems. . . . I can be a real introvert around people I don't know well . . . I worry a lot about what others my age who are not my closest friends must think of me, probably that I'm a total dork. (Harter, 2006, p. 531)

Notice, also, that early adolescents unify separate traits ("smart," "curious") into more abstract descriptors ("intelligent"). But these generalizations about the self are not interconnected and are often contradictory. For example, 12- to 14-year-olds might mention opposing traits—"intelligent" and "dork," "extrovert" and "introvert." These disparities result from the expansion of adolescents' social world, which creates pressure to display different selves in different relationships. Traits mentioned for different social contexts actually become increasingly dissimilar over the teenage years. As their awareness of these inconsistencies grows, adolescents frequently agonize over "which is the real me" (Harter, 1998, 2003, 2006).

From middle to late adolescence, cognitive changes enable teenagers to combine their traits into an organized system. Their use of qualifiers ("I have a *fairly* quick temper," "I'm not *thoroughly* honest") reveals growing awareness and acceptance that psychological qualities often change from one situation to the next. Older adolescents also add integrating principles that make sense of formerly troublesome contradictions. "I'm very adaptable," one young person remarked. "When I'm around my friends, who think what I say is important, I'm very talkative; but around my family I'm quiet because they're never interested enough to really listen to me" (Damon, 1990, p. 88).

Compared with school-age children, teenagers place more emphasis on social virtues, such as being friendly, considerate, kind, and cooperative—traits that reflect adolescents' increasing concern with being viewed positively by others (Damon & Hart, 1988). Among older adolescents, personal and moral standards also appear as key themes. For example, here is how a 17-year-old described herself:

> I'm a pretty conscientious person. . . . Eventually I want to go to law school, so developing good study habits and getting top grades are both essential . . . I'd like to be an ethical person who treats other people fairly. That's the kind of lawyer I'd like to be, too. I don't always live up to that standard; that is, sometimes I do something that doesn't feel ethical. When that happens, I get a little depressed because I don't like myself as a person. But I tell myself that it's natural to make mistakes, so I don't really question the fact that deep down inside, the real me is a moral person. . . . While I am basically an introvert, especially on a date when I get pretty self-conscious, in the right social situation, like watching a ball game with my friends, I can be pretty extroverted. . . . I'm looking forward to leaving home and going to college, where I can be more independent, although I'm a little ambivalent. I love my parents, and really want to stay connected to them, plus, what they think about me is still important to how I feel about myself as a person. (Harter, 2006, pp. 545–546)

This well-integrated account of personal traits and values differs from the fragmented, listlike self-descriptions typical of children. As adolescents revise their views of themselves to include enduring beliefs and plans, they move toward the kind of unity of self that is central to identity development.

In adolescence, self-esteem usually rises. This 14-year-old feels especially good about her athletic capabilities and peer relationships.

Changes in Self-Esteem

Self-esteem, the evaluative side of self-concept, continues to differentiate in adolescence. To the self-evaluations of middle childhood—academic competence, social competence, physical/athletic competence, and physical appearance—teenagers add new dimensions: close friendship, romantic appeal, and job competence. These reflect important concerns of this new period (Harter, 1999, 2003, 2006).

Level of self-esteem changes as well. Though some adolescents experience temporary declines after school transitions (see Chapter 15, pages 579–580), self-esteem rises for most young people, who report feeling especially good about their peer relationships and athletic capabilities (Cole et al., 2001; Twenge & Campbell, 2001). Teenagers often assert that they have become more mature, capable, personable, and attractive than in the past. In a study of adolescents in 13 industrialized nations, most were optimistic, felt a strong sense of control over their personal and vocational futures, and expressed confidence in their ability to cope with life's problems (Grob & Flammer, 1999).

At the same time, individual differences in self-esteem become increasingly stable in adolescence (Trzesniewski, Donnellan, & Robins, 2003). And positive relationships among self-esteem, valuing of various activities, and success at those activities strengthen. For example, academic self-esteem is a powerful predictor of teenagers' judgments of the importance and usefulness of school subjects, their willingness to exert effort, and their eventual career choice (Bleeker & Jacobs, 2004; Jacobs et al., 2002; Valentine, DuBois, & Cooper, 2004).

Certain self-esteem factors are more strongly related to adjustment. Teenagers who feel highly dissatisfied with parental relationships often are aggressive and antisocial. Those with poor academic self-esteem tend to be anxious and unfocused, and those with negative peer relationships are anxious and depressed (Leadbeater et al., 1999; Marsh, Parada, & Ayotte, 2004). And although virtually all teenagers become increasingly concerned about others' opinions, those who are overly dependent on social approval place their self-worth continually "on the line" and, as a result, report frequent self-esteem shifts—on average, about once a week (Harter & Whitesell, 2003). Let's take a closer look at factors that affect adolescents' self-esteem—both its level and its stability.

identity achievement The identity status of individuals who have explored and committed themselves to self-chosen values and goals.

identity moratorium The identity status of individuals who are exploring, but not yet committed to, self-chosen values and goals.

identity foreclosure The identity status of individuals who do not engage in exploration but, instead, are committed to ready-made values and goals chosen for them by authority figures.

identity diffusion The identity status of individuals who do not engage in exploration and do not commit themselves to self-chosen values and goals.

Influences on Self-Esteem

In Chapters 14 and 15 we saw that adolescents who are off time in pubertal development, who are heavy drug users, and who fail in school feel poorly about themselves. And as in middle childhood, girls score lower than boys in overall sense of self-worth, though the difference remains slight (Cole et al., 2001; Shapka & Keating, 2005; Young & Mroczek, 2003). Nevertheless, of those young people whose self-esteem declines in adolescence, most are girls. Recall that teenage girls worry more than teenage boys about their physical appearance and feel more insecure about their abilities. At the same time, girls outscore boys on self-esteem dimensions of close friendship and social acceptance.

But the contexts in which young people find themselves can modify these group differences. The ingredients of authoritative parenting—warmth, approval, appropriate expectations for maturity, and positive problem solving—predict stable, favorable self-esteem in adolescence, just as they did in childhood. Encouragement from teachers is linked to a positive self-image as well (Carlson, Uppal, & Prosser, 2000; Steinberg, Darling, & Fletcher, 1995; Wilkinson, 2004). In contrast, teenagers whose parents are critical and insulting tend to have highly unstable and generally low self-esteem (Kernis, 2002). Feedback that is largely negative, inconsistent, or not contingent on performance causes these young people to feel, at best, uncertain of their capacities and, at worst, incompetent and unloved. As a result, they are constantly in need of reassurance, and their self-worth fluctuates with every evaluative remark by an adult or peer. Teenagers who experience this type of parenting tend to rely heavily on peers rather than on adults to affirm their self-esteem—a risk factor for adjustment difficulties (DuBois et al., 1999, 2002a).

The larger social environment also influences self-esteem. Sustaining a middle-childhood trend, Caucasian-American adolescents' self-esteem is less positive than that of African Americans, who benefit from warm, extended families and ethnic pride (Gray-Little & Hafdahl, 2000). And collectivist valuing of modesty and self-effacement leads Asians to score increasingly low in self-esteem relative to Caucasians as adolescence progresses (Twenge & Crocker, 2002). Finally, teenagers who attend schools or live in neighborhoods where their SES or ethnic group is well represented have fewer self-esteem problems (Gray-Little & Carels, 1997). Schools and communities that accept the young person's cultural heritage support a positive sense of self-worth as well as a solid and secure personal identity.

Paths to Identity

Adolescents' well-organized self-descriptions and expanded sense of self-esteem provide the cognitive foundation for forming an identity. Using a clinical interviewing procedure devised by James Marcia (1980) or briefer questionnaire measures, researchers commonly evaluate progress in identity development on two key criteria derived from Erikson's theory: *exploration* and *commitment.* Their various combinations yield four *identity statuses:* **identity achievement,** commitment to values, beliefs, and goals following a period of exploration; **identity moratorium,** exploration without having reached commitment; **identity foreclosure,** commitment in the absence of exploration; and **identity diffusion,** an apathetic state characterized by lack of both exploration and commitment. Table 16.1 summarizes these identity statuses.

Identity development follows many paths. Some young people remain in one status; others experience many status transitions. And the pattern often varies across *identity domains.* For example, in junior high school, Louis accepted his parents' religious beliefs (foreclosure) and gave little thought to a vocational direction (diffusion). In his last two years of high school, he

TABLE 16.1   The Four Identity Statuses

IDENTITY STATUS	DESCRIPTION	EXAMPLE
Identity achievement	Having already explored alternatives, identity-achieved individuals are committed to a clearly formulated set of self-chosen values and goals. They feel a sense of psychological well-being, of sameness through time, and of knowing where they are going.	When asked how willing she would be to give up going into her chosen occupation if something better came along, Darla responded, "Well, I might, but I doubt it. I've thought long and hard about law as a career. I'm pretty certain it's for me."
Identity moratorium	*Identity moratorium* means "delay or holding pattern." These individuals have not yet made definite commitments. They are in the process of exploring—gathering information and trying out activities, with the desire to find values and goals to guide their lives.	When asked whether he had ever had doubts about his religious beliefs, Ramon said, "Yes, I guess I'm going through that right now. I just don't see how there can be a God and yet so much evil in the world."
Identity foreclosure	Identity-foreclosed individuals have committed themselves to values and goals without exploring alternatives. They accept a ready-made identity that authority figures (usually parents but sometimes teachers, religious leaders, or romantic partners) have chosen for them.	When asked if she had ever reconsidered her political beliefs, Hillary answered, "No, not really, our family is pretty much in agreement on these things."
Identity diffusion	Identity-diffused individuals lack clear direction. They are not committed to values and goals or actively trying to reach them. They may never have explored alternatives or may have found the task too threatening and overwhelming.	When asked about his attitude toward nontraditional gender roles, Joel responded, "Oh, I don't know. It doesn't make much difference to me. I can take it or leave it."

began exploring these issues. Like Louis, most adolescents change from "lower" statuses (foreclosure or diffusion) to "higher" statuses (moratorium or achievement) between their mid-teens and mid-twenties, but some move in the reverse direction (Kroger, 2001, 2005; Meeus, 1996). And the number of domains explored and the intensity with which they are examined vary widely, depending on the contexts young people want to enter and the importance they attach to them. Almost all grapple with work, close relationships, and family. Others add political, religious, community, and leisure-time commitments, with certain commitments being more central to their identity than others.

Because attending college provides many opportunities to explore career options and lifestyles, college students make more progress toward formulating an identity than they did in high school (Meeus et al., 1999). And as we will see in Chapter 17, after college, young people often sample a broad range of life experiences before choosing a life course. Those who go to work immediately after high school graduation often settle on a self-definition earlier than college-educated youths. But young people who find it difficult to realize their occupational goals because of lack of training or vocational choices (see Chapter 15) are at risk for long-term identity foreclosure or diffusion (Eccles et al., 2003).

At one time, researchers thought that adolescent girls postponed the task of establishing an identity and focused instead on Erikson's next stage, intimacy development. Some girls do show more sophisticated reasoning in identity domains related to intimacy, such as sexuality and family versus career priorities. Otherwise, late adolescents of both sexes typically make progress on identity concerns before experiencing genuine intimacy in relationships (Berman et al., 2006; Meeus et al., 1999).

Identity Status and Psychological Well-Being

According to identity theorists, individuals who move away from foreclosure and diffusion toward moratorium and achievement build a well-structured identity that integrates various domains. As a result, they experience a gratifying sense of personal continuity and social connection—of being the same person across time and contexts and a competent member of the adult community (Snarey & Bell, 2003; van Hoof & Raaijmakers, 2003). A wealth of research supports the conclusion that both identity achievement and moratorium are psychologically healthy routes to a mature self-definition, whereas long-term foreclosure and diffusion are maladaptive.

Although adolescents in moratorium are often anxious about the challenges they face, they resemble identity-achieved individuals in using an active, *information-gathering cognitive style* when making personal decisions and solving problems. That is, they seek out relevant information, evaluate it carefully, and critically reflect on and revise their views (Berzonsky, 2003; Berzonsky & Kuk, 2000). Young people who are identity-achieved or exploring have higher self-esteem, feel more in control of their own lives, are more likely to view school and work as feasible avenues for realizing their aspirations, and are more advanced in moral reasoning (Adams & Marshall, 1996; Kroger, 2002; Serafini & Adams, 2002). When asked for a "turning point" narrative (an account of a past event that they view as important in understanding themselves), identity-achieved individuals tell stories with more sophisticated personal insights and in which negative life events are followed by good outcomes—personal renewal, improvement, and enlightenment (McLean & Pratt, 2006).

Adolescents who get stuck in either foreclosure or diffusion are passive in the face of identity concerns and have adjustment difficulties. Foreclosed individuals display a *dogmatic, inflexible cognitive style* in which they internalize the values and beliefs of parents and others without deliberate evaluation and are closed to information that might threaten their position (Berzonsky & Kuk, 2000). Most fear rejection by people on whom they depend for affection and self-esteem. A few foreclosed teenagers who are alienated from their families and society may join cults or other extremist groups, uncritically adopting a way of life different from their past.

Long-term diffused teenagers are the least mature in identity development. They typically use a *diffuse-avoidant cognitive style* in which they avoid dealing with personal decisions and problems and, instead, allow current situational pressures to dictate their reactions (Berzonsky & Kuk, 2000; Krettenauer, 2005). Taking an "I don't care" attitude, they entrust themselves to luck or fate and tend to go along with the "crowd." As a result, they often experience time-management and academic difficulties and, of all young people, are the most likely to commit antisocial acts and to use and abuse drugs (Archer & Waterman, 1990; Schwartz et al., 2005). Often at the heart of their apathy and impulsiveness is a sense of hopelessness about the future. Many are at risk for serious depression and suicide—problems we will address in the final section of this chapter.

Influences on Identity Development

Adolescent identity formation begins a lifelong dynamic process influenced by a wide variety of factors related to both personality and context. A change in either the individual or the context opens up the possibility of reformulating identity (Kunnen & Bosma, 2003). Many factors influence identity development.

PERSONALITY ■ Identity status, as we saw in the previous section, is both cause and consequence of personality characteristics. Adolescents who assume that absolute truth is always attainable tend to be foreclosed, whereas those who doubt that they will ever feel certain about anything are more often identity-diffused. Young people who appreciate that they can use rational criteria to choose among alternatives are likely to be in a state of moratorium or identity achievement (Berzonsky & Kuk, 2000; Boyes & Chandler, 1992). This flexible, open-minded approach helps them greatly in identifying and pursuing educational, vocational, and other life goals.

As this teenager gathers information about events in the news, he becomes more aware of a diversity of viewpoints. A flexible, open-minded approach to grappling with competing beliefs and values fosters identity development.

FAMILY ■ Recall from Chapter 7 that toddlers with a healthy sense of self have parents who provide both emotional support and freedom to explore. Similarly, identity development is enhanced for teenagers whose families serve as a "secure base" from which they can confidently move out into the wider world. In families of diverse ethnicities, adolescents who feel attached to their parents but also feel free to voice their own opinions tend to be in a state of moratorium or identity achievement (Grotevant & Cooper, 1998; Luyckx et al., 2006; Schwartz et al., 2005). Foreclosed teenagers usually have close bonds with parents but lack opportunities for healthy separation. And diffused young people report the lowest levels of parental support and warm, open communication (Reis & Youniss, 2004; Zimmerman & Becker-Stoll, 2002).

Recall that parents who engage in positive problem solving—who resolve conflicts by seeking their child's input and collaborating on a solution—foster high self-esteem. Notice, also, how this approach promotes the balance between family relatedness and autonomy that supports identity development (Deci & Ryan, 2002).

PEERS ■ Through interaction with a variety of peers, adolescents' exposure to ideas and values expands. As young people jointly participate in school and community activities, they encourage one another's exploration of values and role possibilities (Barber et al., 2005).

Close friends also help young people explore options by providing emotional support and role models of identity development. In one study, 15-year-olds with warm, trusting peer ties were more involved in exploring relationship issues—for example, thinking about what they valued in close friends and in a life partner (Meeus, Oosterwegel, & Vollebergh, 2002). In another study, college students' attachment to friends predicted career exploration and progress in choosing a career (Felsman & Blustein, 1999). In sum, friends—like parents—can serve as a "secure base" as adolescents grapple with possibilities.

SCHOOL, COMMUNITY, AND SOCIETY ■ Identity development also depends on schools and communities that offer rich and varied opportunities for exploration. Schools can foster identity development in many ways—through classrooms that promote high-level thinking, extracurricular and community activities that permit teenagers to take on responsible roles,

Applying What We Know

Supporting Healthy Identity Development

STRATEGY	EXPLANATION
Engage in warm, open communication.	Provides both emotional support and freedom to explore values and goals.
Initiate discussions that promote high-level thinking at home and at school.	Encourages rational and deliberate selection among competing beliefs and values.
Provide opportunities to participate in extracurricular activities and vocational training programs.	Permits young people to explore the real world of adult work.
Provide opportunities to talk with adults and peers who have worked through identity questions.	Offers models of identity achievement and advice on how to resolve identity concerns.
Provide opportunities to explore ethnic heritage and learn about other cultures in an atmosphere of respect.	Fosters identity achievement in all areas and ethnic tolerance, which supports the identity explorations of others.

ethnic identity A sense of ethnic group membership as an enduring aspect of the self.

acculturative stress Psychological distress resulting from conflict between the minority culture and the host culture.

bicultural identity The identity constructed by individuals who explore and adopt values from both their family's subculture and the dominant culture.

teachers and counselors who encourage low-SES and ethnic minority students to go to college, and vocational training programs that immerse adolescents in the real world of adult work (Cooper, 1998; McIntosh, Metz, & Youniss, 2005).

Culture strongly influences the way adolescents deal with an aspect of mature identity that is not captured by the identity-status approach: constructing a sense of self-continuity despite major personal changes. In one study, researchers asked Canadian-Aboriginal and cultural-majority 12- to 20-year-olds to describe themselves in the past and in the present and then to justify why they regarded themselves as the same continuous person (Lalonde & Chandler, 2005). Responses of both groups increased in complexity with age, but their strategies differed. Most cultural-majority adolescents used an individualistic approach: they described an *enduring personal essence,* a core self that remained the same despite change. In contrast, Aboriginal youths took an interdependent approach that emphasized a constantly transforming self, resulting from new roles and relationships. They typically constructed a *coherent narrative* in which they linked together various time slices of their life with a thread explaining how they had changed in meaningful ways.

Finally, societal forces are also responsible for the special challenges faced by gay, lesbian, and bisexual youths (see Chapter 14) and by ethnic minority adolescents in forming a secure identity (see the Cultural Influences box on the following page). Applying What We Know above summarizes ways that adults can support adolescents in their quest for identity.

Ask Yourself

●**Review**   List personal and contextual factors that promote identity development.

●**Apply**   Return to the conversation between Louis and Darryl at the beginning of this chapter. Which identity status best characterizes the two boys? How can you tell?

●**Connect**   Explain how changes in self-concept and self-esteem at adolescence pave the way for identity development.

●**Reflect**   How would you characterize your identity status? Does it vary across the domains of sexuality, close relationships, vocation, religious beliefs, and political values? Describe your identity development in an important domain, along with factors that may have influenced it.

Cultural Influences

Identity Development among Ethnic Minority Adolescents

Most adolescents are aware of their cultural ancestry but relatively unconcerned about it. But for teenagers who are members of minority groups, **ethnic identity**—a sense of ethnic group membership and attitudes and feelings associated with that membership—is central to the quest for identity, and it presents complex challenges. As they develop cognitively and become more sensitive to feedback from the social environment, minority youths become painfully aware that they are targets of prejudice and discrimination. This discovery complicates their efforts to develop a sense of cultural belonging and a set of personally meaningful goals.

Minority youths often feel caught between the standards of the larger society and the traditions of their culture of origin. In many immigrant families from collectivist cultures, adolescents' commitment to obeying their parents and fulfilling family obligations lessens the longer the family has been in the immigrant-receiving country—a circumstance that induces **acculturative stress**, psychological distress resulting from conflict between the minority and the host culture (Phinney, Ong, & Madden, 2000). When immigrant parents tightly restrict their teenagers through fear that assimilation into the larger society will undermine their cultural traditions, their youngsters often rebel, rejecting aspects of their ethnic background.

Other minority teenagers react to years of shattered self-esteem, school failure, and barriers to success in the mainstream culture by defining themselves in contrast to majority values. A Mexican-American teenager who had given up on school commented, "Mexicans don't have a chance to go on to college and make something of themselves" (Matute-Bianche, 1986, pp. 250–251). At the same time, discrimination can interfere with forming a positive ethnic identity. In one study, Mexican-American youths who had experienced more discrimination were less likely to explore their ethnicity and to report feeling good about it. Those with low ethnic pride showed a sharp drop in self-esteem in the face of discrimination (Romero & Roberts, 2003).

With age, some ethnic minority young people progress from ethnic-identity diffused or foreclosed through moratorium to ethnic-identity achieved. But because the process of forging an ethnic identity can be painful and confusing, others show no change, and still others regress (Seaton, Scottham, & Sellers, 2006). Young people with parents of different ethnicities face extra challenges. In a large survey of high school students, part-black biracial teenagers reported as much discrimination as their monoracial black counterparts, yet they felt less positively about their ethnicity. And compared with monoracial minorities, many biracials—including black–white, black–Asian, white–Asian, black–Hispanic, and white–Hispanic—regarded ethnicity as less central to their identities (Herman, 2004). Perhaps these adolescents felt as if they did not belong to any ethnic group, so they discounted the significance of ethnic identity and (in the case of part-black biracials) viewed their minority background somewhat negatively.

When family members encourage them to behave proactively by disproving stereotypes of low achievement or antisocial behavior, adolescents typically surmount the threat that discrimination poses to a favorable ethnic identity. These young people manage experiences of unfair treatment effectively, by seeking social support and engaging in direct problem solving (Phinney & Chavira, 1995; Scott, 2003). Also, adolescents whose families taught them the history, traditions, values, and language of their ethnic group and who frequently interact with same-ethnicity peers are more likely to forge a favorable ethnic identity (McHale et al., 2006; Hughes et al., 2006).

How can society help minority adolescents resolve identity conflicts constructively? Here are some relevant approaches:

- Promote effective parenting, in which children and adolescents benefit from family ethnic pride yet are encouraged to explore the meaning of ethnicity in their own lives.
- Ensure that schools respect minority youths' native languages, unique learning styles, and right to a high-quality education.
- Foster contact with peers of the same ethnicity, along with respect between ethnic groups (García Coll & Magnuson, 1997).

These adolescents celebrate their cultural heritage by participating in a Filipino Parade in New York City. When minority youths encounter respect for their cultural heritage in schools and communities, they are more likely to retain ethnic values and customs as an important part of their identity.

A strong, secure ethnic identity is associated with higher self-esteem, optimism, a sense of mastery over the environment, and more positive attitudes toward one's ethnicity (Carlson, Uppal, & Prosser, 2000; St. Louis & Liem, 2005; Worrell & Gardner-Kitt, 2006). For these reasons, adolescents with a positive connection to their ethnic group are better-adjusted. They cope more effectively with stress, show higher achievement in school, and have fewer emotional and behavior problems than agemates who identify only weakly with their ethnicity (Greene, Way, & Pahl, 2006; Seaton, Scottham, & Sellers, 2006; Umana-Taylor & Alfaro, 2006; Yip, Seaton, & Sellers, 2006). For teenagers faced with adversity, ethnic identity is a powerful source of resilience.

Forming a **bicultural identity**—by exploring and adopting values from both the adolescent's subculture and the dominant culture—offers added benefits. Biculturally identified adolescents tend to be achieved in other areas of identity as well. And their relations with members of other ethnic groups are especially favorable (Phinney et al., 2001; Phinney & Kohatsu, 1997). In sum, achievement of ethnic identity enhances many aspects of psychological development.

Through changes in cognition and social experience, teenagers—like these high school students gathering donated clothing for victims of Hurricane Katrina—gain an understanding of larger social structures that govern moral responsibilities in complex societies.

Moral Development

Eleven-year-old Sabrina sat at the kitchen table reading the Sunday newspaper, her eyes wide with interest. "You gotta see this," she said to 16-year-old Louis, who sat munching cereal. Sabrina held up a page of large photos showing a 70-year-old woman standing in her home. The floor and furniture were piled with stacks of newspapers, cardboard boxes, tin cans, glass containers, food, and clothing. The accompanying article described crumbling plaster on the walls, frozen pipes, and nonfunctioning sinks, toilet, and furnace. The headline read: "Loretta Perry: My Life Is None of Their Business."

"Look what they're trying to do to this poor lady," exclaimed Sabrina. "They wanna throw her out of her house and tear it down! Those city inspectors must not care about anyone. Here it says, 'Mrs. Perry has devoted much of her life to doing favors for people.' Why doesn't someone help *her?*"

"Sabrina, you missed the point," Louis responded. "Mrs. Perry is violating 30 building code standards. The law says you're supposed to keep your house clean and in good repair."

"But Louis, she's old, and she needs help. She says her life will be over if they destroy her home."

"The building inspectors aren't being mean, Sabrina. Mrs. Perry is stubborn. She's refusing to obey the law. And she's not just a threat to herself—she's a danger to her neighbors, too. Suppose her house caught on fire. You can't live around other people and say your life is nobody's business."

"You don't just knock someone's home down," Sabrina replied angrily. "Why aren't her friends and neighbors over there fixing up that house? You're like those building inspectors, Louis. You've got no feelings!"

Louis and Sabrina's disagreement over Mrs. Perry's plight illustrates the tremendous advances in moral understanding that occur in adolescence. Changes in cognition and social experience permit teenagers to better understand larger social structures—institutions and law-making systems—that govern moral responsibilities in complex societies. As their grasp of social arrangements expands, adolescents construct new ideas about what ought to be done when the needs and desires of people conflict. As a result, they move toward increasingly just, fair, and balanced solutions to moral problems.

Kohlberg's Theory of Moral Development

Early work by Piaget (1932/1965) on the moral judgment of the child inspired Lawrence Kohlberg's more comprehensive theory of the development of moral understanding. Kohlberg used a clinical interviewing procedure in which he presented a sample of 10- to 16-year-old boys with hypothetical *moral dilemmas*—stories presenting a conflict between two moral values—and asked them what the main actor should do and why. Then he followed the participants longitudinally, reinterviewing them at 3- to 4-year intervals over the next 20 years. The best known of these stories, the "Heinz dilemma," pits the value of obeying the law (not stealing) against the value of human life (saving a dying person):

> In Europe a woman was near death from cancer. There was one drug that the doctors thought might save her. A druggist in the same town had discovered it, but he was charging ten times what the drug cost him to make. The sick woman's husband, Heinz, went to everyone he knew to borrow the money, but he could only get together half of what it cost. The druggist refused to sell the drug for less or let Heinz pay later. So Heinz got desperate and broke into the man's store to steal the drug for his wife. Should Heinz have done that? Why? (paraphrased from Colby et al., 1983, p. 77)

Kohlberg emphasized that it is *the way an individual reasons* about the dilemma, not *the content of the response* (whether to steal or not), that determines moral maturity. Individuals who believe that Heinz should steal the drug and those who think he should not can be found at each of Kohlberg's first four stages. Only at the highest two stages do moral reasoning and content come together in a coherent ethical system (Kohlberg, Levine, & Hewer, 1983). Given a choice between obeying the law and preserving individual rights, the most advanced moral thinkers support individual rights (in the Heinz dilemma, stealing the drug to save a life). **TAKE A MOMENT...** Does this remind you of adolescents' effort to formulate a sound, well-organized set of personal values in constructing an identity? According to some theorists, the development of identity and moral understanding are part of the same process (Bergman, 2004; Blasi, 1994).

For more efficient gathering and scoring of moral reasoning, researchers have devised short-answer questionnaires. The most recent, the *Sociomoral Reflection Measure–Short Form* (SRM-SF), poses 11 questions that (like Kohlberg's clinical interview) ask individuals to evaluate the importance of moral values and to reason about them—for example: "Let's say a friend of yours needs help and may even die, and you're the only person who can save him or her. How important is it for a person (without losing his or her own life) to save the life of a friend?" For each question, participants rate the importance of the value it addresses (from "very important," to "not important") and write a brief explanation. Their explanations are coded according to a revised version of Kohlberg's stages. Scores on the SRM-SF correlate well with those obtained from Kohlberg's clinical interview but are far less time-consuming to obtain (Gibbs, Basinger, & Grime, 2003).

KOHLBERG'S STAGES OF MORAL UNDERSTANDING ■ Kohlberg organized moral development into three levels, each with two stages, yielding six stages in all. He believed that moral understanding is promoted by the same factors Piaget thought were important for cognitive development: (1) actively grappling with moral issues and noticing weaknesses in one's current reasoning, and (2) gains in perspective taking, which permit individuals to resolve moral conflicts in more effective ways. Kohlberg's moral stages are related to Selman's perspective-taking stages, described on page 492 in Chapter 13. **TAKE A MOMENT...** As we examine Kohlberg's developmental sequence in light of possible responses to the Heinz dilemma, look for changes in perspective taking that each stage assumes.

The Preconventional Level.   At the **preconventional level,** morality is externally controlled: Children accept the rules of authority figures and judge actions by their consequences. Behaviors that result in punishment are viewed as bad, those that lead to rewards as good.

■ **Stage 1: The punishment and obedience orientation.** Children at this stage, while recognizing that others may have different thoughts and feelings, still find it difficult to consider two points of view in a moral dilemma. As a result, they overlook people's intentions. Instead, they focus on fear of authority and avoidance of punishment as reasons for behaving morally.

  Prostealing: "If you let your wife die, you will . . . be blamed for not spending the money to help her and there'll be an investigation of you and the druggist for your wife's death." (Kohlberg, 1969, p. 381)

  Antistealing: "You shouldn't steal the drug because you'll be caught and sent to jail if you do. If you do get away, [you'd be scared that] the police would catch up with you any minute." (Kohlberg, 1969, p. 381)

■ **Stage 2: The instrumental purpose orientation.** Children at this stage realize that people can have different perspectives in a moral dilemma, but at first this understanding is very concrete. They view right action as flowing from self-interest and understand reciprocity as equal exchange of favors: "You do this for me, and I'll do that for you."

  Prostealing: "[I]f Heinz decides to risk jail to save his wife, it's his life he's risking; he can do what he wants with it. And the same goes for the druggist; it's up to him to decide what he wants to do." (Rest, 1979, p. 26)

  Antistealing: "[Heinz] is running more risk than it's worth [to save a wife who is near death]." (Rest, 1979, p. 27)

preconventional level
Kohlberg's first level of moral development, in which moral understanding is based on rewards, punishments, and the power of authority figures.

The Conventional Level. At the **conventional level,** individuals continue to regard conformity to social rules as important, but not for reasons of self-interest. Rather, they believe that actively maintaining the current social system ensures positive human relationships and societal order.

■ **Stage 3: The "good boy–good girl" orientation, or the morality of interpersonal cooperation.** The desire to obey rules because they promote social harmony first appears in the context of close personal ties. Stage 3 individuals want to maintain the affection and approval of friends and relatives by being a "good person"—trustworthy, loyal, respectful, helpful, and nice. The capacity to view a two-person relationship from the vantage point of an impartial, outside observer supports this new approach to morality. At this stage, individuals understand *ideal reciprocity:* They express the same concern for the welfare of another as they do for themselves—a standard of fairness summed up by the Golden Rule: "Do unto others as you would have them do unto you."

Prostealing: "No one will think you're bad if you steal the drug, but your family will think you're an inhuman husband if you don't. If you let your wife die, you'll never be able to look anyone in the face again." (Kohlberg, 1969, p. 381)

Antistealing: "It isn't just the druggist who will think you're a criminal, everyone else will too. . . . [Y]ou'll feel bad thinking how you've brought dishonor on your family and yourself." (Kohlberg, 1969, p. 381)

■ **Stage 4: The social-order-maintaining orientation.** At this stage, the individual takes into account a larger perspective—that of societal laws. Moral choices no longer depend on close ties to others. Instead, rules must be enforced in the same evenhanded fashion for everyone, and each member of society has a personal duty to uphold them. The Stage 4 individual believes that laws must be obeyed under all circumstances because they are vital for ensuring societal order and cooperation between people.

Prostealing: "Heinz has a duty to protect his wife's life; it's a vow he took in marriage. But it's wrong to steal, so he would have to take the drug with the idea of paying the druggist for it and accepting the penalty for breaking the law later."

Antistealing: "Even if his wife is dying, it's still [Heinz's] duty as a citizen to obey the law. . . . If everyone starts breaking the law in a jam, there'd be no civilization, just crime and violence." (Rest, 1979, p. 30)

The Postconventional or Principled Level. Individuals at the **postconventional level** move beyond unquestioning support for the laws and rules of their own society. They define morality in terms of abstract principles and values that apply to all situations and societies.

■ **Stage 5: The social contract orientation.** At Stage 5, individuals regard laws and rules as flexible instruments for furthering human purposes. They can imagine alternatives to their own social order, and they emphasize fair procedures for interpreting and changing the law. When laws are consistent with individual rights and the interests of the majority, each person follows them because of a *social contract orientation*—free and willing participation in the system because it brings about more good for people than if it did not exist.

Prostealing: "Although there is a law against stealing, the law wasn't meant to violate a person's right to life. . . . If Heinz is prosecuted for stealing, the law needs to be reinterpreted to take into account situations in which it goes against people's natural right to keep on living."

Antistealing: At this stage, there are no antistealing responses.

■ **Stage 6: The universal ethical principle orientation.** At this highest stage, right action is defined by self-chosen ethical principles of conscience that are valid for all people, regardless of law and social agreement. Stage 6 individuals typically mention such abstract principles as respect for the worth and dignity of each person.

Prostealing: "It doesn't make sense to put respect for property above respect for life itself. [People] could live together without private property at all. Respect for human life and personality is absolute, and accordingly [people] have a mutual duty to save one another from dying." (Rest, 1979, p. 37)

Antistealing: At this stage, there are no antistealing responses.

Young people make up a large part of public demonstrations over moral issues. These protestors in Los Angeles express their opposition to anti-immigrant legislation. In imagining an alternative social order, they convey a principled level of morality.

conventional level
Kohlberg's second level of moral development, in which moral understanding is based on conforming to social rules to ensure positive human relationships and maintain societal order.

postconventional level
Kohlberg's highest level of moral development, in which individuals define morality in terms of abstract principles and values that apply to all situations and societies.

RESEARCH ON KOHLBERG'S STAGE SEQUENCE ■ Kohlberg's original research and other longitudinal studies provide the most convincing evidence for his stage sequence. With few exceptions, individuals move through the first four stages in the predicted order (Colby et al., 1983; Dawson, 2002; Walker & Taylor, 1991b). Moral development is slow and gradual: Reasoning at Stages 1 and 2 decreases in early adolescence, while Stage 3 reasoning increases through midadolescence and then declines. Stage 4 reasoning rises over the teenage years until, by early adulthood, it is the typical response.

Few people move beyond Stage 4. In fact, postconventional morality is so rare that no clear evidence exists that Kohlberg's Stage 6 actually follows Stage 5. This poses a key challenge to Kohlberg's theory: If people must reach Stages 5 and 6 to be considered truly morally mature, few individuals anywhere would measure up! According to one reexamination of Kohlberg's stages, moral maturity can be found in a revised understanding of Stages 3 and 4. These stages are not "conventional"—based on social conformity—as Kohlberg assumed. Rather, they require profound moral constructions—an understanding of ideal reciprocity as the basis for relationships (Stage 3) and for widely accepted moral standards, set forth in rules and laws (Stage 4). In this view, "postconventional" morality is a highly reflective endeavor achieved only by a handful of individuals who have attained advanced education, usually in philosophy. (Gibbs, 1991, 2003).

TAKE A MOMENT... In reading the Heinz dilemma, you probably came up with your own solution. Now, think of an actual moral dilemma you faced recently. How did you solve it? Did your reasoning fall at the same stage as your thinking about Heinz? Real-life conflicts, such as whether to continue helping a friend who is taking advantage of you, often elicit moral reasoning below a person's actual capacity because they involve practical considerations and mix cognition with intense emotion (Carpendale, 2000). Although adolescents and adults still mention reasoning as their most frequent strategy for resolving these dilemmas, they also refer to other strategies—talking through issues with others, relying on intuition, and calling on religious and spiritual ideas. And they report feeling drained, confused, and torn by temptation—an emotional side of moral judgment not tapped by hypothetical situations (Walker, 2004). As one person observed, "It's a lot easier to be moral when you have nothing to lose" (Walker et al., 1995, p. 381).

The influence of situational factors on moral judgments suggests that, like Piaget's cognitive stages, Kohlberg's moral stages are loosely organized and overlapping. Rather than developing in a neat, stepwise fashion, people draw on a range of moral responses that vary with context. With age, this range shifts upward as less mature moral reasoning is gradually replaced by more advanced moral thought.

Are There Sex Differences in Moral Reasoning?

As we have seen, real-life moral dilemmas highlight the role of emotion in moral judgment. Return again to the moral discussion between Sabrina and Louis on page 606. Sabrina's moral argument focuses on caring and commitment to others, while Louis's takes a more impersonal approach based on competing rights and justice.

Carol Gilligan (1982) is the best-known of those who have argued that Kohlberg's theory—originally formulated on the basis of interviews with males—does not adequately represent the morality of girls and women. Gilligan believes that feminine morality emphasizes an "ethic of care" that Kohlberg's system devalues. For example, Sabrina's reasoning falls at Stage 3 because it is based on mutual trust and affection, whereas Louis's is at Stage 4 because he emphasizes the importance of obeying the law to ensure societal order. According to Gilligan, a concern for others is a *different* but no less valid basis for moral judgment than a focus on impersonal rights.

Many studies have tested Gilligan's claim that Kohlberg's approach underestimates the moral maturity of females. Most do not support it (Turiel, 2006). On hypothetical dilemmas as well as everyday moral problems, adolescent and adult females display reasoning at the same stage as their male counterparts—or, sometimes, a higher stage. Themes of justice and caring appear in the responses of both sexes, and when girls do raise interpersonal concerns, they are not downgraded in Kohlberg's system

Adolescents, whether male or female, express themes of both justice and caring in their moral responses. But some evidence shows that females place greater emphasis on care, especially when reasoning about real-life dilemmas. This teenage girl cares for and comforts her elderly grandmother, who has Alzheimer's disease.

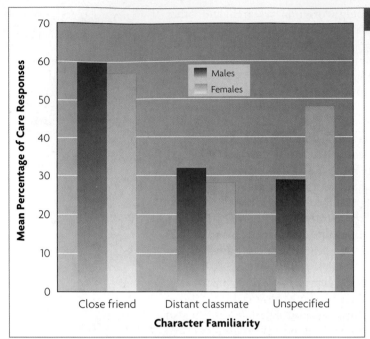

FIGURE 16.1

Relationship of familiarity of the main character in a moral dilemma to care responses. Australian university students were presented with one of three variations of a moral dilemma in which familiarity of the main character varied: close friend, distant classmate, and unspecified. Both male and female participants gave more care responses when considering a close friend than a distant classmate. Sex differences appeared only in the unspecified condition, where females may have assumed greater familiarity. (From M. K. Ryan, B. David, & K. J. Reynolds, 2004, "Who Cares? The Effect of Gender and Context on the Self and Moral Reasoning," *Psychology of Women Quarterly, 28,* 246–255. Copyright © 2004 by the American Psychological Association. Reprinted by permission.)

(Jadack et al., 1995; Kahn, 1992; Walker, 1995). These findings suggest that although Kohlberg emphasized justice rather than caring as the highest moral ideal, his theory taps both sets of values.

Still, Gilligan makes a powerful claim that research on moral development has been limited by too much attention to rights and justice (a "masculine" ideal) and too little to caring and responsiveness (a "feminine" ideal). Some evidence shows that although the morality of males and females taps both orientations, females do tend to emphasize care, or empathic perspective taking, whereas males either stress justice or focus equally on justice and care (Jaffee & Hyde, 2000; Wark & Krebs, 1996; Weisz & Black, 2002). This difference in emphasis, which appears more often in real-life dilemmas than in hypothetical ones, may reflect women's greater involvement in daily activities involving care and concern for others.

Indeed, both cultural and situational contexts profoundly affect use of a care orientation. In one study, U.S. and Canadian 17- to 26-year-old females showed more complex reasoning about care issues than their male counterparts. But Norwegian males were just as advanced as Norwegian females in care-based understanding (Skoe, 1998). Perhaps Norwegian culture, which explicitly endorses gender equality, induces boys and men to think deeply about interpersonal obligations. And in an Australian investigation, researchers presented 18- to 38-year-old university students with one of three versions of a moral dilemma, in which the main character varied in familiarity: (1) a close friend in class, (2) a person "known only vaguely" from class, and (3) a classmate whose relationship was unspecified (Ryan, David, & Reynolds, 2004). When asked whether they would permit the character, who was in danger of failing the course, to borrow a copy of their recently completed assignment despite risk of cheating, participants of both genders gave more care responses when considering a close friend than a socially distant classmate. As Figure 16.1 above shows, gender differences emerged only in the unspecified condition, where women—who tend to forge closer relationships—may have assumed greater familiarity.

Coordinating Moral, Social-Conventional, and Personal Concerns

Adolescents' moral advances are also evident in their reasoning about situations that raise competing moral, social-conventional, and personal issues. In diverse Western and non-Western cultures, teenagers express great concern with matters of personal choice—a reflection of their quest for identity and strengthening independence (Neff & Helwig, 2002; Nucci, 2002).

More firmly than at younger ages, adolescents assert that dress, hairstyle, diary records, and friendships are solely the province of the individual and not subject to control by authority figures (such as parents) (Nucci, 2001, 2005). In countries varying widely in individualism versus collectivism—such as the United States and Japan—teenagers indicate that such matters should be theirs to decide alone. U.S. and Japanese adolescents whose parents frequently intrude into the personal domain report greater psychological stress (Hasebe, Nucci, & Nucci, 2004). In contrast, teenagers in both cultures believe that parents have a right to tell them what to do in moral and social-conventional situations and, when these spark disagreements, are less likely to challenge parental authority (Smetana & Daddis, 2002).

As they enlarge the range of issues they regard as personal, adolescents think more intently about conflicts between personal choice and community obligations—whether, and under what conditions, it is permissible for laws to restrict speech, religion, marriage, childbearing, group membership, and other individual rights (Helwig, 1995; Wainryb, 1997). Teenagers display more subtle thinking than school-age children on such issues. For example, when asked if it is OK to exclude a child from a peer group on the basis of race or gender, fourth graders usually say exclusion is always unfair. But by tenth grade, young people, though increasingly mindful of fairness, indicate that under certain conditions—within friendship more often than peer groups, and on the basis of gender more often than race—exclusion is OK (Killen et al., 2002). In explaining, they mention the right to personal choice as well as concerns about effective group functioning. Justifying why she thought members of an all-boys music club need not let a girl in, one tenth grader said, "It's not nice . . . but it's their club." Another commented, "[The girl and the boys] probably wouldn't relate on very many things" (p. 62).

As adolescents integrate personal rights with ideal reciprocity, they demand that the protections they want for themselves extend to others. Similarly, they are increasingly mindful of the overlap between moral imperatives and social conventions. Eventually they realize that violating strongly held conventions—showing up at a wedding in a T-shirt, talking out of turn at a student council meeting—can harm others, either by inducing distress or by undermining fair treatment. Over time, as their grasp of fairness deepens, young people realize that social conventions are not just dictates of authority figures but vital for maintaining a just and peaceful society (Nucci, 2001). Notice how this understanding is central to Kohlberg's Stage 4, which is typically attained as adolescence draws to a close.

Influences on Moral Reasoning

Many factors affect the maturity of moral reasoning, including the young person's personality and a wide range of social experiences—child-rearing practices, peer interaction, schooling, and aspects of culture. Growing evidence suggests that, as Kohlberg believed, these experiences work by presenting young people with cognitive challenges, which stimulate them to think about moral problems in more complex ways.

PERSONALITY ■ A flexible, open-minded approach to new information and experiences is linked to gains in moral reasoning, just as it is to identity development (Hart et al., 1998; Matsuba & Walker, 1998). Because open-minded young people are more socially skilled, they have more opportunities for social participation. A richer social life enhances exposure to others' perspectives, and open-mindedness helps adolescents derive moral insights from that exposure. In contrast, adolescents who have difficulty adapting to new experiences are less likely to be interested in others' moral ideas and justifications.

CHILD-REARING PRACTICES ■ As in childhood, moral understanding in adolescence is fostered by warm parenting and discussion of moral concerns. Teenagers whose parents listen sensitively, ask clarifying questions, and present higher-level reasoning gain most in moral reasoning (Pratt, Skoe, & Arnold, 2004; Wyatt & Carlo, 2002). In contrast, young people whose parents lecture, use threats, or make sarcastic remarks show little or no change (Walker & Taylor, 1991a). In sum, parents facilitate moral understanding by using an authoritative approach that is affectionate, rational, verbal, and respectful, and that promotes a cooperative style of family life. Notice that these are similar to the characteristics—discussed in Chapter 10—that promote moral internalization in young children.

SCHOOLING ■ Years of schooling completed is a powerful predictor of movement to Kohlberg's Stage 4 or higher (Dawson et al., 2003; Speicher, 1994). Attending college introduces young people to social issues that extend beyond personal relationships to entire political and cultural groups. Consistent with this idea, college students who report more academic perspective-taking opportunities (for example, classes that emphasize open discussion of opinions) and who indicate that they have become more aware of social diversity tend to be advanced in moral reasoning (Mason & Gibbs, 1993a, 1993b).

PEER INTERACTION ■ Research supports Piaget's belief that interaction among peers who confront one another with differing viewpoints promotes moral understanding. When children and adolescents negotiate and compromise with agemates, they realize that social life can be based on cooperation between equals rather than authority relations (Killen & Nucci, 1995). Young people who report more close friendships, more often participate in conversations with their friends, and are viewed as leaders by classmates score higher in moral reasoning (Schonert-Reichl, 1999). The mutuality and intimacy of friendship, which fosters decision making based on consensual agreement, may be particularly important for moral development.

Peer discussions and role playing of moral problems have provided the basis for interventions aimed at improving high school and college students' moral understanding. For these discussions to be effective, young people must be highly engaged—confronting, critiquing, and attempting to clarify one another's viewpoints, as Sabrina and Louis did when they argued over Loretta Perry's plight (Berkowitz & Gibbs, 1983). And because moral development is a gradual process, many peer interaction sessions over weeks or months typically are needed to produce moral change.

CULTURE ■ Individuals in industrialized nations move through Kohlberg's stages more quickly and advance to a higher level than individuals in village societies, who rarely move beyond Stage 3. One explanation of these cultural differences is that in village societies, moral cooperation is based on direct relations between people and does not allow for the development of advanced moral understanding (Stages 4 to 6), which depends on appreciating the role of larger social structures, such as laws and government institutions (Gibbs, Basinger, & Grime, 2005; Snarey, 1995).

In support of this view, in cultures where young people participate in the institutions of their society at early ages, moral reasoning is advanced. For example, on *kibbutzim,* small but technologically complex agricultural settlements in Israel, children receive training in the governance of their community in middle childhood. By third grade, they mention more concerns about societal laws and rules when discussing moral conflicts than do Israeli city-reared or U.S. children (Fuchs et al., 1986). During adolescence and adulthood, a greater percentage of kibbutz than American individuals reach Kohlberg's Stages 4 and 5 (Snarey, Reimer, & Kohlberg, 1985).

Growing up in an isolated village in India, these adolescents view moral cooperation as based on direct relations between people. Their moral reasoning is likely to emphasize a close connection between individual and group responsibility.

© SUCHETA DAS/REUTERS/CORBIS

A second possible reason for cultural variation is that responses to moral dilemmas in collectivist cultures (including village societies) are often more other-directed than in Western Europe and North America (Miller, 1997). Consistent with this explanation, in both village and industrialized cultures that highly value interdependency, statements portraying the individual as vitally collected to the social group are common. In one study, both male and female Japanese adolescents, who almost always integrated care- and justice-based reasoning, placed greater weight on caring, which they regarded as a communal responsibility. As one boy remarked, *yasashii* (kindness/gentleness) and *omoiyari* (empathy) are "something 'normal' that everyone shows" (Shimizu, 2001). Similarly, in research conducted in India, even highly educated people (expected to have attained Kohlberg's Stages 4 and 5) viewed solutions to moral dilemmas as the responsibility of the entire society, not of a single person (Miller & Bersoff, 1995).

These findings raise the question of whether Kohlberg's highest level represents not a universal way of thinking but a culturally specific one, limited to Western societies that emphasize individualism and an appeal to an inner, private conscience. At the same time, a common justice-based morality is clearly evident in the dilemma responses of people from vastly different cultures.

Moral Reasoning and Behavior

According to Kohlberg, moral thought and action should come together at the higher levels of moral understanding. Mature moral thinkers realize that behaving in line with their beliefs is vital for creating and maintaining a just social world (Gibbs, 2003). Consistent with this idea, adolescents who are more advanced in moral reasoning more often act prosocially by helping, sharing, and defending victims of injustice (Carlo et al., 1996; Comunian & Gielan, 2000). Also, they less often engage in cheating, aggression, and other antisocial behaviors (Gregg, Gibbs, & Fuller, 1994; Taylor & Walker, 1997).

Yet the connection between more mature moral reasoning and action is only moderate. As we saw in earlier chapters, moral behavior is influenced by many factors besides cognition, including the emotions of empathy, sympathy, and guilt; individual differences in temperament; and a long history of experiences that affect moral choice and decision making. **Moral self-relevance**—the degree to which morality is central to self-concept—also affects moral behavior (Walker, 2004). In a study of low-SES African-American and Hispanic teenagers, those who emphasized moral traits and goals in their self-descriptions displayed exceptional levels of community service, but they did not differ from their agemates in moral reasoning (Hart & Fegley, 1995). The capacity to empathize with groups of people subjected to unfavorable life conditions (the homeless, the chronically ill) increases in adolescence (Hoffman, 2000). Perhaps these highly prosocial young people developed this advanced form of empathic responding to an especially high degree.

Research has yet to discover the origins of a sense of moral self-relevance, or just how thought combines with other influences to foster moral commitment. Close relationships with parents, teachers, and friends may play vital roles by modeling prosocial behavior and fostering morally relevant emotions of empathy and guilt, which combine with moral cognition to powerfully motivate moral action. Another possibility is that *just educational environments*—in which teachers guide students in democratic decision making and rule setting, resolving disputes civilly, and taking responsibility for others' welfare—are influential (Atkins, Hart, & Donnelly, 2004). Schools may also promote moral self-relevance by expanding students' opportunities for civic engagement. As the Social Issues: Education box on page 614 reveals, encouraging civic responsibility in young people can help them see the connection between their personal interests and the public interest—an insight that may foster all aspects of morality. Finally, as we will see next, religious affiliation has a broad-ranging impact on moral development as well.

Religious Involvement and Moral Development

Recall that in resolving real-life moral dilemmas, many people express notions of religion and spirituality. Religion is especially important in North American family life. In recent national polls, nearly two-thirds of Americans and about one-half of Canadians reported being religious, compared with one-third of those in Great Britain and Italy and even fewer elsewhere in Europe (Adams, 2003; Jones, 2003). People who are affiliated with a church, synagogue, or mosque and regularly attend religious services include many parents with children. During adolescence, formal religious involvement declines—for U.S. youths, from 55 percent at ages 13 to 15 to 40 percent at ages 17 to 18 (Donahue & Benson, 1995; Kerestes & Youniss, 2003). The drop coincides with increased autonomy and efforts to construct a personally meaningful religious identity—a task usually not resolved until the late teens or twenties, as Chapter 17 will reveal (Hunsberger, Pratt, & Pancer, 2001).

But adolescents who remain part of a religious community are advantaged in moral values and behavior. Compared with nonaffiliated youths, they are more involved in community service activities aimed at helping the less fortunate (Kerestes, Youniss, & Metz, 2004). And religious involvement promotes responsible academic and social behavior and discourages

© JEFF GREENBERG / PHOTOEDIT

This teenager clearly has a warm relationship with the two young girls she teaches at their vacation bible school. Adolescents who are part of a religious community tend to be advanced in moral development and are more likely to be involved in community service.

moral self-relevance The degree to which morality is central to an individual's self-concept.

Social Issues: Education

Development of Civic Responsibility

On Thanksgiving day, Jules, Martin, Louis, and Sabrina joined their parents at a soup kitchen, serving holiday dinners to poverty-stricken people. Throughout the year, Sabrina volunteered on Saturday mornings at a nursing home, where she conversed with bedridden elders. In the months before a congressional election, Martin and Louis attended special youth meetings with candidates and raised concerns. "What's your view on preserving our environment?" Martin asked. "How would you prevent the proposed tax cut from mostly benefiting the rich?" Louis chimed in. At school, Louis and his girlfriend Cassie formed an organization devoted to promoting ethnic and racial tolerance.

Already, these young people have a strong sense of *civic responsibility*—a complex capacity that combines cognition, emotion, and behavior. Civic responsibility involves *knowledge* of political issues and the means through which citizens can resolve differing views fairly; *feelings* of attachment to the community, of wanting to make a difference in its welfare; and *skills* for achieving civic goals, such as how to contact and question public officials and how to conduct meetings so that all participants have a voice (Flanagan & Faison, 2001).

When young people engage in community service that exposes them to people in need

or to public issues, they are especially likely to report reexamining their beliefs and attitudes and to express a commitment to future service and working toward societal goals, such as eradicating poverty or ethnic prejudice (Metz, McLellan, & Youniss, 2003; Reinders & Youniss, 2006). New research reveals that family, school, and community experiences contribute to adolescents' civic responsibility.

Family Influences

Teenagers whose parents have encouraged them to form opinions about controversial issues are more knowledgeable and interested in civic issues and better able to see them from more than one perspective (Santoloupo & Pratt, 1994). Also, adolescents who report that their parents engage in community service and emphasize compassion for the less fortunate tend to hold socially responsible values. When asked what causes such social ills as unemployment, poverty, and homelessness, these teenagers more often mention situational and societal factors (lack of education, government policies, or the state of the economy) than individual factors (low intelligence or personal problems). Youths who endorse situational and societal causes, in turn, have more altruistic life goals, such as working to eradicate poverty or to preserve the earth for future generations (Flanagan & Tucker, 1999).

School and Community Influences

A democratic climate at school—one in which teachers set high academic and moral standards for all students, promote discussion of controversial issues, and insist that students listen to and respect one another—fosters a sense of civic responsibility. Teenagers who say their teachers engage in these practices are more aware of political issues, better able to analyze them critically, and more committed to social causes (Flanagan & Faison, 2001).

Participation in extracurricular activities at school and in youth organizations is also associated with civic commitment that persists into adulthood (see Chapter 15, page 588). Two aspects of these involvements seem to account for their lasting impact. First, they introduce adolescents to the vision and skills required for mature civic engagement. Within student government, clubs, teams, and other groups, young

people see how their actions affect the wider school and community. They realize that collectively they can achieve results greater than any one person can achieve alone. And they learn to work together, balancing strong convictions with compromise (Atkins, Hart, & Donnelly, 2004; Youniss, McLellan, & Yates, 1997). Second, while producing a weekly newspaper, participating in a dramatic production, or implementing a service project, young people explore political and moral ideals. Often they redefine their identities to include a responsibility to combat the misfortunes of others (Wheeler, 2002).

The power of family, school, and community to promote civic responsibility may lie in discussions, educational practices, and activities that jointly foster moral thought, emotion, and behavior. In a comparison of nationally representative samples of 14-year-olds in 28 nations, North American young people excelled at community service, with more than 50 percent of U.S. students reporting membership in organizations devoted to volunteering (Torney-Purta, 2002).

Currently, 66 percent of U.S. public schools provide students with community service opportunities. And nearly half of these schools have *service-learning programs*, which integrate service activities into the academic curriculum. About one-third of students enroll, applying academic knowledge to service projects and engaging in regular, organized reflection on and evaluation of their efforts. Still, most principals in U.S. schools offering service learning say that neither their school nor their district has policies encouraging or requiring service learning (Scales & Roehlkepartain, 2004). In Canada, the province of Ontario requires 40 hours of community service for high school graduation, with schools arranging placements that match students' interests and skills.

Nevertheless, low-SES, inner-city youths—although they express high interest in contributing to society—score substantially lower than higher-SES youths in civic knowledge and participation (Balsano, 2005). A broad societal commitment to fostering civic character must pay special attention to supportive school and community experiences for these young people, so their eagerness to make a difference can be realized.

© NANCY RICHMOND/THE IMAGE WORKS

During adolescence, young people develop a stronger sense of connection to their communities. These teenage volunteers gather food donations for the needy outside a grocery store on "Make a Difference Day."

misconduct (Dowling et al., 2004). It is associated with lower levels of drug and alcohol use, early sexual activity, and delinquency (Regnerus, Smith, & Fritsch, 2003).

A variety of factors probably contribute to these favorable outcomes. In a study of inner-city high school students, religiously involved young people were more likely to report trusting relationships with parents, other adults, and friends who hold similar worldviews. The more activities they shared with this network, the higher they scored in empathy and prosocial behavior (King & Furrow, 2004). Furthermore, religious education and youth activities directly teach concern for others and provide opportunities for moral discussions and civic engagement. And adolescents who feel connected to a higher being may develop certain inner strengths, including moral self-relevance, that help them translate their thinking into action (Furrow, King, & White, 2004).

Because most teenagers, regardless of formal affiliation, identify with a religious denomination and say they believe in a higher being, religious institutions may be uniquely suited to foster moral and prosocial commitments and discourage risky behaviors (Bridges & Moore, 2002). For youths in inner-city neighborhoods with few alternative sources of social support, outreach by religious institutions can lead to life-altering involvement (Jang & Johnson, 2001). An exception is seen in religious cults, where rigid indoctrination into the group's beliefs, suppression of individuality, and estrangement from society all work against moral maturity.

Gender Typing

As Sabrina entered adolescence, some aspects of her thinking and behavior became more gender-typed. For example, she began to place more emphasis on excelling in the traditionally feminine subjects of language, art, and music than in math and science. And when with peers, Sabrina worried about how she should walk, talk, eat, dress, laugh, and compete, judged according to accepted social standards for maleness and femaleness.

Early adolescence is a period of **gender intensification**—increased gender stereotyping of attitudes and behavior, and movement toward a more traditional gender identity (Basow & Rubin, 1999; Galambos, Almeida, & Petersen, 1990). Gender intensification occurs in both sexes but is stronger for girls. Recall from earlier chapters that girls are less gender-typed than boys during childhood, a difference that extends into the teenage years. But early adolescent girls feel less free to experiment with "other-gender" activities and behavior than they did in middle childhood (Huston & Alvarez, 1990).

What accounts for gender intensification? Biological, social, and cognitive factors are involved. As puberty magnifies sex differences in appearance, teenagers spend more time thinking about themselves in gender-linked ways. Pubertal changes also prompt gender-typed pressures from others. Parents—especially those with traditional gender-role beliefs—may encourage "gender-appropriate" activities and behavior more than they did in middle childhood (Crouter, Manke, & McHale, 1995). When adolescents start to date, they often become more gender-typed as a way of increasing their attractiveness (Maccoby, 1998). Finally, cognitive changes—in particular, greater concern with what others think—make young teenagers more responsive to gender-role expectations.

Gender intensification declines by middle to late adolescence, but not all young people move beyond it to the same degree. The social environment is a primary force in promoting gender-role flexibility, just as it was at earlier ages. Teenagers who are encouraged to explore non-gender-typed options and to question the value of gender stereotypes are more likely to build an androgynous gender identity (see Chapter 10, page 395). Overall, androgynous adolescents, especially girls, tend to be psychologically healthier—more self-confident, more willing to speak their own mind, better-liked by peers, and identity-achieved (Dusek, 1987; Harter, 2006).

In early adolescence, young people, especially girls, move toward more traditional gender identities. But by their late teens, these girls may shift toward greater gender-role flexibility, expanding their interests beyond a stereotypically feminine focus on appearance and popularity.

gender intensification The increased gender stereotyping of attitudes and behavior and movement toward a more traditional gender identity, typical of early adolescence.

Ask Yourself

Review   In our discussion of Kohlberg's theory, why were examples of both prostealing and antistealing responses to the Heinz dilemma presented for Stages 1 through 4, but only prostealing responses for Stages 5 and 6?

Apply   Tam grew up in a small village culture, Lydia in a large industrial city. At age 15, Tam reasons at Kohlberg's Stage 3, Lydia at Stage 4. What factors might account for the difference?

Connect   What experiences that promote mature moral reasoning are also likely to foster identity development?

Reflect   In early adolescence, did you and your friends display gender intensification? Cite examples. When did this concern with gender appropriateness decline?

The Family

Franca and Antonio remember Louis's freshman year of high school as a difficult time. Because of a demanding project at work, Franca spent many evenings and weekends away from home. In her absence, Antonio took over, but when business picked up at his hardware store, he, too, had less time for the family. That year, Louis and two friends used their computer know-how to crack the code of a long-distance telephone service. From the family basement, they made calls around the country. Louis's grades fell, and he often left the house without saying where he was going. Franca and Antonio began to feel uncomfortable about the long hours Louis was spending in the basement and their lack of contact with him. Finally, when the telephone company traced the illegal calls to the family's phone number, they knew they had cause for concern.

Development at adolescence involves striving for **autonomy**—a sense of oneself as a separate, self-governing individual. Autonomy first became a major issue in toddlerhood, but now it is revisited on a higher plane. Teenagers strive to rely more on themselves and less on parents for guidance and decision making (Collins & Laursen, 2004; Steinberg & Silk, 2002). A major way that teenagers seek greater self-directedness is to shift their attention away from family to peers, with whom they explore new courses of action. Nevertheless, parent–child relationships remain vital for helping adolescents become autonomous, responsible individuals.

Parent–Child Relationships

Adolescent autonomy receives support from a variety of changes within the adolescent. In Chapter 11, we saw that puberty triggers psychological distancing from parents. Further, as young people look more mature, parents give them more independence and responsibility. Cognitive development also paves the way toward autonomy: Gradually, adolescents solve problems and make decisions more effectively. And an improved ability to reason about social relationships leads teenagers to *deidealize* their parents, viewing them as "just people." Consequently, they no longer bend as easily to parental authority as they did when younger. Yet as Franca and Antonio's episode with Louis reveals, teenagers still need guidance and, at times, protection from dangerous situations.

autonomy At adolescence, a sense of oneself as a separate, self-governing individual, which involves relying more on oneself and less on parents for direction and guidance and engaging in careful, well-reasoned decision making.

TAKE A MOMENT... Think back to what we said earlier about the type of parenting that fosters academic achievement (Chapter 15), identity formation, and moral maturity. You will find a common theme: Effective parenting of adolescents strikes a balance between *connection* and *separation*. In diverse ethnic groups, SES levels, nationalities, and family structures (including single-parent, two-parent, and stepparent), warm, supportive parent–adolescent

Applying What We Know

Parenting Practices That Foster Adolescent Competence

PARENTING PRACTICE	ADOLESCENT OUTCOMES
Project warmth and acceptance.	Promotes high self-esteem, identity exploration and achievement, prosocial behavior, and more positive parent–adolescent communication.
Monitor activities.	Promotes high self-esteem and reduced likelihood of engaging in antisocial behavior. Most effective when parents have a cooperative relationship with the adolescent and modify their supervision to fit the young person's increasing competence.
Engage in democratic decision making, verbal give-and-take.	Promotes self-esteem and self-reliant, responsible behavior.
Establish firm control and consistent discipline.	When accompanied by warmth, explanations, and verbal give-and-take, promotes self-reliant, responsible behavior. (Firm control without explanations that clarify the legitimacy of parents' rules can undermine self-reliance and responsibility.)
Provide information and model effective skills.	Promotes competencies as diverse as academic achievement and conflict resolution; protects against high-risk behaviors, such as sex without contraception and substance use.

Sources: Collins & Steinberg, 2006; Steinberg & Silk, 2002.

ties that make appropriate demands for maturity while allowing young people to explore ideas and social roles foster autonomy—predicting high self-reliance, effortful control, work orientation, academic achievement, dating competence, favorable self-esteem, advanced identity development, and ease of separation in transitioning to college (Bean, Barber, & Crane, 2007; Eisenberg et al., 2005; Steinberg & Silk, 2002; Vazsonyi, Hibbert, & Snider, 2003). Note that these are features of the authoritative style. See Applying What We Know above for a summary of practices emanating from authoritative parenting that promote adolescent cognitive and social development.

Conversely, parents who are coercive or psychologically controlling (for example, by belittling teenagers) interfere with the development of autonomy. These tactics can breed intense, negative emotional exchanges between parent and teenager (Caples & Barrera, 2006; Kim et al., 2001). Research in Africa, Asia, Europe, the Middle East, and North and South America shows that parental coercion and control are linked to low self-esteem, depression, substance use, and antisocial behavior among teenagers—outcomes that often persist into adulthood (Barber, Stolz, & Olsen, 2005; Bronte-Tinkew, Moore, & Carrano, 2006; Wissink, Deković, & Meijer, 2002).

In Chapter 2 we described the family as a *system* that must adapt to changes in its members. The rapid physical and psychological changes of adolescence trigger conflicting expectations in parent–child relationships—a major reason that many parents find rearing teenagers to be stressful.

Earlier we noted that interest in making choices about personal matters strengthens in adolescence. Yet parents and teenagers—especially young teenagers—differ sharply on the appropriate age for granting certain privileges, such as control over clothing, school courses, going out with friends, and dating (Smetana, 2002). Consistent parental monitoring of the young person's daily activities, through a cooperative relationship in which the adolescent willingly discloses information, predicts favorable adjustment. Besides preventing delinquency, it is linked to other positive outcomes—a reduction in sexual activity, improved school performance, and positive psychological well-being (Crouter & Head, 2002; Jacobson & Crockett, 2000; Stattin & Kerr, 2000).

Parents' own development can also lead to friction with teenagers. While their children face a boundless future and a wide array of choices, middle-aged parents must come to terms with the fact that their own possibilities are narrowing (Holmbeck, 1996). Often parents can't understand why the adolescent wants to skip family activities to be with peers. And teenagers fail to appreciate that parents want the family to spend as much time together as possible because an important period in their adult life—child rearing—will soon end.

This teenager and his father share an affectionate moment. Although adolescents may resist parental authority, especially in matters of personal choice such as dress, most maintain close family ties. This is especially likely when parents make appropriate demands for autonomy while still giving teenagers the freedom to explore ideas and social roles.

Immigrant parents from cultures that place a high value on family closeness and obedience to authority have greater difficulty adapting to their teenagers' push for autonomy. Compared with nonimmigrant parents, they often react more strongly to adolescent disagreement. When they do, their youngsters are more dissatisfied with daily life (Phinney & Ong, 2001). Furthermore, over time, adolescents' growing exposure to the host culture's language and individualistic values may prompt parental criticism and a drop in youths' reliance on the family network for social support. The resulting *acculturative stress* (see page 605) is associated with a rise in deviant behavior—for example, increased alcohol use among Hispanic adolescents and delinquency among Chinese youths (Crane et al., 2005; de la Rosa et al., 2005; Gil, Wagner, & Vega, 2000; Warner et al., 2006).

Throughout adolescence, the quality of the parent–child relationship is the single most consistent predictor of mental health—higher self-esteem, assertiveness, and dating competence as well as more advanced identity development. In well-functioning families, young people remain attached to parents and seek their advice, but they do so in a context of greater freedom (Collins & Steinberg, 2006; Steinberg, 2001). The mild conflict that arises facilitates adolescent identity development and autonomy by helping family members express and tolerate disagreement. Conflicts also inform parents of teenagers' changing needs and expectations, signaling that adjustments in the parent–child relationship are necessary.

By middle to late adolescence, most parents and children achieve this mature, mutual relationship, and harmonious interaction is on the rise. The reduced time that Western teenagers spend with their families—for U.S. youths, a drop from 33 percent of waking hours in fifth grade to 14 percent in twelfth grade—has little to do with conflict (Larson et al., 1996). Rather, it results from the large amount of unstructured time available to teenagers in North America and Western Europe—on average, nearly half their waking hours (Larson, 2001). Young people tend to fill these free hours with activities that take them away from home—part-time jobs, a growing array of leisure and volunteer pursuits, and time with friends.

But this drop in family time is not universal. In one study, urban low- and middle-SES African-American youths showed no decline from childhood to adolescence in hours spent at home with family—a typical pattern in cultures with collectivist values (Larson et al., 2001). Furthermore, teenagers living in risky neighborhoods tend to have warmer, more trusting relationships with parents and adjust more favorably when their parents maintain tighter control and pressure them not to engage in worrisome behaviors (McElhaney & Allen, 2001). In harsh surroundings, young people seem to interpret more measured granting of autonomy as a sign of parental caring.

Family Circumstances

As Franca and Antonio's experience with Louis reminds us, adult life stresses can interfere with warm, involved child rearing and, in turn, with children's adjustment at any phase of development. But maternal employment or a dual-earner family does not by itself reduce parental time with teenagers, nor is it harmful to adolescent development (Richards & Duckett, 1994). To the contrary, parents who are financially secure, not overloaded with job pressures, and content with their marriages find it easier to grant their teenagers appropriate autonomy and experience less conflict with them. Their children, in turn, report higher levels of psychological well-being (Cowan & Cowan, 2002; Crouter & Bumpus, 2001). When Franca and Antonio's work stress eased and they recognized Louis's need for more involvement and guidance, his problems subsided.

Less than 10 percent of families with adolescents have seriously troubled relationships—chronic, escalating levels of conflict and repeated arguments over serious issues. Of these, most have difficulties that began in childhood (Collins & Laursen, 2004). Table 16.2 summarizes family conditions considered in earlier chapters that pose challenges for adolescents. Teenagers who develop well despite family stresses continue to benefit from factors that fostered resilience in earlier years: an appealing, easygoing disposition; a parent who combines warmth with high expectations; and (especially if parental supports are lacking) bonds with prosocial adults outside the family who care deeply about the adolescent's well-being (Masten, 2001).

Siblings

Like parent–child relationships, sibling interactions adapt to change at adolescence. As younger siblings mature and become more self-sufficient, they accept less direction from their older brothers and sisters. Consequently, teenage siblings relate to one another on a more equal footing. Furthermore, as adolescents become more involved in friendships and romantic relationships, they invest less time and energy in their siblings, who are part of the family from

TABLE 16.2	Family Circumstances with Implications for Adolescent Adjustment
FAMILY CIRCUMSTANCE	**TO REVIEW, TURN TO . . .**
Type of Family	
Adoptive	Chapter 2, pages 65–68
Never-married, single parent	Chapter 13, page 509
Divorced	Chapter 13, pages 509–512
Blended	Chapter 13, pages 512–514
Employed mother and dual-earner	Chapter 13, pages 514–516
Gay and lesbian	Chapter 13, page 508
Family Conditions	
Child maltreatment	Chapter 10, pages 401–405 Chapter 13, pages 517–518
Economic hardship	Chapter 2, pages 74–75
Adolescent parenthood	Chapter 14, pages 555–559

which they are trying to establish autonomy. As a result, sibling relationships often become less intense, in both positive and negative feelings, during adolescence (Cole & Kerns, 2001; Hetherington, Henderson, & Reiss, 1999).

Despite a drop in companionship, attachment between siblings, like closeness to parents, remains strong for most young people. Brothers and sisters who established a positive bond in early childhood continue to display greater affection and caring during the teenage years—an outcome linked to more favorable emotional and social adjustment (Branje et al., 2004; Dunn, Slomkowski, & Beardsall, 1994). Older siblings with whom relations are positive provide advice as young people face challenges in romantic relationships, schoolwork, and decisions about the future. In a study of Israeli Arab girls, a culturally prescribed role of older sister as caregiver helped teenage siblings adapt to social conditions radically different from their parents' traditional way of life. Older sisters assisted in academic and peer-relationship areas, where mothers were least helpful (Seginer, 1992).

Sibling interaction at adolescence continues to be affected by other relationships, and vice versa. As at earlier ages, teenagers whose parents are warm and supportive and who have a history of caring friendships have more positive sibling ties (Bussell et al., 1999; Kramer & Kowal, 2005). And in bidirectional fashion, warm adolescent sibling relationships contribute to more gratifying friendships (Yeh & Lempers, 2004). Finally, mild sibling differences in perceived parental affection no longer trigger jealousy but, rather, predict increasing sibling warmth (Feinberg et al., 2003). Perhaps adolescents interpret a unique parental relationship, as long as it is generally accepting, as a gratifying sign of their own individuality.

Peer Relations

As adolescents spend less time with family members, peers become increasingly important. In industrialized societies, young people spend most of each weekday with agemates in school. Teenagers also spend much out-of-class time together, more in some cultures than others. For example, U.S. young people have about 50 hours of free time per week, Europeans about 45 hours, and East Asians about 33 hours (Larson, 2001). A shorter school year and less demanding academic standards, which lead American youths to spend far less time than Western European and Asian youths on schoolwork (especially homework), account for this difference (see Figure 16.2 on page 620).

FIGURE 16.2

Weekly free time and time devoted to homework by adolescents in the United States, Europe, and East Asia. Figures are averages of those reported in many studies. American teenagers have more free time available to spend with peers than their European and, especially, Asian counterparts, a difference largely explained by American adolescents spending far less time doing homework. (Adapted from Larson, 2001.)

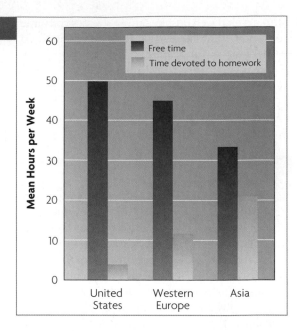

In the following sections, we will see that adolescent peer relations can be both positive and negative. At their best, peers serve as crucial bridges between the family and adult social roles.

Friendships

Adolescents report their most favorable moods when in the company of friends (Larson & Richards, 1991). The number of "best friends" declines from about four to six in early adolescence to one or two in adulthood (Hartup & Stevens, 1999). At the same time, the nature of the relationship changes.

CHARACTERISTICS OF ADOLESCENT FRIENDSHIPS ■ When asked about the meaning of friendship, teenagers stress two characteristics. The first and most important is *intimacy.* Adolescents seek psychological closeness, trust, and mutual understanding from their friends—the reason that self-disclosure (exchanges of private thoughts and feelings) between friends increases steadily over the adolescent years (see Figure 16.3). Second, more than younger children, teenagers want their friends to be *loyal*—to stick up for them and not leave them for somebody else (Buhrmester, 1996; Hartup & Abecassis, 2004).

As frankness and faithfulness increase in friendships, teenagers get to know each other better as personalities. Cooperation and mutual affirmation between friends also rise—changes that may reflect greater effort and skill at preserving the relationship as well as increased sensitivity to a friend's needs and desires (Phillipsen, 1999). Teenagers are less possessive of their friends than they were in childhood (Parker et al., 2005). Desiring a certain degree of autonomy for themselves, they recognize that friends need this, too.

In addition to the many characteristics that school-age friends share (see Chapter 13, page 499), adolescent friends tend to be alike in identity status, educational aspirations, political beliefs, and willingness to try drugs and engage in lawbreaking acts. Over time, they become more similar in these ways (Akers, Jones, & Coyl, 1998; Berndt & Murphy, 2002). Friendship similarity partly reflects the way adolescents' social world is organized. Most teenagers live in neighborhoods segregated by income, ethnicity, and belief systems. Through tracking, schools sort them further. Teenagers may also choose companions like themselves to increase the supportiveness of friendship.

Occasionally, however, adolescents choose friends who differ in some ways from themselves. As they forge an identity, they give themselves room to explore new attitudes and values within the security of a compatible relationship. Furthermore, ethnicity affects friendship similarity. For example, African-American friends are less similar than Caucasian-American friends in school achievement. Many African-American adolescents seem to minimize academic performance in favor of identification with their ethnic group as a basis for friendship (Hamm, 2000).

Intimacy and loyalty are defining features of friendship in adolescence. Girls place special emphasis on emotional closeness, often gathering to "just talk" and exchange private thoughts and feelings.

Adolescent friendships are fairly stable and become more so with age (Degirmencioglu et al., 1998). Nevertheless, the transition to middle or junior high school brings friendship changes as teenagers encounter new peers and become interested in romantic relationships (Hardy, Bukowski, & Sippola, 2002). And for a time, they sacrifice similarity for admiration of superficial features—whether a potential friend is popular, physically attractive, or athletically skilled. Young teenagers of both sexes are attracted to aggressive boys as friends—a trend that contributes to a rise in antisocial behavior (Bukowski, Sippola, & Newcomb, 2000). Girls' tendency to strike up friendships with virile, aggressive boys who fit a stereotype of masculinity can lead to negative experiences in their first dating relationships. Over time, preference for friends who are prominent in the peer system subsides, and adolescents return to seeking friends whose traits, interests, and values resemble their own.

SEX DIFFERENCES IN FRIENDSHIP QUALITY ■ TAKE A MOMENT . . . Ask several adolescent girls and boys to describe their close friendships. You are likely to find a consistent sex difference. Emotional closeness is more common between girls (Markovitz, Benenson, & Dolenszky, 2001). Girls frequently get together to "just talk," and their exchanges contain more self-disclosure and mutually supportive statements. In contrast, boys more often gather for an activity—usually sports and competitive games. Boys' conversations usually focus on accomplishments and mastery issues, such as attainments in sports and school, and involve more competition and conflict (Brendgen et al., 2001; Rubin, Bukowski, & Parker, 2006).

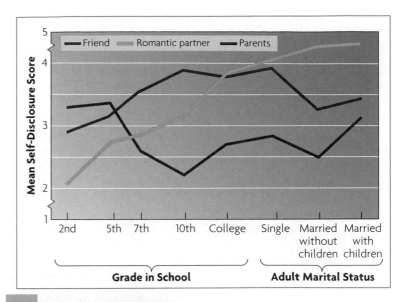

FIGURE 16.3

Age changes in reported self-disclosure to parents and peers, based on data from several studies. Self-disclosure to friends increases steadily during adolescence, reflecting intimacy as a major basis of friendship. Self-disclosure to romantic partners also rises. However, not until the college years does it surpass intimacy with friends. Self-disclosure to parents declines in early adolescence, a time of mild parent–child conflict. As family relationships readjust to the young person's increasing autonomy, self-disclosure to parents rises. (From D. Buhrmester, 1996, "Need Fulfillment, Interpersonal Competence, and the Developmental Contexts of Early Adolescent Friendship," in W. M. Bukowski, A. F. Newcomb, & W. W. Hartup, Eds., *The Company They Keep: Friendship in Childhood and Adolescence*, New York: Cambridge University Press, p. 168. Reprinted by permission.)

In line with gender-role expectations, girls' friendships typically focus on communal concerns, boys' on achievement and status. Boys do form close friendship ties, but the quality of their friendships is more variable than girls'. The intimacy of boys' friendships is related to gender identity. Androgynous boys are just as likely as girls to form intimate same-sex ties, whereas boys with a "masculine" identity are less likely to do so (Jones & Dembo, 1989).

Closeness in friendship, though usually beneficial, can have costs as well as benefits. When adolescent friends focus on their innermost thoughts and feelings, they tend to *coruminate,* or repeatedly mull over problems and negative feelings—an activity that contributes to friendship quality but also may spark anxiety and depression—symptoms more common among girls (Rose, 2002). Also, when conflict arises between intimate friends, more potential exists for one party to harm the other through relational aggression—for example, by divulging sensitive personal information to outsiders. Partly for this reason, girls' closest same-sex friendships tend to be of shorter duration than boys' (Benenson & Christakos, 2003). Also, whereas boys often resolve conflicts by minimizing their importance ("It's no big deal"), this strategy tends to lead to friendship break-up among girls (Bowker, 2004). In an emotionally intense bond, minimizing rather than confronting disagreement may restore harmony on the surface but engender avoidance of self-disclosure, making the friendship less stable.

In early adolescence, young people who are either very popular or very unpopular are more likely to have other-sex friends. Boys have more other-sex friends than do girls, whose desire for closeness leads to a preference for same-sex friendships. Among boys without same-sex friends, having an other-sex friend is associated with feelings of competence. Among girls

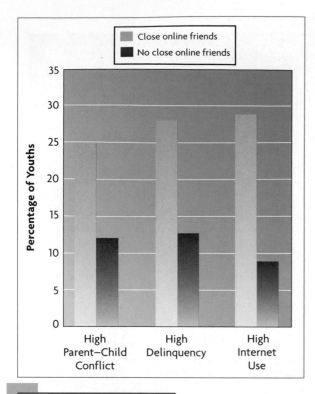

FIGURE 16.4

Association of close online friendships with parent–child conflict, delinquency, and high Internet use. In this survey of a nationally representative sample of 1,500 U.S. Internet-using 10- to 17-year-olds, those who reported that they had formed close online friendships or romances were more likely to be troubled youths who spent much time on the Internet. (Adapted from Wolak, Mitchell, & Finkelhor, 2003.)

who lack same-sex friends, other-sex friendships are linked to less positive well-being (Bukowski, Sippola, & Hoza, 1999). Perhaps these girls are especially likely to befriend boys with negative traits, such as aggression.

FRIENDSHIPS ON THE INTERNET ■ Teenagers frequently use the Internet to communicate, and instant messaging—their preferred means of online interaction—seems to support friendship closeness. In one study, as amount of instant messaging increased, so did young people's perceptions of intimacy in the relationship (Hu et al., 2004).

Besides communicating with friends they know, adolescents use the Internet to meet new young people. As they strive for autonomy and identity, building relationships in cyberspace is appealing because it opens up vast alternatives beyond their families, schools, and communities. But although online ties give some teens sources of support, they also pose dangers. In a survey of a nationally representative sample of 1,500 U.S. 10- to 17-year-olds, 14 percent reported online close friendships or romances (Wolak, Mitchell, & Finkelhor, 2003). Although some adolescents who formed these bonds were well-adjusted, many were youths who reported high levels of conflict with parents, peer victimization, depression, and delinquency, and who spent extensive time on the Internet (see Figure 16.4). They were more likely to have been asked by online friends for face-to-face meetings and to have attended those meetings—without telling their parents.

The Internet's value for enabling convenient and satisfying communication among teenage friends must be weighed against its potential for facilitating harmful social experiences. Parents are wise to point out the risks of Internet communication, including harassment and exploitation (see pages 502 and 517 in Chapter 13).

BENEFITS OF ADOLESCENT FRIENDSHIPS ■ As long as adolescent friendships are not characterized by jealousy, relational aggression, or attraction to antisocial behavior, they are related to many aspects of psychological health and competence in emerging adulthood (Bagwell et al., 2001; Bukowski, 2001). The reasons are several:

- *Close friendships provide opportunities to explore the self and develop a deep understanding of another.* Through open, honest communication, adolescent friends become sensitive to each other's strengths and weaknesses, needs and desires—a process that supports the development of self-concept, identity, and perspective taking.
- *Close friendships provide a foundation for future intimate relationships.* Look again at Figure 16.3, and you will see that self-disclosure to friends precedes disclosure to romantic partners. Sexuality and romance are common topics of discussion between teenage friends—conversations that, along with the intimacy of friendship itself, may help adolescents establish and work out problems in romantic partnerships (Connolly & Goldberg, 1999).
- *Close friendships help young people deal with the stresses of adolescence.* Because supportive, prosocial friendships enhance sensitivity to and concern for another, they promote empathy, sympathy, and positive social behavior. As a result, friendships contribute to involvement in constructive youth activities, avoidance of antisocial acts, and psychological well-being (Lansford et al., 2003; Wentzel, Barry, & Caldwell, 2004).
- *Close friendships can improve adolescents' attitudes toward and involvement in school.* Close friendships promote good school adjustment, academically and socially, in both middle- and low-SES students (Berndt & Murphy, 2002; Wentzel, Barry, & Caldwell, 2004). When teenagers enjoy interacting with friends at school, they may begin to view all aspects of school life more positively.

Cliques and Crowds

In early adolescence, *peer groups* (see Chapter 13) become increasingly common and tightly structured. They are organized into **cliques**—groups of about five to seven members who are good friends and, therefore, tend to resemble one another in family background, attitudes, values, and interests. At first, cliques are limited to same-sex members. Among girls but not boys, being in a clique predicts academic and social competence. Clique membership is more important to girls, who use it as a context for expressing emotional closeness and support (Henrich et al., 2000). By midadolescence, mixed-sex cliques are common.

These high school cheerleaders form a crowd. Unlike the more intimate clique, the larger, more loosely organized crowd grants adolescents an identity within the larger social structure of the school.

Often several cliques with similar values form a larger, more loosely organized group called a **crowd.** Membership in a crowd—unlike the more intimate clique—is based on reputation and stereotype, granting the adolescent an identity within the larger social structure of the school. Prominent crowds in a typical high school might include "brains" (nonathletes who enjoy academics), "jocks" (who are very involved in sports), "populars" (class leaders who are highly social and involved in activities), "partyers" (who value socializing but care little about schoolwork), "nonconformists" (who like unconventional clothing and music), "burnouts" (who cut school and get into trouble), and "normals" (average to good students who get along with most other peers) (Kinney, 1999; Stone & Brown, 1999).

What influences the assortment of teenagers into cliques and crowds? Crowd affiliations are linked to strengths in adolescents' self-concepts, which reflect their abilities and interests (Prinstein & LaGreca, 2002). Family factors are important, too. In a study of 8,000 ninth to twelfth graders, adolescents who described their parents as authoritative were members of "brain," "jock," and "popular" groups that accepted both adult and peer reward systems. In contrast, boys with permissive parents aligned themselves with "partyers" and "burnouts," suggesting lack of identification with adult reward systems (Durbin et al., 1993).

These findings indicate that many peer-group values are extensions of values acquired at home. Once adolescents join a clique or crowd, it can modify their beliefs and behavior. In a study of the relationship between crowd affiliation and health-risk behaviors, brains were the lowest risk takers, populars and jocks were intermediate, and nonconformists and burnouts were the highest, often engaging in substance use and unprotected sex and agreeing that they would "do anything on a dare" (LaGreca, Prinstein, & Fetter, 2001). But the positive impact of having competent, self-controlled peers is greatest for teenagers whose own parents are authoritative. And the negative impact of associating with antisocial, drug-using agemates is strongest for teenagers whose parents use less effective child-rearing styles (Mounts & Steinberg, 1995). In sum, family experiences affect the extent to which teenagers become like their peer associates over time.

As interest in dating increases, boys' and girls' cliques come together. Mixed-sex cliques provide boys and girls with models for how to interact with the other sex and a chance to do so without having to be intimate (Connolly et al., 2004). Gradually, the larger group divides into couples, several of whom spend time going out together. By late adolescence, when boys and girls feel comfortable about approaching each other directly, the mixed-sex clique disappears (Connolly & Goldberg, 1999).

As adolescents settle on personal values and goals, they no longer feel a need to broadcast who they are through dress, language, and preferred activities, and crowds decline in importance. From tenth to twelfth grade, about half of young people switch crowds, mostly in favorable directions. "Brains" and "normal" crowds grow and deviant crowds lose members as teenagers focus more on their future (Strouse, 1999).

Both cliques and crowds serve vital functions. The clique provides a context for acquiring social skills and experimenting with values and roles. The crowd offers adolescents the security of a temporary identity as they separate from the family and construct a coherent sense of self (Newman & Newman, 2001).

clique A small group of about five to seven members who are good friends and, therefore, tend to resemble one another in family background, attitudes, and values.

crowd A large, loosely organized group consisting of several cliques, with membership based on reputation and stereotype.

Dating

The hormonal changes of puberty increase sexual interest (see Chapter 14), but cultural expectations determine when and how dating begins. Asian youths start dating later and have fewer dating partners than young people in Western societies, which tolerate and even encourage romantic involvements between teenagers from middle school on (see Figure 16.5). At age 12 to 14, these relationships last only briefly, but by age 16 and older, they continue, on average, for nearly two years (Carver, Joyner, & Udry, 2003). Transformations in teenagers' dating goals account for this change: Early adolescents date largely for superficial reasons—recreation, peer status, and exploration of sexuality. By late adolescence, as young people become ready for greater psychological intimacy, they look for someone who offers personal compatibility, companionship, affection, and social support (Brown, 2004; Collins & Van Dulmen, 2006a).

The achievement of intimacy between dating partners typically lags behind that of friends. And positive relationships with parents and friends contribute to the development of warm romantic ties, whereas conflict-ridden parent–adolescent and peer relationships forecast hostile dating interactions (Connolly, Furman, & Konarski, 2000; Linder & Collins, 2005). Recall from Chapter 7 that according to ethological theory, early attachment bonds lead to an *internal working model,* or set of expectations about attachment figures, that guides later close relationships. Consistent with this idea, secure attachment to parents in infancy and childhood—together with recollections of that security in adolescence—predicts quality of teenagers' and young adults' friendships and romantic ties (Collins & Van Dulmen, 2006b; Weimer, Kerns, & Oldenburg, 2004). In a study of high school seniors, supportive interactions with parents, and secure models of attachment to parents, predicted adolescents' warm interaction with friends and secure models of friendship. Teenagers' images of friendship security, in turn, were related to their images of security in romantic relationships (Furman et al., 2002).

Perhaps because early adolescent dating relationships are shallow and stereotyped, they do not foster social maturity. To the contrary, early, frequent dating is related to drug use, delinquency, and poor academic achievement (Zimmer-Gembeck, Siebenbruner, & Collins, 2001). These factors, along with a history of abusive family relationships, increase the likelihood of dating violence. About 10 to 20 percent of adolescents are physically or sexually abused by dating partners, with boys and girls equally likely to report being victims and violence by one partner often returned by the other (Arriaga & Foshee, 2004; Cyr, McDuff, & Wright, 2006). Mental health consequences are severe, including increased anxiety, depression, suicide attempts, risky sexual behavior, and—in girls—unhealthy weight control (vomiting and use of laxatives) (Carver, Joyner, & Udry, 2003; Silverman et al., 2001; Werkerle & Avgoustis, 2003). Furthermore, whereas early adolescent boys who date gain in status among same-sex peers, girls often experience conflict due to competition and jealousy of other girls. For all these reasons, sticking with group activities, such as parties and dances, before becoming involved with a steady boyfriend or girlfriend is best for young teenagers.

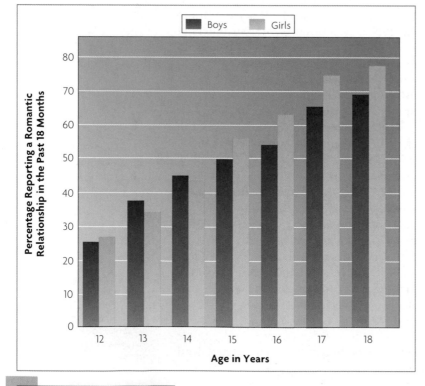

FIGURE 16.5

Increase in romantic relationships during adolescence. More than 16,000 American youths responded to an interview in which they indicated whether they had been involved in a romantic relationship in the past 18 months. Romantic involvements increased steadily with age. At 12 years, about one-fourth of young people reported them, a figure that rose to about three-fourths at age 18. (Adapted from Carver, Joyner, & Udry, 2003.)

Homosexual youths face special challenges in initiating and maintaining visible romances. Their first dating relationships seem to be short-lived and to involve little emotional commitment, but for reasons different from those of heterosexuals: They fear peer harassment and rejection (Diamond & Lucas, 2004). Recall from Chapter 14 that because of intense prejudice, homosexual adolescents often retreat into heterosexual dating. In addition, many have difficulty finding a same-sex partner because their homosexual peers have not yet come out. Often their first contacts with other sexual-minority youths occur in support groups, where they are free to date publicly and can discuss concerns about coming out (Diamond, 2003).

As long as it does not begin too soon, dating provides lessons in cooperation, etiquette, and dealing with people in a wide range of situations. Among older teenagers, close romantic ties promote enhanced sensitivity, empathy, intimacy, self-esteem, and identity development. In addition, teenagers' increasing capacity for interdependence and compromise within dating probably enhances the quality of other peer relationships (Collins, 2003; Furman & Shaffer, 2003).

Still, first romances usually serve as practice for later, more mature bonds. About half of heterosexual romances do not survive high school graduation, and those that do usually become less satisfying (Shaver, Furman, & Buhrmester, 1985). Because young people are still forming their identities, high school couples often find that they have little in common later. Nevertheless, warm, caring romantic ties in adolescence can have long-term implications. In a German study, they were positively related to gratifying, committed relationships in early adulthood (Seiffge-Krenke, 2003).

As long as dating does not begin too soon, it extends the benefits of adolescent friendships. Besides being fun, dating promotes sensitivity, empathy, and identity development as teenagers relate to someone whose needs differ from their own.

Peer Pressure and Conformity

When Franca and Antonio discovered Louis's lawbreaking during his freshman year of high school, they began to worry about the negative side of adolescent peer networks. Although conformity to peer pressure is greater during adolescence than in childhood or early adulthood, it is a complex process, varying with the adolescent's age, current situation, need for social approval, and culture.

A study of several hundred American junior and senior high school students revealed that adolescents felt greatest pressure to conform to the most obvious aspects of the peer culture—dress, grooming, and participation in social activities. Peer pressure to engage in proadult behavior, such as cooperating with parents and getting good grades, was also strong (Brown, Lohr, & McClenahan, 1986). Many teenagers said that their friends actively discouraged antisocial acts. In similar research conducted in Singapore, a culture that emphasizes family loyalty, outcomes were similar, except that peer pressure to meet family and school obligations exceeded pressure to join in peer-culture pursuits (Sim & Koh, 2003). As these findings reveal, adults and peers often act in concert, toward desirable ends!

Perhaps because of greater concern with what their friends think of them, early adolescents are more likely than older or younger individuals to give in to peer pressure to engage in drug taking and delinquent acts (Brown, Clasen, & Eicher, 1986; McIntosh, MacDonald, & McKeganey, 2006). Yet when parents and peers disagree, even young teenagers do not consistently rebel against the family. Whereas peers exert more influence on teenagers' day-to-day personal choices, such as dress, music, and friendships, parents have more impact on basic life values and educational plans. Adolescents' personal characteristics also make a difference: Young people who feel competent and worthwhile, who score lower in sensation-seeking, and who are more effective decision makers are less likely to succumb to negative peer pressure (Crocket, Raffaelli, & Shen, 2006; Steinberg, 2001).

Finally, authoritative child rearing is related to resistance to peer pressure. When their parents are supportive and exert appropriate oversight, teenagers respect them—an attitude that fosters mature autonomy and that acts as an antidote to unfavorable peer pressure (Dorius et al.,

2004; Masten, 2001). In contrast, adolescents who experience extremes of parental behavior—either too much or too little control—tend to be highly peer-oriented (Mason et al., 1996; Pettit et al., 1999). Youths who bend easily to peer influence display wide-ranging problems, including unstable friendships, drug taking, aggression, delinquency, and declining peer popularity and increasing depressive symptoms over time (Allen, Porter, & McFarland, 2006).

Ask Yourself

Review   Cite the distinct positive functions of friendships, cliques, and crowds in adolescence. What factors lead some friendships and peer-group ties to be harmful?

Apply   Thirteen-year-old Mattie's parents are warm, firm in their expectations, and consistent in monitoring her activities. At school, Mattie met some girls who want her to tell her parents she's going to a friend's house and then, instead, to join them at the beach for a party. Is Mattie likely to comply? Explain.

Connect   How might gender intensification, discussed on page 615, contribute to the shallow quality of early adolescent dating relationships?

Reflect   How did family experiences influence your crowd membership in high school? How did crowd membership influence your behavior?

Problems of Development

Although most young people move through adolescence with little disturbance, we have seen that some encounter major disruptions in development, such as premature parenthood, substance abuse, and school failure. In each instance, biological and psychological changes, families, schools, peers, communities, and culture combine to produce particular outcomes. Serious difficulties rarely occur in isolation but are usually interrelated—as is apparent in three additional problems of the teenage years: depression, suicide, and delinquency.

Depression in teenagers should not be dismissed as a temporary side effect of puberty. It can lead to long-term life disruption and adjustment problems.

Depression

Depression—feeling sad, frustrated, and hopeless about life, accompanied by loss of pleasure in most activities and disturbances in sleep, appetite, concentration, and energy—is the most common psychological problem of adolescence. Among North American teenagers, about 20 to 50 percent experience mild to moderate feelings of depression, bouncing back after a short time. Others display a more worrisome picture. About 15 to 20 percent have had one or more major depressive episodes, a rate comparable to that of adults. From 2 to 8 percent are chronically depressed—gloomy and self-critical for many months and sometimes years. Serious depression affects only 1 to 3 percent of children (more boys than girls), most of whom remain depressed in adolescence. Depressive symptoms increase sharply between ages 13 and 15, when—as Figure 16.6 shows—the sex difference reverses, with many more girls in industrialized nations reporting depression. Adolescent girls are twice as likely as adolescent boys to experience persistent depressed mood, a difference sustained throughout the lifespan (Hankin & Abela, 2005; Nolen-Hoeksema, 2002).

If allowed to continue, depression prevents young people from mastering crucial developmental tasks. Adolescent depression disrupts identity development and is also associated with persistent anxiety, poor school performance, drug abuse, law-breaking, and auto accidents. Without treatment, depressed teenagers are likely to

FIGURE 16.6

Change in depressive symptoms from age 12 to age 20 in a cross-sectional study of over 12,000 Norwegian adolescents. Girls showed a more rapid rise in depression around the time of puberty than boys. Similar trends occur in other industrialized nations. (From L. Wichstrøm, 1999, "The Emergence of Gender Difference in Depressed Mood During Adolescence: The Role of Intensified Gender Socialization," *Developmental Psychology, 35*, p. 237. Copyright © 1999 by the American Psychological Association. Reprinted by permission of the publisher and author.)

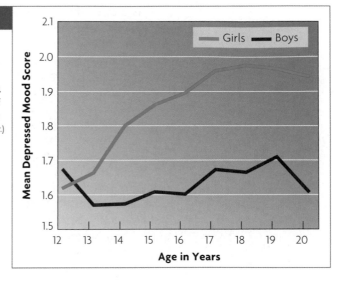

become depressed adults with persistent problems in work, family life, and social life (Fergusson & Woodward, 2002).

Unfortunately, because of the popular stereotype of adolescence as a period of storm and stress, teachers and parents tend to minimize the seriousness of adolescents' depressive symptoms, interpreting depression as just a passing phase. As a result, the overwhelming majority of depressed teenagers do not receive treatment (Asarnow et al., 2005).

FACTORS RELATED TO ADOLESCENT DEPRESSION ■ The precise combination of biological and environmental factors leading to depression varies from one individual to the next. Kinship studies reveal that heredity plays an important role (Glowinski et al., 2003). Genes can induce depression by affecting the balance of neurotransmitters in the brain, the development of brain regions involved in inhibiting negative emotion, or the body's hormonal response to stress (Kaufman & Charney, 2003).

But experience can also activate depression, promoting any of these biological changes. A high incidence of depression and other psychological disorders is seen in parents of depressed children and adolescents. Although a genetic risk may be passed from parent to child, in earlier chapters we saw that depressed or otherwise stressed parents often form insecure attachments with their children and engage in maladaptive child rearing. As a result, their child's emotional self-regulation, working models of attachment, and self-esteem are likely to be impaired, with serious consequences for many cognitive and social skills (Abela et al., 2005; Margolese, Markiewicz, & Doyle, 2005). Depressed youths usually display a learned-helpless attributional style (see Chapter 13), viewing positive academic and social outcomes as beyond their control (Graber, 2004). In a vulnerable young person, numerous negative life events can spark depression—for example, failing at something important, parental divorce, the end of a close friendship or romantic partnership, or the challenges of school transition.

SEX DIFFERENCES ■ Why are girls more prone to depression than boys? Biological changes associated with puberty cannot be a major factor because the gender difference is limited to industrialized nations. In developing countries, rates of depression are similar for males and females and occasionally higher in males (Culbertson, 1997). Even when females do exceed males in depression, the size of the difference varies. For example, it is smaller in China than in North America, perhaps because of decades of efforts by the Chinese government to eliminate gender inequalities (Greenberger et al., 2000).

Instead, stressful life events and gender-typed coping styles seem to be involved. Early-maturing girls are especially prone to depression (see Chapter 14). And the gender intensification of early adolescence often strengthens passivity and dependency—maladaptive approaches to the tasks expected of teenagers in complex cultures. Consistent with this explanation, adolescents who identify strongly with "feminine traits" are more depressed, regardless of their sex (Wichstrøm, 1999). Also, girls who repeatedly feel overwhelmed develop an overly reactive physiological stress response and cope more poorly with challenges in the future (Nolen-Hoeksema, 2002, 2006). In this way, stressful experiences and stress reactivity feed on one another, sustaining depression.

As indicated in previous chapters, child abuse, especially sexual abuse, is related to severe depression (Schraedley, Gotlib, & Hayward, 1999). Adolescent girls are more likely than boys to be sexually abused in family and dating relationships. As abuse alters the young person's stress reactivity (see Chapter 10, page 404), victims may respond maladaptively to many stressors of daily life, worsening their feelings of helplessness.

Profound depression in adolescence predicts depression in adulthood and serious impairments in work, family life, and social life. And depression often leads to suicidal thoughts, which all too often are translated into action.

Suicide

Compared with his sister, who was an outstanding student, 17-year-old Brad couldn't measure up. Brad's parents had been critical of his school performance for years. Now, with adulthood just around the corner, they berated him for his lack of direction. "At your age, you oughta have a clue about where you're going!" Brad's father shouted one day. "Pick a college, get a trade—just stop sitting around!"

All through high school, Brad had been a loner. He excelled in art class, but his parents never showed much interest in his drawings, which were piled in a corner of his room. Brad spent hours alone there, sketching. Though Brad's parents worried that he seemed unhappy and didn't have many friends, they consoled themselves that at least he wasn't getting into trouble like some kids.

One day, Brad got up enough nerve to ask a girl out. His father, encouraged by Brad's interest in dating, gave him permission to use the family car. But when Brad arrived to pick up the girl, she wasn't home. Several hours later, Brad's parents got a call from the police. He had been picked up for speeding, "driving under the influence," and evading the police. The chase through city streets ended when Brad drove off the road into a ditch. Although he wasn't injured, the car was totaled. A terrible argument followed between Brad and his parents.

Over the next two days, Brad was somber and withdrawn. Then, after dinner one night, he seemed resolved to make things better. "I've taken care of things, and I won't cause any more problems," he told his parents. Handing several of his favorite drawings to his sister, he said, "Here, I want you to have these—for keeps, to think of me." Early the next morning, Brad's parents found him hanging from a rope in his room.

FACTORS RELATED TO ADOLESCENT SUICIDE ■ The suicide rate increases from childhood to old age, but it jumps sharply at adolescence. Currently, suicide is the third-leading cause of death (after motor vehicle collisions and homicides) among American youths and the second-leading cause (after motor vehicle collisions) among Canadian youths. Perhaps because North American teenagers experience more stresses and fewer social supports than in the past, adolescent suicide tripled in the United States and Canada between the mid-1960s and the mid-1990s, followed by a slight decline (Spirito & Esposito-Smythers, 2006) At the same time, rates of adolescent suicide vary widely among industrialized nations—low in Greece, Italy, the Netherlands, and Spain; intermediate in Australia, Canada, Japan, and the United States; and high in Finland, New Zealand, and Singapore (Bridge, Goldstein, & Brent, 2006). These international differences remain unexplained.

Striking sex differences in suicidal behavior exist. Despite girls' higher rates of depression, the number of boys who kill themselves exceeds the number of girls by a ratio of 3 or 4 to 1. Girls make more unsuccessful suicide attempts, using methods from which they are more likely to be revived, such as a sleeping pill overdose. In contrast, boys tend to choose techniques that lead to instant death, such as firearms or hanging. Gender-role expectations may contribute; less tolerance exists for feelings of helplessness and failed efforts in males than in females (Canetto & Sakinofsky, 1998).

Perhaps because of higher levels of support from extended families, African Americans and Hispanics have slightly lower suicide rates than Caucasian Americans (see Figure 16.7). Recently, however, suicide has risen among African-American adolescent males; the current rate approaches that of Caucasian-American males. And Native-American and Canadian-

FIGURE 16.7

Suicide rates among 15- to 19-year-olds in the United States and Canada by sex and ethnicity Suicide rates are high among Native-American and, especially, Canadian-Aboriginal youths. Although African-American and Hispanic youth have suicide rates slightly lower than those of Caucasian Americans, the African-American adolescent male rate has recently risen. (From Statistics Canada, 2003d; U.S. Census Bureau, 2007b.)

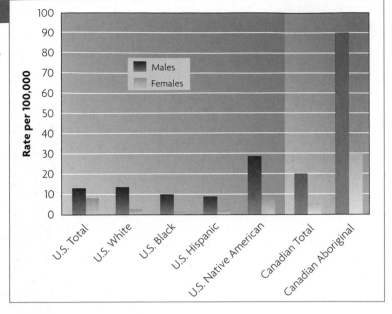

Aboriginal youths commit suicide at rates 2 to 6 times national averages (Health Canada, 2003; U.S. Census Bureau, 2007b). High rates of profound family poverty, school failure, alcohol and drug use, and depression probably underlie these trends—factors that also make homeless, runaway, and imprisoned youths prone to suicide (Spirito & Esposito-Smythers, 2006). Gay, lesbian, and bisexual youths also are at high risk, attempting suicide three times as often as other adolescents. Those who have tried to kill themselves report more family conflict over their gender-atypical behavior, inner turmoil about their sexuality, problems in romantic relationships, and peer victimization due to their sexual orientation (D'Augelli et al., 2005).

Suicide tends to occur in two types of young people. The first group includes adolescents much like Brad—highly intelligent but solitary, withdrawn, and unable to meet their own standards or those of important people in their lives. Members of the second, larger group show antisocial tendencies and express their despondency through bullying, fighting, stealing, increased risk taking, and drug abuse (Evans, Hawton, & Rodham, 2004; Fergusson, Woodward, & Horwood, 2000). Besides being hostile and destructive toward others, they turn their anger and disappointment inward.

Biology and environment jointly contribute to suicidal behavior. As we have just seen, personality traits—either high introversion or high impulsivity and recklessness—are predisposing factors. A family history of emotional and antisocial disorders and of suicide is often present, and frequently the teenager has been diagnosed with a mental disorder. In addition, suicidal young people are more likely to have experienced multiple stressful life events, including economic disadvantage, parental separation and divorce, absence of family warmth, frequent parent–child conflict, and abuse and neglect. Stressors typically increase during the period preceding a suicide attempt or completion (Beautrais, 2003; Pfeffer, 2006). Triggering events include parental blaming of the teenager for family problems, the breakup of an important peer relationship, or the humiliation of having been caught engaging in antisocial acts.

Why does suicide increase in adolescence? Teenagers' improved ability to plan ahead seems to be involved. Although some act impulsively, many young people, like Brad, take purposeful steps to kill themselves (McKeown et al., 1998). Furthermore, depressed youths learned helplessness greatly increases the likelihood that, when faced with a stressful event, their despair, hopelessness, and isolation will deepen. Suicidal behavior often recurs, with about 10 percent of attempters trying again within 6 months and more than 40 percent within 21 months (Hawton, Zahl, & Weatherall, 2003).

PREVENTION AND TREATMENT ■ Picking up on the signals that a troubled teenager sends is a crucial first step in suicide prevention. Parents and teachers must be trained to recognize warning signs (see Table 16.3 on page 630). Schools and recreational and religious organizations can provide sympathetic counselors, peer support groups, and information about telephone hot lines (Spirito et al., 2003). Once a teenager takes steps toward suicide, essential help includes staying with the young person, listening, and expressing compassion and concern until professional help

TABLE 16.3   Warning Signs of Suicide

Efforts to put personal affairs in order—smoothing over troubled relationships, giving away treasured possessions

Verbal cues—saying goodbye to family members and friends, making direct or indirect references to suicide ("I won't have to worry about these problems much longer"; "I wish I were dead")

Feelings of sadness, despondency, "not caring" anymore

Extreme fatigue, lack of energy, boredom

No desire to socialize; withdrawal from friends

Easily frustrated

Emotional outbursts—spells of crying or laughing, bursts of energy

Inability to concentrate, distractible

Decline in grades, absence from school, discipline problems

Neglect of personal appearance

Sleep change—loss of sleep or excessive sleepiness

Appetite change—eating more or less than usual

Physical complaints—stomachaches, backaches, headaches

can be obtained. Applying What We Know below offers suggestions for how to respond to a young person who might be suicidal.

Intervention with depressed and suicidal adolescents takes many forms, from antidepressant medication to individual, family, and group therapy. Sometimes hospitalization is necessary to ensure the teenager's safety and swift entry into treatment. Until the adolescent improves, removing weapons, knives, razors, scissors, and drugs from the home is vital. Strengthening social supports and providing training in effective strategies for coping with stress and depressed mood are essential ingredients of resilience that prevent repeated suicide attempts (Asarnow et al., 2005; Kalafat, 2005). On a broader scale, gun-control legislation that limits adolescents' access to the most frequent and deadly suicide method in the United States would greatly reduce both the number of suicides and the high teenage homicide rate (Commission on Adolescent Suicide Prevention, 2005).

After a suicide, family and peer survivors need support to help them cope with grief, anger, and guilt over their inability to help the victim. Teenage suicides often occur in clusters, with one death increasing the likelihood of others among depressed peers who knew the young person or heard about the death through the media (Bearman & Moody, 2004; Gould, Jamieson, & Romer, 2003). In view of this trend, an especially watchful eye must be kept on vulnerable adolescents after a suicide happens. Restraint by journalists in reporting teenage suicides on television and in newspapers also aids prevention.

Applying What We Know

Ways to Respond to a Young Person Who Might Be Suicidal

STRATEGY	DESCRIPTION
Be psychologically and physically available.	Grant the young person your full attention; indicate when and where you can be located, and emphasize that you are always willing to talk.
Communicate a caring, capable attitude.	Such statements as "I'm concerned. I care about you" encourage the adolescent to discuss feelings of despair. Conveying a capable attitude helps redirect the young person's world of confusion toward psychological order.
Assess the immediacy of risk.	Gently inquire into the young person's motives with such questions as "Do you want to harm yourself? Do you want to die or kill yourself?" If the answer is yes, ask about the adolescent's plan. If it is specific (involves a method and a time), the risk of suicide is high.
Empathize with the young person's feelings.	Empathy, through such statements as "I understand your confusion and pain," increases your persuasive power and defuses the adolescent's negative emotion.
Oppose the suicidal intent.	Communicate sensitively but firmly that suicide is not an acceptable solution and that you want to help the adolescent explore other options.
Offer a plan for help.	Offer to assist the young person in finding professional help and in telling others, such as parents and school officials, who need to know about the problem.
Obtain a commitment.	Ask the adolescent to agree to the plan. If he or she refuses, negotiate a promise to contact you or another supportive person if and when suicidal thoughts return.

Source: Kirk, 1993.

Delinquency

Juvenile delinquents are children or adolescents who engage in illegal acts. Although North American youth crime has declined since the mid-1990s, U.S. and Canadian 12- to 17-year-olds account for a substantial proportion of police arrests—about 15 percent in the United States and 23 percent in Canada (Statistics Canada, 2005b; U.S. Department of Justice, 2006). When teenagers are asked directly and confidentially about lawbreaking, almost all admit to having committed an offense of some sort—usually a minor crime, such as petty stealing or disorderly conduct (Flannery et al., 2003).

Both police arrests and self-reports show that delinquency rises over adolescence, then declines (Farrington, 2004; U.S. Department of Justice, 2006). What accounts for this trend? Recall that among young teenagers, antisocial behavior increases as a result of a desire for peer approval. Over time, peers become less influential, decision making and moral reasoning improve, and young people enter social contexts (such as higher education, work, career, and marriage) that are less conducive to lawbreaking.

For most adolescents, a brush with the law does not forecast long-term antisocial behavior. But repeated arrests are cause for concern. Teenagers are responsible for 13 percent of violent crimes in the United States and for 8 percent in Canada (Statistics Canada, 2005b; U.S. Department of Justice, 2006). A small percentage become recurrent offenders, who commit most of these crimes, and some enter a life of crime. As the Biology and Environment box on pages 632–633 reveals, childhood-onset conduct problems are far more likely to persist than conduct problems that first appear in adolescence.

Delinquency rises during early adolescence, remains high during middle adolescence, and then declines. Most delinquency involves petty stealing and disorderly conduct, but a small percentage of young people repeatedly engage in serious offenses and are at risk for a life of crime.

FACTORS RELATED TO DELINQUENCY ■ In adolescence, the gender gap in overt aggression widens (Chesney-Lind, 2001). Although girls account for about 18 percent of adolescent arrests for violent crimes—a larger proportion than a decade ago—their offenses are largely limited to simple assault (such as pushing), the least serious category. Once labeled status offenses (noncriminal behavior), today these acts are more likely to lead to arrests, especially in physical exchanges with parents, who may report the youth's behavior to the police (Chesney-Lind & Belknap, 2004). Serious violent crime continues to be mostly the domain of boys (Dahlberg & Simon, 2006).

SES and ethnicity are strong predictors of arrests, but they are only mildly related to teenagers' self-reports of antisocial acts. The difference is due to the tendency to arrest, charge, and punish low-SES ethnic minority youths more often than their higher-SES white and Asian counterparts (Farrington, 2004; U.S. Department of Justice, 2006). In isolation from other life circumstances, ethnicity tells us little about youths' propensity to engage in violence and other lawbreaking acts.

Difficult temperament, low intelligence, and a history of poor school performance, peer rejection, and association with antisocial peers are linked to chronic delinquency (Laird et al., 2005). How do these factors fit together? One of the most consistent findings about delinquent youths is that their families are low in warmth, high in conflict, and characterized by inconsistent discipline and low monitoring (Barnes et al., 2006; Capaldi et al., 2002). Because marital transitions often contribute to disrupted parenting, boys who experience parental separation and divorce are especially prone to delinquency (Farrington, 2004). And youth crime peaks on weekdays between 2:00 and 8:00 P.M., when many teenagers are unsupervised (U.S. Department of Justice, 2006).

Our discussion on page 388 in Chapter 10 explained how ineffective parenting can promote and sustain children's aggression. Boys are more likely than girls to be targets of angry, inconsistent discipline because they are more active and impulsive and therefore harder to control. When children who are extreme in these characteristics are exposed to inept parenting,

Biology and Environment

Two Routes to Adolescent Delinquency

Persistent adolescent delinquency follows two paths of development, one with an onset of conduct problems in childhood, the second with an onset in adolescence. Research reveals that the early-onset type is far more likely to lead to a life-course pattern of aggression and criminality (Farrington & Loeber, 2000). In contrast, the late-onset type usually does not persist beyond the transition to young adulthood.

Both childhood-onset and adolescent-onset youths engage in serious offenses; associate with deviant peers; participate in substance abuse, unsafe sex, and dangerous driving; and spend time in correctional facilities. Why does antisocial activity more often continue and escalate into violence in the first group than in the second? Longitudinal studies yield similar answers to this question. So far, findings are clearest for boys, who are the focus of most research. But several investigations report that girls who were physically aggressive in childhood are also at risk for later problems—occasionally violent delinquency, but more often other norm-violating behaviors and psychological disorders (Broidy et al., 2003; Chamberlain, 2003). And early relational aggression is linked to adolescent conduct problems as well.

Early-Onset Type

Early-onset youngsters seem to inherit traits that predispose them to aggressiveness (Pettit, 2004). For example, violence-prone boys are distinguished by their difficult and fearless temperamental style; they are emotionally negative, restless, willful, and physically aggressive as early as age 2. They also show subtle deficits in cognitive functioning that seem to contribute to disruptions in the development of language, memory, and cognitive and emotional self-regulation (Moffitt, 2006; Shaw et al., 2003). Some have attention-deficit hyperactivity disorder (ADHD), which compounds their learning and self-control problems (see Chapter 12, page 444).

Yet these biological risks are not sufficient to sustain antisocial behavior: Most early-onset boys decline in aggression over time and do not display serious delinquency followed by adult criminality. Those who avoid the life-course path benefit from better reading achievement in first grade and an interrelated set of protective factors in middle school—parental monitoring, avoidance of deviant peer relationships, higher family income, and better-quality neighborhoods (Petras et al., 2004).

Among youths who do follow the life-course path, inept parenting transforms their undercontrolled style into hostility, defiance, and persistent aggression—a strong predictor of violent delinquency in adolescence (Brame, Nagin, & Tremblay, 2001; Broidy et al., 2003). As they fail academically and are rejected by peers, they befriend other deviant youths, who facilitate one another's violent behavior while relieving loneliness (see Figure 16.8) (Lacourse et al., 2003). Early-onset teenagers' limited cognitive and social skills result in high rates of school dropout and unemployment, contributing further to their antisocial involvements. Often these boys experience their first arrest before age 14, a good indicator that they will be chronic offenders by age 18 (Patterson & Yoerger, 2002).

Preschoolers high in relational aggression also tend to be hyperactive and frequently in conflict with peers and adults (Willoughby, Kupersmidt, & Bryant, 2001). As these behaviors trigger peer rejection, relationally aggressive girls befriend other girls high in relational hostility, and their relational aggression rises (Werner & Crick, 2004). Adolescents high in relational aggression are often angry, vengeful, and defiant of adult rules. Among teenagers

aggression rises during childhood, leads to violent offenses in adolescence, and persists into adulthood (again, see the Biology and Environment box).

Disruptive, peer-rejected children and adolescents relieve their loneliness by seeking out antisocial friends, who facilitate one another's violent, antisocial behavior (Lacourse et al., 2003). But compared to youths with conventional friends, adolescents with deviant friends are more depressed—due to their history of unfavorable family, school, and peer experiences and high rates of conflict in their friendships (Brendgen, Vitaro, & Bukowski, 1998). Delinquent youths seem to stick with these friends to avoid social isolation and to bolster their fragile self-esteem. Indeed, many aggressive youths report overly high self-esteem. When their arrogant, cocky behavior prompts others to challenge their inflated but vulnerable self-image, they lash out in anger (Baumeister, Smart, & Boden, 1996; Costello & Dunaway, 2003).

Teenagers commit more crimes in poverty-stricken neighborhoods with limited recreational and employment opportunities and high adult criminality (Kroneman, Loeber, & Hipwell, 2004). In such neighborhoods, adolescents have easy access to deviant peers, drugs, and firearms and are likely to be recruited into antisocial gangs, whose members commit the vast majority of violent delinquent acts. Furthermore, schools in these locales typically fail to meet students' developmental needs (Flannery et al., 2003). Large classes, weak instruction, and rigid rules with harsh consequences for infractions may increase teenagers' inclination toward defiance and aggression.

Zero tolerance policies—which severely punish all disruptive and threatening behaviors, major and minor, usually with suspension or expulsion—have become increasingly common in

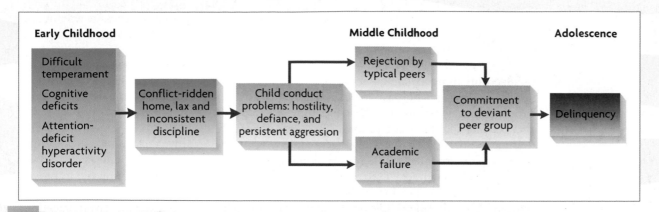

FIGURE 16.8

Path to chronic delinquency for adolescents with childhood-onset antisocial behavior. Difficult temperament and cognitive deficits characterize many of these youths in early childhood; some have attention-deficit hyperactivity disorder. Inept parenting transforms biologically based self-control difficulties into hostility and defiance.

who combine physical and relational hostility, these oppositional reactions intensify, increasing the likelihood of serious antisocial activity (Prinstein, Boergers, & Vernberg, 2001).

Late-Onset Type

Other youths first display antisocial behavior around the time of puberty, gradually increasing their involvement. Their conduct problems arise from the peer context of early adolescence, not from biological deficits and a history of unfavorable development. For some,

quality of parenting may decline for a time, perhaps because of family stresses or the challenges of disciplining an unruly teenager (Moffitt et al., 1996). But when age brings gratifying adult privileges, these youths draw on prosocial skills mastered before adolescence and give up their antisocial ways.

A few late-onset youths, however, continue to engage in antisocial acts. The seriousness of their adolescent offenses seems to trap them in situations that close off opportunities for responsible behavior. Being employed or in school and

forming positive, close relationships predict an end to criminal offending by age 20 to 25 (Clingempeel & Henggeler, 2003; Stouthamer-Loeber et al., 2004). In contrast, the longer antisocial young people spend in prison, the more likely they are to sustain a life of crime.

These findings suggest a need for a fresh look at policies aimed at stopping youth crime. Keeping youth offenders locked up for many years disrupts their vocational lives and access to social support during a crucial period of development, committing them to a bleak future.

North American schools. Yet often they are implemented inconsistently: Low-SES minority students are two to three times as likely to be punished, especially for minor misbehaviors, which constitute the majority of problematic acts in schools (Robbins, 2005). No evidence exists that zero tolerance—in focusing on punishment rather than prevention and intervention—achieves its objective of reducing youth aggression and other forms of misconduct (Skiba & Rausch, 2006; Stinchcomb, Bazemore, & Riestenberg, 2006). To the contrary, some studies find that by excluding students from school, zero tolerance often heightens dropout and delinquency.

PREVENTION AND TREATMENT ■ Because delinquency often has roots in childhood and results from events in several contexts, prevention must start early and take place at multiple levels (DeMatteo & Marczyk, 2005). Positive family relationships, authoritative parenting, high-quality teaching in schools, well-designed work–study vocational education programs, and communities with healthy economic and social conditions go a long way toward reducing adolescent criminality.

Treating serious offenders also requires an approach that recognizes the multiple determinants of delinquency. Insofar as possible, adolescents are best kept in their own homes and communities to increase the possibility that treatment changes will transfer to their daily lives. Treatment models include individual therapies, halfway houses, day treatment centers, work experience programs, and summer camps. However, delinquents who engage in serious, violent crimes often must be removed from the community and placed in a correctional facility. Regardless of where treatment takes place, the most effective approaches are lengthy and intensive, encompassing parent training, social understanding, and instruction in cognitive and social skills needed to overcome peer and school difficulties (Heilbrun, Lee, & Cottle, 2005).

In a program called EQUIP, *positive peer culture*—an adult-guided but adolescent-conducted small-group approach aimed at creating a climate in which prosocial acts replace antisocial behavior—served as the basis for treatment. By themselves, peer-culture groups do not reduce antisocial behavior—in fact, they sometimes increase it by perpetuating deviant peer influences (Dodge, Dishion, & Lansford, 2006). But in EQUIP, the approach is supplemented with training in social skills, anger management, correction of cognitive distortions (such as misperceiving others' intentions as hostile or blaming victims), and moral reasoning (Gibbs, 2004; DiBiase, Gibbs, & Potter, 2005). Delinquents who participated in EQUIP displayed improved social skills and conduct during the following year compared with controls receiving no intervention. Also, the more advanced moral reasoning that emerged during group meetings seemed to have a long-term impact on antisocial youths' ability to inhibit lawbreaking behavior (Leeman, Gibbs, & Fuller, 1993).

Yet even multidimensional treatments can fall short if adolescents remain embedded in hostile home lives, poor-quality schools, antisocial peer groups, and violent neighborhoods. In another program, called multisystemic therapy, therapists trained parents in communication, monitoring, and discipline skills; integrated violent youths into positive school, work, and leisure activities; and disengaged them from deviant peers. Compared with conventional services or individual therapy, the intervention led to improved parent–child relations, a dramatic drop in number of arrests over a four-year period, and—when participants did commit crimes—a reduction in their severity (Huey & Henggeler, 2001). Efforts to create nonaggressive environments—at the family, community, and cultural levels—are needed to help delinquent youths and to foster healthy development of all young people.

Ask Yourself

Review Why are adolescent girls at greater risk for depression and adolescent boys at greater risk for suicide?

Review Explain how biology and environment jointly contribute to the development of violent delinquency.

Apply Zeke had been well-behaved in elementary school, but around age 13 he started spending time with the "wrong crowd." At age 16, he was arrested for property damage. Is Zeke likely to become a long-term offender? Why or why not?

Connect Reread the sections on adolescent pregnancy and substance abuse in Chapter 14. What factors do these problems have in common with suicide and chronic delinquency?

At the Threshold

The complex and rapid changes of development that occur during adolescence make teenagers vulnerable to certain problems. Most teenagers, however, do not show serious depression, suicidal tendencies, or persistent antisocial behavior. As we look back on the demands, expectations, dangers, and temptations of the adolescent period, the strength and vitality of young people are all the more remarkable. On a daily basis, adolescents must decide how vigorously to apply themselves in school, what kinds of friends to make, and whether to adopt risky behaviors, such as experimentation with sex and drugs. These short-term choices can profoundly affect the long-term paths they pursue.

Societies have good reason to treasure their youths as a rich national resource. Adolescents' ability to think seriously and deeply about possibilities, to commit themselves to idealistic causes, to be loyal to one another, and to experiment and take risks, while sometimes hazardous to themselves, energizes progress. But to realize their potential, teenagers must have family, school, and community environments that nurture personal strengths while limiting exposure to adversity. To factors that foster resilience considered in earlier chapters (see Chapter 13, page 521) we can now add the following resources, which are particularly beneficial in adolescence:

- A balance between family connection and separation
- Effective family problem solving that models and encourages rational decision making
- Parental monitoring and school involvement
- Close, supportive friendships
- High-quality vocational education
- A culturally sensitive school and community that foster a secure ethnic or bicultural identity
- Affiliation with a religious organization
- Opportunities to participate in extracurricular activities, youth organizations, and community service

As we turn now to the conclusion of our developmental journey, we will see that many young people in industrialized nations face more complex choices today than even several decades ago. Consequently, researchers have begun to investigate a new period that stands between adolescence and young adulthood. The support provided during the first 18 years is crucial for preparing young people to embrace the challenges of this transition. At no other time of life will the scope of possibilities and the freedom to experiment and make independent decisions be greater.

Summary

Erikson's Theory: Identity versus Role Confusion

According to Erikson, what is the major personality achievement of adolescence?

- Erikson's theory emphasizes **identity** as the major personality achievement of adolescence. Young people who successfully resolve the psychological conflict of **identity versus role confusion** construct a solid self-definition consisting of self-chosen values and goals.

Self-Understanding

Describe changes in self-concept and self-esteem during adolescence.

- The cognitive changes of adolescence enable teenagers to describe themselves in more organized and consistent ways. They place more emphasis on social virtues, and personal and moral standards gradually appear as key themes. Self-esteem continues to differentiate, and young people add new dimensions reflecting important concerns of the teenage years: close friendship, romantic appeal, and job competence.

- For most adolescents, self-esteem rises. At the same time, individual differences in self-esteem become more stable. Self-esteem factors strongly related to adjustment include parental relationships, academic competence, and peer relationships. The

ingredients of authoritative parenting—warmth, approval, appropriate expectations for maturity, and positive problem solving—support self-esteem. Schools and neighborhoods where the young person's SES or ethnic group is well represented also have a positive impact.

Describe the four identity statuses, along with factors that promote identity development.

- In complex societies, a period of exploration followed by commitment is necessary to form a personally meaningful identity. **Identity achievement** (exploration followed by commitment) and **identity moratorium** (exploration without having reached commitment) are psychologically healthy identity statuses. Long-term **identity foreclosure** (commitment without exploration) and **identity diffusion** (lack of both exploration and commitment) are related to adjustment difficulties.

- Adolescents who use a flexible, open-minded approach to grappling with competing beliefs and values and who feel attached to parents but free to voice their own opinions are likely to be advanced in identity development. Close friends support young people in exploring options.

- Schools and communities that provide young people of all backgrounds with rich and varied opportunities for exploration also foster identity achievement. Ethnic minority youths may experience **acculturative stress** resulting from conflict between their family's culture and that of the larger society. But those who construct a strong, secure **ethnic identity** or a **bicultural identity** are advantaged in many aspects of emotional and social development.

Moral Development

Describe Kohlberg's theory of moral development, and evaluate its accuracy.

■ By examining how responses to moral dilemmas change with growing maturity, Kohlberg concluded that moral reasoning advances through three levels, each containing two stages: (1) the **preconventional level,** in which morality is viewed as controlled by rewards, punishments, and the power of authority figures; (2) the **conventional level,** in which conformity to laws and rules is regarded as necessary to preserve positive interpersonal relationships and maintain societal order; and (3) the **postconventional level,** in which individuals define morality in terms of abstract, universal principles of justice.

■ Development of moral reasoning is slow and gradual, extending into adulthood. A reexamination of Kohlberg's stages suggests that moral maturity can be found at Stages 3 and 4. Because it focuses on hypothetical moral dilemmas, Kohlberg's theory emphasizes rational weighing of alternatives, while overlooking other strategies that affect moral judgment in everyday life. The influence of situational factors on moral reasoning suggests that Kohlberg's moral stages are best viewed as a loosely organized sequence.

Evaluate claims that Kohlberg's theory does not adequately represent the morality of females.

■ Contrary to Gilligan's claim, Kohlberg's theory does not underestimate the moral maturity of females. Both justice and caring moralities coexist but vary in emphasis between males and females, across cultures, and with degree of familiarity with the people involved.

■ Compared with children, teenagers display more subtle reasoning about conflicts between personal choice and community obligations. They are also increasingly mindful of the moral implications of following social conventions.

Describe influences on moral reasoning and the relationship of moral reasoning to behavior.

■ A flexible, open-minded approach to new information and experiences is linked to gains in moral reasoning. Warm, rational parenting, years of schooling, and peer discussion of moral issues also contribute. Young people in industrialized nations advance to higher levels of moral understanding than young people in village societies. Responses to moral dilemmas in collectivist cultures are often more other-directed.

■ Maturity of moral reasoning is modestly related to positive social behaviors. Other factors that affect moral action include the emotions of empathy and guilt, the individual's history of morally

relevant experiences, and **moral self-relevance**— the extent to which morality is central to self-concept.

■ Although formal religious involvement declines during adolescence, young people who remain part of a religious community are advantaged in moral values and behavior. Religious affiliation is linked to community service, responsible behavior, and avoidance of misconduct.

Gender Typing

Why is early adolescence a period of gender intensification?

■ Biological, social, and cognitive factors contribute to the **gender intensification** of early adolescence. Physical changes, gender-typed pressures from parents and peers, and increased concern with what others think prompt teenagers to view themselves in gender-linked ways. Young people who eventually build an androgynous gender identity tend to be psychologically healthier.

The Family

Discuss changes in parent–child relationships during adolescence.

■ Adapting family interaction to meet adolescents' need for **autonomy** is especially challenging. As teenagers deidealize their parents, they often question parental authority. And because both adolescents and parents are undergoing major life transitions, they approach situations from different perspectives. Effective parenting requires an authoritative style that strikes a balance between connection and separation. Consistent parental monitoring, through a cooperative relationship, predicts favorable adjustment.

■ Parents who are financially secure, not overloaded with job pressures, and content with their marriages usually find it easier to grant teenagers appropriate autonomy. When parents and adolescents have seriously troubled relationships, the difficulties usually began in childhood.

How do sibling relationships change during adolescence?

■ Sibling relationships become less intense as adolescents separate from the family and turn toward peers, but for most young people, attachment to siblings remains strong. Teenagers whose parents are warm and supportive have more positive sibling ties. Warm sibling relationships, in turn, contribute to more gratifying friendships.

Peer Relations

Describe adolescent friendships and their consequences for development.

■ During adolescence, friendship changes, moving toward greater intimacy and loyalty. Adolescent friends generally resemble one another in many ways. Although early adolescence is a period of change in friendships, teenagers' friendships are fairly stable and become more so with age.

- Girls' friendships place greater emphasis on emotional closeness, boys' on joint activities, mastery issues, and competition. Among boys without same-sex friends, other-sex friendships are linked to feelings of competence. But among girls who lack same-sex friends, other-sex friendships are associated with less positive well-being.

- Adolescents use the Internet to communicate with friends and to meet new people. Instant messaging is especially common and seems to support friendship closeness. But for some young people, online relationships pose risks of harmful social experiences, including harassment and exploitation.

- As long as they are not characterized by jealousy or aggression, adolescent friendships promote self-concept, identity, perspective taking, and the capacity for intimate relationships. They also help young people deal with stress and can foster improved attitudes toward and involvement in school.

Describe peer groups and dating relationships in adolescence.

- Adolescent peer groups are organized into **cliques**, small groups of friends with common interests, attitudes, and values. Often several cliques form a larger, more loosely organized group called a **crowd**, which grants the adolescent an identity within the larger social structure of the school.

- Although teenagers' interests and abilities affect group membership, parenting practices are also influential. Many peer-group values are extensions of values taught at home.

- Mixed-sex cliques provide a supportive context for boys and girls to get to know one another. Intimacy in dating relationships lags behind that in friendships, and early, frequent dating is linked to adjustment problems. Positive relationships with parents and friends contribute to the development of warm romantic ties, which enhance emotional and social development in older teenagers. Because of intense prejudice, initiating and maintaining visible romances is especially challenging for homosexual youths. First romances generally dissolve or become less satisfying after graduation from high school.

Discuss conformity to peer pressure in adolescence.

- Peer conformity is greater during adolescence than in either childhood or early adulthood. Young teenagers are more likely than older teenagers to give in to peer pressure for antisocial behavior. However, most peer pressure is consistent with adult values. Authoritative parenting is related to resistance to unfavorable peer pressure.

Problems of Development

Describe factors related to adolescent depression and suicide.

- Depression is the most common psychological problem of the teenage years. Various combinations of biological and environmental factors can lead to depression. Although heredity is involved, maladaptive parenting and stressful life events may trigger it. Depression is more common in girls than boys—a difference believed to be due to stressful life events and gender-typed coping styles.

- Profound depression in adolescence predicts depression in adulthood and often leads to suicidal thoughts. The suicide rate increases sharply at adolescence. Boys account for most teenage deaths by suicide, while girls make more unsuccessful suicide attempts. Teenagers at risk for suicide may be solitary and withdrawn but more often are antisocial. Again, biology and environment jointly contribute; risk factors include a highly introverted or impulsive personality, economic disadvantage, family conflict, and abuse and neglect.

Discuss factors related to delinquency.

- Delinquency rises over adolescence and then declines. Only a few teenagers are serious repeat offenders, most often boys with a childhood history of conduct problems.

- Childhood-onset antisocial behavior is linked to difficult temperament, cognitive deficits, and inept parenting—a pattern likely to result in persistent aggression, peer rejection, academic failure, association with antisocial peers, and chronic, violent delinquency. Adolescent-onset antisocial behavior typically arises from peer pressures of the teenage years. It usually subsides by young adulthood.

- Factors beyond the family and peer group contribute to delinquency. Schools that fail to meet adolescents' developmental needs and poverty-stricken neighborhoods with high crime rates and few constructive alternatives to antisocial activity promote adolescent lawbreaking. Zero-tolerance policies for misbehavior, which have become increasingly common in North American schools, do not reduce and may even heighten delinquency.

At the Threshold

Review factors that foster resilience in adolescence.

- To develop optimally, adolescents require family, school, and community contexts that foster personal strengths while reducing adversity. In addition to factors mentioned in earlier chapters, the following resources foster resilience in adolescence: a balance between family connection and separation, effective family problem solving, parental monitoring and school involvement, close friendships, high-quality vocational education, culturally sensitive schools and communities, religious affiliation, and opportunities to participate in extracurricular activities and community service.

Important Terms and Concepts

Milestones
Development in Adolescence

Early adolescence 11–14

PHYSICAL

- If a girl, reaches peak of growth spurt. (535)
- If a girl, adds more body fat than muscle. (532)
- If a girl, starts to menstruate. (535)
- If a boy, begins growth spurt. (535)
- If a boy, starts to ejaculate seminal fluid. (535–536)
- Likely is aware of sexual orientation. (551)
- If a girl, motor performance gradually increases and then levels off. (533–534)
- Synaptic growth and myelination of neural fibers accelerate, especially between the frontal lobes and other brain areas, supporting diverse cognitive skills. (537)
- Neurons in the brain become more responsive to excitatory neurotransmitters, heightening stress response and novelty-seeking. (538)
- Sleep "phase delay" strengthens. (538)

COGNITIVE

- Shows gains in hypothetico-deductive reasoning and propositional thought. (566–567)
- Improves in scientific reasoning—coordinating theory with evidence—on complex, multivariable tasks. (569–570)
- Becomes more self-conscious and self-focused. (571–572)

- Becomes more idealistic and critical. (573)
- Metacognition and self-regulation continue to improve (574)
- Evaluates vocational options in terms of interests. (583)

LANGUAGE

- Metalinguistic awareness improves further. (577)
- Vocabulary continues to increase as abstract words are added. (577–578)
- Grasps irony, sarcasm, and figurative language, such as proverbs. (577–578)
- Understanding and use of complex grammatical constructions improves further. (578)
- Capacity to adjust speech style, depending on the situation, improves. (578)

EMOTIONAL/SOCIAL

- Moodiness and parent–child conflict tend to increase. (616)
- Self-concept includes abstract descriptors, but these are often contradictory and not interconnected. (599)
- Shows gender intensification—increased gender stereotyping of attitudes and behavior. (615)
- In striving for autonomy, spends less time with parents and siblings, more time with peers. (619)

- Friendships decline in number and are based on intimacy and loyalty. (620)
- Peer groups become organized around same-sex cliques. (623)
- Cliques with similar values form crowds. (623)
- Conformity to peer pressure increases. (625)

Middle adolescence 14–16

PHYSICAL

- If a girl, completes growth spurt. (535)
- If a boy, reaches peak of growth spurt. (535)
- If a boy, voice deepens. (535)
- If a boy, adds muscle while body fat declines. (533)
- May have had sexual intercourse. (547–550)
- If a boy, motor performance improves dramatically. (533–534)

COGNITIVE

- Continues to improve in hypothetico-deductive reasoning and propositional thought. (566–567)
- Continues to improve in scientific reasoning, following a similar sequential order on different types of tasks. (569–570)
- Becomes less self-conscious and self-focused. (571–572)
- Improves in everyday decision making. (573)
- Evaluates vocational options in terms of interests, abilities, and values. (583)

■ Engages in more subtle reasoning about conflicts between moral, social-conventional, and personal-choice issues. (610–611)

■ Gender intensification declines. (615)

■ Mixed-sex cliques are common. (623)

■ Has probably started dating. (624)

■ Conformity to peer pressure may decline. (625)

LANGUAGE

■ Can read and interpret adult literary works. (578)

■ More effectively analyzes and corrects grammar. (578)

Late adolescence 16–18

PHYSICAL

■ If a boy, completes growth spurt. (535)

■ If a boy, gains in motor performance continue. (534)

EMOTIONAL/SOCIAL

■ Combines features of the self into an organized self-concept. (598)

■ Self-esteem differentiates further and tends to rise. (600)

■ In forming an identity, likely begins to change from "lower" to "higher" statuses. (600–602)

■ Is likely to engage in societal perspective taking. (608)

■ Increasingly emphasizes ideal reciprocity and societal laws as the basis for resolving moral dilemmas. (611)

EMOTIONAL/SOCIAL

■ Self-concept emphasizes personal and moral standards. (599)

■ Continues to construct an identity. (601)

■ Continues to advance in maturity of moral reasoning. (607)

■ Cliques and crowds decline in importance. (623)

■ Romantic ties last longer. (624)

COGNITIVE

■ Continues to improve in metacognition, scientific reasoning, and decision making. (537)

■ Narrows vocational options. (589)

Note: Numbers in parentheses indicate the page or pages on which each milestone is discussed.

Chapter 17

In this mural painted on a downtown San Francisco building, an emerging adult expresses a multitude of thoughts and feelings on his return from volunteer service in El Salvador. Scenes of daily life—a young woman struggling to care for her son after her husband had gone to find work in the United States, people gathered for an enjoyable meal at an outdoor restaurant, a family out for a relaxed stroll—coexist with images of horror that recall the bloody civil war that raged in the 1980s. In the mountains and rivers and on the walls are depictions of massacres and lost loved ones, each inspired by a real story that a Salvadoran related to the artist.

Reprinted with permission from Joel Bergner

"A Past That Still Lives"
Joel Bergner
25 years, United States

Emerging Adulthood

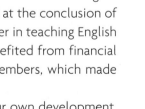

emerging adulthood A new period of development, extending from the late teens to the twenties, during which young people have left adolescence but have not yet assumed the enduring responsibilities of adults.

Recently, David and Peter—my two grown sons—asked me how old I was when I got married, knew what I wanted to do for a career, and earnestly began to prepare for my life's work. To their surprise, I responded that I had attained all of these widely accepted markers of adulthood by age 22—and that nearly all my friends of several decades ago had done so as well.

My sons' experiences were vastly different. Throughout college and for several years beyond, they explored possibilities. David, for example, completed a bachelor's degree in chemistry and pursued a master's degree in public health. Then he made another about-face. After volunteering for several months in an elementary school, at age 24 he returned to graduate school to become a teacher. Peter also vacillated after college about a vocational direction. Following a "year off" that included an internship, he settled on law school. Both young men deferred romance while they launched their work lives.

Similarly, few of David's and Peter's friends made lasting career or romantic commitments in their late teens and early twenties. To the contrary, their experimentation became more varied and deliberate. After graduating from college, one traveled the world for eight months, explaining that she wanted "to experience as much as possible." Another accepted a Peace Corps assignment in a remote region of Peru, forged a romance with a Peruvian man that she ended at the conclusion of her tour of duty, then returned to school to prepare for a career in teaching English to newly arrived immigrants. Each of these young people benefited from financial and other forms of support from parents and other family members, which made possible their extended explorations.

TAKE A MOMENT... Think, for a moment, about your own development. Do you consider yourself to have reached adulthood? When a large sample of North American 18- to 25-year-olds was asked this question, the majority gave an ambiguous answer: "yes and no" (see Figure 17.1 on page 642). Only after reaching their late twenties and early thirties did most feel that they were truly adult (Arnett, 1997, 2001, 2003). The life pursuits and subjective judgments of many contemporary youths indicate that the transition to adult roles has become so delayed and prolonged that it has spawned a new transitional period, extending from the late teens to the mid-twenties, called **emerging adulthood.**

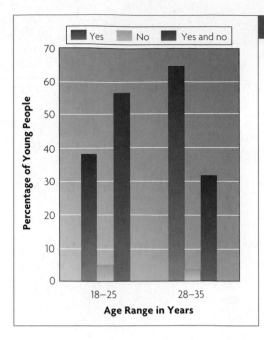

FIGURE 17.1

North American young people's responses to the question, "Do you feel that you have reached adulthood?" Between ages 18 and 25, the majority answered "yes and no," reflecting their view that they had left adolescence but were not yet fully adult. Even in their late twenties and early thirties, about one-third of young people judged that they had not completed the transition to adulthood. (Adapted from Arnett, 2001.)

Emerging adults have left adolescence but are still some distance from taking on adult responsibilities. Rather, young people who have the economic resources to do so explore alternatives in education, work, personal values, and love more intensely than they did as teenagers (Arnett, 2006). Many are working on advanced degrees and credentials—accumulating experiences and mastering practical skills so that they can land a personally and financially rewarding job in an ever-more-complex labor market. Those who are less economically privileged, however, often struggle to acquire the skills needed for a job that will provide a decent standard of living for the family they desire—or may have already begun (see the discussion of non-college-bound youths on pages 591–593 in Chapter 15).

A Period of Unprecedented Exploration

Emerging adulthood is a time of great challenge and uncertainty. During this period, many young people make frequent changes in educational paths, jobs, and love partners. Adult milestones—finishing school, living on one's own, launching a career, and building a lasting intimate partnership—are highly diverse in timing and order across individuals (Cohen et al., 2003). Consequently, it is harder to make general statements about development during emerging adulthood than for any other period.

Today, more college students than in past generations draw out their education, pursuing it in a nonlinear way. Only about half of U.S. and one-third of Canadian young people who enroll in higher education have earned their bachelor's degree by age 25. Some take a few courses while working part-time. Others leave school temporarily to work full-time or travel. Most change their majors several times as they try out career options. After graduation, about one-third enter graduate school, taking even more years to settle into their desired career track (Statistics Canada, 2003e; U.S. Department of Education, 2006b).

Young people are postponing marriage, as well. In 1950, the average age of first marriage was about 20 for women and 23 for men. Currently, the comparable ages are 25 and 27 in the United States and 28 and 30 in Canada (Statistics Canada, 2007; U.S. Census Bureau, 2007b). Similar delays have occurred in other industrialized nations, allowing for a longer period of experimentation with sexuality and intimacy. A half-century ago, North Americans viewed marriage and parenthood as crucial markers of adult status. Today, the majority view these milestones as personal choices and endorse the people's right to alternative lifestyles (Furstenberg et al., 2004).

Together, extended education, delayed career entry, and later marriage lead to great residential instability. North American 18- to 25-year-olds are "on the move," more than at any other time of life. About one-third move in and out of residence halls, fraternity and sorority houses, and apartments during college. And more than half move in with a romantic partner, choosing *cohabitation* as their preferred way of entering into a committed intimate partnership (Le Bourdais & Lapierre-Adamcyk, 2004; U.S. Census Bureau, 2007b).

Furthermore, nearly half of 18- to 25-year-olds return to their parents' home for brief periods after first leaving (Goldscheider & Goldscheider, 1999). Usually, role transitions, such as the end of college, bring young people back. For others, tight job markets, high housing

The U.S. couple of the 1950s on the left were married in their early twenties and became parents soon after. Today, young people in industrialized nations often postpone marriage and parenthood to pursue higher education and explore life options. A recent college graduate, the emerging adult on the right has set aside two years to serve as a Peace Corps volunteer in a Guatemalan village and to travel.

costs, or failures in work or love prompt a temporary return home. As they encounter unexpected twists and turns on the road to adulthood, the parental home serves as a safety net and base of operations for launching adult life.

Economically well-off emerging adults are more likely to live independently than those from lower-SES and ethnic minority families. Among African-American, Hispanic, Native-American, and Canadian-Aboriginal groups, poverty and a cultural tradition of extended family living lead to lower rates of leaving home, even among young people who are in college or working (Fussell & Furstenberg, 2005). Unmarried Asian emerging adults also tend to live with their parents. But the longer Asian families have lived in North America, where they are exposed to individualistic values, the more likely young people are to move out earlier, following the pattern of their Caucasian agemates. These emerging adults, however, usually remain financially dependent on parents (Goldscheider & Goldscheider, 1999; Lindsay, Almey, & Normand, 2002). Indeed, without parents' economic support, including coresidence, few emerging adults would be able to advance their education, explore career possibilities, or regroup when they encounter difficulties (Aquilino, 2006).

In Chapter 16, we noted that college students make more progress than high school students in shaping their identities (see page 602). Notice how emerging adulthood greatly prolongs identity development. And changes in reasoning capacity permit emerging adults to revise, and sometimes replace, their political and religious perspectives (Arnett, 2000a). Then they modify these philosophies further as they continue their explorations. What explains the recent appearance of this rich, complex bridge between adolescence and assumption of adult responsibilities? Rapid cultural change seems to be the answer: Research suggests that emerging adulthood is a *cultural construction*.

Cultural Change and Emerging Adulthood

As the economies of industrialized nations have become more technical and information based, the amount of education required to enter complex, well-paid careers has increased. In response, young people of the twenty-first century are pursuing higher education in record numbers. In 1950, only 14 percent of North Americans enrolled in colleges and universities in the first year after graduating from high school; today, about two-thirds do so. And nearly half

In developing countries, most young people do not experience emerging adulthood. This Qeqci Indian couple in Peten, Guatemala, have not yet reached age 20. Yet they are already married, with two children. They have entered fully into adult roles.

of the U.S. and Canadian early-twenties population attends an educational institution full-time (ACT, 2006; Service Canada, 2005). This massive expansion of higher education has delayed financial independence and career commitment—trends that grant far more time for exploring options.

Dramatic gains in life expectancy in prosperous nations have also contributed to emerging adulthood. A North American born in 1900 could expect to live to age 50. By 1950, life expectancy had increased to age 68. Today, it is 78 in the United States and 80 in Canada (Statistics Canada, 2006c; U.S. Census Bureau, 2007b). Nations with abundant wealth and longer-living populations have no pressing need for young people's labor, freeing 18- to 25-year-olds for the extended moratorium of emerging adulthood (Arnett, 2000a).

Recall from Chapter 14 that all societies, no matter how simple, have at least a brief period of adolescence. In contrast, emerging adulthood is limited to cultures that postpone entry into adult roles until the twenties. In developing countries such as China and India, only a privileged few—usually those admitted to universities—experience emerging adulthood. Moreover, the overwhelming majority of young people in traditional, non-Western countries—those who have few economic resources or who remain in the rural regions where they grew up—do not experience emerging adulthood. With limited education, they typically enter marriage, parenthood, and lifelong work early. In India, for example, only 60 percent of boys and 40 percent of girls complete elementary school; in Kenya, the figures are 34 and 30 percent, respectively; in Guatemala, 41 and 38 percent (UNICEF, 2007).

In industrialized nations, where a great many young people benefit from this transitional period, they nevertheless vary in their beliefs about what it means to become an adult. Reflecting the self-searching of these years, most emphasize psychological qualities, especially self-sufficiency—accepting responsibility for one's actions, deciding on personal beliefs and values, establishing an equal relationship with parents, and becoming financially independent. Youths from collectivist minority groups also attach great importance to becoming more considerate of others, to attaining certain roles, and to self-control.

For example, African-American and Hispanic young people point to supporting and caring for a family as a major marker of adulthood (Arnett, 2003). Mormon youths believe that becoming less self-oriented and conducting oneself responsibly are as important as self-sufficiency, and they rate family commitments a close second (Nelson, 2003). And in a survey of Canadian-Aboriginal college students, "avoiding drunk driving" ranked high, sparked by awareness that alcohol abuse is a widespread response to poverty and discrimination in Native-Canadian communities. Also, Aboriginal students who identified strongly with their cultural heritage regarded "good control over emotions" and "capable of supporting parents financially" as more important than did those with less cultural identification. And both groups of Aboriginal students placed greater weight on financial self-sufficiency and on interdependent qualities (such as making lifelong commitments to others) than did Canadian white students (Cheah & Nelson, 2004).

Nevertheless, for the many low-SES young people in Western nations who are burdened by early parenthood, do not finish high school, are otherwise academically unprepared for college, or do not have access to vocational training, emerging adulthood is limited or nonexistent (see Chapters 14 and 15). Instead of excitement and personal expansion, these youths encounter a "floundering period" during which they alternate between unemployment and dead-end, low-paying jobs (Cohen et al., 2003; Eccles et al., 2003).

Still, some theorists predict that emerging adulthood will become increasingly common as *globalization*—the exchange of ideas, information, trade, and immigration among nations—accelerates. Contact between industrialized and developing countries fosters economic progress. It also heightens awareness of events, lifestyles, and practices in faraway places. As globalization proceeds, gains in financial security and higher education and the formation of a common "global identity" among young people may lead to the spread of emerging adulthood (Arnett, 2002; Saraswathi & Larson, 2002). Eventually, this period may become a typical experience on the path to adult life around the world.

Development in Emerging Adulthood

A wide array of demanding experiences and tasks await emerging adults. To make a successful transition to adulthood, they must acquire a wealth of new knowledge and skills.

Cognitive Changes

Piaget (1967) acknowledged the possibility that important advances in thinking follow the attainment of formal operations. He observed that adolescents prefer an idealistic, internally consistent perspective on the world to one that is vague, contradictory, and adapted to particular circumstances (see page 573 in Chapter 15). Researchers who study **postformal thought**—cognitive development beyond Piaget's formal operational stage—have shown that college students make impressive strides in cognition. This is not surprising, since college serves as a "developmental testing ground," a time when full attention can be devoted to exploring alternative roles, values, and behaviors. To facilitate exploration, college exposes students to a form of culture shock—encounters with new ideas and beliefs, new freedoms and opportunities, and new academic and social demands. These social experiences combine with personal effort to spark increasingly rational, flexible, and practical ways of thinking that accept uncertainties and vary across situations.

DEVELOPMENT OF EPISTEMIC COGNITION ■ The work of William Perry (1981, 1970/1988) provided the starting point for an expanding research literature on the development of *epistemic cognition. Epistemic* means "of or about knowledge," and **epistemic cognition** refers to our reflections on how we arrived at facts, beliefs, and ideas. When mature, rational thinkers reach conclusions that differ from those of others, they consider the justifiability of these conclusions. When they cannot justify their approach, they revise it, seeking a more balanced, adequate route to acquiring knowledge.

Perry wondered why students respond in dramatically different ways to the diversity of ideas they encounter in college. To find out, he interviewed Harvard University undergraduates at the end of each of their four years, asking "what stood out" during the previous year. Responses indicated that students' reflections on knowing changed as they experienced the complexities of university life and moved closer to adult roles—findings confirmed in many subsequent studies (King & Kitchener, 1994; Magolda, 2002; Moore, 2002).

Younger students regarded knowledge as made up of separate units (beliefs and propositions), whose truth can be determined by comparing them to objective standards—standards that exist apart from the thinking person and his or her situation. As a result, they engaged in **dualistic thinking,** dividing information, values, and authority into right and wrong, good and bad, we and they. As one college freshman put it, "When I went to my first lecture, what the man said was just like God's word. I believe everything he said because he is a professor ... and this is a respected person" (Perry, 1981, p. 81). When asked, "If two people disagree on the interpretation of a poem, how would you decide which one is right?" a sophomore replied, "You'd have to ask the poet. It's his poem" (Clinchy, 2002, p. 67).

Older students, in contrast, had moved toward **relativistic thinking,** viewing all knowledge as embedded in a framework of thought. Aware of a diversity of opinions on many topics, they abandoned the possibility of absolute truth in favor of multiple truths, each relative to its context. As a result, their thinking became more flexible and tolerant. As one college senior put it, "Just seeing how [famous philosophers] fell short of an all-encompassing answer, [you realize] that ideas are really individualized. And you begin to have respect for how great their thought could be, without its being absolute" (Perry, 1970/1998, p. 90). Relativistic thinking leads to the realization that one's own beliefs are often subjective, since several frameworks may satisfy the criterion of internal logical consistency (Moore, 2002; Sinnott, 2003). Thus, the relativistic thinker is acutely aware that each person, in arriving at a position, creates her own "truth."

Eventually, the most mature individuals progress to **commitment within relativistic thinking.** Instead of choosing between opposing views, they try to formulate a more satisfying

postformal thought
Development beyond Piaget's formal operational stage.

epistemic cognition
Reflections on how one arrived at facts, beliefs, and ideas.

dualistic thinking The view that knowledge is made up of separate beliefs and propositions, whose truth can be determined by comparing them with objective standards.

relativistic thinking The view that knowledge is embedded in a framework of thought and that multiple truths can exist, each *relative* to its context.

commitment within relativistic thinking The mature individual's formulation of a perspective that synthesizes contradictions between opposing views, rather than choosing between them.

When college students challenge one another's reasoning while tackling realistic, ambiguous problems, they are likely to gain in epistemic cognition. Peer discussion of alternatives encourages reflection on one's own thinking, evaluation of competing ideas and strategies, and coordination of opposing perspectives into a new, more effective structure.

perspective that synthesizes contradictions. When considering which of two theories studied in a college course is better or which of several movies most deserves an Oscar, the individual moves beyond the stance that everything is a matter of opinion and generates rational criteria against which options can be evaluated (Moshman, 2003, 2005). Few college students reach this extension of relativism. Those who do generally display a more sophisticated approach to learning, in which they actively seek differing perspectives to advance their knowledge and understanding. Attainment of commitment within relativism occurs more often among young people who pursue advanced graduate education (King & Kitchener, 2002).

IMPORTANCE OF PEER INTERACTION AND REFLECTION ■ Advances in epistemic cognition depend on further gains in metacognition, which are likely to occur in situations that challenge young people's perspectives and induce them to consider the rationality of their thought processes (Moshman, 2005). In a study of the college learning experiences of seniors scoring low and high in epistemic cognition, high-scoring students frequently reported activities that encouraged them to struggle with realistic but ambiguous problems in a supportive environment, in which faculty offered encouragement and guidance. For example, an engineering major, describing an airplane-design project that required advanced epistemic cognition, noted his discovery that "you can design 30 different airplanes and each one's going to have its benefits and there's going to be problems with each one" (Marra & Palmer, 2004, p. 116). Low-scoring students rarely mentioned such experiences.

When students tackle challenging, ill-structured problems, interaction among individuals who are roughly equal in knowledge and authority is beneficial because it prevents acceptance of another's reasoning simply because of greater power or expertise. When college students were asked to devise the most effective solution to a difficult logical problem, only 3 out of 32 students (9 percent) in a "work-alone" condition succeeded. But in an "interactive" condition, 15 out of 20 small groups (75 percent) arrived at the best answer following extensive discussion (Moshman & Geil, 1998). Whereas few students working alone reflected on their solution strategies, most groups engaged in a process of "collective rationality" in which members challenged one another to justify their reasoning and collaborated in working out the most effective strategy. Of course, reflection on one's own thinking can also occur individually. But peer interaction fosters the necessary type of individual reflection: arguing with oneself over competing ideas and strategies and coordinating opposing perspectives into a new, more effective structure. **TAKE A MOMENT...** Return to page 469 in Chapter 12 to review how peer collaboration fosters cognitive development in childhood. It remains a highly effective basis for education in emerging adulthood.

Emotional and Social Changes

During college, students' attitudes and values broaden. They express increased interest in literature, the performing arts, and philosophical and historical issues and greater tolerance for ethnic and cultural diversity. And as noted in Chapter 16, college leaves its mark on moral reasoning by fostering greater concern with individual rights and human welfare, sometimes expressed in political activism. Furthermore, exposure to multiple viewpoints encourages young people to look more closely at themselves. As a result, they develop a more complex self-concept that includes awareness of their own changing traits and values over time, along with enhanced self-esteem (Labouvie-Vief, 2006; Montgomery & Côté, 2003; Pascarella & Terenzini, 1991). Together, these developments contribute to advances in identity development.

In emerging adulthood, young people refine their approach to constructing an identity. Besides exploring *in breadth* (weighing multiple possibilities), they also explore *in depth*—

evaluating existing commitments (Luyckx et al., 2006). For example, if you have not yet selected your major, you may be taking classes in a broad array of disciplines. Once you choose a major, you are likely to embark on an in-depth evaluation of your choice—reflecting on your interest, motivation, and performance and on your career prospects as you take additional classes in that field. Depending on the outcome of your evaluation, either your commitment to your major strengthens, or you return to a broad exploration of options.

In a longitudinal study extending over first two years of college, most students cycled between making commitments and evaluating commitments in various identity domains. Fluctuations in students' certainty about their commitments sparked movement between these two states (Luyckx, Goossens, & Soenens, 2006). **TAKE A MOMENT...** Think about your own identity progress. Does it fit this *dual-cycle model,* in which identity formation is a lengthy process of feedback loops? Notice how the model helps explain the movement between identity statuses displayed by many young people, described in Chapter 16. Emerging adults who move toward exploration in depth and certainty of commitment are higher in self-esteem and in academic and social adjustment. Those who spend much time exploring in breadth without making commitments tend to be poorly adjusted—depressed and higher in drug use (Luyckx et al., 2006).

Many aspects of the life course that were once socially structured—marriage, parenthood, religious beliefs, career paths—are increasingly left to individuals to decide on their own. As a result, emerging adults are required to "individualize" their identities—a process that requires a sense of self-efficacy, purpose, confidence in overcoming obstacles and responsibility for outcomes (Côté & Schwartz, 2002). Among emerging adults of diverse ethnicities and SES levels, this set of qualities, termed *personal agency,* is positively related to an information-gathering cognitive style, identity exploration, and commitment and negatively related to a diffuse-avoidant cognitive style and identity diffusion (Schwartz, Côté, & Arnett, 2005). Now let's turn to development in three main identity domains of this period: love, work, and worldviews.

By exposing young people to multiple viewpoints, attending college encourages them to reflect on their traits and values and to develop a more complex self concept. This student listens attentively at a campus demonstration highlighting concerns about global warming.

LOVE ■ Return to Chapter 1, pages 14–16, to review the description of Erikson's psychosocial theory, which identifies *intimacy* as a major task of these years. The increasing closeness of dating relationships in late adolescence extends further in emerging adulthood. With age, emerging adults' romantic ties last longer and involve greater trust, support, emotional closeness, and commitment. Frequently, they lead to cohabitation (Collins & van Dulmen, 2006; Montgomery, 2005). Also, conceptions of close relationships become more complex, expressing a wider array of desired qualities and responses from others and from the self—a trend that reflects both a more differentiated self-concept and increased experience with close peer bonds (Waldinger et al., 2002). One emerging adult described this change: "Now you know what it means to support your partner, to be with him, to understand him. Today it is deeper, we discuss matters, we negotiate" (Shulman & Kipnis, 2001, p. 342). Whereas the adolescent asks, "With whom would I like to spend time now?" many emerging adults address a more serious question: "Whom do I want as a partner in life?" (Arnett, 2000a).

Emerging adults take their time about forging a committed relationship; many say they don't feel ready to make this choice and want to experience a variety of personal relationships before settling on one (Arnett, 2004). At the end of high school, about half of North American young people are sexually active, but by age 25 nearly all have become so, and the gender and SES differences in sexual activity that were apparent in adolescence (see pages 549–550 in Chapter 14) have diminished. Although emerging adults have more sexual partners and engage in casual sex more often than adults over age 25, about 60 percent have had only one partner in the previous year (Lefkowitz & Gillen, 2006).

Finding a lifelong intimate partner is a major milestone, with profound consequences for psychological well-being. On average, married couples are physically and mentally healthier, are financially better-off, and have more frequent and satisfying sex than their single counterparts—including single emerging adults (Lansford et al., 2005; Marks, Bumpass, & Jun, 2004). Two

Romantic ties in emerging adulthood last longer than those in adolescence and involve a deeper sense of emotional closeness. Still, many emerging adults say they don't feel ready to settle on a life partner.

interrelated factors increase the chances that an intimate bond forged in emerging adulthood will be mutually satisfying and last a lifetime: partner similarity and good communication.

Partner Similarity Young people who establish happy, lasting intimate relationships rarely meet at bars or through personal ads. Instead, they meet in conventional ways: Family members or friends introduce them, or they get to know each other at work, school, or social events where people similar to themselves congregate (Laumann et al., 1994). Sustaining an intimate tie is easier when couples share interests and values and when people they know approve of the match. Over the past decade, Internet dating services have become an increasingly popular and widely accepted way to initiate relationships. Although success rates are lower than with conventional strategies, adults who form an online relationship and then meet face-to-face often go on to see each other again, with 18 percent of such ties lasting for more than a year (Gavin, Scott, & Duffield, 2005).

Contrary to the popular belief that "opposites attract," lovers tend to resemble each other—in attitudes, personality, intelligence, educational plans, physical attractiveness, ethnicity, and (to a lesser extent) religion. The more alike two people are, the more satisfied they tend to be with their relationship, and the more likely they are to stay together (Blackwell & Lichter, 2004; Caspi & Herbener, 1990; Lucas et al., 2004).

Good Communication. Lasting romantic relationships are based on good communication. Couples who sustain warm, tender expressions of intimacy and who decide to stay together, despite difficult moments, are more likely to express increased happiness over time. An important feature of their commitment is constructive conflict resolution—directly expressing wishes and needs, listening patiently, asking for clarification, compromising, accepting responsibility, and avoiding the escalation of negative emotion sparked by criticism, contempt, and defensiveness (Gottman et al., 1998; Schneewind & Gerhard, 2002).

As with best friendships and dating partners in adolescence (see page 624 in Chapter 16), a secure *internal working model* of attachment relationships fosters gratifying intimate ties in emerging adulthood. Young people who recall their attachment experiences with parents as warm and supportive tend to describe both their friendships and their romantic partnerships as trusting and happy (Cassidy, 2001; Collins & van Dulmen, 2006). Their behaviors toward their partner are more supportive and their conflict resolution strategies more constructive than those of young people who describe their attachment histories as insecure. They are also more at ease in turning to their partner for comfort and assistance and report mutually initiated, enjoyable sexual activity (Creasey, 2002; Creasey & Ladd, 2004; Roisman et al., 2001)

However, memories of early attachments are only one of several influences on the quality of emerging adults' romantic relationships. Characteristics of the partner and current life conditions also make a difference. When one partner feels secure and behaves considerately, the other is likely to respond in kind (Cook, 2000). And young people who are content with progress in other aspects of their lives probably approach their love relationships with a more positive, relaxed state of mind.

Finally, although half of American and Canadian young couples cohabit, their relationships are more likely to break up within two years than those of Western European cohabiters (Brown, 2000; Kiernan, 2001). In the Netherlands, Norway, and Sweden, cohabitation is thoroughly integrated into society. Between 70 and 90 percent of young people live together before marriage, and cohabiting couples are nearly as committed to each other as married people (Fussell & Gauthier, 2005; Ramsøy, 1994). In North America, societal attitudes toward cohabitation, though more tolerant than in the past, are not as positive as in Western Europe. Consequently, North American emerging adults who cohabit prior to engagement tend to have less conventional values. They have had more sexual partners and are more politically liberal, less religious, and more androgynous. In addition, a larger number have parents who divorced (Axinn & Barber, 1997). Perhaps the nature of North American cohabiting relationships—

more open-ended than in Western Europe—reduces motivation to develop effective conflict-resolution skills. Consequently, these unions often dissolve when problems arise.

WORK ■ Recall from Chapter 15 that North American teenagers rarely have access to meaningful paid work activities. Most view their part-time work merely as a way to obtain spending money. In emerging adulthood, work experiences increasingly focus on preparation for adult work roles. Young people eagerly seek apprenticeships with experts and internships in companies and community agencies to resolve vocational identity issues. They ask, What kind of work am I good at, and what will I find personally rewarding? Their selection of college courses also addresses these questions. They try out various possibilities, often changing majors several times. And graduate school permits them to switch directions again.

Conducting in-depth interviews, Daniel Levinson (1978, 1996) asked middle-aged men and women to describe the challenges they had encountered in making the transition from adolescence to adulthood. Most reported that between ages 18 and 22, they constructed a *dream,* an image of themselves in the adult world that guided their decision making. For men, the dream usually emphasized an independent achiever in a career role. In contrast, most career-oriented women displayed "split dreams," in which both marriage and career were prominent.

To help realize their dream, young people generally formed a relationship with a *mentor*—a person several years older who was experienced in the career the young person wanted to enter. Most of the time, professors and senior colleagues filled this role. Occasionally, knowledgeable friends or relatives provided mentoring. Mentors sometimes acted as teachers who enhanced the person's career-related skills. At other times, they served as guides who acquainted the person with the values and customs of the work setting.

Gender. Identity achievement in the vocational realm is more challenging for women than for men. During college, women's career ambitions often decline, partly because of unresolved questions about their abilities and partly because of concerns about combining work with parenthood. Low self-efficacy on the part of many college women about succeeding in male-dominated fields further limits their occupational choices. Research indicates that many mathematically talented college women settle on nonscience majors. And those who remain in the sciences are more likely than their male counterparts to choose medicine or other health professions rather than engineering, math, or physical science (Benbow et al., 2000; Wigfield et al., 2002, 2006).

Women who do pursue male-dominated careers usually have "masculine traits"—high achievement orientation, self-reliance, and a belief that their efforts will result in success (Petersen & Gonzales, 1999). But even those with high self-efficacy are less certain than their male counterparts that they can overcome barriers to career success (Lindley, 2005). Because men dominate these latter fields, women are less available to serve as mentors. Although mentor support is similar in same-sex and other-sex mentoring relationships, women with female mentors tend to be more successful (Goldstein, 1979; O'Neill, Horton, & Crosby, 1999). Perhaps female mentors are more likely to be perceived as role models and to provide guidance on the unique educational and workplace challenges that women encounter.

Despite obstacles to success, most young women prefer to blend work and family. They seem to realize that a rewarding career will bring higher levels of life satisfaction—an outcome confirmed by research (Burke, 2001). Those who continue to achieve usually have four experiences in common:

- A college environment that values the accomplishments of women and that addresses women's historical and current experiences in its curriculum
- Frequent interaction with faculty and professionals in their chosen fields

During college, many women begin to doubt their ability to compete in male-dominated fields. Others become concerned about combining work with child rearing. Those who continue to achieve often have mentors, especially accomplished women who serve as role models and guides to overcoming educational and workplace challenges.

■ The opportunity to test their abilities in supportive extracurricular, internship, and work environments

■ Models of accomplished women who have successfully dealt with family–career role conflict (Pascarella et al., 1997; Swanson & Fouad, 1999)

Ethnic Minorities. Ethnic minority young people from low-SES families also arrive at emerging adulthood with past experiences that compromise their self-confidence and academic preparedness for college and career success (see, for example, Chapter 15, pages 583–585). Consequently, they are at increased risk of dropping out of college, with most dropouts leaving during the first year and many within the first six weeks (ACT, 2005; Montgomery & Côté, 2003). Reflecting this trend, the U.S. graduation rate for African Americans is 43 percent, compared with 63 percent for white students (U.S. Department of Education, 2006b). These young people have few alternatives to college as a means of successful entry into the workforce. As a result, they often end up in low-paid jobs or unemployed, with seriously compromised long-term work and earning prospects.

Preparing young people in childhood and adolescence with the necessary visions and skills can do much to improve college success. In a study that followed nearly 700 young people from sixth grade until two years after high school graduation, a set of factors—grade point average, academic self-concept, persistence in the face of challenge, parental SES and valuing of a college education, and the individual's plans to attend college—predicted college attendance at age 20 (Eccles, Vida, & Barber, 2004). Although parental SES is difficult to modify, improving parents' attitudes and behaviors and students' academic motivation and educational aspirations is within reach, through a wide array of strategies considered in Chapters 15 and 16.

Once emerging adults enroll in college, reaching out to them is crucial, especially in the early weeks and throughout the first year. Colleges that do little to help high-risk students, through developmental courses and other support services, have a higher percentage of dropouts (Moxley, Najor-Durack, & Dumbrigue, 2001). Programs that forge bonds between teachers and students and that provide academic support, part-time work opportunities, and meaningful extracurricular roles increase retention. Membership in campus-based social and religious organizations is especially helpful in strengthening minority students' sense of belonging (Fashola & Slavin, 1998). Young people who feel that they have entered a college community that is concerned about them as individuals are far more likely to graduate.

Despite laws guaranteeing equality of opportunity, racial bias in career opportunities remains strong, even for college graduates. In one study, researchers responded to more than 1,300 help-wanted newspaper ads with fictitious résumés, some containing higher qualifications and some lower qualifications. Half the résumés were assigned a white-sounding name ("Emily Walsh," "Brendan Baker") and half a black-sounding name ("Lakisha Washington," "Jamal Jones"). At all job levels, résumés with "white" names evoked 50 percent more callbacks than those with "black" names. And although whites with high-quality résumés received substantially more callbacks than those with low-quality résumés, having a high-quality résumé made little difference for blacks (see Figure 17.2). As the researchers noted, "Discrimination appears to bite twice, making it harder for African Americans to find a job and to improve their employability" (Bertrand & Mullainathan, 2004, p. 4).

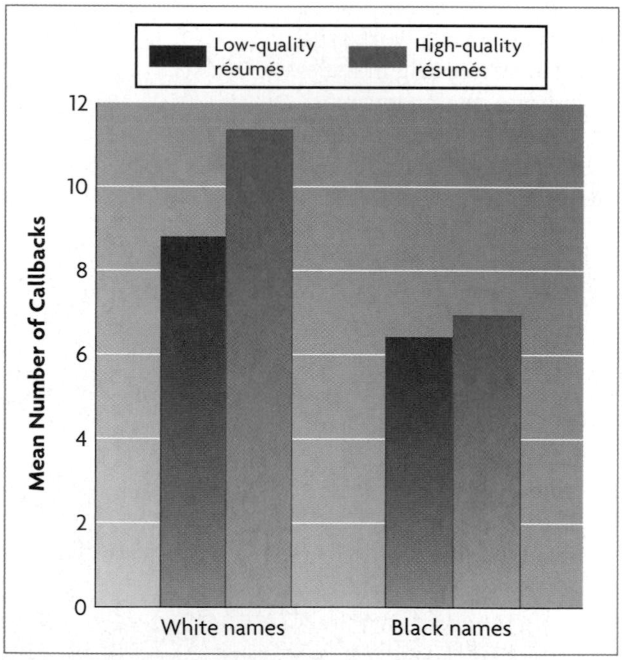

FIGURE 17.2

Relationship of ethnicity of job applicant's name to employer callbacks. Researchers responded to help-wanted newspaper ads with fictitious résumés, some having white-sounding names and others black-sound names. Résumés with "white" names evoked many more callbacks than résumés with "black" names. When résumés were high in quality, callbacks to whites increased, but those to blacks showed little change. (Adapted from Bertrand & Mullainathan, 2004.)

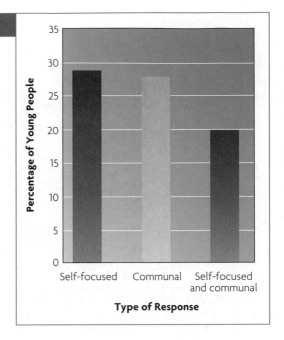

FIGURE 17.3

North American young people's responses to the question, What values do you think are most important to pass on to the next generation? Although nearly one-third of this sample of 20- to 29-year-olds gave self-focused responses, just as many emphasized communal values, or commitments and responsibilities to others. And a substantial number combined the two sets of values. Most young people do not construct a one-sided, egoistic worldview, as older adults often believe. (Adapted from Arnett, Ramos, & Jensen, 2001.)

Ethnic minority women must surmount combined gender and racial discrimination to realize their career potential. Those who succeed often develop an unusually high sense of self-efficacy, attacking problems head-on despite repeated obstacles to achievement (Byars & Hackett, 1998). In interviews with African-American women who had become leaders in diverse fields, all reported intense persistence, fueled by supportive relationships with other women, including teachers and peers. And many described their mothers as inspiring role models who had set high standards for them. Others mentioned support from their African-American communities, stating that a deep sense of connection to their people had empowered them (Richie et al., 1997).

WORLDVIEWS ■ Emerging adults say that constructing a *worldview,* or set of beliefs and values to live by, is essential for attaining adult status—even more important than finishing their education and settling into a career and marriage (Arnett, 1997, 1998, 2001). Do today's young people forge worldviews that focus on concern for the self—as older adults who speak of the "me generation" believe they do?

To answer this question, researchers asked a mostly Caucasian sample of North Americans in their twenties, "What values do you think are most important to pass on to the next generation?" As Figure 17.3 shows, many did give self-focused responses, referring to the importance of positive self-esteem, independence, and living life to the fullest—central concerns of this period. But an equal number emphasized communal values, or commitments and responsibilities to others. And almost as many combined self and communal concerns (Arnett, Ramos, & Jensen, 2001).

Civic and Political Commitments. Other evidence supports the view that many emerging adults want to improve their communities, nation, and world. Compared to older people, they are more likely to be involved in organizations devoted to specific issues of concern to them, such as protecting the environment, combating racial and gender discrimination, and eradicating poverty. And in a national survey of U.S. college students, 30 percent reported engaging in some form of volunteer work—a rate twice as great as that of young people not enrolled in higher education (Dote et al., 2006).

But compared with previous generations, far fewer American, Canadian, and Western European young people vote or engage in political party activities, such as campaigning for candidates (Flanagan et al., 1999; U.S. Census Bureau, 2007b). Many seem to have lost faith in the conventional political process, perhaps because they see it as having made little progress on social problems that concern them.

Religion and Spirituality. During the late teens and early twenties, attendance at religious services drops to its lowest level throughout the lifespan, as departure from home reduces parental pressure to attend and as young people continue to question the beliefs they acquired in their families (Lefkowitz, 2005). Still, about 30 percent of American and 25 percent of Canadian emerging adults sustain regular, formal religious activities (Bibby, 2000; Jones, 2003; Kerestes & Youniss, 2003). But whether or not they are involved in organized religion, many young

These young adults participate in a church-sponsored service mission, building homes for poverty-stricken rural families. Through religious involvement, emerging adults encounter frequent reminders of social injustices and the importance of community service.

people begin to construct their own individualized faith, often by weaving together beliefs and practices from a variety of sources, including Eastern and Western religious traditions, science, and popular culture. Often they struggle to reconcile religious or spiritual beliefs with scientific principles (Shipman et al., 2002). One emerging adult who grew up as a devout Catholic described his up-and-coming belief system:

. . . all these religions, Mohammed and Buddha and Jesus, all the patterns there are very similar. . . . And I believe that there's a spirit, an energy. Not necessarily a guy or something like that, but maybe just a power force. Like in *Star Wars*—the Force. . . that makes it possible to live. (Arnett & Jensen, 2002, p. 460)

Emerging adults who feel securely attached to their parents and who view them as having used an authoritative child-rearing style are more likely to hold religious or spiritual beliefs similar to those of their parents (Okagaki, Hammond, & Seamon, 1999). The warmth, explanations, and autonomy-granting of authoritative parenting seem to provide young people with a fuller understanding of their parents' religious ideology, as well as with greater freedom to evaluate it against alternatives. Consequently, they are more likely to integrate their parents' perspectives into their own worldview.

As with adolescents, emerging adults who view religion as important in their lives engage in more community service. Religion seems to serve as a reminder of social injustices and the importance of helping others in need. Also, as emerging adults seek their place in an increasingly complex, ever-changing world, religion helps anchor them. It offers a link between the past and the present, a transcendent system through which they can view stressful, confusing events, and an image of an ideal future toward which they can strive (Kerestes & Youniss, 2003).

Some young people think that their agemates who are religious are compliant and narrow-minded, but this is inaccurate. Rather, most are energetic, self-reliant individuals for whom religion is part of a broader approach to life (Youniss, McLellan, & Yates, 1999).

Risk and Resilience in Emerging Adulthood

In grappling with momentous choices, emerging adults play a more active role in their own development than at any earlier time. They must choose and coordinate demanding life roles and refine the skills necessary to succeed in those roles (Arnett, 2006; Eccles et al., 2003). As they experiment, they often encounter disappointments in love and work that require them to adjust, and sometimes radically change, their life path.

Emerging adults' vigorous explorations also extend earlier risks, including unprotected sexual activity, substance use, and hazardous driving behavior. And certain risks increase. For example, drug taking peaks between ages 19 and 22. Eager to try a wide range of experiences before settling down to the responsibilities of adulthood, young people of this age are more likely than younger or older individuals to smoke cigarettes, chew tobacco, engage in binge drinking, and experiment with prescription and illegal drugs, at times with tragic consequences (U.S. Department of Health and Human Services, 2006).

Living on their own and making frequent moves, 18- to 24-year-olds spend more time by themselves than any other age group younger than 40. Consequently, feelings of loneliness peak during the late teens and early twenties (see Figure 17.4). As they move through school and employment settings, emerging adults must constantly separate from friends and develop new relationships (Rokach, 2001). Extreme loneliness is associated with self-defeating attitudes and behavior, including low self-esteem and socially withdrawn and insensitive behaviors (Brehm, 2002; Jones, 1990). But as long as loneliness is not overwhelming, it can motivate young people to reach out to others. It can also encourage them to find ways to be comfortably alone and to use this time to understand themselves better.

Longitudinal research shows that the personal attributes and social supports listed in Applying What We Know below foster successful passage through this period, as indicated by completing a college education, forging a warm, stable intimate relationship, finding and keeping a well-paying job, and volunteering in one's community (Benson et al., 2006; Eccles & Gootman, 2002). Notice how the factors in the table overlap with ones discussed in earlier chapters that promote development through *resilience*, the capacity to overcome challenge and adversity. Young people with more of these resources—and with resources in all three categories—probably make an especially smooth transition to adulthood. But many emerging adults with only a few resources also fare well.

As in childhood and adolescence, certain resources strengthen others. Relationships with parents have an especially wide-ranging influence. A secure, affectionate parent–emerging adult bond that extends the balance of connection and separation established in adolescence promotes many aspects of adaptive functioning: favorable self-esteem, identity progress, successful transition

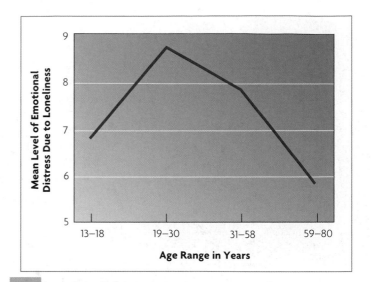

FIGURE 17.4

Changes in loneliness over the lifespan. More than 700 Canadian 13- to 80-year-olds responded to a questionnaire assessing the extent to which they experienced emotional distress due to loneliness. Loneliness peaked in the late teens and twenties, the period of emerging adulthood. (Adapted from Rokach, 2001.)

Applying What We Know

Resources That Foster Resilience in Emerging Adulthood

TYPE OF RESOURCE	DESCRIPTION
Cognitive attributes	Effective planning and decision making
	Information-gathering cognitive style
	Good school performance
	Knowledge of vocational options and skills
Emotional and social attributes	Positive self-esteem
	Good emotional self-regulation and flexible coping strategies
	Good conflict-resolution skills
	Confidence in one's ability to reach one's goals
	Sense of personal responsibility for outcomes
	Persistence and good use of time
	Healthy identity development—movement toward exploration in depth and commitment certainty
	Strong moral character
	Sense of meaning and purpose in life, engendered by religion, spirituality, or other sources
	Desire to contribute meaningfully to one's community
Social supports	Positive relationships with parents, peers, teachers, and mentors
	Sense of connection to social institutions, such as school, church, workplace, and community center

Sources: Benson et al., 2006; Eccles and Gootman, 2002.

Warm relationships with parents promote resilience in emerging adulthood. As she moves out of her parents' home to live on her own, this young woman clearly feels connected to her parents. She knows she can count on their emotional support and, if needed, their practical help.

to college life, higher academic achievement, more rewarding friendships and romantic ties, and reduced anxiety, depression, loneliness, and drug abuse. As one reviewer of research concluded, "What seems advantageous for emerging adults' achievement of independence is feeling connected, secure, understood, and loved in their families, and having the willingness to call on parental resources" (Aquilino, 2006, p. 201).

In contrast, exposure to multiple negative life events—family conflict, abusive intimate relationships, repeated romantic breakups, academic or employment difficulties, and financial strain—undermines development, even in emerging adults whose childhood and adolescence prepared them well for this transition (Cui & Vaillant, 1996). In sum, supportive family, school, and community environments are crucial, just as they were at earlier ages. The overwhelming majority of young people with access to these resources are highly optimistic about their future (Arnett, 2000b, 2006). Although they worry about grim aspects of their world, such crime, war, and environmental destruction, they nevertheless are convinced that they will someday arrive at where they want to be in life: secure enough financially and happy in work and close relationships.

Ask Yourself

Review What cultural changes have led to the appearance of the period known as emerging adulthood?

Apply List supports that your college environment offers emerging adults in its health and counseling services, academic advising, residential living, and extracurricular activities. How does each help young people master the challenges of this period?

Connect What family, school, and community experiences in adolescence increase the chances that emerging adults will engage in volunteer work? (See Chapter 16, page 614.)

Reflect Give an example of how your thinking has become more relativistic. Which college experiences probably contributed to this change?

Summary

A Period of Unprecedented Exploration

What is emerging adulthood?

■ In Western nations, **emerging adulthood** is a new transitional period extending from the late teens to the mid-twenties, during which young people have moved beyond adolescence but have not yet taken on full adult responsibilities. Rather, emerging adults prolong identity development as they explore alternatives in education, work, personal values, and love.

Cultural Change and Emerging Adulthood

How has cultural change contributed to the appearance of emerging adulthood?

■ As the amount of education required to enter complex, well-paid careers has increased, young people have pursued higher education in record numbers. In addition, gains in economic prosperity and life expectancy mean that developed nations have no pressing need for young people's labor. This frees emerging adults to experiment with options. Many low-SES and ethnic minority youths, however, do not have access to the benefits of this period.

■ Globalization may result in the spread of emerging adulthood. Eventually, this period may become a typical experience around the world.

Development in Emerging Adulthood

What cognitive, emotional, and social changes take place during emerging adulthood?

■ Studies of **postformal thought** reveal that as college students explore new ideas and beliefs, their reasoning becomes more rational, flexible, and practical. Their **epistemic cognition**—reflections on how they arrived at facts, beliefs, and ideas—advances. As a result, they move away from **dualistic thinking** toward **relativistic thinking,** in which they accept the existence of multiple truths, each relative to its context. Eventually, the most mature individuals arrive at **commitment within relativistic thinking,** the ability to synthesize contradictions into a more satisfying perspective.

■ Attending college leads to gains in epistemic cognition by providing situations that challenge young people's perspectives. College also offers opportunities to tackle problems collaboratively with others who are roughly equal in knowledge and authority, which promotes reflection on one's own thinking.

■ College students' attitudes and values broaden, enhancing their self-understanding and self-esteem. They refine their approach to constructing an identity, exploring not just in breadth but also in depth, cycling between making commitments and evaluating commitments in various identity domains. Those who move toward exploration in depth and certainty of commitments tend to be high in personal agency and show more favorable academic and social adjustment.

■ Emerging adults' romantic ties last longer and are more emotionally intimate than adolescents' dating relationships. Partner similarity and good communication, especially constructive conflict resolution, predict happy, lasting relationships. A secure internal working model of attachment, a considerate partner, and contentment with other aspects of life also contribute to gratifying intimate bonds.

■ Emerging adults' work experiences increasingly focus on preparation for adult work roles. Most construct a dream, typically emphasizing career for men and marriage and career for women. Then they form a relationship with a mentor to help realize their dream. Identity achievement in the vocational realm is more challenging for women, who often question their abilities and express concerns about combining work with child rearing.

■ Despite self-focused themes in their worldviews, most emerging adults also want to improve their communities, nation, and world. They are more likely than older people to be involved in organizations devoted to specific causes of concern to them. Whether or not they remain involved in formal religious activities, most young people begin to construct their own, individualized faith. Those who view religion as important in their lives engage in more community service.

Risk and Resilience in Emerging Adulthood

What risks do emerging adults face, and what factors foster a successful transition to adulthood?

■ In trying out possibilities, emerging adults must adjust to disappointments in love and work and, sometimes, radically change their life path. Their explorations also extend risky behaviors of adolescence, such as unprotected sexual activity and substance use. Also, loneliness peaks in emerging adulthood.

■ During this time of great challenge, repeated exposure to negative life events can undermine well-being, even in well-adjusted young people. A wide array of personal attributes and social supports in families, schools, and communities, many of which were also important at earlier ages, foster resilience and successful passage into adulthood.

Important Terms and Concepts

Glossary

Aboriginal Head Start
A Canadian federally funded preschool intervention program providing First Nations, Inuit, and Métis children younger than age 6 with educational, nutritional, and health services and encouraging parent involvement in children's learning and development. (p. 351)

academic preschool and kindergarten programs
Educational programs in which teachers structure children's learning, teaching academic skills through formal lessons, often using repetition and drill. Distinguished from *child-centered preschool and kindergarten programs.* (p. 350)

accommodation
That part of adaptation in which new schemes are created and old ones adjusted to produce a better fit with the environment. Distinguished from *assimilation.* (p. 208)

acculturative stress
Psychological distress resulting from conflict between the minority culture and the host culture. (p. 605)

acquired immune deficiency syndrome (AIDS)
A viral infection that destroys the immune system and that is spread through transfer of body fluids from one person to another; it can be transmitted prenatally. (p. 114)

adaptation
In Piaget's theory, the process of building schemes through direct interaction with the environment. Made up of two complementary processes: *assimilation* and *accommodation.* (p. 208)

adolescence
The transition between childhood and adulthood. (p. 529)

affordances
The action possibilities that a situation offers an organism with certain motor capabilities. Discovering affordances plays a major role in perceptual differentiation. (p. 202)

age of viability
The earliest age at which the fetus can survive if born prematurely, occurring sometime between 22 and 26 weeks. (p. 102)

alcohol-related neurodevelopmental disorder (ARND)
The least severe form of fetal alcohol spectrum disorder, involving brain injury, but with typical physical growth and absence of facial abnormalities. (p. 111)

allele
Each of two forms of a gene located at the same place on the autosomes. (p. 56)

amnion
The inner membrane that encloses the prenatal organism. (p. 99)

amniotic fluid
The fluid that fills the amnion, helping to keep temperature constant and to provide a cushion against jolts caused by the mother's movement. (p. 99)

amodal sensory properties
Information that overlaps two or more sensory systems, such as common rate, rhythm, and duration in visual and auditory input. (p. 202)

analgesics
Mild pain-relieving drugs. (p. 136)

androgyny
The gender identity held by individuals who score high on both traditionally masculine and traditionally feminine personality characteristics. (p. 395)

anesthetics
Strong painkillers that block sensation. (p. 136)

animistic thinking
The belief that inanimate objects have lifelike qualities, such as thoughts, wishes, feelings, and intentions. (p. 325)

anorexia nervosa
An eating disorder in which young people, mainly girls, starve themselves because of a compulsive fear of getting fat. (p. 544)

A-not-B search error
The error made by 8- to 12-month-olds who, after an object has been moved from hiding place A to hiding place B, search for it incorrectly in the first hiding place (A). (p. 211)

anoxia
Inadequate oxygen supply. (p. 139)

Apgar Scale
A rating used to assess the newborn baby's physical condition immediately after birth. (p. 132)

assimilation
That part of adaptation in which the external world is interpreted in terms of current schemes. Distinguished from *accommodation.* (p. 208)

associative play
A form of true social interaction, in which children engage in separate activities but interact by exchanging toys and commenting on one another's behavior. Distinguished from *nonsocial activity, parallel play,* and *cooperative play.* (p. 374)

asthma
A chronic illness in which, in response to a variety of stimuli, highly sensitive bronchial tubes fill with mucus and contract, leading to episodes of coughing, wheezing, and serious breathing difficulties. (p. 422)

attachment
The strong affectionate tie that humans have for special people in their lives. (p. 268)

Attachment Q-Sort
A method for assessing the quality of attachment between ages 1 and 5 years through home observations of a variety of attachment-related behaviors. (p. 271)

attention-deficit hyperactivity disorder
A childhood disorder involving inattention, impulsivity, and excessive motor activity, often resulting in academic failure and social problems. (p. 444)

attribution retraining
An intervention that uses adult feedback to encourage learned-helpless children to believe that they can overcome failure through effort. (p. 488)

attributions
Common, everyday explanations of the causes of behavior. (p. 486)

authoritarian child-rearing style
A child-rearing style that is low in acceptance and involvement, is high in coercive control, and restricts rather than grants autonomy. Distinguished from *authoritative, permissive,* and *uninvolved child-rearing styles.* (p. 399)

authoritative child-rearing style
A child-rearing style that is high in acceptance and involvement, emphasizes firm control with explanations, and includes gradual, appropriate autonomy granting. Distinguished from *authoritarian, permissive,* and *uninvolved child-rearing styles.* (p. 399)

autobiographical memory
Representations of special, one-time events that are long-lasting because they are imbued with personal meaning. (p. 224)

autonomy
At adolescence, a sense of oneself as a separate, self-governing individual, which involves relying more on oneself and less on parents for direction and guidance and engaging in careful, well-reasoned decision making. (p. 616)

autonomy versus shame and doubt
In Erikson's theory, the psychological conflict of toddlerhood, which is resolved positively when parents provide young children with suitable guidance and reasonable choices. (p. 252)

autosomes
The 22 matching chromosome pairs in each human cell. (p. 54)

avoidant attachment
The attachment pattern characterizing infants who seem unresponsive to the parent when she is present, are usually not distressed when she leaves, and avoid the parent when she returns. Distinguished from *secure, resistant,* and *disorganized/disoriented attachment.* (p. 270)

babbling
Repetition of consonant–vowel combinations in long strings, beginning around 6 months of age. (p. 240)

basic emotions
Emotions such as happiness, interest, surprise, fear, anger, sadness, and disgust that are universal in humans and other primates and have a long evolutionary history of promoting survival. (p. 254)

basic trust versus mistrust
In Erikson's theory, the psychological conflict of infancy, which is resolved positively when caregiving, especially during feeding, is sympathetic and loving. (p. 252)

behavior modification
Procedures that combine conditioning and modeling to eliminate undesirable behaviors and increase desirable responses. (p. 18)

behavioral genetics
A field devoted to uncovering the contributions of nature and nurture to the diversity in human traits and abilities. (p. 83)

behaviorism
An approach that regards directly observable events—stimuli and responses—as the appropriate focus of study and that views the development of behavior as taking place through classical and operant conditioning. (p. 16)

bicultural identity
The identity constructed by individuals who explore and adopt values from both their family's subculture and the dominant culture. (p. 605)

blastocyst
The zygote 4 days after fertilization, when the tiny mass of cells forms a hollow, fluid-filled ball. (p. 99)

blended, or reconstituted, family
A family structure formed through cohabitation or remarriage that includes parent, child, and steprelatives. (p. 513)

body image
A person's conception of and attitude toward his or her physical appearance. (p. 542)

bonding
Parents' feelings of affection and concern for the newborn baby. (p. 146)

brain plasticity
The capacity of various parts of the cerebral cortex to take over functions of damaged regions. Declines as hemispheres of the cerebral cortex lateralize. (p. 172)

breech position
A position of the baby in the uterus that would cause the buttocks or feet to be delivered first. (p. 138)

Broca's area
A structure located in the left frontal lobe of the cerebral cortex that supports grammatical processing and language production. (p. 237)

bulimia nervosa
An eating disorder in which young people engage in strict dieting and excessive exercise accompanied by binge eating, often followed by deliberate vomiting and purging with laxatives. (p. 545)

canalization
The tendency of heredity to restrict the development of some characteristics to just one or a few outcomes. (p. 86)

cardinality
The principle stating that the last number in a counting sequence indicates the quantity of items in the set. (p. 348)

carrier
A heterozygous individual who can pass a recessive gene to his or her children. (p. 56)

categorical self
Classification of the self according to prominent ways in which people differ, such as age, sex, physical characteristics, and competencies, that develops between 18 and 30 months. (p. 285)

central executive
The conscious part of working memory that directs the flow of information through the mental system by deciding what to attend to, coordinating incoming information with information already in the system, and selecting, applying, and monitoring strategies. (p. 221)

centration
The tendency to focus on one aspect of a situation, neglecting other important features. Distinguished from *decentration.* (p. 325)

cephalocaudal trend
An organized pattern of physical growth that proceeds from head to tail. (p. 166)

cerebellum
A brain structure that aids in balance and control of body movement. (p. 298)

cerebral cortex
The largest, most complex structure of the human brain, responsible for the highly developed intelligence of the human species. (p. 171)

cerebral palsy
A general term for a variety of problems, all involving muscle coordination, that result from brain damage before, during, or just after birth. (p. 139)

cesarean delivery
A surgical delivery in which the doctor makes an incision in the mother's abdomen and lifts the baby out of the uterus. (p. 138)

child development
A field of study devoted to understanding all aspects of human constancy and change from conception through adolescence. (p. 4)

child-centered preschool and kindergarten programs
Educational programs in which teachers provide activities from which children select, and most of the day is devoted to play. Distinguished from *academic preschool and kindergarten programs.* (p. 350)

child-directed speech (CDS)
A form of language adults use to speak to young children, consisting of short sentences with high-pitched, exaggerated expression, clear pronunciation, distinct pauses between speech segments, clear gestures to support verbal meaning, and repetition of new words in a variety of contexts. (p. 245)

child-rearing styles
Combinations of parenting behaviors that occur over a wide range of situations, creating an enduring child-rearing climate. (p. 398)

chorion
The outer membrane that surrounds the amnion and sends out tiny, fingerlike villi, from which the placenta begins to develop. (p. 99)

chromosomes
Rodlike structures in the cell nucleus that store and transmit genetic information. (p. 52)

chronosystem
In ecological systems theory, temporal changes in children's environments, which produce new conditions that affect development. These changes can be imposed externally or arise from within the child. (p. 27)

circular reaction
In Piaget's theory, a means of building schemes in which infants try to repeat a chance event caused by their own motor activity. (p. 209)

classical conditioning
A form of learning that involves associating a neutral stimulus with a stimulus that leads to a reflexive response. (p. 183)

clinical interview
An interview method in which the researcher uses a flexible, conversational style to probe for the participant's point of view. (p. 33)

clinical, or case study, method
A method in which the researcher attempts to understand an individual child by combining interview data, observations, and sometimes test scores. (p. 34)

clique
A small group of about five to seven members who are good friends and, therefore, tend to resemble one another in family background, attitudes, and values. (p. 623)

cognitive maps
Mental representations of familiar, large-scale spaces, such as school or neighborhood. (p. 438)

cognitive self-regulation
The process of continuously monitoring progress toward a goal, checking outcomes, and redirecting unsuccessful efforts. (p. 448)

cognitive-developmental theory
An approach introduced by Piaget that views children as actively constructing knowledge as they manipulate and explore their world and that regards cognitive development as taking place in stages. (p. 18)

cohort effects
The effects of cultural-historical change on the accuracy of longitudinal and cross-sectional findings. Children born in a particular time period are influenced by a particular set of cultural and historical conditions. (p. 40)

collectivist societies
Societies in which people define themselves as part of a group and stress group over individual goals. Distinguished from *individualistic societies*. (p. 77)

commitment within relativistic thinking
The mature individual's formulation of a perspective that synthesizes contradictions between opposing views, rather than choosing between them. (p. 645)

communities of learners
Classrooms in which both teachers and students have the authority to define and resolve problems, drawing on the expertise of one another and of others as they work toward project goals, which often address complex real-world issues. (p. 469)

compliance
Voluntary obedience to adult requests and commands. (p. 285)

comprehension
In language development, the words and word combinations that children understand. Distinguished from *production*. (p. 243)

concordance rate
The percentage of instances in which both members of a twin pair show a trait when it is present in one pair member, used to study the contribution of heredity to emotional and behavior disorders. (p. 84)

concrete operational stage
Piaget's third stage, extending from about 7 to 11 years, in which thought becomes logical, flexible, and organized in its application to concrete information. (p. 438)

conditioned response (CR)
In classical conditioning, an originally reflexive response that is produced by a conditioned stimulus. (p. 184)

conditioned stimulus (CS)
In classical conditioning, a neutral stimulus that, through pairing with an unconditioned stimulus, leads to a new response. (p. 184)

conservation
The understanding that certain physical characteristics of objects remain the same, even when their outward appearance changes. (p. 325)

constructivist classroom
A classroom in which students are active learners who are encouraged to construct their own knowledge, the teacher guides and supports in response to children's needs, and students are evaluated by considering their progress in relation to their own prior development. Distinguished from *traditional classroom* and *social-constructivist classroom*. (p. 467)

contexts
Unique combinations of personal and environmental circumstances that can result in markedly different paths of development. (p. 8)

continuous development
A view that regards development as a cumulative process of gradually augmenting the same types of skills that were there to begin with. Distinguished from *discontinuous development*. (p. 8)

contrast sensitivity
A general principle accounting for early pattern preferences, which states that if babies can detect a difference in contrast between two or more patterns, they will prefer the one with more contrast. (p. 196)

control deficiency
The inability to control, or execute, a mental strategy consistently. Distinguished from *production deficiency, utilization deficiency,* and *effective strategy use*. (p. 443)

controversial children
Children who get many votes, both positive and negative, on assessments of peer acceptance. Distinguished from *popular, rejected,* and *neglected children*. (p. 500)

conventional level
Kohlberg's second level of moral development, in which moral understanding is based on conforming to social rules to ensure positive human relationships and maintain societal order. (p. 608)

convergent thinking
Thinking that involves arriving at a single correct answer to a problem; emphasized on intelligence tests. Distinguished from *divergent thinking*. (p. 473)

cooing
Pleasant vowel-like noises made by infants, beginning around 2 months of age. (p. 240)

cooperative learning
Collaboration on a task by a small group of students who resolve differences of opinion, share responsibility, consider one another's ideas, and work toward common goals. (p. 470)

cooperative play
A type of social interaction in which children orient toward a common goal, such as acting out a make-believe theme or working on a project together. Distinguished from *nonsocial activity, parallel play,* and *associative play*. (p. 374)

core knowledge perspective
A perspective that states that infants are born with a set of innate knowledge systems, or core domains of thought, each of which permits a ready grasp of new, related information. (p. 217)

coregulation
A form of supervision in which parents exercise general oversight while letting children take charge of moment-by-moment decision making. (p. 506)

corpus callosum
The large bundle of fibers connecting the two hemispheres of the brain. (p. 299)

correlation coefficient
A number, ranging from +1.00 to −1.00, that describes the strength and direction of the relationship between two variables. (p. 37)

correlational design
A research design in which the researcher gathers information on individuals without altering participants' experiences and then examines relationships between variables. Does not permit inferences about cause and effect. (p. 35)

creativity
The ability to produce work that is original yet appropriate—something that others have not thought of but that is useful in some way. (p. 473)

crossing over
During meiosis, the exchange of genes between chromosomes next to each other. (p. 53)

cross-sectional design
A research design in which groups of people differing in age are studied at the same point in time. Distinguished from *longitudinal design*. (p. 41)

crowd
A large, loosely organized group consisting of several cliques, with membership based on reputation and stereotype. (p. 623)

decentration
The ability to focus on several aspects of a problem at once and relate them. Distinguished from *centration*. (p. 438)

deferred imitation
The ability to remember and copy the behavior of models who are not present. (p. 212)

delay of gratification
Ability to wait for an appropriate time and place to engage in a tempting act. (p. 285)

deoxyribonucleic acid (DNA)
Long, double-stranded molecules that make up chromosomes. (p. 52)

dependent variable
The variable the investigator expects to be influenced by the independent variable in an experiment. (p. 37)

developmental cognitive neuroscience
An area of investigation that brings together researchers from psychology, biology, neuroscience, and medicine to study the relationship between changes in the brain and the developing child's cognitive processing and behavior patterns. (p. 22)

developmental quotient, or DQ
A score on an infant intelligence test, computed in the same manner as an IQ but based primarily on perceptual and motor responses. (p. 231)

developmental science
An interdisciplinary field devoted to the study of all changes we experience throughout the lifespan. (p. 4)

developmentally appropriate practice
Research-based standards devised by the National Association for the Education of Young Children that specify program characteristics that meet the developmental and individual needs of young children of varying ages. (p. 233)

differentiation theory
The view that perceptual development involves the detection of increasingly fine-grained, invariant features in the environment. (p. 202)

difficult child
A child whose temperament is characterized by irregular daily routines, slow acceptance of new experiences, and a tendency to react negatively and intensely. Distinguished from *easy child* and *slow-to-warm-up child*. (p. 260)

dilation and effacement of the cervix
Widening and thinning of the cervix during the first stage of labor. (p. 131)

discontinuous development
A view of development as a process in which new ways of understanding and responding to the world emerge at specific times. Distinguished from *continuous development*. (p. 8)

disorganized/disoriented attachment
The attachment pattern reflecting the greatest insecurity, characterizing infants who show confused, contradictory behaviors when reunited with the parent after a separation. Distinguished from secure, *avoidant,* and *resistant attachment*. (p. 271)

distributive justice
Beliefs about how to divide material goods fairly. (p. 492)

divergent thinking
Thinking that involves generating multiple and unusual possibilities when faced with a task or problem; associated with creativity. Distinguished from *convergent thinking*. (p. 473)

divorce mediation
A series of meetings between divorcing adults and a trained professional aimed at reducing family conflict, including legal battles over property division and child custody. (p. 512)

dominance hierarchy
A stable ordering of group members that predicts who will win when conflict arises. (p. 432)

dominant cerebral hemisphere
The hemisphere of the brain responsible for skilled motor action. In right-handed individuals, the left hemisphere is dominant. (p. 297)

dominant–recessive inheritance
A pattern of inheritance in which, under heterozygous conditions, the influence of only one allele is apparent. (p. 56)

dual representation
The ability to view a symbolic object as both an object in its own right and a symbol. (p. 324)

dualistic thinking
The view that knowledge is made up of separate beliefs and propositions, whose truth can be determined by comparing them with objective standards. (p. 645)

dynamic assessment
An approach to testing in which an adult introduces purposeful teaching into the testing situation to find out what the child can attain with social support. (p. 460)

dynamic systems perspective
A view that regards the child's mind, body, and physical and social worlds as a dynamic, integrated system. A change in any part of the system leads the child to reorganize his behavior so the various components of the system work together again but in a more complex and effective way. (p. 27)

dynamic systems theory of motor development
A theory that views new motor skills as reorganizations of previously mastered skills, which lead to more effective ways of exploring and controlling the environment. Each new skill is a joint product of central nervous system development, the body's movement possibilities, the child's goals, and environmental supports for the skill. (p. 188)

easy child
A child whose temperament is characterized by establishment of regular routines in infancy, general cheerfulness, and easy adaptation to new experiences. Distinguished from *difficult child* and *slow-to-warm-up child*. (p. 260)

ecological systems theory
Bronfenbrenner's approach, which views the child as developing within a complex system of relationships affected by multiple levels of the surrounding environment, from immediate settings of family and school to broad cultural values and programs. (p. 25)

educational self-fulfilling prophecies
Teachers' positive or negative views of individual children, who tend to adopt and start to live up to these views. (p. 470)

effective strategy use
Consistent use of a mental strategy, leading to improvement in performance. Distinguished from *production deficiency, control deficiency,* and *utilization deficiency*. (p. 443)

effortful control
The self-regulatory dimension of temperament, involving voluntary suppression of a dominant, reactive response in order to plan and execute a more adaptive response. (p. 261)

egocentrism
Failure to distinguish the symbolic viewpoints of others from one's own. (p. 325)

elaboration
A memory strategy that involves creating a relationship, or shared meaning, between two or more pieces of information that are not members of the same category. (p. 446)

embryo
The prenatal organism from 2 to 8 weeks after conception—the period when the groundwork is laid for all body structures and internal organs. (p. 100)

embryonic disk
A small cluster of cells on the inside of the blastocyst, from which the new organism will develop. (p. 99)

emergent literacy
Young children's active efforts to construct literacy knowledge through informal experiences. (p. 346)

emerging adulthood
A new period of development, extending from the late teens to the twenties, during which young people have left adolescence but have not yet assumed the enduring responsibilities of adults. (p. 641)

emotional intelligence
A set of emotional abilities that enable individuals to process and adapt to emotional information. (p. 457)

emotional self-regulation
Strategies for adjusting our emotional state to a comfortable level of intensity so we can accomplish our goals. (p. 258)

emotion-centered coping
An approach to coping with stress that is internal, private, and aimed at controlling distress when little can be done to change an outcome. Distinguished from *problem-centered coping*. (p. 490)

empathy
The ability to understand another's emotional state and respond emotionally in a similar way—"feeling with" that person. (p. 284)

epigenesis
Development of the individual resulting from ongoing, bidirectional exchanges between heredity and all levels of the environment. (p. 88)

epiphyses
Growth centers in the bones where new cartilage cells are produced and gradually harden. (p. 166)

episodic memory
Memory for everyday experiences. (p. 340)

epistemic cognition
Reflections on how one arrived at facts, beliefs, and ideas. (p. 645)

ethnic identity
A sense of ethnic group membership, and attitudes and feelings associated with that membership, as an enduring aspect of the self. (p. 605)

ethnography
A method in which the researcher attempts to understand the unique values and social processes of a culture or a distinct social group through participant observation—living with its members and taking field notes over an extended period of time. (p. 34)

ethological theory of attachment
Bowlby's theory that the infant's emotional tie to the caregiver is an evolved response that promotes survival. (p. 269)

ethology
An approach concerned with the adaptive, or survival, value of behavior and its evolutionary history. (p. 34)

evolutionary developmental psychology
An approach that seeks to understand the adaptive value of species-wide cognitive,

emotional, and social competencies as those competencies change with age. (p. 24)

exosystem
In ecological systems theory, social settings that do not contain children but that affect children's experiences in immediate settings. Examples are parents' workplace, health and welfare services available in the community, and parents' social networks. (p. 26)

expansions
Adult responses that elaborate on children's speech, increasing its complexity. (p. 360)

experience-dependent brain growth
New growth and refinement of brain structures as a result of specific learning experiences that vary widely across individuals and cultures. (p. 176)

experience-expectant brain growth
The young brain's rapidly developing organization, which depends on ordinary experiences—opportunities to see and touch objects, to hear language and other sounds, and to move about and explore the environment. (p. 176)

experimental design
A research design in which the investigator randomly assigns participants to treatment conditions. Permits inferences about cause and effect. (p. 37)

expressive style
A style of early language learning in which toddlers use language mainly to talk about their own feelings and needs and those of other people, with an emphasis on social formulas and pronouns. Distinguished from *referential style*. (p. 244)

extended-family household
A household in which parent and child live with one or more adult relatives. (p. 77)

fantasy period
The period of vocational development in which young children fantasize about career options through make-believe play. (p. 589)

fast mapping
Connecting a new word with an underlying concept after only a brief encounter. (p. 356)

fetal alcohol spectrum disorder (FASD)
A range of physical, mental, and behavioral outcomes caused by prenatal alcohol exposure. (p. 222)

fetal alcohol syndrome (FAS)
The most severe form of fetal alcohol spectrum disorder, distinguished by slow physical growth, facial abnormalities, and brain injury; usually seen in children whose mothers consumed large amounts of alcohol during most or all of pregnancy. (p. 111)

fetal monitors
Electronic instruments that track the baby's heart rate during labor. (p. 136)

fetus
The prenatal organism from the ninth week to the end of pregnancy—the period when body structures are completed and dramatic growth in size occurs. (p. 102)

fontanels
Six gaps, or "soft spots," separating the bones of the skull at birth. (p. 168)

forceps
Metal clamps placed around a baby's head to pull the infant from the birth canal. (p. 137)

formal operational stage
Piagetian stage beginning around age 11, in which young people develop the capacity for abstract, systematic, scientific thinking. (p. 566)

fraternal, or dizygotic, twins
Twins resulting from the release and fertilization of two ova. They are genetically no more alike than ordinary siblings. Distinguished from *identical, or monozygotic, twins*. (p. 55)

gametes
Human sperm and ova, which contain half as many chromosomes as regular body cells. (p. 53)

gender constancy
The understanding that sex is biologically based, remaining the same over time even if clothing, hairstyle, and play activities change. (p. 396)

gender identity
An image of oneself as relatively masculine or feminine in characteristics. (p. 395)

gender intensification
The increased gender stereotyping of attitudes and behavior and movement toward a more traditional gender identity, typical of early adolescence. (p. 615)

gender schema theory
An information-processing approach to gender typing that explains how environmental pressures and children's cognitions work together to shape gender-role development. (p. 396)

gender typing
Any association of objects, activities, roles, or traits with one sex or the other in ways that conform to cultural stereotypes. (p. 391)

gene
A segment of a DNA molecule that contains hereditary instructions. (p. 52)

general growth curve
Curve representing overall changes in body size—rapid growth during infancy, slower gains in early and middle childhood, and rapid growth again during adolescence. (p. 296)

genetic counseling
A communication process designed to help couples assess their chances of giving birth to a baby with a hereditary disorder and choose the

best course of action in view of risks and family goals. (p. 63)

genetic–environmental correlation
The idea that heredity influences the environments to which individuals are exposed. (p. 86)

genetic imprinting
A pattern of inheritance in which alleles are imprinted, or chemically marked, in such a way that one pair member is activated, regardless of its makeup. (p. 59)

genotype
An individual's genetic makeup. (p. 51)

gifted
Displaying exceptional intellectual strengths, including high IQ, creativity, or talent. (p. 472)

glial cells
Cells that are responsible for myelination and, in certain instances, also participate directly in neural communication. (p. 168)

goodness-of-fit model
Thomas and Chess's model, which states that an effective match, or "good fit," between a child's temperament and the child-rearing environment leads to more adaptive functioning, whereas a "poor fit" results in adjustment problems. (p. 266)

growth hormone (GH)
A pituitary hormone that affects the development of all body tissues except the central nervous system and the genitals. (p. 301)

growth spurt
A rapid gain in height and weight that is the first outward sign of puberty. (p. 532)

guided participation
Shared endeavors between more expert and less expert participants, regardless of the precise features of communication. (p. 335)

habituation
A gradual reduction in the strength of a response as a result of repetitive stimulation. (p. 185)

heritability estimate
A statistic that measures the extent to which individual differences in complex traits in a specific population are due to genetic factors. (p. 83)

heterozygous
Having two different alleles at the same place on a pair of chromosomes. Distinguished from *homozygous*. (p. 56)

hierarchical classification
The organization of objects into classes and subclasses on the basis of similarities and differences. (p. 326)

hippocampus
An inner-brain structure that plays a vital role in memory and in spatial images we use to help us find our way. (p. 299)

Home Observation for Measurement of the Environment (HOME)
A checklist for gathering information about the quality of children's home lives through observation and parental interview. (p. 231)

homozygous
Having two identical alleles at the same place on a pair of chromosomes. Distinguished from *heterozygous*. (p. 56)

hostile aggression
Aggression intended to harm another person. Distinguished from *instrumental aggression*. (p. 387)

hypothetico-deductive reasoning
A formal operational problem-solving strategy that begins with a hypothesis, from which logical inferences can be deduced and then tested by systematically isolating and combining variables. (p. 566)

identical, or monozygotic, twins
Twins that result when a zygote, during the early stages of cell duplication, divides in two. They have the same genetic makeup. Distinguished from *fraternal, or dizygotic, twins*. (p. 55)

identity
A well-organized conception of the self that defines who one is, what one values, and what directions one wants to pursue in life. (p. 598)

identity achievement
The identity status of individuals who have explored and committed themselves to self-chosen values and goals. Distinguished from *identity moratorium, identity diffusion*, and *identity foreclosure.*. (p. 601)

identity diffusion
The identity status of individuals who do not engage in exploration and do not commit themselves to self-chosen values and goals. Distinguished from *identity achievement, identity moratorium*, and *identity foreclosure*. (p. 601)

identity foreclosure
The identity status of individuals who do not engage in exploration but, instead, are committed to ready-made values and goals chosen for them by authority figures. Distinguished from *identity achievement, identity moratorium*, and *identity foreclosure*. (p. 601)

identity moratorium
The identity status of individuals who are exploring, but not yet committed to, self-chosen values and goals. Distinguished from *identity achievement, identity foreclosure*, and *identity diffusion*. (p .601)

identity versus role confusion
In Erikson's theory, the psychological conflict of adolescence, which is resolved positively when adolescents attain an identity after successful outcomes of earlier stages. (p. 598)

imaginary audience
Adolescents' belief that they are the focus of others' attention and concern. (p. 572)

imitation
Learning by copying the behavior of another person. Also called *modeling* or *observational learning*. (p. 186)

implantation
Attachment of the blastocyst to the uterine lining, which occurs 7 to 9 days after fertilization. (p. 99)

inclusive classrooms
Classrooms in which students with learning difficulties learn alongside typical students in a regular educational setting. (p. 472)

incomplete dominance
A pattern of inheritance in which both alleles are expressed in the phenotype, resulting in a combined trait, or one that is intermediate between the two. (p. 57)

independent variable
The variable the researcher expects to cause changes in another variable in an experiment. (p. 37)

individualistic societies
Societies in which people think of themselves as separate entities and are largely concerned with their own personal needs. Distinguished from *collectivist societies*. (p. 77)

induced labor
A labor started artificially by breaking the amnion and giving the mother a hormone that stimulates contractions. (p. 137)

induction
A type of discipline in which an adult helps make the child aware of feelings by pointing out the effects of the child's misbehavior on others. (p. 381)

industry versus inferiority
In Erikson's theory, the psychological conflict of middle childhood, which is resolved positively when experiences lead children to develop a sense of competence at useful skills and tasks. (p. 482)

infant mortality
The number of deaths in the first year of life per 1,000 live births. (p. 144)

infantile amnesia
The inability of most people to recall events that happened to them before age 3. (p. 224)

information processing
An approach that views the human mind as a symbol-manipulating system through which information flows and that regards cognitive development as a continuous process. (p. 21)

inhibited, or shy, child
A child who tends to react negatively to and withdraw from novel stimuli. Distinguished from *uninhibited, or sociable, child*. (p. 262)

initiative versus guilt
In Erikson's theory, the psychological conflict of early childhood, which is resolved positively through play experiences that foster a healthy sense of initiative and through the development of a superego, or conscience, that is not overly strict and/or guilt-ridden. (p. 366)

instrumental aggression
Aggression aimed at obtaining an object, privilege, or space with no deliberate intent to harm another person. Distinguished from *hostile aggression*. (p. 387)

intelligence quotient, or IQ
A score that reflects an individual's performance on an intelligence test compared with the performances of other individuals of the same age. (p. 230)

intentional, or goal-directed, behavior
A sequence of actions in which schemes are deliberately combined to solve a problem. (p. 210)

interactional synchrony
A form of communication in which the caregiver responds to infant signals in a well-timed, rhythmic, appropriate fashion and both partners match emotional states, especially positive ones. (p. 274)

intermodal perception
Integration of simultaneous stimulation from more than one sensory system, resulting in perception of such input as an integrated whole. (p. 202)

internal working model
A set of expectations, derived from early caregiving experiences, about the availability of attachment figures, their likelihood of providing support during times of stress, and the self's interaction with those figures, which becomes a guide for all future close relationships. (p. 270)

intersubjectivity
The process whereby two participants who begin a task with different understandings arrive at a shared understanding. (p. 335)

irreversibility
The inability to mentally go through a series of steps in a problem and then reverse direction, returning to the starting point. Distinguished from *reversibility*. (p. 325)

I-self
The self as knower and actor, which is separate from the surrounding world, remains the same person over time, has a private inner life not accessible to others, and can control its own thoughts and actions. Distinguished from *me-self*. (p. 366)

joint attention
A state in which child and caregiver attend to the same object or event and the caregiver comments on what the child sees. (p. 241)

joint custody
A legal arrangement that grants divorced parents equal say in important decisions about their children's upbringing. (p. 512)

kinship studies
Studies comparing the characteristics of family members to determine the importance of heredity in complex human characteristics. (p. 83)

kwashiorkor
A disease caused by a diet low in protein that usually appears after weaning, with symptoms including an enlarged belly, swollen feet, hair loss, skin rash, and irritable, listless behavior. (p. 181)

language acquisition device (LAD)
In Chomsky's theory, an innate system containing a universal grammar, or set of rules common to all languages, that permits children to understand and speak in a rule-oriented fashion as soon as they have learned enough words. (p. 237)

lanugo
White, downy hair that covers the entire body of the fetus, helping the vernix stick to the skin. (p. 102)

lateralization
Specialization of functions in the two hemispheres of the cerebral cortex. (p. 172)

learned helplessness
The view that success is due to external factors, such as luck, while failure is due to ability, which cannot be improved by trying hard. Distinguished from *mastery-oriented attributions*. (p. 487)

learning disabilities
Specific learning disorders that lead children to achieve poorly in school. (p. 472)

logical necessity
The idea that the accuracy of conclusions drawn from premises rests on the rules of logic, not on real-world confirmation. A basic property of propositional thought. (p. 568)

longitudinal design
A research design in which participants are studied repeatedly at different ages. Distinguished from *cross-sectional design*. (p. 40)

long-term memory
In information processing, the part of the mental system that contains our permanent knowledge base. (p. 221)

macrosystem
In ecological systems theory, cultural values, laws, customs, and resources that influence experiences and interactions at inner levels of the environment. (p. 27)

make-believe play
A type of play in which children pretend, acting out everyday and imaginary activities. (p. 212)

malocclusion
A condition in which the upper and lower teeth do not meet properly. (p. 414)

marasmus
A disease usually appearing in the first year of life, caused by a diet low in all essential nutrients, that leads to a wasted condition of the body. (p. 181)

mastery-oriented attributions
Attributions that credit success to ability, which can be improved by trying hard, and failure to insufficient effort. Distinguished from *learned helplessness*. (p. 486)

matters of personal choice
Concerns that do not violate rights and are up to each individual, such as choice of friends or color of clothing. (p. 386)

maturation
A genetically determined, naturally unfolding course of growth. (p. 12)

meiosis
The process of cell division through which gametes are formed and in which the number of chromosomes in each cell is halved. (p. 53)

memory strategies
Deliberate mental activities that improve the likelihood of remembering. (p. 339)

menarche
Scientific name for first menstruation, from the Greek word arche, meaning "beginning." (p. 535)

mental representation
Internal depictions of information that the mind can manipulate. (p. 211)

mental strategies
In information processing, procedures that operate on and transform information, thereby increasing the efficiency and flexibility of thinking and the chances that information will be retained. (p. 220)

me-self
The self as an object of knowledge and evaluation, consisting of all physical, psychological, and social characteristics that make the self unique. Distinguished from *I-self*. (p. 366)

mesosystem
In ecological systems theory, connections between children's immediate settings. (p. 26)

metacognition
Thinking about thought; awareness of mental activities. (p. 342)

metalinguistic awareness
The ability to think about language as a system. (p. 462)

microgenetic design
A research design in which investigators present children with a novel task and follow their mastery over a series of closely spaced sessions. (p. 43)

microsystem
In ecological systems theory, the innermost level of the environment, consisting of activities and interaction patterns in the child's immediate surroundings. (p. 26)

mitosis
The process of cell duplication, in which each new cell receives an exact copy of the original chromosomes. (p. 52)

modifier genes
Genes that can enhance or dilute the effects of other genes. (p. 56)

moral imperatives
Standards that protect people's rights and welfare. (p. 386)

moral self-relevance
The degree to which morality is central to an individual's self-concept. (p. 613)

mutation
A sudden but permanent change in a segment of DNA. (p. 61)

mutual exclusivity bias
Children's assumption in early vocabulary growth that words refer to entirely separate categories. (p. 356)

myelination
A process in which neural fibers are coated with an insulating fatty sheath, myelin, that improves the efficiency of message transfer. (p. 168)

myopia
Nearsightedness; inability to see distant objects clearly. (p. 415)

natural, or prepared, childbirth
An approach designed to reduce pain and medical intervention and to make childbirth a rewarding experience for parents. (p. 134)

naturalistic observation
A method in which the researcher goes into the natural environment to observe the behavior of interest. Distinguished from *structured observation.* (p. 31)

nature–nurture controversy
Debate among theorists about whether genetic or environmental factors are more important in development. (p. 8)

neglected children
Children who are seldom mentioned, either positively or negatively, on assessments of peer acceptance. Distinguished from *popular, controversial,* and *rejected children.* (p. 500)

Neonatal Behavioral Assessment Scale (NBAS)
A test developed to assess the behavior of a newborn infant in terms of reflexes, muscle tone, state changes, responsiveness to physical and social stimuli, and other reactions. (p. 157)

neonatal mortality
The number of deaths in the first month of life per 1,000 live births. (p. 144)

neural tube
The primitive spinal cord that develops from the ectoderm, the top of which swells to form the brain during the period of the embryo. (p. 100)

neurons
Nerve cells that store and transmit information. (p. 168)

neurotransmitters
Chemicals released by neurons that cross the synapse to send messages to other neurons. (p. 168)

niche-picking
A type of genetic–environmental correlation in which individuals actively choose environments that complement their heredity. (p. 87)

noble savage
Rousseau's view of the child as naturally endowed with a sense of right and wrong and an innate plan for orderly, healthy growth. (p. 12)

nocturnal enuresis
Repeated bedwetting during the night. (p. 422)

nonorganic failure to thrive
A growth disorder, usually present by 18 months of age, caused by lack of affection and stimulation. (p. 182)

non-rapid-eye-movement (NREM) sleep
A "regular" sleep state in which the body is quiet and heart rate, breathing, and brain-wave activity are slow and regular. Distinguished from *rapid-eye-movement (REM) sleep.* (p. 150)

nonsocial activity
Unoccupied, onlooker behavior and solitary play. Distinguished from *parallel play, associative play,* and *cooperative play.* (p. 374)

normal distribution
A bell-shaped distribution that results when individual differences are measured in large samples. (p. 230)

normative approach
An approach in which age-related averages are computed to represent typical development. (p. 13)

obesity
A greater-than-20-percent increase over healthy body weight, based on body mass index, a ratio of weight to height associated with body fat. (p. 417)

object permanence
The understanding that objects continue to exist when they are out of sight. (p. 210)

operant conditioning
A form of learning in which a spontaneous behavior is followed by a stimulus that influences the probability that the behavior will occur again. (p. 184)

ordinality
Relationships of order (more than and less than) between quantities. (p. 348)

organization
In Piaget's theory, the internal rearrangement and linking together of schemes so that they form a strongly interconnected cognitive system. In information processing, a memory strategy that involves grouping related items, which dramatically improves recall. (pp. 208, 445)

overextension
An early vocabulary error in which a word is applied too broadly, to a wider collection of objects and events than is appropriate. Distinguished from *underextension.* (p. 242)

overlapping-waves theory
The theory of problem solving that states that when given challenging problems, children try various strategies and gradually select those that are fastest and most accurate. (p. 341)

overregularization
Overextension of regular grammatical rules to words that are exceptions. (p. 358)

parallel play
A limited form of social participation in which a child plays near other children with similar materials but does not try to influence their behavior. Distinguished from *associative play, cooperative play,* and *nonsocial activity.* (p. 374)

partial fetal alcohol syndrome (p-FAS)
A form of fetal alcohol spectrum disorder characterized by facial abnormalities and brain injury, but less severe than fetal alcohol syndrome; usually seen in children whose mothers drank alcohol in smaller quantities during pregnancy. (p. 111)

peer acceptance
The extent to which a child is viewed by a group of agemates as a worthy social partner. (p. 500)

peer groups
Social units of peers who generate unique values and standards for behavior and a social structure of leaders and followers. (p. 498)

peer victimization
A destructive form of peer interaction in which certain children become frequent targets of verbal and physical attacks or other forms of abuse. (p. 502)

permissive child-rearing style
A child-rearing style that is high in acceptance but either overindulging or inattentive, low in control, and inappropriately lenient in autonomy granting. Distinguished from *authoritative, authoritarian,* and *uninvolved child-rearing styles.* (p. 400)

personal fable
Adolescents' inflated opinion of their own importance—the belief that they are special and unique and that others cannot possibly understand their thoughts and feelings. (p. 572)

perspective taking
The capacity to imagine what other people are thinking and feeling. (p. 491)

phenotype
The individual's physical and behavioral characteristics, which are determined by both genetic and environmental factors. (p. 51)

phobia
An intense, unmanageable fear that leads to persistent avoidance of the feared situation. (p. 516)

phonics approach
An approach to beginning reading instruction that emphasizes coaching children on phonics, the basic rules for translating written symbols into sounds. Distinguished from *whole-language approach*. (p. 449)

phonological awareness
The ability to reflect on and manipulate the sound structure of spoken language, as indicated by sensitivity to changes in sounds within words, to rhyming, and to incorrect pronunciation. (p. 346)

physical aggression
A form of hostile aggression that harms others through physical injury to individuals or their property. Distinguished from *verbal* and *relational aggression*. (p. 387)

pincer grasp
The well-coordinated grasp that emerges at the end of the first year, involving thumb and index finger opposition. (p. 190)

pituitary gland
A gland located near the base of the brain that releases hormones affecting physical growth. (p. 301)

placenta
The organ that permits exchange of nutrients and waste products between the bloodstreams of the mother and the embryo, while also preventing the mother's and embryo's blood from mixing directly. (p. 99)

planning
Thinking out a sequence of acts ahead of time and allocating attention accordingly to reach a goal. (p. 339)

polygenic inheritance
A pattern of inheritance in which many genes affect the characteristic in question. (p. 61)

popular children
Children who get many positive votes on assessments of peer acceptance. Distinguished from *rejected*, *controversial*, and *neglected children*. (p. 500)

popular-antisocial children
A subtype of popular children consisting of "tough," athletically skilled but defiant, trouble-causing boys and of relationally aggressive boys and girls who are admired for their sophisticated but devious social skills. Distinguished from *popular-prosocial children*. (p. 500)

popular-prosocial children
A subtype of popular children who combine academic and social competence. Distinguished from *popular-antisocial children*. (p. 500)

postconventional level
Kohlberg's highest level of moral development, in which individuals define morality in terms of abstract principles and values that apply to all situations and societies. (p. 608)

postformal thought
Development beyond Piaget's formal operational stage. (p. 645)

postpartum depression
Feelings of sadness and withdrawal that develop shortly after childbirth and continue for weeks or months. (p. 159)

pragmatics
The practical, social side of language, concerned with how to engage in effective and appropriate communication. (p. 359)

preconventional level
Kohlberg's first level of moral development, in which moral understanding is based on rewards, punishments, and the power of authority figures. (p. 607)

prenatal diagnostic methods
Medical procedures that permit detection of developmental problems before birth. (p. 63)

preoperational stage
Piaget's second stage, extending from about 2 to 7 years, in which rapid growth in representation takes place but thought is not yet logical. (p. 322)

prereaching
The poorly coordinated, primitive reaching movements of newborn babies. (p. 190)

preterm infants
Infants born several weeks or more before their due date. (p. 140)

primary sexual characteristics
Characteristics of the reproductive organs—ovaries, uterus, and vagina in females; penis, scrotum, and testes in males. Distinguished from *secondary sexual characteristics*. (p. 535)

private speech
Self-directed speech that children use to plan and guide their own behavior. (p. 334)

problem-centered coping
An approach to coping with stress in which the individual appraises the situation as changeable, identifies the difficulty, and decides what to do about it. Distinguished from *emotion-centered coping*. (p. 490)

production
In language development, the words and word combinations that children use. Distinguished from *comprehension*. (p. 243)

production deficiency
The failure to produce a mental strategy when it could be helpful. Distinguished from *control deficiency*, *utilization deficiency*, and *effective strategy use*. (p. 443)

Project Head Start
The most extensive federally funded preschool intervention program in the United States, providing low-SES children with a year or two of preschool education, along with nutritional and medical services, and encouraging parent involvement in children's learning and development. (p. 351)

propositional thought
A type of formal operational reasoning involving the ability to evaluate the logic of propositions without referring to real-world circumstances. (p. 567)

prosocial, or altruistic, behavior
Actions that benefit another person without any expected reward for the self. (p. 373)

proximodistal trend
An organized pattern of physical growth that proceeds from the center of the body outward. (p. 166)

psychoanalytic perspective
Freud's view of personality development, in which children move through a series of stages in which they confront conflicts between biological drives and social expectations. The way these conflicts are resolved determines psychological adjustment. (p. 14)

psychological control
Parental behaviors that intrude on and manipulate children's verbal expression, individuality, and attachments to parents. (p. 399)

psychosexual theory
Freud's theory, which emphasizes that how parents manage children's sexual and aggressive drives in the first few years of life is crucial for healthy personality development. (p. 14)

psychosocial dwarfism
A growth disorder, observed between 2 and 15 years of age, characterized by very short stature, decreased GH secretion, immature skeletal age, and serious adjustment problems. Caused by emotional deprivation. (p. 302)

psychosocial theory
Erikson's theory, which emphasizes that at each Freudian stage, individuals not only develop a unique personality but also acquire attitudes and skills that help them become active, contributing members of their society. (p. 14)

puberty
A flood of biological events leading to an adult-size body and sexual maturity. (p. 529)

public policies
Laws and government programs designed to improve current conditions. (p. 79)

punishment
In operant conditioning, removal of a desirable stimulus or presentation of an unpleasant stimulus, which decreases the occurrence of a response. (p. 184)

random assignment
An unbiased procedure for assigning participants to treatment groups, which increases the chances that participants' characteristics will be equally distributed across treatment conditions in an experiment. (p. 38)

range of reaction
Each person's unique, genetically determined response to a range of environmental conditions. (p. 85)

rapid-eye-movement (REM) sleep
An "irregular" sleep state in which brain-wave activity is similar to that of the waking state. Distinguished from *non-rapid-eye-movement (NREM) sleep*. (p. 150)

realistic period
The period of vocational development in which adolescents focus on a general vocational category and, within it, experiment for a time before settling on a single occupation. (p. 589)

recall
The type of memory that involves remembering something without perceptual support. (p. 223)

recasts
Adult responses that restructure children's grammatically inaccurate speech into correct form. (p. 360)

reciprocal teaching
A teaching method in which a teacher and two to four students form a cooperative group, within which dialogues occur that create a zone of proximal development. (p. 468)

recognition
The simplest form of memory, which involves noticing whether a new experience is identical or similar to a previous one. (p. 223)

recovery
Following habituation, an increase in responsiveness to a new stimulus. (p. 185)

referential style
A style of early language learning in which toddlers use language mainly to label objects. Distinguished from *expressive style*. (p. 244)

reflex
An inborn, automatic response to a particular form of stimulation. (p. 147)

rehearsal
A memory strategy that involves repeating information to oneself. (p. 445)

reinforcer
In operant conditioning, a stimulus that increases the occurrence of a response. (p. 184)

rejected children
Children who are actively disliked and get many negative votes on assessments of peer acceptance. Distinguished from *popular, controversial*, and *neglected children*. (p. 500)

rejected-aggressive children
A subtype of rejected children who show high rates of conflict, physical and relational aggression, and hyperactive, inattentive, and impulsive behavior. Distinguished from *rejected-withdrawn children*. (p. 501)

rejected-withdrawn children
A subtype of rejected children who are passive, socially awkward, and overwhelmed by social anxiety. Distinguished from *rejected-aggressive children*. (p. 501)

relational aggression
A form of hostile aggression that damages another's peer relationships through social exclusion, malicious gossip, or friendship manipulation. Distinguished from *physical* and *verbal aggression*. (p. 387)

relativistic thinking
The view that knowledge is embedded in a framework of thought and that multiple truths can exist, each relative to its context. (p. 645)

resilience
The ability to adapt effectively in the face of threats to development. (p. 10)

resistant attachment
The attachment pattern characterizing infants who seek closeness to the parent before her departure, are usually distressed when she leaves, and combine clinginess with angry, resistive behavior when she returns. Distinguished from *secure, avoidant*, and *disorganized/disoriented attachment*. (p. 270)

respiratory distress syndrome
A disorder of preterm infants in which the lungs are so immature that the air sacs collapse, causing serious breathing difficulties. (p. 140)

reticular formation
A brain structure that maintains alertness and consciousness. (p. 298)

reversibility
The ability to go through a series of steps in a problem and then mentally reverse direction, returning to the starting point. Distinguished from *irreversibility*. (p. 438)

Rh factor incompatibility
A condition that arises when the fetus's blood contains the Rh protein but the mother's blood does not, causing the mother to build up antibodies, which, if they return to the fetus's system, destroy red blood cells, reducing the oxygen supply to organs and tissues. (p. 118)

rooming in
An arrangement in which the newborn baby stays in the mother's hospital room all or most of the time. (p. 147)

rough-and-tumble play
A form of peer interaction involving friendly chasing and play-fighting that, in our evolutionary past, may have been important for the development of fighting skill. (p. 431)

rubella
Three-day, or German, measles; responsible for a wide variety of prenatal abnormalities, especially when it strikes during the embryonic period. (p. 114)

scaffolding
Adjusting the assistance offered during a teaching session to fit the child's current level of performance. As competence increases, the adult gradually and sensitively withdraws support, turning responsibility over to the child. (p. 335)

scheme
In Piaget's theory, a specific structure, or organized way of making sense of experience that changes with age. (p. 208)

scripts
General descriptions of what occurs and when it occurs in a particular situation, used to organize and interpret repeated events. (p. 340)

secondary sexual characteristics
Features visible on the outside of the body that serve as signs of sexual maturity, including breast development in females and the appearance of underarm and pubic hair in both sexes. Distinguished from *primary sexual characteristics*. (p. 535)

secular trends in physical growth
Changes in body size from one generation to the next. (p. 413)

secure attachment
The attachment pattern characterizing infants who are distressed by parental separation but are easily comforted by the parent when she returns. Distinguished from *avoidant, resistant*, and *disorganized/disoriented attachment*. (p. 270)

secure base
Role of the familiar caregiver as a point from which the infant explores the environment, returning for emotional support. (p. 256)

self-care children
Children who regularly look after themselves during after-school hours. (p. 515)

self-concept
The set of attributes, abilities, attitudes, and values that an individual believes defines who he or she is. (p. 367)

self-conscious emotions
Emotions such as shame, embarrassment, guilt, envy, and pride that involve injury to or enhancement of the sense of self. (p. 257)

self-esteem
The judgments individuals make about their own worth and the feelings associated with those judgments. (p. 368)

semantic bootstrapping
Using word meanings to figure out grammatical rules. (p. 359)

sensitive caregiving
Caregiving that involves prompt, consistent, and appropriate responses to infant signals. (p. 273)

sensitive period
A time that is optimal for certain capacities to emerge and in which the individual is especially responsive to environmental influences. (p. 23)

sensorimotor stage
Piaget's first stage, spanning the first two years of life, during which infants and toddlers "think" with their eyes, ears, hands, and other sensorimotor equipment. (p. 208)

sensory register
The part of the mental system in which sights and sounds are represented directly and stored briefly before they decay or are transferred to working memory. (p. 220)

separation anxiety
An infant's distressed reaction to the departure of the familiar caregiver. (p. 269)

sequential design
A research design in which several similar cross-sectional or longitudinal studies (called sequences) are conducted at varying times. (p. 42)

seriation
The ability to order items along a quantitative dimension, such as length or weight. (p. 438)

sex chromosomes
The twenty-third pair of chromosomes, which determines the sex of the child—in females, called XX; in males, called XY. (p. 54)

shape constancy
Perception of an object's shape as the same, despite changes in the shape projected on the retina. (p. 201)

size constancy
Perception of an object's size as the same, despite changes in the size of its retinal image. (p. 201)

skeletal age
An estimate of physical maturity based on development of the bones of the body. (p. 166)

slow-to-warm-up child
A child whose temperament is characterized by inactivity; mild, low-key reactions to environmental stimuli; negative mood; and slow adjustment to new experiences. Distinguished from *easy child* and *difficult child*. (p. 260)

small-for-date infants
Infants whose birth weight is below normal when length of the pregnancy is taken into account. (p. 140)

social comparisons
Children's assessments of their own appearance, abilities, and behavior in relation to those of others. (p. 483)

social conventions
Customs such as table manners that are determined by consensus within a society. (p. 386)

social learning theory
An approach that emphasizes the role of modeling, or observational learning, in the development of behavior. (p. 17)

social problem solving
Generating and applying strategies that prevent or resolve disagreements, leading to outcomes that are both acceptable to others and beneficial to the self. (p. 377)

social referencing
Active seeking of emotional information from a trusted person in deciding how to respond in an uncertain situation. (p. 257)

social smile
The smile evoked by the stimulus of the human face, which first appears between 6 and 10 weeks. (p. 255)

social-constructivist classroom
A classroom in which children participate in a wide range of challenging activities with teachers and peers, with whom they jointly construct understandings. Distinguished from *traditional classroom* and *constructivist classroom*. (p. 467)

sociocultural theory
Vygotsky's theory, in which children acquire the ways of thinking and behaving that make up a community's culture through cooperative dialogues with more knowledgeable members of their society. (p. 24)

sociodramatic play
Children's make-believe play with others. (p. 323)

socioeconomic status (SES)
A measure of a family's social position and economic well-being that combines three related variables: years of education, the prestige of and skill required by one's job, and income. (p. 71)

spermarche
Scientific name for first ejaculation. (p. 536)

stage
A qualitative change in thinking, feeling, and behaving that characterizes a specific period of development. (p. 8)

standardization
The practice of giving an intelligence test to a large, representative sample, which serves as the standard for interpreting individual scores. (p. 230)

states of arousal
Different degrees of sleep and wakefulness. (p. 149)

stereotype threat
The fear of being judged on the basis of a negative stereotype, which can trigger anxiety that interferes with performance. (p. 459)

Strange Situation
A laboratory method used to assess the quality of attachment between age 1 and 2 years by observing the baby's responses to eight short episodes, in which brief separations from and reunions with the caregiver occur in an unfamiliar playroom. (p. 270)

stranger anxiety
Expression of fear in response to unfamiliar adults, which appears in many babies in the second half of the first year. (p. 256)

structured interview
An interview method in which each participant is asked the same questions in the same way. (p. 33)

structured observations
A method in which the investigator sets up a laboratory situation that evokes the behavior of interest so that every participant has an equal opportunity to display the response. Distinguished from *naturalistic observation*. (p. 31)

subculture
A group of people with beliefs and customs that differ from those of the larger culture. (p. 77)

sudden infant death syndrome (SIDS)
The unexpected death, usually during the night, of an infant younger than 1 year of age that remains unexplained after thorough investigation. (p. 151)

sympathy
Feelings of concern or sorrow for another's plight. (p. 373)

synapses
The gaps between neurons, across which chemical messages are sent. (p. 168)

synaptic pruning
Loss of connective fibers by seldom-stimulated neurons, thereby returning them to an uncommitted state so they can support future development. (p. 168)

syntactic bootstrapping
Discovering word meanings by observing how words are used in the structure of sentences. (p. 357)

tabula rasa
Locke's view of the child as a "blank slate" whose character is shaped entirely by experience. (p. 11)

talent
Outstanding performance in a specific field. (p. 473)

telegraphic speech
Toddlers' two-word utterances that, like a telegram, omit smaller and less important words. (p. 243)

temperament
Early-appearing, stable individual differences in the quality and intensity of emotional reaction, activity level, attention, and emotional self-regulation. (p. 260)

tentative period
The period of vocational development in which adolescents start to think about careers in more complex ways, evaluating vocational options in terms of their interests, abilities, and values. (p. 589)

teratogen
Any environmental agent that causes damage during the prenatal period. (p. 105)

thalidomide
A sedative widely available in the early 1960s that produced gross deformities of the embryo's arms and legs when taken by expectant mothers 4 to 6 weeks after conception. (p. 107)

theory
An orderly, integrated set of statements that describes, explains, and predicts behavior. (p. 6)

theory of multiple intelligences
Gardner's theory, which proposes at least eight independent intelligences on the basis of distinct sets of processing operations that permit individuals to engage in a wide range of culturally valued activities. (p. 455)

thyroid-stimulating hormone (TSH)
A pituitary hormone that stimulates the thyroid gland to release thyroxine, which is necessary for normal brain development and body growth. (p. 302)

time out
A form of mild punishment in which children are removed from the immediate setting until they are ready to act appropriately. (p. 384)

toxemia
An illness of the last half of pregnancy, also known as preeclampsia, in which the mother's blood pressure increases sharply; if untreated, it can cause convulsions in the mother and death of the fetus. (p. 119)

toxoplasmosis
A parasitic disease caused by eating raw or undercooked meat or through contact with the feces of infected cats; during the first trimester, it leads to eye and brain damage. (p. 115)

traditional classroom
An elementary school classroom in which the teacher is the sole authority for knowledge, rules, and decision making and students are relatively passive learners who are evaluated in relation to a uniform set of standards. Distinguished from *constructivist classroom* and *social-constructivist classroom*. (p. 467)

transition
Climax of the first stage of labor, in which the frequency and strength of contractions are at their peak and the cervix opens completely. (p. 131)

transitive inference
The ability to seriate—or order items along a quantitative dimension—mentally. (p. 438)

triarchic theory of successful intelligence
Sternberg's theory, which identifies three broad, interacting intelligences—analytical, creative, and practical—that must be balanced to achieve success according to one's personal goals and the requirements of one's cultural community. (p. 454)

trimesters
Three equal time periods in prenatal development, each lasting three months. (p. 102)

trophoblast
The thin outer ring of cells of the blastocyst, which will become the structures that provide protective covering and nourishment to the new organism. (p. 99)

ulnar grasp
The clumsy grasp of the young infant, in which the fingers close against the palm. (p. 190)

umbilical cord
The long cord that connects the prenatal organism to the placenta, delivering nutrients and removing waste products. (p. 100)

unconditioned response (UCR)
In classical conditioning, a reflexive response that is produced by an unconditioned stimulus. (p. 183)

unconditioned stimulus (UCS)
In classical conditioning, a stimulus that leads to a reflexive response. (p. 183)

underextension
An early vocabulary error in which a word is applied too narrowly, to a smaller number of objects and events than is appropriate. Distinguished from *overextension*. (p. 242)

uninhibited, or sociable, child
A child who tends to display positive emotion and to approach novel stimuli. Distinguished from *inhibited*, or *shy, child*. (p. 262)

uninvolved child-rearing style
A child-rearing style that combines low acceptance and involvement with little control and indifference to autonomy granting. Distinguished from *authoritative*, *authoritarian*, and *permissive child-rearing styles*. (p. 400)

utilization deficiency
The inability to improve performance despite consistent use of a mental strategy. Distinguished from *control deficiency, production deficiency*, and *effective strategy use*. (p. 443)

vacuum extractor
A plastic cup attached to a suction tube, used to help deliver a baby. (p. 137)

verbal aggression
A form of hostile aggression that harms others through threats of physical aggression, name-calling, or hostile teasing. Distinguished from *physical* and *relational aggression*. (p. 387)

vernix
A white, cheeselike substance that covers the fetus, preventing the skin from chapping due to constant exposure to amniotic fluid. (p. 102)

violation-of-expectation method
A method in which researchers habituate infants to a physical event and then determine whether they recover to (look longer at) an expected event (a variation of the first event that conforms to physical laws) or an unexpected event (a variation that violates physical laws). Recovery to the unexpected event suggests awareness of that aspect of physical reality. (p. 212)

visual acuity
Fineness of visual discrimination. (p. 155)

Wernicke's area
A structure located in the left temporal lobe of the cerebral cortex that plays a role in comprehending word meaning. (p. 237)

whole-language approach
An approach to beginning reading instruction that parallels children's natural language learning through the use of reading materials that are whole and meaningful. Distinguished from *phonics approach*. (p. 449)

working, or short-term, memory
The part of the mental system where we actively "work" on a limited amount of information, applying mental strategies to ensure that it will be retained. (p. 220)

X-linked inheritance
A pattern of inheritance in which a recessive gene is carried on the X chromosome, so that males are more likely to be affected. (p. 57)

zone of proximal development
In Vygotsky's theory, a range of tasks that the child cannot yet handle alone but can accomplish with the help of more skilled partners. (p. 227)

zygote
The newly fertilized cell formed by the union of sperm and ovum at conception. (p. 53)

References

Abbott, S. (1992). Holding on and pushing away: Comparative perspectives on an eastern Kentucky child-rearing practice. *Ethos, 20,* 33–65.

Abel, E. (2004). Paternal contribution to fetal alcohol syndrome. *Addiction Biology, 9,* 127–133.

Abela, J. R. Z., Hankin, B. L., Haigh, E. A. P., Adams, P., Vinokuroff, T., & Trayhern, L. (2005). Interpersonal vulnerability to depression in high-risk children: The role of insecure attachment and reassurance seeking. *Journal of Clinical Child and Adolescent Psychology, 34,* 182–192.

Abikoff, H. B., Jensen, P. S., Arnold, L. L., Hoza, B., Hechtman, L., et al. (2002). Observed classroom behavior of children with ADHD: Relationship to gender and comorbidity. *Journal of Abnormal Child Psychology, 30,* 349–359.

Aboud, F. E. (2003). The formation of in-group favoritism and out-group prejudice in young children: Are they distinct attitudes? *Developmental Psychology, 39,* 48–60.

Aboud, F. E., & Amato, M. (2001). Developmental and socialization influences on intergroup bias. In R. Brown & S. Gaertner (Eds.), *Blackwell handbook of social psychology: Intergroup processes.* Oxford, UK: Blackwell.

Aboud, F. E., & Doyle, A. (1996). Parental and peer influences on children's racial attitudes. *International Journal of Intercultural Relations, 20,* 371–383.

Abraham, R. (2005). Emotional intelligence in the workplace: A review and synthesis. In R. Schulze & R. D. Roberts (Eds.), *Emotional intelligence: An international handbook* (pp. 255–270). Göttingen, Germany: Hogrefe & Huber.

Abramovitch, R., Freedman, J. L., Henry, K., & Van Brunschot, M. (1995). Children's capacity to consent to participation in psychological research: Some empirical findings. *Child Development, 62,* 1100–1109.

Accutane Action Group Forum. (2003, October). *General archive area.* Retrieved from http://www.xsorbit1.com/users

Achenbach, T. M., Phares, V., Howell, C. T., Rauh, V. A., & Nurcombe, B. (1990). Seven-year outcome of the Vermont program for low-birthweight infants. *Child Development, 61,* 1672–1681.

Acker, M. M., & O'Leary, S. G. (1996). Inconsistency of mothers' feedback and toddlers' misbehavior and negative affect. *Journal of Abnormal Child Psychology, 24,* 703–714.

ACT (American College Testing). (2005). *Retention trends.* Retrieved from www.act.org/path/postsec/droptables/index.html

ACT (American College Testing). (2006). *Retention trends.* Retrieved from www.act.org/psath/postsec/droptables/index.html

Adams, G. R., & Marshall, S. (1996). A developmental social psychology of identity: Understanding the person in context. *Journal of Adolescence, 19,* 429–442.

Adams, M. (2003). *Fire and ice: The United States, Canada, and the myth of converging values.* Toronto: Penguin.

Adams, R., & Laursen, B. (2001). The organization and dynamics of adolescent conflict with parents and friends. *Journal of Marriage and the Family, 63,* 97–110.

Adams, R. J., & Courage, M. L. (1998). Human newborn color vision: Measurement with chromatic stimuli varying in excitation purity. *Journal of Experimental Child Psychology, 68,* 22–34.

Adolph, K. (2002). Learning to keep balance. In R. V. Kail (Ed.), *Advances in child development and behavior* (Vol. 30, pp. 1–40). Boston: Academic Press.

Adolph, K. E. (2000). Specificity of learning: Why infants fall over a veritable cliff. *Psychological Science, 11,* 290–295.

Adolph, K. E., & Berger, S. E. (2006). Motor development. In D. Kuhn & R. Siegler (Eds.), *Handbook of child psychology: Vol. 2. Cognition, perception, and language* (6th ed., pp. 161–213). Hoboken, NJ: Wiley.

Adolph, K. E. A., Vereijken, B., & Shrout, P. E. (2003). What changes in infant walking and why. *Child Development, 74,* 475–497.

Afifi, T. O., Brownridge, D. A., Cox, B. J., & Sareen J. (2006). Physical punishment, childhood abuse and psychiatric disorders. *Child Abuse and Neglect, 30,* 1093–1103.

Aguiar, A., & Baillargeon, R. (1999). 2.5-month-old infants' reasoning about when objects should and should not be occluded. *Cognitive Psychology, 39,* 116–157.

Aguiar, A., & Baillargeon, R. (2002). Developments in young infants' reasoning about occluded objects. *Cognitive Psychology, 45,* 267–336.

Ahlgren, M., Melbye, M., Wohlfahrt, J., & Sørensen, T. I. (2004). Growth patterns and the risk of breast cancer in women. *New England Journal of Medicine, 351,* 1619–1626

Ahmed, A., & Ruffman, T. (1998). Why do infants make A not B errors in a search task, yet show memory for the location of hidden objects in a nonsearch task? *Developmental Psychology, 34,* 441–453.

Aikins, J. W., Bierman, K. L., & Parker, J.G. (2005). Navigating the transition to junior high school: The influence of pre-transition friendship and self-system characteristics. *Social Development, 14,* 42–60.

Ainsworth, M. D. S., Blehar, M. C., Waters, E., & Wall, S. (1978). *Patterns of attachment.* Hillsdale, NJ: Erlbaum.

Akers, J. F., Jones, R. M., & Coyl, D. D. (1998). Adolescent friendship pairs: Similarities in identity status development, behaviors, attitudes, and intentions. *Journal of Adolescent Research, 13,* 178–201.

Akhtar, N., & Montague, L. (1999). Early lexical acquisition: The role of cross-situational learning. *First Language, 19,* 347–358.

Akhtar, N., & Tomasello, M. (2000). The social nature of words and word learning. In R. Golinkoff & K. Hirsh-Pasek (Eds.), *Becoming a word learner: A debate on lexical acquisition.* Oxford, U.K.: Oxford University Press.

Akimoto, S. A., & Sanbinmatsu, D. M. (1999). Differences in self-effacing behavior between European and Japanese Americans: Effect on competence evaluations. *Journal of Cross-Cultural Psychology, 30,* 159–177.

Aksan, N., & Kochanska, G. (2004). Heterogeneity of joy in infancy. *Infancy, 6,* 79–94.

Akshoomoff, N. A., Feroleto, C. C., Doyle, R. E., & Stiles, J. (2002). The impact of early unilateral brain injury on perceptual organization and visual memory. *Neuropsychologia, 40,* 539–561.

Alan Guttmacher Institute. (2001). *Can more progress be made? Teenage sexual and reproductive behavior in developed countries.* Retrieved from www.guttmacher.org

Alan Guttmacher Institute. (2004). *Teen sexuality: Stats & facts.* Retrieved from www.fotf.ca/familyfacts/issues/teensexuality/stats.html

Alan Guttmacher Institute. (2005). *Facts in brief: Contraceptive use.* Retrieved from www.guttmacher.org/pubs/fb_contr_use.html

Alan Guttmacher Institute. (2006). *U.S. teenage pregnancy statistics: National and state trends and trends by race and ethnicity.* New York: Author. Retrieved from www.guttmacher.org/pubs/2006/09/12/USTPstats.pdf

Alcohol Concern. (2004). *Advertising alcohol.* Retrieved from www.alcoholconcern.org.uk

Aldridge, M. A., Stillman, R. D., & Bower, T. G. R. (2001). Newborn categorization of vowel-like sounds. *Developmental Science, 4,* 220–232.

Alessandri, S. M., Bendersky, M., & Lewis, M. (1998). Cognitive functioning in 8- to 18-month-old drug-exposed infants. *Developmental Psychology, 34,* 565–573.

Alexander, J. M., Fabricius, W. V., Fleming, V. M., Zwahr, M., & Brown, S. A. (2003). The development of metacognitive causal explanations. *Learning and Individual Differences, 13,* 227–238.

Alexandre-Bidon, D., & Lett, D. (1997). *Les enfants au Moyen Age, Ve–XVe siecles.* Paris: Hachette.

Ali, L., & Scelfo, J. (2002, December 9). Choosing virginity. *Newsweek,* pp. 60–65.

Aligne, C. A., Moss, M. E., Auinger, P., & Weitzman, M. (2003). Association of pediatric dental caries with passive smoking. *Journal of the American Medical Association, 289,* 1258–1264.

Allen, J. P., Philliber, S., Herrling, S., & Kuperminc, G. P. (1997). Preventing teen pregnancy and academic failure: Experimental evaluation of a developmentally based approach. *Child Development, 64,* 729–742.

Allen, J. P., Porter, M. R., & McFarland, F. C. (2006). Leaders and followers in adolescent close friendships: Susceptibility to peer influence as a predictor of risky behavior, friendship instability, and depression. *Development and Psychopathology, 18,* 155–172.

Allen, M., & Burrell, N. (1996). Comparing the impact of homosexual and heterosexual parents on children: Meta-analysis of existing research. *Journal of Homosexuality, 32,* 19–35.

Allen, S. E. M., & Crago, M. B. (1996). Early passive acquisition in Inukitut. *Journal of Child Language, 23,* 129–156.

Allison, B. N., & Schultz, J. B. (2004). Parent–adolescent conflict in early adolescence. *Adolescence, 39,* 101–119.

Al-Namlah, A. S., Fernyhough, C., & Meins, E. (2006). Sociocultural influences on the development of verbal mediation: Private speech and phonological recoding in Saudi Arabian and British samples. *Developmental Psychology, 42,* 117–131.

Alsaker, F. D. (1995). Timing of puberty and reactions to pubertal changes. In M. Rutter (Ed.), *Psychosocial disturbances in young people: Challenges for prevention* (pp. 37–82). New York: Cambridge University Press.

Amano, S., Kezuka, E., & Yamamoto, A. (2004). Infant shifting attention from an adult's face to an adult's hand: A precursor of joint attention. *Infant Behavior and Development, 27,* 64–80.

Amato, P. R. (2001). Children of divorce in the 1990s: An update of the Amato and Keith (1991) meta-analysis. *Journal of Family Psychology, 15,* 355–370.

Amato, P. R. (2006). Marital discord, divorce, and children's well-being: Results from a 20-year longitudinal study of two generation. In A. Clarke-Stewart & J. Dunn (Eds.), *Families count: Effects on child and adolescent development* (pp. 179–202). New York: Cambridge University Press.

Amato, P. R., & Cheadle, J. (2005). The long reach of divorce: Divorce and child well-being across three generations. *Journal of Marriage and Family, 67,* 191–206.

Amato, P. R., & Fowler, F. (2002). Parenting practices, child adjustment, and family diversity. *Journal of Marriage and the Family, 64,* 703–716.

Amato, P. R., & Sobolewski, J. M. (2004). The effects of divorce on fathers and children: Nonresidential fathers and stepfathers. In M. E. Lamb (Ed.), *The role of the father in child development* (4th ed., pp. 341–367). Hoboken, NJ: Wiley.

Ambert, A.-M. (2005). *Same-sex couples and same-sex parent families: Relationships, parenting, and issues of marriage.* Ontario: Vanier Institute of the Family. Retrieved from www.vifamily.ca/library/publications/samesexd.html

Ambert, A.-M. (2006). *One-parent families: Characteristics, causes, consequences, and issues.* Ontario, Canada: Vanier Institute of the Family.

American Academy of Pediatrics. (2005a). Breastfeeding and the use of human milk. *Pediatrics, 115,* 496–506.

American Academy of Pediatrics. (2005b). Use of performance-enhancing substances. *Pediatrics, 115,* 1103–1106.

American Academy of Pediatrics, Subcommittee on Attention-Deficit Hyperactivity Disorder. (2005c). Treatment of attention-deficit hyperactivity disorder. *Pediatrics, 115,* e749–e757.

American Academy of Pediatrics. (2006). Folic acid for the prevention of neural tube defects. *Pediatrics, 104,* 325–327.

American Psychiatric Association. (1994). *Diagnostic and statistical manual of mental disorders* (4th ed.). Washington, DC: Author.

American Psychological Association. (2002). Ethical principles of psychologists and code of conduct. *American Psychologist, 57,* 1060–1073.

Amsel, E., Cottrell, J., Sullivan, J., & Bowden, T. (2005). Anticipating and avoiding regret as a model of adolescent decision-making. In J. Jacobs & P. Kaczynski (Eds.), *The development of judgment and decision-making in children and adolescents* (pp. 119–154). Mahwah, NJ: Erlbaum.

Anand, S. S., Yusuf, S., Jacobs, R., Davis, A. D., Yi, Q., & Gerstein, H. (2001). Risk factors, arteriosclerosis, and cardiovascular disease among Aboriginal people in Canada: The study of health assessment and risk evaluation in Aboriginal peoples (SHARE-AP). *Lancet, 358,* 1147–1153.

Ances, B. M. (2002). New concerns about thalidomide. *Obstetrics and Gynecology, 99,* 125–128.

Anderman, E. M., Eccles, J. S., Yoon, K. S., Roeser, R., Wigfield, A., & Blumenfeld, P. (2001). Learning to value mathematics and reading: Relations to mastery and performance-oriented instructional practices. *Contemporary Educational Psychology, 26,* 76–95.

Andersen, E. (2000). Exploring register knowledge: The value of "controlled improvisation." In L. Menn & N. B. Ratner (Eds.), *Methods for studying language production* (pp. 225–248). Mahwah, NJ: Erlbaum.

Anderson, C. A., Berkowitz, L., Donnerstein, E., Huesmann, R., Johnson, J. D., Linz, D., Malamuth, N. M., & Wartella, E. (2003). The influence of media violence on youth. • *Psychological Science in the Public Interest, 4*(3), 81–106.

Anderson, D. M., Huston, A. C., Schmitt, K. L., Linebarger, D. L., & Wright, J. C. (2001). Early childhood television viewing and adolescent behavior. *Monographs of the Society for Research in Child Development, 66*(1, Serial No. 264).

Anderson, L. L., Morgan, J. L., & White, K. S. (2003). A statistical basis for speech sound discrimination. *Language and Speech, 46,* 155–182.

Anderson, M. E., Johnson, D. C., & Batal, H. A. (2005). Sudden infant death syndrome and prenatal maternal smoking: Rising attributed risk in the Back to Sleep era. *BMC Medicine, 3,* 4.

Anderson, P. M., Butcher, K. F., & Levine, P. B. (2003). Maternal employment and overweight children. *Journal of Health Economics, 22,* 477–504.

Anderson, S. E., Dallal, G. E., & Must, A. (2003). Relative weight and race influence average age at menarche: Results from two nationally representative surveys of U.S. girls studied 25 years apart. *Pediatrics, 111,* 844–850.

Anderson, V. A., Catroppa, C., Dudgeon, P., Morse, S. A., Haritou, F., & Rosenfeld, J. V. (2006). Understanding predictors of functional recovery and outcome 30 months following early childhood head injury. *Neuropsychology, 20,* 42–57.

Andersson, B.-E. (1989). Effects of public day care—A longitudinal study. *Child Development, 60,* 857–866.

Andersson, B.-E. (1992). Effects of day care on cognitive and socioemotional competence of thirteen-year-old Swedish schoolchildren. *Child Development, 63,* 20–36.

Andersson, T., & Magnusson, D. (1990). Biological maturation in adolescence and the development of drinking habits and alcohol abuse among young males: A prospective longitudinal study. *Journal of Youth and Adolescence, 19,* 33–41.

Andresen, M. (2006). Accutane registry compulsory in U.S., but not Canada. *Canadian Medical Association Journal, 174,* 1701.

Andrews, G., & Halford, G. S. (1998). Children's ability to make transitive inferences: The importance of premise integration and structural complexity. *Cognitive Development, 13,* 479–513.

Andrews, G., & Halford, G. S. (2002). A cognitive complexity metric applied to cognitive development. *Cognitive Psychology, 45,* 475–506.

Andrews, R., Torgerson, C., Beverton, S., Locke, T., Low, G., Robinson, A., & Zhu, D. (2006). *The effect of grammar teaching (syntax) on 5 to 16-year-olds' accuracy and quality in written composition.* York, UK: Department of Educational Studies. Retrieved from www.york.ac.uk /depts/educ/ResearchPaperSeries/English%20Grammar%20(Syntax).pdf

Anglin, J. M. (1993). Vocabulary development: A morphological analysis. *Monographs of the Society for Research in Child Development, 58*(10, Serial No. 238).

Anisfeld, M., Turkewitz, G., Rose, S. A., Rosenberg, F. R., Shelber, F. J., Couturier-Fagan, D. A., Ger, J. S., & Sommer I. (2001). No compelling evidence that newborns imitate oral gestures. *Infancy, 2,* 111–122.

Annett, M. (2002). *Handedness and brain asymmetry: The right shift theory.* Hove, U.K.: Psychology Press.

Anslow, P. (1998). Birth asphyxia. *European Journal of Radiology, 26,* 148–153.

Antshel, K. M. (2003). Timing is everything: Executive functions in children exposed to elevated levels of phenylalanine. *Neuropsychology, 17,* 458–468.

Apgar, V. (1953). A proposal for a new method of evaluation in the newborn infant. *Current Research in Anesthesia and Analgesia, 32,* 260–267.

Aquilino, W. S. (2006). Family relationships and support systems in emerging adulthood. In J. J. Arnett & J. L. Tanner (Eds.), *Emerging adults in America: Coming of age in the 21st century* (pp. 193–218). Washington, DC: American Psychological Association.

Aram, D., & Levin, I. (2001). Mother– child joint writing in low SES: Sociocultural factors, maternal mediation, and emergent literacy. *Cognitive Development, 16,* 831–852.

Aram, D., & Levin, I. (2002). Mother– child joint writing and storybook reading: Relations with literacy among low SES kindergartners. *Merrill-Palmer Quarterly, 48,* 202–224.

Archer, S. L., & Waterman, A. S. (1990). Varieties of identity diffusions and foreclosures: An exploration of subcategories of the identity statuses. *Journal of Adolescent Research, 5,* 96–111.

Archibald, A. B., Graber, J. A., & Brooks-Gunn, J. (2006). Pubertal processes and physiological growth in adolescence. In G. R. Adams & M. D. Berzonsky (Eds.), *Blackwell handbook of adolescence* (pp. 24–48). Malden, MA: Blackwell.

Archibald, A. B., Linver, M. R., Graber, J. A., & Brooks-Gunn, J. (2002). Parent–adolescent relationships and girls' unhealthy eating: testing reciprocal effects. *Journal of Research on Adolescence, 12,* 451–461.

Ardila-Rey, A., & Killen, M. (2001). Middle-class Colombian children's evaluations of personal, moral, and social-conventional interactions in the classroom. *International Journal of Behavioral Development, 25,* 246–255.

Arija, V., Esparó, G., Fernández-Ballart, J., Murphy, M. M., Biarnés, E., & Canals, J. (2006). Nutritional status and performance in test of verbal and nonverbal intelligence in 6 year old children. *Intelligence, 34,* 141–149.

Arnett, J. J. (1997). Young people's conceptions of the transition to adulthood. *Youth and Society, 29,* 1–23.

Arnett, J. J. (1998). Learning to stand alone: The contemporary American transition to adulthood in cultural and historical context. *Human Development, 41,* 295–315.

Arnett, J. J. (2000a). Emerging adulthood: A theory of development from the late teens through the twenties. *American Psychologist, 55,* 469–480.

Arnett, J. J. (2000b). High hopes in a grim world: Emerging adults' view of their futures and of "Generation X." *Youth and Society, 31,* 267–286.

Arnett, J. J. (2001). Conceptions of the transition to adulthood: Perspectives from adolescence to midlife. *Journal of Adult Development, 8,* 133–143.

Arnett, J. J. (2002). The psychology of globalization. *American Psychologist, 57,* 774–783.

Arnett, J. J. (2003). Conceptions of the transition to adulthood among emerging adults in American ethnic groups. In J. J. Arnett & N. L. Galambos (Eds.), *Exploring cultural conceptions of the transitions to adulthood* (New directions for child and adolescent development, No. 100, pp. 63–75). San Francisco: Jossey-Bass.

Arnett, J. J. (2004). *Emerging adulthood: The winding road from the late teens through the twenties.* New York: Oxford University Press.

Arnett, J. J. (2006). Emerging adulthood: Understanding the new way of coming of age. In J. J. Arnett & J. L. Tanner (Eds.), *Emerging adults in America: Coming of age in the 21st century* (pp. 3–19). Washington, DC: American Psychological Association.

Arnett, J. J., & Jensen, L. A. (2002). A congregation of one: Individualized religious beliefs among emerging adults. *Journal of Adolescent Research, 17,* 451–467.

Arnett, J. J., Ramos, K. D., & Jensen, L. A. (2001). Ideological views in emerging adulthood: Balancing autonomy and community. *Journal of Adult Development, 8,* 69–79.

Arnett, J. J., & Tanner, J. L. (Eds.). (2006). *Emerging adults in America: Coming of age in the 21st century.* Washington, DC: American Psychological Association.

Arnold, D. H., Fisher, P. H., Doctoroff, G. L., & Dobbs, J. (2002). Accelerating math development in Head Start classrooms. *Journal of Educational Psychology, 94,* 762–770.

Arnold, P. (1999). Emotional disorders in deaf children. In V. L. Schwean & D. H. Saklofske (Eds.), *Handbook of psychosocial characteristics of exceptional children* (pp. 493–522). New York: Kluwer.

Arnon, S., Shapsa, A., Forman, L., Regev, R., Bauer, S., & Litmanovitz, I. (2006). Live music is beneficial to preterm infants in the neonatal intensive care unit. *Birth, 33,* 131–136.

Aronson, A. A., & Henderson, S. O. (2006). Pediatrics, otitis media. *eMedicine Specialties, Pediatrics.* Retrieved from www.emedicine.com/emerg/topic393.htm

Arora, S., McJunkin, C., Wehrer, J., & Kuhn, P. (2000). Major factors influencing breastfeeding rates: Mother's perception of father's attitude and milk supply. *Pediatrics, 106,* e67.

Arriaga, X. B., & Foshee, V. A. (2004). Adolescent dating violence: Do adolescents follow in their friends or their parents' footsteps? *Journal of Interpersonal Violence, 19,* 162–184.

Arsenio, W., & Fleiss, K. (1996). Typical and behaviourally disruptive children's understanding of the emotional consequences of socio-moral events. *British Journal of Developmental Psychology, 14,* 173–186.

Arterberry, M. E., Craton, L. G., & Yonas, A. (1993). Infants' sensitivity to motion-carried information for depth and object properties. In C. E. Granrud (Ed.), *Visual perception and cognition in infancy* (pp. 215– 234). Hillsdale, NJ: Erlbaum.

Artman, L., & Cahan, S. (1993). Schooling and the development of transitive inference. *Developmental Psychology, 29,* 753–759.

Artman, L., Cahan, S., & Avni-Babad, D. (2006). Age, schooling, and conditional reasoning. *Cognitive Development, 21,* 131–145.

Asakawa, K. (2001). Family socialization practices and their effects on the internationalization of educational values for Asian and white American adolescents. *Applied Developmental Science, 5,* 184–194.

Asarnow, J. R., Jaycox, L. H., Duan, N., LaBorde, A. P., Rea, M. M., & Murray, P. (2005). Effectiveness of a quality improvement intervention for adolescent depression in primary care clinics. *Journal of the American Medical Association, 293,* 311–319.

Asbjornsen, A. E., Obrzut, J. E., Boliek, C. A., Myking, E., Holmefjord, A., & Reisaeter, S. (2005). Impaired auditory attention skills following middle-ear infections. *Child Neuropsychology, 11,* 121–133.

Asher, S. R., & Rose, A. J. (1997). Promoting children's social-emotional adjustment with peers. In P. Salovey & D. J. Sluyter (Eds.), *Emotional development and emotional intelligence* (pp. 193–195). New York: Basic Books.

Aslin, R. N., Jusczyk, P. W., & Pisoni, D. B. (1998). Speech and auditory processing during infancy: Constraints on and precursors to language. In D. Kuhn & R. S. Siegler (Eds.), *Handbook of child psychology: Vol. 2. Cognition, perception, and language* (5th ed., pp. 147–198). New York: Wiley.

Astington, J. W., & Jenkins, J. M. (1995). Theory of mind development and social understanding. *Cognition and Emotion, 9,* 151–165.

Astington, J. W., & Pelletier, J. (2005). Theory of mind, language, and learning in the early years: Developmental origins of school readiness. In B. D. Homer & C. S. Tamis-LeMonda (Eds.), *The development of social cognition and communication* (pp. 205–230). Mahwah, NJ: Erlbaum.

Astington, J. W., Pelletier, J., & Homer, B. (2002). Theory of mind and epistemological development: The relation between children's second-order false belief

understanding and their ability to reason about evidence. *New Ideas in Psychology, 20,* 131–144.
Atanackovic, G., & Koren, G. (1999). Fetal exposure to oral isotretinoin: Failure to comply with the Pregnancy Prevention Program. *Canadian Medical Association Journal, 160,* 1719–1720.
Atance, C. M., & Meltzoff, A. N. (2005). My future self: Young children's ability to anticipate and explain future states. *Cognitive Development, 20,* 341–361.
Aten, M. J., Siegel, D. M., Enaharo, M., & Auinger, P. (2002). Keeping middle school students abstinent: Outcomes of a primary prevention intervention. *Journal of Adolescent Health, 31,* 70–78.
Atkins, R., Hart, D., & Donnelly, T. M. (2004). Moral identity development and school attachment. In D. Narvaez & D. Lapsley (Eds.), *Moral development, self, and identity* (pp. 65–82). Mahwah, NJ: Erlbaum.
Atkinson, R. C., & Shiffrin, R. M. (1968). Human memory: A proposed system and its control processes. In K. W. Spence & J. T. Spence (Eds.), *Advances in the psychology of learning and motivation* (Vol. 2, pp. 90–195). New York: Academic Press.
Au, T. K., Sidle, A. L., & Rollins, K. B. (1993). Developing an intuitive understanding of conservation and contamination: Invisible particles as a plausible mechanism. *Developmental Psychology, 29,* 286–299.
Aunola, K., Stattin, H., & Nurmi, J.-E. (2000). Parenting styles and adolescents' achievement strategies. *Journal of Adolescence, 23,* 205–222.
Aunola, K., Stattin, H., & Nurmi, J.-E. (2000). Parenting styles and adolescents' achievement strategies. *Journal of Adolescence, 23,* 205–222.
Averhart, C. J., & Bigler, R. S. (1997). Shades of meaning: Skin tone, racial attitudes, and constructive memory in African-American children. *Journal of Experimental Child Psychology, 67,* 368–388.
Avis, J., & Harris, P. L. (1991). Belief– desire reasoning among Baka children: Evidence for a universal conception of mind. *Child Development, 62,* 460–467.
AWC (American Women's Club) Oslo. (2005). *Health care in Norway.* Retrieved from www.awcoslo.org/Sections/LivingInOslo/health_care_in_norway.htm
Axia, G., Bonichini, S., & Benini, F. (1999). Attention and reaction to distress in infancy: A longitudinal study. *Developmental Psychology, 35,* 500–504.
Axinn, W. G., & Barber, J. S. (1997). Living arrangements and family formation attitudes in early adulthood. *Journal of Marriage and the Family, 59,* 595–611.
Azar, S. T., & Wolfe, D. A. (1998). Child physical abuse and neglect. In E. J. Mash & R. A. Barkley (Eds.), *Treatment of childhood disorders* (2nd ed., pp. 501–544). New York: Guilford.
Azurmendi, A., Braza, F., Garcia, A., Braza, P., Munoz, J. M., & Sanchez-Martin, J. R. (2006). Aggression, dominance, and affiliation: Their relationships with androgen levels and intelligence in 5-year-old children. *Hormones and Behavior, 50,* 132–140.
Bach-y-Rita, P. (2001). Theoretical and practical considerations in the restoration of function after stroke. *Topics in Stroke Rehabilitation, 8,* 1–15.
Baddeley, A. (2000). Short-term and working memory. In E. Tulving & R. I. M. Craik (Eds.), *The Oxford handbook of memory* (pp. 77–92). New York: Oxford University Press.
Bader, A. P. (1995). Engrossment revisited: Fathers are still falling in love with their newborn babies. In J. L. Shapiro, M. J. Diamond, & M. Greenberg (Eds.), *Becoming a father* (pp 224–233). New York: Springer.
Bader, A. P., & Phillips, R. D. (2002). Fathers' recognition of their newborns by visual-facial and olfactory cues. *Psychology of Men and Masculinity, 3,* 79–84.
Baenninger, M., & Newcombe, N. (1995). Environmental input to the development of sex-related differences in spatial and mathematical ability. *Learning and Individual Differences, 7,* 363–379.
Baer, J. (2002). Is family cohesion a risk or protective factor during adolescent development? *Journal of Marriage and Family, 64,* 668–675.
Baer, J. S., Sampson, P. D., Barr, H. M., Connor, P. D., & Streissguth, A. P. (2003). A 21-year longitudinal analysis of the effects of prenatal alcohol exposure on young adult drinking. *Archives of General Psychiatry, 60,* 377–385.
Bagwell, C. L., & Coie, J. D. (2004). The best friendships of aggressive boys: Relationship quality, conflict management, and rule-breaking behavior. *Journal of Experimental Child Psychology, 88,* 5–24.
Bagwell, C. L., Coie, J. D., Terry, R. A., & Lochman, J. E. (2000). Peer clique participation and social status in preadolescence. *Merrill-Palmer Quarterly, 46,* 280–305.
Bagwell, C. L., Newcomb, A. F., & Bukowski, W. M. (1998). Preadolescent friendship and peer rejection as predictors of adult adjustment. *Child Development, 69,* 140–153.
Bagwell, C. L., Schmidt, M. E., Newcomb, A. F., & Bukowski, W. M. (2001). Friendship and peer rejection as predictors of adult adjustment. In D. W. Nangle & C. A. Erdley (Eds.), *The role of friendship in psychological adjustment* (pp. 25–49). San Francisco: Jossey-Bass.
Bahrick, L. E., Gogate, L. J., & Ruiz, I. (2002). Attention and memory for faces and actions in infancy: The salience of actions over faces in dynamic events. *Child Development, 73,* 1629–1643.
Bahrick, L. E., Hernandez-Reif, M., & Flom, R. (2005). The development of infant learning about specific face–voice relations. *Developmental Psychology, 41,* 541–552.
Bahrick, L. E., Hernandez-Reif, M., & Pickens, J. N. (1997). The effect of retrieval cues on visual preferences and memory in infancy: Evidence for a four-phase attention function. *Journal of Experimental Child Psychology, 67,* 1–20.
Bahrick, L. E., Lickliter, R., & Flom, R. (2004). Intersensory redundancy guides the development of selective attention, perception, and cognition in infancy. *Current Directions in Psychological Science, 13,* 99–102.
Bahrick, L. E., Netto, D., & Hernandez-Reif, M. (1998). Intermodal perception of adult and child faces and voices by infants. *Child Development, 69,* 1263–1275.
Bahrick, L. E., & Pickens, J. N. (1995). Infant memory for object motion across a period of three months: Implications for a four-phase attention function. *Journal of Experimental Child Psychology, 59,* 343–371.
Bai, D. L., & Bertenthal, B. I. (1992). Locomotor status and the development of spatial search skills. *Child Development, 63,* 215–226.
Bailey, J. M., Bobrow, D., Wolfe, M., & Mikach, S. (1995). Sexual orientation of adult sons of gay fathers. *Developmental Psychology, 31,* 124–129.
Bailey, J. M., Dunne, M. P., & Martin, N. G. (2000). Genetic and environmental influences on sexual orientation and its correlates in an Australian twin sample. *Journal of Personality and Social Psychology, 78,* 524–536.
Bailey, R. C. (1991). The comparative growth of Efe pygmies and African farmers from birth to age 5 years. *Annals of Human Biology, 18,* 113–120.
Baillargeon, R. (2000). Reply to Bogartz, Shinskey, and Schilling: Schilling; and Cashon and Cohen. *Infancy, 1,* 447–462.
Baillargeon, R. (2004). Infants' reasoning about hidden objects: Evidence for event-general and event-specific expectations. *Developmental Science, 7,* 391–424.
Baillargeon, R., & DeVos, J. (1991). Object permanence in young infants: Further evidence. *Child Development, 62,* 1227–1246.
Bainbridge, J., Meyers, M. K., Tanaka, S., & Waldfogel, J. (2005). Who gets an early education? Family income and the enrollment of three- to five-year-olds from 1968 to 2000. *Social Science Quarterly, 86,* 724–745.
Baker, J. A. (2006). Contributions of teacher–child relationships to positive school adjustment during elementary school. *Journal of School Psychology, 44,* 211–229.
Baker, J. L., Michaelsen, K. F., Rasmussen, K. M., & Sørensen, T. I. (2004). Maternal prepregnant body mass index, duration of breastfeeding, and timing of complementary food introduction are associated with infant weight gain. *American Journal of Clinical Nutrition, 80,* 1579–1588.
Bakermans-Kranenburg, M. J., van IJzendoorn, M. H., & Juffer, F. (2003). Less is more: Meta-analyses of sensitivity and attachment interventions in early childhood. *Psychological Bulletin, 129,* 195–215.
Balsano, A. B. (2005). Youth civic engagement in the United States: Understanding and addressing the impact of social impediments on positive youth and community development. *Applied Developmental Science, 9,* 188–201.
Band, G. P. H., van der Molen, M. W., Overtoom, C. C. E., & Verbaten, M. N. (2000). The ability to activate and inhibit speeded responses: Separate developmental trends. *Journal of Experimental Child Psychology, 75,* 263–290.
Bandura, A. (1977). *Social learning theory.* Englewood Cliffs, NJ: Prentice-Hall.
Bandura, A. (1992). Perceived selfefficacy in cognitive development and functioning. *Educational Psychologist, 28,* 117–118.
Bandura, A. (1999). Social cognitive theory of personality. In L. A. Pervin (Ed.), *Handbook of personality: Theory and research* (2nd ed., pp. 154–196). New York: Guilford.
Bandura, A. (2001). Social cognitive theory: An agentic perspective. *Annual Review of Psychology, 52,* 1–26.
Banish, M. T. (1998). Integration of information between the cerebral hemispheres. *Current Directions in Psychological Science, 7,* 32–37.
Banish, M. T., & Heller, W. (1998). Evolving perspectives on lateralization of function. *Current Directions in Psychological Science, 7,* 1–2.
Banks, M. S. (1980). The development of visual accommodation during early infancy. *Child Development, 51,* 157–173.
Banks, M. S., & Ginsburg, A. P. (1985). Early visual preferences: A review and new theoretical treatment. In H. W. Reese (Ed.), *Advances in child development and behavior* (Vol. 19, pp. 207–246). New York: Academic Press.
Banks, M. S., & Salapatek, P. (1983). Infant visual perception. In M. M. Haith & J. J. Campos (Eds.), *Handbook of child psychology: Vol. 2. Infancy and developmental psychobiology* (4th ed., pp. 435–571). New York: Wiley.
Barakat, L. P., & Kazak, A. E. (1999). Family issues. In R. T. Brown (Ed.), *Cognitive aspects of chronic illness in children* (pp. 333–354). New York: Guilford.
Barber, B. K., & Harmon, E. L. (2002). Violating the self: Parental psychological control of children and adolescents. In B. K. Barber (Ed.), *Intrusive parenting: How psychological control affects children and adolescents* (pp. 15–52). Washington, DC: American Psychological Association.
Barber, B. K., & Olsen, J. A. (1997). Socialization in context: Connection, regulation, and autonomy in the family, school, and neighborhood, and with peers. *Journal of Adolescent Research, 12,* 287–315.
Barber, B. K., & Olsen, J. A. (2004). Assessing the transitions to middle and high school. *Journal of Adolescent Research, 19,* 3–30.
Barber, B. K., Stolz, H. E., & Olsen, J. A. (2005). Parental support, psychological control, and behavioral control: Assessing relevance across time, culture, and method. *Monographs of the Society for Research in Child Development, 70*(4, Serial No. 282).
Barber, B. L., Stone, M. R., Hunt, J. E., & Eccles, J. S. (2005). Benefits of activity participation: The roles of identity affirmation and peer group norm sharing. In J. L. Mahoney, R. W. Larson, & J. S. Eccles (Eds.), *Organized activities as contexts of development: Extracurricular activities, after-school and community programs* (pp. 185–210). Mahwah, NJ: Erlbaum.
Barber, J. S. (2001a). Ideational influences on the transition to parenthood: Attitudes toward childbearing and competing alternatives. *Social Psychology Quarterly, 64,* 101–127.
Barber, J. S. (2001b). The intergenerational transmission of age at first birth among married and unmarried men and women. *Social Sciences Research, 30,* 219–247.
Bard, K. A., Todd, B. K., Bernier, C., Love, J., & Leavens, D. A. (2006). Self-awareness in human and chimpanzee infants: What is measured and what is meant by the mark and mirror test? *Infancy, 9,* 191–219.
Barenbaum, J., Ruchkin, V., & Schwab-Stone, M. (2004). The psychosocial aspects of children exposed to war: Practice and policy initiatives. *Journal of Child Psychology and Psychiatry, 45,* 41–62.
Barker, D. (2002). Fetal programming of coronary heart disease. *Trends in Endocrinology and Metabolism, 13,* 364.
Barkley, R. A. (2001). Executive functions and self-regulation: An evolutionary neuropsychological perspective. *Neuropsychology Review, 11,* 1–29.
Barkley, R. A. (2002a). Psychosocial treatments of attention-deficit/hyperactivity disorder in children. *Journal of Clinical Psychology, 63*(Suppl. 12), 36–43.
Barkley, R. A. (2002b). Major life activity and health outcomes associated with attention-deficit/hyperactivity disorder. *Journal of Clinical Psychiatry, 63*(Suppl. 12), 10–15.

Barkley, R. A. (2003). Attention-deficit/hyperactivity disorder. In E. J. Mash & R. A. Barkley (Eds.), *Child psychopathology* (2nd ed., pp. 75–143). New York: Guilford.

Barkley, R. A. (2006). Attention-deficit/hyperactivity disorder. In R. A. Barkley, D. A. Wolfe, & E. J. Mash (Eds.), *Behavioral and emotional disorders in adolescents: Nature, assessment, and treatment* (pp. 91–152). New York: Guilford.

Barnea-Goraly, N., Menon, V., Eckert, M., Tamm, L., Bammer, R., & Karchemskiy, A. (2005). White matter development during childhood and adolescence: A cross-sectional diffusion tensor imaging study. *Cerebral Cortex, 15,* 1848–1854.

Barnes, G. M., Hoffman, J. H., Welte, J. W., Farrell, M. P., & Dintcheff, B. A. (2006). Effects of parental monitoring and peer deviance on substance use and delinquency. *Journal of Marriage and Family, 68,* 1084–1104.

Barnes-Josiah, D., & Augustin, A. (1995). Secular trend in the age at menarche in Haiti. *American Journal of Human Biology, 7,* 357–362.

Barnet, B., Arroyo, C., Devoe, M., & Duggan, A. K. (2004). Reduced school dropout rates among adolescent mothers receiving school-based prenatal care. *Archives of Pediatric and Adolescent Medicine, 158,* 262–268.

Barnett, D., Ganiban, J., & Cicchetti, D. (1999). Maltreatment, negative expressivity, and the development of Type D attachments from 12 to 24 months of age. In J. I. Vondra & D. Barnett (Eds.), *Atypical attachment in infancy and early childhood among children at developmental risk. Monographs of the Society for Research in Child Development, 64*(3, Serial No. 258), pp. 97–118.

Barnett, D., & Vondra, J. I. (1999). Atypical patterns of early attachment: Theory, research, and current directions. In J. I. Vondra & D. Barnett (Eds.), *Atypical attachment in infancy and early childhood among children at developmental risk. Monographs of the Society for Research in Child Development, 64*(3, Serial No. 258), pp. 1–24.

Baron-Cohen, S., Baldwin, D. A., & Crowson, M. (1997). Do children with autism use the speaker's direction of gaze strategy to crack the code of language? *Child Development, 68,* 48–57.

Baron-Cohen, S., & Belmonte, M. K. (2005). Autism: A window onto the development of the social and the analytic brain. *Annual Review of Neuroscience, 28,* 109–126.

Barr, H. M., Streissguth, A. P., Darby, B. L., & Sampson, P. D. (1990). Prenatal exposure to alcohol, caffeine, tobacco, and aspirin: Effects on fine and gross motor performance in 4-year-old children. *Developmental Psychology, 26,* 339–348.

Barr, R., & Hayne, H. (1999). Developmental changes in imitation from television during infancy. *Child Development, 70,* 1067–1081.

Barr, R., & Hayne, H. (2003). It's not what you know, it's who you know: Older siblings facilitate imitation during infancy. *International Journal of Early Years Education, 11,* 7–21.

Barr, R., Marrott, H., & Rovee-Collier, C. (2003). The role of sensory preconditioning in memory retrieval by preverbal infants. *Learning and Behavior, 31,* 111–123.

Barr, R. G. (2001). "Colic" is something infants do, rather than a condition they "have": A developmental approach to crying phenomena patterns, pacification and (patho)genesis. In R. G. Barr, I. St James- Roberts, & M. R. Keefe (Eds.), *New evidence on unexplained infant crying* (pp. 87–104). St. Louis: Johnson & Johnson Pediatric Institute.

Barr, R. G., Paterson, J. A., MacMartin, L. M., & Lehtonen, L. (2005). Prolonged and unsoothable crying bouts in infants with and without colic. *Journal of Developmental and Behavioral Pediatrics, 26,* 14–23.

Barratt, M. S., Roach, M. A., & Leavitt, L. A. (1996). The impact of low-risk prematurity on maternal behaviour and toddler outcomes. *International Journal of Behavioral Development, 19,* 581–602.

Barrett, J. L. (2002). Do children experience God as adults do? In J. Andresen (Ed.), *Religion in mind* (pp. 173–190). New York: Cambridge University Press.

Barrett, J. L., Richert, R. A., & Driesenga, A. (2001). God's beliefs versus mother's: The development of nonhuman agent concepts. *Child Development, 72,* 50–65.

Barrett, J. L., & Van Orman, B. (1996). The effects of the use of images in worship on God concepts. *Journal of Psychology and Christianity, 15,* 38–45.

Barrett, K. C. (2005). The origins of social emotions and self-regulation in toddlerhood: New evidence. *Cognition and Emotion, 19,* 953–979.

Bartgis, J., Lilly, A. R., & Thomas, D. G. (2003). Event-related potential and behavioral measures of attention in 5-, 7-, and 9-year-olds. *Journal of General Psychology, 130,* 311–335.

Barton, M. E., & Strosberg, R. (1997). Conversational patterns of two-year-old twins in mother–twin–twin triads. *Journal of Child Language, 24,* 257–269.

Barton, M. E., & Tomasello, M. (1991). Joint attention and conversation in mother–infant–sibling triads. *Child Development, 62,* 517–529.

Bartrip, J., Morton, J., & de Schonen, S. (2001). Responses to mother's face in 3-week to 3-month-old infants. *British Journal of Developmental Psychology, 19,* 219–232.

Bartsch, K., & Wellman, H. (1995). *Children talk about the mind.* New York: Oxford University Press.

Basow, S. A., & Rubin, L. R. (1999). Gender influences on adolescent development. In N. G. Johnson & M. C. Roberts (Eds.), *Beyond appearance: A new look at adolescent girls* (pp. 25–52). Washington, DC: American Psychological Association.

Bass, J. L., Corwin, M., Gozal, D., Moore, C., Nishida, H., Parker, S., Schonwald, A., Wilker, R. E., Stehle, S., & Kinane, T. B. (2004). The effect of chronic or intermittent hypoxia on cognition in childhood: A review of the evidence. *Pediatrics, 114,* 805–816.

Bates, E. (2004). Explaining and interpreting deficits in language development across clinical groups: Where do we go from here? *Brain and Language, 88,* 248–253.

Bates, E., & MacWhinney, B. (1987). Competition, variation, and language learning. In B. MacWhinney (Ed.), *Mechanisms of language acquisition* (pp. 157–193). Hillsdale, NJ: Erlbaum.

Bates, E., Marchman, V., Thal, D., Fenson, L., Dale, P., Reznick, J. S., Reilly, J., & Hartung, J. (1994). Developmental and stylistic variation in the composition of early vocabulary. *Journal of Child Language, 21,* 85–123.

Bates, E., Wilson, S. M., Saygin, A. P., Dick, F., Sereno, M. I., Knight, R. T., & Dronkers, N. F. (2003). Voxel-based lesion-symptom mapping. *Nature Neuroscience, 6,* 448–450.

Bates, J. E., Wachs, T. D., & Emde, R. N. (1994). Toward practical uses for biological concepts. In J. E. Bates & T. D. Wachs (Eds.), *Temperament: Individual differences at the interface of biology and behavior* (pp. 275–306). Washington, DC: American Psychological Association.

Bauer, C. R., Langer, J. C., Shakaran, S., Bada, H. S., & Lester, B. (2005). Acute neonatal effects of cocaine exposure during pregnancy. *Archives of Pediatrics and Adolescent Medicine, 159,* 824–834.

Bauer, P. J. (1997). Development of memory in early child-hood. In N. Cowan (Ed.), *The development of memory in childhood* (pp. 83–111). Hove, U.K.: Psychology Press.

Bauer, P. J. (2002a). Early memory development. In U. Goswami (Ed.), *Blackwell handbook of child cognitive development* (pp. 127–150). Malden, MA: Blackwell.

Bauer, P. J. (2002b). Long-term recall memory: Behavioral and neuro-developmental changes in the first 2 years of life. *Current Directions in Psychological Science, 11,* 137–141.

Bauer, P. J. (2006). Event memory. In D. Kuhn & R. Siegler (Eds.), *Handbook of child psychology: Vol. 2. Cognition, perception, and language* (6th ed., pp. 373–425). Hoboken, NJ: Wiley.

Bauer, P. J., Wiebe, S. A., Carver, L. J., Lukowski, A. F., Haight, J. C., Waters, J. M., & Nelson, C. A. (2006). Electrophysiological indexes of encoding and behavioral indexes of recall: Examining relations and developmental change late in the first year of life. *Developmental Neuropsychology, 29,* 293–320.

Baumeister, R. F. (1998). Inducing guilt. In J. Bybee (Ed.), *Guilt and children* (pp. 185–213). San Diego: Academic Press.

Baumeister, R. F., Campbell, J. D., Krueger, J. I., & Vohs, K. D. (2003). Does high self-esteem cause better performance, interpersonal success, happiness, or healthier lifestyles? *Psychological Science in the Public Interest, 4*(1), 1–44.

Baumeister, R. F., Smart, L., & Boden, J. M. (1996). Relation of threatened egotism to violence and aggression: The dark side of high self-esteem. *Psychological Review, 103,* 5–33.

Baumrind, D. (1971). Current patterns of parental authority. *Developmental Psychology Monograph, 4* (No. 1, Pt. 2).

Baumwell, L., Tamis-LeMonda, C. S., & Bornstein, M. H. (1997). Maternal verbal sensitivity and child language comprehension. *Infant Behavior and Development, 20,* 247–258.

Bauserman, R. (2002). Child adjustment in joint-custody versus sole-custody arrangements: A metaanalytic review. *Journal of Family Psychology, 16,* 91–102.

Baydar, N., Greek, A., & Brooks-Gunn, J. (1997). A longitudinal study of the effects of the birth of a sibling during the first 6 years of life. *Journal of Marriage and the Family, 59,* 939–956.

Bayley, N. (1969). *Bayley Scales of Infant Development.* New York: Psychological Corporation.

Bayley, N. (1993). *Bayley Scales of Infant Development* (2nd ed.). New York: Psychological Corporation.

Bayley, N. (2005). *Bayley Scales of Infant and Toddler Development* (3rd ed.). (Bayley III). San Antonio, TX: Harcourt Assessment.

Beals, D. E. (2001). Eating and reading: Links between family conversations with preschoolers and later language and literacy. In D. K. Dickinson & P. O. Tabors (Eds.), *Beginning literacy with language: Young children learning athome and school* (pp. 75–92). Baltimore, MD: Paul H. Brookes.

Bean, R. A., Barber, B. K., & Crane, D. R. (2007). Parental support, behavioral control, and psychological control among African American youth: The relationships to academic grades, delinquency, and depression. *Journal of Family Issues, 27,* 1335–1355.

Bearer, C. F., Stoler, J. M., Cook, J. D., & Carpenter, S. J. (2005). *Biomarkers of alcohol use in pregnancy.* National Institute on Alcohol Abuse and Alcoholism. Retrieved from pubs.niaaa.nih.gov/publications/arh28-1/38-43.htm

Bearman, P. S., & Moody, J. (2004). Suicide and friendships among American adolescents. *American Journal of Public Health, 94,* 89–95.

Beatty, W. W. (1992). Gonadal hormones and sex differences in nonreproductive behaviors. In A. A. Gerall, H. Moltz, & I. L. Ward (Eds.), *Handbook of behavioral neurobiology: Vol. 11. Sexual differentiation* (pp. 85–128). New York: Plenum.

Beautrais, A. L. (2003). Life course factors associated with suicidal behaviors in young people. *American Behavioral Scientist, 46,* 1137–1156.

Becker, G., Beyene, Y., Newsome, E., & Mayen, N. (2003). Creating continuity through mutual assistance: Intergenerational reciprocity in four ethnic groups. *Journal of Gerontology, 38B,* S151–S159.

Beckett, C., Maughan, B., Rutter, M., Castle, J., Colvert, E., & Groothues, C. (2006). Do the effects of early severe deprivation on cognition persist into early adolescence? Findings from the English and Romanian adoptees study. *Child Development, 77,* 696–711.

Bedford, O. A. (2004). The individual experience of guilt and shame in Chinese culture. *Culture and Psychology, 10,* 29–52.

Beekhoven, S., & Dekkers, H. (2005). Early school leaving in the lower vocational track: Triangulation of qualitative and quantitative data. *Adolescence, 40,* 197–213.

Behnke, M., Eyler, F. D., Garvan, C. W., & Wobie, K. (2001). The search for congenital malformations in newborns with fetal cocaine exposure. *Pediatrics, 107,* e74.

Behnke, M., Eyler, F. D., Warner, T. D., Garvan, C. W., Hou, W., & Wobie, K. (2006). Outcome from a prospective, longitudinal study of prenatal cocaine use: Preschool development at 3 years of age. *Journal of Pediatric Psychology, 31,* 41–49.

Behrman, R. E., Kliegman, R. M., & Arvin, A. M. (1996). *Nelson textbook of pediatrics* (15th ed.). Philadelphia: Saunders.

Behrman, R. E., Kliegman, R. M., & Jenson, H. B. (2000). *Nelson textbook of pediatrics* (16th ed.). Philadelphia: Saunders.

Beilin, H. (1992). Piaget's enduring contribution to developmental psychology. *Developmental Psychology, 28,* 191–204.

Beitel, A. H., & Parke, R. D. (1998). Paternal involvement in infancy: The role of maternal and paternal attitudes. *Journal of Family Psychology, 12,* 268–288.

Bell, J. H., & Bromnick, R. D. (2003). The social reality of the imaginary audience: A grounded theory approach. *Adolescence, 38,* 205–219.

Bell, M. A. (1998). Frontal lobe function during infancy: Implications for the development of cognition and attention. In J. E. Richards (Ed.), *Cognitive neuroscience of attention: A developmental perspective* (pp. 327–362). Mahwah, NJ: Erlbaum.

Bell, M. A., & Fox, N. A. (1996). Crawling experience is related to changes in cortical organization during infancy: Evidence from EEG coherence. *Developmental Psychobiology, 29,* 551–561.

Bellamy, C. (2004). *The state of the world's children: 2004.* New York: UNICEF.

Bellamy, C. (2005). *The state of the world's children 2005.* New York: UNICEF.

Bellinger, D. C. (2005). Teratogen update: Lead and pregnancy. *Birth Defects Research: Part A, Clinical and Molecular Teratology, 73,* 409–420.

Bellinger, D. C., Leviton, A., & Sloman, J. (1990). Antecedents and correlates of improved cognitive performance in children exposed in utero to low levels of lead. *Environmental Health Perspectives, 89,* 5–11.

Belsky, J. (2001). Emanuel Miller Lecture: Developmental risks (still) associated with early child care. *Journal of Child Psychology and Psychiatry, 42,* 845–859.

Belsky, J. (2005). Attachment theory and research in ecological perspective: Insights from the Pennsylvania Infant and Family Development Project and the NICHD Study of Early Child Care. In K. E. Grossmann, K. Grossmann, & E. Waters (Eds.), *Attachment from infancy to adulthood: The major longitudinal studies* (pp. 71–97). New York: Guilford.

Belsky, J., Campbell, S. B., Cohn, J. F., & Moore, G. (1996). Instability of infant–parent attachment security. *Developmental Psychology, 32,* 921–924.

Belsky, J., & Fearon, R. M. P. (2002a). Early attachment security, subsequent maternal sensitivity, and later child development: Does continuity in development depend on caregiving? *Attachment and Human Development, 4,* 361–387.

Belsky, J., & Fearon, R. M. P. (2002b). Infant–mother attachment security, contextual risk, and early development: A moderational analysis. *Development and Pathology, 14,* 293–310.

Belsky, J., & Hsieh, K.-H. (1998). Patterns of marital change during the early childhood years: Parent personality, coparenting, and division-of-labor correlates. *Journal of Family Psychology, 12,* 511–528.

Bempechat, J., & Drago-Severson, E. (1999). Cross-national differences in academic achievement: Beyond etic conceptions of children's understandings. *Review of Educational Research, 69,* 287–314.

Benbow, C. P., Lubinski, D., Shea, D. L., & Eftekhara-Sanjani, H. (2000). Sex differences in mathematical reasoning ability at age 13: Their status 20 years later. *Psychological Science, 11,* 474–480.

Benbow, C. P., & Stanley, J. C. (1983). Sex differences in mathematical reasoning: More facts. *Science, 222,* 1029–1031.

Benenson, J. F., & Christakos, A. (2003). The greater fragility of females' versus males' closest same-sex friendships. *Child Development, 74,* 1123–1129.

Bengtson, H. (2005). Children's cognitive appraisal of others' distressful and positive experiences. *International Journal of Behavioral Development, 29,* 457–466.

Benigno, J. P., & Ellis, S. (2004). Two is greater than three: Effects of older siblings on parental support of preschoolers' counting in middle-income families. *Early Childhood Research Quarterly, 19,* 4–20.

Bennett, K. E., Haggard, M. P., Silva, P. A., & Stewart, I. A. (2001). Behaviour and developmental effects of otitis media with effusion into the teens. *Archives of Disease in Childhood, 85,* 91–95.

Bennett, M., Barrett, M., Karakozov, R., Kipiani, G., Lyons, E., Pavlenko, V., & Riazanova, T. (2004). Young children's evaluations of the ingroup and outgroups: A multi-national study. *Social Development, 13,* 124–141.

Bennett, S. E., & Assefi, N. P. (2005). School-based teenage pregnancy prevention programs: A systematic review of randomized controlled trials. *Journal of Adolescent Health, 36,* 72–81.

Benson, P. L., Scales, P. C., Hamilton, S. F., & Sesma, A., Jr. (2006). Positive youth development: Theory, research, and applications. In R. M. Lerner (Ed.), *Handbook of child psychology: Vol. 1. Theoretical models of human development* (6th ed., pp. 894–941). Hoboken, NJ: Wiley.

Ben-Zeev, T., Carrasquillo, C. M., Ching, A. M. L., Patton, G. E., Stewart, T. D., & Stoddard, T. (2005). "Math is hard!" (Barbie™, 1994): Responses of threat vs. challenge-mediated arousal to stereotypes alleging intellectual inferiority. In A. M. Gallagher & J. C. Kaufman (Eds.), *Gender differences in mathematics: An integrative psychological approach* (pp. 189–206). New York: Cambridge University Press.

Berenbaum, S. A. (2001). Cognitive function in congenital adrenal hyperplasia. *Endocrinology and Metabolism Clinics of North America, 30,* 173–192.

Bergen, D., & Mauer, D. (2000). Symbolic play, phonological awareness, and literacy skills at three age levels. In K. A. Roskos & J. F. Christie (Eds.), *Play and literacy in early childhood: Research from multiple perspectives* (pp. 45–62). Mahwah, NJ: Erlbaum.

Berger, A., Tzur, G., & Posner, M. I. (2006). Infant brains detect arithmetic errors. *Proceedings of the National Academy of Sciences, 103,* 12649–12653.

Bergman, R. (2004). Identity as motivation. In D, K. Lapsley & D. Narvaez (Eds.), *Moral development, self, and identity* (pp. 21–46). Mahwah, NJ: Erlbaum.

Berk, L. E. (1985). Relationship of caregiver education to child-oriented attitudes, job satisfaction, and behaviors toward children. *Child Care Quarterly, 14,* 103–129.

Berk, L. E. (1992). The extracurriculum. In P. W. Jackson (Ed.), *Handbook of research on curriculum* (pp. 1002–1043). New York: Macmillan.

Berk, L. E. (2001a). *Awakening children's minds: How parents and teachers can make a difference.* New York: Oxford University Press.

Berk, L. E. (2001b). Private speech and self-regulation in children with impulse-control difficulties: Implications for research and practice. *Journal of Cognitive Education and Psychology, 2*(1), 1–21.

Berk, L. E. (2004). *Conversations with children.* Normal, IL: Illinois State University.

Berk, L. E. (2005). Why parenting matters. In S. Olfman (Ed.), *Childhood lost: How American culture is failing our kids* (pp. 19–53). New York: Guilford.

Berk, L. E. (2006a). Looking at kindergarten children. In D. Gullo (Ed.), *K today: Teaching and learning in the kindergarten year* (pp. 11–25). Washington, DC: National Association for the Education of Young Children.

Berk, L. E. (2006b). Make-believe play: Wellspring for development of self-regulation. In D. Singer, K. Hirsh-Pasek, & R. Golinkoff (Eds.), *Play = learning.* New York: Oxford University Press.

Berk, L. E., & Harris, S. (2003). Vygotsky, Lev. In L. Nadel (Ed.), *Encyclopedia of cognitive science.* London: Macmillan.

Berk, L. E., Mann, T., & Ogan, A. (2006). Make-believe play: Wellspring for development of self-regulation. In D. Singer, K. Hirsh-Pasek, & R. Golinkoff (Eds.), *Play=learning* (pp. 74–100). New York: Oxford University Press.

Berk, L. E., & Spuhl, S. T. (1995). Maternal interaction, private speech, and task performance in preschool children. *Early Childhood Research Quarterly, 10,* 145–169.

Berkowitz, C. M. (2004). *Talking to your kids about sex.* Somerville, NJ: Somerset Medical Center. Retrieved from www.somersetmedicalcenter.com/18417.cfm

Berkowitz, M. W., & Gibbs, J. C. (1983). Measuring the developmental features of moral discussion. *Merrill-Palmer Quarterly, 29,* 399–410.

Berkowitz, R. J., & Stunkard, A. J. (2002). Development of childhood obesity. In T. A. Wadden & A. J. Stunkard (Eds.), *Handbook of obesity treatment* (pp. 515–531). New York: Guilford.

Berkowitz, R. L., Roberts, J., & Minkoff, H. (2006). Challenging the strategy of maternal age-based prenatal genetic counseling. *Journal of the American Medical Association, 295,* 1446–1448.

Berman, P. W. (1980). Are women more responsive than men to the young? A review of developmental and situational variables. *Psychological Bulletin, 88,* 668–695.

Berman, S. L., Weems, C. F., Rodriguez, E. T., & Zamora, I. J. (2006). The relation between identity status and romantic attachment style in middle and late adolescence. *Journal of Adolescence, 29,* 737–748.

Berndt, T. J. (2004). Children's friendships: Shifts over a half-century in perspectives on their development and effects. *Merrill-Palmer Quarterly, 50,* 206–223.

Berndt, T. J., & Keefe, K. (1995). Friends' influence on adolescents' adjustment to school. *Child Development, 66,* 1312–1329.

Berndt, T. J., & Murphy, L. M. (2002). Influences of friends and friendships: Myths, truths, and research recommendations. In R. V. Kail (Ed.), *Advances in child development and behavior* (Vol. 30, pp. 275–310). San Diego, CA: Academic Press.

Bernier, J. C., & Siegel, D. H. (1994). Attention-deficit hyperactivity disorder: A family ecological systems perspective. *Families in Society, 75,* 142–150.

Bernier, L., & Grégoire, D. (2004). Reproductive and therapeutic cloning, germline therapy, and purchase of gametes and embryos: Comments on Canadian legislation governing reproduction technologies. *Journal of Medical Ethics, 30,* 527–532.

Berninger, V. W. (2006). A developmental approach to learning disabilities. In K. A. Renninger & I. E. Sigel (Eds.), *Handbook of child psychology: Vol. 4. Child psychology in practice* (6th ed., pp. 420–452). Hoboken, NJ: Wiley.

Berninger, V. W., Vermeulen K., Abbott, R. D., McCutchen, D., Cotton, S., & Cude, J. (2003). Naming speed and phonological awareness as predictors of reading development. *Journal of Educational Psychology, 95,* 452–464.

Bertenthal, B. I. (1993). Infants' perception of biomechanical motions: Intrinsic image and knowledge-based constraints. In C. Granrud (Ed.), *Visual percpetion and cognition in infancy* (pp. 175–214). Hillsdale, NJ: Erlbaum.

Berthier, N. E., Bertenthal, B. I., Seaks, J. D., Sylvia, M. R., Johnson, R. L., & Clifton, R. K. (2001). Using object knowledge in visual tracking and reaching. *Infancy, 2,* 257–284.

Bertrand, M., & Mullainathan, S. (2004). *Are Emily and Brendan more employable than Lakisha and Jamal? A field experiment on labor market discrimination.* Unpublished manuscript, University of Chicago.

Berzonsky, M. D. (2003). Identity style and well-being: Does commitment matter? *Identity: An International Journal of Theory and Research, 3,* 131–142.

Berzonsky, M. D., & Kuk, L. S. (2000). Identity status, identity processing style, and the transition to university. *Journal of Adolescent Research, 15,* 81–98.

Best, D. L. (2001). Gender concepts: Convergence in cross-cultural research and methodologies. *Cross-cultural Research: The Journal of Comparative Social Science, 35,* 23–43.

Beyers, J. M., Bates, J. E., Pettit, G. S., & Dodge, K. A. (2003). Neighborhood structure, parenting processes, and the development of youths' externalizing behaviors: A multilevel analysis. *American Journal of Community Psychology, 31,* 35–53.

Beyth-Marom, R., & Fischhoff, B. (1997). Adolescents' decisions about risks: A cognitive perspective. In J. Schulenberg, J. L. Maggs, & K. Hurrelmann (Eds.), *Health risks and developmental transitions during adolescence* (pp. 110–135). New York: Cambridge University Press.

Bhandari, N., Bahl, R., Taneja, S., Strand, T., & Mølbak, K. (2002). Substantial reduction in severe diarrheal morbidity by daily zinc supplementation in young North Indian children. *Pediatrics, 109,* e86–e92.

Bhanot, R., & Jovanovic, J. (2005). Do parents' academic gender stereotypes influence whether they intrude on their children's homework? *Sex Roles, 52,* 597–607.

Bhat, A., Heathcock, J., & Galloway, J. C. (2005). Toy-oriented changes in hand and joint kinematics during the emergence of purposeful reaching. *Infant Behavior and Development, 28,* 445–465.

Bhatt, R. S., Rovee-Collier, C., & Weiner, S. (1994). Developmental changes in the interface between perception and memory retrieval. *Developmental Psychology, 30,* 151–162.

Bhatt, R. S., Wilk, A., Hill, D., & Rovee-Collier, C. (2004). Correlated attributes and categorization in the first half-year of life. *Developmental Psychobiology, 44,* 103–115.

Bialystok, E. (2001). *Bilingualism in development: Language, literacy, and cognition.* New York: Cambridge University Press.

Bialystok, E., & Martin, M. M. (2003). Notation to symbol: Development in children's understanding of print. *Journal of Experimental Child Psychology, 86,* 223–243.

Bialystok, E., & Martin, M. M. (2004). Attention and inhibition in bilingual children: Evidence from the dimensional change card sort task. *Developmental Science, 7,* 325–339.

Bialystok, E., McBride-Chang, C., & Luk, G. (2005). Bilingualism, language proficiency, and learning to read in two writing systems. *Journal of Educational Psychology, 97,* 580–590.

Bialystok, E., & Senman, L. (2004). Executive processes in appearance–reality tasks: The role of inhibition of attention and symbolic representation. *Child Development, 75,* 562–579.

Bianchi, D. W. (2005). Prenatal genetic diagnosis. In H. W. Taeusch, R. A. Ballard, & C. A. Gleason (Eds.), *Avery's diseases of the newborn* (pp. 57–70). Philadelphia: Saunders.

Bianco, A., Stone, J., Lynch, L., Lapinski, R., Berkowitz, G., & Berkowitz, R. L. (1996). Pregnancy outcome at age 40 and older. *Obstetrics and Gynecology, 87,* 917–922.

Bibace, R., & Walsh, M. E. (1980). Development of children's concepts of illness. *Pediatrics, 66,* 912–917.

Bibby, R. W. (2000). *Restless gods: The renaissance of religion in Canada.* Toronto: Stoddart.

Biederman, J., & Spencer, T. J. (2000). Genetics of childhood disorders: XIX, ADHD, part 3: Is ADHD a noradrenergic disorder? *Journal of the American Academy of Child and Adolescent Psychiatry, 39,* 1330–1333

Biederman, J., Kwon, A., Aleardi, M., Chouinard, V.-A., Marino, T., & Cole, H. (2005). Absence of gender effects on attention-deficit hyperactivity disorder: Findings in nonreferred subjects. *American Journal of Psychiatry, 162,* 1083–1089.

Bielawska-Batorowicz, E., & Kossakowska-Petrycka, K. (2006). Depressive mood in men after the birth of their offspring in relation to a partner's depression, social support, fathers' personality and prenatal expectations. *Journal of Reproductive and Infant Psychology, 24,* 21–29.

Bielinski, J., & Davison, M. L. (1998). Gender differences by item difficulty interactions in multiple-choice mathematics items. *American Educational Research Journal, 35,* 455–476.

Bigelow, A. (1992). Locomotion and search behavior in blind infants. *Infant Behavior and Development, 15,* 179–189.

Bigelow, A. E. (2003). The development of joint attention in blind infants. *Development and Psychopathology, 15,* 259–275.

Bigler, R. S., Brown, C. S., & Markell, M. (2001). When groups are not created equal: Effects of group status on the formation of intergroup attitudes in children. *Child Development, 72,* 1151–1162.

Bigler, R. S., & Liben, L. S. (1992). Cognitive mechanisms in children's gender stereotyping: Theoretical and educational implications of a cognitive-based intervention. *Child Development, 63,* 1351–1363.

Bimmel, N., Juffer, F. van IJzendoorn, M. H., & Bakermans-Kranenburg, M. J. (2003). Problem behavior of internationally adopted adolescents: A review and meta-analysis. *Harvard Review of Psychiatry, 11,* 64–77.

Bioethics Consultative Committee. (2003). *Comparison of ethics legislation in Europe.* Retrieved from www.synapse.net.mt/bioethics/euroleg1.htm

Birch, E. E. (1993). Stereopsis in infants and its developmental relation to visual acuity. In K. Simons (Ed.), *Early visual development: Normal and abnormal* (pp. 224–236). New York: Oxford University Press.

Birch, L. L. (1999). Development of food preferences. *Annual Review of Nutrition, 19,* 41–62.

Birch, L. L., & Fisher, J. A. (1995). Appetite and eating behavior in children. *Pediatric Clinics of North America, 42,* 931–953.

Birch, L. L., Fisher, J. O., & Davison, K. K. (2003). Learning to overeat: Maternal use of restrictive feeding practices promotes girls' eating in the absence of hunger. *American Journal of Clinical Nutrition, 78,* 215–220.

Birch, L. L., Zimmerman, S., & Hind, H. (1980). The influence of social-affective context on preschool children's food preferences. *Child Development, 51,* 856–861.

Birch, S. A. J., & Bloom, P. (2003). Children are cursed: An asymmetric bias in mental-state attribution. *Psychological Science, 14,* 283–285.

Birch, S. H., & Ladd, G. W. (1998). Children's interpersonal behaviors and the teacher–child relationship. *Developmental Psychology, 34,* 934–946.

Bird, A., & Reese, E. (2006). Emotional reminiscing and the development of an autobiographical self. *Developmental Psychology, 42,* 613–626.

Biringen, Z., Emde, R. N., Campos, J. J., & Appelbaum, M. I. (1995). Affective reorganization in the infant, the mother, and the dyad: The role of upright locomotion and its timing. *Child Development, 66,* 499–514.

Birken, C. S., Parkin, P. C., To, T., & Macarthur, C. (2006). Trends in rates of death from unintentional injury among Canadian children in urban areas: Influence of socioeconomic status. *Canadian Medical Association Journal, 175,* 867–868.

Birney, D. P., Citron-Pousty, J. H., Lutz, D. J., & Sternberg, R. J. (2005). The development of cognitive and intellectual abilities. In M. H. Bornstein & M. E. Lamb (Eds.), *Developmental science: An advanced textbook* (5th ed., pp. 327–358). Mahwah, NJ: Erlbaum.

Bjorklund, D., & Blasi, C. (2005). Evolutionary developmental psychology. In D. Buss (Ed.), *Handbook of evolutionary psychology* (pp. 828–850). Hoboken, NJ: Wiley.

Bjorklund, D. F. (2004). *Children's thinking* (4th ed.). Belmont, CA: Wadsworth.

Bjorklund, D. F., & Douglas, R. N. (1997). The development of memory strategies. In N. Cowan (Ed.), *The development of memory in childhood* (pp. 83–111). Hove, U.K.: Psychology Press.

Bjorklund, D. F., & Pellegrini, A. D. (2002). *The origins of human nature: Evolutionary developmental psychology.* Washington, DC: American Psychological Association.

Bjorklund, D. F., Schneider, W., Cassel, W. S., & Ashley, E. (1994). Training and extension of a memory strategy: Evidence for utilization deficiencies in high- and low-IQ children. *Child Development, 65,* 951–965.

Black, M. M. (2005). Failure to thrive. In M. C. Roberts (Ed.), *Handbook of pediatric psychology and psychiatry* (3rd ed., pp. 499–511). New York: Guilford.

Black, R. E., Williams, S. M., Jones, I. E., & Goulding, A. (2002). Children who avoid drinking cow milk have low dietary calcium intakes and poor bone health. *American Journal of Clinical Nutrition, 76,* 675–680.

Blackwell, D. L., & Lichter, D. T. (2004). Homogamy among dating, cohabiting, and married couples. *Sociological Quarterly, 45,* 719–737.

Blakemore, J. E. O. (2003). Children's beliefs about violating gender norms: Boys shouldn't look like girls, and girls shouldn't act like boys. *Sex Roles, 48,* 411–419.

Blakemore, S.-J., & Choudhury, S. (2006). Development of the adolescent brain: Implications for executive function and social cognition. *Journal of Child Psychology and Psychiatry, 47,* 296–312.

Blanchard, R., & Bogaert, A. F. (2004). Proportion of homosexual men who owe their sexual orientation to fraternal birth order: An estimate based on two national probability samples. *American Journal of Human Biology, 16,* 151–157.

Blasi, A. (1994). Moral identity: Its role in moral functioning. In B. Puka (Ed.), *Fundamental research in moral development: A compendium* (Vol. 2, pp. 123–167). New York: Garland.

Blasi, C. H., & Bjorklund, D. F. (2003). Evolutionary developmental psychology: A new tool for better understanding human ontogeny. *Human Development, 46,* 259–281.

Blass, E. M. (1999). Savoring sucrose and suckling milk: Easing pain, saving calories, and learning about mother. In M. Lewis & D. Ramsay (Eds.), *Soothing and stress* (pp. 79–107). Mahwah, NJ: Erlbaum.

Blass, E. M., Ganchrow, J. R., & Steiner, J. E. (1984). Classical conditioning in newborn humans 2–48 hours of age. *Infant Behavior and Development, 7,* 223–235.

Blatchford, P., Bassett, P., Goldstein, H., & Martin, C. (2003). Are class size differences related to pupils' educational progress and classroom processes? Findings from the Institute of Education Class Size Study of children aged 5–7 years. *British Educational Research Journal, 29,* 709–730.

Blazek-O'Neill, B. (2005). Complementary and alternative medicine in allergy, otitis media, and asthma. *Current Allergy and Asthma Reports, 5,* 313–318.

Bleeker, M. M., & Jacobs, J. E. (2004). Achievement in math and science: Do mothers' beliefs matter 12 years later? *Journal of Educational Psychology, 96,* 97–109.

Blewitt, P. (1994). Understanding categorical hierarchies: The earliest levels of skills. *Child Development, 65,* 1279–1298.

Blickstein, I. (2002). Normal and abnormal growth of multiples. *Seminars in Neonatology, 7,* 177–185.

Bliss, L. S., McCabe, A., & Miranda, A. E. (1998). Narrative assessment profile: Discourse analysis for school-age children. *Journal of Communication Disorders, 31,* 347–363.

Bloom, L. (1998). Language acquisition in its developmental context. In D. Kuhn & R. S. Siegler (Eds.), *Handbook of child psychology: Vol. 2. Cognition, perception, and language* (5th ed., pp. 309–370). New York: Wiley.

Bloom, L. (2000). The intentionality model of language development: How to learn a word, any word. In R. Golinkoff, K. Hirsh-Pasek, N. Akhtar, L. Bloom, G. Hollich, L. Smith, M. Tomasello, & A. Woodward (Eds.), *Becoming a word learner: A debate on lexical acquisition.* New York: Oxford University Press.

Bloom, P. (1999). The role of semantics in solving the bootstrapping problem. In R. Jackendoff & P. Bloom (Eds.), *Language, logic, and concepts* (pp. 285–309). Cambridge, MA: MIT Press.

Blotner, R., & Bearison, D. J. (1984). Developmental consistencies in socio-moral knowledge: Justice reasoning and altruistic behavior. *Merrill-Palmer Quarterly, 30,* 349–367.

Blum, N. J., & Nemeth, N. (2003). Relationship between age at initiation of toilet training and duration of training: A prospective study. *Pediatrics, 111,* 810–814.

Blumberg, M. S., & Lucas, D. E. (1996). A developmental and component analysis of active sleep. *Developmental Psychobiology, 29,* 1–22.

Blumenfeld, P. C., Marx, R. W., & Harris, C. J. (2006). Learning environments. In K. A. Renninger & I. E. Sigel (Eds.), *Handbook of child psychology: Vol. 4. Child psychology in practice* (6th ed., pp. 297–342). Hoboken, NJ: Wiley.

Boardman, J. D. (2004). Stress and physical health: The role of neighborhoods as mediating and moderating mechanisms. *Social Science and Medicine, 58,* 2473–2483.

Bodrova, E., & Leong, D. J. (2006). *Tools of the mind: The Vygotskian approach to early childhood education.* Upper Saddle River, NJ: Merrill Prentice Hall.

Bodrova, E., & Leong, D. J. (2007). *Tools of the mind: The Vygotskian approach to early childhood education* (2nd ed.). Upper Saddle River, NJ: Merrill Prentice Hall.

Bogaert, A. F. (2005). Age at puberty and father absence in a national probability sample. *Journal of Adolescence, 28,* 541–546.

Bogartz, R. S., Shinskey, J. L., & Schilling, T. H. (2000). Object permanence in five-and-a-half-month-old infants. *Infancy, 1,* 403–428.

Bogin, B. (2001). *The growth of humanity.* New York: Wiley-Liss.

Bogin, B., Smith, P., Orden, A. B., Varela, S., & Loucky, J. (2002). Rapid change in height and body proportions of Maya American children. *American Journal of Human Biology, 14,* 753–761.

Bohannon, J. N., & Bonvillian, J. D. (2005). Theoretical approaches to language acquisition. In J. B. Gleason (Ed.), *The development of language* (6th ed., pp. 230–291). Boston: Allyn and Bacon.

Bohannon, J. N., III, & Stanowicz, L. (1988). The issue of negative evidence: Adult responses to children's language errors. *Developmental Psychology, 24,* 684–689.

Bohnert, A. M., Crnic, K., & Lim, K. G. (2003). Emotional competence and aggressive behavior in school-age children. *Journal of Abnormal Child Psychology, 31,* 79–91.

Boldizar, J. P. (1991). Assessing sex typing and androgyny in children: The children's sex role inventory. *Developmental Psychology, 27,* 505–515.

Bolen, R. M. (2001). *Child sexual abuse.* New York: Kluwer Academic.

Boller, K., Grabelle, M., & Rovee-Collier, C. (1995). Effects of postevent information on infants' memory for a central target. *Journal of Experimental Child Psychology, 59,* 372–396.

Bollmer, J. M., Milich, R., Harris, M. J., & Maras, M. A. (2005). A friend in need: The role of friendship quality as a protective factor in peer victimization and bullying. *Journal of Interpersonal Violence, 20,* 701–712.

Bolzani, L. H., Messinger, D. S., Yale, M., & Dondi, M. (2002). Smiling in infancy. In M. H. Abel (Ed.), *An empirical reflection on the smile* (pp. 111–136). Lewiston, NY: Edwin Mellen Press.

Bonilla, S., Kehl, S., Kwong, K. Y., Morphew, T., Kachru, R., & Jones, C. A. (2005). School absenteeism in children with asthma in a Los Angeles inner-city school. *Journal of Pediatrics, 147,* 802–806.

Bono, M. A., & Stifter, C. A. (2003). Maternal attention-directing strategies and infant focused attention during problem solving. *Infancy, 4,* 235–250.

Book, A. S., Starzyk, K. B., & Quinsey, V. L. (2001). The relationship between testosterone and aggression: A meta-analysis. *Aggression and Violent Behavior, 6,* 579–599.

Bookstein, F. L., Sampson, P. D., Connor, P. D., & Streissguth, A. P. (2002). Midline corpus callosum is a neuroanatomical focus of fetal alcohol damage. *Anatomical Record, 269,* 162–174.

Borke, H. (1975). Piaget's mountains revisited: Changes in the egocentric landscape. *Developmental Psychology, 11,* 240–243.

Borkowski, J. G., & Muthukrishna, N. (1995). Learning environments and skill generalization: How contexts facilitate regulatory processes and efficacy beliefs. In F. Weinert & W. Schneider (Eds.), *Memory performances and competence: Issues in growth and development* (pp. 283– 300). Mahwah, NJ: Erlbaum.

Bornstein, M. H. (1989). Sensitive periods in development: Structural characteristics and causal interpretations. *Psychological Bulletin, 105,* 179–197.

Bornstein, M. H. (2002). Parenting infants. In M. H. Bornstein (Ed.), *Handbook of parenting: Vol. 1* (2nd ed., pp. 3–44). Mahwah, NJ: Erlbaum.

Bornstein, M. H. (2006). Parenting science and practice. In K. Renninger & I. E. Sigel (Eds.), *Handbook of child psychology: Vol. 4. Child psychology in practice* (6th ed., pp. 893–949). Hoboken, NJ: Wiley.

Bornstein, M. H., & Arterberry, M. E. (1999). Perceptual development. In M. H. Bornstein & M. E. Lamb (Eds.), *Developmental psychology: An advanced textbook* (pp. 231–274). Mahwah, NJ: Erlbaum.

Bornstein, M. H., & Arterberry, M. E. (2003). Recognition, discrimination, and categorization of smiling by 5-month-old infants. *Developmental Science, 6,* 585–599.

Bornstein, M. H., & Cote, L. R. (2004). Cross-linguistic analysis of vocabulary in young children: Spanish, Dutch, French, Hebrew, Italian, Korean, and American English. *Child Development, 75,* 1115–1139.

Bornstein, M. H., Haynes, O. M., Pascual, L., Painter, K. M., & Galperin, C. (1999a). Play in two societies: Pervasiveness of process, specificity of structure. *Child Development, 70,* 317–331.

Bornstein, M. H., Selmi, A. M., Haynes, O. M., Painter, K. M., & Marx, E. S. (1999b). Representational abilities and the hearing status of child/mother dyads. *Child Development, 70,* 833–852.

Bornstein, M. H., Vibbert, M., Tal, J., & O'Donnell, K. (1992b). Toddler language and play in the second year: Stability, covariation, and influences of parenting. *First Language, 12,* 323–338.

Boroughs, D. S. (2004). Female sexual abusers of children. *Children and Youth Services Review, 26,* 481–487.

Borst, C. G. (1995). *Catching babies: The professionalization of childbirth, 1870–1920.* Cambridge, MA: Harvard University Press.

Bortolus, R., Parazzini, F., Chatenoud, L., Benzi, G., Bianchi, M. M., & Marini, A. (1999). The epidemiology of multiple births. *Human Reproduction Update, 5,* 179–187.

Bos, H. M. W., van Balen, F., & van den Boom, D. C. (2004). Experience of parenthood, couple relationship, social support, and child-rearing goals in planned lesbian mother families. *Journal of Child Psychology and Psychiatry, 25,* 755–764.

Bosacki, S. L., & Moore, C. (2004). Preschoolers' understanding of simple and complex emotions: Links with gender and language. *Sex Roles, 50,* 659–675.

Bosch, L., & Sebastian-Galles, N. (2001). Evidence of early language discrimination abilities in infants from bilingual environments. *Infancy, 2,* 29–49.

Bouchard, T. J. (2004). Genetic influence on human psychological traits: A survey. *Current Directions in Psychological Science, 13,* 148–151.

Bouchard, T. J., & Loehlin, J. C. (2001). Genes, evolution, and personality. *Behavior Genetics, 31,* 243–274.

Boukydis, C. F. Z., & Lester, B. M. (1998). Infant crying, risk status and social support in families of preterm and term infants. *Early Development and Parenting, 7,* 31–39.

Bouldin, P. (2006). An investigation of the fantasy predisposition and fantasy style of children with imaginary companions. *Journal of Genetic Psychology, 167,* 17–29.

Boulton, M. J. (1996). A comparison of 8- and 11-year-old girls' and boys' participation in specific types of rough-and-tumble play and aggressive fighting: Implications for functional hypotheses. *Aggressive Behavior, 22,* 271–287.

Boulton, M. J. (1999). Concurrent and longitudinal relations between children's playground behavior and social preference, victimization, and bullying. *Child Development, 70,* 944–954.

Boulton, M. J., & Smith, P. K. (1992). The social nature of play-fighting and play-chasing: Mechanisms and strategies underlying cooperation and compromise. In J. H. Barkow, L. Cosmides, & J. Tooby (Eds.), *The adapted mind* (pp. 429–444). New York: Oxford University Press.

Bowen, N. K., Bowen, G. L., & Ware, W. B. (2002). Neighborhood social disorganization, families, and the educational behavior of adolescents. *Journal of Adolescent Research, 17,* 468–490.

Bower-Russa, M. E., Knutson, J. F., & Winebarger, A. (2001). Disciplinary history, adult disciplinary attitudes, and risk for abusive parenting. *Journal of Community Psychology, 29,* 219–240.

Bowker, A. (2004). Predicting friendship stability during early adolescence. *Journal of Early Adolescence, 24,* 85–112.

Bowlby, J. (1969). *Attachment and loss: Vol. 1. Attachment.* New York: Basic Books.

Bowlby, J. (1980). *Attachment and loss: Vol. 3. Loss.* New York: Basic Books.

Bowlby, J. W., & McMullen, K. (2002). *At a crossroads: First results for the 18- to 20-year-old cohort of the Youth in Transition Survey.* Ottawa, Canada: Human Resources Development Canada.

Bowman, S. A., Gortmaker, S. L., Ebbeling, C. B., Pereira, M. A., & Ludwig, D. S. (2004). Effects of fast-food consumption on energy intake and diet quality among children in a national household survey. *Pediatrics, 113,* 112–113.

Boyce, W. M., Doherty, M., MacKinnon, D., & Fortin, C. (2003*). Canadian Youth, Sexual Health, HIV/AIDS Study: Factors influencing knowledge, attitudes and behaviours.* Toronto, Ontario: Council of Ministers of Education, Canada.

Boyd-Franklin, N. (2006). *Black families in therapy* (2nd ed.). New York: Guilford.

Boyer, K., & Diamond, A. (1992). Development of memory for temporal order in infants and young children. In A. Diamond (Ed.), *Development and neural bases of higher cognitive function* (pp. 267– 317). New York: New York Academy of Sciences.

Boyer, T. W. (2006). The development of risk-taking: A multi-perspective review. *Developmental Review, 26,* 291–345.

Boyes, M. C., & Chandler, M. (1992). Cognitive development, epistemic doubt, and identity formation in adolescence. *Journal of Youth and Adolescence, 21,* 277–304.

Boyle, M. H., & Lipman, E. L. (2002). Do places matter? Socioeconomic disadvantage and behavioral problems of children in Canada. *Journal of Consulting and Clinical Psychology, 70,* 378–389.

Boysson-Bardies, B. de, & Vihman, M. M. (1991). Adaptation to language: Evidence from babbling and first words in four languages. *Language, 67,* 297–319.

Bracci, R., Perrone, S., & Buonocore, G. (2006). The timing of neonatal brain damage. *Biology of the Neonate, 90,* 145–155.

Brackbill, Y., McManus, K., & Woodward, L. (1985). *Medication in maternity: Infant exposure and maternal information.* Ann Arbor: University of Michigan Press.

Bracken, B. A. (2000). *The psychoeducational assessment of preschool children.* Boston: Allyn and Bacon.

Bradford, K., Barber, B. K., Olsen, J. A., Maughan, S. L., Erickson, L. D., Ward, D., & Stolz, H. E. (2003). A multi-national study of interparental conflict, parenting, and adolescent functioning: South Africa, Bangladesh, China, India, Bosnia, Germany, Palestine, Colombia, and the United States. *Marriage and Family Review, 35,* 107–137.

Bradley, P. J., & Bray, K. H. (1996). The Netherlands' Maternal-Child Health Program: Implications for the United States. *Journal of Obstetric, Gynecologic, and Neonatal Nursing, 25,* 471–475.

Bradley, R. H. (1994). The HOME Inventory: Review and reflections. In H. W. Reese (Ed.), *Advances in child development and behavior* (Vol. 25, pp. 241–288). San Diego: Academic Press.

Bradley, R. H., & Caldwell, B. M. (1982). The consistency of the home environment and its relation to child development. *International Journal of Behavioral Development, 5,* 445–465.

Bradley, R. H., & Corwyn, R. F. (2003). Age and ethnic variations in family process mediators of SES. In M. H. Bornstein & R. H. Bradley (Eds.), *Socioeconomic status, parenting, and child development* (pp. 161–188). Mahwah, NJ: Erlbaum.

Bradley, R. H., Corwyn, R. F., McAdoo, H. P., & García Coll, C. (2001). The home environments of children in the United States. Part I: Variations by age, ethnicity, and poverty status. *Child Development, 72,* 1844–1867.

Bradley, R. H., Whiteside, L., Mundfrom, D. J., Casey, P. H., Kelleher, K. J., & Pope, S. K. (1994). Contribution of early intervention and early caregiving experiences to resilience in low-birthweight, premature children living in poverty. *Journal of Clinical Child Psychology, 23,* 425–434.

Bradshaw, R. A., & Burlingame, A. L. (2005). From proteins to proteomics. *IUBMB Life, 57,* 267–272.

Braet, C., & Crombez, G. (2003). Cognitive interference due to food cues in childhood obesity. *Journal of Clinical Child and Adolescent Psychology, 32,* 32–39.

Braine, L. G., Schauble, L., Kugelmass, S., & Winter, A. (1993). Representation of depth by children: Spatial strategies and lateral biases. *Developmental Psychology, 29,* 466–479.

Braine, M. D. S. (1994). Is nativism sufficient? *Journal of Child Language, 21,* 1–23.

Brainerd, C. J. (2003). Jean Piaget, learning, research, and American education. In B. J. Zimmerman (Ed.), *Educational psychology: A century of contributions* (pp. 251–287). Mahwah, NJ: Erlbaum.

Brame, B., Nagin, D. S., & Tremblay, R. E. (2001). Developmental trajectories of physical aggression from school entry to late adolescence. *Journal of Child Psychology and Psychiatry, 42,* 503–512.

Branca, F., & Ferrari, M. (2002). Impact of micronutrient deficiencies on growth: The stunting syndrome. *Annals of Nutrition and Metabolism, 46*(Suppl. 1), 8–17.

Branje, S. J. T., van Lieshout, C. F. M., van Aken, M. A. G., & Haselager, G. J. T. (2004). Perceived support in sibling relationships and adolescent adjustment. *Journal of Child Psychology and Psychiatry, 45,* 1385–1396.

Braswell, G. S., & Callanan, M. A. (2003). Learning to draw recognizable graphic representations during mother–child interactions. *Merrill-Palmer Quarterly, 49,* 471–494.

Bratt, R. G. (2002). Housing: The foundation of family life. In F. Jacobs, D. Wertlieb, & R. M. Lerner (Eds.), *Handbook of applied developmental science* (Vol. 2, pp. 445–468). Thousand Oaks, CA: Sage.

Bray, J. H. (1999). From marriage to remarriage and beyond: Findings from the Developmental Issues in Stepfamilies Research Project. In E. M. Hetherington (Ed.), *Coping with divorce, single parenting, and remarriage: A risk and resiliency perspective* (pp. 295–319). Mahwah, NJ: Erlbaum.

Brazelton, T. B., Koslowski, B., & Tronick, E. (1976). Neonatal behavior among urban Zambians and Americans. *Journal of the American Academy of Child Psychiatry, 15,* 97–107.

Brazelton, T. B., & Nugent, J. K. (1995). *Neonatal Behavioral Assessment Scale.* London: Mac Keith Press.

Brazelton, T. B., Nugent, J. K., & Lester, B. M. (1987). Neonatal Behavioral Assessment Scale. In J. D. Osofsky

(Ed.), *Handbook of infant development* (2nd ed., pp. 780–817). New York: Wiley.

Brazelton, T. B., & Sparrow, J. D. (2004). Toilet learning: The child's role. In T. B. Brazelton (Ed.), *Toilet training the Brazelton way.* Cambridge, MA: Da Capo Press.

Bredekamp, S., & Copple, C. (Eds.). (1997). *Developmentally appropriate practice in early childhood programs* (rev. ed.). Washington, DC: National Association for the Education of Young Children.

Brehm, S. S. (2002). *Intimate relationships* (3rd ed.). New York: McGraw-Hill.

Bremner, A. J., & Mareschal, D. (2004). Reasoning . . . what reasoning? *Developmental Science, 7,* 419–421.

Brendgen, M., Markiewicz, D., Doyle, A. B., & Bukowski, W. M. (2001). The relations between friendship quality, ranked-friendship preference, and adolescents' behavior with their friends. *Merrill-Palmer Quarterly, 47,* 395–415.

Brendgen, M., Vitaro, F., & Bukowski, W. M. (1998). Deviant friends and early adolescents' emotional and behavioral adjustment. *Journal of Research on Adolescence, 10,* 173–189.

Brennan, R. T., Kim, J., Wenz-Gross, M., & Siperstein, G. N. (2001). The relative equitability of high-stakes testing versus teacher-assigned grades: An analysis of the Massachusetts Comprehensive Assessment System (MCAS). *Harvard Educational Review, 71,* 173–216.

Brennan, W. M., Ames, E. W., & Moore, R. W. (1966). Age differences in infants' attention to patterns of different complexities. *Science, 151,* 354–356.

Brenner, E., & Salovey, P. (1997). Emotional regulation during childhood: Developmental, interpersonal, and individual considerations. In P. Salovey & D. Sluyter (Eds.), *Emotional literacy and emotional development* (pp. 168–192). New York: Basic Books.

Brenner, R. A. (2003). Prevention of drowning in infants, children, and adolescents. *Pediatrics, 112,* 440–445.

Brenner, R. A., Simons-Morton, B. G., Bhaskar, B., Revenis, M., Das, A., & Clemens, J. D. (2003). Infant–parent bed sharing in an inner-city population. *Archives of Pediatrics and Adolescent Medicine, 157,* 33–39.

Bretherton, I., Fritz, J., Zahn-Waxler, C., & Ridgeway, D. (1986). Learning to talk about emotions: A functionalist perspective. *Child Development, 57,* 529–548.

Bretherton, I., & Munholland, K. A. (1999). Internal working models in attachment relationships: A construct revisited. In J. Cassidy & P. R. Shaver (Eds.), *Handbook of attachment* (pp. 89–111). New York: Guilford.

Brewaeys, A., Ponjaert, I., Van Hall, E. V., & Golombok, S. (1997). Donor insemination: Child development and family functioning in lesbian mother families. *Human Reproduction, 12,* 1349–1359.

Bridge, J. A., Goldstein, T. R., & Brent, D. A. (2006). Adolescent suicide and suicidal behavior. *Journal of Child Psychology and Psychiatry, 47,* 372–394.

Bridges, L. J., & Moore, K. A. (2002). Religious involvement and children's well-being: What research tells us (and what it doesn't). *Child Trends Research Brief.* Retrieved from http://www.childtrends.org

Briefel, R. R., Reidy, K., Karwe, V., & Devaney, B. (2004). Feeding Infants and Toddlers study: Improvements needed in meeting infant feeding recommendations. *Journal of the American Dietetic Association, 104*(Suppl. 1), s31–s37.

Briggs, F. (2000). *Children's views of the world.* Magill, Australia: University of South Australia.

Briggs, F. (2002). *To what extent can Keeping Ourselves Safe protect children?* Wellington, NZ: New Zealand Police.

Bright, J. E. H., Pryor, R. G. L., Wilkenfeld, S., & Earl, J. (2005). The role of social context and serendipitous events in career decision making., *International Journal for Educational and Vocational Guidance, 5,* 19–36.

British Columbia Reproductive Care Program. (2003). *Guidelines for perinatal care manual: Perinatal cocaine use: Care of the newborn.* Retrieved from mdm.ca /cpgsnew/cpgs-f/search/French/help/2bcrcp.htm

Broberg, A. G., Wessels, H., Lamb, M. E., & Hwang, C. P. (1997). Effects of day care on the development of cognitive abilities in 8-year-olds: A longitudinal study. *Developmental Psychology, 33,* 62–69.

Brody, G. H., & Flor, D. L. (1998). Maternal resources, parenting practices, and child competence in rural, single-parent African American families. *Child Development, 69,* 803–816.

Brody, G. H., Ge, X., Kim, S. Y., Murry, V. M., Simons, R. L., & Gibbons, F. X. (2003). Neighborhood disadvantage moderates associations of parenting and older sibling problem attitudes and behavior with conduct disorders in African American children. *Journal of Consulting and Clinical Psychology, 71,* 211–222.

Brody, G. H., & Murry, V. M. (2001). Sibling socialization of competence in rural, single-parent African American families. *Journal of Marriage and the Family, 63,* 996–1008.

Brody, G. H., Stoneman, Z., & Flor, D. (1996a). Family wages, family processes, and youth competence in rural married African American families. In E. M. Hetherington & E. A. Blechman (Eds.), *Stress, coping, and resiliency in children and families. Family research consortium: Advances in family research* (pp. 173–188). Mahwah, NJ: Erlbaum.

Brody, G. H., Stoneman, Z., & Flor, D. (1996b). Parental religiosity, family processes, and youth competence in rural, two-parent African-American families. *Developmental Psychology, 32,* 696–706.

Brody, G. H., Stoneman, Z., & McCoy, J. K. (1992). Associations of maternal and paternal direct and differential behavior with sibling relationships: Contemporaneous and longitudinal analyses. *Child Development, 63,* 82–92.

Brody, G. H., Stoneman, Z., & McCoy, J. K. (1994). Forecasting sibling relationships in early adolescence from child temperament and family processes in middle childhood. *Child Development, 65,* 771–784.

Brody, L. (1999). *Gender, emotion, and the family.* Cambridge, MA: Harvard University Press.

Brody, M. (2006). Child psychiatry, drugs, and the corporation. In S. Olfman (Ed.), *No child left different* (pp. 89–105). Westport, CT: Praeger.

Brody, N. (1997). Intelligence, schooling, and society. *American Psychologist, 52,* 1046–1050.

Brodzinsky, D. M., & Pinderhughes, E. (2002). Parenting and child development in adoptive families. In M. H. Bornstein (Ed.), *Handbook of parenting: Vol. 1* (2nd ed., pp. 279–311). Mahwah, NJ: Erlbaum.

Broidy, L. M., Nagin, D. S., Tremblay, R. E., Bates, J. E., Brame, B., Dodge, K. A., Fergusson, D., Horwood, J. L., Loeber, R., Laird, R., Lynam, D. R., Moffitt, T. E., Pettit, G. S., & Vitaro, F. (2003). Developmental trajectories of childhood disruptive behaviors and adolescent delinquency: A six-site, cross-national study. *Developmental Psychology, 39,* 222–245.

Broidy, L. M., Nagin, D. S., Tremblay, R. E., Brame, B., Dodge, K. A., & Fergusson, D. (2003). Developmental trajectories of childhood disruptive behaviors and adolescent delinquency: A six-site, cross-national study. *Developmental Psychology, 39,* 222–245.

Bronfenbrenner, U. (Ed.). (2005). *Making human beings human.* Thousand Oaks, CA: Sage.

Bronfenbrenner, U., & Morris, P. A. (2006). The bioecological model of human development. In R. M. Lerner (Ed.), *Handbook of child psychology: Vol. 1. Theoretical models of human development* (6th ed., pp. 793–828). Hoboken, NJ: Wiley.

Bronson, G. W. (1994). Infant's transitions toward adult-like scanning. *Child Development, 65,* 1243–1261.

Bronson, M. B. (1995). *The right stuff for children birth to 8.* Washington, DC: National Association for the Education of Young Children.

Bronte-Tinkew, J., Moore, K. A., & Carrano, J. (2006). The father–child relationship, parenting styles, and adolescent risk behaviors in intact families. *Journal of Family Issues, 27,* 850–881.

Brooks, K., Xu, X., Chen, W., Zhou, K., Neale, B., & Lowe, N. (2006). The analysis of 51 genes in DSM-IV combined type attention deficit hyperactivity disorder: Association signals in DRD4, DAT1, and 16 other genes. *Molecular Psychiatry, 11,* 935–953.

Brooks, P. J., Hanauere, J. B., Padowska, B., & Rosman, H. (2003). The role of selective attention in preschoolers' rule use in a novel dimensional card sort. *Cognitive Development, 18,* 195–215.

Brooks, R., & Meltzoff, A. N. (2005). The development of gaze following and its relation to language. *Developmental Science, 8,* 535–543.

Brooks-Gunn, J. (1988). Antecedents and consequences of variations in girls' maturational timing. *Journal of Adolescent Health Care, 9,* 365–373.

Brooks-Gunn, J. (2003). Do you believe in magic? What we can expect from early childhood intervention programs. *Social Policy Report of the Society for Research in Child Development, 27*(1).

Brooks-Gunn, J. (2004). Intervention and policy as change agents for young children. In P. L. Chase-Lansdale, K. Kiernan, & R. J. Friedman (Eds.), *Human development across lives and generations: The potential for change* (pp. 293–340). New York: Cambridge University Press.

Brooks-Gunn, J., Han, W.-J., & Waldfogel, J. (2002). Maternal employment and child cognitive outcomes in the first three years of life: The NICHD study of early child care. *Child Development, 73,* 1052–1072.

Brooks-Gunn, J., Klebanov, P. K., Smith, J., Duncan, G. J., & Lee, K. (2003). The black-white test score gap in young children. Contributions of test and family characteristics. *Applied Developmental Science, 7,* 239–252.

Brooks-Gunn, J., Schley, S., & Hardy, J. (2002). Marriage and the baby carriage: Historical change and intergenerational continuity in early parenthood. In L. J. Crockett & R. K. Sibereisen (Eds.), *Negotiating adolescence in times of social change* (pp. 36–57). New York: Cambridge University Press.

Brown, A. L. (1997). Transforming schools into communities of thinking and learning about serious matters. *American Psychologist, 52,* 399–413.

Brown, A. M., & Miracle, J. A. (2003). Early binocular vision in human infants: Limitations on the generality of the Superposition Hypothesis. *Vision Research, 43,* 1563–1574.

Brown, A. S., & Susser, E. S. (2002). In utero infection and adult schizophrenia. *Mental Retardation and Developmental Disabilities Research Reviews, 8,* 51–57.

Brown, B. (2004). Adolescents' relationships with peers. In R. Lerner & L. Steinberg (Eds.), *Handbook of adolescent psychology* (2nd ed., pp. 363–394). Hoboken, NJ: Wiley.

Brown, B. B., Clasen, D., & Eicher, S. (1986). Perceptions of peer pressure, peer conformity dispositions, and self-reported behavior among adolescents. *Developmental Psychology, 22,* 521–530.

Brown, B. B., Lohr, M. J., & McClenahan, E. L. (1986). Early adolescents' perceptions of peer pressure. *Journal of Early Adolescence, 6,* 139–154.

Brown, C. S., & Bigler, R. S. (2004). Children's perceptions of gender discrimination. *Developmental Psychology, 40,* 714–726.

Brown, J. L., Roderick, T., Lantieri, L., & Aber, J. L. (2004). The Resolving Conflict Creatively Program: A school-based social and emotional learning program. In J. E. Zins, R. P. Weissberg, M. C. Wang, & H. J. Walberg (Eds.), *Building academic success on social and emotional learning: What does the research say?* (pp. 151–169). New York: Teachers Colllege Press.

Brown, J. R., Donelan-McCall, N., & Dunn, J. (1996). Why talk about mental states? The significance of children's conversations with friends, siblings, and mothers. *Child Development, 67,* 836–849.

Brown, J. R., & Dunn, J. (1996). Continuities in emotion understanding from 3 to 6 years. *Child Development, 67,* 789–802.

Brown, R. T., Reynolds, C. R., & Whitaker, J. S. (1999). Bias in mental testing since *Bias in Mental Testing. School Psychology Quarterly, 14,* 208–238.

Brown, R. W. (1973). *A first language: The early stages.* Cambridge, MA: Harvard University Press.

Brown, S. A., & Ramo, D. E. (2005). Clinical course of youth following treatment for alcohol and drug problems. In. H. A. Liddle & C. L. Rowe (Eds.), *Adolescent substance abuse: Research and clinical advances* (pp. 79–103). Cambridge: Cambridge University Press.

Brown, S. L. (2000). Union transitions among cohabiters: The significance of relationship assessments and expectations. *Journal of Marriage and the Family, 62,* 833–846.

Brown, T. E. (2005). *Attention deficit disorder: The unfocused mind in children and adults.* New Haven, CT: Yale University Press.

Brown, T. E. (2006). Executive functions and attention deficit hyperactivity disorder: Implications of two conflicting views. *International Journal of Disability, Development and Education, 53,* 35–46.

Browne, J. V., & Talmi, A. (2005). Family-based intervention to enhance infant–parent relationships in the neonatal

intensive care unit. *Journal of Pediatric Psychology, 30,* 667–677.
Brownell, C.A., & Carriger, M. S. (1990). Changes in cooperation and self–other differentiation during the second year. *Child Development, 61,* 1164–1174.
Bruch, H. (2001). *The golden cage: The enigma of anorexia nervosa.* Cambridge, MA: Harvard University Press.
Bruck, M., & Ceci, S. J. (2004). Forensic developmental psychology: Unveiling four common misconceptions. *Current Directions in Psychological Science, 13,* 229–232.
Bruer, J. T. (1999). *The myth of the first three years.* New York: Free Press.
Bruschweiler-Stern, N. (2004). A multifocal neonatal intervention. In A. J. Sameroff, S. C. McDonough, & K. L. Rosenblum (Eds.), *Treating parent–infant relationship problems* (pp. 188–212). New York: Guilford.
Bruzzese, J., & Fisher, C. B. (2003). Assessing and enhancing the research consent capacity of children and youth. *Applied Developmental Science, 7,* 13–26.
Bryant, B. K., Zvonkovic, A. M., & Reynolds, P. (2006). Parenting in relation to child and adolescent vocational development. *Journal of Vocational Behavior, 69,* 149–175.
Bryant, P., & Nunes, T. (2002). Children's understanding of mathematics. In U. Goswami (Ed.), *Blackwell handbook of childhood cognitive development* (pp. 412–439). Malden, MA. Blackwell.
Buchanan, A. (1996). *Cycles of child maltreatment.* Chichester, U.K.: Wiley.
Buchanan, C. M., Eccles, J. S., & Becker, J. B. (1992). Are adolescents the victims of raging hormones? Evidence for activational effects of hormones on moods and behaviors at adolescence. *Psychological Bulletin, 111,* 62–107.
Buchanan, C. M., & Holmbeck, G. N. (1998). Measuring beliefs about adolescent personality and behavior. *Journal of Youth and Adolescence, 27,* 609–629.
Buchanan, C. M., Maccoby, E. E., & Dornbusch, S. M. (1996). *Adolescents after divorce.* Cambridge, MA: Harvard University Press.
Buchanan-Barrow, E., & Barrett, M. (1998). Children's rule discrimination within the context of the school. *British Journal of Developmental Psychology, 16,* 539–551.
Buescher, E. S. (2001). Anti-inflammatory characteristics of human milk: How, where, why. *Advances in Experimental Medicine and Biology, 501,* 207–222.
Bugental, D. B., Ellerson, P. C., Lin, E. K., Rainey, B., & Kokotovic, A. (2002). A cognitive approach to child abuse prevention. *Journal of Family Psychology, 16,* 243–258.
Bugental, D. B., & Grusec, J. E. (2006). Socialization processes. In N. Eisenberg (Ed.), *Handbook of child psychology: Vol. 3. Social, emotional, and personality development* (6th ed., pp. 366–428). Hoboken, NJ: Wiley.
Bugental, D. B., & Happaney, K. (2004). Predicting infant maltreatment in low-income families: The interactive effects of maternal attributions and child status at birth. *Developmental Psychology, 40,* 234–243.
Buhrmester, D. (1996). Need fulfillment, interpersonal competence, and the developmental contexts of early adolescent friendship. In W. M. Bukowski & A. F. Newcomb (Eds.), *The company they keep: Friendship in childhood and adolescence* (pp. 158–185). New York: Cambridge University Press.
Buhrmester, D., & Furman, W. (1990). Perceptions of sibling relationships during middle childhood and adolescence. *Child Development, 61,* 1387–1398.
Buhs, E. S., & Ladd, G. W. (2001). Peer rejection as antecendent of young children's school adjustment: An examination of mediating processes. *Developmental Psychology, 37,* 550–560.
Buhs, E. S., Ladd, G. W., & Herald, S. L. (2006). Peer exclusion and victimization: Processes that mediate the relation between peer group rejection and children's classroom engagement and achievement. *Journal of Educational Psychology, 98,* 1–13.
Bukowski, W. M. (2001). Friendship and the worlds of childhood. In D. W. Nangle & C. A. Erdley (Eds.), *The role of friendship in psychological adjustment* (pp. 93–105). San Francisco: Jossey-Bass.
Bukowski, W. M., Sippola, L. K., & Hoza, B. (1999). Same and other: Interdependency between participation in same- and other-sex friendships. *Journal of Youth and Adolescence, 28,* 439–459.
Bukowski, W. M., Sippola, L. K., & Newcomb, A. F. (2000). Variations in patterns of attraction of same- and other-sex peers during early adolescence. *Developmental Psychology, 36,* 147–154.
Bullock, M., & Lutkenhaus, P. (1990). Who am I? The development of self-understanding in toddlers. *Merrill-Palmer Quarterly, 36,* 217–238.
Bunting, L., & McAuley, C. (2004). Teenage pregnancy and parenthood: The role of fathers. *Child and Family Social Work, 9,* 295–303.
Burden, M. J., Jacobson, S. W., & Jacobson, J. L. (2005). Relation of prenatal alcohol exposure to cognitive processing speed and efficiency in childhood. *Alcoholism: Clinical and Experimental Research, 29,* 1473–1483.
Burhans, K. K., & Dweck, C. S. (1995). Helplessness in early childhood: The role of contingent worth. *Child Development, 66,* 1719–1738.
Burke, R. J. (2001). Organizational values, work experiences, and satisfactions among managerial and professional women. *Journal of Managerial Development, 20,* 346–354.
Burns, C. E. (2000). *Pediatric primary care: A handbook for nurse practitioners.* Philadelphia: Saunders.
Burts, D. C., Hart, C. H., Charlesworth, R., Fleege, P. O., Mosley, J., & Thomasson, R. H. (1992). Observed activities and stress behaviors of children in developmentally appropriate and inappropriate kindergarten classrooms. *Early Childhood Research Quarterly, 7,* 297–318.
Bushman, B. J., & Huesmann, L. R. (2001). Effects of televised violence of aggression. In D. G. Singer & J. L. Singer (Eds.), *Handbook of children and the media* (pp. 223–254). Thousand Oaks, CA: Sage.
Bushnell, E. W., & Boudreau, J. P. (1993). Motor development and the mind: The potential role of motor abilities as a determinant of aspects of perceptual development. *Child Development, 64,* 1005–1021.
Bushnik, T., Barr-Telford, L., & Bussiére, P. (2004). *In and out of high school: First results from the second cycle of the Youth in Transition Survey, 2002.* Ottawa, ON: Statistics Canada.
Bussell, D. A., Neiderhiser, J. M., Pike, A., Plomin, R., Simmens, S., Howe, G. W., Hetherington, E. M., Carroll, E., & Reiss, D. (1999). Adolescents' relationships to siblings and mothers: A multivariate genetic analysis. *Developmental Psychology, 35,* 1248–1259.
Bussey, K. (1992). Lying and truthfulness: Children's definitions, standards, and evaluative reactions. *Child Development, 63,* 129–137.
Bussey, K. (1999). Children's categorization and evaluation of different types of lies and truths. *Child Development, 70,* 1338–1347.
Butler, M., & Meaney, J. (Eds.). (2005). *Genetics of developmental disabilities.* Boca Raton, FL: Taylor & Francis.
Butler, R. (1998). Age trends in the use of social and temporal comparison for self-evaluation: Examination of a novel developmental hypothesis. *Child Development, 69,* 1054–1073.
Butler, R., & Ruzany, N. (1993). Age and socialization effects on the development of social comparison motives and normative ability assessment in kibbutz and urban children. *Child Development, 64,* 532–543.
Butler, R. J., Golding, J., & Heron, J. (2005). Nocturnal enuresis: A survey of parental coping strategies at 7_ years. *Child: Care, Health and Development, 31,* 659–667.
Byard, R. W., & Krous, H. F. (2003). Sudden infant death syndrome: Overview and update. *Perspectives on Pediatric Pathology, 6,* 112–127.
Byars, A. M., & Hackett, G. (1998). Applications of social cognitive theory to the career development of women of color. *Applied and Preventive Psychology, 7,* 255–267.
Bybee, J., Merisca, R., & Velasco, R. (1998). The development of reactions to guilt-producing events. In J. Bybee (Ed.), *Guilt and children* (pp. 185–213). San Diego: Academic Press.
Byrnes, J. P. (2002). The development of decision-making. *Journal of Adolescent Health, 31,* 208–215.
Cabrera, N. J., & García-Coll, C. (2004). Latino fathers: Uncharted territory in need of much exploration. In M. E. Lamb (Ed.), *The role of the father in child development* (4th ed., pp. 98–120). Hoboken, NJ: Wiley.
Cabrera, N. J., Tamis-LeMonda, C. S., Bradley, R. H., Hoferth, S., & Lamb, M. E. (2000). Fatherhood in the twenty-first century. *Child Development, 71,* 127–136.
Cain, K. M., & Dweck, C. S. (1995). The relation between motivational patterns and achievement cognitions through the elementary school years. *Merrill-Palmer Quarterly, 41,* 25–52.
Caine, N. (1986). Behavior during puberty and adolescence. In G. Mitchell & J. Erwin (Eds.), *Comparative primate biology: Vol. 2A. Behavior, conservation, and ecology* (pp. 327–361). New York: Liss.
Cairns, R., Xie, H., & Leung, M.-C. (1998). The popularity of friendship and the neglect of social networks: Toward a new balance. In W. M. Bukowski & A. H. Cillessen (Eds.), *Sociometry then and now: Building on six decades of measuring children's experiences with the peer group* (pp. 25–53). San Francisco: Jossey-Bass.
Cairns, R. B., & Cairns, B. D. (2006). The making of developmental psychology. In R. M. Lerner (Ed.), *Handbook of child psychology: Vol. 1. Theoretical models of human development* (6th ed., pp. 89–165). Hoboken, NJ: Wiley.
Caldwell, B. M., & Bradley, R. H. (1994). Environmental issues in developmental follow-up research. In S. L. Friedman & H. C. Haywood (Eds.), *Developmental follow-up* (pp. 235–256). San Diego: Academic Press.
Caldwell, J. (1999). Paths to lower fertility. *British Medical Journal, 319,* 985–987.
Calkins, S. D. (2002). Does aversive behavior during toddlerhood matter? The effects of difficult temperament on maternal perceptions and behavior. *Infant Mental Health Journal, 23,* 381–402.
Callaghan, T., Rochat, P., Lillard, A., Claux, M. L., Odden, H., Itakura, S., Tapanya, S., & Singh, S. (2005). Synchrony in the onset of mental-state reasoning: Evidence from five cultures. *Psychological Science, 16,* 378–384.
Callaghan, T. C. (1999). Early understanding and production of graphic symbols. *Child Development, 70,* 1314–1324.
Callaghan, T. C., & Rankin, M. P. (2002). Emergence of graphic symbol functioning and the question of domain specificity: A longitudinal training study. *Child Development, 73,* 359–376.
Callanan, M. A., & Sabbagh, M. A. (2004). Multiple labels for objects in conversations with young children: Parents' language and children's developing expectations about word meanings. *Developmental Psychology, 40,* 746–763.
Calle, E. E., Rodriguez, C., Walker-Thurmond, K., & Thun, M. J. (2003). Overweight, obesity, and mortality from cancer in a prospectively studied cohort of U.S. adults. *New England Journal of Medicine, 348,* 1625–1638.
Cameron, C. A., & Lee, K. (1997). The development of children's telephone communication. *Journal of Applied Developmental Psychology, 18,* 55–70.
Cameron, J. A., Alvarez, J. M., Ruble, D. N., & Fuligni, A. J. (2001). Children's lay theories about in-groups and out-groups: Reconceptualizing research on prejudice. *Personality and Social Psychology Review, 5,* 118–128.
Cameron, M. B., & Wilson, B. J. (1990). The effects of chronological age, gender, and delay of entry on academic achievement and retention: Implications for academic redshirting. *Psychology in the Schools, 27,* 260–263.
Cameron-Faulkner, T., Lieven, E., & Tomasello, M. (2003). A construction based analysis of child-directed speech. *Cognitive Science, 27,* 843–873.
Cammu, H., Martens, G., Ruyssinck, G., & Amy, J. J. (2002). Outcome after elective labor induction in nulliparous women: A matched cohort study. *American Journal of Obstetrics and Gynecology, 186,* 240–244.
Campa, M. I., & Eckenrode, J. J. (2006). Pathways to intergenerational adolescent childbearing in a high-risk sample. *Journal of Marriage and Family, 68,* 558–572.
Campbell, A., Shirley, L., & Candy, J. (2004). A longitudinal study of gender-related cognition and behaviour. *Developmental Science, 7,* 1–9.
Campbell, F. A., Pungello, E. P., Miller-Johnson, S., Burchinal, M., & Ramey, C. T. (2001). The development of cognitive and academic abilities: Growth curves from an early childhood educational experiment. *Developmental Psychology, 37,* 231–242.
Campbell, F. A., Ramey, C. T., Pungello, E., Sparling, J., & Miller-Johnson, S. (2002). Early childhood education: Young adult outcomes from the Abecedarian Project. *Applied Developmental Science, 6,* 42–57.
Campbell, S. B., Brownell, C. A., Hungerford, A., Spieker, S. J., Mohan, R., & Blessing, J. S. (2004). The course of maternal depressive symptoms and maternal sensitivity

as predictors of attachment security at 36 months. *Development and Psychopathology, 16*, 231–252.

Campos, J., Frankel, C., & Camras, L. (2004). On the nature of emotion regulation. *Child Development, 75*, 377–394.

Campos, J. J., Anderson, D. I., Barbu-Roth, M. A., Hubbard, E. M., Hertenstein, J. J., & Witherington, D. (2000). Travel broadens the mind. *Infancy, 1*, 149–219.

Campos, J. J., Kermoian, R., & Zumbahlen, M. R. (1992). Socioemotional transformation in the family system following infant crawling onset. In N. Eisenberg & R. A. Fabes (Eds.), *New directions for child development* (No. 55, pp. 25–40). San Francisco: Jossey-Bass.

Campos, R. G. (1989). Soothing pain-elicited distress in infants with swaddling and pacifiers. *Child Development, 60*, 781–792.

Camras, L. A. (1992). Expressive development and basic emotions. *Cognition and Emotion, 6*, 267–283.

Camras, L. A., Oster, H., Campos, J. J., & Bakeman, R. (2003). Emotional facial expressions in European-American, Japanese, and Chinese infants. *Annals of the New York Academy of Sciences, 1000*, 1–17

Camras, L. A., Oster, H., Campos, J. J., Miyake, K., & Bradshaw, D. (1992). Japanese and American infants' responses to arm restraint. *Developmental Psychology, 28*, 578–583.

Camras, L. A., Oster, H., Campos, J., Campos, R., Ujie, T., Miyake, K., Wang, L., & Meng, Z. (1998). Production of emotional and facial expressions in European American, Japanese, and Chinese infants. *Developmental Psychology, 34*, 616–628.

Canada Campaign 2000. (2003). *Poverty amidst prosperity—building a Canada for all children: 2002 report card.* Ottawa: House of Commons.

Canada Campaign 2000. (2005). *Decision time for Canada: Lets make child poverty history. 2005 Report Card on Child Poverty in Canada.* Retrieved from www.campaign2000.ca/rc/rc05/05NationalReportCard.pdf

Canadian Broadcast Standards Council. (2003). *Voluntary code regarding violence in television programming.* Retrieved from http://www.cbsc.ca/english/codes/violence/violence.htm

Canadian Fitness and Lifestyle Research Institute. (2005a). *A case for daily physical education.* Retrieved from www.cflri.ca/eng/lifestyle/1995/daily_pe.php

Canadian Fitness and Lifestyle Research Institute. (2005b). *Survey of physical activity in Canadian schools.* Retrieved from www.cflri.ca/cflri/pa/surveys/2001survey/2001survey.html

Canadian Institute for Health Information. (2005). *Proportion of deliveries by caesarean section, excluding stillbirths.* Retrieved from www.cihi.ca

Canadian Paediatric Society. (2005). Youth and firearms in Canada. *Paediatrics and Child Health, 10*, 473–477.

Canadian Psychological Association. (2000). *Canadian code of ethics for psychologists.* Ottawa, ON: Author. Retrieved from www.cpa.ca/ethics2000.html

Candy-Gibbs, S., Sharp, K., & Petrun, C. (1985). The effects of age, object, and cultural/religious background on children's concepts of death. *Omega, 15*, 329–345.

Canetto, S. S., & Sakinofsky, I. (1998). The gender paradox in suicide. *Suicide and Life-Threatening Behavior, 28*, 1–23.

Canobi, K. H. (2004). Individual differences in children's addition and subtraction knowledge. *Cognitive Development, 19*, 81–93.

Canobi, K. H., Reeve, R. A., & Pattison, P. E. (1998). The role of conceptual understanding in children's addition problem solving. *Developmental Psychology, 34*, 882–891.

Canobi, K. H., Reeve, R. A., & Pattison, P. E. (2003). The role of conceptual understanding in children's addition problem solving. *Developmental Psychology, 39*, 521–534.

Capaldi, D., DeGarmo, D., Patterson, G. R., & Forgatch, M. (2002). Contextual risk across the early life span and association with antisocial behavior. In J. B. Reid, G. R. Patterson, & J. Snyder (Eds.), *Antisocial behavior in children and adolescents* (pp. 123–145). Washington, DC: American Psychological Association.

Capelli, C. A., Nakagawa, N., & Madden, C. M. (1990). How children understand sarcasm: The role of context and intonation. *Child Development, 61*, 1824–1841.

Capirci, O., Contaldo, A., Caselli, M. C., & Volterra, V. (2005). From action to language through gesture. *Gesture, 5*, 155–177.

Caplan, M., Vespo, J., Pedersen, J., & Hay, D. F. (1991). Conflict and its resolution in small groups of one- and two-year-olds. *Child Development, 62*, 1513–1524.

Caples, H. S., & Barrera, M., Jr. (2006). Conflict, support and coping as mediators of the relation between degrading parenting and adjustment. *Journal of Youth and Adolescence, 35*, 603–615.

Carbonaro, W. (2005). Tracking, students' effort, and academic achievement. *Sociology of Education, 78*, 27–49.

Carey, S. (1995). On the origins of causal understanding. In D. Sperber, D. Premack, & A. J. Premack (Eds.), *Causal cognition* (pp. 268–308). Oxford, U.K.: Clarendon Press.

Carey, S. (1999). Sources of conceptual change. In E. K. Scholnick, K. Nelson, S. A. Gelman, & P. H. Miller (Eds.), *Conceptual development: Piaget's legacy* (pp. 293–326). Mahwah, NJ: Erlbaum.

Carey, S., & Markman, E. M. (1999). Cognitive development. In B. M. Bly & D. E. Rumelhart (Eds.), *Cognitive science* (pp. 201–254). San Diego: Academic Press.

Carlo, G., Koller, S. H., Eisenberg, N., Da Silva, M., & Frohlich, C. (1996). A cross-national study on the relations among prosocial moral reasoning, gender role orientations, and prosocial behaviors. *Developmental Psychology, 32*, 231–240.

Carlson, C., Uppal, S., & Prosser, E. (2000). Ethnic differences in processes contributing to the selfesteem of early adolescent girls. *Journal of Early Adolescence, 20*, 44–67.

Carlson, S. M., Moses, L. J., & Claxton, S. J. (2004). Individual differences in executive functioning and theory of mind: An investigation of inhibitory control and planning ability. *Journal of Experimental Child Psychology, 87*, 299–319.

Carlson, V. J., & Harwood, R. L. (2003). Attachment, culture, and the caregiving system: The cultural patterning of everyday experiences among Anglo and Puerto Rican mother–infant pairs. *Infant Mental Health Journal, 24*, 53–73.

Carmichael, S. L., & Shaw, G. M. (2000). Maternal life stress and congenital anomalies. *Epidemiology, 11*, 30–35.

Carolson, C., Uppal, S., & Prosser, E. C. (2000). Ethnic differences in processes contributing to the self-esteem of early adolescent girls. *Journal of Early Adolescence, 20*, 44–67.

Carpendale, J. I., & Chandler, M. J. (1996). On the distinction between false belief understanding and subscribing to an interpretive theory of mind. *Child Development, 67*, 1686–1706.

Carpendale, J. I. M. (2000). Kohlberg and Piaget on stages and moral reasoning. *Developmental Review, 20*, 181–205.

Carpenter, M., Akhtar, N., & Tomasello, M. (1998). Fourteen- through eighteen-month-old infants differentially imitate intentional and accidental actions. *Infant Behavior and Development, 21*, 315–330.

Carpenter, M., Nagel, K., & Tomasello, M. (1998). Social cognition, joint attention, and communicative competence. *Monographs of the Society for Research in Child Development, 63*(4, Serial No. 255).

Carpenter, T. P., Fennema, E., Fuson, K., Hiebert, J., Human, P., & Murray, H. (1999). Learning basic number concepts and skills as problem solving. In E. Fennema & T. A. Romberg (Eds.), *Mathematics classrooms that promote understanding: Studies in mathematical thinking and learning series* (pp. 45–61). Mahwah, NJ: Erlbaum.

Carr, D., & Friedman, M. A. (2005). Is obesity stigmatizing? Body weight, perceived discrimination, and psychological well-being in the United States. *Journal of Health and Social Behavior, 46*, 244–256.

Carr, J. (2002). Down syndrome. In P. Howlin & O. Udwin (Eds.), *Outcomes in neurodevelopmental and genetic disorders* (pp. 169–197). New York: Cambridge University Press.

Carruth, B. R., Ziegler, P. J., Gordon, A., & Henricks, K. (2004). Developmental milestones and self-feeding behaviors in infants and toddlers. *Journal of the American Dietetic Association, 104*(Suppl. 1), S51–S56.

Carskadon, M. A., Acebo, C., & Jenni, O. G. (2004). Regulation of adolescent sleep: Implications for behavior. In R. E. Dahl & L. P. Spear (Eds.), *Adolescent brain development: Vulnerabilities and opportunities* (pp. 276–291). New York: New York Academy of Sciences.

Carskadon, M. A., Harvey, K., Duke, P., Anders, T. F., Litt, I. F., & Dement, W. C. (2002). Pubertal changes in daytime sleepiness. *Sleep, 25*, 525–605.

Carta, J. J., Atwater, J. B., Greenwood, C. R., McConnell, S. R., & McEvoy, M. A. (2001). Effects of cumulative prenatal substance exposure and environmental risks on children's developmental trajectories. *Journal of Clinical Psychology, 30*, 327–337.

Carver, K., Joyner, K., & Udry, J. R. (2003). National estimates of adolescent romantic relationships. In P. Florsheim (Ed.), *Adolescent romantic relations and sexual behavior: Theory, research, and practical implications* (pp. 23–56). Mahwah, NJ: Erlbaum.

Carver, P. R., Egan, S. K., & Perry, D. G. (2004). Children who question their heterosexuality. *Developmental Psychology, 40*, 43–53.

Casasola, M., Cohen, L. B., & Chiarello, E. (2003). Six-month-old infants' categorization of containment spatial relations. *Child Development, 74*, 679–693.

Casby, M. W. (2001). Otitis media and language development: A meta-analysis. *American Journal of Speech-Language Pathology, 10*, 65–80.

Case, R. (1996). Introduction: Reconceptualizing the nature of children's conceptual structures and their development in middle childhood. In R. Case & Y. Okamoto (Eds.), The role of central conceptual structures in the development of children's thought. *Monographs of the Society for Research in Child Development, 246*(61, Serial No. 246), pp. 1–26.

Case, R. (1998). The development of conceptual structures. In D. Kuhn & R. S. Siegler (Eds.), *Handbook of child psychology: Vol. 2. Cognition, perception, and language* (pp. 745– 800). New York: Wiley.

Case, R., & Okamoto, Y. (Eds.). (1996). The role of central conceptual structures in the development of children's thought. *Monographs of the Society for Research in Child Development, 61*(1–2, Serial No. 246).

Casey, B. J., Thomas, K. M., Davidson, M. C., Kunz, K., & Franzen, P. L. (2002). Dissociating striatal and hippocampal function developmentally with a stimulus-response compatibility task. *Journal of Cognitive Neuroscience, 22*, 8647–8652.

Casey, B. M. (1986). Individual differences in selective attention among prereaders: A key to mirror-image confusions. *Developmental Psychology, 22*, 824–831.

Casey, B. M., Nuttall, R. L., & Pezaris, E. (2001). Spatial-mechanical reasoning skills versus mathematics self-confidence as mediators of gender differences on mathematics subtests using cross-national gender-based items. *Journal for Research in Mathematics Education, 32*, 28–57.

Casey, M. B., Nuttall, R. L., & Pezaris, E. (1997). Mediators of gender differences in mathematics college entrance test scores: A comparison of spatial skills with internalized beliefs and anxieties. *Developmental Psychology, 33*, 669–680.

Cashon, C. H., & Cohen, L. B. (2000). Eight-month-old infants' perceptions of possible and impossible events. *Infancy, 1*, 429–446.

Casper, L. M., & Smith, K. E. (2002). Dispelling the myths: Self-care, class, and race. *Journal of Family Issues, 23*, 716–727.

Caspi, A. (2000). The child is father of the man: Personality continuities from childhood to adulthood. *Journal of Personality and Social Psychology, 78*, 158–172.

Caspi, A., Elder, G. H., Jr., & Bem, D. J. (1987). Moving against the world: Life-course patterns of explosive children. *Developmental Psychology, 23*, 308–313.

Caspi, A., Elder, G. H., Jr., & Bem, D. J. (1988). Moving away from the world: Life-course patterns of shy children. *Developmental Psychology, 24*, 824–831.

Caspi, A., Harrington, H., Milne, B., Amell, J. W., Theodore, R. F., & Moffitt, T. E. (2003). Children's behavioral styles at age 3 are linked to their adult personality traits at age 26. *Journal of Personality, 71*, 495–513.

Caspi, A., & Herbener, E. (1990). Continuity and change: Assortative marriage and the consistency of personality in adulthood. *Journal of Personality and Social Psychology, 58*, 250–258.

Caspi, A., Lynam, D., Moffitt, T. E., & Silva, P. A. (1993). Unraveling girls' delinquency: Biological, dispositional, and contextual contributions to adolescent misbehavior. *Developmental Psychology, 29*, 19–30.

Caspi, A., McClay, J., Moffitt, T. E., Mill, J., Martin, J., & Craig, I. W. (2002). Role of genotype in the cycle of violence in maltreated children. *Science, 297*, 851–854.

Caspi, A., Moffitt, T. E., Morgan, J., Rutter, M., Taylor, A., Kim-Cohen, J., & Polo-Tomas, M. (2004). Maternal expressed emotion predicts children's antisocial behavior problems: Using monozygotic-twin differences to identify environmental effects on behavioral development. *Developmental Psychology, 40*, 149–161.

Caspi, A., & Roberts, B. W. (2001). Personality development across the life course: The argument for change and continuity. *Psychological Inquiry, 12*, 49–66.

Caspi, A., & Shiner, L. (2006). Personality development. In N. Eisenberg (Ed.), *Handbook of child psychology: Vol. 3. Social, emotional, and personality development* (6th ed., pp. 300–365). Hoboken, NJ: Wiley.

Cassia, V. M., Turati, C., & Simion, F. (2004). Can a nonspecific bias toward top-heavy patterns explain newborns' face preference? *Psychological Science, 15*, 379–383.

Cassidy, J. (2001). Adult romantic attachments: A developmental perspective on individual differences. *Review of General Psychology, 4*, 111-131.

Cassidy, J., & Berlin, L. J. (1994). The insecure/ambivalent pattern of attachment: Theory and research. *Child Development, 65*, 971–991.

Castellanos, F. X., Lee, P. P., Sharp, W., Jeffries, N. O., Greenstein, D. K., & Clasen, L. S. (2002). Developmental trajectories of brain volume abnormalities in children and adolescents with attention-deficit/hyperactivity disorder. *Journal of the American Medical Association, 288*, 1740–1748.

Castellanos, F. X., Sharp, W. S., Gottesman, R. F., Greenstein, D. K., Giedd, J. N., & Rapoport, J. L. (2003). Anatomic brain abnormalities in monozygotic twins discordant for attention-deficit hyperactivity disorder. *American Journal of Psychiatry, 160*, 1693–1695.

Catalano, R., Bruckner, T., Anderson, E., & Gould, J. B. (2005). Fetal death sex ratios: A test of the economic stress hypothesis. *International Journal of Epidemiology, 34*, 944–948.

Catalano, R. A. (2003). Sex ratios in the two Germanies: A test of the economic stress hypothesis. *Human Reproduction, 18*, 1972–1975.

Caton, D., Corry, M. P., Frigoletto, F. D., Hopkins, D. P., Liberman, E., & Mayberry, L. (2002). The nature and management of labor pain: Executive summary. *American Journal of Obstetrics and Gynecology, 186*, S1–S15.

Cavadini, C., Siega-Riz, A. M., & Popkin, B. M. (2000). U.S. adolescent food intake trends from 1965 to 1996. *Archives of Diseases in Childhood, 83*, 18–24.

Ceci, S. J. (1991). How much does schooling influence general intelligence and its cognitive components? A reassessment of the evidence. *Developmental Psychology, 27*, 703–722.

Ceci, S. J. (1999). Schooling and intelligence. In S. J. Ceci & W. M. Williams (Eds.), *The nature–nurture debate: The essential readings* (pp. 168–175). Oxford: Blackwell.

Ceci, S. J., Bruck, M., & Battin, D. (2000). The suggestibility of children's testimony. In Bjorklund, D. (Ed) *False-memory creation in children and adults* (pp. 169–201) Mahwah, NJ: Erlbaum.

Ceci, S. J., Fitneva, S. A., & Gilstrap, L. L. (2003). Memory development and eyewitness testimony. In A. Slater & G. Bremner (Eds.), *An introduction to developmental psychology* (pp. 283–310). Malden MA: Blackwell.

Ceci, S. J., & Roazzi, A. (1994). The effects of context on cognition: Postcards from Brazil. In R. J. Sternberg (Ed.), *Mind in context* (pp. 74–101). New York: Cambridge University Press.

Ceci, S. J., Rosenblum, T. B., & Kumpf, M. (1998). The shrinking gap between high- and low-scoring groups: Current trends and possible causes. In U. Neisser (Ed.), *The rising curve: Long-term gains in IQ and related measures* (pp. 287–302). Washington, DC: American Psychological Association.

Ceci, S. J., & Williams, W. M. (1997). Schooling, intelligence, and income. *American Psychologist, 52*, 1051–1058.

Cecil, J. E., Watt, P., Murrie, I. S. L., Wrieden, W., Wallis, D. J., Hetherington, M. M., Bolton-Smith, C., & Palmer, C. N. A. (2005). Childhood obesity and socioeconomic status: A novel role for height growth limitation. *International Journal of Obesity, 29*, 1199–1203.

Center for Communication and Social Policy. (Ed.). (1998). *National Television Violence Study* (Vol. 2). Newbury Park, CA: Sage.

Center for Effective Discipline. (2005). *Worldwide bans on corporal punishment.* Retrieved from www.stophitting.com/disatschool/facts.php

Centers for Disease Control and Prevention. (2005). *Preventing lead poisoning in young children.* Atlanta: Author.

Cernoch, J. M., & Porter, R. H. (1985). Recognition of maternal axillary odors by infants. *Child Development, 56*, 1593–1598.

Cervantes, C. A., & Callanan, M. A. (1998). Labels and explanations in mother–child emotion talk: Age and gender differentiation. *Developmental Psychology, 34*, 88–98.

Chall, J. S. (1983). *Stages of reading development.* New York: McGraw-Hill.

Chalmers, J. B., & Townsend, M. A. R. (1990). The effects of training in social perspective taking on socially maladjusted girls. *Child Development, 61*, 178–190.

Chamberlain, P. (2003). Antisocial behavior and delinquency in girls. In P. Chamberlain (Ed.), *Treating chronic juvenile offenders* (pp. 109–127). Washington, DC: American Psychological Association.

Champion, T. B. (2003a). "A matter of vocabulary": Performances of low-income African-American Head Start children on the Peabody Picture Vocabulary Test. *Communication Disorders Quarterly, 24*, 121–127.

Champion, T. B. (2003b). *Understanding storytelling among African-American children: A journey from Africa to America.* Mahwah, NJ: Erlbaum.

Chan, R. W., Raboy, B., & Patterson, C. J. (1998). Psychosocial adjustment among children conceived via donor insemination by lesbian and heterosexual mothers. *Child Development, 69*, 443–457.

Chandra, R. K. (1991). Interactions between early nutrition and the immune system. In *Ciba Foundation Symposium No. 156* (pp. 77–92). Chichester, U.K.: Wiley.

Chang, F., Dell, G. S., & Bock, K. (2006). Becoming syntactic. *Psychological Review, 113*, 234–272.

Chang, L., Schwartz, D., Dodge, D. A., & McBride-Chang, C. (2003). Harsh parenting in relation to child emotion regulation and aggression. *Journal of Family Psychology, 17*, 598–606.

Chao, R. K. (1994). Beyond parental control and authoritarian parenting style: Understanding Chinese parenting through the cultural notion of training. *Child Development, 65*, 1111–1119.

Chao, R. K. (2001). Extending research on the consequences of parenting style for Chinese Americans and European Americans. *Child Development, 72*, 1832–1843.

Chapman, R. S. (2000). Children's language learning: An interactionist perspective. *Journal of Child Psychology and Psychiatry, 41*, 33–54.

Charchut, S. W., Allred, E. N., & Needleman, H. L. (2003). The effects of infant feeding patterns on the occlusion of the primary dentition. *Journal of Dentistry for Children, 70*, 197–203.

Charman, T., Baron-Cohen, S., Swettenham, J., Baird, G., Cox, A., & Drew, A. (2001). Testing joint attention, imitation, and play as infancy precursors to language and theory of mind. *Cognitive Development, 15*, 481–49.

Charpak, N., Ruiz-Peláez, J. G., & Figueroa, Z. (2005). Influence of feeding patterns and other factors on early somatic growth of healthy, preterm infants in home-based kangaroo mother care: A cohort study. *Journal of Pediatric Gastroenterology and Nutrition, 41*, 430–437.

Chase-Lansdale, P. L., Brooks-Gunn, J., & Zamsky, E. S. (1994). Young African-American multigenerational families in poverty: Quality of mothering and grandmothering. *Child Development, 65*, 373–393.

Chase-Lansdale, P. L., Gordon, R., Brooks-Gunn, J., & Klebanov, P. K. (1997). Neighborhood and family influences on the intellectual and behavioral competence of preschool and early school-age children. In J. Brooks-Gunn, G. Duncan, & J. L. Aber (Eds.), *Neighborhood poverty: Context and consequences for development* (pp. 79–118). New York: Russell Sage Foundation.

Chassin, L., Hussong, A., Barrera, M., Jr., Molina, B. S. G., Trim, R., & Ritter, J. (2004). Adolescent substance use. In R. M. Lerner & L. Steinberg (Eds.), *Handbook of adolescent psychology* (2nd ed., pp. 665–696). Hoboken, NJ: Wiley.

Chauhan, G. S., Shastri, J., & Mohite, P. (2005). Development of gender constancy in preschoolers. *Psychological Studies, 50*, 62–71.

Chavajay, P., & Rogoff, B. (1999). Cultural variation in management of attention by children and their caregivers. *Developmental Psychology, 35*, 1079–1090.

Chavajay, P., & Rogoff, B. (2002). Schooling and traditional collaborative social organization of problem solving by Mayan mothers and children. *Developmental Psychology, 38*, 55–66.

Cheah, C. S. L., & Nelson, L. J. (2004). The role of acculturation in the emerging adulthood of aboriginal college students. *International Journal of Behavioral Development, 28*, 495–507.

Checkley, W., Epstein, L. D., Gilman, R. H., Cabrera, L., & Black, R. E. (2003). Effects of acute diarrhea on linear growth in Peruvian children. *American Journal of Epidemiology, 157*, 166–175.

Chen, D. W., Fein, G. G., Killen, M., & Tam, H.-P. (2001). Peer conflicts of preschool children: Issues, resolution, incidence, and age-related patterns. *Early Education and Development, 12*, 523–544.

Chen, D. W., Fein, G., & Tam, H. P. (2001). Peer conflicts of preschool children: Issues, resolution, incidence, and age-related patterns. *Early Education and Development, 12*, 523–544.

Chen, J. J. (2005). Relation of academic support from parents, teachers, and peers to Hong Kong adolescents' academic achievement: The mediating role of academic engagement. *Genetic, Social, and General Psychology Monographs, 131*, 77–127.

Chen, M. (2003). Wombs for rent: An examination of prohibitory and regulatory approaches to governing preconception arrangements. *Health Law in Canada, 23*, 33–50.

Chen, X., Cen, G., Li, D., & He, Y. (2005). Social functioning and adjustment in Chinese children: The imprint of historical time. *Child Development, 76*, 182–195.

Chen, X., DeSouza, A. T., Chen, H., & Wang, L. (2006). Reticent behavior and experiences in peer interactions in Chinese and Canadian children. *Developmental Psychology, 42*, 656–665.

Chen, X., Hastings, P. D., Rubin, K. H., Chen, H., Cen, G., & Stewart, S. L. (1998). Child-rearing attitudes and behavioral inhibition in Chinese and Canadian toddlers: A cross-cultural study. *Developmental Psychology, 34*, 677–686.

Chen, X., Rubin, K. H., & Li, Z. (1995). Social functioning and adjustment in Chinese children: A longitudinal study. *Developmental Psychology, 31*, 531–539.

Chen, Y.-C., Yu, M.-L., Rogan, W., Gladen, B., & Hsu, C.-C. (1994). A 6-year follow-up of behavior and activity disorders in the Taiwan Yu-cheng children. *American Journal of Public Health, 84*, 415–421.

Chen, Y.-J., & Hsu, C.-C. (1994). Effects of prenatal exposure to PCBs on the neurological function of children: A neuropsychological and neurophysiological study. *Developmental Medicine and Child Neurology, 36*, 312–320.

Chen, Z., Sanchez, R. P., & Campbell, T. (1997). From beyond to within their grasp: The rudiments of analogical problem solving in 10- to 13-month-olds. *Developmental Psychology, 33*, 790–801.

Chen, Z., & Siegler, R. S. (2000). Across the great divide: Bridging the gap between understanding of toddlers' and older children's thinking. *Monographs of the Society for Research in Child Development, 65*(2, Serial No. 261).

Cheng, T. L., Fields, C. B., Brenner, R. A., Wright, J. L., Lomax, T., Scheidt, P. C., & the District of Columbia Child/Adolescent Injury Research Network. (2000). Sports injuries: An important cause of morbidity in urban youth. *Pediatrics, 105*, e32.

Chesney-Lind, M. (2001). Girls, violence, and delinquency: Popular myths and persistent problems. In S. O. White (Ed.), *Handbook of youth and justice* (pp. 135–158). New York: Kluwer Academic.

Chesney-Lind, M., & Belknap, J. (2004). Trends in delinquent girls' aggression and violent behavior. In M. Putallaz & K. L. Bierman (Eds.), *Aggression, antisocial behavior, and violence among girls: A developmental perspective* (pp. 203–220). New York: Guilford.

Chess, S., & Thomas, A. (1984). *Origins and evolution of behavior disorders.* New York: Brunner/Mazel.

Child Care Advocacy Association of Canada. (2004). *Family living costs in Manitoba, 2004, and cost of raising a child.* Retrieved from www.action.web.ca/home/ccaac/alerts/shtm?x=67753

Child Trends. (2005). *Facts at a glance.* Washington, DC: Author.

Child Trends. (2007). *Late or no prenatal care.* Retrieved from www.childtrendsdatabank.org/indicators /25PrenatalCare.cfm

Children's Defense Fund. (2006). *The state of America's children: 2005.* Washington, DC: Author.

Chin, D. G., Schonfeld, D. J., O'Hare, L. L., Mayne, S. T., Salovey, P., Showalter, D. R., & Cicchetti, D. V. (1998). Elementary school-age children's developmental understanding of the causes of cancer. *Developmental and Behavioral Pediatrics, 19,* 397–403.

Chisholm, J. S. (1989). Biology, culture, and the development of temperament: A Navajo example. In J. K. Nugent, B. M. Lester, & T. B. Brazelton (Eds.), *Biology, culture, and development* (Vol. 1, pp. 341–364). Norwood, NJ: Ablex.

Choi, J., & Silverman, I. (2003). Processes underlying sex differences in route-learning strategies in children and adolescents. *Personality and Individual Differences, 34,* 1153–1166.

Choi, S., & Gopnik, A. (1995). Early acquisition of verbs in Korean: A cross-linguistic study. *Journal of Child Language, 22,* 497–529.

Choi, S., McDonough, L., Bowerman, M., & Mandler, J. M. (1999). Early sensitivity to language-specific spatial categories in English and Korean. *Cognitive Development, 14,* 241–268.

Chomsky, C. (1969). *The acquisition of syntax in children from five to ten.* Cambridge, MA: MIT Press.

Chomsky, N. (1957). *Syntactic structures.* The Hague: Mouton.

Chordirker, B., Cadrin, C., Davies, G., Summers, A., Wilson, R., Winsor, E., & Young, D. (2001). Genetic indications for prenatal diagnosis. *Journal of the Society of Obstetricians and Gynaecologists of Canada, 23,* 525–531.

Chorzempa, B. F., & Graham, S. (2006). Primary-grade teachers' use of within-class ability grouping in reading. *Journal of Educational Psychology, 98,* 529–541.

Chouinard, M. M., & Clark, E. V. (2003). Adult reformulations of child errors as negative evidence. *Journal of Child Language, 30,* 637–669.

Christenson, S. L., & Sheridan, S. M. (2001). *Schools and families.* New York: Guilford.

Christenson, S. L., & Thurlow, M. L. (2004). School dropouts: Prevention considerations, interventions, and challenges. *Current Directions in Psychological Science, 13,* 36–39.

Christophersen, E. R., & Mortweet, S. L. (2003). *Parenting that works: Building skills that last a lifetime.* Washington, DC: American Psychological Association.

Chudley, A. E., Conry, J., Cook, J. L., Loock, C., Rosales, T., & LeBlanc, N. (2005). Fetal alcohol spectrum disorder: Canadian guidelines for diagnosis. *Canadian Medical Association Journal, 172,* S1–S21.

Chumlea, W. C., Schubert, C. M., Roche, A. F., Kulin, H. E., Lee, P. A., Himes, J. H., & Sun, S. S. (2003). Age at menarche and racial comparisons in U.S. girls. *Pediatrics, 111,* 110–113.

Chung, H. H. (2006). Code switching as a communicative strategy: A case study of Korean–English bilinguals. *Bilingual Research Journal, 30,* 293–307.

Cicchetti, D. (2003). Neuroendocrine functioning in maltreated children. In D. Cicchetti & E. F. Walker (Eds.), *Neurodevelopmental mechanisms in psychopathology* (pp. 345–365). New York: Cambridge University Press.

Cicchetti D., & Toth, S. L. (2006). Developmental psychopathology and preventive intervention. In K. A. Renninger & I. E. Sigel (Eds.), *Handbook of child psychology: Vol. 4. Child psychology in practice* (6th ed., pp. 497–547). Hoboken, NJ: Wiley.

Cillessen, A. H. N., & Bellmore, A. D. (2004). Social skills and interpersonal perception in early and middle childhood. In P. K. Smith & C. H. Hart (Eds.), *Blackwell handbook of childhood social development* (pp. 355–374). Malden, MA: Blackwell.

Cillessen, A. H. N., & Mayeux, L. (2004). From censure to reinforcement: Developmental changes in the association between aggression and social status. *Child Development, 75,* 147–163.

Clapp, J. F., III, Kim, H., Burciu, B., Schmidt, S., Petry, K., & Lopez, B. (2002). Continuing regular exercise during pregnancy: Effect of exercise volume on fetoplacental growth. *American Journal of Obstetrics and Gynecology, 186,* 142–147.

Clark, E. V. (1995). The lexicon and syntax. In J. L. Miller & P. D. Eimas (Eds.), *Speech, language, and communication* (pp. 303–337). San Diego: Academic Press.

Clark, K. E., & Ladd, G. W. (2000). Connectedness and autonomy support in parent–child relationships: Links to children's socioemotional orientation and peer relationships. *Developmental Psychology, 36,* 485–498.

Clark, L. A., Kochanska, G., & Ready, R. (2000). Mothers' personality and its interaction with child temperament as predictors of parenting. *Journal of Personality and Social Psychology, 79,* 701–719.

Clarke-Stewart, K. A. (1998). Historical shifts and underlying themes in ideas about rearing young children in the United States: Where have we been? Where are we going? *Early Development and Parenting, 7,* 101–117.

Clarke-Stewart, K. A., Allhusen, V., & Goossens, F. (2001). Day care and the Strange Situation. In A. Göncue & E. L. Klein (Eds.), *Children in play, story, and school* (pp. 241–266). New York: Guilford.

Clarke-Stewart, K. A., & Hayward, C. (1996). Advantages of father custody and contact for the psychological well-being of school-age children. *Journal of Applied Developmental Psychology, 17,* 239–270.

Clarkson, T. W., Magos, L., & Myers, G. J. (2003). The toxicology of mercury—current exposures and clinical manifestations. *New England Journal of Medicine, 349,* 1731–1737.

Clausen, J. A. (1975). The social meaning of differential physical and sexual maturation. In S. E. Dragastin & G. H. Elder (Eds.), *Adolescence in the life cycle: Psychological change and the social context* (pp. 25–47). New York: Halsted.

Claxton, L. J., Keen, R., & McCarty, M. E. (2003). Evidence of motor planning in infant reaching behavior. *Psychological Science, 14,* 354–356.

Clements, D. H., & Sarama, J. (2003). Young children and technology: What does the research say? *Young Children, 58*(6), 34–40.

Cleveland, E. S., & Reese, E. (2005). Maternal structure and autonomy support in conversations about the past: Contributions to children's autobiographical memory. *Developmental Psychology, 41,* 376–388.

Clifford, R. M., Barbarin, O., Chang, F., Early, D., Bryant, D., Howes, C., Burchinal, M., & Pianta, R. (2005). What is pre-kindergarten? Characteristics of public pre-kindergarten programs. *Applied Developmental Science, 9,* 126–143.

Clifton, R. K., Rochat, P., Robin, D. J., & Berthier, N. E. (1994). Multimodal perception in the control of infant reaching. *Journal of Experimental Psychology: Human Perception and Performance, 20,* 876–886.

Clinchy, B. M. (2002). Revisiting women's ways of knowing. In B. K. Hofer & P. R. Pintrich (Eds.), *Personal epistemology: The psychological beliefs about knowledge and knowing* (pp. 63–87). Mahwah, NJ: Erlbaum.

Clingempeel, W. G., & Henggeler, S. W. (2003). Aggressive juvenile offenders transitioning into emerging adulthood: Factors discriminating persistors and desistors. *American Journal of Orthopsychiatry, 73,* 310–323.

Cloud, N., Genesee, F., & Hamayan, E. (2000). *Dual language instruction: A handbook for enriched education.* Boston, MA: Heinle & Heinle.

Cohen, L. B. (2003). Commentary on Part I: Unresolved issues in infant categorization. In D. H. Rakison & L. M. Oakes (Eds.), *Early category and concept development: Making sense of the blooming, buzzing confusion* (pp. 193–209). New York: Oxford University Press.

Cohen, L. B., & Cashon, C. H. (2001). Infant object segregation implies information integration. *Journal of Experimental Child Psychology, 78,* 75–83.

Cohen, L. B., & Cashon, C. H. (2006). Infant cognition. In D. Kuhn & R. Siegler (Eds.), *Handbook of child psychology: Vol. 2. Cognition, perception, and language* (6th ed., pp. 214–251). Hoboken, NJ: Wiley.

Cohen, L. B., & Marks, K. S. (2002). How infants process addition and subtraction events. *Developmental Science, 5,* 186–201.

Cohen, P., Kasen, S., Chen, H., Harmrk, C., & Gordon, K. (2003). Variations in patterns of developmental transitions in the emerging adulthood period. *Developmental Psychology, 39,* 657–669.

Cohen, S., & Herbert, T. B. (1996). Health psychology: Psychological factors and physical disease from the perspective of human psychoneuroimmunology. *Annual Review of Psychology, 47,* 113–142.

Coholl, A., Kassotis, J., Parks, R., Vaughan, R., Bannister, H., & Northridge, M. (2001). Adolescents in the age of AIDS: Myths, misconceptions, and misunderstandings regarding sexually transmitted diseases. *Journal of the National Medical Association, 93,* 64–69.

Coie, J. D., & Dodge, K. A. (1998). Aggression and antisocial behavior. In N. Eisenberg (Ed.), *Handbook of child psychology: Vol. 3. Social, emotional, and personality development* (5th ed., pp. 779–862). New York: Wiley.

Coie, J. D., Dodge, K. A., & Coppotelli, H. (1982). Dimensions and types of social status: A cross-age perspective. *Developmental Psychology, 18,* 557–570.

Colapinto, J. (2001). *As nature made him: The boy who was raised as a girl.* New York: Perennial.

Colby, A., Kohlberg, L., Gibbs, J., & Lieberman, M. (1983). A longitudinal study of moral judgment. *Monographs of the Society for Research in Child Development, 48*(1–2, Serial No. 200).

Cole, A., & Kerns, K. A. (2001). Perceptions of sibling qualities and activities of early adolescents. *Journal of Early Adolescence, 21,* 204–226.

Cole, D. A., Martin, J. M., Peeke, L. A., Seroczynski, A. D., & Fier, J. (1999). Children's over- and underestimation of academic competence: A longitudinal study of gender differences, depression, and anxiety. *Child Development, 70,* 459–473.

Cole, D. A., Maxwell, S. E., Martin, J. M., Peeke, L. G., Seroczynski, A. D., & Tram, J. M. (2001). The development of multiple domains of child and adolescent self-concept: A cohort sequential longitudinal design. *Child Development, 72,* 1723–1746.

Cole, M. (1990). Cognitive development and formal schooling: The evidence from cross-cultural research. In L. C. Moll (Ed.), *Vygotsky and education* (pp. 89–110). New York: Cambridge University Press.

Cole, M. (2005). Culture in development. In M. H. Bornstein & M. E. Lamb (Ed.), *Developmental science: An advanced textbook* (5th ed., pp. 45–102). Mahwah, NJ: Erlbaum.

Cole, M. (2006). Culture and cognitive development in phylogenetic, historical, and ontogenetic perspective. In D. Kuhn & R. S. Siegler (Eds.), *Handbook of child psychology: Vol. 2. Cognition, perception, and language* (6th ed., pp. 636–685). Hoboken, NJ: Wiley.

Cole, P. M., Bruschi, C. J., & Tamang, B. L. (2002). Cultural differences in children's emotional reactions to difficult situations. *Child Development, 73,* 983–996.

Cole, P. M., & Tamang, B. L. (1998). Nepali children's ideas about emotional displays in hypothetical challenges. *Developmental Psychology, 34,* 640–648.

Cole, P. M., Tamang, B. L., & Shrestha, S. (2006). Cultural variations in the socialization of young children's anger and shame. *Child Development, 77,* 1237–1251.

Cole, T. J. (2000). Secular trends in growth. *Proceedings of the Nutrition Society, 59,* 317–324.

Coleman, P. K. (2003). Perceptions of parent–child attachment, social self-efficacy, and peer relationships in middle childhood. *Infant and Child Development, 12,* 351–368.

Coley, R. L. (1998). Children's socialization experiences and functioning in single-mother households: The importance of fathers and other men. *Child Development, 69,* 219–230.

Coley, R. L., Morris, J. E., & Hernandez, D. (2004). Out-of-school care and problem behavior trajectories among low-income adolescents: Individual, family, and neighborhood characteristics as added risks. *Child Development, 75,* 948–965.

Collaer, M. L., & Hill, E. M. (2006). Large sex difference in adolescents on a timed line judgment task: Attentional contributors and task relationship to mathematics. *Perception, 35,* 561–572.

Collaer, M. L., & Hines, M. (1995). Human behavioral sex differences: A role for gonadal hormones during early development? *Psychological Bulletin, 118,* 55–107.

Collie, R., & Hayne, H. (1999). Deferred imitation by 6- and 9-month-old infants: More evidence for declarative memory. *Developmental Psychobiology, 35,* 83–90.

Collins, W. A. (1983). Children's processing of television content: Implications for prevention of negative effects. *Prevention in Human Services, 2,* 53–66.

Collins, W. A. (2003). More than myth: The developmental significance of romantic relationships during adolescence. *Journal of Research on Adolescence, 13,* 1–24.

Collins, W. A., & Laursen, B. (2004). Parent–adolescent relationships and influences. In R. M. Lerner & L. Steinberg (Eds.), *Handbook of adolescent psychology* (2nd ed., pp. 331–361). New York: Wiley.

Collins, W. A., Maccoby, E. E., Steinberg, L., Hetherington, E. M., & Bornstein, M. H. (2000). Contemporary research on parenting: The case for nature and nurture. *American Psychologist, 52,* 218–232.

Collins, W. A., Madsen, S. D., & Susman-Stillman, A. (2002). Parenting during middle childhood. In M. H. Bornstein (Ed.), *Handbook of parenting: Vol. 1. Children and parenting* (2nd ed., pp. 73–101). Mahwah, NJ: Erlbaum.

Collins, W. A., & Russell, G. (1991). Mother–child and father–child interactions in middle childhood and adolescence. *Developmental Review, 11,* 99–136.

Collins, W. A., & Steinberg, L. (2006). Adolescent development in interpersonal context. In N. Eisenberg (Ed.), *Handbook of child psychology: Vol. 3. Social, emotional, and personality development* (6th ed., pp. 1003–1067). Hoboken, NJ: Wiley.

Collins, W. A., & Van Dulmen, M. (2006a). Friendships and romantic relationships in emerging adulthood: Continuities and discontinuities. In J. J. Arnett & J. Tanner (Eds.), *Emerging adults in America: Coming of age in the 21st century* (pp. 219–234). Washington, DC: American Psychological Association.

Collins, W. A., & Van Dulmen, M. (2006b). "The course of true love(s) . . .": Origins and pathways in the development of romantic relationships. In A. Booth & A. Crouter (Eds.), *Romance and sex in adolescence and emerging adulthood: Risks and opportunities* (pp. 63–86). Mahwah, NJ: Erlbaum.

Collins, W. K., & Steinberg, L. (2006). Adolescent development in interpersonal context. In N. Eisenberg (Ed.), *Handbook of child psychology: Vol. 3. Social, emotional, and personality development* (6th ed., pp. 1003–1067). Hoboken, NJ: Wiley.

Colman, L. L., & Colman, A. D. (1991). *Pregnancy: The psychological experience.* Noonday Press.

Colombo, J. (1995). On the neural mechanisms underlying developmental and individual differences in visual fixation in infancy. *Developmental Review, 15,* 97–135.

Colombo, J. (2002). Infant attention grows up: The emergence of a developmental cognitive neuroscience perspective. *Current Directions in Psychological Science, 11,* 196–199.

Colombo, J., Shaddy, D. J., Richman, W. A., Maikranz, J. M., & Blaga, O. M. (2004). The developmental course of habituation in infancy and preschool outcome. *Infancy, 5,* 1–38.

Coltrane, S. (1990). Birth timing and the division of labor in dual-earner families. *Journal of Family Issues, 11,* 157–181.

Coltrane, S. (1996). *Family man.* New York: Oxford University Press.

Commission on Adolescent Suicide Prevention. (2005). Targeted youth suicide prevention programs. In D. L. Evans, E. B. Foa, R. E. Gur, H. Hending, & C. P. O'Brien (Eds.), *Treating and preventing adolescent mental health disorders: What we know and what we don't know* (pp. 463–469). New York: Oxford University Press.

Comstock, G., & Scharrer, E. (2006). Media and popular culture. In K. A. Renninger & I. E. Sigel (Eds.), *Handbook of child psychology: Vol. 4. Child psychology in practice* (6th ed., pp. 817–863). Hoboken, NJ: Wiley.

Comunian, A. L., & Gielen, U. P. (2000). Sociomoral reflection and prosocial and antisocial behavior: Two Italian studies. *Psychological Reports, 87,* 161–175.

Conboy, B. T., & Thal, D. J. (2006). Ties between the lexicon and grammar: Cross-sectional and longitudinal studies of bilingual toddlers. *Child Development, 77,* 712–735.

Conchas, G. Q. (2006). *The color of success: Race and high-achieving urban youth.* New York: Teachers College Press.

Conger, R., Wallace, L., Sun, Y., Simons, L., McLoyd, V., & Brody, G. (2002). Economic pressure in African American families: A replication and extension of the family stress model. *Developmental Psychology, 38,* 179–193.

Conger, R. D., & Conger, K. J. (2002). Resilience in Midwestern families: Selected findings from the first decade of a prospective, longitudinal study. *Journal of Marriage and the Family, 64,* 361–373.

Connell, M. W., Sheridan, K., & Gardner, H. (2003). On abilities and domains. In R. J. Sternberg & E. Grigorenko (Eds.), *Perspectives on the psychology of abilities, competencies, and expertise* (pp. 126–155). New York: Cambridge University Press.

Conner, D. B., & Cross, D. R. (2003). Longitudinal analysis of the presence, efficacy, and stability of maternal scaffolding during informal problem-solving interactions. *British Journal of Developmental Psychology, 21,* 315–334.

Connolly, J., Craig, W., Goldberg, A., & Pepler, D. (2004). Mixed-gender groups, dating, and romantic relationships in early adolescence. *Journal of Research on Adolescence, 14,* 185–207.

Connolly, J., & Goldberg, A. (1999). Romantic relationships in adolescence: The role of friends and peers in their emergence and development. In W. Furman, B. B. Brown, & C. Feiring (Eds.), *The development of romantic relationships in adolescence* (pp. 266–290). New York: Cambridge University Press.

Connolly, J., Furman, W., & Konarski, R. (2000). The role of peers in the emergence of romantic relationships in adolescence. *Child Development, 71,* 1395–1408.

Connolly, J. A., & Doyle, A. B. (1984). Relations of social fantasy play to social competence in preschoolers. *Developmental Psychology, 20,* 797–806.

Connor, J. M. (2003). Physical activity and well-being. In M. H. Bornstein, L. Davidson, C. L. M. Keyes, K. A. Moore, & the Center for Child Well-Being (Eds.), *Well-being: Positive development across the life course* (pp. 65–79). Mahwah, NJ: Erlbaum.

Connor, P. D., Sampson, P. D., Streissguth, A. P., Bookstein, F. L., & Barr, H. M. (2006). Effects of prenatal alcohol exposure on fine motor coordination and balance: A study of two adult samples. *Neuropsychologia, 44,* 744–751.

Conti-Ramsden, G., & Pérez-Pereira, M. (1999). Conversational interactions between mothers and their infants who are congenitally blind, have low vision, or are sighted. *Journal of Visual Impairment and Blindness, 93,* 691–703.

Conway, A. R. A., Kane, M. J., & Engle, R. W. (2003). Working memory capacity and its relation to general intelligence. *Trends in Cognitive Sciences, 7,* 547–552.

Conyers, C., Miltenberger, R., Maki, A., Barenz, R., Jurgens, M., Sailer, A., Haugen, M., & Kopp, B. (2004). A comparison of response cost and differential reinforcement of other behaviors to reduce disruptive behavior in a preschool classroom. *Journal of Applied Behavior Analysis, 37,* 411–415.

Cook, W. L. (2000). Understanding attachment security in family context. *Journal of Personality and Social Psychology, 78,* 285–294.

Cooper, C. R. (1998). *The weaving of maturity: Cultural perspectives on adolescent development.* New York: Oxford University Press.

Cope-Farrar, K. M., & Kunkel, D. (2002). Sexual messages in teens' favorite prime-time television programs. In J. D. Brown, J. R. Steele, & K. Walsh-Childers (Eds.), *Sexual teens, sexual media* (pp. 59–78). Mahwah, NJ: Erlbaum.

Coplan, R. J., Bowker, A., & Cooper, S. M. (2003). Parenting daily hassles, child temperament, and social adjustment in preschool. *Early Childhood Research Quarterly, 18,* 376–395.

Coplan, R. J., Gavinsky-Molina, M. H., Lagace-Seguin, D., & Wichmann, C. (2001). When girls versus boys play alone: Nonsocial play and adjustment in kindergarten. *Developmental Psychology, 37,* 464–474.

Coplan, R. J., Prakash, K., O'Neil, K., & Armer, M. (2004). Do you "want" to play? Distinguishing between conflicted shyness and social disinterest in early childhood. *Developmental Psychology, 40,* 244–258.

Corenblum, B. (2003). What children remember about ingroup and outgroup peers: Effects of stereotypes on children's processing of information about group members. *Journal of Experimental Child Psychology, 86,* 32–66.

Cornelius, J. R., Maisto, S. A., Pollock, N. K., Martin, C. S., Salloum, I. M., Lynch, K. G., & Clark, D. B. (2003). Rapid relapse generally follows treatment for substance use disorders among adolescents. *Addictive Behaviors, 28,* 381–386.

Correa-Chavez, M., Rogoff, B., & Arauz, R. M. (2005). Cultural patterns in attending to two events at once. *Child Development, 76,* 664–678.

Cortese, D. A., & Smith, H. C. (2003). *Mayo Clinic family health book* (3rd ed.). New York:

Cory-Slechta, D. A. (2003). Lead-induced impairments in complex cognitive function: Offerings from experimental studies. *Child Neuropsychology, 9,* 64–75.

Cosden, M., Peerson, S., & Elliott, K. (1997). Effects of prenatal drug exposure on birth outcomes and early child development. *Journal of Drug Issues, 27,* 525–539.

Costello, B. J., & Dunaway, R. G. (2003). Egotism and delinquent behavior. *Journal of Interpersonal Violence, 18,* 572–590.

Costello, E. J., & Angold, A. (1995). Developmental epidemiology. In D. Cicchetti & D. Cohen (Eds.), *Developmental psychopathology: Vol. 1. Theory and method* (pp. 23–56). New York: Wiley.

Costigan, C. L., Cox, M. J., & Cauce, A. M. (2003). Work–parenting linkages among dual-earner couples at the transition to parenthood. *Journal of Family Psychology, 17,* 397–408.

Costos, D., Ackerman, R., & Paradis, L. (2002). Recollections of menarche: Communication between mothers and daughters regarding menstruation. *Sex Roles, 46,* 49–59.

Côté, J. E., & Schwartz, S. J. (2002). Comparing psychological and sociological approaches to identity: Identity status, identity capital, and the individualization process. *Journal of Adolescence, 25,* 571–586.

Coté, S., Zoccolillo, M., Tremblay, R., Nagin, D., & Vitaro, F. (2001). Predicting girls' conduct disorder in adolescence from childhood trajectories of disruptive behaviors. *Journal of the American Academy of Child and Adolescent Psychiatry, 40,* 678–684.

Cotinot, C., Pailhoux, E., Jaubert, F., & Fellous, M. (2002). Molecular genetics of sex determination. *Seminars in Reproductive Medicine, 20,* 157–168.

Cotton, A., Stanton, K. R., Acs, Z. J., & Lovegrove, M. (2006). *The UB Obesity Report Card: An overview.* Retrieved from www.ubalt.edu/experts/obesity

Coulton, C. J., Korbin, J. E., & Su, M. (1999). Neighborhoods and child maltreatment: A multi-level study. *Child Abuse and Neglect, 23,* 1019–1040.

Courage, M. L., & Howe, M. L. (1998). The ebb and flow of infant attentional preferences: Evidence for long-term recognition memory in 3-month-olds. *Journal of Experimental Child Psychology, 18,* 98–106.

Courage, M. L., & Howe, M. L. (2002). From infant to child: The dynamics of cognitive change in the second year of life. *Psychological Bulletin, 128,* 250–277.

Courchesne, E., Carper, R., & Akshoomoff, N. (2003). Evidence of brain overgrowth in the first year of life in autism. *Journal of the American Medical Association, 290,* 337–344.

Couturier, J. L., & Lock, J. (2006). Denial and minimization in adolescents with anorexia nervosa. *International Journal of Eating Disorders, 39,* 212–216.

Covington, C. Y., Nordstrom-Klee, B., Ager, J., Sokol, R., & Delaney-Black, V. (2002). Birth to age 7 growth of children prenatally exposed to drugs: A prospective cohort study. *Neurotoxicology and Teratology, 24,* 489–496.

Cowan, C. P., & Cowan, P. A. (1997). Working with couples during stressful transitions. In S. Dreman (Ed.), *The family on the threshold of the 21st century* (pp. 17–47). Mahwah, NJ: Erlbaum.

Cowan, C. P., & Cowan, P. A. (2000). *When partners become parents.* Mahwah, NJ: Erlbaum.

Cowan, P. A., & Cowan, C. P. (2002). Interventions as tests of family systems theories: Marital and family relationships in children's development and psychopathology. *Development and Psychopathology, 14,* 731–759.

Cowan, P. A., & Cowan, C. P. (2004). From family relationships to peer rejection to antisocial behavior in middle childhood. In J. B. Kupersmidt & K. A. Dodge (Eds.), *Children's peer relations: From development to intervention* (pp. 159–177). Washington, DC: American Psychological Association.

Cox, C. E., Kotch, J. B., & Everson, M. D. (2003). A longitudinal study of modifying influences in the relationship between domestic violence and child maltreatment. *Journal of Family Violence, 18,* 5–17.

Cox, M. J., Owen, M. T., Henderson, V. K., & Margand, N. A. (1992). Prediction of infant–father and infant–mother attachment. *Developmental Psychology, 28,* 474–483.

Cox, M. J., Paley, B., & Harter, K. (2001). Interparental conflict and parent–child relationships. In J. H. Grych & F. D. Fincham (Eds.), *Interparental conflict and child development: Theory, research, and applications* (pp. 249–272). New York: Cambridge University Press.

Cox, S. M., Hopkins, J., & Hans, S. L. (2000). Attachment in preterm infants and their mothers: Neonatal risk status and maternal representations. *Infant Mental Health Journal, 21,* 464–480.

Coyle, T. R., & Bjorklund, D. F. (1997). Age differences in, and consequences of, multiple- and variable-strategy use on a multitrial sort-recall task. *Developmental Psychology, 33,* 372–380.

Crago, M. B., Annahatak, B., & Ningiuruvik, L. (1993). Changing patterns of language socialization in Inuit homes. *Anthropology and Education Quarterly, 24,* 205–223.

Craig, C. M., & Lee, D. N. (1999). Neonatal control of sucking pressure: Evidence for an intrinsic Ů-guide. *Experimental Brain Research, 124,* 371–382.

Crain, W. (2005). *Theories of development* (5th ed.). Upper Saddle River, NJ: Prentice-Hall.

Crair, M. C., Gillespie, D. C., & Stryker, M. P. (1998). The role of visual experience in the development of columns in the cat visual cortex. *Science, 279,* 566–570.

Crane, D. R., Ngai, S. W., Larson, J. H., & Hafen, M., Jr. (2005). The influence of family functioning and parent–adolescent acculturation on North American Chinese adolescent outcomes. *Family Relations, 54,* 400–410.

Cratty, B. J. (1986). *Perceptual and motor development in infants and children* (3rd ed.). Englewood Cliffs, NJ: Prentice-Hall.

Crawford, J. (1997). *Best evidence: Research foundations of the bilingual ecucation act.* Washington, DC: National Clearinghouse for Bilingual Education.

Creasey, G. (2002). Associations between working models of attachment and conflict management behavior in romantic couples. *Journal of Counseling Psychology, 49,* 365–375.

Creasey, G., & Ladd, A. (2004). Negative mood regulation expectancies and conflict behaviors in late adolescent college student romantic relationships: The moderating role of generalized attachment representations. *Journal of Research on Adolescence, 14,* 235–255.

Creasey, G. L., Jarvis, P. A., & Berk, L. E. (1998). Play and social competence. In O. N. Saracho & B. Spodek (Eds.), *Multiple perspectives on play in early childhood education* (pp. 116–143). Albany: State University of New York Press.

Crick, N. R. (1996). The role of overt aggression, relational aggression, and prosocial behavior in children's future social adjustment. *Child Development, 67,* 2317–2327.

Crick, N. R., Casas, J. F., & Nelson, D. A. (2002). Toward a more comprehensive understanding of peer maltreatment: Studies of relational victimization. *Current Directions in Psychological Science, 11,* 98–101.

Crick, N. R., & Dodge, K. A. (1994). A review and reformulation of social information-processing mechanisms in children's social adjustment. *Psychological Bulletin, 115,* 74–101.

Crick, N. R., & Nelson, D. A. (2002). Relational and physical victimization within friendships: Nobody told me there'd be friends like these. *Journal of Abnormal Child Psychology, 30,* 599–607.

Crick, N. R., Ostrov, J. M., Appleyard, K., Jansen, E., & Casas, J. F. (2004). Relational aggression in early childhood: You can't come to my birthday party unless … In M. Putallaz & K. Bierman (Eds.), *Duke series in child development and public policy: Aggressive antisocial behavior and violence among girls: A developmental perspective* (Vol. 1, pp. 71–89). New York: Guilford.

Crick, N. R., Ostrov, J. M., & Werner, N. E. (2006). A longitudinal study of relational aggression, physical aggression, and social-psychological adjustment. *Journal of Abnormal Child Psychology, 34,* 131–142.

Critser, G. (2003). *Fat land.* Boston: Houghton Mifflin.

Crittenden, P. (2000). A dynamic-maturational approach to continuity and change in patterns of attachment. In P. Crittenden & A. Claussen (Eds.), *The organization of attachment relationships* (pp. 343–358). New York: Cambridge University Press.

Crockenberg, S., & Leerkes, E. (2000). Infant social and emotional development in family context. In C. H. Zeanah, Jr. (Ed.), *Handbook of infant mental health* (2nd ed., pp. 60–90). New York: Guilford.

Crockenberg, S., & Leerkes, E. (2003). Infant negative emotionality, caregiving, and family relationships. In A. C. Crouter & A. Booth (Eds.), *Children's influence on family dynamics* (pp. 57–78). Mahwah, NJ: Erlbaum

Crockenberg. S. C., & Leerkes, E. M. (2003). Parental acceptance, postpartum depression, and maternal sensitivity: Mediating and moderating processes. *Journal of Family Psychology, 17,* 80–93.

Crockenberg, S. C., & Leerkes, E. M. (2004). Infant and maternal behaviors regulate infant reactivity to novelty at 6 months. *Developmental Psychology, 40,* 1123–1132.

Crockett, L. J., Raffaelli, M., & Shen, Y.-L. (2006). Linking self-regulation and risk-proneness to risky sexual behavior: Pathways through peer pressure and early substance use. *Journal of Research on Adolescence, 16,* 503–525.

Croninger, R. G., & Lee, V. E. (2001). Social capital and dropping out of high school: Benefits to at-risk students of teachers' support and guidance. *Teachers College Record, 103,* 548–581.

Crosno, R., Kirkpatrick, M., & Elder, G. H., Jr. (2004). Intergenerational bonding in school: The behavioral and contextual correlates of student–teacher relationships. *Sociology of Education, 77,* 60–81.

Crouter, A. C., & Bumpus, M. F. (2001). Linking parents' work stress to children's and adolescents' psychological adjustment. *Current Directions in Psychological Science, 10,* 156–159.

Crouter, A. C., & Head, M. R. (2002). Parental monitoring and knowledge of children. In M. H. Bornstein (Ed.), *Handbook of parenting: Vol. 3. Being and becoming a parent* (2nd ed., pp. 461–483). Mahwah, NJ: Erlbaum.

Crouter, A. C., Helms-Erikson, H., Updegraff, K., & McHale, S. M. (1999). Conditions underlying parents' knowledge about children's daily lives in middle childhood: Between- and within-family comparisons. *Child Development, 70,* 246–259.

Crouter, A. C., Manke, B. A., & McHale, S. M. (1995). The family context of gender intensification in early adolescence. *Child Development, 66,* 317–329.

Crowhurst, M. (1990). Teaching and learning the writing of persuasive/argumentative discourse. *Canadian Journal of Education, 15,* 348–359.

Csikszentmihalyi, M. (1999). Implications of a systems perspective for the study of creativity. In R. J. Sternberg (Ed.), *Handbook of creativity* (pp. 313–335). Cambridge, U.K.: Cambridge University Press.

Csoti, M. (2003). *School phobia, panic attacks, and anxiety in children.* London: Jessica Kingsley.

Cuddy-Casey, M., & Orvaschel, H. (1997). Children's understanding of death in relation to child suicidality and homicidality. *Clinical Psychology Review, 17,* 33–45.

Cui, X., & Vaillant, G. E. (1996). Antecedents and consequences of negative life events in adulthood: A longitudinal study. *American Journal of Psychiatry, 153,* 21–26.

Cuijpers, P. (2002). Effective ingredients of school-based drug prevention programs: A systematic review. *Addictive Behaviors, 27,* 1009–1023.

Culbertson, F. M. (1997). Depression and gender: An international review. *American Psychologist, 52,* 25–51.

Culnane, M., Fowler, M. G., Lee, S. S., McSherry, G., Brady, M., & O'Donnell, K. (1999). Lack of long-term effects of in utero exposure to zidovudine among uninfected children born to HIV-infected women. *Journal of the American Medical Association, 281,* 151–157.

Cummings, E. M., & Davies, P. T. (1994). Maternal depression and child development. *Journal of Child Psychology and Psychiatry, 35,* 73–112.

Cunningham, A. E., & Stanovich, K. E. (1998). What reading does for the mind. *American Educator,* Spring/Summer, 8–15.

Curran, M., Hazen, N., Jacobvitz, D., & Feldman, A. (2005). Representations of early family relationships predict marital maintenance during the transition to parenthood. *Journal of Family Psychology, 19,* 189–197.

Cutrona, C. E., Hessling, R. M., Bacon, P. L., & Russell, D. W. (1998). Predictors and correlates of continuing involvement with the baby's father among adolescent mothers. *Journal of Family Psychology, 12,* 369–387.

Cyr, M., McDuff, P., & Wright, J. (2006). Prevalence and predictors of dating violence among adolescent female victims of child sexual abuse. *Journal of Interpersonal Violence, 21,* 1000–1017.

D'Agostino, J. A., & Clifford, P. (1998). Neurodevelopmental consequences associated with the premature neonate. *AACN Clinical Issues, 9,* 11–24.

D'Augelli, A. R. (2002). Mental health problems among lesbian, gay, and bisexual youths ages 14 to 21. *Clinical Child Psychology and Psychiatry, 7,* 433–456.

D'Augelli, A. R. (2006). Developmental and contextual factors and mental health among lesbian, gay, and bisexual youths. In A. M. Omoto & H. S. Howard (Eds.), *Sexual orientation and mental health: Examining identity and development in lesbian, gay, and bisexual people* (pp. 37–53). Washington, DC: American Psychological Association.

D'Augelli, A. R., Grossman, A. H., Salter, N. P., Vasey, J. J., Starks, M. T., & Sinclair, K. O. (2005). Predicting the suicide attempts of lesbian, gay, and bisexual youth. *Suicide and Life-Threatening Behavior, 35,* 646–660.

D'Augelli, A. R., Grossman, A. H., & Starks, M. T. (2005). Parents' awareness of lesbian, gay, and bisexual youths' sexual orientation. *Journal of Marriage and Family, 67,* 474–482.

Dabrowska, E. (2000). From formula to schema: The acquisition of English questions. *Cognitive Linguistics, 11,* 1–20.

Dahl, R. E. (2004). Adolescent brain development: A period of vulnerabilities and opportunities. In R. E. Dahl & L. P. Spear (Eds.), *Adolescent brain development: Vulnerabilities and opportunities* (pp. 1–22). New York: New York Academy of Sciences.

Dahl, R. E., & Lewin, D. S. (2002). Pathways to adolescent health: Sleep regulation and behavior, *Journal of Adolescent Health, 31*(6 Suppl.), 175–184.

Dahl, R. E., Scher, M. S., Williamson, D. E., Robles, N., & Day, N. (1995). A longitudinal study of prenatal marijuana use: Effects on sleep and arousal at age 3 years. *Archives of Pediatric and Adolescent Medicine, 149,* 145–150.

Dahlberg, L. L., & Simon, T. R. (2006). Predicting and preventing youth violence: Developmental pathways and risk. In L. L. Dahlberg & T. R. Simon (Eds.), *Preventing violence: Research and evidence-based intervention strategies* (pp. 97–124). Washington, DC: American Psychological Association.

Dal Santo, J. A., Goodman, R. M., Glik, D., & Jackson, K. (2004). Childhood unintentional injuries: Factors predicting injury risk among preschoolers. *Journal of Pediatric Psychology, 29,* 273–283.

Dales, L., Hammer, S. J., & Smith, N. J. (2001). Time trends in autism and MMR immunization coverage in California. *Journal of the American Medical Association, 285,* 1183–1185.

Daley, K. C. (2004). Update on sudden infant death syndrome. *Current Opinion in Pediatrics, 16,* 227–232.

Damashek, A., & Peterson, L. (2002). Unintentional injury prevention efforts for young children: Levels, methods, types, and targets. *Developmental and Behavioral Pediatrics, 23,* 443–455.

Damon, W. (1977). *The social world of the child.* San Francisco: Jossey-Bass.

Damon, W. (1988). *The moral child.* New York: Free Press.

Damon, W. (1990). Self-concept, adolescent. In R. M. Lerner, A. C. Petersen, & J. Brooks-Gunn (Eds.), *The encyclopedia of adolescence* (Vol. 2, pp. 87–91). New York: Garland.

Damon, W. (1995). *Greater expectations: Overcoming the culture of indulgence in America's homes and schools.* New York: Free Press.

Damon, W., & Hart, D. (1988). *Self-understanding in childhood and adolescence.* New York: Cambridge University Press.

Daniels, D. H. (1998). Age differences in concepts of self-esteem. *Merrill-Palmer Quarterly, 44,* 234–259.

Daniels, D. H., Kalkman, D. L., & McCombs, B. L. (2001). Young children's perspectives on learning and teacher practices in different classroom contexts: Implications for motivation. *Early Education and Development, 12,* 253–273.

Daniels, P., Noe, G. F., & Mayberry, R. (2006). Barriers to prenatal care among black women of low socioeconomic status. *American Journal of Health Behavior, 30,* 188–198.

Dannemiller, J. L., & Stephens, B. R. (1988). A critical test of infant pattern preference models. *Child Development, 59,* 210–216.
Dapretto, M., & Bjork, E. L. (2000). The development of word retrieval abilities in the second year and its relation to early vocabulary growth. *Child Development, 71,* 635–648.
Darling, N., & Steinberg, L. (1997). Community influences on adolescent achievement and deviance. In J. Brooks-Gunn, G. Duncan, & L. Aber (Eds.), *Neighborhood poverty: Context and consequences for children: Conceptual, ethological, and policy approaches to studying neighborhoods* (Vol. 2, pp. 120–131). New York: Russell Sage Foundation.
Darroch, J. E., Frost, J. J., & Singh, S. (2001). *Teenage sexual and reproductive behavior in developed countries: Can more progress be made?* New York: Alan Guttmacher Institute.
Das, D. A., Grimmer, D. A., Sparnon, A. L., McRae, S. E., & Thomas, B. H. (2005). The efficacy of playing a virtual reality game in modulating pain for children with acute burn injuries: A randomized controlled trial. *BMC Pediatrics, 5*(1), 1–10.
Davidov, M., & Grusec, J. E. (2006). Untangling the links of parental responsiveness to distress and warmth to child outcomes. *Child Development, 77,* 44–58.
Davidson, R. J. (1994). Asymmetric brain function, affective style, and psychopathology: The role of early experience and plasticity. *Development and Psychopathology, 6,* 741–758.
Davies, P. A., & Lindsay, L. L. (2004). Everyday marital conflict and child aggression. *Journal of Abnormal Child Psychology, 32,* 191–202.
Davis, K. F., Parker, K. P., & Montgomery, G. L. (2004). Sleep in infants and young children. Part 1: Normal sleep. *Journal of Pediatric Health Care, 18,* 65–71.
Davison, K. K., & Birch, L. L. (2002). Obesigenic families: Parents' physical activity and dietary intake patterns predict girls' risk of overweight. *International Journal of Obesity and Related Metabolic Disorders, 26,* 1186–1193.
Dawson, G., Ashman, S. B., Panagiotides, H., Hessl, D., Self, J., Yamada, E., & Embry, L. (2003). Preschool outcomes of children of depressed mothers: Role of maternal behavior, contextual risk, and children's brain activity. *Child Development, 74,* 1158–1175.
Dawson, T. L. (2002). New tools, new insights: Kohlberg's moral judgment stages revisited. *International Journal of Behavioral Development, 26,* 154–166.
Day, N. L., Leach, S. L., Richardson, G. A., Cornelius, M. D., Robles, N., & Larkby, C. (2002). Prenatal alcohol exposure predicts continued deficits in offspring size at 14 years of age. *Alcoholism: Clinical and Experimental Research, 26,* 1584–1591.
de Bruyn, E. H. (2005). Role strain, engagement and academic achievement in early adolescence. *Educational Studies, 31,* 15–27.
De Bruyn, E. H., Dekovic´, M., & Meijnen, G. W. (2003). Parenting, goal orientations, classroom behavior, and school success in early adolescence. *Journal of Applied Developmental Psychology, 24,* 393–412.
De Corte, E., & Verschaffel, L. (2006). Mathematical thinking and learning. In K. A. Renninger & I. E. Sigel (Eds.), *Handbook of child psychology: Vol. 4. Child psychology in practice* (6th ed., pp. 103–152). Hoboken, NJ: Wiley.
de Haan, M., & Johnson, M. H. (2003). Mechanisms and theories of brain development. In M. de Haan & M. H. Johnson (Eds.), *The cognitive neuroscience of development* (pp. 1–18). Hove, UK: Psychology Press.
de Haan, M., Bauer, P. J., Georgieff, M. K., & Nelson, C. A. (2000). Explicit memory in low-risk infants aged 19 months born between 27 and 42 weeks of gestation. *Developmental Medicine and Child Neurology, 42,* 304–312.
de la Rosa, M. R., Holleran, L. K., Rugh, D., & MacMaster, S. A. (2005). Substance abuse among U.S. Latinos: A review of the literature. *Journal of Social Work Practice in the Addictions, 5,* 1–20.
De Lisi, R., & Gallagher, A. M. (1991). Understanding gender stability and constancy in Argentinean children. *Merrill-Palmer Quarterly, 37,* 483–502.
de Muinck Keizer-Schrama, S. M. P. F., & Mul, D. (2001). Trends in pubertal development in Europe. *Human Reproduction Update, 7,* 287–291.
de Pree-Geerlings, B., de Pree, I. M., & Bulk-Bunschoten, A. M. (2001). 1901–2001: 100 years of physicians of infant and toddler welfare centers in the Netherlands. *Netherlands Tijdschrift Voor Geneeskunde, 145,* 2461–2465.
de Ribaupierre, A., & Lecerf, T. (2006). Relationships between working memory and intelligence from a developmental perspective: Convergent evidence from a neo-Piagetian and a psychometric approach. *European Journal of Cognitive Psychology, 18,* 109–137.
De Schipper, J. C., Tavecchio, L. W. C., van IJzendoorn, M. H., & van Zeijl, J. (2004). Goodness-of-fit in center day care: Relations of temperament, stability, and quality of care with the child's adjustment. *Early Childhood Research Quarterly, 19,* 257–272.
De Schipper, J. C., van IJzendoorn, M. H., & Tavecchio, L. W. C. (2004). Stability in center day care: Relations with children's well-being and problem behavior in day care. *Social Development, 13,* 531–550.
de Villiers, J. G., & de Villiers, P. A. (1973). A cross-sectional study of the acquisition of grammatical morphemes in child speech. *Journal of Psycholinguistic Research, 2,* 267–278.
de Villiers, J.G., & de Villiers, P. A. (1999). Language development. In M. H. Bornstein & M. E. Lamb (Eds.), *Developmental psychology: An advanced textbook* (4th ed., pp. 313–373). Mahwah, NJ: Erlbaum.
de Villiers, J. G., & de Villiers, P. A. (2000). Linguistic determinism and the understanding of false beliefs. In P. Mitchell & K. J. Riggs (Eds.), *Children's reasoning and the mind* (pp. 87–99). Hove, U.K.: Psychology Press.
de Waal, F. B. M. (1993). Sex differences in chimpanzee (and human) behavior: A matter of social values? In M. Hechter, L. Nadel, & R. E. Michod (Eds.), *The origin of values* (pp. 285– 303). New York: Aldine de Gruyter.
de Weerd, A. W., & van den Bossche, A. S. (2003). The development of sleep during the first months of life. *Sleep Medicine Reviews, 7,* 179–191.
de Weerth, C., & Buitelaar, J. K. (2005). Physiological stress reactivity in human pregnancy—a review. *Neuroscience and Biobehavioral Reviews, 29,* 295–312.
de Winter, M., Balledux, M., & de Mare, J. (1997). A critical evaluation of Dutch preventive child health care. *Child: Care, Health and Development, 23,* 437–446.
De Wolff, M. S., & van IJzendoorn, M. H. (1997). Sensitivity and attachment: A meta-analysis on parental atnecedents of infant attachment. *Child Development, 68,* 571–591.
Deafness Research Foundation. (2005). *Hear us: Incidence of deafness in newborns.* Retrieved from www.hearinghealth.com
Deák, G. O. (2000). Hunting the fox of word learning: Why "constraints" fail to capture it. *Developmental Review, 20,* 29–80.
Deák, G. O., Ray, S. D., & Brenneman, K. (2003). Children's perseverative appearance–reality errors are related to emerging language skills. *Child Development, 74,* 944–964.
Deák, G. O., Yen, L., & Pettit, J. (2001). By any other name: When will preschoolers produce several labels for a reference? *Journal of Child Language, 28,* 787–804.
Dearing, E., McCartney, K., & Taylor, B. A. (2006). Within-child associations between family income and externalizing and internalizing problems. *Developmental Psychology, 42,* 237–252.
Deary, I. J. (2001). *g* and cognitive elements of information progressing: An agnostic view. In R. J. Sternberg & E. L. Grigorenko (Eds.), *The general factor of intelligence: How general is it?* (pp. 447–479). Mahwah, NJ: Erlbaum.
Deater-Deckard, K., Lansford, J. E., Dodge, K. A., Pettit, G. S., & Bates, J. E. (2003). The development of attitudes about physical punishment: An 8-year longitudinal study. *Journal of Family Psychology, 17,* 351–360.
Deater-Deckard, K., Pickering, K., Dunn, J. F., & Golding, J. (1998). Family structure and depressive symptoms in men preceding and following the birth of a child. *American Journal of Psychiatry, 155,* 818–823.
Deater-Deckard, K., Pike, A., Petrill, S. A., Cutting, A. L., Hughes, C., & O'Connor, T. G. (2001). Nonshared environmental processes in social-emotional development: An observational study of identical twin differences in the preschool period. *Developmental Science, 4,* F1–F6.
DeBerry, K. M., Scarr, S., & Weinberg, R. (1996). Family racial socialization and ecological competence: Longitudinal assessments of African-American transracial adoptees. *Child Development, 67,* 2375–2399.
DeCasper, A. J., & Spence, M. J. (1986). Prenatal maternal speech influences newborns' perception of speech sounds. *Infant Behavior and Development, 9,* 133–150.
Deci, E. L., & Ryan, R. M. (2002). Self-determination research: Reflections and future directions. In E. L. Deci & R. M. Ryan (Eds.), *Handbook of self-determination research* (pp. 431–441). Rochester, NY: University of Rochester Press.
Degirmencioglu, S. M., Urberg, K. A., Tolson, J. M., & Richard, P. (1998). Adolescent friendship networks: Continuity and change over the school year. *Merrill-Palmer Quarterly, 44,* 313–337.
Dekovi´c, M., & Buist, K. L. (2005). Multiple perspectives within the family: Family relationship patterns. *Journal of Family Issues, 26,* 467–490.{COMP: The accent goes over the c in Dekovic}
Dekovic´, M., Noom, M. J., & Meeus, W. (1997). Expectations regarding development during adolescence: Parent and adolescent perceptions. *Journal of Youth and Adolescence, 26,* 253–271. .{COMP: The accent goes over the c in Dekovic}
Delemarre-van de Waal, H. A. (2002). Regulation of puberty. *Best Practice and Research in Clinical Endocrinology and Metabolism, 16,* 1–12.
Delemarre-van de Waal, H. A., van Coeverden, S. C., & Rotteveel, J. (2001). Hormonal determinants of pubertal growth. *Journal of Pediatric Endocrinology and Metabolism, 14,* 1521–1526.
Delgado-Gaitan, C. (1994). Socializing young children in MexicanAmerican families: An intergenerational perspective. In P. Greenfield & R. Cocking (Eds.), *Cross-cultural roots of minority child development* (pp. 55–86). Hillsdale, NJ: Erlbaum.
Dell, D. L. (2001). Adolescent pregnancy. In N. L. Stotland & D. E. Stewart (Eds.), *Psychological aspects of women's health care* (pp. 95–116). Washington, DC: American Psychiatric Association.
DeLoache, J. S. (1987). Rapid change in symbolic functioning of very young children. *Science, 238,* 1556–1557.
DeLoache, J. S. (2000). Dual representation and children's use of scale models. *Child Development, 71,* 329–338.
DeLoache, J. S. (2002). The symbol-mindedness of young children. In W. Hartup & R. A. Weinberg (Eds.), *Minnesota symposia on child psychology* (Vol. 32, pp. 73–101). Mahwah, NJ: Erlbaum.
DeLoache, J. S., & Todd, C. M. (1988). Young children's use of spatial categorization as a mnemonic strategy. *Journal of Experimental Child Psychology, 46,* 1–20.
Delville, Y. (1999). Exposure to lead during development alters aggressive behavior in golden hamsters. *Neurotoxicology and Teratology, 21,* 445–449.
DeMarie, D., Miller, P. H., Ferron, J., & Cunningham, W. R. (2004). Path analysis tests of theoretical models of children's memory performance. *Journal of Cognition and Development, 5,* 461–492.
DeMatteo, D., & Marczyk, G. (2005). Risk factors, protective factors, and the prevention of antisocial behavior among juveniles. In K. Heilbrun, N. E. S. Goldstein, & R. E. Redding (Eds.), *Juvenile delinquency: Prevention, assessment, and intervention* (pp. 19–44). New York: Oxford University Press.
Demetriou, A., Christou, C., Spanoudis, G., & Platsidou, M. (2002). The development of mental processing: Efficiency, working memory, and thinking. *Monographs of the Society for Research in Child Development, 67*(1, Serial No. 268).
Demetriou, A., Efklides, A., Papadaki, M., Papantoniou, G., & Economou, A. (1993). Structure and development of causal–experimental thought: From early adolescence to youth. *Developmental Psychology, 29,* 480–497.
Demetriou, A., & Kazi, S. (2001). *Unity and modularity in the mind and the self: Studies on the relationships between self-awareness, personality, and intellectual development from childhood to adolescence.* London: Routledge.
Dempster, F. N., & Corkill, A. J. (1999). Interference and inhibition in cognition and behavior: Unifying themes for educational psychology. *Educational Psychology Review, 11,* 1–88.
Denham, S. (1998). *Emotional development in young children.* New York: Guilford.
Denham, S., & Kochanoff, A. T. (2002). Parental contributions to preschoolers' understanding of emotion. *Marriage and Family Review, 34,* 311–343.

Denham, S. A. (2005). Emotional competence counts: Assessment as support for school readiness. In K. Hirsh-Pasek, A. Kochanoff, N. S. Newcombe, & J. de Villiers (Eds.), Using scientific knowledge to inform preschool assessment. *Social Policy Report of the Society for Research in Child Development, 19*(No.1), 12.

Denham, S. A. (2006). Emotional competence: Implications for social functioning. In J. L. Luby (Ed.), *Handbook of preschool mental health: Development, disorders, and treatment* (pp. 23–44). New York: Guilford.

Denham, S. A., Blair, K., Schmidt, M., & DeMulder, E. (2002). Compromised emotional competence: Seeds of violence sown early? *American Journal of Orthopsychiatry, 72,* 70–82.

Denham, S. A., & Burton, R. (2003). *Social and emotional prevention and intervention programming for preschoolers.* New York: Kluwer-Plenum.

Dennis, W. (1960). Causes of retardation among institutionalized children: Iran. *Journal of Genetic Psychology, 96,* 47–59.

Dennison, B. A., Straus, J. H., Mellits, D., & Charney, E. (1998). Childhood physical fitness tests: Predictor of adult physical activity levels? *Pediatrics, 82,* 342–330.

Department of Justice Canada. (2006a). *Child abuse: A fact sheet.* Retrieved from justice.gc.ca/en/ps/fm/childafs.html#widespread

Department of Justice Canada. (2006b). *Parenting after divorce.* Retrieved from www.justice.gc.ca/en/ps/pad/resources/index.html

deRegnier, R.-A. (2005). Neurophysiologic evaluation of early cognitive development in high-risk infants and toddlers. *Mental Retardation and Developmental Disabilities, 11,* 317–324.

Derom, C., Thiery, E., Vlietinck, R., Loos, R., & Derom, R. (1996). Handedness in twins according to zygosity and chorion type: A preliminary report. *Behavior Genetics, 26,* 407–408.

DeRosier, M. E., & Thomas, J. M. (2003). Strengthening sociometric prediction: Scientific advances in the assessment of children's peer relations. *Child Development, 75,* 1379–1392.

Deutsch, F. M., Ruble, D. N., Fleming, A., Brooks-Gunn, J., & Stangor, C. (1988). Information-seeking and maternal self-definition during the transition to motherhood. *Journal of Personality and Social Psychology, 55,* 420–431.

Deutsch, W., & Pechmann, T. (1982). Social interaction and the development of definite descriptions. *Cognition, 11,* 159–184.

DeVries, R. (2001). Constructivist education in preschool and elementary school: The sociomoral atmosphere as the first educational goal. In S. L. Golbeck (Ed.), *Psychological perspectives on early childhood education* (pp. 153–180). Mahwah, NJ: Erlbaum.

Dexter, E., LeVine, S., & Velasco, P. (1998). Maternal schooling and health-related language and literacy skills in rural Mexico. *Comparative Education Review, 42,* 139–162.

Diamond, A. (2000). Close interrelation of motor development and cognitive development and of the cerebellum and prefrontal cortex. *Child Development, 71,* 44–56.

Diamond, A. (2004). Normal development of prefrontal cortex from birth to young adulthood: Cognitive functions, anatomy, and biochemistry. In D. T. Stuff & R. T. Knight (Eds.), *Principles of frontal lobe function* (pp. 466–503). New York: Oxford University Press.

Diamond, A., Cruttenden, L., & Neiderman, D. (1994). AB with multiple wells: 1. Why are multiple wells sometimes easier than two wells? 2. Memory or memory + inhibition. *Developmental Psychology, 30,* 192–205.

Diamond, A., & Taylor, C. (1996). Development of an aspect of executive control: Development of the abilities to remember what I said and to "do as I say, not as I do." *Developmental Psychobiology, 29,* 315–334.

Diamond, L. M. (1998). Development of sexual orientation among adolescent and young adult women. *Developmental Psychology, 34,* 1085–1095.

Diamond, L. M. (2003). Love matters: Romantic relationships among sexual-minority adolescents. In P. Florsheim (Ed.), *Adolescent romantic relations and sexual behavior* (pp. 85–108). Mahwah, NJ: Erlbaum.

Diamond, L. M., & Lucas, S. (2004). Sexual-minority and heterosexual youths' peer relationships: Experiences,

expectations, and implications for well-being. *Journal of Research on Adolescence, 14,* 313–340.

Diamond, M., & Sigmundson, H. K. (1999). Sex reassignment at birth. In S. J. Ceci & W. M. Williams (Eds.), *The nature–nurture debate* (pp. 55–75). Malden, MA: Blackwell.

Dias, M. G., & Harris, P. (1988). The effect of make-believe play on deductive reasoning. *British Journal of Developmental Psychology, 6,* 207–221.

Dias, M. G., & Harris, P. (1990). The influence of the imagination on reasoning by young children. *British Journal of Developmental Psychology, 8,* 305–318.

DiBiase, A., Gibbs, J. C., & Potter, G. B. (2005). *EQUIP for educators: Teaching youth (grades 5–8) to think and act responsibly.* Champaign, IL: Research Press.

DiCenso, A., Guyatt, G., Willan, A., & Griffith, L. (2002). Interventions to reduce unintended pregnancies among adolescents: Systematic review of randomized controlled trials. *British Medical Journal, 324,* 1426–1430.

Dick, D. M., Rose, R. J., Viken, R. J., & Kaprio, J. (2000). Pubertal timing and substance use: Associations between and within families across late adolescence. *Developmental Psychology, 36,* 180–189.

Dick, F., Dronkers, N. F., Pizzamiglio, L., Saygin, A. P., Small, S. L., Wilson, S. (2004). Language and the brain. In M. Tomasello & D. I Slobin (Eds.), *Beyond nature–nurture: Essays in honor of Elizabeth Bates* (pp. 237–260). Mahwah, NJ: Erlbaum.

Dickens, W. T., & Flynn, J. R. (2001). Heritability estimates versus large environmental effects: The IQ paradox resolved. *Psychological Review, 108,* 346–369.

Dickens, W. T., & Flynn, J. R. (2006). Black Americans reduce the racial IQ gap: Evidence from standardization samples. *Psychological Science, 17,* 913–920.

Dickinson, D. K., & McCabe, A. (2001). Bringing it all together: The multiple origins, skills, and environmental supports of early literacy. *Learning Disabilities Research and Practice, 16,* 186–202.

Dickinson, D. K., McCabe, A., Anastasopoulos, L., Peisner-Feinberg, E. S., & Poe, M. D. (2003). The comprehensive language approach to early literacy: The interrelationships among vocabulary, phonological sensitivity, and print knowledge among preschool-age children. *Journal of Educational Psychology, 95,* 465–481.

Dickinson, D. K., & Sprague, K. E. (2001). The nature and impact of early childhood care environments on the language and early literacy development of children from low-income families. In S. B. Neuman & D. K. Dickinson (Eds.), *Handbook of early literacy research.* New York: Guilford.

Dick-Read, G. (1959). *Childbirth without fear.* New York: Harper & Brothers.

Dickson, K. L., Fogel, A., & Messinger, D. (1998). The development of emotion from a social process view. In M. F. Mascolo (Ed.), *What develops in emotional development?* (pp. 253–271). New York: Plenum.

Diehr, S. (2003). How effective is desmopressin for primary nocturnal enuresis? *Journal of Family Practice, 52,* 568–569.

Diener, E., Suh, E. M., Lucas, R. E., & Smith, H. L. (1999). Subjective well-being: Three decades of progress. *Psychological Bulletin, 125,* 276–302.

Diener, M. L., Goldstein, L. H., & Mangelsdorf, S. C. (1995). The role of prenatal expectations in parents' reports of infant temperament. *Merrill-Palmer Quarterly, 41,* 172–190.

Dietrich, K. N., Ris, M. D., Succop, P. A., Berger, O. G., & Bornschein, R. L. (2001). Early exposure to lead and juvenile delinquency. *Neurotoxicology and Teratology, 23,* 511–518.

Dietrich, K. N., Ware, J. H., Salganik, M., Radcliffe, J., Rogan, W. J., & Rhoads, G. C. (2004). Effect of chelation therapy on the neuropsychological and behavioral development of lead-exposed children after school entry. *Pediatrics, 114,* 19–26.

Dietz, T. L. (1998). An examination of violence and gender-role portrayals in video games: Implications for gender socialization and aggressive behavior. *Sex Roles, 38,* 425–444.

Dildy, G. A., Jackson, G. M., Fowers, G. K., Oshiro, B. T., Varner, M. W., & Clark, S. L. (1996). Very advanced maternal age: Pregnancy after age 45. *American Journal of Obstetrics and Gynecology, 175,* 668–674.

DiMatteo, M. R., & Kahn, K. L. (1997). Psychosocial aspects of childbirth. In S. J. Gallant, G. P. Keita, & R. Royak-Schaler (Eds.), *Health care for women: Psychological, social, and behavioral influences* (pp. 175–186). Washington, DC: American Psychological Association.

Dion, K. K. (1995). Delayed parenthood and women's expectations about the transition to parenthood. *International Journal of Behavioral Development, 18,* 315–333.

DiPietro, J. A., Bornstein, M. H., Costigan, K. A., Pressman, E. K., Hahn, C.-S., & Painter, K. (2002). What does fetal movement predict about behavior during the first two years of life? *Developmental Psychobiology, 40,* 358–371.

DiPietro, J. A., Hodgson, D. M., Costigan, K. A., & Hilton, S. C. (1996). Fetal neurobehavioral development. *Child Development, 67,* 2553–2567.

Dirks, J. (1982). The effect of a commercial game on children's Block Design scores on the WISC–R test. *Intelligence, 6,* 109–123.

Dishion, T. J., Andrews, D. W., & Crosby, L. (1995). Antisocial boys and their friends in early adolescence: Relationship characteristics, quality, and interactional processes. *Child Development, 66,* 139–151.

Dodd, V. L. (2005). Implications of kangaroo care for growth and development in preterm infants. *JOGNN, 34,* 218–232.

Dodge, K. A., Coie, J. D., & Lynam, D. (2006). Aggression and antisocial behavior in youth. In N. Eisenberg (Ed.), *Handbook of child psychology: Vol. 3. Social, emotional, and personality development* (6th ed., pp. 719–788). Hoboken, NJ: Wiley.

Dodge, K. A., Dishion, T. J., & Lansford, J. E. (2006). Deviant peer influences in intervention and public policy for youth. *Social Policy Report of the Society for Research in Child Development, 20*(1), 3–19.

Dodge, K. A., Lansford, J. E., Burks, V. S., Bates, J. E., Pettit, G. S., Fontaine, R., & Price, J. M. (2003). Peer rejection and social information-processing factors in the development of aggressive behavior problems in children. *Child Development, 74,* 374–393.

Dodge, K. A., McLoyd, V. C., & Lansford, J. E. (2006). The cultural context of physically disciplining children. In V. C. McLoyd, N. E. Hill, & K A. Dodge (Eds.), *African-American family life: Ecological and cultural diversity* (pp. 245–263). New York: Guilford.

Dodge, K. A., Pettit, G. S., McClaskey, C. L., & Brown, M. M. (1986). Social competence in children. *Monographs of the Society for Research in Child Development, 51*(2, Serial No. 213).

Doeker, B., Simic-Schleicher, A., Hauffa, B. P., & Andler, W. (1999). Psychosozialer Kleinwuchs maskiert als Wachstumshormonmangel. [Psychosocially stunted growth masked as growth hormone deficiency]. *Klinische Padiatrie, 211,* 394–398.

Doherty, G., Lero, D. S., Goelman, H., Tougas, J., & LaGrange, A. (2000). *You bet I care! Caring and learning environments: Quality in regulated family child care across Canada.* Guelph, Ontario: Centre for Families, Work and Well-Being, University of Guelph.

Doherty, N. N., & Hepper, P. G. (2000). Habituation in fetuses of diabetic mothers. *Early Human Development, 59,* 85–93.

Dohnt, H., & Tiggemann, M. (2005). Peer influences on body image and dieting awareness in young girls. *British Journal of Developmental Psychology, 23,* 103–116.

Dohnt, H., & Tiggemann, M. (2006). The contribution of peer and media influences to the development of body satisfaction and self-esteem in young girls: A prospective study. *Developmental Psychology, 42,* 929–936.

Dombrowski, K. J., Lantz, P. M., & Freed, G. L. (2004). Risk factors for delay in age-appropriate vaccination. *Public Health Reports, 119,* 144–155.

Donahue, M. J., & Benson, P. L. (1995). Religion and the well-being of adolescents. *Journal of Social Issues, 51,* 145–160.

Donatelle, R. (2004). *Health: The basics* (6th ed.). San Francisco: Benjamin Cummings.

Dondi, M., Simion, F., & Caltran, G. (1999). Can newborns discriminate between their own cry and the cry of another newborn infant? *Developmental Psychology, 35,* 418–426.

Donnellan, M. B., Trzesniewski, K. H., Robins, R. W., Moffitt, T. E., & Caspi, A. (2005). Low self-esteem is related to aggression, antisocial behavior, and delinquency. *Psychological Science, 16,* 328–335.

Donnerstein, E., Slaby, R. G., & Eron, L. D. (1994). The mass media and youth aggression. In L. D. Eron, J. H. Gentry, & P. Schlegel (Eds.), *Reason to hope: A psychosocial perspective on violence and youth* (pp. 219–250). Washington, DC: American Psychological Association.

Dorius, C. J., Bahr, S. J., Hoffman, J. P., Harmon, E. L. (2004). Parenting practices as moderators of the relationship between peers and adolescent marijuana use. *Journal of Marriage and Family, 66,* 163–178.

Dornbusch, S. M., & Glasgow, K. L. (1997). The structural context of family–school relations. In A. Booth & J. F. Dunn (Eds.), *Family–school links: How do they affect educational outcomes?* (pp. 35–55). Mahwah, NJ: Erlbaum.

Dornbusch, S. M., Glasgow, K. L., & Lin, I.-C. (1996). The social structure of schooling. *Annual Review of Psychology, 47,* 401–429.

Dornbusch, S. M., Ritter, P. L., Mont-Reynaud, R., & Chen, Z. (1990). Family decision making and academic performance in a diverse high school population. *Journal of Adolescent Research, 5,* 143–160.

Dorris, M. (1989). *The broken cord.* New York: Harper & Row.

Dote, L., Cramer, K., Dietz, N., & Grimm, R., Jr. (2006). *College students helping America.* Washington, DC: Corporation for National & Community Service.

Dovidio, J. F., Gaertner, S. L., Nier, J. A., Kawakami, K., & Hodson, G. (2004). Contemporary racial bias: When good people do bad things. In G. A. Miller (Ed.), *The social psychology of good and evil* (pp. 141–167). New York: Guilford.

Dowling, E. M., Gestsdottir, S., Anderson, P. M., von Eye, A., Almerigi, J., & Lerner, R. M. (2004). Structural relations among spirituality, religiosity, and thriving in adolescence. *Applied Developmental Psychology, 8,* 7–16.

Downs, A. C., & Fuller, M. J. (1991). Recollections of spermarche: An exploratory investigation. *Current Psychology: Research and Reviews, 10,* 93–102.

Dozier, M., Stovall, K. C., Albus, K. E., & Bates, B. (2001). Attachment for infants in foster care: The role of caregiver state of mind. *Child Development, 72,* 1467–1477.

Drabman, R. S., Cordua, G. D., Hammer, D., Jarvie, G. J., & Horton, W. (1979). Developmental trends in eating rates of normal and overweight preschool children. *Child Development, 50,* 211–216.

Drotar, D., Pallotta, J., & Eckerle, D. (1994). A prospective study of family environments of children hospitalized for nonorganic failure-to-thrive. *Developmental and Behavioral Pediatrics, 15,* 78–85.

Dubé, E. M., Savin-Williams, R. C., & Diamond, L. M. (2001). Intimacy development, gender, and ethnicity among sexual-minority youths. In A. R. D'Augelli & C. J. Patterson (Eds.), *Lesbian, gay, and bisexual identities and youth* (pp. 129–152). New York: Oxford University Press.

Dublin, S., Lydon-Rochelle, M., Kaplan, R. C., Watts, D. H., & Crichlow, C. W. (2000). Maternal and neonatal outcomes after induction of labor without an identified indication. *American Journal of Obstetrics and Gynecology, 183,* 986–994.

DuBois, D. L., Burk-Braxton, C., Swenson, L. P., Tevendale, H. D., Lockerd, E. M., & Moran, B. L. (2002a). Getting by with a little help from self and others: Selfesteem and social support as resources during early adolescence. *Developmental Psychology, 38,* 822–939.

DuBois, D. L., Felner, R. D., Brand, S., & George, G. R. (1999). Profiles of self-esteem in early adolescence: Identification and investigation of adaptive correlates. *American Journal of Community Psychology, 27,* 899–932.

Duckworth, A. L., & Seligman, M. E. P. (2005). Self-discipline outdoes IQ in predicting academic performance of adolescents. *Psychological Science, 12,* 939–944.

Dueker, G. L., Modi, A., & Needham, A. (2003). 4.5-month-old infants' learning, retention and use of object boundary information. *Infant Behavior and Development, 26,* 588–605.

Duggan, A., McFarlane, E., Fuddy, L., Burrell, L., Higman, S. M., Windham, A., & Sia, C. (2004). Randomized trial of a statewide home visiting program: Impact in preventing child abuse and neglect. *Child Abuse and Neglect, 28,* 597–622.

Duncan, G. J., & Brooks-Gunn, J. (2000). Family poverty, welfare reform, and child development. *Child Development, 71,* 188–196.

Duncan, G. J., & Magnuson, K. A. (2003). Off with Hollingshead: Socioeconomic resources, parenting, and child development. In M. H. Bornstein & R. H. Bradley (Eds.), *Socioeconomic status, parenting, and child development* (pp. 83–106). Mahwah, NJ: Erlbaum.

Dunham, Y., Baron, A. S., & Banaji, M. R. (2006). From American city to Japanese village: A cross-cultural investigation of implicit race attitudes. *Child Development, 77,* 1129–1520.

Dunifon, R., Kalil, A., & Danziger, S. K. (2003). Maternal work behavior under welfare reform: How does the transition from welfare to work affect child development? *Children and Youth Services Review, 25,* 55–82.

Duniz, M., Scheer, P. J., Trojovsky, A., Kaschnitz, W., Kvas, E., & Macari, S. (1996). *European Child and Adolescent Psychiatry, 5,* 93–100.

Dunn, J. (1989). Siblings and the development of social understanding in early childhood. In P. G. Zukow (Ed.), *Sibling interaction across cultures* (pp. 106–116). New York: Springer-Verlag.

Dunn, J. (1994). Temperament, siblings, and the development of relationships. In W. B. Carey & S. C. McDevitt (Eds.), *Prevention and early intervention* (pp. 50–58). New York: Brunner/Mazel.

Dunn, J. (2002). The adjustment of children in stepfamilies: Lessons from community studies. *Child and Adolescent Mental Health, 7,* 154–161.

Dunn, J. (2004). Sibling relationships. In P. K. Smith & C. H. Hart (Eds.), *Handbook of childhood social development* (pp. 223–237). Malden, MA: Blackwell.

Dunn, J. (2005). Moral development in early childhood and social interaction in the family. In M. Killen & J. G. Smetana (Eds.), *Handbook of moral development* (pp. 331–350). Mahwah, NJ: Erlbaum.

Dunn, J., Bretherton, I., & Munn, P. (1987). Conversations about feeling states between mothers and their young children. *Developmental Psychology, 23,* 132–139.

Dunn, J., Brown, J. R., & Maguire, M. (1995). The development of children's moral sensibility: Individual differences and emotion understanding. *Developmental Psychology, 31,* 649–659.

Dunn, J., Cheng, H., O'Connor, T. G., & Bridges, L. (2004). Children's perspectives on their relationships with their nonresident fathers: Influences, outcomes and implications. *Journal of Child Psychology and Psychiatry, 45,* 553–566.

Dunn, J., Cutting, A. L., & Fisher, N. (2002). Old friends, new friends: Predictors of children's perspective on their friends at school. *Child Development, 73,* 621–635.

Dunn, J., Slomkowski, C., & Beardsall, L. (1994). Sibling relationships from the preschool period through middle childhood and early adolescence. *Developmental Psychology, 30,* 315–324.

Durbin, D. L., Darling, N., Steinberg, L., & Brown, B. B. (1993). Parenting style and peer group membership among European-American adolescents. *Journal of Research on Adolescence, 3,* 87–100.

Durkin, M. S., Laraque, D., Lubman, I., & Barlow, B. (1999). Epidemiology and prevention of traffic injuries to urban children and adolescents. *Pediatrics, 103,* e74.

Durlach, J. (2004). New data on the importance of gestational Mg deficiency. *Journal of the American College of Nutrition, 23,* 694S-700S.

Durrant, J., Broberg, A., & Rose-Krasnor, L. (2000). Predicting use of physical punishment during mother–child conflicts in Sweden and Canada. In P. Hastings & C. Piotrowski (Eds.), *Conflict as a context for understanding maternal beliefs about child rearing and children's misbehavior: New directions for child development.* San Francisco: Jossey-Bass.

Durston, S., Pol, H. E. H., Schnack, H. G., Buitelaar, J. K., Steenhuis, M. P., & Minderaa, R. B. (2004). Magnetic resonance imaging of boys with attention-deficit/ hyperactivity disorder and their unaffected siblings. *Journal of the American Academy of Child and Adolescent Psychiatry, 43,* 332–340.

Dusek, J. B. (1987). Sex roles and adjustment. In D. B. Carter (Ed.), *Current conceptions of sex roles and sex typing* (pp. 211–222). New York: Praeger.

Dweck, C. S. (2002). Messages that motivate: How praise molds students' beliefs, motivation, and performance (in surprising ways). In J. Aronson (Ed.), *Improving academic achievement: Impact of psychological factors on education* (pp. 37–60). San Diego, CA: Academic Press.

Dworkin, J. B., Larson, R., & Hansen, D. (1993). Adolescents' accounts of growth experiences in youth activities. *Journal of Youth and Adolescence, 32,* 17–26.

Dykman, R., Casey, P. H., Ackerman, P. T., & McPherson, W. B. (2001). Behavioral and cognitive status in school-aged children with a history of failure to thrive during early childhood. *Clinical Pediatrics, 40,* 63–70.

Dzurova, D., & Pikhart, H. (2005). Down syndrome, paternal age and education: Comparison of California and the Czech Republic. *BMC Public Health, 5,* 69.

East, P. L., & Felice, M. E. (1996). *Adolescent pregnancy and parenting: Findings from a racially diverse sample.* Mahwah, NJ: Erlbaum.

Eaves, L., Silberg, J., Foley, D., Bulik, C., Maes, H., & Erkanli, A. (2004). Genetic and environmental influences on the relative timing of pubertal change. *Twin Research, 7,* 471–481.

Ebeling, K. S., & Gelman, S. A. (1994). Children's use of context in interpreting "big" and "little." *Child Development, 65,* 1178–1192.

Eberhard, J., Stein, S., & Geissbuehler, V. (2005). Experience of pain and analgesia with water and land births. *Journal of Psychosomatic Obstetrics and Gynecology, 26,* 127–133.

Eberhart-Phillips, J. E., Frederick, P. D., & Baron, R. C. (1993). Measles in pregnancy: A descriptive study of 58 cases. *Obstetrics and Gynecology, 82,* 797–801.

Eccles, J. S. (2004). Schools, academic motivation, and stage–environment fit. In R. M. Lerner & L. Steinberg (Eds.), *Handbook of adolescent psychology* (2nd ed., pp. 125–154). Hoboken, NJ: Wiley.

Eccles, J. S., & Gootman, J. (Eds.). (2002). *Community programs to promote youth development.* Washington, DC: National Academy Press.

Eccles, J. S., & Harold, R. D. (1991). Gender differences in sport involvement: Applying the Eccles expectancy-value model. *Journal of Applied Sport Psychology, 3,* 7–35.

Eccles, J. S., Jacobs, J., & Harold, R. D. (1990). Gender-role stereotypes, expectancy effects, and parents' role in the socialization of gender differences in self-perceptions and skill acquisition. *Journal of Social Issues, 46,* 183–201.

Eccles, J. S., Templeton, J., Barber, B., & Stone, M. (2003). Adolescence and emerging adulthood: The critical passage ways to adulthood. In M. H. Bornstein, L. Davidson, C. L. M. Keyes, K. A. Moore, & the Center for Child Well-Being (Eds.), *Well-being: Positive development across the life course* (pp. 383–406). Mahwah, NJ: Erlbaum.

Eccles, J. S., Vida, M. N., & Barber, B. (2004). The relation of early adolescents' college plans and both academic ability and task-value beliefs to subsequent college enrollment. *Journal of Early Adolescence, 24,* 63–77.

Eckerman, C. O., & Peterman, K. (2001). Peers and infant social/communicative development. In G. Bremner & A. Fogel (Eds.), *Blackwell handbook of infant development* (pp. 326–350). Malden, MA: Blackwell.

Eckerman, C. O., & Whitehead, H. (1999). How toddler peers generate coordinated action: A cross-cultural exploration. *Early Education and Development, 10,* 241–266.

Eder, R. A., & Mangelsdorf, S. C. (1997). The emotional basis of early personality development: Implications for the emergent self-concept. In R. Hogan, J. Johnson, & S. Briggs (Eds.), *Handbook of personality psychology* (pp. 209–240). San Diego, CA: Academic Press.

Egan, S. K., Monson, T. C., & Perry, D. G. (1998). Social-cognitive influences on change in aggression over time. *Developmental Psychology, 34,* 996–1006.

Egeland, B., Jacobvitz, D., & Sroufe, L. A. (1988). Breaking the cycle of abuse. *Child Development, 59,* 1080–1088.

Eichstedt, J. A., Serbin, L. A., Poulin-Dubois, D., & Sen, M. G. (2002). Of bears and men: Infants' knowledge of conventional and metaphorical gender stereotypes. *Infant Behavior and Development, 25,* 296–310.

Eisbach, A. O. (2004). Children's developing awareness of diversity in people's trains of thought. *Child Development, 75,* 1694–1707.

Eisenberg, N. (2003). Prosocial behavior, empathy, and sympathy. In M. H. Bornstein & L. Davidson (Eds.), *Well-being: Positive development across the life course* (pp. 253–265). Mahwah, NJ: Erlbaum.

Eisenberg, N., Cumberland, A., & Spinrad, T. L. (1998). Parental socialization of emotion. *Psychological Inquiry, 9,* 241–273.

Eisenberg, N., Fabes, R. A., Shepard, S. A., Murphy, B. C., Jones, S., & Guthrie, I. K. (1998). Contemporaneous and longitudinal prediction of children's sympathy from dispositional regulation and emotionality. *Developmental Psychology, 34,* 910–924.

Eisenberg, N., Fabes, R. A., & Spinrad, T. L. (2006). Prosocial development. In N. Eisenberg (Ed.), *Handbook of child psychology: Vol. 3. Social, emotional, and personality development* (6th ed., pp. 646–718). Hoboken, NJ: Wiley.

Eisenberg, N., Gershoff, E. T., Fabes, R. A., Shepard, S. A., Cumberland, A. J., & Losoya, S. H. (2001). Mothers' emotional expressivity and children's behavior problems and social competence: Mediation through children's regulation. *Developmental Psychology, 37,* 475–490.

Eisenberg, N., & McNally, S. (1993). Socialization and mothers' and adolescents' empathy-related characteristics. *Journal of Research on Adolescence, 3,* 171–191.

Eisenberg, N., & Morris, A. S. (2002). Children's emotion-related regulation. In R. Kail (Ed.), Advances in child development and behavior (Vol. 30, pp. 190–229). San Diego, CA: Elsevier.

Eisenberg, N., Sadovsky, A., Spinrad, T. L., Fabes, R. A., Losoya, S., & Valiente, C. (2005). The relations of problem behavior status to children's negative emotionality, effortful control, and impulsivity: Concurrent relations and prediction of change. *Developmental Psychology, 41,* 193–211.

Eisenberg, N., Smith, C. L., Sadovsky, A., & Spinrad, T. L. (2004a). Effortful control: Relations with emotion regulation, adjustment, and socialization in childhood. In R. Baumeister & K. D. Vohs (Eds.), *Handbook of self-regulation: Research, theory, and applications* (pp. 259–282). New York: Guilford.

Eisenberg, N., & Spinrad, T. L. (2004). Emotion-related regulation: Sharpening the definition. *Child Development, 75,* 334–339.

Eisenberg, N., Spinrad, T., Fabes, R., Reiser, M., Cumberland, A., & Shepard, S. (2004b). The relations of effortful control and impulsivity to children's resiliency and adjustment. *Child Development, 75,* 25–46.

Eisenberg, N., Zhou, Q., Spinrad, T. L., Valiente, C., Fabes, R. A., & Liew, J. (2005). Relations among positive parenting, children's effortful control, and externalizing problems: A three-wave longitudinal study. *Child Development, 76,* 1055–1071.

Ekman, P. (2003). *Emotions revealed.* New York: Times Books.

Ekman, P., & Friesen, W. (1972). Constants across culture in the face and emotion. *Journal of Personality and Social Psychology, 17,* 124–129.

Elfenbein, D. S., & Felice, M. E. (2003). Adolescent pregnancy. *Pediatric Clinics of North America, 50,* 781–800.

Eliakim, A., Friedland, O., Kowen, G., Wolach, B., & Nemet, D. (2004). Parental obesity and higher pre-intervention BMI reduce the likelihood of a multidisciplinary childhood obesity program to succeed: A clinical observation. *Journal of Pediatric Endocrinology and Metabolism, 17,* 1055–1061.

Elias, C. L., & Berk, L. E. (2002). Self-regulation in young children: Is there a role for sociodramatic play? *Early Childhood Research Quarterly, 17,* 1–17.

Elias, M. J., Parker, S., & Rosenblatt, J. L. (2005). Building educational opportunity. In S. Goldstein & R. B. Brooks (Eds.), *Handbook of resilience in children* (pp. 315–336). New York: Kluwer Academic.

Elicker, J., Englund, M., & Sroufe, L. A. (1992). Predicting peer competence and peer relationships in childhood from early parent–child relationships. In R. D. Parke & G. W. Ladd (Eds.), *Family–peer relationships: Modes of linkage* (pp. 77–106). Hillsdale, NJ: Erlbaum.

Elkind, D. (1994). *A sympathetic understanding of the child: Birth to sixteen* (3rd ed.). Boston: Allyn and Bacon.

Elkind, D., & Bowen, R. (1979). Imaginary audience behavior in children and adolescents. *Developmental Psychology, 15,* 33–44.

Ellickson, P. L., D'Amico, E. J., Collins, R. L., & Klein, D. J. (2005). Marijuana use and later problems: When

frequency of recent use explains age of initiation effects. *Substance Use and Misuse, 40,* 343–359.

Elliott, D. S., Wilson, W. J., Huizinga, D., Sampson, R. J., Elliott, A., & Rankin, B. (1996). The effects of neighborhood disadvantage on adolescent development. *Journal of Research in Crime and Delinquency, 33,* 389–426.

Elliott, J. G. (1999). School refusal: Issues of conceptualization, assessment, and treatment. *Journal of Child Psychology and Psychiatry and Allied Disciplines, 40,* 1001–1012.

Ellis, B. J. (2004). Timing of pubertal maturation in girls: An integrated life history approach. *Psychological Bulletin, 130,* 920–958.

Ellis, B. J., Bates, J. E., Dodge, K. A., Fergusson, D. M., Horwood, L. J., Pettit, G. S., & Woodward, L. (2003). Does father absence place daughters at special risk for early sexual activity and teenage pregnancy? *Child Development, 74,* 801–821.

Ellis, L., & Bonin, S. L. (2003). Genetics and occupation-related preferences: Evidence from adoptive and non-adoptive families. *Personality and Individual Differences, 35,* 929–937.

Elman, J. L. (2001). Connectionism and language acquisition. In M. Tomasello & E. Bates (Eds.), *Language development* (pp. 295–306). Oxford, U.K.: Blackwell.

Else-Quest, N. M., Hyde, J. S., Goldsmith, H. H., & Van Hulle, C. A. (2006). Gender differences in temperament: A meta-analysis. *Psychological Bulletin, 132,* 33–72.

El-Sheikh, M., Cummings, E. M., & Reiter, S. (1996). Preschoolers' responses to ongoing interadult conflict: The role of prior exposure to resolved versus unresolved arguments. *Journal of Abnormal Child Psychology, 24,* 665–679.

Eltzschig, H. K., Lieberman, E. S., & Camann, W. R. (2003). Regional anesthesia and analgesia for labor and delivery. *New England Journal of Medicine, 384,* 319–332.

Ely, R. (2005). Language development in the school years. In J. B. Gleason (Ed.), *The development of language* (5th ed., pp. 395–443). Boston: Allyn and Bacon.

Emery, R. E., Laumann-Billings, L., Waldron, M. C., Sbarra, D. A., & Dillon, P. (2001). Child custody mediation and litigation: Custody, contact, and coparenting 12 years after initial dispute resolution. *Journal of Consulting and Clinical Psychology, 69,* 323–332.

Emery, R. E., Sbarra, D., & Grover, T. (2005). Divorce mediation: Research and reflections. *Family Court Review, 43,* 22–37.

Emory, E. K., Schlackman, L. J., & Fiano, K. (1996). Drug–hormone interactions on neurobehavioral responses in human neonates. *Infant Behavior and Development, 19,* 213–220.

Engle, R. A., & Conant, F. R. (2002). Guiding principles for fostering productive disciplinary engagement: Explaining an emergent argument in a community of learners classroom. *Cognition and Instruction, 20,* 399–483.

Engler, A. J., Ludington-Hoe, S. M., Cusson, R. M., Adams, R., Bahnsen, M., & Brumbaugh, E. (2002). Kangaroo care: National survey of practice, knowledge, barriers, and perceptions. *American Journal of Maternal and Child Nursing, 27,* 146–153.

Entwisle, D. R., Alexander, K. L., & Olson, L. S. (2005). First grade and educational attainment by age 22: A new story. *American Journal of Sociology, 110,* 1458–1502.

Epstein, J. L. (2001). *School, family, and community partnerships: Preparing educators and improving schools.* Boulder, CO: Westview.

Epstein, J. L., & Sanders, M. G. (2002). Family, school, and community partnerships. In M. H. Bornstein (Ed.), *Handbook of parenting: Vol. 5. Practical issues in parenting* (2nd ed., pp. 407–437). Mahwah, NJ: Erlbaum.

Epstein, L. H., Roemmich, J. N., & Raynor, H. A. (2001). Behavioral therapy in the treatment of pediatric obesity. *Pediatric Clinics of North America, 48,* 981–983.

Epstein, L. H., Saelens, B. E., & O'Brien, J. G. (1995). Effects of reinforcing increases in active versus decreases in sedentary behavior for obese children. *International Journal of Behavioral Medicine, 2,* 41–50.

Epstein, L. H., Saelens, B. E., Myers, M. D., & Vito, D. (1997). Effects of decreasing sedentary behaviors on activity choice in obese children. *Health Psychology, 16,* 107–113.

Erickson, J. D., Patterson, J. M., Wall, M., & Neumark-Sztainer, D. (2005). Risk behaviors and emotional well-being in youth with chronic health conditions. *Children's Health Care, 34,* 181–192.

Erikson, E. H. (1950). *Childhood and society.* New York: Norton.

Erikson, E. H. (1968). *Identity, youth, and crisis.* New York: Norton.

Ernst, M., Moolchan, E. T., & Robinson, M. L. (2001). Behavioral and neural consequences of prenatal exposure to nicotine. *Journal of the American Academy of Child and Adolescent Psychiatry, 40,* 630–641.

Eshel, Y., & Kohavi, R. (2003). Perceived classroom control, self-regulated learning strategies, and academic achievement. *Educational Psychology, 23,* 249–260.

Espy, K. A., Molfese, V. J., & DiLalla, L. F. (2001). Effects of environmental measures on intelligence in young children: Growth curve modeling of longitudinal data. *Merrill-Palmer Quarterly, 47,* 42–73.

Estourgie-van Burk, G. F., Bartels, M., van Beijsterveldt, T. C., Delemarre-van de Waal, H. A., & Boomsma, D. I. (2006). Body size in five-year-old twins: Heritability and comparison to singleton standards. *Twin Research and Human Genetics, 9,* 646–655.

Ethier, K. A., Kershaw, T., Niccolai, L., Lewis, J. B., & Ickovics, J. R. (2003). Adolescent women underestimate their susceptibility to sexually transmitted infections. *Sexually Transmitted Infections, 79,* 408–411.

Evans, A. M., & Scutter, S. D. (2004). How common are "growing pains" in young children? *Journal of Pediatrics, 145,* 255–258.

Evans, E., Hawton, K., & Rodham, K. (2004). Factors associated with suicidal phenomena in adolescents: A systematic review of population-based studies. *Clinical Psychology Review, 24,* 957–979.

Evans, G. W. (2006). Child development and the physical environment. *Annual Review of Psychology, 57,* 424–451.

Evans, G. W., Maxwell, L. E., & Hart, B. (1999). Parental language and verbal responsiveness to children in crowded homes. *Developmental Psychology, 35,* 1020–1023.

Everman, D. B., & Cassidy, S. B. (2000). Genetics of childhood disorders: XII. Genomic imprinting: Breaking the rules. *Journal of the American Academy of Child and Adolescent Psychiatry, 38,* 386–389.

Fabes, R. A., Eisenberg, N., Hanish, L. D., & Spinrad, T. L. (2001). Preschoolers' spontaneous emotion vocabulary: Relations to likability. *Early Education and Development, 12,* 11–27.

Fabes, R. A., Eisenberg, N., McCormick, S. E., & Wilson, M. S. (1988). Preschoolers' attributions of the situational determinants of others' naturally occurring emotions. *Developmental Psychology, 24,* 376–385.

Fabes, R. A., Martin, C. L., & Hanish, L. D. (2003). Young children's play qualities in same-, other-, and mixed-sex peer groups. *Child Development, 74,* 921–932.

Fagan, J. F., III. (1973). Infants' delayed recognition memory and forgetting. *Journal of Experimental Child Psychology, 16,* 424–450.

Fagard, J., & Pezé, A. (1997). Age changes in interlimb coupling and the development of bimanual coordination. *Journal of Motor Behavior, 29,* 199–208.

Fagot, B. I. (1984). The child's expectations of differences in adult male and female interactions. *Sex Roles, 11,* 593–600.

Fagot, B. I. (1985). Changes in thinking about early sex role development. *Developmental Review, 5,* 83–98.

Fagot, B. I., & Hagan, R. I. (1991). Observations of parent reactions to sex-stereotyped behaviors: Age and sex effects. *Child Development, 62,* 617–628.

Fagot, B. I., & Leinbach, M. D. (1989). The young child's gender schema: Environmental input, internal organization. *Child Development, 60,* 663–672.

Fahrmeier, E. D. (1978). The development of concrete operations among the Hausa. *Journal of Cross-Cultural Psychology, 9,* 23–44.

Fairburn, C. G. (2005). Evidence-based treatment of anorexia nervosa. *International Journal of Eating Disorders, 37,* S26–S30.

Fairburn, C. G., & Harrison, P. J. (2003). Eating disorders. *Lancet, 361,* 407–416.

Faircloth, B. S., & Hamm, J. V. (2005). Sense of belonging among high school students representing four ethnic groups. *Journal of Youth and Adolescence, 34,* 293–309.

Falbo, T. (1992). Social norms and the one-child family: Clinical and policy implications. In F. Boer & J. Dunn (Eds.), *Children's sibling relationships* (pp. 71–82). Hillsdale, NJ: Erlbaum.

Falbo, T., & Poston, D. L., Jr. (1993). The academic, personality, and physical outcomes of only children in China. *Child Development, 64,* 18–35.

Falbo, T., Poston, D. L., Jr., Triscari, R. S., & Zhang, X. (1997). Self-enhancing illusions among Chinese schoolchildren. *Journal of Cross-Cultural Psychology, 28,* 172–191.

Falck-Ytter, T., Gredebäck, G., & von Hofsten, C. (2006). Infants predict other people's action goals. *Nature Neuroscience, 9,* 878–879.

Fantz, R. L. (1961, May). The origin of form perception. *Scientific American, 204*(5), 66–72.

Farmer, T. W., Leung, M., Pearl, R., Rodkin, P. C., Cadwallader, T. W., & Van Acker, R. (2002). Deviant or diverse peer groups? The peer affiliations of aggressive elementary students. *Journal of Educational Psychology, 94,* 611–620.

Farrant, K., & Reese, E. (2000). Maternal style and children's participation in reminiscing: Stepping stones in children's autobiographical memory development. *Journal of Cognition and Development, 1,* 193–225.

Farrington, D. P. (2004). Conduct disorder, aggression, and delinquency. In R. M. Lerner & L. Steinberg (Eds.), *Handbook of adolescent psychology* (2nd ed., pp. 627–664). New York: Wiley.

Farrington, D. P., & Loeber, R. (2000). Epidemiology of juvenile violence. *Juvenile Violence, 9,* 733–748.

Farroni, T., Csibra, G., Simion, F., & Johnson, M. H. (2002). Eye contact detection in humans from birth. *Proceedings of the National Academy of Sciences, 99,* 9602–9605.

Farver, J. M., & Branstetter, W. H. (1994). Preschoolers' prosocial responses to their peers' distress. *Developmental Psychology, 30,* 334–341.

Farver, J. M., Kim, Y. K., & Lee, Y. (1995). Cultural differences in Korean- and Anglo-American preschoolers' social interaction and play behaviors. *Child Development, 66,* 1099–1099.

Farver, J. M., & Wimbarti, S. (1995). Indonesian children's play with their mothers and older siblings. *Child Development, 66,* 1493–1503.

Fashola, O. S., & Slavin, R. E. (1998). Effective dropout prevention and college attendance programs for students placed at risk. *Journal of Education for Students Placed at Risk, 3,* 159–183.

Fasig, L. G. (2000). Toddlers' understanding of ownership: Implications for self-concept development. *Social Development, 9,* 370–382.

Fasula, A. M., & Miller, K. S. (2006). African-American and Hispanic adolescents' intentions to delay first intercourse: Parental communication as a buffer for sexually active peers. *Journal of Adolescent Health, 38,* 193–200.

Fattibene, P., Mazzei, F., Nuccetelli, C., & Risica, S. (1999). Prenatal exposure to ionizing radiation: Sources, effects, and regulatory aspects. *Acta Paediatrica, 88,* 693–702.

Faulkner, G., & Goodman, J. (2007). Participation in high school physical education—Ontario, Canada, 1999–2005. *Morbidity and Mortality Weekly Report, 56,* 52–56.

Federal Interagency Forum on Child and Family Statistics. (2006a). *America's Children in Brief: Key National Indicators of Well-Being.* Retrieved from www.childstats.gov/americaschildren/tables.asp

Federal Interagency Forum on Child and Family Statistics. (2006b). *Family structure and children's living arrangements.* Retrieved from www.childstats.gov/americaschildren/pop6.asp

Federenko, I. S., & Wadhwa, P. D. (2004). Women's mental health during pregnancy influences fetal and infant developmental and health outcomes. *CNS Spectrums, 9,* 198–206.

Feeney, J. A., Hohaus, L., Noller, P., & Alexander, R. P. (2001). *Becoming parents: Exploring the bonds between mothers, fathers, and their infants.* New York: Cambridge University Press.

Feinberg, M. E., McHale, S. M., Crouter, A. C., & Cumsille, P. (2003). Sibling differentiation: Sibling and parent relationship trajectories in adolescence. *Child Development, 74,* 1261–1274.

Feiring, C., Taska, L., & Lewis, M. (1999). Age and gender differences in children's and adolescents' adaptation to sexual abuse. *Child Abuse and Neglect, 23,* 115–128.

Feiring, C., & Taska, L. S. (1996). Family self-concept: Ideas on its meaning. In B. Bracken (Ed.), *Handbook of self-concept* (pp. 317–373). New York: Wiley.

Feldkámper, M., & Schaeffel, F. (2003). Interactions of genes and environment in myopia. *Developmental Ophthalmology, 37,* 34–49.

Feldman, R. (2002). Parents' convergence on sharing and marital satisfaction, father involvement, and parent–child relationship in the transition to parenthood. *Infant Mental Health Journal, 21,* 176–191.

Feldman, R. (2003). Infant–mother and infant–father synchrony: The coregulation of positive arousal. *Infant Mental Health Journal, 24,* 1–23.

Feldman, R. (2006). From biological rhythms to social rhythms: Physiological precursors of mother–infant synchrony. *Developmental Psychology, 42,* 175–188.

Feldman, R., & Eidelman, A. I. (2003). Skin-to-skin contact (kangaroo care) accelerates autonomic and neurobehavioral maturation in preterm infants. *Developmental Medicine and Child Neurology, 45,* 274–281.

Feldman, R., Eidelman, A., Sirota, L., & Weller, A. (2002). Comparison of skin-to-skin (kangaroo) and traditional care: Parenting outcomes and preterm infant development. *Pediatrics, 110,* 16–26.

Feldman, R., Greenbaum, C. W., & Yirmiya, N. (1999). Mother–infant affect synchrony as an antecedent of the emergence of self-control. *Developmental Psychology, 35,* 223–231.

Feldman, R., & Klein, P. S. (2003). Toddlers' self-regulated compliance to mothers, caregivers, and fathers: Implications for theories of socialization. *Developmental Psychology, 39,* 680–692.

Feldman, R., Sussman, A. L., & Zigler, E. (2004). Parental leave and work adaptation at the transition to parenthood: Individual, marital, and social correlates. *Journal of Applied Developmental Psychology, 25,* 459–479.

Feldman, R., Weller, A., Sirota, L., & Eidelman, A. I. (2003). Testing a family intervention hypothesis: The contribution of mother–infant skin-to-skin contact (kangaroo care) to family interaction, proximity, and touch. *Journal of Family Psychology, 17,* 94–107.

Felner, R. D., Favazza, A., Shim, M., Brand, S., Gu, K., & Noonan, N. (2002). Whole school improvement and restructuring as prevention and promotion: Lessons from STEP and the Project on High Performance Learning Communities. *Journal of School Psychology, 39,* 177–202.

Felsman, D. E., & Blustein, D. L. (1999). The role of peer relatedness in late adolescent career development. *Journal of Vocational Behavior, 54,* 279–295.

Feng, Q. (2005). Postnatal consequences of prenatal cocaine exposure and myocardial apoptosis: Does cocaine in utero imperil the adult heart? *British Journal of Pharmacology, 144,* 887–888.

Fennema, E., Carpenter, T. P., Jacobs, V. R., Franke, M. L., & Levi, L. W. (1998). A longitudinal study of gender differences in young children's mathematical thinking. *Educational Researcher, 27,* 6–11.

Fenson, L., Dale, P. S., Reznick, J. S., Bates, E., Thal, D. J., & Pethick, S. J. (1994). Variability in early communicative development. *Monographs of the Society for Research in Child Development, 59*(5, Serial No. 242).

Ferguson, T. J., Stegge, H., & Damhuis, I. (1991). Children's understanding of guilt and shame. *Child Development, 62,* 827–839.

Ferguson, T. J., Stegge, H., Miller, E. R., & Olsen, M. E. (1999). Guilt, shame, and symptoms in children. *Developmental Psychology, 35,* 347–357.

Fergusson, D. M., & Horwood, J. (2003). Resilience to childhood adversity: Results of a 21-year study. In S. S. Luthar (Ed.), *Resilience and vulnerability* (pp. 130–155). New York: Cambridge University Press.

Fergusson, D. M., & Woodward, L. J. (1999). Breast-feeding and later psychosocial adjustment. *Paediatric and Perinatal Epidemiology, 13,* 144–157.

Fergusson, D. M., & Woodward, L. J. (2002). Mental health, educational, and social role outcomes of adolescents with depression. *Archives of General Psychiatry, 59,* 225–231.

Fergusson, D. M., Woodward, L. J., & Horwood, L. J. (2000). Risk factors and life processes associated with the onset of suicidal behaviour during adolescence and early adulthood. *Psychological Medicine, 30,* 23–39.

Fernald, A., Perfors, A., & Marchman, V. A. (2006). Picking up speed in understanding: Speech processing efficiency and vocabulary growth across the 2nd year. *Developmental Psychology, 42,* 98–116.

Fernald, L. C., & Grantham-McGregor, S. M. (1998). Stress response in school-age children who have been growth-retarded since early childhood. *American Journal of Clinical Nutrition, 68,* 691–698.

Fernyhough, C., & Fradley, E. (2005). Private speech on an executive task: Relations with task difficulty and task performance. *Cognitive Development, 20,* 103–120.

Ficca, G., Fagioli, I., Giganti, F., & Salzarulo, P. (1999). Spontaneous awakenings from sleep in the first year of life. *Early Human Development, 55,* 219–228.

Field, T. (2001). Massage therapy facilitates weight gain in preterm infants. *Current Directions in Psychological Science, 10,* 51–54.

Field, T., Hernandez-Reif, M., & Freedman, J. (2004) Stimulation programs for preterm infants. *Social Policy Report of the Society for Research in Child Development, 18*(1).

Field, T. M. (1998). Massage therapy effects. *American Psychologist, 53,* 1270–1281.

Fingerhut, L. A., & Christoffel, K. K. (2002). Firearm-related death and injury among children and adolescents. *Future of Children, 12,* 25–37.

Finn, J. D., Gerber, S. B., & Boyd-Zaharias, J. (2005). Small classes in the early grades, academic achievement, and graduating from high school. *Journal of Educational Psychology, 97,* 214–233.

Finn, J. D., Pannozzo, G. M., & Achilles, C. M. (2003). The "why's" of class size: Student behavior in small classes. *Review of Educational Research, 73,* 321–368.

Finnilä, K., Mahlberga, N., Santtilia, P., & Niemib, P. (2003). Validity of a test of children's suggestibility for predicting responses to two interview situations differing in degree of suggestiveness. *Journal of Experimental Child Psychology, 85,* 32–49.

Fisch, H., Hyun, G., Golden, R., Hensle, T. W., Olsson, C. A., & Liberson, G. L. (2003). The influence of paternal age on Down syndrome. *Journal of Urology, 169,* 2275–2278.

Fisch, S. M., Truglio, R. T., & Cole, C. F. (1999). The impact of Sesame Street on preschool children: A review and synthesis of 30 years' research. *Media Psychology, 1,* 165–190.

Fischer, K., & Bidell, T. (1991). Constraining nativisit inferences about cognitive capacities. In S. Carey & R. Gelman (Eds.), *The epigenesis of mind: Essays on biology and cognition* (pp. 199–235). Hillsdale, NJ: Erlbaum.

Fischer, K. W., & Bidell, T. R. (1998). Dynamic development of psychological structures in action and thought. In R. M. Lerner (Ed.), *Handbook of child psychology: Vol. 1. Theoretical models of human development* (5th ed., pp. 467–562). New York: Wiley.

Fischer, K. W., & Bidell, T. R. (2006). Dynamic development of action and thought. In R. M. Lerner (Ed.), *Handbook of child psychology: Vol. 1. Theoretical models of human development* (6th ed., pp. 313–399). Hoboken, NJ: Wiley.

Fischman, M. G., Moore, J. B., & Steele, K. H. (1992). Children's one-hand catching as a function of age, gender, and ball location. *Research Quarterly for Exercise and Sport, 63,* 349–355.

Fish, M. (2004). Attachment in infancy and preschool in low socioeconomic status rural Appalachian children: Stability and change and relations to preschool and kindergarten competence. *Development and Psychopathology, 16,* 293–312.

Fisher, C. B. (1993, Winter). Integrating science and ethics in research with high-risk children and youth. *Social Policy Report of the Society for Research in Child Development, 4*(4).

Fisher, C. B., Hoagwood, K., Boyce, C., Duster, T., Frank, D. A., & Grisso, T. (2002). Research ethics for mental health science involving ethnic minority children and youths. *American Psychologist, 57,* 1024–1040.

Fisher, J. O., Mitchell, D. S., Smiciklas-Wright, H., & Birch, L. L. (2001). Maternal milk consumption predicts the tradeoff between milk and soft drinks in young girls' diets. *Journal of Nutrition, 131,* 246–250.

Fisher, J. O., Rolls, B. J., & Birch, L. L. (2003). Children's bite size and intake of an entrée are greater with large portions than with ageappropriate or self-selected portions. *American Journal of Clinical Nutrition, 77,* 1164–1170.

FitzGerald, D. P., & White, K. J. (2003). Linking children's social worlds: Perspective-taking in parent–child and peer contexts. *Social Behavior and Personality, 31,* 509–522.

Fivush, R. (2001). Owning experience: Developing subjective perspective in autobiographical narratives. In C. Moore & K. Lemmon (Eds.), *The self in time: Developmental perspectives* (pp. 35–52). Mahwah, NJ: Erlbaum.

Fivush, R., & Haden, C. A. (2005). Parent–child reminiscing and the construction of a subjective self. In B. D. Homer & C. S. Tamis-LeMonda (Eds.), *The development of social cognition and communication* (pp. 315–336). Mahwah, NJ: Erlbaum.

Fivush, R., & Reese, E. (2002). Reminiscing and relating: The development of parent–child talk about the past. In J. D. Webster & B. K. Haight (Eds.), *Critical advances in reminiscence work: From theory to application* (pp. 109–122). New York: Springer.

Flake, A. W. (2003). Surgery in the human fetus: The future. *Journal of Physiology, 547,* 45–51.

Flaks, D. K., Ficher, I., Masterpasqua, F., & Joseph, G. (1995). Lesbians choosing motherhood: A comparative study of lesbian and heterosexual parents and their children. *Developmental Psychology, 31,* 105–114.

Flanagan, C. A., & Faison, N. (2001). Youth civic development: Implications of research for social policy and programs. *Social Policy Report of the Society for Research in Child Development, 15*(1).

Flanagan, C. A., Jonsson, B., Botcheva, L., Csapo, B., Bowes, J., Macek, P., Averina, I., & Sheblanova, E. (1999). Adolescents and the social contract: Developmental roots of citizenship in seven countries. In M. Yates & J. Youniss (Eds.), *Roots of civic identity: International perspectives on community service and activism in youth* (pp. 135–155). New York: Cambridge University Press.

Flanagan, C. A., & Tucker, C. J. (1999). Adolescents' explanations for political issues: Concordance with their views of self and society. *Developmental Psychology, 35,* 1198–1209.

Flannery, D. J., Hussey, D. L., Biebelhausen, L., & Wester, K. L. (2003). Crime, delinquency, and youth gangs. In G. R. Adams & M. D. Berzonsky (Eds.), *Blackwell handbook of adolescence* (pp. 502–522). Malden, MA: Blackwell.

Flannery, K. A., & Liederman, J. (1995). Is there really a syndrome involving the co-occurrence of neurodevelopmental disorder, talent, non-right handedness and immune disorder among children? *Cortex, 31,* 503–515.

Flavell, J. H. (1999). Cognitive development: Children's knowledge about the mind. *Annual Review of Psychology, 50,* 21–45.

Flavell, J. H., Flavell, E. R., & Green, F. L. (2001). Development of children's understanding of connections between thinking and feeling. *Psychological Science, 12,* 430–432.

Flavell, J. H., Flavell, E. R., Green, F. L., & Korfmacher, J. E. (1990). Do young children think of television images as pictures or real objects? *Journal of Broadcasting and Electronic Media, 34,* 339–419.

Flavell, J. H., Green, F. L., & Flavell, E. R. (1987). Development of knowledge about the appearance–reality distinction. *Monographs of the Society for Research in Child Development, 51*(1, Serial No. 212).

Flavell, J. H., Green, F. L., & Flavell, E. R. (1993). Children's understanding of the stream of consciousness. *Child Development, 64,* 387–398.

Flavell, J. H., Green, F. L., & Flavell, E. R. (1995). Young children's knowledge about thinking. *Monographs of the Society for Research in Child Development, 60*(1, Serial No. 243).

Flavell, J. H., Green, F. L., Flavell, E. R., & Grossman, J. B. (1997). The development of children's knowledge about inner speech. *Child Development, 68,* 39–47.

Fletcher-Flinn, C. M., & Gravatt, B. (1995). The efficacy of computer-assisted instruction (CAI): A meta-analysis. *Journal of Educational Computing Research, 12,* 219–242.

Floccia, C., Christophe, A., & Bertoncini, J. (1997). Highamplitude sucking and newborns: The quest for underlying mechanisms. *Journal of Experimental Child Psychology, 64,* 175–198.

Flom, R., & Pick, A. D. (2003). Verbal encouragement and joint attention in 18-month-old infants. *Infant Behavior and Development, 26,* 121–134.

Florian, V., & Kravetz, S. (1985). Children's concepts of death: A cross-cultural comparison among Muslims, Druze, Christians, and Jews in Israel. *Journal of Cross-Cultural Psychology, 16,* 174–179.

Flouri, E., & Buchanan, A. (2004). Early father's and mother's involvement and child's later educational outcomes. *British Journal of Educational Psychology, 74,* 141–153.

Flynn, J. R. (1999). Searching for justice: The discovery of IQ gains over time. *American Psychologist, 54,* 5–20.

Flynn, J. R. (2003). Movies about intelligence: The limitations of *g. Current Directions in Psychological Science, 12,* 95–99.

Focus on the Family Canada. (2004). *Substance abuse: What every family should know.* Retrieved from www.fotf.ca/familyfacts/analysis/010902.html

Fogel, A. (1993). *Developing through relationships: Origins of communication, self and culture.* New York: Harvester Wheatsheaf.

Fogel, A. (2000). Systems, attachment, and relationships. *Human Development, 43,* 314–320.

Fomon, S. J., & Nelson, S. E. (2002). Body composition of the male and female reference infants. *Annual Review of Nutrition, 22,* 1–17.

Fordham, K., & Stevenson-Hinde, J. (1999). Shyness, friendship quality, and adjustment during middle childhood. *Journal of Child Psychology and Psychiatry, 40,* 757–768.

Forman, D. R., Aksan, N., & Kochanska, G. (2004). Toddlers' responsive imitation predicts preschool-age conscience. *Psychological Science, 15,* 699–704.

Forman, D. R., O'Hara, M. W., Larsen, K., Coy, K. C., Gorman, L. L., & Stewart, S. (2003). Infant emotionality: Observational methods and the validity of maternal reports. *Infancy, 4,* 541–565.

Foster, M. A., Lambert, R., Abbott-Shim, M., McCarty, F., & Franze, S. (2005). A model of home learning environment and social risk factors in relation to children's emergent literacy and social outcomes. *Early Childhood Research Quarterly, 20, 13*–36.

Fowden, A. L., Giussani, D. A., & Forhead, A. J. (2005). Endocrine and metabolic programming during intrauterine development. *Early Human Development, 81,* 723–734.

Fowles, D. C., & Kochanska, G. (2000). Temperament as a moderator of pathways to conscience in children: The contribution of electrodermal activity. *Psychophysiology, 37,* 788–795.

Fox, C. L., & Boulton, M. J. (2006). Friendship as a moderator of the relationship between social skills problems and peer victimization. *Aggressive Behavior, 32,* 110–121.

Fox, N. A. (1991). If it's not left, it's right: Electroencephalograph asymmetry and the development of emotion. *American Psychologist, 46,* 863–872.

Fox, N. A., & Calkins, S. D. (2003). The development of self-control of emotion: Intrinsic and extrinsic influences. *Motivation and Emotion, 27,* 7–26.

Fox, N. A., & Davidson, R. J. (1986). Taste-elicited changes in facial signs of emotion and the asymmetry of brain electrical activity in newborn infants. *Neuropsychologia, 24,* 417–422.

Foy, J. G., & Mann, V. (2003). Home literacy environment and phonological awareness in preschool children: Differential effects for rhyme and phoneme awareness. *Applied Psycholinguistics, 24,* 59–88.

Fraiberg, S. (1971). *Insights from the blind.* New York: Basic Books.

Franco, P., Chabanski, S., Szliwowski, H., Dramaiz, M., & Kahn, A. (2000). Influence of maternal smoking on autonomic nervous system in healthy infants. *Pediatric Research, 47,* 215–220.

Franco, P., Danias, A. P., Akamine, E. H., Kawamoto, E. M., Fortes, Z. B., Scavone, C., & Tostes, R. C. (2002). Enhanced oxidative stress as a potential mechanism underlying the programming of hypertension in utero. *Journal of Cardiovascular Pharmacology, 40,* 501–509.

Frank, D. A., Rose-Jacobs, R., Beeghly, M., Wilbur, M., Bellinger, D., & Cabral, H. (2005). Level of prenatal cocaine exposure and 48-month IQ: Importance of preschool enrichment. *Neurotoxicology and Teratology, 27,* 15–28.

Frederiksen-Goldsen, K. I., & Sharlach, A. E. (2000). *Families and work: New directions in the twenty-first century.* New York: Oxford University Press.

Fredricks, J. A., & Eccles, J. S. (2002). Children's competence and value beliefs from childhood through adolescence: Growth trajectories in two male-sex-typed domains. *Developmental Psychology, 38,* 519–533.

Fredricks, J. A., & Eccles, J. S. (2005). Developmental benefits of extracurricular involvement: Do peer characteristics mediate the link between activities and youth outcomes? *Journal of Youth and Adolescence, 34,* 507–520.

Fredricks, J. A., & Eccles, J. S. (2006). Is extracurricular participation associated with beneficial outcomes? Concurrent and longitudinal relations. *Developmental Psychology, 42,* 698–713.

Freedman, D. S., Khan, L. K., Serdula, M. K., Dietz, W. H., Srinivasan, S. R., & Berenson, G. S. (2002). Relation of age at menarche to race, time period, and anthropometric dimensions: The Bogalusa Heart Study. *Pediatrics, 110,* e43–e49.

Freedman, D. S., Khan, L. K., Serdula, M. K., Srinivasan, S. R., & Berenson, G. S. (2000). Secular trends in height among children during 2 decades: The Bogalusa Heart Study. *Archives of Pediatric and Adolescent Medicine, 154,* 155–161.

Freedman-Doan, C., Wigfield, A., Eccles, J. S., Blumenfeld, P., Arbreton, A., & Harold, R. D. (2000). What am I best at? Grade and gender differences in children's beliefs about ability improvement. *Journal of Applied Developmental Psychology, 21,* 379–402.

Freeman, C. E. (2004). *Trends in educational equity of girls and women: 2004.* U.S. Department of Education, National Center for Education Statistics. Washington, DC: U.S. Government Printing Office.

Freeman, D. (1983). *Margaret Mead and Samoa: The making and unmaking of an anthropological myth.* Cambridge, MA: Harvard University Press.

Freud, A. (1969). Adolescence as a developmental disturbance. In G. Caplan & S. Lebovici (Eds.), *Adolescence* (pp. 5–10). New York: Basic Books.

Freud, S. (1973). *An outline of psychoanalysis.* London: Hogarth. (Original work published 1938)

Freud, S. (1974). *The ego and the id.* London: Hogarth. (Original work published 1923)

Fried, P. A. (1993). Prenatal exposure to tobacco and marijuana: Effects during preganancy, infancy, and early childhood. *Clinical Obstetrics and Gynecology, 36,* 319–337.

Fried, P. A., Watkinson, B., & Gray, R. (2003). Differential effects on cognitive functioning in 13- to 16-year-olds prenatally exposed to cigarettes and marijuana. *Neurotoxicology and Teratology, 25* 427–436.

Friedman, J. M. (1996). *The effects of drugs on the fetus and nursing infant: A handbook for health care professionals.* Baltimore: Johns Hopkins University Press.

Friedman, S. L., & Scholnick, E. K. (1997). An evolving "blueprint" for planning: Psychological requirements, task characteristics, and social–cultural influences. In S. L. Friedman & E. K. Scholnick (Eds.), *The developmental psychology of planning: Why, how, and when do we plan?* (pp. 3–22). Mahwah, NJ: Erlbaum.

Frijda, N. (2000). The psychologist's point of view. In M. Lewis & J. M. Haviland-Jones (Eds.), *Handbook of emotions* (pp. 59–74). New York: Guilford.

Frith, L. (2001). Gamete donation and anonymity: The ethical and legal debate. *Human Reproduction, 16,* 818–824.

Frith, U. (2003). *Autism: Explaining the enigma* (2nd ed.). Malden, MA: Blackwell.

Frith, U., & Happé, F. (1994). Autism: Beyond "theory of mind." *Cognition, 50,* 115–132.

Fuchs, D., Fuchs, L.S., Mathes, P. G., & Martinez, E. A. (2002b). Preliminary evidence on the standing of students with learning disabilities in PALS and No-PALS classrooms. *Learning Disabilities Research and Practice, 17,* 205–215.

Fuchs, I., Eisenberg, N., Hertz-Lazarowitz, R., & Sharabany, R. (1986). Kibbutz, Israeli city, and American children's moral reasoning about prosocial moral conflicts. *Merrill-Palmer Quarterly, 32,* 37–50.

Fuchs, L. S., Fuchs, D., Yazdian, L., & Powell, S. R. (2002a). Enhancing first-grade children's mathematical development with peer-assisted learning strategies. *School Psychology Review, 31,* 569–583.

Fulhan, J., Collier, S., & Duggan, C. (2003). Update on pediatric nutrition: Breastfeeding, infant nutrition, and growth. *Current Opinion in Pediatrics, 15,* 323–332.

Fuligni, A. J. (1998). Authority, autonomy, and parent–adolescent conflict and cohesion: A study of adolescents from Mexican, Chinese, Filipino, and European backgrounds. *Developmental Psychology, 34,* 782–792.

Fuligni, A. J. (1998). The adjustment of children from immigrant families. *Current Directions in Psychological Science, 7,* 99–103.

Fuligni, A. J. (2004). The adaptation and acculturation of children from immigrant families. In U. P. Gielen & J. Roopnarine (Eds.), *Childhood and adolescence: Cross-cultural perspectives* (pp. 297–318). Westport, CT: Praeger.

Fuligni, A. J., Yip, T., & Tseng, V. (2002). The impact of family obligation on the daily activities and psychological well-being of Chinese-American adolescents. *Child Development, 73,* 302–314.

Fuligni, A. J., & Yoshikawa, H. (2003). Socioeconomic resources, parenting, and child development among immigrant families. In M. H. Bornstein & R. H. Bradley (Eds.), *Socioeconomic status, parenting, and child development* (pp. 107–124). Mahwah, NJ: Erlbaum.

Fuligni, A. S., Han, W.-J., & Brooks-Gunn, J. (2004). The Infant-Toddler HOME in the 2nd and 3rd years of life. *Parenting: Science and Practice, 4,* 139–159.

Fuller, C., Keller, L., Olson, J., Plymale, A., & Gottesman, M. (2005). Helping preschoolers become healthy eaters. *Journal of Pediatric Health Care, 19,* 178–182.

Fuller-Thomson, E. (2005). Canadian First Nations grandparents raising grandchildren: A portrait in resilience. *International Journal of Aging and Human Development, 60,* 331–342.

Fuller-Thomson, E., & Minkler, M. (2005). Native American grandparents raising grandchildren: Findings from the Census 2000 Supplementary Survey and implications for social work practice. *Social Work, 50,* 131–139.

Furman, W., & Buhrmester, D. (1992). Age and sex differences in perceptions of networks of personal relationships. *Child Development, 63,* 103–115.

Furman, W., & Shaffer, L. (2003). The role of romantic relationships in adolescent development. In P. Florsheim (Ed.), *Adolescent romantic relations and sexual behavior* (pp. 3–22). Mahwah, NJ: Erlbaum.

Furman, W., Simon, V. A., Shaffer, L., & Bouchey, H. A. (2002). Adolescents' working models and styles for relationships with parents, friends, and romantic partners. *Child Development, 73,* 241–255.

Furrow, J. L., King, P. E., & White, K. (2004). Religion and positive youth development: Identity, meaning, and prosocial concerns. *Applied Developmental Science, 8,* 17–26.

Furstenberg, F. F., Jr., & Harris, K. M. (1993). When and why fathers matter: Impact of father involvement on children of adolescent mothers. In R. I. Lerman & T. J. Ooms (Eds.), *Young unwed fathers* (pp. 117–138). Philadelphia: Temple University Press.

Furstenberg, F. F., Jr., Kennedy, S., McLoyd, V. C., Rumbaut, R. G., & Settersten, R. A., Jr. (2004). Growing up is harder to do. *Contexts, 3*(3), 33–41.

Fuson, K. C., & Burghard, B. H. (2003). Multidigit addition and subtraction methods invented in small groups and teacher support of problem solving and reflection. In A. J. Baroody & A. Dowker (Eds.), *The development of arithmetic concepts and skills* (pp. 267–304). Mahwah, NJ: Erlbaum.

Fussell, E., & Furstenberg, F. F., Jr. (2005). The transition to adulthood during the twentieth century. In R. A. Settersten, Jr., F. F. Furstenberg, Jr., & R. G. Rumbaut (Eds.), *On the frontier of adulthood* (pp. 29–75). Chicago: University of Chicago Press.

Fussell, E., & Gauthier, A. H. (2005). American women's transition to adulthood in comparative perspective. In R. A. Settersten, Jr., F. F. Furstenberg, Jr., & R. G. Rumbaut (Eds.), *On the frontier of adulthood: Theory, research, and public policy* (pp. 76–109). Chicago: University of Chicago Press.

Gagnon, J. C., & Leone, P. E. (2002). Alternative strategies for school violence prevention. In R. J. Skiba & G. G. Noam (Eds.), *Zero tolerance: Can suspension and expulsion keep school safe?* (pp. 101–125). San Francisco: Jossey-Bass.

Galambos, N. L., Almeida, D. M., & Petersen, A. C. (1990). Masculinity, femininity, and sex role attitudes in early adolescence: Exploring gender intensification. *Child Development, 61,* 1905–1914.

Galambos, S. J., & Maggs, J. L. (1991). Children in self-care: Figures, facts and fiction. In J. V. Lerner & N. L. Galambos (Eds.), *Employed mothers and their children* (pp. 131–157). New York: Garland.

Gallagher, A. M., & Kaufman, J. C. (2005). Gender differences in mathematics: What we know and what we need to know. In A. M. Gallagher & J. C. Kaufman (Eds.), *Gender differences in mathematics: An integrative psychological approach* (pp. 316–331). New York: Cambridge University Press.

Galler, J. R., Ramsey, C. F., Morley, D. S., Archer, E., & Salt, P. (1990). The long-term effects of early kwashiorkor compared with marasmus. IV. Performance on the National High School Entrance Examination. *Pediatric Research, 28,* 235–239.

Galloway, J. C., & Thelen, E. (2004). Feet first. Object exploration in young infants. *Infant Behavior and Development, 27,* 107-112

Gandy, J. (2004). *Children explain God.* Retrieved from http://www. geocities.com/jonathangandy.geo/chilren-describeGod.html

Ganger, J., & Brent, M. R. (2004). Reexamining the vocabulary spurt. *Developmental Psychology, 40,* 621–632.

Ganji, V., Hampl, J. S., & Betts, N. M. (2003). Race-, gender-, and age-specific differences in dietary micronutrient intakes of U.S. children. *International Journal of Food Sciences and Nutrition, 54,* 485–490.

Ganong, L. H., & Coleman, M. (1994). *Remarried family relationships.* Thousand Oaks, CA: Sage.

Garcia, M. M., Shaw, D. S., Winslow, E. B., & Yaggi, K. E. (2000). Destructive sibling conflict and the development of conduct problems in young boys. *Developmental Psychology, 36,* 44–53.

García Coll, C., & Magnuson, K. (1997). The psychological experience of immigration: A developmental perspective. In A. Booth, A. C. Crouter, & N. Landale (Eds.), *Immigration and the family* (pp. 91–131). Mahwah, NJ: Erlbaum.

Gardner, H. (1980). *Artful scribbles: The significance of children's drawings.* New York: Basic Books.

Gardner, H. (1983). *Frames of mind: The theory of multiple intelligences.* New York: Basic Books.

Gardner, H. (1993). *Multiple intelligences: The theory in practice.* New York: Basic Books.

Gardner, H. (1998). Extraordinary cognitive achievements (ECA): A symbol systems approach. In R. M. Learner (Ed.), *Handbook of child psychology: Vol. 1. Theoretical models of human development* (5th ed., pp. 415–466). New York: Wiley.

Gardner, H. E. (2000). *Intelligence reframed: Multiple intelligences for the twenty-first century.* New York: Basic Books.

Gardner, W. (2005). Just one click—Sexual abuse of children and young people through the Internet and mobile phone technology. *Child Abuse Review, 14,* 448–449.

Garner, P. W. (1996). The relations of emotional role taking, affective/moral attributions, and emotional display rule knowledge to low-income school-age children's social competence. *Journal of Applied Developmental Psychology, 17,* 19–36.

Garner, P. W. (2003). Child and family correlates of toddlers' emotional and behavioral responses to a mishap. *Infant Mental Health Journal, 24,* 580–596.

Garner, P. W., & Estep, K. (2001). Emotional competence, emotion socialization, and young children's peer-related social competence. *Early Education and Development, 12,* 29–48.

Garnier, H. E., Stein, J. A., & Jacobs, J. K. (1997). The process of dropping out of high school: A 19-year perspective. *American Educational Research Journal, 34,* 395–419.

Garrett, P., Ng'andu, N., & Ferron, J. (1994). Poverty experiences of young children and the quality of their home environments. *Child Development, 65,* 331–345.

Garrison, M. M., & Christakis, D. A. (2005). *A teacher in the living room? Educational media for babies, toddlers, and preschoolers.* Menlo Park, CA: Henry J. Kaiser Family Foundation.

Gartstein, M. A., & Rothbart, M. K. (2003). Studying infant temperament via the revised infant behavior questionnaire. *Infant Behavior and Development, 26,* 64–86.

Gartstein, M. A., Slobodskaya, H. R., & Kinsht, I. A. (2003). Cross-cultural differences in temperament in the first year of life: United States of America (U.S.) and Russia. *International Journal of Behavioral Development, 27,* 316–328.

Gasden, V. (1999). Black families in intergenerational and cultural perspective. In M. E. Lamb (Ed.), *Parenting and child development in "nontraditional" families* (pp. 221–246). Mahwah, NJ: Erlbaum.

Gaskins, S. (1999). Children's daily lives in a Mayan village: A case study of culturally constructed roles and activities. In R. Göncü (Ed.), *Children's engagement in the world: Sociocultural perspectives* (pp. 25– 61). Cambridge, U.K.: Cambridge University Press.

Gaskins, S. (2000). Children's daily activities in a Mayan village: A culturally grounded description. *Cross-Cultural Research, 34,* 375–389.

Gathercole, S. E., Adams, A.-M., & Hitch, G. (1994). Do young children rehearse? An individual-differences analysis. *Memory and Cognition, 22,* 201–207.

Gathercole, V., Sebastián, E., & Soto, P. (1999). The early acquisition of Spanish verbal morphology: Across-the-board or piecemeal knowledge? *International Journal of Bilingualism, 3,* 133–182.

Gaultney, J. F., & Gingras, J. L. (2005). Fetal rate of behavioral inhibition and preference for novelty during infancy. *Early Human Development, 81,* 379–386.

Gauvain, M. (2004). Bringing culture into relief: Cultural contributions to the development of children's planning skills. In R. V. Kail (Ed.), *Advances in child development and behavior* (pp. 39–71). San Diego, CA: Elsevier.

Gauvain, M., de la Ossa, J. L., & Hurtado-Ortiz, M. T. (2001). Parental guidance as children learn to use cultural tools: The case of pictorial plans. *Cognitive Development, 16,* 551–575.

Gauvain, M., & Huard, R. D. (1999). Family interaction, parenting style, and the development of planning: A longitudinal analysis using archival data. *Journal of Family Psychology, 13,* 75–92.

Gauvain, M., & Rogoff, B. (1989a). Collaborative problem solving and children's planning skills. *Developmental Psychology, 25,* 139–151.

Gauvain, M., & Rogoff, B. (1989b). Ways of speaking about space: The development of children's skill in communicating spatial knowledge. *Cognitive Development, 4,* 295–307.

Gavin, J., Scott, A., & Duffield, J. (2005. *Internet dating more successful than thought.* Retrieved from www.sciencedaily .com/releases/2005/02/050218125144.htm

Gawlitzek-Maiwald, I., & Tracy, R. (1996). Bilingual bootstrapping. *Linguistics, 34,* 901–926.

Gaylor, E. E., Burnham, M. M., Goodlin-Jones, B. L., & Anders, T. (2005). A longitudinal follow-up study of young children's sleep patterns using a developmental classification system. *Behavioral Sleep Medicine, 3,* 44–61.

Gazelle, H., & Rudolph, K. D. (2004). Moving toward and away from the world: Social approach and avoidance trajectories in anxious and solitary youth. *Child Development, 75,* 829–849.

Ge, X., Brody, G. H., Conger, R. D., Simons, R. L., & Murry, V. (2002). Contextual amplification of the effects of pubertal transition on African American children's deviant peer affiliation and externalized behavioral problems. *Developmental Psychology, 38,* 42–54.

Ge, X., Conger, R. D., & Elder, G. H., Jr. (1996). Coming of age too early: Pubertal influences on girls' vulnerability to psychological distress. *Child Development, 67,* 3386–3400.

Ge, X., Conger, R. D., & Elder, G. H., Jr. (2001). The relation between puberty and psychological distress in adolescent boys. *Journal of Research on Adolescence, 11,* 49–70.

Ge, X., Kim, I. J., Brody, G. H., Conger, R. D., & Simons, R. L. (2003). It's about timing and change: pubertal transition effects on symptoms of major depression among African American youths. *Developmental Psychology, 39,* 430–439.

Geary, D. C. (1999). Evolution and developmental sex differences. *Current Directions in Psychological Science, 8,* 115–120.

Geary, D. C. (2006). Development of mathematical understanding. In D. Kuhn & R. Siegler (Eds.), *Handbook of child psychology: Vol. 2. Cognition, perception, and language* (6th ed., pp. 777–810). Hoboken, NJ: Wiley.

Geary, D. C., Bow-Thomas, C. C., Liu, F., & Siegler, R. S. (1996). Development of arithmetical competencies in Chinese and American children: Influence of age, language, and schooling. *Child Development, 67,* 2022–2044.

Geary, D. C., Saults, J. S., Liu, F., & Hoard, M. K. (2000). Sex differences in spatial cognition, computational fluency, and arithmetic reasoning. *Journal of Experimental Child Psychology, 77,* 337–353.

Gee, C. B., & Rhodes, J. E. (2003). Adolescent mothers' relationship with their children's biological fathers: Social support, social strain, and relationship continuity. *Journal of Family Psychology, 17,* 370–383.

Geerts, M., Steyaert, J., & Fryns, J. P. (2003). The XYY syndrome: A follow-up study on 38 boys. *Genetic Counseling, 14,* 267–279.

Gellin, B. G., Maibach, E. W., & Marcuse, E. K. (2000). Do parents understand immunizations? A national telephone survey. *Pediatrics, 106,* 1097–1102.

Gelman, R. (1972). Logical capacity of very young children: Number invariance rules. *Child Development, 43,* 75–90.

Gelman, R., & Shatz, M. (1978). Appropriate speech adjustments: The operation of conversational constraints on talk to two-year-olds. In M. Lewis & L. A. Rosenblum (Eds.), *Interaction, conversation, and the development of language* (pp. 27–61). New York: Wiley.

Gelman, S. A. (2003). *The essential child.* New York: Oxford University Press.

Gelman, S. A. (2006). Early conceptual development. In K. McCartney & D. Phillips (Eds.), *Blackwell handbook of early childhood development* (pp. 149–166). Malden, MA: Blackwell.

Gelman, S. A., & Kalish, C. W. (2006). Conceptual development. In D. Kuhn & R. Siegler (Eds.), *Handbook of child psychology: Vol. 2. Cognition, perception, and language* (6th ed., 687–733). New York: Wiley.

Gelman, S. A., & Koenig, M. A. (2003). Theory-based categorization in early childhood. In D. H. Rakison & L. M. Oakes (Ed.), *Early category and concept development* (pp. 330–359). New York: Oxford University Press.

Gelman, S. A., & Opfer, J. E. (2002). Development of the animate– inanimate distinction. In U. Goswami (Ed.), *Blackwell handbook of childhood cognitive development* (pp. 151–166). Malden, MA: Blackwell.

Gelman, S. A., Taylor, M. G., & Nguyen, S. P. (2004). Mother–child conversations about gender. *Monographs of the Society for Research in Child Development, 69*(1, Serial No. 275), pp. 1–127.

Genesee, F. (2001). Portrait of the bilingual child. In V. Cook (Ed.), *Portraits of the second language user* (pp. 170–196). Clevedon, U.K.: Multilingual Matters.

Gennetian, L. A., & Morris, P. A. (2003). The effects of time limits and make-work-pay strategies on the well-being of children: Experimental evidence from two welfare reform programs. *Children and Youth Services Review, 25,* 17–54.

Gentner, D., & Namy, L. L. (2004). The role of comparison in children's early word learning. In D. G. Hall & S. R. Waxman (Eds.), *Weaving a lexicon* (pp. 533–568). Cambridge, MA: MIT Press.

Gerardi-Caulton, G. (2000). Sensitivity to spatial conflict and the development of self-regulation in children 24–36 months of age. *Developmental Science, 3,* 397–404.

Gergely, G., Bekkering, H., & Király, I. (2003). Rational imitation in preverbal infants. *Nature, 415,* 755.

Gergely, G., & Watson, J. (1999). Early socio-emotional development: Contingency perception and the social-biofeedback model. In P. Rochat (Ed.), *Early social cognition: Understanding others in the first months of life* (pp. 101–136). Mahwah, NJ: Erlbaum.

Gershoff, E. T. (2002). Corporal punishment, physical abuse, and the burden of proof: Reply to Baumrind, Larzelere, and Cowan (2002), Holden (2002), and Parke (2002). *Psychological Bulletin, 128,* 602–611.

Gerten, K. A., Coonrod, D. V., Bay, R. C., & Chambliss, L. R. (2005). Cesarean delivery and respiratory distress syndrome: Does labor make a difference? *American Journal of Obstetrics and Gynecology, 193,* 1061–1064.

Gertner, S., Greenbaum, C. W., Sadeh, A., Dolfin, Z., Sirota, L. & Ben-Nun, Y. (2002). Sleep-wake patterns in preterm infants and 6 month's home environment: Implications for early cognitive development. *Early Human Development, 68,* 93–102.

Gervai, J., Turner, P. J., & Hinde, R. A. (1995). Gender-related behaviour, attitudes, and personality in parents of young children in England and Hungary. *International Journal of Behavioral Development, 18,* 105–126.

Geschwind, D. H., Boone, K. B., Miller, B. L., & Swerdloff, R. S. (2000). Neurobehavioral phenotype of Klinefelter syndrome. *Mental Retardation and Developmental Disabilities Research Reviews, 6,* 107–116.

Gesell, A. (1933). Maturation and patterning of behavior. In C. Murchison (Ed.), *A handbook of child psychology.* Worcester, MA: Clark University Press.

Gessner, B. D., & Porter, T. J. (2006). Bed sharing with unimpaired parents is not an important risk for sudden infant death syndrome. *Pediatrics, 117,* 990–991.

Gest, S. D., Graham-Bermann, S. A., & Hartup, W. W. (2001). Peer experience: Common and unique features of number of friendships, social network, centrality, and socioeconomic status. *Social Development, 10,* 23–40.

Geurts, H. M., Verte, S., Oosterlaan, J., Roeyers, H., Sergeant, J. A., & Geurts, H. M. (2004). How specific are executive functioning deficits in attention-deficit hyperactivity disorder and autism? *Journal of Child Psychology and Psychiatry, 45,* 836–854.

Ghim, H.R. (1990). Evidence for perceptual organization in infants: Perception of subjective contours by young infants. *Infant Behavior and Development, 13,* 221–248.

Gibbons, A. (1998). Which of our genes make us human? *Science, 281,* 1432–1434

Gibbons, R., Dugaiczyk, L. J., Girke, T., Duistermars, B., Zielinski, R., & Dugaiczyk, A. (2004). Distinguishing humans from great apes with AluYb8 repeats. *Journal of Molecular Biology, 339,* 721–729.

Gibbs, J. C. (1991). Toward an integration of Kohlberg's and Hoffman's theories of morality. In W. M. Kurtines & J. L. Gewirtz (Eds.), *Handbook of moral behavior and development* (Vol. 1, pp. 183–222). Hillsdale, NJ: Erlbaum.

Gibbs, J. C. (2003). *Moral development and reality: Beyond the theories of Kohlberg and Hoffman.* Thousand Oaks, CA: Sage.

Gibbs, J. C. (2004). Moral reasoning training. In A. P. Goldstein, R. Nensen, B. Daleflod, & M. Kalt (Eds.), *New perspectives on aggression replacement training* (pp. 51–72). West Sussex, UK: Wiley.

Gibbs, J. C., Basinger, K. S., & Grime, R. L. (2003). Moral judgment maturity: From clinical to standard measures. In S. J. Lopez & C. R. Snyder (Eds.), *Handbook of positive psychological assessment* (pp. 361–373). Washington, DC: American Psychological Association.

Gibbs, J. C., Basinger, K. S., & Grime, R. L. (2005, August). Cross-cultural research using the SRM–SF. In J. Comunian (Chair), *Cross-cultural research on morality using different assessment instruments.* Symposium conducted at the meeting of the American Psychological Association, Washington, DC.

Gibson, E. J. (1970). The development of perception as an adaptive process. *American Scientist, 58,* 98–107.

Gibson, E. J. (2000). Perceptual learning in development: Some basic concepts. *Ecological Psychology, 12,* 295–302.

Gibson, E. J. (2003). The world is so full of a number of things: On specification and perceptual learning. *Ecological Psychology, 15,* 283–287.

Gibson, E. J., & Walk, R. D. (1960). The "visual cliff." *Scientific American, 202,* 64–71.

Gibson, J. J. (1979). *The ecological approach to visual perception.* Boston: Houghton Mifflin.

Gil, A. G., Wagner, E. F., & Vega, W. A. (2000). Acculturation, familism and alcohol use among Latino adolescent males: Longitudinal relations. *Journal of Community Psychology, 28,* 443–458.

Giles, J. W., & Heyman, G. D. (2005). Young children's beliefs about the relationship between gender and aggressive behavior. *Child Development, 76,* 107–121.

Gillies, R. M. (2002). The residual effects of cooperative-learning experiences: A two-year follow-up. *Journal of Educational Research, 96,* 15–20.

Gillies, R. M. (2003). Structuring co-operative learning experiences in primary school. In R. M. Gillies & A. F. Ashman (Eds.), *Co-operative learning: The social and intellectual outcomes of learning in groups* (pp. 36–53). New York: Routledge.

Gillies, R. M. (2003). The behaviors, interactions, and perceptions of junior high school students during small-group learning. *Journal of Educational Psychology, 95,* 137–147.

Gillies, R. M., & Ashman, A. F. (1996). Teaching collaborative skills to primary school children in classroom-based workgroups. *Learning and Instruction, 6,* 187–200.

Gilligan, C. F. (1982). *In a different voice.* Cambridge, MA: Harvard University Press.

Gilliom, M., Shaw, D. S., Beck, J. E., Schonberg, M. A., & Lukon, J. L. (2002). Anger regulation in disadvantaged preschool boys: Strategies, antecedents, and the development of self-control. *Developmental Psychology, 38,* 222–235.

Ginsburg-Block, M. D., Rohrbeck, C. A., & Fantuzzo, J. W. (2006). A meta-analytic review of social, self-concept, and behavioral outcomes of peer-assisted learning. *Journal of Educational Psychology, 98,* 732–749.

Giuliani, A., Schöll, W. M., Basver, A., & Tasmussino, K. F. (2002). Mode of delivery and outcome of 699 term singleton breech deliveries at a single center. *American Journal of Obstetrics and Gynaecology, 187,* 1694–1698.

Glade, A. C., Bean, R. A., & Vira, R. (2005). A prime time for marital/relational intervention: A review of the transition to parenthood literature with treatment recommendations. *American Journal of Family Therapy, 33,* 319–336.

Gladstone, I. M., & Katz, V. L. (2004). The morbidity of the 34- to 35-week gestation: Should we reexamine the paradigm? *American Journal of Perinatology, 21,* 9–13.

Gladwell, M. (1998, February 2). The Pima paradox. *The New Yorker,* pp. 44–57.

Glasgow, K. L., Dornbusch, S. M., Troyer, L., Steinberg, L., & Ritter, P. L. (1997). Parenting styles, adolescents' attributions, and educational outcomes in nine heterogeneous high schools. *Child Development, 68,* 507–523.

Gleason, T. R. (2002). Social provisions of real and imaginary relationships in early childhood. *Developmental Psychology, 38,* 979–992.

Gleason, T. R., & Hohmann, L. M. (2006). Concepts of real and imaginary friendships in early childhood. *Social Development, 15,* 128–144.

Gleason, T. R., Sebanc, A. M., & Hartup, W. W. (2000). Imaginary companions of preschool children. *Developmental Psychology, 36,* 419–428.

Gleitman, L. R., Cassidy, K., Nappa, R., Papfragou, A., & Trueswell, J. C. (2005). Hard words. *Language Learning and Development, 1,* 23–64.

Gleitman, L. R., & Newport, E. (1996). *The invention of language by children.* Cambridge, MA: MIT Press.

Glover, V., & O'Connor, T. G. (2005). Effects of antenatal maternal stress or anxiety: From fetus to child. In B. Hopkins & S. P. Johnson (Eds.), *Prenatal development of postnatal functions* (pp. 221–245). Westport, CT: Praeger.

Glowinski, A. L., Madden, P. A. F., Bucholz, K. K., Lynskey, M. T., & Heath, A. C. (2003). Genetic epidemiology of self-reported lifetime DSM-IV major depressive disorder in a population-based twin sample of female adolescents. *Journal of Child Psychology and Psychiatry and Allied Disciplines, 44,* 988–996.

Gluckman, P. D., Sizonenko, S. V., & Bassett, N. S. (1999). The transition from fetus to neonate—an endocrine perspective. *Acta Paediatrica Supplement, 88*(428), 7–11.

Gnepp, J. (1983). Children's social sensitivity: Inferring emotions from conflicting cues. *Developmental Psychology, 19,* 805–814.

Godart, N. T., Perdereau, F., Curt, F., Rein, Z., Lang, F., & Venisse, J. L. (2006). Is major depressive episode related to anxiety disorders in anorexics and bulimics? *Comprehensive Psychiatry, 47,* 91–98.

Godfrey, K. M., & Barker, D. J. (2000). Fetal nutrition and adult disease. *American Journal of Clinical Nutrition, 71,* 1344S–1352S.

Godfrey, K. M., & Barker, D. J. (2001). Fetal programming and adult health. *Public Health Nutrition, 4,* 611–624.

Goelman, H., Doherty, G., Lero, D. S., LaGrange, A., & Tougas, J. (2000). *You bet I care! Caring and learning environments: Quality in child care centers across Canada.* Guelph, Ontario: Centre for Families, Work and Well-Being, University of Guelph.

Goering, J. (Ed.). (2003). Choosing a better life? *How public housing tenants selected a HUD experiment to improve their lives and those of their children: The Moving to Opportunity Demonstration Program.* Washington, DC: Urban Institute Press.

Goetz, T., Frenzel, A. C., Pekrun, R., & Hall, N. (2005). Emotional intelligence in the context of learning and achievement. In R. Schulze & R. D. Roberts (Eds.), *Emotional intelligence: An international handbook* (pp. 233–253). Göttingen, Germany: Hogrefe & Huber.

Gogate, L. J., & Bahrick, L. E. (1998). Intersensory redundancy facilitates learning of arbitrary relations between vowel sounds and objects in seven-month-old infants. *Journal of Experimental Child Psychology, 69,* 133–149.

Gogate, L. J., & Bahrick, L. E. (2001). Intersensory redundancy and 7-month-old infants' memory for arbitrary syllable–object relations. *Infancy, 2,* 219–231.

Goldberg, A. E., & Perry-Jenkins, M. (2003). Division of labor and working-class women's well-being across the transition to parenthood. *Journal of Family Psychology, 18,* 225–236.

Goldberg, M. C., Maurer, D., & Lewis, T. L. (2001). Developmental changes in attention: The effects of endogenous cueing and of distractors. *Developmental Science, 4,* 209–219.

Goldberg, S., Benoit, D., Blokland, K., & Madigan, S. (2003). Atypical maternal behavior, maternal representations, and infant disorganized attachment. *Development and Psychopathology, 15,* 239–257.

Goldbloom, R. B. (2004). *Screening for hemoglobinopathies in Canada.* Hamilton: McMaster University Medical Centre.

Goldenberg, C., Gallimore, R., Reese, L., & Garnier, H. (2001). Cause or effect? Immigrant Latino parents' aspirations and expectations, and their children's school performance. *American Educational Research Journal, 38,* 547–582.

Goldfield, B. A. (1987). Contributions of child and caregiver to referential and expressive language. *Applied Psycholinguistics, 8,* 267–280.

Goldin-Meadow, S., & Butcher, S. (2003). Pointing toward two-word speech in young children. In S. Kita (Ed.), *Pointing: Where language, culture, and cognition meet* (pp. 85–107). Mahwah, NJ: Erlbaum.

Goldscheider, F., & Goldscheider, C. (1999). *The changing transition to adulthood: Leaving and returning home.* Thousand Oaks, CA: Sage.

Goldschmidt, L., Richardson, G. A., Cornelius, M. D., & Day, N. L. (2004). Prenatal marijuana and alcohol exposure and academic achievement at age 10. *Neurotoxicology and Teratology, 26,* 521–532.

Goldsmith, L. T. (2000). Tracking trajectories of talent: Child prodigies growing up. In R. C. Friedman & B. M. Shore (Eds.), *Talents unfolding: Cognition and development* (pp. 89–122). Washington, DC: American Psychological Association.

Goldstein, E. (1979). Effect of same-sex and cross-sex role models on the subsequent academic productivity of scholars. *American Psychologist, 34,* 407–410.

Goldstein, S. E., Davis-Kean, P. E., & Eccles, J. S. (2005). Parents, peers, and problem behavior: A longitudinal investigation of the impact of relationship perceptions and characteristics on the development of adolescent problem behavior. *Developmental Psychology, 41,* 401–413.

Goleman, D. (1998). *Working with emotional intelligence.* New York: Bantam.

Golfier, F., Vaudoyer, F., Ecochard, R., Champion, F., Audra, P., & Raudrant, D. (2001). Planned vaginal delivery versus elective caesarean section in singleton term breech presentation: A study of 1116 cases. *European Journal of Obstetrics and Gyncecology, 98,* 186–192.

Golinkoff, R. M., & Hirsh-Pasek, K. (2006). Baby wordsmith: From associationist to social sophisticate. *Current Directions in Psychological Science, 15,* 30–33.

Golomb, C. (2004). *The child's creation of a pictorial world* (2nd ed.). Mahwah, NJ: Erlbaum.

Golombok, S., Lycett, E., MacCallum, F., Jadva, V., Murray, C., Rust, J., Abdalla, H., Jenkins, J., & Margar, R. (2004). Parenting of infants conceived by gamete donation. *Journal of Family Psychology, 18,* 443–452.

Golombok, S., & MacCallum, F. (2003). Practitioner review: Outcomes for parents and children following non-traditional conception: What do clinicians need to know? *Journal of Child Psychology and Psychiatry, 44,* 303–315.

Golombok, S., Perry, B., Burston, A., Murray, C., Mooney-Somers, J., Stevens, M., & Golding, J. (2003). Children with lesbian parents: A community study. *Developmental Psychology, 39,* 20–33.

Golombok, S., & Tasker, F. L. (1996). Do parents influence the sexual orientation of their children? Findings from a longitudinal study of lesbian families. *Developmental Psychology, 32,* 3–11.

Golub, M. S. (1996). Labor analgesia and infant brain development. Pharmacology, *Biochemistry, and Behavior, 55,* 619–628.

Gomez-Perez, E., & Ostrosky-Solis, F. (2006). Attention and memory evaluation across the life span: Heterogeneous effects of age and education. *Journal of Clinical and Experimental Neuropsychology, 28,* 477–494.

Gómez-Sanchiz, M., Canete, R., Rodero, I., Baeza, J. E., & Avilo, O. (2003). Influence of breast-feeding on mental

and psychomotor development. *Clinical Pediatrics, 42,* 35–42.

Göncü, A. (1993). Development of intersubjectivity in the dyadic play of preschoolers. *Early Childhood Research Quarterly, 8,* 99–116.

Göncü, A., Patt, M. B., & Kouba E. (2004). Understanding young children's pretend play in context. In P. K. Smith & C. H. Hart (Eds.), *Blackwell handbook of childhood social development* (pp. 418–437). Malden, MA: Blackwell.

Gonzales, N. A., Cauce, A. M., Friedman, R. J., & Mason, C. A. (1996). Family, peer, and neighborhood influences on academic achievement among African-American adolescents: One-year prospective effects. *American Journal of Community Psychology, 24,* 365–387.

Good, T. L., & Brophy, J. (2003). *Looking in classrooms* (9th ed.). Boston: Allyn and Bacon.

Goodlin-Jones, B. L., Burnham, M. M., & Anders, T. F. (2000). Sleep and sleep disturbances: Regulatory processes in infancy. In A. J. Sameroff, M. Lewis, & S. M. Miller (Eds.), *Handbook of developmental psychology* (2nd ed., pp. 309–325). New York: Kluwer.

Goodlin-Jones, B. L., Tassone, F., Gane, L. W., & Hagerman, R. J. (2004). Autistic spectrum disorder and the fragile X permutation. *Journal of Developmental and Behavioral Pediatrics, 25,* 392–398.

Goodman, G. S., Quas, J. A., Bulkley, J., & Shapiro, C. (1999). Innovations for child witnesses: A national survey. *Psychology, Public Policy, and Law, 5,* 255, 281.

Goodman, S. H., Gravitt, G. W., Jr., & Kaslow, N. J. (1995). Social problem solving: A moderator of the relation between negative life stress and depression symptoms in children. *Journal of Abnormal Child Psychology, 23,* 473–485.

Goodwin, M. H. (1998). Games of stance: Conflict and footing in hopscotch. In S. Hoyle & C. T. Adger (Eds.), *Language practices of older children* (pp. 23–46). New York: Oxford University Press.

Gootman, E. (2005, January 16). New York City: the politics of promotion. *New York Times.* Retrieved from www.nytimes.com/2005/01/16/education/edlife/EDGOOT.html

Gopnik, A., & Choi, S. (1990). Do linguistic differences lead to cognitive differences? A cross-linguistic study of semantic and cognitive development. *First Language, 11,* 199–215.

Gopnik, A., & Meltzoff, A. N. (1986). Relations between semantic and cognitive development in the one-word stage: The specificity hypothesis. *Child Development, 57,* 1040–1053.

Gopnik, A., & Meltzoff, A. N. (1987). The development of categorization in the second year and its relation to other cognitive and linguistic developments. *Child Development, 58,* 1523–1531.

Gopnik, A., & Nazzi, T. (2003). Words, kinds, and causal powers: A theory theory perspective on early naming and categorization. In D. H. Rakison & L. M. Oakes (Eds.), *Early category and concept development* (pp. 303–329). New York: Oxford University Press.

Gopnik, A., & Wellman, H. M. (1994). The 'theory' theory. In L. A. Hirschfeld & S. A. Gelman (Eds.), *Mapping the mind: Domain specificity in cognition and culture* (pp. 257–293). Cambridge, U.K.: Cambridge University Press.

Gordon, D. (2003). *The distribution of child poverty in the developing world: Report to UNICEF.* Bristol, U.K.: Centre for International Poverty Research, University of Bristol.

Gordon, R. A., Chase-Lansdale, P. L., & Brooks-Gunn, J. (2004). Extended households and the life course of young mothers: Understanding the associations using a sample of mothers with premature, low-birth-weight babies. *Child Development, 75,* 1013–1038.

Gore, S. A., Foster, J. A., DiLillo, V. G., Kirk, K., & West, D. S. (2003). Television viewing and snacking. *Eating Behaviors, 4,* 399–405.

Gormally, S., Barr, R. G., Wertheim, L., Alkawaf, R., Calinoiu, N., & Young, S. N. (2001). Contact and nutrient caregiving effects on newborn infant pain responses. *Developmental Medicine and Child Neurology, 43,* 28–38.

Goss, D. A., & Rainey, B. B. (1998). Relation of childhood myopia progression rates to time of year. *Journal of the American Optometric Association, 69,* 262–266.

Goswami, U. (1996). Analogical reasoning and cognitive development. In H. Reese (Ed.), *Advances in child*

development and behavior (Vol. 26, pp. 91–138). New York: Academic Press.

Goswami, U. (2000). Phonological and lexical processes. In M. L. Kamil & P. B. Mosenthal (Eds.), *Handbook of reading research* (Vol. 3, pp. 251–284). Mahwah, NJ: Erlbaum.

Gott, V. L. (1998). Antoine Marfan and his syndrome: One hundred years later. *Maryland Medical Journal, 47,* 247–252.

Gottesman, I. I. (1963). Genetic aspects of intelligent behavior. In N. Ellis (Ed.), *Handbook of mental deficiency* (pp. 253–296). New York: McGraw-Hill.

Gottesman, I. I. (1991). *Schizophrenia genetics: The origins of madness.* New York: Freeman.

Gottfredson, L. S. (2005). Applying Gottfredson's theory of circumscription and compromise in career guidance and counseling. In S. D. Brown & R. W. Lent (Eds.), *Career development and counseling* (pp. 71–100). Hoboken, NJ: Wiley.

Gottfried, A. E., Gottfried, A. W., & Bathurst, K. (2002). Maternal and dual-earner employment status and parenting. In M. H. Bornstein (Ed.), *Handbook of parenting: Vol. 3. Being and becoming a parent* (2nd ed., pp. 207–230). Mahwah, NJ: Erlbaum.

Gottlieb, G. (1998). Normally occurring environmental and behavioral influences on gene activity: From central dogma to probabilistic epigenesis. *Psychological Review, 105,* 792–802.

Gottlieb, G. (2000). Environmental and behavioral influences on gene activity. *Current Directions in Psychological Science, 9,* 93–97.

Gottlieb, G. (2002). *Individual development and evolution: The genesis of novel behavior.* New York: Oxford University Press.

Gottlieb, G. (2003). On making behavioral genetics truly developmental. *Human Development, 46,* 337–355.

Gottlieb, G., Wahlsten, D., & Lickliter, R. (2006). The significance of biology for human development: A developmental psychobiological systems of view. In R. M. Lerner (Ed.), *Handbook of child psychology: Vol. 1. Theoretical models of human development* (6th ed., pp. 210–257). Hoboken, NJ: Wiley.

Gottman, J., Coan, J., Carrere, S., & Swanson, C. (1998). Predicting marital happiness and stability from newlywed interactions. *Journal of Marriage and the Family, 60,* 5–22.

Gould, J. L., & Keeton, W. T. (1996). *Biological science* (6th ed.). New York: Norton.

Gould, M., Jamieson, P., & Romer, D. (2003). Media contagion and suicide among the young. *American Behavioral Scientist, 46,* 1269–1284.

Govaerts, P. J., De Beukelaer, C., Daemers, K., De Ceulaer, G., Yperman, M., Somers, T., Schatteman, I., & Offeciers, F. E. (2002). Outcome of cochlear implantation at different ages from 0 to 6 years. *Otology and Neurotology, 23,* 885–890.

Graber, J. A. (2003). Puberty in context. In C. Hayward (Ed.), *Gender differences at puberty* (pp. 307–325). New York: Cambridge University Press.

Graber, J. A. (2004). Internalizing problems during adolescence. In R. M. Lerner & L. Steinberg (Eds.), *Handbook of adolescent psychology* (2nd ed., pp. 587–626). Hoboken, NJ: Wiley.

Graber, J. A., Brooks-Gunn, J., & Warren, M. P. (2006). Pubertal effects on adjustment in girls: Moving from demonstrating effects to identifying pathways. *Journal of Youth and Adolescence, 35,* 413–423.

Graber, J. A., Lewinsohn, P. M., Seeley, J. R., & Brooks-Gunn, J. (1997). Is psychopathology associated with the timing of pubertal development? *Journal of the American Academy of Child and Adolescent Psychiatry, 36,* 1768–1776.

Graber, J. A., Seeley, J. R., Brooks-Gunn, J., & Lewinsohn, P. M. (2004). Is pubertal timing associated with psychopathology in young adulthood? *Journal of the American Academy of Child and Adolescent Psychiatry, 43,* 718–726.

Grady, M. A., & Bloom, K. C. (2004). Pregnancy outcomes of adolescents enrolled in a CenteringPregnancy program. *Journal of Midwifery and Women's Health, 49,* 412–420.

Gralinski, J. H., & Kopp, C. B. (1993). Everyday rules for behavior: Mothers' requests to young children. *Developmental Psychology, 29,* 573–584.

Granic, I., Hollenstein, T., Dishion, T. J., & Patterson, G. R. (2003). Longitudinal analysis of flexibility and reorganization in early adolescence: A dynamic systems study of family interactions. *Developmental Psychology, 39,* 606–617.

Granier-Deferre, C., Bassereau, S., Ribeiro, A., Jacquet, A.-Y., & Lecanuet, J.-P. (2003). *Cardiac "orienting" response in fetuses and babies following in utero melody-learning.* Paper presented at the 11th European Conference on Developmental Psychology, Milan, Italy.

Granillo, T., Jones-Rodriguez, G., & Carvajal, S. C. (2005). Prevalence of eating disorders in Latina adolescents: Associations with substance use and other correlates. *Journal of Adolescent Health, 36,* 214–220.

Granot, M., Spitzer, A., Aroian, K. J., Ravid, C., Tamir, B., & Noam, R. (1996). Pregnancy and delivery practices and beliefs of Ethiopian immigrant women in Israel. *Western Journal of Nursing Research, 18,* 299–313.

Grant, H., & Dweck, C. S. (2001). Cross-cultural response to failure: Considering outcome attributions with different goals. In F. Salili & C. Chiu (Eds.), *Student motivation: The culture and context of learning* (pp. 203–219). New York: Plenum.

Grant, K., O'Koon, J., Davis, T., Roache, N., Poindexter, L., & Armstrong, M. (2000). Protective factors affecting low-income urban African American youth exposed to stress. *Journal of Early Adolescence, 20,* 388–418.

Grantham-McGregor, S., & Ani, C. (2001). A review of studies on the effect of iron deficiency on cognitive development in children. *Journal of Nutrition, 131,* 649S–668S.

Grantham-McGregor, S., Powell, C., Walker, S., Chang, S., & Fletcher, P. (1994). The long-term follow-up of severely malnourished children who participated in an intervention program. *Child Development, 65,* 428–439.

Grantham-McGregor, S., Schofield, W., & Powell, C. (1987). Development of severely malnourished children who received psychosocial stimulation: Six-year follow-up. *Pediatrics, 79,* 247–254.

Grantham-McGregor, S. M., Walker, S. P., & Chang, S. (2000). Nutritional deficiencies and later behavioral development. *Proceedings of the Nutrition Society, 59,* 47–54.

Grattan, M. P., De Vos, E., Levy, J., & McClintock, M. K. (1992). Asymmetric action in the human newborn: Sex differences in patterns of organization. *Child Development, 63,* 273–289.

Graue, M. E., & DiPerna, J. (2000). Redshirting and early retention: Who gets the "gift of time" and what are its outcomes? *American Educational Research Journal, 37,* 509–534.

Gray, K. A., Day, N. L., Leech, S., & Richardson, G. A. (2005). Prenatal marijuana exposure: Effect on child depressive symptoms at ten years of age. *Neurotoxicology and Teratology, 27,* 439–448.

Gray, M. R., & Steinberg, L. (1999). Unpacking authoritative parenting: Reassessing a multidimensional construct. *Journal of Marriage and the Family, 61,* 574–587.

Gray-Little, B., & Carels, R. (1997). The effects of racial and socioeconomic consonance on self-esteem and achievement in elementary, junior high, and high school students. *Journal of Research on Adolescence, 7,* 109–131.

Gray-Little, B., & Hafdahl, A. R. (2000). Factors influencing racial comparisons of self-esteem: A quantitative review. *Psychological Bulletin, 126,* 26–54.

Green, G. E., Irwin, J. R., & Gustafson, G. E. (2000). Acoustic cry analysis, neonatal status and long-term developmental outcomes. In R. G. Barr, B. Hopkins, & J. A. Green (Eds.), *Crying as a sign, a symptom, and a signal* (pp. 137–156). Cambridge, U.K.: Cambridge University Press.

Greenberger, E., Chen, C., Tally, S. R., & Dong, Q. (2000). Family, peer, and individual correlates of depressive symptomatology among U.S. and Chinese adolescents. *Journal of Counseling and Clinical Psychology, 68,* 209–219.

Greenberger, E., O'Neil, R., & Nagel, S. K. (1994). Linking workplace and homeplace: Relations between the nature of adults' work and their parenting behaviors. *Developmental Psychology, 30,* 990–1002.

Greendorfer, S. L., Lewko, J. H., & Rosengren, K. S. (1996). Family and gender-based socialization of children and adolescents. In F. L. Smoll & R. E. Smith (Eds.), *Children and youth in sport: A biopsychological perspective* (pp. 89–111). Dubuque, IA: Brown & Benchmark.

Greene, K., Krcmar, M., Walters, L. H., Rubin, D. L., Hale, J., & Hale, L. (2000). Targeting adolescent risk-taking behaviors: The contributions of egocentrism and sensationseeking. *Journal of Adolescence, 23,* 439–461.

Greene, M. L., Way, N., & Pahl, K. (2006). Trajectories of perceived adult and peer discrimination among Black, Latino, and Asian American adolescents: Patterns and psychological correlates. *Developmental Psychology, 42,* 218–238.

Greene, S. M., Anderson, E., Hetherington, E. M., Forgath, M. S., & DeGarmo, D. S. (2003). Risk and resilience after divorce. In R. Walsh (Ed.), *Normal family processes* (pp. 96–120). New York: Guilford.

Greenfield, P. M. (1992, June). *Notes and references for developmental psychology.* Conference on Making Basic Texts in Psychology More Culture-Inclusive and CultureSensitive, Western Washington University, Bellingham, WA.

Greenfield, P. M. (2004). *Weaving generations together: Evolving creativity in the Maya of Chiapas.* Santa Fe, NM: School of American Research.

Greenfield, P. M., Keller, H., Fuligni, A., & Maynard, A. (2003). Cultural pathways through universal development. *Annual Review of Psychology, 54,* 461–490.

Greenfield, P. M., Maynard, A. E., & Childs, C. P. (2000). History, culture, learning, and development. *Cross-Cultural Research, 34,* 351–374.

Greenfield, P. M., Suzuki, L. K., & Rothstein-Fish, C. (2006). Cultural pathways through human development. In K. A. Renninger & I. E. Sigel (Eds.), *Handbook of child psychology: Vol. 4. Child psychology in practice* (6th ed., pp. 655–699). Hoboken, NJ: Wiley.

Greenhill, L. L., Halperin, J. M., & Abikoff, H. (1999). Stimulant Medications. *Journal of the American Academy of Child and Adolescent Psychiatry, 38,* 503–512.

Greenough, W. T., & Black, J. E. (1992). Induction of brain structure by experience: Substrates for cognitive development. In M. Gunnar & C. A. Nelson (Eds.), *Minnesota symposia on child psychology* (pp. 155–200). Hillsdale, NJ: Erlbaum.

Greenspan, S. I., & Shanker, S. G. (2004). *The first idea: How symbols, language, and intelligence evolved from our primate ancestors to modern humans.* Cambridge, MA: Da Capo Press.

Greer, T., & Lockman, J. J. (1998). Using writing instruments: Invariances in young children and adults. *Child Development, 69,* 888–902.

Gregg, V., Gibbs, J. C., & Fuller, D. (1994). Patterns of developmental delay in moral judgment by male and female delinquents. *Merrill-Palmer Quarterly, 40,* 538–553.

Gregory, A., & Weinstein, R. S. (2004). Connection and regulation at home and in school: predicting growth in achievement for adolescents. *Journal of Adolescent Research, 19,* 405–427.

Gregory, A. M., Eley, T. C., O'Connor, T. G., & Plomin, R. (2004). Etiologies of associations between childhood sleep and behavioral problems in a large twin sample. *Journal of the American Academy of Child and Adolescent Psychiatry, 43,* 744–751.

Grief, G. L., Hrabowski, F. A., & Maton, K. I. (1998). African-American fathers of high-achieving sons: Using outstanding members of an at-risk population to guide intervention. *Families in Society, 79,* 45–52.

Griffin, K. W., Botvin, G. J., Nichols, T. R., & Doyle, M. M. (2003). Effectiveness of a universal drug abuse prevention approach for youth at high risk for substance use initiation. *Preventive Medicine, 36,* 1–7.

Grigorenko, E. L. (2000). Heritability and intelligence. In R. J. Sternberg (Ed.), *Handbook of intelligence* (pp. 53–91). Cambridge, U.K.: Cambridge University Press.

Grigorenko, E. L., & Sternberg, R. J. (1998). Dynamic testing. *Psychological Bulletin, 124,* 75–111.

Grob, A., & Flammer, A. (1999). Macrosocial context and adolescents' perceived control. In F. D. Alsaker & A. Flammer (Eds.), *The adolescent experience* (pp. 99–114). Mahwah, NJ: Erlbaum.

Grody, W. W. (1999). Cystic fibrosis: Molecular diagnosis, population screening, and public policy. *Archives of Pathology and Laboratory Medicine, 123,* 1041–1046.

Grolnick, W. S., Bridges, L. J., & Connell, J. P. (1996). Emotion regulation in two-year-olds: Strategies and emotional expression in four contexts. *Child Development, 67,* 928–941.

Grolnick, W. S., Kurowski, C. O., Dunlap, K. G., & Hevey, C. (2000). Parental resources and the transition to junior high. *Journal of Research on Adolescence, 10,* 466–488.

Groome, L. J., Swiber, M. J., Holland, S. B., Bentz, L. S., Atterbury, J. L., & Trimm, R. F., III. (1999). Spontaneous motor activity in the perinatal infant before and after birth: Stability in individual differences. *Developmental Psychobiology, 35,* 15–24.

Grossmann, K., Grossmann, K. E., Fremmer-Bombik, E., Kindler, H., Scheuerer-Englisch, H., & Zimmermann, P. (2002). The uniqueness of the child–father attachment relationship: Fathers' sensitive and challenging play as a pivotal variable in a 16-year longitudinal study. *Social Development, 11,* 307–331.

Grossmann, K., Grossmann, K. E., Spangler, G., Suess, G., & Unzner, L. (1985). Maternal sensitivity and newborns' orientation responses as related to quality of attachment in Northern Germany. In I. Bretherton & E. Waters (Eds.), Growing points of attachment theory and research. *Monographs of the Society for Research in Child Development, 50*(1–2, Serial No. 209).

Grotevant, H. D. (1998). Adolescent development in family contexts. In N. Eisenberg (Ed.), *Handbook of child psychology: Vol. 3. Social, emotional, and personality development* (5th ed., pp. 1097–1149). New York: Wiley.

Grotevant, H. D., & Cooper, C. R. (1998). Individuality and connectedness in adolescent development: Review and prospects for research on identity, relationships, and context. In E. Skoe & A. von der Lippe (Eds.), *Personality development in adolescence.* London: Routledge & Kegan Paul.

Grotpeter, J. K., & Crick, N. R. (1996). Relational aggression, overt aggression, and friendship. *Child Development, 67,* 2328–2338.

Grow-Maienza, J., Hahn, D.-D., & Joo, C.-A. (2001). Mathematics instruction in Korean primary schools: Structures, processes, and a linguistic analysis of questioning. *Journal of Educational Psychology, 93,* 363–376.

Grunau, R. E., Whitfield, M. F., & Fay, T. B. (2004). Psychosocial and academic characteristics of extremely low birth weight ([Unknown character: Geneva 178]800g) adolescents who are free of major impairment compared with term-born control subjects. *Pediatrics, 114,* E725–E732.

Grusec, J. E. (1988). *Social development: History, theory, and research.* New York: Springer-Verlag.

Grusec, J. E., & Goodnow, J. J. (1994). Impact of parental discipline methods on the child's internalization of values: A reconceptualization of current points of view. *Developmental Psychology, 30,* 4–19.

Grych, J. H., & Clark, R. (1999). Maternal employment and development of the father–infant relationship in the first year. *Developmental Psychology, 35,* 893–903.

Guay, F., Marsh, H. W., & Boivin, M. (2003). Academic self-concept and academic achievement: Developmental perspectives on their causal ordering. *Journal of Educational Psychology, 95,* 124–136.

Guilford, J. P. (1985). The structure-of-intellect model. In B. B. Wolman (Ed.), *Handbook of intelligence* (pp. 225–266). New York: Wiley.

Guilleminault, C., Palombini, L., Pelayo, R., & Chervin, R. D. (2003). Sleepwalking and sleep terrors in prepubertal children: What triggers them? *Pediatrics, 111,* e17–e25.

Gullone, E. (2000). The development of normal fear: A century of research. *Clinical Psychology Review, 20,* 429–451.

Gunn, A. J. (2000). Cerebral hypothermia for prevention of brain injury following perinatal asphyxia. *Current Opinion in Pediatrics, 12,* 111–115.

Gunnar, M. R., & Cheatham, C. L. (2003). Brain and behavior interfaces: Stress and the developing brain. *Infant Mental Health Journal, 24,* 195–211.

Gunnar, M. R., Morison, S. J., Chisholm, K., & Schuder, M. (2001). Salivary cortisol levels in children adopted from Romanian orphanages. *Development and Psychopathology, 13,* 611–628.

Gunnar, M. R., & Nelson, C. A. (1994). Event-related potentials in year-old infants: Relations with emotionality and cortisol. *Child Development, 65,* 80–94.

Gunnoe, M. L., & Mariner, C. L. (1997). Toward a developmental-contextual model of the effects of parental spanking on children's aggression. *Archives of Pediatrics and Adolescent Medicine, 151,* 768–775.

Guo, G., & VanWey, L. K. (1999). Sibship size and intellectual development: Is the relationship causal? *American Sociological Review, 64*, 169–187.

Gure, A., Ucanok, Z., & Sayil, M. (2006). The associations among perceived pubertal timing, parental relations and self-perception in Turkish adolescents. *Journal of Youth and Adolescence, 35*, 541–550.

Gustafson, G. E., Green, J. A., & Cleland, J. W. (1994). Robustness of individual identity in the cries of human infants. *Developmental Psychobiology, 27*, 1–9.

Gustafson, G. E., Wood, R. M., & Green, J. A. (2000). Can we hear the causes of infants' crying? In R. G. Barr & B. Hopkins (Eds.), *Crying as a sign, a symptom, and a signal: Clinical, emotional, and developmental aspects of infant and toddler crying* (pp. 8–22). New York: Cambridge University Press.

Gutman, L. M., & Midgley, C. (2000). The role of protective factors in supporting the academic achievement of poor African-American students during the middle school transition. *Journal of Youth and Adolescence, 29*, 223–248.

Gutman, L. M., Sameroff, A. J., & Cole, R. (2003). Academic growth curve trajectories from 1st grade to 12th grade: Effects of multiple social risk factors and preschool child factors. *Developmental Psychology, 39*, 777–790.

Guttentag, R., & Ferrell, J. (2004). Reality compared with its alternatives: Age differences in judgments of regret and relief. *Developmental Psychology, 40*, 764–775.

Guyda, H. J. (1999). Four decades of growth hormone therapy for short children: What have we achieved? *Journal of Clinical Endocrinology and Metabolism, 84*, 4307–4316.

Gwiazda, J., & Birch, E. E. (2001). Perceptual development: Vision. In E. B. Goldstein (Ed.), *Blackwell handbook of perception* (pp. 636–668). Oxford, U.K.: Blackwell.

Hack, M., Flannery, D. J., Schluchter, M., Cartar, L., Borawski, E., & Klein, N. (2002). Outcomes in young adulthood for very-low-birth-weight infants. *New England Journal of Medicine, 346*, 149–157.

Hack, M., & Klein, N. (2006). Young adult attainments of preterm infants. *Journal of the American Medical Association, 295*, 695–696.

Hacker, D. J. (1997). Comprehension monitoring of written discourse across early-to-middle adolescence. *Reading and Writing, 9*, 207–240.

Hagekull, B., Bohlin, G., & Rydell, A. (1997). Maternal sensitivity, infant temperament, and the development of early feeding problems. *Infant Mental Health Journal, 18*, 92–106.

Haight, W. L., & Miller, P. J. (1993). *Pretending at home: Early development in a sociocultural context.* Albany: State University of New York Press.

Hainline, L. (1998). The development of basic visual abilities. In A. Slater (Ed.), *Perceptual development: Visual, auditory, and speech perception in infancy* (pp. 37–44). Hove, U.K.: Psychology Press.

Haith, M. M. (1999). Some thoughts about claims for innate knowledge and infant physical reasoning. *Developmental Science, 2*, 153–156.

Hakuta, K. (1999). The debate on bilingual education. *Developmental and Behavioral Pediatrics, 20*, 36–37.

Hakuta, K., Bialystok, E., & Wiley, E. (2003). Critical evidence: A test of the critical period hypothesis for second-language acquisition. *Psychological Science, 14*, 31–38.

Halberstadt, A. G., Denham, S. A., & Dunsmore, J. C. (2001). Affective social competence. *Social Development, 10*, 79–119.

Hale, C. M., & Tager-Flusberg, H. (2003). The influence of language on theory of mind: A training study. *Developmental Science, 6*, 346–359.

Hales, V. N., & Ozanne, S. E. (2003). The dangerous road of catch-up growth. *Journal of Physiology, 547*, 5–10.

Halfon, N., & McLearn, K. T. (2002). Families with children under 3: What we know and implications for results and policy. In N. Halfon & K. T. McLearn (Eds.), *Child rearing in America: Challenges facing parents with young children* (pp. 367–412). New York: Cambridge University Press.

Halford, G. S. (2002). Information-processing models of cognitive development. In U. Goswami (Ed.), *Blackwell handbook of childhood cognitive development* (pp. 555–574). Malden, MA: Blackwell.

Halford, G. S. (2005). Development of thinking. In K. J. Holyoak & R. G. Morrison (Eds.), *The Cambridge handbook of thinking and reasoning* (pp. 529–558). New York: Cambridge University Press.

Halford, G. S., & Andrews, G. (2006). Reasoning and problem solving. In D. Kuhn & R. Siegler (Eds.), *Handbook of child psychology: Vol. 2. Cognition, perception, and language* (6th ed., pp. 557–608). Hoboken, NJ: Wiley.

Halford, G. S., Wilson, W. H., Phillips, S. (1998). Processing capacity defined by relational complexity: Implications for comparative, developmental, and cognitive psychology. *Behavioral and Brain Sciences, 21*, 803–864.

Hall, D. G., Burns, T., & Pawluski, J. (2003). Input and word learning: Caregivers' sensitivity to lexical category distinctions. *Journal of Child Language, 30*, 711–729.

Hall, D. G., & Graham, S. A. (1999). Lexical form class information guides word-to-object mapping in preschoolers. *Child Development, 70*, 78–91.

Hall, G. S. (1904). *Adolescence.* New York: Appleton-Century-Crofts.

Hall, J. G. (2003). Twinning. *Lancet, 362*, 735–743.

Halle, T. G. (2003). Emotional development and well-being. In M. H. Bornstein, L. Davidson, C. L. M. Keyes, K. A. Moore, & the Center for Child Well-Being (Eds.), *Well-being: Positive development across the life course* (pp. 125–138). Mahwah, NJ: Erlbaum.

Haller, J. (2005). Vitamins and brain function. In H. R. Lieberman, R. B. Kanarek, & C. Prasad (2005). *Nutritional neuroscience* (pp. 207–233). Philadelphia: Taylor & Francis.

Hallett, M. (2000). Brain plasticity and recovery from hemiplegia. *Journal of Medical Speech-Language Pathology, 9*, 107–115.

Halliday, J. L., Watson, L. F., Lumley, J., Danks, D. M., & Sheffield, L. S. (1995). New estimates of Down syndrome risks at chorionic villus sampling, amniocentesis, and live birth in women of advanced maternal age from a uniquely defined population. *Prenatal Diagnosis, 15*, 455–465.

Hallinan, M. T., & Kubitschek, W. N. (1999). Curriculum differentiation and high school achievement. *Social Psychology of Education, 3*, 41–62.

Halpern, C. T., Udry, J. R., & Suchindran, C. (1997). Testosterone predicts initiation of coitus in adolescent females. *Psychosomatic Medicine, 59*, 161–171.

Halpern, D. F. (2000). *Sex differences in cognitive abilities* (3rd ed.). Mahwah, NJ: Erlbaum.

Halpern, D. F. (2004). A cognitive-process taxonomy for sex differences in cognitive abilities. *Current Directions in Psychological Science, 13*, 135–139.

Halpern, D. F., & Collaer, M. L. (2005). Sex differences in visuospatial abilities: More than meets the eye. In P. Shah & A. Miyake (Eds.), *Handbook of visuospatial thinking* (pp. 170–212). New York: Cambridge University Press.

Halpern, D. F., Wai, J., & Saw, A. (2005). A psychobiosocial model: Why females are sometimes greater than and sometimes less than males in math achievement. In D. F. Halpern, J. Wai, & A. Saw (Eds.), *Gender differences in mathematics: An integrative psychological approach* (pp. 48–72). New York: Cambridge University Press.

Halpern-Felsher, B. L., Biehl, M., Kropp, R. Y., & Rubinstein, M. L. (2004). Perceived risks and benefits of smoking: Differences among adolescents with different smoking experiences and intentions. *Preventive Medicine, 39*, 559–567.

Halpern-Felsher, B. L., & Cauffman, E. (2001). Costs and benefits of a decision: Decision-making competence in adolescents and adults. *Journal of Applied Developmental Psychology, 22*, 257–273.

Hamer, D. H., Hu, S., Magnuson, V. L., Hu, N., & Pattatucci, A. M. L. (1993). A linkage between DNA markers on the X chromosome and male sexual orientation. *Science, 261*, 321–327.

Hamilton, B. E., Ventura, S. J., Martin, J. A., & Sutton, P. D. (2005). Preliminary births for 2004. *Health E-Stats.* Retrieved from www.cdc.gov/nchs/products/pubs/pubd/hestats/prelim_births/prelim_births04.htm

Hamilton, C. E. (2000). Continuity and discontinuity of attachment from infancy through adolescence. *Child Development, 71*, 690–694.

Hamilton, H. A. (2005). Extended families and adolescent well-being. *Journal of Adolescent Health, 36*, 260–266.

Hamilton, S. F., & Hamilton, M. A. (2000). Research, intervention, and social change: Improving adolescents' career opportunities. In L. J. Crockett & R. K. Silbereisen (Eds.), *Negotiating adolescence in times of social change* (pp. 267–283). New York: Cambridge University Press.

Hamm, J. V. (2000). Do birds of a feather flock together? The variable bases for African American, Asian American, and European American adolescents' selection of similar friends. *Developmental Psychology, 36*, 209–219.

Hammes, B., & Laitman, C. J. (2003). Diethylstilbestrol (DES) update: Recommendations for the identification and management of DES-exposed individuals. *Journal of Midwifery and Women's Health, 48*, 19–29.

Han, W.-J., & Waldfogel, J. (2003). Parental leave: The impact of recent legislation on parents' leave taking. *Demography, 40*, 191–200.

Hanawalt, B. A. (1993). *Growing up in medieval London: The experience of childhood in history.* New York: Oxford University Press.

Hanawalt, B. A. (2003). The child in the Middle Ages and the Renaissance. In W. Koops & M. Zuckerman (Eds.), *Beyond the century of childhood: Cultural history and developmental psychology.* Philadelphia: University of Pennsylvania Press.

Hanel, M. L., & Wevrick, R. (2001). The role of genomic imprinting in human developmental disorders: Lessons from Prader-Willi syndrome. *Clinical Genetics, 59*, 156–164.

Hanke, W., Sobala, W., & Kalinka, J. (2004). Environmental tobacco smoke exposure among pregnant women: Impact on fetal biometry at 20–24 weeks of gestation and newborn child's birth weight. *International Archives of Occupational and Environmental Health, 77*, 47–52.

Hankin, B. L., & Abela, J. R. Z. (2005). Depression from childhood through adolescence and adulthood.: A developmental vulnerability and stress perspective. In B. L. Hankin & J. R. Z. Abela (Eds.), *Development of psychopathology: A vulnerability-stress perspective* (pp. 245–288). Thousand Oaks, CA: Sage.

Hannon, E. E., & Johnson, S. P. (2004). Infants use meter to categorize rhythms and melodies: Implications for musical structure learning. *Cognitive Psychology, 50*, 354–377.

Hannon, E. E., & Trehub, S. E. (2005a). Metrical categories in infancy and adulthood. *Psychological Science, 16*, 48–55.

Hannon, E. E., & Trehub, S. E. (2005b). Tuning in to musical rhythms: Infants learn more readily than adults. *Proceedings of the National Academy of Sciences, 102*, 12639–12643.

Hannon, T. S., Rao, G., & Arslanian, S. A. (2005). Childhood obesity and Type 2 diabetes mellitus. *Pediatrics, 116*, 473–480.

Hansen, M., Janssen, I., Schiff, A., Zee, P. C., & Dubocovich, M. L. (2005). The impact of school daily schedule on adolescent sleep. *Pediatrics, 115*, 1555–1561.

Hanson, T. N., Corbet, A., & Ballard, R. A. (2005). Disorders of the chest wall, pleural cavity, and diaphragm. In H. W. Taeusch, R. A. Ballard & C. A. Gleason (Eds.), *Avery's diseases of the newborn* (pp. 57–70). Philadelphia: Saunders.

Hanvey, L., & Kunz, J. L. (2000). *Immigrant youth in Canada.* Toronto, ON: Canadian Council on Social Development.

Harari, M. D., & Moulden, A. (2000). Nocturnal enuresis: What is happening? *Journal of Paediatrics and Child Health, 36*, 78–81.

Hardre, P. L., & Reeve, J. (2003). A motivational model of rural students' intentions to persist in, versus drop out of, high school. *Journal of Educational Psychology, 95*, 347–356.

Hardy, C. L., Bukowski, W. M., & Sippola, L. K. (2002). Stability and change in peer relationships during the transition to middle-level school. *Journal of Early Adolescence, 22*, 117–142.

Hardy, J. B., Astone, N. M., Brooks-Gunn, J., Shapiro, S., & Miller, T. L. (1998). Like mother, like child: Intergenerational patterns of age at first birth and associations with childhood and adolescent characteristics and adult outcomes in the second generation. *Developmental Psychology, 34*, 1220–1232.

Harley, B., & Jean, G. (1999). Vocabulary skills of French immersion students in their second language. *Zeitschrift für Interkulterellen Fremdsprachenunterricht, 4*(2). Retrieved from www.ualberta.ca

Harley, K., & Reese, E. (1999). Origins of autobiographical memory. *Developmental Psychology, 35*, 1338–1348.

Harlow, H. F., & Zimmerman, R. (1959). Affectional responses in the infant monkey. *Science, 130,* 421–432.

Harold, G. T., Shelton, K. H., Goeke-Morey, M. C., & Cummings, E. M. (2004). Marital conflict, child emotional security about family relationships, and child adjustment. *Social Development, 13,* 350–376.

Harris, G. (1997). Development of taste perception and appetite regulation. In G. Bremner, A. Slater, & G. Butterworth (Eds.), *Infant development: Recent advances* (pp. 9–30). East Sussex, U.K.: Erlbaum.

Harris, J. R. (1998). *The nurture assumption: Why children turn out the way they do.* New York: Free Press.

Harris, P. L. (2006). Social cognition. In D. Kuhn, & R. S. Siegler (Eds.), *Handbook of child psychology: Vol. 2: Cognition, perception, and language* (6th ed., pp. 811–858). Hoboken, NJ: Wiley.

Harris, P. L., Brown, E., Marriott, C., Whitall, S., & Harmer, S. (1991). Monsters, ghosts and witches: Testing the limits of the fantasy–reality distinction in young children. *British Journal of Developmental Psychology, 9,* 105–123.

Harris, P. L., & Leevers, H. J. (2000). Reasoning from false premises. In P. Mitchell & K. J. Riggs (Eds.), *Children's reasoning and the mind* (pp. 67–99). Hove, U.K.: Psychology Press.

Harris, Y. R., & Graham, J. A. (2007). *The African American child: Development and challenges.* New York: Springer.

Harrison, A. O., Wilson, M. N., Pine, C. J., Chan, S. Q., & Buriel, R. (1994). Family ecologies of ethnic minority children. In G. Handel & G. G. Whitchurch (Eds.), *The psychosocial interior of the family* (pp. 187–210). New York: Aldine De Gruyter.

Harrist, A. W., Zaia, A. F., Bates, J. E., Dodge, K. A., & Pettit, G. S. (1997). Subtypes of social withdrawal in early childhood: Sociometric status and social-cognitive differences across four years. *Child Development, 68,* 278–294.

Hart, B. (2004). What toddlers talk about. *First Language, 24,* 91–106.

Hart, B., & Risley, T. R. (1995). *Meaningful differences in the everyday experience of young American children.* Baltimore: Paul H. Brookes.

Hart, C. H., Burts, D. C., Durland, M. A., Charlesworth, R., DeWolf, M., & Fleege, P. O. (1998). Stress behaviors and activity type participation of preschoolers in more and less developmentally appropriate classrooms: SES and sex differences. *Journal of Research in Childhood Education, 13.*

Hart, C. H., Newell, L. D., & Olsen, S. F. (2003). Parenting skills and social–communicative competence in childhood. In J. O. Greene & B. R. Burleson (Eds.), *Handbook of communication and social interaction skills* (pp. 753–797). Mahwah, NJ: Erlbaum.

Hart, C. H., Yang, C., Charlesworth, R., & Burts, D. C. (2003, April). *Kindergarten teaching practices: Associations with later child academic and social/emotional adjustment to school.* Paper presented at the biennial meeting of the Society for Research in Child Development, Tampa, FL.

Hart, C. H., Yang, C., Nelson, L. J., Robinson, C. C., Olsen, J. A., Nelson, D. A., et al. (2000). Peer acceptance in early childhood and subtypes of socially withdrawn behavior in China, Russia and the United States. *International Journal of Behavioral Development, 24,* 73–81.

Hart, D., & Fegley, S. (1995). Prosocial behavior and caring in adolescence: Relations to self-understanding and social judgment. *Child Development, 66,* 1346–1359.

Hart, S., Field, T., & Roitfarb, M. (1999). Depressed mothers' assessments of their neonates' behaviors. *Infant Mental Health Journal, 20,* 200–210.

Harter, S. (1998). The development of self-representations. In N. Eisenberg (Ed.), *Handbook of child psychology: Vol. 3. Social, emotional, and personality development* (5th ed., pp. 553–618). New York: Wiley.

Harter, S. (1999). *The construction of self: A developmental perspective.* New York: Guilford.

Harter, S. (2003). The development of self-representations during childhood and adolescence. In M. R. Leary & J. P. Tangney (Eds.), *Handbook of self and identity* (pp. 610–642). New York: Guilford.

Harter, S. (2006). The self. In N. Eisenberg (Ed.), *Handbook of child psychology: Vol. 3. Social, emotional, and personality development* (6th ed., pp. 505–570). Hoboken, NJ: Wiley.

Harter, S., & Whitesell, N. (1989). Developmental changes in children's understanding of simple, multiple, and blended emotion concepts. In C. Saarni & P. Harris (Eds.), *Children's understanding of emotion* (pp. 81–116). Cambridge, U.K.: Cambridge University Press.

Harter, S., & Whitesell, N. R. (2003). Beyond the debate: Why some adolescents report stable self-worth over time and situation, whereas others report changes in self-worth. *Journal of Personality, 71,* 1027–1058.

Hartshorn, K., Rovee-Collier, C., Gerhardstein, P., Bhatt, R. S., Klein, P. J., Aaron, F., Wondoloski, T. L., & Wurtzel, N. (1998a). Developmental changes in the specificity of memory over the first year of life. *Developmental Psychobiology, 33,* 61–78.

Hartshorn, K., Rovee-Collier, C., Gerhardstein, P., Bhatt, R. S., Wondoloski, T. L., Klein, P., Gilch, J., Wurtzel, N., & Campos-deCarvalho, M. (1998b). The ontogeny of long-term memory over the first year-and-a-half of life. *Developmental Psychobiology, 32,* 69–89.

Hartup, W. W. (1999). Peer experience and its developmental significance. In M. Bennett (Ed.), *Developmental psychology: Achievements and prospects* (pp. 106–125). Philadelphia, PA: Psychology Press.

Hartup, W. W., & Abecassis, M. (2004). Friends and enemies. In P. K. Smith & C. H. Hart (Eds.), *Blackwell handbook of childhood social development* (pp. 285–306). Malden, MA: Blackwell.

Hartup, W. W., & Stevens, N. (1999). Friendships and adaptation across the life span. *Current Directions in Psychological Science, 8,* 76–79.

Harvey, M. W. (2001). Vocational-technical education: A logical approach to dropout prevention for secondary special education. *Preventing School Failure, 45,* 108–113.

Harwood, M. D., & Farrar, M. J. (2006). Conflicting emotions: The connection between affective perspective taking and theory of mind. *British Journal of Developmental Psychology, 24,* 401–418.

Harwood, R., Leyendecker, B., Carlson, V., Asencio, M., & Miller, A. (2002). Parenting among Latino families in the U.S. In M. H. Bornstein (Ed.), *Handbook of parenting: Vol. 4* (2nd ed., 2146). Mahwah, NJ: Erlbaum.

Hasebe, Y., Nucci, L., & Nucci, M. S. (2004). Parental control of the personal domain and adolescent symptoms of psychopathology: A cross-national study in the United States and Japan. *Child Development, 75,* 815–828.

Haskett, M. E., Scott, S. S., Grant, R., Ward, C. S., & Robinson, C. (2003). Child-related cognitions and affective functioning of physically abusive and comparison parents. *Child Abuse and Neglect, 27,* 663–686.

Hassan, M. A., & Killick, S. R. (2003). Effect of male age on fertility: Evidence for the decline in male fertility with increasing age. *Fertility and Sterility, 79,* 1520–1527.

Hatton, D. D., Bailey, D. B., Jr., Burchinal, M. R., & Ferrell, K. A. (1997). Developmental growth curves of preschool children with vision impairments. *Child Development, 68,* 788–806.

Hauck, F. R., Herman, S. M., Donovan, M., Iyasu, S., Merrick Moore, C., & Donoghue, E. (2003). Sleep environment and the risk of sudden infant death syndrome in an urban population: The Chicago Infant Mortality Study. *Pediatrics, 111,* 1207–1214.

Hauck, F. R., Omojokun, O. O., & Siadaty, M. S. (2005). Do pacifiers reduce the risk of sudden infant death syndrome? A meta-analysis. *Pediatrics, 116,* e716–e723.

Hausenblas, H. A., & Downs, D. S. (2005). Prospective examination of leisure-time exercise behavior during pregnancy. *Journal of Applied Psychology, 17,* 240–246.

Hauser-Cram, P., Warfield, M. E., Stadler, J., & Sirin, S. R. (2006). School environments and the diverging pathways of students living in poverty. In A. C. Huston & M. N. Ripke (Eds.), *Developmental contexts in middle childhood* (pp. 198–216). New York: Cambridge University Press.

Hausfather, A., Toharia, A., LaRoche, C., & Engelsmann, F. (1997). Effects of age of entry, day-care quality, and family characteristics on preschool behavior. *Journal of Child Psychology and Psychiatry, 38,* 441–448.

Hawke, S., & Knox, D. (1978). The one-child family: A new life-style. *The Family Coordinator, 27,* 215–219.

Hawkins, J. N. (1994). Issues of motivation in Asian education. In H. F. O'Neil, Jr., & M. Drillings (Eds.), *Motivation: Theory and research* (pp. 101–115). Hillsdale, NJ: Erlbaum.

Hawton, K., Zahl, D., & Weatherall, R. (2003). Suicide following deliberate self-harm: Long-term follow-up of patients who presented to a general hospital. *British Journal of Psychiatry, 182,* 537–542.

Hay, D. F., Pawlby, S., Angold, A., Harold, G. T., & Sharp, D. (2003). Pathways to violence in the children of mothers who were depressed postpartum. *Developmental Psychology, 39,* 1983–1094.

Hay, D. F., Payne, A., & Chadwick, A. (2004). Peer relations in childhood. *Journal of Child Psychology and Psychiatry, 45,* 84–108.

Hayne, H. (2002). Thoughts from the crib: Meltzoff and Moore (1994) alter our views of mental representation during infancy. *Infant Behavior and Development, 25,* 62–64.

Hayne, H. (2004). Infant memory development: Implications for childhood amnesia. *Developmental Review, 24,* 33–73.

Hayne, H., Boniface, J., & Barr, R. (2000). The development of declarative memory in human infants: Age-related changes in deferred imitation. *Behavioral Neuroscience, 114,* 77–83.

Hayne, H., & Rovee-Collier, C. K. (1995). The organization of reactivated memory in infancy. *Child Development, 66,* 893–906.

Hayne, H., Rovee-Collier, C., & Perris, E. E. (1987). Categorization and memory retrieval by three-month-olds. *Child Development, 58,* 750–767.

Hayslip, B., Jr. (1994). Stability of intelligence. In R. J. Sternberg (Ed.), *Encyclopedia of human intelligence* (Vol. 2, pp. 1019–1026). New York: Macmillan.

Hayslip, B., Emick, M. A., Henderson, C. E., & Elias, K. (2002). Temporal variations in the experiences of custodial grandparenting: A short-term longitudinal study. *Journal of Applied Gerontology, 21,* 139–156.

Haywood, K. M., & Getchell, N. (2001). *Life span motor development* (3rd ed.). Champaign, IL: Human Kinetics.

Haywood, K. M., & Getchell, N. (2005). *Life span motor development* (4th ed.). Champaign, IL: Human Kinetics.

Head Start Bureau. (2006). *Head Start fact sheet.* Retrieved from www.acf.hhs.gov/programs/hsb/research/2006.htm

Health Canada. (2002). *Proceedings of a meeting of the Expert Advisory Group on Rubella in Canada.* Retrieved from http://www.hc-sc.gc.ca/pphb-dgspsp/publicat/ccdr-rmtc/02vol28/28s4

Health Canada. (2003). *Acting on what we know: Preventing youth suicide in First Nations.* Ottawa: Author.

Health Canada. (2004a). *Aboriginal Head Start: Program overview.* Retrieved from www.phac-aspc.gc.ca/dca-dea/programs-mes/ahs_overview_e.html#allocation

Health Canada. (2004b). *Canadian perinatal health report 2004.* Ottawa: Minister of Public Works and Government Services.

Health Canada. (2004c). *Exclusive breastfeeding duration—2004 Health Canada recommendation.* Retrieved from *www.hc-sc.gc.ca/hpfb-dgpsa/onpp*-bppn/exclusive_breastfeeding_duration_e.html

Health Canada. (2004d). *Healthy Canadians: A federal report on comparable health indicators.* Retrieved from www.hc-sc.gc.ca/iacb-dgiac/arad-draa/english/accountability/indicators/html#high

Health Canada. (2005a). *Childhood injury: Deaths and hospitalizations in Canada.* Retrieved from www.hc-sc.ca

Health Canada. (2005b). *Injury surveillance.* Retrieved from dsol-smed.phac-aspc.gc.ca/dsol-smed/is-sb/c_mech_e.html

Health Canada. (2005c, July 5). 2004 Canadian Community Health Survey: Nutrition. *The Daily.* Retrieved from www.statcan.ca/Daily/English/050706/d050706a.htm

Health Canada. (2006a). *Canada Prenatal Nutrition Program (CPNP).* Retrieved from www.phac-aspc.gc.ca/dca-dea/programs-mes/cpnp_main_e.html

Health Canada. (2006b). *Fetal alcohol spectrum disorder.* Retrieved from www.hc-sc.gc.ca/iyh-vsv/diseases-maladies/fasd-etcaf_e.html

Health Canada. (2006c). *Lead information package.* Retrieved from www.hc-sc.gc.ca/ewh-semt/contaminants/lead-plomb/index_e.html

Health Canada. (2006d). *Sexually transmitted infections surveillance and epidemiology.* Retrieved from www.phac-aspc.gc.ca/sti-its-surv-epi/surveillance_e.html

Healy, B. (2005, September 5). Pledging for Accutane. *U.S. News and World Report,* p. 63.

Hearing Foundation of Canada. (2006). *Newborn screening*. Retrieved from www.thfc.ca/NewbornScreening.asp

Heath, S. B. (1990). The children of Trackton's children: Spoken and written language in social change. In J. Stigler, G. Herdt, & R. A. Shweder (Eds.), *Cultural psychology: Essays on comparative human development* (pp. 496–519). New York: Cambridge University Press.

Hebert, M., & Tourigny, M. (2004). Child sexual abuse prevention: A review of evaluative studies and recommendations for program development. In S. P. Serge (Eds.), *Advances in psychology research* (Vol. 29, pp. 123–155). Hauppauge, NY: Nova Science Publishers.

Heckman, J. J., & Masterov, D. V. (2004). *The productivity argument for investing in young children*. Working Paper 5, Invest in Kids Working Group, Committee for Economic Development. Retrieved from jenni.uchicago.edu/Invest

Hedges, L. V., & Nowell, A. (1998). Black–white test score convergence since 1995. In C. Jencks & M. Phillips (Eds.), *The black–white test score gap* (pp.149–181). Washington, DC: Brookings Institution.

Hediger, M. L., Overpeck, M. D., Ruan, W. J., & Troendle, J. F. (2002). Birthweight and gestational age effects on motor and social development. *Paediatric and Perinatal Epidemiology, 16*, 33–46.

Heilbrun, K., Lee, R., & Cottle, C. C. (2005). Risk factors and intervention outcomes: Meta-analyses of juvenile offending. In K. Heilbrun, N. E. S. Goldstein, & R. E. Redding (Eds.), *Juvenile delinquency: Prevention, assessment, and intervention* (pp. 111–133). New York: Oxford University Press.

Heinz, W. R. (1999a). Introduction: Transitions to employment in a cross-national perspective. In W. R. Heinz (Ed.), *From education to work: Cross-national perspectives* (pp. 1–21). New York: Cambridge University Press.

Heinz, W. R. (1999b). Job-entry patterns in a life-course perspective. In W. R. Heinz (Ed.), *From education to work: Cross-national perspectives* (pp. 214–231). New York: Cambridge University Press.

Helburn, S. W. (Ed.). (1995). *Cost, quality and child outcomes in child care centers*. Denver: University of Colorado.

Helwig, C. C. (1995). Adolescents' and young adults' conceptions of civil liberties: Freedom of speech and religion. *Child Development, 66*, 152–166.

Helwig, C. C., Arnold, M. L., Tan, D., & Boyd, D. (2003). Chinese adolescents' reasoning about democratic and authority-based decision making in peer, family, and school contexts. *Child Development, 74*, 783–800.

Helwig, C. C., & Jasiobedzka, U. (2001). The relation between law and morality: Children's reasoning about socially beneficial and unjust laws. *Child Development, 72*, 1382–1393.

Helwig, C. C., & Kim, S. (1999). Children's evaluations of decision making procedures in peer, family, and school contexts. *Child Development, 70*, 502–512.

Helwig, C. C., & Prencipe, A. (1999). Children's judgments of flags and flag-burning. *Child Development, 70*, 132–143.

Helwig, C. C., & Turiel, E. (2002). Civil liberties, autonomy, and democracy: Children's perspective. *International Journal of Law and Psychiatry, 25*, 253–270.

Helwig, C. C., & Turiel, E. (2004). Children's social and moral reasoning. In P. K. Smith & C. H. Hart (Eds.), *Blackwell handbook of childhood social development* (pp. 476–490). Malden, MA: Blackwell.

Helwig, C. C., Zelazo, P. D., & Wilson, M. (2001). Children's judgments of psychological harm in normal and canonical situations. *Child Development, 72*, 66–81.

Henderson, H. A., Marshall, P. J., Fox, N. A., & Rubin, K. H. (2004). Psychophysiological and behavioral evidence for varying forms and functions of nonsocial behavior in preschoolers. *Child Development, 75*, 251–263.

Henrich, C. C., Brookmeyer, K. A., Shrier, L. A., & Shahar, G. (2006). Supportive relationships and sexual risk behavior in adolescence: An ecological–transactional approach. *Journal of Pediatric Psychology, 31*, 286–297.

Henrich, C. C., Kuperminc, G. P., Sack, A., Blatt, S. J., & Leadbeater, B. J. (2000). Characteristics and homogeneity of early adolescent friendship groups: A comparison of male and female clique and nonclique members. *Applied Developmental Science, 4*, 15–26.

Henricsson, L., & Rydell, A.-M. (2004). Elementary school children with behavior problems: Teacher–child

relations and self-perception. A prospective study. *Merrill-Palmer Quarterly, 50*, 111–138.

Herbert, J., & Hayne, H. (2000). The ontogeny of long-term retention during the second year of life. *Developmental Science, 3*, 50–56.

Hergenrather, J. R., & Rabinowitz, M. (1991). Age-related differences in the organization of children's knowledge of illness. *Developmental Psychology, 27*, 952–959.

Herman, M. (2004). Forced to choose: Some determinants of racial identification in multiracial adolescents. *Child Development, 75*, 730–748.

Hernandez, F. D., & Carter, A. S. (1996). Infant response to mothers and fathers in the still-face paradigm. *Infant Behavior and Development, 19*, 502.

Herrera, E., Reissland, N., & Shepherd, J. (2004). Maternal touch and maternal child-directed speech: Effects of depressed mood in the postnatal period. *Journal of Affective Disorders, 81*, 29–39.

Herrnstein, R. J., & Murray, C. (1994). *The bell curve*. New York: Free Press.

Hertenstein, M. J., & Campos, J. J. (2004). The retention effects of an adult's emotional displays on infant behavior. *Child Development, 75*, 595–613.

Herzog, D. B., Eddy, K. T., & Beresin, E. V. (2006). Anorexia and bulimia nervosa. In M. K. Dulcan & J. M. Wiener (Eds.), *Essentials of child and adolescent psychiatry* (pp. 527–560). Washington, DC: American Psychiatric Publishing.

Hespos, S. J., & Baillargeon, R. (2001). Reasoning about containment events in very young infants. *Cognition, 78*, 207–245.

Hesse, E., & Main, M. (2000). Disorganized infant, child, and adult attachment: Collapse in behavioral and attentional strategies. *Journal of the American Psychoanalytic Association, 48*, 1097–1127.

Hetherington, E. M. (1999). Should we stay together for the sake of the children? In E. M. Hetherington (ed.), *Coping with divorce, single parenting, and remarriage: A risk and resiliency perspective* (pp. 93–116). Hillsdale, NJ: Erlbaum.

Hetherington, E. M. (2003). Social support and the adjustment of children in divorced and remarried families. *Childhood, 10*, 237–254

Hetherington, E. M., Henderson, S. H., & Reiss, D. (1999). Adolescent siblings in stepfamilies: Family functioning and adolescent adjustment. *Monographs of the Society for Research in Child Development, 64*(4, Serial No. 259).

Hetherington, E. M., & Jodl, K. M. (1994). Stepfamilies as settings for child development. In A. Booth & J. Dunn (Eds.) *Stepfamilies: Who benefits? Who does not?* (pp. 55–79). Hillsdale, NJ: Erlbaum.

Hetherington, E. M., & Kelly, J. (2002). *For better or for worse: Divorce reconsidered*. New York: Norton.

Hetherington, E. M., & Stanley-Hagan, M. (1999). The adjustment of children with divorced parents: A risk and resiliency perspective. *Journal of Child Psychology and Psychiatry, 40*, 129–140.

Hetherington, E. M., & Stanley-Hagan, M. (2000). Diversity among stepfamilies. In D. H. Demo, K. R. Allen, & M. A. Fine (Eds.), *Handbook of family diversity* (pp. 173–196). New York: Oxford University Press.

Hetherington, E. M., & Stanley-Hagan, M. (2002). Parenting in divorced and remarried families. In M. H. Bornstein (Ed.), *Handbook of parenting: Vol. 3. Being and becoming a parent* (2nd ed., pp. 287–315). Mahwah, NJ: Erlbaum.

Hewlett, B. S. (1992). Husband–wife reciprocity and the father–infant relationship among Aka pygmies. In B. S. Hewlett (Ed.), *Father–child relations: Cultural and biosocial contexts* (pp. 153– 176). New York: Aldine De Gruyter.

Hewlett, B. S. (2004). Fathers in forager, farmer, and pastoral cultures. In M. E. Lamb (Ed.), *The role of the father in child development* (4th ed., pp. 182–195). Hoboken, NJ: Wiley.

Hewlett, S. (2003). *Creating a life*. New York: Miramax.

Heyman, G. D., & Dweck, C. S. (1998). Children's thinking about traits: Implications for judgments of the self and others. *Child Development, 69*, 391–403.

Heyman, G. D., Dweck, C. S., & Cain, K. M. (1992). Young children's vulnerability to self-blame and helplessness: Relationship to beliefs about goodness. *Child Development, 63*, 401–415.

Heyman, G. D., & Gelman, S. A. (1999). The use of trait labels in making psychological inferences. *Child Development, 70*, 604–619.

Heyman, G. D., & Gelman, S. A. (2000). Preschool children's use of trait labels to make inductive inferences. *Journal of Experimental Child Psychology, 77*, 1–19.

Heyman, G. D., & Legare, C. H. (2004). Children's beliefs about gender differences in the academic and social domains. *Sex Roles, 50*, 227–239.

Hibell, B. (2001). *European School Survey Project on Alcohol and Drugs*. Stockholm: Swedish Council for Information on Alcohol and Other Drugs.

Hickling, A. K., & Wellman, H. M. (2001). The emergence of children's causal explanations and theories: Evidence from everyday conversation. *Developmental Psychology, 37*, 668–683.

Higgins, C., & Duxbury, L. (2002). *The 2001 National Work-Life Conflict Study: Report One*. Retrieved from www.phac-aspc.gc.ca/publicat/work-travail/report1/index.html

High, P. C., LaGasse, L., Becker, S., Ahlgren, I., & Gardner, A. (2000). Literacy promotion in primary care pediatrics: Can we make a difference? *Pediatrics, 105*, 927–934.

Hildreth, K., & Rovee-Collier, C. (2002). Forgetting functions of reactivated memories over the first year of life. *Developmental Psychobiology, 41*, 277–288.

Hildreth, K., Sweeney, B., & Rovee-Collier, C. (2003). Differential memory-preserving effects of reminders at 6 months. *Journal of Experimental Child Psychology, 84*, 41–62.

Hilgers, K. K., Akridge, M., Scheetz, J. P., & Kinance, D. E. (2006). Childhood obesity and dental development. *Pediatric Dentistry, 28*, 18–22.

Hill, J. L., Brooks-Gunn, J., & Waldfogel, J. (2003). Sustained effects of high participation in an early intervention for low-birth-weight premature infants. *Developmental Psychology, 39*, 730–744.

Hill, N. E., Bush, K. R., & Roosa, M. W. (2003). Parenting and family socialization strategies and children's mental health: Low-income Mexican-American and Euro-American mothers and children. *Child Development, 74*, 189–204.

Hill, N. E., & Taylor, I. C. (2004). Parental school involvement and children's academic achievement: Pragmatics and issues. *Current Directions in Psychological Science, 13*, 161–164.

Hillis, S. D., Anda, R. F., Dube, S. R., Felitti, V. J., Marchbanks, P. A., & Marks, J. S. (2004). The association between adverse childhood experiences and adolescent pregnancy, long-term psychosocial consequences, and fetal death. *Pediatrics, 113*, 320–327.

Hilt, L. M. (2004). Attribution retaining for therapeutic change: Theory, practice, and future directions. *Imagination, Cognition, and Personality, 23*, 289–307.

Hinde, R. A. (1992). Ethological relationships and approaches. In R. Vasta (Ed.), *Six theories of child development* (pp. 251–285). Philadelphia, PA: Jessica Kingsley.

Hines, M., Golombok, S., Rust, J., Johnston, K. J., Golding, J., & the ALSPAC Study Team. (2002). Testosterone during pregnancy and gender role behavior of preschool children: A longitudinal, population study. *Child Development, 73*, 1678–1687.

Hinojosa, T., Sheu, C.-F., & Michael, G. F. (2003). Infant hand-use preference for grasping objects contributes to the development of a hand-use preference for manipulating objects. *Developmental Psychobiology, 43*, 328–334.

Hirsh-Pasek, K., & Golinkoff, R. M. (2003). *Einstein never used flash cards*. New York: Rodale.

Hjälmäs, K. (1998). Nocturnal enuresis: Basic facts and new horizons. *European Urology, 33*(Suppl. 3), 53–57.

Hoch-Espada, A., Ryan, E., & Deblinger, E. (2006). Child sexual abuse. In J. E. Fisher & W. T. O'Donohue (Eds.), *Practitioner's guide to evidence-based psychotherapy* (pp. 177–188). New York: Springer.

Hock, H. S., Park, C. L., & Bjorklund, D. F. (1998). Temporal organization in children's strategy formation. *Journal of Experimental Child Psychology, 70*, 187–206.

Hodges, J., & Tizard, B. (1989). Social and family relationships of exinstitutional adolescents. *Journal of Child Psychology and Psychiatry, 30*, 77–97.

Hodges, R. M., & French, L. A. (1988). The effect of class and collection labels on cardinality, class-inclusion, and number conservation tasks. *Child Development, 59*, 1387–1396.

Hodgson, J., & Spriggs, M. (2005). A practical account of autonomy: Why genetic counseling is especially well suited to the facilitation of informed autonomous decision making. *Journal of Genetic Counseling, 14*, 89–97.

Hoff, E. (2003). The specificity of environmental influence: Socioeconomic status affects early vocabulary development via maternal speech. *Child Development, 74*, 1368–1378.

Hoff, E., Laursen, B., & Tardif, T. (2002). Socioeconomic status and parenting. In M. H. Bornstein (Ed.), *Handbook of parenting: Vol. 2. Biology and ecology of parenting* (pp. 231–252). Mahwah, NJ: Erlbaum.

Hoff, E., & Naigles, L. (2002). How children use input to acquire a lexicon. *Child Development, 73*, 418–433.

Hoff, E. V. (2005). A friend living inside me: The forms and functions of imaginary companions. *Imagination, Cognition and Personality, 24*, 151–189.

Hofferth, S. L., & Anderson, K. G. (2003). Are all dads equal? Biology versus marriage as a basis for paternal investment. *Journal of Marriage and the Family, 65*, 213–232.

Hoffman, L. W. (2000). Maternal employment: Effects of social context. In R. D. Taylor & M. C. Wang (Eds.), *Resilience across contexts: Family, work, culture, and community* (pp. 147–176). Mahwah, NJ: Erlbaum.

Hoffman, L. W., & Youngblade, L. M. (1999). *Mothers at work: Effects on children's well-being.* New York: Cambridge University Press.

Hoffman, M. K., Vahratian, A., Sciscione, A. C., Troendle, J. F., & Zhang, J. (2006). Comparison of labor progression between induced and noninduced multiparous women. *Obstetrics and Gynecology, 107*, 1029–1034.

Hoffman, M. L. (2000). *Empathy and moral development.* New York: Cambridge University Press.

Hoffman, S., & Hatch, M. C. (1996). Stress, social support and pregnancy outcome: A reassessment based on research. *Paediatric and Perinatal Epidemiology, 10*, 380–405.

Hoffmann, W. (2001). Fallout from the Chernobyl nuclear disaster and congenital malformations in Europe. *Archives of Environmental Health, 56*, 478–483.

Hoffner, C., & Badzinski, D. M. (1989). Children's integration of facial and situational cues to emotion. *Child Development, 60*, 411–422.

Hofstadter, M., & Reznick, J. S. (1996). Response modality affects human infant delayed-response performance. *Child Development, 67*, 646–658.

Hokoda, A., & Fincham, F. D. (1995). Origins of children's helpless and mastery achievement patterns in the family. *Journal of Educational Psychology, 87*, 375–385.

Holcomb, T. F. (1990). Fourth graders' attitudes toward AIDS issues: A concern for the elementary school counselor. *Elementary School Guidance and Counseling, 25*, 83–90.

Holden, G. W., Coleman, S. M., & Schmidt, K. L. (1995). Why 3-year-old children get spanked: Determinants as reported by collegeeducated mothers. *Merrill-Palmer Quarterly, 41*, 431–452.

Holditch-Davis, D., Belyea, M., & Edwards, L. J. (2005). Prediction of 3-year developmental outcomes from sleep development over the preterm period. *Infant Behavior and Development, 79*, 49–58.

Holland, A. L. (2004). Plasticity and development. *Brain and Language, 88*, 254–255.

Holland, J. L. (1985). *Making vocational choices: A theory of vocational personalities and work environments.* Englewood Cliffs, NJ; Prentice-Hall.

Holland, J. L. (1997). *Making vocational choices: A theory of vocational personalities and work environments* (3rd ed.). Odessa, FL: Psychological Assessment Resources.

Hollich, G. J., Hirsh-Pasek, K., & Golinkoff, R. M. (2000). Breaking the language barrier: An emergentist coalition model for the origins of word learning. *Monographs of the Society for Research in Child Development, 65*(3, Serial No. 262).

Holliday, R. E. (2003). Reducing misinformation effects in children with cognitive interviews: Dissociating recollection and familiarity. *Child Development, 74*, 728–751.

Holmbeck, G. N. (1996). A model of family relational transformations during the transition to adolescence: Parent–adolescent conflict and adaptation. In J. A. Graber, J. Brooks-Gunn, & A. C. Petersen (Eds.), *Transitions through adolescence* (pp. 167–199). Mahwah, NJ: Erlbaum.

Holmbeck, G. N., Paikoff, R. L., & Brooks-Gunn, J. (1995). Parenting adolescents. In M. H. Bornstein (Ed.), *Handbook of parenting: Vol. 1. Children and parenting* (pp. 91–118). Mahwah, NJ: Erlbaum.

Holobow, N., Genesee, F., & Lambert, W. (1991). The effectiveness of a foreign language immersion program for children from different ethnic and social class backgrounds: Report 2. *Applied Psycholinguistics, 12*, 179–198.

Holowka, S., Brosseau-Lapré, F., & Petitto, L. A. (2002). Semantic and conceptual knowledge underlying bilingual babies' first signs and words. *Language Learning, 52*, 205–262.

Holsen, I., Kraft, P., & Vittersø, J. (2000). Stability in depressed mood in adolescence: Results from a 6-year longitudinal study. *Journal of Youth and Adolescence, 29*, 61–78.

Holtkamp, K., Muller, B., Heussen, N., Remschmidt, H., & Herpertz-Dahlmann, B. (2005). Depression, anxiety, and obsessionality in long-term recovered patients with adolescent-onset anorexia nervosa. *European Child and Adolescent Psychiatry, 14*, 106–110.

Honein, M. A., Moore, C. A., Lyon Daniel, K., & Erickson, J. D. (2002). Problems with informing women adequately about teratogen risk: Some barriers to preventing exposures to known teratogens. *Teratology, 66*, 202–204.

Honein, M. A., Paulozzi, L. J., & Erickson, J. D. (2001). Continued occurrence of Accutane-exposed pregnancies. *Teratology, 64*, 142–147.

Hong, G., & Raudenbush, S. W. (2005). Effects of kindergarten retention policy on children's cognitive growth in reading and mathematics. *Educational Evaluation and Policy Analysis, 27*, 205–224.

Hong, Z.-R., Veach, P. M., & Lawrenz, F. (2003). An investigation of the gender stereotyped thinking of Taiwanese secondary school boys and girls. *Sex Roles, 48*, 495–504.

Hood, B. M. (2004). Is looking good enough or does it beggar belief? *Developmental Science, 7*, 415–417.

Hood, B. M., Atkinson, J., & Braddick, O. J. (1998). Selection-for-action and the development of orienting and visual attention. In J. E. Richards (Ed.), *Cognitive neuroscience of attention: A developmental perspective* (pp. 219–251). Mahwah, NJ: Erlbaum.

Hope, S., Power, C., & Rodgers, B. (1999). Does financial hardship account for elevated psychological distress in lone mothers? *Social Science and Medicine, 29*, 381–389.

Hopkins-Golightly, T., Raz, S., & Sander, C. J. (2003). Influence of slight to moderate risk for birth hypoxia on acquisition of cognitive and language function in the preterm infant: A cross-sectional comparison with preterm-birth controls. *Neuropsychology, 17*, 3–13.

Horgan, D. (1978). The development of the full passive. *Journal of Child Language, 5*, 65–80.

Horne, R. S. C., Franco, P., Adamson, T. M., Grosswasser, J., & Kahn, A. (2004). Influences of maternal cigarette smoking on infant arousability. *Early Human Development, 79*, 49–58.

Horner, S. L., & Gaither, S. M. (2004). Attribution retraining instruction with a second-grade class. *Early Childhood Education Journal, 31*, 165–170.

Horner, T. M. (1980). Two methods of studying stranger reactivity in infants: A review. *Journal of Child Psychology and Psychiatry, 21*, 203–219.

Houlihan, J., Kropp, T., Wiles, R., Gray, S., & Campbell, C. (2005). *Body burden: The pollution in newborns.* Washington, DC: Environmental Working Group.

Houts, A. C. (2003). Behavioral treatment for enuresis. In A. E. Kazdin (Ed.), *Evidence-based psychotherapies for children and adolescents* (pp. 389–406). New York: Guilford.

Hoven, C. W., Mandell, D., & Duarte, C. S. (2003). Mental health of New York City public school children after 9/11: An epidemiologic investigation. In S. W. Coates & J. L. Rosenthal (Eds.), *September 11: Trauma and human bonds* (pp. 51–74). Hillsdale, NJ: Analytic Press.

Howard, A. W. (2002). Automobile restraints for children: A review for clinicians. *Canadian Medical Association Journal, 167*, 769–773.

Howard, B. J., & Wong, J. (2001). Sleep disorders. *Pediatrics in Review, 22*, 327–342.

Howard, D. E., & Wang, M. Q. (2004). Multiple sexual-partner behavior among sexually active U.S. adolescent girls. *American Journal of Health Behavior, 28*, 3–12.

Howe, N., Aquan-Assee, J., & Bukowski, W. M. (2001). Predicting sibling relations over time: Synchrony between maternal management styles and sibling relationship quality. *Merrill-Palmer Quarterly, 47*, 121–141.

Howe, N., Aquan-Assee, J., Bukowski, W. M., Lehoux, P. M., & Rinaldi, C. M. (2001). Siblings as confidants: Emotional understanding, relationship warmth, and sibling self-disclosure. *Social Development, 10*, 439–454.

Howell, K. K., Lynch, M. E., Platzman, K. A., Smith, G. H., & Coles, C. D. (2006). Prenatal alcohol exposure and ability, academic achievement, and school functioning in adolescence: A longitudinal follow-up. *Journal of Pediatric Psychology, 31*, 116–126.

Howes, C., & Hamilton, C. E. (1993). The changing experience of child care: Changes in teachers and in teacher–child relationships and children's social competence with peers. *Early Childhood Research Quarterly, 8*, 15–32.

Howes, C., & James, J. (2002). Children's social development within the socialization context of child care and early childhood education. In P. Smith & C. H. Hart (Eds.), *Blackwell handbook of childhood social development* (pp. 137–155). New York: Blackwell.

Howes, C., & Matheson, C. C. (1992). Sequences in the development of competent play with peers: Social and social pretend play. *Developmental Psychology, 28*, 961–974.

Hoza, B., Gerdes, A. C., Hinshaw, S. P., Bukowski, W. M., Gold, J. A., Kraemer, H. C., Pelham, W. E., Jr., Wigal, T., & Arnold, L. E. (2005). What aspects of peer relationships are impaired in children with attention-deficit/hyperactivity disorder? *Journal of Consulting and Clinical Psychology, 73*, 411–423.

Hu, Y., Wood, J. F., Smith, V., & Westbrook, N. (2004). Friendships through IM: Examining the relationship between instant messaging and intimacy. *Journal of Computer-Mediated Communication, 10*(1). Retrieved from jcmc.indiana.edu/vol10/issue1

Hubbs-Tait, L., Nation, J. R., Krebs, N. F., & Bellinger, D. C. (2005). Nuerotoxicants, micronurtrients, and social environments: Individual and combined effects on children's development. *Psychological Science in the Public Interest, 6*, 57–121.

Hubbs-Tait, L., Nation, J. R., Krebs, N. F., & Bellinger, D. C. (2006). Neurotoxicants, micronutrients, and social environments: Individual and combined effects on children's development. *Psychological Science in the Public Interest, 6*, 57–121.

Huddleston, J., & Ge, X. (2003). Boys at puberty: Psychosocial implications. In C. Hayward (Ed.), *Gender differences at puberty* (pp. 113–134). New York: Cambridge University Press.

Hudson, J. A., Fivush, R., & Kuebli, J. (1992). Scripts and episodes: The development of event memory. *Applied Cognitive Psychology, 6*, 483–505.

Hudson, J. A., Sosa, B. B., & Shapiro, L. R. (1997). Scripts and plans: The development of preschool children's event knowledge and event planning. In S. L. Friedman & E. K. Scholnick (Eds.), *The developmental psychology of planning* (pp. 77–102). Mahwah, NJ: Erlbaum.

Huesmann, L. R. (1986). Psychological processes promoting the relation between exposure to media violence and aggressive behavior by the viewer. *Journal of Social Issues, 42*, 125–139.

Huesmann, L. R., Moise-Titus, J., Podolski, C., & Eron, L. D. (2003). Longitudinal relations between children's exposure to TV violence and their aggressive and violent behavior in young adulthood: 1977–1992. *Developmental Psychology, 39*, 201–221.

Huey, S. J., Jr., & Henggeler, S. W. (2001). Effective community-based interventions for antisocial and delinquent adolescents. In J. N. Hughes & A. M. La Greca (Eds.), *Handbook of psychological services for children and adolescents* (pp. 301–322). London: Oxford University Press.

Hughes, C. (1998). Finding your marbles: Does preschoolers' strategic behavior predict later understanding of mind? *Developmental Psychology, 34*, 1326–1339.

Hughes, C., & Dunn, J. (1998). Understanding mind and emotion: Longitudinal associations with mental-state talk between young friends. *Developmental Psychology, 34*, 1026–1037.

Hughes, C. A., & Filbert, M. (2000). Computer-assisted instruction in reading for students with learning

disabilities: A research synthesis. *Education and Treatment of Children, 23,* 173–183.
Hughes, D., Rodriguez, J., Smith, E. P., Johnson, D. J., Stevenson, H. C., & Spicer, P. (2006). Parents' ethnic-racial socialization practices: A review of research and directions for future study. *Developmental Psychology, 42,* 747–770.
Hughes, D. C., & Ng, S. (2003). Reducing health disparities among children. *Future of Children, 13,* 153–167.
Hughes, J. N., Cavell, T. A., & Grossman, P. B. (1997). A positive view of self: Risk or protection for aggressive children? *Development and Psychopathology, 9,* 75–94.
Hughes, J. N., & Kwok, O. (2006). Classroom engagement mediates the effect of teacher–student support on elementary students' peer acceptance. *Journal of School Psychology, 43,* 465–480.
Hughes, J. N., Zhang, D., & Hill, C. R. (2006). Peer assessments of normative and individual teacher–student support predict social acceptance and engagement among low-achieving children. *Journal of School Psychology, 43,* 447–463.
Huizink, A. C., & Mulder, E. J. (2006). Maternal smoking, drinking or cannabis use during pregnancy and neurobehavioral and cognitive functioning in human offspring. *Neuroscience and Biobehavioral Reviews, 30,* 24–41.
Humphrey, T. (1978). Function of the nervous system during prenatal life. In U. Stave (Ed.), *Perinatal physiology* (pp. 651– 683). New York: Plenum.
Hunnius, S., & Geuze, R. H. (2004a). Developmental changes in visual scanning of dynamic faces and abstract stimuli in infants: A longitudinal study. *Infancy, 6,* 231–255.
Hunnius, S., & Geuze, R. H. (2004b). Gaze shifting in infancy: A longitudinal study using dynamic faces and abstract stimuli. *Infant Behavior and Development, 27,* 397–416.
Hunsberger, B., Pratt, M., & Pancer, S. M. (2001). Adolescent identity formation: Religious exploration and commitment. *Identity, 1,* 365–386.
Huotilainen, M., Kujala, A., Hotakainen, M., Parkkonen, L., Taulu, S., & Simola, J. (2005). Short-term memory functions of the human fetus recorded with magnetoencephalography. *Neuroreport, 16,* 81–84.
Hurewitz, F., Brown-Schmidt, S., Thorpe, K., Gleitman, L. R., & Trueswell, J. C. (2000). One frog, two frog, red frog, blue frog: Factors affecting children's syntactic choices in production and comprehension. *Journal of Psycholinguistic Research, 29,* 597–626.
Hurt, H., Brodsky, N. L., Roth, H., Malmud, E., & Giannetta, J. M. (2005). School performance of children with gestational cocaine exposure. *Neurotoxicology and Teratology, 27,* 203–211.
Huston, A. C., & Alvarez, M. M. (1990). The socialization context of gender role development in early adolescence. In R. Montemayor, G. R. Adams, & T. P. Gullotta (Eds.), *From childhood to adolescence: A transitional period?* (pp. 156– 179). Newbury Park, CA: Sage.
Huston, A. C., Wright, J. C., Marquis, J., & Green, S. B. (1999). How young children spend their time: Television and other activities. *Developmental Psychology, 35,* 912–925.
Hutinger, P. L., Bell, C., Beard, M., Bond, J., Johanson, J., & Terry, C. (1998). *The early childhood emergent literacy technology research study: Final report.* Macomb, IL: Western Illinois University. ERIC ED 418545.
Huttenlocher, P. R. (2000). Synaptogenesis in human cerebral cortex and the concept of critical periods. In N. A. Fox, L. A. Leavitt, & J. G. Warhol (Eds.), *The role of early experience in infant development* (pp. 15–28). St. Louis, MO: Johnson & Johnson Pediatric Institute.
Huttenlocher, P. R. (2002). *Neural plasticity: The effects of environment on the development of the cerebral cortex.* Cambridge, MA: Harvard University Press.
Huyck, M. H. (1996). Continuities and discontinuities in gender identity in midlife. In V. L. Bengtson (Ed.), *Adulthood and aging* (pp. 98–121). New York: Springer-Verlag.
Hyde, J. S., Essex, M. J., Clark, R., & Klein, M. H. (2001). Maternity leave, women's employment, and marital incompatibility. *Journal of Family Psychology, 15,* 476–491.
Hymel, S., LeMare, L., Ditner, E., & Woody, E. Z. (1999). Assessing self-concept in children: Variations across self-concept domains. *Merrill-Palmer Quarterly, 45,* 602–623.
Hyppönen, E., Power, C., & Smith, G. D. (2003). Prenatal growth, BMI, and risk of type 2 diabetes by early midlife. *Diabetes Care, 26,* 2512–2517.
Ickovics, J., Kershaw, T., Westdahl, C., Rising, S. S., Klima, C., & Reynolds, H. (2003). Group prenatal care and preterm birth weight: Results from a matched cohort study at public clinics. *Obstetrics and Gynecology, 102,* 1051–1057.
Iglowstein, I., Jenni, O. G., Molinari, L., & Largo, R. H. (2003). Sleep duration from infancy to adolescence: Reference values and generational trends. *Pediatrics, 111,* 302–307.
Imai, M., & Haryu, E. (2004). The nature of word-learning biases and their roles for lexical development: From a cross-linguistic perspective. In D. G. Hall & S. R. Waxman (Eds.), *Weaving a lexicon* (pp. 411–444). Cambridge, MA: MIT Press.
Inhelder, B., & Piaget, J. (1958). *The growth of logical thinking from childhood to adolescence: An essay on the construction of formal operational structures.* New York: Basic Books. (Original work published 1955)
International Human Genome Sequencing Consortium. (2004). Finishing the euchronmatic sequence of the human genome. *Nature, 21,* 931–945.
Iocaboni, M., Molnar-Szakacs, I., Gallese, V., Buccino, G., & Mazziotta, J. C. (2005). Grasping the intentions of others with one's own mirror neuron system. *Public Library of Science: Biology, 3*(3), e79.
Isabella, R. (1993). Origins of attachment: Maternal interactive behavior across the first year. *Child Development, 64,* 605–621.
Isabella, R., & Belsky, J. (1991). Interactional synchrony and the origins of infant–mother attachment: A replication study. *Child Development, 62,* 373–384.
Israel, M. Johnson, C., & Brooks, P. J. (2000). From states to events: The acquisition of English passive participles. *Cognitive Linguistics, 11,* 103–129.
Izard, C. E. (1979). *The maximally discriminative facial movement scoring system.* Unpublished manuscript, University of Delware.
Izard, C. E., & Ackerman, B. P. (2000). Motivational, organizational, and regulatory functions of discrete emotions. In M. Lewis & J. M. Haviland-Jones (Eds.), *Handbook of emotions* (2nd ed., pp. 253–264). New York: Guilford.
Izard, C. E., Trentacosta, C. J., King, K. A., & Mostow, A. J. (2004). An emotion-based prevention program for Head Start children. *Early Education and Development, 15,* 407–422.
Jaakkola, J. J., & Gissler, M. (2004). Maternal smoking in pregnancy, fetal development, and childhood asthma. *American Journal of Public Health, 94,* 136–140.
Jaccard, J., Dittus, P., & Gordon, V. V. (2000). Parent–adolescent congruency in reports of adolescent sexual behavior and in communications about sexual behavior. *Child Development, 69,* 247–261.
Jaccard, J., Dodge, T., & Dittus, P. (2002). Parent–adolescent communication about sex and birth control: A conceptual framework. In S. S. Feldman & D. A. Rosenthal (Eds.), *Talking sexuality: Parent–adolescent communication* (pp. 9–41). San Francisco: Jossey-Bass.
Jaccard, J., Dodge, T., & Dittus, P. (2003). Maternal discussions about pregnancy and adolescents' attitudes toward pregnancy. *Journal of Adolescent Health, 33,* 84–87.
Jackson, R. A., Gibson, K. A., & Wu, Y. W. (2004). Perinatal outcomes in singletons following in vitro fertilization: A meta-analysis. *Obstetrics and Gynecology, 103,* 551–563.
Jacobs, J. E., & Klaczynski, P. A. (2002). The development of judgment and decision making during childhood and adolescence. *Current Directions in Psychological Science, 11,* 145–149.
Jacobs, J. E., Lanza, S., Osgood, D. W., Eccles, J. S., & Wigfield, A. (2002). Changes in children's selfcompetence and values: Gender and domain differences across grades one through twelve. *Child Development, 73,* 509–527.
Jacobs, J. E., & Weisz, V. (1994). Gender stereotypes: Implications for gifted education. *Roeper Review, 16,* 152–155.
Jacobson, J. L., & Jacobson, S. W. (2003). Prenatal exposure to polychlorinated biphenyls and attention at school age. *Journal of Pediatrics, 143,* 780–788.
Jacobson, K. C., & Crockett, L. J. (2000). Parental monitoring and adolescent adjustment: An ecological perspective. *Journal of Research on Adolescence, 10,* 65–97.
Jacobson, S. W., Jacobson, J. L., Sokol, R. J., Chiodo, L. M., & Corobana, R. (2004). Maternal age, alcohol abuse history, and quality of parenting as moderators of the effects of prenatal alcohol exposure on 7.5-year intellectual function. *Alcoholism, Clinical and Experimental Research, 28,* 1732–1745.
Jacquet, P. (2004). Sensitivity of germ cells and embryos to ionizing radiation. *Journal of Biological Regulators and Homeostatic Agents, 18,* 106–114.
Jadack, R. A., Hyde, J. S., Moore, C. F., & Keller, M. L. (1995). Moral reasoning about sexually transmitted diseases. *Child Development, 66,* 167–177.
Jaffe, J., Beebe, B., Feldstein, S., Crown, C. L., & Jasnow, M. D. (2001). Rhythms of dialogue in infancy. *Monographs of the Society for Research in Child Development, 66*(2, Serial No. 265).
Jaffee, S. R., Caspi, A., Moffitt, T. E., Belsky, J., & Silva, P. (2001). Why are children born to teen mothers at risk for adverse outcomes in young adulthood? *Development and Psychopathology, 13,* 377–397.
Jaffee, S. R., & Hyde, J. S. (2000). Gender differences in moral orientation: A meta-analysis. *Psychological Bulletin, 126,* 703–706.
Jaffee, S. R., Moffitt, T. E., Caspi, A., & Taylor, A. (2003). Life with (or without) father: The benefits of living with two biological parents depend on the father's antisocial behavior. *Child Development, 74,* 109–126.
Jain, A., Concat, J., & Leventhal, J. M. (2002). How good is the evidence linking breastfeeding and intelligence? *Pediatrics, 109,* 1044–1053.
Jambunathan, S., Burts, D. C., & Pierce, S. (2000). Comparisons of parenting attitudes among five ethnic groups in the United States. *Journal of Comparative Family Studies, 31,* 395–406.
James, W. (1890). *Principles of psychology.* Chicago: Encyclopedia Britannica.
Jamieson, J. R. (1995). Interactions between mothers and children who are deaf. *Journal of Early Intervention, 19,* 108–117.
Jang, S. J., & Johnson, B. R. (2001). Neighborhood disorder, individual religiosity, and adolescent use of illicit drugs: A test of multilevel hypotheses. *Criminology, 39,* 109–143.
Jankowski, J. J., Rose, S. A., & Feldman, J. F. (2001). Modifying the distribution of attention in infants. *Child Development, 72,* 339–351.
Janosz, M., Le Blanc, M., Boulerice, B., & Tremblay, R. E. (2000). Predicting different types of school dropouts: A typological approach with two longitudinal samples. *Journal of Educational Psychology, 92,* 171–190.
Jansen, A., Theunissen, N., Slechten, K., Nederkoorn, C., Boon, B., Mulkens, S., & Roefs, A. (2003). Overweight children overeat after exposure to food cues. *Eating Behaviors, 4,* 197–209.
Janssens, J. M. A. M., & Dekovic´, M. (1997). Child rearing, prosocial moral reasoning, and prosocial behavior. *International Journal of Behavioral Development, 20,* 509–527.
Jatana, M., Singh, I., Singh, A. K., & Jenkins, D. (2006). Combination of systemic hypothermia and N-acetylcysteine attenuates hypoxic-ischemic brain injury in neonatal rats. *Pediatric Research, 59,* 684–689.
Jayakody, R., & Kalil, A. (2002). Social fathering in low-income, African-American families with preschool children. *Journal of Marriage and the Family, 64,* 504–516.
Jeffrey, J. (2004, November). Parents often blind to their kids' weight. *British Medical Journal Online.* Retrieved from content.health.msn.com/content/article/97/104292.htm
Jenkins, J. M., & Astington, J. W. (1996). Cognitive factors and family structure associated with theory of mind development in young children. *Developmental Psychology, 32,* 70–78.
Jenkins, J. M., & Astington, J. W. (2000). Theory of mind and social behavior: Causal models tested in a longitudinal study. *Merrill-Palmer Quarterly, 46,* 203–220.
Jenkins, J. M., Rasbash, J., & O'Connor, T. G. (2003). The role of the shared family context in differential parenting. *Developmental Psychology, 39,* 99–113.
Jenkins, J. M., Turrell, S. L., Kogushi, Y., Lollis, S., & Ross, H. S. (2003). A longitudinal investigation of the dynamics of mental state talk in families. *Child Development, 74,* 905–920.

Jensen, A. R. (1969). How much can we boost IQ and scholastic achievement? *Harvard Educational Review, 39,* 1–123.

Jensen, A. R. (1985). The nature of the black–white difference on various psychometric tests: Spearman's hypothesis. *Behavioral and Brain Sciences, 8,* 193–219.

Jensen, A. R. (1998). *The g factor: The science of mental ability.* New York: Praeger.

Jensen, A. R. (2001). Spearman's hypothesis. In J. M. Collis & S. Messick (Eds.), *Intelligence and personality: Bridging the gap in theory and measurement* (pp. 3–24). Mahwah, NJ: Erlbaum.

Jensen, A. R. (2002). Galton's legacy to research on intelligence. *Journal of Biosocial Science, 34,* 145–172.

Jiao, S., Ji, G., & Jing, Q. (1996). Cognitive development of Chinese urban only children and children with siblings. *Child Development, 67,* 387–395.

Jimerson, S. R., Graydon, K., Fletcher, S. M., Schnurr, B., Kundert, D., & Nickerson, A. (2006). Grade retention and promotion. In G. G. Bear & K. M. Minke (Eds.), *Children's needs III: Development, prevention, and intervention* (pp. 601–613). Washington, DC: National Association of School Psychologists.

Joh, A. S., & Adolph, K. E. (2006). Learning from falling. *Child Development, 77,* 89–102.

Johnson, D. E. (2000). Medical and developmental sequelae of early childhood institutionalization in Eastern European adoptees. In C. A. Nelson (Ed.), *Minnesota symposia on child psychology* (Vol. 31, pp. 113–162). Mahwah, NJ: Erlbaum.

Johnson, D. E. (2002). Adoption and the effect on children's development. *Early Human Development, 68,* 39–54.

Johnson, J. G., Cohen, P., Smailes, E. M., Kasen, S., & Brook, J. S. (2002). Television viewing and aggressive behavior during adolescence and adulthood. *Science, 295,* 2468–2471.

Johnson, J. H., Figueroa, R., Garry, D., & Elimian, A. (2004). Immediate maternal and neonatal effects of forceps and vacuum-assisted deliveries. *Obstetrics and Gynecology, 103,* 513–518.

Johnson, K. C., & Daviss, B.-A. (2005). Outcomes of planned home births with certified professional midwives: Large prospective study in North America. *British Medical Journal, 330,* 1416.

Johnson, M. (1991). Infant and toddler sleep: A telephone survey of parents in one community. *Developmental and Behavioral Pediatrics, 12,* 108–114.

Johnson, M. H. (1998). The neural basis of cognitive development. In D. Kuhn & R. S. Siegler (Eds.), *Handbook of child psychology: Vol. 2. Cognition, perception, and language* (5th ed., pp. 1–49). New York: Wiley.

Johnson, M. H. (1999). Ontogenetic constraints on neural and behavioral plasticity: Evidence from imprinting and face processing. *Canadian Journal of Experimental Psychology, 55,* 77–90.

Johnson, M. H. (2001a). The development and neural basis of face recognition: Comment and speculation. *Infant and Child Development, 10,* 31–33.

Johnson, M. H. (2001b). Infants' initial "knowledge" of the world: A cognitive neuroscience perspective. In F. Lacerda, C. von Hofsten, & M. Heimann (Eds.), *Emerging cognitive abilities in early infancy* (pp. 53–72). Mahwah, NJ: Erlbaum.

Johnson, M. H. (2005). Developmental neuroscience, psychophysiology, and genetics. In M. H. Bornstein & M. E. Lamb (Eds.), *Developmental science: An advanced textbook* (5th ed., pp. 187–222). Mahwah, NJ: Erlbaum.

Johnson, S. P. (1997). Young infants' perception of object unity: Implications for development of attentional and cognitive skills. *Current Directions in Psychological Science, 6,* 5–11.

Johnson, S. P. (2004). Development of perceptual completion in infancy. *Psychological Science, 15,* 769–775.

Johnson, S. P., Amso, D., & Slemmer, J. A. (2003). Development of object concepts in infancy: Evidence for early learning in an eye-tracking paradigm. *Proceedings of the National Academy of Sciences, 100,* 10568–10753.

Johnson, S. P., Bremner, J. G., Slater, A. M., Mason, U. C., & Foster, K. (2002). Young infants' perception of unity and form in occlusion displays. *Journal of Experimental Child Psychology, 81,* 358–374.

Johnson, S. P., Bremner, J. G., Slater, A., Mason, U., Foster, K., & Cheshire, A. (2003). Infants' perception of object trajectories. *Child Development, 74,* 94–108.

Johnson, S. P., Slemmer, J. A., & Amso, D. (2004). Where infants look determines how they see: Eye movements and object perception performance in 3-month-olds. *Infancy, 6,* 185–201.

Johnston, L. D., O'Malley, P. M., Bachman, J. G., & Schulenberg, J. E. (2006). *Monitoring the Future: National results on adolescent drug use: Overview of key findings 2006.* Bethesda, MD: U.S. Department of Health and Human Services.

Johnston, M. V., Nishimura, A., Harum, K., Pekar, J., & Blue, M. E. (2001). Sculpting the developing brain. *Advances in Pediatrics, 48,* 1–38.

Jones, C. M., Braithwaite, V. A., & Healy, S. D. (2003). The evolution of sex differences in spatial ability. *Behavioral Neuroscience, 117,* 403–411.

Jones, E. F., & Thompson, N. R. (2001). Action perception and outcome valence: Effects on children's inferences of intentionality and moral and liking judgments. *Journal of Genetic Psychology, 162,* 154–166.

Jones, F. (2003). Religious commitment in Canada, 1997 and 2000. *Religious Commitment Monograph No. 3.* Ottawa: Christian Commitment Research Institute.

Jones, G. P., & Dembo, M. H. (1989). Age and sex role differences in intimate friendships during childhood and adolescence. *Merrill-Palmer Quarterly, 35,* 445–462.

Jones, J., Lopez, A., & Wilson, M. (2003). Congenital toxoplasmosis. *American Family Physician, 67,* 2131–2137.

Jones, M. C., & Mussen, P. H. (1958). Self-conceptions, motivations, and interpersonal attitudes of early- and late-maturing girls. *Child Development, 29,* 491–501.

Jones, R. K., Purcell, A., Singh, S., & Finer, L. B. (2005). Adolescents' reports of parental knowledge of adolescents' use of sexual health services and their reactions to mandated parental notification for prescription contraceptives. *Journal of the American Medical Association, 293,* 340–348.

Jones, W. H. (1990). Loneliness and social exclusion. *Journal of Social and Clinical Psychology, 9,* 214–220.

Jongbloet, P. H., Zielhuis, G. A., Groenewoud, H. M., & Pasker-De Jong, P. C. (2001). The secular trends in male:female ratio at birth in postwar industrialized countries. *Environmental Health Perspectives, 109,* 749–752.

Jordan, B. (1993). *Birth in four cultures.* Prospect Heights, IL: Waveland.

Jorgensen, K. M. (1999). Pain assessment and management in the newborn infant. *Journal of PeriAnesthesia Nursing, 14,* 349–356.

Jose, P., Huntsinger, C., Huntsinger, P., & Liaw, F.-R. (2000). Parental values and practices relevant to young children's social development in Taiwan and the United States. *Journal of Cross-Cultural Psychology, 31,* 677–702.

Joseph, R. M., & Tager-Flusberg, H. (2004). The relationship of theory of mind and executive functions to symptom type and severity in children with autism. *Development and Psychopathology, 16,* 137–155.

Joshi, P. T., O'Donnell, D. A., Cullins, L. M., & Lewin, S. (2006). Children exposed to war and terrorism. In M. M. Feerick & G. B. Silverman (Eds.), *Children exposed to violence* (pp. 53–84). Baltimore: Paul H. Brookes.

Joyner, M. H., & Kurtz-Costes, B. (1997). Metamemory development. In W. Schneider & F. E. Weinert (Eds.), *Memory performance and competencies: Issues in growth and development* (pp. 275–300). Hillsdale, NJ: Erlbaum.

Jusczyk, P. W. (2001). In the beginning was the word… In F. Lacerda & C. von Hofsten (Eds.), *Emerging cognitive abilities in early infancy* (pp. 173–192). Mahwah, NJ: Erlbaum.

Jusczyk, P. W. (2002). Some critical developments in acquiring native language sound organization. *Annals of Otology, Rhinology and Laryngology, 189,* 11–15.

Jusczyk, P. W., & Hohne, E. A. (1997). Infants' memory for spoken words. *Science, 277,* 1984–1986.

Jusczyk, P. W., Johnson, S. P., Spelke, E. S., & Kennedy, L. J. (1999). Synchronous change and perception of object unity: Evidence from adults and infants. *Cognition, 71,* 257–288.

Jusczyk, P. W., & Luce, P. A. (2002). Speech perception. In H. Pashler & S. Yantis (Eds.), *Steven's handbook of experimental psychology: Vol. 1. Sensation and perception* (3rd ed., pp. 493–536). New York: Wiley.

Justice for Children and Youth. (2003). *Corporal punishment.* Toronto: Canadian Foundation for Children, Youth, and the Law. Retrieved from http://www.jfcy.org/corporalp/corporalp.html

Justice, E. M. (1986). Developmental changes in judgments of relative strategy effectiveness. *British Journal of Developmental Psychology, 4,* 75–81.

Justice, E. M., Baker-Ward, L., Gupta, S., & Jannings, L. R. (1997). Means to the goal of remembering: Developmental changes in awareness of strategy use–performance relations. *Journal of Experimental Child Psychology, 65,* 293–314.

Kagan, J. (1998). Biology and the child. In N. Eisenberg (Ed.), *Handbook of child psychology: Vol. 3. Social, emotional, and personality development* (5th ed., pp. 177–236). New York: Wiley.

Kagan, J. (2003). Behavioral inhibition as a temperamental category. In R. J. Davidson, K. R. Scherer, & H. H. Goldsmith (Eds.), *Handbook of affective sciences* (pp. 320–331). New York: Oxford University Press.

Kagan, J., Arcus, D., Snidman, N., Feng, W. Y., Hendler, J., & Greene, S. (1994). Reactivity in infants: A cross-national comparison. *Developmental Psychology, 30,* 342–345.

Kagan, J., & Fox, N. A. (2006). Biology, culture, and temperamental biases. In N. Eisenberg (Ed.), *Handbook of child psychology: Vol. 3. Social, emotional, and personality development* (6th ed., pp. 167–225). Hoboken, NJ: Wiley.

Kagan, J., & Saudino, K. J. (2001). Behavioral inhibition and related temperaments. In R. N. Emde & J. K. Hewitt (Eds.), *Infancy to early childhood: Genetic and environmental influences on developmental change* (pp. 111–119). New York: Oxford University Press.

Kagan, J., & Snidman, N. (2004). *The long shadow of temperament.* Cambridge, MA: Belknap Press.

Kagan, J., Snidman, N., Zentner, M., & Peterson, E. (1999). Infant temperament and anxious symptoms in school-age children. *Development and Psychopathology, 11,* 209–224.

Kahn, P. H., Jr. (1992). Children's obligatory and discretionary moral judgments. *Child Development, 63,* 416–430.

Kail, R. (2000). Speed of information processing: Developmental change and links to intelligence. *Journal of School Psychology, 38,* 51–61.

Kail, R., & Park, Y. (1992). Global developmental change in processing time. *Merrill-Palmer Quarterly, 38,* 525–541.

Kail, R., & Park, Y. (1994). Processing time, articulation time, and memory span. *Journal of Experimental Child Psychology, 57,* 281–291.

Kail, R. V. (2003). Information processing and memory. In M. H. Bornstein, L. Davidson, C. L. M. Keyes, K. A. Moore, and the Center for Child Well-Being (Eds.), *Well-being: Positive development across the life course* (pp. 269–280). Mahwah, NJ: Erlbaum.

Kaisa, A., Stattin, H., & Nurmi, J. (2000). Parenting styles and adolescents' achievement strategies. *Journal of Adolescence, 23,* 205–222.

Kaitz, M., Good, A., Rokem, A. M., & Eidelman, A. I. (1987). Mothers' recognition of their newborns by olfactory cues. *Developmental Psychobiology, 20,* 587–591.

Kaitz, M., Good, A., Rokem, A. M., & Eidelman, A. I. (1988). Mothers' and fathers' recognition of their newborns' photographs during the postpartum period. *Journal of Developmental and Behavioral Pediatrics, 9,* 223–226.

Kaitz, M., Meirov, H., Landman, I., & Eidelman, A. I. (1993a). Infant recognition by tactile cues. *Infant Behavior and Development, 16,* 333–341.

Kaitz, M., Shiri, S., Danziger, S., Hershko, Z., & Eidelman, A. I. (1993b). Fathers can also recognize their newborns by touch. *Infant Behavior and Development, 17,* 205–207.

Kalafat, J. (2005). Suicide. In T. P. Gullotta & G. R. Adams (Eds.), *Handbook of adolescent behavioral problems: Evidence-based approaches to prevention and treatment* (pp. 231–254). New York: Springer.

Kalies, H., Heinrich, J., Borte, N., Schaaf, B., von Berg, A., & von Kries, R. (2005). The effect of breastfeeding on weight gain in infants: Results of a birth cohort study. *European Journal of Medical Research, 10,* 36–42.

Kalil, A., Levine, J. A., & Ziol-Guest, K. M. (2005). Following in their parents' footsteps: How characteristics of parental work predict adolescents' interest in parents' jobs. In B. Schneider & L. J. Waite (Eds.), *Being together, working apart: Dual-career families and the work-life balance* (pp. 422–442). New York: Cambridge University Press.

Kalil, A., Schweingruber, H., & Seefeldt, K. (2001). Correlates of employment among welfare recipients: Do psychological characteristics and attitudes matter? *American Journal of Community Psychology, 29,* 701–723.

Kaltiala-Heino, R., Kosunen, E., & Rimpelä, M. (2003). Pubertal timing, sexual behaviour and self-reported depression in middle adolescence. *Journal of Adolescence, 26,* 531–545.

Kamerman, S. (2000). Early childhood intervention policies: An international perspective. In J. P. Shonkoff & S. J. Meisels (Eds.), *Handbook of early childhood intervention* (2nd ed., pp. 316–329). New York: Cambridge University Press.

Kamerman, S. B. (1993). International perspectives on child care policies and programs. *Pediatrics, 91,* 248–252.

Kandall, S. R., Gaines, J., Habel, L., Davidson, G., & Jessop, D. (1993). Relationship of maternal substance abuse to subsequent sudden infant death syndrome in offspring. *Journal of Pediatrics, 123,* 120–126.

Kane, C. M. (2000). African-American family dynamics as perceived by family members. *Journal of Black Studies, 30,* 691–702.

Kane, P., & Garber, J. (2004). The relations among depression in fathers, children's psychopathology, and father–child conflict: A meta-analysis. *Clinical Psychology Review, 24,* 339–360.

Kaplowitz, P. (2006). Pubertal development in girls: Secular trends. *Current Opinion in Obstetrics and Gynecology, 18,* 487–491.

Karadsheh, R. (1991). *This room is a junkyard!: Children's comprehension of metaphorical language.* Paper presented at the biennial meeting of the Society for Research in Child Development, Seattle, WA.

Karafantis, D. M., & Levy, S. R. (2004). The role of children's lay theories about the malleability of human attributes in beliefs about and volunteering for disadvantaged groups. *Child Development, 75,* 236–250.

Karpati, A. M., Rubin, C. H., Kieszak, S. M., Marcus, M., & Troiano, R. P. (2002). Stature and pubertal stage assessment in American boys: The 1988–1994 Third National Health and Nutrition Examination Survey. *Journal of Adolescent Health, 30,* 205–212.

Karrass, J., & Braungart-Rieker, J. M. (2005). Effects of shared parent–infant book reading on early language acquisition. *Applied Developmental Psychology, 26,* 133–148.

Kasmauski, K., & Jaret, P. (2003). *Impact: On the frontlines of global health.* Washington, DC: National Geographic.

Kassel, J. D., Weinstein, S., Skitch, S. A., Veilleux, J., & Mermelstein, R. (2005). The development of substance abuse in adolescence: Correlates, causes, and consequences. In J. D. Kassel, S. Weinstein, S. A. Skitch, J. Veilleux, & R. Mermelstein (Eds.), *Development of psychopathology: A vulnerability-stress perspective* (pp. 355–384). Thousand Oaks, CA: Sage.

Kato, I., Franco, P., Groswasser, J., Scaillet, S., Kelmanson, I., Togari, H., & Kahn, A. (2003). Incomplete arousal processes in infants who were victims of sudden death. *American Journal of Respiratory and Critical Care, 168,* 1298–1303.

Katz, L. F., & Windecker-Nelson, B. (2004). Parental meta-emotion philosophy in families with conduct-problem children: Links with peer relations. *Journal of Abnormal Child Psychology, 32,* 385–398.

Katzman, D. K. (2005). Medical complications in adolescents with anorexia nervosa: A review of the literature. *International Journal of Eating Disorders, 37,* S52–S59.

Katzmarzyk, P. T., & Leonard, W. R. (1998). Climatic influences on human body size and proportions: Ecological adaptations and secular trends. *American Journal of Physical Anthropology, 106,* 483–503.

Kaufman, J., & Charney, D. (2001). Effects of early stress on brain structure and function: Implications for understanding the relationship between child maltreatment and depression. *Development and Psychopathology, 13,* 451–471.

Kaufman, J., & Charney, D. (2003). The neurobiology of child and adolescent depression: Current knowledge and future directions. In D. Cicchetti & E. Walker (Eds.), *Neurodevelopmental mechanisms in psychopathology* (pp. 461–490). New York: Cambridge University Press.

Kaufman, J., Csibra, G., & Johnson, M. H. (2005). Oscillatory activity in the infant brain reflects object maintenance. *Proceedings of the National Academy of Sciences, 102,* 15271–15274.

Kavanaugh, R. D., & Engel, S. (1998). The development of pretense and narrative in early childhood. In O. N. Saracho & B. Spodek (Eds.), *Multiple perspectives on play in early childhood education* (pp. 80–99). Albany: State University of New York Press.

Kavsek, M. (2004). Predicting later IQ from infant visual habituation and dishabituation: A meta-analysis. *Journal of Applied Developmental Psychology, 25,* 369–393.

Kaye, K., & Marcus, J. (1981). Infant imitation: The sensory-motor agenda. *Developmental Psychology, 17,* 258–265.

Kaye, W. H., Frank, G. K., Bailer, U. F., & Henry, S. E. (2005). Neurobiology of anorexia nervosa: Clinical implications of alterations of the function of serotonin and other neuronal systems. *International Journal of Eating Disorders, 37,* S15–S19.

Kazdin, A. E. (2003). Problem-solving skills training and parent management training for conduct disorder. In A. E. Kazdin & J. R. Weisz (Eds.), *Evidence-based psychotherapies for children and adolescents* (pp. 241–262). New York: Guilford.

Kazdin, A. E., & Whitley, M. E. (2003). Treatment of parental stress to enhance therapeutic change among children referred for aggressive and antisocial behavior. *Journal of Consulting and Clinical Psychology, 71,* 504–515.

Kearins, J. M. (1981). Visual spatial memory in Australian aboriginal children of desert regions. *Cognitive Psychology, 13,* 434–460.

Keating, D. (1979). Adolescent thinking. In J. Adelson (Ed.), *Handbook of adolescent psychology* (pp. 211–246). New York: Wiley.

Keating, D. (1990). Adolescent thinking. In S. S. Feldman & G. R. Elliott (Eds.), *At the threshold* (pp. 54–89). Cambridge, MA: Harvard University Press.

Keating, D. P. (2004). Cognitive and brain development. In R. M. Lerner & L. Steinberg (Eds.), *Handbook of adolescent psychology* (2nd ed., pp. 45–45–84). Hoboken, NJ: Wiley.

Keating-Lefler, R., Hudson, D. B., Campbell-Grossman, C., Fleck, M. O., & Westfall, J. (2004). Needs, concerns, and social support of single, low-income mothers. *Issues in Mental Health Nursing, 25,* 381–401.

Keefe, M. R., Barbosa, G. A., & Froese-Fretz, A., Kotzer, A. M., & Lobo, M. (2005). An intervention program for families with irritable infants. *American Journal of Maternal/Child Nursing, 30,* 230–236.

Keil, F. C., & Lockhart, K. L. (1999). Explanatory understanding in conceptual development. In E. K. Scholnick, K. Nelson, S. A. Gelman, & P. H. Miller (Eds.), *Conceptual development: Piaget's legacy* (pp. 103–130). Mahwah, NJ: Erlbaum.

Keith, T. Z., Keith, P. B., Quirk, K. J., Sperduto, J., Santillo, S., & Killings, S. (1998). Longitudinal effects of parent involvement on high school grades: Similarities and differences across gender and ethnic groups. *Journal of School Psychology, 36,* 335–363.

Keller, H. (2003). Socialization for competence: Cultural models of infancy. *Human Development, 46,* 288–311.

Keller, S. N., & Brown, J. D. (2002). Media interventions to promote responsible sexual behavior. *Journal of Sex Research, 39,* 67–72.

Kelley, S. A., Brownell, C. A., & Campbell, S. B. (2000). Mastery motivation and self-evaluative affect in toddlers: Longitudinal relations with maternal behavior. *Child Development, 71,* 1061–1071.

Kelley, S. S., Borawski, E. A., Flocke, S. A., & Keen, K. J. (2003). The role of sequential and concurrent sexual relationships in the risk of sexually transmitted diseases among adolescents. *Journal of Adolescent Health, 32,* 296–305.

Kellman, P. J., & Arterberry, M. E. (2006). Infant visual perception. In D. Kuhn & R. Siegler (Eds.), *Handbook of child psychology: Vol. 2. Cognition, perception, and language* (6th ed., pp. 109–160). Hoboken, NJ: Wiley.

Kelly, F. W., Terry, R., & Naglieri, R. (1999). A review of alternative birthing positions. *Journal of the American Osteopathic Association, 99,* 470–474.

Kelly, N., & Norwich, B. (2004). Pupils' perceptions of self and of labels: Moderate learning difficulties in mainstream and special schools. *British Journal of Educational Psychology, 74,* 411–435.

Kemeny, M. E. (2003). The psychobiology of stress. *Current Directions in Psychological Science, 12,* 124–129.

Kempe, C. H., Silverman, B. F., Steele, P. W., Droegemueller, P. W., & Silver, H. K. (1962). The battered-child

syndrome. *Journal of the American Medical Association, 181,* 17–24.

Kendall, G., & Peebles, D. (2005). Acute fetal hypoxia: The modulating effect of infection. *Early Human Development, 81,* 27–34.

Kendler, K. S., Thornton, L. M., Gilman, S. E., & Kessler, R. C. (2000). Sexual orientation in a U.S. national sample of twin and non-twin sibling pairs. *American Journal of Psychiatry, 157,* 1843–1846.

Kennell, J. H., Klaus, M., McGrath, S., Robertson, S., & Hinkley, C. (1991). Continuous emotional support during labor in a U.S. hospital. *Journal of the American Medical Association, 265,* 2197–2201.

Kenney-Benson, G. A., Pomerantz, E. M., Ryan, A. M., & Patrick, H. (2006). Sex differences in math performance: The role of children's approach to schoolwork. *Developmental Psychology, 42,* 11–26.

Kenyon, B. L. (2001). Current research in children's conceptions of death: A critical review. *Omega, 43,* 63–91.

Kerckhoff, A. C. (2002). The transition from school to work. In J. T. Mortimer & R. Larson (Eds.), *The changing adolescent experience* (pp. 52–87). New York: Cambridge University Press.

Keren, M., Feldman, R., Namdari-Weinbaum, I., Spitzer, S., & Tyano, S., (2005). Relations between parents' interactive style in dyadic and triadic play and toddlers' symbolic capacity. *American Journal of Orthopsychiatry, 75,* 599–607.

Kerestes, M., & Youniss, J. E. (2003). Rediscovering the importance of religion in adolescent development. In R. M. Lerner, F. Jacobs, & D. Wertlieb (Eds.), *Handbook of applied developmental science* (Vol. 1, pp. 165–184). Thousand Oaks, CA: Sage.

Kerestes, M., Youniss, J., & Metz, E. (2004). Longitudinal patterns of religious perspective and civic integration. *Applied Developmental Science, 8,* 39–46.

Kernis, M. H. (2002). Self-esteem as a multifaceted construct. In T. M. Brinthaupt & R. P. Lipka (Eds.), *Understanding early adolescent self and identity* (pp. 57–88). Albany, NY: State University of New York Press.

Kerpelman, J. L., Shoffner, M. F., & Ross-Griffin, S. (2002). African American mothers' and daughters' beliefs about possible selves and their strategies for reaching the adolescents' future academic and career goals. *Journal of Youth and Adolescence, 31,* 289–302.

Kerr, D. C. R., Lopez, N. L., Olson, S. L., & Sameroff, A. J. (2004). Parental discipline and externalizing behavior problems in early childhood: The roles of moral regulation and child gender. *Journal of Abnormal Child Psychology, 32,* 369–383.

Kessen, W. (1967). Sucking and looking: Two organized congenital patterns of behavior in the human newborn. In H. W. Stevenson, E. H. Hess, & H. L. Rheingold (Eds.), *Early behavior: Comparative and developmental approaches* (pp. 147–179). New York: Wiley.

Kessler, R. C., Adler, L. A., Barkley, R., Biederman, J., Conners, C. K., & Demler, O. (2006). The prevalence and correlates of adult ADHD in the United States: Results from the National Comorbidity Survey Replication. *American Journal of Psychiatry, 163,* 716–723.

Kessler, R. C., Adler, L. A., Barkley, R., Biederman, J., Conners, C. K., & Faraone, S. V. (2005). Patterns and predictors of attention-deficit/hyperactivity disorder persistence into adulthood: Results from the National Comorbidity Survey Replication. *Biological Psychiatry, 57,* 1442–1451.

Kidd, S. A., & Scrimenti, K. (2004). Evaluating child and youth homelessness: The example of New Haven, Connecticut. *Evaluation Review, 28,* 325–341.

Kieras, J. E., Tobin, R. M., Graziano, W. G., & Rothbart, M. K. (2005). You can't always get what you want: Effortful control and children's responses to undesirable gifts. *Psychological Science, 16,* 391–396.

Kiernan, K. (2001). European perspectives on nonmarital childbearing. In L. L. Wu & B. Wolfe (Eds.), *Out of wedlock: Causes and consequences of nonmarital fertility* (pp. 77–108). New York: Russell Sage Foundation.

Killen, M., Crystal, D., & Watanabe, H. (2002). The individual and the group: Japanese and American children's evaluations of peer exclusion, tolerance of difference, and prescriptions for conformity. *Child Development, 73,* 1788–1802.

Killen, M., Lee-Kim, J., McGlothlin, H., & Stangor, C. (2002). How children and adolescents evaluate gender

and racial exclusion. *Monographs of the Society for Research in Child Development, 67*(4, Serial No. 271).
Killen, M., & Nucci, L. P. (1995). Morality, autonomy, and social conflict. In M. Killen & D. Hart (Eds.), *Morality in everyday life: Developmental perspectives* (pp. 52–86). Cambridge, U.K.: Cambridge University Press.
Killen, M., & Smetana, J. G. (1999). Social interactions in preschool classrooms and the development of young children's conceptions of the personal. *Child Development, 70,* 486–501.
Killen, M., & Stangor, M. (2001). Children's social reasoning about inclusion and exclusion in gender and race peer group contexts. *Child Development, 72,* 174–186.
Kilpatrick, S. W., & Sanders, D. M. (1978). Body image stereotypes: A developmental comparison. *Journal of Genetic Psychology, 132,* 87–95.
Kim, J., & Cicchetti, D. (2006). Longitudinal trajectories of self-system processes and depressive symptoms among maltreated and nonmaltreated children. *Child Development, 77,* 624–639.
Kim, J. M. (1998). Korean children's concepts of adult and peer authority and moral reasoning. *Developmental Psychology, 34,* 947–955.
Kim, J. M., & Turiel, E. (1996). Korean children's concepts of adult and peer authority. *Social Development, 5,* 310–329.
Kim, K. J., Conger, R. D., Lorenz, F. O., & Elder, G. H., Jr. (2001). Parent– adolescent reciprocity in negative affect and its relation to early adult social development. *Developmental Psychology, 37,* 775–790.
Kim, M., McGregor, K. K., & Thompson, C. K. (2000). Early lexical development in English- and Korean-speaking children: Language-general and language-specific patterns. *Journal of Child Language, 27,* 225–254.
King, E. M., & Mason, A. D. (2001). *Engendering development: Through gender equality in rights, resources, and voice.* Washington, DC: UNICEF.
King, P. E., & Furrow, J. L. (2004). Religion as a resource for positive youth development: Religion, social capital, and moral outcomes. *Developmental Psychology, 40,* 703–713.
King, P. M., & Kitchener, K. S. (1994). *Developing reflective judgment: Understanding and promoting intellectual growth and critical thinking in adolescents and adults.* San Francisco: Jossey-Bass.
King, P. M., & Kitchener, K. S. (2002). The reflective judgment model: Twenty years of research on epistemic cognition. In B. K. Hofer & P. R. Pintrich (Eds.), *Personal epistemology: The psychological beliefs about knowledge and knowing* (pp. 37–61). Mahwah, NJ: Erlbaum.
Kinney, D. (1999). From "headbangers" to "hippies": Delineating adolescents' active attempts to form an alternative peer culture. In J. A. McLellan & M. J. V. Pugh (Eds.), *The role of peer groups in adolescent social identity: Exploring the importance of stability and change* (pp. 21–35). San Francisco: Jossey-Bass.
Kirby, D. (2002a). Antecedents of adolescent initiation of sex, contraceptive use, and pregnancy. *American Journal of Health Behavior, 26,* 473–485.
Kirby, D. (2002b). Effective approaches to reducing adolescent unprotected sex, pregnancy, and childbearing. *Journal of Sex Research, 39,* 51–57.
Kirby, D. (2002c). The impact of schools and school programs upon adolescent sexual behavior. *Journal of Sex Research, 39,* 27–33.
Kirchner, G. (2000). *Children's games from around the world.* Boston: Allyn and Bacon.
Kirk, K. M., Bailey, J. M., Dunne, M. P., & Martin, N. G. (2000). Measurement models for sexual orientation in a community twin sample. *Behavior Genetics, 30,* 345–356.
Kirk, W. G. (1993). *Adolescent suicide.* Champaign, IL: Research Press.
Kirkham, N. Z., Cruess, L., & Diamond, A. (2003). Helping children apply their knowledge to their behavior on a dimension-switching task. *Developmental Science, 6,* 449–476.
Kirkham, N. Z., Slemmer, J. A., & Johnson, S. P. (2002). Visual statistical learning in infancy: Evidence for a domain general learning mechanism. *Cognition, 83,* B35–B42.
Kirkman, M., Rosenthal, D. A., & Feldman, S. S. (2002). Talking to a tiger: Fathers reveal their difficulties in communicating about sexuality with adolescents. In S. S. Feldman & D. A. Rosenthal (Eds.), *Talking sexuality: Parent–adolescent communication* (pp. 57–74). San Francisco: Jossey-Bass.
Kisilevsky, B. S., Hains, S. M. J., Lee, K., Muir, D. W., Xu, F., Fu, G., Zhao, Z. Y., & Yang, R. L. (1998). The still-face effect in Chinese and Canadian 3- to 6-month-old infants. *Developmental Psychology, 34,* 629–639.
Kisilevsky, B. S., Hains, S. M. J., Lee, K., Xie, X., Huang, H., Ye, H. H., Zhang, K., & Wang, Z. (2003). Effects of experience on fetal voice recognition. *Psychological Science, 14,* 220–224.
Kisilevsky, B. S., & Low, J. A. (1998). Human fetal behavior: 100 years of study. *Developmental Review, 18,* 1–29.
Kitzmann, K. M., & Beech, B. M. (2006). Family-based interventions for pediatric obesity: Methodological and conceptual challenges from family psychology. *Journal of Family Psychology, 20,* 175–189.
Kitzmann, K. M., Cohen, R., & Lockwood, R. L. (2002). Are only children missing out? Comparison of the peer-related social competence of only children and siblings. *Journal of Social and Personal Relationships, 19,* 299–316.
Klaczynski, P. A. (1997). Bias in adolescents' everyday reasoning and its relationships with intellectual ability, personal theories, and self-serving motivation. *Developmental Psychology, 33,* 273–283.
Klaczynski, P. A. (2001). Analytic and heuristic processing influences on adolescent reasoning and decision-making. *Child Development, 72,* 844–861.
Klaczynski, P. A., & Narasimham, G. (1998a). Development of scientific reasoning biases: Cognitive versus ego-protective explanations. *Developmental Psychology, 34,* 175–187.
Klaczynski, P. A., & Narasimham, G. (1998b). Representations as mediators of adolescent deductive reasoning. *Developmental Psychology, 34,* 865–881.
Klaczynski, P. A., Schuneman, M. J., & Daniel, D. B. (2004). Theories of conditional reasoning: A developmental examination of competing hypotheses. *Developmental Psychology, 40,* 559–571.
Klahr, D., & MacWhinney, B. (1998). Information processing. In D. Kuhn & R. S. Siegler (Eds.), *Handbook of child psychology: Vol. 2. Cognition, perception, and language* (5th ed., pp. 631–678). New York: Wiley.
Klahr, D., & Nigam, M. (2004). The equivalence of learning paths in early science instruction: Effects of direct instruction and discovery learning. *Psychological Science, 15,* 661–667.
Klaus, M. H., & Kennell, J. H. (1982). *Parent–infant bonding.* St. Louis: Mosby.
Klaw, E. L., Rhodes, J. E., & Fitzgerald, L. F. (2003). Natural mentors in the lives of African-American adolescent mothers: Tracking relationships over time. *Journal of Youth and Adolescence, 32,* 223–232.
Klebanoff, M. A., Levine, R. J., Clemens, J. D., & Wilkins, D. G. (2002). Maternal serum caffeine metabolites and small-for-gestational-age birth. *American Journal of Epidemiology, 155,* 32–37.
Klebanov, P. K., Brooks-Gunn, J., McCarton, C., & McCormick, M. C. (1998). The contribution of neighborhood and family income to developmental test scores over the first three years of life. *Child Development, 69,* 1420–1436.
Klein, P. J., & Meltzoff, A. N. (1999). Long-term memory, forgetting, and deferred imitation in 12-month-old infants. *Developmental Science, 2,* 102–113.
Klenberg, L., Korkman, M., & Lahti-Nuuttila, P. (2001). Differential development of attention and executive functions in 3- to 12-year-old Finnish children. *Developmental Neuropsychology, 20,* 407–428.
Klesges, L. M., Johnson, K. C., Ward, K. D., & Barnard, M. (2001). Smoking cessation in pregnant women. *Obstetrics and Gynecology Clinics of North America, 28,* 269–282.
Klibanoff, R. S., Levine, S. C., Huttenlocher, J., Vasilyeva, M., & Hedges, L. V. (2006). Preschool children's mathematical knowledge: The effect of teacher "math talk." *Developmental Psychology, 42,* 59–69.
Kliewer, W., Fearnow, M. D., & Miller, P. A. (1996). Coping socialization in middle childhood: Tests of maternal and paternal influences. *Child Development, 67,* 2339–2357.
Klimes-Dougan, B., & Kistner, J. (1990). Physically abused preschoolers' responses to peers' distress. *Developmental Psychology, 26,* 599–602.
Klingman, A. (2006). Children and war trauma. In K. A. Renninger & I. E. Sigel (Eds.), *Handbook of child psychology: Vol. 4. Child psychology in practice* (6th ed., pp. 619–652). Hoboken, NJ: Wiley.
Klingner, J. K., Vaughn, S., Hughes, M. T., Schumm, J. S., & Elbaum, B. (1998). Outcomes for students with and without learning disabilities in inclusive classrooms. *Learning Disabilities Research and Practice, 13,* 153–161.
Klitzing, K. von, Simoni, H., Amsler, F., & Buergin, D. (1999). The role of the father in early family interactions. *Infant Mental Health Journal, 20,* 222–237.
Klomsten, A. T., Skaalvik, E. M., & Espnes, G. A. (2004). Physical self-concept and sports: Do gender differences exist? *Sex Roles, 50,* 119–127.
Klump, K. L., Kaye, W. H., & Strober, M. (2001). The evolving genetic foundations of eating disorders. *Psychiatric Clinics of North America, 24,* 215–225.
Knafo, A., & Plomin, R. (2006). Parental discipline and affection and children's prosocial behavior: Genetic and environmental links. *Journal of Personality and Social Psychology, 90,* 147–164.
Knight, N., Sousa, P., Barrett, J. L., & Atran, S. (2004). Children's attributions of beliefs to humans and God: Cross-cultural evidence. *Cognitive Science, 28,* 117–126.
Knobloch, H., & Pasamanick, B. (Eds.). (1974). *Gesell and Amatruda's Developmental Diagnosis.* Hagerstown, MD: Harper & Row.
Knoers, N., van den Ouweland, A., Dreesen, J. Verdijk, M., Monnens, L. S., & van Oost, B. A. (1993). Nephrongenic diabetes inspidus: Identification of the genetic defect. *Pediatric Nephrology, 7,* 685–688.
Knopf, M., Kraus, U., & Kressley-Mba, R. A. (2006). Relational information processing of novel unrelated actions by infants. *Infant Behavior and Development, 29,* 44–53.
Kobayashi, T., Hiraki, K., & Hasegawa, T. (2005). Auditory-visual intermodal matching of small numerosities in 6-month-old infants. *Developmental Science, 8,* 409–419.
Kobayashi, T., Kazuo, H., Ryoko, M., & Hasegawa, T. (2004). Baby arithmetic: One object plus one tone. *Cognition, 91,* B23–B34.
Kobayashi, Y. (1994). Conceptual acquisition and change through social interaction. *Human Development, 37,* 233–241.
Kochanska, G. (1991). Socialization and temperament in the development of guilt and conscience. *Child Development, 62,* 1379–1392.
Kochanska, G., Aksan, N., & Carlson, J. J. (2005). Temperament, relationships, and young children's receptive cooperation with their parents. *Developmental Psychology, 41,* 648–660.
Kochanska, G., Aksan, N., & Nichols, K. E. (2003). Maternal power assertion in discipline and moral discourse contexts: Commonalities, differences, and implications for children's moral conduct and cognition. *Developmental Psychology, 39,* 949–963.
Kochanska, G., Casey, R. J., & Fukumoto, A. (1995). Toddlers' sensitivity to standard violations. *Child Development, 66,* 643–656.
Kochanska, G., Forman, D. R., Aksan, N., & Dunbar, S. B. (2005). Pathways to conscience: Early mother–child mutually responsive orientation and children's moral emotion, conduct, and cognition. *Journal of Child Psychology and Psychiatry, 46,* 19–34.
Kochanska, G., Forman, D. R., & Coy, K. C. (1999). Implications of the mother–child relationship in infancy for socialization in the second year of life. *Infant Behavior and Development, 22,* 249–265.
Kochanska, G., Gross, J. N., Lin, M.-H., & Nichols, K. E. (2002). Guilt in young children: Development, determinants, and relations with broader system standards. *Child Development, 73,* 461–482.
Kochanska, G., & Knaack, A. (2003). Effortful control as a personality characteristic of young children: Antecedents, correlates, and consequences. *Journal of Personality, 71,* 1087–1112.
Kochanska, G., Murray, K. T., & Harlan, E. T. (2000). Effortful control in early childhood: Continuity and change, antecedents, and implications for social development. *Developmental Psychology, 36,* 220–232.
Kochenderfer-Ladd, B. (2003). Identification of aggressive and asocial victims and the stability of their peer victimization. *Merrill-Palmer Quarterly, 49,* 401–425.
Kochenderfer-Ladd, B., & Wardrop, J. L. (2001). Chronicity and instability of children's peer victimization experiences as predictors of loneliness and social satisfaction trajectories. *Child Development, 72,* 134–151.

Koelsch, S., Gunter, T., von Cramon, D., Zysset, S., Lohmann, G., & Friederici, A. (2002). Bach speaks: A cortical "language-network" serves the processing of music. *NeuroImage, 17,* 956–966.

Koestner, R., Franz, C., & Weinberger, J. (1990). The family origins of empathic concern: A 26-year longitudinal study. *Journal of Personality and Social Psychology, 58,* 709–717.

Kohen, D., Hunter, T., Pence, A., & Goelman, H. (2000). The Victoria Day Care Research Project: Overview of a longitudinal study of child care and human development in Canada. *Canadian Journal of Research in Early Childhood Education, 8,* 49–54.

Kohen, D. E., Brooks-Gunn, J., Leventhal, T., & Hertzman, C. (2002). Neighborhood income and physical and social disorder in Canada: Associations with young children's competencies. *Child Development, 73,* 1844–1860.

Kohlberg, L. (1966). A cognitivedevelopmental analysis of children's sex-role concepts and attitudes. In E. E. Maccoby (Ed.), *The development of sex differences* (pp. 82–173). Stanford, CA: Stanford University Press.

Kohlberg, L. (1969). Stage and sequence: The cognitivedevelopmental approach to socialization. In D. A. Goslin (Ed.), *Handbook of socialization theory and research* (pp. 347–480). Chicago: Rand McNally.

Kohlberg, L., Levine, C., & Hewer, A. (1983). *Moral stages: A current formulation and a response to critics.* Basel, Switzerland: Karger.

Kolb, B., & Gibb, R. (2001). Early brain injury, plasticity, and behavior. In C. A. Nelson & M. Luciana (Eds.), *Handbook of developmental cognitive neuroscience* (pp. 175–190). Cambridge, MA: MIT Press.

Kolomer, S. R., & McCallion, P. (2005). Depression and caregiver mastery in grandfathers caring for their grandchildren. *International Journal of Aging and Human Development, 60,* 283–294.

Kolominsky, Y., Igumnov, S., & Drozdovitch, V. (1999). The psychological development of children from Belarus exposed in the prenatal period to radiation from the Chernobyl atomic power plant. *Journal of Child Psychology and Psychiatry, 40,* 299–305.

Konold, T. R., & Pianta, R. C. (2005). Empirically-derived, person-oriented patterns of school readiness in typically developing children: Description and prediction to first-grade achievement. *Applied Developmental Science, 9,* 174–187.

Kontic-Vucinic, O., Sulovic, N., & Radunovic, N. (2006). Micronutrients in women's reproductive health: II. Minerals and trace elements. *International Journal of Fertility and Women's Medicine, 51,* 116–124.

Kontos, A. P. (2004). Perceived risk, risk taking, estimation of ability and injury among adolescent sport participants. *Journal of Pediatric Psychology, 29,* 447–455.

Kopp, C. B., & Neufeld, S. J. (2003). Emotional development during infancy. In R. Davidson, K. R. Scherer, & H. H. Goldsmith (Eds.), *Handbook of affective sciences* (pp. 347–374). Oxford, UK: Oxford University Press.

Korkman, M., Kettunen, S., & Autti-Raemoe, I. (2003). Neurocognitive impairment in early adolescence following prenatal alcohol exposure of varying duration. *Child Neurology, 9,* 117–128.

Kornhaber, M., Orfield, G., & Kurlaender, M. (2001). *Raising standards or raising barriers? Inequality and high-stakes testing in public education.* New York: Century Foundation Press.

Kornhaber, M. L. (2004). Using multiple intelligences to overcome cultural barriers to identification for gifted education. In D. Boothe & J. C. Stanley (Eds.), *In the eyes of the beholder: Critical issues for diversity in gifted education* (pp. 215–225). Waco, TX: Prufrock Press.

Kotchick, B. A., Dorsey, S., & Heller, L. (2005). Predictors of parenting among African-American single mothers: Personal and contextual factors. *Journal of Marriage and Family, 67,* 448–460.

Kouvonen, A., & Kivivuori, J. (2001). Part-time jobs, delinquency, and victimization among Finnish adolescents. *Journal of Scandinavian Studies in Criminology and Crime Prevention, 2,* 191–212.

Kozer, E., Costei, A. M., Boskovic, R., Nulman, I., Nikfar, S., & Koren, G. (2003). Effects of aspirin consumption during pregnancy on pregnancy outcomes: Meta-analysis. *Birth Defects Research: Part B, Developmental and Reproductive Toxicology, 68,* 70–84.

Kozulin, A. (Ed.). (2003). *Vygotsky's educational theory in cultural context.* Cambridge, U.K.: Cambridge University Press.

Kraemer, H. C., Yesavage, J. A., Taylor, J. L., & Kupfer, D. (2000). How can we learn about developmental processes from cross-sectional studies, or can we? *American Journal of Psychiatry, 157,* 163–171.

Krafft, K., & Berk, L. E. (1998). Private speech in two preschools: Significance of open-ended activities and make-believe play for verbal self-regulation. *Early Childhood Research Quarterly, 13,* 637–658.

Kramer, L., & Kowal, A. K. (2005). Sibling relationship quality from birth to adolescence: The enduring contributions of friends. *Journal of Family Psychology, 19,* 503–511.

Kramer, M. S., Guo, T., Platt, R. W., Sevkowskaya, Z., Dzikovich, I., & Collet, J. P. (2003). Infant growth and health outcomes associated with 3 compared with 6 mo. of exclusive breastfeeding. *American Journal of Clinical Nutrition, 78,* 291–295.

Kramer, M. S., Guo, T., Platt, R. W., Shapiro, S., Collet, J. P., & Chalmers, B. (2002). Breastfeeding and infant growth: Biology or bias? *Pediatrics, 110,* 343–347.

Krascum, R. M., & Andrews, S. (1998). The effects of theories on children's acquisition of family-resemblance categories. *Child Development, 69,* 333–346.

Krebs, N. F., & Jacobson, M. S. (2003). Prevention of pediatric overweight and obesity. *Pediatrics, 112,* 424–430.

Krettenauer, T. (2005). The role of epistemic cognition in adolescent identity formation: Further evidence. *Journal of Youth and Adolescence, 34,* 185–198.

Krevans, J., & Gibbs, J. C. (1996). Parents' use of inductive discipline: Relations to children's empathy and prosocial behavior. *Child Development, 67,* 3263–3277.

Kroger, J. (2001). What transits in an identity status transition: A rejoinder to commentaries. *Identity, 3,* 291–304.

Kroger, J. (2002). *Identity development: Adolescence through adulthood.* Thousand Oaks, CA: Sage.

Kroger, J. (2005). *Identity in adolescence: The balance between self and other.* New York: Routledge.

Kroneman, L., Loeber, R., & Hipwell, A. E. (2004). Is neighborhood context differently related to externalizing problems and delinquency for girls compared with boys? *Clinical Child and Family Psychology Review, 7,* 109–122.

Kruger, A. C. (1993). Peer collaboration: Conflict, cooperation, or both? *Social Development, 2,* 165–182.

Krumhansl, C. L., & Jusczyk, P. W. (1990). Infants' perception of phrase structure in music. *Psychological Science, 1,* 70–73.

Kubik, M. Y., Lytle, L. A., Hannan, P. J., Perry, C. L., & Story, M. (2003). The association of the school food environment with dietary behaviors of young adolescents. *American Journal of Public Health, 93,* 1168–1173.

Kuchner, J. (1989). *Chinese-American and European-American mothers and infants: Cultural influences in the first three months of life.* Paper presented at the biennial meeting of the Society for Research in Child Development, Kansas City, MO.

Kuczynski, L. (1984). Socialization goals and mother–child interaction: Strategies for long-term and short-term compliance. *Developmental Psychology, 20,* 1061–1073.

Kuczynski, L. (2003). Beyond bidirectionality. In L. Kuczynski (Ed.), *Handbook of dynamics in parent–child relations* (pp. 3–24). Thousand Oaks, CA: Sage.

Kuczynski, L., & Lollis, S. (2002). Four foundations for a dynamic model of parenting. In J. R. M. Gerris (Ed.), *Dynamics of parenting.* Hillsdale, NJ: Erlbaum.

Kuebli, J., Butler, S., & Fivush, R. (1995). Mother–child talk about past emotions: Relations of maternal language and child gender over time. *Cognition and Emotion, 9,* 265–283.

Kugelmass, J., & Ainscow, M. (2004). Leadership for inclusion: A comparison of international practices. *Journal of Research in Special Educational Needs, 4,* 133–141.

Kuhl, P. K., Tsao, F.-M., & Liu, H.-M. (2003). Foreign-language experience in infancy: Effects of short-term exposure and social interaction on phonetic learning. *Proceedings of the National Academy of Sciences, 100,* 9096–9101.

Kuhn, D. (1989). Children and adults as intuitive scientists. *Psychological Review, 96,* 674–689.

Kuhn, D. (1993). Connecting scientific and informal reasoning. *Merrill-Palmer Quarterly, 39,* 74–103.

Kuhn, D. (1995). Microgenetic study of change: What has it told us? *Psychological Science, 6,* 133–139.

Kuhn, D. (1999). Metacognitive development. *Current Directions in Psychological Science, 9,* 178–181.

Kuhn, D. (2000a). Theory of mind, metacognition, and reasoning: A life-span perspective. In P. Mitchell & K. J. Riggs (Eds.), *Children's reasoning and the mind* (pp. 301–326). Hove, U.K.: Psychology Press.

Kuhn, D. (2000b). Why development does (and does not) occur: Evidence from the domain of inductive reasoning. In R. Siegler & J. McClelland (Eds.), *Mechanisms of cognitive development* (pp. 221–249). Mahwah, NJ: Erlbaum.

Kuhn, D. (2002). What is scientific thinking, and how does it develop? In U. Goswami (Ed.), *Blackwell handbook of childhood cognitive development* (pp. 371–393). Malden, MA: Blackwell.

Kuhn, D., Amsel, E., & O'Loughlin, M. (1988). *The development of scientific thinking skills.* Orlando, FL: Academic Press.

Kuhn, D., & Dean, D. (2004). Connecting scientific reasoning and causal inference. *Journal of Cognition and Development, 5,* 261–288.

Kuhn, D., & Franklin, S. (2006). The second decade: What develops (and how)? In D. Kuhn & R. S. Siegler (Eds.), *Handbook of child psychology: Vol. 2. Cognition, perception, and language* (6th ed., pp. 953–994). Hoboken, NJ: Wiley.

Kuhn, D., & Pearsall, S. (2000). Developmental origins of scientific thinking. *Journal of Cognition and Development, 1,* 113–129.

Kuklinski, M. R., & Weinstein, R. S. (2001). Classroom and developmental differences in a path model of teacher expectancy effects. *Child Development, 72,* 1554–1578.

Kumar, S., & O'Brien, A. (2004). Recent developments in fetal medicine. *British Medical Journal, 328,* 1002–1006.

Kumpfer, K. L., & Alvarado, R. (2003). Family-strengthening approaches for the prevention of youth problem behaviors. *American Psychologist, 58,* 457–465.

Kunnen, E. S., & Bosma, H. A. (2003). Fischer's skill theory applied to identity development: A response to Kroger. *Identity, 3,* 247–270.

Kunzinger, E. L., III. (1985). A short-term longitudinal study of memorial development during early grade school. *Developmental Psychology, 21,* 642–646.

Kurdek, L. A., & Fine, M. A. (1994). Family acceptance and family control as predictors of adjustment in young adolescents: Linear, curvilinear, or interactive effects? *Child Development, 65,* 1137–1146.

Kuriyama, K., & Yoshida, H. (1995). Representational structure of numbers in mental addition. *Japanese Journal of Educational Psychology, 43,* 402–410.

Kushman, J. W., Sieber, C., & Heariold-Kinney, P. (2000). This isn't the place for me: School dropout. In D. Capuzzi & D. R. Gross (Eds.), *Youth risk: A prevention resource for counselors, teachers, and parents* (3rd ed., pp. 471–507). Alexandria, VA: American Counseling Association.

Kyratzis, A., & Guo, J. (2001). Preschool girls' and boys' verbal conflict strategies in the United States and China. *Research on Language and Social Interaction, 34,* 45–74.

La Ferle, C., Edwards, S. M., & Lee, W. N. (2000). Teens' use of traditional media and the Internet. *Journal of Advertising Research, 40,* 55–65.

Laberge, L., Petit, D., Simard, C., Vitaro, F., & Tremblay, R. E. (2001). Development of sleep patterns in early adolescence. *Journal of Sleep Research, 10,* 59–67.

Labouvie-Vief, G. (2006). Emerging structures of adult thought. In J. J. Arnett & J. L. Tanner (Eds.), *Emerging adults in America: Coming of age in the 21st century* (pp. 59–84). Washington, DC: American Psychological Association.

Lacourse, E., Nagin, D., Tremblay, R. E., Vitaro, F., & Claes, M. (2003). Developmental trajectories of boys' delinquent group membership and facilitation of violent behaviors during adolescence. *Development and Psychopathology, 15,* 183–197.

Ladd, G. W., Birch, S. H., & Buhs, E. S. (1999). Children's social and scholastic lives in kindergarten: Related spheres of influence? *Child Development, 70,* 1373–1400.

Ladd, G. W., Buhs, E. S., & Seid, M. (2000). Children's initial sentiments about kindergarten: Is school liking an antecedent of early classroom participation and achievement? *Merrill-Palmer Quarterly, 46*, 255–279.

Ladd, G. W., & Burgess, K. B. (1999). Charting the relationship trajectories of aggressive, withdrawn, and aggressive/withdrawn children during early grade school. *Child Development, 70*, 910–929.

Ladd, G. W., Herald, S. L., & Kochel, K. P. (2006). School readiness: Are there social prerequisites? *Early Education and Development, 17*, 115–150.

Ladd, G. W., LeSieur, K., & Profilet, S. M. (1993). Direct parental influences on young children's peer relations. In S. Duck (Ed.), *Learning about relationships* (Vol. 2, pp. 152–183). London: Sage.

Ladd, G. W., & Pettit, G. S. (2002). Parenting and the development of children's peer relationships. In M. Bornstein (Ed.), *Handbook of parenting: Vol. 5. Practical issues in parenting* (2nd ed., pp. 269–309). Mahwah, NJ: Erlbaum.

Ladd, G. W., & Price, J. M. (1987). Predicting children's social and school adjustment following the transition from preschool to kindergarten. *Child Development, 58*, 1168–1189.

Ladd, G. W., & Troop-Gordon, W. (2003). The role of chronic peer difficulties in the development of children's psychological adjustment problems. *Child Development, 74*, 1344–1367.

LaFontana, K. M., & Cillessen, A. H. N. (1999). Children's interpersonal perceptions as a function of sociometric and peer perceived popularity. *Journal of Genetic Psychology, 160*, 225–242.

Lagattuta, K. H., Wellman, H. M., & Flavell, J. H. (1997). Preschoolers' understanding of the link between thinking and feeling: Cognitive cuing and emotional change. *Child Development, 68*, 1081–1104.

Lagercrantz, H., & Slotkin, T. A. (1986). The "stress" of being born. *Scientific American, 254*, 100–107.

Lagnado, L. (2001, November 2). Kids confront Trade Center trauma. *Wall Street Journal*, pp. B1, B6.

LaGreca, A. M., Prinstein, M. J., & Fetter, M. D. (2001). Adolescent peer crowd affiliation: Linkages with health-risk behaviors and close friendships. *Journal of Pediatric Psychology, 26*, 131–143.

Laible, D. (2004). Mother–child discourse in two contexts: Links with child temperament, attachment security, and socioemotional competence. *Developmental Psychology, 40*, 979–992.

Laible, D., & Song, J. (2006). Constructing emotional and relational understanding: The role of affect and mother–child discourse. *Merrill-Palmer Quarterly, 52*, 44–69.

Laible, D. J., & Thompson, R. A. (2002). Mother–child conflict in the toddler years: Lessons in emotion, morality, and relationships. *Child Development, 73*, 1187–1203.

Laird, J. (2003). Lesbian and gay families. In F. Walsh (Ed.), *Normal family processes* (pp. 176–209). New York: Guilford.

Laird, R. D., Jordan, K. Y., Dodge, K. A., Pettit, G. S., & Bates, J. E. (2001). Peer rejection in childhood, involvement with antisocial peers in early adolescence, and the development of externalizing behavior problems. *Development and Psychopathology, 13*, 337–354.

Laird, R. D., Pettit, G. S., Dodge, K. A., & Bates, J. E. (2005). Peer relationship antecedents of delinquent behavior in late adolescence: Is there evidence of demographic group differences in developmental processes? *Development and Psychopathology, 17*, 127–144.

Laird, R. D., Pettit, G. S., Mize, J., & Lindsey, E. (1994). Mother–child conversations about peers: Contributions to competence. *Family Relations, 43*, 425–432.

Lalonde, C., & Chandler, M. (2005). Culture, selves, and time: Theories of personal persistence in native and non-native youth. In C. Lightfoot, C. Lalonde, & M. Chandler (Eds.), *Changing conceptions of psychological life* (pp. 207–229). Mahwah, NJ: Erlbaum.

Lamarche, V., Brendgen, M., Boivin, M., Vitaro, F., Perusse, D., & Dionne, G. (2006). Do friendships and sibling relationships provide protection against peer victimization in a similar way? *Social Development, 15*, 373–393.

Lamaze, F. (1958). *Painless childbirth*. London: Burke.

Lamb, M. (1994). Infant care practices and the application of knowledge. In C. B. Fisher & R. M. Lerner (Eds.),

Applied developmental psychology (pp. 23–45). New York: McGraw-Hill.

Lamb, M. E. (1997). The development of father–infant relationships. In M. E. Lamb (Ed.), *The role of the father in child development* (3rd ed., pp. 104–120). New York: Wiley.

Lamb, M. E., & Ahnert, L. (2006). Nonparental child care: Context, concepts, correlates, and consequences. In K. A. Renninger & I. E. Sigel (Eds.), *Handbook of child psychology: Vol. 4. Child psychology in practice* (6th ed., pp. 700–778). Hoboken, NJ: Wiley.

Lamb, M. E., & Lewis, C. (2004). The development and significance of father–child relationships in two-parent families. In M. E. Lamb (Ed.), *The role of the father in child development* (4th ed., pp. 272–306). Hoboken, NJ: Wiley.

Lamb, M. E., & Oppenheim, D. (1989). Fatherhood and father–child relationships: Five years of research. In S. H. Cath, A. Gurwitt, & L. Gunsberg (Eds.), *Fathers and their families* (pp. 11–26). Hillsdale, NJ: Erlbaum.

Lamb, M. E., Sternberg, K. J., & Prodromidis, M. (1992). Nonmaternal care and the security of infant–mother attachment: A reanalysis of the data. *Infant Behavior and Development, 15*, 71–83.

Lamb, M. E., Thompson, R. A., Gardner, W., Charnov, E. L., & Connell, J. P. (1985). Infant–mother attachment: The origins and developmental significance of individual differences in the Strange Situation: Its study and biological interpretation. *Behavioral and Brain Sciences, 7*, 127–147.

Lammers, C., Ireland, M., Resnick, M., & Blum, R. (2000). Influences on adolescents' decisions to postpone onset of sexual intercourse: A survival analysis of virginity among youths aged 13 to 18 years. *Journal of Adolescent Health, 26*, 42–48.

Lamphear, B. P., Hornung, R., Khoury, J., Yolton, K., Baghurst, P., & Bellinger, D. C. (2005). Low-level environmental lead exposure and children's intellectual function: An international pooled analysis. *Environmental Health Perspectives, 113*, 894–899.

Lampl, M. (1993). Evidence of saltatory growth in infancy. *American Journal of Human Biology, 5*, 641–652.

Lampl, M., Veldhuis, J. D., & Johnson, M. L. (1992). Saltation and stasis: A model of human growth. *Science, 258*, 801–803.

Landry, S. H., Smith, K. E., Swank, P. R., & Miller-Loncar, C. L. (2000). Early maternal and child influences on children's later independent cognitive and social functioning. *Child Development, 71*, 358–375.

Langer, J., Gillette, P., & Arriaga, R. I. (2003). Toddlers' cognition of adding and subtracting objects in action and in perception. *Cognitive Development, 18*, 233–246.

Lansford, J. E., Antonucci, T. C., Akiyama, H., & Takahashi, K. (2005). A quantitative and qualitative approach to social relationships and well-being in the United States and Japan. *Journal of Comparative Family Studies, 36*, 1–22.

Lansford, J. E., Criss, M. M., Pettit, G. S., Dodge, K. A., & Bates, J. E. (2003). Friendship quality, peer group affiliation, and peer antisocial behavior as moderators of the link between negative parenting and adolescent externalizing behavior. *Journal of Research on Adolescence, 13*, 161–184.

Lansford, J. E., Deater-Deckard, K., Dodge, K. A., Bates, J. E., & Pettit, G. S. (2004). Ethnic differences in the link between physical discipline and later adolescent externalizing behaviors. *Journal of Child Psychology and Psychiatry, 45*, 801–812.

Lansford, J. E., Malone, P. S., Castellino, D. R., Dodge, K. A., Pettit, G., & Bates, J. E. (2006). Trajectories of internalizing, externalizing, and grades for children who have and have not experienced their parents' divorce or separation. *Journal of Family Psychology, 20*, 292–301.

Lantieri, L. (2003). Waging peace in our schools: The Resolving Conflict Creatively Program. In M. J. Elias & H. Arnold (Eds.), *EQ + IQ = best leadership practices for caring and successful schools* (pp. 76–88). Thousand Oaks, CA: Corwin.

Lapsley, D. K., Jackson, S., Rice, K., & Shadid, G. (1988). Self-monitoring and the "new look" at the imaginary audience and personal fable: An ego-developmental analysis. *Journal of Adolescent Research, 3*, 17–31.

Laptook, A. R., O'Shea, T. M., Shankaran, S., & Bhaskar, B. (2005). Adverse neurodevelopmental outcomes among extremely low birth weight infants with a normal head

ultrasound: Prevalence and antecedents. *Pediatrics, 115*, 673–680.

Largo, R. H., Caflisch, J. A., Hug, F., Muggli, K., Molnar, A. A., & Molinari, L. (2001). Neuromotor development from 5 to 18 years. Part 1: Timed performance. *Developmental Medicine and Child Neurology, 43*, 436–443.

Larson, R., & Ham, M. (1993). Stress and "storm and stress" in early adolescence: The relationship of negative events with dysphoric affect. *Developmental Psychology, 29*, 130–140.

Larson, R., & Lampman-Petraitis, C. (1989). Daily emotional states as reported by children and adolescents. *Child Development, 60*, 1250–1260.

Larson, R. W. (2001). How U.S. children and adolescents spend time: What it does (and doesn't) tell us about their development. *Current Directions in Psychological Science, 10*, 160–164.

Larson, R. W., Moneta, G., Richards, M. H., & Wilson, S. (2002). Continuity, stability, and change in daily emotional experience across adolescence. *Child Development, 73*, 1151–1165.

Larson, R. W., & Richards, M. H. (1991). Daily companionship in late childhood and early adolescence: Changing developmental contexts. *Child Development, 62*, 284–300.

Larson, R. W., & Richards, M. H. (1998). Waiting for the weekend: Friday and Saturday night as the emotional climax of the week. In A. C. Crouter & R. Larson (Eds.), *Temporal rhythms in adolescence: Clocks, calendars, and the coordination of daily life* (pp. 37–51). San Francisco: Jossey-Bass.

Larson, R. W., Richards, M. H., Moneta, G., Holmbeck, G., & Duckett, E. (1996). Changes in adolescents' daily interactions with their families from ages 10 to 18: Disengagement and transformation. *Developmental Psychology, 32*, 744–754.

Larson, R. W., Richards, M. H., Sims, B., & Dworkin, J. (2001). How urban African-American young adolescents spend their time: Time budgets for locations, activities, and companionship. *American Journal of Community Psychology, 29*, 565–597.

Larzelere, R. E., Schneider, W. N., Larson, D. B., & Pike, P. L. (1996). The effects of discipline responses in delaying toddler misbehavior recurrences. *Child and Family Behavior Therapy, 18*, 35–7.

Lattimore, K. A., Donn, S. M., Kaciroti, N., Kemper, A. R., Neal, C. R., Jr., & Vazquez, D. M. (2005). Selective serotonin reuptake inhibitor (SSRI) use during pregnancy and effects on the fetus and newborn: A meta-analysis. *Journal of Perinatology, 25*, 595–604.

Latz, S., Wolf, A. W., & Lozoff, B. (1999). Sleep practices and problems in young children in Japan and the United States. *Archives of Pediatric and Adolescent Medicine, 153*, 339–346.

Laucht, M., Esser, G., & Schmidt, M. H. (1997). Developmental outcome of infants born with biological and psychosocial risks. *Journal of Child Psychology and Psychiatry, 38*, 843–853.

Lauer, J. A., Betrán, A. P., Victora, C. G., de Onís, M., & Barros, A. J. D. (2004). Breastfeeding patterns and exposure to suboptimal breastfeeding among children in developing countries: Review and analysis of nationally representative surveys. *BMC Medicine, 2*, 26.

Laumann, E. O., Gagnon, J. H., Michael, R. T., & Michaels, S. (1994). *The social organization of sexuality*. Chicago: University of Chicago Press.

Laursen, B., Coy, K., & Collins, W. A. (1998). Reconsidering changes in parent–child conflict across adolescence: A meta-analysis. *Child Development, 69*, 817–832.

Lavelli, M., & Fogel, A. (2005). Developmental changes in the relationship between the infant's attention and emotion during early face-to-face communication: The 2-month transition. *Developmental Psychology, 41*, 265–280.

Law, K. L., Stroud, L. R., Niaura, R., LaGasse, L. L., Liu, J., & Lester, B. M. (2003). Smoking during pregnancy and newborn neurobehavior. *Pediatrics, 111*, 1318–1323.

Law, K. S., Wong, C.-S., Song, L. J., & Law, K. S. (2004). The construct and criterion validity of emotional intelligence and its potential utility for management studies. *Journal of Applied Psychology, 89*, 483–496.

Lawrence, K., Kuntsi, J., Coleman, M., Campbell, R., & Skuse, D. (2003). Face and emotion recognition deficits in Turner syndrome: A possible role for X-linked genes in amygdala development. *Neuropsychology, 17*, 39–49.

Lawson, K. R., & Ruff, H. A. (2004). Early attention and negative emotionality predict later cognitive and behavioral function. *International Journal of Behavioral Development, 28,* 157–165.

Lazar, I., & Darlington, R. (1982). Lasting effects of early education: a report from the Consortium for Longitudinal Studies. *Monographs of the Society for Research in Child Development, 47*(2–3, Serial No. 195).

Lazarus, R. S., & Lazarus, B. N. (1994). *Passion and reason.* New York: Oxford University Press.

Le Bourdais, C., & Lapierre-Adamcyk, E. (2004). Changes in conjugal life in Canada: Is cohabitation progressively replacing marriage? *Journal of Marriage and Family, 66,* 929–942.

Le Grand, R., Mondloch, C. J., Maurer, D., & Brent, H. P. (2001). Early visual experience and face processing. *Nature, 410,* 890.

Le Grand, R., Mondloch, C. J., Maurer, D., & Brent, H. P. (2003). Expert face processing requires input to the right hemisphere during infancy. *Nature Neuroscience, 6,* 1108–1112.

Leadbeater, B., & Hoglund, W. (2006). Changing the social texts of peer victimization. *Journal of the Canadian Academy of Child and Adolescent Psychiatry, 15,* 21–26.

Leadbeater, B. J., Kuperminc, G. P., Blatt, S. J., & Herzog, C. (1999). A multivariate model of gender differences in adolescents' internalizing and externalizing problems. *Developmental Psychology, 35,* 1268–1282.

Leaper, C. (1994). Exploring the correlates and consequences of gender segregation: Social relationships in childhood, adolescence, and adulthood. In C. Leaper (Ed.), *New directions for child development* (No. 65, pp. 67–86). San Francisco: Jossey-Bass.

Leaper, C. (2000). Gender, affiliation, assertion, and the interactive context of parent–child play. *Developmental Psychology, 36,* 381–393.

Leaper, C., Anderson, K. J., & Sanders, P. (1998). Moderators of gender effects on parents' talk to their children: A meta-analysis. *Developmental Psychology, 34,* 3–27.

Leaper, C., Leve, L., Strasser, T., & Schwartz, R. (1995). Mother–child communication sequences: Play activity, child gender, and marital status effects. *Merrill-Palmer Quarterly, 41,* 307–327.

Leaper, C., Tenenbaum, H. R., & Shaffer, T. G. (1999). Communication patterns of African-American girls and boys from low-income, urban backgrounds. *Child Development, 70,* 1489–1503.

Learmonth, A. E., Lamberth, & Rovee-Collier, C. (2004). Generalization of deferred imitation during the first year of life. *Journal of Experimental Child Psychology, 88,* 297–318.

LeBlanc, L. A., Goldsmith, T., & Patel, D. R. (2003). Behavioral aspects of chronic illness in children and adolescents. *Pediatric Clinics of North America, 50,* 859–878.

Lecanuet, J.-P., Granier-Deferre, C., & DeCasper, A. (2005). Are we expecting too much from prenatal sensory experiences? In B. Hopkins & S. P. Johnson (Eds.), *Prenatal development of postnatal functions* (pp. 31–49). Westport, CT: Praeger.

Lecanuet, J.-P., Granier-Deferre, C., Jacquet, A.-Y., Capponi, I., & Ledru, L. (1993). Prenatal discrimination of a male and female voice uttering the same sentence. *Early Development and Parenting, 2,* 217–228.

Lederer, J. M. (2000). Reciprocal teaching of social studies in inclusive elementary classrooms. *Journal of Learning Disabilities, 33,* 91–106.

Lee, C. L., & Bates, J. E. (1985). Mother–child interaction at age two years and perceived difficult temperament. *Child Development, 56,* 1314–1325.

Lee, E. A., Torrance, N., & Olson, D. R. (2001). Young children and the say/mean distinction: Verbatim and paraphrase recognition in narrative and nursery rhyme contexts. *Journal of Child Language, 28,* 531–543.

Lee, K., Cameron, C., Xu, F., Fu, G., & Board, J. (1997). Chinese and Canadian children's evaluations of lying and truth telling: Similarities and differences in the context of pro- and antisocial behaviors. *Child Development, 68,* 924–934.

Lee, S. J., Ralston, H. J., Partridge, J. C., & Rosen, M. A. (2005). Fetal pain: A systematic multidisciplinary review of the evidence. *Journal of the American Medical Association, 294,* 947–954.

Lee, V. E., & Burkam, D. T. (2002). *Inequality at the starting gate.* Washington, DC: Economic Policy Institute.

Lee, V. E., & Burkam, D. T. (2003). Dropping out of high school: The role of school organization and structure. *American Educational Research Journal, 40,* 353–393.

Leeman, L. W., Gibbs, J. C., & Fuller, D. (1993). Evaluation of a multi-component group treatment program for juvenile delinquents. *Aggressive Behavior, 19,* 281–292.

Lefebvre, F., Mazurier, E., & Tessier, R. (2005). Cognitive and educational outcomes in early adulthood for infants weighing 1000 grams or less at birth. *Acta Paediatrica, 94,* 733–740.

Lefkowitz, E. S. (2005). "Things have gotten better": Developmental changes among emerging adults after the transition to university. *Journal of Adolescent Research, 20,* 40–63.

Lefkowitz, E. S., Boone, T. L., Sigman, M., & Au, T. K. (2002). He said, she said: Gender differences in mother–adolescent conversations about sexuality. *Journal of Research on Adolescence, 12,* 217–242.

Lefkowitz, E. S., & Gillen, M. M. (2006). "Sex is just a normal part of life": Sexuality in emerging adulthood. In J. J. Arnett & J. L. Tanner (Eds.), *Emerging adults in America* (pp. 235–256). Washington, DC: American Psychological Association.

Lefkowitz, E. S., Sigman, M., & Au, T. K. (2000). Helping mothers discuss sexuality and AIDS with adolescents. *Child Development, 71,* 1383–1394.

Lehman, D. R., & Nisbett, R. E. (1990). A longitudinal study of the effects of undergraduate training on reasoning. *Developmental Psychology, 26,* 952–960.

Lehman, E. B., Steier, A., Guidash, K. M., & Wanna, S. Y. (2002). Predictors of compliance in toddlers: Child temperament, maternal personality, and emotional availability. *Early Child Development and Care, 172,* 301–310.

Leiferman, J. A., & Evenson, K. R. (2003). The effect of regular leisure physical activity on birth outcomes. *Maternal and Child Health Journal, 7,* 59–64.

Lemche, E., Lennertz, I., Orthmann, C., Ari, A., Grote, K., Hafker, J., & Klann-Delius, G. (2003). Emotion-regulatory process in evoked play narratives: Their relation with mental representations and family interactions. *Praxis der Kinderpsychologie und Kinderpsychiatrie, 52,* 156–171.

Lempert, H. (1989). Animacy constraints on preschoolers' acquisition of syntax. *Child Development, 60,* 237–245.

Lempert, H. (1990). Acquisition of passives: The role of patient animacy, salience, and lexical accessibility. *Journal of Child Language, 17,* 677–696.

Lengua, L. J., Wolchik, S., Sandler, I. N., & West, S. G. (2000). The additive and interactive effects of parenting and temperament in predicting problems of children of divorce. *Journal of Clinical Psychology, 29,* 232–244.

Lenhart, A., Rainie, L., & Lewis, O. (2001). *Teenage life online: The rise of the instant-message generation and the Internet's impact on friendships and family relationships.* Washington, DC: Pew Internet & American Life Project. Retrieved from www.pewinternet.org/reports/toc?aspReport=36

Lenroot, R. K., & Giedd, J. N. (2006). Brain development in children and adolescents: Insights from anatomical magnetic resonance imaging. *Neuroscience and Biobehavioral Reviews, 30,* 718–729.

Leon, K. (2003). Risk and protective factors in young children's adjustment to parental divorce: A review of the research. *Family Relations, 52,* 258–270.

Lerner, R. M. (2006). Developmental science, developmental systems, and contemporary theories of human development. In R. M. Lerner (Ed.), *Handbook of child psychology: Vol. 1. Theoretical models of human development* (6th ed., pp. 1–17). Hoboken, NJ: Wiley.

Lerner, R. M., Fisher, C. B., & Weinberg, R. A. (2000). Toward a science for and of the people: Promoting civil society through the application of developmental science. *Child Development, 71,* 11–20.

Lerner, R. M., Rothbaum, F., Boulos, S., & Castellino, D. R. (2002). Developmental systems perspective on parenting. In M. H. Bornstein (Ed.), *Handbook of parenting: Vol. 2. Biology and ecology of parenting* (2nd ed., pp. 315–344). Mahwah, NJ: Erlbaum.

Leslie, A. M. (2004). Who's for learning? *Developmental Science, 7,* 417–419.

Lester, B. M. (1985). Introduction: There's more to crying than meets the ear. In B. M. Lester & C. F. Z. Boukydis (Eds.), *Infant crying* (pp. 1–27). New York: Plenum.

Lester, B. M., ElSohly, M., Wright, L. L., Smeriglio, V. L., Verter, J., & Bauer, C. R. (2001). The maternal lifestyle study: Drug use by meconium toxicology and maternal self-report. *Pediatrics, 107,* 309–317.

Lester, B. M., Kotelchuck, M., Spelke, E., Sellers, M. J., & Klein, R. E. (1974). Separation protest in Guatemalan infants: Cross-cultural and cognitive findings. *Developmental Psychology, 10,* 79–85.

Lester, B. M., LaGasse, L., Seifer, R., Tronick, E. Z., Bauer, C., & Shankaran, S. (2003). The maternal lifestyle study (MLS): Effects of prenatal cocaine and/or opiate exposure on auditory brain response at one month. *Journal of Pediatrics, 142,* 279–285.

Lester, B. M., & Tronick, E. Z. (2004). *NICU Network Neurobehavioral Scale (NNNS).* Baltimore, MD: Brookes.

Lett, D. (1997). *L'enfant des miracles: Enfance et société au Moyen Age (XIIe–XIIIe siecle).* Paris: Aubier.

LeVay, S. (1993). *The sexual brain.* Cambridge, MA: MIT Press.

Leventhal, T., & Brooks-Gunn, J. (2003). Children and youth in neighborhood contexts. *Current Directions in Psychological Science, 12,* 27–31.

Levin, I., & Bus, A. G. (2003). How is emergent writing based on drawing? Analyses of children's products and their sorting by children and mothers. *Developmental Psychology, 39,* 891–905.

Levine, L. E. (1983). Mine: Selfdefinition in 2-year-old boys. *Developmental Psychology, 19,* 544–549.

Levine, L. J. (1995). Young children's understanding of the causes of anger and sadness. *Child Development, 66,* 697–709.

LeVine, R., LeVine, S. E., Rowe, M. L., & Schnell-Anzola, B. (2004). Maternal literacy and health behavior: A Nepalese case study. *Social Science and Medicine, 58,* 863–877.

LeVine, R. A., Dixon, S., LeVine, S., Richman, A., Leiderman, P. H., Keefer, C. H., & Brazelton, T. B. (1994). *Child care and culture: Lessons from Africa.* New York: Cambridge University Press.

LeVine, R. A., LeVine, S., Richman, A., Tapia Uribe, M. R., Sunderland Correa, C., & Miller, P. (1991). Women's schooling and child care in the demographic transition: A Mexican case study. *Population and Development Review, 17,* 459–496.

LeVine, R. A., LeVine, S. E., & Schnell, B. (2001). "Improve the women": Mass schooling, female literacy, and worldwide social change. *Harvard Educational Review, 71,* 1–50.

Levine, S. C., Huttenlocher, J., Taylor, A., & Langrock, A. (1999). Early sex differences in spatial skill. *Developmental Psychology, 35,* 940–949.

Levinson, D. J. (1978). *The seasons of a man's life.* New York: Knopf.

Levinson, D. J. (1996). *The seasons of a woman's life.* New York: Knopf.

Levtzion-Korach, O., Tennenbaum, A., Schnitzer, R., & Ornoy, A. (2000). Early motor development of blind children. *Journal of Paediatric and Child Health, 36,* 226–229.

Levy, G. D., Taylor, M. G., & Gelman, S. A. (1995). Traditional and evaluative aspects of flexibility in gender roles, social conventions, moral rules, and physical laws. *Child Development, 66,* 515–531.

Levy, S. R., & Dweck, C. S. (1999). The impact of children's static vs. dynamic conceptions of people on stereotype information. *Child Development, 70,* 1163–1180.

Levy-Shiff, R., & Israelashvili, R. (1988). Antecedents of fathering: Some further exploration. *Developmental Psychology, 24,* 434–440.

Lewis, C., Freeman, N. H., Kyriadidou, C., Maridakikasso-taki, K., & Berridge, D. M. (1996). Social influences on false belief access—specific sibling influences or general apprenticeship? *Child Development, 67,* 2930–2947.

Lewis, M. (1992). *Shame: The exposed self.* New York: Free Press.

Lewis, M. (1995). Embarrassment: The emotion of self-exposure and evaluation. In J. P. Tangney & K. W. Fischer (Eds.), *Self-conscious emotions* (pp. 198–218). New York: Guilford.

Lewis, M. (1997). *Altering fate: Why the past does not predict the future.* New York: Guilford.

Lewis, M. (1998). Emotional competence and development. In D. Pushkar, W. M. Bukowski, A. E. Schwartzman, E. M. Stack, & D. R. White (Eds.), *Improving competence across the lifespan* (pp. 27–36). New York: Plenum.
Lewis, M., & Brooks-Gunn, J. (1979). *Social cognition and the acquisition of self.* New York: Plenum.
Lewis, M., Feiring, C., & Rosenthal, S. (2000). Attachment over time. *Child Development, 71,* 707–720.
Lewis, M., & Ramsay, D. (2002). Cortisol response to embarrassment and shame. *Child Development, 73,* 1034–1045
Lewis, M., Ramsay, D. S., & Kawakami, K. (1993). Differences between Japanese infants and Caucasian American infants in behavioral and cortisol response to inoculation. *Child Development, 64,* 1722–1731.
Lewis, M., Sullivan, M. W., Stanger, C., & Weiss, M. (1989). Self development and self-conscious emotions. *Child Development, 60,* 146–156.
Lewis, M. D. (2000). The promise of dynamic systems approaches for an integrated account of human development. *Child Development, 71,* 36–43.
Li, Q. (2006). Cyberbullying in schools: A research of gender differences. *School Psychology International, 27,* 157–170.
Li, R., Darling, N., Maurice, E., Barker, L., & Grummer-Strawn, L. M. (2005). Breastfeeding rates in the United States by characteristics of the child, mother, or family: The 2002 National Immunization Survey. *Pediatrics, 115,* e31–e37.
Li, S.-C., Lindenberger, U., Hommel, B., Aschersleben, G., Prinz, W., & Baltes, P. B. (2004). Transformation in the couplings among intellectual abilities and constituent cognitive processes across the life span. *Psychological Science, 15,* 155–163.
Li, W., Han, S., Gregg, T. R., Kemp, F. W., Davidow, A. L., & Louria, D. B. (2003). Lead exposure potentiates predatory attack behavior in the cat. *Environmental Research, 92,* 197–206.
Liben, L. (2006). Education for spatial thinking. In K. A. Renninger & I. E. Sigel (Eds.), *Handbook of child psychology: Vol. 4. Child psychology in practice* (6th ed., pp. 197–247). Hoboken, NJ: Wiley.
Liben, L. S. (1999). Developing an understanding of external spatial representations. In I. E. Sigel (Ed.), *Development of mental representation* (pp. 297–321). Mahwah, NJ: Erlbaum.
Liben, L. S., & Bigler, R. S. (2002). The developmental course of gender differentiation: Conceptualizing, measuring, and evaluating constructs and pathways. *Monographs of the Society for Research in Child Development, 67*(2, Serial No. 269).
Liben, L. S., Bigler, R. S., & Krogh, H. R. (2001). Pink and blue collar jobs: Children's judgments of job status and job aspirations in relation to sex of worker. *Journal of Experimental Child Psychology, 79,* 346–363.
Liben, L. S., & Downs, R. M. (1993). Understanding person-space-map relations: Cartographic and developmental perspectives. *Developmental Psychology, 29,* 739–752.
Liben, L. S., & Signorella, M. L. (1993). Gender-schematic processing in children: The role of initial interpretations of stimuli. *Developmental Psychology, 29,* 141–149.
Lickliter, R., & Bahrick, L. E. (2000). The development of infant intersensory perception: Advantages of a comparative convergent-operations approach. *Psychological Bulletin, 126,* 260–280.
Lidz, C. S. (2001). Multicultural issues and dynamic assessment. In L. A. Suzuki & J. G. Ponterotto (Eds.), *Handbook of multicultural assessment: Clinical, psychological, and educational applications* (2nd ed., pp. 523–539). San Francisco: Jossey-Bass.
Lidz, J., Gleitman, H., & Gleitman, L. (2004). Kidz in the 'hood: Syntactic bootstrapping and the mental lexicon. In D. G. Hall & S. R. Waxman (Eds.), *Weaving a lexicon* (pp. 603–636). Cambridge, MA: MIT Press.
Lieven, E., Pine, J., & Baldwin, G. (1997). Lexically based learning and early grammatical development. *Journal of Child Language, 24,* 187–220.
Lillard, A. (2007). *Montessori: The science behind the genius.* New York: Oxford University Press.
Lillard, A., & Else-Quest, N. (2006). Evaluating Montessori education. *Science, 313,* 1893–1894.
Lillard, A. S. (2003). Pretend play and cognitive development. In U. Goswami (Ed.), *Blackwell handbook of childhood cognitive development* (pp. 189–205). Malden, MA: Blackwell.
Lin, C. C., Hsiao, C. K., & Chen, W. J. (1999). Development of sustained attention assessed using the continuous performance test among children 6–15 years. *Journal of Abnormal Child Psychology, 27,* 403–412.
Lin, Z. L., Yu, H. M., Chen, S. Q., Liang, Z. Q., & Zhang, Z. Y. (2006). Mild hypothermia via selective head cooling as neuroprotective therapy in term neonates with perinatal asphyxia: An experience from a single neonatal intensive care unit. *Journal of Perinatology, 26,* 180–184.
Linder, J. R., & Collins, W. A. (2005). Parent and peer predictors of physical aggression and conflict management in romantic relationships in early adulthood. *Journal of Family Psychology, 19,* 252–262.
Lindley, L. D. (2005). Perceived barriers to carreer development in the context of social-cognitive career theory. *Journal of Career Assessment, 13,* 271–287.
Lindsay-Hartz, J., de Rivera, J., & Mascolo, M. F. (1995). Differentiating guilt and shame and their effects on motivation. In J. P. Tangney & K. W. Fischer (Eds.), *Self-conscious emotions* (pp. 274–300). New York: Guilford.
Lindsey, D., & Martin, S. K. (2003). Deepening child poverty: The not so good news about welfare reform. *Children and Youth Services Review, 25,* 165–173.
Lindsey, E. W., & Colwell, M. J. (2003). Preschoolers' emotional competence: Links to pretend and physical play. *Child Study Journal, 33,* 39–52.
Lindsey, E. W., & Mize, J. (2000). Parent–child physical and pretense play: Links to children's social competence. *Merrill-Palmer Quarterly, 46,* 565–591.
Linn, M. C., & Petersen, A. C. (1985). Emergence and characterization of sex differences in spatial ability: A meta-analysis. *Child Development, 56,* 1479–1498.
Linscheid, T. R., Budd, K. S., & Rasnake, L. K. (2005). Pediatric feeding problems. In M. C. Roberts (Ed.), *Handbook of pediatric psychology and psychiatry* (3rd ed., pp. 481–488). New York: Guilford.
Linver, M. R., Brooks-Gunn, J., & Kohen, D. E. (2002). Family processes as pathways from income to young children's development. *Developmental Psychology, 38,* 719–734.
Linver, M. R., Martin, A., & Brooks-Gunn, J. (2004). Measuring infants' home environment: The IT-HOME for infants between birth and 12 months in four national data sets. *Parenting: Science and Practice, 4,* 115–137.
Lipman, E. L., Boyle, M. H., Dooley, M. D., & Offord, D. R. (2002). Child well-being in single-mother families. *Journal of the American Academy of Child and Adolescent Psychiatry, 41,* 75–82.
Lipsitt, L. P. (2003). Crib death: A biobehavioral phenomenon? *Psychological Science, 12,* 164–170.
Lipton, J. S., & Spelke, E. S. (2003). Origins of number sense: Large-number discrimination in human infants. *Psychological Science, 14,* 396–401.
Liston, R., Crane, J., Hamilton, E., Hughes, O., Kuling, S., & MacKinnon, C. (2002). Fetal health surveillance during labour. *Journal of Obstetrics and Gynecology of Canada, 24,* 250–276.
Liszkowski, U., Carpenter, M., Henning, A., Striano, T., & Tomasello, M. (2004). Twelve-month-olds point to share attention and interest, *Developmental Science, 7,* 297–307.
Litovsky, R. Y., & Ashmead, D. H. (1997). Development of binaural and spatial hearing in infants and children. In R. H. Gilkey & T. R. Anderson (Eds.), *Binaural and spatial hearing in real and virtual environments* (pp. 571–592). Mahwah, NJ: Erlbaum.
Little, C., & Carter, A. S. (2005). Negative emotional reactivity and regulation in 12-month-olds following emotional challenge: Contributions of maternal–infant emotional availability in a low-income sample, *Infant Mental Health Journal, 26,* 354–368.
Liu, J., Raine, A., Venables, P. H., Dalais, C., & Mednick, S. A. (2003). Malnutrition at age 3 years and lower cognitive ability at age 11 years. *Archives of Paediatric and Adolescent Medicine, 157,* 593–600.
Liu, J., Raine, A., Venables, P. H., & Mednick, S. A. (2004). Malnutrition at age 3 years and externalizing behavior problems at ages 8, 11, and 17 years. *American Journal of Psychiatry, 161,* 2005–2013.
Lloyd, L. (1999). Multi-age classes and high ability students. *Review of Educational Research, 69,* 187–212.
Lochman, J. E., & Dodge, K. A. (1998). Distorted perceptions in dyadic interactions of aggressive and nonaggressive boys: Effects of prior expectations, context, and boys' age. *Development and Psychopathology, 10,* 495–512.
Locke, J. (1892). Some thoughts concerning education. In R. H. Quick (Ed.), *Locke on education* (pp. 1–236). Cambridge, U.K.: Cambridge University Press. (Original work published 1690)
Lockhart, R. S., & Craik, F. I. M. (1990). Levels of processing: A retrospective commentary on a framework for memory research. *Canadian Journal of Psychology, 44,* 87–112.
Loeb, S., Fuller, B., Kagan, S. L., & Carrol, B. (2004). Child care in poor communities: Early learning effects of type, quality, and stability. *Child Development, 75,* 47–65.
Loehlin, J. C., Horn, J. M., & Willerman, L. (1997). Heredity, environment, and IQ in the Texas Adoption Project. In R. J. Sternberg & E. L. Grigorenko (Eds.), *Intelligence, heredity, and environment* (pp. 105–125). New York: Cambridge University Press.
Loehlin, J. C., & Martin, N. G. (2001). Age changes in personality traits and their heritabilities during the adult years: Evidence from Australian twin registry samples *Personality and Individual Differences, 30,* 1147–1160.
Loganovskaja, T. K., & Loganovsky, K. N. (1999). EEG, cognitive and psychopathological abnormalities in children irradiated in utero. *International Journal of Psychophysiology, 34,* 213–224.
Lohman, D. F. (2000). Measures of intelligence: Cognitive theories. In A. E. Kazdin (Ed.), *Encyclopedia of psychology: Vol. 5* (pp. 147–150). Washington, DC: American Psychological Association.
Longstaffe, S., Moffatt, M. E., & Whalen, J. C. (2000). Behavioral and self-concept changes after six months of enuresis treatment: A randomized, controlled trial. *Pediatrics, 105,* 935–940.
Loock, C., Conry, J., Cook, J. L., Chudley, A. E., & Rosales, T. (2005). Identifying fetal alcohol spectrum disorder in primary care. *Canadian Medical Association Journal, 172,* 628–630.
Looker, D., & Thiessen, V. (2003). *The digital divide in Canadian schools: Factors affecting student access to and use of information technology.* Ottawa: Canadian Education Statistics Council.
Loots, G., & Devise, I. (2003). The use of visual-tactile communication strategies by deaf and hearing fathers and mothers of deaf infants. *Journal of Deaf Studies and Deaf Education, 8,* 31–42.
Lord, R. H., & Kozar, B. (1996). Overuse injuries in young athletes. In F. L. Smoll & R. E. Smith (Eds.), *Children and youth in sport: A biopsychological perspective* (pp. 281–294). Dubuque, IA: Brown & Benchmark.
Lorenz, K. Z. (1952). *King Solomon's ring.* New York: Crowell.
LoTurco, J. J. (2000). Neural circuits in the 21st century: Synaptic networks of neurons and glia. *Proceedings of the National Academy of Sciences, 97,* 8196–8197.
Louie, V. (2001). Parents' aspirations and investment: The role of social class in the educational experiences of 1.5- and second-generation Chinese Americans. *Harvard Educational Review, 71,* 438–474.
Louis, J., Cannard, C., Bastuji, H., & Challamel, M.-J. (1997). Sleep ontogenesis revisited: A longitudinal 24-hour home polygraphic study on 15 normal infants during the first two years of life. *Sleep, 20,* 323–333.
Lourenco, O. (2003). Making sense of Turiel's dispute with Kohlberg: The case of the child's moral competence. *New Ideas in Psychology, 21,* 43–68.
Love, J. M., Harrison, L., Sagi-Schwartz, A., van IJzendoorn, M. H., Ross, C., & Ungerer, J. A. (2003). Child care quality matters: How conclusions may vary with context. *Child Development, 74,* 1021–1033.
Love, J. M., Kisker, E. E., Ross, C., Raikes, H., Constantine, J., Boller, K., & Brooks-Gunn, J. (2005). The effectiveness of early Head Start for 3-year-old children and their parents: Lessons for policy and programs. *Developmental Psychology, 41,* 885–901.
Lozoff, B., Klein, N. K., Nelson, E. C., McClish, D. K., Manuel, M., & Chacon, M. E. (1998). Behavior of infants with iron-deficiency anemia. *Child Development, 69,* 24–36.
Lucas, S. R., & Behrends, M. (2002). Sociodemographic diversity, correlated achievement, and de facto tracking. *Sociology of Education, 75,* 328–348.

Lucas, T. W., Wendorf, C. A., Imamoglu, E. O., Shen, J., Parkhill, M. R., Weisfeld, C. C., & Weisfeld, G. E. (2004). Marital satisfaction in four cultures as a function of homogamy, male dominance, and female attractiveness. *Sexualities, Evolution & Gender, 6,* 97–130.

Luciana, M., Sullivan, J., & Nelson, C. A. (2001). Associations between phenylalanine-to-tyrosine ratios and performance on tests of neuropsychological function in adolescents treated early and continuously for phenylketonuria. *Child Development, 72,* 1637–1652.

Ludemann, P. M. (1991). Generalized discrimination of positive facial expressions by seven- and ten-month-old infants. *Child Development, 62,* 55–67.

Luna, B., Garver, K. E., Urban, T. A., Lazar, N. A., & Sweeney, J. A. (2004). Maturation of cognitive processes from late childhood to adulthood. *Child Development, 75,* 1357–1372.

Luna, B., Thulborn, K. R., Monoz, D. P., Merriam, E. P., Garver, K. E., Minshew, N. J., Keshavan, M. S., Genovese, C. R., Eddy, W. F., & Sweeney, J. A. (2001). Maturation of widely distributed brain function subserves cognitive development. *Neuroimage, 13,* 786–793.

Lundy, B. L. (2002). Paternal socio-psychological factors and infant attachment: The mediating role of synchrony in father–infant interactions. *Infant Behavior and Development, 25,* 221–236.

Lundy, B. L. (2003). Father- and mother-infant face-to-face interactions: Differences in mind-related comments and infant attachment? *Infant Behavior and Development, 26,* 200–212.

Luo, Y., & Baillargeon, R. (2005). When the ordinary seems unexpected: Evidence for incremental physical knowledge in young infants. *Cognition, 95,* 297–328.

Luria, A. R. (1976). *Cognitive development: Its cultural and social foundations.* Cambridge, MA: Harvard University Press.

Lussier, G., Deater-Deckard, K., Dunn, J., & Davies, L. (2002). Support across two generations: Children's closeness to grandparents following parental divorce and remarriage. *Journal of Family Psychology, 16,* 363–376.

Luster, T., & Haddow, J. L. (2005). Adolescent mothers and their children: An ecological perspective. In T. Luster & J. L. Haddow (Eds.), *Parenting: An ecological perspective* (2nd ed., pp. 73–101). Mahwah, NJ: Erlbaum.

Luster, T., & McAdoo, H. (1996). Family and child influences on educational attainment: A secondary analysis of the High/Scope Perry Preschool data. *Developmental Psychology, 32,* 26–39.

Luthar, S. S., & Becker, B. E. (2002). Privileged but pressured: A study of affluent youth. *Child Development, 73,* 1593–1610.

Luthar, S. S., Cushing, T. J., & McMahon, T. J. (1997). Interdisciplinary interface: Developmental principles brought to substance abuse research. In S. S. Luthar, J. A. Burack, D. Cicchetti, & Weisz, J. R. (1997). *Developmental psychopathology* (pp. 437–456). Cambridge: Cambridge University Press.

Luthar, S. S., & Latendresse, S. J. (2005a). Children of the affluent: Challenges to well-being. *Current Directions in Psychological Science, 14,* 49–53.

Luthar, S. S., & Latendresse, S. J. (2005b). Comparable "risks" at the socioeconomic status extremes: Preadolescents' perceptions of parenting. *Development and Psychopathology, 17,* 207–230.

Luthar, S. S., & Sexton, C. (2004). The high price of affluence. In R. V. Kail (Ed.), *Advances in child development* (Vol. 32, pp. 126–162). San Diego, CA: Academic Press.

Luxembourg Income Study. (2005). *Household income surveys, 2000.* Retrieved from www.lisproject.org

Luyckx, K., Goossens, L., & Soenens, B. (2006). A developmental contextual perspective on identity construction in emerging adulthood: Change dynamics in commitment formation and commitment evaluation. *Developmental Psychology, 42,* 366–380.

Luyckx, K., Goossens, L., Soenens, B., & Beyers, W. (2006). Unpacking commitment and exploration: Preliminary validation of an integrative model of late adolescent identity formation. *Journal of Adolescence, 29,* 361–378.

Lynch, S. K., Turkheimer, E., D'Onofrio, B. M., Mendle, J., Emery, R. E., Slutske, W. S., & Martin, N. G. (2006). A genetically informed study of the association between harsh punishment and offspring behavioral problems. *Journal of Family Psychology, 20,* 190–198.

Lyon, T. D., & Flavell, J. H. (1994). Young children's understanding of "remember" and "forget." *Child Development, 65,* 1357–1371.

Lyons-Ruth, K. (1996). Attachment relationships among children with aggressive behavior problems: The role of disorganized early attachment patterns. *Journal of Consulting and Clinical Psychology, 64,* 64–73.

Lyons-Ruth, K., Bronfman, E., & Parsons, E. (1999). Maternal frightened, frightening, or aytpical behavior and disorganized infant attachment patterns. *Monographs of the Society for Research in Child Development, 64*(3, Serial No. 258), 67–96.

Lyons-Ruth, K., Easterbrooks, A., & Cibelli, C. (1997). Infant attachment strategies, infant mental lag, and maternal depressive symptoms: Predictors of internalizing and externalizing problems at age 7. *Developmental Psychology, 33,* 681–692.

Lytton, H., & Gallagher, L. (2002). Parenting twins and the genetics of parenting. In M. H. Bornstein (Ed.), *Handbook of parenting: Vol. 1. Children and Parenting* (pp. 227–253). Mahwah, NJ: Erlbaum.

Maberly, G. F., Haxton, D. P., & van der Haar, F. (2003). Iodine deficiency: Consequences and progress toward elimination. *Food and Nutrition Bulletin, 24,* S91–S98.

Maccoby, E. E. (1984). Middle childhood in the context of the family. In W. A. Collins (Ed.), *Development during middle childhood* (pp. 184– 239). Washington, DC: National Academy Press.

Maccoby, E. E. (1998). *The two sexes: Growing up apart, coming together.* Cambridge, MA: Belknap/Harvard University Press.

Maccoby, E. E. (2000). Perspectives on gender development. *International Journal of Behavioral Development, 24,* 398–406.

Maccoby, E. E. (2002). Gender and group process: A developmental perspective. *Current Directions in Psychological Science, 11,* 54–58.

Machin, G. A. (2005). Multiple birth. In H. W. Taeusch, R. A. Ballard, & C. A. Gleason (Eds.), *Avery's diseases of the newborn* (8th ed., pp. 57–62). Philadelphia: Saunders.

Mackey, K., Arnold, M. K., & Pratt, M. W. (2001). Adolescents' stories of decision making in more and less authoritative families: Representing the voices of parents in narrative. *Journal of Adolescent Research, 16,* 243–268.

MacWhinney, B. (2005). Language development. In M. H. Bornstein & M. E. Lamb (Eds.), *Developmental science: An advanced textbook* (5th ed., pp. 359–387). Mahwah, NJ: Erlbaum.

Madom, S., Jussim, L., & Eccles, J. (1997). In search of the powerful self-fulfilling prophecy. *Journal of Personality and Social Psychology, 72,* 791–809.

Magnuson, K. A., & Duncan, G. J. (2002). Parents in poverty. In M. H. Bornstein (Ed.), *Handbook of parenting: Vol. 4. Social conditions and applied parenting* (pp. 95–122). Mahwah, NJ: Erlbaum.

Magnusson, D. (1999). Holistic interactionism: A perspective for research on personality development. In L. A. Pervin & O. P. John (Eds.), *Handbook of personality: Theory and research* (2nd ed., pp. 219–247). New York: Guilford.

Magolda, M. B. B. (2002). Epistemological reflection: The evolution of epistemological assumptions from age 18 to 30. In B. K. Hofer & P. R. Pintrich (Eds.), *Personal epistemology* (pp. 89–102). Mahwah, NJ: Erlbaum.

Mahon, M. M., Goldberg, E. Z., & Washington, S. K. (1999). Concept of death in a sample of Israeli kibbutz children. *Death Studies, 23,* 43–59.

Mahoney, J. L., & Magnusson, D. (2001). Parent participation in community activities and the persistence of criminality. *Development and Psychopathology, 13,* 123–139.

Mahoney, J. L., Schweder, A. E., & Stattin, H. (2002). Structured after-school activities as a moderator of depressed mood for adolescents with detached relations to their parents. *Journal of Community Psychology, 30,* 69–86.

Mahoney, J. L., & Stattin, H. (2000). Leisure activities and antisocial behavior: The role of structure and social context. *Journal of Adolescence, 23,* 113–127.

Mahoney, J. L., Stattin, H., & Magnusson, D. (2001). Youth recreation centre participation and criminal offending: A 20-year longitudinal study of Swedish boys. *International Journal of Behavioral Development, 25,* 509–520.

Main, M. (2000). The organized categories of infant, child, and adult attachment: Flexible vs. inflexible attention under attachment-related stress. *Journal of the American Psychoanalytic Association, 48,* 1055–1096.

Main, M., & Cassidy, J. (1988). Categories of response to reunion with the parent at age 6: Predictable from infant attachment classifications and stable over a 1-month period. *Developmental Psychology, 24,* 415–426.

Main, M., & Solomon, J. (1990). Procedures for identifying infants as disorganized/disoriented during the Ainsworth Strange Situation. In M. Greenberg, D. Cicchetti, & M. Cummings (Eds.), *Attachment in the preschool years: Theory, research, and intervention* (pp. 121–160). Chicago: University of Chicago Press.

Majnemer, A., & Barr, R. G. (2005). Influence of supine sleep positioning on early motor milestone acquisition. *Developmental Medicine and Child Neurology, 47,* 370–376.

Major, B., Spencer, S., Schmader, T., Wolfe, C., & Crocker, J. (1998). Coping with negative stereotypes about intellectual performance: The role of psychological disengagement. *Personality and Social Psychology Bulletin, 24,* 34–50.

Makin, J. E., Fried, P. A., & Watkinson, B. (1991). A comparison of active and passive smoking during pregnancy: Long-term effects. *Neurotoxicology and Teratology, 13,* 5–12.

Malatesta, C. Z., Grigoryev, P., Lamb, C., Albin, M., & Culver, C. (1986). Emotion socialization and expressive development in preterm and full-term infants. *Child Development, 57,* 316–330.

Malcom, N. L. (2006). "Shaking it off" and "toughing it out": Socialization to pain and injury in girls' softball. *Journal of Contemporary Ethnography, 35,* 495–525.

Malina, R. M., & Beunen, G. (1996). Matching of opponents in youth sports. In O. Bar-Or (Ed.), *The child and adolescent athlete* (pp. 202–213). Oxford: Blackwell.

Malina, R. M., & Bouchard, C. (1991). *Growth, maturation, and physical activity.* Champaign, IL: Human Kinetics.

Mandler, J. M. (2004a). *The foundations of mind.* New York: Oxford University Press.

Mandler, J. M. (2004b). Thought before language. *Trends in Cognitive Sciences, 8,* 508–513.

Mandler, J. M., & McDonough, L. (1993). Concept formation in infancy. *Cognitive Development, 8,* 291–318.

Mandler, J. M., & McDonough, L. (1998). On developing a knowledge base in infancy. *Developmental Psychology, 34,* 1274–1288.

Mangelsdorf, S. C., Schoppe, S. J., & Buur, H. (2000). The meaning of parental reports: A contextual approach to the study of temperament and behavior problems. In V. J. Molfese & D. L. Molfese (Eds.), *Temperament and personality across the life span* (pp. 121–140). Mahwah, NJ: Erlbaum.

Manlove, J. (1997). Early motherhood in an intergenerational perspective: The experiences of a British cohort. *Journal of Marriage and the Family, 59,* 263–279.

Manlove, J., Franzetta, K., Ryan, S., & Moore, K. (2006). Adolescent sexual relationships, contraceptive consistency, and pregnancy prevention approaches. In A. C. Crouter & A. Booth (Eds.), *Romance and sex in adolescence and emerging adulthood: Risks and opportunities* (pp. 181–212). Mahwah, NJ: Erlbaum.

Manlove, J., Ryan, S., & Franzetta, K. (2003). Patterns of contraceptive use within teenagers' first sexual relationships. *Perspectives on Sexual and Reproductive Health, 35,* 246–255.

Manson, J. E., Skerrett, P. J., Greenland, P., & VanItallie, T. B. (2004). The escalating pandemics of obesity and sedentary lifestyle: A call to action for clinicians. *Archives of Internal Medicine, 164,* 249–258.

Mao, A., Burnham, M. M., Goodlin-Jones, B. L., Gaylor, E. E., & Anders, T. F. (2004). A comparison of the sleep–wake patterns of cosleeping and solitary-sleeping infants. *Child Psychiatry and Human Development, 35,* 95–105.

Maratsos, M. (1998). The acquisition of grammar. In D. Kuhn & R. S. Siegler (Eds.), *Handbook of child psychology: Vol. 1. Theoretical models of human development* (5th ed., pp. 255–308). New York: Wiley.

Maratsos, M. (2000). More overregularizations after all: New data and discussion on Marcus, Pinker, Ullman, Hollander, Rosen, & Xu. *Journal of Child Language, 27,* 183–212.

Marchman, V. A., & Thal, D. J. (2005). Words and grammar. In M. Tomasello & D. I. Slobin (Eds.), *Beyond nature–nurture: Essays in honor of Elizabeth Bates* (pp. 141–164). Mahwah, NJ: Erlbaum.

Marcia, J. E. (1980). Identity in adolescence. In J. Adelson (Ed.), *Handbook of adolescent psychology* (pp. 159–187). New York: Wiley.

Marcon, R. A. (1999a). Differential impact of preschool models on development and early learning of inner-city children: A three-cohort study. *Developmental Psychology, 35,* 358–375.

Marcon, R. A. (1999b). Positive relationships between parent–school involvement and public school inner-city preschoolers' development and academic performance. *School Psychology Review, 28,* 395–412.

Marcus, G. F. (1995). Children's overregularization of English plurals: A quantitative analysis. *Journal of Child Language, 22,* 447–459.

Marcus, G. F., Fernandes, K. J., & Johnson, S. P. (2007). Infant rule learning facilitated by speech. *Psychological Science, 18,* pp. 387–391.

Marcus, G. F., Vijayan, S., Rao, S. B., & Vishton, P. M. (1999). Rule learning by seven-month-old infants. *Science, 283,* 77–80.

Mardh, P. A. (2002). Influence of infection with *Chlamydia trachomatis* on pregnancy outcome, infant health and life-long sequelae in infected offspring. *Best Practices in Clinical Obstetrics and Gynaecology, 16,* 847–964.

Margolese, S. K., Markiewicz, D., & Doyle, A. B. (2005). Attachment to parents, best friend, and romantic partner: Predicting different pathways to depression in adolescence. *Journal of Youth and Adolescence, 34,* 637–650.

Mariano, K. A., & Harton, H. C. (2005). Similarities in aggression, inattention/hyperactivity, depression, and anxiety in middle childhood friendships. *Journal of Social and Clinical Psychology, 24,* 471–496.

Markman, E. M. (1992). Constraints on word learning: Speculations about their nature, origins, and domain specificity. In M. R. Gunnar & M. P. Maratsos (Eds.), *Minnesota Symposia on Child Psychology* (Vol. 25, pp. 59–101). Hillsdale, NJ: Erlbaum.

Markovits, H., & Barrouillet, P. (2002). The development of conditional reasoning: A Piagetian reformulation of mental models theory. *Merrill-Palmer Quarterly, 39,* 131–158.

Markovits, H., Benenson, J., & Dolenszky, E. (2001). Evidence that children and adolescents have internal models of peer interactions that are gender differentiated. *Child Development, 72,* 879–886.

Markovits, H., Schleifer, M., & Fortier, L. (1989). Development of elementary deductive reasoning in young children. *Developmental Psychology, 25,* 787–793.

Markovits, H., & Vachon, R. (1990). Conditional reasoning, representation, and level of abstraction. *Developmental Psychology, 26,* 942–951.

Marks, G. N., Cresswell, J., & Ainley, J. (2006). Explaining socioeconomic inequalities in student achievement: The role of home and school factors. *Educational Research and Evaluation, 12,* 105–128.

Marks, N. F., Bumpass, L. L., & Jun, H. (2004). Family roles and well-being during the middle life course. In O. G. Brim, C. D. Ryff, & R. C. Kessler (Eds.), *How healthy are we? A national study of well-being at midlife* (pp. 514–549). Chicago: University of Chicago Press.

Markus, H. R., & Kitayama, S. (1991). Culture and the self: Implications for cognition, emotion, and motivation. *Psychological Review, 98,* 224–253.

Marlier, L., & Schaal, B. (2005). Human newborns prefer human milk: Conspecific milk odor is attractive without postnatal exposure. *Child Development, 76,* 155–168.

Marlier, L., Schaal, B., & Soussignan, R. (1998). Neonatal responsiveness to the odor of amniotic and lacteal fluids: A test of perinatal chemosensory continuity. *Child Development, 69,* 611–623.

Marra, R., & Palmer, B. (2004). Encouraging intellectual growth: Senior college student profiles. *Journal of Adult Development, 11,* 111–122.

Marsh, H., & Kleitman, S. (2005). Consequences of employment during high school: Character building, subversion of academic goals, or a threshold? *American Educational Research Journal, 42,* 331–369.

Marsh, H. W. (1990). The structure of academic self-concept: The Marsh/Shavelson model. *Journal of Educational Psychology, 82,* 623–636.

Marsh, H. W., & Ayotte, V. (2003). Do multiple dimensions of self-concept become more differentiated with age? The differential distinctiveness hypothesis. *Journal of Educational Psychology, 95,* 687–706.

Marsh, H. W., Craven, R., & Debus, R. (1998). Structure, stability, and development of young children's self-concepts: A multicohort– multioccasion study. *Child Development, 69,* 1030–1053.

Marsh, H. W., Ellis, L. A., & Craven, R. G. (2002). How do preschool children feel about themselves? Unraveling measurement and multidimensional self-concept structure. *Developmental Psychology, 38,* 376–393.

Marsh, H. W., & Hau, K.-T. (2003). Big-fish–little-pond effect on academic self-concept: A cross-cultural (26-country) test of the negative effects of academically selective schools. *American Psychologist, 58,* 364–376.

Marsh, J. S., & Daigneault, J. P. (1999). The young athlete. *Current Opinion in Pediatrics, 11,* 84–88.

Marsh, M. W., Parada, R. H., & Ayotte, V. (2004). A multidimensional perspective of relations between self-concept (Self Description Questionnaire II) and adolescent mental health (Youth Self Report). *Psychological Assessment, 16,* 27–41.

Marshall-Baker, A., Lickliter, R., & Cooper, R. P. (1998). Prolonged exposure to a visual pattern may promote behavioral organization in preterm infants. *Journal of Perinatal and Neonatal Nursing, 12,* 50–62.

Martin, C. L., Eisenbud, L., & Rose, H. (1995). Children's gender-based reasoning about toys. *Child Development, 66,* 1453–1471.

Martin, C. L., & Fabes, R. A. (2001). The stability and consequences of young children's same-sex peer interactions. *Developmental Psychology, 37,* 431–446.

Martin, C. L., Fabes, R. A., Evans, S. M., & Wyman, H. (1999). Social cognition on the playground: Children's beliefs about playing with girls versus boys and their relations to sex segregated play. *Journal of Social and Personal Relationships, 16,* 751–771.

Martin, C. L., & Halverson, C. F. (1987). The role of cognition in sex role acquisition. In D. B. Carter (Ed.), *Current conceptions of sex roles and sex typing: Theory and research* (pp. 123–137). New York: Praeger.

Martin, C. L., & Ruble, D. (2004). Children's search for gender cues: Cognitive perspectives on gender development. *Current Directions in Psychological Science, 13,* 67–70.

Martin, C. L., Ruble, D. N., & Szkrybalo, J. (2002). Cognitive theories of early gender development. *Psychological Bulletin, 128,* 903–933.

Martin, G. L., & Pear, J. (2007). *Behavior modification: What it is and how to do it* (8th ed.). Upper Saddle River, NJ: Prentice-Hall.

Martin, J. A., Hamilton, B. E., Menacker, F., Sutton, P. D., & Mathews, T. J. (2006, November). Preliminary births. *Health E-Stats.* Retrieved from www.cdc.gov/nchs/about /major/nhcs/nhcs_newsclippings.htm

Martin, J. A., Hamilton, B. E., Ventura, S. J., Menacker, F., & Park, M. M. (2002). *Births: Final data for 2001. National Vital Statistics Reports, Vol. 51, No. 2.* Hyattsville, MD: National Center for Health Statistics.

Martin, K. A. (1996). *Puberty, sexuality and the self: Girls and boys at adolescence.* New York: Routledge.

Martinez, C. R., & Forgatch, M. S. (2002). Adjusting to change: Linking family structure transitions with parenting and boys' adjustment. *Journal of Family Psychology, 16,* 107–117.

Martins, C., & Gaffan, E. A. (2000). Effects of maternal depression on patterns of infant–mother attachment: A meta-analytic investigation. *Journal of Child Psychology and Psychiatry, 41,* 737–746.

Martins, P. A., Hoffman, D. J., Fernandes, M. T., Nascimento, C. R., Roberts, S. B., Sesso, R., & Sawaya, A. L. (2004). Stunted children gain less lean body mass and more fat mass than their non-stunted counterparts: A prospective study. *British Journal of Nutrition, 92,* 819–825.

Martlew, M., & Connolly, K. J. (1996). Human figure drawings by schooled and unschooled children in Papua New Guinea. *Child Development, 67,* 2743–2762.

Martyn, C. N., Barker, D. J. P., & Osmond, C. (1996). Mothers' pelvic size, fetal growth, and death from stroke and coronary heart disease in men in the UK. *Lancet, 348,* 1264–1268.

Marzolf, D. P., & DeLoache, J. S. (1994). Transfer in young children's understanding of spatial representations. *Child Development, 65,* 1–15.

Masataka, N. (1996). Perception of motherese in a signed language by 6-month-old deaf infants. *Developmental Psychology, 32,* 874–879.

Mascolo, M. F., & Fischer, K. W. (1995). Developmental transformations in appraisals for pride, shame, and guilt. In J. P. Tangney & K. W. Fischer (Eds.), *Self-conscious emotions* (pp. 114–139). New York: Guilford.

Mason, C. A., Cauce, A. M., Gonzales, N., & Hiraga, Y. (1996). Neither too sweet nor too sour: Problem peers, maternal control, and problem behavior in African-American adolescents. *Child Development, 67,* 2115–2130.

Mason, M. G., & Gibbs, J. C. (1993a). Role-taking opportunities and the transition to advanced moral judgment. *Moral Education Forum, 18,* 1–12.

Mason, M. G., & Gibbs, J. C. (1993b). Social perspective taking and moral judgment among college students. *Journal of Adolescent Research, 8,* 109–123.

Massey, Z., Rising, S. S., & Ickovics, J. (2006). CenteringPregnancy group prenatal care: Promoting relationship-centered care. *JOGNN, 35,* 286–294.

Masten, A. S. (2001). Ordinary magic: Resilience processes in development. *American Psychologist, 56,* 227–238.

Masten, A. S., Coatsworth, J. D., Neemann, J., Gest, S. D., Tellegen, A., & Garmezy, N. (1995). The structure and coherence of competence from childhood through adolescence. *Child Development, 66,* 1635–1659.

Masten, A. S., & Gewirtz, A. H. (2006). Vulnerability and resilience in early child development. In K. McCartney & D. Phillips (Eds.), *Blackwell handbook of early childhood development* (pp. 22–43). Malden, MA: Blackwell.

Masten, A. S., & Powell, J. L. (2003). A resilience framework for research, policy, and practice. In S. S. Luthar (Ed.), *Resilience and vulnerability* (pp. 1–25). New York: Cambridge University Press.

Masten, A. S., & Reed, M. J. (2002). Resilience in development. In C. R. Snyder & S. J. Lopez (Eds.), *Handbook of positive psychology* (pp. 74–88). New York: Oxford University Press.

Masten, A. S., & Shaffer, A. (2006). How families matter in child development: Reflections from research on risk and resilience. In A. S. Masten & A. Shaffer (Eds.), *Families count: Effects on child and adolescent development* (pp. 5–25). New York: Cambridge University Press.

Mastropieri, D., & Turkewitz, G. (1999). Prenatal experience and neonatal responsiveness to vocal expressions of emotion. *Developmental Psychobiology, 35,* 204–214.

Masur, E. F., McIntyre, C. W., & Flavell, J. H. (1973). Developmental changes in apportionment of study time among items in a multi-trial free recall task. *Journal of Experimental Child Psychology, 15,* 237–246.

Masur, E. F., & Rodemaker, J. E. (1999). Mothers' and infants' spontaneous vocal, verbal, and action imitation during the second year. *Merrill-Palmer Quarterly, 45,* 392–412.

Matheny, A. P., Jr. (1991). Children's unintentional injuries and gender: Differentiation and psychosocial aspects. *Children's Environment Quarterly, 8,* 51–61.

Mathews, F., Yudkin, P., & Neil, A. (1999). Influence of maternal nutrition on outcome of pregnancy: Prospective cohort study. *British Medical Journal, 319,* 339–343.

Mathews, T. J., & MacDorman, M. F. (2006, May). Infant mortality statistics from the 2003 period linked birth/infant death data set. *National Vital Statistics Reports, 54*(16), 1–29.

Maticka-Tyndale, E. (2001). Sexual health and Canadian youth: How do we measure up? *Canadian Journal of Human Sexuality, 10*(1–2), 1–17.

Matsuba, M. K., & Walker, L. J. (1998). Moral reasoning in the context of ego functioning. *Merrill-Palmer Quarterly, 44,* 464–483.

Matsuda, Y., Maeda, T., & Kouno, S. (2003). Comparison of neonatal outcome including cerebral palsy between placenta abruptio and placenta previa. *European Journal of Obstetrics, Gynecology, and Reproductive Biology, 106*, 125–129.

Matute-Bianchi, M. E. (1986). Ethnic identities and patterns of school success and failure among Mexican-descent and Japanese-American students in a California high school: An ethnographic analysis. *American Journal of Education, 95*, 233–255.

Maupin, R., Lyman, R., Fatsis, J., Prystowiski, E., Nguyen, A., & Wright, C. (2004). Characteristics of women who deliver with no prenatal care. *Journal of Maternal-Fetal and Neonatal Medicine, 16*, 45–50.

Maurer, D., Lewis, T. L., Brent, H. P., & Levin, A. V. (1999). Rapid improvement in the acuity of infants after visual input. *Science, 286*, 108–110.

Mayberry, R. I. (1994). The importance of childhood to language acquisition: Evidence from American Sign Language. In J. C. Goodman & H. C. Nusbaum (Eds.), *The development of speech perception: The transition from speech sounds to spoken words* (pp. 57–90). Cambridge, MA: MIT Press.

Mayeiux, L., & Cillessen, A. H. N. (2003). Development of social problem solving in early childhood: Stability, change, and associations with social competence. *Journal of Genetic Psychology, 164*, 153–173.

Mayer, J. D., Salovey, P., & Caruso, D. R. (2003). *Mayer-Salovey-Caruso Emotional Intelligence Test (MSCEIT): User's manual.* Toronto, Canada: Multi-Health Systems.

Mayes, L. C. (1999). Reconsidering the concept of vulnerability in children using the model of prenatal cocaine exposure. In T. B. Cohen & E. M. Hossein (Eds.), *The vulnerable child* (Vol. 3, pp. 35–54). Madison, CT: International Universities Press.

Mayes, L. C., & Zigler, E. (1992). An observational study of the affective concomitants of mastery in infants. *Journal of Child Psychology and Psychiatry, 33*, 659–667.

Maynard, A. E. (2002). Cultural teaching: The development of teaching skills in Maya sibling interactions. *Child Development, 73*, 969–982.

Maynard, A. E., & Greenfield, P. M. (2003). Implicit cognitive development in cultural tools and children: Lessons from Maya Mexico. *Cognitive Development, 18*, 489–510.

Maynard, A. E., Subrahmanyam, K., & Greenfield, P. M. (2005). Technology and the development of intelligence: From the loom to the computer. In R. J. Sternberg & D. D. Preiss (Eds.), *Intelligence and technology: The impact of tools on the nature and development of human abilities* (pp. 29–53). Mahwah, NJ: Erlbaum.

McBride-Chang, C., & Kail, R. V. (2002). Cross-cultural similarities in the predictors of reading acquisition. *Child Development, 73*, 1392–1407.

McCabe, A. (1997). Developmental and cross-cultural aspects of children's narration. In M. Bamberg (Ed.), *Narrative development: Six approaches* (pp. 137–174). Mahwah, NJ: Erlbaum.

McCabe, A. E., & Peterson, C. (1988). A comparison of adults' versus children's spontaneous use of *because* and *so. Journal of Genetic Psychology, 149*, 257–268.

McCall, R. B. (1993). Developmental functions for general mental performance. In D. K. Detterman (Ed.), *Current topics in human intelligence* (Vol. 3, pp. 3–29). Norwood, NJ: Ablex.

McCall, R. B., & Carriger, M. S. (1993). A meta-analysis of infant habituation and recognition memory performance as predictors of later IQ. *Child Development, 64*, 57–79.

McCartney, K., Harris, M. J., & Bernieri, F. (1990). Growing up and growing apart: A developmental meta-analysis of twin studies. *Psychological Bulletin, 107*, 226–237.

McCartney, K., Owen, M., Booth, C., Clarke-Stewart, A., & Vandell, D. (2004). Testing a maternal attachment model of behavior problems in early childhood. *Journal of Child Psychology and Psychiatry, 45*, 765–778.

McCarton, C. (1998). Behavioral outcomes in low birth weight infants. *Pediatrics, 102*, 1293–1297.

McCarty, M. E., & Ashmead, D. H. (1999). Visual control of reaching and grasping in infants. *Developmental Psychology, 35*, 620–631.

McCarty, M. E., & Keen, R. (2005). Facilitating problem-solving performance among 9- and 12-month-old infants. *Journal of Cognition and Development, 6*, 209–228.

McCormack, V. A., dos Santos Silva, I., Koupil, I., Leon, D. A., & Lithell, H. O. (2005). Birth characteristics and adult cancer incidence: Swedish cohort of over 11,000 men and women. *International Journal of Cancer, 115*, 611–617.

McCune, L. (1993). The development of play as the development of consciousness. In M. H. Bornstein & A. O'Reilly (Eds.), *New directions for child development* (No. 59, pp. 67–79). San Francisco: Jossey-Bass.

McDaniel, J., Purcell, D., & D'Augelli, A. R. (2001). The relationship between sexual orientation and risk for suicide: Research findings and future directions for research and prevention. *Suicide and Life-Threatening Behavior, 31*, 84–105.

McDonagh, M. S., Osterweil, P., & Guise, J. M. (2005). The benefits and risks of inducing labour in patients with prior cesarean delivery: A systematic review. *BJOG, 112*, 1007–10-15.

McDonough, L. (1999). Early declarative memory for location. *British Journal of Developmental Psychology, 17*, 381–402.

McDowell, D. J., & Parke, R. D. (2000). Differential knowledge of display rules for positive and negative emotions: Influences from parents, influences on peers. *Social Development, 9*, 415–432.

McElhaney, K. B., & Allen, J. P. (2001). Autonomy and adolescent social functioning: The moderating effect of risk. *Child Development, 72*, 220–235.

McGee, G. (1997). Legislating gestation. *Human Reproduction, 12*, 407–408.

McGee, L. M., & Richgels, D. J. (2004). *Literacy's beginnings* (4th ed.). Boston: Allyn and Bacon.

McGill-Franzen, A., Lanford, C., & Adams, E. (2002). Learning to be literate: A comparison of five urban early childhood programs. *Journal of Educational Psychology, 94*, 443–464.

McGillicuddy-De Lisi, A. V., Daly, M. & Neal, A. (2006). Children's distributive justice judgments: Aversive racism in Euro-American children? *Child Development, 77*, 1063–1080.

McGillicuddy-De Lisi, A. V., Watkins, C., & Vinchur, A. J. (1994). The effect of relationship on children's distributive justice reasoning. *Child Development, 65*, 1694–1700.

McGlothlin, H., & Killen, M. (2005). Children's perceptions of intergroup and intragroup similarity and the role of social experience. *Applied Developmental Psychology, 26*, 680–698.

McGuffin, P., & Sargeant, M. P. (1991). Major affective disorder. In P. McGuffin & R. Murray (Eds.), *The new genetics of mental illness* (pp. 165–181). London: Butterworth-Heinemann.

McHale, J. P., Kazali, C., Rotman, T., Talbot, J., Carleton, M., & Lieberson, R. (2004). The transition to coparenthood: Parents' prebirth expectations and early coparental adjustment at 3 months postpartum. *Development and Psychopathology, 16*, 711–733.

McHale, J. P., Lauretti, A., Talbot, J., & Pouquette, C. (2002). Retrospect and prospect in the psychological study of coparenting and family group process. In J. P. McHale & W. S. Grolnick (Eds.), *Retrospect and prospect in the psychological study of families* (pp. 127–165). Mahwah, NJ: Erlbaum.

McHale, J. P., Vinden, P. G., Bush, L., Richer, D., Shaw, D., & Smith, B. (2005). Patterns of personal and social adjustment among sport-involved and noninvolved urban middle-school children. *Sociology of Sport Journal, 22*, 119–136.

McHale, S. M., Crouter, A. C., Kim, J.-Y., Burton, L. M., Davis, K. D., Dotterer, A. M., & Swanson, D. P. (2006). Mothers' and fathers' racial socialization in African-American families: Implications for youth. *Child Development, 77*, 1387–1402.

McHale, S. M., Updegraff, K. A., Helms-Erikson, H., & Crouter, A. C. (2001). Sibling influences on gender development in middle childhood and early adolescence: A longitudinal study. *Developmental Psychology, 37*, 115–125.

McIntosh, H., Metz, E., & Youniss, J. (2005). Community service and identity formation in adolescents. In J. S. Mahoney, R. W. Larson, & J. S. Eccles (Eds.), *Organized activities as contexts of development: Extracurricular activities, after-school and community programs* (pp. 331–351). Mahwah, NJ: Erlbaum.

McIntosh, J., MacDonald, F., & McKeganey, N. (2006). Why do children experiment with illegal drugs? The declining role of peer pressure with increasing age. *Addiction Research and Theory, 14*, 275–287.

McKelvie, P., & Low, J. (2002). Listening to Mozart does not improve children's spatial ability: Final curtains for the Mozart effect. *British Journal of Developmental Psychology, 20*, 241–258.

McKenna, J. J. (2001). Why we never ask "Is it safe for infants to sleep alone?" *Academy of Breast Feeding Medicine News and Views, 7*(4), 32, 38.

McKenna, J. J. (2002, September/October). Breastfeeding and bedsharing still useful (and important) after all these years. *Mothering, 114*. Retrieved from www.mothering.com/articles/new_baby/sleep/mckenna.html

McKenna, J. J., & McDade, T. (2005). Why babies should never sleep alone: A review of the co-sleeping controversy in relation to SIDS, bedsharing, and breastfeeding. *Paediatric Respiratory Reviews, 6*, 134–152.

McKeown, R. E., Garrison, C. Z., Cuffe, S. P., Waller, J. L., Jackson, K. L., & Addy, C. L. (1998). Incidence and predictors of suicidal behaviors in a longitudinal sample of young adolescents. *Journal of the American Academy of Child and Adolescent Psychiatry, 37*, 612–619.

McKown, C., & Weinstein, R. S. (2002). Modeling the role of child ethnicity and gender in children's differential response to teacher expectations. *Journal of Applied Social Psychology, 32*, 159–184.

McKown, C., & Weinstein, R. S. (2003). The development and consequences of stereotype consciousness in middle childhood. *Child Development, 74*, 498–515.

McKusick, V. A. (2002). *Online Mendelian inheritance in man: A catalog of human genes and genetic disorders.* Baltimore: Johns Hopkins University Press. Retrieved from www.ncbi.nlm.nih.gov/entrez/query.fcgi?db=OMIM

McLanahan, S. (1999). Father absence and the welfare of children. In E. M. Hetherington (Ed.), *Coping with divorce, single parenting, and remarriage: A risk and resiliency perspective* (pp. 117–145). Mahwah, NJ: Erlbaum.

McLanahan, S. S., & Carlson, M. J. (2002). Welfare reform, fertility, and father involvement. *Future of Children, 12*, 111–115.

McLean, K. C., & Pratt, M. W. (2006). Life's little (and big) lessons: identity statuses and meaning-making in the turning point narratives of emerging adults. *Developmental Psychology, 42*, 714–722.

McLeod, C. (2007). *Obesity of China's kids stuns officials.* Retrieved from www.usatoday.com/news/world/2007-01-08-chinese-obesity_x.htm

McLoyd, V. C., Aikens, N. L., & Burton, L. M. (2006). Childhood poverty, policy, and practice. In K. A. Renninger & I. E. Sigel (Eds.), *Handbook of child psychology: Vol. 4. Child psychology in practice* (6th ed., pp. 700–778). Hoboken, NJ: Wiley.

McLoyd, V. C., & Smith, J. (2002). Physical discipline and behavior problems in African-American, European-American, and Hispanic children: Emotional support as a moderator. *Journal of Marriage and the Family, 64*, 40–53.

McManus, I. C., Sik, G., Cole, D. R., Mellon, A. F., Wong, J., & Kloss, J. (1988). The development of handedness in children. *British Journal of Developmental Psychology, 6*, 257–273.

McNamee, S., & Peterson, J. (1986). Young children's distributive justice reasoning, behavior, and role taking: Their consistency and relationship. *Journal of Genetic Psychology, 146*, 399–404.

MCR Vitamin Study Research Group. (1991). Prevention of neural tube defects: Results of the Medical Research Council Vitamin Study. *Lancet, 338*, 131–137.

Mead, G. H. (1934). *Mind, self, and society.* Chicago: University of Chicago Press.

Mead, M. (1928). *Coming of age in Samoa.* Ann Arbor, MI: Morrow.

Mead, M., & Newton, N. (1967). Cultural patterning of perinatal behavior. In S. Richardson & A. Guttmacher (Eds.), *Childbearing: Its social and psychological aspects* (pp. 142–244). Baltimore: Williams & Wilkins.

Mechelli, A., Crinion, J. T., Noppeney, U., O'Doherty, J., Ashburner, J., Frackowiak, R. S., & Price, C. J. (2004). Structural plasticity in the bilingual brain: Proficiency in a second language and age at acquisition affect grey-matter density. *Nature, 431,* 757.

Media Awareness Network. (2001). *Parental awareness of Canadian children's Internet use.* Retrieved from www.media-awareness.ca

Medina, A. L. (2006). The parallel bar: Writing assessment and instruction. In J. S. Schumm (Ed.), *Reading assessment and instruction for all learners* (pp. 381–430). New York: Guilford Press.

Meeus, W. (1996). Studies on identity development in adolescence: An overview of research and some new data. *Journal of Youth and Adolescence, 25,* 569–598.

Meeus, W., Iedema, J., Helsen, M., & Vollebergh, W. (1999). Patterns of adolescent identity development: Review of literature and longitudinal analysis. *Developmental Review, 19,* 419–461.

Meeus, W., Oosterwegel, A., & Vollebergh, W. (2002). Parental and peer attachment and identity development in adolescence. *Journal of Adolescence, 25,* 93–106.

Mehlmadrona, L., & Madrona, M. M. (1997). Physician- and midwifeattended home births—effects of breech, twin, and post-dates outcome data on mortality rates. *Journal of Nurse-Midwifery, 42,* 91–98.

Meins, E., Fernyhough, C., Russell, J., & Clark-Carter, D. (1998). Security of attachment as a predictor of symbolic and mentalizing abilities: A longitudinal study. *Social Development, 7,* 1–24.

Meins, E., Fernyhough, C., Wainwright, R., Clark-Carter, D., Gupta, M. D., Fradley, E., & Tucker, M. (2003). Pathways to understanding mind: Construct validity and predictive validity of maternal mind-mindedness. *Child Development, 74,* 1194–1211.

Meisels, S. J., Dichtelmiller, M., & Liaw, F. R. (1993). A multidimensional analysis of early childhood intervention programs. In C. H. Zeanah (Ed.), *Handbook of infant mental health* (pp. 361–385). New York: Guilford.

Melton, G. B. (2005). Treating children like people: A framework for research and advocacy. *Journal of Clinical Child and Adolescent Psychology, 34,* 646–657.

Meltzoff, A. N. (1995). Understanding the intentions of others: Reenactment of intended acts by 18-month-old children. *Developmental Psychology, 31,* 838–850.

Meltzoff, A. N., & Decety, J. (2003). What imitation tells us about social cognition: A rapprochement between developmental psychology and cognitive neuroscience. *Philosophical Transactions of the Royal Society of London, Series B, Biological Sciences, 358,* 491–500.

Meltzoff, A. N., & Moore, M. (1998). Object representation, identity, and paradox of early permanence: Steps toward a new framework. *Infant Behavior and Development, 21,* 201–235.

Meltzoff, A. N., & Moore, M. K. (1977). Imitation of facial and manual gestures by human neonates. *Science, 198,* 75–78.

Meltzoff, A. N., & Moore, M. K. (1994). Imitation, memory, and the representation of persons. *Infant Behavior and Development, 17,* 83–99.

Meltzoff, A. N., & Moore, M. K. (1999). Persons and representation: Why infant imitation is important for theories of human development. In J. Nadel & G. Butterworth (Eds.), *Imitation in infancy* (pp. 9–35). Cambridge, U.K.: Cambridge University Press.

Menendez, M. (2005). Down syndrome, Alzheimer's disease and seizures. *Brain and Development, 27,* 246–252.

Mennella, J. A., & Beauchamp, G. K. (1998). Early flavor experiences: Research update. *Nutrition Reviews, 56,* 205–211.

Ment, L. R., Vohr, B., Allan, W., Katz, K. H., Schneider, K. C., Westerveld, M., Cuncan, C. C., & Makuch, R. W. (2003). Change in cognitive function over time in very low-birth-weight infants. *Journal of the American Medical Association, 289,* 705–711.

Menyuk, P., Liebergott, J. W., & Schultz, M. C. (1995). *Early language development in full-term and premature infants.* Hillsdale, NJ: Erlbaum.

Meredith, N. V. (1978). *Human body growth in the first ten years of life.* Columbia, SC: State Printing.

Meredith, W. H., Wang, A., & Zheng, F. M. (1993). Determining constructs of self-perception for children in Chinese cultures. *School Psychology International, 14,* 371–380.

Mervis, C. B., Pani, J. R., & Pani, A. M. (2003). Transaction of child cognitive-linguistic abilities and adult input in the acquisition of lexical categories at the basic and subordinate levels. In D. H. Rakison & L. M. Oakes (Ed.), *Early category and concept development* (pp. 242–274). New York: Oxford University Press.

Metz, E., McLellan, J., & Youniss, J. (2003). Types of voluntary service and adolescents' civic development. *Journal of Adolescent Research, 18,* 188–203.

Meyer, P. A., Pivetz, T., Dignam, T. A., Hma, D. M., Schoonover, J., & Brody, D. (2003). Surveillance for elevated blood lead levels among children—United States, 1997–2001. *Morbidity and Mortality Weekly Report, 52*(No. SS-10), 1–21.

Meyer-Bahlburg, H. F. L., Ehrhardt, A. A., Rosen, L. R., Gruen, R. S., Veridiano, N. P., Vann, F. H., & Neuwalder, H. F. (1995). Prenatal estrogens and the development of homosexual orientation. *Developmental Psychology, 31,* 12–21.

Meyers, C., Adam, R., Dungan, J., & Prenger, V. (1997). Aneuploidy in twin gestations: When is maternal age advanced? *Obstetrics and Gynecology, 89,* 248–251.

Meyers, M. K., Rosenbaum, D., Ruhm, C., & Waldfogel, J. (2004). Inequality in early childhood education and care: What do we know? In K. Neckerman (Ed.), *Social inequality.* New York: Russell Sage Foundation.

Mezulis, A. H., Hyde, J. S., & Clark, R. (2004). Father involvement moderates the effect of maternal depression during a child's infancy on child behavior problems in kindergarten. *Journal of Family Psychology, 18,* 575–588.

Miccio, A. W., Yont, K. M., Clemons, H. L., & Vernon-Feagans, L. (2002). Otitis media and the acquisition of consonants. In F. Windsor & M. L. Kelly (Eds.), *Investigations in clinical phonetics and linguistics* (pp. 429– 235). Mahwah, NJ: Erlbaum.

Miceli, P. J., Whitman, T. L., Borkowski, J. G., Braungart-Riekder, J., & Mitchell, D. W. (1998). Individual differences in infant information processing: The role of temperamental and maternal factors. *Infant Behavior and Development, 21,* 119–136.

Michael, A., & Eccles, J. S. (2003). When coming of age means coming undone: Links between puberty and psychosocial adjustment among European American and African American girls. In C. Hayward (Ed.), *Gender differences at puberty* (pp. 277–303). New York: Cambridge University Press.

Michael, R. T., Gagnon, J. H., Laumann, E. O., & Kolata, G. (1994). *Sex in America.* Boston: Little, Brown.

Michaels, G. Y. (1988). Motivational factors in the decision and timing of pregnancy. In G. Y. Michaels & W. A. Goldberg (Eds.), *The transition to parenthood: Current theory and research* (pp. 23–61). New York: Cambridge University Press.

Milberger, S., Biederman, J., Faraone, S. V., Guite, J., & Tsuang, M. T. (1997). Pregnancy, delivery and infancy complications and attention-deficit hyperactivity disorder: Issues of gene–environment interaction. *Biological Psychiatry, 41,* 65–75.

Miles, H. L. (1999). Symbolic communication with and by great apes. In S. T. Parker, R. W. Mitchell, & H. L. Miles (Eds.), *The mentalities of gorillas and orangutans* (pp. 197– 210). Cambridge, U.K.: Cambridge University Press.

Millar, W. J., & Hill, G. (2004). Pregnancy and smoking. *Health Reports, 15,* 53–56.

Miller, C. J., Sanchez, J., & Hynd, G. W. (2003). Neurological correlates of reading disabilities. In H. L. Swanson, K. R. Harris, & S. Graham (Eds.), *Handbook of learning disabilities* (pp. 242–255). New York: Guilford.

Miller, J. G. (1997). Culture and self: uncovering the cultural grounding of psychological theory. In J. G. Snodgrass & R. L. Thompson (Eds.), *Annals of the New York Academy of Sciences* (Vol. 18, pp. 217–231). New York: New York Academy of Sciences.

Miller, J. G., & Bersoff, D. M. (1995). Development in the context of everyday family relationships: Culture, interpersonal morality, and adaptation. In M. Killen & D. Hart (Eds.), *Morality in everyday life: Developmental perspectives* (pp. 259–282). Cambridge, U.K.: Cambridge University Press.

Miller, K. S., Forehand, R., & Kotchick, B. (1999). Adolescent sexual behavior in two ethnic minority samples: The role of family variables. *Journal of Marriage and the Family, 61,* 85–98.

Miller, L. T., & Vernon, P. A. (1992). The general factor in short-term memory, intelligence, and reaction time. *Intelligence, 16,* 5–29.

Miller, P. A., Eisenberg, N., Fabes, R. A., & Shell, R. (1996). Relations of moral reasoning and vicarious emotion to young children's prosocial behavior toward peers and adults. *Developmental Psychology, 32,* 210–219.

Miller, P. H. (2000). How to best utilize a deficiency. *Child Development, 71,* 1013–1017.

Miller, P. H., & Bigi, L. (1979). The development of children's understanding of attention. *Merrill-Palmer Quarterly, 25,* 235–250.

Miller, P. J., Fung, H., & Mintz, J. (1996). Self-construction through narrative practices: A Chinese and American comparison of early socialization. *Ethos, 24,* 1–44.

Miller, P. J., Hengst, J. A., & Wang, S. (2003). Ethnographic methods: Applications from developmental cultural psychology. In P. M. Camic & J. E. Rhodes (Eds.), *Qualitative research in psychology* (pp. 219– 242). Washington, DC: American Psychological Association.

Miller, P. J., Wang, S., Sandel, T., & Cho, G. E. (2002). Self-esteem as folk theory: A comparison of European American and Taiwanese mothers' beliefs. *Parenting: Science and Practice, 2,* 209–239.

Miller, P. J., Wiley, A. R., Fung, H., & Liang, C.-H. (1997). Personal storytelling as a medium of socialization in Chinese and American families. *Child Development, 68,* 557–568.

Miller, R. B. (2000). Do children make a marriage unhappy? *Family Science Review, 13,* 60–73.

Miller, S. A., Hardin, C. A., & Montgomery, D. E. (2003). Young children's understanding of the conditions for knowledge acquisition. *Journal of Cognition and Development, 4,* 325–356.

Mills, D., Plunkett, K., Prat, C., & Schafer, G. (2005). Watching the infant brain learn words: Effects of language and experience. *Cognitive Development, 20,* 19–31.

Mills, R., & Grusec, J. E. (1989). Cognitive, affective, and behavioral consequences of praising altruism. *Merrill-Palmer Quarterly, 35,* 299–326.

Mills, R. S. L. (2005). Taking stock of the developmental literature on shame. *Developmental Review, 25,* 26–63.

Mills, T. L., Gomez-Smith, Z., & De Leon, J. M. (2005). Skipped generation families: Sources of psychological distress among grandmothers of grandchildren who live in homes where neither parent is present. *Marriage and Family Review, 37,* 191–212.

Minde, K. (2000). Prematurity and serious medical conditions in infancy: Implications for development, behavior, and intervention. In C. H. Zeanah, Jr. (Ed.), *Handbook of infant mental health* (pp. 176–194). New York: Guilford.

Mindell, J. A. (2005). *Sleeping through the night.* New York: HarperResource.

Mindell, J. A., Owens, J. A., & Carskadon, M. A. (1999). Developmental features of sleep. *Child and Adolescent Psychiatric Clinics of North America, 8,* 695–725.

Minkler, M., & Fuller-Thomson, E. (2005). African American grandparents raising grandchildren: A national study using the Census 2000 American Community Survey. *Journal of Gerontology, 60B,* S82–S92.

Mischel, W., & Liebert, R. M. (1966). Effects of discrepancies between observed and imposed reward criteria on their acquisition and transmission. *Journal of Personality and Social Psychology, 3,* 45–53.

Mistry, R. S., Biesanz, J. C., Taylor, L. C., Burchinal, M., & Cox, M. J. (2004). Family income and its relation to preschool children's adjustment for families in the NICHD Study of Early Child Care. *Developmental Psychology, 40,* 727–745.

Mitchell, A., & Boss, B. J. (2002). Adverse effects of pain on the nervous systems of newborns and young children: A review of the literature. *Journal of Neuroscience Nursing, 34,* 228–235.

Miura, I. T., & Okamoto, Y. (2003). Language supports for mathematics understanding and performance. In A. J. Baroody & A. Dowker (Eds.), *The development of arithmetic concepts and skills* (pp. 229–242). Mahwah, NJ: Erlbaum.

Mize, J., & Pettit, G. S. (1997). Mothers' social coaching, mother–child relationship style, and children's peer competence–Is the medium the message? *Child Development, 68,* 312–332.

Moerk, E. L. (2000). *The guided acquisition of first language skills.* Westport, CT: Ablex.

Moffitt, T. E. (2006). Life-course-persistent versus adolescence-limited antisocial behavior. In D. Cicchetti & D. J. Cohen (Eds.), *Developmental psychopathology: Vol. 3. Risk, disorder, and adaptation* (2nd ed., pp. 570–598). Hoboken, NJ: Wiley.

Moffitt, T. E., Caspi, A., Dickson, N., Silva, P., & Stanton, W. (1996). Childhood-onset versus adolescent-onset antisocial conduct problems in males: Natural history from ages 3 to 18 years. *Development and Psychopathology, 8,* 399–424.

Mokdad, A. H., Bowman, B. A., Ford, E. S., Vinicor, F., Marks, J. S., & Koplan, J. P. (2001). The continuing epidemics of obesity and diabetes in the United States. *Journal of the American Medical Association, 286,* 1195–1200.

Moll, I. (1994). Reclaiming the natural line in Vygotsky's theory of cognitive development. *Human Development, 37,* 333–342.

Monastersky, R. (2005, March 4). Primed for numbers: Are boys born better at math? Experts try to divide the influences of nature and nurture. *Chronicle of Higher Education,* pp. A1, A12–A14.

Mondloch, C. J., Lewis, T., Budreau, D. R., Maurer, D., Dannemillier, J. L., Stephens, B. R., & Kleiner-Gathercoal, K. A. (1999). Face perception during early infancy. *Psychological Science, 10,* 419–422.

Mondoza, C. (2006). Inside today's classrooms: Teacher voices on No Child Left Behind and the education of gifted children. *Roeper Review, 29,* 28–31.

Monk, C., Fifer, W. P., Myers, M. M., Sloan, R. P., Trien, L., & Hurtado, A. (2000). Maternal stress responses and anxiety during pregnancy: Effects on fetal heart rate. *Developmental Psychobiology, 36,* 67–77.

Monk, C., Sloan, R., Myers, M. M., Ellman, L., Werner, E., Jeon, J., Tager, F., & Fifer, W. P. (2004). Fetal heart rate reactivity differs by women's psychiatric status: An early marker for developmental risk? *Journal of the American Academy of Child and Adolescent Psychiatry, 43,* 283–290.

Montague, D. P. F., & Walker-Andrews, A. S. (2001). Peekaboo: A new look at infants' perception of emotion expressions. *Developmental Psychology, 37,* 826–838.

Montemayor, R., & Eisen, M. (1977). The development of selfconceptions from childhood to adolescence. *Developmental Psychology, 13,* 314–319.

Montgomery, M. J. (2005). Psychosocial intimacy and identity: From early adolescence to emerging adulthood. *Journal of Adolescent Research, 20,* 346–374.

Montgomery, M. J., & Côté, J. E. (2003). College as a transition to adulthood. In G. R. Adams & M. D. Berzonsky (Eds.), *Blackwell handbook of adolescence* (pp. 150–172). Malden, MA: Blackwell.

Moon, C., Cooper, R. P., & Fifer, W. P. (1993). Two-day-old infants prefer their native language. *Infant Behavior and Development, 16,* 495–500.

Moon, S. M., & Feldhusen, J. F. (1994). The Program for Academic and Creative Enrichment (PACE): A follow-up study ten years later. In R. F. Subotnik & K. D. Arnold (Eds.), *Beyond Terman: Contemporary longitudinal studies of giftedness and talent* (pp. 375–400). Norwood, NJ: Ablex.

Moonie, D. A., Sterling, D. A., Figgs, L., & Castro, M. (2006). Asthma status and severity affects missed school days. *Journal of School Health, 76,* 18–24.

Moore, D. R., & Florsheim, P. (2001). Interpersonal processes and psychopathology among expectant and nonexpectant adolescent couples. *Journal of Consulting and Clinical Psychology, 69,* 101–113.

Moore, E. G. J. (1986). Family socialization and the IQ test performance of traditionally and transracially adopted black children. *Developmental Psychology, 22,* 317–326.

Moore, G. A., Cohn, J. E., & Campbell, S. B. (2001). Infant affective responses to mother's still face at 6 months differentially predict externalizing and internalizing behaviors at 18 months. *Developmental Psychology, 37,* 706–714.

Moore, K. A., Morrison, D. R., & Green, A. D. (1997). Effects on the children born to adolescent mothers. In R. A. Maynard (Ed.), *Kids having kids* (pp. 145–180). Washington, DC: Urban Institute.

Moore, K. A., Myers, D. E., Morrison, D. R., Nord, C. W., Brown, B., & Edmonston, B. (1993). Age at first childbirth and later poverty. *Journal of Research on Adolescence, 3,* 393–422.

Moore, K. L., & Persaud, T. V. N. (2003). *Before we are born* (6th ed.). Philadelphia: Saunders.

Moore, M. K., & Meltzoff, A. N. (1999). New findings on object permanence: A developmental difference between two types of occlusion. *British Journal of Developmental Psychology, 17,* 563–584.

Moore, M. K., & Meltzoff, A. N. (2004). Object permanence after a 24-hr delay and leaving the locale of disappearance: The role of memory, space, and identity. *Developmental Psychology, 40,* 606–620.

Moore, W. S. (2002). Understanding learning in a postmodern world: Reconsidering the Perry scheme of ethical and intellectual development. In B. K. Hofer & P. R. Pintrich (Eds.), *Personal epistemology* (pp. 17–36). Mahwah, NJ: Erlbaum.

Moran, G. F., & Vinovskis, M. A. (1986). The great care of godly parents: Early childhood in Puritan New England. *Monographs of the Society for Research in Child Development, 50*(4–5, Serial No. 211).

Moran, S., & Gardner, H. (2006). Extraordinary achievements: A developmental and systems analysis. In D. Kuhn & R. S. Siegler (Eds.), *Handbook of child psychology: Vol. 2. Cognition, perception, and language* (6th ed., pp. 905–949). Hoboken, NJ: Wiley.

Morelli, G., Rogoff, B., Oppenheim, D., & Goldsmith, D. (1992). Cultural variation in infants' sleeping arrangements: Questions of independence. *Developmental Psychology, 28,* 604–613.

Morelli, G. A., Rogoff, B., & Angelillo, C. (2003). Cultural variation in young children's access to work or involvement in specialized child-focused activities. *International Journal of Behavioral Development, 27,* 264–274.

Morgan, B., Maybery, M., & Durkin, K. (2003). Weak central coherence, poor joint attention, and low verbal ability: Independent deficits in early autism. *Developmental Psychology, 39,* 646–656.

Morgane, P. J., Austin-LaFrance, R., Bronzino, J., Tonkiss, J., Diaz-Cintra, S., Cintra, L., Kemper, T., & Galler, J. R. (1993). Prenatal malnutrition and development of the brain. *Neuroscience and Biobehavioral Reviews, 17,* 91–128.

Mori, L., & Peterson, L. (1995). Knowledge of safety of high and low active–impulsive boys: Implications for child injury prevention. *Journal of Clinical Child Psychology, 24,* 370–376.

Morrongiello, B. A., Fenwick, K. D., & Chance, G. (1998). Crossmodal learning in newborn infants: Inferences about properties of auditory-visual events. *Infant Behavior and Development, 21,* 543–554.

Morrongiello, B. A., & Kiriakou, S. (2004). Mothers' home-safety practices for preventing six types of childhood injuries: What do they do, and why? *Journal of Pediatric Psychology, 29,* 285–297.

Morrongiello, B. A., Midgett, C., & Shields, R. (2001). Don't run with scissors: Young children's knowledge of home safety rules. *Journal of Pediatric Psychology, 26,* 105–115.

Morrongiello, B. A., Ondejko, L., & Littlejohn, A. (2004). Understanding toddlers' in-home injuries: I. Context, correlates, and determinants. *Journal of Pediatric Psychology, 29,* 415–431.

Morrongiello, B. A., & Rennie, H. (1998). Why do boys engage in more risk taking than girls? The role of attributions, beliefs, and risk appraisals. *Journal of Pediatric Psychology, 23,* 33–43.

Morrow, D. F. (2006). Gay, lesbian, and transgender adolescents. In D. F. Morrow & L. Messinger (Eds.), *Sexual orientation and gender expression in social work practice* (pp. 177–195). New York: Columbia University Press.

Mosby, L., Rawls, A. W., Meehan, A. J., Mays, E., & Pettinari, C. J. (1999). Troubles in interracial talk about discipline: An examination of African American child rearing narratives. *Journal of Comparative Family Studies, 30,* 489–521.

Mosely-Howard, G. S., & Evans, C. B. (2000). Relationships and contemporary experiences of the African-American family: An ethnographic case study. *Journal of Black Studies, 30,* 428–451.

Moses, L. J., Baldwin, D. A., Rosicky, J. G., & Tidball, G. (2001). Evidence for referential understanding in the emotions domain at twelve and eighteen months. *Child Development, 72,* 718–735.

Moshman, D. (1998). Cognitive development beyond childhood. In D. Kuhn & R. S. Siegler (Eds.), *Handbook of child psychology: Vol. 2. Cognition, perception, and language* (5th ed., pp. 947– 978). New York: Wiley.

Moshman, D. (1999). *Adolescent psychological development: Rationality, morality, and identity.* Mahwah, NJ: Erlbaum.

Moshman, D. (2003). Developmental change in adulthood. In J. Demick & C. Andreoletti (Eds.), *Handbook of adult development* (pp. 43–61). New York: Plenum.

Moshman, D. (2005). *Adolescent psychological development: Rationality, morality, and identity* (2nd ed.). Mahwah, NJ: Erlbaum.

Moshman, D., & Franks, B. A. (1986). Development of the concept of inferential validity. *Child Development, 57,* 153–165.

Moshman, D., & Geil, M. (1998). Collaborative reasoning: Evidence for collective rationality. *Thinking and Reasoning, 4,* 231–248.

Moss, E., Bureau, J.-F., Cyr, C., Mongeau, C., & St.-Laurent, D. (2004). Correlates of attachment at age 3: Construct validity of the preschool attachment classification system. *Developmental Psychology, 40,* 323–334.

Moss, E., Cyr, C., Bureau, J.-F., Tarabulsy, G. M., & Dubois-Comtois, K. (2005). Stability of attachment during the preschool period. *Developmental Psychology, 41,* 773–783.

Moss, E., Cyr, C., & Dubois-Comtois, K. (2004). Attachment at early school age and developmental risk: Examining family contexts and behavior problems of controlling-caregiving, controlling-punitive, and behaviorally disorganized children. *Developmental Psychology, 40,* 519–532.

Moss, E., Smolla, N., Guerra, I., Mazzarello, T., Chayer, D., & Berthiaume, C. (2006). Attachment and self-reported internalizing and externalizing behavior problems in a school period. *Canadian Journal of Behavioural Science, 38,* 142–157.

Moss, E., St.-Laurent, D., Dubois-Comtois, K., & Cyr, C. (2005). Quality of attachment at school age: Relations between child attachment behavior, psychosocial functioning, and school performance. In K. A. Kerns & R. A. Richardson (Eds.), *Attachment in middle childhood* (pp. 189–211). New York: Guilford.

Mosteller, F. (1995). The Tennessee Study of Class Size in the Early School Grades. *Future of Children, 5*(2), 113–127.

Mota, J., Silva, P., Santos, M. P., Ribeiro, J. C., Oliveira, J., & Duarte, J. A. (2005). Physical activity and school recess time: Differences between the sexes and the relationship between children's playground physical activity and habitual physical activity. *Journal of Sports Sciences, 23,* 269–275.

Motl, R. W., Dishman, R. K., Saunders, R. P., Dowda, M., Felton, G., Ward, D. S., & Pate, R. R. (2002). Examining social–cognitive determinants of intention and physical activity among black and white adolescent girls using structural equation modeling. *Health Psychology, 21,* 459–467.

Mounts, N. S., & Steinberg, L. (1995). An ecological analysis of peer influence on adolescent grade point average and drug use. *Developmental Psychology, 31,* 915–922.

Moxley, D. P., Najor-Durack, A., & Dumbrigue, C. (2001). *Keeping students in higher education.* London: Kogan Page.

Mrug, S., Hoza, B., & Gerdes, A. C. (2001). Children with attention-deficit/hyperactivity disorder: Peer relationships and peer-oriented interventions. In D. W. Nangle & C. A. Erdley (Eds.), *The role of friendship in psychological adjustment* (pp. 51–77). San Francisco: Jossey-Bass.

Mueller, C. M., & Dweck, C. S. (1998). Intelligence praise can undermine motivation and performance. *Journal of Personality and Social Psychology, 75,* 33–52.

Mueller, R. A., Rothermel, R., Behen, M., Muzik, O., Mangner, T., & Chugani, H. (1998). Differential patterns of language and motor reorganization following early left hemisphere injury. *Archives of Neurology, 55,* 1113–1119.

Mulder, E. J. H., Robles de Medina, P. G., Huizink, A. C., Van den Bergh, B. R. H., Buitelaar, J. K., & Visser, G. H. A. (2002). Prenatal maternal stress: Effects on pregnancy and the (unborn) child. *Early Human Development, 70,* 3–14.

Muller, F., Rebiff, M., Taillandier, A., Qury, J. F., & Mornet, E. (2000). Parental origin of the extra chromosome in prenatally diagnosed fetal trisomy. *Human Genetics, 106,* 340–344.

Müller, O., & Krawinkel, M. (2005). Malnutrition and health in developing countries. *Canadian Medical Association Journal, 173,* 279–286.

Müller, U., Overton, W. F., & Reene, K. (2001). Development of conditional reasoning: A longitudinal study. *Journal of Cognition and Development, 2,* 27–49.

Mumme, D. L., Bushnell, E. W., DiCorcia, J. A., & Lariviere, L. A. (2007). Infants' use of gaze cues to interpret others' actions and emotional reactions. In R. Flom, K. Lee, & D. Muir (Eds.), *Gaze-following: Its development and significance* (pp. 143–170). Mahwah, NJ: Erlbaum.

Mumme, D. L., Fernald, A., & Herrera, C. (1996). Infants' responses to facial and vocal emotional signals in a social referencing paradigm. *Child Development, 67,* 3219–3237.

Munakata, Y. (2001). Task-dependency in infant behavior: Toward an understanding of the processes underlying cognitive development. In F. Lacerda, C. von Hofsten, & M. Heimann (Eds.), *Emerging cognitive abilities in early infancy* (pp. 29–52). Mahwah, NJ: Erlbaum.

Munakata, Y. (2006). Information processing approaches to development. In D. Kuhn & R. S. Siegler (Eds.), *Handbook of child psychology: Vol. 2. Cognition, perception, and language* (6th ed., pp. 426–463). Hoboken, NJ: Wiley.

Munakata, Y., & Stedron, J. M. (2002). Modeling infants' perception of object unity: What have we learned? *Developmental Science, 5,* 176.

Munakata, Y., Casey, B. J., & Diamond, A. (2004). Developmental cognitive neuroscience: Progress and potential. *Trends in Cognitive Sciences, 8,* 122–128.

Mundy, P. (2003). The neural basis of social impairments in autism: The role of the dorsal medial-frontal cortex and anterior cingulated system. *Journal of Child Psychology and Psychiatry and Allied Disciplines, 44,* 793–809.

Mundy, P., & Stella, J. (2000). Joint attention, social orienting, and nonverbal communication in autism. In A. M. Wetherby & B. M. Prizant (Eds.), *Autism spectrum disorders* (Vol. 9, pp. 55–77). Baltimore, MD: Paul H. Brookes.

Munroe, R. L., & Romney, A. K. (2006). Gender and age differences in same-sex aggregation and social behavior. *Journal of Cross-Cultural Psychology, 37,* 3–19.

Muret-Wagstaff, S., & Moore, S. G. (1989). The Hmong in America: Infant behavior and rearing practices. In J. K. Nugent, B. M. Lester, & T. B. Brazelton (Eds.), *Biology, culture, and development* (Vol. 1, pp. 319–339). Norwood, NJ: Ablex.

Muris, P., Merckelbach, H., Gadet, B., & Moulaert, V. (2000). Fears, worries, and scary dreams in 4- to 12-year-old children: their content, developmental pattern, and origins. *Journal of Clinical Child Psychology, 29,* 43–52.

Muris, P., Merckelbach, H., Ollendick, T. H., King, N. J., & Bogie, N. (2001). Children's nighttime fears: Parent–child ratings of frequency, content, origins, coping behaviors and severity. *Behaviour Research and Therapy, 39,* 13–28.

Murray, A. D. (1985). Aversiveness is in the mind of the beholder. In B. M. Lester & C. F. Z. Boukydis (Eds.), *Infant crying* (pp. 217–239). New York: Plenum.

Murray, F. B., & Zhang, Y. (2005). The role of necessity in cognitive development. *Cognitive Development, 20,* 235–241.

Mussen, P., & Eisenberg-Berg, N. (1977). *Roots of caring, sharing, and helping.* San Francisco: Freeman.

Mustanski, B. S., Viken, R. J., Kaprio, J., Pulkkinen, L., & Rose, R. J. (2004). Genetic and environmental influences on pubertal development: Longitudinal data from Finnish twins at ages 11 and 14. *Developmental Psychology, 40,* 1188–1198.

Mustillo, S., Worthman, C., Erkanli, A., Keeler, G., Angold, A., & Costello, E. J. (2003). Obesity and psychiatric disorder: Developmental trajectories. *Pediatrics, 111,* 851–859.

Mutti, D. O., Mitchell, G. L., Moeschberger, M. L., Jones, L. A., & Zadnik, K. (2002). Parental myopia, near work, school achievement, and children's refractive error. *Investigative Ophthalmology and Visual Science, 43,* 3633–3640.

Myant, K. A., & Williams, J. M. (2005). Children's concepts of health and illness: Understanding of contagious illnesses, noncontagious illnesses and injuries. *Journal of Health Psychology, 10,* 805–819.

Myers, M. G., Brown, S. A., Tate, S., Abrantes, A., & Tomlinson, K. (2001). *Adolescents, alcohol, and substance abuse* (pp. 275–296). New York: Guilford.

Myowa-Yamakoshi, M., Tomonaga, M., Tanaka, M., & Matsuzawa, T. (2004). Imitation in neonatal chimpanzees (Pan troglodytes). *Developmental Science, 7,* 437–442.

Nadel, J., Prepin, K., & Okanda, M. (2005). Experiencing contingency and agency: First step toward self-understanding in making a mind? *Interaction Studies, 6,* 447–462.

Nafstad, P., Hagen, J. A., Øie, L., Magnus, P., & Jaakkola, J. J. K. (1999). Day care centers and respiratory health. *Pediatrics, 103,* 753–758.

Nagin, D., & Tremblay, R. E. (1999). Trajectories of boys' physical aggression, opposition, and hyperactivity on the path to physically violent and nonviolent juvenile delinquency. *Child Development, 70,* 1181–1196.

Nagy, W. E., & Scott, J. A. (2000). Vocabulary processes. In M. L. Kamil & P. B. Mosenthal (Eds.), *Handbook of reading research* (Vol. 3, pp. 269–284). Mahwah, NJ: Erlbaum.

Nánez, J., Sr., & Yonas, A. (1994). Effects of luminance and texture motion on infant defensive reactions to optical collision. *Infant Behavior and Development, 17,* 165–174.

Narayan, D., Chambers, R., Shah, M. K., & Peteesch, P. (2000). *Voices of the poor: Crying out for change.* New York: Oxford University Press for the World Bank.

Nastasi, B. K., & Clements, D. H. (1994). Effectance motivation, perceived scholastic competence, and higher-order thinking in two cooperative computer environments. *Journal of Educational Computing Research, 10,* 249–275.

Natale, R., & Dodman, N. (2003). Birth can be a hazardous journey: Electronic fetal monitoring does not help. *JOGC, 25,* 1007–1009.

National Association for the Education of Young Children. (1998). *Accreditation criteria and procedures*

National Association for Sport and Physical Education. (2002). *Active start: Physical activity for children birth to 5 years.* Reston, VA: Author.

National Council of Youth Sports. (2005). *Report on trends and participation in youth sports.* Stuart, FL: Author.

National Diabetes Education Program, Diabetes in Children and Adolescents Work Group. (2004). An update on type 2 diabetes in youth from the National Diabetes Education Program. *Pediatrics, 114,* 259–263.

National Federation of State High School Associations. (2006). *High school athletic participation survey.* Kansas City, MO: Author.

National Forum on Welfare to Work. (2004). *Welfare to work: The next generation. A national forum.* St. John's, Newfoundland: Author.

National Institutes of Health. (2006). *Genes and disease.* Retrieved from www.ncbi.nlm.nih.gov/disease

National Safe Kids Campaign. (2005). *Report to the nation: Trends in unintentional childhood injury mortality: 1987–2000.* Washington, DC: Author.

National Sleep Foundation. (2004). *Sleep in America poll.* Retrieved from www.sleepfoundation.org/hottopics /index.php?secid=16

Navarrete, C., Martinez, I., & Salamanca, F. (1994). Paternal line of transmission in chorea of Huntington with very early onset. *Genetic Counseling, 5,* 175–178.

Needleman, H. L., MacFarland, C., Ness, R. B., Reinberg, S., & Tobin, M. J. (2002). Bone lead levels in adjudicated delinquents: A case control study. *Neurotoxicology and Teratology, 24,* 711–717.

Neff, K. D., & Helwig, C. C. (2002). A constructivist approach to understanding the development of reasoning about rights and authority within cultural contexts. *Cognitive Development, 17,* 1429–1450.

Neitzel, C., & Stright, A. D. (2003). Mothers' scaffolding of children's problem solving: Establishing a foundation of academic selfregulatory competence. *Journal of Family Psychology, 17,* 147–159.

Nelson, C. A. (2000). Neural plasticity and human development: The role of early experience in sculpting memory systems. *Developmental Science, 3,* 115–130.

Nelson, C. A. (2002). Neural development and lifelong plasticity. In R. M. Lerner, F. Jacobs, & D. Wertlieb (Eds.), *Handbook of applied developmental science* (Vol. 1, pp. 31–60). Thousand Oaks, CA: Sage.

Nelson, C. A., & Bosquet, M. (2000). Neurobiology of fetal and infant development: Implications for infant mental

health. In C. H. Zeanah, Jr. (Ed.), *Handbook of infant mental health* (2nd ed., pp. 37–59). New York: Guilford.

Nelson, C. A., III, Thomas, K. M., & de Haan, M. (2006). Neural bases of cognitive development. In D. Kuhn & R. Siegler (Eds.), *Handbook of child psychology: Vol. 2. Cognition, perception, and language* (6th ed., pp. 3–57). Hoboken, NJ: Wiley.

Nelson, D. A., Hart, C. H., Yang, C., Olsen, J. A., & Jin, S. (2006). Aversive parenting in China: Associations with child physical and relational aggression. *Child Development, 77,* 554–572

Nelson, D. A., Nelson, L. J., Hart, C. H., Yang, C., & Jin, S. (2005). Parenting and peer-group behavior in cultural context. In X. Chen, B. Schneider, & D. French (Eds.), *Peer relations in cultural context.* New York Cambridge University Press.

Nelson, D. A., Robinson, C. C., & Hart, C. H. (2005). Relational and physical aggression of preschool-age children: Peer status linkages across informants. *Early Education and Development, 16,* 115–139.

Nelson, E. A. S., Schiefenhoevel, W., & Haimerl, F. (2000). Child care practices in nonindustrialized societies. *Pediatrics, 105,* e75.

Nelson, J. (1996). *Positive discipline.* New York: Ballantine.

Nelson, K. (1973). Structure and strategy in learning to talk. *Monographs of the Society for Research in Child Development, 38*(1–2, Serial No. 149).

Nelson, K. (2001). Language and the self: From the "experiencing I" to the "continuing me." In C. Moore & K. Lemmon (Eds.), *The self in time* (pp. 15–33). Mahwah NJ: Erlbaum.

Nelson, K. (2003). Narrative and the emergence of a consciousness of self. In G. D. Fireman & T. E. McVay, Jr. (Eds.), *Narrative and consciousness: Literature, psychology, and the brain* (pp. 17–36). London: Oxford University Press.

Nelson, K., & Fivush, R. (2004). The emergence of autobiographical memory: A social cultural developmental theory. *Developmental Review, 111,* 486–511.

Nelson, L. J. (2003). Rites of passage in emerging adulthood: Perspectives of young Mormons. In J. J. Arnett & N. L. Galambos (Eds.), *Exploring cultural conceptions of the transitions to adulthood (New directions for child and adolescent development,* No. 100, pp. 33–49). San Francisco: Jossey-Bass.

Nemet, D., Barkan, S., Epstein, Y., Friedland, O., Kowen, G., & Eliakim, A. (2005). Short- and long-term beneficial effects of a combined dietary–behavioral–physical activity intervention for the treatment of childhood obesity. *Pediatrics, 115,* e443–e449.

Neuman, S. B. (1999). Books make a difference: A study of access to literacy. *Reading Research Quarterly, 34,* 286–311.

Neuman, S. B. (2003). From rhetoric to reality: The case for high-quality compensatory prekindergarten programs. *Phi Delta Kappan, 85*(4), 286–291.

Neumark-Sztainer, D., Hannan, P. J., Story, M., Croll, J., & Perry, C. (2003). Family meal patterns: Associations with sociodemographic characteristics and improved dietary intake among adolescents. *Journal of the American Dietetic Association, 103,* 317–322.

Neurath, C. (2005). Tooth decay trends for 12 year olds in nonfluoridated and fluoridated countries. *Flouride, 1,* 324–325.

Neville, H. J., & Bavelier, D. (2002). Human brain plasticity: Evidence from sensory deprivation and altered language experience. In M. A. Hofman, G. J. Boer, A. J. G. D. Holtmaat, E. J. W. van Someren, J. Berhaagen, & D. F. Swaab (Eds.), *Plasticity in the adult brain: From genes to neurotherapy* (pp. 177–188). Amsterdam: Elsevier Science.

Neville, H. J., & Bruer, J. T. (2001). Language processing: How experience affects brain organization. In D. B. Bailey, Jr., J. T. Bruer, F. J. Symons, & J. W. Lichtman (Eds.), *Critical thinking about critical periods* (pp. 151–172). Baltimore: Paul H. Brookes.

Nevin, R. (2000). How lead exposure relates to temporal changes in IQ, violent crime, and unwed pregnancy. *Environmental Research, 83,* 1–22.

Newachek, P., Hung, Y.-Y., Hochstein, M., & Halfon, N. (2002). Access to health care for disadvantaged young children. *Journal of Early Intervention, 25,* 1–11.

Newcomb, A. F., Bukowski, W. M., & Pattee, L. (1993). Children's peer relations: A meta-analytic review of popular, rejected, neglected, controversial, and average sociometric status. *Psychological Bulletin, 113,* 99–128.

Newcomb, M. D., Abbott, R. D., Catalano, R. F., Hawkins, J. D., Battin-Pearson, S., & Hill, K. (2002). Mediational and deviance theories of late high school failure: Process roles of structural strains, academic competence, and general versus specific problem behavior. *Journal of Counseling Psychology, 49,* 172–186.

Newcombe, N., & Huttenlocher, J. (1992). Children's early ability to solve perspective-taking problems. *Developmental Psychology, 28,* 635–643.

Newcombe, N. S., & Huttenlocher, J. (2006). Development of spatial cognition. In D. Kuhn & R. Siegler (Eds.), *Handbook of child psychology: Vol. 2. Cognition, perception, and language* (6th ed., pp. 734–776). Hoboken, NJ: Wiley.

Newcombe, N. S., Sluzenski, J., & Huttenlocher, J. (2005). Preexisting knowledge versus on-line learning: What do young infants really know about spatial location? *Psychological Science, 16,* 222–227.

Newcombe, P. A., & Boyle, G. J. (1995). High school students' sports personalities: Variations across participation level, gender, type of sport, and success. *International Journal of Sports Psychology, 26,* 277–294.

Newman, A. J., Bavelier, D., Corina, D., Jezzard, P., & Neville, H. J. (2002). A critical period for right hemisphere recruitment in American sign language processing. *Nature Neuroscience, 5,* 76–80.

Newman, B. M., & Newman, P. R. (2001). Group identity and alienation: Giving the we its due. *Journal of Youth and Adolescence, 30,* 515–538.

Newman, C., Atkinson, J., & Braddick, O. (2001). The development of reaching and looking preferences in infants to objects of different sizes. *Developmental Psychology, 37,* 561–572.

Newnham, J. P., Evans, S. F., Michael, C. A., Stanley, F. J., & Landau, L. I. (1993). Effects of freqeunt ultrasound during pregnancy: A randomized controlled trial. *Lancet, 342,* 887–890.

Newport, E. L. (1991). Contrasting conceptions of the critical period for language. In S. Carey & R. Gelman (Eds.), *The epigenesis of mind: Essays on biology and cognition* (pp. 111–130). Hillsdale, NJ: Erlbaum.

Newport, E. L., & Aslin, R. N. (2000). Innately constrained learning: Blending old and new approaches to language acquisition. In S. C. Howell, S. A. Fish, & T. Keith-Lucas (Eds.), *Proceedings of the 24th Annual Boston University Conference on Language Development* (pp. 1–21). Somerville, MA: Cascadilla Press.

Newson, J., & Newson, E. (1975). Intersubjectivity and the transmission of culture: On the social origins of symbolic functioning. *Bulletin of the British Psychological Society, 28,* 437–446.

Ni, Y. (1998). Cognitive structure, content knowledge, and classificatory reasoning. *Journal of Genetic Psychology, 159,* 280–296.

Niccolai, L. M., Ethier, K. A., Kershaw, T. S., Lewis, J. B., Meade, C. S., & Ickovics, J. R. (2004). New sex partner acquisition and sexually transmitted disease risk among adolescent females. *Journal of Adolescent Health, 34,* 216–223.

NICHD (National Institute for Child Health and Development) Early Child Care Research Network. (1997). The effects of infant child care on infant–mother attachment security: Results of the NICHD Study of Early Child Care. *Child Development, 68,* 860–879.

NICHD (National Institute for Child Health and Human Development) Early Child Care Research Network. (1999). Child care and mother–child interaction in the first 3 years of life. *Developmental Psychology, 35,* 1399–1413.

NICHD (National Institute of Child Health and Human Development) Early Child Care Research Network. (2000a). Characteristics and quality of child care for toddlers and preschoolers. *Applied Developmental Science, 4,* 116–135.

NICHD (National Institute of Child Health and Human Development) Early Child Care Research Network. (2000b). The relation of child care to cognitive and language development. *Child Development, 71,* 960–980.

NICHD (National Institute of Child Health and Human Development) Early Child Care Research Network. (2001). Before Head Start: Income and ethnicity, family characteristics, child care experiences, and child development. *Early Education and Development, 12,* 545–575.

NICHD (National Institute of Child Health and Human Development) Early Child Care Research Network. (2002a). Child-care structure → process → outcome: Direct and indirect effects of child-care quality on young children's development. *Psychological Science, 13,* 199–206.

NICHD (National Institute of Child Health and Human Development) Early Child Care Research Network. (2002b). The interaction of child care and family risk in relation to child development at 24 and 36 months. *Applied Developmental Science, 6,* 144–156.

NICHD (National Institute of Child Health and Human Development) Early Child Care Research Network. (2003a). Does amount of time spent in child care predict socioemotional adjustment during the transition to kindergarten? *Child Development, 74,* 976–1005.

NICHD (National Institute of Child Health and Human Development) Early Child Care Research Network. (2003b). Does quality of child care affect child outcomes at age *Developmental Psychology, 39,* 451–469.

NICHD (National Institute of Child Health and Human Development) Early Child Care Research Network. (2004a). Are child development outcomes related to before- and after-school care arrangements? Results from the NICHD Study of Early Child Care. *Child Development, 75,* 280–295.

NICHD (National Institute of Child Health and Human Development) Early Child Care Research Network. (2004b). Type of child care and children's development at 54 months. *Early Childhood Research Quarterly, 19,* 203–230.

NICHD (National Institute of Child Health and Development) Early Child Care Research Network. (2006). Child-care effect sizes for the NICHD Study of Early Child Care and Youth Development. *American Psychologist, 61,* 99–116.

Nichols, K. E., Fox, N., & Mundy, P. (2005). Joint attention, self-recognition, and neurocognitive function in toddlers. *Infancy, 7,* 35–51.

Nicholson, C. (2006, September). Thinking it over: fMRI and psychological science. *APS Observer,* pp. 21–25.

Nickman, S. L., Rosenfeld, A. A., & Fine, P. (2005). Children in adoptive families: Overview and update. *Journal of the American Academy of Child and Adolescent Psychiatry, 44,* 987–995.

Nickman, S. L., Rosenfeld, A. A., Fine, P., MacIntyre, J. C., Pilowsky, D. J., & Howe, R.-A. (2005). Children in adoptive families: Overview and update. *Journal of the American Academy of Child and Adolescent Psychiatry, 44,* 987–995.

Niehaus, M. D., Moore, S. R., Patrick, P. D., Derr, L. L., Lorntz, B., Lima, A. A., & Gurerrant, R. L. (2002). Early childhood diarrhea is associated with diminished cognitive function 4 to 7 years later in children in a northeast Brazilian shantytown. *American Journal of Tropical Medicine and Hygiene, 66,* 590–593.

Nielsen, S. J., & Popkin, B. M. (2003). Patterns and trends in food portion sizes. *Journal of the American Medical Association, 289,* 450–453.

Nippold, M. A. (1999). Word definition in adolescents as a function of reading proficiency: A research note. *Child Language Teaching and Therapy, 15,* 171–176.

Nippold, M. A. (2000). Language development during the adolescent years: Aspects of pragmatics, syntax, and semantics. *Topics in Language Disorders, 20,* 15–28.

Nippold, M. A., Allen, M. M., & Kirsch, D. I. (2001). Proverb comprehension as a function of reading proficiency in preadolescents. *Language, Speech and Hearing Services in the Schools, 32,* 90–100.

Nippold, M. A., Taylor, C. L., & Baker, J. M. (1996). Idiom understanding in Australian youth: A cross-cultural comparison. *Journal of Speech and Hearing Research, 39,* 442–447.

Nisbett, R. E. (1998). Race, genetics, and IQ. In C. Jencks & M. Phillips (Eds.), *The black–white test score gap* (pp. 86–102). Washington, DC: Brookings Institution.

Nix, R. L., Pinderhughes, E. E., Dodge, K. A., Bates, J. E., Pettit, G. S., & McFadyen-Ketchum, S. A. (1999). The relation between mothers' hostile attribution tendencies and children's externalizing behavior problems: The mediating role of mothers' harsh discipline practices. *Child Development, 70,* 896–909.

Noland, J. S., Singer, L. T., Short, E. J., Minnes, S., Arendt, R. E., & Krichner, H. L. (2005). Prenatal drug exposure and selective attention in preschoolers. *Neurotoxicology and Teratology, 27,* 429–438.

Nolen-Hoeksema, S. (2002). Gender differences in depression. In I. H. Gotlib & C. L. Hammen (Eds.), *Handbook of depression* (pp. 492–509). New York: Guilford.

Nolen-Hoeksema, S. (2006). The etiology of gender differences in depression. In C. M. Mazure, G. P. Keita, & G. Puryear (Eds.), *Understanding depression in women: Applying empirical research to practice and policy* (pp. 9–43). Washington, DC: American Psychological Association.

Noonan, C. W., Kathman, S. J., Sarasua, S. M., & White, M. C. (2003). Influence of environmental zinc on the association between environmental and biological measures of lead in children. *Journal of Exposure Analysis and Environmental Epidemiology, 13,* 318–323.

Norgaard, J. P., Djurhuus, J. C., Watanabe, H., Stenberg, A., & Lettgen, B. (1997). Experience and current status of research into the pathophysiology of nocturnal enuresis. *British Journal of Urology, 79,* 825–835.

Noterdaeme, M., Mildenberger, K., Minow, F., & Amorosa, H. (2002). Evaluation of neuromotor deficits in children with autism and children with a specific speech and language disorder. *European Child and Adolescent Psychiatry, 11,* 219–225.

Nucci, L. (2001). *Education in the moral domain.* New York: Cambridge University Press.

Nucci, L. (2005). Culture, context, and the psychological sources of human rights concepts. In W. Edelstein & G. Nunner-Winkler (Eds.), *Morality in context* (pp. 365–394). Amsterdam, Netherlands: Elsevier.

Nucci, L. P. (1996). Morality and the personal sphere of action. In E. Reed, E. Turiel, & T. Brown (Eds.), *Values and knowledge* (pp. 41–60). Hillsdale, NJ: Erlbaum.

Nucci, L. P. (2002). The development of moral reasoning. In U. Goswami (Ed.), *Blackwell handbook of childhood cognitive development* (pp. 303–325). Malden, MA: Blackwell.

Nuttal, R. L., Casey, M. B., & Pezaris, E. (2005). Spatial ability as a mediator of gender differences on mathematics tests: A biological–environmental framework. In A. M. Gallagher & C. J. Kaufman (Eds.), *Gender differences in mathematics: An integrated psychological approach* (pp. 121–142). New York: Cambridge University Press.

Nye, B., Hedges, L. V., & Konstantopoulos, S. (2001). Are effects of small classes cumulative? Evidence from a Tennessee experiment. *Journal of Educational Research, 94,* 336–345.

Oakes, L. M., Coppage, D. J., & Dingel, A. (1997). By land or by sea: The role of perceptual similarity in infants' categorization of animals. *Developmental Psychology, 33,* 396–407.

Oakes, L. M., & Madole, K. L. (2003). Principles of developmental change in infants' category formation. In D. H. Rakison & L. M. Oakes (Eds.), *Early category and concept development: Making sense of the blooming, buzzing confusion* (pp. 132–158). New York: Oxford University Press.

Obeidallah, D., Brennan, R. T., Brooks-Gunn, J., & Earls, F. (2004). Links between pubertal timing and neighborhood contexts: Implications for girls' violent behavior. *Journal of the American Academy of Child and Adolescent Psychiatry, 43,* 1460–1468.

Obler, L. K. (2005). Language in adulthood. In J. B. Gleason (Ed.), *Development of language* (6th ed., pp. 444–458). Boston: Allyn and Bacon.

Obradovi´c, J., & Masten, A. S. (2007). Developmental antecedents of young adult civic engagement. *Applied Developmental Science, 11,* 2–19. {COMP: The accent goes over the c in Obradovic}

O'Callaghan, M. J., Burn, Y. R., Mohay, H. A., Rogers, Y., & Tudehope, D. I. (1993). The prevalence and origins of left hand preference in high risk infants, and its implications for intellectual, motor, and behavioral performance at four and six years. *Cortex, 29,* 617–627.

O'Connor, A. R., Stephenson, T., Johnson, A., Tobin, M. J., Ratib, S., Ng, Y., & Fielder, A. R. (2002). Long-term ophthalmic outcome of low birth weight children with and without retinopathy of prematurity. *Pediatrics, 109,* 12–18.

O'Connor, C. (1997). Dispositions toward (collective) struggle and educational resilience in the inner city: A case analysis of six African-American high school students. *American Educational Research Journal, 34,* 593–629.

O'Connor, T. G., & Croft, C. M. (2001). A twin study of attachment in preschool children. *Child Development, 72,* 1501–1511.

O'Connor, T. G., Deater-Deckard, K., Fulker, D., Rutter, M., & Plomin, R. (1998). Genotype–environment correlations in late childhood and early adolescence: Antisocial behavioral problems and coercive parenting. *Developmental Psychology, 34,* 970–981.

O'Connor, T. G., Marvin, R. S., Rutter, M., Olrich, J. T., Britner, P. A., & the English and Romanian Adoptees Study Team. (2003). Child–parent attachment following early institutional deprivation. *Development and Psychopathology, 15,* 19–38.

O'Connor, T. G., Rutter, M., Beckett, C., Keaveney, L., Dreppner, J. M., & the English and Romanian Adoptees Study Team. (2000). The effects of global severe privation on cognitive competence: Extension and longitudinal follow-up. *Child Development, 71,* 376–390.

O'Dea, J. A. (2003). Why do kids eat healthful food? Perceived benefits of and barriers to healthful eating and physical activity among children and adolescents. *Journal of the American Dietetic Association, 103,* 497–501.

OECD (Organisation for Economic Cooperation and Development). (2005). *Education at a glance: OECD indicators 2005.* Paris: Author.

Ogbu, J. U. (1997). Understanding the school performance of urban blacks: Some essential background knowledge. In H. J. Walberg, O. Reyes, & R. P. Weissberg (Eds.), *Children and youth: Interdisciplinary perspectives* (pp. 190–222). Thousand Oaks, CA: Sage.

Ogbu, J. U. (2003). *Black American students in an affluent suburb: A study of academic disengagement.* Mahwah, NJ: Erlbaum.

Ogden, C. L., Carroll, M. D., McDowell, M., Tabak, C. J., & Flegal, K. M. (2006). Prevalence of overweight and obesity in the United States, 1999–2004. *Journal of the American Medical Association, 295,* 1549–1555.

Ohgi, S., Arisawa, K., Takahashi, T., Kusumoto, T., Goto, Y., Akiyama, T., & Saito, H. (2003a). Neonatal behavioral assessment scale as a predictor of later developmental disabilities of low-birth-weight and/or premature infants. *Brain and Development, 25,* 313–321.

Ohgi, S., Takahashi, T., Nugent, J. K., Arisawa, K., & Akiyama, T. (2003b). Neonatal behavioral characteristics and later behavioral problems. *Clinical Pediatrics, 42,* 679–686.

Okagaki, L., Hammond, K. A., & Seamon, L. (1999). Socialization of religious beliefs. *Journal of Applied Developmental Psychology, 20,* 273–294.

Okagaki, L., & Sternberg, R. J. (1993). Parental beliefs and children's school performance. *Child Development, 64,* 36–56.

Okami, P., Weisner, T., & Olmstead, R. (2002). Outcome correlates of parent–child bedsharing: An eighteen-year longitudinal study. *Developmental and Behavioral Pediatrics, 23,* 244–253.

O'Keefe, M. J., O'Callaghan, M., Williams, G. M., Najman, J. M., & Bor, W. (2003). Learning, cognitive, and attentional problems in adolescents born small for gestational age. *Pediatrics, 112,* 301–307.

Olafson, E., & Boat, B. W. (2000). Long-term management of the sexually abused child: Considerations and challenges. In R. M. Reece (Ed.), *Treatment of child abuse: Common ground for mental health, medical, and legal practitioners* (pp. 14–35). Baltimore: Johns Hopkins University Press.

O'Laughlin, E. M., & Anderson, V. N. (2001). Perceptions of parenthood among young adults: Implications for career and family planning. *American Journal of Family Therapy, 29,* 95–108.

Oldershaw, L. (2002). *A national survey of parents of young children.* Toronto: Invest in Kids.

Ollendick, T. H., King, N. J., & Muris, P. (2002). Fears and phobias in children: Phenomenology, epidemiology, and aetiology. *Child and Adolescent Mental Health, 7,* 98–106.

Oller, D. K. (2000). *The emergence of the speech capacity.* Mahwah, NJ: Erlbaum.

Oller, D. K., Eilers, R. E., Neal, A. R., & Schwartz, H. K. (1999). Precursors to speech in infancy: The prediction of speech and language disorders. *Journal of Communication Disorders, 32,* 223–245.

Olson, S. L., Bates, J. E., Sandy, J. M., & Lantheir, R. (2000). Early development precursors of externalizing behavior in middle childhood and adolescence. *Journal of Abnormal Child Psychology, 28,* 119–133.

Omar, H., McElderry, D., & Zakharia, R. (2003). Educating adolescents about puberty: What are we missing? *International Journal of Adolescent Medicine and Health, 15,* 79–83.

O'Neill, M., Bard, K. A., Kinnell, M., & Fluck, M. (2005). Maternal gestures with 20-month-old infants in two contexts. *Developmental Science, 8,* 352–359.

O'Neill, R., Welsh, M., Parke, R. D., Wang, S., & Strand, C. (1997). A longitudinal assessment of the academic correlates of early peer acceptance and rejection. *Journal of Clinical Child Psychology, 26,* 290–303.

O'Neill, R. M., Horton, S. S., & Crosby, F. J. (1999). Gender issues in developmental relationships. In A. J. Murrell, F. J. Crosby, & R. J. Ely (Eds.), *Mentoring dilemmas* (pp. 63–80). Mahwah, NJ: Erlbaum.

Ong, K. K., Ahmed, M. L., & Dunger, D. B. (2006). Lessons from large population studies on timing and tempo of puberty (secular trends and relation to body size): the European trend. *Molecular and Cellular Endocrinology, 254–255,* 8–12.

Ong, W., Allison, J., & Haladyna, T. M. (2000). Student achievement of third graders in comparable single-age and multiage classrooms. *Journal of Research in Childhood Education, 14,* 205–215.

Oosterwegel, A., & Openheimer, L. (1993). *The self-system: Developmental changes between and within self-concepts.* Hillsdale, NJ: Erlbaum.

O'Rahilly, R., & Müller, F. (2001). *Human embryology and teratology.* New York: Wiley-Liss.

Orbio de Castro, B., Veerman, J. W., Koops, W., Bosch, J. D., & Monshouwer, H. J. (2002). Hostile attribution of intent and aggressive behavior: A meta-analysis. *Child Development, 73,* 916–934.

O'Reilly, A. W. (1995). Using representations: Comprehension and production of actions with imagined objects. *Child Development, 66,* 999–1010.

Osborne, J. (1994). Academics, selfesteem, and race: A look at the underlying assumption of the disidentification hypothesis. *Personality and Social Psychology Bulletin, 21,* 449–455.

Osherson, D. N., & Markman, E. M. (1975). Language and the ability to evaluate contradictions and tautologies. *Cognition, 2,* 213–226.

Oshima-Takane, Y., & Robbins, M. (2003). Linguistic environment of secondborn children. *First Language, 23,* 21–40.

OSSTF (Ontario Secondary School Teachers' Federation). (2006). Update on testing: Current results. *OSSTF Critical Issues, Monograph #32.* Retrieved from www.osstf.ca/adx/aspx/adxGetMedia.aspx?DocID=770,765,550,541,442,365,Documents&MediaID=696&Filename=monograph-32.pdf

Ostrov, J. M., Crick, N. R., & Stauffacher, K. (2006). Relational aggression in sibling and peer relationships during early childhood. *Applied Developmental Psychology, 27,* 241–253.

Ostrov, J. M., Gentile, D. A., & Crick, N. R. (2006). Media exposure, aggression, and prosocial behavior during early childhood: A longitudinal study. *Social Development, 15,* 612–627.

Otis, N., Grouzet, F. M. E., & Pelletier, L. G. (2005). Latent motivational change in an academic setting: A three-year longitudinal study. *Journal of Educational Psychology, 97,* 170–183.

Ovando, C. J., & Collier, V. P. (1998). *Bilingual and ESL classrooms: Teaching in multicultural contexts.* Boston: McGraw-Hill.

Ovelese, Y., & Ananth, C. V. (2006). Placental abruption. *Obstetrics and Gynecology, 108,* 1005–1016.

Ovelese, Y., & Smulian, J. C. (2006). Placenta previa, placenta accreta, and vasa previa. *Obstetrics and Gynecology, 107,* 927–941.

Owen-Kostelnik, J., Reppucci, N. D., & Meyer, J. R. (2006). Testimony and interrogation of minors: Assumptions about maturity and morality. *American Psychologist, 61,* 286–304.

Owens, E. B., & Shaw, D. S. (2003). Predicting growth curves of externalizing behavior across the preschool years. *Journal of Abnormal Child Psychology, 31,* 575–590.

Owens, J. A., Rosen, C. L., & Mindell. J. A. (2003). Medication use in the treatment of pediatric insomnia: Results of a survey of community-based pediatricians. *Pediatrics, 111,* e628–e635.

Owens, R. E. (2005). *Language development: An introduction.* Boston: Allyn and Bacon.

Oyserman, D., Bybee, D., Mowbray, C., & Hart-Johnson, T. (2005). When mothers have serious mental health problems: Parenting as a proximal mediator. *Journal of Adolescence, 28,* 443–463.

Pacella, R., McLellan, M., Grice, K., Del Bono, E. A., Wiggs, J. L., & Gwiazda, J. E. (1999). Role of genetic factors in the etiology of juvenile-onset myopia based on a longitudinal study of refractive error. *Optometry and Vision Science, 76,* 381–386.

Pagani, L., Tremblay, R. E., Vitaro, F., Boulerice, B., & McDuff, P. (2001). Effects of grade retention on academic performance and behavioral development. *Development and Psychopathology, 13,* 297–315.

Paladino, J. (2006). *Private speech in children with autism: Developmental course and functional utility.* Unpublished doctoral dissertation, Illinois State University.

Palda, V., Guise, J.-M., & Wathen, N., with the Canadian Task Force on Preventive Health Care. (2004). Interventions to promote breast-feeding: Applying the evidence in clinical practice. *Canadian Medical Association Journal, 170,* 976–978.

Palincsar, A. S. (2003). Advancing a theoretical model of learning and instruction. In B. J. Zimmerman (Ed.), *Educational psychology: A century of contributions* (pp. 459–475). Mahwah, NJ: Erlbaum.

Palincsar, A. S., & Herrenkohl, L. R. (1999). Designing collaborative contexts: Lessons from three research programs. In A. M. O'Donnell & A. King (Eds.), *Cognitive perspectives on peer learning. The Rutgers Invitational Symposium on Education Series* (pp. 151–177). Mahwah, NJ: Erlbaum.

Palmer, J. R., Hatch, E. E., Rao, R. S., Kaufman, R. H., Herbst, A. L., & Noller, K. L. (2001). Infertility among women exposed prenatally to diethylstilbestrol. *American Journal of Epidemiology, 154,* 316–321.

Pan, B. A., & Snow, C. E. (1999). The development of conversation and discourse skills. In M. Barrett (Ed.), *The development of language* (pp. 229–249). Hove, U.K.: Psychology Press.

Pan, H. W. (1994). Children's play in Taiwan. In J. L. Roopnarine, J. E. Johnson, & F. H. Hooper (Eds.), *Children's play in diverse cultures* (pp. 31–50). Albany, NY: SUNY Press.

Paquette, D. (2004). Theorizing the father–child relationship: Mechanisms and developmental outcomes. *Human Development, 47,* 193–219.

Parameswaran, G. (2003). Experimenter instructions as a mediator in the effects of culture on mapping one's neighborhood. *Journal of Environmental Psychology, 23,* 409–417.

Pardeck, J. T. (2005). An exploration of child maltreatment among homeless families: Implications for family policy. *Early Child Development and Care, 175,* 335–342.

Pardun, C. J., L'Engle, K. L., & Brown, J. D. (2005). Linking exposure to outcomes: Early adolescents' consumption of sexual content in six media. *Mass Communication and Society, 87,* 75–91.

Parent, A., Teilmann, G., Juul, A., Skakkebaek, N. E., Toppari, J., & Bourguignon, J. (2003). The timing of normal puberty and the age limits of sexual precocity: Variations around the world, secular trends, and changes after migration. *Endocrine Reviews, 24,* 668–693.

Paris, S. G., & Paris, A. G. (2006). Assessments of early reading. In K. A. Renninger & I. E. Sigel (Eds.), *Handbook of child psychology: Vol. 4. Child psychology in practice* (6th ed., pp. 48–74). Hoboken, NJ: Wiley.

Parke, R. D. (2002). Fathers and families. In M. H. Bornstein (Ed.), *Handbook of parenting: Vol. 3* (2nd ed., pp. 27–73). Mahwah, NJ: Erlbaum.

Parke, R. D., & Buriel, R. (2006). Socialization in the family: Ethnic and ecological perspectives. In N. Eisenberg (Ed.), *Handbook of child psychology: Vol. 3. Social, emotional, and personality development* (6th ed., pp. 429–504). Hoboken, NJ: Wiley.

Parke, R. D., Coltrane, S., Fabricius, W., Powers, J., & Adams, M. (2004). Assessing father involvement in Mexican-American families. In R. Day & M. E. Lamb

(Eds.), *Conceptualizing and measuring paternal involvement* (pp. 17–38). Mahwah, NJ: Erlbaum.

Parke, R. D., Simpkins, S. D., McDowell, D. J., Kim, M., Killian, C., Dennis, J., Flyr, M. L., Wild, M., & Rah, Y. (2004). Relative contributions of families and peers to children's social development. In P. K. Smith & C. H. Hart (Eds.), *Blackwell handbook of childhood social development* (pp. 156–177). Malden, MA: Blackwell.

Parke, R. D., & Tinsley, B. R. (1981). The father's role in infancy: Determinants of involvement in caregiving and play. In M. E. Lamb (Ed.), *The role of the father in child development* (pp. 429–458). New York: Wiley.

Parker, F. L., Boak, A. Y., Griffin, K. W., Ripple, C., & Peay, L. (1999). Parent–child relationship, home learning environment, and school readiness. *School Psychology Review, 28,* 413–425.

Parker, J. G., Low, C. M., Walker, A. R., & Gamm, B. K. (2005). Friendship jealousy in young adolescents: Individual differences and links to sex, self-esteem, aggression, and social adjustment. *Developmental Psychology, 41,* 235–250.

Parker, J. G., Rubin, K. H., Price, J., & DeRosier, M. E. (1995). Peer relationships, child development, and adjustment: A developmental psychopathology perspective. In D. Cicchetti & D. Cohen (Eds.), *Developmental psychopathology: Vol. 2. Risk, disorder, and adaptation* (pp. 96–161). New York: Wiley.

Parker, S. W., Nelson, C. A., & the Bucharest Early Intervention Project Core Group. (2005). The impact of early institutional rearing on the ability to discriminate facial expressions of emotion: An event-related potential study. *Child Development, 76,* 54–72.

Parten, M. (1932). Social participation among preschool children. *Journal of Abnormal and Social Psychology, 27,* 243–269.

Pascalis, O., de Haan, M., & Nelson, C. A. (1998). Long-term recognition memory for faces assessed by visual paired comparison in 3- and 6-month-old infants. *Journal of Experimental Psychology: Learning, Memory, and Cognition, 24,* 249–260.

Pascalis, O., de Haan, M., & Nelson, C. A. (2002). Is face processing species-specific during the first year of life? *Science, 296,* 1321–1323.

Pascarella, E. T., & Terenzini, P. T. (1991). *How college affects students.* San Francisco: Jossey-Bass.

Pascarella, E. T., Whitt, E. J., Edison, M. I., Nora, A., Hagedorn, L. S., Yeager, P. M., & Terenzini, P. T. (1997). Women's perceptions of a "chilly climate" and their cognitive outcomes during the first year of college. *Journal of College Student Development, 38,* 109–124.

Pasterski, V. L., Geffner, M. E., Brain, C., Hindmarsh, P., Brook, C., & Hines, M. (2005). Prenatal hormones and postnatal socialization by parents as determinants of male-typical toy play in girls with congenital adrenal hyperplasia. *Child Development, 76,* 264–278.

Patel, D. R., Pratt, H. D., & Greydanus, D. E. (2003). Treatment of adolescents with anorexia nervosa. *Journal of Adolescent Research, 18,* 244–260.

Paterson, D. S., Trachtenberg, F. L., Thompson, E. G., Belliveau, R. A., Beggs, A. H., & Darnall, R. (2006). Multiple serotonergic brainstem abnormalities in sudden infant death syndrome. *Journal of the American Medical Association, 296,* 2124–2132.

Patrick, E., & Abravanel, E. (2000). The self-regulatory nature of preschool children's private speech in a naturalistic setting. *Applied Psycholinguistics, 21,* 45–61.

Pattenden, S., Antova, T., Neuberger, M., Nikiforov, B., De Sario, M., Grize, L., & Heinrich, J. (2006). Parental smoking and children's respiratory health: Independent effects of prenatal and postnatal exposure. *Tobacco Control, 15,* 294–301.

Patterson, C. J. (2000). Family relationships of lesbians and gay men. *Journal of Marriage and the Family, 62,* 1052–1069.

Patterson, G. R., & Fisher, P. A. (2002). Recent developments in our understanding of parenting: Bidirectional effects, causal models, and the search for parsimony. In M. H. Bornstein (Ed.), *Handbook of parenting* (Vol. 5, pp. 59–88). Mahwah, NJ: Erlbaum.

Patterson, G. R., & Yoerger, K. (2002). A developmental model for early- and late-onset delinquency. In J. B. Reid & G. R. Patterson (Eds.), *Antisocial behavior in children and adolescents* (pp. 147–172). Washington, DC: American Psychological Association.

Patton, G. C., Selzer, R., Coffey, C., Carlin, J. B., & Wolfe, R. (1999). Onset of adolescent eating disorders: Population based cohort study over 3 years. *British Medical Journal, 318,* 765–768.

Paul, J. J., & Cillessen, A. H. N. (2003). Dynamics of peer victimization in early adolescence: Results from a four-year longitudinal study. *Journal of Applied School Psychology, 19,* 25–43.

PCA America. (2006). *Health Families America FAQ.* Retrieved from www.healthyfamiliesamerica.org /about_us/faq.shtml

Pearl, P. L., Capp, P. K., Novotny, E. J., & Gibson, K. M. (2005). Inherited disorders of neurotransmitters in children and adults. *Clinical Biochemistry, 38,* 1051–1058.

Pearlman, D. N., Zierler, S., Meersman, S., Kim, H. K., Viner-Brown, & Caron, C. (2006). Race disparities in childhood asthma: Does where you live matter? *Journal of the National Medical Association, 98,* 239–247.

Pebody, R. G., Edmunds, W. J., Conyn-van Spaendonck, M., Olin, P., Berbers, G., & Rebiere, I. (2000). The seroepidemiology of rubella in Western Europe. *Epidemiology and Infections, 125,* 347–357.

Pederson, D. R., Gleason, K. E., Moran, G., & Bento, S. (1998). Maternal attachment representations, maternal sensitivity, and the infant–mother attachment relationship. *Developmental Psychology, 34,* 925–933.

Pederson, D. R., & Moran, G. (1996). Expressions of the attachment relationship outside of the Strange Situation. *Child Development, 67,* 915–927.

Pedlow, R., Sanson, A., Prior, M., & Oberklaid, F. (1993). Stability of maternally reported temperament from infancy to 8 years. *Developmental Psychology, 29,* 998–1007.

Peirano, P., Algarin, C., & Uauy, R. (2003). Sleep–wake states and their regulatory mechanisms throughout early human development. *Journal of Pediatrics, 143,* S70–S79.

Peisner-Feinberg, E. S., Burchinal, M. R., Clifford, R. M., Culkin, M. L., Howes, C., Kagan, S. L., & Yazijian, N. (2001). The relation of preschool child-care quality to children's cognitive and social developmental trajectories through second grade. *Child Development, 72,* 1534–1553.

Pellegrini, A. D. (1992). Kindergarten children's social cognitive status as a predictor of first grade success. *Early Childhood Research Quarterly, 7,* 565–577.

Pellegrini, A. D. (2003). Perceptions and functions of play and real fighting in early adolescence. *Child Development, 74,* 1522–1533.

Pellegrini, A. D. (2004). Rough-and-tumble play from childhood through adolescence: Development and possible functions. In P. K. Smith & C. H. Hart (Eds.), *Blackwell handbook of childhood social development* (pp. 438–453). Malden, MA: Blackwell.

Pellegrini, A. D. (2005). *Recess: Its role in development and education.* Mahwah, NJ: Erlbaum.

Pellegrini, A. D., & Holmes, R. M. (2006). The role of recess in primary school. In D. G. Singer, R. M. Golinkoff, & K. Hirsh-Pasek (Eds.), *Play=learning* (pp. 36–53). New York: Oxford University Press.

Pellegrini, A. D., Huberty, P. D., & Jones, I. (1995). The effects of recess timing on children's playground and classroom behaviors. *American Educational Research Journal, 32,* 845–864.

Pellegrini, A. D., Kato, K., Blatchford, P., & Baines, E. (2002). A short-term longitudinal study of children's playground games across the first year of school: Implications for social competence and adjustment to school. *American Educational Research Journal, 39,* 991–1015.

Pellegrini, A. D., & Smith, P. K. (1998). Physical activity play: The nature and function of a neglected aspect of play. *Child Development, 69,* 577–598.

Pellicano, E., Maybery, M., Durkin, K., & Maley, A. (2006). Multiple cognitive capabilities/deficits in children with an autism spectrum disorder: "Weak" central coherence and its relationship to theory of mind and executive control. *Development and Psychopathology, 18,* 77–98.

Peña, R., Wall, S., & Person, L. (2000). The effect of poverty, social inequality, and maternal education on infant mortality in Nicaragua, 1988–1993. *American Journal of Public Health, 90,* 64–69.

Penner, A. M. (2003). International gender item difficulty interactions in mathematics and science achievement tests. *Journal of Educational Psychology, 95,* 650–655.

Pepler, D., Craig, W., Yuile, A., & Connolly, J. (2004). Girls who bully: A developmental and relational perspective. In M. Putallaz & K. L. Bierman (Eds.), *Aggression, antisocial behavior, and violence among girls: A developmental perspective* (pp. 90–109). New York: Guilford.

Peralta de Mendoza, O. A., & Salsa, A. M. (2003). Instruction in early comprehension and use of a symbol–referent relation. *Cognitive Development, 18,* 269–284.

Perie, M., Sherman, J. D., Phillips, G., & Riggan, M. (2000). Elementary and secondary education: An international perspective. *Education Statistics Quarterly.* Retrieved from http://www.nces.ed.gov/pubs2000/quarterly/sum-mer/5int/q51.html

Perkins, D. F., Jacobs, J. E., Barber, B. L., & Eccles, J. S. (2004). Childhood and adolescent sports participation as predictors of participation in sports and physical fitness activities during young adulthood. *Youth and Society, 35,* 495–520.

Perlman, M., & Ross, H. S. (1997). The benefits of parent intervention in children's disputes: An examination of concurrent changes in children's fighting styles. *Child Development, 64,* 690–700.

Perlmutter, M. (1984). Continuities and discontinuities in early human memory: Paradigms, processes, and performances. In R. V. Kail, Jr., & N. R. Spear (Eds.), *Comparative perspectives on the development of memory* (pp. 253–287). Hillsdale, NJ: Erlbaum.

Perren, S., von Wyl, A., Burgin, D., Simoni, H., & Von Klitzing, K. (2005). Intergenerational transmission of marital quality across the transition to parenthood. *Family Process, 44,* 441–459.

Perry, C. L., McGuire, M. T., Neumark-Sztainer, D., & Story, M. (2002). Adolescent vegetarians: How well do their dietary patterns meet the Healthy People 2010 objectives? *Archives of Pediatric and Adolescent Medicine, 156,* 431–437.

Perry, W. G. (1998). *Forms of intellectual and ethical development in the college years: A scheme.* San Francisco: Jossey-Bass. (Originally published 1970.)

Perry, W. G., Jr. (1970). *Forms of intellectual and ethical development in the college years.* New York: Holt, Rinehart and Winston.

Perry, W. G., Jr. (1981). Cognitive and ethical growth. In A. Chickering (Ed.), *The modern American college* (pp. 76–116). San Francisco: Jossey-Bass.

Peshkin, A. (1978). *Growing up American: Schooling and the survival of the community.* Chicago: University of Chicago Press.

Peshkin, A. (1994). *Growing up American: Schooling and the survival of community.* Prospect Heights, IL: Waveland Press.

Peshkin, A. (1997). *Places of memory: Whiteman's schools and Native American communities.* Mahwah, NJ: Erlbaum.

Peters, R. D. (2005). A community-based approach to promoting resilience in young children, their families, and their neighborhoods. In R. D. Peters, B. Leadbeater, & R. J. McMahon (Eds.), *Resilience in children, families, and communities: Linking context to practice and policy* (pp. 157–176). New York: Kluwer Academic.

Peters, R. D., Petrunka, K., & Arnold, R. (2003). The Better Beginnings, Better Futures Project: A universal, comprehensive, community-based prevention approach for primary school children and their families. *Journal of Clinical Child and Adolescent Psychology, 32,* 215–227.

Petersen, N., & Gonzales, R. C. (1999). *Career counseling models for diverse populations.* Belmont, CA: Wadsworth.

Peterson, C., & Roberts, C. (2003). Like mother, like daughter: Similarities in narrative style. *Developmental Psychology, 39,* 551–562.

Peterson, C. C. (2001). Influence of siblings' perspectives on theory of mind. *Cognitive Development, 15,* 435–455.

Petinou, K. C., Schwartz, R. G., Gravel, J. S., & Raphael, L. J. (2001). A preliminary account of phonological and morphological perception in young children with and without otitis media. *International Journal of Language and Communication Disorders, 36,* 21–42.

Petitto, L. A., Holowka, S., Sergio, L. E., Levy, B., & Ostry, D. J. (2004). Baby hands that move to the rhythm of language: Hearing babies acquiring sign languages babble silently on the hands. *Cognition, 93,* 43–73.

Petitto, L. A., Holowka, S., Sergio, L. E., & Ostry, D. (2001). Language rhythms in babies' hand movements. *Nature, 413,* 35–36.

Petitto, L. A., & Marentette, P. F. (1991). Babbling in the manual mode: Evidence for the ontogeny of language. *Science, 251,* 1493–1496.

Petras, H., Schaeffer, C. M., Ialongo, N., Hubbard, S., Muthén, B., & Lambert, S. F. (2004). When the course of aggressive behavior in childhood does not predict antisocial outcomes in adolescence and young adulthood: An examination of potential explanatory variables. *Development and Psychopathology, 16,* 919–941.

Petrill, S. A., & Deater-Deckard, K. (2004). The heritability of general cognitive ability: A within-family adoption design. *Intelligence, 32,* 403–409.

Petrovich, O. (1997). Understanding non-natural causality in children and adults: The case against artificialism. *Psyche en Geloof, 8,* 151–165.

Pettit, G. S. (2004). Violent children in developmental perspective. *Current Directions in Psychological Science, 13,* 194–197.

Pettit, G. S., Bates, J. E., Dodge, K. A., & Meece, D. W. (1999). The impact of after-school peer contact on early adolescent externalizing problems is moderated by parental monitoring, perceived neighborhood safety, and prior adjustment. *Child Development, 70,* 768–778.

Pettit, G. S., Brown, E. G., Mize, J., & Lindsey, E. (1998). Mothers' and fathers' socializing behaviors in three contexts: Links with children's peer competence. *Merrill-Palmer Quarterly, 44,* 173–193.

Pfeffer, C. R. (2006). Suicide and suicidality. In M. K. Dulcan & J. M. Wiener (Eds.), *Essentials of child and adolescent psychiatry* (pp. 621–632). Washington, DC: American Psychiatric Publishing.

Phillips, D. A., Howes, C., & Whitebook, M. (1992). The social policy context of child care: Effects on quality. *American Journal of Community Psychology, 20,* 25–51.

Phillips, M. (1997). What makes schools effective? A comparison of the relationships of communitarian climate and academic climate to mathematics achievement and attendance during middle school. *American Educational Research Journal, 34,* 633–662.

Phillipsen, L. C. (1999). Associations between age, gender, and group acceptance and three components of friendship quality. *Journal of Early Adolescence, 19,* 438–464.

Phinney, J. S., & Chavira, V. (1995). Parental ethnic socialization and adolescent outcomes in ethnic minority families. *Journal of Research on Adolescence, 5,* 31–53.

Phinney, J. S., Horenczyk, G., Liebkind, K., & Vedder, P. (2001). Ethnic identity, immigration, and well-being: An interactional perspective. *Journal of Social Issues, 57,* 493–510.

Phinney, J. S., & Kohatsu, E. L. (1997). Ethnic and racial identity development and mental health. In J. Schulenberg, J. L. Maggs, & K. Hurrelmann (Eds.), *Health risks and developmental transitions during adolescence* (pp. 420–443). Cambridge, U.K.: Cambridge University Press.

Phinney, J. S., & Ong, A. (2001). Family obligations and life satisfaction among adolescents from immigrant and non-immigrant families: Direct and moderated effects. Unpublished manuscript, California State University, Los Angeles.

Phinney, J. S., Ong, A., & Madden, T. (2000). Cultural values and intergenerational value discrepancies in immigrant and non-immigrant families. *Child Development, 71,* 528–539.

Piaget, J. (1926). *The language and thought of the child.* New York: Harcourt, Brace & World. (Original work published 1923)

Piaget, J. (1930). *The child's conception of the world.* New York: Harcourt, Brace, & World. (Original work published 1926)

Piaget, J. (1951). *Play, dreams, and imitation in childhood.* New York: Norton. (Original work published 1945)

Piaget, J. (1952). *The origins of intelligence in children.* New York: International Universities Press. (Original work published 1936)

Piaget, J. (1965). *The moral judgment of the child.* New York: Free Press. (Original work published 1932)

Piaget, J. (1967). *Six psychological studies.* New York: Vintage.

Piaget, J. (1971). *Biology and knowledge.* Chicago: University of Chicago Press.

Pianta, R., Egeland, B., & Erickson, M. F. (1989). The antecedents of maltreatment: Results of the Mother–Child Interaction Research Project. In D.

Cicchetti & V. Carlson (Eds.), *Child maltreatment* (pp. 203–253). New York: Cambridge University Press.

Pianta, R., Howes, C., Burchinal, M., Bryant, D., Clifford, R., Early, D., & Barbarin, O. (2005). Features of pre-kindergarten programs, classrooms, and teachers: Do they predict observed classroom quality and child–teacher interactions? *Applied Developmental Science, 9,* 144–159.

Pianta, R. C., Hamre, B., & Stuhlman, M. (2003). Relationships between teachers and children. In W. M. Reynolds & G. E. Miller (Eds.), *Handbook of psychology: Educational psychology* (Vol. 7, pp. 199–234). New York: Wiley.

Pickens, J., Field, T., & Nawrocki, T. (2001). Frontal EEG asymmetry in response to emotional vignettes in preschool age children. *International Journal of Behavioral Development, 25,* 105–112.

Pickett, K. E., Luo, Y., & Lauderdale, D. S. (2005). Widening social inequalities in risk for sudden infant death syndrome. *American Journal of Public Health, 95,* 1976–1981.

Pierce, K. M., Hamm, J. V., & Vandell, D. L. (1999). Experiences in after-school programs and children's adjustment in first-grade classrooms. *Child Development, 70,* 756–767.

Pierce, S. H., & Lange, G. (2000). Relationships among metamemory, motivation and memory performance in young school-age children. *British Journal of Developmental Psychology, 18,* 121–135.

Pietz, J., Peter, J., Graf, R., Rauterberg, R. I., Rupp, A., & Sontheimer, D. (2004). Physical growth and neurodevelopmental outcome of nonhandicapped low-risk children born preterm. *Early Human Development, 79,* 131–143.

Pillow, B. (2002). Children's and adults' evaluation of the certainty of deductive inferences, inductive inferences, and guesses. *Child Development, 73,* 779–792.

Pinderhughes, E. E., Dodge, K. A., Bates, J. E., Pettit, G. S., & Zelli, A. (2000). Discipline responses: Influences of parents' socioeconomic status, ethnicity, beliefs about parenting, stress, and cognitive-emotional processes. *Journal of Family Psychology, 14,* 380–400.

Pinderhughes, E. E., Nix, R., Foster, E. M., Jones, D., & the Conduct Problems Prevention Research Group. (2001). Parenting in context: Impact of neighborhood poverty, residential stability, public services, social networks, and danger on parental behaviors. *Journal of Marriage and the Family, 63,* 941–953.

Pine, J. M. (1995). Variation in vocabulary development as a function of birth order. *Child Development, 66,* 272–281.

Ping, Y., & Berryman, D. L. (1996). The relationship among self-esteem, acculturation, and recreation participation of recently arrived Chinese immigrant adolescents. *Journal of Leisure Research, 28,* 251–273.

Pinker, S. (1989). *Learnability and cognition.* Cambridge, MA: MIT Press.

Pinker, S. (1999). *Words and rules: The ingredients of language.* New York: Basic Books.

Pinker, S., Lebeaux, D. S., & Frost, L. A. (1987). Productivity and constraints in the acquisition of the passive. *Cognition, 26,* 195–267.

Pipp, S., Easterbrooks, M. A., & Brown, S. R. (1993). Attachment status and complexity of infants' self- and other-knowledge when tested with mother and father. *Social Development, 2,* 1–14.

Pipp, S., Easterbrooks, M. A., & Harmon, R. J. (1992). The relation between attachment and knowledge of self and mother in one-year-old infants to three-year-old infants. *Child Development, 63,* 738–750.

Pitts, V. P. (1976). Drawing the invisible: Children's conceptualization of God. *Character Potential, 8,* 12–24.

Pivarnik, J. M. (1998). Potential effects of maternal physical activity on birth weight: Brief review. *Medicine and Science in Sports and Exercise, 30,* 407–414.

Pleck, J. H., & Masciadrelli, B. P. (2004). Paternal involvement by U.S. residential fathers: Levels, sources, and consequences. In M. E. Lamb (Ed.), *The role of the father in child development* (4th ed., pp. 222–271). Hoboken, NJ: Wiley

Plomin, R. (1994). *Genetics and experience: The interplay between nature and nurture.* Thousand Oaks, CA: Sage.

Plomin, R. (2003). General cognitive ability. In R. Plomin & J. C. DeFries (Eds.), *Behavioral genetics in the*

postgenomic era (pp. 183–201). Washington, DC: American Psychological Association.

Plomin, R. (2005). *Finding genes in child psychology and psychiatry: When are we going to be there?* Unpublished manuscript. London: King's College.

Plomin, R., DeFries, J. C., Craig, I. W., & McGuffin, P. (2003). Behavioral genomics. In R. Plomin, J. C. DeFries, I. W. Craig, & P. McGuffin (Eds.), *Behavioral genetics in the postgenomic era* (pp. 531–540). Washington, DC: American Psychological Association.

Plomin, R., DeFries, J. C., McClearn, G. E., & McGuffin, P. (2001). *Behavioral genetics* (4th ed.). New York: Worth.

Plomin, R., Fulker, D. W., Corley, R., & DeFries, J. C. (1997). Nature, nurture and cognitive development from 1 to 16 years: A parent–offspring study. *Psychological Science, 8,* 442–447.

Plomin, R., & Spinath, F. M. (2004). Intelligence: Genetics, genes, and genomics. *Journal of Personality and Social Psychology, 86,* 112–129.

Plumert, J. M., Pick, H. L., Jr., Marks, R. A., Kintsch, A. S., & Wegesin, D. (1994). Locating objects and communicating about locations: Organizational differences in children's searching and direction-giving. *Developmental Psychology, 30,* 443–453.

Poehlmann, J. (2003). An attachment perspective on grandparents raising their very young grandchildren: Implications for intervention and research. *Infant Mental Health Journal, 24,* 149–173.

Poehlmann, J., & Fiese, B. H. (2001). The interaction of maternal and infant vulnerabilities on developing attachment relationships. *Development and Psychopathology, 13,* 1–11.

Pogarsky, G., Thornberry, T. P., & Lizotte, A. J. (2006). Developmental outcomes for children of young mothers. *Journal of Marriage and Family, 68,* 332–344.

Pohl, R. (2001). *Homelessness in Canada: Part 1— An introduction.* Ottawa: Innercity Ministries.

Pohl, R. (2002). *Poverty in Canada.* Ottawa: Innercity Ministries.

Polka, L., & Rvachew, S. (2005). The impact of otitis media with effusion on infant phonetic perception. *Infancy, 8,* 101–117.

Polka, L., & Werker, J. F. (1994). Developmental changes in perception of non-native vowel contrasts. *Journal of Experimental Psychology: Human Perception and Performance, 20,* 421–435.

Pollitt, E. (1996). A reconceptualization of the effects of undernutrition on children's biological, psychosocial, and behavioral development. *Social Policy Report of the Society for Research in Child Development, 10*(5).

Pollitt, E. (2001). The developmental and probabilistic nature of the functional consequences of iron-deficiency anemia in children. *Journal of Nutrition, 131*(Suppl. 2), 669S–675S.

Pomerantz, E. M., & Dong, W. (2006). Effects of mothers' perceptions of children's competence: The moderating role of mothers' theories of competence. *Developmental Psychology, 42,* 950–961.

Pomerantz, E. M., & Eaton, M. M. (2000). Developmental differences in children's conceptions of parental control: "They love me, but they make me feel incompetent." *Merrill-Palmer Quarterly, 46,* 140–167.

Pomerantz, E. M., & Ruble, D. N. (1998). The role of maternal control in the development of sex differences in child self-evaluative factors. *Child Development, 69,* 458–478.

Pomerantz, E. M., & Saxon, J. L. (2001). Conceptions of ability as stable and self-evaluative processes: A longitudinal examination. *Child Development, 72,* 152–173.

Pomerleau, A., Scuccimarri, C., & Malcuit, G. (2003). Mother–infant behavioral interactions in teenage and adult mothers during the first six months postpartum: Relations with infant development. *Infant Mental Health Journal, 24,* 495–509.

Pons, F., Lawson, J., Harris, P. L., & de Rosnay, M. (2003). Individual differences in children's emotion understanding: Effects of age and language. *Scandinavian Journal of Psychology, 44,* 347–353.

Portes, A., & Rumbaut, R. G. (2005). Introduction: The second generation and the children of immigrants longitudinal study. *Ethnic and Racial Studies, 28,* 983–999.

Posada, G., Carbonell, O. A., Alzate, G., & Plata, S. J. (2004). Through Colombian lenses: Ethnographic and conventional analyses of maternal care and their associations with secure base behavior. *Developmental Psychology, 40*, 508–518.

Posada, G., Jacobs, A., Richmond, M. K., Carbonell, O. A., Alzate, G., Bustamante, M. R., & Quiceno, J. (2002). Maternal caregiving and infant security in two cultures. *Developmental Psychology, 38*, 67–78.

Posner, J. K., & Vandell, D. L. (1994). Low-income children's after-school care: Are there beneficial effects of after-school programs? *Child Development, 64*, 440–456.

Poudevigne, M. S., O'Connor, P. J., Laing, E. M., Wilson, A. M. R., Modlesky, C. M., & Lewis, R. D. (2003). Body images of 4–8-year-old girls at the outset of their first artistic gymnastics class. *International Journal of Eating Disorders, 34*, 325–344.

Poulin-Dubois, D., Serbin, L. A., Eichstedt, J. A., Sen, M. G., & Beissel, C. F. (2002). Men don't put on make-up: Toddlers' knowledge of the gender stereotyping of household activities. *Social Development, 11*, 166–181.

Poulin-Dubois, D., Serbin, L. A., Kenyon, B., & Derbyshire, A. (1994). Infants' intermodal knowledge about gender. *Developmental Psychology, 30*, 436–442.

Povinelli, D. J. (2001). The self—Elevated in consciousness and extended in time. In C. Moore & K. Lemmon (Eds.), *The self in time: Developmental perspectives* (pp. 75–95). Mahwah, NJ: Erlbaum.

Powlishta, K. K., Serbin, L. A., & Moller, L. C. (1993). The stability of individual differences in gender typing: Implications for understanding gender segregation. *Sex Roles, 29*, 723–737.

Powls, A., Botting, N., Cooke, R. W. I., & Marlow, N. (1996). Handedness in very-low-birthweight (VLBW) children at 12 years of age: Relation to perinatal and outcome variables. *Developmental Medicine and Child Neurology, 38*, 594–602.

Pratt, M. W., Skoe, E. E., & Arnold, M. L. (2004). Care reasoning development and family socialization patterns in later adolescence: A longitudinal analysis. *International Journal of Behavioral Development, 28*, 139–147.

Prechtl, H. F. R. (1958). Problems of behavioral studies in the newborn infant. In D. S. Lehrmann, R. A. Hinde, & E. Shaw (Eds.), *Advances in the study of behavior* (Vol. 1, pp. 75–98). New York: Academic Press.

Prechtl, H. F. R., & Beintema, D. (1965). *The neurological examination of the full-term newborn infant.* London: Heinemann Medical.

Preisler, G. M. (1991). Early patterns of interaction between blind infants and their sighted mothers. *Child: Care, Health and Development, 17*, 65–90.

Preisler, G. M. (1993). A descriptive study of blind children in nurseries with sighted children. *Child: Care, Health and Development, 19*, 295–315.

Preissler, M. A., & Carey, S. (2004). Do both pictures and words function as symbols for 18- and 24-month-old children? *Journal of Cognition and Development, 5*, 185–212.

Pressley, M., & Hilden, D. (2006). Cognitive strategies. In D. Kuhn & R. Siegler (Eds.), *Handbook of child psychology: Vol. 2. Cognition, perception, and language* (6th ed., pp. 511–556).

Pressley, M., Wharton-McDonald, R., Raphael, L. M., Bogner, K., & Roehrig, A. (2002). Exemplary first-grade teaching. In B. M. Taylor & P. D. Pearson (Eds.), *Teaching reading: Effective schools, accomplished teachers* (pp. 73–88). Mahwah, NJ: Erlbaum.

Prevatt, F. (2003). Dropping out of school: A review of intervention programs. *Journal of School Psychology, 41*, 377–399.

Prevatt, F., & Kelly, F. D. (2003). Dropping out of school: A review of intervention programs. *Journal of School Psychology, 41*, 377–395.

Previc, F. H. (1991). A general theory concerning the prenatal origins of cerebral lateralization. *Psychological Review, 98*, 299–334.

Priddy, K. D. (2004). Is there logic behind fetal monitoring? *Journal of Obstetric, Gynecologic, and Neonatal Nursing, 33*, 550–553.

Prinstein, M. J., Boergers, J., & Spirito, A. (2001). Adolescents' and their friends' health-risk behavior: Factors that alter or add to peer influence. *Journal of Pediatric Psychology, 26*, 287–298.

Prinstein, M. J., Boergers, J., & Vernberg, E. M. (2001). Overt and relational aggression in adolescents: Social–psychological adjustment of aggressors and

victims. *Journal of Clinical Child Psychology, 30*, 479–491.

Prinstein, M. J., & La Greca, A. (2004). Childhood peer rejection and aggression as predictors of adolescent girls' externalizing and health risk behaviors: A 6-year longitudinal study. *Journal of Consulting and Clinical Psychology, 72*, 103–112.

Prinstein, M. J., & La Greca, A. M. (2002). Peer crowd affiliation and internalizing distress in childhood and adolescence: A longitudinal follow-back study. *Journal of Research on Adolescence, 12*, 325–351.

Prinstein, M. J., Meade, C. S., & Cohen, G. L. (2003). Adolescent oral sex, peer popularity, and perceptions of best friends' sexual behavior. *Journal of Pediatric Psychology, 28*, 243–249.

Proctor, M. H., Moore, L. L. Gao, D., Cupples, L. A., Bradlee, M. L., Hood, M. Y., & Ellison, R. C. (2003). Television viewing and change in body fat from preschool to early adolescence: The Framingham Children's Study. *International Journal of Obesity, 27*, 827–833.

Programme for International Student Assessment. (2003). *Learning for tomorrow's world: First results from Programme for International Student Assessment 2003.* Retrieved from www.pisa.oecd.org

Programme for International Student Assessment. (2005). *School factors related to quality and equity.* Retrieved from www.pisa.oecd.org

Provins, K. A. (1997). Handedness and speech: A critical reappraisal of the role of genetic and environmental factors in the cerebral lateralization of function. *Psychological Review, 104*, 554–571.

Pruett, M. K., Williams, T. Y., Insabella, G., & Little, T. D. (2003). Family and legal indicators of child adjustment to divorce among families with young children. *Journal of Family Psychology, 17*, 169–180.

Pryor, J. B., & Reeder, G. D. (1993). Collective and individual representations of HIV/AIDS stigma. In J. B. Pryor & G. D. Reeder (Eds.), *The social psychology of HIV infection* (pp. 263–286). Hillsdale, NJ: Erlbaum.

Prysak, M., Lorenz, R. P., & Kisly, A. (1995). Pregnancy outcome in nulliparous women 35 years and older. *Obstetrics and Gynecology, 85*, 65–70.

Purcell-Gates, V. (1996). Stories, coupons, and the TV guide: Relationships between home literacy experiences and emergent literacy knowledge. *Reading Research Quarterly, 31*, 406–428.

Putnam, F. W. (2003). Ten-year research update review: Child sexual abuse. *Journal of the American Academy of Child and Adolescent Psychiatry, 42*, 269–278.

Putnam, S. P., Samson, A. V., & Rothbart, M. K. (2000). Child temperament and parenting. In V. J. Molfese & D. L. Molfese (Eds.), *Temperament and personality across the life span* (pp. 255–277). Mahwah, NJ: Erlbaum.

Putta, L. V., & Spencer, J. P. (2000). Assisted vaginal delivery using the vacuum extractor. *American Family Physician, 62*, 1316–1320.

Quinn, C. T., Rogers, Z. R., & Buchanan, G. R. (2004). Survival of children with sickle cell disease. *Blood, 103*, 4023–4027.

Quinn, T. C., & Overbaugh, J. (2005). HIV/AIDS in women: An expanding epidemic. *Science, 308*, 1582–1583.

Quist, J. F., & Kennedy, J. L. (2001). Genetics of childhood disorders: XXIII. ADHD, part 7: The serotonin system. *Journal of the American Academy of Child and Adolescent Psychiatry, 40*, 253–256.

Quyen, G. T., Bird, H. R., Davies, M., Hoven, C., Cohen, P., Jensen, P. S., & Goodman, S. (1998). Adverse life events and resilience. *Journal of the American Academy of Child and Adolescent Psychiatry, 37*, 1191–1200.

Radecki, C. M., & Jaccard, J. (1995). Perceptions of knowledge, actual knowledge, and information search behavior. *Journal of Experimental Social Psychology, 31*, 107–138.

Radelet, M. A., Lephart, S. M., Rubinstein, E. N., & Myers, J. B. (2002). Survey of the injury rate for children in community sports. *Pediatrics, 110*, e28.

Radziszewska, B., & Rogoff, B. (1988). Influence of adult and peer collaboration on the development of children's planning skills. *Developmental Psychology, 24*, 840–848.

Raffaelli, M., Bogenschneider, K., & Flood, M. F. (1998). Parent–teen communication about sexual topics. *Journal of Family Issues, 19*, 315–333.

Raffaelli, M., & Green, S. (2003). Parent–adolescent communication about sex: Retrospective reports by

Latino college students. *Journal of Marriage and Family, 65*, 474–481.

Raffaelli, M., & Ontai, L. L. (2001). 'She's 16 years old and there's boys calling over to the house: An exploratory study of sexual socialization in Latino families. *Culture, Health and Sexuality, 3*, 295–310.

Rahman, Q., & Wilson, G. D. (2003). Born gay? The psychobiology of human sexual orientation. *Personality and Individual Differences, 34*, 1337–1382.

Raikes, H. A., & Thompson, R. A. (2005). Links between risk and attachment security: Models of influence. *Journal of Applied Developmental Psychology, 26*, 440–455.

Raikes, H. A., & Thompson, R. A. (2006). Family emotional climate, attachment security, and young children's emotion knowledge in a high-risk sample. *British Journal of Developmental Psychology, 24*, 89–104.

Rakoczy, H., Tomasello, M., & Striano, T. (2004). Young children know that trying is not pretending: A test of the "behaving-as-if" construal of children's early concept of pretense. *Developmental Psychology, 40*, 388–399.

Ralph, K., Harrington, K., & Pandha, H. (2004). Recent developments and current status of gene therapy using viral vectors in the United Kingdom. *British Medical Journal, 329*, 839–842.

Ram, A., & Ross, H. S. (2001). Problem-solving, contention, and struggle: How siblings resolve a conflict of interests. *Child Development, 72*, 1710–1722.

Raman, L., & Gelman, S. A. (2004). A cross-cultural developmental analysis of children's and adults' understanding of illness in South Asia (India) and the United States. *Journal of Cognition and Culture, 4*, 293–317.

Ramchandani, P., Stein, A., Evan, J., O'Connor, T. G., & the ALSPAC Study Team. (2005). Paternal depression in the postnatal period and child development: A prospective population study. *Lancet, 365*, 2201–2205.

Ramey, C. T., Ramey, S. L., & Lanzi, R. G. (2006). Children's health and education. In K. A. Renninger & I. E. Sigel (Eds.), *Handbook of child psychology: Vol. 4. Child psychology in practice* (6th ed., pp. 864–892). Hoboken, NJ: Wiley.

Ramey, S. L., & Ramey, C. T. (1999). Early experience and early intervention for children "at risk" for developmental delay and mental retardation. *Mental Retardation and Developmental Disabilities, 5*, 1–10.

Ramos, E., Frontera, W. R., Llopart, A., & Feliciano, D. (1998). Muscle strength and hormonal levels in adolescents: Gender related differences. *International Journal of Sports Medicine, 19*, 526–531.

Ramos, M. C., Guerin, D. W., Gottfried, A. W., Bathurst, K., & Oliver, P. H. (2005). Family conflict and children's behavior problems: The moderating role of child temperament. *Structural Equation Modeling, 12*, 278–298.

Ramsay, L. J., Moreton, G., Gorman, D. R., Blake, E., Goh, D., & Elton, R. A. (2003). Unintentional home injury in preschool-aged children: Looking for the key—an exploration of the inter-relationship and relative importance of potential risk factors. *Public Health, 117*, 404–411.

Ramsøy, N. R. (1994). Non-marital cohabitation and change in norms: The case of Norway. *Acta Sociologica, 37*, 23–37.

Ramus, F. (2002). Language discrimination by newborns: Teasing apart phonotactic, rhythmic, and intonational cues. *Annual Review of Language Acquisition, 2*, 85–115.

Rangel, M. C., Gavin, L., Reed, C., Fowler, M. G., & Lee, L. M. (2006). Epidemiology of HIV and AIDS among adolescents and young adults in the United States. *Journal of Adolescent Health, 39*, 156–163.

Raskind, W. H., Igo, R. P. Jr., Chapman, N. H., Berninger, V. W., Thomson, J. B., Matsushita, M., & Brkanac, Z. (2005). A genome scan in multigenerational families with dyslexia: Identification of a novel locus on chromosome 2q that contributes to phonological decoding efficiency. *Molecular Psychiatry, 10*, 699–711.

Rasmussen, C., Ho, E., & Bisanz, J. (2003). Use of the mathematical principle of inversion in young children. *Journal of Experimental Child Psychology, 85*, 89–102.

Rasmussen, C., Neuman, R. J., Heath, A. C., Levy, F., Hay, D. A., & Todd, R. D. (2004). Familial clustering of latent class and DSM-IV defined attention-deficit hyperactivity disorder (ADHD) subtypes. *Journal of Child Psychology and Psychiatry, 45*, 589–598.

Rast, M., & Meltzoff, A. N. (1995). Memory and representation in young children with Down syndrome:

Exploring deferred imitation and object permanence. *Development and Psychopathology, 7,* 393–407.

Rathunde, K., & Csikszentmihalyi, M. (2005). The social context of middle school: Teachers, friends, and activities in Montessori and traditional school environments. *Elementary School Journal, 106,* 59–79.

Rauber, M. (2006, May 18). Parents aren't sitting still as recess disappears. *Parents in Action.* Retrieved from www.parentsaction.org/news/parents-in-action/index.cfm?i=410

Rauscher, F. H., Shaw, G. L., & Ky, K. N. (1993). Music and spatial task performance. *Nature, 365,* 611.

Raver, C. C. (2003). Does work pay psychologically as well as economically? The role of employment in predicting depressive symptoms and parenting among low-income families. *Child Development, 74,* 1720–1736.

Ravid, D., & Tolchinsky, L. (2002). Developing linguistic literacy: A comprehensive model. *Journal of Child Language, 29,* 417–447.

Ray, N., & Gregory, R. (2001). School experiences of the children of lesbian and gay parents. *Family Matters, 59,* 28–35.

Rayner, K., & Pollatsek, A. (1989). *The psychology of reading.* Englewood Cliffs, NJ: Prentice-Hall.

Rayner, K., Pollatsek, A., & Starr, M. S. (2003). Reading. In A. F. Healy & R. W. Proctor (Eds.). (2003). *Handbook of psychology: Experimental psychology* (Vol. 4, pp. 549–574). New York: Wiley.

Raz, S., Shah, F., & Sander, C. J. (1996). Differential effects of perinatal hypoxic risk on early developmental outcome: A twin study. *Neuropsychology, 10,* 429–436.

Reddin, J. (1997). High-achieving women: Career development patterns. In H. S. Farmer (Ed.), *Diversity and women's career development* (pp. 95–126). Thousand Oaks, CA: Sage.

Regnerus, M., Smith, C., & Fritsch, M. (2003). *Religion in the lives of American adolescents: A review of the literature.* Chapel Hill, NC: National Study of Youth and Religion.

Reifman, A., Villa, L. C., Amans, J. A., Rethinam, V., & Telesca, T. Y. (2001). Children of divorce in the 1990s: A meta-analysis. *Journal of Divorce and Remarriage, 36,* 27–36.

Reifsnider, E., & Gill, S. L. (2000). Nutrition for the childbearing years. *Journal of Obstetrics, Gynecology, and Neonatal Nursing, 29,* 43–55.

Reilly, J., Losh, M., Bellugi, U., & Wulfeck, B. (2004). "Frog, where are you?" Narratives in children with specific language impairment, early focal brain injury, and Williams syndrome. *Brain and Language, 88,* 229–247.

Reilly, J. S., Bates, E. A., & Marchman, V. A. (1998). Narrative discourse in children with early focal brain injury. *Brain and Language, 61,* 335–375.

Reilly, T. P., Hasazi, J. E., & Bond, L. A. (1983). Children's concepts of death and personal mortality. *Journal of Paediatric Psychology, 8,* 21–31.

Reinders, H., & Youniss, J. (2006). School-based required community service and civic development in adolescents. *Applied Developmental Science, 10,* 2–12.

Reis, O., & Youniss, J. (2004). Patterns in identity change and development in relationships with mothers and friends. *Journal of Adolescent Research, 19,* 31–44.

Reis, S. M. (2004). We can't change what we don't recognize: Understanding the special needs of gifted females. In S. Baum (Ed.), *Twice-exceptional and special populations of gifted students* (pp. 67–80). Thousand Oaks, CA: Corwin Press.

Reisman, J. E. (1987). Touch, motion, and proprioception. In P. Salapatek & L. Cohen (Eds.), *Handbook of infant perception: Vol. 1. From sensation to perception* (pp. 265–303). Orlando, FL: Academic Press.

Reiss, A. L., & Dant, C. C. (2003). The behavioral neurogenetics of fragile X syndrome: Analyzing gene–brain–behavior relationships in child developmental psychopathologies. *Development and Psychopathology, 15,* 927–968.

Reiss, D. (2003). Child effects on family systems: Behavioral genetic strategies. In A. C. Crouter & A. Booth (Eds.), *Children's influence on family dynamics* (pp. 3–36). Mahwah, NJ: Erlbaum.

Renninger, K. A. (1998). Developmental psychology and instruction: Issues from and for practice. In I. Sigel & K. A. Renninger (Eds.), *Handbook of child psychology: Vol. 4. Child psychology and practice* (pp. 211–274). New York: Wiley.

Repacholi, B. M. (1998). Infants' use of attentional cues to identify the referent of another person's emotional expression. *Developmental Psychology, 34,* 1017–1025.

Repacholi, B. M., & Gopnik, A. (1997). Early reasoning about desires: Evidence from 14- and 18-month-olds. *Developmental Psychology, 33,* 12–21.

Repke, J. T. (1992). Drug supplementation in pregnancy. *Current Opinion in Obstetrics and Gynecology, 4,* 802–806.

Resnick, M., & Silverman, B. (2005). *Some reflections on designing construction kits for kids.* Proceedings of the Conference on Interaction Design and Children, Boulder, CO.

Resnick, M. B., Gueorguieva, R. V., Carter, R. L., Ariet, M., Sun, Y., Roth, J., Bucciarelli, R. L., Curran, J. S., & Mahan, C. S. (1999). The impact of low birth weight, perinatal conditions, and sociodemographic factors on educational outcome in kindergarten. *Pediatrics, 104,* e74.

Rest, J. R. (1979). *Development in judging moral issues.* Minneapolis: University of Minnesota Press.

Reyna, V. F., & Farley, F. (2006). Risk and rationality in adolescent decision making: Implications for theory, practice, and public policy. *Psychological Science in the Public Interest, 7,* 1–44.

Reynolds, A. J., & Ou, S.-R. (2004). Alterable predictors of child well-being in the Chicago Longitudinal Study. *Children and Youth Services Review, 26,* 1–14.

Reynolds, A. J., & Temple, J. A. (1998). Extended early childhood intervention and school achievement: Age thirteen findings from the Chicago Longitudinal Study. *Child Development, 69,* 231–246.

Reynolds, C. R., & Kaiser, S. M. (1990). Test bias in psychological assessment. In T. B. Gutkin & C. R. Reynolds (Eds.), *The handbook of school psychology* (pp. 487–525). New York: Wiley.

Reynolds, M. A., Schieve, L. A., Martin, J. A., Meng, G., & Macaluso, M. (2003). Trends in multiple births conceived using assisted reproductive technology, United States, 1997–2000. *Pediatrics, 111,* 1159–1162.

Richards, M. (2004). Assisted reproduction, genetic technologies, and family life. In J. Scott, J. Treas, & M. Richards (Eds.), *The Blackwell companion to the sociology of families* (pp. 478–498). Malden, MA: Blackwell.

Richards, M. H., & Duckett, E. (1994). The relationship of maternal employment to early adolescent daily experience with and without parents. *Child Development, 65,* 225–236.

Richert, R. A., & Barrett, J. L. (2005). Do you see what I see? Young children's assumptions about God's perceptual abilities. *International Journal for the Psychology of Religion, 15,* 283–295.

Richie, B. S., Fassinger, R. E., Linn, S. G., Johnson, J., Prosser, J., & Robinson, S. (1997). Persistence, connection, and passion: A qualitative study of the career development of highly achieving African American black and white women. *Journal of Counseling Psychology, 44,* 133–148.

Richler, J., Luyster, R., Risi, S., Hsu, W.-L., Dawson, G., & Bernier, R. (2006). Is there a 'regressive phenotype' of autism spectrum disorder associated with the measles-mumps-rubella vaccine? A CPEA study. *Journal of Autism and Developmental Disorders, 36,* 299–316.

Rideout, V. J., Vandewater, E. A., & Wartella, E. A. (2003). *Zero to six: Electronic media in the lives of toddlers and preschoolers.* Menlo Park, CA: Henry J. Kaiser Foundation.

Rietvelt, M. J. H., Hudziak, J. J., Bartels, M., van Beijsterveldt, C. E. M., & Boomsma, D. I. (2004). Heritability of attention problems in children: Longitudinal results from a study of twins, age 3 to 12. *Journal of Child Psychology and Psychiatry, 45,* 577–588.

Rigby, K. (2004). Bullying in childhood. In P. K. Smith & C. H. Hart (Eds.), *Blackwell handbook of childhood social development* (pp. 549–568). Malden, MA: Blackwell.

Riggs, K. J., & Peterson, D. M. (2000). Counterfactual thinking in preschool children: Mental state and causal inferences. In P. Mitchell & K. J. Riggs (Eds.), *Children's reasoning and the mind* (pp. 87–99). Hove, U.K.: Psychology Press.

Rijsdijk, F. V., & Boomsma, D. I. (1997). Genetic mediation of the correlation between peripheral nerve conduction velocity and IQ. *Behavior Genetics, 27,* 87–98.

Riley, E. P., McGee, C. L., & Sowell, E. R. (2004). Teratogenic effects of alcohol: A decade of brain imaging. *American Journal of Medical Genetics: Part C, Seminars in Medical Genetics, 127,* 35–41.

Riordan, J., Gross, A., Angeron, J., Drumwiede, B., & Melin, J. (2000). The effect of labor pain relief medication on neonatal suckling and breastfeeding duration. *Journal of Human Lactation, 16,* 7–12.

Ripple, C. H., & Zigler, E. (2003). Research, policy, and the federal role in prevention initiatives for children. *American Psychologist, 58,* 482–490.

Ris, M. D., Dietrich, K. N., Succop, P. A., Berger, O. G., & Bornschein, R. L. (2004). Early exposure to lead and neuropsychological outcome in adolescence. *Journal of the International Neuropsychological Society, 10,* 261–270.

Riva, D., & Giorgi, C. (2000). The cerebellum contributes to higher functions during development: Evidence from a series of children surgically treated for posterior fossa tumors. *Brain, 123,* 1051–1061.

Rivera, S. M., Wakeley, A., & Langer, J. (1999). The drawbridge phenomenon: Representational reasoning or perceptual preference? *Developmental Psychology, 35,* 427–435.

Rivkees, S. A. (2003). Developing circadian rhythmicity in infants. *Pediatrics, 112,* 373–381.

Rizzolatti, G., & Craighero, L. (2004). The mirror-neuron system. *Annual Review of Neuroscience, 27,* 169–192.

Roazzi, A., & Bryant, P. (1997). Explicitness and conservation: Social class differences. *International Journal of Behavioral Development, 21,* 51–70.

Robb, A. S., & Dadson, M. J. (2002). Eating disorders in males. *Child and Adolescent Psychiatric Clinics of North America, 11,* 399–418.

Robbins, C. G. (2005). Zero tolerance and the politics of racial injustice. *Journal of Negro Education, 74,* 2–17.

Roberts, B. W., & DelVecchio, W. F. (2000). The rank-order consistency of personality traits from childhood to old age: A quantitative review of longitudinal studies. *Psychological Bulletin, 126,* 3–25.

Roberts, D. F., Foehr, U. G., & Rideout, V. (2005). *Generation M: Media in the lives of 8–18 year olds.* Menlo Park, CA: Henry J. Kaiser Family Foundation.

Roberts, D. F., Henriksen, L., & Foehr, U. G. (2004). Adolescents and media. In R. M. Lerner & L. Steinberg (Eds.), *Handbook of adolescent psychology* (2nd ed., pp. 627–664). Hoboken, NJ: Wiley.

Roberts, J. E., Burchinal, M. R., & Durham, M. (1999). Parents' report of vocabulary and grammatical development of American preschoolers: Child and environment associations. *Child Development, 70,* 92–106.

Roberts, J. E., Burchinal, M. R., Zeisel, S. A., Neebe, E. C., Hooper, S. R., Roush, J., Bryant, D., Mundy, M., & Henderson, F. W. (1998). Otitis media, the caregiving environment, and language and cognitive outcomes at 2 years. *Pediatrics, 102,* 346–354.

Roberts, J. M., & Masten, A. S. (2004). Resilience in context. In R. D. Peters, R. McMahon, & B. Leadbeater (Eds.), *Resilience in children, families, and communities: Linking context to practice and policy* (pp. 13–25). New York: Kluwer Academic.

Roberts, R. J., Jr., & Aman, C. J. (1993). Developmental differences in giving directions: Spatial frames of reference and mental rotation. *Child Development, 64,* 1258–1270.

Robertson, J. A., Martinez, L. P., Gallegos, S., Leen-Mitchell, M. J., & Garcia, V. (2002). Accutane cases: A teratogen information service's approach. *Teratology, 66,* 1–2.

Robin, D. J., Berthier, N. E., & Clifton, R. K. (1996). Infants' predictive reaching for moving objects in the dark. *Developmental Psychology, 32,* 824–835.

Robins, R. W., Tracy, J. L., Trzesniewski, K., Potter, J., & Gosling, S. D. (2001). Personality correlates of self-esteem. *Journal of Research in Personality, 35,* 463–482.

Robinson, C. C., Anderson, G. T., Porter, C. L., Hart, C. H., & Wouden-Miller, M. (2003). Sequential transition patterns of preschoolers' social interactions during child-initiated play: Is parallel-aware play a bi-directional bridge to other play states? *Early Childhood Research Quarterly, 18,* 3–21.

Rochat, P. (1989). Object manipulation and exploration in 2- to 5-month-old infants. *Developmental Psychology, 25,* 871–884.

Rochat, P. (1998). Self-perception and action in infancy. *Experimental Brain Research, 123,* 102–109.

Rochat, P. (2001). *The infant's world.* Cambridge, MA: Harvard University Press.

Rochat, P. (2003). Five levels of self-awareness as they unfold early in life. *Consciousness and Cognition, 12,* 717–731.

Rochat, P., & Goubet, N. (1995). Development of sitting and reaching in 5- to 6-month-old infants. *Infant Behavior and Development, 18*, 53–68.

Rochat, P., & Hespos, S. J. (1997). Differential rooting responses by neonates: Evidence for an early sense of self. *Early Development and Parenting, 6*, 105–112.

Rochat, P., Querido, J. G., & Striano, T. (1999). Emerging sensitivity to the timing and structure of protoconversation. *Developmental Psychology, 35*, 950–957.

Rochat, P., & Striano, T. (2002). Who's in the mirror? Self–other discrimination in specular images by four- and nine-month-old infants. *Child Development, 73*, 35–46.

Rochat, P., Striano, T., & Blatt, L. (2002). Differential effects of happy, neutral, and sad still-faces on 2-, 4-, and 6-month-old infants. *Infant and Child Development, 11*, 289–303.

Rodgers, J. L., Cleveland, H. H., van den Oord, E., & Rowe, D. C. (2000). Resolving the debate over birth order, family size, and intelligence. *American Psychologist, 55*, 599–612.

Rodkin, P. C., Farmer, T. W., Pearl, R., & Van Acker, R. (2000). Heterogeneity of popular boys: Antisocial and prosocial configurations. *Developmental Psychology, 36*, 14–24.

Rodkin, P. C., Farmer, T. W., Pearl, R., & Van Acker, R. (2006). They're cool: Social status and peer group supports for aggressive boys and girls. *Social Development, 15*, 175–204.

Roelfsema, N. M., Hop, W. C., Boito, S. M., & Wladimiroff, J. W. (2004). Three-dimensional sonographic measurement of normal fetal brain volume during the second half of pregnancy. *American Journal of Obstetrics and Gynecology, 190*, 275–280.

Roeser, R. W., Eccles, J. S., & Freedman-Doan, C. (1999). Academic functioning and mental health in adolescence: Patterns, progressions, and routes from childhood. *Journal of Adolescent Research, 14*, 135–174.

Roeser, R. W., Eccles, J. S., & Sameroff, A. J. (2000). School as a context of early adolescents' academic and social-emotional development: A summary of research findings. *Elementary School Journal, 100*, 443–471.

Rogan, W. J., Dietrich, K. N., Ware, J. H., Dockery, D. W., Salganik, M., & Radcliffe, J. (2001). The effect of chelation therapy with succimer on neuropsychological development in children exposed to lead. *New England Journal of Medicine, 344*, 1421–1426.

Rogers, L. J. (2000). Evolution of hemispheric specialization: Advantages and disadvantages. *Brain and Language, 73*, 236–253.

Rogge, M. M., Greenwald, M., & Golden, A. (2004). Obesity, stigma, and civilized oppression. *Advances in Nursing Science, 27*, 301–315.

Roggman, L. A., Langlois, J. H., Hubbs-Tait, L., & Rieser-Danner, L. A. (1994). Infant day-care, attachment, and the "file drawer problem." *Child Development, 65*, 1429–1443.

Rogoff, B. (1986). The development of strategic use of context in spatial memory. In M. Perlmutter (Ed.), *Perspectives on intellectual development* (pp. 107–123). Hillsdale, NJ: Erlbaum.

Rogoff, B. (1996). Developmental transitions in children's participation in sociocultural activities. In A. J. Sameroff & M. M. Haith (Eds.), *The five to seven year shift: The age of reason and responsibility,* (pp. 273–294). Chicago: University of Chicago Press.

Rogoff, B. (1998). Cognition as a collaborative process. In D. Kuhn & R. S. Siegler (Eds.), *Handbook of child psychology: Vol. 2. Cognition, perception, and language* (5th ed., pp. 679–744). New York: Wiley.

Rogoff, B. (2003). *The cultural nature of human development.* New York: Oxford University Press.

Rogoff, B., & Chavajay, P. (1995). What's become of research on the cultural basis of cognitive development? *American Psychologist, 50*, 859–877.

Rogoff, B., Malkin, C., & Gilbride, K. (1984). Interaction with babies as guidance in development. In B. Rogoff & J. V. Wertsch (Eds.), *Children's learning in the "zone of proximal development" (New directions for child development,* No. 23, pp. 31–44). San Francisco: Jossey-Bass.

Rogoff, B., Paradise, R., Arauz, R. M., Correa-Chávez, M., & Angelillo, C. (2003). Firsthand learning through intent participation. *Annual Review of Psychology, 54*, 175–203.

Rogol, A. D., Roemmich, J. N., & Clark, P. A. (2002). Growth at puberty. *Journal of Adolescent Health, 31*, 192–200.

Rohner, R., & Brothers, S. (1999). Perceived parental rejection, psychological maladjustment, and borderline personality disorder. *Journal of Emotional Abuse, 1*, 81–95.

Rohner, R. P., & Veneziano, R. A. (2001). The importance of father love: History and contemporary evidence. *Review of General Psychology, 5*, 382–405.

Roid, G. (2003). *The Stanford-Binet Intelligence Scales, Fifth Edition, interpretive manual.* Itasca, IL: Riverside Publishing.

Roisman, G. I., Madsen, S. D., Hennighausen, K. H., Sroufe, L. A., & Collins, W. A. (2001). The coherence of dyadic behavior across parent–child and romantic relationships as mediated by the internalized representation of experience. *Attachment and Human Development, 3*, 156–172.

Roizen, N. J., & Patterson, D. (2003). Down's syndrome. *Lancet, 361*, 1281–1289.

Rojewski, J. W., & Hill, R. B. (1998). Influence of gender and academic risk behavior on career decision making and occupational choice in early adolescence. *Journal of Education for Students Placed at Risk, 3*, 265–287.

Rokach, A. (2001). Perceived causes of loneliness in adulthood. *Journal of Social Behavior and Personality, 15*, 67–84.

Rolls, B. J., Morris, E. L., & Roe, L. S. (2002). Portion size of food affects energy intake in normal-weight and overweight men and women. *American Journal of Clinical Nutrition, 6*, 1207–1213.

Romans, S. E., Martin, M., Gendall, K., & Herbison, G. P. (2003). Age of menarche: The role of some psychosocial factors. *Psychological Medicine, 33*, 933–939.

Rome-Flanders, T., & Cronk, C. (1995). A longitudinal study of infant vocalizations during mother– infant games. *Journal of Child Language, 22*, 259–274.

Romero, A. J., & Roberts, R. E. (2003). The impact of multiple dimensions of ethnic identity on discrimination and adolescents' self-esteem. *Journal of Applied Social Psychology, 33*, 2288–2305.

Rönnqvist, L., & Hopkins, B. (1998). Head position preference in the human newborn: A new look. *Child Development, 69*, 13–23.

Roopnarine, J. L., & Evans, M. E. (2007). Family structural organization, mother–child and father–child relationships and psychological outcomes in English-speaking African Caribbean and Indo Caribbean families. In M. Sutherland (Ed.), *Psychology of development in the Caribbean.* Kingston, Jamaica: Ian Randle.

Roopnarine, J. L., Hossain, Z., Gill, P., & Brophy, H. (1994). Play in the East Indian context. In J. L. Roopnarine, J. E. Johnson, & F. H. Hooper (Eds.), *Children's play in diverse cultures* (pp. 9–30). Albany, NY: SUNY Press.

Roopnarine, J. L., Krishnakumar, A., Metindogan, A., & Evans, M. (2006). Links between parenting styles, parent–child academic interaction, parent–school interaction, and early academic skills and social behaviors in young children of English-speaking Caribbean immigrants. *Early Childhood Research Quarterly, 21*, 238–252.

Roopnarine, J. L., Lasker, J., Sacks, M., & Stores, M. (1998). The cultural contexts of children's play. In O. N. Saracho & B. Spodek (Eds.), *Multiple perspectives on play in early childhood education* (pp. 194–219). Albany: State University of New York Press.

Rosander, K., & von Hofsten, C. (2002). Development of gaze tracking of small and large objects. *Experimental Brain Research, 146*, 257–264.

Rosander, K., & von Hofsten, C. (2004). Infants' emerging ability to represent occluded object motion. *Cognition, 91*, 1–22.

Rose, A. J. (2002). Co-rumination in the friendships of girls and boys. *Child Development, 73*, 1830–1843.

Rose, A. J., & Asher, S. R. (1999). Children's goals and strategies in response to conflicts within a friendship. *Developmental Psychology, 35*, 69–79.

Rose, A. J., Swenson, L. P., & Waller, E. M. (2004). Overt and relational aggression and perceived popularity: Developmental differences in concurrent and prospective relations. *Developmental Psychology, 40*, 378–387.

Rose, L. (2000). Fathers of full-term infants. In N. Tracey (Ed.), *Parents of premature infants: Their emotional world* (pp. 105–116). London: Whurr.

Rose, S. A., Feldman, J. F., & Janowski, J. J. (2001). Attention and recognition memory in the 1st year of life: A longitudinal study of preterm and full-term infants. *Developmental Psychology, 37*, 135–151.

Rose, S. A., Feldman, J. F., & Wallace, I. F. (1992). Infant information processing in relation to six-year cognitive outcomes. *Child Development, 63*, 1126–1141.

Rose, S. A., Jankowski, J. J., & Senior, G. J. (1997). Infants' recognition of contour-deleted figures. *Journal of Experimental Psychology: Human Perception and Performance, 23*, 1206–1216.

Rosen, A. B., & Rozin, P. (1993). Now you see it, now you don't: The preschool child's conception of invisible particles in the context of dissolving. *Developmental Psychology, 29*, 300–311.

Rosen, D. (2003). Eating disorders in children and young adolescents: Etiology, classification, clinical features, and treatment. *Adolescent Medicine: State of the Art Reviews, 14*, 49–59.

Rosengren, K. S., & Hickling, A. K. (2000). The development of children's thinking about possible events and plausible mechanisms. In K. S. Rosengren, C. N. Johnson, & P. L. Harris (Eds.), *Imagining the impossible* (pp. 75–98). Cambridge, U.K.: Cambridge University Press.

Rosenshine, B., & Meister, C. (1994). Reciprocal teaching: A review of nineteen experimental studies. *Review of Educational Research, 64*, 479–530.

Ross, C. M., & Harrison, P. L. (2006). Ability grouping. In G. G. Bear & K. M. Minke (Eds.), *Children's needs III: Development, prevention, and intervention* (pp. 579–588). Washington, DC: National Association of School Psychologists.

Ross, H. S., Conant, C., Cheyne, J. A., & Alevizos, E. (1992). Relationships and alliances in the social interactions of kibbutz toddlers. *Social Development, 1*, 1–17.

Rotenberg, K. J., McDougall, P., Boulton, M. J., Vaillancourt, T., Fox, C., & Hymel, S. (2004). Cross-sectional and longitudinal relations among peer-reported trustworthiness, social relationships, and psychological adjustment in children and early adolescents from the United Kingdom and Canada. *Journal of Experimental Child Psychology, 88*, 46–67.

Roth, J., Brooks-Gunn, J., Murray, L., & Foster, W. (1998). Promoting healthy adolescents: Synthesis of youth development program evaluations. *Journal of Research on Adolescence, 8*, 423–459.

Rothbart, M. K. (2003). Temperament and the pursuit of an integrated developmental psychology. *Merrill-Palmer Quarterly, 50*, 492–505.

Rothbart, M. K., Ahadi, S. A., & Evans, D. E. (2000). Temperament and personality: Origins and outcome. *Journal of Personality and Social Psychology, 78*, 122–135.

Rothbart, M. K., & Bates, J. E. (2006). Temperament. In N. Eisenberg (Ed.), *Handbook of child psychology: Vol. 3. Social, emotional, and personality development* (6th ed., pp. 99–166). Hoboken, NJ: Wiley.

Rothbart, M. K., & Mauro, J. A. (1990). Questionnaire approaches to the study of infant temperament. In J. W. Fagen & J. Colombo (Eds.), *Individual differences in infancy: Reliability, stability and prediction* (pp. 411–429). Hillsdale, NJ: Erlbaum.

Rothbart, M. K., Posner, M. I., & Kieras, J. (2006). Temperament, attention, and the development of self-regulation. In K. McCartney & D. Phillips (Eds.), *Blackwell handbook of early childhood development* (pp. 338–357). Malden, MA: Blackwell.

Rothbaum, F., Pott, M., Azuma, H., Miyake, K., & Weisz, J. (2000a). The development of close relationships in Japan and the United States: Paths of symbiotic harmony and generative tension. *Child Development, 71*, 1121–1142.

Rothbaum, F., Weisz, J., Pott, M., Miyake, K., & Morelli, G. (2000b). Attachment and culture: Security in the United States and Japan. *American Psychologist, 55*, 1093–1104.

Rouselle, L., Palmers, E., & Noël, M.-P. (2004). Magnitude comparison in preschoolers: What counts? Influence of perceptual variables. *Journal of Experimental Child Psychology, 87*, 57–84.

Rovee-Collier, C. (1999). The development of infant memory. *Current Directions in Psychological Science, 8*, 80–85.

Rovee-Collier, C., & Barr, R. (2001). Infant learning and memory. In G. Bremner & A. Fogel (Eds.), *Blackwell handbook of infant development* (pp. 139–168). Oxford, U.K.: Blackwell.

Rovee-Collier, C. K., & Bhatt, R. S. (1993). Evidence of long-term memory in infancy. *Annals of Child Development, 9,* 1–45.

Rovet, J., Netley, C., Keenan, M., Bailey, J., & Stewart, D. (1996). The psychoeducational profile of boys with Klinefelter syndrome. *Journal of Learning Disabilities, 29,* 180–196.

Rowe, D. (1994). *The limits of family influence: Genes, experience, and behavior.* New York: Guilford.

Rowe, R., Maughan, B., & Goodman, R. (2004). Childhood psychiatric disorder and unintentional injury: Findings from a national cohort study. *Journal of Pediatric Psychology, 29,* 119–130.

Rowe, S., & Wertsch, J. V. (2002). Vygotsky's model of cognitive development. In G. Bremner & A. Fogel (Eds.), *Blackwell handbook of infant development* (pp. 538–554). Oxford, U.K.: Blackwell.

Rowland, C., & Pine, J. M. (2000). Subject-auxiliary inversion errors and wh-question acquisition: "What children do know?" *Journal of Child Language, 27,* 157–181.

Rubel, E. W., & Ryals, B. M. (1982). Patterns of hair cell loss in chick basilar papilla after intense auditory stimulation: Exposure duration and survival time. *Acta Otolaryngologica, 93,* 31–41.

Rubel, E. W., & Ryals, B. M. (1983). Development of the place principle: Acoustical trauma. *Science, 219,* 512–514.

Rubin, K. H., Bukowski, W. M., & Parker, J. G. (2006). Peer interactions, relationships, and groups. In N. Eisenberg (Ed.), *Handbook of child psychology: Vol. 3. Social, emotional, and personality development* (6th ed., pp. 571–645). Hoboken, NJ: Wiley.

Rubin, K. H., Burgess, K. B., & Coplan, R. (2002). Social withdrawal and shyness. In P. K. Smith & C. H. Hart (Eds.), *Blackwell handbook of child social development* (pp. 329–352). Oxford: Blackwell.

Rubin, K. H., Burgess, K. B., Dwyer, K. M., & Hastings, P. D. (2003). Predicting preschoolers' externalizing behaviors from toddler temperament, conflict, and maternal negativity. *Developmental Psychology, 39,* 164–176.

Rubin, K. H., Burgess, K. B., & Hastings, P. D. (2002). Stability and social-behavioral consequences of toddlers' inhibited temperament and parenting behaviors. *Child Development, 73,* 483–495.

Rubin, K. H., Coplan, J., Chen, X., Buskirk, A. A., & Wojslawowicz, J. C. (2005). Peer relationships in childhood. In M. H. Bornstein & M. E. Lamb (Eds.), *Developmental science: An advanced textbook* (pp. 469–512). Mahwah, NJ: Erlbaum.

Rubin, K. H., & Coplan, R. J. (1998). Social and nonsocial play in childhood: An individual differences perspective. In O. N. Saracho & B. Spodek (Eds.), *Multiple perspectives on play in early childhood education* (pp. 144–170). Albany, NY: State University of New York Press.

Rubin, K. H., Fein, G. G., & Vandenberg, B. (1983). Play. In E. M. Hetherington (Ed.), *Handbook of child psychology: Vol. 4. Socialization, personality, and social development* (4th ed., pp. 693–744). New York: Wiley.

Rubin, K. H., Hastings, P. D., Stewart, S. L., Henderson, H. A., & Chen, X. (1997). The consistency and concomitants of inhibition: Some of the children, all of the time. *Child Development, 68,* 467–483.

Rubin, K. H., Stewart, S. L., & Coplan, R. J. (1995). Social withdrawal in childhood: Conceptual and empirical perspectives. In T. H. Ollendick & R. J. Prinz (Eds.), *Advances in clinical child psychology* (Vol. 17, pp. 157–196). New York: Plenum.

Rubin, K. H., Watson, K. S., & Jambor, T. W. (1978). Free-play behaviors in preschool and kindergarten children. *Child Development, 49,* 539–536.

Ruble, D. N., Alvarez, J., Bachman, M., Cameron, J., Fuligni, A., Garcia Coll, C. T., & Rhee, E. (2004). The development of a sense of "we": The emergence and implications of children's collective identity. In M. Bennett & F. Sani (Eds.), *The development of the social self* (pp. 29–76). Hove, U.K.: Psychology Press.

Ruble, D. N., & Flett, G. L. (1988). Conflicting goals in self-evaluative information seeking: Developmental and ability level analyses. *Child Development, 59,* 97–106.

Ruble, D. N., Martin, C. L., & Berenbaum, S. A. (2006). Gender development. In N. Eisenberg (Ed.), *Handbook of child Psychology: Vol. 3. Social, emotional, and personality development* (6th ed., pp. 858–932). Hoboken, NJ: Wiley.

Rudolph, D. K., & Heller, T. L. (1997). Interpersonal problem solving, externalizing behavior, and social competence in preschoolers: A knowledge-performance discrepancy? *Journal of Applied Developmental Psychology, 18,* 107–117.

Rudolph, D. K., Lambert, S. F., Clark, A. G., & Kurlakowsky, K. D. (2001). Negotiating the transition to middle school: The role of self-regulatory processes. *Child Development, 72,* 929–946.

Ruff, C. (2002). Variation in human body size and shape. *Annual Review of Anthropology, 31,* 211–232.

Ruff, H. A., & Capozzoli, M. C. (2003). Development of attention and distractibility in the first 4 years of life. *Developmental Psychology, 39,* 877–890.

Ruff, H. A., & Rothbart, M. K. (1996). *Attention in early development.* New York: Oxford University Press.

Ruffman, T. (1999). Children's understanding of logical inconsistency. *Child Development, 70,* 872–886.

Ruffman, T., & Langman, L. (2002). Infants' reaching in a multi-well A not B task. *Infant Behavior and Development, 25,* 237–246.

Ruffman, T., Perner, J., Olson, D. R., & Doherty, M. (1993). Reflecting on scientific thinking: Children's understanding of the hypothesis– evidence relation. *Child Development, 64,* 1617–1636.

Ruffman, T., Slade, L., Devitt, K., & Crowe, E. (2006). What mothers say and what they do: The relation between parenting, theory of mind, language, and conflict/cooperation. *British Journal of Developmental Psychology, 24,* 105–124.

Runco, M. A. (1992). Children's divergent thinking and creative ideation. *Developmental Review, 12,* 233–264.

Rushton, J. P., & Jensen, A. R. (2005). Thirty years of research on race differences in cognitive ability. *Psychology, Public Policy, and Law, 11,* 235–294.

Rushton, J. P., & Jensen, A. R. (2006). The totality of available evidence shows the race IQ gap still remains. *Psychological Science, 17,* 921–924.

Russell, A., Mize, J., & Bissaker, K. (2004). Parent–child relationships. In P. K. Smith & C. H. Hart (Eds.), *Blackwell handbook of childhood social development* (pp. 204–222). Malden, MA: Blackwell.

Russell, A., Pettit, G. S., & Mize, J. (1998). Horizontal qualities in parent–child relationships: Parallels with and possible consequences for children's peer relationships. *Developmental Review, 18,* 313–352.

Russell, J. A. (1990). The preschooler's understanding of the causes and consequences of emotion. *Child Development, 61,* 1872–1881.

Russell, J. A., Douglas, A. J., & Ingram, C. D. (2001). Brain preparations for maternity–Adaptive changes in behavioral and neuroendocrine systems during pregnancy and lactation: An overview. *Progress in Brain Research, 133,* 1–38.

Russell, R. B., Petrini, J. R., Damus, K., Mattison, D. R., & Schwarz, R. H. (2003). The changing epidemiology of multiple births in the United States. *Obstetrics and Gynecology, 101,* 129–135.

Rust, J., Golombok, S., Hines, M., Johnston, K., Golding, J., & the ALSPAC Study Team. (2000). The role of brothers and sisters in the gender development of preschool children. *Journal of Experimental Child Psychology, 77,* 292–303.

Rutter, M. (1996). Maternal deprivation. In M. H. Bornstein (Ed.), *Handbook of parenting: Vol. 4. Applied and practical parenting* (pp. 3–31). Mahwah, NJ: Erlbaum.

Rutter, M. (2002). Nature, nurture, and development: From evangelism through science toward policy and practice. *Child Development, 73,* 1–21.

Rutter, M. (2006a). *Genes and behavior: Nature–nurture interplay explained.* Malden, MA: Blackwell.

Rutter, M. (2006b). The psychological effects of early institutional rearing. In P. J. Marshall & N. A. Fox (Eds.), *The development of social engagement: Neurobiological perspectives* (pp. 355–391). New York: Oxford University Press.

Rutter, M., & the English and Romanian Adoptees Study Team. (1998). Developmental catch-up, and deficit, following adoption after severe global early privation. *Journal of Child Psychology and Psychiatry, 39,* 465–476.

Rutter, M., O'Connor, T. G., and the English and Romanian Adoptees Study Team. (2004). Are there biological programming effects for psychological development? Findings from a study of Romanian adoptees. *Developmental Psychology, 40,* 81–94.

Rutter, M., Pickles, A., Murray, R., & Eaves, L. (2001). Testing hypotheses on specific environmental causal effects on behavior. *Psychological Bulletin, 127,* 291–324.

Ryan, A. M. (2001). The peer group as a context for the development of young adolescent motivation and achievement. *Child Development, 72,* 1135–1150.

Ryan, A. M., & Patrick, H. (2001). The classroom social environment and changes in adolescents' motivation and engagement during middle school. *American Educational Research Journal, 38,* 437–460.

Ryan, M. K., David, B., & Reynolds, K. J. (2004). Who cares? The effect of gender and context on the self and moral reasoning. *Psychology of Women Quarterly, 28,* 246–255.

Ryan, R. M., Fauth, R. C., & Brooks-Gunn, J. (2006). Childhood poverty: Implications for school readiness and early childhood education In B. Spodek & O. N. Saracho (Eds.), *Handbook of research on the education of young children* (2nd ed., pp. 323–346). Mahwah, NJ: Erlbaum.

Ryding, M., Konradsson, K., Kalm, O., & Prellner, K. (2002). Auditory consequences of recurrent acute purulent otitis media. *Annals of Otology, Rhinology, and Laryngology, 111*(3, Pt. 1), 261–266.

Saarni, C. (1999). *The development of emotional competence.* New York: Guilford.

Saarni, C. (2000). Emotional competence: A developmental perspective. In R. Bar-On & J. D. A. Parker (Eds.), *Handbook of emotional intelligence* (pp. 68–91). San Francisco: Jossey-Bass.

Saarni, C., Campos, J. J., Camras, L. A., & Witherington, D. (2006). Emotional development: Action, communication, and understanding. In N. Eisenberg (Ed.), *Handbook of child psychology: Vol. 3. Social, emotional, and personality development* (6th ed., pp. 226–299). Hoboken, NJ: Wiley.

Sabbagh, M. A., Xu, F., Carlson, S. M., Moses, L. J., & Lee, K. (2006). The development of executive functioning and theory of mind: A comparison of Chinese and U.S. preschoolers. *Psychological Science, 17,* 74–81.

Sacks, P. (1999). *Standardized minds: The high price of America's testing culture and what we can do to change it.* Cambridge, MA: Perseus.

Sacks, P. (2005). "No child left": What are schools for in a democratic society? In S. Olfman (Ed.), *Childhood lost: How American culture is failing our kids* (pp. 185–202). Westport, CT: Praeger.

Sadeh, A. (1997). Sleep and melatonin in infants: A preliminary study. *Sleep, 20,* 185–191.

Sadler, T. W. (2006). *Langman's medical embryology* (10th ed.). Baltimore: Williams & Wilkins.

Saenger, P. (2003). Dose effects of growth hormone during puberty. *Hormone Research, 60*(Suppl. 1), 52–57.

Safe Kids Worldwide. (2002). *Childhood injury worldwide: Meeting the challenge.* Retrieved from http://www.safekidsworldwide.org

Saffran, J. R., Aslin, R. N., & Newport, E. L. (1996). Statistical learning by 8-month-old infants. *Science, 27,* 1926–1928.

Saffran, J. R., & Thiesen, E. D. (2003). Pattern induction by infant language learners. *Developmental Psychology, 39,* 484–494.

Saffran, J. R., Werker, J. F., & Werner, L. A. (2006). The infant's auditory world: Hearing, speech, and the beginnings of language. In D. Kuhn & R. Siegler (Eds.), *Handbook of child psychology: Vol. 2. Cognition, perception, and language* (6th ed., pp. 58–108). Hoboken, NJ: Wiley.

Sagi, A., van IJzendoorn, M. H., Aviezer, O., Donnell, F., Koren-Karie, N., Joels, T., & Harel, Y. (1995). Attachments in a multiple-caregiver and multiple-infant environment: The case of the Israeli kibbutzim. In E. Waters, B. E. Vaughn, G. Posada, & K. Kondo-Ikemura (Eds.), *Caregiving, cultural, and cognitive perspectives on secure-base behavior and working models: New growing points in attachment theory and research. Monographs of the Society for Research in Child Development, 60*(1, Serial No. 244), 71–91.

Saginak, K. A., & Saginak, M. A. (2005). Balancing work and family: Equity, gender, and marital satisfaction. *Counseling and Therapy for Couples and Families, 13,* 162–166.

Saha, C., Riner, M. E., & Liu, G. (2005). Individual and neighborhood-level factors in predicting asthma. *Archives of Pediatrics and Adolescent Medicine, 159,* 759–763.

Saigal, S., Stoskopf, B., Streiner, D., Boyle, M., Pinelli, J., & Paneth, N. (2006). Transition of extremely low-birth-weight infants from adolescence to young adulthood.

Journal of the American Medical Association, 295, 667–675.

Saitta, S. C., & Zackai, E. H. (2005). Specific chromosome disorders in newborns. In H. W. Taeusch, R. A. Ballard, & C. A. Gleason (Eds.), *Avery's diseases of the newborn* (8th ed., pp. 204–215). Philadelphia: Saunders.

Salbe, A. D., Weyer, C., Harper, I., Lindsay, R. S., Ravussin, E., & Tataranni, P. A. (2002a). Assessing risk factors for obesity between childhood and adolescence: II. Energy metabolism and physical activity. *Pediatrics, 110,* 307–314.

Salbe, A. D., Weyer, C., Lindsay, R. S., Ravussin, E., & Tataranni, P. A. (2002b). Assessing risk factors for obesity between childhood and adolescence: I. Birth weight, childhood adiposity, parental obesity, insulin, and leptin. *Pediatrics, 110,* 299–306.

Salerno, M., Micillo, M., Di Maio, S., Capalbo, D., Ferri, P., & Lettiero, T. (2001). Longitudinal growth, sexual maturation and final height in patients with congenital hypothyroidism detected by neonatal screening. *European Journal of Endocrinology, 145,* 377–383.

Salihu, H. M., Shumpert, M. N., Slay, M., Kirby, R. S., & Alexander, G. R. (2003). Childbearing beyond maternal age 50 and fetal outcomes in the United States. *Obstetrics and Gynecology, 102,* 1006–1014.

Salmela-Aro, K., Nurmi, J., Saisto, T., & Halmesmaki, E. (2000). Women's and men's personal goals during the transition to parenthood. *Journal of Family Psychology, 14,* 171–186.

Salmivalli, C., & Voeten, M. (2004). Connections between attitudes, group norms, and behaviour in bullying situations. *International Journal of Behavioral Development, 28,* 246–258.

Salovey, P., & Pizzaro, D. A. (2003). The value of emotional intelligence. In R. J. Sternberg, J. Lautrey, & T. I. Lubart (Eds.), *Models of intelligence: International perspectives* (pp. 263–278). Washington, DC: American Psychological Association.

Salter, D., McMillan, D., Richards, M., Talbot, T., Hodges, J., Bentovim, A., & Hastings, R. (2003). Development of sexually abusive behavior in sexually victimized males: A longitudinal study. *Lancet, 361,* 471–476.

Sameroff, A. (2006). Identifying risk and protective factors for healthy child development. In A. Clarke-Stewart & J. Dunn (Eds.), *Families count: Effects on child and adolescent development* (pp. 53–76). New York: Cambridge University Press.

Samuels, M. (2003). Viruses and sudden infant death. *Peaediatric Respiratory Review, 4,* 178–183.

Sanchez-Ramos, L. (2005). Induction of labor. *Obstetrics and Gynecology Clinics of North America, 32,* 181–200.

Sandberg, D. E., & Voss, L. D. (2002). The psychosocial consequences of short stature: A review of the evidence. *Best Practice and Research in Clinical Endocrinology and Metabolism, 16,* 449–463.

Sandberg, J. F., & Hofferth, S. L. (2001). Changes in children's time with parents: United States, 1981–1997. *Demography, 38,* 423–436.

Sanderson, J. A., & Siegal, M. (1988). Conceptions of moral and social rules in rejected and nonrejected preschoolers. *Journal of Clinical Child Psychology, 17,* 66–72.

Sandler, J. C. (2006). Alternative methods of child testimony: A review of law and research. In C. R. Bartol & A. M. Bartol (Eds.), *Current perspectives in forensic psychology and criminal justice* (pp. 203–212). Thousand Oaks, CA: Sage.

Sandstrom, M. J., & Cillessen, A. H. N. (2003). Sociometric status and children's peer experiences: Use of the daily diary method. *Merrill-Palmer Quarterly, 49,* 427–452.

Sansavini, A., Bertoncini, J., & Giovanelli, G. (1997). Newborns discriminate the rhythm of multisyllabic stressed words. *Developmental Psychology, 33,* 3–11.

Santoloupo, S., & Pratt, M. (1994). Age, gender, and parenting style variations in mother–adolescent dialogues and adolescent reasoning about political issues. *Journal of Adolescent Research, 9,* 241–261.

Sapp, F., Lee, K., & Muir, D. (2000). Three-year-olds' difficulty with the appearance–reality distinction: Is it real or is it apparent? *Developmental Psychology, 36,* 547–560.

Saraswathi, T. S., & Larson, R. (2002). Adolescence in global perspective: An agenda for social policy. In B. B. Frown, R. Larson, & T. S. Saraswathi (Eds.), *The world's youth* (pp. 344–362). New York: Cambridge University Press.

Sarnecka, B. W., & Gelman, S. A. (2004). Six does not just mean a lot: Preschoolers see number words as specific. *Cognition, 92,* 329–352.

Sarrazin, G. (1999). WISC-III, *Échelle d'intelligence de Wechs pour enfants, troisième édition, adaptation canadienne-française, Manuel d'administration.* Toronto: Psychological Corporation.

Saucier, J. F., Sylvestre, R., Doucet, H., Lambert, J., Frappier, J. Y., Charbonneau, L., & Malus, M. (2002). Cultural identity and adaptation to adolescence in Montreal. In F. J. C. Azima & N. Grizenko (Eds.), *Immigrant and refugee children and their families: Clinical, research, and training issues* (pp. 133–154). Madison, WI: International Universities Press.

Saudino, K. J. (2003). Parent ratings of infant temperament: Lessons from twin studies. *Infant Behavior and Development, 26,* 100–107.

Saudino, K. J., & Cherny, S. S. (2001). Sources of continuity and change in observed temperament. In R. N. Emde & J. K. Hewitt (Eds.), *Infancy to early childhood: Genetic and environmental influences on developmental change* (pp. 89–110). New York: Oxford University Press.

Saudino, K. J., & Plomin, R. (1997). Cognitive and temperamental mediators of genetic contributions to the home environment during infancy. *Merrill-Palmer Quarterly, 43,* 1–23.

Sauls, D. J. (2002). Effects of labor support on mothers, babies, and birth outcomes. *Journal of Obstetric, Gynecologic, and Neonatal Nursing, 31,* 733–741.

Savin-Williams, R. C. (2001). A critique of research on sexual-minority youths. *Journal of Adolescence, 24,* 5–13.

Savin-Williams, R. C. (2003). Lesbian, gay, and bisexual youths' relationships with their parents. In L. D. Garnets & D. C. Kimmel (Eds.), *Psychological perspectives on lesbian, gay, and bisexual experiences* (2nd ed., pp. 299–326). New York: Columbia University Press.

Savin-Williams, R. C., & Diamond, L. M. (2004). Sex. In R. M. Lerner & L. Steinberg (Eds.), *Handbook of adolescent development* (2nd ed., pp. 189–231). Hoboken, NJ: Wiley.

Savin-Williams, R. C., & Ream, G. L. (2003). Sex variations in the disclosure to parents of same-sex attractions. *Journal of Family Psychology, 17,* 429–438.

Saw, S. M., Carkeet, A., Chia, K. S., Stone, R. A., & Tan, D. T. (2002). Component dependent risk factors for ocular parameters in Singapore Chinese children. *Ophthalmology, 109,* 2065–2071.

Saxe, G. B. (1988, August–September). Candy selling and math learning. *Educational Researcher, 17*(6), 14–21.

Saygin, A. P., Wilson, S. M., Dronkers, N. F., & Bates, E. (2004). Action comprehension in aphasia: Linguistic and non-linguistic deficits and their lesion correlates. *Neuropsychologia, 42,* 1788–1804.

Saylor, C. F., Cowart, B. L., Lipovsky, J. A., Jackson, C., & Finch, A. J., Jr. (2003). Media exposure to September 11: Elementary school students' experiences and posttraumatic symptoms. *American Behavioral Scientist, 46,* 1622–1642.

Saylor, M. M., Baldwin, D. A., & Sabbagh, M. A. (2005). Word learning: A complex product. In G. Hall & S. Waxman (Eds.), *Weaving a lexicon.* Cambridge, MA: MIT Press.

Saylor, M. M., Sabbagh, M. A., & Baldwin, D. A. (2002). Children use whole–part juxtaposition as a pragmatic cue to word meaning. *Developmental Psychology, 38,* 993–1003.

Saywitz, K. J., Goodman, G. S., & Lyon, T. D. (2002). Interviewing children in and out of court: Current research and practice implications. In J. E. B. Myers & L. Berliner (Eds.), *The APSAC handbook on child maltreatment* (2nd ed., pp. 349–377). Thousand Oaks, CA: Sage.

Scales, P. C., & Roehlkepartain, E. C. (2004). *Community service and service learning in U.S. public schools, 2004. Findings from a national survey.* St. Paul, MN: National Youth Leadership Council.

Scarr, S., & McCartney, K. (1983). How people make their own environments: A theory of genotype–environment effects. *Child Development, 54,* 424–435.

Scarr, S., & Weinberg, R. A. (1983). The Minnesota adoption studies: Genetic differences and malleability. *Child Development, 54,* 260–267.

Schaal, B., Marlier, L., & Soussignan, R. (2000). Human fetuses learn odours from their pregnant mother's diet. *Chemical Senses, 25,* 729–737.

Scharrer, E., & Comstock, G. (2003). Entertainment televisual media: Content patterns and themes. In E. L. Palmer & B. M. Young (Eds.), *The faces of televisual media: Teaching violence, selling to children* (pp. 161–193). Mahwah, NJ: Erlbaum.

Schauwers, K., Gillis, S., Daemers, K., De Beukelaer, C., De Ceulaer, G., Yperman, M., & Govaerts, P. J. (2004). Normal hearing and language development in a deaf-born child. *Otology and Neurotology, 25,* 924–929.

Schellenberg, E. G. (2004). Music lessons enhance IQ. *Psychological Science, 15,* 511–514.

Schellenberg, E. G. (2005). Music and cognitive abilities. *Current Directions in Psychological Science, 14,* 317–320.

Scher, A., Epstein, R., & Tirosh, E. (2004). Stability and changes in sleep regulation: A longitudinal study from 3 months to 3 years. *International Journal of Behavioral Development, 28,* 268–274.

Scher, A., Tirosh, E., Jaffe, M., Rubin, L., Sadeh, A., & Lavie, P. (1995). Sleep patterns of infants and young children in Israel. *International Journal of Behavioral Development, 18,* 701–711.

Schieber, R. A., & Sacks, J. J. (2001). Measuring community bicycle helmet use among children. *Public Health Reports, 116,* 113–121.

Schilling, T. (2000). Infants' looking at possible and impossible screen rotations: The role of familiarization. *Infancy, 1,* 389–402.

Schlagmüller, M., & Schneider, W. (2002). The development of organizational strategies in children: Evidence from a microgenetic longitudinal study. *Journal of Experimental Child Psychology, 81,* 298–319.

Schlegel, A., & Barry, H., III. (1991). *Adolescence: An anthropological inquiry.* New York: Free Press.

Schmid, R. G., Tirsch, W. S., & Scherb, H. (2002). Correlation between spectral EEG parameters and intelligence test variables in school-age children. *Clinical Neurophysiology, 113,* 1647–1656.

Schmitz, S., Fulker, D. W., Plomin, R., Zahn-Waxler, C., Emde, R. N., & DeFries, J. C. (1999). Temperament and problem behaviour during early childhood. *International Journal of Behavioral Development, 23,* 333–355.

Schneewind, K. A., & Gerhard, A. (2002). Relationship personality, conflict resolution, and marital satisfaction in the first 5 years of marriage. *Family Relations, 51,* 63–71.

Schneider, B. H., Atkinson, L., & Tardif, C. (2001). Child–parent attachment and children's peer relations: A quantitative review. *Developmental Psychology, 37,* 86–100.

Schneider, W. (1986). The role of conceptual knowledge and metamemory in the development of organizational processes in memory. *Journal of Experimental Child Psychology, 42,* 218–236.

Schneider, W. (2002). Memory development in childhood. In U. Goswami (Ed.), *Blackwell handbook of childhood cognitive development* (pp. 236–256). Malden, MA: Blackwell.

Schneider, W., & Bjorklund, D. F. (1992). Expertise, aptitude, and strategic remembering. *Child Development, 63,* 461–473.

Schneider, W., & Bjorklund, D. F. (1998). Memory. In D. Kuhn & R. S. Siegler (Eds.), *Handbook of child psychology: Vol. 2. Cognition, perception, and language* (5th ed., pp. 467–521). New York: Wiley.

Schneider, W., & Pressley, M. (1997). *Memory development between two and twenty* (2nd ed.). Mahwah, NJ: Erlbaum.

Scholl, B. J., & Leslie, A. M. (2000). Minds, modules, and meta-analysis. *Child Development, 72,* 696–701.

Scholl, T. O., Hediger, M. L., & Belsky, D. (1996). Prenatal care and maternal health during adolescent pregnancy: A review and meta-analysis. *Journal of Adolescent Health, 15,* 444–456.

Schonert-Reichl, K. A. (1999). Relations of peer acceptance, friendship adjustment, and social behavior to moral reasoning during early adolescence. *Journal of Early Adolescence, 19,* 249–279.

Schoon, I., & Parsons, S. (2002). Teenage aspirations for future careers and occupational outcomes. *Journal of Vocational Behavior, 60,* 262–288.

Schor, J. B. (2002). Time crunch among American parents. In S. A. Hewlett, N. Rankin, & C. West (Eds.), *Taking parenting public* (pp. 83–102). Boston: Rowman & Littlefield.

Schott, J. M., & Rossor, M. N. (2003). The grasp and other primitive reflexes. *Journal of Neurological and Neurosurgical Psychiatry, 74,* 558–560.

Schraedley, P. K., Gotlib, I. H., & Hayward, C. (1999). Gender differences in correlates of depressive symptoms in adolescents. *Journal of Adolescent Health, 25,* 98–108.

Schuetze, P., & Eiden, R. D. (2006). The association between maternal cocaine use during pregnancy and physiological regulation in 4- to 8-week-old infants: An examination of possible mediators and moderators. *Journal of Pediatric Psychology, 31,* 15–26.

Schull, W. J. (2003). The children of atomic bomb survivors: A synopsis. *Journal of Radiological Protection, 23,* 369–394.

Schulman, J. D., & Black, S. H. (1997). Screening for Huntington disease and certain other dominantly inherited disorders: A case for preimplantation genetic testing. *Journal of Medical Screening, 4,* 58–59.

Schulte, L. E., Shanahan, S., Anderson, T. D., & Sides, J. (2003). Student and teacher perceptions of their middle and high schools' sense of community. *School Community Journal, 13,* 7–33.

Schultz, D., Izar, C. E., Ackerman, B. P., & Youngstrom, E. A. (2001). Emotion knowledge in economically disadvantaged children: Self-regulatory antecedents and relations to social difficulties and withdrawal. *Development and Psychopathology, 13,* 53–67.

Schunk, D. H., & Pajares, F. (2005). Competence perceptions and academic functioning. In A. J. Andrew & C. S. Dweck (Eds.), *Handbook of competence and motivation* (pp. 85–104). New York: Guilford.

Schwalb, D. W., Nakazawa, J., Yamamoto, T., & Hyun, J.-H. (2004). Fathering in Japanese, Chinese, and Korean cultures: A review of the literature. In M. E. Lamb (Ed.), *The role of the father in child development* (4th ed., pp. 146–181). Hoboken, NJ: Wiley.

Schwanenflugel, P. J., Henderson, R. L., & Fabricius, W. V. (1998). Developing organization of mental verbs and theory of mind in middle childhood: Evidence from extensions. *Developmental Psychology, 34,* 512–524.

Schwartz, C. E., Wright, C. I., Shin, L. M., Kagan, J., & Rauch, S. L. (2003). Inhibited and uninhibited infants "grown up": Adult amygdalar response to novelty. *Science, 300,* 1952–1953.

Schwartz, D., Proctor, L. J., & Chien, D. H. (2001). The aggressive victim of bullying: Emotional and behavioral dysregulation as a pathway to victimization by peers. In J. Juonen & S. Graham (Eds.), *Peer harassment in school: The plight of the vulnerable and victimized* (pp. 147–174). New York: Guilford.

Schwartz, S. J., Côté, J. E., & Arnett, J. J. (2005). Identity and agency in emerging adulthood: Two developmental routes in the individualization process. *Youth and Society, 37,* 201–229.

Schwartz, S. J., Pantin, H., Prado, G., Sullivan, S., & Szapocznik, J. (2005). Family functioning, identity, and problem behavior: Immigrant early adolescents. *Journal of Early Adolescence, 25,* 392–420.

Schwarz, N. (1999). Self-reports: How the questions shape the answers. *American Psychologist, 54,* 93–105.

Schwebel, D. C., & Bounds, M. L. (2003). The role of parents and temperament on children's estimation of physical ability: Links to unintentional injury prevention. *Journal of Pediatric Psychology, 28,* 505–516.

Schwebel, D. C., Brezausek, C. M., Ramey, S. L., & Ramey, C. T. (2004). Interactions between child behavior patterns and parenting: Implications for children's unintentional injury risk. *Journal of Pediatric Psychology, 29,* 93–104.

Schwebel, D. C., Hodgens, J. B., & Sterling, S. (2006). How mothers parent their children with behavior disorders: Implications for unintentional injury risk. *Journal of Safety Research, 37,* 167–173.

Schweiger, W. K., & O'Brien, M. (2005). Special needs adoption: An ecological systems approach. *Family Relations, 54,* 512–522.

Schweinhart, L. J., Montie, J., Xiang, Z., Barnett, W. S., & Belfield, C. R. (2004). *Lifetime effects: The High/Scope Perry Preschool Study through age 40.* Boston, MA: Strategies for Children. Retrieved from www.highscope.org/Research/PerryProject/perrymain.htm

Schweizer, K., Moosbrugger, H., & Goldhammer, F. (2006). The structure of the relationship between attention and intelligence. *Intelligence, 33,* 589–611.

Schwimmer, J. B., Burwinkle, T. M., & Varni, J. W. (2003). Health-related quality of life of severely obese children and adolescents. *Journal of the American Medical Association, 289,* 1813–1819.

Scott, C. S., Arthur, D., Owen, R., & Panizo, M. I. (1989). Black adolescents' emotional response to menarche. *Journal of the National Medical Association, 81,* 285–290.

Scott, K. D., Berkowitz, G., & Klaus, M. (1999). A comparison of intermittent and continuous support during labor: A meta-analysis. *American Journal of Obstetrics and Gynecology, 180,* 1054–1059.

Scott, L. D. (2003). The relation of racial identity and racial socialization to coping with discrimination among African Americans. *Journal of Black Studies, 20,* 520–538.

Scrutton, D. (2005). Influence of supine sleeping positioning on early motor milestone acquisition. *Developmental Medicine and Child Neurology, 47,* 364.

Seaton, E. K., Scottham, K. M., & Sellers, R. M. (2006). The status model of racial identity development in African American adolescents: Evidence of structure, trajectories, and well-being. *Child Development, 77,* 1416–1426.

Sebanc, A. (2003). The friendship features of preschool children: Links with prosocial behavior and aggression. *Social Development, 12,* 249–268.

Seccombe, K. (2002). "Beating the odds" versus "changing the odds": Poverty, resilience, and family policy. *Journal of Marriage and the Family, 64,* 384–394.

Seginer, R. (1992). Sibling relationships in early adolescence: A study of Israeli Arab sisters. *Journal of Early Adolescence, 12,* 96–110.

Seidman, E., Aber, J. L., & French, S. E. (2004). Assessing the transitions to middle and high school. *Journal of Adolescent Research, 19,* 3–30.

Seidman, E., Lambert, L. E., Allen, L., & Aber, J. L. (2003). Urban adolescents' transition to junior high school and protective family transactions. *Journal of Early Adolescence, 23,* 166–193.

Seifer, R., & Schiller, M. (1995). The role of parenting sensitivity, infant temperament, and dyadic interaction in attachment theory and assessment. In E. Waters, B. E. Vaughn, G. Posada, & K. Kondo-Ikemura K. (Eds.), *Caregiving, cultural, and cognitive perspectives on secure-base behavior and working models: New growing points of attachment theory and research. Monographs of the Society for Research in Child Development, 60*(2–3, Serial No. 244).

Seiffge-Krenke, I. (2003). Testing theories of romantic development from adolescence to young adulthood: Evidence of a developmental sequence. *International Journal of Behavioral Development, 27,* 519–531.

Seinhausen, H. (2002). The outcome of anorexia nervosa in the 20th century. *American Journal of Psychiatry, 159,* 1284–1293.

Seitz, V., & Apfel, N. H. (2005). Creating effective school-based interventions for pregnant teenagers. In R. DeV. Peters, B. Leadbeater, & R. J. McMahon (Eds.), *Resilience in children, families, and communities: Linking context to practice and policy* (pp. 65–82). New York: Kluwer Academic.

Selman, R. L. (1976). Social-cognitive understanding: A guide to educational and clinical practice. In T. Lickona (Ed.), *Moral development and behavior: Theory, research, and social issues* (pp. 299–316). New York: Holt, Rinehart, & Winston.

Selman, R. L. (1980). *The growth of interpersonal understanding.* New York: Academic Press.

Selman, R. L., & Byrne, D. F. (1974). A structural-developmental analysis of levels of role taking in middle childhood. *Child Development, 45,* 803–806.

Sen, M. G., Yonas, A., & Knill, D. C. (2001). Development of infants' sensitivity to surface contour information for spatial layout. *Perception, 30,* 167–176.

Senechal, M., & LeFevre, J. (2002). Parental involvement in the development of children's reading skill: A five-year longitudinal study. *Child Development, 73,* 445–460.

Serafini, T. E., & Adams, G. R. (2002). Functions of identity: Scale construction and validation. *Identity: An International Journal of Theory and Research, 2,* 361–389.

Serbin, L. A., Powlishta, K. K., & Gulko, J. (1993). The development of sex typing in middle childhood. *Monographs of the Society for Research in Child Development, 58*(2, Serial No. 232).

Sermon, K., Van Steirteghem, A., & Liebaers, I. (2004). Preimplantation genetic diagnosis. *Lancet, 363,* 1633–1641.

Serpell, R., Sonnenschein, S., Baker, L., & Ganapathy, H. (2002). Intimate culture of families in the early socialization of literacy. *Journal of Family Psychology, 16,* 391–405.

Service Canada. (2005). *Canadian youth: Who are they and what do they want?* Retrieved from www.youth.gc.ca

Sesame Workshop. (2005). *Sesame workshop.* Retrieved from www.sesameworkshop.org

Seward, R. R., Yeats, D. E., & Zottarelli, L. K. (2002). Parental leave and father involvement in child care: Sweden and the United States. *Journal of Comparative Family Studies, 33,* 387–399.

Seymour, S. C. (1999). *Women, family, and child care in India.* Cambridge, UK: Cambridge University Press.

Shahar, S. (1990). *Childhood in the Middle Ages.* London: Routledge & Kegan Paul.

Shainess, N. (1961). A re-evaluation of some aspects of femininity through a study of menstruation: A preliminary report. *Comparative Psychiatry, 2,* 20–26.

Shanahan, M. J., Mortimer, J. T., & Krüger, H. (2002). Adolescence and adult work in the twenty-first century. *Journal of Research on Adolescence, 12,* 99–120.

Shankaran, S., Laptook, A. R., Ehrenkranz, R. A., Tyson, J. E., McDonald, S. A., & Donovan, E. F. (2005). Whole-body hypothermia for neonates with hypoxic–ischemic encephalopathy. *New England Journal of Medicine, 353,* 1574–1584.

Shapiro, A. E., Gottman, J. M., & Carrere, S. (2000). The baby and the marriage: Identifying factors that buffer against decline in marital satisfaction after the first baby arrives. *Journal of Family Psychology, 14,* 59–70.

Shapka, J. D., & Keating, D. P. (2005). Structure and change in self-concept during adolescence. *Canadian Journal of Behavioural Science, 37,* 83–96.

Sharma, S. K., & Leveno, K. J. (2003). Regional analgesia and progress of labor. *Clinical Obstetrics and Gynecology, 46,* 633–645.

Shaver, P., Furman, W., & Buhrmester, D. (1985). Transition to college: Network changes, social skills, and loneliness. In S. Duck & D. Perlman (Eds.), *Understanding personal relationships: An interdisciplinary approach* (pp. 193–219). London: Sage.

Shaw, D. S., Gilliom, M., Ingoldsby, E. M., & Nagin, D. S. (2003). Trajectories leading to school-age conduct problems. *Developmental Psychology, 39,* 189–200.

Shaw, D. S., Winslow, E. B., & Flanagan, C. (1999). A prospective study of the effects of marital status and family relations on young children's adjustment among African-American and European-American families. *Child Development, 70,* 742–755.

Shea, B. T., & Bailey, R. C. (1996). Allometry and adaptation of body proportions and stature in African pygmies. *American Journal of Physical Anthropology, 100,* 311–340.

Shedler, J., & Block, J. (1990). Adolescent drug use and psychological health: A longitudinal inquiry. *American Psychologist, 45,* 612–630.

Sheehan, G., Darlington, Y., Noller, P., & Feeney, J. (2004). Children's perceptions of their sibling relationships during parental separation and divorce. *Journal of Divorce and Remarriage, 41,* 69–94.

Sheehy, A., Gasser, T., Molinari, L., & Largo, R. H. (1999). An analysis of variance of the pubertal and midgrowth spurts for length and width. *Annals of Human Biology, 26,* 309–331.

Sheldon, J. P. (2004). Gender stereotypes in educational software for young children. *Sex Roles, 51,* 433–444.

Shenkin, J. D., Broffitt, B., Levy, S. M., & Warren, J. J. (2004). The association between environmental tobacco smoke and primary tooth caries. *Journal of Public Health Dentistry, 64,* 184–186.

Sherrill, C. L., & Pinderhughes, E. E. (1999). Conceptions of family and adoption among older adoptees. *Adoption Quarterly, 2,* 21–48.

Sherry, B., McDivitt, J., Brich, L. L., Cook, F. H., Sanders, S., Prish, J. L., Francis, L. A., & Scanlon, K. S. (2004). Attitudes, practices, and concerns about child feeding and child weight status among soicioeconomically diverse white, Hispanic, and African-American mothers. *Journal of the American Dietetic Association, 104,* 215–221.

Shimizu, H. (2001). Japanese adolescent boys' senses of empathy (omoiyari) and Carol Gilligan's perspectives on the morality of care: A phenomenological approach. *Culture and Psychology, 7*, 453–475.

Shipman, H. L., Brickhouse, N. W., Dagher, Z., & Letts, W. J., IV. (2002). Changes in student views of religion and science in a college astronomy course. *Science Education, 86*, 526–547.

Shipman, K. L., Zeman, J., Nesin, A. E., & Fitzgerald, M. (2003). Children's strategies for displaying anger and sadness: What works with whom? *Merrill-Palmer Quarterly, 49*, 100–122.

Shonk, S. M., & Cicchetti, D. (2001). Maltreatment, competency deficits, and risk for academic and behavioral maladjustment. *Developmental Psychology, 37*, 3–17.

Shonkoff, J., & Phillips, D. (Eds.). (2001). *Neurons to neighborhoods: The science of early childhood development.* Washington, DC: National Academy Press.

Shulman, S., & Kipnis, O. (2001). Adolescent romantic relationships: A look from the future. *Journal of Adolescence, 24*, 337–351.

Shure, M. B., & Aberson, B. (2005). Enhancing the process of resilience through effective thinking. In S. Goldstein & R. B. Brooks (Eds.), *Handbook of resilience in children* (pp. 373–394). New York: Kluwer Academic.

Shweder, R. A., Goodnow, J. J., Hatano, G., LeVine, R. A., Markus, H. R., & Miller, P. J. (2006). The cultural psychology of development: One mind, many mentalities. In R. M. Lerner (Ed.), *Handbook of child psychology: Vol. 1. Theoretical models of human development* (6th ed., pp. 716–792). Hoboken, NJ: Wiley.

Sidebotham, P., Heron, J., & the ALSPAC Study Team. (2003). Child maltreatment in the "children of the nineties": The role of the child. *Child Abuse and Neglect, 27*, 337–352.

Siegler, R. S. (1995). How does change occur? A microgenetic study of number conservation. *Cognitive Psychology, 28*, 225–273.

Siegler, R. S. (1996). *Emerging minds: The process of change in children's thinking.* New York: Oxford University Press.

Siegler, R. S. (2002). Microgenetic studies of self-explanation. In N. Granott & J. Parziale (Eds.), *Microdevelopment: Transition processes in development and learning* (pp. 31–58). New York: Cambridge University Press.

Siegler, R. S. (2006). Microgenetic analyses of learning. In D. Kuhn & R. Siegler (Eds.), *Handbook of child psychology: Vol. 2. Cognition, perception, and language* (6th ed., pp. 464–510). Hoboken, NJ: Wiley.

Siegler, R. S., & Alibali, M. W. (2005). *Children's thinking* (4th ed.). Upper Saddle River, NJ: Prentice-Hall.

Siegler, R. S., & Booth, J. L. (2004). Development of numerical estimation in young children. *Child Development, 75*, 428–444.

Siegler, R. S., & Crowley, K. (1991). The microgenetic method: A direct means for studying cognitive development. *American Psychologist, 46*, 606–620.

Siegler, R. S., & Jenkins, E. A. (1989). *How children discover new strategies.* Hillsdale, NJ: Erlbaum.

Siegler, R. S., & Svetina, M. (2006). What leads children to adopt new strategies? A microgenetic/cross-sectional study of class inclusion. *Child Development, 77*, 997–1015.

Siervogel, R. M., Maynard, L. M., Wisemandle, W. A., Roche, A. F., Guo, S. S., Chumlea, W. C., & Towne, B. (2000). Annual changes in total body fat and fat-free mass in children from 8 to 18 years in relation to changes in body mass index: The Fels Longitudinal Study. *Annals of the New York Academy of Sciences, 904*, 420–423.

Sigman, M. (1995). Nutrition and child development: More food for thought. *Current Directions in Psychological Science, 4*, 52–55.

Sigman, M. (1999). Developmental deficits in children with Down syndrome. In H. Tager-Flusberg (Ed.), *Neurodevelopmental disorders: Developmental cognitive neuroscience* (pp. 179–195). Cambridge, MA: MIT Press.

Sigman, M., Cohen, S. E., & Beckwith, L. (1997). Why does infant attention predict adolescent intelligence? *Infant Behavior and Development, 20*, 133–140.

Signorielli, N. (2001). Television's gender-role images and contribution to stereotyping. In D. G. Singer & J. L. Singer (Eds.), *Handbook of children and the media* (pp. 341–358). Thousand Oaks, CA: Sage.

Silberglitt, B., Appleton, J. J., Burns, M. K., & Jimerson, S. R. (2006). Examining the effects of grade retention on student reading performance: A longitudinal study. *Journal of School Psychology, 44*, 255–270.

Silk, J. S., Morris, A. S., Kanaya, T., & Steinberg, L. D. (2003). Psychological control and autonomy granting: Opposite ends of a continuum or distinct constructs? *Journal of Research on Adolescence, 13*, 113–128.

Silva, I. dos Santos, De Stavola, B. L., Hardy, R. J., Kuh, D. J., McCormack, V. A., & Wadsworth, M. E. J. (2004). Is the association of birth weight with premenopausal breast cancer risk mediated through childhood growth? *British Journal of Cancer, 91*, 519–524.

Silvén, M. (2001). Attention in very young infants predicts learning of first words. *Infant Behavior and Development, 24*, 229–237.

Silver, E. J., & Bauman, L. J. (2006). The association of sexual experience with attitudes, beliefs, and risk behaviors of inner-city adolescents. *Journal of Research on Adolescence, 16*, 29–45.

Silverman, B. E., Goodine, W. M., Ladouceur, M. G., & Quinn, J. (2001). Learning needs of nurses working in Canada's First Nations communities and hospitals. *Journal of Continuing Education in Nursing, 32*, 38–45.

Silverman, J. G., Raj, A., Mucci, L. A., & Hathaway, J. E. (2001). Dating violence against adolescent girls and associated substance use, unhealthy weight control, sexual risk behavior, pregnancy, and suicidality. *Journal of the American Medical Association, 286*, 572–579.

Sim, T. N., & Koh, S. F. (2003). A domain conceptualization of adolescent susceptibility to peer pressure. *Journal of Research on Adolescence, 13*, 57–80.

Simcock, G., & Hayne, H. (2002). Breaking the barrier? Children fail to translate their preverbal memories into language. *Psychological Science, 13*, 225–231.

Simcock, G., & Hayne, H. (2003). Age-related changes in verbal and nonverbal memory during early childhood. *Developmental Psychology, 39*, 805–814.

Simion, F., Cassia, V. M., Turati, C., & Valenza, E. (2001). The origins of face perception: Specific versus non-specific mechanisms. *Infant and Child Development, 10*, 59–65.

Simoneau, M., & Markovits, H. (2003). Reasoning with premises that are not empirically true: Evidence for the role of inhibition and retrieval. *Developmental Psychology, 39*, 964–975.

Simons, D. J., & Keil, F. C. (1995). An abstract to concrete shift in the development of biological thought: The insider story. *Cognition, 56*, 129–163.

Simons, R. L., Whitbeck, L. B., Conger, R. D., & Chyi-In, W. (1991). Intergenerational transmission of harsh parenting. *Developmental Psychology, 27*, 159–171.

Simons-Morton, B. G., & Haynie, D. L. (2003). Growing up drug free: A developmental challenge. In M. H. Bornstein, L. Davidson, C. L. M. Keyes, K. A. Moore, & the Center for Child Well-Being (Eds.), *Well-being: Positive development across the life course* (pp. 109–122). Mahwah, NJ: Erlbaum.

Simpson, J. A., Rholes, W. S., Campbell, L., Tran, S., & Wilson, C. L. (2003). Adult attachment, the transition to parenthood, and depressive symptoms. *Journal of Personality and Social Psychology, 84*, 1172–1187.

Simpson, J. L., de la Cruz, F., Swerdloff, R. S., Samango-Sprouse, C., Skakkebaek, N. E., & Graham, J. M., Jr. (2003). Klinefelter syndrome: Expanding the phenotype and identifying new research directions. *Genetic Medicine, 5*, 460–468.

Simpson, J. M. (2001). Infant stress and sleep deprivation as an aetiological basis for the sudden infant death syndrome. *Early Human Development, 61*, 1–43.

Singer, D. G., & Singer, J. L. (2005). *Imagination and play in the electronic age.* Cambridge, MA: Harvard University Press.

Singer, L. T., Arendt, R., Minnes, S., Farkas, K., Salvator, A., Kirchner, H. L., & Kliegman, R. (2002a). Cognitive and motor outcomes of cocaine-exposed infants. *Journal of the American Medical Association, 287*, 1952–1960.

Singer, L. T., Minnes, S., Short, E., Arendt, R., Farkas, K., Lewis, B., & Klein, N. (2004). Cognitive outcomes of preschool children with prenatal cocaine exposure. *Journal of the American Medical Association, 291*, 2448–2456.

Singer, L. T., Salvator, A., Arendt, R., Minnes, S., Farkas, K., & Kliegman, R. (2002b). Effects of cocaine/polydrug exposure and maternal psychological distress on infant birth outcomes. *Neurotoxicology and Teratology, 24*, 127–135.

Singleton, J. L., & Newport, E. L. (2004). When learners surpass their models: The acquisition of American Sign Language from inconsistent input. *Cognitive Psychology, 49*, 370–407.

Sinkkonen, J., Anttila, R., & Siimes, M. A. (1998). Pubertal maturation and changes in self-image in early adolescent Finnish boys. *Journal of Youth and Adolescence, 27*, 209–218.

Sinnott, J. D. (2003). Postformal thought and adult development: Living in balance. In J. Demic & C. Andreoletti (Eds.), *Handbook of adult development* (pp. 221–238). New York: Kluwer Academic.

Skiba, R. J., & Rausch, M. K. (2006). Zero tolerance, suspension, and expulsion: Questions of equity and effectiveness. In C. M. Evertson & C. S. Weinstein (Eds.), *Handbook of classroom management: Research, practice, and contemporary issues* (pp. 1063–1089). Mahwah, NJ: Erlbaum.

Skinner, B. F. (1957). *Verbal behavior.* New York: Appleton-Century-Crofts.

Skinner, E. A., Zimmer-Gembeck, M. J., & Connell, J. P. (1998). Individual differences and the development of perceived control. *Monographs of the Society for Research in Child Development, 63*(2–3, Serial No. 254).

Skoe, E. S. A. (1998). The ethic of care: Issues in moral development. In E. E. A. Skoe & A. L. von der Lippe (Eds.), *Personality development in adolescence* (pp. 143–171). London: Routledge.

Slack, K. S., & Yoo, J. (2005). Food hardship and child behavior problems among low-income children. *Social Service Review, 79*, 511–536.

Slade, A., Belsky, J., Aber, J. L., & Phelps, J. L. (1999). Mothers' representations of their relationships with their toddlers: Links to adult attachment and observed mothering. *Developmental Psychology, 35*, 611–619.

Slater, A. (2001). Visual perception. In G. Bremner & A. Fogel (Eds.), *Blackwell handbook of infant development* (pp. 5–34). Malden, MA: Blackwell.

Slater, A., Bremner, G., Johnson, S. P., Sherwood, P., Hayes, R., & Brown, E. (2000). Newborn infants' preference for attractive faces: The role of internal and external facial features. *Infancy, 1*, 265–274.

Slater, A., Brown, E., Mattock, A., & Bornstein, M. H. (1996). Continuity and change in habituation in the first 4 months from birth. *Journal of Reproductive and Infant Psychology, 14*, 187–194.

Slater, A., & Johnson, S. P. (1999). Visual sensory and perceptual abilities of the newborn: Beyond the blooming, buzzing confusion. In A. Slater & S. P. Johnson (Eds.), *The development of sensory, motor and cognitive capacities in early infancy* (pp. 121–141). Hove, U.K.: Sussex Press.

Slater, A., & Quinn, P. C. (2001). Face recognition in the newborn infant. *Infant and Child Development, 10*, 21–24.

Slaughter, V., Jaakkola, R., & Carey, S. (1999). Constructing a coherent theory: Children's biological understanding of life and death. In M. Siegel & C. C. Petersen (Eds.), *Children's understanding of biology and health* (pp. 71–96). Cambridge, U.K.: Cambridge University Press.

Slaughter, V., & Lyons, M. (2003). Learning about life and death in early childhood. *Cognitive Psychology, 46*, 1–30.

Slavin, R. E., Cooper, R. (1999). Improving intergroup relations: Lessons learned from cooperative learning programs. *Journal of Social Issues, 55*, 647–633.

Sleet, D. A., & Mercy, J. A. (2003). Promotion of safety, security, and well-being. In M. H. Bornstein, L. Davidson, C. M. M. Keyes, K. A. Moore, & the Center for Child Well-Being (Eds.), *Well-being: Positive development across the life course* (pp. 81–97). Mahwah, NJ: Erlbaum.

Slobin, D. I. (1985). Cross-linguistic evidence for language-making capacity. In D. I. Slobin (Ed.), *The cross-linguistic study of language acquisition: Vol. 2. Theoretical issues* (pp. 1157–1256). Hillsdale, NJ: Erlbaum.

Slobin, D. I. (1997). On the origin of grammaticalizable notions: Beyond the individual mind. In D. I. Slobin (Ed.), *The cross-linguistic study of language acquisition: Vol. 5* (pp. 265–324). Hillsdale, NJ: Erlbaum.

Sluzenski, J., Newcombe, N. S., & Kovacs, S. L. (2006). Binding, relational memory, and recall of naturalistic events: A developmental perspective. *Journal of Experimental Psychology: Learning, Memory, and Cognition, 32,* 89–100.

Slyper, A. H. (2006). The pubertal timing controversy in the USA, and a review of possible causative factors for the advance in timing of onset of puberty. *Clinical Endocrinology, 65,* 1–8.

Small, M. (1998). *Our babies, ourselves.* New York: Anchor.

Smetana, J., & Daddis, C. (2002). Domain-specific antecedents of parental psychological control and monitoring: The role of parenting beliefs and practices. *Child Development, 73,* 563–580.

Smetana, J. G. (2002). Culture, autonomy, and personal jurisdiction in adolescent–parent relationships. In R. V. Kail & H. W. Reese (Eds.), *Advances in child development and behavior* (Vol. 29, pp. 51–87). San Diego, CA: Academic Press.

Smetana, J. G. (2006). Social-cognitive domain theory: Consistencies and variations in children's moral and social judgments. In M. Killen & J. G. Smetana (Eds.), *Handbook of moral development* (pp. 119–154). Mahwah, NJ: Erlbaum.

Smith, B. H., Barkley, R. A., & Shapiro, C. J. (2006). Attention-deficit/hyperactivity disorder. In E. J. Mash & R. A. Barkley (Eds.), *Treatment of childhood disorders* (3rd ed., pp. 65–136). New York: Guilford.

Smith, G. C. S., Pell, J. P., Cameron, A. D., & Dobbie, R. (2002b). Risk of perinatal death associated with labor after previous cesarean delivery in uncomplicated term pregnancies. *Journal of the American Medical Association, 287,* 2684–2690.

Smith, J., Duncan, G. J., & Lee, K. (2003). The black–white test score gap in young children: Contributions of test and family characteristics. *Applied Developmental Science, 7,* 239–252.

Smith, J. R., Brooks-Gunn, J., Kohen, D., & McCarton, C. (2001). Transitions on and off AFDC: Implications for parenting and children's cognitive development. *Child Development, 72,* 1512–1533.

Smith, K. E., Landry, S. H., Swank, P. R., Baldwin, C. D., Denson, S. E., & Wildin, S. (1996). The relation of medical risk and maternal stimulation with preterm infants' development of cognitive, language, and daily living skills. *Journal of Child Psychology and Psychiatry, 37,* 855–864.

Smith, L. B., Jones, S. S., Landau, B., Gershkoff-Stowe, L., & Samuelson, L. (2002a). Object name learning provides on-the-job training for attention. *Psychological Science, 13,* 13–19.

Smith, P., Perrin, S., Yule, W., & Rabe-Hesketh, S. (2001). War exposure and maternal reactions in the psychological adjustment of children from Bosnia-Hercegovina. *Journal of Child Psychology and Psychiatry and Allied Disciplines, 42,* 395–404.

Smith, P. K. (2003). Play and peer relations. In A. Slater & G. Bremner (Eds.), *An introduction to developmental psychology* (pp. 311–333). Malden, MA: Blackwell.

Smith, P. K., Ananiadou, K., & Cowie, H. (2003). Interventions to reduce school bullying. *Canadian Journal of Psychiatry, 48,* 591–599.

Smith, R. (1999). The timing of birth. *Scientific American, 280*(3), 68–75.

Smylie, J. (2001). A guide for health professionals working with Aboriginal peoples. *Journal of the Society of Obstetricians and Gynaecologists of Canada, 100,* 2–15.

Snarey, J. (1995). In a communitarian voice: The sociological expansion of Kohlbergian theory, research, and practice. In W. M. Kurtines & J. L. Gewirtz (Eds.), *Moral development: An introduction* (pp. 109–134). Boston: Allyn and Bacon.

Snarey, J. R., & Bell, D. (2003). Distinguishing structural and functional models of human development: A response to "what transits in an identity status transition?" *Identity, 3,* 221–230.

Snarey, J. R., Reimer, J., & Kohlberg, L. (1985). The development of social– moral reasoning among kibbutz adolescents: A longitudinal cross-cultural study. *Developmental Psychology, 21,* 3–17.

Snell, E. K., Adam, E. K., & Duncan, G. J. (2007). Sleep and the body mass index and overweight status of children and adolescents. *Child Development, 78,* 309–323.

Snidman, N., Kagan, J., Riordan, L., & Shannon, D. C. (1995). Cardiac function and behavioral reactivity. *Psychophysiology, 32,* 199–207.

Snow, C. E., & Kang, J. Y. (2006). Becoming bilingual, biliterate, and bicultural. In K. A. Renninger & I. E. Sigel (Eds.), *Handbook of child psychology: Vol. 4. Child psychology in practice* (6th ed., pp. 75–102). Hoboken, NJ: Wiley.

Snow, C. E., Pan, B. A., Imbens-Bailey, A., & Herman, J. (1996). Learning how to say what one means: A longitudinal study of children's speech act use. *Social Development, 5,* 56–84.

Snyder, J., Brooker, M., Patrick, M. R., Snyder, A., Schrepferman, L., & Stoolmiller, M. (2003). Observed peer victimization during early elementary school: Continuity, growth, and relation to risk for child antisocial and depressive behavior. *Child Development, 74,* 1881–1898.

Sobel, D. M. (2006). How fantasy benefits young children's understanding of pretense. *Developmental Science, 9,* 63–75.

Society for Research in Child Development. (1993). Ethical standards for research with children. In *Directory of Members* (pp. 337–339). Ann Arbor, MI: Author.

Soderstrom, M., Seidl, A., Nelson, D. G. K., & Jusczyk, P. W. (2003). The prosodic bootstrapping of phrases: Evidence from prelinguistic infants. *Journal of Memory and Language, 49,* 249–267.

Solomon, G. B., & Bredemeier, B. J. L. (1999). Children's moral conceptions of gender stratification in sport. *International Journal of Sport Psychology, 30,* 350–368.

Solomon, G. E. A., & Johnson, S. C. (2000). Conceptual change in the classroom: Teaching young children to understand biological inheritance. *British Journal of Development Psychology, 18,* 81–96.

Sondergaard, C., Henriksen, T. B., Obel, C., & Wisborg, K. (2002). Smoking during pregnancy and infantile colic. *Journal of the American Academy of Child and Adolescent Psychiatry, 41,* 147.

Sophian, C. (1995). Representation and reasoning in early numerical development: Counting, conservation, and comparisons between sets. *Child Development, 66,* 559–577.

Sørensen, T. I., Holst, C., & Stunkard, A. J. (1998). Adoption study of environmental modifications of the genetic influences on obesity. *International Journal of Obesity and Related Metabolic Disorders, 22,* 73–81.

Sosa, R., Kennell, J., Klaus, M., Robertson, S., & Urrutia, J. (1980). The effect of a supportive companion on perinatal problems, length of labor, and mother–infant interaction. *New England Journal of Medicine, 303,* 597–600.

Sowell, E. R., Trauner, D. A., Camst, A., & Jernigan, T. (2002). Development of cortical and subcortical brain structures in childhood and adolescence: A structural MRI study. *Developmental Medicine and Child Neurology, 44,* 4–16.

Spätling, L., & Spätling, G. (1988). Magnesium supplementation in pregnancy: A double-blind study. *British Journal of Obstetrics and Gynecology, 95,* 120–125.

Spear, L. P. (2004). Adolescent brain development and animal models. In R. E. Dahl & L. P. Spear (Eds.), *Adolescent brain development: Vulnerabilities and opportunities* (pp. 23–26). New York: New York Academy of Sciences.

Speece, D. L., Ritchey, K. D., Cooper, D. H., Roth, F. P., & Schatschneider, C. (2004). Growth in early reading skills from kindergarten to third grade. *Contemporary Educational Psychology, 29,* 312–332.

Speece, M. W., & Brent, S. B. (1996). The development of children's understanding of death. In C. A. Corr & D. M. Corr (Eds.), *Handbook of childhood death and bereavement* (pp. 29–50). New York: Springer.

Speicher, B. (1994). Family patterns of moral judgment during adolescence and early adulthood. *Developmental Psychology, 30,* 624–632.

Spelke, E. (2000). Core knowledge. *American Psychologist, 55,* 1233–1242.

Spelke, E. S., & Hermer, L. (1996). Early cognitive development: Objects and space. In R. Gelman & T. K. Au (Eds.), *Perceptual and cognitive development* (pp. 71–114). San Diego: Academic Press.

Spelke, E. S., & Newport, E. L. (1998). Nativism, empiricism, and the development of knowledge. In R. M. Lerner (Ed.), *Handbook of child psychology: Vol. 1. Theoretical models of human development* (5th ed., pp. 199–254). New York: Wiley.

Spence, M. J., & DeCasper, A. J. (1987). Prenatal experience with lowfrequency maternal voice sounds influences neonatal perception of maternal voice samples. *Infant Behavior and Development, 10,* 133–142.

Spencer, J. P., & Schöner, G. (2003). Bridging the representational gap in the dynamic systems approach to development. *Developmental Science, 6,* 392–412.

Spencer, J. P., Verejiken, B., Diedrich, F. J., & Thelen, E. (2000). Posture and the emergence of manual skills. *Developmental Science, 3,* 216–233.

Spencer, P. E. (2000). Looking without listening: Is audition a prerequisite for normal development of visual attention in infancy? *Journal of Deaf Studies and Education, 5,* 291–302.

Spencer, P. E., & Lederberg, A. (1997). Different modes, different models: Communication and language of young deaf children and their mothers. In L. B. Adamson & M. Romski (Eds.), *Communication and language acquisition: Discoveries from atypical development* (pp. 203–230). Baltimore: Paul H. Brookes.

Spencer, P. E., & Meadow-Orlans, K. P. (1996). Play, language, and maternal responsiveness: A longitudinal study of deaf and hearing infants. *Child Development, 67,* 3176–3191.

Spera, C. (2005). A review of the relationship among parenting practices, parenting styles, and adolescent school achievement. *Educational Psychology Review, 17,* 125–146.

Sperduto, R. D., Hiller, R., Podgor, M. J., Freidlin, V., Milton, R. C., Wolf, P. A., Myers, R. H., Dagostine, R. B., Roseman, M. J., Stockman, M. E., & Wilson, P. W. (1996). Familial aggregation and prevalence of myopia in the Framingham Offpring Eye Study. *Archives of Ophthalmology, 114,* 326–333.

Spere, K. A., Schmidt, L. A., Theall-Honey, L. A., & Martin-Chang, S. (2004). Expressive and receptive language skills of temperamentally shy preschoolers. *Infant and Child Development, 13,* 123–133.

Spirito, A., & Esposito-Smythers, C. (2006). Attempted and completed suicide. *Annual Review of Clinical Psychology, 2,* 237–266.

Spirito, A., Valeri, S., Boergers, J., & Donaldson, D. (2003). Predictors of continued suicidal behavior in adolescents following a suicide attempt. *Journal of Clinical Child and Adolescent Psychology, 32,* 284–289.

Spitz, R. A. (1946). Anaclitic depression. *Psychoanalytic Study of the Child, 2,* 313–342.

Spock, B., & Needlman, R. (2004). *Dr. Spock's baby and child care* (8th ed.). New York: Pocket.

Spokane, A. R., & Cruza-Guet, M. C. (2005). Holland's theory of vocational personalities in work environments. In S. D. Brown & R. W. Lent (Eds.), *Career development and counseling* (pp. 24–41). Hoboken, NJ: Wiley.

Sport Canada. (2003). *Youth participation in sport.* Retrieved from www.pch.gc.ca/progs/sc/info-fact/youth_e.cfm

Spruijt-Metz, D., Lindquist, C. H., Birch, L. L., Fisher, J. O., & Goran, M. I. (2002). Relation between mothers' child-feeding practices and children's adiposity. *American Journal of Clinical Nutrition, 75,* 581–586.

Sridhar, D., & Vaughn, S. (2001). Social functioning of students with learning disabilities. In D. P. Hallahan & B. K. Keogh (Eds.), *Research and global perspectives in learning disabilities* (pp. 65–91). Mahwah, NJ: Erlbaum.

Sroufe, L. A. (2002). From infant attachment to promotion of adolescent autonomy: Prospective, longitudinal data on the role of parents in development. In J. G. Borkowski & S. L. Ramey (Eds.), *Parenting and the child's world* (pp. 187–202). Mahwah, NJ: Erlbaum.

Sroufe, L. A., Egeland, B., Carlson, E., & Collins, W. (2005). *Minnesota Study of Risk and Adaptation from birth to maturity: The development of the person.* New York: Guilford.

Sroufe, L. A., Egeland, B., & Kreutzer, T. (1990). The fate of early experience following developmental change: Longitudinal approaches to individual adaptation. *Child Development, 61,* 1363–1373.

Sroufe, L. A., & Waters, E. (1976). The ontogenesis of smiling and laughter: A perspective on the organization of development in infancy. *Psychological Review, 83,* 173–189.

Sroufe, L. A., & Wunsch, J. P. (1972). The development of laughter in the first year of life. *Child Development, 43,* 1324–1344.

St James-Roberts, I., Goodwin, J., Peter, B., Adams, D., & Hunt, S. (2003). Individual differences in responsivity to a neurobehavioural examination predict crying patterns of 1-week-old infants at home. *Developmental Medicine and Child Neurology, 45,* 400–407.

St. Louis, G. R., & Liem, J. H. (2005). Ego identity, ethnic identity, and the psychosocial well-being of ethnic minority and majority college students. *Identity, 5,* 227–246.

Stacey, J., & Biblarz, T. (2001). (How) Does the sexual orientation of parents matter? *American Sociological Review, 66,* 159–183.

Stack, D. M., & Muir, D. W. (1992). Adult tactile stimulation during face-to-face interactions modulates five-month-olds' affect and attention. *Child Development, 63,* 1509–1525.

Staff, J., & Uggen, C. (2003). The fruits of good work: Early work experiences and adolescent deviance. *Journal of Research in Crime and Delinquency, 40,* 263–290.

Stams, G. J. M., Juffer, F., & van IJzendoorn, M. H. (2002). Maternal sensitivity, infant attachment, and temperament in early childhood predict adjustment in middle childhood: The case of adopted children and their biologically unrelated parents. *Developmental Psychology, 38,* 806–821.

Standley, J. M. (1998). The effect of music and multimodal stimulation on responses of premature infants in neonatal intensive care. *Pediatric Nursing, 24,* 532–538.

Stanley, C., Murray, L., & Stein, A. (2004). The effect of postnatal depression on mother–infant interaction, infant response to the still-face perturbation, and performance on an instrumental learning task. *Development and Psychopathology, 16,* 1–18.

Stanovich, K. E. (2004). *How to think straight about psychology* (7th ed.). Boston: Allyn and Bacon.

Starky, S. (2005, July 15). *The obesity epidemic in Canada.* Ottawa: Parliamentary Information and Research Service. Retrieved from www.parl.gc.ca/information /library/PRBpubs/prb0511-e.htm#prevalencetxt

Statistics Canada. (2003a). *Age groups, number of grandparents, and sex for grandchildren living with grandparents with no parent present, 2001.* Retrieved from www12.statcan.ca/English/census01/products /analytic/companion/fam/provs.cfm

Statistics Canada. (2003b). *Language composition of Canada, 2001 census.* Retrieved from www.statcan.ca /english/IPS/Data

Statistics Canada. (2003c). *National Longitudinal Survey of Children and Youth: Challenges of late adolescence.* Retrieved from www.statcan.ca/Daily/English/030616 /d030616a.htm

Statistics Canada. (2003d). Suicide deaths and suicide attempts. *Health Reports 13*(2), 9–22.

Statistics Canada. (2003e). *Who goes to postsecondary education and when: Pathways chosen by 20-year-olds.* Retrieved from http://www. statcan.ca/english/IPS/Data /81-595-MIE2003006.htm

Statistics Canada. (2003f). *Women in Canada: Work chapter updates.* Retrieved from www.statcan.ca/cgi-bin /downpub/freepub.cgi

Statistics Canada. (2004a, July 8). Household Internet use survey. *The Daily.* Retrieved from www.statcan.ca/Daily /English/040708/d040708a.htm

Statistics Canada. (2004b). *Information and communications technologies in schools survey.* Retrieved from www.statcan.ca/Daily/English/040610/d040610b.htm

Statistics Canada. (2004c, June 16). Youth in Transition Survey: Education and labor market pathways of young adults. *The Daily.* Retrieved from www.statcan.ca/Daily /English/040616/d040616b.htm

Statistics Canada. (2005a, February 7). Child care. *The Daily.* Retrieved from www.statcan.ca/Daily/English /050207/d050207b.htm

Statistics Canada. (2005b, July 21). Crime statistics. *The Daily.* Retrieved from www.statcan.ca/Daily/English /050721/d050721a.htm

Statistics Canada. (2005c) *Divorces.* Retrieved from www.statcan.ca

Statistics Canada. (2005d, December 16). Education matters: Trends in dropout rates among the provinces. *The Daily.* Retrieved from www.statcan.ca/Daily /English/051216/d051216c.htm

Statistics Canada. (2005e, May 3). Food insecurity in Canadian households. *The Daily.* Retrieved from www.statcan.ca/Daily/English/050503/d050503b.htm

Statistics Canada. (2005f). *Infant mortality rates.* Retrieved from www.statcan.ca/english/Pgdb/health21.htm

Statistics Canada. (2005g). *Statistics Canada data bank and analysis of television viewing in Canada.* Retrieved from www.ctatcan.ca/english/freepub/87-008-GIE/sect /tvmain.htm

Statistics Canada. (2005h, October 11). University enrolment. *The Daily.* Retrieved from www.statcan.ca /Daily/English/051011/d051011b.htm

Statistics Canada. (2006a). *Canadian vital statistics, births.* Retrieved from www.statcan.ca/bsolc/english/bsolc ?catno=84F0210XIE#olcinfopanel

Statistics Canada. (2006b). *Education indicators in Canada: Report of the Pan-Canadian Education Indicators Program 2005.* Retrieved from www.statcan.ca/english /freepub/81-582-XIE/81-582-XIE2006001.htm

Statistics Canada. (2006c). *Population.* Retrieved from www.statcan.ca

Statistics Canada. (2006d). *Vital statistics—birth database.* Retrieved from www.statcan.ca/cgi-bin

Statistics Canada. (2007, January 17). Marriages. *The Daily.* Retrieved from www.statcan.ca/Daily/English/070117 /d070117a.htm

Stattin, H., & Kerr, M. (2000). Parental monitoring: A reinterpretation. *Child Development, 71,* 1072–1085.

Stattin, H., & Magnusson, D. (1990). *Pubertal maturation in female development.* Hillsdale, NJ: Erlbaum.

Staub, F. C., & Stern, E. (2002). The nature of teachers' pedagogical content beliefs matters for students' achievement gains: Quasi-experimental evidence from elementary mathematics. *Journal of Educational Psychology, 94,* 344–355.

Stearns, E., & Glennie, E. J. (2006). When and why dropouts leave high school. *Youth and Society, 38,* 29–57.

Steele, C. M. (1997). A threat in the air: How stereotypes shape intellectual identity and performance. *American Psychologist, 52,* 613–629.

Steele, J. (2003). Children's gender stereotypes about math: The role of stereotype stratification. *Journal of Applied Social Psychology, 33,* 2587–2606.

Steele, S., Joseph, R. M., Tager-Flusberg, H. (2003). Developmental change in theory of mind abilities in children with autism. *Journal of Austism and Developmental Disorders, 33,* 461–467.

Stehr-Green, P., Tull, P., Stellfeld, M., Mortenson, P. B., & Simpson, D. (2003). Autism and thimerosal-containing vaccines: Lack of consistent evidence for an association. *American Journal of Preventive Medicine, 25,* 101–106.

Stein, J. H., & Reiser, L. W. (1994). A study of white middle-class adolescent boys' responses to "semenarche" (the first ejaculation). *Journal of Youth and Adolescence, 23,* 373–384.

Stein, N., & Levine, L. J. (1999). The early emergence of emotional understanding and appraisal: Implications for theories of development. In T. Dalgleish & M. J. Power (Eds.), *Handbook of cognition and emotion* (pp. 383–408). Chichester, U.K.: Wiley.

Stein, Z., Susser, M., Saenger, G., & Marolla, F. (1975). *Famine and human development: The Dutch hunger winter of 1944–1945.* New York: Oxford.

Steinberg, L. (1986). Latchkey children and susceptibility to peer pressure: An ecological analysis. *Developmental Psychology, 22,* 433–439.

Steinberg, L. (2001). We know some things: Parent–adolescent relationships in retrospect and prospect. *Journal of Research on Adolescence, 11,* 1–19.

Steinberg, L., & Morris, A. S. (2001). Adolescent development. *Annual Review of Psychology, 52,* 83–110.

Steinberg, L., & Silk, J. S. (2002). Parenting adolescents. In M. H. Bornstein (Ed.), *Handbook of parenting: Vol. 1. Children and parenting* (pp. 103–134). Mahwah, NJ: Erlbaum.

Steinberg, L. D., Darling, N. E., & Fletcher, A. C. (1995). Authoritative parenting and adolescent development: An ecological journey. In P. Moen, G. H. Elder, Jr., & K. Luscher (Eds.), *Examining lives in context* (pp. 423–466). Washington, DC: American Psychological Association.

Steinberg, S., & Bellavance, F. (1999). Characteristics and treatment of women with antenatal and postpartum depression. *International Journal of Psychiatry in Medicine, 29,* 209–233.

Steiner, J. E. (1979). Human facial expression in response to taste and smell stimulation. In H. W. Reese & L. P. Lipsitt

(Eds.), *Advances in child development and behavior* (Vol. 13, pp. 257–295). New York: Academic Press.

Steiner, J. E., Glaser, D., Hawilo, M. E., & Berridge, D. C. (2001). Comparative expression of hedonic impact: Affective reactions to taste by human infants and other primates. *Neuroscience and Biobehavioral Review, 25,* 53–74.

Steinhausen, C. (2006). Eating disorders: Anorexia nervosa and bulimia nervosa. In C. Gillberg, R. Harrington, & H. Steinhausen (Eds.), *A clinician's handbook of child and adolescent psychiatry* (pp. 272–303). New York: Cambridge University Press.

Stenberg, C., & Campos, J. (1990). The development of anger expressions in infancy. In N. Stein, B. Leventhal, & T. Trabasso (Eds.), *Psychological and biological approaches to emotion* (pp. 247–282). Hillsdale, NJ: Erlbaum.

Stenberg, G. (2003). Effects of maternal inattentiveness on infant social referencing. *Infant and Child Development, 12,* 399–419.

Stern, D. (1985). *The interpersonal world of the infant.* New York: Basic Books.

Stern, M., & Karraker, K. H. (1989). Sex stereotyping of infants: A review of gender labeling studies. *Sex Roles, 20,* 501–522.

Sternberg, R. J. (2001). Beyond *g*: The theory of successful intelligence. In R. J. Sternberg & E. L. Grigorenko (Eds.), *The general factor of intelligence: How general is it?* (pp. 447–479). Mahwah, NJ: Erlbaum.

Sternberg, R. J. (2002). Intelligence is not just inside the head: The theory of successful intelligence. In J. Aronson (Ed.), *Improving academic achievement* (pp. 227–244). San Diego, CA: Academic Press.

Sternberg, R. J. (2003a). A broad view of intelligence: The theory of successful intelligence. *Consulting Psychology Journal: Practice and Research, 55,* 139–154.

Sternberg, R. J. (2003b). The development of creativity as a decision-making process. In R. K. Sawyer, V. John-Steiner, S. Moran, R. J. Sternberg, D. H. Feldman, J. Nakamura, & M. Csikszentmihalyi (Eds.), *Creativity and development* (pp. 91–138). New York: Oxford University Press.

Sternberg, R. J. (2005). The triarchic theory of successful intelligence. In D. P. Flanagan & P. L. Harrison (Eds.), *Contemporary intellectual assessment: Theories, tests, and issues* (pp. 103–119). New York: Guilford.

Sternberg, R. J., Forsythe, G. B., Hedlund, J., Horvath, J. A., Wagner, R. K., Williams, W. M., Snook, S. A., & Grigorenko, E. L. (2000). *Practical intelligence in everyday life.* Cambridge, U.K.: Cambridge University Press.

Sternberg, R. J., & Grigorenko, E. L. (2002). *Dynamic testing.* New York: Cambridge University Press.

Sternberg, R. J., & Jarvin, L. (2003). Alfred Binet's contributions as a paradigm for impact in psychology. In R. J. Sternberg (Ed.), *The anatomy of impact: What makes the great works of psychology great* (pp. 89– 107). Washington, DC: American Psychological Association.

Sternberg, R. J., & Lubart, T. I. (1995). *Defying the crowd.* New York: Basic Books.

Sternberg, R. J., & Lubart, T. I. (1996). Investing in creativity. *American Psychologist, 51,* 677–688.

Stetsenko, A., Little, T. D., Gordeeva, T., Grasshof, M., & Oettingen, G. (2000). Gender effects in children's beliefs about school performance. *Child Development, 21,* 517–527.

Stettler, N., Stallings, V. A., Troxel, A. B., Zhao, J., Schinnar, R., Nelson, S. E., Ziegler, E. E., & Strom, B. L. (2005). Weight gain in the first week of life and overweight in adulthood: A cohort study of European American subjects fed infant formula. *Circulation, 111,* 1897–18903.

Stevenson, H. W. (1994). Extracurricular programs in East Asian schools. *Teachers College Record, 95,* 389–407.

Stevenson, H. W., Lee, S., & Mu, X. (2000). Successful achievement in mathematics: China and the United States. In C. F. M. van Lieshout & P. G. Heymans (Eds.), *Developing talent across the lifespan* (pp. 167– 183). Philadelphia: Psychology Press.

Stevenson, R., & Pollitt, C. (1987). The acquisition of temporal terms. *Journal of Child Language, 14,* 533–545.

Stevens-Simon, C., Sheeder, J., & Harter, S. (2005). Teen contraceptive decisions: Childbearing intentions are the tip of the iceberg. *Women and Health, 42,* 55–73.

Steward, D. K. (2001). Behavioral characteristics of infants with nonorganic failure to thrive during a play interaction. *American Journal of Maternal Child Nursing, 26,* 79–85.

Stewart, P., Reihman, J., Lonky, E., Darvill, T., & Pagano, J. (2000). Prenatal PCB exposure and neonatal behavioral assessment scale (NBAS) performance. *Neurotoxicology and Teratology, 22,* 21–29.

Stewart, R. B., Jr. (1990). *The second child: Family transition and adjustment.* Newbury Park, CA: Sage.

Stice, E. (2003). Puberty and body image. In C. Hayward (Ed.), *Gender differences at puberty* (pp. 61–76). New York: Cambridge University Press.

Stice, E., Presnell, K., & Bearman, S. K. (2001). Relation of early menarche to depression, eating disorders, substance abuse, and comorbid psychopathology among adolescent girls. *Developmental Psychology, 37,* 608–619.

Stifter, C. A., Coulehan, C. M., & Fish, M. (1993). Linking employment to attachment: The mediating effects of maternal separation anxiety and interactive behavior. *Child Development, 64,* 1451–1460.

Stiles, J. (2001a). Neural plasticity in cognitive development. *Developmental Neuropsychology, 18,* 237–272.

Stiles, J. (2001b). Spatial cognitive development. In C. A. Nelson & M. Luciana (Eds.), *Handbook of developmental cognitive neuroscience* (pp. 399–414). Cambridge, MA: MIT Press.

Stiles, J., Bates, E. A., Thal, D., Trauner, D. A., & Reilly, J. (2002). Linguistic and spatial cognitive development in children with pre- and perinatal focal brain injury: A ten-year overview from the San Diego longitudinal project. In M. H. Johnson & Y. Munakata (Eds.), *Brain development and cognition: A reader* (2nd ed., pp. 272–291). Malden, MA: Blackwell.

Stiles, J., Moses, P., Roe, K., Akshoomoff, N. A., Trauner, D., & Hesselink, J. (2003). Alternative brain organization after prenatal cerebral injury: Convergent fMRI and cognitive data. *Journal of the International Neuropsychological Society, 9,* 604–622.

Stiles, J., Reilly, J., Paul, B., & Moses, P. (2005). Cognitive development following early brain injury: Evidence for neural adaptation. *Trends in Cognitive Sciences, 9,* 136–143.

Stilson, S. R., & Harding, C. G. (1997). Early social context as it relates to symbolic play: A longitudinal investigation. *Merrill-Palmer Quarterly, 43,* 682–693.

Stinchcomb, J. B., Bazemore, G., & Riestenberg, N. (2006). Beyond zero tolerance: Restoring justice in secondary schools. *Youth Violence and Juvenile Justice, 4,* 123–147.

Stipek, D. (1995). The development of pride and shame in toddlers. In J. P. Tangney & K. W. Fischer (Eds.), *Self-conscious emotions* (pp. 237–252). New York: Guilford.

Stipek, D. (2002). At what age should children enter kindergarten? A question for policy makers and parents. *Social Policy Report of the Society for Research in Child Development, 16*(3).

Stipek, D. (2004). Teaching practices in kindergarten and first grade: Different strokes for different folks. *Early Childhood Research Quarterly, 19,* 548–568.

Stipek, D. J., & Byler, P. (1997). Early childhood education teachers: Do they practice what they preach? *Early Childhood Research Quarterly, 12,* 305–326.

Stipek, D. J., & Byler, P. (2001). Academic achievement and social behaviors associated with age of entry into kindergarten. *Journal of Applied Developmental Psychology, 22,* 175–189.

Stipek, D. J., Gralinski, J. H., & Kopp, C. B. (1990). Self-concept development in the toddler years. *Developmental Psychology, 26,* 972–977.

Stoch, M. B., Smythe, P. M., Moodie, A. D., & Bradshaw, D. (1982). Psychosocial outcome and CT findings after growth undernourishment during infancy: A 20-year developmental study. *Developmental Medicine and Child Neurology, 24,* 419–436.

Stocker, C. J., Arch, J. R., & Cawthorne, M. A. (2005). Fetal origins of insulin resistance and obesity. *Proceedings of the Nutrition Society, 64,* 143–151.

Stockman, N. K. A., Schenkel, T. C., Brown, J. N., & Duncan, A. M. (2005). Comparison of energy and nutrient intakes among meals and snacks of adolescent males. *Preventive Medicine, 41,* 203–210.

Stone, M. R., & Brown, B. B. (1999). Identity claims and projections: Descriptions of self and crowds in secondary school. In J. A. McLellan & M. J. V. Pugh (Eds.), *The role of peer groups in adolescent social identity:*

Exploring the importance of stability and change (pp. 7–20). San Francisco: Jossey-Bass.

Stone, R. (2005). *Best classroom management practices for reaching all learners: What award-winning classroom teachers do.* Thousand Oaks, CA: Corwin Press.

Storch, S. A., & Whitehurst, G. J. (2001). The role of family and home in the literacy development of children from low-income backgrounds. In P. R. Britto & J. Brooks-Gunn (Eds.), *The role of family literacy environments in promoting young children's emerging literacy skills (New directions for child and adolescent development,* No. 92, pp. 53–71). San Francisco: Jossey-Bass.

Storey, A. E., Walsh, C. J., Quinton, R. L., & Wynn-Edwards, K. E. (2000). Hormonal correlates of paternal responsiveness in new and expectant fathers. *Evolution and Human Behavior, 21,* 79–95.

Stormshak, E. A., Bierman, K. L., McMahon, R. J., Lengua, L. J., & the Conduct Problems Prevention Research Group. (2000). Parenting practices and child disruptive behavior problems in early elementary school. *Journal of Clinical Child Psychology, 29,* 17–29.

Stouthamer-Loeber, M., Wei, E., Loeber, R., & Masten, A. S. (2004). Desistance from persistent serious delinquency in the transition to adulthood. *Development and Psychopathology, 16,* 897–918.

Strachan, T., & Read, A. (2004). *Human molecular genetics* (3rd ed.). New York: Garland Science.

Strapp, C. M., & Federico, A. (2000). Imitations and repetitions: What do children say following recasts? *First Language, 20,* 273–290.

Strassberg, Z. (1995). Social information processing in compliance situations by mothers of behavior-problem boys. *Child Development, 66,* 376–389.

Straus, M. A., & Stewart, J. H. (1999). Corporal punishment by American parents: National data on prevalence, chronicity, severity, and duration, in relation to child and family characteristics. *Clinical Child and Family Psychology Review, 2,* 55–70.

Strauss, R. S., & Pollack, H. A. (2003). Social marginalization of overweight children. *Archives of Pediatric and Adolescent Medicine, 157,* 746–752.

Strayer, L., & Roberts, W. (2004). Children's anger, emotional expressiveness, and empathy: Relations with parents' empathy, emotional expressiveness, and parenting practices. *Social Development, 13,* 229–254.

Streissguth, A. P., Bookstein, F. L., Barr, H. M., Sampson, P. D., O'Malley, K., & Young, J. K. (2004). Risk factors for adverse life outcomes in fetal alcohol syndrome and fetal alcohol effects. *Journal of Developmental and Behavioral Pediatrics, 25,* 228–238.

Streissguth, A. P., Treder, R., Barr, H. M., Shepard, T., Bleyer, W. A., Sampson, P. D., & Martin, D. (1987). Aspirin and acetaminophen use by pregnant women and subsequent child IQ and attention decrements. *Teratology, 35,* 211–219.

Streri, A. (2005). Touching for knowing in infancy: The development of manual abilities in very young infants. *European Journal of Developmental Psychology, 2,* 325–343.

Streri, A., Lhote, M., & Dutilleul, S. (2000). Haptic perception in newborns. *Developmental Science, 3,* 319–327.

Stretesky, P. B., & Lynch, M. J. (2001). The relationship between lead exposure and homicide. *Archives of Pediatrics and Adolescent Medicine, 155,* 579–582.

Striano, T., & Rochat, P. (2000). Emergence of selective social referencing in infancy. *Infancy, 1,* 253–264.

Striano, T., Tomasello, M., & Rochat, P. (2001). Social and object support for early symbolic play. *Developmental Science, 4,* 442–455.

Stright, A. D., Neitzel, C., Sears, K. G., & Hoke-Sinex, L. (2002). Instruction begins in the home: Relations between parental instruction and children's self-regulation in the classroom. *Journal of Educational Psychology, 93,* 456–466.

Strohschein, L. (2005). Parental divorce and child mental health trajectories. *Journal of Marriage and Family, 67,* 1286–1300.

Strouse, D. L. (1999). Adolescent crowd orientations: A social and temporal analysis. In J. A. McLellan & M. J. V. Pugh (Eds.), *The role of peer groups in adolescent social identity: Exploring the importance of stability and change* (pp. 37–54). San Francisco: Jossey-Bass.

Stryer, B. K., Tofler, I. R., & Lapchick, R. (1998). A developmental overview of child and youth sports in

society. *Child and Adolescent Psychiatric Clinics of North America, 7,* 697–719.

Studelska, J. V. (2006, Spring). At home in birth. *Midwifery Today,* pp. 32–33.

Styne, D. M. (2003). The regulation of pubertal growth. *Hormone Research, 60*(Suppl.1), 22–26.

Suárez-Orozco, C., & Suárez-Orozco, M. M. (2001). *Children of immigration.* Cambridge, MA: Harvard University Press.

Suarez-Orozco, C., Todorova, I., & Qin, D. B. (2006). The well-being of immigrant adolescents: A longitudinal perspective on risk and protective factors. In F. A. Villarruel & T. Luster (Eds.), *The crisis in youth mental health: Critical issues and effective programs: Vol. 2. Disorders in adolescence* (pp. 53–83). Westport, CT: Praeger.

Subbotsky, E. (2004). Magical thinking in judgments of causation: Can anomalous phenomena affect ontological causal beliefs in children and adults? *British Journal of Developmental Psychology, 22,* 123–152.

Subbotsky, E. V. (1994). Early rationality and magical thinking in preschoolers: Space and time. *British Journal of Developmental Psychology, 12,* 97–108.

Subrahmanyam, K., Greenfield, P., Kraut, R., & Gross, E. (2001). The impact of computer use on children's and adolescents' development. *Applied Developmental Psychology, 22,* 7–30.

Subrahmanyam, K., & Greenfield, P. M. (1996). Effect of video game practice on spatial skills in girls and boys. In P. M. Greenfield & R. R. Cocking (Eds.), *Interacting with video* (pp. 95–114). Norwood, NJ: Ablex.

Sullivan, M. W., & Lewis, M. (2003). Contextual determinants of anger and other negative expressions in young infants. *Developmental Psychology, 39,* 693–705.

Sullivan, S., & Glanz, J. (2006). *Building effective learning communities: Strategies for leadership, learning, and collaboration.* Thousand Oaks, CA: Corwin Press.

Sullivan, S. A., & Birch, L. L. (1990). Pass the sugar, pass the salt: Experience dictates preference. *Developmental Psychology, 26,* 546–551.

Super, C. M. (1981). Behavioral development in infancy. In R. H. Monroe, R. L. Monroe, & B. B. Whiting (Eds.), *Handbook of cross-cultural human development* (pp. 181–270). New York: Garland.

Super, D. (1980). A life-span, life-space approach to career development. *Journal of Vocational Behavior, 16,* 282–298.

Super, D. (1984). Career and life development. In D. Brown & L. Brooks (Eds.), *Career choice and development* (pp. 192–234). San Francisco: Jossey-Bass.

Susman, E. J., & Rogol, A. (2004). Puberty and psychological development. In R. M. Lerner & L. Steinberg (Eds.), *Handbook of adolescent psychology* (2nd ed., pp.15–44). Hoboken, NJ: Wiley.

Sutcliffe, A. G. (2002). Health risks in babies born after assisted reproduction. *British Medical Journal, 325,* 117–118.

Sutton, M. J., Brown, J. D., Wilson, K. M., & Klein, J. D. (2002). Shaking the tree of forbidden fruit: Where adolescents learn about sexuality and contraception. In J. D. Brown, J. R. Steele, & K. Walsh-Childers (Eds.), *Sexual teens, sexual media* (pp. 25–55). Mahwah, NJ: Erlbaum.

Svensson, A. (2000). Computers in school: Socially isolating or a tool to promote collaboration. *Journal of Educational Computing Research, 22,* 437–453.

Svirsky, M. A., Teoh, S. W., & Neuburger, H. (2004). Development of language and speech perception in congenitally profoundly deaf children as a function of age at cochlear implantation. *Audiology and Neuro-Otology, 9,* 224–233.

Swanson, J. L., & Fouad, N. A. (1999). Applying theories of person– environment fit: The transition from school to work. *Career Development Quarterly, 47,* 337–347.

Sweet, M. A., & Appelbaum, M. L. (2004). Is home visiting an effective strategy? A meta-analytic review of home visiting programs for families with young children. *Child Development, 75,* 1435–1456.

Symons, D. K. (2001). A dyad-oriented approach to distress and mother–child relationship outcomes in the first 24 months. *Parenting: Science and Practice, 1,* 101–122.

Szaflarski, J. P., Binder, J. R., Possing, E. T., McKiernan, K. A., Ward, B. D., & Hammeke, T. A. (2002). Language lateralization in left-handed and ambidextrous people: fMRI data. *Neurology, 59,* 238–244.

Szepkouski, G. M., Gauvain, M., & Carberry, M. (1994). The development of planning skills in children with and without mental retardation. *Journal of Applied Developmental Psychology, 15,* 187–206.

Szkrybalo, J., & Ruble, D. N. (1999). "God made me a girl": Sex-category constancy judgments and explanations revisited. *Developmental Psychology, 35,* 392–402.

Tacon, A., & Caldera, Y. (2001). Attachment and parental correlates in late adolescent Mexican American women. *Hispanic Journal of Behavioral Sciences, 23,* 71–88.

Taga, G., Asakawa, K., Maki, A., Konishi, Y., & Koizumi, H. (2003). Brain imaging in awake infants by near-infrared optical tomography. *Proceedings of the National Academy of Sciences, 100,* 10722–10727.

Tager-Flusberg, H. (2005). Putting words together: Morphology and syntax in the preschool years. In J. B.Gleason (Ed.), *The development of language* (5th ed., pp. 148–190). Boston: Allyn and Bacon.

Takahashi, K. (1990). Are the key assumptions of the "Strange Situation" procedure universal? A view from Japanese research. *Human Development, 33,* 23–30.

Takala, M. (2006). The effects of reciprocal teaching on reading comprehension in mainstream and special (SLI) education. *Scandinavian Journal of Educational Research, 50,* 559–576.

Tamis-LeMonda, C. S., & Bornstein, M. H. (1989). Habituation and maternal encouragement of attention in infancy as predictors of toddler language, play, and representational competence. *Child Development, 60,* 738–751.

Tamis-LeMonda, C. S., Shannon, J. D., Cabrera, N. J., & Lamb, M. E. (2004). Fathers and mothers at play with their 2- and 3-year-olds: Contributions to language and cognitive development. *Child Development, 75,* 1806–1820.

Tammelin, T., Näyhä, S., Hills, A. P., & Järvelin, M. (2003). Adolescent participation in sports and adult physical activity. *American Journal of Preventive Medicine, 24,* 22–28.

Tamminen, K. (1991). *Religious development in childhood and youth.* Helsinki, Finland: Gummerus Kirjapaino Oy.

Tamrouti-Makkink, I. D., Dubas, J. S., Gerris, J. R. M., & van Aken, A. G. (2004). The relation between the absolute level of parenting and differential parental treatment with adolescent siblings' adjustment. *Journal of Child Psychology and Psychiatry, 45,* 1397–1406.

Tandon, S. D., Parillo, K. M., & Keefer, M. (2005). Hispanic women's perceptions of patient-centeredness during prenatal care: A mixed-method study. *Birth, 32,* 312–317.

Tangney, J. P. (2001). Constructive and destructive aspects of shame and guilt. In A. C. Bohart & D. J. Stipek (Eds.), *Constructive and destructive behavior* (pp. 127–145). Washington, DC: American Psychological Association.

Tanner, J. M. (1990). *Foetus into man* (2nd ed.). Cambridge, MA: Harvard University Press.

Tanner, J. M., Healy, M., & Cameron, N. (2001). *Assessment of skeletal maturity and prediction of adult height* (3rd ed.). Philadelphia: Saunders.

Tardif, T., Gelman, S. A., & Xu, F. (1999). Putting the "noun bias" in context: A comparison of English and Mandarin. *Child Development, 70,* 620–635.

Tardif, T., Wellman, H. M., & Cheung, K. M. (2004). False belief understanding in Cantonese-speaking children. *Journal of Child Language, 31,* 779–800.

Tasker, F. (2005). Lesbian mothers, gay fathers, and their children: A review. *Developmental and Behavioral Pediatrics, 26,* 224–240.

Taumoepeau, M., & Ruffman, T. (2006). Mother and infant talk about mental states relates to desire language and emotion understanding. *Child Development, 77,* 465–481.

Taylor, E. (2004). ADHD is best understood as a cultural construct. *British Journal of Psychiatry, 184,* 8–9.

Taylor, J. H., & Walker, L. J. (1997). Moral climate and the development of moral reasoning: The effects of dyadic discussions between young offenders. *Journal of Moral Education, 26,* 21–43.

Taylor, J. S. (2002). Caregiver support for women during childbirth: Does the presence of a labor-support person affect maternal–child outcomes? *American Family Physician, 66,* 1205–1206.

Taylor, M. (1996). The development of children's beliefs about the social and biological aspects of gender differences. *Child Development, 67,* 1555–1571.

Taylor, M., & Carlson, S. M. (1997). The relation between individual differences in fantasy and theory of mind. *Child Development, 68,* 436–455.

Taylor, M., & Carlson, S. M. (2000). The influence of religious beliefs on parental attitudes about children's fantasy behavior. In K. S. Rosengren, C. N. Johnson, & P. L. Harris (Eds.), *Imagining the impossible* (pp. 247–268). New York: Cambridge University Press.

Taylor, M., Carlson, S. M., Maring, B. L., Gerow, L., & Charley, C. M. (2004). The characteristics and correlates of fantasy in school-age children: Imaginary companions, impersonation, and social understanding. *Developmental Psychology, 40,* 1173–1187.

Taylor, M., Esbensen, B. M., & Bennett, R. T. (1994). Children's understanding of knowledge acquisition: The tendency for children to report that they have always known what they have just learned. *Child Development, 65,* 1581–1604.

Taylor, R. D., & Roberts, D. (1995). Kinship support and maternal and adolescent well-being in economically disadvantaged African-American families. *Child Development, 66,* 1585–1597.

Taylor, R. L. (2000). Diversity within African-American families. In D. H. Demo & K. R. Allen (Eds.), *Handbook of family diversity* (pp. 232– 251). New York: Oxford University Press.

Teicher, M. H., Dumont, N. L., Ito, Y., Vaituzis, C., Giedd, J., & Andersen, S. L. (2004). Childhood neglect is associated with reduced corpus callosum area. *Biological Psychiatry, 56,* 80–85.

Telama, R., Yang, X., Viikari, J., Valimaki, I., Wanne, O., & Raitakari, O. (2005). Physical activity from childhood to adulthood: A 21-year tracking study. *American Journal of Preventive Medicine, 28,* 267–273.

Tellings, A. (1999). Psychoanalytical and genetic-structuralistic approaches of moral development: Incompatible views? *Psychoanalytic Review, 86,* 903–914.

Temple, C. M., & Carney, R. A. (1995). Patterns of spatial functioning in Turner's syndrome. *Cortex, 31,* 109–118.

Tenenbaum, H. R., & Leaper, C. (2002). Are parents' gender schemas related to their children's gender-related cognitions? A meta-analysis. *Developmental Psychology, 38,* 615–630.

Tenenbaum, H. R., & Leaper, C. (2003). Parent–child conversations about science: The socialization of gender inequities? *Developmental Psychology, 39,* 34–57.

Tenenbaum, H. R., Snow, C. E., Roach, K. A., & Kurland, B. (2005). Talking and reading science: Longitudinal data on sex differences in mother–child conversations in low-income families. *Journal of Applied Developmental Psychology, 26,* 1–19.

Terlecki, M. S., & Newcombe, N. S. (2005). How important is the digital divide? The relations of computer and videogame usage to gender differences in mental rotation ability. *Sex Roles, 53,* 433–441.

Terwel, J., Gillies, R. M., van den Eeden, P., & Hoek, D. (2001). Cooperative learning processes of students: A longitudinal multilevel perspective. *British Journal of Educational Psychology, 71,* 619–645.

Tessier, R., Cristo, M., Velez, S., Giron, M., Nadeau, L., & Figueroa, Z. (2003). Kangaroo mother care: A method of protecting high-risk premature infants against developmental delay. *Infant Behavior and Development, 26,* 384–397.

Teti, D. M., Gelfand, D. M., Messinger, D. S., & Isabella, R. (1995). Maternal depression and the quality of early attachment: An examination of infants, preschoolers, and their mothers. *Developmental Psychology, 31,* 364–376.

Teyber, E. (1992). *Helping children cope with divorce.* New York: Lexington Books.

Teyber, E. (2001). *Helping children cope with divorce* (rev. ed.). San Francisco: Jossey-Bass.

Thacker, S. B., & Stroup, D. F. (2003). Revisiting the use of the electronic fetal monitor. *Lancet, 361,* 445–446.

Thapar, A., Fowler, T., Rice, F., Scourfield, J., van den Bree, M., Thomas, H., Harold, G., & Hay, D. (2003). Maternal smoking during pregnancy and attention deficit hyperactivity disorder symptoms in offspring. *American Journal of Psychiatry, 160,* 1985–1989.

Tharpar, N., & Sanderson, I. R. (2004). Diarrhea in children: An interface between developing and developed countries. *Lancet, 363,* 641–653.

Tharpe, A. M., & Ashmead, D. H. (2001). A longitudinal investigation of infant auditory sensitivity. *American Journal of Audiology, 10,* 104–112.

Thatcher, R. W., Lyon, G. R., Rumsey, J., & Krasnegor, J. (1996). *Developmental neuroimagining.* San Diego, CA: Academic Press.

Thatcher, R. W., Walker, R. A., & Giudice, S. (1987). Human cerebral hemispheres develop at different rates and ages. *Science, 236,* 1110–1113.

Theil, S. (2006, September 4). Beyond babies. *Newsweek: International Edition.* Retrieved from www.msnbc.msn.com/id/14535863/site/newsweek

Thelen, E. (1989). The (re)discovery of motor development: Learning new things from an old field. *Developmental Psychology, 25,* 946–949.

Thelen, E., & Adolph, K. E. (1992). Arnold Gesell: The paradox of nature and nurture. *Developmental Psychology, 28,* 368–380.

Thelen, E., & Corbetta, D. (2002). Microdevelopment and dynamic systems: Applications to infant motor development. In N. Granott & J. Parziale (Eds.), *Microdevelopment: Transition processes in development and learning* (pp. 59–79). New York: Cambridge University Press.

Thelen, E., Corbetta, D., & Spencer, J. (1996). The development of reaching during the first year: The role of movement speed. *Journal of Experimental Psychology: Human Perception and Performance, 22,* 1059–107

Thelen, E., Fisher, D. M., & Ridley-Johnson, R. (1984). The relationship between physical growth and a newborn reflex. *Infant Behavior and Development, 7,* 479–493.

Thelen, E., Schöner, G., Scheier, C., & Smith, L. B. (2001). The dynamics of embodiment: A field theory of infant perseverative reaching. *Behavioral and Brain Sciences, 24,* 1–34.

Thelen, E., & Smith, L. B. (1994). *A dynamic systems approach to the development of cognition and action.* Cambridge, MA: Cambridge University Press.

Thelen, E., & Smith, L. B. (2006). Dynamic systems theories. In R. M. Lerner (Ed.), *Handbook of child psychology: Vol. 1. Theoretical models of human development* (6th ed., pp. 258–312). Hoboken, NJ: Wiley.

Théoret, H., Halligan, E., Kobayashi, M., Fregni, F., Tager-Flusberg, H., & Pascual-Leone, A. (2005). Impaired motor facilitation during action observation in individuals with autism spectrum disorder, *Current Biology, 15,* R84–R85.

Thiedke, C. C. (2001). Sleep disorders and sleep problems in childhood. *American Family Physician, 63,* 277–284.

Thiedke, C. C. (2003). Nocturnal enuresis. *American Family Physician, 67,* 1499–1506.

Thiessen, E. D., & Saffran, J. R. (2003). When cues collide: Use of stress and statistical cues to word boundaries by 7- to 9-month-old infants. *Developmental Psychology, 39,* 709–716.

Thoeni, A., Zech, N., Moroder, L., & Ploner, F. (2005). Review of 1600 water births. Does water birth increase the risk of neonatal infection? *Journal of Maternal-Fetal and Neonatal Medicine, 17,* 357–361.

Thoman, E., & Ingersoll, E. W. (1993). Learning in premature infants. *Developmental Psychology, 29,* 692–700.

Thomas, A., & Chess, S. (1977). *Temperament and development.* New York: Brunner/Mazel.

Thomas, A., Chess, S., & Birch, H. G. (1968). *Temperament and behavior disorders in children.* New York: New York University Press.

Thomas, J. R., & French, K. E. (1985). Gender differences across age in motor performance: A metaanalysis. *Psychological Bulletin, 98,* 260–282.

Thomas, R. M. (2005). *Comparing theories of child development* (6th ed.). New York: New York University Press.

Thompson, A., Hollis, C., & Richards, D. (2003). Authoritarian parenting attitudes as a risk for conduct problems: Results of a British national cohort study. *European Child and Adolescent Psychiatry, 12,* 84–91.

Thompson, L. A., Goodman, D. C., & Little, G. A. (2002). Is more neonatal intensive care always better? Insights from a cross-national comparison of reproductive care. *Pediatrics, 109,* 1036–1043.

Thompson, P. M., Giedd, J. N., Woods, R. P., MacDonald, D., Evans, A. C., & Toga, A. W. (2000a). Growth patterns in the developing brain detected by using continuum mechanical tensor maps. *Nature, 404,* 190–192.

Thompson, P. M., Giedd, J. N., Woods, R. P., MacDonald, D., Evans, A. C., & Toga, A. W. (2000b). Is more neonatal intensive care always better? Insights from a cross-sectional comparison of reproductive care. *Pediatrics, 109,* 1036–1043.

Thompson, R. A. (1990a). On emotion and self-regulation. In R. A. Thompson (Ed.), *Nebraska Symposia on Motivation* (Vol. 36, pp. 383–483). Lincoln: University of Nebraska Press.

Thompson, R. A. (1990b). Vulnerability in research: A developmental perspective on research risk. *Child Development, 61,* 1–16.

Thompson, R. A. (2000). The legacy of early attachments. *Child Development, 71,* 145–152.

Thompson, R. A. (2006). The development of the person: Social understanding, relationships, conscience, self. In N. Eisenberg (Ed.), *Handbook of child psychology: Vol. 3. Social, emotional, and personality development* (6th ed., pp. 24–98). Hoboken, NJ: Wiley.

Thompson, R. A., Easterbrooks, M. A., & Padilla-Walker, L. M. (2003). Social and emotional development in infancy. In R. M. Lerner & M. A. Easterbrooks (Eds.), *Social and emotional development in infancy* (pp. 91–112). New York: Wiley.

Thompson, R. A., & Limber, S. (1991). "Social anxiety" in infancy: Stranger wariness and separation distress. In H. Leitenberg (Ed.), *Handbook of social and evaluation anxiety* (pp. 85–137). New York: Plenum.

Thompson, R. A., Meyer, S., & McGinley, M. (2006). Understanding values in relationships: The development of conscience. In M. Killen & J. G. Smetana (Eds.), *Handbook of moral development* (pp. 267–298). Mahwah, NJ: Erlbaum.

Thompson, R. A., & Nelson, C. A. (2001). Developmental science and the media. *American Psychologist, 56,* 5–15.

Thompson, R. A., & Raikes, H. A. (2003). Toward the next quarter-century: Conceptual and methodological challenges for attachment theory. *Development and Psychopathology, 15,* 691–718.

Thornton, S. (1999). Creating conditions for cognitive change: The interaction between task structures and specific strategies. *Child Development, 70,* 588–603.

Thorpy, M. J., & Yager, J. (2001). *Encyclopedia of sleep and sleep disorders.* New York: Facts on File.

Tienari, P., Wynne, L. C., Laksy, K., Moring, J., Nieminen, P., & Sorri, A. (2003). Genetic boundaries of the schizophrenia spectrum: Evidence from the Finnish adoptive family study of schizophrenia. *American Journal of Psychiatry, 160,* 1587–1594.

Tiggemann, M., & Anesbury, T. (2000). Negative stereotyping of obesity in children: The role of controllability beliefs. *Journal of Applied Social Psychology, 30,* 1977–1993.

Tincoff, R., & Jusczyk, P. W. (1999). Some beginnings of word comprehension in 6-month-olds. *Psychological Science, 10,* 172–175.

Tinsley, B. J. (2003). *How children learn to be healthy.* Cambridge, U.K.: Cambridge University Press.

Tizard, B., & Rees, J. (1975). The effect of early institutional rearing on the behaviour problems and affectional relationships of four-year-old children. *Journal of Child Psychology and Psychiatry, 16,* 61–73.

Tofler, I. R., Knapp, P. K., & Drell, M. J. (1998). The achievement by proxy spectrum in youth sports: Historical perspective and clinical approach to pressured and high-achieving children and adolescents. *Child and Adolescent Psychiatric Clinics of North America, 7,* 803–820.

Tomasello, M. (1999). Having intentions, understanding intentions, and understanding communicative intentions. In P. D. Zelazo, J. W. Astington, & J. Wilde (Eds.), *Developing theories of intention: Social understanding and self-control* (pp. 63–75). Mahwah, NJ: Erlbaum.

Tomasello, M. (2000). Do young children have adult syntactic competence? *Cognition, 74,* 209–253.

Tomasello, M. (2003). *Constructing a language: A usage-based theory of language acquisition.* Cambridge, MA: Harvard University Press.

Tomasello, M. (2006). Acquiring linguistic constructions. In D. Kuhn & R. Siegler (Eds.), *Handbook of child psychology: Vol. 2: Cognition, perception, and language* (6th ed., pp. 255–298). Hoboken, NJ: Wiley.

Tomasello, M., & Akhtar, N. (1995). Two-year-olds use pragmatic cues to differentiate reference to objects and actions. *Cognitive Development, 10,* 201–224.

Tomasello, M., Akhtar, N., Dodson, K., & Rekau, L. (1997). Differential productivity in young children's use of nouns and verbs. *Journal of Child Language, 24,* 373–387.

Tomasello, M., & Brooks, P. (1999). Early syntactic development: A construction grammar approach. In M. Barrett (Ed.), *The development of language* (pp. 161–190). London: UCL Press.

Tomasello, M., Call, J., & Hare, B. (2003). Chimpanzees understand psychological states—the question is which ones and to what extent. *Trends in Cognitive Sciences, 7,* 153–156.

Tomasello, M., & Rakoczy, H. (2003). What makes human cognition unique? From individual to shared to collective intentionality. *Mind and Language, 18,* 121–147.

Tomasello, M., Striano, T., & Rochat, P. (1999). Do young children use objects as symbols? *British Journal of Developmental Psychology, 17,* 563–584.

Tong, S., McMichael, A. J., & Baghurst, P. A. (2000). Interactions between environmental lead exposure and sociodemographic factors on cognitive development. *Archives of Environmental Health, 55,* 330–335.

Toomela, A. (1999). Drawing development: Stages in the representation of a cube and a cylinder. *Child Development, 70,* 1141–1150.

Toomela, A. (2002). Drawing as a verbally mediated activity: A study of relationships between verbal, motor, visuospatial skills and drawing in children. *International Journal of Behavioral Development, 26,* 234–247.

Torney-Purta, J. (2002). The school's role in developing civic engagement: A study of adolescents in twenty-eight countries. *Applied Developmental Science, 6,* 203–212.

Torrance, E. P. (1988). The nature of creativity as manifest in its testing. In R. J. Sternberg (Ed.), *The nature of creativity: Contemporary psychological perspectives* (pp. 43–75). New York: Cambridge University Press.

Torrey, E. F., Bower, A. E., Taylor, E. H., & Gottesman, I. I. (1994). *Schizophrenia and manic-depressive disorder: The biological roots of mental illness as revealed by the landmark study of identical twins.* New York: Basic Books.

Touwen, B. C. L. (1984). Primitive reflexes—conceptual or semantic problem? In H. F. R. Prechtl (Ed.), *Continuity of neural functions from prenatal to postnatal life* (Clinics in Developmental Medicine No. 94, pp. 115–125). Philadelphia: Lippincott.

Towner, E., & Towner, J. (2002). UNICEF's child injury league table. An analysis of legislation: More mixed messages. *Injury Prevention, 8,* 97–100.

Toyamo, N. (2000). "What are food and air like inside our bodies?" Children's thinking about digestion and respiration. *International Journal of Behavioral Development, 24,* 222–230.

Trahms, C. M., & Pipes, P. L. (1997). *Nutrition in infancy and childhood* (6th ed.). New York: McGraw-Hill.

Trapp, D. (2007, January 15). Congress plugs SCHIP funding gap but deficits still loom in 14 states. *amednews.com.* Retrieved from www.ama-assn.org/amednews/2007/01/15/gvl10115.htm

Trautner, H. M., Gervai, J., & Nemeth, R. (2003). Appearance–reality distinction and development of gender constancy understanding in children. *International Journal of Behavioral Development, 27,* 275–283.

Trautner, H. M., Ruble, D. N., Cyphers, L., Kirsten, B., Behrendt, R., & Hartman, P. (2005). Rigidity and flexibility of gender stereotypes in childhood: Developmental or differential? *Infant and Child Development, 14,* 365–381.

Trautwein, U., Ludtke, O., Marsh, H. W., Koller, O., & Baumert, J. (2006). Tracking, grading, and student motivation: Using group composition and status to predict self-concept and interest in ninth-grade mathematics. *Journal of Educational Psychology, 98,* 788–806.

Treasure, J., & Schmidt, U. (2004). Anorexia nervosa. *Clinical Evidence, 13,* 1148–1157.

Trehub, S. E. (2001). Musical predispositions in infancy. *Annals of the New York Academy of Sciences, 930,* 1–16.

Tremblay, L., & Frigon, J.-Y. (2005). Precocious puberty in adolescent girls: A biomarker of later psychosocial adjustment problems. *Child Psychiatry and Human Development, 36,* 73–94.

Tremblay, R. E. (2000). The development of aggressive behavior during childhood: What have we learned in the past century? *International Journal of Behavioral Development, 24,* 129–141.

Tremblay, R. E. (2002). Prevention of injury by early socialization of aggressive behavior. *Injury Prevention, 8*(Suppl. IV), 17–21.

Tremblay, R. E., Japel, C., Perusse, D., Voivin, M., Zoccolillo, M., Montplaisir, J., & McDuff, P. (1999). The search for the age of "onset" of physical aggression: Rousseau and Bandura revisited. *Criminal Behavior and Mental Health, 9,* 8–23.

Trent, K., & Harlan, S. L. (1994). Teenage mothers in nuclear and extended households. *Journal of Family Issues, 15,* 309–337.

Trevarthen, C. (2003). Infant psychology is an evolving culture. *Human Development, 46,* 233–246.

Triandis, H. C. (1995). *Individualism and collectivism.* Boulder, CO: Westview Press.

Triandis, H. C. (1998, May). *Crosscultural versus cultural psychology: A synthesis?* Colloquium presented at Illinois Wesleyan University, Bloomington, Illinois.

Trickett, P. K., Noll, J., Reiffman, A., & Putnam, F. (2001). Variants of intrafamilial sexual abuse experiences: Implications for short-and long-term development. *Development and Psychopathology, 13,* 1001–1019.

Trickett, P. K., & Putnam, F. W. (1998). Developmental consequences of child sexual abuse. In P. K. Trickett & C. J. Schellenbach (Eds.), *Violence against children in the family and community* (pp. 39–56). Washington, DC: American Psychological Association.

Trocomé, N., & Wolfe, D. (2002). *Child maltreatment in Canada: The Canadian Incidence Study of Reported Child Abuse and Neglect.* Retrieved from http://www.hc-sc.gc.ca/pphb-dgspsp/cm-vee

Tronick, E., Morelli, G., & Ivey, P. (1992). The Efe forager infant and toddler's pattern of social relationships: Multiple and simultaneous. *Developmental Psychology, 28,* 568–577.

Tronick, E. Z., Thomas, R. B., & Daltabuit, M. (1994). The Quechua manta pouch: A caretaking practice for buffering the Peruvian infant against the multiple stressors of high altitude. *Child Development, 65,* 1005–1013.

Troop-Gordon, W., & Asher, S. R. (2005). Modifications in children's goals when encountering obstacles to conflict resolution. *Child Development, 76,* 568–582.

True, M. M., Pisani, L., & Oumar, F. (2001). Infant–mother attachment among the Dogon of Mali. *Child Development, 72,* 1451–1466.

Trusty, J. (1999). Effects of eighth-grade parental involvement on late adolescents' educational expectations. *Journal of Research and Development in Education, 32,* 224–233.

Trzesniewski, K. H., Donnellan, M. B., & Robins, R. W. (2003). Stability of self-esteem across the life span. *Journal of Personality and Social Psychology, 84,* 205–220.

Tuchfarber, B. S., Zins, J. E., & Jason, L. A. (1997). Prevention and control of injuries. In R. Weissberg, T. P. Gullotta, R. L. Hampton, B. A. Ryan, & G. R. Adams (Eds.), *Enhancing children's wellness* (pp. 250–277). Thousand Oaks, CA: Sage.

Tucker, C. J., McHale, S. M., & Crouter, A. C. (2001). Conditions of sibling support in adolescence. *Journal of Family Psychology, 15,* 254–271.

Tudge, J. R. H. (1992). Processes and consequences of peer collaboration: A Vygotskian analysis. *Child Development, 63,* 1364–1397.

Tudge, J. R. H., Hogan, D. M., Snezhkova, I. A., Kulakova, N. N., & Etz, K. E. (2000). Parents' child-rearing values and beliefs in the United States and Russia: The impact of culture and social class. *Infant and Child Development, 9,* 105–121.

Tunmer, W. E., & Chapman, J. W. (2002). The relation of beginning readers' reported word identification strategies to reading achievement, reading-related skills, and academic self-perceptions. *Reading and Writing, 15,* 341–358.

Turati, C. (2004). Why faces are not special to newborns: An account of the face preference. *Current Directions in Psychological Science, 13,* 5–8.

Turiel, E. (2006). The development of morality. In N. Eisenberg (Ed.), *Handbook of child psychology: Vol. 3.*

Social, emotional, and personality development (6th ed., pp. 789–857). Hoboken, NJ: Wiley.

Turkheimer, E., Haley, A., Waldron, M., D'Onofrio, B., & Gottesman, I. I. (2003). Socioeconomic status modifies heritability of IQ in young children. Psychological Science, 14, 623–628.

Turnbull, M., Hart, D., & Lapkin, S. (2003). Grade 6 French immersion students' performance on large-scale reading, writing, and mathematics tests: Building explanations. Alberta Journal of Educational Research, 49, 6–23.

Turner, P. J., & Gervai, J. (1995). A multidimensional study of gender typing in preschool children and their parents: Personality, attitudes, preferences, behavior, and cultural differences. Developmental Psychology, 31, 759–772.

Tuss, P., Zimmer, J., & Ho, H.-Z. (1995). Causal attributions of underachieving fourth-grade students in China, Japan, and the United States. Journal of Cross-Cultural Psychology, 26, 408–425.

Tuyen, J. M., & Bisgard, K. (2003). Community setting: Pertussis outbreak. Atlanta, GA: U.S. Centers for Disease Control and Prevention. Retrieved from www.cdc.gov/nip/publications/pertussis/chapter10.pdf

Twenge, J. M., & Campbell, W. K. (2001). Age and birth cohort differences in self-esteem: A crosstemporal meta-analysis. Personality and Social Psychology Review, 5, 321–344.

Twenge, J. M., & Crocker, J. (2002). Race and self-esteem: Meta-analyses comparing whites, blacks, Hispanics, Asians, and American Indians and comment on Gray-Little and Hafdahl (2000). Psychological Bulletin, 128, 371–408.

Tyrka, A. R., Graber, J. A., & Brooks-Gunn, J. (2000). The development of disordered eating: Correlates and predictors of eating problems in the context of adolescence. In A. J. Sameroff & M. Lewis (Eds.), Handbook of developmental psychopathology (2nd ed., pp. 607–624). New York: Kluwer.

Tzuriel, D. (2001). Dynamic assessment of young children. New York: Kluwer Academic.

Tzuriel, D., & Kaufman, R. (1999). Mediated learning and cognitive modifiability: Dynamic assessment of young Ethiopian immigrant children to Israel. Journal of Cross-Cultural Psychology, 30, 359–380.

Ullrich-French, S., & Smith, A. L. (2006). Perceptions of relationships with parents and peers in youth sport: Independent and combined prediction of motivational outcomes. Psychology of Sport and Exercise, 7, 193–214.

Umana-Taylor, A. J., & Alfaro, E. C. (2006). Ethnic identity among U.S. Latino adolescents: Measurement and implications for well-being. In F. A. Villarruel & T. Luster (Eds.), The crisis in youth mental health: Critical issues and effective programs: Vol. 2. Disorders in adolescence (pp. 195–211). Westport, CT: Praeger.

Underwood, M. K. (2003). Social aggression in girls. New York: Guilford.

UNICEF (United Nations Children's Fund). (2001). Teenage births in rich nations. Innocenti Report Card No. 3. Florence, Italy: UNICEF Innocenti Research Centre.

UNICEF (United Nations Children's Fund). (2005a). Child poverty in rich countries 2005. Florence, Italy: Innocenti Research Centre.

UNICEF (United Nations Children's Fund). (2005b). Children under threat. New York: Author.

UNICEF (United Nations Children's Fund). (2006). Immunization summary 2006. Geneva, Switzerland: World Health Organization.

UNICEF (United Nations Children's Fund). (2007). State of the world's children. New York: Author.

United Nations. (2000). The world's women: Trends and statistics. New York: United Nations.

United Nations. (2002). The world's women: Trends and statistics. New York: United Nations.

United Nations. (2006). Preventing HIV in women and infants. Retrieved from www.unfpa.org/hiv/transmission.htm

United Nations Development Programme. (2002). Human development report 2002. New York: Oxford University Press.

U.S. Census Bureau. (2007a). International data base. Retrieved from www.census.gov/ipc/www/idbsum.html

U.S. Census Bureau. (2007b). Statistical abstract of the United States (127th ed.). Washington, DC: U.S. Government Printing Office.

U.S. Centers for Disease Control and Prevention. (2006). Sexually transmitted disease (STD) surveillance. Retrieved from www.cdc.gov/std

U.S. Department of Agriculture. (2005a). Expenditures on children by families, 2005. Miscellaneous Publication Number 1528-2005. Retrieved from www.usda.gov/cnpp/Crc/crc2005.pdf

U.S. Department of Agriculture. (2005b). Food insecurity in households with children. Washington, DC: Author.

U.S. Department of Agriculture. (2005c). Frequently asked questions about the Special Supplemental Nutrition Program for Women, Infants, and Children (WIC). Retrieved from www.ers.usda.gov/Briefing/WIC

U.S. Department of Education. (2003). NAEP High School Transcript Study: The Nation's Report Card. Retrieved from http://nces.ed.gov/nationsreportcard/

U.S. Department of Education. (2005a). The condition of education, 2000–2005. Washington, DC: U.S. Government Printing Office.

U.S. Department of Education. (2005b). Trial urban district report cards in reading and mathematics, 2005. Retrieved from nces.ed.gov/nationsreportcard/nrc/tuda_reading_mathematics_2005

U.S. Department of Education. (2006a). Calories in, calories, out: Food and exercise in public elementary schools, 2005. Retrieved from nces.ed.gov/Pubs2006/nutrition

U.S. Department of Education. (2006b). Digest of education statistics 2005. Washington, DC: U.S. Government Printing Office.

U.S. Department of Education. (2006c). Long-term trend: Trends in average mathematics scale scores by gender. The Nation's Report Card. Retrieved from nces.ed.gov/nationsreportcard/ltt/results2005/sub-mathematics-gender.asp

U.S. Department of Education. (2006d). Long-term trend: Trends in average mathematics scale scores by race/ethnicity. The Nation's Report Card. Retrieved from nces.ed.gov/nationsreportcard/ltt/results2005/sub_mathematics_race2.asp

U.S. Department of Education. (2006e). Long-term trend: Trends in average reading scale scores by gender. The Nation's Report Card. Retrieved from nces.ed.gov/nationsreportcard/ltt/results2005/sub-reading-gender.asp

U.S. Department of Education. (2006f). Long-term trend: Trends in average reading scale scores by race/ethnicity. The Nation's Report Card. Retrieved from nces.ed.gov/nationsreportcard/ltt/results2005/sub_reading_race2.asp

U.S. Department of Education. (2006g). Long-term trend: Trends in average writing scale scores by gender. The Nation's Report Card. Retrieved from nces.ed.gov/nationsreportcard/ltt/results2005/sub-writing-gender.asp

U.S. Department of Education. (2007). Digest of educational statistics, 2006. Washington, DC: U.S. Government Printing Office.

U.S. Department of Health and Human Services. (2005a). Abortion surveillance—United States, 2002. Retrieved from www.cdc.gov/mmwr/preview/mmwrhtml/ss5407a1.htm

U.S. Department of Health and Human Services. (2005b). Breastfeeding—Best for baby, best for mom. Retrieved from www.womenshealth.gov/breastfeeding/index.cfm?page=home

U.S. Department of Health and Human Services. (2005c). Health United States. Washington, DC: U.S. Government Printing Office.

U.S. Department of Health and Human Services. (2005d). SHPPS 2000 fact sheets: Physical education and activity 2000. Retrieved from www.cdc.gov/HealthyYouth/shpps/factsheets/pe.htm

U.S. Department of Health and Human Services. (2006a). Child maltreatment 2004: Summary of key findings. Retrieved from www.childwelfare.gov/pubs/factsheets/canstats.cfm

U.S. Department of Health and Human Services. (2006b). FASTATS: Births—Methods of delivery. Retrieved from www.cdc.gov/nchs/fastats/delivery.htm

U.S. Department of Health and Human Services. (2006c). FASTATS: Births—Unmarried childbearing. Retrieved from www.cdc.gov/nchs/fastats/unmarry.htm

U.S. Department of Health and Human Services. (2006d). Health United States and injury chartbook. Washington, DC: U.S. Government Printing Office.

U.S. Department of Health and Human Services. (2006e). Health, United States, 2006, with chartbook on trends in the health of Americans. Retrieved from www.cdc.gov/nchs/data/hus/hus06.pdf

U.S. Department of Health and Human Services. (2006f). Impaired fecundity by age and selected characteristics. Washington, DC: U.S. Government Printing Office.

U.S. Department of Health and Human Services. (2006g). National Household Survey on Drug Use and Health. Retrieved from www.oas.samhsa.gov/nsduhLatest.htm

U.S. Department of Health and Human Services. (2006h, September 15). National, state, and urban area vaccination levels among children aged 19 to 35 months: United States 2005. Morbidity and Mortality Weekly Report, 55, 988–993.

U.S. Department of Health and Human Services. (2006i). Prenatal care. Retrieved from www.cdc.gov/nchs/fastats/prenatal.htm

U.S. Department of Health and Human Services. (2006j). Youth risk behavior surveillance—United States, 2005. Morbidity and Mortality Weekly Report, 55(No. SS-5).

U.S. Department of Health and Human Services. (2007). Overweight and obesity: Obesity trends. Retrieved from www.cdc.gov/nccdphp/dnpa/obesity/trend/maps/

U.S. Department of Justice. (2006). Uniform crime reports: Preliminary report, 2005. Retrieved from www.fbi.gov/ucr/ucr.htm

Updegraff, K. A., McHale, S. M., & Crouter, A. C. (1996). Gender roles in marriage: What do they mean for girls' and boys' school achievement? Journal of Youth and Adolescence, 25, 73–88.

Uribe, F. M. T., LeVine, R. A., & LeVine, S. E. (1994). Maternal behavior in a Mexican community: The changing environments of children. In P. M. Greenfield & R. R. Cocking (Eds.), Cross-cultural roots of minority child development (pp. 41–54). Hillsdale, NJ: Erlbaum.

Vaillancourt, T., Hymel, S., & McDougall, P. (2003). Bullying is power: Implications for school-based intervention strategies. Journal of Applied Social Psychology, 19, 157–176.

Vaish, A., & Striano, T. (2004). Is visual reference necessary? Contributions of facial versus vocal cues in 12-month-olds' social referencing behavior. Developmental Science, 7, 261–269.

Valdés, G. (1997). Dual-language immersion programs: A cautionary note concerning the education of language-minority students. Harvard Educational Review, 67, 391–429.

Valdés, G. (1998). The world outside and inside schools: Language and immigrant children. Educational Researcher, 27(6), 4–18.

Valentine, J. C., DuBois, D. L., & Cooper, H. (2004). The relation between self-beliefs and academic achievement: A meta-analytic review. Educational Psychologist, 39, 111–133.

Valian, V. (1999). Input and language acquisition. In W. C. Ritchie & T. K. Bhatia (Eds.), Handbook of child language acquisition (pp. 497–530). San Diego: Academic Press.

Valiente, C., Eisenberg, N., Fabes, R. A., Shepard, S. A., Cumberland, A., & Losoya, S. H. (2004). Prediction of children's empathy-related responding from their effortful control and parents' expressivity. Developmental Psychology, 40, 911–926.

Van den Bergh, B. R. H. (2004). High antenatal maternal anxiety is related to ADHD symptoms, externalizing problems, and anxiety in 8- and 9-year-olds. Child Development, 75, 1085–1097.

Van den Bergh, B. R. H., & De Rycke, L. (2003). Measuring the multidimensional self-concept and global self-worth of 6- to 8-year-olds. Journal of Genetic Psychology, 164, 201–225.

van den Boom, D. C., & Hoeksma, J. B. (1994). The effect of infant irritability on mother–infant interaction: A growth-curve analysis. Developmental Psychology, 30, 581–590.

van der Meer, A. L. (1997). Keeping the arm in the limelight: Advanced visual control of arm movements in neonates. European Journal of Paediatric Neurology, 4, 103–108.

Van der Woerd, K. A., & Cox, D. N. (2001, June). Assessing academic competence and the well-being of Aboriginal students in British Columbia. Poster presented at the American Psychological Association, Atlanta.

Van Doesum, K. T. M., Hosman, C. M. H., & Riksen-Walraven, J. M. (2005). A model-based intervention for depressed mothers and their infants. *Infant Mental Health Journal, 26,* 157–176.

Van Esbroeck, R., Tibos, K., & Zaman, M. (2005). A dynamic model of career choice development. *International Journal for Educational and Vocational Guidance, 5,* 5–18.

Van Goozen, S. H. M., Cohen-Kettenis, P. T., Gooren, I. J. G., Frijda, N. H., & Van De Poll, N. E. (1995). Gender differences in behaviour: Activating effects of cross-sex hormones. *Psychoneuroendocrinology, 20,* 171–177.

van Hoof, A., & Raaijmakers, Q. A. W. (2003). The search for the structure of identity formation. *Identity, 3,* 271–289.

van IJzendoorn, M. H. (1995). Adult attachment representations, parental responsiveness, and infant attachment: A meta-analysis on the predictive validity of the Adult Attachment Interview. *Psychological Bulletin, 117,* 387–403.

van IJzendoorn, M. H., & Hubbard, F. O. A., (2000). Are infant crying and maternal responsiveness during the first year related to infant–mother attachment at 15 months? *Attachment and Human Development, 2,* 371–391.

van IJzendoorn, M. H., Juffer, F., & Poelhuis, C. W. K. (2005). Adoption and cognitive development: A meta-analytic comparison of adopted and nonadopted children's IQ and school performance. *Psychological Bulletin, 131,* 301–316.

van IJzendoorn, M. H., & Kroonenberg, P. M. (1988). Cross-cultural patterns of attachment: A meta-analysis of the Strange Situation. *Child Development, 59,* 147–156.

van IJzendoorn, M. H., & Sagi, A. (1999). Cross-cultural patterns of attachment. In J. Cassidy & P. R. Shaver (Eds.), *Handbook of attachment: Theory, research, and clinical applications* (pp. 713–734). New York: Guilford.

van IJzendoorn, M. H., Schuengel, C., & Bakermans-Kranenburg, M. J. (1999). Disorganized attachment in early childhood: Meta-analysis of precursors, concomitants, and sequelae. *Development and Psychopathology, 11,* 225–249.

van IJzendoorn, M. H., Vereijken, C. M. J. L., Bakermans-Kranenburg, M. J., & Riksen-Walraven, J. M. (2004). Assessing attachment security with the Attachment Q Sort: Meta-analytic evidence for the validity of the Observer AQS. *Child Development, 75,* 1188–1213.

Van Keer, H. (2004). Fostering reading comprehension in fifth grade by explicit instruction in reading strategies and peer tutoring. *British Journal of Educational Psychology, 74,* 37–70.

Vandell, D. L. (1999). When school is out: Analysis and recommendations. *Future of Children, 9*(2). Retrieved from www.futureofchildren.org

Vandell, D. L., & Mueller, E. C. (1995). Peer play and friendships during the first two years. In H. C. Foot, A. J. Chapman, & J. R. Smith (Eds.), *Friendship and social relations in children* (pp. 181–208). New Brunswick, NJ: Transaction.

Vandell, D. L., & Posner, J. K. (1999). Conceptualization and measurement of children's after-school environments. In S. L. Friedman & T. D. Wachs (Eds.), *Measuring environment across the life span* (pp. 167–196). Washington, DC: American Psychological Association.

Vandell, D. L., & Shumow, L. (1999). After-school child care programs. *Future of Children, 9*(2), 64–80.

Vandenberg, B. (1998). Real and not real: A vital developmental dichotomy. In O. N. Saracho & B. Spodek (Eds.), *Multiple perspectives on play in early childhood education* (pp. 295–305). Albany: State University of New York Press.

Varendi, H., Christensson, K., Porter, R. H., & Winberg, J. (1998). Soothing effect of amniotic fluid smell in newborn infants. *Early Human Development, 51,* 47–55.

Varendi, H., & Porter, R. H. (2001). Breast odour as the only maternal stimulus elicits crawling toward the odour source. *Acta Paediactrica, 90,* 372–375.

Varnhagen, C. (2007). Children and the Internet. In J. Gackenbach (Ed.), *Psychology and the Internet* (2nd ed., pp. 37–54). Amsterdam: Elsevier.

Vartanian, L. R. (1997). Separation– individuation, social support, and adolescent egocentrism: An exploratory study. *Journal of Early Adolescence, 17,* 245–270.

Vartanian, L. R., & Powlishta, K. K. (1996). A longitudinal examination of the social-cognitive foundations of adolescent egocentrism. *Journal of Early Adolescence, 16,* 157–178.

Vatten, L. J., Maehle, B. O., Lund, N. T., Treti, S., Hsieh, C. C., Trichopoulos, D., & Stuver, S. O. (2002). Birth weight as a predictor of breast cancer: A case-control study in Norway. *British Journal of Cancer, 86,* 89–91.

Vaughn, B. E., & Bost, K. K. (1999). Attachment and temperament: Redundant, independent, or interacting influences on interpersonal adaptation and personality development? In J. Cassidy & P. Shaver (Eds.), *Handbook of attachment: Theory, research, and clinical applications* (pp. 265–286). New York: Guilford.

Vaughn, B. E., Colvin, T. N., Azria, M. R., Caya, L., & Krzysik, L. (2001). Dyadic analyses of friendship in a sample of preschool-age children attending Head Start: Correspondence between measures and implications for social competence. *Child Development, 72,* 862–878.

Vaughn, B. E., Kopp, C. B., & Krakow, J. B. (1984). The emergence and consolidation of self-control from eighteen to thirty months of age: Normative trends and individual differences. *Child Development, 55,* 990–1004.

Vaughn, B. E., Vollenweider, M., Bost, K. K., Azria-Evans, M. R., & Snider, J. B. (2003). Negative interactions and social competence for preschool children in two samples: Reconsidering the interpretation of aggressive behavior for young children. *Merrill-Palmer Quarterly, 49,* 245–278.

Vaughn, S., & Klingner, J. K. (1998). Students' perceptions of inclusion and resource room settings. *Journal of Special Education, 32,* 79–88.

Vazsonyi, A. T., Hibbert, J. R., & Snider, J. B. (2003). Exotic enterprise no more? Adolescent reports of family and parenting processes from youth in four countries. *Journal of Research on Adolescence, 13,* 129–160.

Vedam, S. (2003). Home birth versus hospital birth: Questioning the quality of the evidence on safety. *Birth, 30,* 57–63.

Velderman, M. K., Bakermans-Kranenburg, M. J., Juffer, F., & van IJzendoorn, M. H. (2006). Effects of attachment-based interventions on maternal sensitivity and infant attachment: Differential susceptibility of highly reactive infants. *Journal of Family Psychology, 20,* 266–274.

Velleman, R. D. B., Templeton, L. J., & Copello, A. G. (2005). The role of the family in preventing and intervening with substance use and misuse: A comprehensive review of family interventions, with a focus on young people. *Drug and Alcohol Review, 24,* 93–109.

Venet, M., & Markovits, H. (2001). Understanding uncertainty with abstract conditional premises. *Merrill-Palmer Quarterly, 47,* 74–99.

Venezia, M., Messinger, D. S., Thorp, D., & Mundy, P. (2004). The development of anticipatory smiling. *Infancy, 6,* 397–406.

Veneziano, R. A. (2003). The importance of paternal warmth. *Cross-Cultural Research, 37,* 265–281.

Vereijken, B., & Adolph, K. E. (1999). Transitions in the development of locomotion. In G. J. P. Savelsbergh, H. L. J. van der Maas, & P. C. L. van Geert (Eds.), *Non-linear analyses of developmental processes* (pp. 137–149). Amsterdam: Elsevier.

Vernon-Feagans, L., Hurley, M., & Yont, K. (2002). The effect of otitis media and daycare quality on mother/child bookreading and language use at 48 months of age. *Journal of Applied Developmental Psychology, 23,* 113–133.

Vidaeff, A. C., Carroll, M. A., & Ramin, S. M. (2005). Acute hypertensive emergencies in pregnancy. *Critical Care Medicine, 33,* S307–S312.

Videon, T. M., & Manning, C. K. (2003). Influences on adolescent eating patterns: The importance of family meals. *Journal of Adolescent Health, 32,* 365–373.

Vik, T., Bakketeig, L. S., Trygg, K. U., Lund-Larsen, K., & Jacobsen, G. (2003). High caffeine consumption in the third trimester of pregnancy: Gender-specific effects on fetal growth. *Paediatric and Perinatal Epidemiology, 17,* 324–331.

Vinden, P. G. (1996). Junín Quechua children's understanding of mind. *Child Development, 67,* 1707–1716.

Vinden, P. G. (2002). Understanding minds and evidence for belief: A study of Mofu children in Cameroon. *International Journal of Behavioral Development, 26,* 445–452.

Visher, E. B., Visher, J. S., & Pasley, K. (2003). Remarriage families and stepparenting. In F. Walsh (Ed.), *Normal family processes: Growing diversity and complexity* (pp. 153–175). New York: Guilford.

Vitaro, F., Larocque, D., Janosz, M., & Tremblay, R. E. (2001). Negative social experiences and dropping out of school. *Educational Psychology, 21,* 401–415.

Vogel, D. A., Lake, M. A., Evans, S., & Karraker, H. (1991). Children's and adults' sex-stereotyped perceptions of infants. *Sex Roles, 24,* 605–616.

Volling, B. L. (2001). Early attachment relationships as predictors of preschool children's emotion regulation with a distressed sibling. *Early Education and Development, 12,* 185–207.

Volling, B. L., & Belsky, J. (1992). Contribution of mother–child and father–child relationships to the quality of sibling interaction: A longitudinal study. *Child Development, 63,* 1209–1222.

Volling, B. L., McElwain, N. L., & Miller, A. L. (2002). Emotion regulation in context: The jealousy complex between young siblings and its relations with child and family characteristics. *Child Development, 73,* 581–600.

von Hofsten, C. (1993). Prospective control: A basic aspect of action development. *Human Development, 36,* 253–270.

von Hofsten, C. (2004). An action perspective on motor development. *Trends in Cognitive Sciences, 8,* 266–272.

von Hofsten, C., & Rosander, K. (1998). The establishment of gaze control in early infancy. In S. Simion & G. Butterworth (Eds.), *The development of sensory, motor and cognitive capacities in early infancy* (pp. 49–66). Hove, U.K.: Psychology Press.

Vondra, J. I., Hommerding, K. D., & Shaw, D. S. (1999). Stability and change in infant attachment in a low-income sample. In J. I Vondra & D. Barnett (Eds.), *Atypical attachment in infancy and early childhood among children at developmental risk. Monographs of the Society for Research in Child Development, 64*(3, Serial No. 258), pp. 119–144.

Vondra, J. I., Shaw, D. S., Searingen, L., Cohen, M., & Owens, E. B. (2001). Attachment stability and emotional and behavioral regulation from infancy to preschool age. *Development and Psychopathology, 13,* 13–33.

Voss, L. D., Mulligan, J., & Betts, P. R. (1998). Short stature at school entry—an index of social deprivation? (The Wessex Growth Study). *Child: Care, Health and Development, 24,* 145–156.

Vostanis, P., Grattan, E., & Cumella, S. (1997). Psychosocial functioning of homeless children. *Journal of the American Academy of Child and Adolescent Psychiatry, 36,* 881–889.

Votruba-Drzal, E., Coley, R. L., & Chase-Lansdale, P. L. (2004). Child care and low-income children's development: Direct and moderated effects. *Child Development, 75,* 296–312.

Vouloumanos, A., & Werker, J. F. (2004). Tuned to the signal: The privileged status of speech for young infants. *Developmental Science, 7,* 270–276.

Voyer, D., Voyer, S., & Bryden, M. P. (1995). Magnitude of sex differences in spatial abilities: A meta-analysis and consideration of critical variables. *Psychological Bulletin, 117,* 250–270.

Vurpillot, E. (1968). The development of scanning strategies and their relation to visual differentiation. *Journal of Experimental Psychology, 6,* 632–650.

Vygotsky, L. S. (1978). *Mind in society: The development of higher psychological processes.* Cambridge, MA: Harvard University Press. (Original works published 1930, 1933, and 1935)

Vygotsky, L. S. (1987). Thinking and speech. In R. W. Rieber, A. S. Carton (Eds.), & N. Minick (Trans.), *The collected works of L. S. Vygotsky: Vol. 1. Problems of general psychology* (pp. 37–285). New York: Plenum. (Original work published 1934)

Wachs, T. D. (1999). The what, why, and how of temperament: A piece of the action. In L. Balter & C. S. Tamis-LeMonda (Eds.), *Child psychology: A handbook of contemporary issues* (pp. 23–44). Philadelphia: Psychology Press.

Wachs, T. D., & Bates, J. E. (2001). Temperament. In G. Bremner & A. Fogel (Eds.), *Blackwell handbook of infant development* (pp. 465–501). Oxford, U.K.: Blackwell.

Waddington, C. H. (1957). *The strategy of the genes.* London: Allen & Unwin.

Wadhwa, P. D., Sandman, C. A., & Garite, T. J. (2001). The neurobiology of stress in human pregnancy: Implications for prematurity and development of the fetal central nervous system. *Progress in Brain Research, 133,* 131–142.

Wahlsten, D. (1994). The intelligence of heritability. *Canadian Psychology, 35,* 244–259.

Wainryb, C. (1997). The mismeasure of diversity: Reflections on the study of cross-cultural differences. In H. D. Saltzstein (Ed.), *New directions for child development* (No. 76, pp. 51–65). San Francisco: Jossey-Bass.

Wainryb, C., & Ford, S. (1998). Young children's evaluations of acts based on beliefs different from their own. *Merrill-Palmer Quarterly, 44,* 484–503.

Wakeley, A., Rivera, S., & Langer, J. (2000). Can young infants add and subtract? *Child Development, 71,* 1477–1720.

Walberg, H. J. (1986). Synthesis of research on teaching. In M. C. Wittrock (Ed.), *Handbook of research on teaching* (3rd ed., pp. 214–229). New York: Macmillan.

Waldenström, U. (1999). Experience of labor and birth in 1111 women. *Journal of Psychosomatic Research, 47,* 471–482.

Waldfogel, J. (2001). International policies toward parental leave and child care. *Future of Children 11,* 52–61.

Waldinger, R. J., Diguer, L., Guastella, F., Lefebrvre, R., Allen, J. P., & Luborsky, L. (2002). The same old song? Stability and change in relationship schemas from adolescence to young adulthood. *Journal of Youth and Adolescence, 31,* 17–44.

Waldman, I. D., Weinberg, R. A., & Scarr, S. (1994). Racial-group differences in IQ in the Minnesota Transracial Adoption Study: A reply to Levin and Lynn. *Intelligence, 19,* 29–44.

Waldron, H. B., Turner, C. W., & Ozechowski, T. J. (2005). Profiles of change in behavioral and family interventions for adolescent substance abuse and dependence. In H. A. Liddle & C. L. Rowe (Eds.), *Adolescent substance abuse: Research and clinical advances* (pp. 357–374). Cambridge: Cambridge University Press.

Wales, R. (1990). Children's pictures. In R. Grieve & M. Hughes (Eds.), *Understanding children* (pp. 140–155). Oxford: Blackwell.

Walker, A., Rosenberg, M., & Balaban-Gil, K. (1999). Neurodevelopmental and neurobehavioral sequelae of selected substances of abuse and psychiatric medications in utero. *Neurological Disorders: Developmental and Behavioral Sequelae, 8,* 845–867.

Walker, L. (1995). Sexism in Kohlberg's moral psychology? In W. M. Kurtines & J. L. Gewirtz (Eds.), *Moral development: An introduction* (pp. 83–107). Boston: Allyn and Bacon.

Walker, L. J. (2004). Progress and prospects in the psychology of moral development. *Merrill-Palmer Quarterly, 50,* 546–557.

Walker, L. J., Pitts, R. C., Hennig, K. H., & Matsuba, M. K. (1995). Reasoning about morality and real-life moral problems. In M. Killen & D. Hart (Eds.), *Morality in everyday life* (pp. 371–407). New York: Cambridge University Press.

Walker, L. J., & Taylor, J. H. (1991a). Family interactions and the development of moral reasoning. *Child Development, 62,* 264–283.

Walker, L. J., & Taylor, J. H. (1991b). Stage transitions in moral reasoning: A longitudinal study of developmental processes. *Developmental Psychology, 27,* 330–337.

Walker-Andrews, A. S. (1997). Infants' perception of expressive behaviors: Differentiation of multimodal information. *Psychological Bulletin, 121,* 437–456.

Walkowiak, J., Wiener, J., Fastabend, A., Heinzow, B., Krämer, U., & Schmidt, E. (2001). Environmental exposure to polychlorinated biphenyls and quality of the home environment: Effects on psychodevelopment in early childhood. *Lancet, 358,* 1602–1607.

Wall, J., Covell, K., & MacIntyre, P. D. (1999). Implications of social supports for adolescents' education and career aspirations. *Canadian Journal of Behavioural Science,* 31, 63–71.

Wallace, J. M., Jr., Bachman, J. G., O'Malley, P. M., Schulenberg, J. E., Cooper, S. M., & Johnston, L. D. (2003). Gender and ethnic differences in smoking, drinking, and illicit drug use among American 8th, 10th, and 12th grade students, 1976–2000. *Addiction, 98,* 225–234.

Wallerstein, J. S., & Lewis, J. M. (2004). The unexpected legacy of divorce: Report of a 25-year study. *Psychoanalytic Psychology, 21,* 353–370.

Walton, G. E., Armstrong, E. S., & Bower, T. G. R. (1998). Newborns learn to identify a face in eight-tenths of a second? *Developmental Science, 1,* 79–84.

Wang, Q. (2004). The emergence of cultural self-constructs: Autobiographical memory and self-description in European American and Chinese children. *Developmental Psychology, 40,* 3–15.

Wang, S., Baillargeon, R., & Paterson, S. (2005). Detecting continuity violations in infancy: A new account and new evidence from covering and tube effects. *Cognition, 95,* 129–173.

Ward, L. M., & Friedman, K. (2006). Using TV as a guide: Associations between television viewing and adolescents' sexual attitudes and behavior. *Journal of Research on Adolescence, 16,* 133–156.

Wark, G. R., & Krebs, D. L. (1996). Gender and dilemma differences in real-life moral judgment. *Developmental Psychology, 32,* 220–230.

Warner, L. A., Valdez, A., Vega, W. A., de la Rosa, M., Turner, R. J., & Canino, G. (2006). Hispanic drug abuse in an evolving cultural context: An agenda for research. *Drug and Alcohol Dependence, 84*(Suppl. 1), S8–S16.

Warnock, F., & Sandrin, D. (2004). Comprehensive description of newborn distress behavior in response to acute pain (newborn male circumcision). *Pain, 107,* 242–255.

Warren, A. R., & Tate, C. S. (1992). Egocentrism in children's telephone conversations. In R. M. Diaz & L. E. Berk (Eds.), *Private speech: From social interaction to self-regulation* (pp. 245–264). Hillsdale, NJ: Erlbaum.

Warren, D. H. (1994). *Blindness and children: An individual difference approach.* New York: Cambridge University Press.

Warren, S. L., & Simmens, S. J. (2005). Predicting toddler anxiety/depressive symptoms: Effects of caregiver sensitivity of temperamentally vulnerable children. *Infant Mental Health Journal, 26,* 40–55.

Wasik, B. A., & Bond, M. A. (2001). Beyond the pages of a book: Interactive book reading and language development in preschool classrooms. *Journal of Educational Psychology, 93,* 243–250.

Wasserman, E. A., & Rovee-Collier, C. (2001). Pick the flowers and mind your As and 2s! Categorization by pigeons and infants. In M. E. Carroll & J. B. Overmier (Eds.), *Animal research and human health: Advancing human welfare through behavioral science* (pp. 263–279). Washington, DC: American Psychological Association.

Watamura, S. E., Donzella, B., Alwin, J., & Gunnar, M. R. (2003). Morning-to-afternoon increases in cortisol concentrations for infants and toddlers at child care: Age differences and behavioral correlates. *Child Development, 74,* 1006–1020.

Waters, E., & Cummings, E. M. (2000). A secure base from which to explore close relationships. *Child Development, 71,* 164–172.

Waters, E., Merrick, S., Treboux, D., Crowell, J., & Albersheim, L. (2000). Attachment security in infancy and early adulthood: A twenty-year longitudinal study. *Child Development, 71,* 684–689.

Waters, E., Vaughn, B. E., Posada, G., & Kondo-Ikemura, K. (Eds.). (1995). Caregiving, cultural, and cognitive perspectives on secure-base behavior and working models: New growing points of attachment theory and research. *Monographs of the Society for Research in Child Development, 60*(2–3, Serial No. 244).

Watkins, W. E., & Pollitt, E. (1998). Iron deficiency and cognition among school-age children. In S. G. McGregor (Ed.), *Recent advances in research on the effects of health and nutrition on children's development and school achievement in the Third World.* Washington, DC: Pan American Health Organization.

Watson, A. C., Nixon, C. L., Wilson, A., & Capage, L. (1999). Social interaction skills and theory of mind in young children. *Developmental Psychology, 35,* 386–391.

Watson, D. J. (1989). Defining and describing whole language. *Elementary School Journal, 90,* 129–141.

Watson, J. B., & Raynor, R. (1920). Conditioned emotional reactions. *Journal of Experimental Psychology, 3,* 1–14.

Watson, M. (1990). Aspects of self development as reflected in children's role playing. In D. Cicchetti & M. Beeghly (Eds.), *The self in transition: Infancy to childhood* (pp. 281–307). Chicago: University of Chicago Press.

Waxman, S., & Lidz, J. L. (2006). Early word learning. In D. Kuhn & R. Siegler (Eds.), *Handbook of child psychology: Vol. 2. Cognition, perception, and language* (6th ed., pp. 464–510). Hoboken, NJ: Wiley.

Waxman, S. R. (2003). Links between object categorization and naming: Origins and emergence in human infants. In D. H. Rakison & L. M. Oakes (Eds.), *Early category and concept development: Making sense of the blooming, buzzing confusion* (pp. 193–209). New York: Oxford University Press.

Waxman, S. R., & Senghas, A. (1992). Relations among word meanings in early lexical development. *Developmental Psychology, 28,* 862–873.

Webb, N. M., Nemer, K. M., & Chizhik, A. W. (1998). Equity issues in collaborative group assessment: Group composition and performance. *American Educational Research Journal, 35,* 607–651.

Webb, S. J., Monk, C. S, & Nelson, C. A. (2001). Mechanisms of postnatal neurobiological development: Implications for human development. *Developmental Neuropsychology, 19,* 147–171.

Weber, C., Hahne, A., Friedrich, M., & Friederici, A. (2004). Discrimination of word stress in early infant perception: Electrophysiological evidence. *Cognitive Brain Research, 18,* 149–161.

Webster-Stratton, C., Reid, J., & Hammond, M. (2001). Social skills and problem-solving training for children with early-onset conduct problems: Who benefits? *Journal of Child Psychology and Psychiatry, 42,* 943–952.

Wechsler, D. (1996). *Canadian supplement manual for the WISC-III.* Toronto: Psychological Corporation.

Wechsler, D. (2002). *WPPSI-III: Wechsler Preschool and Primary Scale of Intelligence* (3rd ed.). San Antonio, TX: Psychological Corporation.

Wechsler, D. (2003). *WISC-IV: Wechsler Intelligence Scale for Children* (4th ed.). San Antonio, TX: Psychological Corporation.

Weems, C. F., & Costa, N. M. (2005). Developmental differences in the expression of childhood anxiety symptoms and fears. *Journal of the American Academy of Child and Adolescent Psychiatry, 44,* 656–663.

Wehren, A., DeLisi, R., & Arnold, M. (1981). The development of noun definition. *Journal of Child Language, 8,* 165–175.

Weikart, D. P. (1998). Changing early childhood development through educational intervention. *Preventive Medicine, 27,* 233–237.

Weimer, B. L., Kerns, K. A., & Oldenburg, C. M. (2004). Adolescents' interactions with a best friend: Associations with attachment style. *Journal of Experimental Child Psychology, 88,* 102–120.

Weinberg, M. K., & Tronick, E. Z. (1994). Beyond the face: An empirical study of infant affective configurations of facial, vocal, gestural, and regulatory behaviors. *Child Development, 65,* 1503–1515.

Weiner, A. (1988). *The Trobrianders of Papua New Guinea.* New York: Holt.

Weiner, J., & Tardif, C. (2004). Social and emotional functioning of children with learning disabilities: Does special education placement make a difference? *Learning Disabilities Research and Practice, 19,* 20–32.

Weinert, F. E., & Hany, E. A. (2003). The stability of individual differences in intellectual development: Empirical evidence, theoretical problems, and new research questions. In R. J. Sternberg & J. Lautrey (Eds.), *Models of intelligence: International perspectives* (pp. 169–181). Washington, DC: American Psychological Association.

Weinert, F. E., & Schneider, W. (Eds.). (1999). *Individual development from 3 to 12: Findings from the Munich Longitudinal Study.* Cambridge, U.K.: Cambridge University Press.

Weinfield, N. S., Sroufe, L. A., & Egeland, B. (2000). Attachment from infancy to early adulthood in a high-risk sample: Continuity, discontinuity, and their correlates. *Child Development, 71,* 695–702.

Weinfield, N. S., Whaley, G. J. L., & Egeland, B. (2004). Continuity, discontinuity, and coherence in attachment from infancy to late adolescence: Sequelae of organization and disorganization. *Attachment and Human Development, 6,* 73–97.

Weinstein, R. S. (2002). *Reaching higher: the power of expectations in schooling.* Cambridge, MA: Harvard University Press.

Weinstock, H., Berman, S., & Cates, W., Jr. (2004). Sexually transmitted diseases among American youth: Incidence and prevalence estimates, 2000. *Perspectives on Sexual and Reproductive Health, 36,* 6–10.

Weisfield, G. (1997). Puberty rites as clues to the nature of human adolescence. *Cross-Cultural Research, 31,* 27–54.

Weisner, T. S., & Wilson-Mitchell, J. E. (1990). Nonconventional family life-styles and sex typing in six-year-olds. *Child Development, 61,* 1915–1933.

Weiss, K. M. (2005). Cryptic causation of human disease: Reading between the germ lines. *Trends in Genetics, 21,* 82–88.

Weisz, A. N., & Black, B. M. (2002). Gender and moral reasoning: African American youths respond to dating dilemmas. *Journal of Human Behavior in the Social Environment, 6,* 17–34.

Weizman, Z. O., & Snow, C. E. (2001). Lexical output as related to children's vocabulary acquisition: Effects of sophisticated exposure and support for meaning. *Developmental Psychology, 37,* 265–279.

Wekerle, C., & Wolfe, D. A. (2003). Child maltreatment. In E. J. Mash & R. A. Barkley (Eds.), *Child psychopathology* (2nd ed., pp. 632–684). New York: Guilford.

Weller, E. B., Kloos, A. L., & Weller, R. A. (2006). Mood disorders. M. K. Dulcan & J. M. Wiener (Eds.), *Essentials of child and adolescent psychiatry* (pp. 267–320). Washington, DC: American Psychiatric Association.

Wellman, H. M. (1990). *The child's theory of mind.* Cambridge, MA: MIT Press.

Wellman, H. M. (2002). Understanding the psychological world: Developing a theory of mind. In U. Goswami (Ed.), *Blackwell handbook of child cognitive development* (pp. 167–187). Malden, MA: Blackwell.

Wellman, H. M., Cross, D., & Watson, J. (2001). Meta-analysis of theory-of-mind development: The truth about false belief. *Child Development, 72,* 655–684.

Wellman, H. M., & Hickling, A. K. (1994). The mind's "I": Children's conception of the mind as an active agent. *Child Development, 65,* 1564–1580.

Wellman, H. M., Somerville, S. C., & Haake, R. J. (1979). Development of search procedures in real-life spatial environments. *Developmental Psychology, 15,* 530–542.

Wen, S. W., Liu, S., Kramer, M. S., Marcoux, S., Ohlsson, A., & Sauvé, R. (2001). Comparison of maternal and infant outcomes between vacuum extraction and forceps deliveries. *American Journal of Epidemiology, 153,* 103–107.

Wentworth, N., Benson, J. B., & Haith, M. M. (2000). The development of infants' reaches for stationary and moving targets. *Child Development, 71,* 576–601.

Wentzel, K. R., Barry, C. M., & Caldwell, K. A. (2004). Friendships in middle school: Influences on motivation and school adjustment. *Journal of Educational Psychology, 96,* 195–203.

Werkerle, C., & Avgoustis, E. (2003). Child maltreatment, adolescent dating, and adolescent dating violence. In P. Florsheim (Ed.), *Adolescent romantic relations and sexual behavior: Theory, research, and practical implications* (pp. 213–242). Mahwah, NJ: Erlbaum.

Werner, E. (2001). *Journeys from childhood to midlife: Risk, resilience, and recovery.* Ithaca, NY: Cornell University Press.

Werner, E. E. (1989, April). Children of the garden island. *Scientific American, 260(4),* 106–111.

Werner, E. E. (2005). What can we learn about resilience from large-scale longitudinal studies? In S. Goldstein & R. B. Brooks (Eds.), *Handbook of resilience in children* (pp. 91–105). New York: Kluwer Academic.

Werner, E. E., & Smith, R. S. (1982). *Vulnerable but invincible: A study of resilient children.* New York: McGraw-Hill.

Werner, E. E., & Smith, R. S. (1992). *Overcoming the odds: High risk children from birth to adulthood.* Ithaca, NY: Cornell University Press.

Werner, E. E., & Smith, R. S. (2001). *Journeys from childhood to midlife: Risk, resilience, and recovery.* Ithaca, NY: Cornell University Press.

Werner, N. E., & Crick, N. R. (2004). Maladaptive peer relationships and the development of relational and physical aggression during middle childhood. *Social Development, 13,* 495–514.

Wheeler, W. (2002). Youth leadership for development: civic activism as a component of youth development programming and a strategy for strengthening civil society. In R. M. Lerner, F. Jacobs, & D. Wertlieb (Eds.), *Handbook of applied developmental science: Vol. 2* (pp. 491–506). Thousand Oaks, CA: Sage.

Whipple, E. E. (2006). Child abuse and neglect: Consequences of physical, sexual, and emotional abuse of children. In H. E. Fitzgerald, B. M. Lester, & B. Zuckerman (Eds.), *The crisis in youth mental health: Vol 1. Childhood disorders* (pp. 205–229). Westport, CT: Praeger.

White, B., & Held, R. (1966). Plasticity of sensorimotor development in the human infant. In J. F. Rosenblith & W. Allinsmith (Eds.), *The causes of behavior* (pp. 60–70). Boston: Allyn and Bacon.

White, M. A., Wilson, M. E., Elander, G., & Persson, B. (1999). The Swedish family: Transition to parenthood. *Scandinavian Journal of Caring Sciences, 13,* 171–176.

Whitehurst, G. J., & Lonigan, C. J. (1998). Child development and emergent literacy. *Child Development, 69,* 848–872.

Whiteside-Mansell, L., Bradley, R. H., Owen, M. T., Randolph, S. M., & Cauce, A. M. (2003). Parenting and children's behavior at 36 months: Equivalence between African-American and European-American mother–child dyads. *Parenting: Science and Practice, 3,* 197–234.

Whiting, B., & Edwards, C. P. (1988a). *Children in different worlds.* Cambridge, MA: Harvard University Press.

Whitington, V., & Ward, C. (1999). Intersubjectivity in caregiver–child communication. In L. E. Berk (Ed.), *Landscapes of development* (pp. 109– 120). Belmont, CA: Wadsworth.

Wichmann, C., Coplan, R. J., & Daniels, T. (2004). The social cognitions of socially withdrawn children. *Social Development, 13,* 377–392.

Wichstrøm, L. (1999). The emergence of gender difference in depressed mood: The role of intensified gender socialization. *Developmental Psychology, 35,* 232–245.

Wichstrom, L. (2006). Sexual orientation as a risk factor for bulimic symptoms. *International Journal of Eating Disorders, 39,* 448–453.

Wideen, M. F., O'Shea, T., Pye, I., & Ivany, G. (1997). High-stakes testing and the teaching of science. *Canadian Journal of Education, 22,* 428–444.

Wiecha, J. L., Sobol, A. M., Peterson, K. E., & Gortmaker, S. L. (2001). Household television access: Associations with screen time, reading, and homework among youth. *Ambulatory Pediatrics, 1,* 244–251.

Wigfield, A., Battle, A., Keller, L. B., & Eccles, J. S. (2002). Sex differences in motivation, self-concept, career aspiration, and career choice: Implications for cognitive development. In A. McGillicudy-De Lisi & R. De Lisi (Eds.), *Biology, society, and behavior: The development of sex differences in cognition* (pp. 93–124). Westport, CT: Ablex.

Wigfield, A., & Eccles, J. S. (1994). Children's competence beliefs, achievement values, and genderal self-esteem change across elementary and middle school. *Journal of Early Adolescence, 14,* 107–138.

Wigfield, A., Eccles, J. S., Schiefele, U., Roeser, R. W., & Davis-Kean, P. (2006). Development of achievement motivation. In N. Eisenberg (Ed.), *Handbook of child psychology: Vol. 3. Social, emotional, and personality development* (6th ed., pp. 933–1002). Hoboken, NJ: Wiley.

Wigfield, A., Eccles, J. S., Yoon, K. S., Harold, R. D., Arbreton, A. J., Freedman-Doan, C., & Blumenfeld, P. C. (1997). Changes in children's competence beliefs and subjective task values across the elementary school years: A three-year study. *Journal of Educational Psychology, 89,* 451–469.

Wilcox, A. J., Weinberg, C. R., & Baird, D. D. (1995). Timing of sexual intercourse in relation to ovulation: Effects on the probability of conception, survival of the pregnancy, and sex of the baby. *New England Journal of Medicine, 333,* 1517–1519.

Wilhelm, O. (2005). Measures of emotional intelligence: Practice and standards. In R. Schulze & R. D. Roberts (Eds.), *Emotional intelligence: An international handbook* (pp. 131–154). Göttingen, Germany: Hogrefe & Huber.

Wilkinson, K., Ross, E., & Diamond, A. (2003). Fast mapping of multiple words: Insights into when "the information provided" does and does not equal "the information perceived." *Applied Developmental Psychology, 24,* 739–762.

Wilkinson, R. B. (2004). The role of parental and peer attachment in the psychological health and self-esteem of adolescents. *Journal of Youth and Adolescence, 33,* 479–493.

Willatts, P. (1999). Development of means–end behavior in young infants: Pulling a support to retrieve a distant object. *Developmental Psychology, 35,* 651–667.

Wille, M. C., Weitz, B., Kerper, P., & Frazier, S. (2004). Advances in preconception genetic counseling. *Journal of Perinatal and Neonatal Nursing, 18,* 28–40.

Williams, C. (2006). Dilemmas in fetal medicine: Premature application of technology or responding to women's choice? *Sociology of Health and Illness, 28,* 1–20.

Williams, J. M., & Currie, C. (2000). Self-esteem and physical development in early adolescence: Pubertal timing and body image. *Journal of Early Adolescence, 20,* 129–149.

Williams, K., Haywood, K. I., & Painter, M. (1996). Environmental versus biological influences on gender differences in the overarm throw for force: Dominant and nondominant arm throws. *Women in Sport and Physical Activity Journal, 5,* 29–48.

Williams, P. E., Weiss, L. G., & Rolfhus, E. (2003). *WISC-IV: Theoretical model and test blueprint.* San Antonio, TX: Psychological Corporation.

Willinger, M., Ko, C.-W., Hoffman, H. J., Kessler, R. C., & Corwin, M. J. (2003). Trends in infant bed sharing in the United States. *Archives of Pediatrics and Adolescent Medicine, 157,* 43–49.

Willms, J. D., Tremblay, M. S., & Katzmarzyk, P. T. (2003). Geographic and demographic variation in the prevalence of overweight Canadian children. *Obesity Research, 11,* 668–673.

Willoughby, J., Kupersmidt, J. B., & Bryant, D. (2001). Overt and covert dimensions of antisocial behavior. *Journal of Abnormal Child Psychology, 29,* 177–187.

Winn, M. (2002). *The plug-in drug: Television, computers, and family life.* New York: Penguin.

Winner, E. (1986, August). Where pelicans kiss seals. *Psychology Today, 20*(8), 25–35.

Winner, E. (1988). *The point of words: Children's understanding of metaphor and irony.* Cambridge, MA: Harvard University Press.

Winner, E. (1996). *Gifted children: Myths and realities.* New York: Basic Books.

Winner, E. (1997). Exceptionally high intelligence and schooling. *American Psychologist, 52,* 1070–1081.

Winner, E. (2000). The origins and ends of giftedness. *American Psychologist, 55,* 159–169.

Winner, E. (2003). Creativity and talent. In M. H. Bornstein, L. Davidson, C. L. M. Keyes, K. A. Moore, & the Center for Child Well-Being, (Eds.), *Well-being: Positive development across the life course* (pp. 371–380). Mahwah, NJ: Erlbaum.

Winsler, A., Abar, B., Feder, M. A., Rubio, D. A., & Schunn, C. D. (2007). Private speech and executive functioning among high functioning children with autism spectrum disorders. *Journal of Autism and Developmental Disorders, Online First™.*

Winsler, A., Diaz, R. M., McCarthy, E. M., Atencio, D. J., & Chabay, L. (1999). Mother–child interaction, private speech, and task performance in preschool children with behavior problems. *Journal of Child Psychology and Psychiatry, 40,* 891–904.

Winsler, A., & Naglieri, J. (2003). Overt and covert verbal problem-solving strategies: Developmental trends in use, awareness, and relations with task performance in children aged 5 to 17. *Child Development, 74,* 659–678.

Winsler, A., Naglieri, J., & Manfra, L. (2006). Children's search strategies and accompanying verbal and motor strategic behavior: Developmental trends and relations with task performance among children age 5 to 17. *Cognitive Development, 21,* 232–248.

Wissink, I. B., Dekoviˊc, M., & Meijer, A. M. (2006). Parenting behavior, quality of the parent–adolescent relationship, and adolescent functioning in four ethnic groups. *Journal of Early Adolescence, 26,* 133–159.

Witherington, D. C. (2005). The development of prospective grasping control between 5 and 7 months: A longitudinal study. *Infancy, 7,* 143–161.

Witherington, D. C., Campos, J. J., Anderson, D. I., Lejeune, L., & Seah, E. (2005). Avoidance of heights on the visual cliff in newly walking infants. *Infancy, 7,* 285–298.

Witherington, D. C., Campos, J. J., & Hertenstein, M. J. (2001). Principles of emotion and its development in infancy. In G. Bremner & A. Fogel (Eds.), *Blackwell handbook of infant development* (pp. 427–464). Malden, MA: Blackwell.

Wolak, J., Mitchell, K. J., & Finkelhor, D. (2003). Escaping or connecting? Characteristics of youth who form close online relationships. *Journal of Adolescence, 26,* 105–119.

Wolak, J., Mitchell, K., & Finkelhor, D. (2007). Unwanted and wanted exposure to online pornography in a national sample of youth Internet users. *Pediatrics, 119,* 247–257.

Wolchik, S. A., Wilcox, K. L., Tein, J.-Y., & Sandler, I. N. (2000). Maternal acceptance and consistency of discipline as buffers of divorce stressors on children's psychological adjustment problems. *Journal of Abnormal Child Psychology, 28,* 87–102.

Wolf, A. W., Jimenez, E., & Lozoff, B. (2003). Effects of iron therapy on infant blood lead levels. *Journal of Pediatrics, 143,* 789–795.

Wolfe, D. A. (2005). *Child abuse* (2nd ed.) Thousand Oaks: Sage.

Wolfe, D. A., Scott, K., Wekerle, C., & Pittman, A. (2001). Child maltreatment: Risk of adjustment problems and dating violence in adolescence. *Journal of the American Academy of Child and Adolescent Psychiatry, 40,* 282–289.

Wolfelt, A. D. (1997). Death and grief in the school setting. In T. N. Fairchild (Ed.), *Crisis intervention strategies for school-based helpers* (2nd ed., pp. 199–244). Springfield, IL: Charles C. Thomas.

Wolff, P. H. (1966). The causes, controls and organization of behavior in the neonate. *Psychological Issues, 5*(1, Serial No. 17).

Wolff, P. H., & Fesseha, G. (1999). The orphans of Eritrea: A five-year follow-up study. *Journal of Child Psychology and Psychiatry and Allied Disciplines, 40,* 1231–1237.

Wolfinger, N. H. (2000). Beyond the intergenerational transmission of divorce: Do people replicate the patterns of marital instability they grew up with? *Journal of Family Issues, 21,* 1061–1086.

Wong, C. A., Eccles, J. S., & Sameroff, A. (2003). The influence of ethnic discrimination and ethnic identification on African American adolescents' school and socioemotional adjustment. *Journal of Personality, 71,* 1197–1232.

Wood, E., Desmarais, S., & Gugula, S. (2002). The impact of parenting experience on gender stereotyped toy play of children. *Sex Roles, 47,* 39–49.

Wood, J. J., Emmerson, N. A., & Cowan, P. A. (2004). Is early attachment security carried forward into relationships with preschool peers? *British Journal of Developmental Psychology, 22,* 245–253.

Woodward, A. L., & Markman, E. M. (1998). Early word learning. In D. Kuhn & R. S. Siegler (Eds.), *Handbook of child psychology: Vol. 2. Cognition, perception, and language* (5th ed., pp. 371–420). New York: Wiley.

Woodward, J., & Ono, Y. (2004). Mathematics and academic diversity in Japan. *Journal of Learning Disabilities, 37,* 74–82.

Woody-Dorning, J., & Miller, P. H. (2001). Children's individual differences in capacity: Effects on strategy production and utilization. *British Journal of Developmental Psychology, 19,* 543–557.

Woolley, J. D. (1997). Thinking about fantasy: Are children fundamentally different thinkers and believers from adults? *Child Development, 68,* 991–1011.

Woolley, J. D. (2000). The development of beliefs about direct mental–physical causality in imagination, magic, and religion. In K. S. Rosengren, C. N. Johnson, & P. L. Harris (Eds.), *Imagining the impossible* (pp. 99–129). New York: Cambridge University Press.

World Education Services. (2007). *World education database.* Retrieved from www.wes.org

World Health Organization. (2003). *Oral Health Country/Area Profile Program.* Retrieved from www.whocollab.od.mah.se/index.html

World Health Organization. (2004). *WHO Oral Health Country/Area Profile Program.* Retrieved from www.whocollab.od.mah.se/sicdata.html

World Health Organization. (2005). *The world health report, 2005.* Geneva, Switzerland: Author.

World Press Review. (2004). *Obesity: A worldwide issue.* Retrieved from www.worldpress.org/Africa/1961.cfm

Worrell, F. C., & Gardner-Kitt, D. L. (2006). The relationship between racial and ethnic identity in black adolescents: The cross-racial identity scale and the multigroup ethnic identity measure. *Identity, 6,* 293–315.

Wright, B. C., & Dowker, A. D. (2002). The role of cues to differential absolute size in children's transitive inferences. *Journal of Experimental Child Psychology, 81,* 249–275.

Wright, J. C., Huston, A. C., Murphy, K. C., St. Peters, M., Pinon, M., Scantlin, R., & Kotler, J. (2001). The relations of early television viewing to school readiness and vocabulary of children from low-income families: The Early Window Project. *Child Development, 72,* 1347–1366.

Wright, J. C., Huston, A. C., Reitz, A. L., & Piemyat, S. (1994). Young children's perceptions of television reality: Determinants and developmental differences. *Developmental Psychology, 30,* 229–239.

Wright, J. W. (Ed.). (1999). *The universal almanac 1999.* Kansas City: Andrews and McMeel.

Wright, M. O., & Masten, A. S. (2005). Resilience processes in development. In S. Goldstein & R. B. Brooks (Eds.), *Handbook of resilience in children* (pp. 17–37). New York: Springer.

Wright, R. O., Tsaih, S. W., Schwartz, J., Wright, R. J., & Hu, H. (2003). Associations between iron deficiency and blood lead level in a longitudinal analysis of children followed in an urban primary care clinic. *Journal of Pediatrics, 142,* 9–14.

Wright, V. C., Schieve, L. A., Reynolds, M. A., Jeng, G., & Kissin, D. (2004). Assisted reproductive technology surveillance—United States 2001. *Morbidity and Mortality Weekly Report, 53,* 1–20.

Wrotniak, B. H., Epstein, L. H., Raluch, R. A., & Roemmich, J. N. (2004). Parent weight change as a predictor of child weight change in family-based behavioral obesity treatment. *Archives of Pediatric and Adolescent Medicine, 158,* 342–347.

Wu, G., Bazer, F. W., Cudd, T. A., Meininger, C. J., & Spencer, T. E. (2004). Maternal nutrition and fetal development. *Journal of Nutrition, 134,* 2169–2172.

Wu, L. L., Bumpass, L. L., & Musick, K. (2001). Historical and life course trajectories of nonmarital childbearing. In L. L. Wu & B. Wolfe (Eds.), *Out of wedlock: Causes and consequences of nonmarital fertility* (pp. 3–48). New York: Russell Sage Foundation.

Wu, P., Robinson, C. C., Yang, C., Hart, C. H., Olsen, S. F., Porter, C. L., Jin, S., Wo, J., & Wu, X. (2002). Similarities and differences in mothers' parenting of preschoolers in China and the United States. *International Journal of Behavioral Development, 26,* 481–491.

Wu, T., Mendola, P., & Buck, G. M. (2002). Ethnic differences in the presence of secondary sex characteristics and menarche among U.S. girls: The Third National Health and Nutrition Examination Survey, 1988–1994. *Pediatrics, 110,* 752–757.

Wu, Y. (2006). Overweight and obesity in China. *British Medical Journal, 333,* 362–363.

Wust, S., Entringer, S., Federenko, I. S., Schlotz, W., Helhammer, D. H. (2005). Birth weight is associated with salivary cortisol responses to psychosocial stress in adult life. *Psychoneuroendocrinology, 30,* 591–598.

Wyatt, J. M., & Carlo, G. (2002). What will my parents think? Relations among adolescents' expected parental reactions, prosocial moral reasoning and prosocial and antisocial behaviors. *Journal of Adolescent Research, 17,* 646–666.

Wynn, K. (1992). Addition and subtraction by human infants. *Nature, 358,* 749–750.

Wynn, K. (2002). Do infants have numerical expectations or just perceptual preferences? Comment. *Developmental Science, 5,* 207–209.

Wynn, K., Bloom, P., & Chiang, W.-C. (2002). Enumeration of collective entities by 5-month-old infants. *Cognition, 83,* B55–B62.

Wynne-Edwards, K. E. (2001). Hormonal changes in mammalian fathers. *Hormones and Behavior, 40,* 139–145.

Xu, F., & Spelke, E. S. (2000). Large number discrimination in 6-month-old infants. *Cognition, 74,* B1–B11.

Xu, X., & Peng, L. (2001). Reflection on parents' educational beliefs in the new century. *Theory and Practice of Education, 21,* 62–63.

Xue, Y., & Meisels, S. J. (2004). Early literacy instruction and learning in kindergarten: Evidence from the early childhood longitudinal study—kindergarten classes of 1998–1999. *American Educational Research Journal, 41,* 191–229.

Yale, M. E., Messinger, D. S., Cobo-Lewis, A. B., Oller, D. K., & Eilers, R. E. (1999). An event-based analysis of the coordination of early infant vocalizations and facial actions. *Developmental Psychology, 35,* 505–513.

Yang, B., Ollendick, T. H., Dong, Q., Xia, Y., & Lin, L. (1995). Only children and children with siblings in the People's Republic of China: Levels of fear, anxiety, and depression. *Child Development, 66,* 1301–1311.

Yang, C., Hart, C. H., Nelson, D. A., Porter, C. L., Olsen, S. F., Robinson, C. C., & Jin, S. (2003). Fathering in the a Beijing Chinese sample: Associations with boys' and girls' negative emotionality and aggression. In R. D. Day & M. E. Lamb (Eds.), *Conceptualizing and measuring father involvement* (pp. 185–215). Mahwah, NJ: Erlbaum.

Yanovski, J. A. (2003). Rapid weight gain during infancy as a predictor of adult obesity. *American Journal of Clinical Nutrition, 77,* 1350–1351.

Yarrow, M. R., Scott, P. M., & Waxler, C. Z. (1973). Learning concern for others. *Developmental Psychology, 8,* 240–260.

Yates, T. M., Egeland, B., & Sroufe, L. A. (2003). Rethinking resilience: A developmental process perspective. In S. S. Luthar (Ed.), *Resilience and vulnerability: Adaptation in the context of childhood adversities* (pp. 243–266). New York: Cambridge University Press.

Yeates, K. O., Schultz, L. H., & Selman, R. L. (1991). The development of interpersonal negotiation strategies in thought and action: A social-cognitive link to behavioral adjustment and social status. *Merrill-Palmer Quarterly, 37,* 369–405.

Yeh, H.-C., & Lempers, J. D. (2004). Perceived sibling relationships and adolescent development. *Journal of Youth and Adolescence, 33,* 133–147.

Yehuda, R., Engel, S. M., Brand, S. R., Seckl, J., Marcus, S. M., & Berkowitz, G. S. (2005). Transgenerational effects of posttraumatic stress disorder in babies of mothers exposed to the World Trade Center attacks during pregnancy. *Journal of Clinical Endocrinology and Metabolism, 90,* 4115–4118.

Yip, R., Scanlon, K., & Trowbridge, F. (1993). Trends and patterns in height and weight status of low-income U.S. children. *Critical Reviews in Food Science and Nutrition, 33,* 409–421.

Yip, T., Seaton, E. K., & Sellers, R. M. (2006). African-American racial identity across the lifespan: Identity status, identity content, and depressive symptoms. *Child Development, 77,* 1504–1517.

Yirmiya, N., Erel, O., Shaked, M., & Solomonica-Levi, D. (1998). Meta-analyses comparing theory of mind abilities of individuals with autism, individuals with mental retardation, and normally developing individuals. *Psychological Bulletin, 124,* 283–307.

Yonas, A., Elieff, C., & Aterberry, M. E. (2002). Emergence of sensitivity to pictorial depth cues: Charting development in individual infants. *Infant Behavior and Development, 25,* 295–514.

Yonas, A., & Granrud, C. E. (2006). Infants' perception of depth from cast shadows. *Perception and Psychophysics, 68,* 154–160.

Yoon, D. P. (2004). Intercountry adoption: The importance of ethnic socialization and subjective well-being for Korean-born adopted children. *Journal of Ethnic and Cultural Diversity in Social Work, 13,* 71–89.

Yoshida, H., & Smith, L. B. (2003). Known and novel noun extensions: Attention at two levels of abstraction. *Child Development, 74,* 564–577.

Yoshinaga-Itano, C. (2003). Early intervention after universal neonatal hearing screening: Impact on outcomes. *Mental Retardation and Developmental Disabilities Research and Reviews, 9,* 252–266.

Young, J. F., & Mroczek, D. K. (2003). Predicting intraindividual self-concept trajectories during adolescence. *Journal of Adolescence, 26,* 589–603.

Youngblade, L. M., & Dunn, J. (1995). Individual differences in young children's pretend play with mother and sibling: Links to relationships and understanding of other people's feelings and beliefs. *Child Development, 66,* 1472–1492.

Youngstrom, E., Wolpaw, J. M., Kogos, J. L., Schoff, K., Ackerman, B., & Izard, C. (2000). Interpersonal problem solving in preschool and first grade: Developmental change and ecological validity. *Journal of Clinical Child Psychology, 29,* 589–602.

Youniss, J., McLellan, J., & Yates, M. (1999). Religion, community service, and identity in American youth. *Journal of Adolescence, 22,* 243–253.

Youniss, J., McLellan, J. A., & Yates, M. (1997). What we know about engendering civic identity. *American Behavioral Scientist, 40,* 620–631.

Yu, R. (2002). On the reform of elementary school education in China. *Educational Exploration, 129,* 56–57.

Yuan, A. S. V., & Hamilton, H. A. (2006). Stepfather involvement and adolescent well-being: Do mothers and nonresidential fathers matter? *Journal of Family Issues, 27,* 1191–1213.

Yuill, N., & Pearson, A. (1998). The developmental bases for trait attribution: Children's understanding of traits as causal mechanisms based on desire. *Developmental Psychology, 34,* 574–586.

Yunger, J. L., Carver, P. R., & Perry, D. G. (2004). Does gender identity influence children's psychological well-being? *Developmental Psychology, 40,* 572–582.

Zafeiriou, D. I. (2000). Plantar grasp reflex in high-risk infants during the first year of life. *Pediatric Neurology, 22,* 75–76.

Zahn-Waxler, C., Kochanska, G., Krupnick, J., & McKnew, D. (1990). Patterns of guilt in children of depressed and well mothers. *Developmental Psychology, 26,* 51–59.

Zahn-Waxler, C., Radke-Yarrow, M., & King, R. M. (1979). Child-rearing and children's prosocial initiations toward victims of distress. *Child Development, 50,* 319–330.

Zahn-Waxler, C., & Robinson, J. (1995). Empathy and guilt: Early origins of feelings of responsibility. In J. P. Tangney & K. W. Fischer (Eds.), *Self-conscious emotions* (pp. 143–173). New York: Guilford.

Zahn-Waxler, C., Schiro, K., Robinson, J. L., Emde, R. N., & Schmitz, S. (2001). Empathy and prosocial patterns in young MZ and DZ twins: Development and genetic and environmental influences. In R. N. Emde & J. K. Hewitt (Eds.), *Infancy to early childhood: Genetic and environmental influences on developmental change* (pp. 141–162). New York: Oxford University Press.

Zaslow, M. J., Weinfield, N. S., Gallagher, M., Hair, E. C., Ogawa, J. R., Egeland, B., Tabors, P. O., & De Temple, J. M. (2006). Longitudinal prediction of child outcomes from differing measures of parenting in a low-income sample. *Developmental Psychology, 42,* 27–37.

Zelazo, N. A., Zelazo, P. R., Cohen, K. M., & Zelazo, P. D. (1993). Specificity of practice effects on elementary neuromotor patterns. *Developmental Psychology, 29,* 686–691.

Zelazo, P. D., Frye, D., & Rapus, T. (1996). An age-related dissociation between knowing rules and using them. *Cognitive Development, 11,* 37–63.

Zelazo, P. D., Muller, U., Frye, D., & Marcovitch, S. (2003). The development of executive function: Cognitive complexity and control—revised. *Monographs of the Society for Research in Child Development, 68*(3), 93–119.

Zeldin, A. L. & Pajares, F. (2000). Against the odds: Self-efficacy beliefs of women in mathematical, scientific, and technological careers. *American Educational Research Journal, 37,* 215–246.

Zeller, M. H., & Modi, A. C. (2006). Predictors of health-related quality of life in obese youth. *Obesity Research, 14,* 122–130.

Zeman, J., Shipman, K., & Suveg, C. (2002). Anger and sadness regulation: Predictions to internalizing and externalizing symptoms in children. *Journal of Clinical Child and Adolescent Psychology, 31,* 393–398.

Zeskind, P. S., & Barr, R. G. (1997). Acoustic characteristics of naturally occurring cries of infants with "colic." *Child Development, 68,* 394–403.

Zeskind, P. S., & Lester, B. M. (2001). Analysis of infant crying. In L. T. Singer & P. S. Zeskind (Eds.), *Biobehavioral assessment of the infant* (pp. 149–166). New York: Guilford.

Zhou, M., & Bankston, C. L. (1998). *Growing up American: How Vietnamese children adapt to life in the United States.* New York: Russell Sage Foundation.

Zhou, M., & Xiong, S. (2005). The multifaceted American experiences of the children of Asian immigrants: Lessons for segmented assimilation. *Ethnic and Racial Studies, 28,* 1119–1152.

Zigler, E. F., & Hall, N. W. (2000). Child development and social policy: Theory and applications. New York: McGraw-Hill.

Zimmer-Gembeck, M. J., Siebenbruner, J., & Collins, W. A. (2001). Diverse aspects of dating: Associations with psychosocial functioning from early to middle adolescence. *Journal of Adolescence, 24,* 313–336.

Zimmerman, B. J., & Risemberg, R. (1997). Self-regulatory dimensions of academic learning and motivation. In G. D. Phye (Ed.), *Handbook of academic learning: Construction of knowledge* (pp. 105–125). San Diego: Academic Press.

Zimmerman, P., & Becker-Stoll, F. (2002). Stability of attachment representations during adolescence: The influence of ego-identity status. *Journal of Adolescence, 25,* 107–124.

Zins, J. E., Garcia, V. F., Tuchfarber, B. S., Clark, K. M., & Laurence, S. C. (1994). Preventing injury in children and adolescents. In R. J. Simeonsson (Ed.), *Risk, resilience, and prevention: Promoting the well-being of all children* (pp. 183–202). Baltimore: Paul H. Brookes.

Zukow-Goldring, P. (2002). Sibling caregiving. In M. H. Bornstein (Ed.), *Handbook of parenting: Vol. 3* (2nd ed., pp. 253–286). Hillsdale, NJ: Erlbaum.

Zur, O., & Gelman, R. (2004). Young children can add and subtract by predicting and checking. *Early Childhood Research Quarterly, 19,* 121–137.

Zuzanek, J. (2000). *The effects of time use and time pressure on child–parent relationships.* Waterloo, ON: Otium.

Name Index

Italic n following page number indicates caption for photograph, illustration, table, or figure.

Subject Index